DOCUMENTARY HISTORY OF THE FIRST FEDERAL CONGRESS OF THE UNITED STATES OF AMERICA

4 March 1789–3 March 1791

SPONSORED BY
THE NATIONAL HISTORICAL PUBLICATIONS AND RECORDS COMMISSION
AND
THE GEORGE WASHINGTON UNIVERSITY

This book has been brought to publication with the generous assistance of the National Historical Publications and Records Commission.

NHPRC
DOCUMENTING DEMOCRACY
National Historical Publications and Records Commission

This volume has been supported by a grant from the National Endowment for the Humanities, an independent federal agency.

NATIONAL
ENDOWMENT
FOR THE
HUMANITIES

PROJECT STAFF
    CHARLENE BANGS BICKFORD, *Co-Editor*
    KENNETH R. BOWLING, *Co-Editor*
    HELEN E. VEIT, *Associate Editor*
    WILLIAM CHARLES DIGIACOMANTONIO, *Associate Editor*

ADMINISTRATIVE ADVISORY COMMITTEE
    ROBERT C. BYRD
    LINDA GRANT DEPAUW, *Chair*
    ELIZABETH FENN
    RICHARD H. KOHN
    CHARLES McC. MATHIAS

VOLUME XVIII

CORRESPONDENCE

SECOND SESSION:
OCTOBER 1789 – 14 MARCH 1790

CHARLENE BANGS BICKFORD

KENNETH R. BOWLING

HELEN E. VEIT

WILLIAM CHARLES DIGIACOMANTONIO

Editors

The Johns Hopkins University Press, Baltimore

This book has been brought to publication with the generous assistance
of the Boone Endowment of the Johns Hopkins University Press.

The Johns Hopkins University Press
2715 North Charles Street
Baltimore, Maryland 21218-4163
www.press.jhu.edu

ISBN-13: 978-0-8018-9445-9 (hardcover: alk. paper)
ISBN-10: 0-8018-9445-X (hardcover: alk. paper)

Library of Congress Control Number: 2009933941

A catalog record for this book is available from the British Library.

*Special discounts are available for bulk purchases of this book. For more information,
please contact Special Sales at 410-516-6936 or specialsales@press.jhu.edu.*

The Johns Hopkins University Press uses environmentally friendly book
materials, including recycled text paper that is composed of at least 30 percent
post-consumer waste, whenever possible. All of our book papers are acid-free,
and our jackets and covers are printed on paper with recycled content.

To
Frank G. Burke, Roger Bruns, and Mary Giunta
for their long-term and steadfast commitment
to the NHPRC's editions program
and the First Federal Congress Project

CONTENTS

ILLUSTRATIONS

INTRODUCTION

The Significance of Congressional Correspondence

The thousands of extant letters to and from members of the First Federal Congress are a monument to one of the most fundamental developments in American political culture. Before the enactment of the Constitution in 1789, the direct constituents of delegates to Congress were the state legislatures that appointed them. Recognizing this, Edmund C. Burnett's *Letters of Members of the Continental Congress* initially aimed at printing only official reports by delegates to their state officials. Even after broadening his selection criteria, Burnett himself acknowledged that the edition's eight volumes were hardly enough to supplement the thirty-four-volume *Journal of the Continental Congress* by conveying "contemporary or nearly contemporary information about the doings of that body," as had been originally intended.[1] The Library of Congress sought to redress the shortcomings of Burnett's pioneering edition by commissioning an expanded twenty-six-volume edition of *Letters of Delegates to Congress, 1774–1789* as part of its American Revolution Bicentennial observance. Although it tripled the number of documents published by Burnett and printed them in their entirety, the newer edition's selection was still limited to outgoing letters.

The nature of the federal government as altered by the Constitution and experienced by members of the First Federal Congress is reflected in the more comprehensive nature of the *Documentary History of the First Federal Congress, 1789–1791 (DHFFC)*. The closed-door proceedings of Congress before 1789 (a secrecy its delegates were solemnly sworn to uphold when directed by a majority vote),[2] its limited powers, and its accountability to state legislatures naturally limited the scope of the exchange between private citizens and their legislators. This changed with the First Federal Congress. Senators continued to be answerable to their state legislatures and met in secret. But the first House of Representatives summarily rejected the authority of formal instructions when it defeated a motion to add the people's right "to instruct their representatives" to the proposed amendments to the Constitution. Representatives would remain directly responsible to an electorate as a whole without intermediaries, and, except on rare occasions, their proceedings and debates could be viewed by any spectator or newspaper reporter. Moreover, both Senators and Representatives were constitutionally endowed with a much broader range of powers, and their reliance on the input of constituents rose correspondingly.

[1] *LDC* 1:v.
[2] *JCC* 23:829.

The flood of requests for constituent services (primarily from petitioners or office seekers) and the opinions expressed on pending legislation attest to the common citizens' perception of their new role. Apart from visits by distant constituents, letters and newspapers from home were the only way congressmen could stay alert to the collective interests they were supposed to be representing. Constituents sometimes mailed their hometown newspapers to their congressmen, but the supply was irregular and unreliable, limiting their impact. Georgia's is the only state government known to have made provision for furnishing its delegation with newspapers from home, and the only known subscription by a member for his hometown paper—Grout's subscription to Worcester's *Massachusetts Spy*—is the exception that proves the rule: members of Congress were desperate to know what their constituents were thinking.[3] Incoming letters are therefore important testimonials to the new role of individual citizens and citizens groups in shaping Congress's legislative agenda as well as the content of legislation.

Realizing that "the people have something else to do than barely to elect," one of Moore's constituents from southwestern Virginia envisioned the creation of a two- or three-member committee in each county to correspond regularly with its Representative, as well as with other county committees of correspondence within the district. There are only a few instances in which citizens groups are known to have approached this level of organization. The three most notable are the marine insurance offices of Massachusetts' North Shore, which regularly corresponded with Goodhue through Michael Hodge; the eleven-member committee of merchants and traders of Portland, Maine, which occasionally corresponded with Thatcher on commercial subjects; and the committee of Philadelphia merchants that corresponded with the Pennsylvania delegation about matters relating to commerce. In July 1789 this last group even submitted a substitute draft Lighthouses Bill [HR-12], which influenced the final text of that act. The higher incidence of correspondence among the New Englanders bears out Fitzsimons's complaint that they were more successful in soliciting and receiving advice from their constituents than were other congressmen.[4]

Every member of the First Federal Congress served the dual function of representing not only the people to the government but the government back to the people. Yet the pressure on congressmen to publicize themselves and their activities was aggravated by the size and dispersion of their constituencies. Representatives (except those elected at large) were accountable

---

[3] Minutes of the Georgia Executive Council, 18 May 1789, State Records, G-Ar; Grout to Isaiah Thomas, 29 Dec. 1789, Thomas Papers, MWA.

[4] Arthur Campbell to Archibald Stuart, [July] 1789, Draper Collection, WHi; Fitzsimons to Tench Coxe, 25 April 1789, Coxe Papers, PHi.

to districts ranging in population from 16,250 (Jackson's Georgia district) to 108,500 (Ashe's North Carolina district) and in size from approximately 400 square miles (Laurance's New York district) to 42,000 square miles (John Sevier's North Carolina district). One result was that "men are brought into Public life upon a very short acquaintance with the People," as one Bostonian wrote to Samuel Russell Gerry. Tucker of South Carolina feared the merely "nominal Representation" that would result from popularly elected congressmen being "totally unknown to nine tenths of their constituents." As a case in point, he might have pointed to Massachusetts' Maine district, where Thatcher was elected Representative with only 588 votes (of 948 cast) in a district of approximately 96,000 inhabitants. Because of these handicaps, a congressman's critical role in transferring legitimacy to and confidence in the new government would have been impossible without the ties nurtured by the exchange of letters.[5]

Newspapers publicizing House debates also helped congressmen explain themselves to their constituents and demystify the workings of the government. It was with placid resignation that Francis Hopkinson—himself a former member of the Continental Congress—wrote Thomas Jefferson in 1785 that "we know little more of Congress here than you do in France, perhaps not so much. They are seldom or ever mentioned in the Papers and are less talked of than if they were in the West Indies Islands." Four years later, the decision to open the doors of the House to the public and the press was seen as heralding a new era in which public affairs were brought "home to the door of every citizen."[6]

Original accounts of congressional debates and proceedings were routine features in several of the seven newspapers published at the seat of government and regularly reappeared in dozens of the ninety-eight newspapers published within the United States in 1789. Thirty-two of these papers were published east of the Hudson, and another twenty-three south of the Potomac; Pennsylvania, with sixteen, had more than any other single state. The number of copies circulated weekly, according to one enterprising New Yorker's estimate in October 1789, was 76,483. Such coverage went far to answer the public's need for information. Since the Confederation, the postmaster general had permitted printers to exchange their newspapers with publishers in other cities free of postage. Congressmen facilitated this process

---

[5] James Sullivan to Gerry, 27 Sept. 1789, Gerry Papers, MHi; Tucker to St. George Tucker, 28 Dec. 1787, *LDC* 24:600; *DHFFE* 1:613.

[6] Hopkinson to Jefferson, 20 April 1785, *PTJ* 8:99; *DHFFC* 10:xi. For more on press access to House debates during the First Federal Congress, see *DHFFC* 10:xi–xl, and Charlene B. Bickford, "Throwing Open the Doors: The First Federal Congress and the Eighteenth Century Media," in Kenneth R. Bowling and Donald R. Kennon, eds., *Inventing Congress: Origins and Establishment of the First Federal Congress* (Athens, Ohio, 1999), pp. 166–90.

by mailing additional issues to their home districts under their "frank," a signature or sign permitting free postage for official mailings. Exercising that congressional privilege made a greater number of newspapers available for redistribution and copying by the local newspapers and ensured their conveyance via the post rider's more reliable official portmanteau. Members' letters frequently refer the recipient to an enclosed newspaper. Not until December 1790 did the First Congress formally resolve to charge the Treasury for supplying members with newspapers published at the seat of government. That practice, begun during the Confederation Congress, seems to have persisted unofficially throughout the First Congress.[7]

Still, many citizens wanted more. George Nicholas on the Kentucky frontier could read about the public actions of Congress in the newspapers, but he sought from Brown's letters "the secret movement" of government. "Pray, Sir, don't let your letter contain mere *news-paper* news," beseeched one of Thatcher's constituents; "give me something that I could not obtain otherwise." "Do let us know how the *Cat Jumps*," begged another . . . or how proceeds "the Continental Waggon" or the drift of "the ship of state," according to the writer's idiom. Many incoming letters contain grateful acknowledgments for past attention and hungry demands for more. Congressmen's letters in fact became coveted tokens, an index of status. More than one correspondent reminded Thatcher that he neglected to write influential constituents at his peril and that they were jealous of the attention he paid to his Antifederalist correspondents.[8]

Letters to and from members of the First Congress were important not only as a medium of political information or influence but as a critical component in the personal life of the member. Long absences from home excluded them from the network of familiar relationships that gave life meaning and pleasure. The "literary visits" that Wingate looked forward to in his correspondence with family members and the "little town news" that Wadsworth relished hearing helped congressmen maintain their mental health by sustaining a lively connection with hearth and home.[9]

---

[7]*GUS,* 14 Oct. 1789; Richard R. John, *Spreading the News: The American Postal System from Franklin to Morse* (Cambridge, Mass., 1995), pp. 32–33; Peter Silvester to Peter Van Schaack, 9 June 1789, Van Schaack Collection, NNC. For background on the subject of newspapers for members, see *DHFFC* 8:676–80.

[8]Nicholas to Brown, 12 Nov. 1789, Kentucky State Historical Society *Register* 41(1943): 3–4; Daniel George to Thatcher, 5 June 1789, Thatcher Papers, MSaE; Daniel Davis to Thatcher, 9 Oct. 1788, Thatcher Family Papers, MHi; William Lithgow, Jr., to Thatcher, 12 Feb. 1789, Thatcher Papers, MSaE; Thatcher to Robert Southgate, 1 July 1789, Scarborough Manuscripts, MeHi; Daniel Cody to Thatcher, 16 May 1789, Chamberlain Collection, MB.

[9]Wingate to Mary Wingate Wiggins, 27 Feb. 1790, Wingate Papers, MH; Wadsworth to Catherine Wadsworth, 20 June 1789, Wadsworth Papers, CtHi.

The Survival of Members' Papers

Although the number of extant letters by and to members documenting the work of the First Federal Congress is impressive, they constitute only a proportion of those actually written. The papers and correspondence of northern members have survived in far greater numbers than have those of southern members. We believe that this has far more to do with those members' sense of history than with the ravages of the Civil War and find it reflected in the contrasting recordkeeping practices of Senate Secretary Samuel A. Otis (of Massachusetts) and House Clerk John Beckley (of Virginia).[10] Not to be forgotten is the powerful influence of a humid climate on even the best paper.

Although we have not attempted to trace in detail what happened to the papers of the men who served in the First Federal Congress, certain information has come to light about how those manuscripts survived (or disappeared) during the more than two centuries since Congress sat. All or portions of the papers of some members were sold on the autograph market (many of these now reside in manuscript repositories): Fitzsimons, Paterson, Gerry, and Langdon are examples. Burke made sure that his papers did not survive by ordering his executor to burn them. Dalton's papers burned in 1794 along with the ship that was transporting his possessions to the future District of Columbia, where he was a partner in the mercantile firm of Tobias Lear and Company. Hawkins's papers, including his diary of Senate proceedings during the first half of the 1790s, was lost when Creek Indians burned his home just after the War of 1812. Giles's papers burned with Richmond, and some of Butler's burned with New Orleans, both during the Civil War. Maclay made efforts to see that his papers survived, but only his diary is extant.

In a few cases the papers of a member—composed of incoming letters and sometimes retained copies of his outgoing letters (usually as drafts or copied into letterbooks) and miscellaneous documents—have survived relatively intact, although not necessarily in one place. The best examples of such collections are the papers of Langdon (most of which arrived at repositories in the 1990s), Adams, Thatcher, Goodhue, Sedgwick, Johnson, Wadsworth, Schuyler, King, Read, R. H. Lee, Madison (unique in that, when organizing papers in his retirement, he asked for and got back his letters to several prominent individuals), Monroe, Johnston, and Butler. Other examples, generally smaller in size and richer in the years before or after 1789–1791, are the papers of Wingate, Gerry, T. Foster, Sherman, Trumbull, Boudinot, Morris, C. Carroll, Stone, Brown, Izard, Smith (S.C.), and Sumter.

---

[10] For a discussion of Beckley's recordkeeping habits, see *DHFFC* 3:vii–xv.

Because it was an age when few people retained copies of outgoing personal and political correspondence, the actual letters written by members of the First Congress are generally found in the collections of their recipients. This is where we located many of the letters of Wingate, Ames, Huntington, Sherman, Clymer, Fitzsimons, Hartley, Wynkoop, Smith (Md.), Bland, R. B. Lee, Page, White, Smith (S.C.), Tucker, and Baldwin. The two most fruitful recipients' collections are the thirty-five letters of Bland, Page, and Tucker in the Tucker-Coleman Papers at the College of William and Mary and the at least sixty-nine letters by members of the Pennsylvania delegation, in addition to a handful by members from seven other states, in the Tench Coxe Papers at the Historical Society of Pennsylvania.

Two other collections once contained dozens of letters written by Pennsylvania members of the First Congress, but they were removed and sold on the autograph letter market. Benjamin Rush's papers were willed to the Library Company of Philadelphia by his son, but before they arrived a family member removed the letters of prominent individuals. These letters were sold in 1943 and 1944; included were 116 letters written during the First Congress by Adams, Boudinot, Madison, Maclay, Clymer, Fitzsimons, and the Muhlenberg brothers. We have been fortunate in locating texts for all but twenty-one of these very revealing political letters. The papers of John Nicholson, comptroller general of Pennsylvania, sat unguarded in the basement of the Pennsylvania capitol for decades after the state sequestered them around 1800.[11] Beginning at least as early as the 1880s, hundreds of letters (particularly those by Morris, a signer of the Declaration of Independence, the Articles of Confederation, and the Constitution) made their way to the New York autograph market. The collection at one time probably contained more than the twenty First Federal Congress letters from Morris, Hartley, Hiester, and Maclay (including drafts of some of his newspaper articles) that we have located.

Whether in their own papers or in the collections of their correspondents, the letter-writing efforts of certain members have survived in greater numbers than have those of others. Goodhue holds the record (more than 150); more than fifty letters each survive from Ames, Fitzsimons, Gerry, Hartley, R. H. Lee, Maclay, Madison, Morris, Sedgwick, Sherman, Smith (Md.), Thatcher, Wingate, and Wynkoop. By contrast, for members who served in all three sessions, none or fewer than five letters survive from Coles, Floyd, A. Foster, Gale, Grout, Gunn, Hathorn, Henry, Huger, Laurance, Mathews, Schureman, Scott, Seney, Sinnickson, Sturges, Sumter, Van Rensselaer, and Vining.

---

[11] For more on the Pennsylvania delegation's letters, see Kenneth R. Bowling, "The Biddle Sale of Rush Papers and Other Letters from Pennsylvania Members of the First Federal Congress to Their Constituents," *Manuscripts* 24(Summer 1972):172–81.

For details on the surviving letters of each member, see the end of the member's biographical sketch in *DHFFC* 14.

Circular Letters

Circular letters bridge the gap between personal letters and newspapers, combining the specificity and immediacy of the first with the periodicity and distribution of the second. Ames's frequent letters to George R. Minot employ an easy, seemingly artless style; he would write, in fact, "as I am used to converse with you."[12] Yet, despite the tone of intimacy, Ames never wrote Minot without knowing that his letters would be shared with the other members of the "Wednesday Night Club," a social gathering of his male friends in Boston. Goodhue's frequent letters to Michael Hodge regularly updated an important audience of businessmen along the North Shore of Massachusetts, while excerpts from Thatcher's letters to his friend Thomas B. Wait regularly and expectedly found their way into the pages of Wait's Portland, Maine, *Cumberland Gazette.* These three examples show how letters to strategically placed sources at home functioned as virtual circular letters.

Only a few First Congress letters share a resemblance to the circular letter format subsequently followed, primarily by southern and western congressmen, during the later Federalist and Jeffersonian eras. Narrowly defined, they were reports and observations on the overall proceedings of Congress, not merely on a single issue. Typically addressed to an unidentified "friend" or "Sir," they were composed intentionally for a wider dissemination and were frequently reprinted in newspapers. Sevier's letter of 10 January 1791 and Steele's of 27 January 1791 are examples of this type. In a broader sense, Sumter's letter of 24 August 1789 also qualifies as a circular letter: it did not circulate initially in print, but it was clearly intended for several readers and ultimately enjoyed wide newspaper distribution, first in Charleston, South Carolina's *City Gazette* and later in at least Boston and Providence, Rhode Island, newspapers.[13]

The Content of the Letters

The correspondence published in this series illuminates several of the fundamental themes that have continued to resonate throughout American political discourse. Letters discussing the issues of the power of removal and the establishment of a national bank reveal the First Congress engaged in

---

[12] Ames to George R. Minot, 23 June 1789, *Ames* 1:54–56.

[13] For a fuller treatment, see Noble E. Cunningham, Jr., ed., *Circular Letters of Congressmen to Their Constituents, 1789–1829,* 3 vols. (Chapel Hill, N.C., 1978), 1:xv–xlix.

the interpretation of the Constitution by legislative construction. When congressmen and their constituents exchanged views on assuming the states' Revolutionary War debts and on the power of the federal courts, federalism and states' rights were at issue. Overt sectionalism peaked for almost a year after the subject of locating the seat of government was formally introduced in August 1789, while distributing the burden of impost duties and peopling and protecting the West sparked sectional conflict almost from the moment Congress convened. Reconciling the powers of the executive and the judiciary with republican ideals, which had fueled so much Antifederalist anxiety during the ratification period, remained a serious concern as Congress turned to the organization of the "great departments," the structure and jurisdiction of the judiciary, and a suitable nonhereditary title for the President. At the same time, keeping Congress's own house in order provoked a highly charged exchange over congressional salaries and the perceived proliferation of congressional officers. Punctuating these broad recurring themes are details about the legislative history of many bills and candid tête-à-tête revelations of behind-the-scenes compromises, as well as procedural maneuvers unrecorded in either the official *Journals* or the unofficial printed debates.

The largest single subject treated in the correspondence is the age-old pursuit of appointed public office. Even would-be "placemen" who personally attended on congressmen at the seat of government often pressed their case with letters of recommendation from the home district. The Constitution calls for the President to nominate federal officials and the Senate to confirm the nominations; consequently, letters of application or recommendation addressed to congressmen were generally forwarded by them to the President. In some cases, applicants launched letter-writing campaigns and congressmen accumulated veritable dossiers on the careers and pretensions of job seekers. Often the only special qualifications cited were patriotism and poverty.

Dim corners previously deemed peripheral to the "public sphere" are illuminated in these letters to show congressmen's multidimensional lives. In addition to their public service and the ideologies that influenced their politics, portions of the letters printed in this series also convey information relating to members' ongoing family, professional, and financial concerns.

A congressman's most intimate correspondence was often with his spouse and kin at home. But leaving out bachelors, widowers, and members who resided with their families at the seat of government, only slightly more than half the members of the First Congress had wives at home, and correspondence is extant for only fourteen of those. The salutations and closings of many of these letters are evidence of the late eighteenth century's significant development of marital partners into "friends." A prudish Congregationalist like Huntington would always address his wife Anne as "Dear

Mrs. Huntington." But others such as Few and Wadsworth consistently addressed their wives as "Dear Friend," while Sedgwick rarely addressed his wife of fifteen years by anything less affectionate than "My Dearest Love." Nicknames playfully convey some of this new collegiality, such as "Affy" for Paterson's wife Euphemia or the more obvious "Getty" for Gertrude Read. Well into middle age Elias and Hannah Boudinot still referred to each other by their courting names, "Narcissus" and "Eugenia."[14]

In her husband's absence, the congressional wife at home exercised considerable autonomy over matters of domestic economy. Yet the letters show that congressmen continued to attempt to exercise some direction over important household matters, such as the education of their children. Butler maintained an iron grip on the education of his only son Thomas, sent at a young age to school in England. Thatcher's approach was probably more representative of those with adolescent children. He accepted the inevitable division of labor and deferred to his wife's implementation of the passages he had begun transcribing for her in February 1789, from his readings of the educational theories of Lord Kames.[15]

Details from business-related correspondence are omitted from this edition. But high among the nonpolitical themes sounded in these letters is the ever-present financial burden some congressmen experienced from the necessary suspension or curtailment of their normal business activities. Large southern plantation owners like Butler and Izard, much of whose business was already in the hands of full-time overseers, were the least inconvenienced by the demands of public office. Lawyers like Sedgwick and Silvester, by contrast, kept their practices alive by corresponding with partners or protégés about caseloads and circuit court appearances scheduled for congressional recesses. Merchants like Morris and manufacturers like Wadsworth continued to manage their affairs by an attenuated but diligent attention to business. Morris was aided by the clerk he kept with him at the seat of government, but other merchant members relied more on their partners or designated proxies. "I would have you do in every particular relating to my business as you think will be for the best," Goodhue wrote his brother Stephen, also a merchant, shortly after arriving for the first session. "Whether it should turn out so or not I shall be content," he added, but hedged his bets by supplying continual advice thereafter about buying and selling shipments of goods.[16]

---

[14] For more on this aspect of congressional history, see William C. diGiacomantonio, "A Congressional Wife at Home: The Case of Sarah Thatcher, 1787–1792," in Kenneth R. Bowling and Donald R. Kennon, eds., *Neither Separate nor Equal: Congress in the 1790s* (Athens, Ohio, 2000), pp. 155–80.

[15] George to Sarah Thatcher, 18, 22 Feb. 1789, Thatcher Family Papers, MHi.

[16] Benjamin to Stephen Goodhue, 8 April 1789, Goodhue Family Papers, MSaE.

Franking and the Mail

The value to the nation of congressional correspondence had been recognized as early as 8 November 1775, when the Second Continental Congress passed an ordinance "that all letters to and from the delegates of the United Colonies, during the sessions of Congress, pass, and be carried free of charge." The ordinance survived subsequent restructuring of the post office department and remained in force up through the First Federal Congress. The one instance in which the practice is known to have been questioned in Congress underscores its importance within the political culture of the time. In December 1782, with franking privileges being extended to a widening circle of civil servants and departmental officers of the army, Congress defeated a call for the total abolition of the frank or its limitation to a set number or weight of letters. Congressmen arguing against the proposal pointed out that delegates and citizens of their respective states would be unjustly taxed by the expense in direct proportion to their distance from the seat of government and that an abridgement of the frank would confine a general knowledge of public affairs to the immediate vicinity of Congress. Both arguments drew force from the looming sectional dispute over the location of the seat of government.[17] In reply to the very practical consideration of lost revenue, congressmen in 1782 maintained that little, if any, additional revenue would be raised if the frank were withdrawn because the number and size of their letters would be correspondingly reduced. They rather disingenuously added that franked letters "however voluminous did not exclude from the mail any private letters" subject to postage. The various resolutions extending the frank to civil servants stipulated that it was only for letters written in an official capacity. Letters "on public service" were expected to bear an endorsement to that effect, until Congress—supposing that the endorsement subtly impugned the honesty of its users—resolved in February 1783 that the frank would no longer be withheld "for want of the words *On public service.*"[18]

A major argument against the frank was revenue loss from its excessive use. Opponents claimed that the losses prevented the post office department from expanding service via post roads into the interior, again linking the debate to underlying sectional tensions. The losses incurred during William Bedlow's tenure as postmaster of New York City while the Confederation Congress resided there from 1785 to 1789 amounted to £475 in arrearages to the government. In March 1790 he was forced to petition the First

---

[17] *JCC* 3:342; Madison's "Notes on Debates," *PJM* 5:371–72.
[18] *JCC* 23:863, 24:157. In anticipation of "numerous letters and packets" being addressed to him "in consequence of his late command, and on matters foreign to his private concerns," George Washington was granted franking privileges for life in April 1784 (*JCC* 26:314).

Congress for a temporary suspension of legal proceedings to recover the debt from his personal estate. Weeks later, in the only explicit reference to the frank known to have been made on the floor during the First Congress, Wadsworth argued that the postal department could be more lucrative "under proper regulation," calculating that seven-eighths of its revenue was lost to private carriers and the frank.[19]

The franking of congressional correspondence was so well established by the time of the First Federal Congress that constituents and congressmen alike invited abuse by applying the broadest possible interpretation of "public service." Congressmen franked letters that were all personal business but for a line or two referring to the anticipated date of adjournment or the final vote on a bill. In violation of the standing post office ordinance engaging them "upon their honour not to frank or enclose any letters but their own,"[20] congressmen often enclosed or forwarded under their frank private letters to or from constituents. Doing so became in effect a type of constituent service, as much as presenting petitions or filing for pension benefits.

A notable example is the merchant Samuel Emery. Residing in Philadelphia and Baltimore in 1789, he frequently wrote franked letters to Thatcher with enclosures for business associates in Boston, which Thatcher dutifully forwarded under his frank. Emery rationalized that he was not subtracting from the post office's revenue because "I assure you If the postage was to be paid I should not write." The newly created justices of the Supreme Court did not enjoy franking privileges, but at least once Dalton compensated for this by franking a letter from Mrs. Sarah Jay to her husband the chief justice, who was then on circuit in New Hampshire.[21]

Preventing abuse of the frank may have been difficult for postal officials, but they were successful in enforcing standards in other ways. Congressmen could receive or mail franked letters only from the seat of government and when Congress was scheduled to be in session (although they did not have to wait for the appearance of a quorum). White left New York City for Virginia before the close of the first session and had to ask House Clerk John Beckley to redirect his mail under Madison's frank. Williamson reminded constituents that they would be charged for letters posted during an upcoming recess. Abigail Adams, who forgot this, sent a long letter to her sister under the Vice President's frank before the second session convened and "had the mortification to receive it back again." Gerry apologized for the expense this temporary suspension imposed on Samuel Hodgdon in Philadelphia for a letter Gerry was forwarding from a mutual friend in New

---

[19] *DHFFC* 13:965. For Bedlow's petition, see *DHFFC* 8:239–40.
[20] *JCC* 3:342.
[21] Emery to Thatcher, 23 April 1789, Thatcher Papers, MHi; Sarah to John Jay, 13 May 1790, Jay Papers, NNC.

York, while Johnson used avoidance of the expense as an excuse for waiting three months before replying to one correspondent. A letter to his son that Johnson had postmarked five days earlier was nevertheless franked one day before the scheduled convening of the second session, suggesting that the postmaster had discretion in such matters.[22]

The convenience of the frank was partially offset by the inherent risks that came with a reliance on the public mail. Not the least of these, in the perception of some congressmen at least, was the threat of deliberate tampering by those "more curious than moral." "I suspect foul play," Joseph Whipple wrote to Langdon, in trying to explain the possible loss of a letter. Goodhue feared the same and routinely enclosed in letters to his brother Stephen letters to others "which I do not chuse should go otherwise." There is a fainter echo of this suspicion in a letter to Anthony Wayne that Madison entrusted to a "casual conveyance" because "it is rendered ineligible by the delay & uncertainty" of the public mail.[23]

During the last days of the Confederation Congress, New York's postmaster customarily delivered members' mail to their desks at City Hall (the future Federal Hall). The practice seems to have been continued into the First Congress, since an editorial writer signed "Look Out" urged the proprietors of the mail stages to arrive by 2:00 P.M. so that members could get their mail before adjourning at 3:00 P.M. (Days later one of the proprietors defended the guild, insisting that the mail had only been late once.) The frequency of scheduled mail pickup and delivery was also tailored to congressmen's convenience. Until the first of May, mail left for and arrived from points south two afternoons per week and points north and east two evenings per week. Thereafter, mail left and arrived three times per week. The first session of Congress having adjourned a week before the post office moved from 8 Wall Street, virtually in the shadow of Federal Hall, members could not participate in the popular outcry raised against the remoteness of the new location at Broadway and Liberty Street, three blocks behind Federal Hall.[24]

---

[22] John Brown to Harry Innes, 28 Sept. 1789, Harry Innes Papers, DLC; White to Madison, 9 Aug. 1789, Madison Papers, DLC; Williamson to John G. Blount, 3 Aug. 1790, Blount Papers, Nc-Ar; Abigail Adams to Mary Cranch, 5 Jan. 1790, Abigail Adams Letters, MWA; Gerry to Hodgdon, 13 Jan. 1790, Mitten Autograph Collection, Indiana Historical Society, Indianapolis; Johnson to (unknown), 8 Jan. 1790, and Johnson to Robert Charles Johnson, 3 Jan. 1790, both in Johnson Papers, CtHi.

[23] Philip to Catherine Schuyler, 24 Feb. 1791, Ford Autograph Collection, Minnesota Historical Society, St. Paul; Whipple to Langdon, 12 Aug. 1789, Sturgis Family Papers, MH; Benjamin to Stephen Goodhue, 20 Aug. 1789, Goodhue Family Papers, MSaE; Madison to Wayne, 31 July 1789, Wayne Manuscripts, PHi.

[24] "Look Out," *NYDA,* 3 June 1789; [Philadelphia] *Federal Gazette,* 12 Jan. 1789; *New York,* pp. 84–85.

How Members Lived

The cultural, social, and physical milieu of New York City in 1789 and 1790 provides the necessary context for understanding the letters congressmen sent forth from that time and place. The city occupied only the extreme southern tip of Manhattan Island from the Battery northward barely one-third of the way to Greenwich Village and east along the East River only as far as the present site of Manhattan Bridge (although city streets were platted up to the site of the Williamsburg Bridge). Readers will find some familiarity with comments describing the seat of government as polluted, odoriferous, crime ridden, and gridlocked.[25]

As many as half of the members of the First Congress found shelter in eight of the city's boarding houses; most of the remaining members took up residence among a dozen other boarding houses. Here they competed for space with the swelling number of pension-, patent-, and office-seekers drawn to the seat of government. Congressmen paid a fixed rate of four to five dollars per week for room and board, with extra charges for liquor, firewood, and candles. Leases were generally signed on the first of February, and moving day was the first of May. Members like Izard, who had brought their families and had the money to house them, rented entire homes. Others may have been persuaded by the rare advertisement offering "a genteel house, within five minutes walk of the Federal Building, fit for three or four gentlemen of Congress." A few members, such as Wynkoop and the Muhlenbergs, stayed with family already residing in New York. Griffin and his wife rented a house on the outskirts of the city. Only two members settled outside the city proper: R. H. Lee lived in Greenwich Village, and Vice President John Adams took possession of Richmond Hill, even farther up the Greenwich Road in the present-day Charlton-King-Vandam Historic District just north of the Holland Tunnel.[26]

A member's official day started when the chambers went into session around eleven in the morning, unless he was serving on a committee, which generally met at nine. Sessions adjourned between three and four in the afternoon. Several congressmen are known to have written from their desks on the floor of the chamber, suggesting the occasional tedium of business

---

[25] The most thorough description of members' daily lives in New York is Kenneth R. Bowling's "New York City, Capital of the United States, 1785–1790," in Stephen Schecter and Wendell Tripp, eds., *World of the Founders: New York Communities in the Federal Period* (Albany, N.Y., 1990), pp. 1–23.

[26] Frank Monaghan and Marvin Lowenthal, *This Was New York: The Nation's Capital in 1789* (Garden City, N.Y., 1943), p. 18; Ebenezer Hazard to John Langdon, 27 Dec. 1788, Langdon Papers, NhPoA; *NYDA*, 26 Mar. 1789; Stephen L. Schechter, ed., *The Reluctant Pillar: New York and the Adoption of the Federal Constitution* (Troy, N.Y., 1985), p. 217.

from which letter writing offered an opportune escape. The lax enforcement of quorum requirements during routine business permitted more literal escapes to meet with other members, lobbyists, or visiting constituents in the lobbies and porticoes of Federal Hall. State delegation caucuses met off the premises, usually at a member's lodging or at any of the city's many taverns. The Pennsylvanians, for example, whose frequent caucusing is well documented by Daniel Hiester and William Maclay, agreed early in the second session to meet every Monday evening at Simons's Tavern, next door to Federal Hall.[27]

Congressmen's letters indicate an eagerness to vary the rhythm of their days through several recreational outlets. Daylong or weekend excursions outside the city included hiking the New Jersey Palisades, exploring the old fortifications at West Point, ferrying to Flatbush, Long Island, and fishing at Sandy Hook, New Jersey. Inside the city, members enjoyed afternoon or evening promenades along Broadway and the Bowling Green or explored the tea gardens and bath houses. Some may have ventured to either of the two "red light" districts located at the extreme margins of town: Topsail Town in the southernmost Dock Ward and the other in the easternmost Out Ward, where the Bowery was born.[28]

New York's John Street Theater was the single most popular public amusement in the city—with the exception of the House gallery itself.[29] In 1789 the theater's resident Old American Company boasted a repertoire of seventy-four comedies, farces, comic operas, tragedies, and pantomimes by William Shakespeare, Joseph Addison, Richard Sheridan, and others. It was a type of entertainment that many congressmen were prevented from enjoying at home until after the widespread repeal of anti-theater laws beginning in Philadelphia in 1789. One New York paper accused the rival city of misplaced zeal for tempting congressmen by legalizing its theaters, since "few members of Congress have countenanced the Theater in this city, which is no small evidence of their steadiness and wisdom." The writer was speaking of members of the departing Confederation Congress, but it is not known how many members of the First Congress deviated from that sober practice. The season offered performances three nights a week from April to December.[30]

Members took stock of each other and the administration not only over daily dinner at their lodgings or taverns but also at the numerous dancing

[27] DHFFC 9:207.

[28] Monaghan and Lowenthal, *This Was New York*, pp. 37, 127.

[29] For a fuller treatment of the members' (and visitors') experiences of Federal Hall, see DHFFC 12:xi–xviii, and "Preparing Federal Hall" DHFFC 15:26–31. For the official record of Congress's use of New York's renovated City Hall, see DHFFC 8:685–91.

[30] Kenneth Silverman, *A Cultural History of the American Revolution* (New York, 1987), pp. 592, 597–98; [Massachusetts] *Salem Mercury*, 17 March 1789; *NYDA*, 10 July 1789; *New York*, pp. 171–72.

balls, presidential dinners, and weekly presidential levees around which the nascent Republican Court revolved. "It is as gay as any Court in Christendom," thought visiting Baltimorean Otho Holland Williams.[31] By the second session, the Court's reception circuit included Monday nights at Abigail Adams's, Tuesdays at Lady Temple's (the wife of the British consul), Wednesdays at Lucy Knox's, and Thursdays at Sarah Jay's; the week culminated in Martha Washington's famous Friday evening levees. Some members felt themselves slaves to the ceremonial parade of receptions, social calls, and obligatory return visits; their letters express a sense of frustration, fatigue, and even scandal at the expense of time and money. But historians of the period are increasingly adept at assessing the influence peddled and brokered at these quasi-political venues.[32]

---

[31] Williams to Philip Thomas, 7 June 1789, Williams Papers, MdHi.

[32] Fine analyses of this important historiographic theme are Catherine Allgor's *Parlor Politics: In Which the Ladies of Washington Help Build a City and a Government* (Charlottesville, Va., 2000) and, for the period of the First Federal Congress and earlier, various unpublished papers presented by Fredrika J. Teute and David S. Shields, including "The Confederation Court," presented at the North American Society for Court Studies Conference, Boston, September 2000, and "The Republican Court and the Historiography of a Women's Domain in the Public Sphere," presented at the Society for Historians of the Early American Republic annual meeting, Boston, July 1994.

Presented here are three volumes of the final series in the *Documentary History of the First Federal Congress, 1789–1791 (DHFFC)*. The eight volumes of official records and the six-volume debate series have illuminated the official actions and words of this seminal Congress. Eight volumes of correspondence and other unofficial documents (three volumes for the Second Session presented here) shed new light on how the founding generation viewed the constitutional issues and sectional conflicts facing it, as well as the challenge of defining federalism. These documents also provide information on the behind-the-scenes political negotiations that laid the foundation for First Federal Congress (FFC) decisions. Particularly important for understanding the evolution of the member-constituent relationship, they show how the people viewed the role of their representatives to the national government and how members saw their jobs as representatives of the people of their districts and states. These letters and documents are vitally important to rounding out the published record of the key institutions and individuals of the Revolutionary and Founding Eras.

The editors of the *DHFFC* have dealt with a tremendous variety of documentary evidence. The diversity of the extant manuscripts and our goal of creating a documentary history, rather than simply a documentary edition, has necessitated a redefinition of editorial method with each new series, and sometimes within a series. This editorial method and its predecessors have been crafted to assist the reader in understanding what is being presented, what editorial choices were made, and why.

Selection

As a documentary history of an institution, the *DHFFC* focuses exclusively upon that institution and its members. Therefore, it does not seek to publish all correspondence to or from the members of the FFC in its entirety, communications about the workings of the other branches of the federal government, or even public opinion about this Congress. More than 13,000 documents have been collected for the FFC correspondence and newspaper files. Our challenge has been to sift through these documents using a selection process that would ensure the inclusion of every piece of information relevant to the history of the FFC. Our selection process for these volumes was governed by the need to use all documents that:

1. Provide insight into the actions of the FFC and its members;
2. Convey information about members' lives on and off the floor, family concerns, character, political philosophies, and other viewpoints;

3. Reveal what constituents, friends, family, and others told members about events and attitudes outside the seat of government relating to the business of Congress; or

4. Demonstrate what constituents expected of their government and their representatives and the responses to those expectations.

Although the editors were tempted to include items that fall into the category of public opinion, such as letters among nonmembers making observations on the actions of the new Congress or the thousands of newspaper opinion pieces published both at and outside the seat of government, we resisted that temptation. In the case of the newspaper pieces, the First Federal Congress Project (FFCP) has prepared an online resource that provides both virtual and intellectual access to these commentaries for the period of the FFC.

Nearly all the documents in these volumes fit into one of the following categories:

1. Letters to or from members;

2. Letters written by an individual at the seat of government that relate information not available from other sources about what went on, on or off the floor of Congress; or

3. Correspondence printed in newspapers that may have been written by or to a member or that presents new information about Congress or its members.

The editors' goal is to present all correspondence as concisely as possible. Therefore, only material relevant to the selection criteria stated above appears in the volumes. Four methods of presentation of the text of, or information from, the correspondence have been employed.

1. Letters that are entirely relevant have been printed in full, with the occasional exception of a very short letter that is summarized and/or quoted in a calendar entry.

2. Relevant portions of other letters are excerpted. To prevent the reader from confusing a spot where text was omitted by the editors with a place where text had been omitted in the copy text (such as an earlier printing of a no longer extant manuscript or an auction catalog summary), we used asterisks to indicate our omissions and ellipses to indicate the omissions of others. Where possible, endnotes indicate where a full printed text of the excerpted letter can be found. These endnotes also indicate the subject of the omitted material (e.g., state politics), if such material might have influenced a member in his personal life or in his role as a legislator.

3. Letters that have only small relevant portions are calendared with both

the location of the original and the source for a printed version, if one exists, provided in the entry. Quotations from such letters are used extensively in the calendars. Letters to members, particularly those from office seekers, are calendared more often than are letters from members. Diary entries are usually calendared, as are members' letters that we know of from other sources but that have not been located.

4. A relatively small number of letters are mostly repetitive of another letter by the same author (primarily Benjamin Goodhue, who sometimes wrote two to four similar letters on the same day). The endnote to the most extensive and informative letter from that individual for that date also deals with these repetitive letters.

Virtually every letter *from* a member of the FFC written during this period has been dealt with in one of these four ways. As a rule, only exclusively business correspondence has been omitted. Representative Jeremiah Wadsworth and Senator Robert Morris, in particular, have extant business correspondence. Occasionally, the business of members intersected with the financial business of the federal government, and we have been careful to include letters that relate to such intersections (e.g., the arrival of member-owned ships containing a cargo about to be subject to a federal impost duty or evidence of speculation in federal debt certificates by members). Other letters that relate primarily to private business but contain some information that meets our standards for inclusion are calendared.

Vice President John Adams presided over the Senate every day as an activist chair, providing his own comments and sometimes striving to steer the course of events. Therefore, we have treated him as a member of the FFC and used the same criteria for selecting correspondence from and to him as for the other members.

Letters *to* members have been selected for what they tell us about topics such as public perceptions of Congress's actions, public expectations of the federal government, how constituents sought to influence legislation, and family matters that could affect the well-being of the member at the seat of government.

One of the unique features of volumes 15–17, and to a lesser extent of volumes 18–22, is the many letters of application for federal offices. Letters relating to the staffing of the new federal government compose a significant part of the extant correspondence, in part because President George Washington preserved them well, and they now constitute series seven of his papers at the Library of Congress. Washington generally did not reply to applicants for office. In cases where the letter was from someone he knew, Washington replied with a standard response, perhaps best seen in his reply to former secretary of foreign affairs Robert R. Livingston:

I plainly foresaw that that part of my duty which obliged me to nominate persons to offices, would, in many instances, be the most irksome and unpleasing; for however desirous I might be of giving a proof of my friendship—and whatever might be his expectations, grounded upon the amity which had subsisted between us, I was fully determined to keep myself free from every engagement that could embarrass me in discharging this part of my administration. I have therefore, uniformly declined giving any decisive answer to the numerous applications which have been made to me; being resolved, whenever I am called upon to nominate persons for those offices which have been created, that I will do it with a sole view to the public good, and shall bring forward those who, upon *every* consideration, and from the best information I can obtain, will in my Judgment be most likely to answer that great end. (ALS, Livingston Papers, NHi)

We do not include office seekers' letters to Washington, other than calendar entries for those letters that mention members of Congress. Many are printed in or commented upon in volumes of *The Papers of George Washington: Presidential Series.* All are calendared in Gaillard Hunt, *Calendar of Applications and Recommendations for Office during the Presidency of George Washington* (Washington, D.C., 1901). Also excluded are office-seeking letters addressed to Vice President Adams, unless they relate to Senate staff positions or mention a member of Congress as a reference.

We include the many office-seeking letters written to congressmen or senators. These are often summarized in the calendars, rather than printed or excerpted, unless the content is of particular interest or importance or other parts of the letter are relevant to the FFC. Letters sent to Washington by FFC members that either forward correspondence from office seekers or support or oppose particular applicants have been printed, as have lists of job applicants from their states that members prepared for the President.

Certain individuals at the seat of government clearly had access to "insider" information because of their interaction with Congress or relationships with members of Congress (e.g., residing at the same boarding house). The relevant letters of the most obvious of these people (George Washington, Thomas Jefferson, and Alexander Hamilton) have already been published elsewhere and will generally only be calendared. Henry Knox's letters, which have not been published, are often excerpted or calendared. A small number of letters from other individuals provide information about the Congress or its members not found elsewhere. Principal among these "people in the know" were presidential assistant William Jackson, Ohio Company lobbyist Manasseh Cutler, Hugh Williamson, North Carolina's agent at the seat of government before becoming a Representative from that state, and New York land speculator and financier William Constable. Other individuals deserve special mention. First Session letters by Senator

Richard Henry Lee's brother, Arthur Lee, a member of the Board of Treasury and one of the most opinionated politicians of the era, contain secondhand information about what occurred behind the Senate's closed doors. During the Second Session, Philadelphian John Pemberton, head of the Quaker delegation that brought petitions to Congress in early 1790, who then stayed to lobby for the cause of regulating the slave trade, is responsible for the longest and most revealing of the letters by people in the know. The Comte de Moustier, French minister to the United States during the First Session, reporting to his government about events in New York and the operation of the new government, wrote the most informative letters of anyone in the diplomatic corps. Moustier's replacement, Louis Guillaume Otto, also wrote interesting and informative reports, some of which are translated for the first time in volumes 18–20.

Occasionally, letters from members or informed visitors to the seat of government were printed in a newspaper in their district or state. The FFCP staff has searched every extant newspaper in publication in the United States during the FFC to locate these letters and will publish all letters datelined to or from New York that reveal information about the Congress or convey information that could influence the public business because they might have been written to or by a member. Additionally, articles from newspapers, particularly those published at the seat of government, that shed light on the actions of Congress or mention its members are included. For all newspaper items we note in the location notes the towns and cities where a reprinting occurred.

Letters or portions of letters that relate solely to petitions sent to the FFC are printed with the petition histories in volumes 7 and 8 of the *DHFFC*. These letters are calendared in this series.

Though Pennsylvania (until 1791), Delaware, and New Hampshire each called their governor "president," we are using the title "governor" for those chief executives to avoid any confusion with the President of the United States.

Members of Congress kept detailed records of their personal expenses at the seat of government. Outstanding as sources for the social history of the early republic, only a few have survived; the most extensive are those of Elias Boudinot (New York Public Library), Pierce Butler (Historical Society of Pennsylvania), and Daniel Hiester (Berks County Historical Society). We are calendaring only those items from these accounts that shed light on the work of the FFC.

Organization

The volumes are arranged chronologically, with each month of a session as a separate chapter. Each day's entry begins with information about the weather, if available, taken from diaries kept at the seat of government. The letters that are printed in full or excerpted appear in alphabetical order by the writer's last name. Relevant diary entries and newspaper articles follow. Each daily entry concludes with a calendar of additional relevant "Other Documents" ordered in the same way as the printed documents. When possible, newspaper pieces have been printed or calendared on the date that the item was written rather than the date of the newspaper's publication. For example, an item printed in the [Philadelphia] *Federal Gazette* on 24 August and headlined "From a Correspondent in New York, 18 August" would appear on 18 August. If the date of the item could not be determined, it appears under the date of the newspaper publication. Each chapter concludes with undated items for that month.

Correspondence from October and November 1789 that relates primarily to Second Session business is printed here. All of the relevant December 1789 intersession correspondence appears in volume 18 as well.

Source Texts and Transcription Policy

The recipient's copy of a letter is our source text of choice. Retained or file copies of letters are used only if a recipient copy could not be located. Contemporary or later printings of the letter have been used if they are the only available source for the text of the letter as it was received. If the editors believe, or at least suspect, that a draft letter was actually turned into a letter that was sent but no text of the letter is extant, the draft is used as the source text. Finally, there are cases where all that is known about a letter is contained in one or more auction catalog entries. As a service to researchers, we are printing all quotes contained in these difficult-to-locate catalog entries in full, even if they do not relate to the FFC.

The *DHFFC* has followed a policy of literal transcription, with only a few exceptions, which have been stated in each section on editorial method. This literal policy is continued in the correspondence series, with the following exceptions:

1. In order to save space and because the information is provided in the headings or endnotes, datelines, salutations, and complimentary closings have been eliminated. Unusual salutations and complimentary closings are quoted in the endnote.

2. Superscript letters have been lowered and periods have been supplied at the end of abbreviations. Abbreviated words with tildes over them have been silently expanded.

3. Periods have been supplied at the end of any paragraph that either had no terminal punctuation or ended with some other mark, such as a dash.

Where there were two forms of punctuation at one place in the manuscript, the editors have chosen between them.

4. Obvious typographical errors in printed documents have been silently corrected.

5. In cases where an opening or closing quotation mark was missing in the manuscript, the editors have provided the missing mark if possible.

6. Words that were inserted above the line were silently lowered and inserted in the text.

Capitalization was frequently a judgment call, but any initial letter that was not clearly lower case was capitalized. Words crossed out in the text are printed with a line through them. Brackets indicate letters or words that are now missing from the document or unreadable but were read by earlier editors. Bracketed and italicized words or phrases describe the original manuscript (e.g., [*torn*]), provide information about names or places (e.g., [*Samuel*] Adams), expand ambiguous abbreviations, or represent the editors' supposition as to the correct reading of words or parts of words that are illegible or physically missing from the document.

Annotation

Each document printed or excerpted is followed by an endnote indicating the type and location of the manuscript or other source text and, when known, the place from which it was written (if not the seat of government), where it was addressed to, by whom it was carried, if it was postmarked and/or franked, and whether it was written over more than one day. As previously stated, the endnotes also contain such additional information as (1) the subject of omitted text if the subject might have influenced a member in his personal life or in his role as a legislator (e.g., state politics); (2) the existence of nearly identical letters composed by the same writer on the same day but for different recipients; (3) cross-references to certain *DHFFC* volumes, particularly volumes 2, 7, and 8; and (4) related information, usually from letters that are not published. Last, the endnote contains any general information about the physical condition of the letter (such as the fact that it is incomplete) and, in the case of excerpted and calendared items, the location of a full printing of the document if available. We do not provide information about other extant manuscript copies (e.g., drafts) unless they include major substantive variations. For calendared selections, this endnote material is incorporated into the entry heading.

The biographical gazetteer that appears in volume 20 is the heart of the annotation for volumes 18–20. The editors have chosen to put all the relevant biographical information about letter writers, recipients, and frequently mentioned persons in this central biographical gazetteer, rather than scatter it in footnotes throughout the volumes. Members of Congress are the exception, since extensive biographies of them, focused upon their FFC careers, have already been published in volume 14. In addition, entries for individuals who were covered in biographical gazetteers in previous volumes provide only basic and new information, with a cross reference to the previous biographical entry or entries.

Footnotes to the documents are intended primarily to clarify historical and literary references and identify contemporary events. Unless they are commonly used today, Latin and other foreign languages are translated; archaic words that we believe readers might have to look up are defined even if they appear in the *Oxford English Dictionary.* Other annotation appears in bracketed and italicized inserts in the text. This format was relied upon principally for providing the full names of identifiable geographical locations and individuals, except members of Congress, congressional staff, the President, and executive department heads.

Because these volumes are intended to be used in close conjunction with other *DHFFC* volumes, particularly the Journals (*DHFFC* 1–3) and the Legislative Histories (*DHFFC* 4–6), cross references are not routinely provided to the House and Senate actions documented there. However, where a letter's reference to a piece of legislation is obscure, bracketed italicized inserts are used to provide the standardized short bill title. Bill numbers are also inserted in cases where identically named bills are under consideration in nearly the same time frame. For example, bracketed inserts identify which of two Settlement of Accounts Bills was being referred to in letters written during the late May–early August 1790 period. A list of these short titles and bill numbers, the long titles that the Congress gave the bills, and the dates when they were introduced and signed, a useful tool for keeping track of what is being discussed, appears before the index to these volumes in volume 20. In addition, lists of dates when the House and Senate were in session, with the subjects considered on those dates, and a list of all federal appointees and the offices to which they were appointed appear in the front matter. A map of lower Manhattan in 1789 keyed to a list of members and the addresses where they lived in New York City appears after the Biographical Gazetteer.

Our aim in these volumes has been to concentrate on the work of the legislative branch of the federal government, and we have made no attempt to follow the actions of the executive, except where they intersect with those of the Congress through either the inclusion of executive documents or our annotation. For a fuller picture of how the new government operated, readers are advised to use the *Papers of George Washington: Presidential Series* in conjunction with the volumes of the *DHFFC.*

ACKNOWLEDGMENTS

This documentary edition would not have been possible without the assistance of numerous institutions and individuals. While the editors have always been very aware of our debt to others, the search for and editing of the documents in the correspondence volumes constantly reminded us of our dependence upon our sponsoring institutions, funders, editorial colleagues, archivists and manuscript curators, librarians, student assistants, and others who have supported and helped us over the life of this project.

The National Historical Publications and Records Commission (NHPRC) took the initiative to do some preliminary work for the First Federal Congress Project (FFCP) in the National Archives in the 1950s and '60s, established it with Dr. Linda Grant DePauw as its director at the George Washington University in 1966, and has cosponsored and funded it since then. We appreciate the faith that commission members, past and present, have had in the FFCP. NHPRC executive directors from Oliver W. Holmes, Jr., to current executive director Kathleen Williams have recognized the value of the *DHFFC* and steadfastly supported this project. We are grateful to them and to the numerous members of the commission's very helpful and professional staff who have assisted us over the years, including Lucy Barber, Timothy Connelly, and Michael Meier.

In recognition of their longtime support for documentary editions and for the *DHFFC* in particular, volume 18 is dedicated to former NHPRC executive director Frank G. Burke, former NHPRC deputy director and occasional acting executive director Roger Bruns, and our longtime program officer Mary Giunta. Their assistance, guidance, encouragement, and even the jokes and puns kept us going during some perilous times.

The George Washington University (GWU) has supported our work through both good times and some very tenuous periods, particularly during the 1980s, when the NHPRC's grant funds were proposed for "zeroing out" in eight consecutive federal budgets. We are grateful for this stable and long-term support and heartily thank former GWU president Stephen Joel Trachtenberg, current president Steven Knapp, former and current vice president for academic affairs Roderick French and Donald Lehman, associate vice president for research and graduate studies Carol Sigelman, former chief research officer Elliot Hirshman, and current and former Office of the Chief Research Officer staff members Kari Aldridge, Sandra Blair, Carol Rine Crane, Carol-Ann Courtney, Hal Gollos, Dan Harter, Patty Keyes, Mary Milbauer, David Razmgar, and Terri Taylor. Numerous other staff members in the Office of the Chief Research Officer have also guided and assisted us over the years, but we want to thank Helen Spencer in particular for her decades of attention to and support for the FFCP.

At GWU the project is part of the History Department in the Columbian College of Arts and Sciences (CCAS). Current dean Peg Barratt, former acting dean Diana Lipscomb, Assistant Dean for Administration Dan Cronin, and Associate Dean for Research and Outreach Geralyn Schulz have been supportive and assisted us with navigating the bureaucracy of research funding. Recent and current History Department chairs Edward Berkowitz, Muriel Atkin, Tyler Anbinder, and William Becker have supported our cause with the university and have taken steps to integrate the project into the department and its academic mission. Two of our current departmental colleagues, David Silverman and Richard Stott, have been particularly helpful in assisting our recruitment of student interns and volunteers, promoting the research opportunities at the FFCP, and providing opportunities for us to lecture to their classes. History Department executive assistant Michael Weeks has been a special friend to and benefactor of this project and cheerfully assists and advises us in numerous ways. Our colleagues at GWU's Eleanor Roosevelt and Human Rights Project, including that project's director, our longtime friend and advisor Allida Black, and assistant editor Mary Jo Binker, have given assistance and support that has been invaluable.

For most of the past two decades, the FFCP has been partially supported by grants from the National Endowment for the Humanities (NEH). The former director of the NEH Research Division, Jim Herbert, was always there to offer advice and support the work of documentary editions. Successive program officers Dan Jones, Michael Hall, and Lydia Medici have all efficiently assisted us during the application and review process. Alice Hudgins, Steve Veneziani, and Peter Scott of the Grants Management Office have been ready to patiently explain the intricacies of grants reporting and provide advice.

Private funding rounds out the financial support for this project. During the period when we were editing these volumes, two funders, the Marpat Foundation and the William Nelson Cromwell Foundation, have either supported special efforts such as the FFCP's online teacher's guide and our "Early American Opinion" website or matched NEH grants for work on the edition. We recognize the special encouragement given this project by Tom Richards, Joan Koven, and the late Ellen Bozman, all former or current members of the Marpat Foundation's board, and John D. Gordan III of the Cromwell Foundation's board.

It is especially pleasing to acknowledge financial contributions by former George Washington University student and friend of the FFCP Edward Buckley and by former George Mason University student Leslie C. Merkle. And we wish to belatedly acknowledge the pro bono contribution of Martin

Moulton in creating a computer-generated map of lower Manhattan in 1789 for volume 17 of the *DHFFC*.

The Johns Hopkins University Press has been committed to the DHFFC from the beginning, and we again thank former director Jack G. Goellner for his unwavering support, current director Kathleen Keane, history editor Bob Brugger, and, in particular, the production editor for these volumes, Linda Forlifer.

The work of documentary editors is made easier by the collegiality of the professionals who work in the field. Even before the founding of the Association for Documentary Editing (ADE) in 1979, there was much exchanging of information and cooperation among those engaged in historical documentary editing. The advent of the ADE served to strengthen that cooperation. We are thankful that our colleagues have assisted in many ways, including answering research questions, searching for FFC documents when visiting a repository, and sharing information about new finds. We are particularly indebted to fellow editors who work in the Revolutionary / Early National period of American history, and our thanks go to all editors who have assisted us: the current editor of the Adams Family Papers, James Taylor, who graciously agreed to publication of much important John Adams correspondence in these volumes, and other past and present editors at that project, including Richard Ryerson, Celeste Walker, and particularly Margaret Hogan; editors at the *Papers of Thomas Jefferson,* including Barbara Oberg, Martha King, James McClure, John Little, and Elaine Pascu; Mary Gallagher and Elizabeth Nuxoll of both the *Robert Morris Papers* and the *Papers of John Jay;* editors at the *Papers of James Madison,* Mary Hackett and David Mattern; the editors of the *Papers of George Washington,* including Theodore Crackel, Philander Chase, William Ferraro, Frank Grizzard, Edward Lengel, Mark Mastromarino, Christine Patrick, and Dorothy Twohig; Dennis Conrad of the *Papers of Nathanael Greene;* Mary Jeske of the *Papers of Charles Carroll;* Maeva Marcus, editor of the *Documentary History of the U.S. Supreme Court, 1789–1800;* the editors of the *Letters of Delegates to Congress, 1774–1789,* Paul H. Smith and Ronald M. Gephart; the editors of *The Documentary History of the First Federal Elections, 1788–1790,* Gordon DenBoer and Lucy Brown; editors Donna Kelly and Lang Baradell of the *Papers of James Iredell;* Melanie Miller of the *Diary of Gouverneur Morris;* Chuck Hobson, editor of the *Papers of John Marshall;* Charles Gehring of the New Netherlands Project; and Mary-Jo Kline, who has been associated with several editorial projects and assisted us in many ways over the decades.

Most importantly, we thank the editors of *The Documentary History of the Ratification of the Constitution.* The FFCP and the Ratification Project have been linked since their inception. In the early days the projects shared an office at the National Archives, and our document searches were joint.

After the projects were divided and relocated at GWU and the University of Wisconsin–Madison, the cooperation continued. We still share research information, search for both projects when visiting a repository, and generally cooperate in every way possible. We are very much indebted to John P. Kaminski for his commitment to maintaining this collegial relationship, as well as Gaspare J. Saladino, Richard Leffler, and Charles Schoenleber for their always willing assistance.

Because they were always there to assist in every way possible and to provide collegial advice, we have dedicated volume 19 to our friends and colleagues at the Founding Era and Founding Fathers projects named above.

The staff of the Independence National Historical Park, in particular Coxey Toogood, shared much information about the FFC's second meeting place and portraits of the members, as did Margaret Christman of the National Portrait Gallery. Jack Warren, Ellen Clark, and Elizabeth Frengel at the Society of the Cincinnati have lent their unique resources and expertise on the American Revolution. Other scholars who have assisted with these volumes are Henry Fulmer of the University of South Carolina, Victoria Harden of the National Institutes of Health, Leo Hershkowitz of Queens College, Mary Rose Kasraie of the American Intercontinental University, Phil Lampi of the American Antiquarian Society, Susan Riggs of the College of William and Mary, and C. Vaughn Stanley of Washington and Lee University.

Several individuals, some of whom have been mentioned before, fall into the category of patron saints of the FFCP. Former editor-in-chief Linda Grant DePauw brought this project to GWU and nurtured it through the publication of the first six volumes. Harvard Law professor Christine Desan has taken a special interest in the project, as well as sharing her enthusiasm for historical research. Stanford professor Jack D. Rakove, who spent weeks researching in our offices, generously shared his insights, wrote letters of support, and assisted in any way possible. Kenneth Bowling's longtime friends from graduate school at the University of Wisconsin, Richard H. Kohn and George M. Curtis III, have encouraged and aided us on a regular basis. Newberry Library President Emeritus Charles T. Cullen and David Chesnutt, formerly of the University of South Carolina, prodded and guided us into the age of technology. Charles was literally our lifeline during our indexing conversion from three-by-five cards to CINDEX and then NLCINDEX software, and he continues to aid and encourage us in numerous ways. David involved the FFCP in the Model Editions Partnership and helped launch us on the Internet. Michael Stevens of the State Historical Society of Wisconsin has gone out of his way to assist our research on several occasions. The well-traveled Constance B. Schulz of the University of South Carolina has always been on the lookout for FFC documents and willing to answer research questions. New York City attorney John D. Gordan III, who was born with history in his genes, always shared what he had discovered and found ways to assist with the FFCP's financial needs. Richard B. Bernstein proclaimed the value of our volumes in numerous book reviews and H-Net listservs. Linda Kerber of the University of Iowa has been a persistent and articulate supporter of this project and advocate for documentary editions.

The dedication for volume 20 recognizes two important supporters of both the National Historical Publications and Records Commission, documentary editions, and the First Federal Congress Project. Former Maryland Senator Charles McC. Mathias served on the project's advisory board from the late 1960s into the twenty-first century and took an active interest in the project's well-being. Several volume publication receptions were held on Capitol Hill with his sponsorship. He was instrumental in the congressional effort to keep the NHPRC's grants program alive during the difficult 1980s and was the lead Senate sponsor on the bill that re-established the National Archives as an independent agency. Retired U.S. Supreme Court Justice David Souter's quiet but firm, intelligent, and well-informed comments and actions during his tenure as a member of the NHPRC were vitally important to the survival of the documentary editions. We are all in his debt.

As is quite typical for these editorial projects, our searching was done on a shoestring budget, and we often found ourselves occupying the guest rooms of friends and family to save money. We want to add the following hosts to the list in volume 15 and thank them for assisting our research: Carla and Bob Baird, Robert Fazekas, Dustin Kahlson, Richard and Lynne Kohn, Michael C. McCarthy, David Miller, Ted and Maryjane Rayhart, Cammeron Richie, Buck and Anne Rhyme, Brian Stacey, and Kenton Williams.

As was true with the First Session correspondence, diplomatic reports back to European capitals revealed new information about and insights into the FFC, and we were fortunate to be able to recruit volunteer translators. We thank Pierre Grange, Nellie Hiemstra, Christoph Loman, and Abou Sy.

One of the advantages of being based at a university is the opportunity it presents for involving students in our work. The following GWU undergraduates and graduate students assisted with these volumes: Daniella Abatelli, Edward Buckley, Anne Dobberteen, Michael Ficht, Rory Ford, Emily French, Andrew Garbarino, Constance Golding, Osama Hanif, David Houpt, Courtney Janes, Jennifer Kenyan, Michael Keough, Noah Klein, Brett Levanto, Conor MacCaffrey, Heather Neviasky, Christopher Perras, Steve Rogers, Brianna Salerno, Brian Siegel, Ted Simonson, Ted Vlachos, Anthony Willshire, and Jonathan Zakheim. George Mason University graduate students Alicia Angelo, Maureen Connors, Johnna Flahive, and Amanda Roberts and University of Maryland graduate student Scott Heerman aided our progress. One graduate student, Paul Polgar, began volunteering at the FFCP soon after his arrival at George Mason University in 2005 and continued as the volunteer/employee in charge of the newspaper Public Opinion Project into 2010. His substantial and continuing commitment to the FFCP is particularly appreciated.

Search

The individuals and institutions mentioned in the acknowledgments in volume 15 of the *DHFFC* (pp. xxxix–xliv) for their contributions to the wide-ranging national and international search for FFC documents contributed to these volumes as well. In addition we acknowledge and thank:

At Dickinson College, James Gerenscer.
At the University of Georgia, Chuck Barber, Steven Brown, Melissa Bush, and Mary Linneman.
At the North Carolina Office of Archives and History, Jeffrey Crow and Dick Langford.

Many FFC letters form parts of private manuscript collections. We acknowledge the generosity of several collectors who wish to remain anonymous, Ned Downing, and, in particular, Seth Kaller, who has been a special friend to the FFCP.

ABBREVIATIONS AND SYMBOLS

Manuscript Types

AL	Autograph Letter
ALS	Autograph Letter Signed
AN	Autograph Note
ANS	Autograph Note Signed
FC	File Copy
FC:dft	File Copy: draft
FC:lbk	File Copy: letterbook
LS	Letter Signed
Ms	Manuscript

Primary Sources

Cutler	Manasseh Cutler Diary, Northwestern University, Chicago, Illinois
Johnson	William Samuel Johnson Diary, Connecticut Historical Society, Hartford, Connecticut
J. B. Johnson	John B. Johnson Diary, Columbia University, New York City
PCC	Papers of the Continental Congress, Record Group 360, National Archives, Washington, D.C.

Printed Sources

AASP	American Antiquarian Society *Proceedings*
Abigail Adams	Stewart Mitchell, ed., *New Letters of Abigail Adams* (Boston, 1947)
Adams	L. H. Butterfield, ed., *The Adams Papers: Diary and Autobiography of John Adams* (4 vols., New York, 1961)
AHA	American Historical Association *Annual Report*
AHR	*American Historical Review*
American Conservatism	David Hackett Fischer, *The Revolution of American Conservatism* (New York, 1965)
Ames	Seth Ames, ed., *Works of Fisher Ames* (2 vols., New York, 1854)
Blount	Alice B. Keith, ed., *John Gray Blount Papers* (3 vols., Raleigh, N.C., 1952–65)
Boston Printers	Benjamin Franklin V, *Boston Printers, Publishers, and Booksellers, 1640–1800* (Boston, 1990)

Boudinot	J. J. Boudinot, ed., *The Life, Public Service, Addresses and Letters of Elias Boudinot* (2 vols., Boston, 1896)
Butler	Malcolm Bell, Jr., *Major Butler's Legacy: Five Generations of a Slaveholding Family* (Athens, Ga., 1987)
Butler Letters	Terry W. Lipscomb, ed., *Letters of Pierce Butler, 1790–1794* (Columbia, S.C., 2007)
CCP	Ronald Hoffman, Sally D. Mason, and Eleanor S. Darcy, eds., *Dear Papa, Dear Charley: The Papers of Charles Carroll of Carrollton, 1748–1782* (3 vols., Chapel Hill, N.C., 2001)
Counter Revolution	Robert L. Brunhouse, *The Counter-Revolution in Pennsylvania, 1776–1790* (Harrisburg, Pa., 1942)
Coxe	Jacob E. Cooke, *Tench Coxe and the Early Republic* (Chapel Hill, N.C., 1978)
CR	*The Congressional Register*
Creation of DC	Kenneth R. Bowling, *The Creation of Washington, D.C.* (Fairfax, Va., 1991)
Cutler	William and Julia Cutler, eds., *Life, Journals, and Correspondence of Rev. Manasseh Cutler* (2 vols., Cincinnati, Oh., 1888)
DGW	Donald Jackson and Dorothy Twohig, eds., *The Diaries of George Washington* (6 vols., Charlottesville, Va., 1976–79)
DHFFC	*Documentary History of the First Federal Congress*
DHFFE	Merrill Jensen, Gordon DenBoer, Lucy T. Brown, and Robert A. Becker, eds., *The Documentary History of the First Federal Elections, 1788–1790* (4 vols., Madison, Wis., 1976–90)
DHROC	Merrill Jensen, John Kaminski, Gaspare J. Saladino, and Richard Leffler, eds., *The Documentary History of the Ratification of the Constitution* (20+ vols., Madison, Wis., 1976–)
DHSCUS	Maeva Marcus, James R. Perry, James M. Buchanan, Christine R. Jordan, William B. R. Daines, Mark G. Hirsch, Natalie Wexler, Robert P. Frankel, Jr., Anthony M. Joseph, Stephen L. Tull, James C. Brandow, and Marc Pachter, eds., *The Documentary History of the Supreme Court of the United States, 1789–1800* (8 vols., New York, 1985–2007)

Drinker	Elaine Forman Crane, ed., *The Diary of Elizabeth Drinker* (3 vols., Boston, 1991)
DVB	John T. Kneebone, Daphne Gentry, and Donald W. Gunter, eds., *Dictionary of Virginia Biography* (3 vols. to date, Richmond, Va., 1998–)
EIHC	Essex Institute *Historical Collections*
Emerging Nation	Mary A. Giunta and J. Dane Hartgrove, eds., *The Emerging Nation: A Documentary History of the Foreign Relations of the United States under the Articles of Confederation, 1780–1789* (3 vols., Washington, D.C., 1996)
Evans	Clifford Shipton and James Mooney, *National Index of American Imprints through 1800, The Short-Title Evans* (2 vols., Worcester, Mass., 1969). An online edition is available by subscription.
Farrand	Max Farrand, ed., *The Records of the Federal Convention of 1787* (rev. ed., 4 vols., New Haven, Conn., 1937); *Supplement* (James H. Hutson and Leonard Rapport, eds., [New Haven, 1987])
FG	[Philadelphia] *Federal Gazette*
FJ	[Philadelphia] *Freeman's Journal*
GA	[Philadelphia] *General Advertiser*
GUS	[New York] *Gazette of the United States*
Harvard Graduates	*John Sibley, Clifford Shipton, Conrad E. Wright, and Edward Hanson, Biographical Sketches of Graduates of Harvard University* (18+ vols., Cambridge, 1873–)
Hening	W. W. Hening, ed., *Statutes at Large . . . of Virginia* (13 vols., Richmond, Va., 1809–23)
Iconography	I. N. Phelps Stokes, *The Iconography of Manhattan Island, 1498–1909* (6 vols., New York, 1915–28)
IG	[Philadelphia] *Independent Gazetteer*
Inns of Court	E. Alfred Jones, *American Members of the Inns of Court* (London, 1924)
Iredell	Griffith J. McRee, *Life and Correspondence of James Iredell* (2 vols., New York, 1857–58)
JCC	Worthington Ford, Gaillard Hunt, John C. Fitzpatrick, and Roscoe R. Hill, eds., *Journals of the Continental Congress, 1774–1789* (34 vols., Washington, D.C., 1904–37)
JER	*Journal of the Early Republic*

John Adams	Charles Francis Adams, ed., *Works of John Adams* (10 vols., Boston, 1850–56)
John Marshall	Herbert A. Johnson, Charles T. Cullen, William C. Stinchcombe, Charles F. Hobson, Fredrika J. Teute, George H. Hoemann, and Ingrid M. Hillinger, eds., *The Papers of John Marshall* (12 vols., Chapel Hill, N.C., 1974–2006)
JQA	Charles Francis Adams, ed., *Life in a New England Town, 1787, 1788: Diary of John Quincy Adams, While a Student in the Office of Theophilus Parsons at Newburyport* (Boston, 1903)
Kentucky in Retrospect	Mrs. William P. Drake, Samuel M. Wilson, and Mrs. William P. Ardery, *Kentucky in Retrospect* (Frankfort, Ky., 1967)
King	Charles R. King, *The Life and Correspondence of Rufus King* (6 vols., New York, 1894–1900)
Lamplugh	George R. Lamplugh, *Politics on the Periphery: Factions and Parties in Georgia, 1783–1806* (Newark, Del., 1986)
Langdon	Alfred Langdon Elwyn, ed., *Letters by Washington, Adams, Jefferson . . . to John Langdon* (Philadelphia, 1880)
LDC	Paul H. Smith, Ronald Gephart, Gerald W. Gawalt, Rosemary Fry Plakas, and Eugene R. Sheridan., eds., *Letters of Delegates to Congress, 1774–1789* (26 vols., Washington, D.C., 1976–2000)
Lee	James C. Ballagh, ed., *The Letters of Richard Henry Lee* (2 vols., New York, 1911–14)
Madison, *Letters*	William C. Rives and Philip R. Fendall, eds., *Letters and Other Writings of James Madison* (4 vols., Philadelphia, 1865)
Maine Bar	William Willis, *A History of the Law, the Courts, and the Lawyers of Maine* (Portland, Me., 1863)
Massachusetts Bar	William T. Davis, *Bench and Bar of the Commonwealth of Massachusetts* (reprint, 2 vols., New York, 1974)
Massachusetts Legislators	John A. Schutz, *Legislators of the Massachusetts General Court, 1691–1780: A Biographical Dictionary* (Boston, 1997)
McGillivray	John Walton Caughey, *McGillivray of the Creeks* (Norman, Okla., 1938)

MHSC	Massachusetts Historical Society *Collections*
MSSR	*Massachusetts Soldiers and Sailors of the Revolutionary War* (17 vols., Boston, 1896–1907)
Murray	Bonnie Hurd Smith, ed., *From Gloucester to Philadelphia in 1790: Observations, Anecdotes & Thoughts from the 18th Century Letters of Judith Sargent Murray* (Cambridge, Mass., 1998)
Naval Documents	William Bell Clark, William James Morgan, and Michael J. Crawford, eds., *Naval Documents of the American Revolution* (11+ vols., Washington, D.C., 1964–)
NEHGR	*New England Historical and Genealogical Register*
New York	Thomas E. V. Smith, *The City of New York in the Year of Washington's Inauguration 1789* (2nd ed., Riverside, Conn., 1972)
NYDA	*The* [New York] *Daily Advertiser*
NYDG	*The New-York Daily Gazette*
NYJ	*The New-York Journal*
NYMP	*The* [New York] *Morning Post*
NYP	*The New-York Packet*
NYWM	*The New-York Weekly Museum*
O'Dwyer	DHFFC modification of Margaret M. O'Dwyer translation, *WMQ*, series 3, 21(1964); translation used by permission. Originals in Correspondance Politique, États-Unis, 35, Ministère des Affairs Étrangères, Archives Nationales, Paris
PAH	Harold C. Syrett and Jacob E. Cooke, eds., *The Papers of Alexander Hamilton* (37 vols., New York, 1961–87)
Patrick Henry	William Wirt Henry, *Patrick Henry* (3 vols., New York, 1891)
PBF	Leonard W. Labaree, William B. Willcox, Claude A. Lopez, Barbara Oberg, and Ellen R. Cohn, eds., *The Papers of Benjamin Franklin* (38+ vols., New Haven, 1959–)
PG	[Philadelphia] *Pennsylvania Gazette*
PGM	Robert A. Rutland, ed., *The Papers of George Mason, 1725–1792* (3 vols., Chapel Hill, N.C., 1970)
PGW	W. W. Abbot, Dorothy Twohig, Jack D. Warren, Mark A. Mastromarino, Robert F. Haggard, Christine Sternberg Patrick, and John C. Pinheiro, eds., *The Papers of George Washington:*

	Presidential Series (13+ vols., Charlottesville, Va., 1987–)
PGW: Confederation	W. W. Abbot, ed., *The Papers of George Washington: Confederation Series* (6 vols., Charlottesville, Va., 1992–97)
PJB	Frank C. Meyers, ed., *The Papers of Josiah Bartlett* (Hanover, N.H., 1979)
PJM	William Hutchinson, William M. E. Rachal, Robert A. Rutland, Charles Hobson, Frederika J. Teute, Frank C. Mevers, and Barbara D. Ripel, eds., *The Papers of James Madison* (17 vols., Chicago and Charlottesville, Va., 1962–91)
PMHB	*Pennsylvania Magazine of History and Biography*
PNG	Richard K. Showman, Dennis M. Conrad, and Roger N. Parks, eds., *The Papers of Nathanael Greene* (13 vols., Providence, R.I., and Chapel Hill, N.C., 1976–2005)
Political Parties	Jackson Turner Main, *Political Parties before the Constitution* (New York, 1973)
Powell	William S. Powell, ed., *Dictionary of North Carolina Biography* (6 vols., Chapel Hill, N.C., 1979–96)
PP	[Philadelphia] *Pennsylvania Packet*
Princetonians	James McLachlan, *Princetonians, 1748–1768, A Biographical Dictionary* (Princeton, N.J., 1976); Richard A. Harrison, *Princetonians, 1769–1775, A Biographical Dictionary* (Princeton, N.J., 1980); *Princetonians, 1776–1783, A Biographical Dictionary* (Princeton, N.J., 1981); Ruth L. Woodward and Wesley Frank Craven, *Princetonians, 1784–1790, A Biographical Dictionary* (Princeton, N.J., 1991); J. Jefferson Looney and Ruth L. Woodward, *Princetonians, 1791–1794: A Biographical Dictionary* (Princeton, N.J., 1991)
PRM	E. James Ferguson, John Catanzariti, Elizabeth M. Nuxoll, Mary A. Gallagher, Francine A. Moskowitz, Nelson S. Dearmont, Herbert Leventhal, Kathleen H. Mullen, and David B. Mattern, eds., *The Papers of Robert Morris* (9 vols., Pittsburgh, 1980–99)
PTJ	Julian Boyd, Charles T. Cullen, John Catanzariti, Barbara Oberg, Eugene R. Sheridan, J. Jefferson

	Looney, Ruth W. Lester, William H. Gaines, Joseph H. Harrison, Mina R. Bryan, Frederick Aandahl, Elizabeth L. Hutter, Alfred L. Bush, and George Hoemann, eds., *The Papers of Thomas Jefferson* (33+ vols., Princeton, N.J., 1950–)
Purse	E. James Ferguson, *The Power of the Purse* (Chapel Hill, N.C., 1961)
Rush	Lyman Butterfield, ed., *Letters of Benjamin Rush* (2 vols., Princeton, N.J., 1951)
SCHM	*South Carolina Historical Magazine*
Sherman's Connecticut	Christopher Collier, *Roger Sherman's Connecticut: Yankee Politics and the American Revolution* (Middletown, Conn., 1971)
Sketches of Kentucky	Lewis Collins, *Historical Sketches of Kentucky* (2 vols., Covington, Ky., 1874)
South Carolina House	N. Louise Bailey and Elizabeth Ivy Cooper, *Biographical Directory of the South Carolina House of Representatives* (3 vols., Columbia, S.C., 1981)
South Carolina Senate	Emily B. Reynolds and Joan R. Faunt, *Biographical Directory of the Senate of the State of South Carolina* (3 vols., Columbia, S.C., 1964)
Steele	Henry M. Wagstaff, ed., *John Steele Papers* (2 vols., Raleigh, N.C., 1924)
VMHB	*Virginia Magazine of History and Biography*
Westward Expansion	Ray Allen Billington, *Westward Expansion: A History of the American Frontier* (New York, 1960)
Wingate	C. E. L. Wingate, *Life and Letters of Paine Wingate* (2 vols., Winchester, Mass., 1930)
WMQ	*William and Mary Quarterly*
Wolcott	George Gibbs, *Memoirs of the Administrations of Washington and Adams* (2 vols., New York, 1846)
Yale Graduates	Franklin Dexter, *Biographical Sketches of the Graduates of Yale College* (6 vols., New York, 1885–1912)

Repositories

CSmH	Henry Huntington Library, San Marino, Cal.
CtHi	Connecticut Historical Society, Hartford
CtY	Manuscripts and Archives, Yale University, New Haven, Conn.
DeU	University of Delaware, Newark
DLC	Library of Congress, Washington, D.C.

DNA	National Archives, Washington, D.C.
DSI	Smithsonian Institute, Washington, D.C.
G-Ar	Georgia State Department of Archives, Atlanta
GHi	Georgia Historical Society, Savannah
GU	University of Georgia, Athens
ICarbS	Southern Illinois University, Carbondale
ICHi	Chicago History Museum, Ill.
IEN	McCormick Library of Special Collections, Northwestern University Library, Evanston, Ill.
M-Ar	Archives Division, Secretary of State, Boston
MB	Rare Books Department, Boston Public Library, Mass.
MDedHi	Dedham Historical Society, Dedham, Mass.
MdHi	H. Furlong Baldwin Library of the Maryland Historical Society, Baltimore
MeHi	Maine Historical Society, Portland
MH	Houghton Library, Harvard College Library, Cambridge, Mass.
MHi	Massachusetts Historical Society, Boston
MiD-B	Detroit Public Library–Benton Collection, Mich.
MiU-C	William L. Clements Library, The University of Michigan, Ann Arbor
Ms-Ar	Mississippi Department of Archives and History, Jackson
MSaE	Phillips Library, Peabody Essex Museum, Salem, Mass.
MSonHi	South Natick Historical Society, Mass.
MWA	American Antiquarian Society, Worcester, Mass.
N	New York State Library, Albany
Nc-Ar	North Carolina State Department of Archives, Raleigh
NcD	Duke University, Durham, N.C.
NcU	Southern Historical Collection, Wilson Library, The University of North Carolina at Chapel Hill
NhHi	New Hampshire Historical Society, Concord
NHi	New-York Historical Society, New York City
NhPoA	Portsmouth Athenaeum, Portsmouth, N.H.
NhPoS	Strawbery Banke, Portsmouth, N.H.
NjMoHP	Morristown National Historic Park, Morristown, N.J.
NjP	Manuscripts Division, Department of Rare Books

	and Special Collections, Princeton University Library, Princeton, N.J.
NjR	Rutgers University, New Brunswick, N.J.
NN	New-York Public Library, New York City
NNC	Rare Book and Manuscript Library, Columbia University, New York City
NNS	New York Society Library, New York City
NRom	Jervis Library, Rome, N.Y.
PDoBHi	Bucks County Historical Society, Doylestown, Pa.
PHarH	Pennsylvania Historical and Museum Commission, Harrisburg, Pa.
PHC	Haverford College, Haverford, Pa.
PHi	Historical Society of Pennsylvania, Philadelphia
PPAmP	American Philosophical Society, Philadelphia
PPIn	Independence National Historic Park, Philadelphia
PPL	Library Company of Philadelphia, Philadelphia
PPRF	Rosenbach Museum and Library, Philadelphia
PRHi	Historical Society of Berks County, Reading, Pa.
PRO	Public Record Office, London
R-Ar	Rhode Island State Archives, Providence
RHi	Rhode Island Historical Society Library, Providence
RPB	Brown University, Providence, R.I.
Sc	South Carolina State Library, Columbia
ScHi	South Carolina Historical Society Collections, Charleston
ScU	South Caroliniana Library, University of South Carolina, Columbia
Uk	British Library, London
Vi	Virginia State Library, Richmond
ViHi	Virginia Historical Society, Richmond
ViLxW	Washington and Lee University, Lexington, Va.
ViMtvL	Mount Vernon Ladies Association of the Union, Mount Vernon, Va.
ViU	Albert H. Small Special Collections Library, University of Virginia, Charlottesville
ViW	Special Collections Research Center, Earl Gregg Swem Library, College of William and Mary, Williamsburg, Va.
WHi	Wisconsin Historical Society, Madison

Ames, Fisher	Massachusetts
Ashe, John Baptista	North Carolina
Baldwin, Abraham	Georgia
Benson, Egbert	New York
Bland, Theodorick	Virginia
(died 1 June 1790)	
Bloodworth, Timothy	North Carolina
Bloudinot, Elias	New Jersey
Bourn, Benjamin	Rhode Island
Brown, John	Virginia
Burke, Aedanus	South Carolina
Cadwalader, Lambert	New Jersey
Carroll, Daniel	Maryland
Clymer, George	Pennsylvania
Coles, Isaac	Virginia
Contee, Benjamin	Maryland
Fitzsimons, Thomas	Pennsylvania
Floyd, William	New York
Foster, Abiel	New Hampshire
Gale, George	Maryland
Gerry, Elbridge	Massachusetts
Giles, William B.	Virginia
(took his seat on 7 December 1790, after being elected to fill the vacancy caused by the death of Theodorick Bland)	
Gilman, Nicholas	New Hampshire
Goodhue, Benjamin	Massachusetts
Griffin, Samuel	Virginia
Grout, Jonathan	Massachusetts
Hartley, Thomas	Pennsylvania
Hathorn, John	New York
Hiester, Daniel, Jr.	Pennsylvania
Huger, Daniel	South Carolina
Huntington, Benjamin	Connecticut
Jackson, James	Georgia
Laurance, John	New York
Lee, Richard Bland	Virginia
Leonard, George	Massachusetts
Livermore, Samuel	New Hampshire
Madison, James, Jr.	Virginia

Mathews, George	Georgia
Moore, Andrew	Virginia
Muhlenberg, Frederick A.	Pennsylvania
Muhlenberg, Peter	Pennsylvania
Page, John	Virginia
Parker, Josiah	Virginia
Partridge, George	Massachusetts
Schureman, James	New Jersey
Scott, Thomas	Pennsylvania
Sedgwick, Theodore	Massachusetts
Seney, Joshua	Maryland
Sevier, John	North Carolina
Sherman, Roger	Connecticut
Silvester, Peter	New York
Sinnickson, Thomas	New Jersey
Smith, William	Maryland
Smith, William	South Carolina
Steele, John	North Carolina
Stone, Michael Jenifer	Maryland
Sturges, Jonathan	Connecticut
Sumter, Thomas	South Carolina
Thatcher, George	Massachusetts
Trumbull, Jonathan	Connecticut
Tucker, Thomas Tudor	South Carolina
Van Rensselaer, Jeremiah	New York
Vining, John	Delaware
Wadsworth, Jeremiah	Connecticut
White, Alexander	Virginia
Williamson, Hugh	North Carolina
Wynkoop, Henry	Pennsylvania

MEMBERS OF THE SENATE

Bassett, Richard	Delaware
Butler, Pierce	South Carolina
Carroll, Charles	Maryland
Dalton, Tristram	Massachusetts
Dickinson, Philemon	New Jersey

(took his seat on 6 December 1790, after being elected to fill
the vacancy caused by the resignation of William Paterson)

Ellsworth, Oliver	Connecticut
Elmer, Jonathan	New Jersey
Few, William	Georgia
Foster, Theodore	Rhode Island
Grayson, William	Virginia
Gunn, James	Georgia
Hawkins, Benjamin	North Carolina
Henry, John	Maryland
Izard, Ralph	South Carolina
Johnson, William Samuel	Connecticut
Johnston, Samuel	North Carolina
King, Rufus	New York
Langdon, John	New Hampshire
Lee, Richard Henry	Virginia
Maclay, William	Pennsylvania
Monroe, James	Virginia

(took his seat on 6 December 1790, after being elected to fill
the vacancy caused by the death of William Grayson)

Morris, Robert	Pennsylvania
Paterson, William	New Jersey

(resigned on 13 November 1790, after being elected governor
of New Jersey)

Read, George	Delaware
Schuyler, Philip	New York
Stanton, Joseph, Jr.	Rhode Island
Strong, Caleb	Massachusetts
Walker, John	Virginia

(appointed to fill the vacancy caused by the death of William
Grayson; served from 31 March through 9 November 1790)

Wingate, Paine	New Hampshire

SUBJECTS DEBATED IN THE HOUSE OF REPRESENTATIVES, AS REPORTED BY THE NEWSPAPERS

8 Jan.	Rules: unfinished business, journal, attendance
9 Jan.	Report on the public credit: form and time of presentation
	Rules: executive communications
	Reply to the State of the Union address
11 Jan.	Enumeration Act [HR-34]
	Rules: unfinished business, petitions
	Petition of Christopher Saddler
12 Jan.	Reply to the State of the Union address
15 Jan.	Newspapers' reporting of debates
	Rules: unfinished business
	Proposals in the State of the Union address
19 Jan.	Foreign Intercourse Bill [HR-35]
	Petition of Christopher Saddler
	Rules: petitions
20 Jan.	Petition of Hannibal W. Dobbyn
	Petition of Charles Markley
	Rules: unfinished business
21 Jan.	Petitions on Revolutionary War claims
22 Jan.	Post Office Bill [HR-42]
	Foreign Intercourse Bill [HR-35]
25 Jan.	Enumeration Act [HR-34]
	Rules: unfinished business
	Copyrights
26 Jan.	Foreign Intercourse Bill [HR-35]
	Enumeration Act [HR-34]
	Petition of James Price
27 Jan.	Foreign Intercourse Bill [HR-35]
	Petition of Hannibal W. Dobbyn
	Rules: unfinished business
28 Jan.	Petition of John Wait
	Petition of Charles Markley
	Rules: unfinished business
	Report on public credit
29 Jan.	Foreign Intercourse Bill [HR-35]
	Courts
1 Feb.	Copyright Bill [HR-39]
	Bankruptcy
2 Feb.	Enumeration Act [HR-34]

11 Mar.	Mitigation of Fines Bill [HR-45]
	Patents Act [HR-41]
12 Mar.	Naturalization Act [HR-40]
	Salaries of Clerks Bill [HR-46]
15 Mar.	Mitigation of Fines Bill [HR-45]
	Patents Act [HR-41]
	Naturalization Act [HR-40]
	Executive business: Northeast boundary dispute with Great Britain
16 Mar.	Mitigation of Fines Bill [HR-45]
	Naturalization Act [HR-40]: land ownership
17 Mar.	Appropriations Act [HR-47]
	Mitigation of Fines Bill [HR-45]
	Naturalization Act [HR-40]: land ownership, suffrage
18 Mar.	Naturalization Act [HR-40]: land ownership
	Appropriations Act [HR-47]
19 Mar.	Mitigation of Fines Bill [HR-45]
	Naturalization Act [HR-40]: land ownership
22 Mar.	Petition of Nathaniel Tracy (Bankruptcy law)
	Petition of John Fitch
	Appropriations Act [HR-47]: doorkeepers' salaries
23 Mar.	Appropriations Act [HR-47]: doorkeepers' salaries
24 Mar.	Appropriations Act [HR-47]: doorkeepers' salaries
	Executive business: Northeast boundary dispute with Great Britain
25 Mar.	Petition of the merchants and traders of Portsmouth (judiciary)
	Memorial of the officers of the late Navy of the United States
29 Mar.	Bailey Bill [HR-44]
	Patents Act [HR-41]
	Petition of John Fitch
	North Carolina Cession Act [S-7]: amendments
30 Mar.	Salaries of Clerks Bill [HR-46]
	Patents Act [HR-41]
	Inspection Act [HR-48]
	Military Establishment Act [HR-50a]
1 Apr.	Pay of Senators
3 Apr.	Pay of Senators
5 Apr.	Patents Act [HR-41]
	Indian Treaty Act [HR-50b]
	Mitigation of Fines Bill [HR-45]

6 Apr.	Military Establishment Act [HR-50a]: compensation of officers
7 Apr.	Southern Territory Act [S-8]
8 Apr.	Collection Act [HR-50]
9 Apr.	Collection Act [HR-50], Southern Territory Act [S-8]
12 Apr.	Southern Territory Act [S-8]
	Mitigation of Fines Bill [HR-45]
	Punishment of Crimes Act [S-6]
13 Apr.	Mitigation of Fines Bill [HR-45]
	Punishment of Crimes Act [S-6]
	Southern Territory Act [S-8]
	Military Establishment Act [HR-50a]
14 Apr.	Southern Territory Act [S-8]
	Punishment of Crimes Act [S-6]
15–16 Apr.	Military Establishment Act [HR-50a]
19 Apr.	Military Establishment Act [HR-50a]
20 Apr.	Military Establishment Act [HR-50a]: title
21 Apr.	Military Establishment Act [HR-50a]: term of (standing army)
22 Apr.	Officers Bill [HR-53]
23 Apr.	Military Establishment Act [HR-50a]: amendment
	Officers Bill [HR-53]
	Mourning for Benjamin Franklin
26–27 Apr.	Courts Act [S-9]
28 Apr.	Rhode Island, provisions respecting
29 Apr.	Senate rules: open doors
30 Apr.	North Carolina Judiciary Bill [S-10]
	Senate rules: open doors
3 May	Joint Rule Salaries-Executive Act [HR-54]
	Foreign Intercourse Act [HR-52]: etiquette, salaries
	North Carolina Judiciary Bill [S-10]
	Mitigation of Forfeitures Act [HR-57]
	Terms of federally elected officials
4 May	Southern Territory Act [S-8]: House amendments
	Mitigation of Forfeitures Act [HR-57]
	Ely Bill [HR-56]
	Authentication Act [HR-58]
	Indian Treaty Act [HR-50b]
	Copyright Act [HR-43]
5 May	Authentication Act [HR-58]
	Invalid Officers Bill [HR-59]

7 May	Foreign Intercourse Act [HR-52]
10 May	Foreign Intercourse Act [HR-52]
	Resolution on Rhode Island
	North Carolina Judiciary Bill [S-10]: House amendments
11 May	Steuben Act [HR-60]
	North Carolina Judiciary Bill [S-10]: House amendments
	Resolution on Rhode Island
12 May	Ely Bill [HR-56]
	North Carolina Judiciary Bill [S-10]
	Copyright Act [HR-43]
13 May	Copyright Act [HR-43]
	Terms of federally elected officials
14 May	Copyright Act [HR-43]
	Terms of federally elected officials
	Rhode Island Trade Bill [S-11]
17 May	Rhode Island Trade Bill [S-11]
	Resolution on Compensation Lists
18 May	Rhode Island Trade Bill [S-11]
	North Carolina Judiciary Bill [S-10]
19–21 May	Resolution on Compensation Lists
24 May	Jenkins Act [HR-67]
	North Carolina Judiciary Act [HR-68]
	Petition of John Calhorda
	Temporary seat of government
25 May	Foreign Intercourse Act [HR-52]
	Steuben Act [HR-60]
26 May	Foreign Intercourse Act [HR-52]
	Steuben Act [HR-60]
	Temporary seat of government
27 May	Jenkins Act [HR-67]
	North Carolina Judiciary Act [HR-68]
	Petition of John Frederick Amelung
	Steuben Act [HR-60]: amendments
28 May	Jenkins Act [HR-67]
	Salaries-Executive Act [HR-54]
	North Carolina Judiciary Act [HR-68]
	Temporary seat of government
31 May	Foreign Intercourse Act [HR-52]
	Residence Act [S-12]
1 June	Jenkins Act [HR-67]
	Residence Act [S-12]
	Temporary seat of government

2 June	Resolution on Publication of Treaties
	Residence Act [S-12]
	Temporary seat of government
	Funding Act [HR-63]
3 June	Funding Act [HR-63]
4 June	McCord Act [HR-70]
	Rhode Island Act [HR-71]
	Residence Act [S-12]
7 June	McCord Act [HR-70]
	Rhode Island Act [HR-71]
	Funding Act [HR-63]
8 June	Joint rules
	Temporary seat of government
	Residence Act [S-12]
9 June	Rhode Island Act [HR-71]
	Funding Act [HR-63]
10 June	Joint rules
	Adjournment
	Funding Act [HR-63]: assumption of state debts
11 June	Petition of Tanners of Philadelphia
	Rhode Island Judiciary Act [HR-73]
	Funding Act [HR-63]: assumption of state debts
14 June	Petition of Congregational clergy
	Funding Act [HR-63]: assumption of state debts
	Temporary seat of government
15 June	Funding Act [HR-63]
16 June	Twining Act [HR-72]
	Funding Act [HR-63]: interest (domestic)
17 June	Funding Act [HR-63]: interest (domestic)
	Foreign Intercourse Act [HR-52]
18 June	Petition of Stephen Moore
	West Point Act [HR-76]
	McCord Act [HR-70]
	Funding Act [HR-63]: interest (domestic)
21 June	Adjournment
	Funding Act [HR-63]: interest (domestic)
22 June	Funding Act [HR-63]: committee report
23 June	Twining Act [HR-72]
	Petition of Sarah Stirling
	Foreign Intercourse Act [HR-52]
	Post Office Bill [HR-74]

24 June	Post Office Bill [HR-74]
	Twining Act [HR-72]
25 June	West Point Act [HR-76]
	Residence Act [S-12]
	Foreign Intercourse Act [HR-52]
28 June	West Point Act [HR-76]
	Residence Act [S-12]: temporary residence
29 June	Gould Bill [HR-79]
	Tonnage Act [HR-78]
	Residence Act [S-12]
30 June	Residence Act [S-12]
	Rhode Island Enumeration Act [HR-75]
	Settlement of Accounts Act [HR-77]
1 July	Merchant Seamen Act [HR-61]
	Settlement of Accounts Act [HR-77]
	Residence Act [S-12]
2 July	Funding Act [HR-63]: assumption of state debts
	Indian Trade Act [HR-65]
	Post Office Bill [HR-74]
3 July	Post Office Bill [HR-74]
5 July	Post Office Bill [HR-74]
6 July	Post Office Bill [HR-74]
	Settlement of Accounts Act [HR-77]
	Gould Bill [HR-79]
	Invalid Pensioners Act [HR-80]
7 July	Settlement of Accounts Act [HR-77]
	Invalid Officers Bill [HR-59]
8 July	Settlement of Accounts Act [HR-77]
	Indian Trade Act [HR-65]
9 July	Indian Treaty Act [HR-50b]
	Settlement of Accounts Act [HR-77]
12 July	Post Office Bill [HR-74]
	Merchant Seamen Act [HR-61]
	Indian Trade Act [HR-65]
	Tonnage Act [HR-78]
13 July	Resolutions on assumption of state debts
14 July	Indian Trade Act [HR-65]
	Settlement of Accounts Act [HR-77]
	Resolutions on assumption of state debts
15 July	Resolutions on assumption of state debts
16 July	Indian Treaty Act [HR-50b]

APPOINTEES TO OFFICE DURING THE SECOND SESSION

(Biographies for those not listed in the Biographical Gazetteer
can be found in *DHFFC* 2:483–556)

Revenue Appointments

District	Port	Office	Appointee
		Massachusetts	
	Marblehead	Collector	Samuel Russell Gerry
		Rhode Island	
	Newport	Collector	William Ellery
		Naval Officer	Robert Crooke
		Surveyor	Daniel Lyman
	Providence	Collector	Jeremiah Olney
		Naval Officer	Theodore Foster
			Ebenezer Thompson
		Surveyor	William Barton
	North Kingston	Surveyor	Daniel Eldridge Updike
	East Greenwich	Surveyor	Job Comstock (declined)
			Thomas Arnold
	Warren and Barrington	Surveyor	Nathaniel Phillips
	Bristol	Surveyor	Samuel Bosworth
	Pawcatuck River	Surveyor	George Stillman
	Patuxet	Surveyor	John Anthony Aborn (declined)
			Zachariah Rhodes
		Connecticut	
	Middletown	Surveyor	Comfort Sage
		New York	
	Albany	Surveyor	Henry Bogart
	Sagg Harbour	Collector	Henry Dering

New Jersey

Great Egg Harbour	Collector	Daniel Benezet, Jr.

Maryland

Cedar Point	Collector	John C. Jones
Lewellensburg	Surveyor	Jeremiah Jordan

Virginia

Hampton	Collector	George Wray
Cherry Stone	Collector	Nathaniel Wilkins
Suffolk	Surveyor	Benjamin Bartlett

North Carolina

Wilmington	Wilmington	Collector	James Read
		Naval Officer	John Walker
		Surveyor	Thomas Callender
	Swansborough	Surveyor	John McCullough
Newbern	Newbern	Collector	John Daves
	Beaufort	Surveyor	John Easton
Washington	Washington	Collector	Nathan Keais
Edenton	Edenton	Collector	Thomas Benbury
	Hartford	Surveyor	Joshua Skinner, Jr.
	Murpheysborough	Surveyor	Hardy Murfree
	Plymouth	Surveyor	Levi Blount (resigned) Thomas Davis Freeman
	Windsor	Surveyor	William Benson
	Skewarkey	Surveyor	Henry Hunter
	Winton	Surveyor	William Wynns
	Bennet's Creek	Surveyor	John Baker
Camden	Plankbridge on Sawyers Creek	Collector	Isaac Gregory
	Nixinton	Surveyor	Hugh Knox
	Indian-town	Surveyor	Thomas Williams
	Currituck Inlet	Surveyor	Samuel Jasper
	Pasquotank River Bridge	Surveyor	Edmund Sawyer
	Newbiggen Creek	Surveyor	Elias Albertson

Georgia

Brunswick	Collector	Christopher Hillary

Kentucky

Louisville	Collector	Richard Taylor

Territorial and Executive Department Appointments

Territory or Department	Office	Appointee
	Treaty Commissioner	Henry Knox
	Commissioners for Settling Accounts	John Taylor Gilman (New Hampshire)
		William Irvine (Pennsylvania)
		John Kean (South Carolina)
	Loan Commissioners	Nathaniel Gilman (New Hampshire)
		Nathaniel Appleton (Massachusetts)
		Jabez Bowen (Rhode Island)
		William Imlay (Connecticut)
		John Cochran (New York)
		James Ewing (New Jersey)
		Thomas Smith (Pennsylvania)
		James Tilton (Delaware)
		Thomas Harwood (Maryland)
		John Hopkins (Virginia)
		William Skinner (North Carolina)
		John Neufville (South Carolina)
		Richard Wylly (Georgia)
Southern Territory	Governor	William Blount
	Secretary	Daniel Smith

Judiciary Appointments

Court or District	Office	Appointee
Supreme Court	Associate Justice	James Iredell (North Carolina)
Rhode Island	District Judge	Henry Marchant
	District Attorney	William Channing
	District Marshal	William Peck
Maryland	District Judge	William Paca

Virginia	District Judge	Cyrus Griffin
	District Attorney	William Nelson, Jr.
South Carolina	District Judge	William Drayton
		Thomas Bee (replaced Drayton, deceased)
North Carolina	District Judge	William R. Davie (declined)
		John Stokes
	District Attorney	John Sitgreaves
	District Marshal	John Skinner
Kentucky	District Attorney	James Brown
Western Territory	Judge	Rufus Putnam
Southern Territory	Judge	David Campbell
	Judge	John McNairy
	Judge	William Peery

Consulate Appointments

Country/Region	Port	Office	Appointee
China	Canton	Consul	Samuel Shaw
Spain	Cadiz	Consul	Richard Harrison
	Bilboa	Consul	Edward Church
	Madeira	Consul	John Marsden Pintard
Great Britain	Liverpool	Consul	James Maury
	Cowes	Vice Consul	Thomas Auldjo
	London	Consul	Joshua Johnson
Ireland	Dublin	Consul	William Knox
France	Marseilles	Vice Consul	Sieur Etienne Cathalan
	Bordeaux	Consul	Joseph Fenwick
	Nantes	Consul	Burrill Carnes
	Rouen	Consul	Nathaniel Barrett
	Havre de Grace	Vice Consul	Sieur de La Motte
Hispaniola	Hispaniola	Consul	Silvanus Bourn
Martinique	Martinique	Consul	Fulwar Skipwith
Germany	Hamburgh	Vice Consul	John Parish
Canary Islands	Teneriffe	Vice Consul	Francisco Sarmento
Azores	Fayal	Vice Consul	John Street
Colony of Guiana	Surinam	Consul	Ebenezer Brush

Military Appointments

Infantry

Rank	Name	State
Lt. Col. Commandant	Josiah Harmar	Pennsylvania
Majors	John Palsgrave Wyllys	Connecticut
	John F. Hamtramck	New York
	Alexander Parker	Virginia
Captains	Jonathan Heart	Connecticut
	David Strong	Connecticut
	John Smith	New York
	John Mercer	New Jersey
	David Ziegler	Pennsylvania
	William McCurdy	Pennsylvania
	Joseph Ashton	Pennsylvania
	Erkuries Beatty	Pennsylvania
	Alexander Trueman	Maryland
	Ballard Smith	Virginia
	Joseph Monfort	North Carolina
	Michael Rudolph	Georgia
Lieutenants	Ebenezer Frothingham	Connecticut
	John Pratt	Connecticut
	Jacob Kingsbury	Connecticut
	William Peters	New York
	William Kersey	New Jersey
	Thomas Doyle	Pennsylvania
	John Armstrong	Pennsylvania
	Ebenezer Denny	Pennsylvania
	Mark McPherson	Maryland
	John Steel	Virginia
	Thomas Pasteur	North Carolina
	Thomas Martin	Georgia
Ensigns	John Jeffers	Connecticut
	Asa Heartshorn	Connecticut
	Abner Prior	New York
	John Morgan	New Jersey
	Cornelius R. Sedam	New Jersey
	Nathan McDowell	Pennsylvania
	Robert Thompson	Pennsylvania
	Jacob Melcher	Pennsylvania
	Richard Archer	Virginia
	Thomas Seayres	Virginia

	Ezekiel Polk	North Carolina
	James Clay	Georgia
Surgeons	John Elliott	New York
	John M. Scott	New Jersey
	Richard Allison	Pennsylvania

Artillery

Major Commandant	John Doughty	New Jersey
Captains	Henry Burbeck	Massachusetts
	Joseph Savage	Massachusetts
	James Bradford	New York
	William Ferguson	Pennsylvania
Lieutenants	John Peirce	Massachusetts
	Moses Porter	Massachusetts
	William Moore	Massachusetts
	Ebenezer Smith Fowle	Massachusetts
	Dirck Schuyler	New York
	Mathew Ernest	New York
	Mahlon Ford	New Jersey
	Edward Spear	Pennsylvania
Surgeon's Mate	Nathan Hayward	Massachusetts

CORRESPONDENCE:
SECOND SESSION

October 1789

Alexander Hamilton to James Madison

I thank you My Dear Sir for the line you was so obliging as to leave for me and for the loan of the book accompanying it; in which I have not yet made sufficient progress to judge of its merit.

I dont know how it was but I took it for granted—That you had left town much earlier than you did; else I should have found an opportunity after your adjournment to converse with you on the subjects committed to me by the house of Representatives.[1] It is certainly important, that a plan as complete and as unexceptionable as possible should be matured by the next meeting of Congress; and for this purpose it could not but be useful that there should be a comparison and [*lined out*] concentration of ideas of those whose duty leads them to a contemplation of the subject.

As I lost the opportunity of a personal communication, May I ask of your friendship to put to paper and send me your thoughts on such objects as may have occurred to you for an additional to our revenue, and also as to any modifications of the public debt which could be made consistent with good faith the interest of the Public and of its Creditors?

In my opinion, in considering plans for the increase of our Revenues, the difficulty lies, not so much in the want of objects as in the prejudices which may be feared with regard to almost every object. The Question is very much What further taxes will be *least* unpopular?

ALS, Madison Papers, DLC. The letter was endorsed as directed to the care of Charles Lee, collector at Alexandria, Virginia, and signed "Yr. Affect[*ionate*]. & Obed[*ient*]. A. Hamilton."

---

[1]On 21 September, the House passed resolutions directing Hamilton to prepare a plan making adequate provision for the support of the public credit, to apply to the governors for statements of their states' debts, the provisions made for their payment, and the amount of government securities in their respective treasuries, and to report on all of these to Congress at its next session.

[*Jeremiah Wadsworth,*] The Observer, No. I

THE value of many civil institutions cannot be known without a familiar acquaintance with the state of some nation wholly destitute of them. By this means strangers travelling in the United States, often discover excellencies in their political constitutions and in the several safe-guards to liberty, which are not noticed by the native inhabitants who have always used them. A Frenchman or a Spainyard educated within the verge of despotic authority, sees with transport a fabrick of freedom, and is much more particular in noticing every part, than the American, who accustomed by habit, thinks them the immediate works of nature, and that the same may be found in all nations—Let Americans thank their God, and admire the wisdom of their ancestors, for the patrimony of civil liberty. A person who means in future to consider himself a citizen of no one nation, but of the world, begs you to know that you are the favored people of the Almighty Father. It is true you are not rich—neither are you poor—there is more poverty and distress in a single city of Europe, than in the whole American dominion. Every honest man may live in a state of competency, and competence to a wise mind is affluence, it is all that human nature can receive. You have no Bastiles or Inquisition[1]—no tyranizing Nobles—None to support but those who are employed in your service. Your rulers are of your own creation—your persons are sacred so long as you are innocent—and the poor have the same access and remedy in your courts of justice as the rich. Your public debt if it can be funded and preserved among yourselves will be a bond of union, and in this way an advantage.

The public debt, under just and fixed regulations, will be an increase of circulating property, very serviceable to the growth of commerce and manufactures—government cannot be supported without a number of officers who for the public dignity must be honorably supported, but in the choice of these officers all men of merit may stand as candidates for appointment—You are not confined as in the old nations of Europe to the beggared sons of noble families, to whom lucrative places are generally given as a means of expensive living, which they can obtain in no other way. You have seen the federal appointments to office made with a suprising sagacity and regard to merit, from a class of men who have had the confidence of the people, and are known to profess eminent genius and integrity in the respective departments they fill. Under such direction the wheels of government cannot fail to move safely and for the benefit of the whole—BUT LET THE PUBLIC BE FOREWARNED that the time is now come, in which jealousy will begin to throw out her suspicions. There have been almost innumerable applicants for public offices, many of them men of no genius, and generally of no industry; who wished to live an easy life on public support. All these are disappointed, and will wish to revenge themselves, by insinuations against the designs of government, and the favored persons who manage our great interests. Like an honest people, let us despise every attempt of this nature, until the government hath had time to operate, we shall then know its excellencies and can remedy its defects if there be any.

[Hartford, Connecticut] *American Mercury*, 12 October. This is the inaugural essay of a tightly organized series of eighteen that appeared in the weekly *American Mercury* (with only one interruption) through 8 February 1790, and that was reprinted (in whole or in part) in newspapers at Salem, Boston, Worcester, Northampton, and Pittsfield, Massachusetts; Norwich, Middletown, Hartford, and Litchfield, Connecticut; Providence, Rhode Island; New York City (*NYDG*, 11 December 1789–12 February 1790; *NYDA*, 16 December 1789–12 February 1790); and Philadelphia. (Observer 19 and 20, printed later in 1790, covered different subjects.) These eighteen essays are being printed, under their respective dates, because they provide background for the second session debate on public credit by an astute writer whom the editors have identified as a member of Congress.

Several clues point to Jeremiah Wadsworth as the author of the Observer essays. From their origins in his hometown press and their strongly nationalist perspective on state economy and politics, it must be assumed the author was a well informed Connecticut Federalist. His authority for disputing (in Observer 18) the attribution of a letter said to be from a member of Congress (in *Boston Gazette*, 11 February, calendared below), might lie in his inclusion among their number. More specific clues are: the author's advocacy (in Observer 9 and 10 respectively) of the creditors' and manufacturing interests, to which Wadsworth was deeply committed; his apparent firsthand knowledge (in Observer 1) of conditions in Europe, where Wadsworth had traveled and conducted business in 1783–84; his support (beginning with Observer 3) for the assumption of the states' war debts, which was the focus of many of Wadsworth's numerous speeches in the second session; and the fact that one of the Observer's critics was certain that its author was in New York when numbers 12 through 18 were first printed at Hartford (An Independent Observer, *NYDG*, 4 March 1790). The most compelling proof of all, however, is a letter to Alexander Hamilton, dated 17 December (printed below), where Wadsworth reveals his control over not only the essays' direction but their very existence, asking for Hamilton's approval of their contents and pledging the unnamed author to continue writing "if none of his projects oppose yours."

---

[1] The Bastille, Paris's infamous prison from the fourteenth century until its demolition in the French Revolution, was a symbol of absolutism and arbitrary punishment. Since 1478, the Spanish Inquisition had been charged with rooting out heresy by censorship, torture, and its notorious autos-da-fé (burning at the stake).

FRIDAY, 16 OCTOBER 1789

Pierce Butler to Weeden Butler

On the breaking up of Congress, I made a short Excursion to Philadelphia; during my stay there I had the satisfaction of Addressing a few lines to You. *** the Reviews[1] are a great treat to me and They at same time inform me of the New Publications—In my last letter to my Boy [*Thomas*] I desired

Him to send me a Thermometer from His own Bank. I do not mean to be long His Debtor, I therefore request the favour of You to pay the Damages. I wish it to be of the best kind.

I have wrote thus far by twilight, before Aurora fairly dawn'd on this Western World.

*** I wish to have the disbursements for my Boy depend as little as possible on Contingency—When mighty Empires are Oeconomising why may not an Individual. ***

I have not yet had leisure to look into Mr. Kates[2] when I peruse Him I have no doubt from Your representation of being highly gratified—If Sheridan shou'd publish His Speech I wish to have it, for tho' His private Character is not amiable, His mind is great—It is not the Man I admire—If Mr. H[*astings*]. is innocent. Messrs. B[*urke*]. and S[*heridan*]. are not so—Is it possible they can be such Monsters of infamy as to filch from Him his good Name?[3]

What think You of matters in France? surely the People are going too far! and may possibly destroy by their Violence the object they Aim at—a free Governmt. Our American Governmt. is geting fast to Rights: Arts and Manufactures are rapidly advancing in several of the States; Some good Artists every now and then find the way over from England.

The Ship is under way, so I must close.

[*P. S.*] When You see my friend [*Dr. Peter*] Spence tell Him I am almost off[*ended?*] at receiving one short letter only from Him since His return to England. Bless my Boy for me.

ALS, Butler Letters, Uk. Addressed to Cheyne Walk, Chelsea, near London; postmarked.

---

[1] *The Monthly Review* was a literary journal of the liberal, Whig persuasion printed in London from 1749 to 1844.

[2] George Keate (1729–97) was a British author of pastoral elegies, satirical poems, and travel literature.

[3] Richard Brinsley Sheridan (1751–1816), the Irish born playwright and famed orator in Parliament (1780–1812), joined Edmund Burke in leading the attack against Warren Hastings (1723–1818) as "plunderer of Bengal" while governor general of British India (1773–84). Impeached by the House of Commons in May 1787, Hastings was tried by the House of Lords in 145 sittings between February 1788 and his acquittal in April 1795. Butler probably refers to Sheridan's most famous speech, delivered on 7 February 1787, during the proceedings that led to Hastings' impeachment. None of Sheridan's speeches was published before 1859.

OTHER DOCUMENTS

George Mason to Thomas Marshall. ALS, Thomas J. Clay Papers, DLC. Written from "Gunston Hall," Fairfax County, Virginia; addressed to Fayette County, Kentucky.

Received a letter from Brown in New York, saying that he had put all his law practice business in the hands of his brother, James Brown.

SATURDAY, 17 OCTOBER 1789

Roger Sherman to Governor Samuel Huntington

The Honorable the General Assembly in January last ordered that one hundred and fifty pounds should be advanced to each of the members of Congress from this state for their expenses to be paid over to the United States on account of the specie requisitions made on this state when they should receive a compensation for their services and expenses. But on consideration of the great expenses incurred by this state in the course of the late war, and advancements of money to the United States, and for supporting invalids since the peace, the members of Congress for this state thought it might be advisable for the state to retain the monies in their own hands, until there should be a final liquidation of their accounts. The sum advanced to me I am willing to repay in such manner as the Honorable Assembly shall direct; but on this occasion I would take the liberty humbly to represent that there is now due to me from the state the sum of 775 pounds and 13 shillings being the balance due for my services and expenses as a member of Congress for their state between the 10th day of May 1775 and sometime in October 1780 as pr. account liquidated by the committee of pay table, which was then due and payable out of the civil list funds, but there not being money in the Treasury to pay it as that time I took a note for it payable in hard money by a special order of the General Assembly which note is dated Nov. 29th 1780 which I expected would be paid at any time when I should have occasion for it after the close of the war, but not being under necessity for it until now, I did not request payment. But I have lately been at considerable expense, by advancements by way of settlement to several of my children, and do really stand in need of some part of it. It would greatly oblige me if the whole of the 150 pounds advanced to me as aforesaid might be offset toward said note, but if only 100 pounds of it shall be advanced to be retained by me for that purpose, or any lesser sum it would afford me some relief.

I loaned some hundred pounds in money to the state for which I have Treasurer's note now due, but that sum that was due for my services and expenses I always considered payable in hard money out of the civil list funds or some other as good. I would humbly request your Excellency to lay this letter before the Honorable the General Assembly that they may take such order thereon as in their wisdom and justice shall seem meet.

Lewis H. Boutel, *The Life of Roger Sherman* (Chicago, 1869), pp. 336–37. Written from New Haven, Connecticut.

Hugh Williamson to John Gray Blount

Since the inclosed was written we learn that Genl. Lincoln & the other Commissioners had the Prospect on their Arrival in Georgia of seeing a vast Body of Indians at the Treaty.[1] The Commissioners are authorised to offer the Indians very good Terms. I think the Indians will infallibly accept of the Terms which must produce a good Peace with those Indians and a Constable will be appointed to keep the Peace viz. a few Continentals. A Treaty with the Cherokees is next in Contemplation & I am in Hopes that our Assembly will not refuse to agree to a very reasonable Proposal which will probably be made to them—whether the [*North Carolina ratification*] Convention confederates or not. The Effects of such Measure will also be a good & firm Peace with the Cherokees. I need not tell you how much to be desired by our Western Friends.

I have just given the Count de Moustier, who sails perhaps tomorrow for France, sundry Propositions respecting our Commerce in Naval Stores as also respecting the Mississippi. I wish greatly to see a regular Trade to France in Naval Stores. If our State confederates & Paper Payments are prohibited I propose forthwith to adventure to a considerable Extent in Commerce, believing that Industry in N.C. promises the Possessors more advantage than in most of the other States for this simple Reason that so few of us possess it.

I do not say that I am weary'd of politics, for if my fellow Citizens are willing to entrust me with some Part of their Confidence either in the Senate or House of Representatives I shall attempt to serve them but I consider this as a very secondary Object I wish to lean on better and more independant Props for the Support of a Family.

I am very sorry that Majr. [*Charles*] Gerrard was not able to see [*lined out*] the Western Lands. I wish very much to know some Thing about the true State of the Soil that has been so much praised—There is a possibility of making settlements in that Country.

ALS, John Gray Blount Papers, Nc-Ar. Addressed to Washington, North Carolina. The enclosure has not been located.

---

[1] Benjamin Lincoln, David Humphreys, and Cyrus Griffin were the federal commissioners appointed in late August to negotiate a peace treaty with the Creek Indians. On 19 September, Georgia's Executive Council officially authorized Few to attend the proceedings on the state's behalf (Executive Council Minutes, G-Ar). Arriving at Rock Landing, a traditional meeting place in the Oconee River in central Georgia, the commissioners and Few found waiting for them anywhere between nine hundred and two thousand Creek headmen and warriors. Talks began on 21 September but ended four days later when the Creeks' chief negotiator, Alexander McGillivray, precipitously broke off the talks and returned home. For more on the negotiations, see *DHFFC* 2:210–41, 17:1468n.

OTHER DOCUMENTS

John Adams to William Cushing. ALS, Robert T. Paine Papers, MHi. Written from Middletown, Connecticut; addressed to "Mr. [*William Walter*] Parsons's," Middletown, Connecticut.

Set out too early to wait on Cushing before leaving; may see him in Braintree or Cambridge; congratulations on his appointment to the "national Bench"; hopes to see him soon in New York City.

John Hamilton to Robert Morris. Copy, Washington Papers, DLC. Written from Edenton, North Carolina; place to which addressed not indicated. For a partial text, see *PGW* 4:401n.

Acknowledges Morris's letter of 29 September, expressing "your wishes on my behalf"; understands that James Iredell, through Williamson, has already made an application to be federal judge of the North Carolina district; asks for Morris's early recommendation for federal attorney, especially as there is a "moral certainty" of North Carolina's ratifying the Constitution in November.

NYDA, 17 October. Wister Butler Papers, PHi. Annotated by Butler to indicate the article for which he retained the issue.

Selection from France's Declaration of Rights (on freedom of religion).

NYDG, 17 October. Wister Butler Papers, PHi. Annotated by Butler to indicate the article for which he retained the issue.

France's Declaration of Rights.

SUNDAY, 18 OCTOBER 1789

Andrew Craigie to Bossenger Foster, Sr. ALS, Craigie Papers, MWA. Addressed to Boston.

"I am acquainted with such facts as leave me no doubt of the rise of Securities."

Hugh Williamson to Abishai C. Thomas. ANS, John Gray Blount Papers, Nc-Ar. Written at 11 A.M.; enclosed in Thomas to J. G. Blount, 19 October. For the full text, see *Blount* 1:512.

Wife (Maria Apthorpe Williamson) delivered a son about an hour earlier; both are well.

MONDAY, 19 OCTOBER 1789

[*Jeremiah Wadsworth,*] The Observer, No. II

The nation which would be served by men of honesty and great abilities,
must pay well

IN my excursions thro' several parts of New England, I have noticed a class of citizens, who complain of the compensations allowed by Congress to the principal officers of government.

The liberal character of the Americans, is an evidence that these complaints arise more from their strong jealousy for liberty, than from parsimony. A jealous concern for public liberty is a noble passion, which will guard the freedom of your posterity, but at the same time it needs the rigid correction of reason. A weak and ignorant administration is one common means of subverting popular rights. Those very principles in the human mind, which make men jealous of their liberty, without restraint will lead into licentiousness.

The end of a good government is to divide out liberty in proper portions to every citizen, that all may be free and none oppressed. In a state of anarchy, every neighbour becomes a tyrant in his own little sphere of afflicting; in absolute governments there are few tyrants, awful in their course, and to approach them is approaching death. If you must be wretched it matters little whether the minister of a prince or an ill-natured neighbour be the instrument. Civil government is the only possible guard against these evils. If you were a nation of slaves, the sword, bayonet, and prison would give efficacy to the measures of weak and unprincipled rulers; but you are free, and if governed at all, men of high talents and approved integrity, your most literary and industrious citizens must be called into employment. Such men never have need to beg business, for the resources of their own minds and their application is a fund of wealth. If the public design to have their service, the reward must be adequate to their abilities and bear some proportion to the gains they make in private life.

No man will leave a private employment, which promises him a thousand dollars per annum, for an office of half the sum, in which he is responsible to the public opinion, and perhaps endangers the loss of his reputation for wisdom, a sacrifice for which no pecuniary satisfaction can be made. Honor or the public notice may with a few be an inducement; but these few are persons of great vanity, and have not the abilities for a difficult or confidential trust. Men of discernment, and such you want, know how to estimate their own consequence in the State, they know that if for the present you employ mean abilities for the sake of being served at a cheap rate, the public system will soon be deranged, and that you must then purchase their aid at such price as they please. It is a better way to commence your government on such principles as will be permanent. Let public officers be few, and make them responsible both for their capacity and honesty. It is too much the custom of this country to pity a man, who says "I did as well as I knew." Ignorance ought to be no excuse before the sacred tribunal of the public. He who accepts an office doth it at his own risque, and there are as many reasons why he should bear the consequence of incapacity as of knavery. Make this the known rule for decision on public characters, and the ignorant seekers of office will become less troublesome in their solicitations. Give an honorable reward which will command the service of your most distinguished citizens, to whatever department they are called. Such men have a character to lose, and ambition will unite with every other consideration to call forth their greatest exertions.

If this proposal doth not please, it is easy to change the system, for in every country there are rogues and dunces in plenty, who will serve you at any price: BUT REMEMBER THAT THE FIRST WILL CHEAT YOU OUT OF THOUSANDS, AND THE LATTER DISSIPATE MILLIONS BY THEIR IGNORANCE.

The compensations determined by Congress, are as small as can possibly command the service of your best characters—a less sum by throwing the execution of your government into unskilful hands would have endangered the whole. The pay of the Senate and Commons great as it may sound in the ears of some, circumstances being all considered, is not extravagant. It is a prevalent idea through the union that these gentlemen shall hold no other office under the empire or particular States—most of them to serve you have relinquished lucrative employment—after the first year Congress will not probably be together more than fifty days in a year—tho' your representatives be encreased, the expence of a legislature will be much less than the sums given by the several States to support the members of the old Congress. Your whole civil list, including every department, would not half defray the houshold expences of an European Prince. The highest officers in your judiciary and revenue have not a better provision than grooms of the stable, noble keepers of hawks and hounds, and dependant still more insignificant than those receive in other nations from the hands of Royalty. Useless officers are the vermin of a State, but some are necessary to its very existence. Let them be few as possible, but men of approved ability—pay them well—make them responsible—and if after this any are unfaithful, demand what atonement you please, it will not be too severe.

[Hartford, Connecticut] *American Mercury*, 19 October. For information on The Observer series, its authorship, and reprintings, see the location note to The Observer, No. I, 12 October, above.

TUESDAY, 20 OCTOBER 1789

James Madison, Memorandum on African Colonization. Ms., hand of Madison, William Thornton Papers, DLC. The editors of *PJM* supply this approximate date, based on Madison's probable meeting with Thornton while at Mary House's Philadelphia boarding house en route home to Virginia. The memo was certainly written by 13 November, when Thornton enclosed it in a letter to the president of the French abolition society, Les Amis des Noirs (*PJM* 12:438n). For the full text, see *PJM* 12:437–38.

> An asylum for freed African Americans on the west coast of Africa might encourage manumission and end slavery in the United States; they could not be permitted to stay and be integrated into American society owing to permanent prejudices among whites, and resettlement in territories occupied by Native Americans would be destroyed owing to the latter's peculiar hatred of Blacks.

WEDNESDAY, 21 OCTOBER 1789

Fisher Ames to Thomas Dwight

No private conveyance offering, this will go by the post. You see, by the date, that I am in Boston, which is busy with preparation and expectation. The President is to appear on a triumphal arch. The Governor begins to take a part in the affair. The gout came so opportunely last Saturday, that it has been doubtful whether his humility would be gratified with the sight of his *superior*. Is it credible that doubts should have existed, whether *he* or the *President* should first visit? that so much honor to one should be supposed to degrade the other? This *inter nos*. Some of his folks have thrown cold water on the ardor of the town, to no purpose. I wish you and all my Springfield friends may be gratified with the sight and conversation of the great and good President. God bless him.

Ames 1:73. Written from Boston; place to which addressed not indicated.

THURSDAY, 22 OCTOBER 1789

William Few to Catherine Few

*** When my mind is a little freed from business and I have leisure to reflect, my imagination extends to you and represents you encircled by your dear and affectionate Parents and Sisters pressing to your lovely bosom the dear little pledge of our mutual affection whose infantile action and gesture already begin to give delight to an indulgent and tender Mother.[1] Those pleasing imaginary Scenes, sometimes act so powerfully on me, that I have almost been induced to close my arrangements here and endeavour to immediately set out for the place of your residence, and there enjoy with you in real[i]ty that pleasure which my imagination has thus painted. But duty, and interest forbid. It is my political duty to be present at the meeting of our next Assembly to give such information respecting the proceedings of Congress and other matters touching the policy of the States, as may be required; and my own interest requires that I should attend to my domestic affairs, which I have not yet been able to properly arrange. I have this year made about 10,000 lb. of Tobacco on my plantation, which I intend to take with me to N. York and the greatest part of it is yet to strip and prize. But these, and all other matters that will make my presence necessary here, I trust will be accomplished in time sufficient to see you by the 10th of Decmr. next which is the day that we appointed for my return and it is the period to which I look forward with some, solicitude; notwithstanding I spend my time here at my peaceful home very agreeably; when my mind is fatigued with reading, I can find abundant amusement in ranging over the fields and woods, and viewing the works of nature and the success of the industry of man. It is harvest with us now, we are gathering in our corn with the fruits of the Summers labor; and it affords to the reflecting mind, the most grateful, and pleasing sensations, to see the bounties of Heaven poured around the industry of man; and here in this mild Climate, and fertile soil, the labor of the husband-man is more than amply compensated— ***

ALS, Few Papers, GU. Written from "Hesperia," Columbia County, Georgia. The omitted text discusses the family's future residence in Georgia and members of the Nicholson family.

[1]Catherine's parents were James and Frances Nicholson. Her sisters included Frances (later Mrs. Seney), Hannah (later Mrs. Albert Gallatin), and Maria. The infant was Frances, born on 30 April 1789.

OTHER DOCUMENTS

Samuel A. Otis to Joseph Otis. ALS, Otis Family Papers, NNC. Written from Boston; addressed to Barnstable, Massachusetts.

Arrived home on 17 October; agrees to sign a bond for Joseph's conduct (as revenue collector at Barnstable).

SUNDAY, 25 OCTOBER 1789

Abigail Adams to John Adams. ALS, Adams Family Manuscript Trust,
MHi. Written from "Richmond Hill," outside New York City.
    Madison is ill at Philadelphia; it is reported that Speaker Muhlenberg
died last week from a burst blood vessel.

MONDAY, 26 OCTOBER 1789

[*Jeremiah Wadsworth,*] The Observer, No. III

The public debt of the union may be so managed as to prove a great national benefit
    Few evils are so great but wisdom and application may derive from them
eventual advantages, which will more than balance the loss at first apprehended. Of all the evils consequent upon your late glorious war, the immense debt incurred by the public hath been esteemed the greatest, and
one for which remedy was the most difficult without doing such injustice
to individuals as must excite the abhorrence of honest men. That this hath
as yet been a perplexed business all will allow—that this debt with its past
management, hath distressed both the people and the creditors is undeniable; but we ought not to impute those distresses to the debt itself, which
have arose almost wholly from impolitic management. The people of this
country were as new in the arts of finance as those of war; in the last you have
excelled and conquered, and in the first may soon become eminent, if some
popular prejudices do not prevent. It is not strange that your finances were
deranged, and the people and creditors both in a state of suffering under an
administration without system or energy, and which was unable to bring
any exertions to a point.
    To load the people with enormous taxes would be wicked and impolitic,
and for this there is no need. In some future numbers of this paper, I shall
endeavour to point out the means of doing such justice to the public creditors, that if reasonable men, they will feel themselves contented, without
burden on the people half as heavy as they have borne. At present I will
mention a number of national benefits to be derived from the public debt,
if managed wisely. There are very few instances in which an individual can
be benefitted by credit beyond his present ability to pay; but with a nation
the case is different. Great Britain lies under the heaviest debt of any nation
on earth[1]—and this very debt hath in a number of instances been the means
of her preservation, by interesting rich subjects to afford their aid, when no
other could be obtained—they advanced new sums to preserve those national funds, in which they had a great property already vested.
    Tho' we hope America will never need to profit by her debt in this way

there are other advantages she may derive. A public debt is a band of union, and interests a powerful and opulent class of citizens to support the government under which it is contracted. An increase of transferable property is another advantage which may be derived from the national debt. Commerce, manufactures, and the conveniences of life require that a certain proportion of property be of such a nature as may be easily negociated or transferred from man to man. Of this kind are articles of barter, gold and silver coins and bills of credit. To determine exactly how great a proportion of this kind of property would be a public advantage is impossible. Many of the best judges imagine that the whole national debt, upon a proper establishment would not be too great for this extensive and growing country. There has been a species of transferal commonly called speculating in public securities, which is but a kind of gaming, and is attended with no advantages to the State: but this has arisen not as much from an undue quantity, as from a distrust of public faith, and a want of system in the finance of the union and of particular States—Let this debt be funded in honor and justice, and it will soon have a regular value, the transferal will no longer be the work of speculators, but take place between citizens of another character, the commercial and the industrious as their own interest may require, and thus become an immense stock for the benefit of trade and manufactures. The true interest of agriculture and commerce naturally embrace each other, and in the state of this country cannot be seperated. All classes of citizens have right to protection for themselves and their property; but if there be any one which hath the best claim to be regarded in public measures, it is the American Farmers, as they constitute the most numerous part of the people. The national debt may be so funded as to produce great consequential advantage to the Farmers, and prove the means of their procuring a much better price for their produce and raw materials, than can otherwise be expected. So far as relates to the present question, a landed property may be considered as fixed and not transferable. In a new country and where land is cheap as in the United States, the inhabitants when they have power to do it, will rest their property in solid soil. The produce of the Farmers land is loose and transferable property, and that it may bear a just price, it is necessary there should be an equal quantity of property within the community, in such a situation that it may be commanded to make pay to the farmer, for the fruit of his toil.

The produce of the country and our raw materials for manufactures, will always command a just price in some part of the world, and it is the business of commerce to collect and transport them to the place in which they are wanted.

If foreigners are under the necessity of coming to us and collecting the articles they need, the price received by the farmer will be limited as they please. Make the supposition that one half the property now in commerce within the

United States, were to be annihilated; tho' our produce might bear the same price in the markets of Europe, it would probably diminish the home price one third. The purchasers would be few—the markets would be over stocked—the produce of your farms being in its nature perishable must be soon vended, and the remaining half of commercial property would command out of your hands nearly the scarce quantity of produce as the whole would have done, if preserved. In this case the loss would be as sensibly felt by the farmers as by the merchant. It is always the case in a new and agricultural country, that the transferable property is in too small quantity for the advantage of those who hold and till the ground. At present the principal of the national debt cannot be paid, but with a little honesty and policy it may be placed in a situation safe for the creditors and beneficial to all classes of citizens.

For the benefit of the agricultural interests, I would not wish the debt to be annihilated, if it were consistent with justice. Let it be honestly funded, it must remain in its nature transferable and will be an immense bank for all kinds of business. The situation of the United States is such, your agriculture so extensive and increasing, and the quantity of your produce so great, that unless by some policy of this kind you fix a certain quantity of property in its nature negociable, the market will be overstocked, and the loss will in the end be borne by the farmer.

Suppose the surplus produce of a farmer beyond his own consumption, to equal one hundred bushels of wheat. If there be a just proportion of negotiable property each bushel will be worth five shillings; but if this proportion be a little lessened, each bushel will command only four shillings, and the whole loss to the farmer will be five pounds; which is a sum four times so great as he need to pay in taxes to place the whole American debt on honorable funds. To execute this business honestly, and great abilities are requisite—the new treasury department promises you both, and I make no doubt but the debt we have lamented, will soon be a great national advantage.

[Hartford, Connecticut] *American Mercury*, 26 October. For information on The Observer series, its authorship, and reprintings, see the location note to The Observer, No. I, 12 October, above.

---

[1] The [Windsor] *Vermont Journal*, 12 May 1790, reported the British debt to be "240 million."

WEDNESDAY, 28 OCTOBER 1789

William Constable to Robert Morris. FC:lbk, Constable-Pierrepont Collection, NN.

Relates a stock transaction involving Morris, Hamilton, and (John Barker?) Church; "I sent your letter to [*William*] Duer with a request that He would call on me at 2 OClk."; Duer has joined John Hopkins in buying up "the soldiers pay" over the previous two months; Duer has "every disposition to oblige you in any thing in his power, & has such reliance on you that He will not hesitate to commit himself in any thing w[*hic*]h. you may recommend—If you will therefore point out to me in your next what You wish him to do, & what You think He may do with safety, I dare answer He will comply with it."

THURSDAY, 29 OCTOBER 1789

Thomas Fitzsimons to Alexander Hamilton. No copy known; mentioned in Hamilton to Fitzsimons, 27 November.

Ebenezer Hazard to Jeremy Belknap. ALS, Belknap Papers, MHi. Addressed to Boston.
    Has just finished an index to the first session's statutes, and is about to make one to the House Journals.

FRIDAY, 30 OCTOBER 1789

A. B. to Mr. Loudon

MIRIFICA!!!

DID you ever hear the story of a very wonderful *bomb*, which is now in the city of New-York? It is one of the most comical machines that ever the eye of curiosity viewed. It is a *bomb, physico—politico—mechanico—chemico—logico—* but its name at full length would take up a paragraph. It is the exact resemblance of an old man's head; or to give you a still better idea of it, it is the very picture of the head of ——. This bomb, you must know, was intended to be charged with *theological* materials, and was to be the load of a *presbyterian* howitzer (alias *pulpit*).[1] But when some sly, pauky presbyters came to examine it, I don't know what was the matter, they did not like it very well; whether they were afraid it would *crack*, or that it was indifferently *charged*, or whatever was the case, they refused to have any thing to do with it. Some others, however, who were not quite so good engineers, and were therefore less scrupulous, determined to employ it. The event proved the first to be the wisest men, for no sooner was it put into the howitzer (which was made of wood and rather large) than it began to *frisk* and *bounce* at such a terrible rate, as threatened to stave the howitzer to pieces, and to drive the fragments about the ears of the spectators, who had come out of curiosity to see it, and who were at length frightened out of the experiment-ground beyond the ramparts (alias the walls of the church). For this and other reasons, it soon became quite useless as a theological instrument. Since that time it has rolled about from one end of the continent to the other, and has gathered a very odd collection of politics, chemistry, mechanism, botany, natural history, theoretic 'farming, malting, brewing, distilling, dying, tanning, baking,' medicine, &c. Now, as these heterogeneous materials were crammed into the bomb, one upon the back of another, and were mixed through each other like the ingredients of a plumb-pudding, a violent heat, and a marvellous explosion might naturally be expected. This was the case, for a daily paper (not a mile from your house) yesterday announced to the public, that on the ——— of September last, the bomb discharged its contents like an eruption of Vesuvius.[2] These contents, *instinctively*, flew at the Latin and Greek languages, and shattered Homers, Ciceros and Virgils, by scores, into non-existence.[3] Nay it is thought that the pieces in their fulminating fury, will break the shins, and put out the eyes of every Latin and Greek schoolar for 8000 miles from New-York, as a centre. It is certainly a very ominous circumstance that, after the *flash* of the bursting bomb, such a cloud of *dust* was raised, as made its effects extremely similar to what Horace calls fumum exfulgore![4]

NYP, 3 November, edited by Samuel Loudon. The title means "wonders" in Latin. The piece is an elaborate satire on Williamson's learning.

[1] Although never ordained, Williamson was licensed to preach before Presbyterian congregations, having studied theology in Connecticut beginning in approximately 1760.
    [2] The eruption in A.D. 79 of Mount Vesuvius on the Bay of Naples buried the cities of Pompeii and Herculaneum.
    [3] The reference is to the widely reprinted and critiqued extract of a letter from Williamson to Johnson (as president of Columbia College), dated 14 September and printed in *NYDA*, 29 October (calendared in *DHFFC* 17:1549). The extract is a long argument based on Williamson's knowledge of history and tightly reasoned pedagogical theories. "I would rescue four or five years from the tyranny of Greek and Latin" as part of an innovative curriculum of "Practical Philosophy." "The difficulties that must occur in executing such a plan," Williamson concluded, "would have pointed it out as a proper object for the national government, if the charge of a public seminary had been expressly committed to their care. This you know was the wish of some gentlemen."
    [4] Latin: the smoke from a lightning bolt. Horace (65–8 B.C.) was a Latin poet.

SATURDAY, 31 OCTOBER 1789

William Few to Catherine Few. ALS, William and Catherine Few Papers, GU. Written from "Hesperia," Columbia County, Georgia; addressed in care of Commodore James Nicholson, New York City. The salutation reads "My Dear Girl."

  Wrote a long letter a few days earlier; "few transactions of my life affords me more pleasing reflections" than contributing to her happiness; complains that he has received no letters from her since his arrival; enquires of (their daughter) Frances; expects to be reunited before the middle of December; has made Catherine's maid Henne his chief cook and washerwoman.

Benjamin Franklin to Jacques-Donatien Leray de Chaumont *fils* (James Le Ray). ALS, Franklin Papers, DLC. Written from Philadelphia; place to which addressed not indicated. The recipient (1760–1840) came to the United States in 1785 with power of attorney for his father, the elder Chaumont (1725–1803), a manufacturer, financier, and strident American supporter at the French Court, who hosted Franklin at his estate at Passy, outside Paris, throughout the latter's tenure as commissioner to France (1776–85) and became deeply involved in the network of commercial transactions co-ordinated by the Deane-Franklin faction in support of the war effort (for example, outfitting John Paul Jones's famous warship named for Franklin, the *Bonhomme Richard*). The unsettled accounts Franklin mentions relate to the petition that Chaumont submitted to Congress in June 1785 on behalf of his father and other French military suppliers seeking compensation for payment in depreciated currency; King, Johnson, and Grayson were on the congressional committee to which it was referred. The accounts were still before the auditor's office on 2 November 1789, but it was apparently these accounts that were settled by a warrant for $9,051.33 that the treasury department issued later in 1790. Chaumont *fils* returned to France that year with his new bride, Grace Coxe, Tench Coxe's sister-in-law, but returned in 1802 as James Le Ray, by which name he is known to history as one of the most famous landed proprietors in northern Pennsylvania and New York State (*Adams* 2:298n, 4:54; Roger G. Kennedy, *Orders From France: The Americans and the French in a Revolutionary World, 1780–1820* [New York, 1989], pp. 39–40; *JCC* 28:489; *PAH* 5:494; *DHFFC* 3:804; *PTJ* 8:89).

Believes that Chaumont's accounts will be among the first debts Congress discharges when they reconvene in January 1790; promises to support Chaumont's application with his strongest interest.

Josiah Thatcher to George Thatcher. ALS, Thomas G. Thatcher Papers, MeHi. Written from Boston; place to which addressed not indicated.

Asks brother (George) to see John R. Livingston about a financial transaction once he is back in New York.

October 1789 Undated

Pierce Butler, Receipt Book. Butler Papers, PHi.

To Weedon Butler, for son Thomas's education (through June 1789), £104.3; for globes, books, etc., £25.7.

November 1789

SUNDAY, 1 NOVEMBER 1789

Letter from a London Merchant to Boston

We fear the period is now near arrived when government will be constrained to assume the duties on pot and pearl ashes and lumber* in general, as paid by foreign powers—yours excepted—The Ambassadors of which powers are continually importuning Administration to exact those duties in common, or allow the produce of their respective kingdoms to be admitted free of duty—as your's. Russia, with whom we are not on the best terms, and with whom we have not now any existing treaty, is foremost in those applications; and we expect they will have weight, as they have reason with them; they have been long silent, but the appearance of your new formed imposts on goods and shipping, in all the public papers, have caught their observation, the ambassadors in question have renewed afresh their importunity, that the exports of their several countries, of the same description, should be placed on an equal footing.

*With respect to our pot and pearl ashes, and lumber, we have not been considered as foreigners in the English ports.

NYDA, 12 January 1790 (the date on which members of Congress would have seen it), from an unlocated Boston newspaper; also reprinted at Portsmouth, New Hampshire; Lansingburgh, New York; Philadelphia; and Baltimore.

OTHER DOCUMENTS

Abigail Adams to Mary Cranch. ALS, Abigail Adams Letters, MWA. Written from "Richmond Hill," outside New York City; addressed to Braintree, Massachusetts. For the full text, see *Abigail Adams*, pp. 31–32.

Asks Cranch to tell Adams that Martha Washington has a present for him when he returns, which she will not show to Abigail.

Thomas Hartley to Anthony Wayne. ALS, Wayne Papers, PHi. Written from York, Pennsylvania; addressed to Savannah, Georgia; carried by Dr. William Montgomery.

Introduces the bearer, son of "our worthy Friend John Montgomery" of Carlisle, Pennsylvania.

MONDAY, 2 NOVEMBER 1789

[*Jeremiah Wadsworth,*] The Observer, No. IV

The people have suffered an immense sum by the deranged state of the national debt

AFTER all that the public have suffered by the confusion of finance in the union and several states, it is not strange that their patience is nearly exhausted. The want of a general government hath cost millions to the people, which are now very happily shared and enjoyed between a set of people who have been very scrupulous about liberty, collectors of the taxes you have paid, and speculators in your disordered funds.

It is time the truth should be fairly spoken to the people at large, and the observer will do it whatever may be the consequence. Some of the same scrupulous people now wish to play over the old game, and fill you with jealousies that they may have a second harvest, but their day is past. For our own preservation it is necessary we should attend to the sources of past confusion. By the national debt I mean all those sums which the union at large, and the particular states stand obligated to pay. These sums were incurred in one common cause, our defence in the general war—it was chance and not option which fixed men's names to the list of continental or State creditors.

The general idea is a true one, that the whole must stand or fall together, and most people had little preference to either kind of security. There is not at present any reason in equity why one class of creditors should be prefered to the other—the whole ought to stand on the same funds, and have equal justice. Soon after the war a new constitution of government was found necessary to set things right, but at that juncture the country was not sufficiently enlightened to obtain it. The consequence was, the continent without any power of creating funds, began in a desultory manner to arrange their own finances. The several states finding the weakness of the union, began to make partial arrangements for that very debt, which on every principle of justice ought to be sustained by the whole nation. Such remedies as these, adopted by different bodies of men, and at distant places and very different times, must in their nature be different and confused.

From this source you have seen more than fifty kinds of paper securities, at one time, within the United States, differing but a small matter in value, but enough to spread confusion over the whole, and betray the honest into the hands of designing men. The people have paid enough to make the creditors contented, had it come to their hands in a regular and equal method;

but in the midst of this darkness nothing has been effected. The members of the old Congress, and your assemblies, were men of wisdom, but what could wisdom do in such different and distant bodies, which had no constitutional connection, and of course could have no general system. Matters of this kind cannot be placed in a numerous body of men, be they ever so wise. A treasury board of proper compass, systematically arranged, and furnished with information, must concert; and the legislature after proper discussions must give the authority to execute.

The first step towards order and light is to reduce the whole national debt to one kind, and one set of regulations, and unless something of this nature takes place, you have millions more to pay without coming any nearer to the desired end. It is impossible that a plain man, who is an industrious and good subject, should distinguish between so many kinds of taxes of different values. Let the whole sum of this debt be brought together—placed on common and similar funds, and regularity introduced to the business—The public will then know their situation—thirty men will do that business for the whole union which now employs thro' the several states two hundred and fifty, all of whom are supported by the people—The creditors will understand a plain and honest plan, and be saved from a thousand impositions—taxes will be of one kind, and the man who purchases to pay them will know the price he ought to give. I can foresee there will be objections to what I advance, and some very cunning men will cry danger! danger! but I never yet saw any evil from simplifying money matters, where all the people have to pay. It is the rolling up together of a number of half made systems, which endangers the people; for they cannot see thro' them, and the man that must borrow his neighbours wits to manage his own affairs, must soon borrow money to pay his debts. The present is a fortunate moment for this country, and the only one they will ever have to simplify their treasury matters. Let one great and inclusive system for the whole be adopted, and your finances may soon be reduced to perfect order. Should the present opportunity be past and the federal system not take in the whole of your national debt, another opportunity must not be expected—confusion will continue—the poor and unsuspicious will be cheated—jealousy will pervade all orders of citizens—there will be no public faith, and your monied men will hide their property—a stable medium for business will be severely wanted—and your future agriculture, manufactures and commerce, be denied that spring which might now be given them.

P. S. In the second number of this paper, some observations were made, on the compensation, the gentlemen of Congress have taken to themselves—I think the public mind must be easy on this subject, when it is understood that the pay they have taken, is not greater than was allowed by the State assemblies to the members of the old Congress—take the State of Connecticut for an example—The assembly of this state until May 1787, allowed their delegates three dollars per diem and their expences—the expences of the delegates were different and from two to four dollars per diem—probably the average of expences was three dollars, which added to the compensation for service, makes the sum now given to the Representatives. Since May 1787, the assembly of Connecticut have allowed five dollars per diem for service and expences. The allowance given by Connecticut, was much smaller than in most of the other States—I am informed that the average allowance made by the assemblies of the thirteen States to their delegates, used to be eight dollars per diem nearly, one fourth more than the gentlemen have allowed themselves—the members might then if they pleased, take a seat and continue under pay the whole year; now it will be but a small part of the year—then they might leave Congress when private business called them; now they are constrained by authority to be present, let their own concerns be ever so urgent—then they might and actually did hold offices of profit under their own States; now it is the popular sense they should not, and many in consequence made a great sacrifice. These facts must justify the present compensation.

[Hartford, Connecticut] *American Mercury*, 2 November. For information on The Observer series, its authorship, and reprintings, see the location note to The Observer, No. I, 12 October, above.

OTHER DOCUMENTS

Francis Taylor, Diary. Vi.
Madison arrived home from Congress.

[Hartford, Connecticut] *American Mercury*, 2 November.
Huntington is a candidate for Council of Assistants in the Connecticut legislature.

TUESDAY, 3 NOVEMBER 1789

Abigail Adams to Mary Cranch

*** For a summer situation this place is delightfull & the House convenient, and except its being Bleak and perhaps difficult of access in some parts of a severe winter, it is more to my mind than any place I ever lived in. in point of oeconomy it would be very advantageous to be able to live at Home part of the year and the winter in particular. wood being the most expensive article here Nut wood, what we call walnut is 7 dollars pr. cord and oak cost me five brought to our door between 40 & 50 cords of which we shall consume in a year, as we are obliged to keep six fires constantly, & occasionally more the hire of servants is an other very heavy article part of which we might spair at Braintree. ***

I have a pretty good Housekeeper a tolerable footman a midling cook, an indifferent steward and a vixen of a House maid, but she has done much better laterly since she finds that the housekeeper will be mistress below stairs, I wish polly [*Tailor*] was in Braintree, and meant to have taken her with me if I had come, but I do not know what to say with regard to her suiting you. She is very far from being a Girl that will turn off work quick, her constitution has been ruined by former hardships, and she is very often laid up, she has not method or regularity with her buisness, all her buisness here is to make 4 or 5 beds, & clean round Rooms which are almost coverd with carpets, all the Brass is cleaned by the footman she helps wash & Iron, but I have been obliged to hire when I have wanted more cleaning than that done in a day, and every days work to pay 3 shilling a day for. I suppose I must keep her till spring unless she should become more than usually quarelsome. with regard to drink I meet with no difficulty with her on that account, and she has an attention to my interest more than any servant I have besides. when Mr. [*John*] Brisler is absent, she keeps no company, and is fond of the children, so that she has her good Qualities, for which I am ready to credit her. ***

I wish Mr. Adams would return with the president, as I know he will be invited to, ***

ALS, Abigail Adams Letters, MWA. Written from "Richmond Hill," outside New York City; addressed to Braintree, Massachusetts. For the full text, see *Abigail Adams*, pp. 33–34.

Pierce Butler to Weeden Butler

Since I last had the satisfaction of addressing You I have been favour'd with Your truly kind and very acceptable letter of the 31st. of August, together with the accompanyments—Never did letters arrive more seasonable—they were more than Medicine to my Dear Mrs. [*Mary Middleton*] Butler who at the time they came to hand was exceedingly indisposed and low Spirited—they were more refreshing to Her than the cooling brook to the hunted Hart—poor Woman She is so attachd to Her Son [*Thomas*] that if She does not hear from Him when She expects, She is wretchd—Indeed You are very good in gratifying Her often—She is sensible of it—there is no better minded woman.

With respect to my Boy, Your goodness leaves me nothing to recommend—You out-run my expectations, though I have sometimes feared that, from the excess of my anxiety, they might in some degree be unreasonable—As I have kept by me all His letters I have lately reviewd them—I have full reason to be satisfied—His progress latterly in writing has been very considerable—In the course of the examination I find He was Stationary for a while in 1786; but He has lately advanced with double rapidity—I am sensible I am indebted to You principaly for this; Nevertheless I wish, through You, to express thanks and return Compliments to Mr. Harper—His former Pupil, my Daughter [Sarah], does Him Creditt I will venture to say that She can write as good a hand as any of Her Sex in America—She is indebted to Mr. Harper for this pleasing and useful acquirement—She is now sedulously Engaged with Astronomy and Natural Philosophy, under the direction of a sensible Man one of the Professors of New York College, a Britoner.[1]

*** I am much obliged by Your intention, respecting the Monthly Reviews No Man feasts on them more than I do—I prefer them to the Critical.[2] I have read Mr. Keate,[3] with inexpressible satisfaction. *** As I love the manners of my friend, I must admire, as far as I have read, those of Mr. Keate—will You present the Respects of a Stranger, nearly as much a Child of Nature, and as much weded to Candor as His Pelew Inhabitants, and thanks for the very great satisfaction I have experienced in Reading His well wrote Book—How just His observations! that Nature, or the God of Nature, made Man open, artless and incapable of disguise! but Civilization teaches distrust—the bane of Society—Highly Civilized in this Sense is part of Europe—I am quite enraptured with the liberality and benevolence of Mr. Keate—I shoud like to have some of His Brittish Works—There is nothing in the literary way here worth your Notice, or I woud Send it—If I meet with a person going to London I will offer You the Journals of Our first Session of Congress—I do not know whether You will read them; Nor do I say they are worth Reading—they are the ground of a larger work, and may hereafter shew the progress of Our Government in Civilization, and the turn it is like to take—I think it is the fact [?] of the Citizen of the United States A pretty accurate knowledge of the principles and tendencies of the different forms of Government—yet I do not oblige You to wade through our Journals—lay them, if You please, on the Shelf—Here is publishd by a Mr. Moss,[4] a Native of One of the States, *the American Geography* I have not looked into it—I will cast my Eye over it, and if I like it I will send a Sett to You.

I have mindfully attended to such Accounts of the progress of the French Revolution as the publick Prints give—I like them not—the Bourgeois are something like a Man long Stinted or Restrained in His diet, they are not only feasting on liberty but imprudently Gormandizing—the result may be Compulsion to return to their Old diet, or possibly a more slender one—It is among the things to be lamented, that Mankind too often abuse the boon

held out to them—I fear it will be the Case in France—Surely the fair Godess, Liberty, requires not such sacrifices to Establish Her throne! such wanton Murders, such repeated Acts of Barbarity! the best friends to the Rights of Mankind must turn their face with abhorrence from them—In this I think the United States have given a lesson to the World—We have Reverted to first Principles, and affected a Revolution in Our form, nay in the Spirit of our Government, not only without bloodshed but even the smallest Strife— Learn from hence Ye more Civilized Nations of Europe a Useful lesson!
***

ALS, Butler Letters, Uk. Addressed to Cheyne Walk, Chelsea near London; postmarked 4 November; answered 5 January 1790.

---

[1] John Kemp (1763–1812), a graduate of the University of Aberdeen (1781) in his native Scotland, immigrated to New York in 1783 and was appointed professor of mathematics and astronomy at Columbia in 1786.

[2] The *Monthly Review*, published in London from 1749 to 1844 was a literary journal allied with the liberal or Whig tradition, while London's *Critical Review; or, Annals of Literature* (1756–1817) espoused Tory, High Church politics.

[3] The British poet and satirist, George Keate (1729–97). Butler refers to Keate's *Account of the Pelew Islands* (London, 1788), drawn from the journals of a famous shipwreck on present-day Pelau, Micronesia, in 1783.

[4] Jedidiah Morse's *American Geography* (Elizabeth, N.J., 1789) earned him the reputation as the "father of American Geography." He petitioned the FFC for copyright protection in May 1789 (*DHFFC* 8:30, 36).

OTHER DOCUMENTS

Abigail Adams to John Adams. ALS, Adams Family Manuscript Trust, MHi. Addressed to Braintree, Massachusetts.

The printers have not sent newspapers since Adams left New York; asks to have them continued.

WEDNESDAY, 4 NOVEMBER 1789

Newspaper Article

PROPOSALS,
FOR PRINTING BY SUBSCRIPTION,
The Adventures
of
A M—m—r of C—ng—ss,

Who lately set out from the seat of Politics in New-Jersey, to *sift* what he could do to establish its permanency: And altho' otherways well informed, he proved rather deficient in what is called, the Knowledge of the World, to which alone we must impute his want of success—and that in his attempt, he got strangely

DONE OVER.

Subscriptions will be taken in at all the Printing-Offices in New-Jersey.

[Elizabethtown] *New-Jersey Journal*, 4 November. The editors cannot determine which member of the New Jersey delegation is the subject of this satirical advertisement. Perth Amboy and Burlington served as the colonial seats of government of East and West New Jersey. After 1776 the legislature met in large taverns in several different towns, but it returned to the colonial practice in October 1789. No member of the delegation lived at either place, but Boudinot, Schureman, and Paterson lived within fifteen miles of Perth Amboy and Cadwallader lived within twenty miles of Burlington (Richard P. McCormick, *Experiment in Independence: New Jersey in the Critical Period, 1781–1789* [New Brunswick, N.J., 1950], pp. 125–26).

THURSDAY, 5 NOVEMBER 1789

Letter from Richmond, Virginia

We learn that the business of the Chicasaw nation to Congress, was, to request they would furnish them with a quantity of powder, lead, and arms, to enable them to go to war with some other tribe which had been troublesome to them. Finding that Congress had adjourned, they have applied to our Assembly, who has come to a resolution to grant them a supply of powder and lead, which we hope they will use towards the protection of our southwest brethren.

NYDG, 16 November.

OTHER DOCUMENTS

Theodore Hopkins to Jeremiah Wadsworth. ALS, Wadsworth Papers, CtHi. Written from London; addressed to Hartford, Connecticut.
　　Encloses last session's last volume of the *Parliamentary Register*; asks "your opinion of the trade to America" and of Hopkins's prospects in seeking a commercial connection there; has sent by Jno. (John) Trumbull an account of the expenses of Silas Deane's funeral.

Plain Sense. *NYP*, 5 November.
　　Defends Williamson against A. B.'s attack of 3 November.

Friday, 6 November 1789

[*Jeremiah Wadsworth,*] The Observer, No. V

The manner of taxation in a number of the American States
oppressive and distressing to the poor

IN every State a certain proportion of property must be devoted to public use, to support the government and defray the expences of general preservation. The contribution designed for these ends, constitutes the national revenue, and ought to be paid by the people in proportion to their ability. Much depends on the manner of apportioning and collecting this contribution. In a very poor country, by a just system of taxation, sufficient sums to answer the public needs, may be collected without injuring any; in the richest nation on earth, small sums may be demanded in such a way as to produce almost general wretchedness. In most nations, there hath been more oppression by the manner of taxation, than by the greatness of the sums demanded. This subject, therefore deserves attention by a people, who are laying the foundations of government and happiness. The resources of this empire are immense—to call them out in a way that is equal and not oppressive to any class of citizens, is the only difficulty. My last number urged the propriety of including in one general system the whole American debt, part of which now stands charged against the Union, and part against particular States. On this plan, all will see there must be some further means of producing a revenue to the United States. In a number of instances, the manner of State taxation is oppressive to those citizens who have small property. Repeated attempts have been made, in most of the States, to amend their respective systems; but with little success. To amend a defective system of finance is next to impossible, and involves more evils than it cures. The present manner of taxation is favourable to a number of opulent members in every Legislature, who tho' they be not a majority can impede any essential alteration; and this is a serious reason, for a transferal of the State debt to the United States, who in the arrangement of a new system, may avoid the oppressive parts of State taxation. In the States of Massachusetts and Connecticut, a Poll tax is in use. In Connecticut, considerable more than one quarter of the whole State revenue, arises from polls. I cannot say how great a proportion in Massachusetts, but believe it is not less. Art cannot contrive a more oppressive mode of drawing money from a people, than by a Poll tax. The frugal and hardy living of the poor generally renders them prolific—their houses are filled with hungry sons, which with great toil they are educating more for the public, than for themselves. Before these sons are arrived to manhood, the father hath a severe Poll tax to pay for them individually. You will often see a poor and industrious family, who earn their bread and their every thing by labouring at a small price per day, or by cultivating the land of others on shares, pay a greater tax to the State than their neighbour of wealth. This is taxing industry and not property—it is making those who must do the labour, pay the expence of public protection. Were the people who inhabit these States brought together, eighteen out of twenty would vote out a poll tax; but it is so interwoven with the State systems, and so many efforts have been made in vain, that I despair of a remedy, but by a general and national arrangement, which I am certain will be on more just principles.

The Poll tax is a discouragement to manufactures, which the true policy of this country ought to promote. It is rare that mechanics arrive at great riches, few of them are able to pay a tax for a large number of apprentices, and this consideration alone prevents many masters, who would otherwise have their shops filled with poor boys learning some art useful to themselves and mankind. This is a discouragement both on manufactures and on the poor.

The taxing of wild and uncultivated lands takes place in a number of States. To tax this property which is absolutely unproductive, is attended with more evils than will be at first imagined. Few men either think equitable, or have the means of paying an annual tribute for dead property. The old countries in the United States are so far cleared that there ought to be an encouragement for preserving wood and timber. Many who would be contented to have their interest lie without use in wild land, not being able to discharge the taxes, have sold them. Even in the agricultural towns our forests are mostly destroyed—the poor unable to pay an advanced price, begin to suffer for fuel, and the dearness of timber and lumber will soon be severely felt by all kinds of people. This piece of State policy, by grasping at a little, for it is only a small sum which any would dare affix on dead property, hath lost much. It would be better policy, in the old countries of America to allow a bounty on the growth of timber. We ought to enrich the cultivation of our improved lands and preserve our wood.

Arbitrary assessment by the opinion of one or several men is an oppressive mode of taxation, and ought not to be the basis of an national revenue. This is practised, in some manner and degree, by most of the States within the union. Justice will not be done through so many prejudices, as are found in the minds of assessors; and if perfect justice could be done the selfishness or ignorance of very many will lead them to suppose they are over assessed. The man thus soured will grumble more at a small tax than for four times the sum imposed on known principles, and where his exact quota is calculated by the letter of the law. Taxing of polls and unproductive property, is an injury to the poor, and calls on those to pay who cannot without making a great sacrifice of their interest. Arbitrary assessment is exposed to injustice, and sours the minds of the people. We hope these things will be considered in the arrangement of federal measures, and that such a plan will be devised by the treasury board, as will invite the people and creditors to throw the debt under their management.

[Hartford, Connecticut] *American Mercury*, 9 November. For information on The Observer series, its authorship, and reprintings, see the location note to The Observer, No. I, 12 October, above.

SATURDAY, 7 NOVEMBER 1789

John Adams to Marston Watson

The Letter you did me the honour to write me on the thirtieth of September, has been to New York; and from thence transmitted to this Place; but it never reached my hand, till the night before last.[1] The sentiment of Esteem for my private Character, expressed by Gentn. who are probably Strangers to me are very obliging: and the approbation of my public Conduct abroad, lays me under still greater obligations.

The Fisheries, are so essential to the commerce and naval Power of this nation that it is astonishing that any one Citizen should ever have been found indifferent about them. But it is certain that at a time when there were reasons to expect that more than one foreign nation would endeavour to deprive us of them, there were many Americans indifferent, and not a few even disposed to give them away. a Knowledge of this was the first and strongest motive with me to embark for Europe a first and a Second time— after all however the final Preservation of the Fisheries was owing to Causes so Providential, that I can never look back upon them without Reverie and Emotion. Your Approbation Sir and that of your Friends of the Part I acted in that Negotiation give me great Pleasure.

The Present of four Boxes of Fish has been received in my Absence by my Family and is in every Point of View very acceptable to me. as an Amateur I shall regale myself and my friends: as a Well Wisher to the Trade I shall endeavour to make the dish fashionable at N.Y. I pray You and your Companions to accept of my Sincere Thanks for the favour; and my best Wishes for their Pleasure Profit and Prosperity in the Prosecution of the Fisheries. May You and they live to see a Commerce and a Naval Power growing out of your occupations, which shall render this, the first and most respectable of maritime nations.

FC, Adams Family Manuscript Trust, MHi; a second copy, in Adams's hand, is in Signers of the Declaration Collection, WHi. Written from Braintree, Massachusetts.

[1] The letter covered a shipment of the "best Table fish" procured by Watson on behalf of "a Fish Club of Gentlemen" in Marblehead (ALS, Adams Family Manuscript Trust, MHi).

MONDAY, 9 NOVEMBER 1789

William Constable to Robert Morris. FC:lbk, Constable-Pierrepont Collection, NN.

"[*William*] Duer talks a good deal of going to Europe next fall—at any rate He will not not continue in the Office longer than that period—I dined with Hamilton on saturday—He is strong in the faith of maintaining public Credit, & is at present employed in an Excise scheme, & as the Impost will not produce 1½ Million Nett Revenue—I tried him on the subject of Indents—'they must no doubt be funded tho it cannot be done immediately' was his Remark—'they must be all put upon a footing'—meaning these as well as the funded Debt."

Letter from Lexington, Kentucky. *NYWM*, 16 January 1790 (the date on which members of Congress would have seen it).

"The Indians on the frontier are still troublesome"; a party of them attacked four men on the Miami River, killing one, with one still missing.

TUESDAY, 10 NOVEMBER 1789

Fisher Ames to John Jay. ALS, Jay Papers, NNC. Written from Boston; postmarked 13 November; received and answered 27 November. For the full text, see *DHSCUS* 1:676–77.

Office seeking: John Tucker for clerk of the Supreme Court.

Phineas Bond to Francis Osborne, Duke of Leeds. ALS, Foreign Office 4/7 p. 253, PRO. Written from Philadelphia; place to which addressed not indicated.

"In a political View, they [*Congress*] see the Expediency of discouraging every Attempt which tends to diffuse the Inhabitants of their Dominion, and transfer Population and consequent Strength, to a greater Distance from the Seat of Government."

FG, 10 November.

Defends Williamson against A. B.'s attack in *NYP*, 3 November.

Letter from Lisbon. *NYP*, 16 February 1790 (the date on which members of Congress would have seen it).

"The [*Portuguese*] Government continues to refuse the privilege to American vessels, of navigating in the Mediterranean under a national flag. This is done in concert with the court of Madrid, to whom the American consuls had applied for the same privilege, and were refused. Three vessels deeply laden with grain for the market of Leghorn [*Livorno, Italy*], are preparing to depart for that place; & as they are stout vessels, carrying 16. guns each, and full of men, they may possibly fight their way through the Barbary corsairs, who are become very numerous."

WEDNESDAY, 11 NOVEMBER 1789

Jeremiah Wadsworth to an Unknown Recipient. Written from Hartford, Connecticut; place to which addressed not indicated. Two page ALS, *Stuart Lutz Historic Documents, Inc. Catalog* [November 2007]:item 137. The letter may have been addressed to Ezra Smith or Salmon Burr; for background on their petitions for invalid pensions, both presented on 19 January 1790, see *DHFFC* 7:336, 339.
"I received your letter just as Congress were closeing [*sic*] the Sessions and had no time to examine the subject. Since my return home I have been constantly occupied with business and attention to a sick family. There can be no allowance made by any existing resolutions of Congress to present your name, but it is not impossible that on his petitioning an allowance made be made—but all the facts must be fully stated and well authenticated which if sent to me with the Petition I will present and see that it has a fair hearing."

THURSDAY, 12 NOVEMBER 1789

Abraham Baldwin, Deposition

As there appears to have been some doubt respecting the supplies which I have received of the state since my absence from it, I have felt it to be my duty to state the fact. No supplies were furnished me on my leaving the state;[1] and for two years and four months, the whole that I received of the state, was 24l. [2?]s. 8d. The first remittances I received from the state since I left it, reached me but a few weeks before I left Congress; but the state of the market, and the price at which the articles were charged was such, that it was out of my power to dispose of any part of them, and I was under the necessity of setting out on my return without receiving any relief from them.

[Georgia] *Augusta Chronicle*, 14 November. See also *DHFFC* 16:986, 1153, 17:1717.

---

[1] Baldwin left Georgia in 1787 to attend the Federal Convention. He remained in the North as a member of the Confederation Congress and a commissioner for settling accounts between the federal and state governments.

Aedanus Burke to Anthony Wayne

*** Your last Letter to me was in August (29th. I think) [4 *June*]. It concluded with a wish of your's to be appointed in some agency in Indian affairs—That letter of your's I perused over & over to see that there was nothing in it improper to be seen by the ~~General~~ President—to whom I was determined to convey your sentiments—I delivered the Letter accordingly to Genl. [*William*] Jackson to shew it to the Prest. under pretence of informing him of some News about the Indians—Let me have acted right or wrong, I did for the best—This was long before any appointments were made.

*** I have to say this, when ever the Election for Pensylva. for Congress comes on, don't you stay in Georgia.

*** Remember me to Gunn & Jackson. ***

ALS, Wayne Papers, PHi. Written from Hilton Head, South Carolina; place to which addressed not indicated. The omitted text relates to Burke's discussion with Governor Thomas Mifflin, whom he describes as "agreeable" and "affectionate," about a Pennsylvania office for Wayne.

Letter from Wheeling, West Virginia, to Georgetown, Maryland

The spirit of emigration to the western regions, rages more than ever, upwards of 3000 persons are encamped near this place, some of which have been here ever since July last: They are detained on account of the high freshets in the river—want of boats, provisions, &c. their situation is truly deplorable, as this part of the country is but thinly settled. This large body of people, with their horses and cattle, have raised the provisions to an alarming height, this has induced many of them who were able to return, while others are spending their little all in expectation to see the waters fall.

But should this not be the case soon, and an early winter set in, the distress of the people will be great indeed; for the principal part of them are very poor, and have disposed of their old home—so that they have no retreat.

The great distress to which thousands of our countrymen expose themselves, by undertaking the journey to Kentucky, at too late a period in the year, should serve as warning to those who intend removing to that country; every head of a family, before he quits a comfortable home, for good and all, should reconnoitre the waters where he intends to embark, build his boats, and lay in a stock of provisions, before he fetches his family, negroes and stock.

We have this moment received intelligence, that a few days ago the Indians took the boat in which a Mr. Thornton, from Augusta county (Virginia), with his family, embarked at Redstone[1] a few days ago.

The boat, it is said, was forced on the Indian shore, by a large raft of trees and logs, floating down the river. The fate of this unfortunate family is as yet unknown. There are, by the best information, large parties of Indians patroling the western banks of the Ohio, in order to intercept the great number of boats now preparing to go down the river.

NYP, 15 December (the date on which members of Congress would have seen it), from a non-extant issue of [Georgetown, Maryland] *Times and Patowmack Packet*; reprinted at Windsor and Bennington, Vermont; Salem, Northampton, Pittsfield, and Stockbridge, Massachusetts; and Augusta, Georgia.

---

[1] Present-day Brownsville, Pennsylvania, on the Monongahela River south of Pittsburgh.

FRIDAY, 13 NOVEMBER 1789

Letter from Baltimore to Philadelphia

The change made in the Post-Office department of this place, has excited the surprise and indignation of the whole community. This office was kept by a lady [*Mary Katherine Goddard*] upwards of fourteen years, whose conduct, during that period, gave uncommon satisfaction; and all the Post-Masters-General have been heard to declare, that the regularity of her accounts and payments were equalled by few, and exceeded by none, upon the continent. The subject of her removal being mentioned, one of these gentlemen observed, that he regretted it much, on her own account, as well as that of the public, who could not possibly be benefited by a change.

As this lady conducted the business during the arduous difficulties attending the depreciation of the continental currency, when its value was not adequate to her trouble, she could not conceive it possible, that any person would cast a wishful eye upon it, at least whilst she wished to enjoy it, and discharged its duties with so much punctuality and satisfaction. And although there are many *worthy officers and citizens of this state*, to whom the emoluments, trifling as they are, might prove a seasonable relief, yet their sense of honor and delicacy has been such, as to disdain every idea of that kind, upon any other terms than that of her own free and voluntary resignation. These gentlemen of course have declined the attempt, and it was reserved for Colonel John White, late Commissary of Accounts, and scarcely known in Baltimore, insidiously to step in and take this lady's living from her—An act which no gentleman in this state, be his necessities ever so pressing, would be mean enough to stoop to for relief.

When the scheme of getting this office was known here, all the merchants and respectable inhabitants joined in an address to be presented to the Post-Master-General, and his Assistant, that this lady should not be disturbed in her office.[1] On White's discovering that the people were unanimously against him, he posted away to meet Mr. [*Jonathan*] Burrell, the Assistant, and informed him thereof. Upon this emergency they concluded to represent the affair as irrecoverably lost; for that Mr. White had actually received his commission, which he would not part with; and by this finesse, it was expected the people of Baltimore would be reconciled to their fate, as a thing irretrievable.

This paltry conduct brings to my remembrance a similar stroke of art, respecting a gentleman of great family interest and connections, who had the misfortune of being put upon trial for his life, before a Judge, well known to have been long at enmity with his predecessors; and this was the first opportunity the conscientious dispenser of justice had of doing any of them an injury. The gentleman, though innocent of the charge, was, through the address of the Judge, found guilty; and whilst he was upon his trial, an apparatus was ordered to be got ready for an immediate execution, from the Court-house windows; which was accordingly done as soon as the jury returned their verdict. This summary way of doing business prevented any application, either for mercy, or a reconsideration of the evidence upon which he was found guilty.

Mr. Burrell, on his arrival at Baltimore, was waited upon by a committee of merchants, who expressed the wish of the town, that this lady should not be removed from office; to whom he was graciously pleased to promise an answer; but on the day appointed for that purpose, Mr. Burrell, like an experienced General treating with an enemy, thought proper to disappear, leaving for answer, that he could not comply with their request. He was equally cautious in avoiding an interview with the poor lady, thus to become a sacrifice to Mr. White's influence. It was not safe to let her know in person any of the incapacities under which she labored, lest she should either confute or obviate them; and Mr. Burrell though three days in town, never came near either her or the office. This is what the vulgar part of the world call travelling to settle and regulate the business of Post-Offices, but which, in this instance, the officer scorned even to look at—for it cannot be supposed that he was ashamed to do his duty. Thus much, however, is certain, that Mr. Burrell was extremely sorry to hear, that "the lady was so strongly recommended on all sides," except his own.

The most disagreeable part of the narrative is, that notwithstanding the number of years she has been indefatigably employed, a variety of heavy losses has swallowed up the fruits of her industry, which renders her totally incapable of sustaining this additional one. Mr. White, her own countryman, has for a long while past often visited her, as an acquaintance, to whom her situation was well known, and her house was the first he came to on his return lately from New-York, when he engaged her office. Little could she suppose that he was employed in supplanting her in a secret, underhand manner, and at the same time visiting her under the garb of friendship; but so it was, be the consequences what they may, either now or hereafter.

This is the first instance known of a military gentleman's seizing and making prize of all the worldly dependence of a female subject and ally. Plunder thus acquired, should make an Algerine pirate blush for meanly tarnishing the honorable profession of arms, with spoils taken from *even* an *enemy* in *petticoats*.

IG, 18 November.

---

[1] This letter to Postmaster General Samuel Osgood, dated 12 November, is printed in *DHFFC* 8:236–37 with background information and other documents relating to the Goddard case.

OTHER DOCUMENTS

Samuel Drake to Jeremiah Wadsworth. ALS, Wadsworth Papers, CtHi. Written from Fort Harmar, at Marietta, Ohio; addressed to Hartford, Connecticut; carried by Capt. John Buell ([1753–1813], captain in the U.S. army; see *DHFFC* 2:483).
    Requests Wadsworth's patronage, "Advice & Directions," if he does not get promoted in the military line within three years.

SATURDAY, 14 NOVEMBER 1789

John Adams to Abigail Adams. Written from Braintree, Massachusetts. ALS, Adams Family Manuscript Trust, MHi.
    Is preparing his books for shipment to New York City; will not be back before three weeks.

Andrew Craigie to William Constable. FC:dft, Craigie Papers, MWA.
    Relies on Morris's and Constable's resources to purchase or borrow $400,000 in securities by 1 January 1790.

Andrew Craigie to Daniel Parker. FC:dft, Craigie Papers, MWA.
    Has not yet heard from Morris, and does not know whether indents and state certificates will be assumed and funded.

John Brown Cutting to William Short. ALS, Short Papers, DLC. Written from London; place to which addressed not indicated.
    Does not think the post of secretary of state was molded for David Humphreys, in support of which he cites a letter from Schuyler to John B.

Church, indicating that the post would be kept vacant pending Jefferson's decision whether to accept it.

SUNDAY, 15 NOVEMBER 1789

Catharine Greene to Jeremiah Wadsworth. ALS, Wadsworth Papers, CtHi. Addressed to Hartford, Connecticut; postmarked.

Is sorry not to have heard from him since his departure; encloses Knox's "sentiments" on her plan (for the settlement of Nathanael Greene's accounts) "for your consideration," and asks to hear any objections he may have; is prepared to pay back his loan.

Moses Myers to Nicholas Low. ALS, Low Papers, DLC. Written from Norfolk, Virginia.

Has heard people complain of Parker's lack of punctuality in meeting financial obligations.

MONDAY, 16 NOVEMBER 1789

[*Jeremiah Wadsworth,*] The Observer, No. VI

Remarks on Taxation

The greatest effects are produced by the most simple causes. A great mind may be distinguished by the simplicity of its conceptions, and the art of managing momentous concerns, by those plain means which others have overlooked. If we examine the history of mankind we shall perceive that the most eminent characters in civil and religious policy, obtained their superiority of reputation, by discerning the opportune moment to sweep away complicated systems the work of those who had been laboriously and minutely wise; and substituting in their place some plain scheme of truth and practice, which the people can understand and see to be for their advantage. In every enlightened country, a majority of the people are willing to do right, or what is the same thing, that which is for their own interest. Intricacy in the measures of government, is a common course of loosing the public confidence; and this ought to be the case, as it exposes the subject to tyranny and fraud, without the means of detection. The manner of raising, collecting and applying a national revenue, has generally been esteemed the most difficult part of government, and doubtless more uneasiness hath arisen from this, than every other source. This difficulty hath generally been imputed to the avarice of the human heart. It hath been said that the people will necessarily be displeased, with every regulation which requires any contribution of their property to the public; but I cannot yet believe that so much both of the fool and knave is essential to human nature. Honesty is known to be the best policy, and the ruling half of an informed people, setting aside moral obligation, will on this account prefer honesty. Let them be convinced the State is honest in its government, and with the same honesty and cheerfulness, they will contribute their quota of the general expence; but the people never can have this evidence of national integrity with such a confusion of schemes as have filled the United States. More than four fifths of the citizens thro' the union are willing to satisfy every demand of justice. The late revolution in government is a proof they have magnanimity sufficient for every event. But in this business a financier who means to lead them, must have a simple and plain system, both of raising and applying the revenue. He must have a permanent system—one which will not need new modelling every session of the supreme Legislature. It is allowed on all hands that taxation hath caused uneasiness in most of the States, but it is not from any want of honesty in the people. Some reasons of this uneasiness were mentioned in my last number, and there are others which deserve notice. When the sums to be paid in the progress of the war became considerable, the State Legislatures through almost the whole union, with the best intentions and a real design to favor the people, set themselves to new modelling those modes of taxation to which they had been respectively used—addition upon addition was made to the tax laws—every year produced something new, which the next was probably repeated, for the sake of some alteration supposed to be better. This fluctuating state of the tax laws became a temptation for particular persons to favor themselves, and their jealousy has been gradually introduced between respectable classes of citizens, whose property is in difficult situations. The people at large are unable to comprehend the design of such frequent alterations—the whole appears to them like confusion, and a game played between the more knowing ones, to promote their own purposes. A frequent violation of funds or appropriations to particular uses, in the application of revenue hath been another ground of uneasiness. The State must be saved at all events, and there may be exigencies of danger which will warrant such violations; but nothing of this kind can amount to a justification, in one quarter of the instances which have happened. A worthy citizen always wishes for an opportunity to glory in the good faith of his country—national justice is his pride—the want of it wounds his feelings and sinks his ambition—he becomes weary of paying when the whole system is a chaos, and the application so variable that none are satisfied, and the public do not obtain the reputation even of trying to be just. Another source of uneasiness, and this I think with great reason, is that part of the public creditors have been wholly neglected and among those who have received some compensation it hath been on various principles, and in different proportions, though all had a right to the same justice. One half of their own securities, have been taxed to pay the interest due to their neighbours, whose notes might run in another name, but had no preferences in equity. They submitted to the necessity of the times with a fortitude almost unparalleled, and it must not be any longer expected from them. There is but one remedy for this evil—let the United States assume the whole public debt—it was incurred for them and in equity they ought to see it funded. The principal ought not to be paid if there was public ability, but the interest should be annually satisfied. This debt will be an advantage to the nation and to individuals, to government, commerce, agriculture and manufactures. I can foresee it will be enquired how shall this be done, will not so vast an amount sink the people? By many their enquiries are honestly made, and by some merely to terrify. Methodize and simplify your whole treasury department and the burden on the people will not be one half of what they have annually borne for fifteen years. The United States have now an impost, the savings of this beyond the support of civil government will amount to a large sum, but other ways and means will doubtless be requisite. In a number of the States there is now an excise, which ought to be banished from all or extended through the whole; and perhaps the latter will be found necessary. An excise is a tax attended with some difficulty in collection, and if not thoroughly gathered proves a discouragement to the honest, who wish to observe all the regulations of government: but notwithstanding this difficulty, there are some reasons both of policy, and equity, which I shall mention in some future number, that may under this mode of revenue [be] expedient. The tax paid by the country planters and farmers ought to be of one kind and on the most simple principles, such that every man may know by his own calculation what will be demanded from him. Among the various expedients of taxation devised by human ingenuity, a land tax of a certain sum per acre on improved grounds, is the most simple and permanent. It admits no altercation concerning the sum to be paid—being placed on stable and immoveable property; the dishonest cannot by any fraud escape payment—it favors the poor who have little property, while a poll tax crushes them, and comes on such as have solid wealth—and the quantity of improved land bears a nearer proportion to the comparative wealth of individuals in the State, than any other articles which can be reduced to taxation. Another thing which favors this mode of taxation in the United States, is that it may be carried into effect with ease, and in an intelligible manner, through every part of the empire. There will be no need of intermedling with the different policies of revenue in the several States, which cannot be reduced into a harmonious system. A very small land tax in addition to the other branches of revenue, would be sufficient, and could it be introduced, by the plainness and simplicity of its operation, would give general content.

[Hartford, Connecticut] *American Mercury*, 16 November. For information on The Observer series, its authorship, and reprintings, see the location note to The Observer, No. I, 12 October, above.

TUESDAY, 17 NOVEMBER 1789

Tobias Lear to Clement Biddle. ALS, Washington-Biddle Correspondence, PHi. Addressed to Philadelphia. For the full text, see *PGW* 4:298–99. For Biddle's reply of 22 November, indicating compliance with the requests mentioned here, see *PGW* 4:314–16.

Asks Biddle, on behalf of Washington, to pay Morris a balance due to Gouverneur Morris for a purchase from France, and to pay Morris himself for floor mats and black satin imported in one of Morris's ships from India in the summer of 1788.

WEDNESDAY, 18 NOVEMBER 1789

Thomas Fitzsimons to Alexander Hamilton

Our Collector [*Sharp Delany*] is much embarrassed on Account of the dutys on the Goods imported into this port, between the 1st. of August when the Continental Impost was to take place and the 7th when he recived his Commission—He Continued to act as an officer of the State, till the latter Period and took bond for the payment of the dutys during that time. I Need not point out to you the difficulty that would arise in Endeavoring to make goods under these Circumstances pay dutys to the United States, nor Remark that if at all practicable, it would operate Unequally as I beleive this is the only port in which the Continental dutys could for that time be Ascertained.

There are some difficultys too on the Score of tonnage—Vessells have entered in Delaware, paid the foreign tonnage there & without haveing taken on board any other goods have proceeded to this place to load—Where a second tonnage is Required I suspect the same thing Must frequently happen in Maryland & Virginia but I suspect probably the officers there are not so particular as ours—If you should be of Opinion, that the Act did not intend to make Vessells thus Circumstanced pay in both places—your directions Will for the Present put an End to the Controversy and, if Necessary, the Act may be altered in that particular, by your instructions to the Collectors they are directed, to make you returns weekly & Monthly—of the Amount of the tonnage & dutys and to Specify the Vessells & M[*erchandi*]ze. would it not be Equally Usefull if the Collectors return was a Genl. one of the Amt.

and that the Naval officer [*lined out*] furnished the particulars of Mze. and the Surveyor of the Tonnage—the one has Copys of all entrys made with the Collector the other Measures the Vessells & Keeps an Acct. of the tonnage—And in this way their returns would form a More perfect check on that of the Collector whose duty is already much greater in proportion than either of the other Officers—and will be much advanced if he is Obliged to make his Returns in the form prescribed, his quarterly return May be agreeable to the present form.

If these hints can be Apply'd you will use them at your discretion.

ALS, Hamilton Papers, DLC. Written from Philadelphia.

THURSDAY, 19 NOVEMBER 1789

James Madison to Alexander Hamilton

I was too much indisposed for some time after the receipt of your favor of the 12 Oct. to comply with the request in it, and since my arrival here and recovery I have till now been without a conveyance to the post office.

The supplemental funds which at present occur to me as on the whole most eligible are 1. an excise on home distilleries. If the tax can be regulated by the size of the Still it will stem every objection that renders excises unpopular or vexatious. Such an experiment was made in Scotland; and as a *Scotch* tax I have not understood that the mode was disapproved. The complaint against it was founded on a comparison with the different mode established in the other part of the Kingdom, by which the burden was rendered disproportionate. 2. an augmentation of the duty on spirituous liquors imported. This will not only be compatible with the former, but in a manner required by it. 3. a Land tax. This seems to be recommended by its simplicity, its certainty, its equity, and the cheapness of collecting it. It may be well also for the General Govt. to espouse this object before a preoccupancy by the States becomes an impediment. When they find It is an essential branch of national revenue; and when once in the hands of the National Govt. the States will of course turn their attention to those miscellaneous objects which can be more easily managed by them than by Congress, and by which they can as they like equalize the burden on their respective Citizens. Some difficulty may perhaps arise from the different rules of Assessment in the different States, but it will only require an adoption of these diversities until the way shall be prepared for uniformity. 4. a Stamp tax on proceedings in the federal Courts, as soon as experience shall have supplied the prerequisite information, and as far as will support make the Establishment support itself.

I do not add a General Stamp tax, because with some it would be obnoxious to prejudices not yet worne out,[1] because it could not be so framed as to fall in due proportion on the States without more information than can be speedily obtained, and because it would not for some time be productive in the State Courts, unless extended to suits for antecedent debts &c., in which case the debtors on whom the tax would fall, would make it a fresh topic of clamor.

The modification of the public debt is a subject on which I ought perhaps to be silent, having not enough revolved it to form any precise ideas. I take it to be the general expectation that the foreign part of the debt is to be put on the most satisfactory footing, and it will no doubt equally gratify the public wish, if it can by that means be turned into a debt ~~bearing~~ bearing a reduced interest. The domestic part is well known to be viewed in different lights by different classes of people. It might be a soothing circumstance to those least favorably disposed, if by some operation the debt could be lessened by purchases made on public account; and particularly if any impression could be made on it by means of the Western lands. This last is a fund which, tho' overrated by many is I think capable of aiding the redemption of the capital of the debt. A further reason for keeping the lands at market is that if the appetite for them be not regularly fed, it may produce licentious settlements, by which the value of the property will not only be lost, but the authority of the laws impaired.

I consider it as very desireable that the provision to be made should be such as will put the debt in a manifest course of extinguishment. There are respectable opinions I know in favor of ~~long~~ prolonging if not perpetuating it. But without entering into the general reasonings on that subject, there are two considerations which give a peculiarity to the case of the U. States—one, that such a policy is disrelished ~~by~~ to a degree that will render heavier burdens for discharging the debt more acceptable than lighter ones not having that for their object—the other, that the debt however modified must, as soon as the interest is provided for, or the permanent views of the Govt. ascertained, slide into the hands of foreigners. As they have more money than the Americans, and less productive ways of laying it out, they can and will pretty generally buy out the Americans.

I need not apprize you that some of the ideas I have hazarded may proceed not only from an inaccurate view of the subject but from a mistake of local for general sentiments with regard to it. The less deserving however I may think them of being communcated to you the more they will prove by their being so, my unwillingness to disobey your commands.

ALS, Hamilton Papers, DLC. Written from Orange, Virginia.

[1] Madison referred to the stamp tax imposed by Great Britain on its North American colonies in 1765. The widespread opposition to the tax, leading to its repeal in 1766, was

widely considered to be the start of the revolutionary movement, and stamp taxes became a byword for government oppression.

FRIDAY, 20 NOVEMBER 1789

John Bondfield to John Adams. ALS, Adams Family Manuscript Trust, MHi. Written from Bordeaux, France.

Office seeking: American agent to sell American flour and wheat to the French government.

SATURDAY, 21 NOVEMBER 1789

William Constable to Jeremiah Wadsworth. ALS, Wadsworth Papers, CtHi. Addressed to Hartford, Connecticut. Constable likely referred to the area known as Mount Pitt, an elevated area on the East River, a mile northeast of Federal Hall.

Has not heard from him since his departure; if Mrs. Mehitable Wadsworth and children came for the winter, offers to find them a "comfortable House," possibly Richard Platt's "on the Mount."

SUNDAY, 22 NOVEMBER 1789

Phineas Bond to Francis Osborne, Duke of Leeds. ALS, Foreign Office 4/7 pp. 339–40, PRO. Written from Philadelphia; place to which addressed not indicated.

"Being seldom at the Seat of Government, my Lord, I have no Opportunity of making fit Inquiries from the Deputies of the different States, which a frequent Intercourse with them, would afford."

John Chaloner to Jeremiah Wadsworth. ALS, Wadsworth Papers, CtHi. Written from Philadelphia; addressed to Hartford, Connecticut; postmarked 23 November.

Will perform anything "of use to Mr. Hamilton & of advantage to myself that would not prevent my pursuing the business I am already in"; Simmons, Wadsworth's coach maker, says he will deliver it with Hamilton's by the time Congress sits.

Thomas Lee Shippen to William Shippen, Jr. ALS, Shippen Family Papers, DLC. Addressed to Philadelphia.

Plans to dine that day with Izard.

MONDAY, 23 NOVEMBER 1789

[*Jeremiah Wadsworth,*] The Observer, No. VII

The fluctuating value of Paper in circulation oppressive to the poor
Every public measure, which subjects needy citizens to the imposition of
the rich, is repugnant to justice. Great numbers of the rich are also generous
to the poor, but it is not the character of all to whom a wise providence hath
distributed wealth. One man of great opulence and a hard heart hath power
to oppress a whole vicinity of needy people. Among the present means of
oppression in the United States, none is greater than a circulating paper of
unsteady and deceitful value; and yet there are those who with a confident
face will assert, that the measures which lead to this are designed as an
easement to the necessitous members of society. Those who are poor and in
backward circumstances unwarily are taken by the fair pretentions—they
are told and believe that it is for their benefit, and bless the measures which
sap the vigor of their industry. The wealthy can make their choice between
several mediums in circulation, and if there be a bad kind of money, we shall
always find it in the hands of those who have least policy and riches; thus
the indigent lie under a double disadvantage, the quantity of their money is
small, and it is of the worst kind, not being in demand to procure the necessaries of life. It is a maxim forever true that the worst kind of circulating
money will in the end fall into the hands of those who are least able to bear a
loss. Those States which have partially funded their debt pay the interest in
paper certificates or indents,[1] which pass into circulation for the payment of
taxes—these certificates are issued as an equivalent for gold and silver coin,
and in every view of the fact they are a depreciated paper money, of very different value at several times of the year and in different districts—they may
be purchased in large sums through most of the States from one hundred to
one hundred and fifty per cent. discount—Taxes issue by authority on the
supposition that this is their real value, and it is their real value to those who
can purchase at the right time of sale; it is also their value to a greater part of
the public creditors, whose distressed situation obliges them to sell on any
terms, the first moment they can obtain the interest from the public. Still
it is fact, that one half the taxable inhabitants purchase them nearly at par
with gold and silver. The poor man and those of little enterprise but industrious, delay purchasing until they are driven by the hour of payment, and
then make the best bargain they can, either with some neighbour, or public
officer, prepared for the *benevolent* purpose of accommodating all such as
could not purchase in time for themselves. In this way provision is made for
the poor, and those whose circumstances are decaying; some of these make
payment in hard labour, and some by promisory bonds, induced by a short

credit they fall into the snare and are effectually ruined. Take the following fact as proof of my assertion. In March 1787, one hundred pounds of specie was sent to Boston to purchase State paper, then receivable in taxes, which paper was put into the hands of a person in one of the western counties of Massachusetts, who returned the principal in November of the same year; with a net profit to the owner of the hundred pounds, of sixty pounds six shillings and one penny. It is to be remembered this agent charged very high for his service and expences, so that it is certain, those who paid the taxes, paid at least forty shillings for every twenty which the State received. These were the very people, who a little before had been scourged into obedience by a military force. For Insurgency they were criminal, and government was right to check their phrenzy by the most coercive means; but to palliate their conduct which we wish to bury in oblivion, let it be remembered that oppression will sometimes make wise men mad. It is but a few articles the poor planter has for sale, and these perhaps not in demand at the time necessity obliges him to sell, so that he can exchange them only for the worst kind of circulating money and that at its highest price. The same necessity obliges him to sell at the lowest price, and between buying and selling he makes a loss of one third. I could mention a thousand ways in which a depreciated circulating medium is oppressive to mankind, but especially to such as have small property; and nature admits not a possibility of remedying the evil, but by wholly removing the cause. No fact can be more fully proved than those I have mentioned, but still there is so strong a propensity in some people to have a cheap kind of money, that they will think the writer hath mischievous schemes in his brains, and that every thing is endangered, until the parish Priest, or town pedagogue, or the incendiary of the neighbourhood, some of whom may chance to remember a phrase of school Latin, shall have sounded the alarm. With wasps and flies the Observer promises great patience and will only drive them gently not aiming at their life, for it is the nature of those insects to buzz round the scent of honey, though they can make none themselves; but should any of the higher class of Peculators, who have grown rich on spoil; under the appearance of much honesty and concern, unwisely throw themselves in his way, he pledges himself to disclose things concerning them which the heart of the public hath not conceived. The old man Abraham was honest, he made payment in the current money of the Merchant, it is the money of the merchants which the poor ought to receive, and no other kind of circulating medium will do justice in the community. Whether this money be gold, silver or paper it is a matter of little consequence, for a fixed value and general demand constitutes its worth. At present it is not possible for the State governments to give this value to their certificates or indents; but the United States, if the whole debt could be brought into one fund, might easily effect it by a Connection with the great merchantile Banks within the empire. Bank money is the money of the merchant, and the whole commercial influence of the country will preserve its value. Suppose the sums of a rich and poor man's taxes to be apportioned according to real wealth and ability; the rich man by purchasing the depreciated medium in proper time and at a small price, makes an easy payment; the poor man purchasing at almost double price finds the demand intolerable, and if to this there be added fees for travel, and others which have no legal name he sinks in ruin. These ye poor and embarrassed citizens are the blessings of a cheap paper money for which too many of you have been advocates.

[Hartford, Connecticut] *American Mercury*, 23 November. For information on The Observer series, its authorship, and reprintings, see the location note to The Observer, No. I, 12 October, above.

---

[1] Indents were a class of federal certificates first issued in 1784 in lieu of the payment of interest on the domestic debt. These promises to pay took their name from being incised or indented along their edges.

OTHER DOCUMENTS

Josiah Burr to Jeremiah Wadsworth. ALS, Wadsworth Papers, CtHi. Written from New Haven, Connecticut; addressed to Hartford, Connecticut; sent by stage coach.

Discusses a negotiation they are conducting with Oliver Phelps and Nathaniel Gorham prior to the next meeting of the Genessee Company; suggests he seek counsel of a lawyer in New York concerning the proper execution of the deeds.

Governor Samuel Johnston to James Iredell. ALS, Iredell Papers, NcD. Written from Fayetteville, North Carolina; completed at 2 P.M.; place to which addressed not indicated. For the full text, see *DHFFE* 4:325.

Was pressed very earnestly, especially by Antifederalist members of the state legislature, to accept election as Senator; has agreed to take the position.

[Worcester] *Massachusetts Spy*, 25 November.

Adams arrived in town on 21 November and left for New York on 23 November.

TUESDAY, 24 NOVEMBER 1789

Benjamin Grymes to Alexander Hamilton. ALS, Hamilton Papers, DLC. Written from "Somerset," near Fredericksburg, Virginia, per stage; postmark illegible. For background on Morris's accounts relating to his chartering the ship *Aurora* on behalf of the secret committee of trade in 1776, see *PRM* 5:6–7n.

Owns one-sixth claim to the *Aurora*; Morris informs him that he will likely get his accounts settled this winter, when he will obtain a certificate for the owners; Morris wants to buy Grymes's share, and as he wishes to sell, inquires the present and prospective future value of such a certificate, and whether Morris has the money to purchase the share.

George Washington to Abigail Adams. AN, hand of Tobias Lear, privately owned in 1976. For the full text, see *PGW* 4:321.
Invites Abigail Adams to a seat in the President's box for that evening's performance (at the John Street Theater's production of *The Toy; or a Trip to Hampton Court*).

[Connecticut] *Litchfield Monitor*, 8 December.
Sherman's brother Josiah died.

WEDNESDAY, 25 NOVEMBER 1789

Timothy Pickering to Peter Anspach. ALS, Pickering Papers, MSaE. Written from Philadelphia. For background on the settlement of Pickering's public accounts as former quartermaster general of the Continental Army, see *DHFFC* 7:486–93.
Has reason to believe, from what Fitzsimons has told him, that Congress will make provision to discharge the balance due on Pickering's accounts.

THURSDAY, 26 NOVEMBER 1789

Edmund Randolph to George Washington. ALS, Washington Papers, DLC. Written from Richmond, Virginia. For the full text, see *PGW* 4:326. Virginia did not ratify the Amendments until 15 December 1791.
Hopes the vote of the Virginia House of Delegates in favor of the first ten proposed Amendments to the Constitution will "efface" the "intemperance" of Grayson's and Lee's letters of 28 September (printed in *DHFFC* 17:1634–35).

FRIDAY, 27 NOVEMBER 1789

Alexander Hamilton to Thomas Fitzsimons

I have been duly favoured with your letters of the 29th of October and 18th instant; though I have been too much hurried sooner to acknowledge either. I thank you for the information contained in the first which corresponds with my general impression: I believe with you that the course of business will not render the arrangements hitherto adopted adequate to the object of drawing the public revenue from the two extremes. Indeed I have been already compelled to have recourse to an auxiliary expedient that is to give drafts for *good notes* with *good indorsers* payable in 30 and sixty days. This I have done both with regard to Boston and Charleston.

When you receive an answer, from your friend in Charleston, I Shall be glad to receive the proposal you intimate.

The circumstance you mention, with regard to Norfolk, applies extensively both in Virginia and Massachusetts. That and other considerations of great force induce me to think that there will be a necessity for an officer in each state, or rather in certain districts of the united states, charged with the overseeing and the receipt of the Revenue. I believe I shall submit a proposition for this purpose. It is neither Safe, nor pleasant, to commit the public money to unauthorised hands; which would be the case, if I should now direct remittances from remote places to a common center of circulation: for instance in the case of Virginia, to Richmond, as you suggest. The idea of a Credit at the end of each month for drafts deposited would be to me an agreeable arrangement.

I feel anxious that it may be found practicable to embrace the pilots in a national system, as I think they might then be made useful to the Revenue; and that there is some danger of their becoming the reverse under a different regulation. I will thank you as you promise for the law of your state on this head.

I expect with impatience the intimations you promise of your ideas respecting new objects of revenue.

With regard to feeling the public pulse about the debt, I have several times had an inclination to the measure, but this inclination has given place to the reflection that bringing on a discussion might be as likely to fix prejudices as to produce good; and that it may be safest to trust to the effect of the Legislative sanction to good measures, and to the reasons that will accompany them at the time.

Before I received yours of the 18th, I had forwarded my opinion respecting the duties on importations between the first of August and the organisation of the custom houses at the respective ports. I was aware of the difficulties; but felt myself concluded by my Sense of the law.

On the Subject of the Tonnage duty I am of opinion that [*text obliterated by seal*] payable at each entry and have given a circular instruction to that effect.

The hint you give respecting returns well deserves consideration. Some of those heretofore directed have been intended only as temporary that is—for present information and will shortly cease.

LS, privately owned in 1973. Place to which written not indicated.

Governor Samuel Johnston to the North Carolina General Assembly

In consequence of my appointment to represent the Legislature of this State in the Senate of the United States, it becomes necessary that I should resign the appointment of first Magestrate for the ensuing year, which the Assembly did me the Honor to confer on me early in the present Session: I do therefore most chearfully and with the utmost gratitude for the high confidence placed in me by the Legislature decline the Honor of serving the State as their Chief Magestrate for the ensuing year, and considering it my duty on all Occasions to submit to the Voice of my Country, do accept the appointment to a Seat in the Senate of the United States.

Should my exertions in the execution of that important trust merit in any degree the approbation of my Fellow Citizens, it will be an ample Recompence for the sacrifices, in my Domestick concerns, which I must necessarily make on this Occasion.

LS, Joint Papers, Resignations, General Assembly Session Records, Nc-Ar. Written from and to Fayetteville, North Carolina. The names "Mr. Brevard" and "Mr. Lindley" are written on the docket page.

OTHER DOCUMENTS

Edward Rutledge to Jeremiah Wadsworth. ALS, Governor Joseph Trumbull Collection, Ct. Written from Charleston, South Carolina; addressed to the care of Knox in New York.

Enquires whether a close friend and relative's two sons, aged eleven and thirteen, can be well educated at New Haven, Connecticut, for what annual sum, whether they can be accepted into Yale College without knowing Greek, and whom Wadsworth would recommend as a tutor.

SATURDAY, 28 NOVEMBER 1789

John Fenno to Joseph Ward. ALS, Ward Papers, ICHi. Addressed to "Land Office," Boston; postmarked 29 November.

Has notified the public that *GUS* will be open for advertisements; has heard rumors that proposals will be made to reduce the interest from six to four percent; payment of the higher rate will not be possible with an excise added to it, which will be proposed in the next session.

Henry Knox to Jeremiah Wadsworth. ALS, Wadsworth Papers, CtHi. Addressed to Hartford, Connecticut; postmarked 29 November.

Encloses five accounts for his signature and requests the relevant receipts;

"Agreeably to your idea when I last saw you," requests the return of warrants unpaid by 15 December, "as I wish to close my accounts with the treasury by that day"; laments developments in France; is sorry to hear that Wadsworth and his children suffer from "the universal influenza."

SUNDAY, 29 NOVEMBER 1789

Samuel Johnston to James Iredell. ALS, Charles E. Johnson Collection, Nc-Ar. Written from Fayette, North Carolina; addressed to New Bern, North Carolina; carried by Thomas Williams. For a partial text, see *DHFFE* 4:329–30.
Is elected Senator; does not know who his colleague will be; should be ready to leave (for New York City?) on Tuesday (1 December), but the Assembly may not agree to his leaving until after they elect a governor; suffers from a cough.

MONDAY, 30 NOVEMBER 1789

Thomas Fitzsimons to Samuel Meredith

I thank you for the papers by Major [*William*] Jackson as well your friendly Letter of the 25th—it was not my intention to give you the trouble of Copying. I could have waited your Convenience but I must trouble you to apply to Howel [*Joseph Howell, Jr.*] for the Statement of the Acct. of the states say the Amt. of the demands—I was fearfull my application for [*Andrew?*] Brown would not be effectual tho I thot. I hazarded nothing in applying to you. I believe his Capacity would render him a Very usefull Assistant if there had been Room for him—I have not often Committed myself on Applications of this Kind once only—and then with some Earnestness but seeing or Rather feeling the Impropriety by the Effect—I have cautiously avoided Such interferences since You will easily see the observation does not Apply to you.
I thank you Kindly for the hint in your last tho no possible Use can be made of it. there are people Near You too soon Acquainted with the transactions of the department to let these Occasions Slip Mr. [*Richard*] Plat & Mr. [*John*] DeLafield have long since had their Agents here to pick up every thing they could Lay their hands on—our gentry who are Sufficently alive to their own Interest exclaim Against this interference & do not Scruple to say that information is obtained Improperly—be that as it may every Species of public securitys are advanceing in Value & the Speculators begin to persuade themselves that their golden dreams are on the point of being Realized. how this will be time only Can tell. I do not perceive that it Amounts to any thing Like certainty. if any thing on this Subject Occurs pray inform

me— *** I begin to suspect too that the Secy. [*Hamilton*] takes more part in your departmt. than is Necessary—tho perhaps this is Merely my suspicion.

The butter shall be got for Daubeny [*Mary Dobiney?*] if possible—I am told it is Scarce Indeed I have been Obliged to order a parcell from Boston for Exportation.

ALS, Dreer Collection, PHi. Written from Philadelphia; postmarked. The omitted text relates to the passing of bank notes.

Newspaper Article

Another correspondent says, that the citizens of America ought to cherish the freedom of the press as the highest security of every interesting concern; he observes, its usefulness in detecting public defaulters and compelling them to account for the public monies entrusted to their disposition, has been strikingly exemplified in regard to the Agent of Commercial Affairs, for the Centinel having, during the discussion of the New Constitution, warned the public of the situation of this officer, as well as others who were zealous *federalists*, the public clamour was excited to such a degree, that Mr. Robert Morris found it necessary to address the public, appologising for not settling his accounts for twelve years, but promising an immediate settlement.[1] A virtuous minority taking advantage of the ferment raised against the public defaulters, led Congress, much against their *secret* inclination, into an investigation of the sums of public monies unaccounted for by individuals;[2] this investigation was artfully intercepted in its passage to this city, and it was a month before it reached us, when it was obtained by a *private hand*; the Centinel immediately improved this official document to confirm his charge against Mr. Morris and other public defaulters—so well supported a charge made the whole city ring again with the enormous delinquency—even the creatures of Mr. Morris were for two days thunder-struck; however, Mr. Morris, like an able general, soon rallied his forces, and lulled the public outcry, by informing, that he had been at New-York, laboring to procure a settlement of his accounts, and that he would do all in his power to bring them to a final settlement before he took his seat in the New Congress[3]—thus driven by a free press, Mr. Morris rendered his accounts to the three late Commissioners of the board of Treasury [*Samuel Osgood, Arthur Lee, and Walter Livingston*]; he could have no hopes now left to veil over the deficiency of the public monies but in their facility; however, they had too high a sense of fidelity or character to balance his accounts without vouchers, and after making every consistent allowance, they have reported a balance due the public by Mr. Robert Morris, of *four hundred and seventy thousand* SPECIE *dollars*; these Commissioners having laid a list before the present Senate of the United States, containing the sums found due by a number of persons, Mr. Morris included, the Honorable Richard Henry Lee, Senator from Virginia, moved that the said public defaulters be called upon to discharge the respective balances ascertained to be due to the United States, on or before the end of nine months; and in failure of such payment, that suits be brought to compel it: when Mr. Morris rose, and said, this was a personal stroke against him, and, astonishing to tell, was able to overpower the motion.[4] After twelve years standing, so moderate a proposition of allowing nine months longer before suits are commenced, was overruled by the interposition of the principal defaulter, whom decency ought to have induced to retire, when the question was agitated, or at least to have been silent. How different the conduct of the Court of Britain on such occasions, who upon a bare suspicion of a defalcation in a public officer, make it a practice to secure his property by a peculiar process, to prevent the public being superceded by *private* creditors—Here this defaulter cannot be meddled with, even after the balance due the public is ascertained; and what is a very alarming circumstance to the people of the United States, this man, sways the general government, and in this state, he and his creatures carry all before them, to the destruction of the best interests of the community.

IG, 30 November. On 17 March 1790 Robert Alexander informed Jonathan Williams, who was in London, that several pieces in the northern press accusing Morris of being a public defaulter who owed the United States $400,000,000 were "understood to have been written by Arthur Lee" (Rush-Biddle-Williams Papers, PPRF). For more on this issue, see *DHFFC* 8:663–75.

[1] Centinel (Samuel Bryan) leveled his accusation against Morris in *IG*, 26 February and 24 March 1788. Morris's reply to the printer appeared in *IG*, 8 April 1788.
[2] On 7 July 1788 the Confederation Congress appointed a committee—that included Williamson—to investigate the accounts of the board of treasury. Its report of 30 September included an investigation into the board's efforts to comply with a congressional resolution of 22 May, ordering it to investigate longstanding unsettled public accounts and bring suit against defaulters within three months. Morris's unsettled accounts as chair of Congress's secret committee of trade in the earliest years of the Revolutionary War were singled out in the report of 30 September (*JCC* 34:171, 300, 562–64).
[3] See Centinel XXIII, dated 17 November 1788 and published in *IG*, 20 November, and Morris's reply to the printer in *IG*, 22 November. For their texts, see *DHFFE* 1:350–53, 354.
[4] For additional information on this incident, see Burke to Samuel Bryan, 5 February, below.

A Philadelphian to Mr. Brown

Be so good as to inform the public, that the facts stated in Mr. Oswald's paper of this morning are not true; and that the writer of this note, does undertake to prove them false. That this proof shall be made in ten days.

The writer assures the public, that he is in no manner whatever connected with Mr. Robert Morris: but that in general politics he is opposed to him: That he has no other view in his present undertaking, than to contradict a falsehood. He doubts not, that Mr. Morris, will, himself, take such notice of the publication as he thinks it deserves, but as a well wisher to the peace of society, and having as he conceives the means of refutation within his power, he thinks it a duty he owes to that Society of which he is a member, thus early to make the promise above stated.

FG, 30 November, edited by Andrew Brown.

Letter from Liverpool, England, to a Merchant at Alexandria, Virginia

In a former letter we mentioned that our laws respecting American shipping are strictly enforced, and, in confirmation of this, we may now add, that a large vessel arrived here from New York, on the 10th of September, but the men not chusing to swear themselves Americans according to the qualifications which our laws require, the vessel was prevented from discharging, and although various applications were made, and much influence exerted for above six weeks, it was, notwithstanding, wholly ineffectual, and the vessel, (after engaging a proper number of American sailors here) proceded to Dublin, and discharged there. Considerable part of her cargo being on freight, the consignees of the vessel were obliged to purchase it at the prices the goods would have sold for here.

This circumstance must suggest the necessity of a very careful attention to the citizenship of the crews of American vessels, for although we still recommend that the crew be severally affirmed or sworn, and the affirmation or oath sent with the vessel, yet, as even this will not avail, if the men do not affirm or swear to the same effect here, it will be further necessary that every possible care be taken, that the affirmation or oath is made on proper grounds with you, and that the characters of the crew be such as to induce a probability that they will not perjure themselves here.

NYMP, 16 April 1790 (the date on which it would have been seen by members of Congress), from [Alexandria] *Virginia Gazette*, 8 April 1790; reprinted at New York City (*NYDG*, 16 April, *NYP*, 17 April) and Lansingburgh, New York; Baltimore; Charleston, South Carolina; and probably elsewhere.

OTHER DOCUMENTS

Edward Fox to Andrew Craigie. ALS, Craigie Papers, MWA. Written from Philadelphia; postmarked.
    Is told that Morris tried unsuccessfully to borrow certificates from Walter Stewart; has undertaken to deny the report in this day's *IG* that Lee made

a motion in the Senate setting a time limit to unsettled public accounts, aimed at Morris, which Morris had negatived; Craigie's confirmation that it is not true may "possibly forward your plan to serve me through M[*orris*]."; asks for verifying documents.

NOVEMBER 1789 UNDATED

John Adams to Abigail Adams. ALS, Adams Family Manuscript Trust. Written from Braintree, Massachusetts.
  Will return to New York with their son Thomas the first week of December, if not sooner.

Pierce Butler to Charles Phillips. FC:lbk, Butler Papers, PHi. Dating is based on internal evidence and the text's location in the letterbook.
  The Indian war has prevented most of the rice planters from making any income for some years.

December 1789

TUESDAY, 1 DECEMBER 1789

William Constable to Robert Morris. FC:lbk, Constable-Pierrepont Collection, NN.

"Your presence here woud ~~I think~~ be of infinite advantage as We might I think find out the intention of the Chancellor of the Exchequer [*Hamilton*]."

Royal Flint to Nathaniel Appleton. ALS, Colborn Collection, MHi. Addressed to "Commiss. Loans," Boston; postmarked 6 December.

Hamilton has not yet prepared his report on public credit; "The Loan Offices will form part in the general System"; has no doubt Congress will discuss it for several months and "all the regulations relative to the publick debt will be critically investigated."

Catharine Greene to Jeremiah Wadsworth. ALS, Wadsworth Papers, CtHi. Written from Savannah, Georgia; addressed to Hartford, Connecticut.

Guarantees repayment of loan; protests her ignorance that Wadsworth was "in *fear*, or want of the Money—You might Naturally have supposed that My children and I would have beged before a friend like You should have suffer'd from your Generosity"; "You talk of going to Europe to settle your affairs. Why should I say a word upon the Subject I have long since lost My influence if ever I had any—it is not all fair play between you and My self—or You are not the Man I have taken You for—some persons I suspect have poisond your Mind against me."

Samuel Johnston to James Iredell. ALS, Charles E. Johnson Collection, Nc-Ar. Written from Fayette, North Carolina; addressed to Edenton, North Carolina. For a partial text, see *DHSCUS* 1:681.

Departure is postponed until the legislature appoints his successor as governor; Samuel Spencer "would condescend to accept an Appointment" as federal judge, and has asked William R. Davie to recommend him to Ellsworth and Johnson and "is to apply to me on the same Subject but has not yet done it"; is susceptible to colds and is troubled by a cough.

George Washington, Diary. Washington Papers, MiD-B.
Adams and all the Senators in town attended levee.

WEDNESDAY, 2 DECEMBER 1789

Theodore Foster to Caleb Strong

The Appointment of a Consul for the United States of America, to reside in the French West Indies is a Matter that probably will soon come into Discussion before Congress. Though I have not the Honor of a particular personal Acquaintance with you, yet presuming on the Benignity of Disposition you are universally acknowledged to possess, and on the Acquaintance you had with my Father [*Jedidiah Foster*] in his Lifetime, who was sometime Second Justice of the Superior Court of Massachusetts, and on your Knowledge of my [*Dwight*] Family Connexions, in the Counties of Hampshire and Berkshire, and on the public Offices I have myself held in this State during the War and since the Peace, I have taken the Liberty of addressing you on the Subject—Hoping that it will not give offence when I assure You that a particular Veneration for your Character in the important Station you hold, and a Regard for the Good of my Country are the Motives of my Conduct herein. The Necessity of Such an appointment is obvious from the Repeated Difficulties and Disputes which have arisen between the Masters of Vessels and others trading to the French West Indies and the Inhabitants and the Officers of their Revenue which probably would have been prevented or more satisfactorily accommodated, had there been any known public Character on the Spot, acquainted with the Laws, Regulations & Customs established according to the Treaties of Alliance and Commerce between the Two Nations, to have applied to, for Information or Assistance. It is the Business of a Consul to keep up a Correspondence with the Government from which he receives his Appointment To Support its Commerce and its Interest: To obtain the Protection of the Laws of the Place, where he resides for those of his Station coming thither for the Purposes of Commerce or otherwise, and to prevent Insults and Impositions upon them on account of thier being Strangers and to take Care that Masters of Vessels, Traders & others who are Citizens of his own Country conduct agreeable to the Orders and Directions they are bound by Treaty or the Laws of thier own Country to observe and in General to promote the Interests of his own Country & his fellow Citizens thereof at all Times, as occasion offers: The most pollitic Commercial Nations have therefore established such

Officers and the Benefits resulting from them have Justified their Appointments—Influenced by Considerations like these and convinced from Experience of the Necessity of the Measure, a Number of Gentlemen concerned in the West India Trade, from different parts of the United States, propose proferring a Petition to his Excellency the President and the Senate of the Union for the Appointment of SAMUEL DUNN Esqr. of this Town to that Office to reside on the Island of Hispaniola. I am personally acquainted with Mr. Dunn—He has a Family in this Place. His Reputation for Integrity & Honor in his Dealings and Business is fair and unimpeached for aught any thing I have heared. He has long been acquainted with the Language, Laws, Customs and Manners of the French in the West Indies in so much That he is considered there as one of their own Nation, and allowed all the Privileges of a Native Citizen. His attachment however to his Native Country is undoubted, and his Abilities are such as will do Credit to the Appointment. This State not being in the Union with the Other States under the present General Government it was thought there would be an impropriety in the Merchants of this Place Signing the Petition which otherwise would have been done. How long we are to remain in this Predicament Heaven only knows—The Leaders of the opposition to our Joining the Union are waiting to See whether the Constitution is adopted by the State of North Carolina and to observe what will then be the Complexion of the Political Hemisphere. Should that much wished for Event take place I suppose it probable that this State will then make Serious Advances towards an Adoption of it likewise. A Measure anxiously wished for by the most enlightend Part of the State. It is hoped that the present Situation of this State will not be an objection to the Appointment of Mr. Dunn. Rhode Island has belonged to the Confederacy. She did her part towards gaining the Independence of our Country. Her Reputation in the Time of the War ought somewhat to influence in her Favour now. There is no Doubt but that she will soon be under the same General Government as her Sister States. Should the Matter of the Appointment of a Consul for these States to Reside in the French West Indies come before the Honorable Board to which you belong and it should be concluded on to establish such an Office I do not think it probable that a more Suitable Person than Mr. Dunn will be found to fill it. I therefore hope you will excuse this Recommendation and Application in his Behalf and that if agreeable to you, you will favour his Appointment.

ALS, formerly at MSonHi. Written from Providence, Rhode Island; place to which addressed not indicated; postmarked Boston, 3 January.

Richard Bland Lee to Robert Carter

After the friendly manner in which you mentioned your approbation of my addresses to your Daughter Sally [*Sarah Fairfax Carter*] I should not have hesitated one moment in renewing my application, as I feel yet the full force of her beauty, and amiable virtues: did I not think it a duty incumbent on me to be assured of the means of maintaining her, should I be fortunate enough to engage her affections, in a stile equal to her birth and deserts. My own patrimony is unequal to this task—and will barely afford me the means of supporting myself in a single state in the first circles of my country. I cannot think therefore of conducting the Lady whom I love to a situation, which it would make me miserable to see her in, & which would be so inferior to her parentage and the just expectations, which on every account she is entitled to form. Duty therefore to her and myself requires, that I should in the first place make known to you, my real situation, & enquire of you, what assistance would be contributed by you, for our mutual happiness. This application is dictated by by the most delicate sentiments of honor, and I hope will find from you a favorable reception, and will be answered by you with that candor which has always manifested itself in your conduct in every transaction of Life.[1] I shall visit my friends at Lee Hall[2] this morning and return to Nominy in the evening, when I hope you will be kind enough fully to explain yourself to me on this interesting subject to us both: that from your explanation, I may able to determine, whether honor will permit me to pursue a passion which I have long felt, and which I am anxious to consummate: or must be compelled from hard necessity to leave unessayed an attempt, in the success of which my future happiness in life is deeply concerned—Whatever may be my fate I devoutly pray that the amiable charmer of my heart may receive the full meed of her virtues both in this life and the life to come. This letter is dictated in haste and in the highest confidence of friendship, and I hope will meet no other eye.

ALS, Miscellaneous Papers, NN. Written from and addressed to "Nomini Hall," Westmoreland County, Virginia.

[1] On 24 December 1790, in response to an article he had read in a Maryland newspaper, Carter wrote Lee that "with such a person [*as you*] I do not propose either intimacy or friendship—therefore I herein refuse to agree to that alliance which you propose" (Louis Morton, *Robert Carter of Nomini Hall* [Williamsburg, Va., 1945], p. 229). Carter may have been referring to one of several articles that appeared in New York, Philadelphia, and Maryland newspapers, criticizing an especially vitriolic dispute carried on for several weeks between Lee and Stephen Thomson Mason in non-extant issues of the [Alexandria] *Virginia Gazette* following the second federal election in September 1790.
[2] The home of "Squire" Richard Lee (ca. 1726–1795).

Oliver Wolcott, Jr. to Oliver Wolcott, Sr.

***

The public Credit of this country is rapidly rising, securities sell at seven shillings on the pound—this is in some degree owing to the speculations of foreigners—the disorders in France, the declining state of the Dutch republic & the enormous debts which oppress all the great nations of Europe are circumstances which give the United States a relative importance and of which I hope we shall profit.

I cannot however help considering all that is doing towards the establishment of government as an experiment of doubtful success—It is certain that the southern States, are far less advanced in political science than the northern, & even there it is certain that the people have by no means prepared themselves for a steady operation of the general government—The Impost will produce about as much as it was estimated at[1]—some additional revenues will be proposed, probably a system for Inland duties on Spirits &c.—to be collected on the first sale from the Wholesale Dealer by regulations which will not be perceived much in the Country—It will probably be also proposed to consolidate the Debts of the Union in the settlement of the States Accounts. This measure though difficult, is I believe necessary, as the States will by Excises or otherwise defeat any general system of revenue which can be proposed, unless this shall be effected.

***

ALS, Wolcott Papers, CtHi. Place to which addressed not indicated. The omitted text relates to the state of public accounts.

[1] The net estimate of $1,364,511, based on statistics provided by the states, was submitted to the House in a select committee report dated 24 September (*DHFFC* 4:81–83).

Letter from an American in London

The prohibition laid last year on the importation of American Wheat, from an apprehension that the Hessian Fly or Weavil might be propagated from it, in this country, has within a few days been taken off: it being now acknowledged that there was no grounds for such an opinion. They have been further induced to this measure from the prospect of a scarcity the ensuing spring.

It must give satisfaction to every American to see the new government get on so well: I trust our country will become respectable and happy under its superintendance. You cannot conceive how much more respectable the government and people appear in the eyes of Europe, than before the united government was put on its present footing.

This country seems anxious to have a commercial treaty with us, and I think an advantageous one may be had.

Will not Congress think it reasonable that the Packets between Falmouth [*England*] and New-York should be alternately British and American? If there were two in each Month commerce would feel the advantage.

GUS, 17 February 1790 (the date on which members of Congress would have seen it); reprinted at least fifteen times at Portland, Maine; Portsmouth, New Hampshire; Pittsfield, Massachusetts; Providence and Newport, Rhode Island; Hartford, Norwich, and New London, Connecticut; Albany, New York; Philadelphia; and Wilmington, Delaware. Another letter of this date from London (*NYDA*, 20 February 1790) reported a rumor in London that the Americans wanted to reunite with Great Britain.

OTHER DOCUMENTS

George Washington, Diary. Washington Papers, MiD-B.
Visited Adams and his family; walked to the Kings' (probably Rufus and Mary) but they were out.

THURSDAY, 3 DECEMBER 1789

Christopher Gore to Rufus King

***

I thank you very sincerely for your offers of information in the mode & form of conducting the duties of my office—and on this subject I shall soon trouble you.

***

Such were the measures adopted by our legislature, & the conviction that followd from the arguments then used in favor of funding the debt, that I entertain no doubt, if the same characters, in the coming session, exert themselves in favor of the plan, it may be carried—shoud this event take place—the Assumption by the national government will be attended with difficulties, perhaps considerd as too trivial by national men—many who favor'd the project of funding the debt, the last session, will not promote [*torn*] ensuing one, if they can feel [*seal*] confidence in the assumption by the U. states—but otherwise they are bound in honor to themselves & obligation to the state creditors to pursue the same measures that were proposed the last session—pray give me your sentiments on this subject.

ALS, King Papers, NHi. Written from Boston; postmarked 2 December.

David Stuart to George Washington

***

During the time of my continuance in Rich[*mon*]d. on the above business, the Session of our Assembly commenced—A very extraordinary letter from our Senators in Congress, complaining of the inefficacy of the proposed amendments, and expressive of their fears, that the State governments would be annihilated; with a strong hint of the insufficiency of our government for so extensive a country, was received and read[1]—I was happy in hearing much indignation expressed at it, by many who were strong Antifederalists, and had voted against the constitution in the Convention—It was generally attributed to an aim at popularity. My belief is, that it was meant by Mr. R. H. Lee to serve his Brother [*Arthur*], who is a Candidate for a Judge's seat in this State, and will no doubt assume the merit with his party, of having been neglected on account of his principles—Grayson's short draft[2] would be a sufficient motive with him to affix his signature to it—The letter was evidently in Mr. Lee's hand—Mr. [*Patrick*] Henry appears to me by no means content—But if the people continue as much satisfyed, as they at present appear to be, he will be soon alone in his sentiments—He however tried to feel the pulse of the House with respect to the Constitution, in two or three instances, and received at length I understood, a very spirited reply from Coll. [*Henry*] Lee. *** The Merchants of Alexandria had yesterday a meeting with the Merchants of Ge[*orge*]town, on the subject of the permanent seat of residence. The result of it, was the appointment of a Joint Committee to correspond with the towns to the Eastward, and give them, the most flaming accounts they can, of the Potomac; and the greater benefits they will derive, from its being fixed there, than on the Susquehana, or the Delaware—As I am one of the Committee, I have my fears, that those sagacious people will laugh at us for our great pains in teaching them their true interests.[3]

ALS, Washington Papers, DLC. Written from "Abingdon," in present-day Arlington County, Virginia. The omitted text relates to personal business affairs and state patronage.

---

[1] Dated 28 September; see *DHFFC* 17:1634.

[2] When the Senators were classed into two, four, and six year terms on 14 May, Grayson drew a two year term.

[3] Stuart crafted the final broadside from partial drafts submitted by several of the ten men who signed it. These drafts are in the Peter Force Collection, DLC. Mailed to town selectmen and other influential New Englanders, it quickly found its way into the newspapers. For the text, see *DHFFC* 6:1785–89.

Peter Allaire, Occurrences from 5 November to 3 December 1789. ALS,
Foreign Office 4/7, pp. 368–69, PRO.
> Discusses Indian threats on the southern frontier; there is talk of aug-
> menting the federal army to 1500 or 2000 as soon as Congress convenes
> in January.

Edward Fox to Andrew Craigie. ALS, Craigie Papers, MWA. Written from
Philadelphia; postmarked.
> The Pennsylvania Assembly has agreed to levy no state taxes for the year;
> the measure is advocated "by the party, called 'Republicans'—or to give
> you a better idea of them: By Mr. Morris, or Fitzsimon's party"; the op-
> position says it is a "meer farce," to allow the federal government to begin
> a "*direct* Tax"; "I have endeavoured to get at Fitzsimon's opinions about
> consolidating the State Debts, with those of the U. States. I find his ideas
> are far beyond what I expected: and that he is for the U. States, taking all
> the Debts, as they originally Stood—as well those which the States may
> have redeemed as those which are not redeemed."

Nathaniel Gilman to Nathaniel Appleton. ALS, Ransom Collection, Litchfield Historical Society, Litchfield, Connecticut. Written from Exeter, New
Hampshire; place to which addressed not indicated.
> Hamilton's circular letter of 12 October to the continental loan officers
> (see *PAH* 5:440) suggests he intends to propose a different method for
> paying interest on the domestic debt; supposes that creditors in every
> state—except where Congress may sit—would oppose sending their
> securities to the seat of government to receive interest; has conversed
> with two New Hampshire congressmen on the subject of interest on the
> domestic debt, "and it appears to be their opinion that it must be paid in
> the several States."

George Washington, Diary. Washington Papers, MiD-B.
> The Schuylers and Daltons, among others, dined with the President.

FRIDAY, 4 DECEMBER 1789

William Judd and Others to Jeremiah Wadsworth

The Subscribers Inhabitants of the Town of Farmington are fully per-
swaded it is necessary for the Post Master General to Establish a Postrider
from the City of New York to the City of Hartford through the Internal part

of the Country Viz. Farmington Litchfield New Milford Danbury Ridge-field &c. to facilitate and maintain the Intercourse between the extreems and the Intermediate Towns, the rout proposed, is distant from the Post road already Established and many disadvantages [*blotted out*] accrue thereby—we take the Liberty to request you, to Use your Influence to Effectuate so Laud-able & beneficial Arangements.

> ALS, Wadsworth Papers, CtHi. Written from Farmington, Connecticut; place to which addressed not indicated. The other signatories were Thomas Lewis, Sam'l. Richards, Jr., Asahel Wadsworth, and Noadiah Hooker.

OTHER DOCUMENTS

Samuel Johnston to North Carolina General Assembly. ALS, Commons Records, Legislative Papers, Nc-Ar. On the same date the General Assembly responded to Johnston, granting him leave to depart. For the full text of these two messages, see *DHFFE* 4:333.

Has completed state business before him and needs to prepare to assume duties as Senator; intends to depart on 5 December unless the General Assembly thinks his presence is essential.

Abigail Rogers to Daniel Denison Rogers. ALS, Miscellaneous Collection, MHi. Addressed to Petersburg, Virginia.

Had tea at Mrs. Adams's last evening; the Vice President returned to New York last Sunday.

SATURDAY, 5 DECEMBER 1789

James Madison to George Washington

Since my last I have been furnished with the inclosed copy of the letter from the Senators of this State to its Legislature. It is well calculated to keep alive the disaffection to the Government, and is accordingly applied to that use by the violent partizans. I understand the letter was written by the first subscriber of it [*R. H. Lee*], as indeed is pretty evident from the stile and strain of it. The other [*Grayson*] *it is said*, subscribed it with reluctance. I am less surprized that this should have been the case, than that he should have subscribed at all.

***

The difficulty started agst. the amendments is really unlucky, and the more to be regretted as it springs from a friend to the Constitution.[1] It is a still greater cause of regret, if the distinction be, as it appears to me, altogether fanciful. If a line can be drawn between the powers granted and the rights retained, it would seem to be the same thing, whether the latter be secured, ~~whether~~ by declaring that they shall ~~be~~ [*lined out*] not be abridged, or that the former shall not be extended. If no line can be drawn a declaration in either form would amount to nothing. If the distinction were just it does not seem to be of sufficient importance to justify the risk of losing the amendts. of furnishing a handle to the disaffected and of arming N[*orth*]. C[*arolina*]. with a pretext, if she be disposed, to prolong her exile from the Union.

ALS, Washington Papers, DLC. Written from Orange, Virginia. The omitted text is an extract copied from Hardin Burnley to James Madison, 28 November 1789, describing recent proceedings and debates of the Virginia House of Delegates. For the full text, see *PJM* 12:458–60.

[1] Madison refers to the Virginia state Senate's rejection of the eleventh and twelfth Amendments submitted to the states for ratification, the present Ninth and Tenth Amendments to the Constitution. Opposition to them was led by Edmund Randolph.

OTHER DOCUMENTS

North Carolina General Assembly to Samuel Johnston. Johnston replied to this message on the same day, agreeing to the legislature's request. Both in Journal of the North Carolina House of Commons, p. 39. For the full text of both messages, see *DHFFE* 4:334–35.

Has reconsidered Johnston's request to depart and now believes that the executive officer should be present in the state until a replacement is chosen; asks him not to leave until either that happens or the General Assembly rises.

Governor Beverley Randolph to Richard Henry Lee and William Grayson. FC, Executive Letterbook, Vi. Written from Richmond, Virginia. The Virginia Assembly's congratulatory address to Washington (see *PGW* 5:350–51) was passed on 28 October 1789. R. H. Lee and Grayson's successor, Walker, did not present the address until 27 April 1790, a time lapse that may be explained by a notation at the bottom of this cover letter: "Duplicate of the Above forwarded 6th. of April 1790."

Transmits Virginia Assembly's Address to the President.

Abigail Rogers to Daniel Denison Rogers. ALS, Miscellaneous Collection, MHi. Addressed to Petersburg, Virginia. Postscript to Rogers's letter of 4 December, above; entry made at 9 P.M.

The Vice President and others passed the evening with her.

William Shepard to George Washington. ALS, Washington Papers, DLC. Written from New Bern, North Carolina; franked; postmarked Philadelphia, 7 January 1790. For the full text, see *PGW* 4:369-70.

Office seeking: naval officer for New Bern; will forward testimonials of his character when Hawkins and Johnston go to New York City.

George Washington, Diary. Washington Papers, MiD-B.

The Adams family dined at the President's.

MONDAY, 7 DECEMBER 1789

Thomas Fitzsimons to Samuel Meredith

As the time Approaches for our winter Campain it is Necessary to turn our attention towards Quarters & I have taken the liberty of inclosing a letter for you to deliver to Mrs. Anderson upon that Subject—the purport of it is that if she Can Accomodate Mr. Clymer & myself *without Incommodeing you* that we will be glad to take possession of our old Quarters on 2 Conditions one that she shd. provide herself with a better Cook the other that she would ascertain What we were to pay when we invited Company—While we were there last summer our Cookery was too bad to be endured—& the Charge for Company was in one instance 12/ head.

Now tho we Neither of us are Epicures nor too attentive to small Matters I Confess I should not like to live in the same way Again nor to be deprived of seeing our friends by the exorbitancy of the Charge & I preferr haveing these points settled beforehand, Rather than have to Complain of them afterwards—the previous Question will be not to disturb or Incommode you—to prevent which Mr. C. & myself will take the 2d floor, leavg. the 1st., for yr. bed chamber & a Room to recive our Comp[*an*]y. & yours if this is any way inconv[*enien*]t. you must say so & one or both will Look out Elsewhere.

If on the Contrary all things are settled we Must Request you to have laid on as much Wood as will serve us—I will send our wine from hence. I hope the session will not be a Long one but the season will be an Inclement one & we must Guard Against it.

We have Nothing New here—the Weather Uncommonly Mild—& Commerce extending beyond all Expectations. Wheat 8/9 bushel flour 45/ ℔ Bbl. I am told a Ship from London in a Very short passage is now Comg. up [*the Delaware River*].

ALS, Dreer Collection, PHi. Written from Philadelphia; postmarked.

Oliver Wolcott, Sr., and Others to Jeremiah Wadsworth

We are informed the subject of establishing a Post Road from New York thro' this Town to Hartford, has been considered by you, & are happy that your opinion is in favor of the measure. The public is certainly interested to effect a matter of this kind thro' such an extensive & populous part of the Country.

We are sensible that many parts of the Road from Litchfield thro' Harwinton are studiously placed over the worst grounds that could have been formed for the purpose; This has long been a subject of Complaint, and upon the Petition of a number of Inhabitants of this Town, our County Court have altered some of the most impassable part of that road, & nothing remains to be done, but to lay out the [*lined out*] alterations, as the Committee for that purpose are appointed.

There are other parts of the road, which we are determined to alter & amend as soon as ~~we~~ it is practicable, and have no doubt of the eventual success of our Exertions. Should a Post Road be established on this Rout, we believe that circumstance, would hasten the necessary amendments: but so ~~So~~ many are the obstacles, & so forcible the prejudices we have to combat, in procuring alterations in roads; that we sincerely hope the Post Roads thro' the union will soon be made subjects of the Supreme Legislative consideration, as we are convinced the business will never be thoroughly done in any other way.

Your acquaintance with the interior parts of this County [*Litchfield*], precludes the necessity of information, as to the general benefits of a Post Road this way; but as to particular parts of the Rout, it may not be improper to state some facts, which you may not be acquainted with. The post Road will doubtless be directed thro' Danbury & thro' this Town, and we have never contemplated any other course from Danbury but that thro' New Milford; when Mr. [*Isaac*] Trowbridge informed us that some people had ideas of forming another rout thro' Newtown Woodbury &c. into this Town, the subject was entirely new; but upon more deliberation we have no objection to that rout—if it should be thought to accommodate the public better than the other: by Mr. Trowbridge's account of the road thro' Newtown, Southbury, Woodbury, & Bethlem to Litchfield, it is not more than 2 miles further, than that thro' New Milford, & is a better road; & most indisputably there is more Wealth & a greater number of Inhabitants on the road thro' Newtown, Woodbury &c. than on the New Milford Road.

We are told Doctr. Johnson has advised to the Newtown & Woodbury road, and thence thro' Litchfield to Hartford.

Trowbridge supposes Mr. [*Samuel*] Ozgood will establish a post Road here, if Dotr. Johnson & you, should suppose the public interest required it;

we have written to the Doctr. requesting his intercession: and should you find it consistent with your Duty & inclination—We request you to write to the Post Master Genl. in favor of such Rout as you judge most proper; as we must be convinced you will think the road should be established thro' this Town, ~~whatever~~ whatever direction it may take in other places; and likewise that you would recommend a Post Office to be fixed in Litchfield.

LS, Wadsworth Papers, CtHi. Written from Litchfield, Connecticut; addressed to Hartford, Connecticut. The letter was also signed by Lynde Lord, Benjn. Tallmadge, Uriah Tracy, Tapping Reeve, Isaac Baldwin, Jr., Ephraim Kirby, Julius Deming, John Allen, and Reuben Smith.

[*Jeremiah Wadsworth,*] The Observer, No. VIII

On the means of preserving Public Liberty

When a system of national freedom hath been established by great exertions, it becomes an interesting enquiry how it shall be best preserved. The speculative Philosopher, and the practical Statesman have united their endeavors to answer this question.

A natural thirst for power in the human mind, with the emoluments springing from authority, tend to a general encroachment on the rights of human nature—Even patriots and honest men have their weakness, passions, and appetites, and in little instances may be tyrants, while they wish for general freedom.

Many systems have been formed which in theory appear almost perfect—many checks have been devised; still there are, and we must expect there will be, abuses of power, until the nature of man is delivered from its present imperfection. In every state some person or persons must be representatives of the public, in whose hands the power of the whole is lodged, for general protections and without this investiture of public authority to restrain and punish, the wicked will be a scourge to all within their reach; and it is also possible, that the very persons who are clothed with public power, may become cruel and unjust. Without power in some national head, anarchy will be the state of man, every one will retaliate and abuse as his passions dictate, which is the worst of tyrannies. With power the rulers of a nation may do injury, for man is frail—great men may misjudge—good men may fall.

To give any man unlimited power, is a greater temptation than ought to be placed before a frail being; at the same time, placing too many checks on rulers is in effect dismembering the body, and destroys its energy of action and of defence, both against foreign enemies and its own evil subjects. So far as we may judge from American experience, a nation of freemen, in modelling their government, are more apt to err in overlimiting, than in giving too great scope to the power of rulers—In both cases the consequence is nearly the same; for when the citizens find their constitutional government cannot protect and do justice, they will throw themselves into the hands of some bold usurper, who promises much to them, but intends only for himself; and in this way very many free states have lost their liberties. The forming a constitution of government is a serious matter—the spirit of deliberation and concession, with which it hath been taken up by the citizens at large, and thus far carried into effect, is a new event in the history of mankind. The present constitution of United States, appears to embrace the essential principles both of freedom and energy in national operations; still very little dependence is to be made on this Constitution, as a future safeguard to the American liberties. I would by no means undervalue those systematic productions, which we call the Constitution of the several states, and of the whole—they express our present ideas of the rulers' power and duty, and the subjects' right—they are a written basis on which national habits will be formed, and in this way will cherish sentiments of freedom and retard the rise of oppression—on these your children will look as maxims of their fathers' wisdom, but if they have no other protection, the lust of those who have opportunity will undermine their privileges. Every generation must assert its own liberties; and for this the collective body of people must be informed. A general diffusion of science, in every class of people, is the true cause of that new series of events which have taken place in the United States. In every other country a great proportion of the people are unacquainted with letters—In several great and civilized kingdoms of Europe, it is but a comparative few who can read and write. The vast number of well meaning and ignorant people, become instruments of superior policy, to oppose every effort of national freedom; but in America there is no order or great number of people, who can be made subservient to such ungenerous purposes. The late war, was a war of the people—general information convinced them of its justice and that their all was endangered; hence sprang their humanity, exertion and patience; and a traitor could in no part of the country find either asylum or aid.

The formation of our present government, by the deliberation of three million citizens, is the highest evidence, and the greatest effect we have yet seen from general information.

The same causes which have given you victory, and a constitution combining the rights of man with the powers of government, will certainly be sufficient to preserve national liberty, and make your children as free as their fathers. A few enlightened citizens may be dangerous; let all be enlightened, and oppression must cease, by the influence of a ruling majority; for it can never be their interest to indulge a system incompatible with the rights of freemen. Those institutions are the most effectual guards to public liberty, which diffuse the rudiments of literature among a people.

Let the most perfect constitution, finite wisdom can devise, be adopted; if succeeding generations become ignorant—if a large part of the people are destitute of letters, their precious patrimony will be cheated from their hands; not, perhaps, by violence, but by a course of artful measures, against which ignorent men have no defence.

A man declaiming for liberty, and suffering his children to grow up without education, acts most absurdly, and prepares them to be licentious but not free.

The road to preferment is open to all, and the common citizen may see his children possess the first offices of state, if endowed with genius, honesty and science; having such incentives to fidelity, the remiss parent is unpardonable. As the best preservative of national liberty, the public ought to patronize institutions to instruct the children of poor people; for, give them knowledge and they will never be the instruments of injuring mankind. A few incautious expressions in our Constitution, or a few salaries of office too great for the contracted feelings of those who do not know the worth of merit and integrity, can never injure the United States, while literature is generally diffused, and the plain citizen and planter reads and judges for himself.

The American legislature could not do an act more favorable to general humanity, liberty and virtue, than to endow the Universities, rising in almost every state, with such funds in the unlocated territory, as would enable them to furnish the best means of instruction, and at an easy rate, to the sons of those who have moderate wealth. Disseminate science thro' all grades of people, and it will forever vindicate your rights, which are now well understood and firmly fixed. Science will do more than this—it will break the chains, and unbolt the prison doors of despotism. At the present moment, France is an instance of its influence—The wealthy subjects of that country are become enlightened, and thus determined to be free, O France! I love thee and thy sons—when my nightly supplication forgets to ask a blessing on thy great exertions, and on thy councils, I shall lose my claim of being a christian. August Empire! Many of thy sons are among the learned; how often have I drank improvement and pleasure from their pens; but I fear, I greatly fear, that the vast mass of thy subjects are not sufficiently informed in the nature of freedom, to receive from Heaven and preserve so rich a gift.

[Hartford, Connecticut] *American Mercury*, 7 December. For information on The Observer series, its authorship, and reprintings, see the location note to The Observer, No. I, 12 October, above.

OTHER DOCUMENTS

John Langdon to James Sullivan. No copy known; acknowledged in Sullivan to Langdon, 11 December.

Thomas Lloyd to John Debrett. FC:lbk, Lloyd Papers, PPAmP. Sent to London. The printers mentioned were also booksellers: Robert Hodge (1746–1813), who emigrated from Edinburgh in 1770 and opened a printing office in New York City in 1773; Thomas Allen, who ran a bookstore in New York from about 1786 to 1799; and Samuel Campbell (1763–1836), who opened a bookstore in New York about 1785 (*New York*, pp. 204–5).

Has regularly forwarded fifty of each issue of *CR* for sale, with requests to know whether it is worth arranging a London printing, and on what terms; has just contracted with three New York City printers and booksellers to print the work; forwards proposal for improving the work by adding laws of the United States.

Henry Van Schaack to Theodore Sedgwick. ALS, Sedgwick Papers, MHi. Written from Pittsfield, Massachusetts; addressed to Stockbridge, Massachusetts.

The people "are cooling fast" about federal salaries; an assumption of the states' war debts would put the United States "on good safe ground," and the man with the greatest role in bringing it about deserves much from his country; if Sedgwick is not zealous and active in the business, it will be a disappointment; the French modeled their revolution after America's, but their temper, good sense, and moderation are not equal.

Boston Gazette, 7 December.

Defends "brave General *Sumpter*" against an attack by A Federalist on his 24 August circular letter and reprints the letter. (For both, see *DHFFC* 16:1395–97.)

TUESDAY, 8 DECEMBER 1789

Edward Trescott to Pierce Butler. ALS, Butler Papers, PHi. Written from Charleston, South Carolina; addressed care of Peter Garbrance, Nassau Street.

Office seeking: revenue collector, if direct taxation is adopted; understands that the President "always consults the Honble. Members of the Senate in all Appointments."

WEDNESDAY, 9 DECEMBER 1789

William Smith (S.C.) to Tench Coxe

Tho greatly obliged to you for your endeavours to procure me information on the Subject of a Bank[*rup*]t. Law, I was a little disappointed in not having received it. The Bill is however drawn & ready to be presented, composed of Such materials as my inquiries have furnished me with & open to such amendmts. as the knowledge of others may suggest. As I have taken for my ground work, the Law of your State,[1] which is a compilation of the English Bank[*ruptc*]y. Laws I have the experience & lights of both countries to guide me & therefore flatter myself it will be less exceptionable than it wo[*ul*]d. otherwise be. I shall be gratefull for any hints on the subject between this & the meeting of Congress & am indebted for those already transmitted which accord perfectly with my Sentimts. & were attended to in the Bill before I receivd. your favor.

Col. [*Nicholas*] Eveleigh desires me to reciprocate his best comp[*limen*]ts. his wife does not come till the Spring.

I am Surprized at not having recd. the Journal of the Convention[2] of which I request you to send me 2 cop[*ie*]s. as soon as it is out. a countryman of mine, Mr. [*William Allen*] Deas, now at Mrs. [*Mary*] House's will probably return here soon & will take charge of any papers you may have to send me. I sho[*ul*]d. be glad to have 2 cops. of the first Session in July last. I am anxious to hear an accot. of the deliberations of your State Convention,[3] if you have any papers containing the debates, you will oblige me by sending them.

The Papers mention the accession of North Carolina, but no official accounts have been received by the President, nor is the intelligence confirmed from Charleston from whence we have late arrivals.

ALS, Coxe Papers, PHi. Addressed to Philadelphia; postmarked 10 December.

[1]"A Supplement to the Several Acts of Assembly for the relief of Insolvent Debtors," adopted by Pennsylvania on 27 March 1789, revised previous acts on the subject.

[2]The thirty-one page *Journal of a Convention of the Protestant Episcopal Church . . . Held in Christ Church, in the City of Philadelphia, From July 28th to August 8th, 1789* was published in Philadelphia by Hall and Sellers in late 1789.

[3]The first session of the convention to amend Pennsylvania's constitution of 1776 met in Philadelphia from 24 November 1789 to 26 February 1790. A 146 page *Minutes of the Convention* was published in Philadelphia by Zachariah Poulson in late 1789.

A Philadelphian to Mr. Brown

In your paper of the 30th ult. I took the liberty to assure the public, that the observations of a correspondent of Oswald's of that date, concerning the public accounts of Mr. Robert Morris were unfounded in fact: and altogether void of merit.[1] I promised to prove them false in ten days. I do now assure the public; that they are false; and challenge the author to prove his assertions. I would not proceed in this mode—but would at once lay such matters before the public as would fully refute all that has been said in the publication alluded to: But that I think it proper, that whatever any man says to the injury of another, he should be called upon to prove it. I will not say that the writer in Oswald's paper has not himself been misinformed, and abused by some other, and that his zeal for the public good induced him to the publication; and therefore I wish to give him an opportunity to lay his documents before the public, and shew his ground for accusing Mr. Morris in so serious a manner. If this should be the case the author will in some measure be acquitted from the charge of a malicious attack upon that gentleman, and will have an opportunity of "fixing the saddle upon the right horse."

If the author declines this challenge the public will believe him wrong— they will believe me right. If he attempts to prove his assertion, I shall meet him at the public bar, with the proofs in my possession.

FG, 11 December, edited by Andrew Brown.

[1] See A Philadelphian to Mr. Brown, in reply to the newspaper article printed in Eleazer Oswald's *IG* earlier that morning, both 30 November, above.

OTHER DOCUMENTS

Archibald Maclaine to James Iredell. ALS, Iredell Papers, NcD. Written from Wilmington, North Carolina; addressed to Edenton, North Carolina. For a partial text, see *DHFFE* 4:339.
> Supposes that Johnston will be with Maclaine before this letter arrives; Johnston "will have numberless applications for the few offices to be distributed in North Carolina" (recommends John Hay as federal attorney for the North Carolina district).

Robert Morris to George Washington. No copy known; acknowledged in Washington to Morris, 14 December.

North Carolina Senate and House Proceedings. *DHFFE* 4:337.
> Hawkins elected Senator.

THURSDAY, 10 DECEMBER 1789

Pierce Butler to Weeden Butler

We are looking out with some anxiety for the October and November Packets, knowing that We shall have a letter or two from Chelsea—I wrote to You the 3d. of last Month.

This letter, Accompanied by Our Journals and Acts of Congress, will be handed to You by Mr. Richards a Gentleman from Jamaica who touched here in His way to London and liking the Country stayd longer than He first intended. He brought letters of introduction to me. I found Him a sensible Young Man.

We Congressional Men have had an Interval of rest—We are to return to Our labours the first of next Month—tranquility, Order and obedience to Law reigns as forcibly at this time in the United states as in any Country on Earth. May the scene long continue! In the Europe the flame appears to spread—I sincerely wish Your Country freedom from it I have expressd myself badly. I mean clear of it. Surely the Bourgois of Paris have gone too far.

ALS, Butler Papers, Uk. Addressed to Cheyne Walk, Chelsea, London, England; answered 1 March 1790.

Thomas Hartley to Jasper Yeates

Mr. Alexander White one of our Profession and a Member of Congress with a very respectable Family of Females goes to New York.

He is a Man of Sense and his Judgment is with the Susquehanna.

He goes to Mr. [*Matthias*] Sloughs and will stay there—from the Number of his Family he would not here nor there go into a *Private House to Lodge.*

You must make it a Point to have them with the Ladies to spend the Evening; I have given them something in the Cold Way and *some Chocolate.*

In this State of the World Circumstances must not be unattended to.

As your Sentiments and myne so fully agree—and the Regard that is to be had [*lined out*] to a respectable Man I hope you will not consider this as an Obtrusion.

ALS, Yeates Papers, PHi. Written from York, Pennsylvania; addressed to Lancaster, Pennsylvania; favored by The Honorable Alexander White.

OTHER DOCUMENTS

George Washington, Diary. Washington Papers, MiD-B.
  Mary King, Catherine Few, and the Griffins dined at the President's.

FRIDAY, 11 DECEMBER 1789

Thomas Hartley to Jasper Yeates

I wrote to you last Night at eleven oClock (without the Knowledge of Mr. White)—the Scrawl which you will probably receive to Day—I think it a great Departure from his usual Prudence for him to take a Family of five Ladies to live at New York for four or five Months—he will find what a handsome Sum it will amount to—I rather call it a bold Stroke.

To Morrow I mean to set off for Chambersburg and will try to pick up a little Cash.

I have Arranged my Affairs for Leaving this Place for New York on Sunday the 3d. of January and will probably stay part of the following Day with you—It is *rather* problematical about the Ladies accompanying me to Lancaster—I fear they will not be able.

Pray have you any account from the [*state constitutional*] Convention?

If you could write me a Line towards the Close of next week and give us some News it would be acceptable.

The Result of the North Caroloina Delibrations we have not yet heard I trust it will be favorable.

ALS, Yeates Papers, PHi. Written from York, Pennsylvania; addressed to Lancaster, Pennsylvania; answered 16 December.

James Sullivan to John Langdon

I have yours of the 7th and thank you for your attention to the small matter in which I begged ~~your attention~~ it.

You mention that you shall proceed toward New York on the 19th or 20th and that we shall have the pleasure of seeing you in Boston. there are a great number of your friends here who wish to see you, and I shall take it as a particular favour, if when you have fixed the Time and manner of your Journey you will give me a line to let me know when we may expect you & how long you shall stay in Boston, & whether your Lady goes on with you.

Your Sister [*Martha Sullivan*] anticipates the pleasure of seeing you, and we hold our house at your Command.

ALS, Langdon-Elwyn Family Papers, NhHi. Written from Boston; place to which addressed not indicated.

OTHER DOCUMENTS

Robert Morris to Gouverneur Morris. LS, Gouverneur Morris Papers, NNC. Written from Philadelphia; place to which addressed not indicated.

For background on the settlement of R. Morris's accounts, see *DHFFC* 8: 663–65.

Private business involving the securities, tobacco, and flour markets in Europe and "the Delaware Works" (R. Morris's recently purchased manufacturing establishment at the Falls of the Delaware, opposite Trenton, New Jersey); dreads leaving home; first object in view after returning to New York City is settlement of his accounts, "respecting which [*Eleazer*] Oswald continues to abuse me, but I hope soon to retort."

George Washington, Diary. Washington Papers, MiD-B.

Because of bad weather, Adams, and no one else, attended Mrs. Washington's levee.

SATURDAY, 12 DECEMBER 1789

William Ellery to Benjamin Huntington

***

I hope you have fully recovered your health, and that you will attend Congress early in the next Session that you will inform me on your arrival at New York, and that I shall have the pleasure and the advantage of a renewal of our correspondence.

The Genl. Assembly of this State is to meet by adjournment, at Providence on the second Monday in January next; but I do not expect that they will then order a Convention to be called. If North-Carolina should adopt the New-Government, of which I am doubtful, it would have a considerable influence upon our Antifeds; but even that happy event would not I think induce them to join the union until the next fall; for until then they will imagine they cannot be made to feel. Then and not before their flax seed, barley, cheese &c. &c. will be ready for exportation, and they cannot I presume suppose that Congress will continue their leniency, and admit into the United States free of duty, if they should admit at all, articles of the growth and manufacture of this State.

I am of the same opinion now, which I have often expressed to you, that if Congress had subjected those articles to the foreign duty this State would have joined the Union: But Congress chose to try to subdue our Antifeds by lenient measures, to draw them by the cords of love. There is indeed something noble and Godlike in this mode of cond[*uct*] and leniency despised will justify rigorous treatment.

But no way I am afraid can be devised to make the Antis feel effectually and suddenly which will not injure the Feds who have already suffered deeply from the refractoriness and fraudulent conduct of the Antis. To prohibit the citizens of this State from an intercourse with the United States, which would seem to be an obvious and a natural way to compel their State to come in, would injure the Feds greatly and immediately, ~~and~~ but would not as hath been already mentioned affect the Antifeds until the fall, and they care not how much the former suffer provided they are unhurt.

A demand of a sum of money to be paid in specie in the course of two or three months, with a declaration that it should be distrained by federal force, unless it were raised by the time assigned would I beleive be the shortest and perhaps as effectual a measure as any to bring the Antifeds to their senses, and would be as little injurious to the Feds as any that could be devised. For notwithstanding the Genl. Assembly in their curious address to Congress, informed them that they were making preparations to pay ~~what they~~ such part of their quota of the public debt as Congress should from time to time require of them;[1] yet such a demand would find them unprepared; for the small sum collected by their impost is and will be in paper, which at the last Session was scaled at fifteen for one, and specie, if at all, cannot be procured for our paper at a much greater discount, and the Antifederal towns if a tax should be laid by the State in pursuance of su[*ch a*] demand, would not be ~~able~~ disposed if they should be ~~disposed~~ able to collect [*thei*]r proportions. The federal towns would exert every [*torn*] to raise their quotas, relying that Congress would not [*torn*] upon those towns, especially upon the federal towns which had furnished their proportions of the requisition, and the Antifeds dreading that their stock might be taken by a military force, and sold at auction in Massachusetts or Connecticut for the payment of their parts of the demand, would I don't doubt, if it should be necessary, force their representatives to call a convention, and hasten into the Union.

I cannot you see, altho' perhaps unseasonably forbe[*ar*] casting my crude notions upon paper, respecting th[*torn*] mode of treating this State in order to compel it [*torn*] its best interest and to do what it ought to do cheerfully.

You will think of them when and as you please.

ALS, Benjamin Huntington Correspondence, 1772–1790, R-Ar. Written from Newport, Rhode Island; addressed to Norwich, Connecticut. The omitted text discusses Huntington's management of Ellery's farm in Colchester, Connecticut.

[1] At the direction of the state legislature, Governor John Collins sent the Address to Congress in September 1789; see *DHFFC* 8:396–98.

James Jackson to Samuel B. Webb

*** I shall be with you by the return of the Jenny—myself only. Mrs. Jackson[1] does not like to venture. The last returns of the Packets in such severe Gales, has made her fearful for her Boys, & many of her Friends with the same apprehensions have induced her to decline it: so that I shall be compelled to risk the cold Climate & Beds of New York by myself in a Batchelor State, which is not very agreeable: most People can console themselves on these occasions with temporary comforts. I have not yet been able to conquer the foolish ideas of the strict ties of matrimonial connections. nor do I wish it. I want again to be near you—What think you of Matthews you & myself taking your House & keeping Batchelors hall together for the session? I do not wish to leave the neighbourhood—I am sincerely fond of my old Friend [*Sebastian*] Bauman & am very happy to hear he has the post Office. If you however do not like that plan, If the upstairs rooms are to let, if the General [*Mathews*] pleases, He & myself will take them: provided we could be furnished with two or three old Chairs &c., as I suppose our old Lodgings are fully occupied.

***

ALS, Fogg Collection, MeHi. Written from Savannah, Georgia; franked by Jackson and sent per sloop *Friendship*, Capt. Joseph Burnham.

[1] Mary Charlotte Young married James Jackson in 1785, and together they had five sons.

Rufus King to George Mason

I thank you for the acquaintance of Mr. [*Joseph*] Fenwick, he appears an agreeable and well informed man, and I.

I am obliged to you for the acquaintance of Mr. Fenwick, he is an agreeable and a modest well informed man, and leaves leaves this place with many prepossessions in his favor the Esteem & Good will of all persons (with whom he has made an acquaintance) who have known had the pleasure to know him.

I consider your Sons your Son [*John Mason*] (whom I recollect with much pleasure) is fortunate in this connection, and so far as I am capable of judging their plan of business promises great success Should if the french revolution has results favorably to the freedom of commerce in that Kingdom, the House of F. M. & Co. from their very respectable connections in this Country and their plan of business can hardly fail of great success—Should Mr. F. hereafter make a visit to the Eastern States eastward or upon his return to F. shd. your Son come this way, it would afford me very sensible pleasure to introduce them to such principal of my friends in New Hamp. & Mass. as might probably be [*lined out*] form beneficial Connection both with their House [*lined out*] Bordeaux and upon the Potomack—in france & america.

I have no doubt that Mr. F. wd. do credit to our Country in the consular

Office, and shd. be very happy to have it in my power to be serviceable to him in procuring an appointment to Bordeaux.

FC:dft, King Papers, NHi.

Civis to Mr. Brown

The numerous publications which have lately appeared against the Hon. Robert Morris, Esq. have given great pain to every friend to the honour and happiness of the state of Pennsylvania.[1]

A writer in your paper has pledged himself to prove an assertion in a late publication against that great and good man, to be false.[2] From the whole tenor of his public and private conduct, there can be no doubt but that every other charge against him which calls his patriotism or integrity in question, is equally without foundation.

It is impossible to review the history of this gentleman's conduct as a patriot, as an officer of government, as a merchant or as a man, without feeling the keenest indignation against those assassins who have for seven years past been trying to ruin his reputation.

The decided part he took with his country in the beginning of the war—his long, faithful, and successful services to his country in the cabinet—the influence of the credit of his name, at one time, in arming, feeding and clothing the American army—the firmness of his mind, under every species of danger and difficulty which he underwent, as financier, and the immense sums he saved to the United States by his economical arrangements; all merit, from his countrymen, more than they are able to bestow. In the opinion of all candid men, he stands second to *General Washington* in his claims upon the esteem and gratitude of the United States.

In his private capacity, honour, integrity, generosity and friendship, have marked every part of his intercourse with his fellow citizens. Where is the tradesman or the mariner that can say he ever suffered wrong, or even an unkindness from him? On the contrary, how many valuable citizens of that description, as well as unfriended young merchants, have owed their prosperity to his benevolence? His goodness has not stopped here—the widows and the orphans of those who have been connected with him in business, have always found a steady and sympathizing friend. Some of them have been saved from ruin, and poverty, and even advanced to competence and independence, by means of his friendship and generosity.

I wish the citizens of Pennsylvania would consider how much their honour, and the credit of our young republic, are concerned in not suffering an ancient and faithful servant of the public to be run down by a few angry and disappointed men. It would be deemed highly disgraceful for the citizens of

Philadelphia to sit still at their doors or windows and see one of their neighbors torn to pieces by a furious animal, without offering to rescue him; and yet we commit the same offence against duty and humanity, by being tame spectators of the attempts to destroy a fellow citizen's character. Who will serve the public? Who will risk life and property to save a sinking country, after reading the volumes of scandal and falsehood that have been published with impunity against a man, to whom America owes so much of the blessings of her liberty and new government?

FG, 12 December, edited by Andrew Brown.

[1] The Centinel (Samuel Bryan) attacked Morris in *IG* on 26 February, 24 March, and 28 November 1788. More recently, Another Correspondent resumed the attack in *IG*, 30 November, above.
[2] A Philadelphian, *FG*, 30 November and 9 December, printed above.

Letter from an American at New Orleans to His Friend at Georgetown, Maryland

The sparks of liberty which were discovered some time past in South America, have now actually broke out into flame. Yes my friend, the American Fever which has shaken to its foundations, the Thrones of enlightened Europe; has found its way to this land of ignorance and superstition: by accounts received over land from Mexico, all bids fair for a revolution. The inhabitants of this rich and fertile Country, who have been the dupes and sport of Priestcraft for Centuries past, begin to open their eyes—they have refused to pay the fourth part of the produce of their Mines to the King, in consequence of which the Viceroy ordered the European troops to take possession of some of the most valuable mines in the neighborhood of the city of Mexico; this happened in October last; and about the 20th of November upwards of 7000 of the inhabitants appeared under arms, amongst which were the most respected characters of the country; they marched and attacked the troops who had taken possession of their property; an engagement took place, the greatest part of the King's troops fell a sacrifice, and the people retook their property; they were afterwards joined by a large body of the Indians (who make the greater part of the inhabitants) and then proceeded to the city of Mexico, where they took possession of the King's Magazines, Arsenals, &c. the Viceroy, the Chief Officers, the Priests and Jesuits, the most obnoxious to the natives, fled towards Carthagena: two expresses arrived here over land; Government wishes to conceal it from the people, but time will disclose the whole of this interesting affair.

NYDG, 3 February 1790 (the date on which members of Congress would have seen it), from the non extant [Georgetown, Maryland] *Times and Patowmack Packet*, 27 January

1790; also reprinted at Windsor and Bennington, Vermont; Portsmouth and Keene, New Hampshire; Newburyport and Salem, Massachusetts; New York City (*NYP*, 4 February, *GUS*, 13 February); Elizabethtown, New Jersey; Edenton, North Carolina; and Charleston, South Carolina.

OTHER DOCUMENTS

Henry Knox to Jeremiah Wadsworth. FC:dft, Knox Papers, Gilder Lehrman Collection, NHi.

Acknowledges receipt of letter of 6 December, enclosing Wadsworth's accounts for provisioning the Springfield arsenal, and requests his payment on an order for $640; rejoices at the recovery of Wadsworth's "amiable family" and hopes they can be induced to spend the winter in New York City as the Knoxes' guests.

MONDAY, 14 DECEMBER 1789

[*Jeremiah Wadsworth,*] The Observer. No. IX

To the Public Creditors

From many of the evils which happen to a good citizen, he extracts a happiness as they pass. The patriotic creditor, who deposited his property with the public, has the happiness of reflecting that his lots contributed to the safety of millions, and laid the foundation of an empire in which we hope science and virtue will perpetuate freedom. There have been many delays and many things done on the part of the public, which ought not to have been; still you have no reason to despair of national justice. Some there may be who would spunge the whole, and obliviate your claims—these men are of small number, and even less influence—they act not from principle and falsely supposing the measure would be popular, have baulked their own expectations of preferment. As the case is circumstanced, if there were no sense of justice, a principle of policy would support your claim with every considerate man; for to drive to despair two hundred thousand creditors and influential citizens, is an event too great to be hazarded, and might produce worse consequences than the most rigorous payment. Convinced of these facts, the creditors ought not to be too hasty in their expectations from the present government. Let it be seen that your patience hath not been the effect of necessity, but from a conviction of the deranged state of the National finances. The mind is apt to vibrate in extremes, and from too great despondency rise into sanguine hopes which never can be realized. Something of this I have observed in the creditors of the nation. To arrange a scheme of finance—to liquidate many unsettled claims—to search from anew, the

resources of this great country, and to adjust the whole into a system beneficial to agriculture, commerce and manufactures, requires great ability and
industry in the official departments, and the most candid indulgence of all
parties concerned. The gentlemen who have these duties in trust possess too
much good sense to hazard their own responsibility in a sudden manner, and
before they can possibly ascertain the means which may be exerted. Returning order in the treasury department, is the first thing necessary—this you
may see, and for the rest, there must be time to adjust measures which will
be durable. If the legislature were to decide without previous information
from its executive, or the executive to endanger its existence by recommending without knowledge, it would betray a want of the proper capacity to
relieve a nation from such confusion as we have experienced. Certainly it will
be for the public advantage to stop the accumulation of interest, on a great
debt, speedily as can be; you may therefore depend on every thing which is
consistent with justice and humanity to the people and more than this ought
not be granted. The resources of the United States are increasing and in a few
years may do what is at present impossible. You have no right to expect that
funds can be suddenly erected and formalized, sufficient to answer the literal
promises of the public; but ought for the present to be satisfied, with what
in this country hath been esteemed small interest for property, on the other
hand, national honor and justice require that the funds provided should be
in their nature increasing ones, that the dividend you receive may increase
with the public ability, until it arrives to the point of equitable interest; after
which, all increase in that national revenue, may become a sinking fund to
do away the general debt, if that be judged best. By funds thus constituted
and sacredly appropriated, a compromise may be made between the nation and its creditors, honorable for one and safe for the other. In a country
of increasing commerce and population, and in which every year brings a
million acres of new land into taxable improvement, there is the best opportunity for funds of the above description. The state creditors appear to
me in the most hazardous situation, and ought immediately to unite their
influence that they may be placed on the same footing with the creditors of
the United States—the measures must take place now or never—you have a
reasonable demand—your property was advanced for the common defence,
and if an application is made in season, you must be heard. I can foresee but
one objection to be made to this measure, which is, that it will increase the
value of State Securities and make them of equal goodness with the Continentals but he must be a churl indeed, who objects on this ground, when it
is considered how much the state creditors have lost in the principal of their
debt, and that the appreciation will arise from the simple circumstances of
giving them a more extended circulation, and placing them on the credit of
a known government, and not from laying any new burdens on the people.

The national and state securities ought to be considered as negotiable Bank Stock, and one circumstance on which its credit and consequent value depends, is the extensiveness of its circulation, and the credit of the government pledged for its redemption. For these reasons, one hundred pounds placed in the funds of the United States, will be of greater value than the same sum bearing the same interest, in the funds of a single State. I am not an advocate for the encreasing demands on the people—they have already been too great, and as a friend of the people, I shall endeavour to shew still more plainly the impositions they have suffered. The people pay a certain sum annually for interest on the state debt, and it is of little consequence to them, whether this centers in the treasury of the United States or of a particular State. If by the adoption of one general system, both people and creditors may be benefitted, every friend of his country will give an influence to complete it.

[Hartford, Connecticut] *American Mercury*, 14 December. For information on The Observer series, its authorship, and reprintings, see the location note to The Observer, No. I, 12 October, above.

OTHER DOCUMENTS

Edward Fox to Andrew Craigie. ALS, Craigie Papers, MWA. Written from Philadelphia; postmarked. On the reverse of the cover sheet, Fox inscribed the key to a numerical coding system, presumably to be used in future correspondence; Morris and Fitzsimons are the only FFC members on the list.

Knox has assured a friend that "those who are most likely to know" say that Hamilton's funding plan will offer four and a half percent to subscribers.

George Washington to Robert Morris. Copy, hand of David Humphreys, Miscellaneous Letters, Miscellaneous Correspondence, State Department Records, Record Group 59, DNA. Sent to Philadelphia. For the full text, see *PGW* 4:400–401.

Acknowledges receipt of Morris's letter of 9 December, enclosing a copy of John Hamilton to Morris, 17 October, above, applying for a federal office, but will preserve freedom of choice by avoiding commitment to any nomination; thanks for offer of a steward, which he declines.

GUS, 30 December.

Burke administered the federal oath at the convening of the federal district court at Charleston, South Carolina.

TUESDAY, 15 DECEMBER 1789

Governor Edward Telfair to the Georgia Delegation

The concurrent Resolutions of the General Assembly that relate to the settlement of the additional claims of this State against the United States,[1] are herewith transmitted, with the Executive order thereon.

To elucidate and accomplish this interesting business of the State, it will require time and application on the part of the Delegation: some of the vouchers may be somewhat defective—this difficulty appears to be fully obviated by the Ordinance of Congress of the 7th. May 1787,[2] as well as that for making provision for interest on all accounts at and after the rate of six per cent. per annum: In every Statement, due regard will doubtless be had to the time of advance, in order to establish a clear statement of Interest on the respective advances.

The Ordinance of Congress referred to, continued to be in full force as far as relates to this State, as will appear by the first enacting clause in the words following "That the several States be and they are hereby limited to the space of six months for exhibiting to the proper Commissioner their claims against the United States, of whatever nature the same may be, and that such States as may neglect to exhibit the same within the period of time after the Commissioner has notified to the supreme Executive thereof, that, he is ready to proceed on the business of his Commission shall be precluded from any future allowance." in order to carry this clause into effect, Mr. [*Guilliam*] Aertsen the Commissioner appointed to liquidate the accounts of South-Carolina and Georgia did on the 21st. August 1787, communicate to the Executive of this State, as follows. "I am appointed Commissioner for liquidating the accounts of the States of South Carolina and Georgia with the United States; and purpose to be at Augusta about the close of December next, when I flatter myself, the necessary papers will be prepared"—The Government of the state at all times eager to enter on the elucidation of this important work, waited with impatience from that period, until the 21st. day of April 1789, when Mr. George Reid appeared, and an official communication having been made to the Executive of his appointment to that office, the Auditor was thereupon requested to exhibit the claims of this State against the United States; and the time between the 21st. day of April and the 25th. day of May thereafter was employed in exhibiting and examining the claims aforesaid; from which it will evidently appear, that so far from six months after due notice by the Commissioner having expired, that he was not even six weeks in the State; it therefore clearly follows, that no part of the delay can or ought to be charged to her, as the Ordinance fully provides in such cases.

It may be justly remarked that Mr. Reid is chargeable with the delay of the papers and vouchers now transmitted; he having alledged, that "he did not think himself authorized to receive the same;" how far any such powers were vested in him, will be better explained by having reference to the 6th. Clause of the said Ordinance, wherein it is provided. "That the said Commissioners be and they are hereby vested with full power and authority to make such allowance for the same as they shall think consistent with the principles of general equity, although such advances or disbursements may not be sanctioned by the Resolves of Congress, or supported by regular vouchers, so as to enable the said Commissioners to make a final adjustment of all the accounts subsisting between the United States, and the several members thereof, agreably to such quota as Congress shall hereafter determine."

This State has laboured under singular disadvantages during the pressure of the late war; she was from the outset of the contest invaded, and partial attacks were made to reduce her, as well by water, as by repeated inroads of the Floridans. in this State of warfare her internal regulations could not be directed at all times by system, and even when an army was raised, a considerable time expired, previous to the establishment of a military chest in the southern department, by which means large advances were made by the State; and from the confusion that arose on the reduction of Savannah in 1778,³ many Persons intrusted with the expenditure of public monies for the support of the military forces acting in defence of the same had their books and papers destroyed, whilst others deserted to the enemy: These are considerations that will doubtless have due force with the Commissioners, when they contemplate that part of their power, which authorizes them to *form decisions* "consistent with the principles of general equity."

The article of supplies ought of right to have a liberal construction in liquidation, as well from the circumstances above recited, as from the following considerations, viz. that of the enemy having from December 1778 until June 1781 had great scope throughout this State to exercise every species of devastation; the spirited opposition that arose within that period, as well as that which took place thereafter and w[hich] caused very great distress to the Citizens, their property being squandered taken and otherwise destroyed; and even what has been liquidated to them, bears little proportion to the damages sustained by the aforementioned ravages.

The quota of this State on a final adjustment of the national expenditure, at the rate of one nineteenth part, is a mat[ter] in which her Citizens are deeply interested, and I trust your exertions will not be wanting in fixing this as a standard for estimation on a final liquidation: the propriety of this will appear from the following reasons:

1st. Because Congress did at no period call upon the States to comply with the 8th. article of the Confederation, which is in the words following "All charges of war, and all other expences that shall be incurred for the common defence or general welfare, and allowed by the United States in Congress assembled, shall be defrayed out of a common Treasury, which shall be supplied by the several States in proportion to the value of all land within each State granted to, or surveyed for any person, as such land and the buildings and improvements thereon shall be estimated, according to such mode as the United States in Congress assembled shall from time to time direct and appoint. The taxes for paying that proportion shall be laid and levied by the authority and direction of the Legislatures of the several States, within the time agreed upon by the United States in Congress assembled." This, being the only basis for taxation must be contended for; should any measures be taken departing from the quota heretofore recited.

2nd Because a ninetieth part has appeared in almost every requisition that has been made by Congress during the war, and it would create an unpleasing reflection in the minds of the people were any deviation now to take place.

3d. Because our being a frontier, and many of our Citizens having lost their all, and the rest who saved a part of their personal property, after returning to the place of their once comfortable habitations, found their houses and other improvements destroyed, and their former fertile fields become a bed of briers: it was under those dark and gloomy encumbrances that many of them once more resumed a settlement.

The occurences that will present themselves to view in the pursuit of the measures recommended to your consideration and the conclusions you will naturally draw upon a retrospect of the whole, may lead to future enquiries: be assured, that nothing on my part, shall be wanting to afford any additional information or aid, that may be in my power to furnish on the part of the State.

FC:lbk, Georgia Executive Council Journal, G-Ar.

[1]On 1 December the Georgia Senate resolved that Auditor John Wereat submit to the general Board of Commissioners the state's accounts and vouchers against the United States for services and expenditures during the Revolutionary War, that Few and Gunn be instructed to explain why the documentation had been delayed and to urge the repeal of the relevant statute of limitation (of 7 May 1787) if necessary, and, if the claims were accepted by the Commissioners, that the Georgia delegation advise the governor whether to appoint someone to arrange and support them before the Board. The House concurred on 4 December, and on 15 December the legislature ordered the governor to forward the claims without further delay.

[2]The ordinance prescribed the mechanisms for settling the accounts between the United States and the individual states, including the appointment of one commissioner to gather

claims in each of five districts (South Carolina and Georgia comprising one district), and the creation of a board of commissioners at the seat of government to adjust those claims (*JCC* 32:262–66).

[3]The British capture of Georgia's capital in December 1778 restored royal government throughout much of the state and left the revolutionary movement with a virtual "government in exile" until the British evacuated in July 1782.

OTHER DOCUMENTS

John Langdon to Henry Knox. ALS, Knox Papers, Gilder Lehrman Collection, NHi.

Predicts he will leave for New York on 22 December.

[Portsmouth] *New Hampshire Spy*, 9 January 1790, from a Charleston, South Carolina, newspaper of 15 December 1789.

Burke still at Charleston.

WEDNESDAY, 16 DECEMBER 1789

Letter from Halifax, North Carolina, to Georgetown, Maryland

The adoption of the New Government has drawn the Anties in a disagreeable situation. An act passed by the General Assembly calls upon all the public officers to settle their accounts before the first day of May.[1] A million of paper money is due to the State; but whether those who have been intrusted with it, will be able to account for it is a Question? Our paper medium is to be redeemed by a Land Office being opened for the Sale of a large Tract of Land, on Cumberland [*River*], in the western Country [*Tennessee*].

If it is true, that "Crowns got by blood must be by blood maintained,"[2] it is equally true that government founded in the wisdom of the people must be by wisdom supported. Hence results the necessity of supporting every channel through [*which*] such information is conveyed to the people. The important transactions which have lately taken place in Europe, may teach a useful and important lesson to Americans. People who have never heard the sound of liberty with emotion, because ignorant of its true principles, and unconscious of its real blessings, when once they get the reins of power into their hands, are apt to rush into the commission of the most flagrant enormities, and commit devastation on the lives and properties of their once lords and masters, under the idea that liberty gives a sanction to their proceedings: when in fact it is but licentiousness.

Kings may learn also, by the present striking lesson which Europe presents, the necessity of cultivating knowledge, and spreading information among their subjects, for experience has fatally shewn that no government be lastingly established, which is not calculated to secure the confidence of the subjects, and the love and esteem of their rulers. In fact no nation, empire or state, can be happy under the bonds of ignorance. 'Tis knowledge, 'tis information on the great subjects of law and government, that make a people happy—The present state of our country loudly testifies to the truth of this; and may the conduct of its citizens continue to evidence it, till time shall be no more.

NYDA, 21 January, from a non extant issue of the [Georgetown, Maryland] *Times and Patowmack Packet*, dated 13 January; reprinted at Philadelphia and Baltimore.

---

[1] "An Act for procuring testimony concerning the Accounts of this state against the United States," adopted in November 1789.

[2] Probably a paraphrase of Shakespeare's *Macbeth*, Act III, scene 4, line 123.

OTHER DOCUMENTS

Tench Coxe to Alexander Hamilton. FC:dft, Coxe Papers, PHi. A docket in an unknown hand states, "Tench Coxe with Notes on Spanish Wool & foreign liquors." The enclosures have not been located.

Encloses rough drafts of papers on "two subjects, one of them of great importance, that may be useful when arranging our affairs with France & Spain"; had intended to have Madison bring them to Jefferson when he returned to New York; of one of them, "it may be useful to converse with Col. J. Wadsworth, whose opportunities in the Branch [*textiles*] it concerns are greater than those of any other person I know among Us."

Henry Knox to Jeremiah Wadsworth. ALS, Wadsworth Papers, CtHi. Written from the War Office; addressed to Hartford, Connecticut; franked; postmarked.

Clothing for federal troops being raised in Springfield, Massachusetts, is directed to be sent via New Haven and Hartford in care of Wadsworth, who should pay for transportation; asks pardon for the trouble given Wadsworth.

Jeremiah Olney to Philip Schuyler. FC, Shipley Library Collection, RHi. Written from Providence, Rhode Island; place to which addressed not indicated.

Office seeking: impost collector for Providence, once Rhode Island ratifies, "which I presume is not far Distant"; intends to wait on Congress in person to obtain the appointment; the letter will be delivered by "our Friend," John S. Dexter.

George Washington, Diary. Washington Papers, MiD-B.
Dined at Governor George Clinton's with the Adamses, among others.

THURSDAY, 17 DECEMBER 1789

Pierce Butler to Governor Charles Pinckney

I was honor'd with Your letter of the 10th. of October by Mr. Pintard—
My inclination led me to write to You before this Day, but Mrs. [*Mary*] Butler's dangerous illness & my own indisposition, occasioned by the Influenza,
totaly disqualified me.

I very sincerely condole with You & Mrs. Pinckney on the sudden death of
Your little Boy[1]—I know from sad experience how unfriendly the Climate
of Carolina is to Children—It is a severe tribute for our attachment to it.

I observe what You say on the Subject of appointments—You know that
the constitution vests the nomination in the President—It is only given to
the Senate to approve or disapprove and tho' it might be our wish, as it realy
was mine, that some of the Gentlemen of So. Carolina shou'd be called to
the Head of some of the Departments, yet it was impossible, on that Ground
alone, to object to the nominations made. It did appear to me that Mr. John
Rutledge [*Sr.*]'s standing gave him a strong claim to be placed at the Head
of the Judiciary, & I mentioned my Opinion I was answered that Mr. Jay
having filled the first Offices under the old Constitution it was impossible
to place him in any secondary station. I believe, entre nous, Mr. Rutledge
has reason given him to think his present appointment is only a step to an
Embassy—either Versailles or the Hauge. With respect to the Laws—situated as You are, You can see & judge better than I possibly can how well
they are liked, & the probability of their meeting with ready obedience—I
have from the first been of opinion that the Judiciary system is not the wisest or most Judicious that could be desired—a little Time will ascertain the
point—That act, as well as some others passed last session, appear to me to
have strongly in intention the annihilation of state Jurisprudence, & finaly
all state Government—I may view them through a wrong medium.

I agree with You that New-York has more than her share of the honors
& emoluments of Office; but I believe it to be more owing to accident than
intention—I mean so far as regards the President of the United States—
That the names who fill the Departments have been din'd into his Ears by a
certain sett of Men I have no doubt, but that he studied the general good I
firmly believe—I thank You my dear Sir, for the friendly manner in which
You express Yourself on this Head—I shall always feel myself obliged by
a free communication of Your sentiments—You ask me what are to be our

European arrangements—I answer you truly, when I say, I am quite in the dark, but from the prevailing opinion of the Senate I shou'd suppose there will be few, if more than two, appointments in the Diplomatick line.

I agree entirely with You, that not only the stability of our Government, but all the advantages to be expected from it depend on the confidence the People place in it; & that confidence can only be secured by a just, impartial & liberal Conduct.

You know, I suppose, before this why the Indian Treaty broke off—because as McGuillvery told the Commissioners,[2] we did not offer as much as the Spaniards—By that is to be understood that we did not bid as high for his Influence as they do—What the result may be I know not—I have not seen the report of the commissioners, tho' I have conversed with them I am told their Report is lengthy & circumstantial—It is possible it may ultimately, I mean the difference with the Indians involve us with Spain, unless the present state of Europe deter them—We shall take up their Business I imagine on making a Senate.

I find that all the Eastern States have renewed their Claims for every Expence incurr'd in defending their individual States[3]—That they have brought forward charges for every   , nay for every hoeful of Earth they threw up in the Shape of Fortifications—Why then shou'd our State refrain from sending forward proper Charges & vouchers for the Expence of fortifying Charleston, erecting Fort Moultry, Fort Johnson,[4] the Works done at Georgetown, the two Frigates bought of the King of France & sunk in the harbour with every other Expence actually incurr'd—I am of opinion it ought in Justice to the state to be done—I wish You wou'd give it consideration—Most of the States have sent forward intelligent agents to attend in the Office of the Commissioners, that have to settle the Accts. of the General Government with the individual States, in order to see that their States have full credit—I strongly recommend this step to So. Carolina; the Sallery given to a proper person will be well bestowed—The State may rely on my giving every possible support to their Agent, & any attention requisite to the Business.

FC:lbk, Butler Papers, PHi. The closing mentions Mary Butler's being "still confined."

---

[1] Sometime after their marriage in April 1788, Charles and Mary Eleanor Laurens Pinckney (1770–94) had a child that they surely named Charles. The boy died in 1789, probably the year he was born (Marty D. Matthews, *Forgotten Founder* [University of South Carolina Press, Columbia, 2004], p. 67; *PJM* 12:34, 36).

[2] Benjamin Lincoln, Cyrus Griffin, and David Humphreys traveled to Georgia in the summer of 1789 to treat with Alexander McGillivray and the Creeks. For the report of the commissioners, see *DHFFC* 2:210–41.

[3] On 7 May 1787 Congress established a three person board of commissioners to settle Revolutionary War accounts between the United States and the individual states. The

Settlement of Accounts Act [HR-13] signed by the President on 5 August 1789 continued the board.

[4] Fort Johnson is located on James Island at the mouth of Charleston harbor. Fort Moultrie was located on Sullivan's Island, across the harbor to the north.

John Dawson to James Madison

I take the liberty of forwarding to you two resolutions which have passed both houses, on the subject of the permanent seat of the General Goverment—to the first of these there was considerable opposition from the South side of James river, under an apprehension that it woud not be advantageous to that part of the State; and from some of the Antis who considerd it as a favour to Congress—they however passed by large majorities, & my only fear is that the money will never be demanded.[1]

The amendments recommended by congress were taken up and all of them passed our house—the Senate amended the resolution by posponing the consideration of the 3rd, 8th, 11th, & 12th, untill the next session of assembly—we adhered, and so did they. A conference took place, and both houses remained obstinate, consequently the whole resolution was lost, and none of the amendments will be adopted by this assembly.

***

You, no doubt have heard of the safe arrival of your friend Mr. Jefferson and of the favourable accounts he gives of France—by the act of Congress establishing the office of Secretary of foreign affairs, I find he is authorisd to appoint an assistant, an office which I have no objection to accept of; and as I am unacquainted with Mr. Jefferson, I must, (if you who know what pretentions I have, think me a proper person) request that you will speak to him shoud you see him, or write to him on the subject—the general assembly on yesterday by a general vote elected me a member of the privey council, which, shoud I accept of it, I shall readily resign to fill the other place, where I shall have an excellent opportunity of acquiring political knowledge.

I shall wish to hear from you as early as possible on this subject, and trust you will continue your communications from New York.

ALS, Madison Papers, DLC. Written from Richmond, Virginia; place to which addressed not indicated. For the full text, see *PJM* 12:461–62. The omitted text relates to amending the state constitution.

[1] On 14 December, the Virginia General Assembly adopted two resolutions regarding the federal seat of government: the first offered at least $120,000 for public buildings if a Potomac site were chosen, and the second directed the governor to provide information to Congress about the navigability of that river; see *DHFFC* 6:1783. For the information provided by the governor, see *DHFFC* 6:1774, 1784–89.

Jeremiah Wadsworth to Alexander Hamilton

Last Night a Man returned from Ruport in the State of Vermont with information that the two Cranes were their & had Counterfeited the Bank Notes of New York. One of them had been taken & let go on his securing the party he had cheated, but the true reason for leting him go was that he was the Second in the business & a plan is laid to catch the principal but I shall delay sending after them till I see you when I will state to you all the facts I knew.[1]

The Author of the Observer has in veiw to procure the good will of the Cittizens of this State to the National Government & to have the State debts adopted.[2] He will go on if none of his projects oppose yours. Have you read him? The next week will produce an observer which proposes a Land tax & reprobates a mode of Collection. I wish you would read them & if you find nothing which you disapprove say so.

The time draws near when Congress meet—I shall be called on for a Militia Bill—you know who I expect it from. Hithertoo the Merchants of this State have been nearly Unanimous in their support of the impost—but they are greatly agitated at the prospect of being oblidged to pay the duties which arose on before the Office was opened. Their will be so many Actions brot. & such disgust given that I fear the evil will be greater good than the good.

ALS, Hamilton Papers, DLC. Written from Hartford, Connecticut; franked.

[1] The Crane brothers, Francis and Adonijah, were eventually arrested for counterfeiting final settlement certificates, but were found not guilty by the New York supreme court in January 1791 ([New Haven] *Connecticut Journal*, 9 February 1791).
[2] See Wadsworth's eighteen Observer essays, October 1789–February 1790, throughout.

OTHER DOCUMENTS

William Constable to Robert Morris. FC:lbk, Constable-Pierrepont Collection, NN.
Regarding their speculations in government certificates; if there is no plan for "a general Consolidation" of the public debt, the impost will not be adequate and "unless their debts are comprehended" the states "will not consent either to an Excise or any direct tax—in either Case the Contin[enta]l. Debt will fall."

Henry Knox to William Samuel Johnson. FC:dft, Knox Papers, Gilder Lehrman Collection, NHi. Written "Thursday Morning."
"You have several times mentioned you desire of having some business transacted at Fort Pitt [*Pittsburg*]"; recommends Lieut. Matthew Ernest for "executing any trust you may please to repose in him."

George Washington, Diary. Washington Papers, MiD-B.
King, the Laurances, Gerry, and Rev. William and Mrs. (Rebecca Blair) Linn dined at the President's. (The [Worcester] *Massachusetts Spy*, 17 December, indicated that Gerry had passed through town sometime during the previous week; the [Springfield, Massachusetts] *Hampshire Chronicle*, 23 December, indicated that Gerry passed through town the previous week.)

FRIDAY, 18 DECEMBER 1789

George Thatcher to Sarah Thatcher

I now begin my correspondence for the ensuing session of Congress; and hope to continue it from mail to mail till my return, once a week at least—and sometimes more frequent.

The afternoon I left Biddeford [*Maine*] I got to Mrs. [*Matthias*] Storers—who was very glad to see me, & enquired affectionately after you & our little body & Girl—She was almost affronted that we should pass them in our return from Boston & not call upon them; & nothing but the great haste we were in & the lateness of the day when we passed Kennebunk [*Maine*] could have served as an apology—I spent little part of that evening at Mr. Browns—and Mr. [*Jonas?*] Clarks—They were very particular in their enquiries when you were coming to see them—Mrs. Brown & Mrs. Clark will rejoice to see you there as likewise Mrs. Storer, this winter—And if you have an opportunity, but I dont see at present how you can get there, I wish you may make them a visit.

I left Mrs. Storer the next morning after breakfast, in company with Mr. [*Daniel?*] Little, who rode with me to Docr. [*Moses*] Hemingways—where we took leave of each other, & I continued my journey to York [*Maine*]—I arrived there about four oClock dined, & put up my horse at Mr. [*Edward*] Emersons—and then went to Judge [*David*] Sewalls—where I drank Tea—The Judge & I went to our friend Deacon Seywards [*Jonathan Sayward*] & spent the evening till ten oClock—I need not tell you how minutely they were in their enquiries & expressions about you and how great were their wishes to see you at York this winter—Mrs. Keiting was there—I lodged at Judge Sewalls & breakfasted with him in the morning—I called to see our good friend Mrs. Tucker & her husband [*Joseph*]—who were second to none of our friends in kindness & friendly enquiries after you & the children—as also in their wishes to see you at York this winter.

I left them about Ten & went to Mr. [*Nathaniel*] Barrells—where I dined—Mr. Barrell had left home on Monday for Boston—Mrs. [*Sally Sayward*] Barrell and the family were, as usual, ready to shew me every possible attention—I spent an hour or two, dined & set off for Portsmouth [*New Hampshire*] where I arrived and put up at Mr. [*John*] Greenliefs about three—where I now write you this—Here I found brother [*George*] Stacey, on his return from the westward—He saw our friends at Newbury [*Massachusetts*]—& will call & see you.

I shall leave this place in the Stage at one oClock—we shall put up at Newbury—consequently I shall spend the evening at our friend Searls [*George Searle's*]—and perhaps may write you again from thence.

Last night was assembly [*dance*] night—and I had several invitations to go—but being weary, & not having much of a relish for such things I tarried at my Lodgings—and read the sermon, which I send you—read it my dear—& keep it—it is a curious thing.

Thus I have giving you a History of my Journey thus far—and must now bid you farewell for the present, Mr. Stacey waits.

ALS, Thatcher Family Papers, MHi. Written from Portsmouth, New Hampshire; place to which addressed not indicated. Written in the morning.

Detector to Mr. Oswald

How long is the credulity of the community to be imposed on, by the artifices and presumptive confidence of a man [*Morris*] whose public stewardship has been so singularly marked by defalcation? Some time ago, I communicated, through your paper,[1] to the public, the daring conduct of this man, in the House of Senate of the United States, upon the occasion of a motion made by the Honorable *Richard Henry Lee*, viz. that compulsory measures be taken, to recover the sums of money ascertained to be due, by the settlement of the Board of Treasury, from the several defaulters contained in the list laid before the Senate, unless they discharged their respective balances, on or before the end of nine months.[2] I stated, that Mr. *Morris*, availing himself of his place as Senator, opposed this very moderate and accommodating motion, although, the balance found due by him, in the capacity Commercial Agent of the United States, amounted, after every consistent allowance being made him, to the enormous sum of four hundred and seventy thousand specie dollars, and more than twelve years had elapsed, since he has withheld this public treasure, not withstanding the public distresses and the burdens of taxation, which might have been considerably relieved, if this man and the other numerous public defaulters, could be made to restore the public monies; and I further stated, that such was his *command* of this Senate, that he prevailed upon a majority of them, to smother the public-spirited motion of the Honorable Richard Henry Lee. I fully expected the old game of *procrastinating* the public opinion upon this serious information, would be again practiced by Mr. Morris, and I have not been disappointed. He, or one of his tools, comes forward, two or three days after my publication, but under an assumed signature,[3] and boldly denies the truth of it, and, to prevent his ambitious schemes, in the present [*state constitutional*] Convention, being marred by this unlucky discovery, he endeavors to dissipate even the shadow of doubt of his innocence, by pledging himself to the public, that he will, in ten days, produce unanswerable documents of the falsity of my charge. Ten days and more, are suffered to glide away, whilst the public opinion is suspended; and his influence in the Convention is unimpaired, when, at last, he appears again on the scene,[4] and, instead of the promised documents, the public are to remain satisfied with his simple, unauthorized assertion, and that under a signature for which he is not responsible. Wishing to see how far this maneuvering would be carried, I silently waited the result, which being construed into a want of evidence to substantiate what Mr. Morris knew to be founded in truth, but hoped was not in my power to obtain; he, or his tool appears again,[5] but still anonymous, and taking it for granted, that the whole of my representation was a falsehood, winds away upon the boasted services of this *great and good man*, for so he is termed, who is said to be second to General *Washington*, in his merits, and artfully endeavors to excite the indignation of the community, against his patriotic opponents, against the faithful centinels of the people, whose vigilance has detected the embezzlement of the public treasures.

How insolent is it to compare this public defaulter with the great Washington, whose conduct has been so diametrically opposite to the former, and whose unexampled services have been rendered to his country gratuitously from the pure impulse of virtuous patriotism, whilst sordid gain has marked the public as well as private career of the other, and finally, a deficiency of upwards of four hundred thousand dollars, specie, found in his public accounts, and that of twelve years standing. I now challenge Mr. Robert Morris to come forward in his own name (not under anonymous signatures, for which he is not responsible) and deny that such a motion, as I have mentioned, was made by the Honorable Richard Henry Lee, and that it was crushed by his undue influence and interposition, which I presume he will not dare to do, as the evidence of the fact is so near at hand, for my information is from Members of the Senate of the United States—gentlemen, whose characters for veracity, and unblemished integrity, have never been yet impeached. Since the shameless effrontery of Mr. Morris's advocates, in denying so public a fact, I have written to these gentlemen, requesting that they would ascertain it beyond all doubt; but as several of the gentlemen are at a considerable distance, I have not received an answer yet but from one of them, who, after expressing his astonishment that an attempt should be made to deceive the public, respecting a transaction of such a public nature, promises to furnish the necessary documents, and I expect similar assistance from the other Senators. I must observe that, from mistake, I misstated the sum found due by Mr. Robert Morris, which I will correct in my next publication; it is not quite so much as four hundred and seventy thousand hard dollars, although it is considerably above *four hundred thousand dollars specie.*

I will ask with what propriety can Mr. Morris be fitting out squadron after squadron to the *East Indies,* freighted with thousands of dollars for the purchase of the costly commodities of the East, and pretend inability to discharge the balance due the public in nine months, after twelve years use of this money? Is it not insulting the people, whose trade and property is taxed for the public exigencies, to observe an individual enabled to monopolize the benefits of commerce and government at their expense, on near a half million of hard dollars of their property?

IG, 18 December, edited by Eleazer Oswald.

[1] See Newspaper Article, 30 November, above.
[2] For more information on Lee's unjournalized motion on public defaulters, see *DHFFC* 8:663–65 and Aedanus Burke to Samuel Bryan, 5 February 1790, below.
[3] See A Philadelphian to Mr. Brown, 30 November, above.
[4] See A Philadelphian to Mr. Brown, 9 December, above.
[5] See Civis to Mr. Brown, 12 December, above.

OTHER DOCUMENTS

George Read to Thomas McKean. ALS, McKean Papers, PHi. Written from New Castle, Delaware; addressed to Philadelphia; received 30 December in "[*Pennsylvania constitutional*] Convention."

Seeks McKean's advice on certain difficulties he has encountered in compiling a collection of the laws of Delaware, as "in business of this kind I am a mere Novice."

Governor Edward Telfair to Georgia Senators and Representatives. Mentioned in Minutes of the Executive Council, G-Ar.

Transmits statements of the state auditor.

Letter from Canton, China. *NYDG,* 19 May 1790 (the date on which members of Congress would have seen it); reprinted at Bennington, Vermont; New London and Litchfield, Connecticut; New York City (*NYP,* 20 May); Philadelphia and Carlisle, Pennsylvania; and Charleston, South Carolina.

Fourteen ships flying American colors are at Canton; the New York schooner has not yet arrived; the one from the northwest coast of North America reports that the Spanish fort at Nootka Sound has taken four or five English ships but "suffer ours to pass unmolested."

SATURDAY, 19 DECEMBER 1789

Ralph Izard to Gabriel Manigault

I have received your Letter of 18th. November, & am very sorry that no opportunity has happened for me to write to you about the Election. Upon maturely considering the matter, I am of opinion that under the present circumstances it will be more for the interest of the Country that I should not serve, & therefore if I should be elected, which I hope may not be the case, I must decline. Had I been returned at the general Election,[1] I could have acted discretionally; but it would now be a declaration of War. The difference between the two cases I am sure must appear very clear to you; & I am very sorry that your Letter, & Mr. E[dward]. Rutledge's did not get to my hands before [Capt. Thomas] Snell sailed. What I said to you here on the subject, should be confined entirely to Mr. E. Rutledge, & yourself. When we have a presumptuous, & malevolent Adversary to deal with, he should be furnished as little as possible with incitements to carry his mischievous projects into execution. [lined out] A certain Cat Fish is in close,* and servile correspondence with him; no doubt for the purpose of obtaining his assistance in gratifying some future scheme of ambition, & would make any communications which might recommend him to favour. We were under considerable anxiety, & uneasiness on account of the length of time which passed before we heard of your arrival. Our affliction since your departure has been great, & it was unlucky that we should have had that addition to it. I hope you visit the Elms[2] now, & then. Let me know, when you write, how things are going on there. Mr. [John] Owen informs me that only 40 Barrels of Rice will be made there. if so the Rains must have done considerable damage. How has my Crowfield Neighbour[3] succeeded? I hope he has been more fortunate.

*I wish you would take an opportunity of communicating this circumstance to Mr. E. Rutledge, that he may be on his guard. It is a subject very disagreeable to me to write upon. The question about the Debts of the States being assumed by Congress will probably be agitated soon after we meet. Unless this measure is adopted, it is my opinion that the Domestic Creditors of our State will not find their Indents of much use to them. I wish a vote in favour of it could be obtained in our Legislature, as my Colleague is against the assumption.

ALS, Izard Papers, ScU. Addressed to Charleston, South Carolina.

[1] Most likely a reference to election to the South Carolina constitutional convention.

[2] "The Elms" was the Goose Creek plantation that Izard inherited upon his father's death in 1749. By 1790 it was the center of his accumulation of rice and indigo plantations totaling 4300 acres and five hundred enslaved Blacks.

[3] "Crowfield" was the 1400 acre Goose Creek rice plantation of John (1753–84) and Frances Motte Middleton, inherited by their only son John (1784–1826) in the year of his birth.

James Lovell to John Adams

Though I know your extreme Delicacy as to any Interference in the *executive* Affairs of the U.Ss. yet to you I must apply; for, Heaven & Secretary [*William*] Jackson know I may be chagrined in an attempt to *address* the President.

I am in Dread least an Action should take Place which will renew the Vigour of the Opponents & damp the Spirit of the the Friends of Government: And, it will be out of Time to await the Motions of a *deliberate* Legislature.

The enclosed Copy of a Letter will explain my Dread.[1] If it appears well-founded and of sufficient Importance to call for a speedy Remedy, a very mild but efficacious one may be suggested. The President may see the circular Instruction of Octr. 31st.[2] and advise that it be immediately followed by another stating the Point "to appear, upon Review, to be of such a Kind as to need, perhaps, Legislative Attention"; and therefore proposing to the Collectors to stay all Proceedings thereon "till they hear again from the Treasury."

I am totally rong in my Conceptions of the Business, or else it may be expected that one single Suit commenced in each of the States would produce a Multitude of News paper Suggestions of a very unpleasant Sort both respecting the General Government and its new Law Courts.

Am I consummately *impudent* in this Application? Whatever may be your Judgement of it, you may be assured I will attribute so much of that Charge to myself as to keep my Doings herein a *profound Secret*.
***

ALS, Adams Family Manuscript Trust, MHi. Written from Boston. The omitted text relates to Lovell's relations with the French consul in Boston and refers to an enclosed issue of Boston's *Herald of Freedom*.

[1]Lovell to Benjamin Lincoln, 17 December, in which Lovell responded to Lincoln's request for a list of imports to Boston between 1 August, when the goods became subject to duty under the Impost Act, and 10 August, when Lincoln assumed his duties as collector. Lovell advises against collecting those duties, as being politically impossible and practically inequitable unless executed consistently by every collector.

[2]Hamilton's circular to all collectors, authorizing them to collect all duties "demandable" after 1 August 1789 (*PAH* 5:478).

Henry Marchant to John Adams

Yours of the 17th. of Sepr. I have been honored with. I truly esteem myself so by every Mark of Your Attention—Your unexpected Visit to Boston prevented an Answer sooner—My Concern as a Friend to my Country is awakened at the Account You give of some disagreable Symptoms attending

Your Breast upon close Attention, and in publick speaking. How We can spare You from the first I scarce can tell—But You must somewhat abate in the Severity of it—As to the latter, Reading &c., I would advise that You let one of the Clerks do all the publick Reading, even every Motion made. I know many Explanations and Observations, Opinions &c. &c. must be expected from the Chair; but You have a peculiar Faculty of speaking multum in parvo.[1]

I was very glad to find upon my Return that my Family had found out your Son:[2] He had taken up Lodgings and could not be tempted to release them. His very agreable Manners and Improvements rendered Him too entertaining to cause any Regret, but that of His too suddenly leaving the Town—We hope Mr. Adams and His, will never pass Us without Notice.

You must be right, and I stand corrected as to the Time of the Prediction &c. I heretofore alluded to—It must have been—I well remember it was at Philadelphia—The Matter, and the Effect of it, as it struck my Mind, and to all Appearances every Member present I never can forget. I have mentioned it a hundred Times, tho' not the Author, save to a very few.

You may remember when I had the Honor of seeing you at New-York last Sept. I informed You, Our Assembly had been called specially, after I left Newport. That it boded no good; and I was confident the Govr. [*John Collins*] had been induced to it, by His Friends who were alarmed at what might take Place in the New House at Octr. Sessions, And therefore were determined by some Means or other, if possible to raise some Difficulty in Thier Way: It turned out so. The special Assembly, (at which I arrived in Time to be mortified with Their Conduct)—directed Town-Meetings to be called to give their new Members Instructions—Those New members had been appointed in Consequence of the Alteration which had greatly taken Place in the Minds of the People as to the Paper Mony System: But the People still not so much relenting in Their Opposition to the New Constitution did indeed instruct Their Members agt. a Convention—Upon Consultation out of the House, we found most of the New Members would have risked giving a Vote for a Convention, if the Disposition of the People had been any way flattering, of Success in a Convention—This not being the Case, it was thought prudent, The Members should conduct agreably to Their Instructions, thereby to continue Their Credit with Their Constituents, till They might be induced to more favourable Sentiments of the New Constitution—With this Opinion the old Fœderal Members politically coincided Our Assembly again sits the second Monday of January—The Ground is considerably changed since the Instructions given last October. The Amendments have been sent forth by Congress, And North Carolina by a very large Majority have acceded to the union And for which I sincerely give You Joy.

What Effect those Circumstances may have we cannot possitively conclude. We have been often deceived in Our Hopes, and I do not wish to be
sanguine—As to interested Motives, I know of none of much Importance,
that we can advance to Our Country Members that have not been already
urged, that will operate till the next Fall upon Them—While Our merchantile Interest on the fifteenth of January will be in a most deplorable State—It
has been an unhappy Circumstance hitherto, that nothing could be done by
which the merchantile and Country Interest should be affected at the same
Time—And unless the merchantile Interest is indulged till next Fall, They
must suffer and severely too, at least nine Months before the Country Interest can be much affected—This however upon the Supposition that there
should not be a voluntary giving up of former Sentiments, or the Measures
of Congress should not prove sufficient Inducements to lead Our People to
a Spirit of Condescention.

I was at New Haven the begining of Novr. where I placed my Son under
President [*Ezra*] Stiles, in the second Year—I arrived there two Hours after
His Excellency THE PRESIDENT, had left the Town on His Return to New
York.

I hope You have refreshed Your Body and Spirits by Your Journey; and
that You found Mrs. Adams & Family well.

ALS, Adams Family Manuscript Trust, MHi. Written from Newport, Rhode Island; place
to which addressed not indicated; answered 20 March.

[1] Much in a little; concisely.
[2] Adverse weather detained John Quincy Adams in Newport from 10 to 14 September
while en route to New York City.

OTHER DOCUMENTS

Joshua Martin to John Langdon. ALS, Langdon Papers, NhPoA. Written
from St. Pierre, Martinique; addressed to New York. Martin commanded
Langdon's ship *Eliza* in 1790.
    Reports slow sales of American goods; little business being done because
all conversation is on troubles in France and liberty.

George Washington, Diary. Washington Papers, MiD-B.
    Committed his thoughts on the militia to paper to send to Knox "to be
worked into the form of a Bill with which to furnish the Committee of
Congress which had been appointed [*on 9 August*] to draught one."

[Springfield, Massachusetts] *Hampshire Chronicle*, 23 December.
    Livermore arrived in town.

NYJ, 24 December.

Samuel A. Otis arrived in town in the evening. (The [Worcester] *Massachusetts Spy*, 17 December, reported that Otis had passed through Worcester the previous week and the [Springfield, Massachusetts] *Hampshire Chronicle*, 23 December, reported that he had passed through Springfield the previous week.)

SUNDAY, 20 DECEMBER 1789

Thomas Fitzsimons to Samuel Meredith

I have delayd to answer your two last favors—that I might not be too great a tax upon Your time. it is proper however that I should inform you Mr. Clymer & I Mean to avail ourselves of your invitation and our good Hostesses Kind intention by Capt. [*Sherlock?*] Watson, who promises to sail tomorrow—You will please to receive a qr. Cask Madeira 1 Case Claret 1 bbl. bottled Porter & if Gray does not disappoint us yr. 2 Casks beer—it will be Necessary to put the Claret where the frost cannot Effect it—& to put into the Madeira half a pint of Milk—placeing it afterwards Where it will be [*illegible*] to come at & free from Pilferage for it is too good for the Servants—as I hope our Session will not be a Long one I expect there will be suff[*icien*]t. of these Articles—I find it Impossible to get the butter for Mrs. Daubeny [*Mary Dobiney*]—tho all possible Inquiry has been Made for it.

I have had no Letter from the Secy. [*of the treasury*] for these two Weeks—do you Know any thing of his plann of finance. I find publick Securitys riseing daily—And am Strongly inclined to sell part of mine at least I avoid asking him (the Secy.) any thing on this Subject. Least I might be Censured for Making an Improper Use of the Information—if Obtained from any other hand that would not be the Case.

I expect. I had allmost s[*ai*]d. hoped. that it will be Late in the Next Mo. before our Members assemble—for I assure you the thots. of leaveing home at this Season is not Very Agreeable.

Y[*ou'l*]l. please Inform Mrs. Anderson our intention of being With her.

ALS, Dreer Collection, PHi. Written from Philadelphia; postmarked 21 December.

Letter from Dublin

The people are every where panting to go to America, to enjoy that freedom and plenty which no part of Europe ground seems longer to afford them. Emissaries from America are at this hour dispersed through

England, Scotland and Ireland, to inveigle our husbandmen and mechanics; and America, like a grateful child, after shaking off all connexion with the mother country, is plundering the nation of its most useful inhabitants. If the Americans would agree to take off only our factious partizans and patriotic imposters, we should have no reason to complain, but to persuade away the quiet and useful members of the community to establish and improve their manufactures, is intolerable. In Scotland there is a general disposition to emigrate, and every one seems to have conversed with an American emissary; at the same time we are of opinion it is not so much the barren solitary tracts of America that allure the people to emigration as the calamities they endure at home from excessive rents, tythes and taxes.

NYDA, 10 March 1790 (the date on which members of Congress would have seen it); reprinted at Portsmouth, New Hampshire; Boston, Worcester, Pittsfield, and Springfield, Massachusetts; Newport, Rhode Island; New York City (*NYWM*, 13 March) and Lansingburgh, New York; and Philadelphia.

OTHER DOCUMENTS

Josiah Burr to Jeremiah Wadsworth. ALS, Wadsworth Papers, CtHi. Written from New Haven, Connecticut; addressed to Hartford, Connecticut.
  "I wonder we do not hear any thing of this Genesee meeting."

Edward Carrington to James Madison. ALS, Madison Papers, DLC. Written from Richmond, Virginia; place to which addressed not indicated. For the full text, see *PJM* 12:462–65. The letter from Virginia's Senators to the House of Delegates is printed in *DHFFC* 17:1634–35.
  Thanks for Madison's "very freindly attention" in securing Carrington's appointment as federal marshal for the Virginia district; Patrick Henry tried to procure the "acknowledgements" of the state's House of Delegates "for the great vigilance of our senators manifested in their letter" of 28 September, "but it not appearing to take well, it was never stirred again"; some of the most violent Antifederalists considered the letter "seditious and highly reprehensible"; discusses the Virginia General Assembly's actions on the Amendments to the Constitution proposed by Congress; asks Madison to continue to send newspapers.

Thomas Fitzsimons to William Constable. No copy known; acknowledged in Constable to Fitzsimons, 25 December.

Robert Morris to Samuel Meredith. ALS, Society Collection, PHi. Written from Philadelphia For background on the settlement of Morris's accounts, see *DHFFC* 8:663–65.

"The Moment I come to N. York I shall apply again for the Settlement of my Accounts & take other decided measures to clear away all the Dirt my Enemies have thrown upon my Character."

[Springfield, Massachusetts] *Hampshire Chronicle*, 23 December.
Livermore attended church and crossed the Connecticut River to West Springfield.

MONDAY, 21 DECEMBER 1789

Stephen Higginson to John Adams

I intended myself the honour of a little conversation with you, before you went to Congress, as to the trade of this State. We are suffering very much for want of a proper inspection of Our exports. that We now have, under the State Laws, is, as to most Articles, worse than none—it serves to conceal & encourage frauds of every kind in preparing Our exports for market. We surely can supplant Ireland in every open market, with Our Beef, pork and Butter; & We can vie with the British in the various kinds of pickled fish, at any foreign port, where We are admitted. in every instance, where the shipper has been personally attentive to have these Articles well put up, We have had the preference, both on account of the quality & price; but, very few of Our exporters are good Judges of those Goods themselves, & fewer still can find time for such attention. I know of no way of getting Our exports into good repute abroad, but by a strict inspection of them; & to effect this, there must be a System with a responsible man of good character & information at the head of it, in each State. let him be answerable to the Shipper who sustains any loss by having bad goods delivered him, that have passed inspection, or been branded by an inspector—let him have the power to appoint & remove persons under him, & oblige him to give large security when he enters into office.

He will then take care, that none but faithful men & such as can give him ample Security shall act under him. Every One then will feel a responsibility; & their interest will induce them all to do their duty. the fees which are now paid to no purpose by the Trade, are nearly sufficient for the purpose. Our exports are such as call for more than common care in fitting them for market; but the attempts made by the State to regulate them have done more hurt than good. the Towns appoint such, & as many as they please, without any regard to character or qualifications; & We can hire, for the fees, the brands of many officers, or obtain their certificates for Goods which they have never seen. Our Beef, pork, Butter, pot & pearl ashes, pickled fish of various kinds, flax seed & Lumber, constitute a large proportion of Our exports in value, as well as in bulk; & all these Articles require inspection.

This must be made a responsible and a respectable department or nothing can be effected. Government can not find proper men in every Seaport in this State for inspectors but a good principal residing here can; nor can the trade bear the expence and loss of time, which must attend Our having only one place of inspection. every facility shd. be given, & every expence saved to the exporter; but the regulation of exports should be such as will give safety and confidence to the Shipper, as to the quality, & tend to bring them into good repute abroad.

I can not but consider your Revenue System as very defective, without such a responsible man at the head of a large district. every petty Collector in our out ports now feels quite independent, having no One within 300 miles that can call his conduct in question; & I am sure that ten times the amount of the salary proper for such an Officer will this year be lost, for want of his influence care & inspection. But this defect I think will soon be remedied—it will be seen by so many, & the loss to the public will be so evident to all who attend to the Subject, that I am persuaded Comptrollers or Inspectors of districts will be appointed. I should think that one man of ability & activity—well acquainted with Our Commerce in all its branches might be sufficient for the N[ew]. E[ngland]. States.

We suffer very much in this State from the unequal trade We now have with the British. They take from us in Our Vessels, even in their home ports, only such articles as they can not do without; and in their Colonies They will not admit us with any thing, on any terms. Our Oil is loaded by them with an enormous duty when in their own bottoms, & prohibited in ours; & yet this is the best market We can find for the most valuable kind. We are totally deprived of the intercourse We had with their Islands, Newfoundland, Canada and Nova Scotia; They are not permitted to draw from us, even in their bottoms, the Supplies They want, except in times of uncommon scarcity, or some particular articles, which They can no where else get without great trouble & expence. But they have nearly the same advantages in Our ports, They used to enjoy. other foreigners do but little interfere with them in carrying Our exports to market; &, they as yet can vie with us, & must have a large share in that branch, the tonnage &c. notwithstanding. This inequality ought not to continue, but the difficulty is how to remove it. Should We at once adopt a resentful, restrictive System, the effect may be to increase the Evil. We may lose their markets for ashes flax seed & white Oil &c., which would injure the trade of this State very much, without gaining any thing to balance it; for we could not much profit by their being excluded Our carrying trade, as We now pursue that branch as far as We have the means, or think it for our interest. The Government of the Union has now so much the appearance of respectibility & efficiency, the British may be brought, perhaps, by wise & prudent measures to view it as meriting attention, & to have some respect for its movements and decissions. I should hope more from open & calm negotiation than retaliation. If We exclude them as Carriers, We must tempt others by high freights to carry Our produce. the no[r]thern States alone can not for a number of years carry off all the produce of America, unless the Business be made much more productive, to call our main efforts & attention that way; & this can not be done without causing a great alarm & much uneasiness in the southern States. the N. E. States, & particularly this feel chiefly the weight of the British restrictions—the others never had much intercourse with Nova Scotia N[*ewfound*]. Land or Canada; & their exports to Britain are not affected like Ours—as the carrying Business is a great Object with the British, We may gain somewhat by negotiation, as an equivalent for their enjoying it; & in this the southern States may feel & go along with us. But if We attempt in the first instance to restrain the British, Our southern friends may get alarmed, & leave us without support; & should We succeed in drawing them into Our Views, We may both be disappointed in the effect produced upon the British. I feel the necessity of having a more equal & reputable trade with the British; but I am not yet satisfied that We can either compel or conciliate them to more reciprocal terms—the latter however at present is, in my mind, more eligible and promising.

I have taken the liberty of suggesting to you in a hasty manner these loose Ideas for your consideration. if they prove of no use, nor throw any new light upon the Subject, you will excuse the manner when assured that the intention is good.

ALS, Adams Family Manuscript Trust, MHi. Written from Boston; place to which addressed not indicated.

Edward Rutledge to Henry Knox

*** I do not know how all of our Delegates will stand affected on the question [*of Catharine Greene's petition*] when it is brought on. Mr. Burke was once the General's [*Nathanael Greene*] Friend. Mr. Smith [*S.C.*] will do his Family Justice. The others I hope will follow his Example. But you must know that Sumter is violently out of temper for some thing that the General is said to have written to the late Governor [*Joseph*] Reed who has very improperly communicated it to Dr. [*William*] Gordon; who has given it a place in his history[1]—You will make the best use of this Hint.

ALS, Knox Papers, The Gilder Lehrman Collection, on Deposit at the New York Historical Society, New York. [GLC 2437.04447] Place from which written not indicated. The dating is based on close similarities to parts of Rutledge's letter to Catharine Greene, written this day, and also in the Knox Papers. The omitted text relates to the state of Greene's finances.

[1] Rutledge was referring to a May 1781 letter quoted in the *History of the Rise, Progress, and Establishment of the Independence of the United States . . .* (3 vols., New York, 1789), in which the British born historian and former Congregational minister of Massachusetts William Gordon (1728–1807) asserted that Sumter's militia had been motivated by plunder rather than the promotion of American independence (see *DHFFC* 16:1397).

[*Jeremiah Wadsworth,*] The Observer—No. X

To the American Planters and Farmers

The gentlemen who possess and cultivate the soil, are in this Country so numerous, and hold so great proportion of property, that they have right to a decided influence in the measures of government. In addressing you I speak to the people, whose will must ultimately determine the system of national police [*policy*]. An enlightened planter is a friend to manufactures, by which his raw materials are prepared for the use of man—he is a friend to commerce, which converts the surplus of his perishable produce into permanent wealth, and mingles the growth of every clime on the board of hospitality: still the agricultural now is, and for a century to come must remain, the prevailing interest in both riches and in influence. The war of independence was yours; and therefore became a war of blows too hard for the common enemy—our present form of government was first delineated by those who roll the tongue and drive the quill; it became a sacred reality by the seal of your suffrages; and the measures of the treasury department must be addressed to your good understanding and sense of national honor to render them successful. Though the nature of your employment is such as precludes the opportunity of collecting information; your judgement must sanctify, and your firmness effectuate the public decrees. The evils resulting from a loss of public credit may effect others first—on you they fall heaviest. Merchants, monied men and those who have great property afloat, are on the watch—they have leisure to collect every information—a correspondence by every post and through half the world advertises them of the evil, and their property by some change in its situation is secured; while you without information and unsuspicious are ensnared. Every possible imposition in public credit will operate thus—either the price of your produce will fall, or the articles you purchase rise, or the deceitful medium center in your hands. When the state of credit, in any country, is such as excites a war of artifice between its citizens, they must be eventual sufferers, whose employment confines them in the field, at a distance from the course of information. The first thing you ought to demand is a stable system for the public debt, which

may be done by placing the whole of every description under one responsible board; the next is a circulating medium of fixed value. To accomplish
this, I am sensible there must be some kind of direct taxation by the United
States, for it is not probable that an impost and excise will equitably fund
the whole debt. Direct taxation is now practised with a heavy hand by the
separate States; and why should the exercise of this power by the general
government be more dangerous, when attended with such circumstances
that a part of the sum you now pay will be sufficient? If a change of system
will remove half the weight you have borne these fifteen years, be not duped
to lose the opportunity, by the artful suggestions of some men, who expect
to gain more by the old game than by a new one. The members of the general
government are your representatives—your friends, and the beings of your
own creation—their existence and popularity are in your hands, and they
have every motive to guard your interests; more cannot be said of the state
legislatures. Still further to remove all suspicions that the writer is acting
an insidious part, I will compare your present situation with what it might
be made, by an interposition of general government.

Every State in the empire is heavily in debt—in each State there are different modes of imposing and collecting taxes, but in all, direct taxation
of some kind is in use—in a few States arbitrary assessment is customary,
which may be set down for the worst kind of imposition—in others every
kind of property specifically is charged at certain rates affixed in the tax
laws—in New England your houses and lands, your cattle of every description, even your sons are taxed before their labour can pay for their support,
and your mechanics are arbitrarily assessed for the labour of their hands.
The tax laws have been varied annually, so that to understand the system of
public demands is next to impossible—these changes in the tax laws, have
opened a succession of speculations destructive and unintelligible to the
unwary citizen—The general taxation of all your property imperceptibly
advances the amount to a grievance—In Connecticut there are one hundred taxgatherers, and in the other States a number proportioned to their
extent—The gentlemen qualified to do this duty, must be men of sagacity, and as such will not forget themselves, nor can we wish they should
serve the public for nothing—An average emolument to themselves of less
than two hundred dollars per annum. would not tempt them to execute the
duty—this emolument arises from a public reward, mileage, forbearance
money, with an opportunity of speculating among the ignorant; and though
it be not charged in the tax bills is eventually paid by the people—I blame
not the collectors, their business requires industry and watching, and is attended with risque, for they must lose the taxes of those who abscond after
their warrants are received; but I accuse a system so expensive to the people.

One hundred tax-gatherers at two hundred dollars each amount to twenty thousand dollars—this sum though not charged in any account whatever, is annually paid by the people of Connecticut—an enormous burthen! for the simple collection of taxes, and all this, on a plan which you have often been told is mighty cheap, and full of economy and liberty. Let us talk no more of the high salaries given by the United States, when our own plan bears so much harder on the people. The employing too many men in any public business, that it may be done at a cheap rate, always proves a spunge in the event. With the great sums you have paid, and collected in this expensive manner; with a general taxation of your whole property, you have not obtained the reputation of being just to your creditors. The evil still remains, and must remain without a general reform of system. Most of my remarks will apply to all the States, and as this publication first appears in Connecticut, I have taken it as an instance to exemplify the whole—Let not these truths excite faction—be calm—reverence government, and public justice, and you will be remedied. Compare with this picture a system I will propose—Let your state debt be assumed by the United States—In addition to the impost and excise give them a direct tax—Let this tax be imposed on the single article of improved land—Three cents per acre, which is two pence currency of New England very nearly, will be sufficient to establish the faith and justice of your country, and content the public creditors, if they are reasonable men—Let this be paid in the money of the merchant, for if there be a depreciated currency in circulation, you will eventually rue the consequences—Eight tax-gatherers will be sufficient to collect an excise and land tax in Connecticut, which now employs one hundred—Make these men responsible; give them the salary of eight hundred dollars per ann. and suffer no kind of fee to be taken from the people. This will make a saving of nearly fourteen thousand dollars in the article of collection, which is principally paid by the poorest citizens; and for which they have no credit in the public opinion. The planter, possessing one hundred acres in fair cultivation, will have to pay annually sixteen shillings New England currency, for the whole amount of his taxes, and without any additional fee to collectors; and those who have less estate in proportion. Every wise planter would compound with the public for this sum—I believe it would be sufficient; and I appeal to the honest cultivators of the earth, whither it be more than one third of the sum they have been used to pay.

My next number shall contain further remarks on a land tax.

[Hartford, Connecticut] *American Mercury*, 21 December. For information on The Observer series, its authorship, and reprintings, see the location note to The Observer, No. I, 12 October, above.

Edward Rutledge to Catharine Greene. ALS, Knox Papers, Gilder Lehrman Collection, NHi. Places to and from which written not indicated.

> Advises against negotiating a loan before petitioning Congress for settlement of her husband's Revolutionary War accounts.

Roger Parker Saunders to Pierce Butler. ALS, Butler Papers, PHi. Place from which written not indicated.

> Office seeking: appointments for a Mr. Brown and for Saunders' uncle (John Parker, Sr.).

John Tracy to Henry Knox. ALS, Knox Papers, Gilder Lehrman Collection, NHi. Written from Newburyport, Massachusetts.

> Office seeking: customs or excise; refers to Dalton and King, "to whom I write on the subject."

Oliver Wolcott, Jr. to Oliver Wolcott, Sr. ALS, Wolcott Papers, CtHi. Addressed to Litchfield, Connecticut.

> The southern members are becoming more federal, as it appears that the states north of the Potomac "are to pay a great proportion of the public Expence."

[Portsmouth] *New Hampshire Spy*, 22 December.

> Wingate left Stratham, New Hampshire, for New York.

[Springfield, Massachusetts] *Hampshire Chronicle*, 23 December.

> Livermore left West Springfield for New York.

TUESDAY, 22 DECEMBER 1789

Very fine (Johnson)

Samuel Hobart to John Langdon. ALS, Langdon Papers, NhPoA. Written from St. Pierre, Martinique; received at Norfolk, Virginia, on 18 January and forwarded by William Lindsay.

> Describes impact of French Revolution in Martinique, where liberty was the predominant passion, business was neglected, the laws were all abolished, and everyone was a law unto himself.

[Portsmouth] *New Hampshire Spy*, 22 December.

> Langdon left for New York.

Modestus to Mr. Loudon. *NYP*, 22 December, edited by Samuel Loudon. Comments on Williamson's attack on the study of classical languages and claims that Johnson never received the letter from Williamson addressed to him on 14 September and printed in *NYDA*, 29 October.

George Washington, Diary. Washington Papers, MiD-B.
Several members of Congress attended the levee.

WEDNESDAY, 23 DECEMBER 1789

Fine (Johnson)

George Thatcher to Sarah Thatcher

About an hour after I took leave of you, in my Letter at Portsmouth [*New Hampshire*], I entered the Stage in company with a Mrs. [*Joseph*] Henderson, wife to the High Sheriff of the County of Suffolk, and Mr. Hall, a Printer in this Town[1]—and drove off for Newbury Port [*Massachusetts*], where we were in great hopes of arriving by sun-set, or a little after—I had proposed, in my own mind, to call upon my friend Dr. [*Daniel*] Killham & take him with me to Mr. Searls [*George Searle*], & there spend the evening—and then return to the Stage house, that I might not get left in the morning—But the roads were so bad, that we did not get to Armsbury [*Amesbury*] ferry till after eight o Clock—And by the time we arrived down to Mrs. [*Sarah Kent*] Atkins's it was nine—I had then concluded to say how do you do? to my friend Dudly [*Atkins Tyng*], & pass on to the Tavern—but he insisted on my tarrying the night with him—He, his mother & sister Becca were seting by the fire enjoying pure tranquil comfort—I told him he wanted nothing but a wife to be as happy as I was myself when at home—He seemed to think it would add to his felicity, & said he proposed to marry in a year or two—He & I chatted till the clock warned us of its being twelve; we then went to bed & there chatted ourselves asleep—We arose little after five next morning, had a dish of Coffee & a good Toast—He then accompanied me to the Stage House where I found the company ready to set off—I wished him good by—steped into the Stage & departed for this Town where we arrived a few moments after sun set—I put up at Coll. [*Daniel*] Colmans in State Street—where I am now writing.

Company has called upon me—& I must for the present leave you—And close by assuring you I am with great affection yours.

ALS, Thatcher Family Papers, MHi. Written from Boston; place to which addressed not indicated. In a postscript written at 10 P.M., Thatcher informed Sarah that he had deposited forty dollars with a merchant on her account, to be spent as she pleased, though he hoped she would buy a bed with it, and promised to send more money by March or April.

[1] Samuel Hall (d. 1807), publisher of the *Courier de Boston* in 1789.

Newspaper Article

Members of Congress now in this city: *Senate*—PRESIDENT of the Senate—Mr. DALTON; Mr. JOHNSON; Mr. SCHUYLER; Mr. KING; Mr. IZARD; Mr. BUTLER. *Representatives*—Mr. GILMAN; Mr. GERRY; Mr. LAWRANCE; Mr. BENSON; Mr. SCOTT; Mr. COLES; Mr. BROWN; Mr. GRIFFIN; Mr. HUGER; Mr. SMITH, of South Carolina.

The public expectation begins to awaken at the approaching sessions of Congress. When we reflect on the various and difficult objects to be accomplished by our legislators, we must suppose their task is weighty and critical. The patience and candor of the people will be equal, we hope, to every reasonable allowance for any delays or errors that inevitably result from circumstances so new and embarrassed.

***

GUS, 23 December. *NYDG* and *NYJ* of this date indicate that Trumbull was also in New York City; *NYJ* also mentioned the presence of White and Otis.

Letter from Havre, France

The ship Pennsylvania, being detained here by contrary winds, will convey you this letter.

Since my last of the 5th inst. the prices of flour are lowered very much; these provisions which a month before were so scarce, are so abundant at present that they seem to arise out of the ground; therefore we thought it proper for your interest and your government to inform you of that revolution.

M. [*Jacques*] Neckar wrote us lately he had given considerable orders on flour in America, but that he, at the same time, had limited the prices of purchase so that it would not cost our government more than 30s. sterling per barrel, free of all expences, and to be delivered in France. This may serve you as a rule if you make any shipments in that article to France.

NYDG, 8 March 1790 (the date on which members of Congress would have seen it); reprinted at Middletown, Connecticut; New York City (*GUS*, 13 March); Elizabethtown, New Jersey; and Philadelphia.

OTHER DOCUMENTS

[Massachusetts] *Salem Mercury*, 22 December.
  Goodhue planned to set out for New York.

[Boston] *Massachusetts Centinel*, 26 December.
  Thatcher and Goodhue passed through Boston after the 23 December
  issue went to press; Ames had already set out for New York.

THURSDAY, 24 DECEMBER 1789

Snow (Johnson)

Pierce Butler to Mrs. Beddy. FC:lbk, Butler Papers, PHi. Sent to Charleston,
South Carolina.
  Mr. Brumfield sailed for England some time ago, so Butler cannot fulfill
  request respecting him; mentions the suffering of Mrs. Beddy's daughter,
  Mrs. Brumfield.

William Constable to Gouverneur Morris. FC:lbk, Constable-Pierrepont
Collection, NN.
  "The Budget will be opened next Month when I am advised that the state
  Debts will be liquidated."

William Davies to Governor Beverley Randolph. ALS, Executive Papers,
Vi. Place to which addressed not indicated.
  Acknowledges receipt of papers entrusted to Beckley to forward and an-
  other box of papers brought by Griffin.

Samuel Savage, Diary. MHi.
  Thatcher left Weston, Massachusetts, for New York.

[Worcester] *Massachusetts Spy*, 24 December. Washington was first presented
to the people of Salem, Massachusetts, from the home of the prominent sil-
versmith Abijah Northey (1741–1816) (Mary C. Crawford, *Among Old New
England Inns* [Boston, 1947], p. 168).
  "One modern example of eloquence, though of a different kind, plays
  upon my feelings: Which is, Mr. Northey's welcome to the President of
  the United States, in the town of Salem, 'Friend Washington, we are glad
  to see thee, and in behalf of the inhabitants bid thee a hearty welcome to
  Salem.' Could a speech couched in the expression of Junius, and spoke by
  a [*Edmund*] Burke, a [*Richard Brinsley*] Sheridan, an Hamilton or an Ames,

have conveyed such a feeling welcome to the sensibility of the illustrious
Washington, as those two plain, simple lines? I think every man of feeling
will join with me and say—'It is worthy of a record.'"

FRIDAY, 25 DECEMBER 1789

Very fine (Johnson)

Thomas Hartley to Jasper Yeates

I received your Favor of the 16th. inst. Our Friend [*Alexander*] White as
you say appears to be tollerable well grounded in his Profession of the Law
and what is (if possible) better—he is a Man of Integrity—I wish he may
have had a safe Journey—Your attentions to him must have been pleasing.

Your Information about our [*state constitutional*] Convention is interesting—and I am glad to understand that there is a proper Understanding
between the Houses of Lancaster and York.[1]

I hope by moderate Temper—a good and useful Constitution may be
formed—but I cannot subscribe to all Mr. [*James*] Willsons Plans—and I
am much surprized to find that the two you mention come from him.

The Cheif [*Wilson?*] appears to most advantage upon the Bench under
the Arms—and he is by no means a little Tyrant—He has some Merit as a
Judge—nay I might say a great deal—but as a Politi[*ci*]an I beleive he does
not excell—Judges like Parsons can't bear Contradiction.

At Chambersburg we had bad Weather and a poor Court—I got Home
with a [*lined out*] cold—but I presume I shall work it off very soon.

If we can arrange Matters with any Kind of Convenience—I believe Mrs.
Hartley & Mrs. Hall[2] would accompany me to Lancaster.

There must be River-Horses &c.—The visit you see depends upon some
Contingencies—but I expect that you will see Me (Solus) ~~and~~ or perhaps
some more of my family on Sunday the 3d. of January on my way to New
York.

ALS, Yeates Papers, PHi. Written from York, Pennsylvania; addressed to Lancaster,
Pennsylvania.

---

[1] England's great dynastic conflict between the Yorkists and the Lancastrians in the fifteenth century was the inspiration for Hartley's reference to York and Lancaster, Pennsylvania.

[2] Hartley's wife Catherine and their daughter Eleanor, who married James Hall in 1787.
For Hall, see *DHFFC* 17:1805.

Letter from Kentucky

I arrived at my friend's T. B. in this country, with my family, about the middle of last month, having met with no considerable accident in our way, except the breaking down of one of the axle-trees of our waggon in crossing a ridge of mountains in about the 38th degree of north latitude, which we were obliged to repair as well as we could, being at a very considerable distance either from blacksmiths or wheelwrights. The country does not deceive my expectations, and you would be astonished to see so recent a settlement in so flourishing a condition. We have nothing yet like winter, vegetation being in the highest perfection, and the wheat fields promising an abundant crop for the ensuing year. The climate I am informed is not subject to severe frosts, but odd as it may seem, becomes colder as you travel eastward towards the mountains. The form of a regular republic is already assumed, we have our parson and our printer, our academy and our court of justice, which latter I am told has had little or nothing to do; as we are in that happy situation where want and necessity do not yet exist to give birth to villainy. Several gentlemen have lately arrived here from the two Carolinas with horses for sale, whom, from several circumstances I conclude to be horse-thieves, although under pretence of seeing and settling in the country.

NYDA, 19 February 1790 (the date on which members of Congress would have seen it); reprinted at Portsmouth, New Hampshire; Boston; New York City (*NYP,* 13 March); and Philadelphia.

OTHER DOCUMENTS

William Constable to Thomas Fitzsimons. FC:lbk, Constable-Pierrepont Collection, NN.
"Your ideas respectg. Indents I believe are perfectly right were I in Cash I shoud act upon that Opinion tho I have no information of the plan proposed but from Conversations which I have had with diff[*eren*]t. Gent[*leme*]n. I have no doubt that they will be funded with the principal"; recommends he exchange his final settlement certificates for indents.

William Grayson to Horatio Gates. ALS, Theodorus Bailey Myers Collection, NN. Written from "Greenwood," Loudoun County, Virginia; addressed to Berkeley (County), West Virginia.
Purchased a half pipe of London's best Madeira wine while in New York, but a change in family circumstances and his intention to leave "Greenwood" immediately induce him to offer it for sale to Gates; he had some in New York and believes it to be the best in their part of the country.

[Worcester] *Massachusetts Spy*, 31 December.
Ames, Langdon, Partridge, Thatcher, and Wingate passed through Worcester.

SATURDAY, 26 DECEMBER 1789

William Samuel Johnson to Robert C. Johnson. ALS, Johnson Papers, NNC. Place to which addressed not indicated.
Advises about a land sale that Robert is handling for his father; "I need not remind you to collect all the Money you can, tho' in truth I do not see how I can live along through the Winter without a considerable sum from thence, as my next Quarter's salary is already almost wholly anticipated"; asks that he write often; "Public securities I am told are falling, without any reason as far as I can Judge so capricious is the public Opinion upon this subject!"; all are well, except Mrs. Anne Beach Johnson, who has "rather a bad Cold."

George Washington, Diary. Washington Papers, MiD-B.
Coles, Gilman, Otis, and Beckley dined at the President's.

GUS, 26 December.
White, Otis, and Beckley in New York for Congress.

PP, 26 December. Wister Butler Papers, PHi. Annotated by Butler to indicate the article for which he retained the issue.
Pennsylvania's proposed constitution (of 1790).

FJ, 29 December.
Frederick A. Muhlenberg was elected president of the German Society of Pennsylvania.

[Springfield, Massachusetts] *Hampshire Chronicle*, 30 December.
Goodhue, Langdon, Thatcher, and Wingate passed through Springfield; Ames arrived.

SUNDAY, 27 DECEMBER 1789

Rain (Johnson)

Pierce Butler to James Jarvis

I was favoured with Your letter of the 25th Inst. A Vessel preparing to Depart for Charleston [*South Carolina*] by which I was under a Necessity of writing several Letters obliged me to defer answering to yours sooner.

You request my opinion on two Points. If that opinion can afford You any light or aid in maturing the Object You so laudably profess to have in View the prosperity of the United States I shall have additional Satisfaction in Complying with Your request.[1]

First You wish to know if the State of So. Carolina woud Guarantee Loans made to Individual Citizens of that State for the purpose of repairing the injuries they Sustained from that Country being long the Theatre of War. I believe if the measure and the many benefits that woud result therefrom were well and Clearly Stated to the Legislature they might be induced to come into it. Tho' there are many Enlightened Men in that State yet few of them have turned their Attention to political Œconomy, or rather to that branch of it—which I can not well Account for knowing that in no part of America does the Amor Patriæ[2] more strongly predominate.

I must therefore believe that they only want to have the many Advantages that woud result from the measure Candidly stated to induce their ready Assent.

Secondly You request to know the Amt. of Our State Debt. As well as my memory serves me the publick Debt of So. Carolina Amts. to from Eight to Nine hundred thousand p[*oun*]ds. after deducting the sett offs.[3] I do not state this to a Certainty but when I go to the Senate Room where my Papers are I can let You know Exactly but I am near the fact I am sure.

You Ask if the Debt has been funded. it has not. Can they be Induced to fund it? I am certain from my long and intimate knowledge of that State that they want no stimulous to induce them to do what is Just and right. I therefore firmly believe that whenever the holders of the publick Debt come forward with any just and Equitable proposal for funding their Claims the Legislature will make no difficulty in agreeing to it. You ask me at what Rate can they be induced to fund their State Debt. I cannot take upon me to say at what Rate of Interest the legislature will fund, but I am persuaded they will do it on liberal principles probably they will be guided by the Example the General Government may set in funding the Fœderal Debt. I think it is more than probable they will; but this is only opinion, not knowing what principles the Fœderal Government may Adopt. But I am Convinced that So. Carolina will be exceeded by none in doing Justice. You request to know in what manner the State can provide for the payment of Interest. Though many of the Individuals of that Country have suffered much by the war and tho' they are now labouring under the inconveniences resulting from the want of a sufficient circulating Medium to facilitate transfer and so represent the real property of the Country. Yet the State is rich in Resource. So. Carolina will this Year in point of Value of Exports be the Second in the Union and will approach nearly to the first. Such a Country can not want Resource. A Tax of half a dollar a head upon the Negroes and a very light Tax on Lands would raise a Sum of £50,000 Yearly which I am persuaded they woud readily agree to appropriate to the payment of the Interest & principal of their Debt. I have confined myself to as concise a mode as I well coud adopt to answer your Querries. If I have been too concise so as to be obscure, You will not attribute to Intention.

FC:lbk, Butler Papers, PHi. Written to and from New York.

[1] Butler's responses may have influenced the ambitious public funding plan Jarvis proposed to Hamilton on 10 February 1790 (*PAH* 6:253–61).
[2] Love of country; in this case, South Carolina.
[3] The amount owed to South Carolina.

George Thatcher to Sarah Thatcher

You would think it strange were I to let pass a sunday in my absence & not write you—And well you might for it has become as habitual to me to write Letters on sunday as it is for other people to dress themselves up & go to meeting—But let me tell you that I have been to meeting this morning & heard Parson [*Nathan*] Strong preach what most people call a very good sermon—and tho' I was not much entertained, or instructed, I must say he did pretty well and said some good things—Indeed I think he is about one haft right! I am now at Mr. Wadsworths where I dined—Mr. Wingate, Langdon & Goodhue dined here, and are now at meeting—I told Mr. Wadsworth that if he would let me have pen, ink & paper to write to you I would stay at home.

To begin where I left off when I wrote you at Boston I must go back to the time of my arrival there, which was a week last night—If I mistake not I told you in my last, that on my arriving to Boston I put up at Coll. [*Daniel*] Colmans in King-Street—I made that my Head quarters while in Town—On sunday I attended Church in the forenoon at Mr. [*James*] Freemans, and dined with him—In the afternoon, for the sake of novelty I went to the old South [*Church*] and heard Mr. Eckla [*Joseph Eckley*]—And then drank Tea with my old friend Dr. [*Aaron*] Dexter—On Monday I dined with him & spent the evening at Mr. [*Henry*] Bass's—they were very happy in seeing me; & requested most affectionately that I would make that my home as long as I tarried in Town—But as I had many things to do in the centre of the Town it would be exceedingly inconvenient; & so excused myself on that account—On Tuesday I dined at Mr. [*John?*] Elliots—Mrs. [*Ann Treadwell*] Elliot enquired after you—The next day, wednesday I dined at Mrs. Barrells—our friend Mr. [*Nathaniel?*] Barrell was there.

I was very often at Mr. [*Thomas*] Dakins and drank Tea there two or three times.

I left in his hands forty dollars for Silas [*Lee*] to take & get a Bed with—unless you shall want it for something else—but as I shall be able to send you money by march—I think it will be prudent for Mr. Lee to get a Bed &c. with the money at Mr. Dakins.

I had not time to go to Weston [*Massachusetts*]; but heard Father & Mother [*Samuel Phillips and Sarah Tyler Savage*] were as usual—On Thursday as I went thro Weston—I called at Brother Amos'[1]—but did not stop a moment—I left your Letters—And Lucy, said Amos had got us some pork & sent it to Boston the day before—she did not know how much—nor the price of it, but only that it come to more money than I left with them last fall—I accordingly put my hand in my pocket & finding four dollars, took it out & gave it to her—and desired her to tell Amos to send the account to me, or you as soon as they could & whatever more should be due, would be discharged.

I forgot to tell you in my last that Cap. [*Elisha*] Thatcher will send down an Hogshead of Molasses—or as much as he can get with what money I could leave him—it is very dear—& it will stand me in two shillings cash a gallon at the least before it gets to our house—therefore you will sell it for three Mr. Paine Bickford is to have about Twenty Gallons—his brother about ten—provided seventy or eighty Gallons should be sent—if not so much you must deal it out accordingly—Mr. Storer, the Blacksmith will want some—I suppose I owe him—Mr. James Staple will want some—And if it holds out Mr. Andrew Staple is to have a few Gallons.

Meeting is done—& the Gentlemen are returning, & I must bid you adieu for the present—But I must just observe—that we have had an agreeable Journey thus far—We shall set off from this place in the morning & if nothing happens, arrive at New-york on wednesday.

Kiss the Children & tell the dear creatures how much their papa loves them—I shall write more about them hereafter.

ALS, Thatcher Family Papers, MHi. Written from Hartford, Connecticut; place to which addressed not indicated.

---

[1] Amos Bigelow (1760–94) of Weston, Massachusetts, married Sarah Thatcher's younger sister Lucy (1761–1834) in 1783.

OTHER DOCUMENTS

Abigail Adams Smith to John Quincy Adams. ALS, Adams Family Manuscript Trust, MHi. Written from "Richmond Hill," outside New York City; place to which addressed not indicated.

Both the President and Dalton have informed the family about John Quincy's safe return to Newburyport [*Massachusetts*] from New York;

brother Charles begins to like New York and brother Thomas has been there with them for some time; members of Congress are assembling daily; "it is reported" that Catherine Thompson, Gerry's sister-in-law, will soon marry Coles, a widower with two children.

MONDAY, 28 DECEMBER 1789

Rain (Johnson)

Jabez Bowen to John Adams

I Congratulate you on the accession of No. Carolina to the general Government. our Antis are Thunderstruck at the News more especially as The Majority was so large. I have waited several Days to find out what they intend to do wheather to agree to Call a Convention or stand out longer in hopes that something would Turn up to perplex the New Government. They are not well agreed among themselves. But the Heads of the party lately proposed (at one of Their Night Meetings) That the Duties on all Goods Imported should be put verry low (say one pr. Cent.) and That our Ports should be opened to all the World (or in other words that Rd. Island should be the St. Estatia of the North).[1] The consequences of such a proceedure can be better seen [*lined out*] to by you Sir than by me. and I have no Idea that Congress will suffer such a set of people to remain *impure* in the verry middle of their Teritorys.

Our Genl. Assembly meets on the second Monday of January when we shall muster all our Forces to procure a Vote for a State Convention: if we faile 'tis proposed by the most Respectable Inhabitants of the Towns of Newport Providence Bristol &c. to separate from the State Government provided Congress will protect us, and we wish to know thro some safe medium wheather This Idea meets the approbation of Congress or wheather some diffrent mode will be adopted to oblige us to submit, when 49 parts out of 50, is for the Adoption, and one half of the 50th part are of the same mind I hope and Intreat that Congress will not think of Restricting our Trade, as that will but Distress the Federal Towns, and will be well pleasing to our *Antis*. in a word we shall be happy to fall in with any measures that will be adopted, by Congress for the Compleating the Union. if Congress would Answer The Letter Received from this State before your Adjournment and State in short the [?] necessity that there was of Their Committing the Consideration of the Federal Governmt. to the People in the way prescribed by The Grand Convention and by the old Congress and perhaps hint that it was necessary that something should be done before the First of April it might bring some of them to consider of the necessity of Acting soon on the Business.

I fully intended to have seen you when at Boston but was prevented by Indisposition.

P. S. in a Letter to the president I lately asked the Question about our seperation. it may not be amis to let him know that I have wrote to you on the same subject &c.

ALS, Adams Family Manuscript Trust, MHi. Written from Providence, Rhode Island; place to which addressed not indicated.

[1] St. Eustatius, a Dutch holding among the Caribbean's Leeward Islands, was a center of the West Indies trade in the eighteenth century. During the Revolutionary War its name became a byword for smuggling and trading in contraband.

[*Jeremiah Wadsworth,*] The Observer—No. XI

Further remarks on a land tax

The writer of this paper, tho' unknown even to suspicion, and distant from fame, wishes to be thought an honest man. Such subjects as he is considering, are not to excite suspicion that some evil is designed; these suspicions may be fomented by the litigious, but with the body of mankind, their origin is from a generous love of freedom, and a determination to vindicate their honest acquirements.

After so many delusions, and ill concerted policies, the Americans would be stupid indeed, did they not watch every proposition of measures as it rises. Next to personal liberty, the preservation of property is the most sacred object which can be affected by government, and taxation is the great instrument by which government acts on the properties of the people. The proposal of a land tax is a weighty subject, and a firm conviction that it is the most direct way of emancipating you from a system, which you can never reduce to calculation, is the reason of my doing it. A citizen is unsafely situated, when the demands made on him by government, cannot be reduced to previous estimation—but can you do this under your several State systems? You cannot determine from year to year the manner, nor the proportion, nor the articles in which you are to be taxed—You choose assembly men once or twice a year, and from long habit, they consider it as justifiable to make sudden alterations—they impose new sums, of which you have not intelligence but by the warrant of a tax gatherer—thus circumstanced, no previous estimate of what you must pay can be made—this I consider as an evil, not of the gentlemen who serve you, but of the system you are pursuing—Warrants go out from the State Treasurer against certain districts for certain sums; subordinate officers make the tax bills against individuals; the law gives them a rule; but not one in ten of the people can tell whether this rule be honestly followed: if the multitude of your tax gatherers are not strictly honest, there will be some over charges, and if discovered, it is easy to call them mistakes. It wounds the feelings of a good subject to wrangle, either with his law givers or collectors, and the thing passes. A simple charge on all lands, can be previously estimated—the planter knows the number of his improved acres, this once ascertained answers forever, he foresees and provides for the exact demand, and there is no possibility of fraud.

I already hear it objected; *the proposal is partial, for improved lands are of unequal value, and some one acre may be worth half a dozen others.*

The same objection lies with greater force against your present system— The tax you now pay on lands suppose them of equal value, only discriminating the kind of cultivation. Your polls are equally assessed; one of these may be sagacious, healthy and rich, and very profitable to the man who carries it; while another is void of all discernment, sickly, poor and an expensive bill to the owner—your cattle are equally taxed; when it is known some one beast, either for sale or improvement, may be worth ten others in the flock—and this is the case with every article in your taxable estate as it now stands.

No kind of property has a greater equality than the soil of the earth, the acres naturally more productive are few, and superior cultivation is the chief thing which gives them an advantage. Taxing high cultivation, in most instances, is but taxing the industry which one man has greater than another; and in this view of the subject, comes near to injustice.

Improvements in the art of husbandry, have made different kinds of soil much nearer in value and profit, than they were half a century past—vast extents of earth, lately supposed of no value, by cropping them suitably are made productive, and daily improvements in husbandry, increases their equality: but if after all, there be any soil so poor it will not pay a small tax, it ought to be dismissed from cultivation and planted with trees, to prevent the scarcity of timber and wood, which will soon become an intolerable evil to the poor, in the ancient parts of this country.

To do fractional justice in a matter of this nature is impossible. That system is the best, which comes nearest to perfect justice, is most intelligible to the people, and may be executed with smallest expence. Suppose the comparative value of your lands were to be appraised; to do justice the appraisment must be frequently repeated, and the expence will more than balance the gain. I dread a system loaded with a prodigious number of subordinate officers; if you pay them a small sum, their number will make an immense amount; if you do not pay them, they will by some artifice pay themselves from the hard earnings of the people; and when public measures pass through an infinitude of managers, you cannot make them responsible, and the citizens under the appearance of protection are pillaged at discretion. Remember the late war! It was the humour of the people to multiply managers—you had prolific officers thro' subordinate grades, innumberable as the leaves of summer, down to captains of a dozen oxen, flourishing with the national cockle in their hats—with all this apparatus, your armies suffered every distress thro' want of the provisions then rotting in store. An absolute monarch is politic in increasing the number of inferior officers for the additional expence creates an influence by which he governs the people; but a republic needs not this policy. A republican government must be grounded on œconomy, on the options and confidence of the people, on general knowledge and happiness; and it ought therefore to avoid a scheme of measures, that is either intricate or expensive.

Another objection to the tax laws, as proposed, will be this—*that the inhabitants in the great towns escape the payment of a sum proportioned to their ability.*

The objection appears with weight, let it be candidly considered. The men of honesty and honor, will not wish to avoid his part of the burthen, whether town or country be his residence. Were a tax on lands, the only means of national revenue, the proposal might work injustice; but by the joint operation of a national impost, excise and land tax, the objection will be obviated. Suppose two persons of equal interest, one a citizen in some great town; the other a planter in the country—the nature of a city life will lead to greater consumption of such articles as are charged with impost and excise, so that the city inhabitant pays double or treble paid by the other.

The inhabitants of a great town must purchase all their food and clothing; and it is not love of luxury, but necessity obliges them to do this; by which means they consume a fourfold share of taxable articles, and duties on commerce must always have this effect, for every man pays in the proportion that he consumes the dutied articles.

The wealth of great towns is generally over rated—they present you with a few instances of great riches, and a thousand of extreme indigence and wretchedness. Were the property of large cities to be equalized among their inhabitants, a share would not be more than an average with the country inhabitants. The parade of business, the show of mercantile property much of which is owned in the back country, and collected for sale, the luxury and idleness of a few, with the general hilarity among a concourse of people, are circumstances when he beholds them, which lead the unacquainted planter to suppose, that the people in great cities might pay a proportion, much greater than they can, without intolerable wretchedness. On this stating of facts, let a land tax be brought into joint operation with a national impost, and excise, I think the objection is obviated.

[Hartford, Connecticut] *American Mercury*, 28 December. For information on The Observer series, its authorship, and reprintings, see the location note to The Observer, No. I, 12 October, above.

OTHER DOCUMENTS

Thomas Fitzsimons to William Constable. No copy known; mentioned in Constable to Fitzsimons, 1 January 1790.

Thomas Harwood to George Washington. Written from Annapolis, Maryland. ALS, Washington Papers, DLC. For the full text, see *PGW* 4:455.
    Office seeking: continuance as loan officer for Maryland, or for any other post, and an office for his brother Benjamin; mentions Morris and the Maryland delegation as references.

Robert Morris to William Constable. No copy known; mentioned in Constable to Fitzsimons, 1 January 1790.

From New York. [Boston] *Massachusetts Centinel*, 6 January 1790.
    Livermore, Sherman, and Tucker have arrived.

TUESDAY, 29 DECEMBER 1789

Snow (Johnson)

Pierce Butler to Rud Portner

*** I shall remain here some years attending the Senate of the United States *** It will give me pleasure to keep up a correspondence with a person who I so highly esteem *** We have nothing new here—Every thing wears the face of peace and satisfaction Our new form of Government is generally approved and cheerfully obeyed—Trade begins agains to flourish; and confidence between man and man to be restored. We shall in the approaching session I believe f[*und*] our publick Debt: Your Country Men have already made much money in buying up our publick securities and much more is still to be made—Messrs. [*Nicholas and Jacob*] Van Staphorsts and some others have cleared a large sum. If You should incline to turn Your mind to them I will render You any service in my Power, for indeed I should be happy in being instrumental in promoting Your welfare.

FC:lbk, Butler Papers, PHi.

Charles Carroll to John Adams

Our Legislature did not rise till late in the night on the 26th inst. I have been obliged to attend the whole Session; constant attendance & application have injured my health; it is now so precarious, & delicate that I am fearful of undertaking a journey to New York, at this inclement Season of the year. If my attendance, for want of a sufficient number of members to compose a Senate, cannot be dispensed with, I shall be under the necessity of resigning my Seat. The executive of this State is authorised to appoint my successor, during the recess of the Assembly, in case of my resignation. I wish to execute, to the best of my power, the trust, with which I have been honored by my country, but I am confident, my fellow citizens would not require me to hazard my life, or health in the execution of it.

I hope to be able to set out for New York in the beginning, or at furthest, by the middle of March. If I can not have leave of absence so long, be pleased Sir, to impart to me the determination of the Senate on this point, that my successor may be appointed without loss of time, who may immediately, or very soon after his appointment repair to New York, to take his seat in the Senate I beg you to present my respectful compliments to the members of the body over whom you preside.

ALS, The Gilder Lehrman Collection, on Deposit at the New York Historical Society, New York. [GLC 8171] Written from Annapolis, Maryland; postmarked 2 January.

Jonathan Grout to Isaiah Thomas

I am at this place on my way to New York.

I intended to have called on you at Worcester but want of Time prevented.

I wish to have you Send (as before) your paper [*Massachusetts Spy*] to me together with any other novelties or any Substantial information of men and things as which you may think beneficial to me or Servisiable to Manking in Geneneral—for which if you will once more take my word I will call and make returns.

ALS, Thomas Papers, MWA. Written from Brookfield, Massachusetts; addressed to Worcester, Massachusetts; franked.

Ralph Izard to Edward Rutledge

I have already written to you by this opportunity. Capt. [*John*] Motley's being detained by contrary winds and bad weather gives me an opportunity of again urging you to procure and send me as soon as possible the sentiments of the members of the Legislature upon the subject of the adoption of our state debt by Congress. If a vote in favor of the measure could be obtained, it would put it in my power to speak with greater confidence than by being possessed simply of the opinions of individuals. I am fully persuaded that it would be of infinite advantage to our State if the measure should be adopted. I have written to Mr. John Hunter, the Member from Little River District on the subject. he is a man of whom I think well; perhaps it may be useful for you to confer with him. When I consider the great loss of time which for several years we have experienced in debating about indents, and many other circumstances which must occur to you, I do not think it possible that you should differ with me on this subject. I am extremely sorry however to find that my Colleague [*Butler*] continues to do so, and I am told that some of our members in the House of Representatives are in sentiment with him. Congress will meet in a few days; but I think the business I have mentioned to you will not be decided until I receive an answer to this letter. Henry [*Rutledge*] is well, is now with me; has this morning received your letter by Capt. Elliot, and says that he intends writing to you by him next week. This will probably find you at Columbia [*South Carolina*]. I hope most sincerely that I may not be mistaken in thinking it will not be for the happiness of the people at large that the Legislature should continue to sit there.

AHR 14(1908–9):777–78. Place to which addressed not indicated.

Other Documents

John Bacon to Elbridge Gerry. ALS, Gerry Papers, MHi. Postscript to letter begun in Stockbridge, Massachusetts, on 17 August and continued 18 November; answered 24 January 1790.
　　Sends condolences on the death of Gerry's son, Thomas.

[Worcester] *Massachusetts Spy*, 31 December.
　　Grout set out for New York.

Wednesday, 30 December 1789

Warm (Johnson)

Benjamin Lincoln to Theodore Sedgwick

I have given your note My dear sir to our mutual friend Docr. [*Andrew*] Craigie I wish you would send me a draught for a like sum on the treasury of the United States It will oblige me by having it done now as we are closing our Accounts for this year.

Let me ask your attention to the debts of the several States in the Union, now or never, in my opinion, if peace and good temper are to be preserved— The excess must go & that immediately & if you do not carry off the the particular debts of the several States the D—l [*Devil*] will be to pay and when he is once roused it will be hard to lay him & all his connexions—they are many and are employed all day besides they work untill late in the evening while many of our good friends are asleep.

ALS, Sedgwick Papers, MHi. Written from Boston; place to which addressed not indicated.

Impartial to Mr. Oswald

I fully expected Mr. *Robert Morris* would have come forward in a manly, ingenuous manner, and accepted the challenge of a DETECTOR,[1] by invalidating the very serious and interesting charge he made against him, especially as, if false, it would have given him so complete a triumph over his accusers, and exculpated him from the suspicion of so immense a defalcation for more than twelve years, which, if he was innocent of it, the high and commanding situation he possesses in the General Congress, would have enabled him, in that case, to do it to full satisfaction from the public documents. But I have been disappointed—no such refutation has appeared. On the contrary, the press is completely muzzled as to Mr. Morris's public accounts, by his ingenuity in commencing a suit against the *Printer* [*Eleazer Oswald*]; for, agreeably to the new doctrine of constructive contempts, introduced and established by *three* of our judges, not any information, further discoveries, or facts, can be published respecting any matter, that a suit is once brought on; so that the veil of secrecy is drawn over Mr. Morris's conduct, as Commercial Agent of the United States, until the issue of the pending suit, although the public is so deeply interested to know what has become of the very large sums of their money intrusted to him above twelve years ago, and which he has so repeatedly promised to account for. I would wish to recall the attention of the public to the various pretexts and promises that Mr. Morris has at different times made to pacify the just clamor of the community, who could not but be anxious to know what had become of so large a portion of the public property. The author of *Common Sense*, before his apostasy from public virtue, stood forth a champion in favor of the community against this COLLOSSUS; and so early as January 5, 1779, (*see Dunlap's paper of that date*) states Mr. Morris's defalcation;[2] and observes, that Mr. Robert Morris had obtained leave of Congress, of which he was then a Member, to retire for six months, on the express pretense of settling his accounts, as Agent to the Secret Committee. In *Dunlap*'s paper of the 9th January, 1779, is Mr. Morris's answer, in which he excuses himself very handsomely, for not completing the accounts, by informing the public, "that the accounts were journalized and posted by his clerks, until the ledger was filled, and no room to open any more accounts in it." "I sent to *Lancaster*," he adds, "to procure paper of the same size, to be sewed into that book that I might go on, but none suitable could be got, and I was obliged to stop." Thus the matter then ended, and the public were so good natured as to be satisfied with his apology. Mr. *Common Sense* adds, "Perhaps it may be said, why do not the Congress do those things?" To which I might by another question, reply, "Why don't you support them when they attempt it? It is not quite so easy a matter to accomplish that point in Congress, as perhaps many conceive. Men will always find friends and connections among the body that appoints them, which will render all such inquiries difficult."

These accounts, one would naturally have supposed, ought to have been closed and rendered as soon as the obstacle of the paper was removed by the termination of the late war; but no such thing happened, and the subject was suffered to fall into oblivion until January or February, 1788, more than eleven years after the receipt of above two million of dollars, nearly equal to specie, when the public attention was again called to the subject: Upon which Mr. Morris again comes forward, and, in a supercilious manner, affects to treat his accusers with contempt. However, he condescends to promise the public he would speedily settle these accounts, about which he was then industriously engaged. The public again seemed to be satisfied. However, the CENTINEL, finding Mr. Morris still very tardy in his movements, and being supported by an investigation of a committee of the old Congress, which ascertained the enormous sum entrusted to the secret committee, whose agent Mr. Morris was, he, at the end of nine months from the last call on Mr. Morris, brings the subject again before the public in his 23rd number, published November 20th, 1788 [*in IG*]; whereupon Mr. Morris again vapors with his usual arrogance, affecting to look down with ineffable contempt upon the public champions, and assures the public, that he will shortly go to New-York, where he will exert every means in his power to settle these accounts before the meeting of the new Congress, of which he was a Member, and which circumstance it was alleged he would avail himself of to prevent the settlement of his accounts.[3] Finally, it having been represented by "Detector," that a year after this further promise and assurance, Mr. Morris's accounts having been laid before the Senate by the Board of Treasury, who had settled them, and found a balance of above four hundred thousand specie dollars due by Mr. Morris to the public and that a motion having been made by the Honorable *Richard Henry Lee*, to compel payment, unless discharged on or before the end of nine months and that this very moderate proposition was over-ruled by Mr. Morris's interposition and undue influence in that body—I say, "Detector," having represented these facts, and called on Mr. Morris to invalidate the truth of them, Mr. Morris, instead of giving the public the least satisfaction, cloaks over the whole *by bringing a suit against the Printer.*

IG, 30 December, edited by Eleazer Oswald; reprinted at Newport, Rhode Island.

---

[1] See Detector to Mr. Oswald, 18 December, above.

[2] While initially taking aim at Silas Deane for his performance as American agent in France, Thomas Paine (1737–1809) also attacked Deane's protector, Robert Morris, in a series of five essays under his best known pseudonym, Common Sense, published in John Dunlap's *PP*, 31 December 1778, and 2, 5, 7, and 9 January 1779. Paine's "apostasy" refers to the fact that on 10 February 1782 Superintendent of Finance Morris, Secretary for Foreign Affairs Robert R. Livingston, and Commander in Chief of the Continental Army George Washington signed a secret agreement to employ Paine with "secret Services" funds to write propaganda in support of Morris's fiscal proposals, most prominently taxation. Morris had first raised the possibility of the relationship with Paine on 18 September 1781 (*PRM* 4:201–2).

[3] See Centinel XXIII, dated 17 November 1788 and published in *IG*, 20 November 1788. Morris's reply to the printer is in *IG*, 22 November 1788. For their texts, see *DHFFE* 1:350–53, 354.

OTHER DOCUMENTS

Thomas B. Wait to George Thatcher. ALS, Thomas G. Thornton Papers, MeHi. Written from Portland, Maine. For the full text, see *DHFFC* 8:414–16.

Relates background to petition of merchants and other inhabitants of Portland regarding the Coasting Act [HR-16]; it was voted to forward the petition to Ames as "you paid no attention to the traders of Portland"; will write "more particularly" with the next post; asks Thatcher to "write me a plan of Study" for a young man Wait has just taken into his office.

Noah Webster, Diary. NN.
Ames passed through Hartford, Connecticut.

GUS, 30 December.
Partridge and Tucker in New York for Congress.

GUS, 30 December.
"The labors of the *Observer* [*Wadsworth*], a writer, whose performances first appear in a Hartford paper, are entitled to the thanks of his countrymen, for unfolding many systems of State policy, which now appear to be a grievous burthen on the people. The speculations of this writer ought to

be read by every citizen; for it is demonstrated by him, that a simplifica-
tion of our numberless State regulations will save millions to the people."

[Springfield, Massachusetts] *Hampshire Chronicle*, 6 January 1790.
   Grout and Strong passed through Springfield; Ames left Springfield, the
home of his fiancé, during the previous week.

THURSDAY, 31 DECEMBER 1789

Rain (Johnson)

William Constable to Thomas Fitzsimons

Your Ideas are all right as far as my intelligence goes—You may Act accordingly—as to So. Carolina one of our principal Brokers has sent 100,000
Dollars in specie there already to buy & Numberless others are pushing at
the same thing—Certificates I take for granted will rise after the Report of
the Secretary of the Treasury & fall again after some time—my opinion is
to buy on time & sell out about the beginning of February.
   I can only drop you this hasty line as the late arrival of Post hardly affords
me time to read yours.

FC:lbk, Constable-Pierrepont Collection, NN.

A Farmer to Dr. B[*enjami*]n R[*u*]sh and Dr. H[*ug*]h W[*illia*]m[*so*]n

THIS address comes to you from one who considers you as very great
Benefactors to the United States of America. I consider you in this light, for
every part of your conduct in public life; but, in a particular manner, for your
late bold, and, I hope, successful attempt to destroy old rooted prejudices,
and to banish the study of foreign languages in general, but above all, the
Greek and Latin, from our places of education. I am myself an example and
proof of some of your remarks. I know the languages to be difficult; and can
remember the time when I was well whipt for forgetting, or misapplying,
the rules of Grammar; for this reason I have had a most cordial hatred at
every thing of the kind since.
   You must know that I was born in Scotland, where they have an unaccountable attachment to learning of all kinds, but especially the Greek
and Latin languages. There I was obliged to go through both school and
college, with very little advantage I assure you: But about my eighteenth

year, I escaped to America, leaving all learning behind me; and now, God be praised, have become a free and independent Farmer, and apply myself wholly to what you have shown ought to be our great and only object in this new and rising country—the cultivation of the soil. I am the more pleased with your attempt, and have the greater hope of its success, when I consider your characters, which are pretty similar, and have been so long and so well known. Had such an attempt been made by a couple of volatile excentric creatures, lovers of whim and singularity, who never could do any thing like other people, nor even like themselves for any length of time, the success would have been much more uncertain: But when the work is undertaken by two gentlemen so remarkable for solidity of judgment, stability of principle, and uniformity of conduct, I think all the efforts of pedantry and bigotry in opposition to it, must be contemptible and fruitless.

So far as you have gone then, Gentlemen, you have done well, and you have my hearty approbation; but the chief reason of my writing to you at this time, is to stir you up to go further, and bring the scheme nearer to perfection. You have left our Seminaries in full possession of the Sciences, and indeed you have recommended them. Now, I humbly conceive, that most of the arguments that you have used, apply with the same, and in many instances, with greater force against the Sciences than against the ancient Languages. Not to mention Logic and Metaphysics, which I suppose you will easily give up, what do you think of the Mathematics, in all their extent; Algebra, with its infinite similes and evanescent quantities; Moral Philosophy, Natural Philosophy, Geography, Astronomy, &c.? The Languages take time, but do not these take much more time, if a man means really to understand them? The Languages are soon forgotten, so are these—The Languages are learned when boys are young, before they are well able to lift a grubbing hoe; but these must be learned when their bodies as well as their understanding are strong, and when they might be either digging the ground, or making shoes for those who do dig it. I must therefore ask, with respect to all the Sciences, *Cui bono*, i.e. To what earthly purpose do they serve? I beg pardon for this Latin phrase; you see how even a little half forgotten learning spoils a man, and leads him into a superfluity of words—what I mean to say is, will the Sciences teach a man how to dress his field, or raise his stock? I trow not—They will rather make him neglect or spoil them. Now have not you justly shown, that our great business in the United States is to cultivate the soil? I agree with you entirely; and am fully of opinion, that Science is like the imported articles of finery, which we should do much better without: It is itself, indeed, an imported article, which, like true Federalists, we should discourage and oppose. If we could but cut off all useless objects of attention and desire, it would greatly simplify our views. Let me ask, what is the substance of all human pursuits? Is it not Industry and Enjoyment, and the first only in order to the last? Therefore what have we to do in the United States, but to plant corn and feed pork, and to eat both?

I beg leave further to observe, that the Sciences are exceedingly dangerous to the Religion and Morals of our young people. It is needless to go through all, Astronomy alone is sufficient to prove this. What can be the effect of the continual mention of Saturn and Jupiter but to give them a Heathenish turn of mind?[1] And if they should take it into their heads to enquire who this Jupiter was, and to learn some of his exploits, though you have forbidden them to read Horace and Juvenal,[2] yet they will get a full account in many English books, which, for brevity and modesty's sake, I do not mention. Mars also is one of the stars, and what can be learned from him, unless it be a disposition to wars and bloodshed? But, above all, what think you of Venus? I am sure she is one of the oldest sinners we have heard or read of—What fine work will it make to excite in boys a curiosity to be informed of her character, temple, rites, votaries, &c. &c.! You will perhaps say that, at any rate, next follows Mercury to repair the devastations made by Venus: But whatever be in this, I will never alter my opinion that they are happiest who know nothing of, and have nothing to do with either the one or the other.

There remains the strongest argument of all against the Sciences, that they are so full of terms derived from the Greek and Latin Languages, that it will be impossible to prevent boys who learn them from looking back, like Lot's wife to Sodom,[3] and falling in love with these Languages, of the pernicious influence of which you have taken so much pains to convince the public. It is impossible to enter upon any of the Sciences without using terms which are in a manner wholly Greek and Latin, some of them not having even an English termination. In Logic, the very name of which is Greek, you have the analytical and synthetical method of reasoning. In Rhetoric you have metaphors and allegory, hyperbole, prosopopeia, epiphonoma, epanathorsis, and how many more Heaven knows, for I am sure I do not. In Mathematics you have the radius, the periphery, the tangent line, and cosine, and others innumerable. In your own Science, I mean the Medical, the prevalence of Latin and Greek, especially the latter, is greater than in any other. I am of opinion, that a regular bred Physician cannot speak at all without Latin and Greek, and the most of them even think that this sort of Language is plainer than English. Of this I give the following example, perfectly authentic. Mr. Broomfield, an eminent surgeon in London, was examined, 27th Feb. 1769, at Surgeons Hall, after he had visited Clark, who got his death wound at one of Mr. Wilkes' election mobs.[4] One or two of the questions and answers are as follow—Q. On what part of the head was the wound? A. On the crown of the head. Q. What do you mean by the crown of the head? A. On the right parietal bone, by the sagittal suture. Again. Q. What do you mean by examining the opposite part? A. I mean the osoccepetis. Again. Q. The extravasation, you say, was under the falx? A. The extravasation was to the right of the falx of the dura mater. I think therefore, Gentlemen, it is plain that if you retain the Sciences, the boys must either learn Greek and Latin, or you will be obliged to find or make words radically English or American, in place of all the terms at present made use of, which I believe will be a very difficult undertaking.

In fine, as you have happily pointed out some eminent and distinguished persons shining at the bar or serving their country, who knew nothing of Latin and Greek, I am able to produce many instances of the like lustre in persons ignorant of the Sciences. One example, instead of more, shall suffice: The great General P—m[5] knew as little of the Sun's paralax, or the Moon's ascending or descending node, as he did of the aoristus, primus or secundus, or the paulo post futurum of the Greek Tongue.[6] Now, I ask this plain question, could not he kill a bear or an Englishman with equal honor to himself & advantage to his country? We know that he did both, and therefore neither Science nor Languages can be of any use to an American Citizen. *Quod erat demonstrandum.*[7]

NYP, 31 December; reprinted at Newport, Rhode Island.

---

[1] Owing to those planets' being named after Roman (pre-Christian) gods.

[2] Juvenal (Decimus Junius Juvenalis) was a Roman satirical poet active in the late first and early second centuries A.D.

[3] Lot's wife was turned into a pillar of salt for looking back as they fled from God's destruction of Sodom and Gomorrah (Genesis 19:26).

[4] John Wilkes (1727–97), the controversial British pamphleteer and champion of civil rights, hand selected John Glynn to serve with him for Middlesex County in a special parliamentary election in December 1768. A "mob for hire" employed by Glynn's opponents created a riot at the polls, during which a lawyer named George Clark was clubbed to death (Arthur H. Cash, *John Wilkes* [New Haven, Conn., 2006], pp. 235–36). London's Barber-Surgeons' Hall was the headquarters of the powerful guild of barbers and surgeons beginning in 1430.

[5] Revolutionary War General Israel Putnam (1718–29 May 1790) achieved folk hero status during his lifetime as a soldier and farmer from Pomfret, Connecticut. The writer may have confused bear killing with the legend in which Putnam killed a wolf in her den with his bare hands.

[6] The first and second aorists are grammatical tenses commonly found in ancient Greek; paulo post futurum, or "a little past the future," was a Latin grammarians' phrase for the future perfect tense.

[7] That which was to be proved.

Philadelphus, An Ode

For the New Year, 1790,
and the
Second Session of the New Congress

HAIL happy morn, that gives new light & joy!
Our pleasures brighten as we forward look;
Sweet cherub, Hope! O, all thy powers employ!
Banish distraction to some wayward nook.

Too long did Discord, with her dismal train,
    With fury-beating wings our peace assail;
Screaming tremendous, they admitance gain,
    Then with foreboding howls each morning hail.
Away with dark distrust—a jealous few,
    With canker'd venom, would destroy our all;
Before the wind let them their venom strew.
    And feed deliciously on their own gall.
Joy springs from love! Behold a patriot train
    Who wish for Concord to maintain her sway;
Who hate to persecute, but will maintain
    The freest government on earth this day.
What more of freedom can wish or hope,
    Unless we have no government at all?
Corinthian pillars are the surest prop—
    And they are beautifully turn'd, tho' small.

IG, 4 January 1790.

OTHER DOCUMENTS

George Thatcher to John Avery, Jr. FC, Chamberlain Collection, MB. Place
to which written not indicated. Thomas Chase (1739–87) had served as
deputy quartermaster general for the eastern department during the Revolutionary War; see also *DHFFC* 15:127.
    Delivered Avery's letter to Jonathan Burrall regarding settlement of
    Thomas Chase's public accounts; conversed with Burrall about proce-
    dures, and that morning delivered the accounts to his office; asks whether
    he is authorized to receive the principal's balance due without the interest.

Ezra Stiles, Diary. CtY.
    Yale's petition for abatement of impost for "phil[*osophical*]. apparatus"
    committed to the care of Sherman. (For background on the petition, see
    DHFFC 8:362–64.)

George Washington, Diary. Washington Papers, MiD-B.
    The Adamses, White, Gerry, Partridge, and Tucker dined at the President's.

DECEMBER 1789 UNDATED

Benjamin Lincoln to Fisher Ames. No copy known; mentioned in Alexander
Hamilton to Lincoln, 20 January 1790. The date is presumed on the basis

of White's speech of 11 January (*DHFFC* 12:10). The subject of the letter was Christopher Saddler's petition praying for relief from penalties imposed on him at Boston for violating the Impost Act; see *DHFFC* 8:421–22. The letter was referred to the secretary of the treasury along with the petition.

Applications for Appointments from North Carolina. AN, hand of Tobias Lear, Washington Papers, DLC. Date based on internal evidence.
    Office seeking: Williamson recommends James Iredell as associate justice of the Supreme Court, and Hawkins and William Blount as commissioners for settling accounts.

1789 UNDATED

Letter from London to Fayetteville, North Carolina. *NYDG*, 6 February 1790 (the date on which members of Congress would have seen it). Originally published in the non extant [Fayetteville] *North Carolina Chronicle*, 28 December; reprinted at Boston; Newport, Rhode Island; New Haven, Connecticut; Philadelphia and York, Pennsylvania; Norfolk and Winchester, Virginia; and Charleston, South Carolina.
    "The new federal duties are smart, but they will assist Congress to bring about an efficient government"; England "will not long tamely submit to America's laying duties on our shipping"; other nations ask the British government why the United States is treated as a most favored nation and not as an alien one like them.

FLEETS Pocket ALMANACK For the Year of our LORD 1790. MeHi. Sedgwick owned a copy of the same almanac (Almanac Collection, MHi).
    Virginia's FFC delegation "is decidedly attached to the Union and the new Constitution, and no doubt they will soon find that their interest and glory will be best connected by a few temporary sacrifices upon the principles of mutual concession."

January 1790

FRIDAY, 1 JANUARY 1790

Very fine (Johnson)

William Constable to Thomas Fitzsimons

I droped you a line yesterday in reply to yours of the 28th. I have since made Enquiry respecting the Loan Office Certificates issued in So. Carolina & find that they were originally given to [*Stephen*] Drayton & others, the date not being filled up, that they have since been issued for state purposes & antidated so as greatly to Alter their value—the Carolina Debt itself in my Opinion will Constitute a much Easier & better Object of speculation, the price of wh. is not above 2/. Many are already gone there to make purchases. I woud Recommend you to employ Geo. Read [*Reid*]—formerly Commissioner there for settling their Acct. with the Continent as your Broker in Case you do any thing in it, direct to him to the Care of R. Hazlehurst Co.

Your Opinion Respectg. Indents is precisely Right in every particular I think—I am making a purchase of them—& wish you to do the same—if you can make an Excha[*nge*]. of a sum in Finals[1] at 9/ for Indents at 6/. I will supply the former. If your Domestic Affairs will not suffer by your absence, the sooner you come on the better, were you on the spott you woud be able to learn the system proposed for the Payment of Interest on the Domestic Debt &ca.—& think We might Conduct some plan of Operations to mutual Advantage.

FC:lbk, Constable-Pierrepont Collection, NN.

---

[1] Final settlement certificates amounting to over $14.7 million were issued by federal commissioners under an act of February 1782 for consolidating and liquidating all civilian and military debts that had been contracted. They were of three types. Most importantly, $11 million in "Pierce's Notes" were issued to Continental Army soldiers as each of their accounts was adjusted by Commissioner John Pierce's clerks between 1783 and 1786. Perhaps as much as $5 million of these represented "commutation," the full pay for five years granted to officers as a pension. Officers, consequently, received "finals" ranging on average from $1500 for lieutenants to $10,000 for generals. Soldiers on average received two or three hundred in finals to cover their back pay and bonuses, as well as claims for rations, clothing, forage, and other items. Another $3.7 million were issued to settle the claims of civilians, a process beginning in 1782 and continuing for a decade. The third type was issued to settle the

accounts of officials who had handled public monies. The total amount of these was comparatively small, but the process of the settlement extended beyond the FFC (*Purse*, pp. 180–93).

Newspaper Article

The company at the President's on New-Year's day,[1] was unusually
crouded and respectable. The members of the senate and house of representatives, the principal officers of the government of the United States, the governor and officers of the state of New York, the mayor and many foreigners
and citizens of distinction paid him their respects, on the commencement of
the New Year. The weather was remarkably fine; and it must have afforded
real pleasure to the contemplative mind, to have beheld the pleasing felicita-
tions of all ranks of citizens, and the general joy that pervaded every breast.

NYJ, 7 January; reprinted at Providence, Rhode Island; Hartford, Connecticut; Philadelphia; and Baltimore.

[1] Washington noted that the event, "to pay the complimts. of the Season," lasted from
noon to 3 P.M. (*DGW* 6:1).

From New York

Congress were to meet on *Monday* next. And although the members arrive
daily—yet it is not expected that the two Houses will be formed for several
days—as since the adoption by *North-Carolina*, it is requisite that there be
THIRTEEN members of the Senate, and THIRTY-THREE members of the
House to form a quorum of each.

[Boston] *Massachusetts Centinel*, 9 January.

From New York

There are now in this city, *Nine* Senators—and *Seventeen* Representatives—so it is expected, that a quorum of both branches will be here on
Thursday next.

There will be a variety of interesting proceedings the ensuing session. The
subject of Finance will require the greatest deliberation and care—and the
state of the Union being known, as it will be, by The PRESIDENT'S speech,
at the opening of the session—the business transacted must be of the utmost
moment. The speech I shall send you as early as possible.

[Boston] *Massachusetts Centinel*, 13 January.

OTHER DOCUMENTS

Jacquelin Ambler to James Madison. ALS, Madison Papers, DLC. Place to and from which written not indicated; franked; postmarked Richmond, Virginia, 5 January. For the full text, see *PJM* 12:465–66.

Cover letter to enclosed bond from Madison to Governor Beverley Randolph for £200 advance as member of Congress, dated 22 August 1789 (attested by Page), and receipt for £100 paid on the bond on 1 January 1790.

Nathan Keais to George Washington. ALS, Washington Papers, DLC. Written from Washington, North Carolina; addressed in care of Williamson.

Office seeking: collector at Bath, North Carolina.

Ezra Stiles, Diary. CtY.

Sherman planned to set out from New Haven, Connecticut, for Congress.

NYDG, 1 January; reprinted as an advertisement in each issue throughout the month.

Letter dated 13 August 1787 from Henry Wynkoop to the president of the Pennsylvania Agricultural Society, advocating the use of plaster of paris as a fertilizer, and accompanied by a certification that Wynkoop was a person of "undoubted good character and worthy of credit."

Letter from London. *GUS*, 20 March (the date on which it would have been seen by members of Congress); reprinted at Windsor, Vermont, and Newburyport, Massachusetts.

Lords Hawkesbury and Grenville are preparing the plan of a commercial treaty with the United States "which I doubt not will *shortly* be fully matured and put into a train of negociation."

SATURDAY, 2 JANUARY 1790

Extreme fine. warm pleasant (Johnson)

William Gray, Jr. to Benjamin Goodhue

Having severall Vessells bound to the Southward, which I intended should go from thence to Europe, I supposed I could not (with propriety) Clear them as Coasters I applyd to the Collr. [*Joseph Hiller*] of this Port to Clear them as Merchant Vessells, they gave me such a Clearance as they thought Proper, but when the Vessells arrived at Virginia, the Collr. there

says they come within the 23d Sec. of the Act of Congress for Regulating
Coasting Trade & as they have no license as Coasters they must pay tonnage;
& that the same as Foreign Ships Fifty Cents ℔ Ton, though I had paid tonnage upon the same Vessell ten days before in this Port.

I think Congress neaver intended this should be the Case.

As the Officers now Construe the 23d Sec[*tion*]. a Vessell bound from this
to Boston, or from a Foreign Port, to Boston, there enters pays Tonnage Impost &c. & takes in part of her Cargo or only one Cask, & comes to this Port
she must pay tonnage again, & that the same as Foreign Ships, unless the
Owner, takes out a license & pays tonnage for one year as a Coaster though
he never intends to employ his a Vessell, as a Coaster but only wants to bring
his Vessell from Boston to Salem after delivering his Cargo at Boston. I think
Congress neaver intended this should be the Case.

I always supposed Congress intended, a Vessell should pay tonnage every
time she enterd from a Foreign Port, but not for going from one dest[*inatio*]n.
to an other.

If any thing can be done to rectify what we suppose an Error, we request
your attention & Interest to have the matter sett right, we Humbly Conceive, that a Vessell ought to have Liberty, to Land a part of her Cargo at
one port upon the Continant, paying impost upon what she Lands, & then
proceed to an other without taking out the whole, leaving a Manifest at the
first Port of the whole Cargo.

We think after Entring, paying Impost, tonnage & every other Charge,
when we come from a Foreign Port we ought to have liberty to proceed to
any other Port upon the Continant to take in our Cargo without paying
tonnage again till we return from a Foreign Port. we cannot think it was
ever intended, that we should pay the same tonnage as Foreigners upon
going from this to the Southward States, when we have Register & every
other Paper than an American Merchant Vessell ought to have, this Matter being sett right imediately (provided the Congress in their wisdom,
should think fitt to ask an Explanation) will very much promote the Interest
of Trade.

ALS, Letters to Goodhue, NNS. Written from Salem, Massachusetts; misdated "1789";
franked.

Robert Morris to Gouverneur Morris

I wish you my Dear Gouverneur a happy New Year and that you may live
to enjoy many, very many of them, Was you here at this moment you would
not only be happy in the Society of your Friends, but in the enjoyment of
the Sweetest air & the mildest day you can possibly conceive, it seems as if

we were to have no Winter for we are arrived to this date without any appearance of Cold Weather.

My Family all join in their good Wishes & unanimously desire me to transmit the Compliments of the Season, the little Captain[1] says he remembers you well, but it is no longer Gover Morris, for he can now pronounce *Governeur* as well as anybody.

*** I visited Doctor [*Benjamin*] Franklyn yesterday, the old Gentn. keeps his bed, but his Face looks strong and wholesome, his Spirits are good, and his Faculties perfect, His body & Limbs are wasting for want of air & exercise and He is frequently in great pain from the Stone & Gravel. Yet from all appearance he may last a good while longer. Oswald has been abusing me very Grosly or rather the Lee's through the Channell of Oswalds Paper, upon the old Topic of my Public Accounts.[2] It unfortunately happened that we could not get through them before the 4th of March last, altho I went to New York solely on that business in October 1788. and in Jany. 1789 and after the 4th March the Commissioner [*Benjamin Walker*] refused to Act, conceiving his Authority at an End as in fact it really was; and I was forced to wait for the New Arrangements. My Enemies taking advantage of this delay have made the grossest misrepresentations and boldly have asserted such bare faced falsehoods, that I determined to bring them to Punishment & shame if possible, I therefore demanded from Oswald the Names of the Authors which he refused, and I have brought an Action of damages against him, in Consequence of which I have no doubt but He will be Severely Trounced in the mean time I have no doubt of getting these Accounts examined & the Settlement compleated during the Coming Session of Congress,[3] and I expect to go for New York in about ten days from this time.

Mr. Jefferson is not come on from Virginia yet and I suppose nothing will be done in regard to Foreign appointments untill he does come, I will forget the doings at Berny,[4] and for several ~~good~~ reasons give way to the good opinion which I have always entertained of Him, consequently I am now prepared to treat him with Respect & attention.

ALS, Robert Morris Papers, DLC. Written from Philadelphia. The omitted text relates to the Pennsylvania constitutional convention.

[1] Probably Morris's youngest son, Henry.

[2] Residual enmity between the Lee clan and Morris dated to the latter's close association with Silas Deane in the Lee-Deane Affair, the source of a serious division in Congress from 1776 to 1779 (*DHFFC* 15:230n). The ongoing feud found an additional outlet in the pages of Philadelphia's *IG*, where editor Eleazer Oswald relentlessly targeted Morris for mismanagement of his accounts as superintendent of finance. See Another Correspondent, 30 November 1789 and Detector, 18 December 1789, above.

[3] For Morris's petition for settlement of his accounts as superintendent of finance, see *DHFFC* 8:663–75.

[4] The French town of Berni was the seat of the French comptroller general, and the site of a meeting of royal councillors and other fiscal experts composing a "Committee on American commerce." On 24 May 1786 the meeting, with Jefferson's urging, decided not to renew Robert Morris's monopoly on the sale of tobacco in France (Dumas Malone, *Jefferson and the Rights of Man* [Boston, 1951], pp. 39–42).

From New York

Members of Congress now in this city: SENATE, President of the Senate. Mr. Dalton. Mr. Johnson. Mr. Schuyler. Mr. King. Mr. Izard. Mr. Butler. Mr. Langdon. Mr. Wingate. Mr. Few.

REPRESENTATIVES, Mr. Gilman. Mr. Gerry. Mr. Lawrance. Mr. Benson. Mr. Scott. Mr. Coles. Mr. Brown. Mr. Griffin. Mr. Huger. Mr. Smith, of South-Carolina. Mr. White. Mr. Partridge. Mr. Tucker. Mr. Goodhue. Mr. Thatcher. Mr. Baldwin.

Mr. Otis, Secretary of the Senate.

Mr. Beckley, Clerk of the House.

GUS, 2 January.

Cat to Mr. Ranlet

I Send you an observation made by a worthy member of Congress, in the debates, which I think I have not seen in your paper.[1] This gentleman was making some remarks that called up the idea of federal and antifederal—He observed, he did not think the idea was properly fixed—that there was many for ratifying the constitution, and many against it—consequently from the word ratifying the constitution, would be more natural to distinguish, by calling those who were in favour of the constitution by the appellation of RATS, & those who were against it ANTI-RATS—Further, your correspondent thinks himself fully authorised to agree with the ingenious gentleman, that the definition is not only more natural, but much more expressive; for by the number of RATS appointed to office under the new government, and their large salaries—it is likely they will consume the greatest part of the public revenue.

[Exeter] *New Hampshire Gazetteer*, 2 January (edited by Henry Ranlet [1762–1807], who settled in Exeter in 1785 and edited newspapers there between 1786 and 1800).

[1] From *CR*'s version of Gerry's speech on Amendments to the Constitution, 15 August 1789 (*DHFFC* 11:1262).

Robert R. Livingston to John Armstrong. ALS, R. R. Livingston Papers, NHi. Place to which addressed not indicated.

"Congress are filling very fast & it is expected will form by tuesday or sooner if Pensilvania comes on [The] funding system seems to gain ground & an Idea pretty generally prevails that the State debts will be adopted."

NYDG, 4 January.

Coles married Catharine Thompson, Bishop Samuel Provoost presiding.

Daniel Hiester, Account Book. PRHi.

Left Reading, Pennsylvania, for Philadelphia en route to New York.

SUNDAY, 3 JANUARY 1790

Very fine (Johnson)

Frederick A. Muhlenberg to Thomas Fitzsimons

With a good deal of Difficulty we reached Elisabeth Town [*New Jersey*] last Evening, & tired of intolerable bad Roads & the jostling of the Waggon we took a Boat at Elisabeth Town this Morning which brot. us to N. York in an hour and a Quarter, where we soon heard that we shall tomorrow already make a House. The Eastern Members are chiefly all arrived. Ames came in this Day. Of the Southern there are Burke Baldwin Tucker Smith [*S.C.*] & Seney—Also White Coles & Brown. Having scarce had Time to leave the House I cannot comunicate any thing new—but wishing You a much pleasanter Journey than we had I soon expect to have the pleasure of seeing You & Mr. Clymer at New York. The Senate I am told have also a Quorum—so that tomorrow we shall probably proceed to Business.

ALS, Gratz Collection, PHi. Addressed to Philadelphia; franked; postmarked 4 January; received 5 January.

George Thatcher to Sarah Thatcher

On wednesday evening about ten oClock I got to the end of my Journey; & put up at my old Lodgings,[1] where I now am.

If I mistake not my last was dated at Hartford [*Connecticut*] on sunday, which place we left early on monday morning, & arrived, that evening, after an agreeable days ride, to New-Haven [*Connecticut*] about six oClock—The next day, Tuesday, about nine, it began to rain, & continued with increasing fury till, three, when it changed into snow—during this time, and while the rain fell in the greatest plenty, we had to pass a ferry, which took us near half an hour—My Cloak was now of singular use—indeed I scarce ever found it so convenient—for having it over my surtout, it shed off the rain so compleatly, that when we had got over and well seated in the Stage, I threw it off & found my other cloaths as dry as tho it had not rained—But the unusual quantity of Rain that fell this day, together with some snow, towards night, rendered the roads so bad that our Horses could only walk—& not more than three miles an Hour—so that we did not get to the place where we intended to put up, till about eleven oClock—The next day, tho clear & moderate, we travled only at the rate of three, or three miles & an half an Hour—but as it closed our Journey, we thought it but a trifle.

We found Mrs. Chadwell & Polly well, & glad to see us returned—They inquired particulary after you, & the Children.

Thus you have the History of my Journey from Biddeford [*Maine*] to New-York—It seems the general opinion of those I have heard speak of the expected length of the ensuing Session, that it will not be longer than april—but this is only a conjecture as yet—I shall be able to form a more certain Judgment in a few days.

You may inform our friends Mr. & Mrs. [*Matthew*] Cobb, that I saw our brother Ned [*Edward Savage*] at Worcester [*Massachusetts*]—He & his little wife were well; but I did not tarry there, one stage, as I expected—Because, I found the travling so uncertain, & the next Stage was like to be so crouded, that I thot it expedient to make the best of my way on.

I am very sorry that I could not spend some time at Weston [*Massachusetts*], as I wanted to provide some school for Phillips [*Thatcher*]; but as I was there only half of a minute, I did not mention the subject—perhaps, however, as you mentioned something about it in your Letter to Lucy, she may write you thereon—If so & you think it will do, & it should be perfectly agreeable to Silas [*Lee*] to take ~~him~~ Phillips with him to Weston, you will do as you think proper.

Are the children well, & clear of the itch?[2] I sometimes itch, & almost doubt whether I ever had the itch—or if I had, that I am not cured of it—But I have not said any thing to a physician—perhaps what I feel is no more than the effects of cold weather—or what is usual after one is cured.

Last evening I recd. a Letter from our Hond. Father [*Samuel Phillips Savage*], dated the 26th. Decr. in which he complains of my not calling upon him—& sais, that if he was going to Portland [*Maine*] he thinks he should not omit calling upon us—He & family were well.

ALS, Thatcher Family Papers, MHi. Place to which addressed not indicated.

---

[1] During the first session, Thatcher lodged with Strong, Goodhue, Grout, Sturges, and Wingate at Philip Mathers's boarding house, 47 Broad Street.
[2] Probably scabies.

OTHER DOCUMENTS

John Fenno to Joseph Ward. ALS, Ward Papers, ICHi. Addressed to "Land office/Boston"; postmarked. For the full text, see *AASP* 89(1979):353.
   "Congress collecting pretty fast—but will hardly make a house to morrow"; subscribers increase but finances "are 0"; asks for new subscriptions to be collected and forwarded.

William Samuel Johnson to Robert Charles Johnson. ALS, Johnson Papers, CtHi. Written "Sundy. Eveng."; addressed to "Fairfield or Stratford," Connecticut; franked; postmarked.
   As Congress is supposed to meet the next day, he intends to try to frank the letter "by way of experiment"; after that point, "there can be no difficulty, & you will direct to me in Senate, & write as often as you can, if it be but two or three lines, as we are all, especially Mamma, unhappy if we do not hear from you often."

George Thatcher to Jeremiah Hill. No copy known; acknowledged in Hill to Thatcher, 26 January.

MONDAY, 4 JANUARY 1790

Still very warm (Johnson)

James Madison to George Washington

After being detained 8 or 10 days beyond the intended commencement of my Journey, by the critical illness of my mother,[1] I am now subjected to a further delay by an attack on my own health. A slight complaint in my bowels which I first felt on the day of my arrival here (friday last) very suddenly took the form of a pretty severe dysentery. With the aid of Doctr. [*David*] Stuart who has been good eno' to see me every day, I have I hope nearly subdued the malignity of the disease, and got into a course of recovery. I find myself however much weakened by the joint operation of the malady

& the medicine, and shall be under the necessity not only of remaining here a few days longer, but of travelling afterwards with some circumspection.

You will probably have seen by the papers that the contest in the [*Virginia*] Assembly on the subject of the amendments ended in the loss of them. The House of Delegates got over the objections to the 11 & 12,[2] but the Senate revived them with an addition of the 3 & 8 articles, and by a vote of adherence prevented a ratification. On some accounts this event is no doubt to be regretted. But it will do no injury to the Genl. Government. On the contrary it will have the effect with many of turning their distrust towards their own Legislature. The miscarriage of the 3d. art. particularly, will have this effect.

A few days before I was allowed to set out for N. York, I took a ride to Monticello. The Answer of Mr. Jefferson to the notification of his appointment will no doubt have explained the state of his mind on that subject.[3] I was sorry to find him so little biased in favor of the domestic service allotted to him, but was glad that his difficulties seemed to result cheifly from what I take to be an erroneous view of the kind and quantity of business annexed to that which constituted the foreign department. He apprehends that it will far exceed the latter which has of itself no terrors to him. On the other hand It was supposed, & I beleive truly that the domestic part will be very trifling, and for that reason improper to be made a distinct department. After all if the whole business can be executed by any one man, Mr. Jefferson must be equal to it; if not he will be relieved by a necessary division of it. All whom I have heard speak on the subject are remarkably solicitous for his acceptance, and I flatter myself that they will not in the final event be disappointed.

In case I should be detained here much longer than I calculate, and any thing should occur, I may trouble you with a few lines further.

ALS, Washington Papers, DLC. Written from Georgetown, Maryland (in present-day Washington, D.C.); marked "private."

[1] Eleanor Rose "Nellie" Conway (1732–1829) married James Madison, Sr., in 1749.
[2] Madison's numbering throughout this letter refers to the twelve articles of Amendment submitted to the states in September 1789, the last ten of which became the Amendments ultimately ratified as the Bill of Rights.
[3] For Jefferson's reply to Washington, 15 December 1789, see *PGW* 4:412–13.

David Sewall to George Thatcher

I take the liberty of inclosing a short Bill respecting the paiment of Costs in Criminal prosecutions. and I think it takes up all the cases that can happen. And it points out a mode of effecting the business, as simple as any that I at present can think of. I presume before this reaches you Congress will be doing Business. By the Judicial Bill The District Court has a Concurrent Jurisdiction with the *Circuit* and *State* Courts, "of all suits at Common law, where the U.S. sue; and the matter in dispute amounts to the Sum or Value of 100. Dollars."[1] Was it the Intention of the legislature that no Common law suit should be commenced in a district Court *for* the U.S. *under* a 100. Dollars? It seems by another Clause that final decrees and judgements in Civil Actions, where the Sum exceeds 50. Dollars may be reexamined, in a Circuit Court upon a Writ of Error.[2]

P. S. my particular respects to the members of the House for this State and when I can hear of Brother Sedgwick, being at N. York—I will endeavour [*lined out*] a Compliance with my Promise at Parting, at Lenox [*Massachusetts*], to Write him. We have no News. ***

ALS, Chamberlain Collection, MB. Written from York, Maine; postmarked Portsmouth, New Hampshire, 5 January. The omitted text includes local weather and mercantile news.

[1] Section 9 of the Judiciary Act [S-1].
[2] Section 22.

Thomas Underwood to James Madison

***

I hear much sed about the British Debts and shall be exceedingly obliged to you for information on that subject, if Congress say nothing about it sure I am our state will be in great confusion shd. the British Creditors bring suits immediately as I am told they will do—it is expected that they should be compell'd to give up the posts and make compensation for the slaves before they can be entitled to recover there Debts.

I shall be glad to hear from you as oft as conv[*enien*]t.

ALS, Madison Papers, DLC. Written from Goochland, Virginia. For the full text, see *PJM* 12:468. The omitted text relates to Underwood's efforts to retrieve prizes won in the lottery established by Congress in November 1776. He was attempting to get official acknowledgment of his ownership of the lost or stolen lottery tickets, and asked Madison "and my other friends in Congress to look into this matter for me and so contrive as that I may get paymt. I suppose it may be done by way of a Petition to Congress on my Agreeing to indemnify Congress and giv[*in*]g. good sec[*urit*]y. therefor which I am willing to do."

[*Jeremiah Wadsworth,*] The Observer—No. XII

On Excise, or duties on inland trade and business

To balance the several branches of a national revenue, in such manner, that no order of citizens may be oppressed, and no kind of useful business discouraged, is the most difficult duty of a financier. Any man who is cloathed with power, and determined on the obtainment of a revenue, may find ways and means to take it from the people; but it is only a great and prudent man, who can combine public and private interests, by enriching the national treasury, in such ways as stimulate general industry, and over-burden no order of people. A genius, natively adapted for such calculations, may fix on leading principles, and conjecture with surprising success; still it is experience which must perfect the system. That rapid growth of empire which we may expect, with such fresh resources as always appear in a new country; under the guidance of a masterly hand and matured by a few years experience, will establish American credit in the opinion of all mankind. But to make a successful beginning, the public must exercise patience, and give time for the several parts of a system, to be brought forward in orderly succession: and when the whole is produced, there will be a fit time to judge, how near the first attempt hath approached to such perfection as we may expect, and wherein alterations may be expedient. No man, who hath abilities to provide otherwise for himself, will long serve a factious people; and when jealousy begins to arise, between the great denominations of citizens, who pursue different employments, it threatens a retirement of those characters, who are most fit to guide. The importing merchants have set a noble example of patriotism, in aiding an impost by their influence; if the retailing merchants and planters discover equal magnanimity, we may defy the predictions of our enemies, that America will be always faithless.

Impost and excise are among the names by which taxes on commerce and business have been called. In the American sense of these words, impost is a tax on merchandise, payable at the port of entry, by the importing merchant; and excise is a tax on certain kinds of business, or a duty on merchandise paid by the retailer after a sale of his goods. Tho' the same article be charged with both duties, there is an obvious reason for seperating the times of imposition and payment. The nature of importation, requires it to be made in larger quantities of the same article, than will command an immediate sale; and an impost must be paid before the merchant can receive any returns by his business. If too high an impost be charged, it in effect prohibits importation, by requiring from the importer a sum greater than he can pay; for tho' he recharges it to the purchaser, there must be a previous advance of the duty, which is beyond his power. This remark will be found true in all mercantile States; but especially in America, from the prevalent custom of giving a long credit to the retailing trader. Were an impost to be imposed of four times the present sum, it would amount to a prohibition on three-fifths of our importing merchants; and throw business into the hands of a few who have great wealth—This would be destructive to many worthy merchants, and operate as a monopoly to raise prices unseasonably on the consumer. There are many articles of Luxury which ought to contribute a large share to the national revenue; among these are wines, and ardent spirits of every kind. The man who will indulge his vanity and appetite, in ways which have a corrupting influence on republican virtue, is a fit subject for such kinds of taxation, as he may avoid or voluntarily take on himself. So great a tax on these articles, at the port of entry or at the distillery, as they ought to pay, would prohibit importation for the reason abovementioned; but divide the tax, let one part be paid on importation, and the other by the retailer, after an actual consumption of the article and the evil is prevented. I care not by what name this last tax is called, for names are arbitrarily imposed, and have such a meaning as the legislature is pleased to give them. Impost and excise do not mean the same thing in any two states on earth. In England, an excise means taxes on various kinds of manufacture and internal business, and is wholly different from those excises used by several states in the union, which are duties on the retail sale of imported articles. In other European countries, impost and excise have meanings as different as the several languages of the people; and by means of our general descent from that country, and a community of language, is an unpopular word in America; for which reason perhaps this name ought not to enter a revenue system in the United States—tho' our duties on inland trade and business, should be established on equitable principles, and with a most sacred regard to the rights of men and citizens, the ideas associated with that word, will not be removed for half a century.

To accomodate myself to the reader's understanding, I have used the word excise in my past Essays, for all duties on inland trade and on certain lucrative branches of business; and I believe it is the sense of the people, that such duties ought to constitute one great branch of the national revenue.

Every principle of national policy requires, that the use of certain foreign articles should be discouraged, by a higher tax, than can be imposed at the port of entry; without forming a virtual monopoly, in favor of a few overgrown importers, or great foreign companies; who would pay any tax, if they might be richly repaid, by a subsequent sale in the country.

Every principle of virtue requires that the superabundant use of certain articles, which are destructive to the morals, health and industry of the people, should be checked by tax laws. If the intemperate, who disturb our neighbourhood, and corrupt our youth, will not benefit the public by their industry and thrift, they should be made subservient to the national good, by contributing largely to its income—So small a quantity of ardent spirit, is necessary for medicine, and the real comfort of life, that a high tax will injure no one, but those who use them to excess; and such have no right to complain of an evil, voluntarily brought on themselves.

Sumptuary laws, or laws against excess in dress and living, have been found necessary in many states, and they are needed in this country. An absolute prince, may prohibit luxury and extravigance in dress, by his positive injunctions; but the experiment will not succeed with a people, who have such ideas of liberty, as prevail in the United States—a more safe method is to discourage foreign superfluities, and encourage our own manufactures by duties judiciously imposed. It is better to enrich our revenue at the expence of prodigality, than of industry—The prodigal are self devoted to ruin, and as the event cannot be prevented, for the contagion of their example, let them make the only possible attonement, a contribution to the necessities of the country which hath protected them. Wrought silks of foreign manufactory, ought to be considered as superfluities in the United States; and a duty on all these would encourage the home cultivation and manufacture, for which the middle and southern states are well adapted. To select all the articles, which ought on these general principles to be dutied, is equally beyond my present design, my information and capacity. Certain branches of business within the country, which are productive to the managers, and firmly established might contribute a share to the national revenue. Our empire extends through a greater variety of climes than any other on earth; in some part of the whole, almost every production of nature may be found, and every work of art will soon be fabricated. Policy leads to a preference of home productions and manufactures, and a mercantile intercourse between the northern, middle and southern states—Untill this takes place we are not an independant people, in so high a sense as we might be; and the encouragement of such intercourse, depends on the regulation of revenue. To take up these general principles and form a system of duties on inland trade, and business, of general benefit, must be a work of time—the task is difficult—the scope is broad, but I firmly believe, the gentlemen, in your treasury department, have an eye of discernment which can measure it.

While on this subject, I cannot refrain mentioning the unpolicy and injustice of those partial systems, which have obtained in a number of States, under the name of excise. That politicians of a little territory, pressed for expedients, should patronize them before the formation of a general government, is not so strange; but that they should persevere at the present crisis is unfortunate—Every thing of this kind is in its nature anti-national, and leads to jealousy and contention between the states—It is contrary to the spirit of our constitution, which wisely provides that commerce, with all its interests shall be under the control of one nurturing parent—and it will give rise to counteracting the scheme of revenue, which will for a time oppress the people, and in the end defeat the whole. It ought further to be observed, that the manner of collecting state excises, has been and will be such, that the rich who purchase in large quantities, escape payment, and the poor who buy of a retailer, in small portions, are submitted to the duty. Certainly this is not good policy or justice.

P. S. Since writing the above, the Observer has heard of a little Treatise, which he would recommend to the perusal of the people of Connecticut. It is entitled *"An enquiry into the Excise Laws of Connecticut"*[1]—and is supposed to be written by a gentleman of known literary merit—in which he hath clearly proved, the impolicy and injustice of all state excises, and local systems of revenue, by commerce, and their inconsistency with the rights of a general government.

[Hartford, Connecticut] *American Mercury*, 4 January. For information on The Observer series, its authorship, and reprintings, see the location note to The Observer, No. 1, 12 October, above.

---

[1] The anonymous pamphlet *Attention! Or, new Thoughts on a Serious Subject* (Hartford, Conn., 1789; Evans 22258) was written by Noah Webster.

OTHER DOCUMENTS

William Constable to John Inglis. FC:lbk, Constable-Pierrepont Collection, NN. For the "late publications," see Another Correspondent, 30 November 1789 and Detector, 18 December 1789, above.

Stocks have risen rapidly due to the faith placed in "the integrity & Abilities of our Pitt, Colo. Hamilton," whose report to Congress, whenever it comes out, will raise the price still higher; and whose friendship Constable is "intimately acquainted & honoured with"; has just learned that "late publications against our friend [*Robert Morris*] have made a great impression [*Eleazer*] Oswald charges him with with owing the U.S. 400,000 Dls. & some person who Came forward to Contradict it has only made it worse"; "these a[*ccoun*]ts. of our Friends must be settled—[*Oliver, Jr.*] Wolcott, who I suppose will have this Business to do appears to be a very liberal man & I think has recd. a right impression from Wadsworth."

William Constable to Robert Morris. FC:lbk, Constable-Pierrepont Collection, NN.

One of the Muhlenbergs says that Morris did not plan to be in New York City before 11 January; advises him, during that interval, to send to Virginia to buy up state debt; "there woud be a senate I am told if You & the Jersey Men were in Town—It only requires 5 Members to Compleat the lower House."

Stephen Drayton to Pierce Butler. ALS, Butler Papers, PHi. Written from Charleston, South Carolina.

Office seeking: surveyor at Charleston, anticipating Edward Weyman's resignation due to ill health.

Christian Charles de Klauman to George Washington. ALS, Washington Papers, DLC. Written from Richmond, Virginia. For the full text, see *PGW* 4:528–29.

Office seeking: some office by which he can make a decent living; has given Bland recommendations from P. Muhlenberg and other military figures.

Hopley Yeaton to John Langdon. ALS, Langdon Papers, NhPoA. Written from Portsmouth, New Hampshire.

Office seeking: something in the "public Line"; "your famerly is all in good helth."

Letter from New York. *PP*, 7 January.

"Congress did not make a House to-day—two Senators and four Representatives wanting."

Letter from a London Merchant. *PP*, 27 March; reprinted at New York City (*GUS*, 31 March, the date on which members of Congress would have seen it).

By an Order in Council the importation of wheat, wheat flour, rye, barley, and oats into England, Wales, and Berwick upon Tweed is allowed "at the low duties" on them.

TUESDAY, 5 JANUARY 1790

Cold (Johnson)

Abigail Adams to Mary Cranch

*** the New Years day in this State, & particularely in this city is celebrated with every mark of pleasure and Satisfaction, the Shops and publick offices are Shut, there is not any market open this day, but every person laying aside Buisness devote the day to the Social purpose of visiting & receiving visits, the churches are open & divine Service performed begining the year in a very proper manner by giving Thanks to the great Governour of the universe for past mercies, & imploring his future Benedictions there is a kind of cake in fashion upon this day call'd New Years cooky, this & cherry Bounce as it is calld is the old Dutch customs of treating their Friends upon the return of every New Year, the common people who are very apt ready to abuse Liberty, on this day are apt to take rather too freely of the good things of this Life, and finding two of my Servants not all together qualified for Buisness. I remonstrated to them, but they excused it Saying it was New Year, & every body was joyous then, the V.P. visited the president & then returned home to receive His Friends. in the Evening I attended the drawing Room, it being mrs. W[*ashington'*]s publick day, it was as much crowded as a Birth Night at St. James,[1] and with Company as Briliantly drest. diamonds & great hoops excepted my Station is always at the right hand of mrs. W. through want of knowing what is right, I find it some times occupied, but on Such an occasion the president never fails of Seeing that it is relinquished for me, and having removed Ladies several times, they have now learnt to rise & give it me, but this between our selves, as *all distinction* you know is unpopular. yet this same p. has ~~the~~ so happy a faculty of appearing to accommodate & yet carrying his point, that if he was not really one of the best intentiond men in the world he might be a very dangerous one, he is polite with dignity, affable without familiarity, distant without Haughtyness, Grave with out Austerity, Modest, Wise, & Good these are traits in his Character which peculiarly fit him for the exalted Station he holds. and God Grant that he may Hold it with the Same applause & universal Satisfaction for many many years—as it is my firm opinion that no other man could rule over this great peopl & consolidate them into one mighty Empire but He who is Set over us.

I thank you my dear-sister for several kind Letters, the reason why I have not written to you has been that the post office would not permit Franks even to the V.P. and I did not think my Letters worth paying for—I wrote you a long Letter a little before mr. Adamss return. but being under Cover to him, I had the mortification to receive it back again. ***

ALS, Abigail Adams Letters, MWA. Place to which written not indicated. For the full text, see *Abigail Adams*, pp. 34–36. The omitted text includes news of various Adams family members. For the postscript, see 10 January, below.

---

[1] Members of the British Court came to St James's Palace to witness, and thereby authenticate, the birth of any potential heir to the throne.

John Brown to Harry Innes

***

Yesterday was the time appointed for the meeting of Congress, only twenty six Members attended & [*since the?*] accession of N. Carolina 33 are re[*quired to make*] a House we shall certainly have [*a quorum?*] tomorrow The Session will be op[*ened with a*] Speech from the President to bot[*h hou*]ses, His communication 'tis expected will be of a very important nature We expect a long Session as a multiplicity of very important Business is already presented to view. Acts relative to Citizenship Militia Bankruptcy Western Lands Public Creditors Crimes & Punishments Law Process Fees &c. must be passed this Session if possible.

The situation of the United States was never so f[*l*]attering as at present Peace & plenty obtain universally our Commerce Manufactures & Population increasing rapidly & our National Character daily becoming more respectable abroad.

I wrote to you from Philada. upon the subject of the N[*avigation of the*] Mississipi—will you ad[*dress the Presid?*]ent & Senate on that head [*Jefferson?*] has arrived in Virga. but has not ye[*t deter*]mined to accept his appointment—'tho' 'tis expected he will—Will Kentucke declair her Independence this Winter? I believe you would not meet with any oppositio[*n he*]re.

I expect to write to you & Colo. [*George*] Nicholas fully by next Post cannot at present as Mr. Benta [*?*] cannot detain..

P. S. I long [*to he*]ar whether you [*have acce*]pted your app[*ointm*]ent.

ALS, Innes Papers, DLC. Addressed to Kentucky. The document has a large hole where it may have been torn when the recipient broke the seal. The omitted text indicates that, en route to New York, Brown had passed through Richmond, Virginia, where he paid a $300 debt.

Hugh Williamson to John Gray Blount

The Bond & Copy of an Oath for the Post Master that I left in your Hands were expected by the Post. I hope they will come by next Post that I may take them with me for I hope to set out within 8 Days from this Date.

I am informed here that Mr. Ch[*arles*]. Johnson does not offer in Person for Congress but offers Mr. [*Stephen*] Cabarrus who in person has ben soliciting Votes. It is zealously objected that my Wife continues to live with me in New York while I am detained there on public Business. The Interest of the State is to be greatly mended in Hands of a Gentleman who together with his Wife were born in a foreign Kingdom & who hardly speaks the Language of this Country. But we hear that Mr. B[*enjamin*]. Williams has promised Mr. Cabarus great Interest in your District.

ALS, John Gray Blount Papers, Nc-Ar. Written from Edenton, North Carolina; addressed to Washington, North Carolina; franked; postmarked 6 January.

Newspaper Article

The weather has been so remarkably temperate for some days past, says a correspondent, that it would seem as if the very seasons conspired with the wishes of the citizens of New-York, it offering every possible accommodation to the members of Congress who had occasion to travel from the different states. No May-day, in its morning dress, could be more beautiful than yesterday, being the day appointed for the meeting of our great National Legislature, which seemed propitious to many contemplative minds.

Several Members met at both Houses, but not a sufficient number to form a quorum.

The arrival of the stages this evening, it is expected, will bring forward several gentlemen, so that it may be supposed there will be a quorum of both Houses to-morrow.

NYDG, 5 January.

OTHER DOCUMENTS

William Bradford, Jr. to Elias Boudinot. ALS, signature clipped, Wallace Papers, PHi. Written from Philadelphia.

Reports encouraging progress of state constitutional convention; Judge Francis Hopkinson's health and reason expected to improve, although a neighbor said "if he should die it will be another instance of the extraordinary good fortune of Genl. Washington!"; "what is the general expectation with you about the funding the national debt? Mr. Fitzsimmons has advanced here, in Company, that a discrimination must be made—But that I think impossible"; family is all well.

Aedanus Burke to Governor Charles Pinckney. ALS, Legislative Papers, Sc. Place to which addressed not indicated.

Could not serve as delegate to South Carolina constitutional convention for the district in the fork between the Broad and Saludi (Saluda) rivers the following May, should Congress still be sitting; therefore, declines.

Aedanus Burke to Benjamin Rush. ALS, Alexander Biddle Collection, PHi. Place to which addressed not indicated.

Arrived on 31 December "after a stormy passage of ten days"; a few days before leaving South Carolina, he read a pamphlet on the dangers of spirituous liquors (*History of Some of the Effects of Hard Drinking* [1789]) by Dr. John Coakley Lettsom (1744–1815), and at a dinner with the governor (Charles Pinckney) and the British consul (George Miller) at Charleston, he accused Lettsom of plagiarizing Rush's own "very ingenious" account of "the diseases, Crimes & punishments which arise from Spirits" (*Enquiry into the Effects of Spirituous Liquors* [1784]).

Samuel W. Stockton to Elias Boudinot. ALS, Stimson-Boudinot Collection, NjP. Written from Trenton, New Jersey; addressed to Elizabeth, New Jersey.

If John Marsden Pintard does not come soon, asks that the remainder of Stockton's set of *CR* be sent to his house; he has received only five.

Caleb Strong and Tristram Dalton to David Cobb, speaker of the Massachusetts House of Representatives. ALS, hand of Dalton, Chamberlain Collection, MB. Addressed to Boston; misdated "1789." On the same day, Strong and Dalton wrote an almost identical misdated letter to Samuel Phillips, Jr., president of the state Senate (Miscellaneous Legislative Papers, Senate Files, M-Ar).

The Massachusetts delegation in Congress presented the state legislature's Address to the President, whose answer it has transmitted to the governor; they are assured that a copy of the Senate journal has been forwarded and transmit, with this letter, for the state House of Representatives, a copy of the acts and resolves of the first session of Congress [Evans 22189].

Jonathan Trumbull to David Trumbull. ALS, Trumbull Papers, CtHi. Written from Hartford, Connecticut; addressed to Lebanon, Connecticut; carried by M. Porter.

Wadsworth left yesterday.

George Washington, Diary. Washington Papers, MiD-B.

Several members of Congress called in the forenoon to pay their respects upon their arrival in town.

[Savannah] *Georgia Gazette*, 7 January.

Jackson sailed for New York on the *Jenny.*

[Stockbridge, Massachusetts] *Western Star,* 5 January.

Sedgwick expected to leave for Congress on 6 January; was detained by his wife's illness.

WEDNESDAY, 6 JANUARY 1790

Cold (Johnson)

Pierce Butler to Weeden Butler

Your favour of the 2d. of Novbr. reachd my hand last week, and that of October, two days ago—By the former I learn with sensible concern that Mrs. Butler was much indisposed. My whole Family participate in Your distress, and anxiously look for more pleasing tidings—May *He* in whose hands are the Issues of all things long spare Her to You, Your Children and my Child [*Thomas Butler*], who woud miss Her nearly as much as Yours—Indeed I shall be uneasy till I hear again of Her situation.

I have two letters from my son—to neither of which can I answer at this time—The Packett sails tomorrow morning—this day Congress are to meet. I am therefore, as You will believe, a little hurried—I shall not be long without writing to Him—He has given me a Clear, distinct and very satisfactory statement of the manner in which He Employs his time—I exceedingly approve of his frequent reading of English Grammer, which He informs he does—"It is well to lay in a good foundation against the time to come"—As I fully purpose to give Him the most liberal Education Judiciously ornamented, it is but right to make strong the foundation by an Intimate knowledge of Grammer rules—I fear I shall tire You with my anxieties on this head, yet you, who as a Father must have similar feelings, can more readily excuse mine.

By a Gentleman Mr. Richards, who sailed from here last Month I sent you a short Letter and the Journals and Acts of Our first session—If they afford You any amusement I will continue them while I continue in Senate—I will in future direct them to be left with the principal Waiter at the New York Coffee-House in the City, to wait your Order—It woud not do to have them put in the Post Office—I think the present session of Our Congress will be a Consequential One to the states; And give a decided Colouring to Our Government—I mean to the Nature of it, or rather the bias—whether it shall be the many or the few—there is not only a Cheerful and Universal Obedience to it at present in the states, but a general Attachment to it— North-Carolina has Joined the Union—Everything here, in short in peace and Order; And Our Governmt. begins to Assume the strong features of a more Antient One—We shall, among the first things, take up the business of the Public Debt in Order to Fund it. American stocks rise rappidly; and the Mynheers I fancy will make Fortunes Out of Our Citizens[1]—they are Engrossing Our Publick securities at 8/ and 9/ in the pound—If I wished to irritate my friend Doctor [*Peter*] Spence I need only recommend to Him to put His surplus Money in Our Funds I think I hear Him pouring forth invectives—Yet in seriousness I am going to sell Lands in Order to buy into them.

My better half who I thank God is on the recovery, and my Daughters desire to be particularly presented to Mrs. Butler and Yourself.

Bless my Boy for me.

ALS, Additional Manuscripts, Butler Papers, Uk. Addressed to Cheyne Walk, Chelsea, "near London"; postmarked; received 3 February.

---

[1] A reference to Dutch bankers, who owned much of the United States' foreign debt.

Edward Fox to Andrew Craigie

***

I hear from the *best* authority that Mr. Hamilton's plan will meet with very considerable opposition. A reduction of Interest and a discrimination between original owners and purch[as]ers will be insisted upon. Mr. Fitzimmons will be for the former—I am not a little astonished at this, and cannot account for his conduct in this particular—more especially as Mr. R. Morris's *outward* professions are otherwise. I have no doubt but the debates upon the subject will be such as to lower the prices. And because they are dishonest impolitic and base ideas, there is a probability of their prevailing.

ALS, Craigie Papers, MWA. Written from Philadelphia. The omitted text includes securities prices.

Stephen Goodhue to Benjamin Goodhue

*** public Securities are at a Stand & I believe falling ~~& not Sale quick Sale be pleased of any to inform if any thing of Consequen~~ the holders of them do not appear to be so elated as when you left home they appeared then to be making hast to be ready but I hope equil Justice will mark the path of Congress be pleased to inform us of any thing of a public Nature & if there is like to be a bankrupt law soon be pleased to inform me. ***

FC:lbk, Goodhue Family Papers, MSaE. Written from Salem, Massachusetts. The omitted text relates to their mercantile business and their grandmother, who "hath recovered her health tolerable well."

Massachusetts Delegation to Governor John Hancock

The Treasurer of our State [*Alexander Hodgdon*] having in the recess of Congress written a letter to Messrs. Dalton & Gerry to be communicated to the other members from Massachusetts, touching the pension accounts of the State, We have embraced the earliest oppertunity for considering the subject & are clearly of opinion that it would be utterly impracticable for any or all the members of Congress from the State to pay that attention to these accounts, & much more so to all that will be exhibited by the State, which Justice demands, & therefore that good policy directs to the appointment of a commissioner on the part of the State to attend the Commissioners of the United State[s] who are entrusted with this business. We are confirmed in this opinion by the Information We have received that several States have adopted similar measures, & have made this communication that if your Excellency should think proper, it may be communicated to the honorable Legislature.

ALS, hand of Gerry, Resolves 1789, Chap. 121, Resolves and Acts, M-Ar. Signed by all members of the delegation except Leonard and Sedgwick, who were not yet in New York City.

Caleb Strong to Samuel Phillips, Sr.

I arrived at this Place on Saturday and a Quorum of the Senate has not appeared before this Day Upon Enquiry we find that the Accounts of Massachusetts will be attended to by the Commissioners in a few Days and that some Person on the Behalf of the State must pay particular Attention to the Subject of those Accounts I am told that their will probably be a considerable Loss to the State unless some Person is authorised to appear on Behalf of this State to arrange & enforce their Claims, the Business will require more Time than either of the members from the State if they attend their Duty in Congress can afford. We have thought of Mr. [*Samuel*] Osgood as well qualified for this Service and the Business may be done by him with far less Expence, than by a Person who should come forward for the sole purpose from the State, some Gentlemen have conversed with him and altho at the last Session of Congress I urged him to consent to undertake the Service & he then declined I am told he ~~now~~ now agrees to do it, if the State should think proper to authorise him—There is not a sufficient Number of Representatives to form a House but the Deficiency will undoubtedly be supplied to morrow—I shall always be happy to communicate any Intelligence to you that can be of ~~any~~ Importance or even gratify your Curiosity and I shall be exceedingly obliged if you will be equally communicative— ***

ALS, Phillips Family Papers, MHi. Place to which addressed not indicated.

Newspaper Article

Post Days at New-York, from January 1st to May 1st, 1790
Southern Mail arrives Tuesday, Wednesday, Thursday, Friday and Saturday, at 4 P.M.
Closes Sunday, Monday, Tuesday, Wednesday, and Thursday, at 9 P.M.
Eastern Mail arrives Wednesday and Saturday, at 6 P.M.
Closes Sunday, at 8, and Wednesday, at 9 P.M.

From May 1st to November 1st
Southern Mail arrives Tuesday, Wednesday, Thursday, Friday and Saturday, at 2 P.M.
Closes Monday, Tuesday, Wednesday, Thursday, and Friday, at 8 A.M.
Eastern Mail arrives Tuesday, Thursday and Saturday, at 7 P.M.
Closes Sunday, at 8, Tuesday and Thursday, at 9 P.M.

NYDG, 6 January.

Letter from New York

The Senators and Representatives are daily collecting. Those I have seen, bring information from their respective States, that the laws of last session give pretty general satisfaction—except the Judicial Bill, which is much censured in Virginia. All agree that the duties are every where collected with an unexpected punctuality.

[Portland, Maine] *Cumberland Gazette*, 18 January. This is probably from a letter written by Thatcher to the newspaper's editor, Thomas B. Wait.

OTHER DOCUMENTS

Elbridge Gerry to Alexander Hodgdon. Listing of ALS, *Libbie Catalog* (17–21 March 1891):item 3773.

Benjamin Goodhue to Stephen Goodhue. ALS, Goodhue Family Papers, MSaE. Addressed to Salem, Massachusetts; franked.
Caught a "violent cold" enroute to New York, but has now recovered; Congress will probably soon proceed to business; $100 will be sent to Benjamin's wife Fanny: $30 for her, and $70 for his own account.

William Samuel Johnson, Diary. Johnson Papers, CtHi.
"Visits."

NYDA, 7 January.
Smith's (S.C.) illness prevented a House quorum.

NYJ, 7 January.
Wadsworth, Ellsworth, and Sturges arrived in the evening.

THURSDAY, 7 JANUARY 1790

Snow Rain (Johnson)

Moses Copeland to George Thatcher

I take the Liberty to trubell you with a few Lines in behalf of the Inhabitants of Thomaston Warren and Cushing Lying on sant. Georges River in the County of Lincoln [*Maine*] theay Lying to the Eastward of the Port of Waldoboro and in the County of Lincoln might Be annexed to the Destrict of Wichcaset and that Warren might be a port of Delivrey as that Lyeth at the Head of Navagation on St. Georges River and a place of the most bisness and Thomaston not being much more then half the distance to Wichcaset then to Penobscut and the Road much befor the Sellect men of Thomaston are about to Right to you on the Subject and the Prinsabell Inhabetants of Warren and Cushing are about sending a petition to Congress on the Subject but for fear thereof Shuld not arive in time I was Desired to Send this Letter[1] and being Sensabell that you wold wish to make the Inhabatents Hapy.

ALS, Chamberlain Collection, MB. Written from Warren, Maine.

[1] On the same subject, Copeland wrote Knox on the same day, elaborating that Francis Cook and John Lee, collectors at Wiscasset and Penobscot, respectively, could not agree where to divide their districts. Knox's endorsement includes a note to "consult Mr. Thatcher thereon" (Knox Papers, Gilder Lehrman Collection, NHi).

Thomas Tudor Tucker to St. George Tucker

I have the Satisfaction to inform you of my Arrival here on the 26th. December, after a very rough & uncomfortable Passage, from the disagreeable Effects of which I have scarcely yet recover'd, for I was most wretchedly sick almost the whole time. We are just about beginning our second Session & have already a Sufficiency of Members to make a Quorum in each House, so that we shall soon proceed to Business. Our Friend, Mr. Page is arrived, & gives me the agreeable Information that he left you perfectly well & also your Family, which was the more pleasing to me as I had heard that you suffer'd severely by the Complaint [*influenza*] which has lately prevail'd throughout the States. I understand that my Friend Richard was to be married the Beginning of this Month. I beg you will offer on my behalf the most hearty Congratulations & good Wishes. I mean to write to him, but the procrastinating Spirit may happen to be powerful & occasion a Delay contrary to my Wishes. By the last Accounts from Bermuda receivd in Charleston our Friends in general were in tolerable Health. Our Sister of Sister of St.

George's[1] still very thin, but much recover'd. I have been extreamly uneasy about her but now flatter myself that she will be restored to Health. I have little to add at present except ~~th~~ my sincere Wishes that every New Year may bring an Increase of Comfort & Happiness to you & your's.

[P. S.] Theod[*orick Bland Randolph*] & John [*Randolph of Roanoke*] are well.

ALS, Tucker-Coleman Papers, Swem Library, ViW. Place to which addressed not indicated.

---

[1] The reference is either to the Tuckers's sister Francis (1740–1825), who continued to live in Bermuda, or to the wife of their brother Henry (1742–1803), who resided at St. George's in Bermuda.

Letter from New York

Yesterday by the arrival of Mr. Henry, of Maryland, and Mr. Maclay, of Pennsylvania, the Senate of the United States formed a quorum, and are now ready to proceed to business; and by the arrival of Mr. Schureman, of New-Jersey, Mr. Lee and Mr. Page, of Virginia, a quorum of the House of Representatives are also in town, but the indisposition of Mr. Smith, of South-Carolina, prevented his attendance yesterday, in consequence whereof the House were unable to proceed to business.

PP, 11 January.

Information from New York

This day there were Members Sufficient to make a Congress. It is said that North-Carolina has chosen Senators, who will speedily be forward, and that they are federal. That State has made it one of her proposed amendments, that Congress shall not assume the State Debts. One might be apt to imagine that the authors of this wretched policy feared that the citizens of America would be too happy, was the necessity of continuing DIRECT TAXES abolished.

[Stockbridge, Massachusetts] *Western Star*, 12 January.

OTHER DOCUMENTS

William Constable to Gouverneur Morris. FC:lbk, Constable-Pierrepont Collection, NN.

Robert Morris has written that he cannot be in New York City until 10 January; a quorum of both "senate & assembly" is expected that day

(7 January); is impatient for Morris's arrival, to consult about securities speculation.

Francis van der Kemp to John Adams. ALS, Adams Family Manuscript Trust, MHi. Written from Kingston, New York.
　　Comments on Adams's *Defense of the Constitutions*; asks for either Congress or the President "to interpose" with the Stadtholder of the United Provinces for the recovery of £7500 he was forced to loan to the Province of Utrecht before he immigrated to the United States; "one Single recommendatory letter to the american agent at the Hage, one note of him to the States general wil do the matter"; "Such an intercession is practised often by the Dutch Republic"; mentions the arrival at New York of Adam Gerard Mappa, and asks Congress to encourage Mappa's type foundry by taxing the importation of foreign letter types; the measure would benefit revenue, "literary performances," and the circulation of cheaper, domestically produced books.

George Washington, Diary. Washington Papers, MiD-B.
　　Joint committee of Congress visited at 1 P.M. to inform him that both houses had achieved a quorum; Senators Langdon, Wingate, Strong, and Few, and Representatives Scott, Livermore, Foster, Ames, Thatcher, Goodhue, Burke, Baldwin, and both Muhlenbergs dined at the President's.

NYDA, 8 January.
　　Paterson arrived at New York.

FRIDAY, 8 JANUARY 1790

Warm (Johnson)

William Samuel Johnson to an Unknown Recipient

　　I did not return an Answer to yr. letter of the 18th. of Octr. because my Power of Franking was suspended during the recess of Congress & no opportunity presented of writing free of Expence. I now enclose you Copy of the Act of Assembly of Connecticut[1] which upon the revision of the Laws of that State after the Revolution was passed without any application or solicitation as far as I know on the part of the Episcop[*alian*]s. or any other denomination of Protestants, but upon pure principles of justice & liberality I am very sorry to find that less liberality & Candor seems at present to prevail in N. Hampshire, & trust that they will soon discover that it is both right & expedient for them to conform to the general sense of Congress & of their sister States upon this subject who evidently intend that there shall be no distinction or preference between any Denominat[*ion*]s. of Christians but that all shall stand upon an equal footing in point of legal Protection. ***

FC:dft, Johnson Papers, CtHi. The omitted text discusses legal titles to unspecified church lands.

[1] The legal code of the state was revised in 1784 and published as *Acts and Laws of the State of Connecticut* (New London, 1784). Evans 18409–10. While maintaining a privileged place for the Congregational Church, the acts ended most discriminations against practitioners of other Christian denominations.

Walter Rutherfurd to John Rutherfurd

*** We continue to have a pleasant Season and are all well. Congress only made Houses yesterday, and this Morning the President delivered his Speech,[1] I was present, he marched thro' the Floor in great Form. the Houses on each Hand, followed by the State Officers, Aids des Camps and Secretaries, the Speech was very long. shall not give the Heads as I expect you will receive it. he has given a splendid Bill of fare, they already say more than they can take up, We had invited Company for to Day. the Chanr. [*Chancellor Robert R. Livingston,*] [*John?*] Watts and Duers [*William and Lady Kitty*], Ph. Livn. [*Philip Livingston*] and [*David Salisbury*] Franks—Paterson and Boudinot ~~were~~ I called on this Morng. and added them to the Party, which was truly brilliant, and much exceeded any I have seen this Season. we kept it up till past seven without a Man stirring. when severall of both Sexes moved to the Drawing room in Cherry street. The Chanr. called on me yesterday, seem'd much alarm'd by a Letter he had received from Elisha Boudinot, wanted to write to you, this morning told him of this Opportunity P[*aterson*]. had told B[*oudinot*]. you would not return Surveys on Ld. S's. [*William Alexander, Lord Stirling*] Warrants. I did not enter on the Merits, he called on R[*obert*]. Morris [*of New Jersey*]—gone to Phila.—You may suppose that we amply discussed, both the general and State Politics, Duer was very learned on the Finances which are now the grand Topick here. P. and B. seem highly pleased with what was done at Amboy last Siting, but still expect that next Sessions will call a Convention,[2] much talk of Pensas. Convention where Debates run high betwixt Wilson and Lewis,[3] the Sherriffs to be still elective by the People but for three Years only. I should have said the Speech was very gracefully delivered. *** Saturday last Miss Thomson was married to [*lined out*] Coll. Cole,[4] they don't see Company till in their own House, formerly Mrs. Bucher's. ***

AL, Rutherfurd Papers, NHi. Addressed to "Tranquillity," Sussex County, New Jersey; carried by Mr. Welles. The letter is misdated 9 January.

---

[1] For the first state of the union address, see *DHFFC* 3:252–54.

[2] New Jersey had no fixed seat of government and the legislature varied its place of meeting, in this case Perth Amboy. While several states replaced their revolutionary constitutions in response to the adoption of the federal Constitution, New Jersey retained its 1776 constitution until 1846.

[3] James Wilson and William Lewis headed opposing divisions within the Republican (anti-constitutionalist) majority at the Pennsylvania constitutional convention of 1789–90. The Wilson Republicans generally favored more democratizing provisions.

[4] Virginia Representative Coles married Catherine Thompson on 2 January.

George Washington, Diary

According to appointment, at 11 Oclock I set out for the City Hall in my Coach—preceeded by Colonel [*David*] Humphreys and Majr. [*William*] Jackson in Uniform (on my two White Horses) & followed by Mesr. [*Tobias*] Lear & [*Thomas*] Nelson in my Chariot & Mr. [*Robert*] Lewis on Horse back following them. In their rear was the Chief Justice of the United States & Secretaries of the Treasury and War Departments in their respective Carriages and in the order they are named. At the outer door of the Hall I was met by the Doorkeepers of the Senate [*Gifford Dalley*] and House [*James Mathers*] and conducted to the Door of the Senate Chamber; and passing from thence to the Chair through the Senate on the right, & House of representatives on the left, I took my Seat. The Gentlemen who attended me followed & took their stand behind the Senators; the whole rising as I entered. After being seated, at which time the members of both Houses also sat, I rose, (as they also did [*lined out*]) and made my Speech; delivering one Copy to the President of the Senate & another to the Speaker of the House of Representatives—after which, and being a few Moments seated, I retired, bowing on each Side to the Assembly (who stood) as I passed, and dessending to the lower Hall attended as before, I returned with them to my House.

Washington Papers, MiD-B.

OTHER DOCUMENTS

Benjamin Goodhue to Joseph Pierce. No copy known; acknowledged in Pierce to Goodhue, 31 January.

William Samuel Johnson, Diary. Johnson Papers, CtHi.
"Visits."

A Citizen, The Federal City ought to be on the Patowmack. [Baltimore] *Maryland Journal*, 8 January; reprinted at Alexandria, Virginia.

In discussing the first session seat of government debate, the author states that one member (Scott) "did not scruple to declare" that, although a Potomac River site was better than a Susquehanna site, he, as a Pennsylvanian, would vote for the latter.

NYDA, 9 January.
Wynkoop arrived at New York.

SATURDAY, 9 JANUARY 1790

Very Fine (Johnson)

Fisher Ames to James Freeman

Nothing is more pleasing to me than the reflection that I may be of some use to those whom I esteem—Your favor of the 2d puts such an occasion in my way. Any agency of mine in promoting the objects of your brother's[1] wishes may be depended upon I met him in the street soon after ~~the~~ my arrival in this city, and requested the favor of his visiting my lodgings, and shall be happy in seeing him often and serving him as much as may be in my power.

Inclosed is the king's speech [*Washington's state of the union address*]—The plan of finance is to be reported by the Secy. [*of the treasury*] next Thursday—It will cause debate in the house, and speculation abroad. The decision will do infinite good or mischief.

ALS, James Freeman Clarke Family Papers, MH. Addressed to Boston; franked; postmarked 10 January.

[1] Two of Freeman's brothers, Ezekial and Constant, Jr., sought federal clerkships during the FFC.

Pierce Butler to John Adams

I feel very sensibly the impropriety of Your Address to me in Senate yesterday[1]—As it was a very indellicate departure from the line of Your Official duty, I did expect that You woud while in the Chair, have made at least the same Apology You did out of it—Namely, that You meant me no offence—The strong desire I have of promoting and preserving harmony in that branch of the Legislature induces me to take no further notice of it at this time, but if ever any thing similar to it takes place again, I shall in justification of my own feelings, and of the situation in which I stand on that floor, be under a necessity of personally resenting it.

AN, Adams Family Manuscript Trust, MHi.

[1] After Washington's annual address on 8 January, the Senate referred it to a select committee, "rather too hastily as Mr. Butler thought, who made some remarks on it, and was called to order by the Chair [*Adams*]." Maclay's diary goes on to record only that Butler "resented the call, and some Altercation ensued" (*DHFFC* 9:180).

John Fitch to William Samuel Johnson

I have the happiness to inform you that we have brought the Steam Boat to a Very considerable degree of perfection,[1] at least so far that no one man can row a Ton, or 30 men 30 Tons, and hold way with us.

In Short Sir at this time we pass the Water as fast as it is possible for two of the stoutest made men to row a light Ships long Boat, which has fully Elucidated the practicability of Navigating the Mississippi by Fire, as it now takes one man to Navigate a Ton up that River.

I calculate that Navigation on the following principles, knowing that no Boat can be worked by the strength of men, with the Same Celerity as it may by the force of Steam.

I will suppose that Slavery is Lawful and commendible, as that is the cheapest way of procureing Manuel Labour, and calculate a Steam Engine suitable to propel a Boat of 60 Tons burthen at £750—I will suppose that Eight young healthy Slaves could be purchased for that money, then ad four men to them, the number that I would take in the Steam Boat, I could transport 60 Ton for the same price that they now can 12 Ton the Engine could also be kept in repair for the one fifth of the expence of maintaining those men, which would keep it in perpetual Repair, while the others would decline and die—This Sir I have ever esteemed, and now am convinced is a scheme of the first importance to the United States.

***

Worthy Sir, we expect that Congress will want a considerable quantity of Copper Cents and other Coin, which they will either ingage with men to do, or will set up a mint of their own—Mr. Voigt is well acquainted with the Business, and has worked in a Mint a considerable time—We flatter ourselves that our moral Characters are such, that we can give Congress every satisfaction that they should reasonably require for our faithful performance to superintend the business—Sir we doubt not your Patronage when you consider the great Sacrifise we have made for the good of our Country.

Permit us Sir, to supplicate you to write a line directed to the Cair of

Mr. Henry Voigt Watchmaker in 2nd. Street Philad., and to give us your opinion what measures will be persued by Congress, and what ought to be persued by us.

ALS, Johnson Papers, CtHi. Written from Philadelphia. The omitted text reaffirms Fitch and Voight's "wish once more to offer our best services to the United States." A postscript indicates that both the delivery of the letter and Johnson's reply were entrusted to "Mrs. Kroft" of Philadelphia.

[1] For more on Fitch's campaign for congressional support for his steamboat, see *DHFFC* 8:39–41, 51–55, 60–73.

Frederick A. Muhlenberg to Benjamin Rush

Before this reaches you I presume you will have seen the presidents Speech to both Houses,[1] which we this Day had before us in a Comittee of the whole House and agreed to prepare an Address in Answer. There is one part of it which I think deserves your particular Attention, I mean that of establishing a national University, and on which I think I heretofore saw a publication in one of our Philada. Papers.[2] If the Subiect was again taken up, and enforced in a more pointed Manner than the president saw fit to express it, it might tend to facilitate a Measure which in my Opinion is of the utmost Importance to America & perhaps pave the Way to obtain the Obiect of our last Conversation at Philada., than which I assure you nothing could give me greater Pleasure. Respecting our public Finances & particularly Certificates a variety of Opinions is held out, the prevailing one, among the Eastern Gentn. is that as the public had the Service or valuable Consideration for them, they ought undoubtedly to be paid—no Matter in whose Hands they were, but when the real Amount of the national Debt is once truly ascertained I think it will make even the boldest shrink. The Secretary of the Treasury is directed to report his plan in writing on Thursday next which will open the Budget. The Southern & [New] York Gentlemen in both Houses strongly contend that with the End of the last Session, all unfinished Business died of Course & that even such pieces of Business as were referred over must be taken up de novo. This Doctrine, taking the Word Session in a strict Sense, may be parliamentary, but I am convinced in [it] never would have been urged were it not intended against the Bill for fixing the permanent Residence of Congress. I am sorry Mr. Morris is absent so long on this as well some other Account. Oswald publications are here,[3] and are read by many with Avidity. They occasion many Sneers & shrewd Hints. As a pennsylvanian I feel myself hurt exceedingly, & wish from the bottom of my Soul that he may by a speedy & satisfactory Settlement of his Acct. put an End to them. How comes on our [*state constitutional*] Convention? I am happy to find Mr. [*James*] Wilson on the popular Side of the Question respecting the Mode of electing Senators. If my Information is right [*Thomas*] Mifflin took the other Side which I do not think will add to his Stock of Popularity which he is endeavouring so anxiously to increase. Habeat sibi[4]—Mr. Maclay lodges with us (we are now agreeably & comfortably situated at Dr. [*John Christopher*] Kunze's) & his constant Company is bothe entertaining & useful to me. I hope & think it will turn to our mutual advantage. Be pleased to remember me to Mr. [*Tench*] Coxe, and to my other Friends if any I have.

ALS, Berol Collection, NNC. Addressed to Philadelphia; franked; postmarked 10 January.

[1] For the address, see *DHFFC* 3:252–54.
[2] Muhlenberg referred to Rush's "To Friends of the Federal Government: A Plan for a Federal University," widely reprinted from *FG*, 29 October 1788.
[3] For the anti-Morris campaign waged in Eleazer Oswald's *IG*, see Another Correspondent and Detector, printed above under 30 November and 18 December, respectively.
[4] May he reap it.

Rufus Putnam to Fisher Ames

In conversation with you at New York in July last (if I recollect right) you made this a question "?can we retain the Western Country within the Government of the United States: and if we can, of what use will it be to them" I confess this subject is far beyond my abilities to do justice to, yet I feel myself so interested in the question that I can not forbear making a few observations thereon. For that those countries may *always* be retained within the Government of the United states and that it will be our interest they should is at present my desisded [*decided*] opinion.

That they may be retained, appears to me evident from the following consideration viz. that it will always be their interest that they should remain connected, now Sir if I can prove this; I conceive that the proposition that they may be retained &c. will be fully established; for it is unreasonable to suppose that a people will pursue measures inconsistent with their Interests: Although it is possible they may; it is true that Flour Hemp Tobacco Iron Pot ash and such bulky articles will go down the Missisippi to New Orleans for Market, and be there sold or shipped to the Atlantic States; Europe and the West Indies and it is also admited that the Countries west of the Mountains and lying below or the southward of the Junction of the Ohio with the Missisippi; may import Goods from New Orleans; and therefore it is absolutely Necessary that the People of the Western Country in some way or other at a proper period shall be possessed of the free Navigation of the Missisippi River But it does not follow from hence that it will be for their Interest to loose their connection with the Atlantic States but the contrary will appear if we consider; that all the Beef, Pork, and Mutton, (from a very Great part of the Western Country) will come to the seaports of Virginia Maryland & Pensylvania to market, as will also most of the furs skins &c. obtained by the Indian Trade to those places, and New York, much more to the advantages of the Western Country People; than they can be sent to New Orleans, or Quebeck. Besides all the Goods for carrying on the Indian Trade, as well as supplying the Inhabitants even to the Kentucky, and Wabash countries, are at present imported into that Country from Philadelphia, Baltimore, Alexandria, &c.—Much cheaper than they can be obtained from New Orleans, or Quebeck—and there is not the least doubt but when the Navigation, of the Potowmack; is completed, with the carrying place to the Monongahala, according to the plan of the undertakers; the transport of Good into the Western Country will be lowered fifty Per cent, and should other communications be opened which there is no doubt but there will be, between the Susquehannah, & Allegheny Rivers—James River, and the great Kenhawa, the expense of transportation will be reduced still lower. In short from the seaports of the United States; to Niagara Detroit, & even to the lake of the Woods, Goods can be Supplied cheaper than from any other quarter.

From this statement of facts which I presume can never be disprov'd, I conceive it fully appears, to be the Interest of the People of the Western Country to remain a part of the United States, if it be said they may be seperated, and yet retain all the advantages of trade here mentioned. I answer that is possible, but by no means probable; for (admit the seperation is not hostile) it is by no means reasonable to suppose, that the Legislature; of the United states; would pay the same attention to the subjects of a Foreign Power, as to their own. Nor is it to be presumed that those People will ever forget that while they remain a part of Union, they will have their voice in all the councils of the Nation, and that no law can pass, but what must affect their bretheren on this side the Mountains, as well as themselves, to be deprived of a commerce with the United states, would be greatly to the Injury, if not the ruin of that country; and to voluntarily deny themselves a voice in the regulation of that commerce, and trust themselves (without any check or controul) in the hands of those, whose Interest would be distant from their own is a folly I trust they never will be guilty of.

But it may be said there are advantages to be gained which will overbalance all this loss. Pray let us attend a little to this matter, ?will they Put themselves under the Vice Roy of Canada? what will be their gain here; a Legislative council of the Kings own appointment; gives Law to the province, except that the whole is under the controul of a Military Govenor. A few by permission from Lord Dorchester, or some body else may carry Good into the Indian country, but the returns must be made to Quebeck, surely this Government can never suit their Genius nor be for their interest Nor are the advantages to be derived from the Spanish Government much better; it is true that New Orleans will be a great mart for their Produce, but it is very doubtfull if they were Spanish subjects whether they would enjoy greater privileges than they might with out; the inhabitants would certainly have no voice in the matter but must be subject to the Despot, they could expectt no indulgence but what should comport with the interest of the Govenor and Spanish court and this they may reasonable expect some [?] should they remain a part of the United States; so if the object be to unite them with great Britton or Spain, I see nothing that is in the least degree worthy their attention.

But perhaps the Idea is that they should set up for a seperate Independent Goverment; this maggot I know is in the heads of some people; therefore we will consider of it a little and see if we can find it for their interest, and for arguments sake we will suppose the united States to consent to all this we will suppose more that they grant a free trade to the Subjects of this new Goverment; then pray tell me what they will be bettered for it—nay? will they not in a much worse situation? will they not incur a great expense to support their new Goverment, beyond what their Proportion to the old can possibly be; ?can it then be for their Interest to [be] seperated.

It may be Said they want a free trade to New Orleans and thence to sea that while they remain a part of the United states this is not like to be obtain'd that the interest of the Old States and theirs in this respect is not consistent with each other, that the Object is first to seperate themselves from the the Union and then to clear the river of the Spaniards, this I have heard is the language of some People at Kentucky; but ?is it rational, will the measure be for their Interest and if not for their interest are we to suppose the the measure will be pursued? have these people considered that the United States are deeply interested in opposing such a seperation? have they consider'd that driving the Spaniards out of the [Mississippi] River will not give them a free trade to sea? do they know that the harbours of Pensacola, and the Havanna, are so situated that a few cruisers from them, send into the Bay; not one vessel in a thousand going from or returning to the Missisippi, would escape falling into their hands. No Sir so far would such a measure be from giving them a free trade to sea; that it would put an end to their present market, and all reasonable proposals of a compensation for the loss. Nor do I conceive that the interest of the Atlantic states, and the Western country, as it respects the navigation, of the Mississippi; by any means interfere for if it is for the interest of the United states; that tobacco, Flour, Potash, Iron, and lumber of all kinds, with ships ready built; should be sent to Europe and the West Indies by way of Remittence for goods obtained from those Countries. If hemp, Flax, Iron and many other raw materials be of any use to be brought into the Atlantic states for the purpose of manufacturing, then it is the interest of those states that the navigation of the Missisippi should be free.

Thus Sir I have endevoured to prove that it is, and always will be, the interest of the Western Country to remain a part of the United States. I do not deny but what shuch circumstances may exist, as shall not only make it the wish of some; but of all the inhabitants of that country, to be seperated from the old States; but what I contend for is that these circumstances do not nor ever can (if I may be allowed the expression) exist naturely, I allow that should Congress, give up her claim to the navigation, of the Mississippi or ceed it to the Spaniards, I believe the People in the Western quarter would Seperate themselves from the United States very soon, such a measure I have no doubt would excite so much rage and disaffection that the People would sooner put themselves under the despotic goverment of Spain, than remain the indented servants of Congress, or should Congress by any means fail to give the inhabitants of that country such protection as their present infant state requires, connected with the interest and dignity of the United States, in that case such events may take place as will oblige the inhabitants of that country, to put themselves under the protection of Great Brittain or Spain; and I know also that in every country there are ambitious minds who paying more attention to the emoluments of office than the Public good may influence People to pursue (as the object of their happiness) measures that will end in their ruin. but these things make nothing against my proposition; for we are not to suppose that Congress will do rong, when it is for their interest to do right, and this brings me to enquire of what use these Countries may be to the United states.

And first the lands of the Western territory, and which are the property of the United States except, what claim, the Natives have to them, amount to at least 169,600,000 acres out of which must be reserved for future sale 14,133,333 acres agreable to the ordinances of the late Congress then 155,466,667 acres remain for Sale, now suppose this sold at half a dollar per acre (which is ⅙ below what any has been sold at as yet) and it amounts to 77,733,333.5 dollars, but it may be said this is the price in Publick Securities, and that the bonds will not fetch more than a quarter that sum in hard money: be it so and then the neat proceeds will amount to 19,433,333.7 Dollars, this sir is no trifling sum; but it is by no means the greatest advantage to be derived from those lands, three lots of one mile square are reserved (by the ordinance of the late Congress[1]) in such Township for the future disposition of Goverment and the local situation of those lots, is such as to command a high price, and at the end of half a Century, (in which time they are to cost Goverment nothing,) it is a very moderate calculation to rate them at four dollars the acre and then they will amount to 56,633,332 dollars, a sum sufficient to build and equip a fleet superior to any a Nation in Europe; we have before hinted that the produce of the Western Country will afford a great source, of remittance, for European, and Westindian Goods; and in a very few years that Country will be able to supply the Atlantic states, with such abundance of Raw Materials for making Duck and Cordage as will prevent all necessity of sending abroad for them, the particular advantages to be derived from the Fur & peltry trade, I am not able to assertain, however this we know that it is considered a very lucrative business, that it affords materials for Manufactories, much to the advantage of the English subject. and the advantage this trade must be to us, would undoubtedly exceed what it is or can be to them in the year 1773 I heard Mr. Chester[2] then Governour of West Florida, say that the duty paid in London on the American peltry, it appeared the Indians paid a tax to the King of two shillings sterling on each poll; encluding men women and children and why a revenue might not be derived to the United States from this qater [*quarter*] I know not.

Again while those countries remain a part of the United States they will pay the same duties on all import Goods, which they consume as the other subjects of the Union, which in case of a Seperation, would be totally lost, and the same observation equally applys to all the good furnished for the Indian trade. at present this revenue may not exceed 20,000 dollars; but in the course of half a century if we only suppose the number of inhabitants to be one million and the goods they shall consume to be at the rate only of three dollars and one third per each Person, (which is a very moderate allowance for an annual consumption). This only at five per cent will amount to 166,500 dollars per annum.

I am sensible that there will be some expence, attending the buisiness for the Indian tribes & presents we will allow 20,000 dollars a year for fifty years, which amounts to no more than one million of dollars. And we will allow three regiments of infantry and an artillary core equal, to a regiment of infantry, in expence and to this we will add a core of horse of like expence, then we shall have the annual expence of five Regiments, and we will allow the pay victualing and clothing of each regiment to annually cost one hundred thousand dollars. then the annual expense of the whole will be half a Million dollars.

This Sir is making a very extravagant charge against that Country for its protection yet when we taken into consideration the value of the lands when sold, the products of the country for remittence, and manufactories, the Peltry trade, with duties on imported goods sent into that country for the Indian trade, and the consumption of its inhabitants, the balance of retaining that territory as a part of the United States, appears evident to be very great. but there is an other point of light in which we ought to consider this matter for if we would know the real advantages, that country must be to this remaining united, we ought to consider what probable mischief will ensue by a division: and among these, may be reconed the loss of more than seventy five million of dollars in the sale of lands, and annual revenue of more than one hundred and sixty thousand dollars on European and West Indias goods; with all the advantages that can possibly arise from the peltry trade.

And what is a matter of serious consideration, it is more than probable (in case of a seperation from the United states,) that country wold be divided between Great Brittian, and Spain; for I can see no reason to suppose they will maintain a seperate existence; and then I suppose the your Western Country, will be the Allegheny Mountains, !a miserable Frontier this (and yet the best to be found if we give up the wester Country) that will require more expence to guard it than the protection of all the wester territory. The natural boundaries of the great lakes, and the Mississippi, added to the inhabitants, of the Western quarter, will give such strenght, and security, to the old states if properly attended to, as they must most forciably, feal the want of; in case of a seperation.

But I have no doubt, but you Sir, and all the members of Congress, will give the subject a full examination; and determin on such measures as will most promote the general good of the nation. and in that case one might I think reasonably hope soon to see the forces of the United States, in the Western Country so increased in number, that if the Brittish Posts, are not given up yet such establishments may be made in the Indian Country as to bring the natives who at present remain hostile into submission, and protect the Nations who are well disposed towards us; not only from their Savage Brethren who are so much under Brittish influence, but also from the people on the frontiers of Pensylvann., & Virginia, too many of whom regard not the orthority of their own states nor yet of congress more than the Savages themselves.

In this place Sir I will take the liberty to inform you, that in the year 1783 a petition was presented, to the then Congress, praying for a grant of land in the Western quarter; that the Utility, and policy, of establishing posts and forming settlements that should extend from the Ohio, to lake Erie, was clearly pointed out, in a letter from the Commander in Chief; and other papers accompaning said petition, & which I presume are now among the files, of the late Congress which I wish you to consult at your pleasure;[3] Beging leave at this time to add that I concieve that the more this subject is examined, the greater will appear the consequence, that it should be effected; as soon as practicable; for from Lake Erie, by a very easy navigation, and short portages, an army may discend by the Allegheny, Muskingum, Sioto, Big Miami, or the Wabash rivers, into any part of the Ohio Country, and so from Lake Erie, as from a common center fall on any part of the Ohio Country, extending more than one thousand miles in length, on that river, and thus the whole Western Territory, is liable to be took by surprise, while on the other hand; were there posts established on or near Lake Erie, even though we were not in possession of Detroit, or Niagara; the Natives disposed to peace would be protected, their numbers and attachments increased, the Indian trade greatly augmented, and that Country soon filled with inhabitants in such a manner that every reasonable fear of loosing it in case of a war, with great Brittain, would be forever banished Was this protection given, we might reasonable hope to see so numerous a body of well informed and well disposed Citizens placing themselves in that quarter, as would be able to counteract all the measures which any might attempt towards a seperation from the old States. And if this protection is given? might we not also hope from the lands already granted for an University, and others, appropriated for the support of schools in general,[4] with some further provisions of little expence; I say might we not hope soon to see such means of Education set on foot, as will have a most favorable aspect, on the manners of the People, of that Country, and remove the danger, that in a state of ignorance, with the art of designing men, they will always be under; to mistake their own true Interest. If Sir the Western Country is to be retain'd as a part of the United states, I conseive the immediate protection, and Peopling, that tract between the Ohio, and Lake Erie, has a direct tendency and is the first link in the chain of arrangment, towards compassing the great object, and if neglected may prove an infinite mischief to the United States for it was in full confidence, that such protection would be afforded that the Ohio, Sioto, and other companies, have contracted for lands, to a very great amount. Now Sir unless this protection is given, these contracts must all fail, (to the loss of many million of dollars to the United States) for of what value are lands, with out inhabitance; and who will wish to inhabit a Country, where no reasonable protection is afforded.

Another Circumstance which renders the present moment important, (in point of giving that district protection,) is the People settling at Muskingum, and the Miami, not having those prejudices, against the Natives which commonly arise from long wars, with them, are led into such a line of conduct, towards them under the wise management of governor [Arthur] St. Clare, and other principle characters, as gives the fairest prospect of Peace and tranquility to the frontier in general. If such military force is established as shall make the Goverment of the United states in the Western territory a terror to evil doers, and a protection, to those as who do well.

I have already exceeded the common bounds of a letter, but there is one circumstance, I can not for bear mentioning, which is the opposition that many New England People and particularly Massachusetts, express against the settlement, of the Western Country, especially by their own Inhabitants removing thither. This opposition I presume arises from two scources viz. the drawing off her inhabitants and preventing the settlement of her Eastern lands [*Maine*].

As to the first I conceive it will make no material odds, for if they do not remove to the Ohio they will emigrate to New York or Vermount. While there are vacant lands to be com[e] at the Population in the cultivated part of the Country will remain nearly the same. I believe in old Massachusetts, the number of pools, has varied very little these many years; and the reason is obvious for within that tract there are no room for new settlements, of any consequence, And as to the Eastern Country it is a very fine Country for lumber, and in that respect is of great service to Massachusetts; but any considerable number of Inhabitants in that district more than to carry on this business, will be a diversion in destroying the timber that ought to be preserving that Country in general is not fit for cultivation, and when this Idea is considered, with the climate, a man ought to consider himself curst, even in this Work who is doomed to inhabit there, as a cultivator, of the land only. However I cannot suppose the Ohio Country, will much affect the settlement of the Eastern Country, because those people, who have not a double curse entail'd to them, will go to New York or Vermount rather than to the Eastward.

Massachusetts is in no danger of being depopulated for the Ohio Country, nor even heaven itself, will not invite them in such multitudes, as to lessen the present numbers. Nor on the other hand, will any policy prevent the migration of her Inhabitants, in such swarms as that her numbers shall not greatly increase, while there are vacant lands in any quarter to be had.

And to what Country, can the Inhabitants of the Massachusetts emigrate so much to their advantage as to the Ohio? is it not for the interest of New-England, that the wester Country should in their manners, morrals, religion, and policy, take the Eastern States, for their model? is the genius education &c. of any other people so favourable to republican Goverment as theirs, and should they not then by throwing in of their Inhabitants endeavour to take the lead and give the tone to the New States forming in the Western quarter.

Besides the products of the Ohio Country, will interfere much less with Massachusetts, or rather they will be of more Utility to it, than to any other of the Atlantic States, Tobacco, Flour, hemp, flax, rice, and Indigo, being the chief articles, for exportation, neither of Which are raised in Massachusetts, in any considerable quantities; but when the navigation of the Mississippi shall become free, will all find their way to the sea ports of that State; and much to the advantage of her Citizens; who shall be concer[n]ed in the trade.

I have only to add that however inaccurate this address may appear, yet none will deny but the subject is important, and I pray God it may have a full, and candid enquiry, by all concer[n]ed in the Councils of the nation.

LS, Putnam Papers, MWA. Written from Rutland, Massachusetts. Ames's docket reads, "a dissertation—Gen. Putnum very good." The editors have silently corrected mistranscriptions using Putnam's draft in his papers at Marietta College, Marietta, Ohio. In a draft letter to Manasseh Cutler, dated from Rutland, Massachusetts, on 21 December 1789, Putnam indicated that he was holding his letter to Ames until Cutler "should first inspect it." For that purpose, as well as "to consult further on the measurs to be taken with Congress" (on the payment for part of the Ohio Company's purchase?), he requests that they meet in Boston on 7 January (Cutler Papers, IEN).

[1] The sale of western lands in the public domain was regulated by the Ordinance of 1785, which reserved to Congress for future sale four of the thirty-six square mile sections into which each township was to be divided (*JCC* 28:375–81).
[2] Peter Chester (1717/18–99), a career soldier in the British army, was the unpopular and ineffective last royal governor of British West Florida, 1770–81.
[3] On 1 July 1783 Congress received a petition of officers of the Continental Army, dated 16 June, praying for their entitlement to lands northwest of the Ohio River (*JCC* 24:421n; Item 42, 6:62–71, PCC, DNA). Washington conveyed the petition with a cover letter, dated 17 June, which also enclosed a letter from Putnam dated the following day, elaborating on the petition (Item 152, 11:321–25, PCC, DNA).
[4] Under the Ordinance of 1785, lot number sixteen of each town's thirty-six one mile square lots was reserved for the purpose of maintaining a public school.

John Cleves Symmes to Elias Boudinot

I wrote you last June but have never been honord by the receipt of an answer—Governor [*Arthur*] St. Clair informs me that he brought out a letter from you for me but that the young gentlemen of his family on whom he depended to put up his papers, had some how unaccountably neglected that letter & left it at Muskingum [*Marietta, Ohio*]—*This misfortune I am sorry for as Capt.* [*Col. Richard*] *Taylor has long been on the ground wishing to hear from you before he attempts a settlement on your land.*[1]

His Excellency the Governor has Organized this purchase into a County by the name of *Hamilton County*, the County town is called *Cincinnata* the same that was formerly Losantiville. Our new Garrison Genl. [*Josiah*] Harmar has named *Fort Washington*. We have three judges of the Common pleas, six justices of the peace, and four companies of Militia of Citizens, viz. two at Columbia,[2] one at Cincinnata and one at this town. Capt. John Brown of Woodbridge is sheriff and Mr. Israel Ludlow is clerk & prothonotary—The settlements have increased considerably since the Ohio was in a state for boating. we number about eight hundred souls at the three villages exclusive of the troops which are about three hundred men.

The Indians are no longer to be soothed by me into peace and friendship as they have been until lately—the last party of Indians that have been in here, left us in October last, promising to return to us again in two Moons. They were as good as their promise—but instead of coming directly into the village as usual, they killed a lad of fifteen as he was hunting his mothers cows in the morning, this was done within the squares of the City—four days after this they murdered two young men of this village about three miles from this place—they have killed one man and carried off two others prisoners from Columbia—all this has been done since the Corn was hard on the stalk, the three last murders which was at this place was done about three weeks ago—These things I know they have done without provocation as I have prevented the Indians being insulted or affronted, almost at the hazard of my life, and loss of the good will of all this western world.

We are now busy in laying out the City at this place agreeable to the Instructions which I have received from the Committe of the proprietors. the plat stretches pretty well over to Miami but some of the squares are very much broken with gutters and short knobs or hills.

There is some uneasiness appears among the people of the town occasioned by the breaking up of the order of the village to make way for the City—one circumstance is in favour of the City, being laid out here; it is that there are several fine springs within the compass of the town—I hope that the proprietors will not fail to proceed in the business of building next season as on this depends the prosperity of the town.

ALS, Gratz Collection, PHi. Written from North Bend, Ohio; addressed to Elizabeth, New Jersey; carried by Daniel Symmes.

---

[1] Symmes was the prime mover behind the 1788 Miami Purchase of one million acres north of the Ohio River between the Great Miami and Little Miami rivers. Boudinot was one of the twenty-four investors and a half interest holder with Symmes in the Purchase's forty thousand acre tract that became North Bend, Ohio (George A. Boyd, *Elias Boudinot: Patriot and Statesman* [Princeton, N.J., 1952], pp. 149–50).

[2] Columbia, within the present-day limits of Cincinnati, was founded on 18 November 1788, at the junction of the Little Miami and Ohio rivers.

Alexander White to Horatio Gates

I delayed writing to you till I should be able to acquaint you that a Congress was formed—which event would have taken place on the day appointed by Law had not the Members from N.Y. N. Jersey and Philadelphia remained at home avowedly till they should hear of the arrival of the more distant Members This induced me to move for a Call of the House, which took place on Tuesday, but it seeming to give uneasiness to a number who were actually in Town, but thought their attendance immaterial. I acquiesced in omitting to enter it on the Journal—Wednesday we had a

Quorum of both Houses but Mr. Smith of S.C. being indisposed, the House of Representatives did not form till Thursday—Yesterday we received the Presidents Communications, and to-day appointed a Committee to prepare an Address in answer to his Speech—The Speech you have enclosed—We have no late European News—the Capture of Belgrade,[1] you have no doubt heard of—and we do not find the State of France materially changed of late—Our Journey was agreeable, considering the advanced Season—We lay by three days only on account of bad Weather—one in Lancaster and two in Philadelphia—and reached N. York that Day Fortnight on which we left home—The Family are much pleased with their Situation.

ALS, Emmet Collection, NN. Addressed to Berkeley County, West Virginia; franked.

---

[1] Belgrade fell to Austrian forces in the fall of 1789, as part of Catherine the Great's Russo-Austrian campaign to expel the Turkish Empire from Europe.

OTHER DOCUMENTS

William Constable to Robert Morris. FC:lbk, Constable-Pierrepont Collection, NN.
   Is convinced that after Hamilton's report on public credit is published, it will be too late to buy up state debt certificates.

Thomas Hartley to Jasper Yeates. AL, Yeates Papers, PHi. Written from Philadelphia; addressed to Lancaster, Pennsylvania; carried by Mr. Dobbins; answered 1 February by post.
   Will not relate news of the state constitutional convention, as Yeates's friends will do it; believes "there is not so much Harmony as could be wished"; encloses business documents.

Thomas Jefferson to James Madison. ALS, Madison Papers, DLC. Written from "Monticello," Virginia. For the full text, see *PJM* 12:469.
   Covers Jefferson's letter of 6 September 1789, which he wrote in Paris and then carried back to Virginia with him (*DHFFC* 17:1477–79).

John Langdon to John Swanwick. No copy known; acknowledged in Swanwick to Langdon, 12 January.

William Maclay to Thomas Ruston. ALS, Coxe Papers, PHi. Addressed to Market Street near eighth Street, Philadelphia; franked; postmarked 10 January.
   Was sorry not to see Ruston when he called on him early on the morning of his departure from Philadelphia; advises about speculation in state

lands, "but must request the favour of You not to mention my having written to You on this business."

Robert Morris to Alexander Donald. ALS, Mss. 2M8337a4, ViHi. Written from Philadelphia; sent to Richmond.
 Must set out for New York in a few days.

Timothy Pickering to Peter Anspach. ALS [?], Pickering Papers, MSaE. Written from Philadelphia; place to which addressed not indicated.
 Encloses letter to Wingate, introducing Anspach as the bearer, and other letters Wingate is requested to forward to Massachusetts; suggests he and Anspach correspond through Wingate.

Governor Beverley Randolph to the Virginia Delegation. FC, Executive Letterbook, Vi. Written from Richmond, Virginia. For the full text (without enclosure), see *PJM* 12:469; for the enclosure, see Hening 13:17–21.
 Cover letter enclosing state act "concerning the erection of the district of Kentucky into an Independant state."

George Thatcher to Governor John Hancock. FC:dft, Thatcher Family Papers, MHi.
 When he saw Hancock on his way to New York, he forgot to give his answer to the request "as I was leaving your house in October," for recommendations for state supreme court judge; provides an extensive reference for William Lithgow, Jr.

SUNDAY, 10 JANUARY 1790

Cold (Johnson)

John Fenno to Joseph Ward

***

The Budget is to be opened next Thursday—It was made a Subject of Debate yesterday whether the Secretary should appear in the House to make a verbal explanation of his plan, and finally a Vote passed that the House would receive his Communication on Thursday—the door is left open for his appearing, but it will be opposed, however I think the probability is that he will be admitted—A Committee is appointed to answer the Presidents Speech some oblique objections to a particular reply to the severall parts were made, on the old score of its being anti republican to *echo*. What *magic* there is in some *words*!

I think Congress will proceed with more decision & dispatch this Session than the last—It is in vain to reason with some characters—and as the public Sentiment is pretty well ascertained, the Antis will be less loquacious upon the subjects of disaffection to the Government &c. I hope for the pleasure of your Company, and think it very probable that your interest may be promoted by it.

*** —if I can weather out the present Winter, I shall make the Gazette productive next Summer I trust—but at present it is hard rubbing—Shall be very much obliged by your assistance in the *Guest*—as the Debates will interfere with my prosecuting it[1]—Your plan of Writing a Father's Advice &c. will be an acquisition to the world—The Weather with you has been fine—it has also with us—and in great favor to me & my family I assure you. ***

ALS, Ward Papers, ICHi. Addressed to Boston; carried by Capt. [*Thomas*] Barnard. For the full text, see *AASP* 89(1979):353–55.

---

[1] "The Guest," a regular feature of Fenno's twice weekly *GUS* beginning on 2 December 1789, was a series of meditations on philosophy, ethics, and fashions written in the form of letters to the editor.

Richard Bland Lee to Charles Lee

You will receive inclosed the President's Speech at the opening of the present session of Congress.[1] It opens an ample field. It will receive the greatest exertion of patriotism and wisdom to place our country in the situation—which seems to be his wish and that of every virtuous citizen. The Secretary of the Treasury is directed to lay before the house of Representatives on Thursday next his plan for establishing the public credit. It is whispered that part of it—is the consolidation of the debts of the states with that of the union—an attempt of this kind—I conceive impracticable at this time—and would I fear put weapons in the hands of the adversaries of the government which might be used very much to it's injury. As soon as it is presented I will forward a copy of it for your perusal—and the information of the town of Alexandria.

You would oblige me by forwarding the inclosed letter to Mr. R[*ichard H.?*]. Lee. Mr. Arthur Lee arrived here yesterday.

Securities ~~have~~ are from 8 to 9/—indents from 6 to 7/.

I have written to Mr. R. Lee that I shall take up the protested Bill which he drew & which I endorsed—you will therefore be pleased to apply part of the resources which may come into your hands on my account to this purpose.

[*P. S.*] Such information and documents as are necessary to enable me to promote the intrests of the Trade of the Potomack ought to be forwarded without delay—and ~~their~~ your opinions respecting the alteration of the districts of the federal courts, ought to be corroborated by a joint memorial from the towns of Georgetown & Alexandria. Col. Wadsworth informed me that the address from Alexa. & Georgetown[2] arrived at Hartford the day before he left it—and that it would be civilly answered.

We have near forty members in the house of Representatives. We have been much alarmed here with accounts of Mr. Madison's illness but were agreeably relieved last night by a letter from himself announcing his convalescence.[3]

ALS, Miscellaneous Papers, NN. Addressed to Alexandria, Virginia; franked; postmarked 11 January.

[1] For the address, see *DHFFC* 3:252–54.

[2] The address was a broadside dated 7 December 1781 and mailed to towns throughout New England to garner support for establishing the permanent seat of government on the Potomac. See *DHFFC* 6:1785–89.

[3] See James Madison to George Washington, 4 January, above.

From New York

***

The question whether the Minister should be admitted on the floor of the House to make verbal explanations was started[1]—and a vote proposed requiring him to commit any explanations which might be deemed necessary to writing—but this clause was finally expunged—and the vote stands simply thus, That Thursday next be assigned to receive his communications, by which you will see the door is left open for his admission—but should it be proposed it will meet with opposition, though I think it probable, that there will be a majority who will not be afraid of the light—Thus you see the budget is to be opened[2] next Thursday.

[Boston] *Massachusetts Centinel*, 20 January; reprinted at Portland, Maine, and Portsmouth, New Hampshire. The omitted text reports procedure relating to the President's state of the union address, and Hamilton's request to know when the House would be ready to receive his report on public credit.

[1] For the printed debate on this question, see *DHFFC* 12:4–7.

[2] "Budget" could refer to a purse or wallet in the late eighteenth century, but the phrase "a budget opened" was employed more specifically, at least as early as 1733, to refer to the

presentation of a finance minister's program. More figuratively, "to open one's budget" meant to speak one's mind, and it may have been in the sense of this double entendre that Maclay entitled his newspaper piece enclosed in his letter to Nicholson dated 30 January, and printed under that date, below.

OTHER DOCUMENTS

Abigail Adams to Mary Cranch. ALS, Abigail Adams Letters, MWA. Place to which written not indicated. This is a postscript to a letter of 5 January, above.

> Complains about the time consumed by public obligations and that living two miles from New York City forces her to close the letter or miss the afternoon church service.

William Bradford, Jr. to Elias Boudinot. ALS, Wallace Papers, PHi. Written from Philadelphia.

> "I shall be glad of information" regarding the views of the members of Congress, particularly on the subject of the national debt; details his exchange of Boudinot's Pennsylvania securities; relates news of Pennsylvania's state constitutional convention; his sister Rachel (1764–1805) sets out with Hartley for New York on Tuesday, 12 January.

William Constable to John Richards, Jr. FC:lbk, Constable-Pierrepont Collection, NN. A John Richards served as Robert Morris's clerk in 1789 (*PAH* 6:15n).

> Morris has not yet arrived; "they have attacked him most unmercifully" in *IG*; "the heavy Charges brought against him as a public defaulter & the large Sums mentioned have made an impression, & even affects the Credit of his Connections as some of us feel."

William Samuel Johnson to Robert Charles Johnson. ALS, Johnson Papers, NNC. Place to which addressed not indicated.

> Received Robert's last letter by Wadsworth; all are well; asks to borrow a copy of *History of the Council of Trent* by Paolo Sarpi (1552–1623) to loan to "yr. friend the Vice President"; encloses newspaper containing the President's speech.

John Page to St. George Tucker. ALS, Tucker-Coleman Papers, ViW. Place to which addressed not indicated. The letter is misdated 1789.

> Arrived on Tuesday night, still troubled by a stiff neck; Thomas Tudor Tucker is pleased to hear of St. George's disposition to marry; Margaret Lowther is pleased with St. George's poetry.

George Read to Henry Latimer. ALS, Carson Collection, Free Library of Philadelphia. Written from New Castle, Delaware; addressed to "Speaker of the House of Assembly," (Dover, Delaware); read to the Assembly on 15 January. The omitted text details the organization of Read's revision of the state statutes.

In accordance with the Delaware legislature's resolution of 24 October 1789, he explains that his slow progress in preparing state statutes for publication is due to ill health; because of illness, "I had hoped that I shod. have been excused from so early an Attendance" at Congress in April 1789, "and that by postponing my going for a time to have nearly completed the Revision above"; ill health upon returning from New York further interrupted progress; expects to be able to complete the task in the next month unless called away to attend the Senate "by Order from that body" or by order of the state Assembly.

Richard Stockton, Jr. to Elias Boudinot. ALS, American Bible Society Boudinot Collection, NjP. Written from "Morven," in Princeton, New Jersey; carried by Capt. (Jonathan) Snowden.

Asks Boudinot to purchase some book titles for him, and to send a copy of the Collection Act [HR-11?], which was not among those previously sent; hopes many days of the new session of Congress will not be wasted by the non-attendance of members; "the public expectation is high" and "the objects which demand your attention are great indeed."

George Thatcher to Jeremiah Hill. No copy known; acknowledged in Hill to Thatcher, 26 January.

George Thatcher to Sarah Thatcher. ALS, Thatcher Family Papers, MHi. Place to which addressed not indicated.

Sarah's letters of 19 and 26 December arrived the evening before; advises her on her difficulty in procuring hay from an "ungenerous" neighbor: "such is the education of some ~~one~~ men, that they are necessarily strangers to every sentiment of generosity—as well as justice & equity—And I dont know but they are to be pitied more than blaimed, since they are thereby as unavoidably out of the reach of the most common pleasures of socibility, as the more refined & exalted feelings of friendship & benevolence"; is happy to hear of the visit from their Portland friends; hopes she will be able to visit them the next winter, but "I fear you will have an arduous piece of business to cure the children & family of the itch—I believe I hinted to you in my last, that I am not without my fears that I am not clear of it myself"; received a "friendly Letter" last night from Na thaniel Fosdick; instructs her to tell King's friends that "he & his family are well—his children grow finely."

Jeremiah Wadsworth to Harriet Wadsworth. ALS, Wadsworth Papers, CtHi. Place to which addressed not indicated; signed, "Your affectionate Friend & Father."
    Trumbull gave him her letter last evening; "I shall attend to the memorandum"; requests some samples of "the fine Cotton"; arrived very well early on the evening of 6 January.

William Samuel Johnson, Diary. Johnson Papers, CtHi.
    "St. Pauls Ordination."

MONDAY, 11 JANUARY 1790

Snow Rain (Johnson)

Tench Coxe to William Paterson

I presume upon the slight acquaintance I had the honor to form with you while you were in Philada. in 1787[1] to enclose you a paper, which is intended to open the public Investigation of a subject of great importance. In consequence of an Application from one of the public departments[2] I have been led into three or four examinations of certain important points in our Customs, Commerce & Manufactures by which it has been manifested, that while our whole Revenues will not neat more than a Million & a half of dollars our imports of *the single article of foreign liquors* exceed *two* Millions & an half annually. To present this alarming fact to the public thro the Medium of a New York or Philada. paper would excite too much attention on and enquiry among my brethren in trade, against the present interest of many of whom it would operate very forcibly. I have therefore determined to broach it upon a smaller scale, & to mix it with other matter. The enclosed paper contains the attempt, in which you will see it is joined with some other points of real Consequence to New Jersey. My wish is that it may be sent by you, if you see no impropriety in it, to the East Jersey Gazette [*Brunswick Gazette*]. You may, if you think proper, inform the printer, that you was requested to put it into his hands without giving him my Name. It seems to be a happy moment to introduce this Subject, when your state legislature are turning their Attention to the promotion of manufactures. If New Jersey intends to maintain its proportion of respectability in the Union, Manufactures appear to be the principal means, for there are in the

State but few vacant tracts of tolerable farming lands. Your population being about 140,000 ~~people~~ and it being supposed we double in 20 Years New Jersey must send out annually near 7000 souls, which is the proportion upon every year. The only relief, at present, from this, is the improvement of the rough lands in the Northern and the sandy tracts in the southern counties, and the Subdivision of your improved farms. Manufactures however may come in aid of them, and as you have many raw Materials of your own growth & produce and as your state is remarkably accessible, both in the Eastern & Western division to foreign importation, there appears to be no impediment. There is one necessary step, which it will not be very easy to accomplish, but which ought to be taken soon. This is to fix your Government in one place, accessible by Sea on account of coal and foreign raw materials, and having a collection of people able to assist in the Business of Manufactures. On the best information I can obtain I am decided in favor of Brunswick & its Vicinity. It is your most safe port being a dozen Miles from any place to which large Men of War can come, and 25 or 30 Miles from the Sea. The competition of New York is more remote~~d~~ than that of Philada. from Burlington or Trenton, as every thing that goes to the two last places must pass by our City. It is on the post road, and is at the N.E. end of the shortest portage from the Waters of Delaware to the great inland Navigation ~~of~~ between East Jersey & Connecticut—In case of a war New York will cease to improve and this Rival of East Jersey may then even lose some of its people in favor of Brunswick, and New Yk. will be kept down by the towns up the Hudson & by the Connecticut ports in some Degree, while Philada. is without any near rival—If any river in your state can be improved to accommodate the heart of it with internal Water Carriage it must be the Rariton tho I do not know how far it may be found practicable. Two or three families here, and ours among them, who have pretty deep concerns in the landed interest of New Jersey, have had serious conversation upon the subject of your Manufactures, as they may be promoted to aid our lands. When I trouble you with so much upon this Subject, I must beg you, Sir, to consider that as my Apology for troubling you ~~with them~~—Permit me to add that as state Jealousies prevail more or less in almost every mind, I wish these Observations to be considered as confidential—You will oblige me by a Jersey ~~paper~~ Gazette containing the papers, if printed.
        ***

ALS, Paterson Papers, NjR. Written from Philadelphia. The omitted text relays greetings from Coxe's father William (1723–1801, a Philadelphia merchant) and the latter's request for aid in a legal matter. The enclosure in question may be the article in the [Philadelphia] *Columbian Magazine* (March 1790), "Address to the Landholders, and other citizens, of New Jersey, showing the practicability, and other advantages, of establishing useful manufactures in that State." Its attribution to Coxe is supported by the existence in the Coxe Papers of an undated draft of the "Address" endorsed by Coxe as "Part of some Essays for N. Jersey, sent to Governor Paterson for publication 1789 or 1790. N.B. some part was republished in the Columbia Magazine" (quoted in *Coxe*, p. 149n). No New Jersey printing has been identified.

[1] The acquaintance formed during Paterson's attendance as a New Jersey delegate to the Federal Convention between 25 May and 23 July 1787.

[2] Coxe undoubtedly alluded to the treasury department, to which he would be appointed assistant secretary less than four months later. Although there is no extant "application" to Coxe prior to that time, an unlocated letter from Hamilton, dated 26 October 1789, included queries to which Coxe responded on 30 November with an enclosure (also unlocated) on the subject of Pennsylvania's commerce (*PAH* 5:461, 569–70n).

Benjamin Goodhue to Samuel Phillips, Jr.

We formed a quorum of both Houses a day or two past, but have not yet enter'd upon any bussines of importance, neither is it probable that We shall, till the Secretary of the Treasury makes his report, on the subject of finance, which he is to do on Thursday, this will open a field of a very extensive, interesting perplexing and as I conceive of a most difficult nature, what his plans are, is kept a secret, but I am apprehensive from what is said, as well as from my own reflections on the subject, that it will embrace the debts of the several States as well as the debt of the Union, should this be the case, or otherwise, I think I can foresee inumerable difficulties to encounter before any measure can be ripened into maturity, of one point I am clearly convinced, that the creditors of the several States being such for the attainment of the same object, for which others became creditors of the Union, they are of consequence equaly worthy of regard and attention, and therefore if by our solicitude for making provision for the latter, the former should be left without any material resourse for its support, we shall be guilty of the greatest injustice and in the issue of perhaps the most ruinous ilpolicy.

As this important bussines unfolds itself, I will endeavour from time to time to give you information. Continental securities are now at 8/6. I shall take it kind if you will now and then drop me a line on the bussines and views of the General Court, and likewise your own observations on the subjects in which you may find us engaged and particularly the one mentioned in this letter.

ALS, Phillips Family Papers, MHi. Place to which addressed not indicated.

Epes Sargent to Benjamin Goodhue

I figure to myself that you are safely arrived at your place of destination, and have begun or are about to take up, the various important matters that will present themselves to you; as one difficulty is cleared another will step in its place, so that you will do well to be armed with an addition to your present stock of patience and resolution; could I be allowed the indulgence of anticipation, I should see you struggling on the great question of permanent residence, and if you are as successfull in the talent of management as heretofore, I augur no great advantages will be taken of you; it appears to me who has nothing to judge of but appearance, if you should be further distant than the susquehannah, that we shall feel like a distant province; not indeed beyond the point of attraction and influence of the great primary, but moved with less velocity than the interior satellites.

The provision to be made for the domestic debt, the liquidation of it, the exploring new resources, the assumption of the individual State debts, the irregularities of their contracting the apportionment of the unequal payments that have been paid by each respectively give a view of such a Chaos, as will require more than human wisdom to avoid being bewildered: added to these the time may not be far distant when you must establish some solid measures for protection and defence by Land and Sea. how will these great and necessary means be established? not easily to accomplish your designs; among them as one I dread the coming forward of a national Bank, it looks like the resurrection of the old pernicious system[1] in a new disguise; should it prove so, farewell faith, Law, government and social happiness; however my confidence in the ability and experience of those at helm, who have travelled over this deceitfull ground is such, that my fears are often eased when I consider tis their interest to avoid it: The review and amendment of your past transactions, will occupy no inconsiderable part of your time; with regard to the revenue, the operation and principle of which I have paid no small attention to, it must be acknowledged that the great outlines of it are drawn most admirably, some retouching might render it more perfect but considered together it may be pronounced a most excellent piece. The forms as prescribed by the Comptroller and decided on by the Secretary will methodize and of course facilitate the transaction of business if they are punctually attended, and I think every Officer must so conform from inclination as well as from interest, I confess there was an intricacy on their first view, but the more they are examined the more pleasure they give similar to what could be derived from the survey of a nice and curious piece of mechanism, when various parts were calculated with great exactness, the result of whose powers would be perfect; tho composed of an almost infinite number of movements. I should on this occasion do injustice to myself not to acknowledge the abilities and minute attention of the Secretary; there is no question I state to him however small, but I am certain of being honoured by his instructions, and those in a clear, decided and pleasing way. the exercise of the great and important department of the Treasury by such a person must afford an agreable presage, that an excellent tone will be given to all the inferior ones, which to the public will be productive of the most benign and salutary effects: the great disease we have laboured under and which has infected every class of people has been the want of punctuality; I think a gradual recovery from this complaint is more and more visible: for the Law like Truth is great and, must prevail; the Temper that was once subject to no controul or if it was manifested the greatest disquietude, subsides; when on enquiry it is well known that the compliance is universal; it is expected and submitted to; sometimes I endeavour to give a due estimate to and hazard some weak reasonings on those great priviledges, few nations enjoy in common with us, if we weigh well the Liberty of the press, freedom of Speech, rights of election and representation, trial by Jury, the independence of the Judicial, they ought to preponderate against a thousand little inconveniences that deserve not to be mentioned: to the inconsiderate clamours of the ignorant I oppose the obvious increase of trade and navigation since the organization of the revenue, contrary to the calculation of its most sanguine friends; besides when it is urged that trade will be *killed*, I remark on the example of the British nation whose trade is extended beyond the limits and encrease of any other people, their famous navigation act founded on the principle that the restraint of the Merchant is a benefitt to commerce has raised them to a summit of opulence and glory unknown in modern or antient day: Time and opinion, Sir, will establish your empire on a base too firm to be shaken.

At some future period I shall state to you the exact fees I have received in Office as well as those I have paid the Surveyor; it is more than I expected and altho' not sufficient to support me, it is better than so much given me, for the time I have been employed might otherwise have been vacant and this of all conditions would have been the most distressing be so good as to enquire at the Book Stores for the Genera Plantarum Linnaeus[2] 1 vol. 8vo Editio sexta. Holmia 1764 and the price.

ALS, Letters to Goodhue, NNS. Written from Gloucester, Massachusetts; franked.

[1] The fiscal system established in England after the Glorious Revolution of 1688.
[2] The *Genera Plantorum* of Swedish botanist and taxonomist Carolus Linnaeus (1707–78), first published in 1737.

[*Jeremiah Wadsworth,*] The Observer—No. XIII

Our national happiness must depend on the perfection of our union
Divide and govern, was the policy of Great-Britain to keep the Americans in subjection, before our emancipation from her authority; and it is now the

policy of those who wish to embarrass our councils and defeat the general government. The success of this artifice is manifest from the strange conceptions of each other, entertained by the inhabitants in the extremes of the United States, before our happy revolution. An intercourse in war and policy, has done much to remove these prejudices of ignorance, and we find that an American, whether he were born in New-Hampshire or Carolina, is a reasonable being, is capable of friendship and honesty, and if he be decently treated will return the civility. Ignorance on this subject is now so far removed, that when I hear any one disseminating prejudices against a distant part of the union, or endeavouring to prove an irreconcileable opposition of interests, I immediately suspect his heart of a political poison; and that a mischievous design against the government, rather than ignorance of men is his motive to asperse.

If there be any who cannot dilate their affections and policy beyond our ancient colonial jurisdictions, they ought immediately to quit the country, and seek an insular situation, where rocks and waves may be an unchangeable boundary to their brotherly love—for such, our parent Isle will be a happy retreat, where a charity and national system of three hundred miles in dimension will overreach the limits of territory.

We often speak of the union—this union now subsists in theory, and to make it permanent must be in feeling and in practice—it must rise superior to local attachments and boundary lines, to the interests and designs of a party—and must grasp the whole. In the policy of a nation the little passions ought to have no concern. In the homebred labourer, who supposes his own district to approach near the extreme limits of human habitation, we forgive the narrow apprehension and its consequences; but in a lawgiver of his country, or in any great public officer, we mark the weakness, and pity him as a man whose mind is less than his employment.

Gentlemen who possess delegated power, ought not to forget the particular interests of their constituents; but this part may be over-acted—a thousand questions of opposite interest, may be invented by a small degree of sagacity; to heal and not aggravate the opposition marks a great politician—to adopt a prevading system, in which sacrifices made by any one part of the union, shall be compensated by equivalent benefits, is the work of a skillful lawgiver. A desire of popularity in their own small districts, with some, proves a temptation to be very curious in discovering local interests; this may succeed for a time, but as the motive is not the most honorable, must in the end defeat the very purposes, which it was designed to promote.

In a country of free electors, where all have some property, there is a worthy pride on this subject, those are most respected, who unite an œconomical care of the peoples' interest, with a magnitude of mind commensurate to national purposes. A good subject had rather loose a few pence annually, than to hear it said his representative is a man of little and selfish views.

In the galleries of State legislation, I have often observed the feelings of every spectator, wounded, by the rising of a member to give information, *that the measure is against the interest of his town or country, and therefore he must oppose it.*

The influence of example is great! We have sanguine expectations, that the magnanimity and enlarged national views, manifested by *all* the gentlemen of our general representation, in their last session, will have a salutary effect on the feelings of those, who legislate for the particular States—When we remember that *every* mind was superior to territorial prepossessions, and enlarged as the empire to which they give law! When we reflect, how they considered themselves acting for a nation, and not for a single state; and that they were not known even to name their own ancient dominions, lest it should be constructed into an antinational meaning! When we observe that this spirit of concession brightened to the very close of their meeting, and shone with most dazzling lustre, on the question of *a permanent seat for government*; we are surprised by such superiority to human weakness! Such examples must be powerful on the feelings of every State! From this moment, a patriotism not confined to little limits will inspire our State councils! And every informed citizen, will consider himself a subject not of one; but of the United States!

The final adjustment of a revenue system, is a subject more exposed than any other, to the intrusion of local views and ancient prepossessions. Both rulers and people must expect to sacrifice some feelings, which were pardonable in our old state of seperation; but in our new state of union are wholly unfit. The man cannot be a good subject, who on a proposition of public measures, first enquires within himself, will this work an exclusive advantage to my own town, county, or State; with this spirit he will be forever grumbling at imaginary wrongs, and his brain will be distracted with political phantoms which have no existence but in his own jealousy and selfishness.

Either break the chain of union, and let every part get what it may, in the general wreck of property and honor; or make the union, as real as it is ostensible; and the only way for this, is to be one in legislation, in a judiciary system, in finance, in public funds, and in the manner of taxation and forming a national revenue. If in this great republic, there are thirteen treasury departments; each jealous of the other, and armed with such hostile cunning as the several States can produce and all of them *most jealous* of the general treasury: If every State is to have a plan of revenue from trade and business, artfully calculated to entrap its neighbours: If each State is to have a seperate debt, for which they must provide, by means the most anti-national in their operation; certainly our union cannot be perfected.

Demagogues and men of dishonest principles but popular views, will take occasions from the disorder to disseminate the seeds of contention between the States—the low passions of the people will be kept alive, and in the hour of passion they will submit to such State measures, as in the end must rob them of prodigious property; for it is not possible for the several States to provide for our debt, in so œconomical a manner, as it may be done by the united power. The old method of requisition on the States hath been found futile in the extreme; and for Congress in taxing the States, to have a motly process adopted to the several modes of assessing and collecting now used in each, will keep alive suspicions of partiality; and prevent order, regularity, and a similarity of decrees in the higher departments of the treasury. Uniformity in the manner of taxing and collecting thro' the whole, I consider as a principal step towards the perfection of our union; and to be uniform, the system of the United States, must overlook all local customs, and stand on its own basis—it must adopt a simple process, which may be understood by every kind of people in the union; and such I conceive is the proposition of a land-tax which I have heretofore made.

There is nothing in the circumstances, either of the eastern, middle or southern States, which in the opinion of an impartial mind, ought to militate against a plan of similar operation thro' the whole. People may have their jealousies; while the States were in treaty with each other, it was necessary to bear them; now we are one people, have a right to the same treatment, and all jealousy ought to be done away.

[Hartford, Connecticut] *American Mercury*, 11 January. For information on The Observer series, its authorship, and reprintings, see the location note to The Observer, No. I, 12 October, above.

[*Jeremiah Wadsworth,*] Observer—No. XIV

Excises and duties on trade, imposed by individual States, inconsistent with the rights of the Federal Constitution—An extract from an enquiry into the excise laws of Connecticut

IT is questioned by many good and sensible men, whether the Excise of a particular State is consistent with the federal Constitution—I will endeavor to examine the subject, with all the candor its magnitude requires.

The clause of the Constitution, on which doubts have arisen, is in the tenth Section of the first Article, in these words, "No State shall, without the consent of Congress, lay any Imposts or duties on imports or exports,

except what may be absolutely necessary for executing its inspection laws,"
The question then resolves itself into this point; whether the Excise of any
State is an *Impost* or *Duty* upon *imports* according to the letter and spirit of
the Constitution. To determine the question, let us first discover the true
meaning of the words, on which the whole depends.

The Taxes laid by government on goods, wares, merchandize or manufactures fall under the following denominations; *Duties, Imposts, Customs, Excise.*
Duties is a word of general import, comprehending every species of Tax
charged by the public upon any goods whatever. All Imposts, Customs, and
Excises, are *Duties. Impost* is strictly speaking a word of the same comprehensive signification. It is from the Latin *impono*, to lay upon or *impose*; or more
accurately from the participle *impositum*, any thing *laid upon* or *imposed*. It is
equivalent to duty, implying any *charge* or *price imposed* upon goods, and *owing*
or payable by law to government. This will be more fully proved afterwards.
Customs is derived from the French *coûtum* or *coust*, from whence we derive our
word *cost.* It signifies originally price, charge, toll or tribute; but according to
the practice of commercial nations, its proper sense is, *Duties* or *Imposts* upon
goods imported from foreign countries, payable by law to government, by
the importing merchant, at the port of entry or delivery. *Excise*, from *excisum*
to cut off, is "an inland imposition, paid sometimes upon the consumption
of the commodity, or frequently upon the retail sale, which is the last stage
before the consumption" Blackstone Com. vol. I. ch. 8.[1] It was originally
intended to be a Duty or Tax distinct from *customs*—customs being laid upon
imports and excise upon *home manufactures.* In general this distinction is still
preserved in England, excises being mostly laid upon articles manufactured
in the kingdom, and paid at the manufacturers. In a few instances, duties
are laid upon imported articles, as upon several kinds of spirits, tea, sugar,
coffee, which duties are called excises; tho' some of them are improperly
so denominated, being collected by the officers of the customs, upon the
articles in bulk. This is the case with liquors imported. See Postlethwaite
Dict. of Commerce vol. I. article *excise.*[2]

The general distinction however observed in England, where we are to recur for the true meaning of these words, is this; duties on imports, payable at
the port of entry or delivery are called *customs*; duties on home manufactures,
which are usually paid at the manufactory, are called *excises.* This distinction is made, where duties are laid on the *same articles*, and by the *same act* of
Parliament. Thus a duty on candles *imported*, laid by 3 Ann. I. is numbered
among the *customs.* A duty on Candles *made in Great Britain*, laid by the same
statute, is called an *Excise.* The same remark applies to skins, hides, soap, and
many other articles. The distinction then between customs and excise is well
established. See Postlethwaite, vol. I. articles, *customs* and *excise.*

What then is the distinction between *Impost* and *Excise*, or is there any distinction? The distinction seems to be this; Impost is a *genus*, of which Excise is a *species*. Impost is a generical term, comprehending every kind of tax. Duty or imposition upon goods, whether imported or home-manufactured. Excise is one species of this tax, viz. a duty on home manufactures, and in three or four instances, has been extended to the retail sale of foreign commodities.

As the foregoing definition of *Impost* is different from the common idea of it in this state, it is necessary to show the grounds on which it stands:

That *Impost* comprehends every species of tax or duty, whether on imports, exports, or manufactures, is decided first, from the derivation of the word; the original denoting any duty, charge or burden upon some person or thing. Secondly, the word has been generally used in this comprehensive sense by the best English writers. If so, then *Excise* is one species of *Impost*, and it is so understood in England.

The best compilers of dictionaries explain *Impost* to be any tax, toll or tribute. A land tax is an *Impost* upon land, in the true sense of the word; and the duty upon the portage of letters, upon chimneys, or hackney coaches, is strictly speaking an *impost* on those articles; the duty is said to be *imposed* by act of Parliament, and that which is so *imposed* is an *Impost* or an *imposition*. This explanation is founded on the best definitions of the word in our language. But not to rest on etymology, let us attend to common practice, or the popular sense of the word.

Postlethwaite, who treats expressly of commerce, defines *Impost* to be, "a tax or duty laid by the sovereign authority, upon such merchandizes as are brought from foreign countries; it is sometimes applied to a tax imposed upon domestic productions and manufactures." It does not appear by this definition, that a particular mode of levying and collecting a tax is necessary to constitute it an *Impost*. On the other hand, it seemes that any tax or duty may be denominated an *Impost*. To come nearer to the point; the Excise itself is called an *Impost*, in an ordinance of the Commons, dated 1649; the "*Impost of Excise;*" and Blackstone's definition of Excise makes it an *Impost*: for he calls it "*an inland imposition;*" imposition here signifying the *thing laid*, is precisely equivalent to *Impost*. So that the best writers on the subject of duties use Impost in the extensive sense before explained.

In this state, we have made a distinction between an *Impost* and an *Excise*; making one to be a duty payable on the first importation; the other a duty payable by the retailer. But the distinction is, in a great measure, a creature of our own; and it arises from our mistaking *Imposts* for *Customs*. We use *Impost* as the English do *Customs*: whereas both *Excise* and *Customs* are equally *Imposts*. Thus the word *Impost* does not make a distinct head of duties in English writers, for it comprehends all. Postlethwait, Blackstone, the Parliamentary register[3] use *Impost* in this general sense, and class the duties payable on importation or exportation, under the head of *Customs*—and the duties paid on the retail sale of tea, coffee, sugar and certain liquors, together with those paid by the manufacturer, under the head of *Excise*. We have, in our practice, confounded terms, using a *generical term* for one of the *species*; and it is a matter of some doubt whether the United States will agree to our sense of the word, in their construction of the Constitution.

But if the word *Impost* did not comprehend *Excise*, so as to restrain the States from laying the duty; yet the word *duty*, which is used in the same clause, would extend the prohibition to every possible method of levying money on imports. This word is universal in its signification, and the Convention, in wording that clause of the Constitution, seem to have been aware of some misconstruction of the word *Impost*, and therefore used the word *Duty* which is of unequivocal meaning. They used two words of general import; "*Imposts* or *Duties*." They could not use them in different senses, for all *Imposts* are *Duties*; but they used *Duties* as an explanatory term more generally understood. Thus far we meet with little difficulty. But an explanation of the subsequent part of the clause is not so easy. The question depends on the true meaning of the words *imports* and *exports*.

An *import* in commerce is an article of goods brought from a foreign country, either by land or water, chiefly by water. An *export* is an article sent from our own to a foreign country. Every article of home produce or manufacture may be exported; but is not considered as an export, unless actually sent abroad. Duties on exports are usually paid on the shipment of the goods.

Now it will be admitted that every article of merchandize brought hither from a foreign country is an *import*, at the time of entry and delivery; and of course, that no state can, without the consent of Congress, lay any tax or duty upon them at the time of importation. But the main question is, whether after the goods are landed, lodged in ware-houses, and opened for sale, they do not lose the name of *imports*. If they do, the States are not prohibited from laying duties upon them at any period, after they have lost that appellation.

I presume to assert that in the common language of merchants, goods imported never lose the name of *imports*. The wholesale merchant, and the smallest retailer, would call the goods in their stores and shops, *imports*; the *imports of the country*; the *imports* from England, Ireland and the West-Indies. These phrases are the usual language of the country. If then the common popular acceptation of a word, used and understood in all commercial countries, is to decide the point, goods brought from abroad never lose the name of *imports*. When should they lose the name? Is it when they are landed? When they are opened? Or when they are sold to the retailer? I confess I am yet to be informed at what particular period or stage of business this change takes place; or by what name the goods shall be called after having lost the name of *imports*. Should it be said that Congress, having exercised their authority over these goods and collected a duty upon them at the time of importation, can have no farther right over them; the goods are then within the jurisdiction of the State Governments, and subject entirely to their laws; this would not operate against my argument. For this unlimited power of the States might interfere with the commerce of the United States, over which Congress are empowered to exercise exclusive authority. Suppose a State should lay a duty upon the retailing of dry goods, of 25 or 30 per cent, the highest possible profit, and should enforce the collection with the most rigorous severity, would not such a duty entirely defeat the commerce of that State? Most clearly. But would not this interfere with the national commerce, which, by a clause of the constitution, is placed solely, under the control of Congress? It certainly would. But suppose three, five or more of the States should take a step, would not Congress have the power to counteract such ruinous measures? By the constitution they undoubtedly have such power. Now admit the principle, that the States can lay any, the smallest duty on imports, under the name of an excise, by the same right, they can lay the largest duties, amounting to an actual prohibition of the articles: And a constitutional power in the States to lay duties on goods imported, under any name whatever, is a power fully competent to ruin the whole commerce of the United States: A power which I am confident, does not exist. A right then in each State to lay *duties on imported articles*, will certainly interfere with our national commerce, but the Constitution of the United States prohibits every such interference, by giving the power of regulating foreign commerce and the commerce between the States, exclusively to Congress. The power then claimed by the States of imposing duties on imported articles in any shape, is directly opposed to the letter, as well as to the spirit of the Constitution.

There is another clause of the Constitution, the spirit of which seems to oppose this power in the States; viz. that "which declares that all duties laid by Congress shall be uniform throughout the United States." The design of this clause is not merely to prevent Congress from laying duties in a partial manner; it has this farther design of preventing one State from having superior advantages to its neighbor, and the infinite number of frauds which always grow out of a difference of prices in different parts of the country. But if the States have power to lay duties on articles of import, the evil is not removed; for some States purchase these articles in other States. If Connecticut can lay duties on dry goods, and call them *excises*; New-York can do the same; and that State also can, as Connecticut has done, define the word *retail* in the most arbitrary manner. The legislature may say that the sale of goods of less value than thirty, forty or fifty pounds shall be deemed a *retail sale*. This is assuming no more than Connecticut has done. But would not this measure lay a duty on goods purchased every day by our traders? The merchants in New-York must evade the duty, or *our* traders must pay it. Would not this be directly repugnant to the federal Constitution; one great end of which is to disarm the States of this power of imposing duties on their neighbors? I presume no man will deny that it would.

In every point of view therefore the *excise* of an individual State is inconsistent with the federal Constitution. It is repugnant to the *words* of it, for every species of *excise* is an *impost*, according to the true meaning of the word; and we may with equal propriety, say, the *impost of customs*, the *impost of tonnage*, the *impost of land tax*, or *the impost of excise*. The last phrase, *impost of excise*, is used by the best writers on the subject.

The duties laid by any State are repugnant to the *spirit* and *intent* of the constitution, for they actually do and may still more interfere with the commerce of the United States; and the power of taxing articles of import at any time or in anyway, if once admitted to exist in the individual States, will amount to a power of embarrassing trade, and even of prohibiting any importation at all. This conclusion is so obvious, that I do not see how it can be denied, for if we admit a principle, we admit all its necessary consequences.

The States seem to have power to lay *excises* according to the true original sense of the word; that is, duties on the produce and manufactures of their own States. Further than this their power does not extend. Congress also have a concurrent power with the States in this particular; "to lay and collect taxes, duties, imposts and excises." These words comprehend every species of tax upon real or personal estate. Monies raised on lands, polls, houses, cattle, &c. are usually called *taxes*. Monies raised on goods imported or exported are called *duties and imposts*. Monies raised on Manufactures and the retailing of liquors are called *excises*. But in a more enlarged sense, *taxes* and *imposts* comprehend ever method of levying money on real or personal estate. *Duties* is usually restricted to taxes on goods, wares and merchandize; *Excise* only being confined to a particular mode of laying duties, and for the most part, to duties on manufactures. These distinctions are well understood in England, and probably will soon be equally established and understood in America.

[Hartford, Connecticut] *American Mercury*, 11 January. For information on The Observer series, its authorship, and reprintings, see the location note to The Observer, No. I, 12 October, above.

---

[1] William Blackstone, *Commentaries on the Laws of England* (4 vols., Oxford, 1765–69).
[2] Malachy Postlethwaite, *Dictionary of Trade and Commerce* (2 vols., London, 1751).
[3] The first *Parliamentary Register*, published in London, began covering the debates of both Houses of Parliament in 1774.

From the Seat of Federal Government

Congress has not yet entered on any business—neither will any of consequence probably be taken up, till the Secretary of the Treasury makes his report (which he is to do next Thursday) on the subject of Finance: this will be opening the budget, and will doubtless contain matter of the most interesting perplexing nature. What his plans are is not even hinted; his communications are expected with impatience. A committee will shortly be appointed for revising the Collection and Coasting Acts; and it is hoped many inconveniences will be remedied, which are now found to attend them.

[Massachusetts] *Salem Gazette*, 19 January. This letter either paraphrases Goodhue's letter of this date to Phillips (printed above), or quotes another letter written by Goodhue.

OTHER DOCUMENTS

Elias Boudinot to Philemon Dickinson. ALS, John Dickinson Papers, PPL at PHi. Addressed to Trenton, New Jersey; franked; postmarked.
"The extreme hurry & Confusion of leaving Home for the Winter" prevented his writing sooner; discusses his management of a property for Dickinson's brother John; in a postscript, asks "what has become of my Brother Cadwallader—There is great Murmurings about the Absence of our Members."

Andrew Craigie to [Samuel Rogers]. FC:dft, Craigie Papers, MWA. The recipient was identified by a cataloguer.
Discusses an investment in public securities; Morris is expected in town "daily," and William Constable "wishes to consult with him respecting the propriety of securing the 400,000 Drs. whole Sum at the present prices"; there is no doubt of the state debts being assumed by Congress and put on "the same respectable footing with the other Debt"; will write again in a few days "& give you the results of the conference" with Morris.

Edward Fox to Andrew Craigie. ALS, Craigie Papers, MWA. Written from Philadelphia; place to which addressed not indicated.
"The Interest which Mr. Fitzimmons holds in our State paper must make him interest himself much in the Business of finance of the United States—if the Business is delayed in Congress—and nothing finally determined for or against Continental Creditors I have no doubt but the State Debt will become of still greater value than it now is—Whereas if the United States debt is funded, our paper can not exceed it much in present value."

Letter from a Member of Congress. *Boston Gazette*, 25 January; reprinted at Portland, Maine; Portsmouth, New Hampshire; Bennington, Vermont; Springfield, Massachusetts; Newport and Providence, Rhode Island, Litchfield and Middletown, Connecticut; New York City (*NYJ*, 4 February, *NYP*,

6 February); Philadelphia; Wilmington, Delaware; and Charleston, South Carolina. Number 18 of the widely reprinted Observer essays doubted that the author of this piece could have been a member of Congress, but the editor of the *Boston Gazette*, 22 February, asserted that he was and "were it necessary, his Name could be mentioned."

> "It is here asserted with great confidence that the Domestic National Debt is five-eighths owned by Foreigners and is thus registered in the Treasury of the United States."

TUESDAY, 12 JANUARY 1790

Snow (Johnson)

William Constable to Gouverneur Morris

*** Hamiltons report will be read on Thursday. It will recommend a general Adoption of the State Debts & an equal provision for the whole viz. an Interest of 4 ℔ ct. & a defered Interest of 2 ℔ ct. after 10 Years at least this I am led to believe is the system—He proposed providing for the Continl. Debt absolutely & the state Debts contingently, but One of his friends with whom I have conversed thinks it will be most safe to put both descriptions on the same footing & by this means He will secure the adoption of his plan by Combining the State Creditors & their Representatives without whose Aid as far as We can count Noses it will be rejected He will not in the first Instance bring forward the Ways & Means, his report Consisting of 100 pages goes largely into reasoning on the proposd taxes &ca. & I am told is very masterly—the Impost has produced 700,000 Nett Dlrs. the first 4 Mos. as Appears by the returns wh. are made Weekly by the Collectors a Moderate Excise on spirits in addition will suffice for the Interest on the whole Consolidated Debt wh. will Amot. to about 80 milns. Dlrs. it is imagined—Returns have only been made by 7 States as yet, so that We cannot ascertain their Amot. Exactly—those returned Amot. to 16 milns. & Comprehend as far as We can conjecture full One half—the Debt of So. Carolina principal is nearly £1,000,000 Sterg. as returned the price by report is said to be 4/. ***

FC:lbk, Constable-Pierrepont Collection, NN.

Nathaniel Gorham to Theodore Sedgwick

The Assumption of the State debts—by the National Government becomes more & more the subject of conversation & beleief—I have conversed with some judicious People from the Country in order to find the sentiments of the People at large on the business—& by what I am able to learn I do not find that there will [be] any objection to it—but on the contrary think it will be a measure pretty generally approved—unless the Antis. beat up a dust in the General Court about it—but even in that point some pretty good judges are of opinion that they will have no success—The most powerfull Engine will be to frighten the people with the idea of Land tax—as some of them by their writings in the papers have shewn—If Congress take the State debts I do not at present se that it can opperate to our prejudice—especially if the measure should be compleated before the first of next April when our second Bond becomes due[1]—because I apprehend that such an interference of a constitutional Goverment would so far vacate the contract as to leave no ~~room~~ rule to find the value but the price of the article at the time of the bargain—especally if the Legislature of Mass. who are one of the contracting parties should take any measure themselves by which the nature of the article is altered—is it possible to have the business in such forwardness as to come before the State Legislatures this Winter—provided it is to come before them at all—for I can easily se that one method may be taken by which they will have nothing to do with it—it is only for Congress to provide for changing the paper at their loan Offices & the business is done—some People here ~~in cas~~ thing [think] in case of an assumption that Mass. ought to give up our Bonds for the benefit of the public—~~that~~ Connecticut thier reserved Lands[?]—& Georgia & N. Caro.—make reasonable Cessions of thier back Country—& that upon this principle N.H. N.Y. Pensyl. & perhaps other States who may not be equally in debt may be brought to vote for the measure—for my part I should very well like the transfer of our Bonds—& I think I could convince Congress that we could close the Matter by making sale of Part of that Country to the public by which they could realize vast sums—you are the best judge whether it will do for you to suggest ~~the~~ to any confidential Friend the propriety of their ~~demanding~~ making the transfer of the Bonds a condition[3]—if I have time I will enclose an open Letter to Mr. Fitzsimonds which when you have read you may seal & deliver to him if you think proper—the propriety of it I submit wholly to ~~me~~ you—I will not write further lest I tire you—but beg you to write me fully by the first Post—& whether you have heard any thing of Ellicut & Chapin.[4]

ALS, Sedgwick Papers, MHi. Written from Boston. On this date, and again on 20 January, Gorham also wrote to Secretary at War Knox regarding this matter (Knox Papers, Gilder Lehrman Collection, NHi).

[1] By their 1788 contract to purchase the six million acre Genessee Tract owned by Massachusetts in western New York State, Gorham and Oliver Phelps agreed to pay £300,000 in depreciated state securities (equivalent to $175,000) in three annual instalments. Gorham

and Phelps later took in a handful of smaller coinvestors, including Wadsworth (Shaw Livermore, *Early American Land Companies* [1938; reprint, New York, 1968], pp. 197–98). Fearing that the federal government's assumption of the state's war debt would inflate the cost of purchasing such securities, Gorham and Phelps aimed for better terms for renegotiating their contract by having their indebtedness transferred to the federal government under the pretexts outlined in the remainder of this letter.

[2] The Western Reserve, in present-day northwestern Ohio, was the four million acres retained by Connecticut when it ceded its western lands to Congress in 1786. Congress understood that the Reserve was in compensation for the loss of Connecticut's claims to land within Pennsylvania that resulted from the December 1782 decision by a special federal arbitration court (*LDC* 23:314–18, 348). Most of it was eventually purchased by the Connecticut Land Company in 1795 for $2.50 an acre.

[3] Gorham floated essentially the same idea in a letter to Knox the same day, adding that Knox ought to refer it to Hamilton, Morris, and Fitzsimons, but "dont mention my having suggested the thing—you know how to manage—I think it would be more convenient for P[*helps*]. & me to be in the hands of Congress" (ALS, Knox Papers, Gilder Lehrman Collection, NHi).

[4] For background on the western boundary line of New York State, surveyed by Andrew Ellicott and Israel Chapin, Sr., in 1790, see *DHFFC* 8:191–94.

Louis Guillaume Otto to Comte de Montmorin

Although the return of Congress was set for the fourth of this month and the very temperate season has favored the journeys of the members, there were only eleven Senators and twenty-five Representatives there that day. It is especially remarkable that none were there from New York and Jersey, in spite of the proximity of their home. It was not until the eighth, the two Houses having a sufficient number of members to begin their deliberations, that the President went to the Senate in order to *open the session* or (according to those who reject English expressions as too favorable [*indulgent*] to royalty) to communicate *with the two Houses*. Ignoring this squeamishness of the exaggerated republicans, the President made his way towards the hall of Congress with the pomp suitable to the first magistrate of a great republic. His carriage harnessed with four horses, preceded by five secretaries on horseback and in American uniform, was followed by the carriages of the Chief Justice of the United States, of the Secretary of the Treasury and of the Secretary of War. He was dressed in a simple cloth of American make. On arriving in the Senate chamber, he occupied a raised seat made in the form of a throne, having at his right the President of the Senate and the Senators, at his left the Speaker and members of the House of Representatives; the rest of the room was filled with citizens and foreigners. He delivered the address, a translation of which I am pleased to annex here,[1] and, after having greeted the two Houses and the audience, he returned with the same retinue to his hotel [*mansion*]. Two days later the members of the two Houses of Congress went with great ceremony to his hotel to respond to his address. These responses contain only an approbation and a repetition of all that the President had said and the promise to occupy themselves at once with the objects which he had recommended. The President thanked them in a few words for their good intentions. Up to that point this ceremony looked completely like that practiced in England between the King and Parliament, but what seems less imitation is that the next day not one voice was raised in the two Houses to attack any part whatever of the address. They limited themselves to naming special committees for each object recommended in order to fulfill as soon as possible the desires of the President.

However little disposed I am, My Lord, to share the Americans' enthusiasm for the rapid progress of their new government, which without doubt is astonishing in several respects, I cannot refrain from observing that the success which the President has had up to now is unique in its own way and that never has the citizen of a free country enjoyed among his compatriots a confidence as pure and as universal. In more than one hundred gazettes, often very licentious, published daily in the United States, his name has constantly been respected; in an assembly composed of so many heterogeneous individuals as is that of Congress, he has always been spoken of with veneration. A success so constant cannot be attributed solely to public prejudice; a real merit and a faithful virtue must be the basis of it.

Although in the speech which I have the honor to send you, My Lord, the President expresses himself with the dignity suitable to the chief of the nation, he never loses sight of the regards which he owes to his fellow citizens. This happy mixture of authority and modesty maintains at the same time respect and confidence. While playing the role of the King of England he mingles in the crowd of his fellow citizens and appears to give them advice rather than orders, to propose doubts to them rather than principles, to indicate to them the road to public prosperity rather than to want to lead them there himself. To do justice to this speech in translation, it would be necessary to calculate carefully the effect of each word and to imbue oneself completely with the spirit of circumspection which characterizes the President in all his measures. He has pushed this scrupulous attention to the point of dating his speech not from *New York* but from the *United States* to indicate that the government had no fixed residence as yet and that all the parties which in the last session have become excited about this subject could still hope to see Congress established in their territory.

In looking over this speech you will undoubtedly observe, My Lord, that in spite of his great modesty and his circumspection the President does not lose sight of the means which ought to assure and extend his power. In this respect the interest of his compatriots agrees perfectly with his own advantage. He insists upon the formation and organization of the troops necessary for the common defense and on the fitness of designating a fund for foreign affairs in order to enable him to fulfill his functions towards the

Powers which could have relations with the United States. This last point is actually of the greatest importance and was entirely neglected by Congress in its first session. It is only by extending his relations to the exterior that the President will be able to affirm his authority in the interior. The House of Representatives is already beginning to take this subject into consideration. Some were for waiting for Mr. Jefferson so that he may give a summary of the posts to be created and the salaries which ought to be attached to them; but the greatest number rightly think that this arrangement must depend on circumstances and be left to the discretion of the President. This last opinion will probably be adopted.

The formation of an army will probably cause long debates and will be accompanied by great difficulties which I shall have the honor to set forth for you, My Lord, when the ideas are a little more mature.

One can read only with the greatest satisfaction the reflections of the President on the necessity of encouraging and watching over public instruction in a free country. They are so true that they impress one at first glance. The most educated people on the continent is that of Massachusetts. It is also the one in which the laws are best observed, the government has the most vigor, and the taxes are proportionately the highest. It is so true that men are never better subjugated than by reason.

To engage the House of Representatives to provide for the needs of the Department of Finances, the President adroitly recalls to them their own resolution. Instead of demanding funds from them, he seems to remember only that they have promised them and he gives to this promise all his approbation. He does more; he recalls their own words and while flattering them he imposes on them a duty to fulfill.

Such are, My Lord, the observations which the President's address suggests in the mind of an impartial foreigner. I would not finish if I applied myself to reporting the praises which the American public gives him.

During the recess of Congress this head of the nation has not been idle. By his orders all the departments have been busy collecting the documents necessary to enlighten the legislature. Never since the war was so much activity seen here. All the bureaus have supplied him with plans and memoranda to prepare the great session which is beginning and the success of which will decide the fate of the confederation. By the number of documents and copies which he had sent to him, it is to be presumed that his object is to form for his private secretariat a depository relating to all parts of the administration in order that he alone hold the thread of that labyrinth which the former Congress was never able to find. No important order is sent from any department whatsoever without having been communicated to him; he himself in his morning excursions inspects the bureaus and if it is impossible for him to see everything, it suffices that the employees are convinced nothing escapes his penetration and vigilance. He enjoys not only the honors of sovereignty, but he also bears its burden.

The first session of Congress has had for its aim only the general organization of the government. The second will be more important and more delicate: it will decide about the purse and the sword. All information relating to finances and to the country's defense has been carefully prepared and will guide the two Houses. It is hoped that their discussion will cause no schism. A third object, much less interesting, may give a more perceptible shock to the new confederation. It is the eternal discussion about the residence. The champions of the two parties are more excited than ever; they come with instructions, plans, offers of territory and even of money. A resolution of the Virginia legislature has again fanned the fire which was on the point of going out. It leaves to Congress the choice of a territory on the Potomac, sends it a copy of the plan of association formed to make this river navigable, offers a subscription of 120,000 dollars to construct the hotels and houses necessary for the reception of Congress, and it invites the legislature of Maryland to pay half of it.[2] The latter answers that it is too busy to consider this project, apparently because it prefers that the government be settled on the Susquehanna. Be that as it may, the Southern party is fortified by the accession of North Carolina whose Senators and Representatives have already arrived here and whose interest is evidently to establish Congress on the Potomac. I so often, My Lord, make mention of this trivial discussion only because it is pursued here very heatedly and because it has already nearly broken up the confederation.

The legislature of New York is also assembled at this moment. This little star which has so often misled the helmsmen of the former government[3] is today eclipsed by the luster of Congress. They hardly trouble themselves about what it is going to do, because they cease to fear it. They know that it is well disposed towards the new government. It has presented to General Washington a respectful address to which he replied very affectionately.[4] These addresses are in America of very great resource in giving importance to the principal personages, but in order to make them more efficacious it would perhaps be prudent to be less prodigal with them. The Virginia legislature has had one of them presented to Monsieur Jefferson by two Senators. Although the merit and the services of this minister are very great, it seems that they could put more nuances between the respects due to the head of the nation and those which they show to a servant of the public.

O'Dwyer, pp. 412–16. Otto's letters included in *DHFFC* were usually written over the course of days, and even weeks, following the day they were begun.

[1] Washington's first state of the union address is printed in *DHFFC* 3:252–54.

[2] Otto refers here to two resolutions passed by the Virginia legislature on 14 December 1789. On 29 January the governor forwarded them, with related enclosures, to Virginia's

delegation in the House, where they were presented and read on 6 July. See *DHFFC* 6:1782–89. The "association" was the Potowmack Company, chartered jointly by Maryland and Virginia in 1785 to improve the navigation of the Potomac River for commercial purposes. The construction of short canals and the removal or bypassing of natural obstructions opened the waterway to traffic by 1802, but other problems—primarily low water levels—hindered its profitability, and the company's charter was revoked, to be transferred to its more famous successor, the C&O (Chesapeake and Ohio) Canal Company, in 1828. George Washington served as the company's first president (1785–89); his will bequeathed his shares to help establish the "national university" he long envisioned for the nation's capital. Other shareholders were FFC members R. H. Lee, White, Stone, and both Carrolls, and frequent correspondents in these volumes, David Stuart, Horatio Gates, and Henry and Charles Lee.

[3] New York's antifederalist reputation was sealed in 1786 by its legislature's lonely refusal to ratify the proposed federal impost plan of 1783, which would have amended the Articles of Confederation by giving Congress power to collect a five percent duty on imported goods for twenty-five years. Despite considerable pressure, the New York legislature refused to yield on the matter of state control over the revenue collectors, and the measure died for lack of the unanimous ratification required under Article XIII (Linda Grant DePauw, *The Eleventh Pillar: New York State and the Federal Constitution* [Ithaca, N.Y., 1966], pp. 31–43).

[4] The New York legislature's congratulatory address to Washington, dated 15 July 1789, was presented to the President on 4 August; for the text and Washington's reply, see *PGW* 16:11–13, 168n.

Alexander White to Mary Rutherford Wood

I wrote you from Philadelphia where we were detained two days by bad weather. When we sat out the first day we reached Trenton 30 miles—2d. Day Brunswick 30 miles—3d. Day Elizabeth Town 20 miles—4th Day (being that Day Fortnight on which we ~~sat out~~ left home) 15 miles to New york—It was then a Fortnight to the Day appointed for the meeting of Congress, but the arrangement of Family affairs, and the reception and return of the Civilities, which the politeness of the inhabitants induced them to show to Strangers ~~was~~ afforded full employment for us—We just entering on business—So that the Ladies[1] will in a great measure will be left to themselves—they have been to one Assembly and once to Mrs. [*Martha*] Washingtons, these are the only Public Places (except the Church) which they have yet been at—the croud at Mrs. Washingtons was so great (being New Years Day) that I could have no conversation with her—Mrs. Washington returned our visit, but unfortunately Mrs. [*Elizabeth*] White and myself were both out—The President appears to be restored to perfect health—I enclose you his Speech at the opening of the Session—I have anxiously awaited to hear from you. My Family have all been blessed with perfect health and have met with no disagreeable Accident since their departure from home.

ALS, Wood-Glass Family Papers, Museum of the Shenandoah Valley Archives, Winchester, Virginia. Addressed to "near Winchester, Virginia"; franked; postmarked.

---

[1] White's wife and daughters.

Paine Wingate to Timothy Pickering

I left home yesterday Three weeks, when my Wife and Children were all well, as were the rest of our friends that way. I lodged one night at your brothers [*John Pickering*]. He is quite as well in health as usual, and seems to enjoy life with a good share of satisfaction. I had not opportunity to visit the several branches of our kindred in salem but was told that they were well. Since I arrived here nothing remarkable has happened. We have yet a thin Congress in both houses, though there was a Quorum of the members in Town on the third day of our meeting. The Presidents speech you have no doubt seen. We have as yet done little business more than to prepare an answer to the Address, which I suppose will be presented tomorrow. It contains little more than a repetition of his own words; and the precise sentiments of the Senate respecting any public measure to be adopted will not be collected from our reply. Next Thursday the Secretary to the treasury is to report his plan respecting the national debt & creditors. This is a matter of great expectation, what will be the result, time only must determine. It is not worth while to venture a conjecture on this subject, which a short time will of course decide. I am told that you are in a hopeful way for establishing a constitution very peaceably in Pennsylvania. I heartily wish you success. I expect this letter will find you at Philadelphia & I hope in good health. I shall be glad to hear from you whenever you have opportunity, and I still hope to see you one time or other, a satisfaction which I have not had for many years. I have no political intelligence to give you that I think of. ***

ALS, Pickering Papers, MHi. Place to which addressed not indicated.

George Washington, Diary

*** I sent written Messages to both Houses of Congress informing them, that the Secretary at War would lay before them a full & complete Statement of the business as it respected the Negotiation with the Creek Indians—My Instructions to, and the Commissioners report of their proceedings with those People—The letters and other papers respecting depredations on the Western Frontiers of Virginia, & District of Kentucky All of which was for their *full* information, but communicated in confidence & under injunction that no Copies be taken, or communications made of such parts as ought to be kept secret.
***
Just before Levee hour a Committee from the House of Representatives called upon me to know when & where they shd. deliver their Address I

named Twelve oclock on thursday, but finding it was there wish that it should be presented at the Federal hall, and offering to surrender the Representatives Chamber for this purpose by retiring into one of the Committee Rooms & there waiting untill I was ready to receive it I would consider on the place, and let them know my determination before the House should sit tomorrow.

Washington Papers, MiD-B.

Other Documents

Nathaniel Barrett to Thomas Jefferson. ALS, Washington Papers, DLC. For a partial text, see *PTJ* 16:102.
> Office seeking: consulship in France; has asked Dalton to deliver this letter and to discuss his application.

Pierce Butler to John Cogdell. FC:lbk, Butler Papers, PHi. Sent to Charleston, South Carolina.
> Office seeking: received Cogdell's letter of 14 August; will render him any service in his power, but heretofore the President has not consulted the members of the Senate on nominations.

Pierce Butler to Edward Trescott. FC:lbk, Butler Papers, PHi. Sent to Charleston, South Carolina.
> Office seeking: acknowledges letter of 8 December; the President has not consulted the Senators when making nominations; there will probably be an increase of appointments for excise officers; if so, Butler will recommend Trescott to the President.

William Constable to Garrett Cottringer. FC:lbk, Constable-Pierrepont Collection, NN.
> *IG*'s attacks on Morris "have travelled this far & made Impressions very unfavourable."

William Few to Governor Edward Telfair. No copy known; mentioned in Telfair to the Georgia delegation, 22 February, and in Georgia Executive Council minutes as read on 22 February.
> On the subject of Indian affairs.

Samuel Meredith to Henry Hill. ALS, John Jay Smith Papers, PPL at PHi. Addressed to Philadelphia.
> Clymer is well.

John Swanwick to John Langdon. ALS, Langdon Papers, NhPoA. Written from Philadelphia.

"You can not do better than by firmly Support[*in*]g. Publick Credit it is the very Basis of National Prosperity & will more than any thing else secure & Strengthen the Government and extend the Commercial & every other Interest of the Union"; encloses letter for Pieter Johan van Berckel.

John Trumbull to Harriet Wadsworth. ALS, Trumbull Collection, CtY. Addressed to Hartford, Connecticut.

"Your Father and your *two old* Uncles [*Jonathan and John Trumbull*] are to take possession of a House tomorrow where they hope to enjoy as much comfort this Winter as three *old* men can find in such a Batchelor style of Existence. They will want one to make buckwheat cakes for them in the morning, & to shorten the tediousness of the long winter Evenings by the addition of a vivacity which some of them begin to lose."

George Washington to John Christopher Kunze. FC:lbk, Washington Papers, DLC. For the full text, as well as background on the German born Lutheran missionary Rev. Anton Theodore Braun (d. 1804) and his solicitation of federal funds to help establish an Indian mission on the United States-Canada border, see *PGW* 4:540–42n.

In reply to Kunze's endorsement of Rev. Braun's suggestion, recommends Kunze judge the proper means of forwarding the business by consulting the opinion "of those Gentlemen in Congress with whom you may be acquainted."

William Samuel Johnson, Diary. Johnson Papers, CtHi.
"Visits."

WEDNESDAY, 13 JANUARY 1790

Rain Cold (Johnson)

Fisher Ames to George R. Minot

I suppose you are beginning, this day, your General Court labors. I wish you may have nothing to record, which a real patriot would not wish to find on the journals. If the spirit of hostility should expire in our State, the new government will not have much opposition to fear from any other quarter. A Mr. Hawkins, a Senator from North Carolina, has arrived. The letter of the Virginia Senators, addressed to that State (Virginia) legislature, was not received with approbation, on account of the antifederal sentiments which it expressed.[1] They would not even order it to be printed, and it was conveyed to the press by a private hand. I suppose you have read it. It seems intended to prevent the amendments giving satisfaction, more radical ones being wanting. Patrick Henry, it is said, advises all his partisans to support the Constitution, and if they wish to be secure against its supposed ill tendency, to get into the government. This is a very ancient mode of proving the faith by the practice. In this State all is quiet. The legislature is federal. The people get too much by the new government to wish it overthrown. I wish the parties in Massachusetts may not wage war again. The question of excise and assumption of State debts may possibly furnish the fuel for fresh heats. I think the assumption will be a serious article of our business in Congress. I wish, from our State, cooperation, not resistance. Our people pay great taxes. In this, and every other State, they are more moderate. They have not raised twenty-five thousand pounds in this State these three years. Their dry taxes[2] are very trifling. Why should our industrious people be crushed, to pay taxes to maintain State credit, and without maintaining it, too, when the United States by excises, &c., equally imposed, can do it effectually? Will they love their fetters so well as to contend against the hand that would set them at liberty? To-morrow the budget is to be opened. The report of the Secretary will excite curiosity, and produce, as every great object will, diversity of sentiment. How the business will issue, cannot be conjectured. I am positive there cannot be a safe and adequate revenue while the States and the United States are in competition for the product of the excises, &c. Wherefore the debts must be assumed.

I have written very dogmatically, and why should I affect doubts, when I entertain none?

Ames 1:72–73. Place to which addressed not indicated.

---

[1] Dated 28 September 1789; see *DHFFC* 17:1634.
[2] Dry taxes are internal taxes, as opposed to a tax on imports (an impost or tariff). They are imposed either as a head tax or as a tax on real or personal property.

Benjamin Goodhue to Stephen Goodhue

The Secry. of the Treasury is to lay before us his plan of Finance tomorrow, what it will be is a secret, tho' from what I hear I make no doubt he will embrace the State debts, but the minds of members are so various on the whole of this great subjects that it must necessarily take much labour and time before any measure is finaly agreed upon—this I think however from present appearances appears pretty clear, vizt. that the interest will not [be] very high for I suppose there are many disposed to give but a small interest, and from conversing with many who are the most liberal, I find few even of those extend their ideas beyond 3 ℔ Ct. I therefore conclude the interest will be likely to be 3 or thereabouts—I do not wish you to communicate my sentiments on this subject—please to deliver the inclosed Letters, without its being Known that I write Mr. [*Elias Hasket*] Derby.

I have it in contemplation to lay in a load of indian Corn against the Brig comes for either Bilboa or Lisbon. the prospect appears flattering and I am advised to it, it will cost about half a dollar to be deliver'd in march.

ALS, Goodhue Family Papers, MSaE. Place to which addressed not indicated.

Benjamin Goodhue to Samuel Phillips, Jr.

In my last I informed you of the pro[*ba*]bility of the report which is to be made tomorrow by the Secry. will in some way or other embrace the Debts of the several States, I am more convinced that will be the case then when I wrote you last, by conversing with several Gentlemen who are as likely to have a knowledge of Mr. Hamitons intentions, as any persons whatever, who make no doubt this will be the case, tho' his plans are yet a sercret—what fate his report will meet with is as uncertain as anything possibly can be, for I perceive Gentlemen have various ideas on this important subject—I make no doubt his plan may strike the minds of many Gentlemen with disgust at its first promulgation, for you Know We are all prone to think ourselves financiers, but yet I am of opinion considering the intricacy of such a bussines, that We may finaly give up our crude and indigested ideas, for a plan which a close and studied application has brought into existance, but I expect this will probably require much time and labour to effect—my mind is pretty much made up on one point, vizt. the rate of interest which will be allowed to the debt when funded—there are many members who I suppose will be zealous for keeping the interest low, and from conversing with several others, who are most liberaly disposed, I find none of them extend their ideas beyond 4 ℔ Ct. and most of them to no more then 3 ℔ Ct., from thence I conclude there is little chance of its being more then 3 and from present appearances will most likely rest at that or thereabouts.
[*P. S.*] You have my liberty to make a communication of those my sentiments in confidence to any of your friends you may think proper.

ALS, Phillips Family Papers, MHi. Place to which addressed not indicated.

William Paterson to Euphemia Paterson

I have not had the pleasure of receiving a Line from you since I left Home, but flatter myself that I shall in a Day or two have that Happiness. I have this

Moment recd. a Letter from Colo. [*John*] Bayard, who informs me, that you
have been low-spirited since my Departure. I left Home with much Regret;
my absence is not a Thing of Choice; it is incidental to my Station, the Duties of which it is incumbent on me to discharge. I am fond, passionately
fond, of the still quiet Scenes of private and domestick Life; I hate Noise
and Bustle; they are not congenial with my Soul. I beg, that you will not
suffer Despondency to have the Ascendant of you, nor a Moment's Gloom
to cloud your Mind on Account of my Absence. Be assured of the Constancy
and Fervor of my Affection, and that neither Absence, Distance, nor Time,
shall abate my Love to you. Remember, that I am in the Path of Duty. I hope,
that these Considerations, aided by your own good Sense, and the Virtues
of your Heart, will instantly restore you to your wonted Cheerfulness of
Temper, and Calmness of Spirit.

Yesterday I paid my Respects to the President and Vice-President; it was
Levee Day. This was the first of my going out, except a Visit of Friendship
to C. Justice Morris [*New York State Chief Justice Richard Morris*], with whom
I dined on Sunday, and another to Doctr. [*John*] Rodgers, who was not at
Home. I went out to Walton's [*Anthony Walton White*] on Saturday, where I
dined, and returned in the Evening. I keep much in my Room; and devote my
Time to reading some Law-Books, which I brought with me; and in prepar-
ing in some Chancery-Cause, which will be argued in the Winter or Spring.

Mr. Alvey,[1] I suppose, has delivered you the Gowns and Stockings, for
which I paid £2.1.6. [*New*] York Money. I did not see them—I hope, that
they are done to your Wish.

My Heart pours out its warmest Affections to you and my dear little Girl
and Boy [*Cornelia and William Paterson*]. I hope, that they are attentive to
their Books. The Improvement of the Mind is the most important Object
in social Life; may they never lose Sight of it.

ALS, Paterson Papers, NjR. Addressed to New Brunswick, New Jersey.

[1] Perhaps Obadiah Allweys, a weaver on Fayette Street, New York City.

William Smith (S.C.) to Tench Coxe

I must apologize to you for not having sooner answd. your several obliging
Letters, accompand. by the Constitn. of Pensa. [*Pennsylvania*] & your Book,
recd. this morng. by Mr. Heister. My thanks for your obliging attention
would have been presented at a much earlier period had I not been so indisposed for some time past as to feel myself incapable of writing. Since I have
attended the House, I have not had leisure to write, & now address you while
attending my duty in the House. Your Convention does not come up to my

expectations in some points, particularly the organiz[*atio*]n. of the Senate, which I fear, on their plan, will not answer the purpose of a check, but being constituted of the same materials, will have the same feelings & sentiments as the Repres[*entative*]s. & be influenced by their prejudices & passions.

The outlines of the Constitn. are pretty good & might have formed a very good basis for an excellt. govermt. Since my last to you, I have recd. a Letter from one of my Constituents,[1] assuring me that a Bankt. [*bankruptcy*] Law is gener[*all*]y. disagreable to the people of So. Cara. & wod. be extremely injurious to them: this intellig[*enc*]e. arriving at the very mom[*en*]t. when I was ready to present the Law, after having bestowed on it a consid[*erabl*]e. degree of patience attention & Labor, has embarassed me not a little: as our House have determined that all business shall commence de novo this Session, I am luckily released from the duty imposed on me the last Session & shall avail myself of that excuse for not proceeding any further in this business at present. The above information is strongly confirmed by my colleagues who have just arrived from home.

Mr. Madison is detain'd on the road by sickness, so that we are deprived of the assistance of that able member. The other members come in very fast. To morrow the Secretary of the Treasy. opens his Budget: various speculations will be occasioned by it & are already anticipated. I am entirely of your opinion respecting the Consolidation of the state Debts & think we shod. reject every plan not founded on that principle. A variety of opinions on this subject have already been broached in private conversations among the members of the two Houses & I apprehend much warmth & opposition from the discussion of this very interesting Subject.

ALS, Coxe Papers, PHi. Addressed to Philadelphia; franked; postmarked.

[1] Edward Rutledge; see Smith to Rutledge, 16 January, below.

George Washington, Diary

After duly considering on the place for receiving the address of the House of Representatives, I concluded, that it would be best to do it at my own House—first, because it seems most consistent with usage & custom—2d. because there is no 3d. place in the Fedl. Hall (*prepared*) to which I could call them, & to go into either of the Chambers appropriated to the Senate or Representatives, did not appear proper; and 3d. because I had appointed my own House for the Senate to deliver theirs in and, accordingly, appointed my own House to receive it.

Washington Papers, MiD-B

Peter to Mr. Fenno

I REQUEST you to re-publish the following tract, with the accompanying observations.

From the review of the Debates of Congress, in the 'Analytical Review, or New Literary Journal,' published by J. Johnston, London.

"Their parliamentary forms, language and constitution, are nearly the same, *mutatis mutandis*,[1] with those of the British and Irish parliaments: but the spirit and air that breathe in their speeches are more candid, sincere and patriotic. The several speakers, it is evident, are less under the influence of prejudice and political faction than ours, and more open to conviction.

The free and republican spirit of America appears in nothing more than in the toleration of taking down the public debates in short hand. This, if the British government shall verge, in process of time, towards republicanism, will be granted by our parliaments: If the genius of monarchy shall, on the contrary, overset the present political balance, the gallery doors will not be so easily opened, and less indulgence will be extended to those who report debates on the strength of memory."

THE liberality of mind which dictated the above, does honor to the human heart—The publication of the debates of Congress, have proved an unbounded source of information, instruction and amusement to the citizens of the United States. And altho from the circumstance of the *novelty* of the business, the various speeches have not been so fully detailed, as some persons have wished, yet upon the whole, more perfect sketches have perhaps never appeared in any country, than many of the publications have been, and the portraits of the speakers in general, have been held up to the view of the people thro this medium, in a very respectable point of light. The National Legislature has been identified, if the expression may be allowed, to the mental eye of every citizen. The transactions of Congress have been "open and above board." The voice of clamor has not been heard, nor have insidious reproaches of intrigues, conclaves, and dark proceedings grated upon our ears. The people have without doubt, been led to entertain the most favorable and honorable sentiments of the Representative body, whose enlightened and candid policy has not only kept the doors of their Gallery open, but suffered their debates to be taken on the floor of the House as a matter of course. Such a privilege once enjoyed (like the precious blessing of freedom) makes an indelible impression on the mind; and it would be infinitely better not to have realized the gratification, than, after having participated [*in*] it for a season, to be deprived of it for ever.

GUS, 13 January, edited by John Fenno; reprinted at Worcester, Massachusetts; Newport, Rhode Island; Baltimore; Fredericksburg and Richmond, Virginia; and Charleston, South

Carolina. The quotation from the *Analytic Review* appeared first in *NYDG*, 9 January. *GUS*'s version is printed here because of Peter's editorial commentary.

[1] All other things being equal.

[*Pelatiah Webster?*] To the Representatives and Senate of the United States, on funding alienated certificates

"*For the* price *of every thing*
Is just as much as it will bring."[1]

THE same may be said of the *worth* of every thing. The public securities of the United States have been sold, at an average, for three and four for one. This then was their real *worth*, as well as price. In this state of their value they were issued. They retained their nominal value no longer than they were retained by the original holder. After he parted with them, they sunk to one third or one fourth of their value. At this rate only they should be redeemed. How many widows and orphans, who put money into the funds, paid to them by law for gold, have been compelled by the scale of depreciation to receive only a tenth or twentieth part of the sum they expected. This was judged necessary to save our country. Now, why should speculators find more generosity, than widows and orphans found *justice* from the public?

But again—If the certificates are to be raised to specie value, pray let the poor soldier and widow, who sold their certificates for six shillings and eight-pence in the pound, be exempt from being taxed to raise them to their nominal value—otherwise you take three shillings and four-pence from that six shillings and eight-pence, which is the height of oppression, such as the King of Prussia would hardly have dared to inflict upon his subjects.

It was remarked during the war, that the greatest distresses of the Americans arose, not from the power or cruelty of Britain, but from the folly or wickedness of our own laws. The same may be said since the peace. It is not the navigation act of Britain[2] that injures us. Our *hard times*—such as, the low price of our lands, the want of employment for our mechanics and sailors, scarcity of money, bad payments, bankruptcies, &c. have all arisen from several of the states having paid eighteen per cent. for money.

The consequences of certificates rising to specie value will be as follows. A few men in every state will be found to possess the greatest part of them. Some will have two hundred, and others three hundred thousand pounds. With these sums they will be able to buy up whole squares of cities, and whole townships and counties in farms. Then we shall have aristocracy in good earnest—a true landed aristocracy, which is the only kind of aristocracy known in the whole world. Then, too, we shall probably have an order of nobility created among us—for the owner of a county could never brook to be called plain Mr. —. He must be the Earl of Clintonshire, or Baron of —shire. Every age and country has its delusions. The crusade expeditions were carried on at an immense expence to preserve the christian faith.[3] Under an equally *false* notion of supporting a *faith* of another kind, our country is to be sold at public vendue to the highest bidder.

It has been said, that if we discriminate between the certificates, who will trust the Congress in case of another war? I answer, this discrimination alone will enable us to bear another war; otherwise our country will be so impoverished, that we shall be unable to resist even a tribe of Indians. Besides, who will ever embark in another war, that recollects that speculators, and Amsterdam and London brokers, alone enjoyed all the benefits of the last, and that a great majority of the people reaped nothing from it but poverty and slavery. There is no injustice done to any body by this discrimination, but infinite injustice by a contrary conduct. Nothing but a discrimination can preserve, not only the credit, but the very existence of the United States.

Let the widows, orphans and original certificate holders look to themselves. They have been misled by joining their claims with the speculators. Let them unite, and petition the Congress for themselves, and justice will be done to them, for all classes of people are willing to pay them honorably, provided they will separate themselves from the speculators.

There is one more consideration that deserves to be attended to upon this subject. If we pay eighteen per cent. on our certificates, a great part of them must soon be bought up by foreigners, who will consider that interest as immense, compared with what they can get in their own country. The consequence of this will be, they will drain our country of all its cash, and in five or six years receive, in interest only, the principal of the purchase money they gave for their certificates.

Whoever wishes to see more upon the subject of a funding law, may consult the seventh Essay upon Finance, published at the time the funding law of Pennsylvania was passed, and written by a citizen of Philadelphia.[4]

PG, 13 January.

---

[1] A paraphrase of Samuel Butler's (1612–80) "The Value of a Thing," his three part satirical poem attacking the Puritans (1663, 1664, 1678).

[2] A general trade policy of England, dating to 1651 and consolidated into the Navigation Act of 1696, that prevented the importation of certain goods into Great Britain except in British vessels. Its enforcement strengthened Britain's merchant marine and led to the attainment of its maritime supremacy in the eighteenth century. England laid the cornerstone of its post Revolutionary War navigation policy toward the United States in an Order in Council dated 2 July 1783. Its principal provision was an exclusion of American ships from the British West Indies so that imports to or exports from the Islands had to be carried in British ships.

[3] Between 1095 and 1272, European Christians launched a series of nine "holy wars," plus

a Children's Crusade in 1212, seeking the forced conversion or death of Muslims and the recapture of Christian sites in the Middle East.

[4] Pelatiah Webster's *Seventh Essay on Free Trade and Finance* (Philadelphia, 1785).

OTHER DOCUMENTS

John Adams to John Trumbull. ALS, MiD-B. Addressed to Hartford, Connecticut; franked; postmarked.

Will no longer delay to write; proposes to him—as "penance" for the "Sin" of reading himself to death—either "a Walk of five miles a day, all at one time before dinner, or a Seat in some house of Representatives, at your option."

Elbridge Gerry to Samuel Hodgdon. ALS, Mitten Collection, Indiana Historical Society, Indianapolis. Addressed to Philadelphia; franked; postmarked.

Acknowledges receipt of several letters waiting for him upon his return from Massachusetts, including a letter from James (?) Thompson and a packet for Salem, Massachusetts, all of which he has forwarded; the post office charged postage because they were delivered during the recess.

Caleb Strong to Theodore Foster. Excerpts of two page ALS, *The Collector*, November 1897, p. 24, and *The Flying Quill*, June 1941, item 51. The address sheet remains in the Foster Papers, RHi; franked; postmarked.

"By the accession of North Carolina you stand alone. The safety of this Government and the collection of its revenue may require that measures disagreeable to your citizens should be adopted." "The idea of a perpetual separation cannot I am sure find place in the mind of one reflecting man. There has been no instance in the history of mankind when two contiguous and unconnected states have existed for a length of time in uninterrupted peace, and the sources of contention in the present case would be numerous."

George Thatcher to Dummer Sewall. No copy known; acknowledged in Sewall to Thatcher, 21 February.

Z to Mr. Wheeler. [Providence, Rhode Island] *United States Chronicle*, 14 January, edited by Bennett Wheeler.

Encloses summary of the Gerry committee report on the estimate of revenues needed by the federal government in 1789 (see *DHFFC* 4:55–58), so that readers can judge the truth of Sumter's letter of 24 August (*DHFFC* 16:1395–97).

From New York. [Boston] *Massachusetts Centinel*, 23 January. The date of the correspondence was mistakenly printed as 15 January. The correction is based on internal evidence.

No business of consequence will be transacted until Hamilton's report is received the next day; "It is not even hinted what his plans are; and they are expected with great impatience"; it is said there will be alterations made to the Collection [HR-11] and Coasting [HR-16] acts; "The confidential communications of the Secretary at War, are said to respect the Indians on our south-western frontier."

Letter from New York. [New Hampshire] *Concord Herald*, 10 February.

"Little business done" since the session convened; two days were taken up reading the report of the treaty commissioners to the Creek Indians and an estimate for protecting the southwestern frontier.

THURSDAY, 14 JANUARY 1790

Snow (Johnson)

Elias Boudinot to Hannah Boudinot

Tho late at Night, I cannot close my Eyes without saying a few words to my beloved wife, and to tell her how I was mortified by Mr. Austin [*David, Jr.*] not calling on me as he promised, by which I was disappointed ~~from~~ in writing a Line.

We had a very long Procession of the House this Morning in Coaches, preceeded by the Serjeant at Arms [*Joseph Wheaton*] on Horseback carrying the Mace, to the Presidents House,[1] to deliver the Address of our House in Answer to his Speech to both Houses at the opening of the Session.

We really cut a splendid Figure—After our Return, the Budget was opened, by reading the Secretary of the Treasury's Report on the funding of the National Debt—It is a very voluminous & well executed performance & does him great Credit, tho' it cuts out an amazing deal of work for us, and makes us look to a much longer Session than we at first apprehended.

I look forward with Anxiety to the first of next week, hoping my amiable Wife will not protract her Visit beyond that Period—If Mr. Austin is not now coming on his own Business, Mardsen [*John Marsden Pintard*] will go over—Mr. Paterson will be with you on Monday to try a Chancery Suit, but will not return till Tuesday and if it is a very fine day on Monday, I should not like you to miss it, otherwise he would be a good Gallant—You will not forget to take Paper Money to pay your ferriage—If the Carriage is not done, insist on bringing it away and I'll get it done here.

Betsy is bravely, and begs you will lend her your Fringe loom while you are here.

I rejoice to find that your Family Affairs go on so well, and hope you will be able to have every Thing very snug—Do pay off all your Debts—do not forget to send Mrs. Neal's £50—Miss [*Rachel*] Bradford I hear is at Princeton [*New Jersey*] on her way to this City, and I suppose will be with you before you set off & perhaps will come with you—Patty left us yesterday she was very well—Mr. L[*ewis*]. Pintard is here & desires to be remembered.

I hope my beloved Wife will not delay her Movements unnecessarily as every Body of your Friends are continually asking after you—I dined at Head Quarters this Day & Mrs. [*Martha*] Washington enquired kindly after you & wished for your coming.

It is just 12 oClock & I am called to go to Bed, tho' I have not my usual incitements to that Pleasure—May the protecting Angel who is commissioned to guard the favourites of Heaven, keep watch over the Sleeping Moments of Her I love—May that God in whom I trust be her defender & Patron in going out & coming in, that we may yet rejoice together in his continued Mercies.

ALS, Stimson Boudinot Collection, NjP. Place to which addressed not indicated; the salutation reads, "My dearest Love."

---

[1] The Washingtons lived at 3 Cherry Street until 23 February, when they moved to larger and more centrally located quarters at 39–41 Broadway. For the House reply, see *DHFFC* 3:260–61.

Paine Wingate to Timothy Pickering

I last Evening received the enclosed book with the letter accompanying it from Capt. [*George?*] Williams, with a desire to forward them to you: He informs me that our friends at Salem [*Massachusetts*] were all well on the 5th instant. I wrote to you two days since & shall only add that this day Colo. Hamilton sent in his report on Finance, to the house of Representatives. It is very long & I am not able to give you any account of the contents, having neither heard nor seen it. I can only say That a gentleman, who was at the coffee house in a large company after they had been in the galleries, told me, that it was the general opinion there, that the public securities would not appretiate but fall some on the report being known. I have no interest in speculations of that kind & can with propriety give no opinion of my own.

ALS, Pickering Papers, MHi. Addressed to Wilkes-Barre, Pennsylvania; franked.

George Washington, Diary

At the hours appointed, the Senate & House of representatives presented their Respective Addresses—The Members of both coming in Carriages and the latter with the Mace preceeding the Speaker. The Address of the Senate was presented by the Vice-President—and that of the House by the Speaker thereof.

The Following Gentlemen dined here to day. viz.

Messrs. Henry & Maclay of the Senate—and Messrs. Wadsworth, Trumbull, Floyd, Boudinot, Wynkoop Seney, Page, Lee, & Mathews of the House of Representatives—and Mr. John Trumbull.

Washington Papers, MiD-B.

A Familiar Epistle

To Mrs. Virginia, alias the Antient Dominion

Dear Sister,

We have lately seen some letters, which two of your confidential servants have sent you, calculated entirely to make mischief in the family.[1] We have always allowed your claim of rank, as our eldest Sister; and when your children and servants have pretended that your power was the greatest, your purse the heaviest, your farm the largest, and yourself a woman of more sense than any of your Sisters, we have never contradicted them, because we did not wish to quarrel about the matter—though we were sensible that a great part of your farm was untenanted and going out of repair, that you were constantly running in debt for your annual expences, and whenever the robbers have broke into your house, you were very poorly able to defend yourself, and could only alarm the neighbourhood, by dismal outcries, of "Help, Murder and Rape." But you ought to remember that we established our Copartnership on terms of perfect equality, and that we have advanced at least our equal shares in the public stock. You cannot therefore pretend any right to govern us in the business. As to your boy, Dicky [*Richard Henry Lee*], we have known him many years. He is a goodnatured fellow when he can have his own way, but as factious as Satan when he is contradicted. Besides, you are sensible, that he never could endure it, that we formerly appointed your Son, George [*Washington*], Steward of the household, and have lately given him a full Power of Attorney to manage the concerns of the company—when Dick, in the simplicity of his heart, always believed himself the fittest man of the two—Whereas you and all the world know, that George is worth as many of him, as Omnipotence could create to all eternity, if it had no other business to attend to. And now Dick and Bill [*William Grayson*] are finding fault with the contract of Copartnership, because it does not give you a controlling power over the whole transactions; and they are out of all patience and temper, because we are not willing to alter it. In the same manner some of your servants lately threatened that you would break your contract, and set up for yourself, unless we would send all our head-servants and agents to reside in your dominion under your immediate eye and inspection.[2] We have always wished to proceed in business in perfect union and equality; and notwithstanding these foolish speeches sometimes thrown out by your people, we have no idea, that you are in the least inclined to follow the example of our profligate Sister, who has run away from the family, and now keeps a house of evil fame, at the Sign of C****ns's [*Governor John Collins*] Head in Rhode-Island. We are still willing, as a matter of etiquette, to allow your superiority in point of age, rank and precedence, but shall not submit to the insults of your domestics. We wish you to take these matters into your serious consideration, and teach some of your servants a little better manners.

We have the honor to be,
With the most cordial esteem,
Your affectionate Sisters,
NEW-ENGLAND,
NEW-YORK,
PENNSYLVANIA,
CAROLINA, &c.

[Hartford] *Connecticut Courant*, 14 January; reprinted at Portsmouth, New Hampshire; Windsor, Vermont; Boston and Northampton, Massachusetts; Litchfield and Middletown, Connecticut; New York City (*GUS, NYDA*, both 20 January); Wilmington, Delaware; Baltimore; Fredericksburg and Richmond, Virginia; and Edenton, North Carolina. Based on "To N.E. N.Y. P. and C.," 5 June, volume 19, the editors believe the piece may have been written by a New England member of Congress. See also the reply dated 10 March, below.

---

[1] For the letters of the Virginia Senators to the Virginia governor and speaker of the House of Delegates, 28 September 1789, see *DHFFC* 17:1634–35.

[2] See the speeches of the Virginia Representatives on 3–4 September 1789 during the debate over the location of the seat of federal government, *DHFFC* 11:1399–1456.

Letter from New York

The budget has been opened—it consists of a very lengthy, systematical, clear report on the national debt, the ways and means: the general outlines are a consolidation of the whole continental and state debts, including principal and interest, without the discrimination even of facilities[1]—five or six different modes of funding to suit the different complexion of creditors. A reduction of interest on terms to 4 per cent. at the election of creditors, who shall become subscribers, by offering temptations to this voluntary act. The foreign debt amounts to about twelve millions of dollars—the domestic debt to about 28 millions, the arrears of interest to about 12 millions—the estimate of the state debts to about 13 millions—in the whole 75 millions—the whole interest at 4 per cent. to about three and a half millions. This is to be provided for with about 600,000 dollars, for current demands, from an additional duty on rum, wine, tea and coffee. In short it is impossible to give you any idea of this well drawn, comprehensive work: I can only say, that on first reading it appears candid, and to proceed wholly on a determined support of public credit. It is ordered to be printed, and shall send you a copy as soon as possible for your opinion.

PP, 18 January; reprinted at Providence, Rhode Island; Elizabethtown, New Jersey; Baltimore; Fredericksburg and Winchester, Virginia; and Edenton, North Carolina. The author was probably a member of Congress.

[1] Indents, a federal certificate indicating interest owed but not yet paid.

OTHER DOCUMENTS

Elias Boudinot to William Bradford, Jr. No copy known; acknowledged in Bradford to Boudinot, 21 January.

William Constable to Gouverneur Morris. FC:lbk, Constable-Pierrepont Collection, NN. Carried by the British ship *Liberty*.
   Hamilton's report on public credit was read that day, "but my attendance at the Bank [*of New York*] prevented me from hearing the greater part of it, & I have not had an Opp[*ortuni*]ty. of Conversing with any since the House Adjourned"; Senator Morris has not yet arrived at Congress; "I wish much for his Counsel how to Act as to the purchase of the Debt."

John Langdon to Hopley Yeaton. No copy known; acknowledged in Yeaton to Langdon, 1 February.

John Marsden Pintard to Elisha Boudinot. ALS, Boudinot-Pintard Papers, NHi. Addressed to Newark, New Jersey; carried by Col. (John Noble) Cumming.
   "Your brother," Elias, thinks Hamilton's funding system will create an opening for "some person or persons being wanted to purchase in Certificates," and that "if you wd. come over immedy. & make personal application in my favor I shd. stand a chance of succeeding."

George Thatcher to Constant Freeman. FC, Thatcher Family Papers, MHi.
Written to Quebec. The recipient is erroneously addressed as "Constantine."
   He knows no one in Quebec, but has been assured by Freeman's son (Ezekial or Constant, Jr.), now in New York, that he may enquire of Freeman
   regarding legal papers possibly located in Quebec, regarding a property
   claim in Maine for which Thatcher is attorney.

Daniel Hiester, Account Book. PRHi.
   Paid five shillings for a hack ride to the President's house for presentation
   of the House response to the state of the union message.

[*Pelatiah Webster*,] A Citizen of Philadelphia, *A Plea for the Poor Soldiers; or an
Essay, to Demonstrate That the Soldiers and Other Public Creditors, Who Really and
Actually Supported the Burden of the Late War, Have Not Been Paid! Ought to Be
Paid! Can Be Paid! and Must Be Paid!* (Philadelphia, 1790). *FG* serialized
it on 14, 15, and 18 January, eliciting responses and a defense by Webster
in its 16, 20, and 21 January issues. According to Webster (to William
Samuel Johnson, 1 February, below), printer Francis Bailey sent a copy to
each member of Congress. For the text, see Addendum, volume 22.

FRIDAY, 15 JANUARY 1790

Rain Thaw (Johnson)

John Lee to George Thatcher

   A presumption that information either of the situation or circumstance
of this part of the Country will be acceptable to you, occations this Address,
and to give you at once a view of the situation of all the several parts of the
District of Penobscot and Frenchmans bay I have Inclosed a correct plan
upon which I have inserted the names by which the several Townships are
now known—And that the information may be as compleat as possible I
have added to this Plan a list of the saw Mills in such District with the names
of the several streams upon which they stand.
   This Country is yet in its infancy the Inhabitants are few and many of
them new beginers in the world, have lately greatly improved their circumstances in the year Eighty five there was but one Vessel that exceeded the
Burden of Fifty Tons owned in the Port of Penobscot there is now twelve
Hundred Tons of Vessels Enrolled with the Collector—From present prospects I think there is not a doubt but what the increase of property will be
still more rapid.

The people in general being convinced of the necessity are disposed to comply with the Laws of the general Government so far as they apply to the circumstances of the Country—There are but *few* Vessels that go foreign Voyages from this District most of them being imployed in the coasting business which at present answers and carrying the wood to Market helps to pay the expence of clearing the land. Therefore the Laws that regulates coasting are of the utmost importance both to this vicinity and the Public— I doubt whether the coas[t]ing Law as it now stands can be Inforc'd so as to answer the expectation of Government. For all Vessels will not make Entry at the Collectors Office as the Law requires, many of them load at the distance of twenty miles from the Collectors Office which is near the center of the District, and a great proportion of these Vessels get their Cargoes from the Islands from which in stormy weather they are not able to pass in Boats and it would often detain them as long to call at the Collectors Office as it usually takes to perform a Voyage—This difficulty has induced some [to] urge that Coasters ought not to be obliged to Enter or Clear or to be subject to any regulation whatever, except that of taking ~~out~~ Licence yearly—But experience has convinced that unless Coasters are well looked too the Impost Law will by no means opperate equally and that by them the Revenue will be greatly injur'd The number of Vessels that are imployed a coasting that visit this District cannot be determined, they are undoubtedly numerous and consist of Vessels of every Burden from twenty to a hunderd and Twenty Tons and supply by far the greatest part of the Cord-wood consumed at Boston and the other sea Port Towns in the vicinity besides a large proportion of the Boards &c. that are Exported from those Ports—I am informed by one of the principal Inhabitants of Islesborough which town contains about seventy five families that there is Shipped yearly from that settlement upwards of one Hundred Cargo[es of?] Cord-wood for Vessels of upwards of fifty Tons Burden which is almost intirely paid for with Goods of Foreign Growth and Manufacture. Under the state Government by far the greatest part of these Vessels found means to avoid the regulation then prescribed—It must ever be very prejudicial for Government to Enact Laws and not have them carried into effect—The permitting Laws to be violated with impunity must injure the cause they ware intended to serve, which must ever be the case in a greater or less degree where Laws do not apply to the circumstance of the Country that they ware ment to bind—Coasters have so long trampled upon the Revenue Laws of this State with impunity that they now think that they are bound by no Laws.

The present sistem I humbly conceive may be improved upon, so as that the Revenue Officers may be able to inforce an observance of the Laws—the attention that I have heretofore paid to the state Revenue has convinced me of the necessity of all Coasting Vessels being obliged to Enter & Clear each

Trip or Voyage that they make. To prove the necessity of paying attention
to all Vessels imployed a Coasting it only need be known that Vessels have
and do frequently when returning from the West Indies touched at some of
the outer Islands upon this shore and have left what part of their Cargo they
thought fit have taken a load of Wood and proceeded to the port to which
the said Vessel belongs or have taken what Cord wood they could upon their
West India Cargo and proceed to the Westward and have landed the whole
without the least suspicion others have when falling in with a light Coaster
at sea shifted their Cargo on board of such light Vessel and have returned to
the Port where owned in Ballast and the Coasters after having taken Wood
to compleat a Cargo have gone and Illicitly landed the whole without the
least suspicion—These are some of the many methods that have been practiced with success to avoid the payment of Duties—In order to prevent as
far as may be such notorious frauds and to put all the seve[r]al parts of this
District upon the same footing and to take away every apology for not complying with the Laws—I humbly submitt the following being as I conceive
adapted to the circumstance of this District. we will suppose that

Fox Island	Sowadabscock
Thomaston Cushing & Warren	Condeskeeg
Camden	Eastern River
Duck Trap	Deer Island
Islesborough	Sedgwick
Belfast	Burntwal Island
Frankfurt	Blue Hill
Marsh Bay	

be each Ports of delivery for all Vessels that are the sole property of Citizens
of the United States and Ports of Entry and delivery for all Vessels employed
in the Coasting Trade that are Licenced agreeable to Law that shall Arrive
from any District in this State or the state of Newhampshire and at each of
these Ports let there be an Office kept by an Inspector to be appointed by
the Collector of the District to whom he is to be accountable which Inspector to have power to admit to an Entry any Vessel that has Licence to Coast
agreeable to Law that shall Arive as aforesaid and deliver to the Master of
such Vessel a Permit to land the Cargo from on board of such Vessel which
Permit shall be signed by the Collector and counter signed by the Inspector
by whom it shall be filled in such a manner as to describe particularly all the
several Packages to be landed and before any such Vessel shall be admitted
to an Entry the master of such Vessel shall make oath to the truth of the
Manifest to be by him exhibited and subscribed except in cases where he is
obliged to produce a manifest [lined out] sworn to from the proper Officer of
the port where he received his cargo—And it shall also [he] the duty of such
Inspector to go on board of all such Vessels as he shall admit to an Entry

where he shall have the least suspicion of fraud and examine whether the Cargo on board is agreeable to the Manifest exhibited by such Master and if he finds any or more Goods than have been Entered unless it should appear to have been a mistake he is to seize and as soon as may be to deposite them with the Collector of the District for the time being for trial—And shall make return weekly of all Entries and Clearances by him made to the Collector of the District. These Inspectors to receive the same Fees demandable by Law for Vessels Licenced to trade between the different Districts, the one Third of which Fees the said Inspectors shall pay once in every month to the Collector of the District the other two thirds to be in full for their services.

There being at each of the abovementioned Ports at least one Inspector besides him that keeps the Office to Aid as circumstances may require—I conceive that the Revenue Laws may be inforced so as that there will be few Evasions—there will then be at least two persons in each Port whose Interest as well as duty it will be to observe the movement of every Vessel—The inconveniency of the Office being at a distance from the extream parts of the District which is now complained of will be removed, And Vessels under fifty Tons Burden will have no reason to complain of being obliged to Enter & Clear to be chargable with only one half the Fees that are paid by larger Vessels—I conceive that at present they have a very great Latitude and that the Public has but very little security for there Good behaviour as almost the only dependence is upon the Oath of the Master who may be only nominal and possible may spent the greatest part of his time at home—These Inspectors thus stationed will know what is doing at all the saw Mills within their Ports by which means without the assistance of Boats they will be able to prevent the most notorious abuses of Law that have been practised both in this and Frenchmans Bay by Vessels from the Brittish Provinces of New Brunswick and Novascotia geting into the by Creeks and Coves where there is saw Mills and but few people and their loading their Vessels and geting to sea before the Collector who is at the distance of Ten or Fifteen miles can possibly unless by accident be informed of any Vessel being upon the coast, A good sale for the Lumber with the advantage of purchasing what they want Cheap and without paying any duties is a sufficient bribe for to induce all concerned in loading such Vessel to keep it a secret.

The Business of this Port was very considerable before the year Eighty five when the Legislature of this state passed a very unfortunate Law that prohibited the Exportation of the produce of this state in foreign Vessels which put an entire stop to the Trade of this Port—We are now happy to find that since the Establishment of the general Government we have a prospect of recovering our business as orders have already been received by the

Gentlemen in trade here, for square Timber sufficient to Load a Thousand Tons of Shipping.

I observe that the 24th Section of the Act of the United States that regulates Coasting directs all Masters of Vessels bound to foreign Ports to deliver to the Collector a Manifest of the Cargo on board of such Vessels &c.[1] This clause appears to be designed to enable Government to obtain an Account of Exports, but how this can be affected while the trade is continued that has been carried on for some ~~past~~ years past from the several Ports in this State to the Bay of Passamaquady With such papers only as Vessel usually have had that trade from Port to Port in this state, they go to the mouth of the River Scooduck [*St. Croix*] which is the Eastern bounds of this State and of the United States where they carry all the several Articles that are usually Exported from this Country—The place they most generally lay with their Vessels while disposing of their Cargoes is at a Cove on the West side of Scootuck directly opposite and within three miles of the Town of St. Andrews which is within the Brittish Government of New-Brunswick. Lumber and other Articles are conveyed to St. Andrews from this Cove with very little Trouble and there sold, Goods in return are brought a cross the River in Boats. The Inhabitants of St. Andrews with those of the other Brittish settlements in the Bay of Passamaquady undoubtedly encourage this Trade it is certainly much in their favor and the Government do not appear to disapprove of it—The Vessels imployed in this Business have all the advantage of a foreign Market in the sale of their Cargoes which makes a great part of the Business that is done in the several Brittish settlements upon that Bay by enabling them to load yearly a number of large Vessels for their West India Islands with the produce of the States—It will be difficult if not impossible for the Collector or other persons appoined to aid the Customs to know the movements of coasting Vessels for the distance and the time that it takes to perform a Voyage from this Port to Boston or to Passamaquady is about the same if the people who navigate the Vessels are silent upon the subject they have little to fear—The amount of foreign Goods Illicitly introduced into the States from this Bay must be very considerable—To prevent which I humbly conceive will [*lined out*] one day merit the attention of Congress.

To give you at once a view of the bay of Passamaquady and of the situation of the Trade there, I have inclosed you a Sketch of that Bay &c.[2]

ALS, Chamberlain Collection, MB. Written from Penobscot, Maine.

---

[1] See *DHFFC* 4:229.
[2] The copy of the "sketch" Lee sent to Thatcher is no longer with the letter, but the copy Lee sent to Hamilton on 29 December is in the Wolcott Papers, CtHi, and appears as an illustration on pp. 222–223 of this volume.

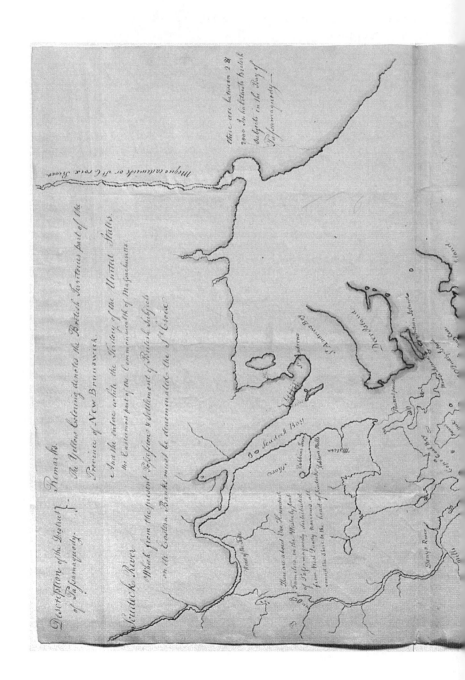

Passamaquoddy Bay. John Lee, federal revenue collector for the district that encompassed the bay, sent a copy of this map to Thatcher on 15 January to illustrate the numerous opportunities for smuggling of goods (primarily lumber) afforded by this congested inlet of the Bay of Fundy between Maine and the Canadian province of New Brunswick. Two weeks earlier Lee had sent this copy of the map to Alexander Hamilton, who evidently passed it to the treasury's auditor, Oliver Wolcott, Jr. in whose papers it remains (*PAH* 6:37). (Courtesy of Connecticut Historical Society.)

William Maclay to John Nicholson

I wrote to you a day or Two ago requesting every possible information respecting the funds of Pennsylvania, or more strictly speaking relating to her late funding System. I repeat the request. The late law however of that State passed in march last,[1] is not in my hands, nor do I recollect ever to have seen it. I beg that it may be among the papers which you send to me. The s[c]heme handed to the Representatives from the Treasury is for funding without discrimination; it is not Yet in print, but will soon be so; when it will be in every hand, and of Course you will see it. I am in Haste.

ALS, Miscellaneous American Autographs, Pierpont Morgan Library, New York City. Addressed to Comptroller General of Pennsylvania, Philadelphia; franked; postmarked 16 January; received 19 January.

[1] "An Act to Repeal So Much of any Act or Acts . . . as Directs the Payment of the New Loan Debt, or the Interest Thereof Beyond the First Day of April Next, and for other Purposes" was adopted on 27 March 1789.

John Page to Thomas Tudor Tucker

Ziff Ybjgure thanks you for your Irefrf & will soon make you a proper Return. feci quod tibi dixi fecirem. & am truely Unccl. I *manœuvered* well. Amicitia sola Fur. long thought was my View. & amicissimè se gessit— Quando me nuper a warry [?] Ybire ostensi, & non frigidum Amicam. Sensibility, Delicacy, Dignity & Pnaqbe were beautifully displayed sum sterum felix Adieu.

W. Cntr

AN, partly in code and Latin, Tucker-Coleman Papers, ViW. A translation (with thanks to Elizabeth Fisher and John Zialkowski, Classics Department, The George Washington University, Washington, D.C.) reads:
"[*Code*] thanks you for your [*code*] & will soon make you a proper Return. I have done what I told you I would do. & am truly [*code: happy?*]. I *manoeuvered* well. [*Margaret Lowther*] long thought only friendship was my View. and she has conducted herself accordingly in a very friendly way. Since I have taken myself from where I was to where I am now [*code*], and not as a cold Friend. Sensibility, Delicacy, Dignity & [*code*] were beautifully displayed I am happy again Adieu. J. Page"

Thomas B. Wait to George Thatcher

I began to fear that ~~my last~~ mine of the 12th ult. had not reached you. I am happy to hear that you have arrived at Newyork, and that your journey was agreeable.

It is a pitty that it does not happen to be in your power to assist Mr. [*Samuel*] Pierson—for in doing this there is no room to doubt but your own interest would have been greatly promoted.

A gentleman at Boston made him an offer, by the last post, of a Store in Wilmington, [*North*] Carolina, but it is a deadly climate—If he goes, I shall expect to see him no more ~~till the great day of Restoration~~.

If the present Session should prove a short one, you are hereby licenced, the very next time we meet, to tell me I was "WRONG."
***

To pray for the abolition of drawbacks appears to be extremely ridiculous—The Petition is a very imperfect piece of composition—~~it is disjointed, and disconnected~~ I am heartily sorry that the resolution of sending it [*to*] Mr. Ames is revoked—You must suffer very much in presenting it. However, there are undoubtedly imperfections in the Revenue Laws, and possibly the petitioners may have stumbled upon some of them—if so— Congress will undoubtedly attend to, & remedy them. When you present it, my friend, speak to it—speak aloud, and speak long—With us Your reputation depends altogether on your speaking—sense or nonsense—no matter—SPEAK.

My mother, my wife, and my little lambs are well—so are yours—We had a letter from Mrs. [*Sarah Savage*] Thatcher last Evening.

ALS, Chamberlain Collection, MB. Written from Portland, Maine. Part of the omitted text relates to a business matter. The remainder, concerning the petition from Portland on the Coasting Act [HR-16], referred to in the conclusion of this excerpt, is printed in *DHFFC* 8:416–17. A postscript dated 16 January is calendared under that date, below.

From New York

No business of consequence will be transacted until the House have the report of the *Secretary of the Treasury*, which will be delivered to-morrow. It is not even hinted what his plans are; and they are expected with great impatience. The Collection [HR-11] and Coasting [HR-16] Acts, it is said, will be revised, and some alterations made in them.

The confidential communications of the Secretary at War, are said to respect the Indians on our south-western frontier.[1]

[Boston] *Massachusetts Centinel*, 23 January.

[1] The House held secret sessions on 12 and 13 January. For the report on the southwestern frontier, see *DHFFC* 5:1279–93.

OTHER DOCUMENTS

Elizur Andrews to Jeremiah Wadsworth. ALS, Wadsworth Papers, CtHi. Written from Southington, Connecticut; franked; postmarked New Haven, 27 January.

Asks to have an order negotiated for him at the war office or returned if it cannot be done.

Lambert Cadwalader to "Madam." ALS, Cadwalader Papers, PHi. Place to which addressed not indicated.

Was unable to write before leaving Trenton, New Jersey, because of the press of business; arrived at New York City Tuesday evening and forwarded to James Monroe papers received from the addressee's brother.

Clement Hall to George Washington. ALS, Washington Papers, DLC. Written from Chowan County, North Carolina. For the full text, see *PGW* 4:584.

Cover letter with enclosures recommending Hall for port surveyor of Edenton, North Carolina, to be delivered by Johnston.

Benjamin Huntington to Governor Samuel Huntington. No copy known; acknowledged in Samuel to Benjamin Huntington, 26 January.

Louis Guillaume Otto to Comte de Montmorin. O'Dwyer, pp. 416–20. Otto's letters included in *DHFFC* were usually written over the course of days, and even weeks, following the day they were begun.

Hamilton has just presented to the House his report on public credit, "His projects, though bold, seem susceptible of prompt execution if the legislature of the United States gives ever so little its approval to them"; Hamilton has employed "a clever mathematician" (Philip Schuyler) to help with the calculations; Otto provides an extensive summary of the report and his observations on it and assures Montmorin that "there no longer remains a doubt for me, My Lord, that this Secretary sincerely desires to reimburse France by means of a loan made in Holland or even in England."

George Washington to Gabriel Dupare, Marquis de Bellegard. FC:lbk, Washington Papers, DLC. Sent to The Netherlands. For the full text, see *PGW* 4:577–78n.

Has "directed enquiries to be made" among the Georgia delegation to Congress, respecting the Marquis's request for information about any land in Georgia that can be claimed by the estate of the late General James Oglethorpe (1696–1785); a Senator from Georgia (Few) mentions having "made every enquiry in his power relative to the matter" upon a request by Jefferson in December 1786, without finding any confiscated land.

William Samuel Johnson, Diary. Johnson Papers, CtHi.
"Visits."

Letter from Providence, Rhode Island. *NYDA*, 21 January.
Congratulates the recipient on the Rhode Island Assembly's vote to call a ratification convention.

SATURDAY, 16 JANUARY 1790

Rain Thaw (Johnson)

Abraham Baldwin to [*Joel Barlow*]

How d'ye two times, I have written you three times before since my return, and write you three more now, for fear you will not find out I am here, and that I shall get none of your chat & politicks. I have learned more of the state of our allies from the brochures which you have sent me than I should have ever known in my life, and more than any body else here knew, I should send you all the news papers, but fear they will incur two much expence in the post office.
***
Hamilton has made a long and sensible report upon finance, which is soon to be taken into consideration. He is strong for the support of public credit. The principal and interest of foreign & domestic debt say 54 million, debt of the several states which we must also assume say 25 million more, by an excise and impost upon a plan which he proposes in an act, can be funded at an interest of 4 ℔ cent. I do not expect it will carry so high as 4 ℔ cent, the uncertainty of the proceeds of impost & excise till we can get returns, and a well grounded fear of falling into our old error of promising more than we are able to perform will make them cautious. Finals are 9/, facilities 7/, runners and packets are sent every where to buy state securities.

The winter is very moderate, wheat 9/ ℔ bushel, people say the times are good and praise the new government.

AL, Baldwin Family Collection, CtY. Place to which addressed not indicated. The addressee was identified from handwriting on the endorsement page and the notation of "No. 20" in a series. The omitted text describes a visit from a mutual friend, Zimri Bradley (1741–1821) of "Greenfield," in present-day Fairfield, Connecticut.

William Maclay to Benjamin Rush

The Budget is now opened and a bulkey one it is. It will not be in print before Thursday next, and I cannot pretend to give you much of it in detail. The late rise of Certificates seems now accounted for. The Speculators are in high Spirits. 'Tis said a Committee of their own body could not have contrived more happy arrangements, than are recommended from the Treasury. I shall be able to say more about it, when I have the perusal of it. Indiscriminate funding is however, said to be the leading feature in it. Perhaps this is the time for those who may be of a different Opinion, to cry aloud and speak out. I have thought that the History of our funding System in Pennsylvania, might be of Use in the Present Crisis. I have therefore thrown together some thoughts on that Subject, which are inclosed.[1] You can enlarge them much from Your own knowledge of that Vile business. at one time I was vain enough to imagine That we would have sunk all the alienated Certificates in Pennsylvania by one stroke of our land office, but while I was absent, in making the Purchase from the Indians, which was a preparatory step, absolutely necessary. Potter and party prevaled, and got me out of the Assembly.[2] and the funding System was engrafted on our Scheme. I have been unluckey enough to begin on an half Sheet of paper, and have not time to write over again. pray write to me often and freely.

ALS, Miscellaneous Manuscripts, NjP. Addressed to Third Street, Philadelphia; franked. This letter was misidentified as Thomas Fitzsimons to Benjamin Rush in *Parke-Bernet Catalog* 499(1944):item 117.

[1] This is probably the piece signed "A Citizen of Pennsylvania," published in *FG*, 25 January, and printed under that date below.
[2] Maclay was a commissioner at the Treaty of Fort Stanwix in October 1784. James Potter (1729–89), an Irish-born settler of Northumberland County, Pennsylvania, was a militia general during the Revolutionary War, vice president of the state (1781–82), member of the Council of Censors (1783–84), and a leader of the state's radical Constitutionalist party. As virtual political "boss" of Northumberland County, Potter would have been principally responsible for engineering the end of Maclay's three year service as a state assemblyman in 1784 (*DHFFE* 1:290n, 425; *DHFFC* 9:436; *Counter Revolution*, pp. 170–71).

William Smith (S.C.) to Edward Rutledge

Your last Letter has occasioned me no little embarassment, & for nothing could be more untimely than your observations on the Bank[rup]t. Law. After all My pains & trouble & inquiries on the subject—after days & weeks have been spent in the acquisition of information on the subject & other days & weeks have afterwards been employed in drawing an endless Bill, when finally my Labors were so far crown'd with success as to have compleated the

Bill & to have procured it the approbation of the Chief Justice of the United States & I was ready to present it to the House, your Letter came upon me like a Clap of thunder & overturned in an instant all my projects; for I could never think of proceeding a step further in the business after reading your observations: I locked up my Bill in my Desk & I went to Congress determined to vote that the business of the last session was entirely done away & that every thing must originate de novo: I was fortunate enough to find a majority of that opinion & a vote passed which established the point that all Committees appointed last session are annihilated; conseq[uentl]y. I shall plead a release from the Duty imposed on me & leave the business to those who wish to amuse themselves with it; I have had my share—I must now however apologize to you for saying that your Letter was untimely—better late than never, & tho you would have saved me a world of trouble & a great waste of time, which I shod. have applied to more valuable purposes, had you communicated this informatn. at an earlier period, yet I return you my thanks for having done it even at the last hour—Miserable shod. I have been had I made myself even the innocent instrument of destroying the tranquillity of my country and (with the best intentions) lent my assistance to destress my fellow-citizens! I communicated your Letter to Mr. Izard & we agreed to postpone the Bill for the present & wait better times when it may be more expedient—there is great force in your remarks & I shall avail myself of them, if called upon for the Bill—I know many people have been anxiously expecting it—some months ago I received a Letter, addressed to me by some debtors in the goal of this City, inquiring why the Bill was not brought forward & assuring me that many distressed persons were looking up to it, as the term of their misery: But Charity begins at home, & I cannot think a moment of contributing to the embarassmt. of my constituents. I have read your brother's [*John Rutledge*] remarks on the Judicy. & will attend to them.[1]

Pray Let me hear from you as soon as you can; I am extremely curious to receive a Letter from Columbia [*South Carolina*]. Having many Letters to write by this Vessel & being much restricted as to time, I am under the necessity of deferring ~~public~~ information on public matters. *** Henry [*Rutledge*] is well—I have been much indisposed, but am recov[ere]d.

ALS, Smith Papers, ScHi. Addressed to South Carolina; franked.

---

[1] Not identified; perhaps enclosed in Edward Rutledge's letter to which this is a reply.

Joseph Willard to Benjamin Goodhue

Some time ago, a present of books was sent by a Gentleman in London, to the University in this place [*Harvard*]. The boxes were reported at the

Custom House in Boston, and the Corporation are called upon by the Officers to pay the duty. I suppose the Officers could not do otherwise, consistently with the letter of the Revenue Acts of the General Government; but I am sure, it could not be the intention of the Congress to tax literature, in public Institutions. Will not your Honorable Body therefore readily make explicit provision, that books imported for the use of public Libraries (which cannot in such case be considered as merchandise) shall be exempted from imposts &ca.? I should be obliged to you, Sir, if you would think upon the subject, and communicate it to your brethren, the Members from this Commonwealth; and should you and they think it expedient, that the matter should be taken up by the Congress, I wish it may be introduced, at as early a period, as it can be with propriety.

You must be sensible, Sir, that I can have no farther view in this application, than the promotion of the general interests of literature, which I am sure will always engage your attention, and that of the Honble. Body to which you belong.

While I am upon a subject which concerns this University, I beg leave to request of you, should a marine Hospital be established in this neighborhood to endeavor that it may be so connected with the medical Institution here,[1] as to promote the interests of medical knowledge. This Institution would become much more useful to the Public, were the Professors able to introduce their Pupils into an Infirmary, to see practice. They might often be witnesses to many curious cases, both in Physic and Surgery. I have not time to enlarge upon the subject. I saw Mr. Gerry and Mr. Ames, some time ago, and discoursed with them upon it. I should be obliged to you, Sir, if you would confer with them, and introduce the matter, as you may have opportunity, to other Members, should the proposal strike you agreeably.

ALS, Letters to Goodhue, NNS. Written from Cambridge, Massachusetts.

[1] Willard's proposal for a medical school was approved in 1782 and the school was established shortly thereafter, remaining at Cambridge until it moved to neighboring Boston in 1810.

Letter from Boston

I never expected that the domestic debt of the United States would be funded at a higher interest than four per cent. nor could I suppose that in making provision for the debts contracted during the late war, and which are the price of the greatest and the happiest revolution that ever marked the page of history, the debts of the several states would be placed in a less favorable situation, than *that* commonly denominated the continental debt—but this will certainly be the case, if the great sources of revenue are diverted into a channel from whence the debts of the several states are to derive no advantage. It is to the general government that the state creditors must now look, as to their only resource—and surely their claims are as well founded, as those of any description of creditors whatever.

I am sensible that many persons have entertained hopes of receiving six per cent. interest, on their securities, and this is particularly the idea of those, who are clamorous for a discrimination between the original holders and those who have *bought* public paper. These persons say that government cannot consistently pay *them* a *less* interest than that expressed on the face of the promise; but at the same time, they can *very clearly* discover the justice of a violation of the *same promise*, expressed in the *same terms*, which happens to be in the hands of some of their neighbors!! Self love strangely blinds people to their own interest—for it is very evident that a violation of the public faith in one instance, would assuredly lead to a violation in the other.

I have said above, that 4 per cent is the highest at which I ever expected that government would fund the debt. My reasons are many, but waiving particulars I shall mention only two. First, This sum is about the average of the general expectation of the creditors; and as the Congress of the United States have proposed to lay the foundation of the government in JUSTICE, they will invariably consider in all their deliberations, that *two parties perfectly equal*, exist in all public contracts—and therefore they will undoubtedly pay attention to the general sentiment—but secondly, I consider 4 per cent. within compass of the ability of the United States. The creditors very well know that it will be in vain to expect an interest beyond this ability—and tho 4 per cent. will be less than the original stipulation, yet *realizing* this diminished rate, will induce a most cordial reliance on a future indemnification for a temporary loss.

GUS, 30 January; reprinted at Litchfield, Connecticut.

OTHER DOCUMENTS

Pierce Butler to Nicholas and Jacob Van Staphorst and Nicholas Hubbard. FC:lbk, Butler Papers, PHi.

> If a copy of Hamilton's report on public credit can be had before the ship carrying this letter sails, he will send it; advises to sell any continental settlement or final settlement securities and use the money in America "for other purposes."

Elbridge Gerry to James Sullivan. No copy known; acknowledged in Sullivan to Gerry, 24 January.

Elbridge Gerry to John Wendell. No copy known; acknowledged in Wendell to Gerry, 3 February.

Stephen Hall to John Langdon. ALS, Langdon Papers, NhPoA. Written from Portland, Maine.

Office seeking: naval officer at Portland; spoke with Langdon when he was last at Portsmouth on "the Conduct of my pretended friend Thatcher," respecting the appointment of Portland's collector; guesses the petition sent by the merchants of Portland would result in appointment of a naval officer there; does not believe Congress "meant to deprive themselves by law of the benefit of a Naval Officer; by giving the Emoluments of both Offices to one person."

Robert R. Livingston to Janet Montgomery. FC:dft, Robert R. Livingston Papers, NHi. Place to which addressed not indicated.

James Thompson "has made a new alliance" by the marriage of his daughter (Catherine) to Coles and it is said Page "is to have the younger."

Theodore Sedgwick to Nathaniel Gorham. No copy known; acknowledged in Gorham to Sedgwick, 27 January.

Theodore Sedgwick to Samuel Henshaw. No copy known; acknowledged in Henshaw to Sedgwick, 27 January.

Theodore Sedgwick to Benjamin Lincoln. No copy known; acknowledged in Lincoln to Sedgwick, 24 January.

Theodore Sedgwick to Henry Van Schaack. No copy known; acknowledged in Van Schaack to Sedgwick, 7 February.

Roger Sherman to Simeon Baldwin. ALS, Sherman Collection, CtY. Place to which addressed not indicated.

Sends newspapers; Hamilton's report on public credit, which proposes assuming the state debts, supposes that additional imports and an excise "modified as to make it easily collected" will pay the annual interest without resorting to direct taxation; will send a copy of the report when it is printed.

Thomas B. Wait to George Thatcher. ALS, Chamberlain Collection, MB. Postscript to letter of 15 January, above. Signed "Yours forever, and ever, and ever."

Asks for a loan of £20 or £30, which would enable him to improve his business's profits and "soon enable me to replace the money in the hands of him [*Thatcher*] to whom I am attached by a thousand obligations of a thousand different kinds."

NYDA, 16 January. Wister Butler Papers, PHi. Annotated by Butler to indicate the article for which he retained the issue.
Observer XIV, on excise duties.

SUNDAY, 17 JANUARY 1790

Rain Fine (Johnson)

Abigail Adams to Cotton Tufts

I think our dear state makes full use of the liberty of the press, but they who write for the benefit of mankind whether learned or unlearned will always find more utility in reasoning than writing; I am led to these observations by several pieces, some in Edes paper, that fountain of Sedition, and a piece in Adams paper signed "a New England man."[1] This same writer and many others will find their hands full, whenever the systems and plans of the Secretary of the Treasury come before them. Many copies [*of the report on public credit*] are ordered to be printed. They are not yet published, but are spoken of by many members of the House, as a performance which does much honour to the abilities of the Secretary. The two Houses are going on upon business and are now pretty full. The *House* condescended to go in a body to the President with their answer to his speech,[2] tho' many of them warmly opposed it, yet as the Senate, with their president at their Head, had done it, they did not know how very well to get over it. But the Senate all rode, & how should they look on foot with a rabble after them splashing through the mud, & this objection was obviated, by a member proposing that the Hackney men[3] should be sent, to supply those with carriages, who had not them of their own.

"Then it looks so monarchial," to go to the president, that they had best send a committee first to know when & where he would receive their answer, this was done, and the president returned for answer, that as the Senate had come to him, he could not think proper to make a distinction, besides it was the usage & custom of particular states to send answers to speeches made them by their Governours, & he would not *wish* to make innovations, and this polite answer being reported, a member moved that as the president had been so very delicate upon the subject, he would not any longer oppose the House going, so the Mountain went to Mahomet, and in style too.

Their Sergeant at Arms preceeded the carriage of the Speaker, bearing his maise [*mace*] before on horse back & carriages followed. Thus this mighty business was accomplished. Pray do not tell anybody from whence you get this story, I dare say it will not be entered upon the journals.

The Ancient Ballad & the Hartford News Boys New Years Address should be bound up together, let those feel the rod who deserve it. Mac Fingal has not yet lost his talent at satire.[4]

I suppose Boston is not behind with New York in speculation. I have thought whether it would not be best to sell the indents & purchase certificates. I suppose they have risen with you, they are seven & six pence here, indents I mean. The little matter you have belonging to me I wish you to dispose of as you would of your own property to the best advantage by changing or selling according to your judgment. The small pittance distributed to the widows is but a mite, my Heart is much larger than my purse and I think I should experience a great pleasure and satisfaction if I could make the Fatherless and widows heart sing for joy. I wish you to order Pratt to carry to Mrs. Palmer[5] a couple of loads of wood, it will be necessary to have fires in all the chimneys in the course of the winter and I wish to give her two cords of wood in that way, for several reasons, and you will order it done in the manner you think best.

Transcript, *The Collector*, vol. 26, 8(June 1913). Place to which addressed not indicated.

---

[1] Benjamin Edes edited the Antifederalist *Boston Gazette*, which at the time was running a series of essays signed "Moderatus" that attacked the Federalists. Thomas Adams edited Boston's *Independent Chronicle*, whose issue of 7 January published a piece by A New-England Man, which attacked The Observer's support for federal taxation.

[2] For the President's annual state of the union speech, delivered on 8 January, see *DHFFC* 3:252–54. The House's reply (*DHFFC* 3:260–61) was presented on 14 January, the Senate's (*DHFFC* 1:219–20) on the same day.

[3] Hired coaches.

[4] The poet John Trumbull was best known for his mock epic "M'Fingal" (1776–82), satirizing British cowardice during the Revolutionary War. "The Anarchiad" was a political satire written in the style of an "Ancient Ballad" and published serially in 1786–87 under the joint authorship of the "Connecticut Wits," Trumbull, David Humphreys, Joel Barlow, and Lemuel Hopkins. For the New Years Address see: *DHFFC* 22:Addenda.

[5] Pratt was a Braintree carpenter. Mary (Cranch) Palmer (d. 1790), sister of the Adamses' brother-in-law Richard Cranch, was the widow of General Joseph Palmer of Germantown, Massachusetts (*Adams* 1:71n, 3:234).

Fisher Ames to William Tudor

The report of the Secretary of the Treasury has set curiosity in motion. It is allowed to be a masterly performance—is very long—is ordered to be printed, and taken up in the committee of the whole on Thursday week. The state debts are proposed to be assumed, and all the debts, except foreign, reloaned at four per cent. It is not to be presumed that any system, especially one so complex and important, can pass without great debate. Perhaps it ought not to be wished.

I hear that Mr. _____ [*John Gardiner*] is going to eat up the bar, not, as the opossum does her young, for protection, but as the turkey-cock eats grasshoppers.[1]

An excise on spirits, wine, teas and coffee is proposed to furnish the cash. How will this suit the fair traders? The other sort of gentry I think will not be suited.

MHSC, series 2, 8(1826):320. Place to which addressed not indicated.

---

[1] This is the first of many references in congressional correspondence during the winter and spring of 1790 to John Gardiner's controversial campaign to reform the legal profession in Massachusetts. The subject had been agitated before the state legislature periodically, with mixed success, throughout the late 1780s. In accordance with notice given on 13 January, Gardiner rose on the floor of the state's House of Representatives on 19 January and spent two full days outlining a bill that proposed, in twenty chapters, to simplify, cheapen, and expedite legal procedures (especially relating to property, contract, and estate law), in many cases alleviating the need for lawyers altogether. On 5 February a House committee reduced much of Gardiner's proposal to four separate bills, of which only one passed, allowing anyone with a power of attorney the right to serve as a lawyer. Gardiner's speeches and proposals, some of which were reprinted far beyond the state line, attracted widespread criticism as being motivated by mere demagoguery, a desire to replace Thatcher, or even an antifederalist plot to destabilize the government by attacking the influence of those seen as the Constitution's strongest supporters ([Boston] *Massachusetts Centinel*, 16, 20, 23, 27, 30 January, 6 February; *JQA*, pp. 57–58; Van Beck Hall, *Politics without Parties: Massachusetts, 1780–1791* [London, 1972], pp. 327–28; Extract of a letter from New York, dated February 2, 1790, [Portland, Maine] *Cumberland Gazette*, 22 February).

William Bradford, Jr. to Elias Boudinot

Your sketch of the Secretary's report was very acceptable. Any information on so interesting a subject is eagerly receivd & I have been called on for an extract for the public prints which I could not refuse. I wait with impatience for the copy which you promise to send me: but if, (as I hear,) it was almost a quire of paper[1] it will take some days to publish it. The idea of embracing the whole debt, state as well as continental has often been spoken of here, & is generally thought a wise measure if it should not swell the amount of the whole beyond the abilities of the Govt. to fund it. It will cut up by the roots all those jealousies & heart-burnings which have taken place between the different states, upon the subject of contribution to the general defence: & by blending all Interests in support of the federal Govt. it will take away these *state interests*, from the operation of which ~~it~~ the Union has most to fear. The general idea of funding the whole, if it can be effected, is a manly & a wise one. If it be possible to provide adequate funds, the effects of it upon the commerce, agriculture & general prosperity of America must be very great. It will be as it were an immense accession of wealth—& by putting an end to the speculations in certificates will leave large capitals at liberty to be employed in improving the manufacturing or landed interests of the Country. As soon as these papers acquire a permanent value Lands must immediately rise in their ~~value~~ price; and I look forward to an era of great prosperity. But I do not yet see where the 3 or 4 millions that ~~are~~ will be annually wanted, are to be drawn from. It is now known that at the utmost the revenue collected in this port will not yield more than 400,000£ probably it will be less–& it is computd that this is the 5th. part of the whole. Additional duties are dangerous things, if they are not managed with great discretion. I do not know why a stamptax would not be a very eligible and productive fund. The bugbear of the name will frighten none but Children, & every duty of this kind is best laid, while the govt. is popular, & before the country is burdened with accumulated Taxes.

    ***

I hope to hear from you as frequently as your Engagements will permit. I suppose that our Mamma [*Hannah Stockton Boudinot*] is with you by this time. Susan [*Boudinot Bradford*] intended to write but has been prevented by a slight indisposition: Not such as confines her—but as renders writing disagreeable. She threatens a long letter next Wednesday: & in the mean time begs to be affectionately remembered.

ALS, Wallace Papers, PHi. Written from Philadelphia. Most of the omitted text relates to Judge Francis Hopkinson's improving health and the proceedings of the Pennsylvania constitutional convention.

[1] Twenty-four sheets.

William Constable to Robert Morris

It seems generally understood that the Contenl. & state Debts are to be put on the same footing precisely—Mr. Hamilton had proposed to make an Absolute provision for the Debt of the U.S. & a Con~~siderable~~ditional One for that of the States, but it is thought most adviseable by his freinds to associate the weight of the state Creditors as otherwise We apprehend the plan woud not be adopted in the Legislature upon the best Calculation We can make—It may ~~Require~~ be worth while to risque a purchase of the [*New*] Jersey Debt if it can be made on time—it is at present Worth 5/.—if it coud be purchased on 12 mo[*nth*]s. Credit even up to 7/. as there are several Years Interest due on the Certificates it woud be an Adviseable speculation—Coud S.O. [*Samuel Ogden*] do any thing in his Native state in the Negotiation—Your presence woud be of infinite Advantage here at this time [*George*] Harrison left this Yesterday.

[*P. S.*] Wrote Jas. Seagrove by Captn. Carpenter who sailed the 15th January.

FC:lbk, Constable-Pierrepont Collection, NN.

Tench Coxe to George Clymer

I wrote you a few lines by the post on Friday relating to the patent bill. From the title of the bill as expressed in the Journal of your house I observe it ~~goes~~ seems ~~seems~~ only to go to the point of securing to original Inventors the benefits of their own proper discoveries, yet from a conversation with Mr. M[*iers*]. Fisher, whom I have employed in some of the writing I find that tho' that is the *title* of the bill ~~yet~~ the enacting clause may be construed to ~~go look~~ extend further. In the present state of the Knowlege of machines in this Country considering also how much they are guarded by pains & penalties ~~& punishments~~ in England, and further how peculiarly adapted to our Circumstances they are it appears to me that the ~~subject~~ Business should be ~~taken up~~ placed by Congress ~~upon~~ on the ground ~~of~~ described in the president's Speech vizt.—that you should give "effectual encouragement as well to the introduction of new[1] & useful inventions from abroad as to the exertions of skill & genius in producing them at home."

The Case in which I shall apply stands thus circumstanced, which for the sake of precision I shall minutely divide.

1st. We shall produce a drawing & model of Arkwrights two first & main movements for *spinning* by Water,[2] applicable as ~~well to~~ we shall shew as well our branches of *wool, flax & hemp* ~~& silk~~ as to his branch of cotton, & to silk of which first movements ~~we~~ we are not the *Inventors*, but the *introducers* there being no model or drawing of these invaluable Movements in the United States.

2dly. We shall produce a drawing & model of ~~the our~~ certain *supplementary* movements & apparatus for the spinning of worsted, and of flaxen & hempen yarn in a manner *invented* by Us, and different from any ~~patent~~ machine in the world.

These two form the Machinery for those Branches complete. vizt. worsted & hempen & flaxen yarn.

3dly. We think we can (tho not immediately) produce a drawing or model of another set of *supplementary* movements & apparatus; which in addition to those specified in No. 1, are equal to the manufactory of cotton goods after the Manner of Arkwrights, & of which we consider him as the Inventor ~~of~~ & ourselves as the *introducers*.

4thly. The supplementary movements & apparatus for the silk ~~Movements Business~~ manufactory, tho ~~patented~~ possessed by people in England we have not yet decided on, but we do not consider ~~it~~ our prospects of either discovering or obtaining it as hopeless, having a person of very great information & capacity in that line, and having ~~two~~ trains of information laid for the purpose of obtaining them.

It may be supposed that considerable expence of money, time & trouble, not ~~unattended~~ without hazard, must be necessary to these attainments in every case, but both the parties, ~~who will be~~ concerned in this application can evince, that with them they have been [*lined out*] actually incur'd. With regard to the foreigner,[3] he has left his country with some necessary parts of the Machines at the risque of a ruinous fine and a long & severe imprisonment without being able to bring his family with him, and he has ~~also~~ moreover sacrificed a ~~good~~ profitable trade & steady employment—also the Business of his wife, who has a separate trade, wch. she must leave as soon as he is ready to receive her—His pretensions to public countenance & support are too great & manifest to require enforcing.

With respect to myself ~~I~~ my attention to this subject is so well known to you that little need be said, but in addition to the overt Circumstances with wch. you are acquainted I have by me an original Contract made in August 1787 wherein I embarked with another person near 1200 Dollars to enable him to go to a particular Kingdom in Europe for the purpose of "procuring the Models & patterns of divers machines, moved by water, fire, horses, or men for preparing & manufacturing *wool, cotton, flax, hemp* & metals or any other raw materials" and after having ~~procured~~ actually expended under that contract 560 dollars as my part and having ~~procured every~~ collected many things of great value, particularly the cotton movements, my plan was entirely defeated by an information & the consequent apprehending of the person employed. [*lined out*] Tho he had been so careful, that nothing but *intention* could be proved ~~upon~~ against him, & he escaped fine & imprisonment, ~~but~~ yet having given a large Security for his good behaviour the package of drawings & models remains ~~unmoved at my order~~ beyond my reach in the place where they were deposited.

I have troubled you Sir with this minute *confidential* information that you might be enabled, so far as you conceive your duty & the public Interests will admit, to procure such alteration in the pending bill if any be necessary as will accommodate it to ~~enterprizes~~ cases of Introduction.[4] ~~Such a~~ [*lined out*] Tho ~~I co~~ I wish some parts of this letter to be confidential, yet I freely leave it in your discretion to communicate the whole of it to whomsoever you think ~~proper~~ fit, under due restrictions Should I not be deceived in my Ideas of the present attainments ~~I think I see~~ I think there is a moral certainty from these and other things ~~that~~ which our enterprize abroad & invention at home will supply, that a capital Manufacturing interest may be established in the United States, without diverting our people from their farms.

It may be [*lined out*] necessary that you should know that ~~from a~~ we shall probably have a drawings prepared by the end of the present Month. You will therefore oblige me by your early [*lined out*] recommendations of such Steps as you may think it advisable to take.

FC:dft, Coxe Papers, PHi. Written from Philadelphia.

[1] Coxe underlined the words "introduction" and "new" but then crossed them out.

[2] Sir Richard Arkwright (1732–92) patented his spinning machine (called a water frame) in 1769. It helped to establish the preeminence of Britain's textile industry.

[3] George Parkinson, with whom Coxe had just signed a partnership a week earlier (*Coxe*, pp. 149–50, 189–90).

[4] The House declared its initial support for rewarding industrial piracy by amending the Copyright Bill [HR-39] in accordance with a motion by Burke on 28 January. The language of the Patents Bill [HR-41] that grew out of it, presented by Burke on 16 February, consequently afforded protection to any "useful" invention "not before known or used within the United States" (*DHFFC* 6:1627). The Senate struck the phrase "within the United States" from the final version of the act, although the smuggling of technology continued to receive quasi-official encouragement from Hamilton and even Jefferson throughout the early 1790s. See Doron Ben-Atar, "Alexander Hamilton's Alternative: Technology Piracy and the Report on Manufactures," in Ben-Atar and Barbara B. Oberg, eds., *Federalists Reconsidered* (Charlottesville, Va., 1998), pp. 41–60.

William Smith (Md.) to Otho H. Williams

The inclosed papers will furnish you with the public transactions here; I have therefore only to add, that the Report, from the Secy. of the Treasury, was delivered to the house of Representatives, on thursday last, which contains Seventy pages with reasons, & calculations, in Support of his plans. The Substance of the whole, as far as my memory Serves, is nearly contained, in one of the papers inclosed. The Report accompanied by a bill, which contains the same number of pages with the report, tables &ca., are with the printer, but cannot be ready before thursday, after which time I will hand you a coppy by the earliest oppertunity. No opinion has yet been expressed, in the House, on the Subject of public credit, but we may reasonably conclude, from the Presidents Speech, & Secrety. report, that continental Securitys will rather rise than fall. it has however occasionaly, raised & lowerd at this market & perhaps the want of money may be the only cause of any decline, tis Said 11/ to 12/6 has been given on a credit of three Months, but I believe not more than 10/ ready money & Sales have been made Since my arrival at 9/ & 9/6 each. The report is to be taken up in a comitee of the whole house, Next thursday week, after which time, some conjecture, may be formed on this head.

The report of the Indian commissioners for the Southern department, bear a very Unfavorable Aspect And I fear the United States will finally be involved in a a war, with the Creek Indians who are probably countenanced And Abetted, by the Spaniards, & Mr. [*Alexander*] McGilvray whose influence appears to be great, has an interest in preventing a Solid & lasting peace from being established. he is not only a Colo. in the Spanish Service, has a considerable Salary allowed him, & what perhaps will Still have greater weight with him, is his being a partner in a considerable trading house, on the head Waters of the Mobile river, which Supplies the Creek Nation with goods to a considerable amount & receives their Furs & Peltry in return.

I hope to hear from you soon.

ALS, Williams Papers, MdHi. Addressed to Baltimore.

Letter from New York

The report of the Secretary of the Treasury, which is now in the press, will explain to the publick the pecuniary situation of our country in a more clear manner than it has hitherto appeared—The whole Debt of the United States, including the arrears of interest upon the demands of the foreign and domestick creditors, amounts to about 54 millions of dollars. The aggregate of the principal and interest of the respective State Debts is about 25 millions of dollars: As the plan proposed by the Secretary of the Treasury contemplates the assumption of all the State Debts, the whole debt of the United States in that case would be about 79 or 80 millions of dollars—Perhaps a revenue of three millions of dollars, or three millions and an half, will be sufficient to support the Government, and pay the annual interest of the National Debt.

This report of the Secretary on the subject of Finance, is universally celebrated here—for the extensiveness of its views—the feasibility of its projects—and for the open, ingenuous and liberal manner, in which the great concerns of the Union are brought to the eye of the publick. His propositions, in general, it is expected will be adopted.

Such hath been the effect of the depreciation of our publick securities heretofore, that it is said near one half of the publick paper of the union are owned in Europe—To get these back, and to prevent the others from following them, is an object worthy attention.

The Hon. Benjamin Hawkins, Esq. one of the Senators of the United States from North Carolina, arrived in this city on Friday, and took his seat.

[Boston] *Massachusetts Centinel*, 27 January; reprinted at Portland, Maine.

OTHER DOCUMENTS

Stephen Austin to Jeremiah Wadsworth. ALS, Wadsworth Papers, CtHi. Written from Philadelphia; postmarked 18 January.

Reports on progress of lead mining and manufacturing in Virginia; "have you any Doubt but Congress will Lay at Least one Cent duty on Shott & Sheet Lead—if Not on Barr Lead—when we make it appear Our daly Production is Ecqual to the Consumtion of this Cuntry."

Silvanus Bourn to John Adams. ALS, Adams Family Manuscript Trust, MHi. Written from Boston; postmarked.

Office seeking: a consulate, or secretary to a diplomat; expects to be in New York City shortly, to prosecute his design.

James Clinton to Isaac Melcher. ALS, Miscellaneous Manuscripts, NHi. Addressed to Philadelphia; postmarked. The Ouaquaga Tract was in Broome County, New York, east of present-day Binghamton. Morris began investing in the area in 1787.

Finds no problem with the deed Melcher has signed over to Morris for part of the "Onnequago Tract on the Susquehanna"; Morris is expected soon; suggests Melcher accompany him to New York.

John Fenno to Joseph Ward. ALS, Ward Papers, ICHi. Addressed to the land office in Boston; carried by Mr. (Nathaniel) Barrett. For the full text, see *AASP* 89(1979):355–56.

Hamilton's report on public credit will be published in eight to ten days; discussion in the House will begin in about three weeks—"not much sooner"; some members will propose three percent interest, but the plan will undergo no "essential alterations"; believes Hamilton "will be called upon to explain his report on the floor of the house"; the report was received "with a most profound attention."

Peter Charles L'Enfant to John Adams. See *DHFFC* 15:35–36.

Regarding nonpayment for Senate furniture.

Thomas McKean to George Washington. Written from Philadelphia. ALS, Washington Papers, DLC. For the full text, see *PGW* 5:4–6.

Office seeking: his son-in-law, Dr. George Buchanan, for superintendent of the marine hospital expected to be established in Baltimore; mentions Charles Carroll and Smith (Md.) as references.

George Thatcher to John Hobby. No copy known; acknowledged in Hobby to Thatcher, 3 February.

John Trumbull to Harriet Wadsworth. ALS, Trumbull Collection, CtY. Addressed to Hartford, Connecticut. This is a postscript to Trumbull to Wadsworth, 12 January, above.

> Apologizes for not yet mailing a copy of George Keate's *Account of the Pelew Islands* (London, 1788), which "your Father and Uncle [*Jonathan Trumbull*] have got possession of" and they "insist that you must wait 'till they have finish'd—you shall receive it as soon as I can get it out of their hands."

William Samuel Johnson, Diary. Johnson Papers, CtHi.
> "S[*t*]. P[*aul's*]."

MONDAY, 18 JANUARY 1790

Thaw (Johnson)

George Clymer to Tench Coxe

Having obtained a printed copy of the bill to promote the progress of the sciences &ca., I have on seeing Cadwalader filled in ~~what~~ the several parts—they are what the Committee proposed to offer when next taken up—When that shall be or on what ground I don't know for by way of setting an example to the other house or getting rid of the Germanton bill [*Seat of Government HR-25*] a question in ours has been carried, implying in some sort that the unfinished business of the former session if taken up at all must be as altogether new.

I am obliged to you for your [*state constitutional*] Convention news about which since knowing the worst in the affair of the Senate my curiosity has a good deal gone off[1]—It was to be the strong hold of the state, but from being an anchor ~~it~~ is to be made a weather cock, and may add to the expence indeed of the government 'tho not much to its security—I deeply regret than an example of wisdom has been thrown before us in vain.

[*P. S.*] I wish you would inform me either as your opinion or from the documents of the Custom house what is the whole value of our exports—that of flour is already known.

ALS, Coxe Papers, PHi. Place to which addressed not indicated. On Coxe and the Patents Act [HR-41], see Coxe to Clymer, 17 January, above.

[1] Clymer may have been referring to the decision in favor of popular election of state senators as opposed to their election by the state House of Representatives (*Counter Revolution*, p. 226).

Benjamin Goodhue to Insurance Offices

The Secry. of the Treasury has made his report on the subject of finance, its very lengthy and its order'd to be printed, as soon as I can procure a Copy, I will transmit you one—from hearing it read once, I am not able to recollect much of it, saving its leading features, as they bear in my memory they are as follows vizt. all discrimination between original and present holders of securities, ~~are~~ is shewn to be unjust and impracticable, the assumption of the State debts is proposed, on the principles of Justice and to prevent an interference between the measures to be adopted by the Union and the several States for the purposes of revenue, which might destroy both, was the assumption not made—but altho' he proposes Congress should make the assumption the present session, yet he is for postponing the provision for the payment of the interest thereon till I think next January, giving opportunity for the holders in the mean time to loan them with the interest due thereon up to that time, and take in lieu thereof a Continental obligation, on the same terms that are held forth as an invitation to holders of Continental securities to reloan theirs—State notes so loaned to the United States and which the U.S. became answerable for are to be charged the particular States, towards a balance which may be found due to them respectively from the United States on a settlement for advances made for carrying on the war which form a part of the aggregate expence of the war which must be born by the Union—indents for interest are to be funded with the principal and on the same terms—he then goes on and proposes five or six different modes or invitations to the Creditors, that they may have their choice of to reloan their securities upon, I do not recollect but one of them perfectly, which is this, that he who loans 100 dollars shall have an obligation for 66⅔ dollars bearing an interest of 6 ℀ ct. and for the other third to have lands @ 20 cents an acre—the other modes are equaly advantageous or meant to be, a Tontine is one of them he then goes on to propose further provision in aid of the present revenue to pay the interest on the present domestic and foreign debt, and the support of civil government, leaving the provision to be made for State debts till this time twelve month, the provision now to be made is by increasing the impost on Teas, Coffee Wines and Spirits, and an excise on Spirits of every discription manufactured within the United States—all these articles he proposes to load with very considerable duties—his report is to be taken up on monday next but what will be its fate either in whole or in part its hard to conjecture, tho' I suspect its as favourably reciev'd as could be expected.

[*P. S.*] It must be remember'd that this statement of his report is from a recollection on its being read once and therefore may be imperfect, tho' I beleive it to be nearly the substance

he estimates the foreign & Domestic debt

including interest on both	54,000,000
the State debts	25,000,000.

ALS, Goodhue Letters, NNS. Addressed to Salem, Massachusetts; franked; postmarked 19 January.

Nathaniel Gorham to Caleb Strong

I hear that Mr. [*Andrew*] Ellicot has returned from Niagara—but I have not heard the result of his doings—do be so kind as to make enquiry and send me such an account of that matter[1] as you are able to obtain.

Mr. Dalton in your last Session sent the Governor [*Hancock*] a copy of Gen. St. Clairs treaty with the Indians[2]—He will lay it before the Legislature tomorrow or next day—do prevent—the ratification for the present & forever if you can—if it is considered as valid & having an opperation upon the title. it will very materially effect us or the State of Massachusetts—If it can be kept of. I think if I was at N. York. I could suggest a plan that would satisfy Pensylvania & the United States—and it is my present intention to be there some time in February—do mention in your Letter to me whether the Legislature of N.Y. are in Session—& if not when they are to meet—I will thank You for your sentiments relative to the assumption of the State debts and indeed to the whole of the system of finance so far as you can consistently give it—some people think that Congress will require the transfer of our Bonds[3] if they take the State debts—If it is just, I should like it—for I think Congress would be reasonable with us.

ALS, formerly at MSonHi. Written from Boston.

[1] On 26 August 1789 Congress authorized Ellicott's continuation of the survey ordered a year earlier, fixing the western boundary of New York State and the national domain that lay beyond, which Congress had already allowed to be annexed by Pennsylvania in September 1788. Gorham's lobbying campaign during the first session had aimed to influence Ellicott's survey by minimizing the acreage of the resulting Erie Triangle, which was to be subtracted from the Genessee Tract purchased in April 1788 by Gorham and Oliver Phelps from Massachusetts (which owned the land, although New York retained jurisdiction). For more background and documents, including Ellicott's own petition to continue the survey, see *DHFFC* 8:191–98.

[2] On 30 September 1789 Dalton forwarded to Governor John Hancock a copy of the Treaty of Fort Harmar, signed by Northwest Territory Governor Arthur St. Clair and representatives of the Six Nations (except the Mohawks) the previous January. The treaty confirmed the Treaty of Fort Stanwix of 1784, which had established the Indians' title to much of what became the western half of the Genessee Tract. As with Ellicott's running of New York State's

western boundary line through the same territory (see n. 1, above), the border confirmed by St. Clair's treaty affected how much land Gorham and Phelps would have to try to extinguish Indian title to, out of the land they had already purchased from Massachusetts the year before. On 26 August 1789 the Senate postponed ratification of the Treaty of Fort Harmar with the Six Nations (except the Mohawks), and it was not taken up again in the FFC (*DHFFC* 2:37, 137–40, 160–63; 17:1643–44).

[3] See Gorham to Sedgwick, 12 January, above.

Thomas Hartley to Jasper Yeates

I arrived here safe on Wednesday last and immediately embarked in Business.

An Indirect attack had been made agst. the Bill about the Federal Seat in our House before I came and the Principle that all the Old Business continued or left unfinished last Settings, must be taken up de novo.

The Bill I refer to is in the other House—but it was intended by this Motion to influence the *other House.*

This I think improper and I brought forward a Motion on Friday to bring on the Question fairly, as you will discover by one of the News Papers which I send you.

As Mr. Fitzsimmons is not here and as it might be thought that I had hurried the Question & tho' it seemed to be absolutely necessary when I made the Motion—I have not stired it to Day—and wish the arrival of Mr. Morris and Mr. Fitzsimmons to assist in supporting their own Grounds.

The News Papers will give you some Idea of what we are about—for my own Part—I am fixed to a tight Committee[1] & have to work double Tides[2]—I suppose it will be good for my Health.

ALS, Yeates Papers, PHi. Addressed to Lancaster, Pennsylvania; franked; postmarked; answered 1 February.

[1] On the Naturalization Bill.
[2] Three days work in two.

Henry Marchant to John Adams

***

The Govr. [*John Collins*] is requested to forward the Proceedings to the President of the United States, with a Request that the Indulgence before granted may be continued, for such Time as Congress shall think proper[1]— The Election of Delegates for a Convention is fixed to the second Monday of February; and the Meeting of the Convention to the first Monday of March— As I have not a reasonable Doubt, but the Constitution will be adopted, and I have never held up any Thing to Congress, but what the Event has justified—I must sincerely wish Congress will gratify Our Wishes—And as some Vessells have sailed since the fifteenth of March for some of the United States and others will sail before such further Indulgence may be granted, I must further wish, that in granting this, They will add, that such Tunnage and Duties as may be paid by Our Vessells, other than are paid by Subjects of the United States may be returned—All this is granting no further than was granted to North Carolina upon Their having appointed a Convention and under the Expectation of an Adoption of the Constitution—I am confident this Indulgence will give Us at least ten Votes in Our Convention; and have a Tendency to reconcile hundreds of Our People—I must be supposed to have a tollerable Idea of the Dispositions of Our Citizens. Few have had greater Opportunities of obtaining such Knowledge—I have not hesitated to give a decided Opinion that Congress would meet Us, with every cordial Mark of Approbation; and almost pledged myself for Success in Our Application—Be so kind Sir, as to present my Respects to the President, and to the Gentlemen of my Acquaintance—And If I have your own favourable Sentiments of this Request, inform Them, that a steady and arduous Friend in this Business begs Their Attention to, and hearty Concurrence in, this Soliscitation.

ALS, Adams Family Manuscript Trust, MHi. Written from East Greenwich, Rhode Island; answered 20 March. The first half of this letter details the maneuvers that led to the Rhode Island legislature's call for a state convention to consider ratifying the Constitution.

¹ The act calling for a ratification convention in Rhode Island and Collins's cover letter (printed in *PGW* 5:7–8) were presented to the House on 28 January. The Collection Act [HR-23], signed into law on 16 September 1789, treated Rhode Island as if it were part of the United States as far as commerce was concerned, thus delaying the implementation of provisions of the Tonnage [HR-5] and Collection [HR-11] Acts. The privilege expired on 15 January 1790. See also *DHFFC* 8:389–98.

Samuel Whittemore to Benjamin Goodhue

I trust you have not been unmind full of the Conversation We had at Salem, and altho' I think I was neglected in the choise of Officers compairing my Self with my Brother officers of this Commonwealth, yet I am Determined to do my Duty in the Office to which I am appointd [*surveyor at Gloucester*], not doubting that Congress will Reward thier Officers according to their Services, and would mention a few Things for your Considiration, Viz.

Whether it is not necessary that some Care should be taken respecting the unloading of Coasters as well as Foreigners and as their are Vessels of a certain description that have Licences, and are exempt from entering and Clearing, unless they have Such a Quantity of Dutible Goods or so much Spirits. others that do enter and Clear, what is there to Prevent thier taking double the Quantity, if some Care is not taken to See what they Deliver, a Vessel may put into Some Eastern Port and put part of her Cargoe on Board Coasters and have it brought up to the westward whereby the Revenue may be greatly defrauded, I have reason to think that would have been the Case here, had there not been great Care taken to Prevent the same, as you may see by the Return I Deliverd to you, and there is no Provision made for that Surveyor for such Services, nor yet for Going or Putting an officer on Board any Vessel on her arival and taking a Manifest required by Law, unless she unloads at the Port whe[re] the Manifest is taken, whether some Allowance ought not to be made for such Services. The Inspectors (and others imployed in the Customs) are allowed one Dollar and one Quarter pr. Day, whose Fees often amount Ten and Sometimes to Twenty Dollars and the Guager and Weigher nearly the same on a Vessel that unloads having a Quanty of Dutible Goods on Board and they are under no Bonds, where as the Surveyor who is und[er] Bonds, and hath the Ovesight of them and is Obligd. to Spend nearly as much Time as they in the Day and often Times to go on Board in the Night, to see that they are on their Duty, hath in general but one Dollar and an half and never more than three Dollars for his Services, if she is Sixteen Days before she is discharged, and there is no Fees on Vessels Clearing out—Whether he might not do the Duty of some of the officers that he hath the oversight off, and receive the Same pay Whether as his Business calls him out Wett and Dry Night and Day he Ought not have the liberty of appointing a Deputy.

ALS, Letters to Goodhue, NNS. Written from Gloucester, Massachusetts.

Paine Wingate to Jeremy Belknap

I have received your favour of the 9th. Instant, and agreeably to your request have forwarded the letter to Dr. [*Benjamin*] Rush. That to Mr. [*Ebenezer*] Hazard I will deliver today. With respect to public securities I will gladly give you any intelligence in my power, as well to gratify your curiosity, as to shew kindness to the female friend you speak of; but I can say nothing at present but mere conjecture. Those securities have not sold for less than 8/3d on the pound in New York since I came here; and I am told that now they are sold from 9/ to 10/, and that the Indents are about 7/. The Secretary of the Treasury has reported as a part of his plan of Finance that the domestic debt should be funded anew to voluntary subscribers at 4 pr. Cent. Interest & include equally both principle & Interest. This it is supposed would appreciate the securities considerably. I think it is doubtful whether the interest will be more than 3 pr. Cent., but a certain revenue will be appropriated for the punctual payment of whatever shall be promised. At this rate of Interest it is the opinion of those who are good judges that the securities will sell for about ten shillings on the pound. I believe that there is no great danger of their being much lower, & they may possibly be something higher. It will be yet a considerable time before this business will be compleated in Congress respecting the new funds, & in the mean time there will be various arts of speculators practiced on one another, as well as on the less knowing. If I was a holder of public securities (which I am not) I should not sell until I knew more of the probable issue of the present plans; but perhaps it may be as advantagous to those who do not choose to be holders in the funds to sell soon after the funds are established as at any after time. This is only my mere opinion in which I am as liable to be deceived as any body—I am not able to give you any tollerable account of Colo. Hamilton's plans, & will not attempt it. By the last of this week, it is expected the pamphlet will be publishd.[1] I am sorry that you are infested at Boston with such kind of Priests as you speak of,[2] but think they cannot prevail much among an enlightened people. I am told that there has been a most extraordinary spirit of fanaticism prevailing last week in this city among the people called Methodists; but hope it will not spread like the influenza.

ALS, Belknap Papers, MHi. Addressed to Boston; franked; postmarked.

[1] Hamilton's report on public credit.
[2] Wingate was echoing the sentiments of outrage in the Boston press about the conduct of a renegade priest, the Abbé de la Poteririe, who tried to disrupt worship at the city's Roman Catholic chapel the previous Christmas Eve. His followers destroyed several pews during this "first known public disturbance" of the Catholic Church in Boston ([Boston] *Massachusetts Centinel*, 26, 30 December; Robert H. Lord, et al., *History of the Archdiocese of Boston, 1604 to 1943* [3 vols., New York, 1944], 1:415, 417–18).

[*Jeremiah Wadsworth*,] The Observer—No. XV

AN assumption of the State debts, is an event which many think must eventually take place; there may be doubts, and difficulties to obviate, which will occasion a delay; but the efforts of the union, and of the States to systematize their treasuries will probably ultimate in this measure.

Doubtless there will be persons enough to raise objections, and with an honest design; for there needs much deliberation to see the propriety of new measures, which will have so extensive an effect. If any of the States should now think the measure against their interest, a short time will open their eyes, by the confusion which must ensue from a continuance in their present

situation. If the State debt should be assumed, it will become a serious question, how shall funds be provided for the aggregate sum? Every possible
revenue from trade will be inadequate, and the treasury of the United States,
must be furnished with other ways and means. The people will chearfully
pay what justice requires, for it must be as much their interest as it is their
duty; and a principal difficulty will be in conciliating the public feelings
to a system of uniform operation thro' the whole. I will mention the several
propositions which have occurred to my hearing. There yet remains a very
small number, who tell us that the old method of requisition is best; leaving
every State to its own way of taxing and collecting the sum demanded—
They say further, that Congress now possesses the power of coercion, and
after a State hath proved delinquent, will be a proper time for the general
government to exert its coercive authority, and enforce a payment.

The very proposition appears to me to be fraught with evil, and must
soon end in a subversion, either of the general, or of the State governments,
and probably of the latter. To make a requisition on the States will be easy;
but there is every reason to suppose some of them will prove delinquent,
which must lead to universal delinquency. In this case who is the subject of
coercion? If it be the delinquent State in its corporate capacity, it can be done
only by levying war on the whole people, and subverting their existence as
a State; if the private citizens considered as subjects of the United States are
to be coerced, the process will be loaded with a thousand difficulties, for
which an antidote cannot be provided. Perhaps the deliquent State has made
a grant of the demanded sum; part is collected and in the State treasury, part
in the hands of speculating collectors, over whom the general government
hath no power, and part unpaid in the hands of the people; some districts
have contributed their whole quota, and others no part of it; in this stage of
the business how shall the general government take hold and force a collection? and to now assess the whole sum on the people, would be a manifest
injustice by the operation of the two governments.

Or suppose the delinquent State neglects to make any grant of the requisition; will it not be an ungrateful business, and have a most powerful
tendency to destroy all respect to State authority, for the United States to
come in and tell the people "we have made our demand on your legislature, and they have not done their duty—they have shewn themselves to
be either ignorant or dishonest; we are therefore under a necessity of taxing
you directly without their intervention, your sister States have paid their
proportion, and criminate your delay, blame not us but your own assembly."
Will a measure of this kind be pacific in its tendency? Will it not look like
a kingdom divided against itself? Will it not be a source of contention, and
either destroy the union, which I think cannot now be done, or anihilate all
respect to the State government where it happens? Ye friends to the dignity

of your own States, be careful how you spread a snare to destroy their legislative reverence! The doctrine of requisition on the States, in every point of view, is a dangerous and impracticable one. Those who tell us, that it is become feasible, since the general government have a power of coercion, either do not foresee consequences, or intend gradually to subvert the government of individual States.

That the general government possesses a coercive power over an individual State, is allowed on all hands; but the matter ought to be so conducted, they may never have occasion to use it. In a conflict of this kind, we know that any one State must ultimately bow to the joint decision of all the others; but I should consider such an event unpropitious. If we intend to preserve a respectableness to the separate States, we must give the United States, original and sole jurisdiction and executive power of all matters in their nature national; and a general system of finance, and providing for the payment of the whole debt, by whatever name called, is conceived to be such. If the general government must ever use coercion, let it be to execute their own laws and grants; and let individuals and not States be the subjects of it. These truths must lead every friend of the union and of the separate States to reject the idea of requisitions. If we design to preserve a respectableness to the State legislature and executive, let us cordially, and in the first instance give up all those matters, which may be better conducted by a national assembly and executive.

I have also heard another proposition, which is this. Let there be an apportionment to each State of its quota of the sum needed; let Congress directly tax the inhabitants, following in each State the mode of taxation and collection, which is used by their own government. This, it is said, will be more familiar and pleasing to the people than any other possible method. On this I observe, that the proposition keeps up the idea of a previous apportionment on the States; which ever hath been, and while continued must be a source of jealousy. By such jealousies nothing is gained and much endangered.

This plan proposes as many modes of taxing and collecting, as there are States, for no two have a similar procedure—there must be thirteen bodies, compleatly organized with limbs, joined to one head, the treasury board of the United States—is it possible for this head to preserve order, controul and give motion to so great a number of bodies? Is it possible for the treasury board to comprehend and act on so complex a system? Is the general government to have a compleat set of officers of their own appointment, or to make use of those appointed by the States? If the former, their number will be immense; if the latter, they will feel no dependence on the union and cannot be brought to account.

The operation of a taxing system is much more expeditious in some, than it is in the other States; in some it often runs into an arrearage of years. Can a general system stand with any punctuality upon such uncertainties? Will it not be in the power of a single State, by altering its own laws, at any time to disconcert the general treasury arrangement? Will the treasury officers ever be able to give an exact account of the national revenue, in whose hands monies are, or whether in a safe situation? I will propose a question which to the people is still a more serious one—Those public officers intrusted with the revenue, and with the disposition of monies, ought to be placed in the most accountable situation; from the integrity of those now in office, we cannot infer the honor or honesty of their successors; and will not so complex a plan as we are now considering, give the greatest room for evasion, and fraud, that can never be detected? Whoever considers these questions, in some of them, will find unanswerable objections, against apportioning to the States and adopting in each one its own method of taxing and collecting.

If neither of the above methods are feasible, the general government must adopt a system of its own, on plain principles, which may operate thro' the whole with equal expedition and justice.

The greatest evil is to be expected from a plan, which either gives discretionary power to subordinate officers of government, in dividing the taxes on the people; or is so complex in its principles and operation that they cannot understand it. No good man will murmer when he sees himself treated on principles of equality; but lawgivers ought to remember, that for the common citizen to see this, the mode of taxation must be very plain. It is but a few, who have a thorough knowledge of the principles and influence of the tax laws in their own States, and this they have acquired by living long under them. Should the general government adopt a complex system, by detaching the most eligible parts, from all the local customs within the union; it would still appear to the people proper object of jealousy, and not seeing an equal operation on others, they would suppose themselves injured. If there be any kind of property which is the basis of wealth throughout the union, and bears a near proportion to the ability of the people who must pay; if this kind of property cannot be secreted, and may be charged on principles of greater equality than any other; if the nature of the property be such that every man may previously calculate his taxes, and detect an overcharge; if it admits a more easy and cheap collection than any other; if its produce must forever be in demand, which will enable the person charged to pay his taxes: this property on some plain principles ought to be the subject of direct taxation.

[Hartford, Connecticut] *American Mercury*, 18 January. For information on The Observer series, its authorship, and reprintings, see the location note to The Observer, No. 1, 12 October, above.

OTHER DOCUMENTS

Abraham Baldwin to Joel Barlow. AN, Baldwin Family Collection, CtY. This note may not have been sent.

Wrote "yesterday or day before to go by this vessel, and promised you some news papers," but only now has heard of a passenger to whom to entrust them; "we are just beginning to make news but have got none done yet that is worth paying postage for."

Josiah Burr to Jeremiah Wadsworth. ALS, Wadsworth Papers, CtHi. Written from New Haven, Connecticut.

Explains why they missed seeing each other when Wadsworth passed through town en route to Congress; asks if he has "something to communicate respecting the genesee business" and asks for advice on the occasion of a meeting of the proprietors. (Wadsworth was one of the small coinvestors in the Gorham-Phelps Genessee Purchase of 1787 [Shaw Livermore, *Early American Land Companies* (1939; reprint, New York, 1968), pp. 197–98].)

Benjamin Goodhue to Stephen Goodhue. ALS, Goodhue Family Papers, MSaE. Addressed to Salem, Massachusetts; franked; postmarked.

"I do not think there is so probability of a Bankrupt law as I did for the person who brought forward the subject last session is sick of it and tells me the people and merchants of Charlestown his Constituents will be ruined as they inform him by the measure"; thinks Hamilton's proposed assumption of state war debts will pass; refers to his letter to the Insurance Offices (above) for a fuller summary of the report on public credit; had thought they would offer no more than three percent interest on the debt, "but I am not so sanguine now but it may amount to 3½."

Benjamin Goodhue to Michael Hodge. ALS, Ebenezer Stone Papers, MSaE. Place to which addressed not indicated. For the full text, see *EIHC* 83(July 1947):218–19. A paraphrase of part of this letter appeared in [Massachusetts] *Salem Gazette*, 26 January.

Summarizes Hamilton's report on public credit; "if any thing in this or any letters I may write you should contain any information worthy of communication you will please to make it, with my compliments to the Gentlemen of Newbury port"; P. S., "I do not wish any of my letters should be printed, tho' I have no objection any extracts from them may when you think proper."

Benjamin Goodhue to Azor Orne. No copy known; acknowledged in Orne to Goodhue, 25 January.

Governor Alexander Martin to George Washington. ALS, Washington Papers, DLC. Written from North Carolina. For the full text, see *PGW* 5:16–18. See also *DHFFC* 2:199–201.

Has been informed that Joseph Martin has been unjustly incriminated by Bennet Ballew before Congress for malpractice as Indian agent.

Theodorick Bland Randolph to St. George Tucker. ALS, Tucker-Coleman Papers, ViHi. Addressed to Williamsburg, Virginia; franked by Thomas Tudor Tucker; postmarked 19 January.

"Since the meeting of congress there has been a great deal of parade made about the President, and to which I am afraid he had no objection."

Theodore Sedgwick to Ephraim Williams. ALS, Sedgwick Papers, MHi. Place to which addressed not indicated.

Asks that Thomas Dwight and (John or Justus?) Ashmun be informed of the value of public securities, which he reports.

Roger Sherman to Justus Mitchell. No copy known; acknowledged in Mitchell to Sherman, 26 January.

[Edenton] *State Gazette of North Carolina*, 23 January.

Johnston left for New York, accompanied by Williamson; "if the prayers of the good and virtuous are heard, a happy and prosperous journey will await him."

Letter from New York. [Massachusetts] *Salem Gazette*, 26 January; reprinted at Portland, Maine. This letter paraphrases Goodhue's letter of this date to the Salem Insurance Offices, printed above.

Mentions several provisions of the report on public credit, including the estimates of the federal and state debts.

TUESDAY, 19 JANUARY 1790

Fogg (Johnson)

Edward Fox to Andrew Craigie

***

I find that Mr. Fitzimons, who with Mr. R. Morris, went on to N. York, this morning: does not like Colo. Hamiltons plan. I had a long conversation with him on Yesterday. His Ideas are that 6 ℔ Cent ought not to be paid,

and that neither houses will ever agree to pay more than 4 ℔ Cent. That in order to save the credit and honor of the Government, the *purchasers* of Certificates ought to make an offer to Congress to relinquish ⅓ of the Interest—he told me that if they would do this, *he* would *undertake* to assure the original holders 6 ℔ Ct. By this it would appear that he has some influential men with him. He has been useing all his art with Mr. [*William*] Bingham, and several other capital holders, to make this offer, but he has not met with any encouragement: at which he seems much hurt. and declares that as they will not see their own Interest; for that by holding out, and insisting on 6 ℔ Ct.—they run considerable risk, and that their not offering the public ⅓ of their Interest, they perhaps will not get even the 4, which he would engage to get them if they would follow his advice. What think you to all this?
***

ALS, Craigie Papers, MWA. Written from Philadelphia; postmarked. The omitted text includes an anxious request for Craigie's observations about Hamilton's report on public credit.

Charles Pettit to Elias Boudinot

The opening of the Budget is considered as a Matter of so much Moment that Curiosity is rather too faint a Term to express the Eagerness with which its Tendency & Contents are enquired after. The Accounts we have yet received of it are too vague to form an Opinion upon. The Letter writers evidently do not understand what they attempt to describe as their Descriptions are not only extremely variant, but contradictory. As a Public Creditor I have my Share of Curiosity about it; and as a Member of the Committee,[1] & one who has taken an active part in behalf of that Class of Citizens, I am much enquired of, without being able to give satisfactory Answers. In a few Days, I presume, the whole Report will be in print. You will much oblige me by sending a Copy as early as may be.

From what I can gather from the various Accounts I have heard, the Plan is founded on those Principles of Honesty on which alone public Credit can be established. But I am apprehensive the Ways & Means for raising the necessary Revenues are too narrow. Impost & Tonnage afford an excellent Source if they are not overstrained; but there may be danger in leaning upon them for more than they can bear. However, I shall spare my Remarks till I see the Plan, as I wish it to have the fairest possible Chances of Success.

At the Request of Col. Hartley I have written a Letter to him on the subject of funding the Debt, which I have no objection to his shewing if he thinks proper. How far my Ideas accord with those of official Men, I am yet to learn; but I hope to find myself nearer to their path than Pelatiah, whose

Pamphlet I am told you are all obliged to read.[2] The Day I hope is past, for the prevalence of such Notions as he most values.

ALS, Old Catalog, Rosenbach Museum and Library, Philadelphia. Written from Philadelphia; postmarked.

[1] Pettit was a member of a committee appointed by the public creditors of Pennsylvania to represent their interests with Congress. For their petition of 21 August 1789, which was an impetus for Hamilton's first report on public credit, see *DHFFC* 8:260–64.

[2] Pelatiah Webster's *Plea for the Poor Soldier* (Philadelphia, 1790). Its printer, Francis Bailey, sent copies to each member of Congress. See Addendum, volume 22.

X. Y.: A Few Reflections,
Humbly Submitted to the Consideration of the Public in General, and in Particular of the Congress of the United States

THOUGH the following reflections come from an individual citizen, no way connected with public business, I hope they will be read with candour and attention. All good conduct proceeds from certain radical principles; and retired theoretical persons certainly may judge as well, perhaps they often judge better, of these, than such as are engaged in the bustle and hurry of an active life, or occupied in the management of particular affairs. Another circumstance encourages me in this hope, that I intend to offer nothing but what shall be beyond the imputation of proceeding either from party attachment or mercenary views.

When the federal constitution was agreed on, it was the fervent desire, I may say the earnest prayer, of many, that it might take place and get into operation with quietness, and under the acquiescence and approbation of the public. This, I think we may say, has happily been the case, so far as we have yet come. The persons chosen to fill the houses of Congress have been generally approved. Perhaps some states, in a few instances, might have made a better choice; but, upon the whole there is little reason to complain. I remember to have heard a gentleman, well acquainted with the subject, say of the former Congress who conducted the war, that he had never known a time in which it did not contain a great plurality of men of integrity, and among these a very respectable number of distinguished abilities. I hope and believe that this is the case at present, and may it always continue to be so.

The measures taken by Congress in their last session have, in general, given satisfaction. I am not ignorant that there have been severe, and in my opinion petulant and insolent, remarks made upon the salaries fixed for public officers, and the compensation allowed for the attendance of members of Congress, especially on the last. I am of opinion, however, that they are both reasonable, and the last at least as reasonable as the first, if not more so. I hope few persons will ever be in Congress, who, devoting their time to the public service, may not well deserve the compensation fixed for them, from their character and talents: and, if they have any lucrative profession or valuable private fortune, these must be deserted for a time, and probably a loss incurred greater than the whole wages. I should also be sorry to hear of any member of Congress, who became rich by the savings above the expence. I know very well that there have been Congress men, and Assembly men too, who have carried home considerable sums out of their wages; but they were such generally as did more good to their families by their penury, than to their country by their political Wisdom.

I come now to what I chiefly intend by this short essay, Much time, of the last session, was spent in debates upon fixing a place for the permanent residence of Congress, and building a federal city. That matter was under the consideration of the former Congress, and was fixed and unfixed, I believe, more than once. It always occasioned great altercation, nor was it possible to tell when it was settled; for whenever Congress changed its members, or the members changed their opinions, everything that had been done was undone. In the last meeting of the federal Congress it seemed to have been finally decided; but, whether by accident or the address of some who were opposed to the decision, it was thrown open again, and is now left as unsettled as ever. I have not met with any body who was sorry, but with many who were happy at this circumstance; and I now sincerely wish that it may be suffered to *sleep* in its present situation, at least for a considerable time, and till some other business of greater and more confessed importance, shall be completely finished. I am now to give my reasons for this opinion.

1. A determination upon that subject is not *necessary*. When I say it is not necessary, I mean that we are not urged to it by any pressing inconveniences or injuries which we have suffered, or are suffering, for want of it. Everybody must own that it would be very expensive; and, indeed, I am one myself who—if it were to be done at all, and there were buildings to be erected which should not belong to any state but to the union—would wish that they should not be barely elegant, but magnificent, that they might not derogate from the dignity of the empire. This is not contrary to the general principle of economy; for it has been observed, that some of the most frugal nations have been most sumptuous in their public edifices, of which the Stadthouse of Amsterdam is an example. Therefore, if the necessity were great, if the public business could not be carried on, or the public authority maintained without it, I should be for submitting to every inconvenience, & would not be deterred even by the expence it felt. But is this really the case? Does it appear to be necessary from the nature of the thing? No. The weight and influence of any deliberative or legislative body, depend much

more on the wisdom of their measures than the splendid apartments in which they are assembled. Does it appear to be necessary, from experience, or the example of other nations? I think not. I can hardly recollect above one or two of the kingdoms or states of Europe, in which the capital is central; and as to confederated republics, some of them have no common capital at all. The Swiss Cantons have no federal city: the Germanic Body has no federal city. The different states of which this last consists have for ages, when they had occasion to meet for common consultation, held their diets at different places. But we need go no further than our own experience. Did not the former Congress carry on the war with Great Britain, defend and secure the liberties of the United States, without a federal city? Was the want of it greatly or deeply felt as an inconvenience? I do not recollect a single complaint made, either in speech or writing, upon the subject.

2. It can be but little *profitable.* The truth is, when I attempt to recollect and enumerate the advantages to be derived from a federal city, in a central place, yet little inhabited, I find them very few and very small. If the American empire were to be one consolidated government, I grant it would be of some consequence that the seat of that government and source of authority should not be too distant from the extremities, for reasons which I need not here mention: but if the particular states are to be preserved, and supported in their constitutional governments, it seems of very little consequence where the Congress, consisting of representatives from these states, shall hold its sessions. There is not only little profit in their being fixed and central, but perhaps some advantages might arise from their being unfixed and ambulatory. This last seems more suitable to the equality of rights of the several states. It is far from being an impossible supposition, that the state in which Congress should be fixed, would think itself entitled to a leading, if not to a domineering, influence over the other states. As to easiness of access, such is the state of this country, living along the sea coast and having so many navigable rivers, that any city whatever, on the coast or great rivers, is easily accessible; and the difference of distances, especially when the payment is to be in proportion to the distance, is not worth mentioning. It is further to be observed, that though buildings may be easily raised for the accommodation of Congress, yet a great city, or a city of opulence or commerce, could not be raised for a long tract of time. It is even uncertain whether the bare residence of Congress during their annual sessions (which it is to be hoped in a few years hence will be but short) independent of other circumstances, will ever raise a great or commercity at all. The Hague, though the residence of the Stadtholder,[1] is far from being the largest, most populous, or most wealthy city in Holland. Now I humbly conceive that, if not residence in, yet nearness to some important commercial city, or cities, will be found to be absolutely necessary for transactions relating to money

or finance: so that if the advantages and disadvantages of a federal city, on the proposed plan, are fairly weighted, I am almost of opinion that the latter would derate.

3. There is reason to fear it may be very *hurtful*. Nothing is of so much consequence to us at present as union; and nothing is so much the desire of all unprejudiced public spirited and virtuous men. The Federal Constitution is but new: it is, we hope, taking place; but cannot yet be said to have taken root. It will, from the nature of things, take some time before it can acquire the respect and veneration necessary in every government from the body of the people, who are always guided by feeling and habit more than by a train of reasoning, however conclusive. Now is there no reason to fear that the disputes on this subject may produce warmth and violence, and perhaps an alienation of mind in some states against others, very prejudicial to public order. The most trifling subjects of dispute have sometimes given birth to divisions, both in larger and smaller political bodies, which have ended in common ruin. If I am rightly informed, the disputes which have already taken place in Congress upon this subject, have been carried on with greater virulence of temper, and acrimony of expression, than have appeared upon any other that has been under their deliberation. This is not to be wondered at, for indeed it is of such a nature that it has a nearer relation to state attachments and local prejudices than any other that can be named. Perhaps in such a question it is lawful, decent, and even necessary, to plead the local interest of particular states; and therefore it is to be expected, that every delegate will contend with earnestness for that of his own. At any rate, whatever ostensible public reasons may be devised by a fertile invention, all unprejudiced hearers will believe that it is local attachment that guides their judgement and inflames their zeal. The only use that it is necessary for me to make of such a remark is, to show that the contention and animosity raised by this dispute will probably extend itself to every other, and that it will not be confined to the contending members in Congress, but will spread itself through all the states whose cause they plead, and whose interest they seem to espouse. This is one of these questions that had much better be decided wrong by general consent, than decided right by a small majority, without convincing or satisfying the opponents.

4. In the last place it is certainly, at least, *unseasonable*, though it were possible fully to answer all the objections I have stated above, I must still say, *there is a time for every thing under the sun*.[2] A measure may be good in itself, and even necessary in a qualified sense; yet, if there be another duty incumbent on the same body, that it is better and more necessary, this surely ought to have the precedence in point of time. Now I think it cannot be denied, and all intelligent persons in the United States seem to be of opinion, that

bringing order into our finances, restoring and establishing public credit, is the important business which the Congress has to do. It is also the most urgent in point of time, because in the interval many public creditors are in a situation truly deplorable; whereas I can think of nobody that is suffering much for want of a federal city. The two designs are also connected together as cause and effect; and I need not tell any body which of these ought to go foremost. What a romantic project will it be to fix on a situation and to form plans for building a number of palaces, before we provide money to build them with, or even before we pay these debts which we have already contracted. This is a matter in which not only all the citizens of America, those who are and those who are not public creditors, are deeply concerned, but on which will depend our future security, our interest and influence among foreign nations, and even the opinion that will be formed of us by posterity itself.

These few reflections, not enlarged upon as they might easily have been, nor swelled or exaggerated by pompous declamation, but simply and nakedly proposed, I leave to the judgment of the impartial public.

NYDG, 19 January.

---

[1] In 1559 William "the Silent" (1533–84) chose The Hague as his provincial capital while serving as Spain's viceroy or stadtholder over three Dutch provinces in the Spanish Netherlands. Under his leadership seven of the Dutch provinces leagued together as the United Provinces and declared their independence from Spain in 1581 (confirmed under the Treaty of Westphalia in 1649). William's successors in the House of Orange became the "stadtholders general" and The Hague continues as the federal seat of government to this day (as well as the provincial capital of South Holland), while Amsterdam serves as the constitutional capital.

[2] Apparently a paraphrase combining Ecclesiastes 1:9 and 3:1.

Epigram

Occasioned by the detention of an Honourable Member from his seat in
    Congress, for some days, on account of the sickness of his Lady.
MARIA, dear Lady, how blest is thy lot,
O'er so noble a Consort to bear SUCH A SWAY!
For sure VERY DEAR must that Woman be thought
Who is valued at more than "SIX DOLLARS A DAY."

[Stockbridge, Massachusetts] *Western Star*, 19 January; reprinted at Portsmouth, New Hampshire; Boston; Providence, Rhode Island; Hartford, Litchfield, New Haven, and New London, Connecticut; New York City (*NYDA*, 25 January); and Elizabethtown, New Jersey. The poem alludes to Sedgwick and his "Lady," Pamela.

[*Charles Pettit*] to [*Thomas Hartley*]

The subject, on which you desired me to write to you, is, in my estimation, of a very great importance to the United States. The stability of the government, the extention of manufactures and commerce, the prosperity of the agricultural interest, and, in short, the welfare of the community in every point of view, cannot fail to be affected by the good or ill state of Public Credit.

That "Public Credit is Public Wealth," is a political axiom which will hardly be controverted. Without counting the numerous advantages which the several States derived from this source, while they were Colonies, we may say it was the great engine by which the revolution was effected; for, although by overloading, we almost destroyed its strength in the course of the struggle, we could have made but a feeble opposition, and must have been crushed at an early period of the contest, without it. It became weak and languid from the want of that nourishment, which our straightened circumstances did not permit us to afford it, during the war; and which our want of experience and order have hitherto prevented us from giving it since the peace: But it has still preserved an existence, and is capable of being easily raised to perfect strength and vigor. There is no country possessed of more ample means to give it a firm establishment, than the United States, nor to which such an establishment would be more extensively useful and beneficial. We are now in the full possession of peace, liberty, and safety, under a government of our own forming, which possesses the confidence of the people in a more eminent degree than, perhaps, any government, of equal age, ever did before. We are a people abounding in plenty, and encreasing in wealth, with fewer exceptions as to individuals, than are to be found in any other country; and want nothing but the complete restoration and establishment of public credit, to render our political situation superior, all things considered, to that of any other on the face of the earth. Public credit, and confidence in the government, being firmly established, private credit and confidence will as naturally result, as vegetation does from the approach of the sun; and will as certainly decay if the former be withdrawn or embarrassed. How highly culpable, then, would it be, in the rulers of the nation, to neglect, or contaminate by tampering with, an ingredient so essential to political and social happiness.

It is a question not uncommonly asked, How is public credit to be established and maintained? There is scarcely an individual in the community that would hesitate a moment about an answer to such a question concerning himself. Every one knows that the purity of his credit depends on an honest compliance with his engagements. The only material difference between the public and an individual, in this respect, is, that if the latter neglects to comply with his engagements, the creditor has a remedy by legal process, which he has not against the former. Hence strict attention to the faith of contracts, is more necessary to the preservation of the credit of the public, than that of an individual. On the other hand, the public may derive greater advantages from preserving its credit unsullied, because it is, in itself, a satisfactory security to the creditors, which needs no auxiliary; and, by means of a regular sinking fund, the payments in discharge of public debts may be made to operate in the ratio of compound interest.

The plain and obvious mode, therefore, of establishing and maintaining public credit, is to fund the public debts, fairly and honestly, on revenues clearly sufficient to pay the interest punctually, and to establish a moderate sinking fund for paying a portion of the principal annually.

The benefits rising to the public, from such a measure, would not be confined to such only as would immediately result to the government from its capability to contract farther debts on the best terms, tho' these benefits would, of themselves, afford sufficient motives, if other motives than justice and good faith were requisite, for the adoption of it. The public debt, thus funded, would become a circulating medium, of equal use to the citizens with so much cash distributed among them, and would, proportionably promote improvements in agriculture, manufactures, and commerce, as well as increase the value of estates, and reduce the interest, or rent of money. These circumstances would at once increase the public revenues, and enable the citizens to pay them with greater ease.

But, it may be asked, By what ways and means are the revenues, necessary for this purpose, to be found? This is a subject which I ought not, perhaps, to say much upon at present, tho' I have no doubt of its practicability. It is referred to an officer of whose abilities and integrity I have a good opinion, and I confidently hope his plans will be good, and adequate to the purpose. I may, however, venture a few cursory remarks on the modes of raising revenues, without danger of improper intrusion on the province of the Secretary.

The impost and tonnage duties will probably produce nearly two millions of dollars per annum. This will increase, as our wealth and numbers increase, and may perhaps be enlarged by additional duties. A stamp duty, judiciously arranged, may raise a considerable sum; and may be made, to a certain degree, as little injurious to the feelings and prejudices of the people, as any mode of taxation. An excise has been mentioned by some. This, however, is a mode of taxation which, under present circumstances, I cannot recommend, because I am apprehensive that any mode of collection, that would be effectual, would be so disgusting to the people as to bring an odium on the government, and probably work more injury than the produce of the tax would be worth. Other sources of revenue may probably be devised; but, for the reasons above suggested, as well as to avoid extending

my letter to too great a length, I decline the pursuit of them at present.
But I cannot entirely dismiss the subject of revenue without a few words on
direct taxation. From this source alone, I think, all the expences of the civil
establishment, or ordinary expences of government ought to be supported.
It is a kind of tax which every citizen ought to pay promptly and cheerfully,
and to know that he pays it as a contribution to the support of the social
compact under which he holds and enjoys the rights of a free citizen. The
expences of war, and other extraordinary circumstances, and the debts occasioned by such extraordinaries, may, with less hazard, be provided for by
means less direct, and less sensibly felt by the people; but taxes, at least to
the amount of the ordinary civil establishments, should openly apply to the
feelings of the citizens. They keep up that direct communication between
the government and the citizens individually, which is necessary to keep
both parties awake to their reciprocal duties, and their proper dependance
on each other, and which I consider as necessary to preserve the government
firm and pure. Lay aside this mode of taxation, and the bulk of the people
will relax into indolent slumbering concerning the affairs of government;
become heedless and negligent about elections, and suffer the government
to slide into the hands of improper men, and to establish precedents, and
adopt measures destructive of the principles which it has cost them so much
pains to establish. These are the sentiments of a private citizen, who wishes
to see the government honourably and amply supported, and who desires
to pay his proportion towards that support. He doubts not the patriotism
of the present administrators of the government, nor entertains a suspicion
that they will designedly swerve from their duty as trustees and guardians
of the peoples' rights; but such are his ideas of the nature and tendency of
all governments, that he is seriously apprehensive a free government cannot
long be preserved in its purity without deriving its support from the open
and sensible contributions of the people.

Revenues amounting to about three millions of dollars annually, may be
requisite to support the present establishments of the United States, and to
fund the ascertained debts, both foreign and domestic.* Revenues to this
amount I suppose may be established with little difficulty. A considerable
part of the domestic debt is offered in the market greatly under par, which
may afford the treasury an opportunity of gaining as much to the public as
will establish a considerable sinking fund, supposing the revenues appropriated to the funding of the debt, to be no more than commensurate with the
annual interest. A new loan may be opened for the reception of a proportion
in certificates, and the residue in cash, and this cash applied to the purchase

*The writer seems to have had in contemplation the certified debts only, independent
of indents and state debts.

of certificates at the market price. But here again I find restraint in mentioning my ideas, lest I should infringe on the province of the secretary. If you examine the origin of the bank of England, and its connexion with, and dependance on the government, you will ready perceive the leading features of a practicable and useful plan.

I have heard of divers schemes of discrimination and reduction of interest. I do not presume to say that these schemes have originated in dishonest motives, though I should consider the adoption of them to be highly injurious to the true interest, as well as to the dignity and honour of the United States.

By discrimination, I understand to be meant, a distinction between original holders of the public certificates, and the purchasers of such as have been alienated. For my own part, if I could conceive the measure practicable, and consistent with honor and sound policy, self interest would prompt me to advocate such discrimination, as I am on the footing of an original holder as to nearly the whole of the certificates I possess. But I consider the scheme as unjust and impolitic in its principles, and impracticable in execution. Unjust, because the purchasers bought the certificates fairly in open market, and paid a valuable consideration for them, proportioned to the general estimation of the risque of delay, or final loss, compared with the prospect of ultimate gain at a distant and uncertain day. The certificates were made payable to bearer, with the avowed design that they might be transferred with facility; every holder of a certificate is therefore as fully possessed of a contract with the public, as the original holder was; and, as the public received full value for the certificates they issued, and explicitly contracted to pay the same to whoever should be the bearer of these evidences of their contracts, they cannot justly refuse such payment. Impolitic, because being a violation of the public faith, it would be destructive of that confidence which ought to be placed in public engagements. And impracticable, because, if it were proper for government to go into the enquiry, they could not possibly discover the value at which the certificates have respectively been transferred from time to time. The loan-office certificates were, many of them, originally taken out of the office in the names of other persons than the lenders of the money; and, being transferable by delivery only, they frequently changed their owners at full value. It would therefore be no less impracticable than improper to investigate the private transactions of the individuals through whose hands they have passed.

The reduction of the interest without the consent of the creditors, whatever plausible appearance might be given to the measure, would be neither more nor less, by an arbitrary act of power, to reduce the value of the principal. Such an act would tarnish the fame of the most despotic government in Europe. It cannot therefore claim a moment's consideration in the councils of the United States. It is true that in England, where they began their funding system at an interest of 8 per cent. they have since reduced it, by different steps, down to 3. But these reductions were never made without the consent of the creditors, to whom an option was always given, from time to time, as the market rate of interest fell, either to receive full payment of principal and interest, or, by a new contract, to continue their loans at the rate proposed; and these proposed rates were always such as would have induced other lenders to furnish the money if the former had declined the acceptance of them. Whenever the government have wanted new loans, if the market rate of interest was higher than that at which the funded debt was established, they continued to borrow at the same rate, *nominally*, in order to avoid odious distinctions among the creditors; but, in *reality*, they paid the full market rate of interest by receiving less than 100 per cent. from the holders, so as to make the market rates of interest on the sum actually, equal to the nominal rate on the nominal sum. Towards the close of the late war, the British government actually received from the lenders but 50 for every hundred of the debt contracted on loan. The market price of stock at 3 per cent. was then about 54 per cent. The market rate of interest in England is now at or under 4 per cent. and the price of 3 per cent. stock near 80, though the legal rate of interest continues, notwithstanding these fluctuations in the market, at 5 per cent. By a strict adherence to justice in dealing with the public creditors indiscriminately, the public credit is so well established in England, that the government can, at any time, borrow any sum they want, at the market rate of interest whatever it may be. By encouraging the buying and selling of stock, it becomes a circulating medium, and is disseminated amongst the people. It is always equal to cash in the hands of the possessor, with the additional advantage of the growing interest. By these means there is always a demand for it, which enables government to contract fresh loans at pleasure. Any attempt to discriminate, or otherwise alter the terms of contract, by an *ex post facto* law, would weaken the confidence of the people, stagnate the circulation, and sicken the public credit to a degree that would probably do more injury to the nation than an unsuccessful war.

I find I have extended this letter to a greater length than I intended, tho' I have aimed at brevity in every part of it. If you should be fatigued by opening more chaff than the few grains of information will compensate, you will be pleased to remember that you invited the task by desiring me to write to you on a subject which cannot be fairly understood without taking into view an extensive field of considerations, which it would require a volume to arrange and illustrate properly. I have confined myself to a few particulars only, and of these I have given rather a syllabus than a description, trusting to your imagination to dilate and apply them.

I have heard that the plan of the Secretary of the Treasury is to be printed: may I ask the favor of you to send me a copy of it? The accounts which have reached us concerning it, are, as yet, too vague to form an opinion upon: They are contradictory of each other in very essential points, and clearly shew that the letter writers do not understand what they undertake to describe.

PP, 10 December 1790. The editors base their identification of the author and recipient on the fact that Pettit indicated in his letter to Boudinot on 17 January that he had written Hartley a letter on the "funding of the debt"; further, the last two sentences in the letter to Hartley appear almost verbatim in the letter to Boudinot. In the newspaper, the letter was preceded by a note to the editors: "The inclosed is a genuine copy of a letter written near twelve months ago. The sentiments and observations it contains, however, may not be inapplicable to present circumstances. It may afford information to some, and entertainment to others, without offence to any. If you view it in this light, you may give it a place in your Paper at a convenient opportunity."

OTHER DOCUMENTS

Louis Guillaume Otto to Comte de Montmorin. Copy, in French, Henry Adams Transcripts, DLC. Received 4 March.
Despite the extreme want and high price of wheat in Ireland, the premium given to American wheat by the government of France will continue to direct it to that kingdom; it is probable that if French consuls had received instructions to encourage the importation of wheat into France and to conclude contracts with the principal American merchants, the supply would have been even more abundant.

David Rittenhouse to James Madison. ALS, Madison Papers, DLC. Written from Philadelphia. For the full text, see *PJM* 12:469–70. For additional information on Bailey and counterfeiting, see *DHFFC* 8:73–84.
Recommends Francis Bailey, who intends to apply for a government job and whose counterfeit-proof method of printing "may perhaps be of use."

Daniel Rodman to George Washington. ALS, Washington Papers, DLC. Written from No. 70 Cherry Street, New York City. For the full text, see *PGW* 5:21–24.
Office seeking: collector of Newport, Rhode Island, or some other port; mentions Connecticut delegation, particularly Huntington, Wadsworth, and Trumbull, as references.

Theodore Sedgwick to Samuel Henshaw. No copy known; acknowledged in Henshaw to Sedgwick, 30 January.

Theodore Sedgwick to the Treasurer of Massachusetts (Alexander Hodgdon). Abstract of two page ALS, *Libbie Catalog*, 17–21 March 1891.
"Relative to the money raised by the State during the war."

South Carolina Instructions, Michael E. Stevens and Christine M. Allen, eds., *Journals of the House of Representatives, 1789–1790* (Columbia, S.C., 1984), pp. 349–51.

> On 19 January, when it ratified all twelve Amendments to the Constitution that had been proposed by Congress in September 1789, the South Carolina legislature instructed its congressional delegation to secure adoption of the amendments proposed by the state's ratification convention in 1788: limits on Congress's power to levy direct taxes and regulate federal elections; the insertion of the word *other* into Article VI, Section 3, of the Constitution, so that it would read, "no *other* religious Test shall ever be required as a Qualification to any Office or public Trust under the United States" than the oath or affirmation that bound them to support the Constitution; and the reservation to the states of all powers not *expressly* delegated to the federal government.

George Thatcher to Jeremiah Hill. No copy known; acknowledged in Hill to Thatcher, 13 February.

FG, 20 January.

> Clymer was elected to the committee of correspondence for the Philadelphia Society for Promoting Agriculture.

WEDNESDAY, 20 JANUARY 1790

Cold (Johnson)

George Rogers Clark to John Brown

***

There is nothing new that hath transpired since my last letter to you of the first of June. The Indians continue their depredations as usual, and will continue to do so until the whole system of our conduct towards them is changed. You will pardon me Sir, for being so free on the subject, but you can hardly mention one single part of our general conduct towards them, meant as pacific measures, but hath had the opposite effect. Invite them to treaties, give them presents, treat them with great respect and humanity, court their friendship, &c. &c.! What is the result of their deliberation upon all this? That we are afraid of them; and their speakers, to prove it to their audience, allude to this general conduct of ours, and say that they can make war and peace with us when they please. Until this idea of theirs is destroyed by our future conduct towards them, we may not expect any better treatment from them than we at present receive. Excell them, if possible, in their own policy, treat them with indifference, make war on them, prosecute it with all the vigor and devastation possible, mention nothing of peace to them, and you would soon have them suing for mercy. Turn the scale upon them and oblige them to give up part of their country to pay for the expense of the war, &c. All other policy in the Indian department, except something similar to this, is the result of the want of judgment or information. I know that we are led to believe that the Indians may be made desperate, that they would even destroy their women and children, that they might have no incumbrance, but continue at war as long as they lived; that they would do things similar to this, for the sake of revenge if an insolent and vigorous conduct was made use of towards them. This was the policy of British Agents, and appears to have descended from them to ours, in order to make the world believe that they, themselves, were men of the greatest importance to the public, by cultivating such a belief of the Indian voracity. This idea hath done us much damage in our public councils and ought to be exploded. The troops you have on this communication, instead of being of service, really encourage the Indians. Their disposition is such, in small parties, at great distance, from each other, that but little could be expected from either. The Indians frequently harassing them without any attempt on their side to retaliate, which the Indians greatly boast of, and encourage their young men to perseverance. If those troops are really designed for the protection of the country, why could they not be so disposed of as to render real service? Embody them, fight their way into the centre of the Indian country, and there take post at the most eligible spot. They might always be secure in what assistance they wished for from the Frontiers. Such a body of troops posted among their towns, sufficiently strong to chastise them at any time, by proper management, would do the business wished for. This would require but little more provisions than the present system, and be no more expensive than a variety of little useless posts, that is of great expense without profit, except a few, as posts of communication. The state of the public funds is not a good excuse for suffering the war to continue; for the credit of Congress would enable them to raise and support what armies they pleased in this country, for that business, without a penny of ready cash. The thoughts of peace, and the prospect of being hereafter paid, would induce the people to give every aid in their power. But could you not, in a few days, establish a fund for the immediate payment of all such expense, and of general good to that class of people that would render their bodily service, and perhaps prevent the loss of a great proportion of them to the Union? Set a moderate price on your lands, pay all those expenses in Land Warrants without destroying their value by confining them to Townships, &c. The people would prefer this to money.

[Frankfort, Kentucky] *The Commonwealth*, 25 July 1838, Draper Collection, WHi. Written from Louisville, Kentucky. The newspaper was edited by Brown's son Orlando, who reported that the text was "from the original letters. We have taken no other liberty with these precious documents than to arrange the punctuation." The omitted text includes thanks for Brown's intervention with Levi Hollingsworth for the payment of a debt owed by Clark, and assurances that Clark will "probably in four or five months" convey papers he has collected for a history of Clark's Revolutionary War campaigns in the Northwest Territory: "If this is to make its appearance in the world, there is no person I could be more happy in their handing the subject than Mr. Madison. You will be pleased to favor me in presenting my most sincere thanks to that gentleman for his expression in my favor."

James Dunn to George Thatcher

Your favors have duly recd.——from appearances I think there is the strongest probability that the subject of a naturalization Law will early occupy the attention of congress——I beg leave just to remark that it seems to me proper that the means of naturalizing should be as accomodating and as little expensive as possible to all, but particularly to those that have resided in this Country four or five years since the War——whether a Certificate of the Character by the Select or Headmen of the Town, afterwards the oath of allegiance before a Justice of peace——or the mode used by the State of pensylvania[1] would be the most accomodating, least expensive, and most eligible is not to be determined by Sir Your most hble. Servt.

ALS, Chamberlain Collection, MB. Written from Portland, Maine.

---

[1] Pennsylvania required only a one year residence and an oath or affirmation of allegiance to the state.

William Samuel Johnson to John Fitch

I recd. yr. favr. of the 9th. Instt. & was extremely glad to find you have been able to make improvements in your steam Boat & have brot. it to the degree of perfection you mention I doubt not you will find it susceptible of still further improvements & that it eventually will be of extensive Utility to Mankind. I wish you could have been properly rewarded for your services, but I cannot say that there is at present much prospect of this. Congress will however no doubt e'er long resume the Consideration of the Act which was before them last session for securing to Discoverers Inventers &c the benifit of their respective Discoveries &c., but in what it will terminate it is difficult at present to say nor can I point out any particular measures for you to pursue, other than that you acquainting as many Members of Congress as you can with your services & sacrifices. For myself, I shall be happy to find it in my power to render you my services, & if Congs. shoud, as it is probable they will take measures for Coining Copper I will as you desire mention Mr. Voit [*Henry Voigt*] as a person acquainted with that business, but you will observe that all Appointments to Office or employment now originate with the President of the U.S. or some of the Execuve. officers of Government to whom application must be made as circumstances may require.

FC:dft, Johnson Papers, CtHi. The recipient is identified from the endorsement on the extant address page of a letter from Fitch to Johnson, 9 January, which is filed with this letter.

Louis Guillaume Otto to Comte de Montmorin

In forming their new government the Americans have taken such good care to balance the different powers that it will be many years before the legislature is able to have the advantage over the executive, or the latter over the legislature. As a result of that vigilance they [*Congress*] have determined almost unanimously that in no circumstance would the secretaries of state be allowed a seat within the legislature, but as in all the great operations of government it is almost impossible that the members of Congress will have the necessary expertise to make a plan, the habit is already established of allowing the secretaries of state and heads of the different departments to report a plan and the legislature to limit itself to debating or rejecting it. It is the legislature itself that ordinarily calls for the work of the executive officers but the President, being aware that several deliberations will be held behind closed doors, begins to use his prerogative of communicating to Congress on his own initiative the projects that seem to merit its attention. In the address with which he opened the present session, he recommended the establishment of a military force, but Congress not seeming disposed to deal with that measure, it was left to him to communicate a [*militia*] plan drawn up by the secretary of war, which has had it published immediately in order to undergo public review. The plan which grants Americans the virtues of the ancient Republics, at least those that biased and pompous historians attribute to them, is more worthy of a scholarly oration than a serious plan of government. Here it recalls the customs and the institutions of the Spanish and the Romans, that is, of the two peoples whose political constitution had not the least affinity to that of the Americans; it stresses the maxim, so foreign to a commercial Republic, that a free people ought to be a nation of soldiers; it wishes not merely that all the citizens might be militarized but that young people might be educated at a national camp for 4 or 5 years, not only to understand the art of war but also to escape the softness of the city and harden their bodies to fatigues, exercises, and privations of all sorts. The author sets forth the danger of a regular [*standing*] army in a free country and he thinks, with all firm democrats, that the [*militia*] forces should always be at the disposal of the executive power exclusively, despite the recent example furnished by the regular troops of France for whom, according to him, discipline had become so slack that their commanders were no longer in a proper state to restrain them. All those arguments, although generally popular, did not make the secretary of war's plan acceptable; he confessed to me in advance that he did not at all expect that view to be acceptable to Congress. The public has not confined itself to censuring it, but has even formed some associations to petition Congress; the object of executive power seems rather to have exceeded democratic principles to the point of rendering the people more sanguine and making them desire precisely the opposite of what he had proposed. In America one knows perfectly well the indirect ways one must guide a people always jealous of their liberty. The dread that it has caused, particularly among the merchants, the idea of a permanent militia has produced the salutary effect of making them desire the establishment of regular troops, which would have been almost unanimously rejected if the executive had had the impudence to propose it. The public seems perfectly prepared at the moment to accept from Congress the establishment of a regular army which, although very small at the start, would be augmented according to circumstances.

I find myself, Sir, in a country fertile with speculations and political experiments of all types, but very barren of results. My pen feels deeply the peculiarity, hardly appropriate, of casting self-interest into my reports. Everything here seems all maxim and no action—and as there are few maxims that may be true at all times and in all places, those that I have the honor to submit to you as a simple historian may be subject to a thousand modifications that I can not contend with, nor justify, nor even anticipate. Time and experience alone will be able to decide. There are also some political experiments that may succeed in all likelihood without nevertheless being exactly proper. In 1787 I did not cease to express my doubts about the establishment of a new American government, yet that revolution has been accomplished, although it is still only *nominal* with the exception of the impost that the States had already granted to the former Congress, although with some restrictions, which obstructed the collection of it. The other powers of the general government still only exist on paper; time will make them effective or illusory. The probabilities and inclinations of the moment are all that I can vouch for, and that experimental government, erected on shifting sand, will yet often change its appearance and deceive the shrewdness of an observer more capable than I.

Copy, in French, Henry Adams Transcripts, DLC. Received 2 July. Otto's letters included in *DHFFC* were usually written over the course of days, and even weeks, following the day they were begun.

Samuel Phillips, Jr. to Benjamin Goodhue

I am much obliged indeed by your favours of the 11th. & 13th. current for the information of what had taken place & your opinion respecting the future, as you do me the honor to ask my opinion on the propriety of the General Governments embracing the debts of the several States, I will just query whether such a measure wont evidently & very materially strengthen that Government, and whether the omission of it, will not have an effect directly the reverse, if this would be the case, the measure cannot be viewed in an indifferent light—another point is very clear, that the Genl. Government, can produce far more (perhaps double & perhaps fourfold) from an excise, than the seperate Legislature, with nearly the same inconvenience to the people—and it is probable if the debts are assumed the chief of the excise will be taken with them; you I am confident, will recollect the embarrassments & perplexities to which we have been subjected by means of different regulations in our Sister States; they have occasioned the passing as many Acts, almost as there have been Sessions of the Generl. Court, since an Excise act first passed,[1] and after all we are at this day ~~of~~ in as disagreable a situation in this respect as ever—The duty is collected very partially & unequally and the loss of a great part of the Revenue is not the greatest evil, for by means of the struggling & evasion of many the fair trader is obliged to relinquish his business or fall in with the General practice—there is now a loud & general call upon the State Legislature to redress the evil, but altho' we all see & lament so great an evil, as that of a public measures operating as a tax upon honesty, & a reward to dishonorable conduct, yet to apply an adequate remedy, is, I fear, beyond the ability of ~~the~~ any seperate Government.
***

ALS, Letters to Goodhue, NNS. Written from Boston. The omitted text briefly describes actions of the Massachusetts legislature on the constitutionality of federal officials holding seats in the state legislature and mentions two unlocated enclosures relating to this issue.

[1] In the late 1780s the Massachusetts legislature passed a series of excise laws: in November 1786, "An Act to Raise a public revenue by excise;" a year later, "An Act in Addition to an Act intitled An Act to Raise a public revenue by excise;" in March 1788, "An Act in Addition to and for the amending of an act intitled An Act to Raise a public revenue by excise;" ten weeks later, "An Act in Addition to the several Acts for raising a Public Revenue by Excises;" and a year later, in June 1789, "An Act in addition to 'An Act to Raise a public revenue by excise'." During February 1790 the legislature debated the issue again and on

3 March replaced all these acts with "An Act to raise a public Revenue by Excise, and to regulate the Collection thereof."

George Lee Turberville to James Madison

An opportunity occurring to a post office—enables me to consign a few lines to you—to assure you that I am still sensible of the obligations that My self my posterity & my fellow citizens are under to you—who have devoted Your life hitherto to the formation of such measures as tend to the promotion of general happiness.

I was not a little disappointed that you did not visit Richmond during the session—I had flatter'd myself once more to have had the pleasure of meeting with you—My retired situation from your walks—almost prohibits the most distant hope of seeing you a Visitant at my Cottage.

A word or two of Politics—how comes it to pass that the secretary of the Treasury has undertaken to repeal a Law of the United States? The Law says that the Duties shall be paid in Actual specie only. The secratary in his Letters[1] to the Naval Officers here (& particularly to Mr. Hudson Muse Collector of Rappahannoc) directs them to receive the notes of the Banks of Newyork & Philadelphia—this may open a speculation—distructive not only to this state by drawing all the specie from it—but ultimately it may be ruinous to the United States. But at any rate the precedent to me is a very disagreeable one.

The fate of the amendments here—you know—Remember that the house of Representatives passed them by a majority of thirteen the senate alone occasion their non-adoption.

We earnestly wish to know whether the senate really are shut up from the world whilst they deliberate as a part of the Legislature—All reports from Newyork assert that they are shut up—but our senator I have been told declares that one door is always open for any persons to listen to their debates through.

***

[P. S.] What news from France?

ALS, Madison Collection, NN. Written from "Epping," Richmond County, Virginia. For the full text, see *PJM* 12:470–71.

---

[1] See *PAH* 5:394–95 (22 September 1789), 444–45 (14 October 1789).

George Walton to John Adams

Being on a circuit of our Superior Courts, & finding a Vessel ready to sail for New-York, I embrace the occasion of congratulating your zeal on the effectual opperation of the federal Government. Its quiet progress to its present stage is a phenomonen in the history of mankind. But in such new and perplexed concerns a perfect combination of the various parts cannot be expected; and it is a problem which experience only will solve, whether some parts of the proceedings of the first Session of the National Congress will not be found to have exceptions. To me it appears that the Judiciary system is too ponderous, expensive and unweildy; and its iron teeth too frightful for the condition of the Southern States. It is too unqualified. The right of the writ of Capias ad Satisfaciendum[1] in the first and last instance, under our circumstances, and without any bankrupt provision, will, I fear, produce much uneasiness. Should the british debts be entirely and at once sued for from Virginia inclusive South, the consequences would be ruinous. That these debts remained so heavy is attributable to the depredations of the War; and I ever thought ought to have been made an object of National consideration. With respect to this State I dont think we are affected, as those debts were confiscated prior to the Treaty of Peace; and all acts of Confiscation already passed were recognized and confirmed by the Treaty.[2] In another capacity I was called upon to give an opinion on this ground last year; and the State of facts made on that occasion I will do myself the pleasure to enclose to you, & shall be particularly obliged by any observations you shall see fit to make thereupon.

The principle of the general Representation in the National Government being according to numbers, this State has lately adopted a measure to encrease hers, by disposing of a part of her vacant territory to three private Companies.[3] This measure will, no doubt, be ascribed to other motives by some: but, although I was not a member of the legislature, I am well assured & believe that the true ground of the cut was what I have mentioned. While human nature continues the same, Governments will always act from a sense of its own Interest and aggrandisemcnt.

I did myself the pleasure to write to you some little time since from Augusta; and the sentiments then expressed will always continue to govern me. I am full of zeal for the prosperity of the United-States; and I am the servant of this State.

Colonel Gunn requests that this letter should be the Vehicle of his respects to you; & that I would add that he is extremely anxious to be with you: but that he was under the necessity of attending the court now sitting. In [*Captain Cornelius*] Schermerhorn he will certainly Sail.

ALS, Adams Family Manuscript Trust, MHi. Written from Savannah, Georgia.

---

[1] A writ restraining the physical liberty of a debtor pending the satisfaction of a debt.
[2] Because the Treaty of Paris (1783) only required Congress to recommend strongly to

the states that they compensate individuals whose property was confiscated, it recognized by implication the legality of the confiscations.

³On 21 December 1789, the Georgia legislature passed an act preempting much of its western territory for three private companies of speculators collectively known as the Yazoo Land Companies. Five million acres in present-day central Mississippi were reserved for the South Carolina Yazoo Company upon payment of $66,964 to the state within two years (payable in Georgia state debt certificates). The Virginia Yazoo Company was to pay $93,741 upon the same terms for seven million acres in northern Mississippi, while the Tennessee Company was offered three and a half million acres in northern Alabama for $46,875. Other provisions of the act were that settlers were to avoid hostilities with the indigenous peoples (primarily Choctaws and Chickasaws), whose title to the same land the Yazoo companies were enjoined to extinguish. For the text of the act (enclosed with Knox's report on the frontiers, submitted to the House on 24 January 1791), see *DHFFC* 5:1371–74. Those designated as assignees under the act included such well connected speculators as Patrick Henry and Huger's brother Isaac. Many other of the companies' "associates" prudently kept their involvement secret, for, as Walton's letter suggested, the Yazoo transaction became highly controversial almost immediately. For more on its impact on congressional politics, see Treaty of New York with the Creeks in Correspondence: Third Session.

Summary View of the Report of the Secretary of the Treasury, submitted to the Hon. House of Representatives of the United States, on Thursday last

THE Report of the Secretary of the Treasury, after premising, in a forcible manner, the importance of the PUBLIC CREDIT, to the character and prosperity of a Nation—the impolicy, as well as the impraticability of making a distinction between the various classes of Public Creditors—the obligation which the public are under, either of discharging the interest due on the debt, or of funding it, on the same terms with the principal—and the propriety of assuming the State Debts, not only on the principles of justice, but in order to facilitate a fair and equitable settlement of accounts between the States and the Union, and of preventing that competition in the raising of Revenue, which would prove either injurious to both, or oppressive to the people—proposes,

That a Loan should be opened for the full amount of the debt, as well of the particular States, as of the Union, upon the following terms, viz.

1st. That for every Hundred Dollars subscribed, payable in the debt, (as well Interest as Principal,) the subscriber should be entitled, to have two thirds funded on an yearly interest of Six per Cent, (the capital redeemable at the pleasure of the Government, by payment of the principal,) and to receive the other third in lands of the Western Territory, at the rate of Twenty Cents per acre—Or,

2d. To have the whole sum funded at a yearly interest of Four per Cent, irredeemable by any payment, exceeding Five Dollars per annum, on account both of the principal and interest, and to receive, as a compensation for the reduction of interest, Fifteen Dollars and Eighty Cents, payable in Lands, as in the preceding case—Or,

3dly. To have Sixty Six and Two Thirds Dollars funded at a yearly interest of Six per Cent. irredeemable also by any payment exceeding Four and Two Thirds Dollars per annum, on account of both of principal and interest—and to have at the end of Ten Years, Twenty Six Dollars and Eighty Eight Cents funded at the like interest, and rate of redemption—Or,

4thly. To have an annuity for the remainder of life, upon the contingency of living to a given age, not less distant than Ten Years, computing interest at Four per Cent.—Or,

5thly. To have an annuity for the remainder of life, on the contingency of the survivorship of the youngest of two persons, computing interest in this case also at Four per Cent.—Or,

6thly. In addition to the foregoing Loans, the Secretary proposes a Loan of Ten Millions Dollars, payable one half in specie, and the other half in the debt, (as well principal as interest,) bearing an interest of Five per Cent. irredeemable by any payment exceeding Six Dollars per annum, both of principal and interest.

And also (by way of experiment) a TONTINE[1] upon the following principles, viz.

THAT the Classes should be Six, composed respectively of persons of the following ages:

First Class. Of those of 20 years and under.

2d. do. Of those above 20, and not exceeding 30.

3d. do. Of those above 30, and not exceeding 40.

4th. do. Of those above 40, and not exceeding 50.

5th. do. Of those above 50, and not exceeding 60.

6th. do. Of those above 60.

Each share to be Two Hundred Dollars. The number of shares in each Class to be indefinite. Persons to be at liberty to subscribe on their own lives, or those of others, nominated by them.

	Dollars.	Cents.
The annuity upon a share in the 1st Class, to be	8	40
Upon a share in the Second,	8	65
Upon a share in the Third,	9	—
Upon a share in the Fourth,	9	65
Upon a share in the Fifth,	10	70
Upon a share in the Sixth,	12	80

The annuities of those who die, to be equally divided among the survivors, until Four Fifths shall be dead, when the principle of survivorship shall cease, and each Annuitant thenceforth enjoy his dividend as a several annuity, during the life upon which it shall depend.

On the Loans where interest is payable, it is proposed, that the payment of the same should be quarterly—not only for the benefit of the creditors, but in order to promote a more rapid circulation of money.

In proposing the foregoing terms, The Secretary appears to have been governed by the following principles:

THAT no change ought to be attempted in the rights of the Creditors, but what is sanctioned by their voluntary consent, and founded on the basis of a fair equivalent.

That the nature of the Public Debt, (being a capital redeemable at the pleasure of the Government, which may avail itself of any fall of interest,) is favorable to the public—unfavorable to the Creditors; and may therefore facilitate an arrangement for the reduction of the present rate of Interest on the basis of a fair equivalent.

That, from the encrease of money arising from the low Rate of Interest in Europe—that of the monied capital of the nation—by funding Seventy Millions of Dollars—the further establishment of Public Credit, and other causes, it is presumable, that the Government rate of interest in the United States will at the expiration of five years, fall to Five per Cent. and in a period not exceeding twenty years, to Four per Cent.

How far the calculations on these various modes of Loan conform to the above principles, it is at present impossible to determine; but from the general accuracy of the report, and the well-known disposition of the Secretary to support the Rights of the Creditors, and the Character of the Nation, there can be no doubt but proper attention has been paid to this point.

The period of the payment of interest on what is at present stiled the National Debt, is proposed to be from the First of January, 1791, and on the State Debts, from the First January, 1792. The funds for the former, (which are the only ones specified in the report) are proposed to accrue from the present duties on Imports and Tonnage, encreased with respect to

Imported Wines,   Tea, and
Spirits,   Coffee,
—and a duty on home made spirits.

These articles (as the Secretary justly observes) are *all* of them in reality luxuries—the greater part of them foreign luxuries, and some of them, in the excess in which they are used, *pernicious luxuries*. Although, (as before observed,) the funds for paying the interest on the aggregate of the State Debts are not pointed out from the few articles which are proposed to constitute those for the present debt of the United States, we have good ground to hope, and believe, that the remainder of the necessary Funds will be easily found without the necessity of having recourse, either to a Land or Poll Tax.

In order that the different loans may be voluntary in *fact*, as well as *name*, provision is made in the report for paying to non-subscribing creditors, a dividend of whatever surplus may remain, after paying the interest of the proposed Loans; with a limitation however to Four per Cent. as the funds immediately to be provided are calculated to produce in that proportion to the entire debt.

The foreign and domestic debt of the United States, with the arrears of interest, together with the debts of the respective States which are estimated at 25,000,000 dollars principal and interest, form a total of about EIGHTY MILLION DOLLARS, the whole amount of the debt of the United States, after the debts of the Individual Governments shall be assumed.

A foreign loan of 12,000,000 of dollars is among the articles proposed: The object of which is, to discharge the arrears of interest due on the foreign debt—to reduce the Interest on that part of the Foreign Debt, which bears an interest of more than 4 per cent.—to form a capital for a National Bank, in order to facilitate the collection of the revenue, and such arrangements as shall be found expedient for reducing the capital of the domestic debt—In aid of this operation, the revenue of the Post Office is proposed as a sinking fund.

It is proposed, that this loan be under the direction of Commissioners to be appointed by Congress.

The report stated, that the Post Office may probably be made to yield a revenue of 100,000 dolls.

So much of the Impost Law as imposes duties on Wines, ardent Spirits, Teas and Coffee, it is proposed should be repealed, after the First of May, for the purpose of enacting a law, laying an enhanced duty on those articles: Those enhanced duties, with the proceeds of the present revenue from Imposts and Tonnage, and a Duty on Distilleries, &c. according to the estimate exhibited, will produce the sum required for the payment of the interest on the present debt of the United States, and the support of government.

The idea of discriminating between *original* Creditors, and those by *purchase*, is reprobated—and every argument in favor of such a plan, in our opinion, is totally exploded.

GUS, 20 January. A few newspapers printed the entire report on public credit and a few others a different summary first published in a non extant New York paper on 16 January. Most, however—well over a third of the one hundred newspapers being published—reprinted this piece from *GUS*: at Windsor, Vermont; Portsmouth, New Hampshire; Newburyport, Salem, Boston, Worcester, Springfield, and Stockbridge, Massachusetts; Providence, Rhode Island; Hartford, Litchfield, Middletown, New Haven, New London, and Norwich, Connecticut; New York City (*NYJ*, 21 January); Elizabethtown, New Jersey; Philadelphia and Carlisle, Pennsylvania; Wilmington, Delaware; Baltimore; Fredericksburg, Richmond, and Winchester, Virginia; Edenton, North Carolina; Charleston, South Carolina; and Augusta and Savannah, Georgia.

---

[1] An annuity shared among the surviving members of a group of investors.

Correspondence from New York

The Secretary of the Treasury has made his Report. The principal objects of the report in which the publick mind is interested, are the assumption of the State Debts, and the proposed rate of interest at FOUR per cent. The former will I presume be adopted, the last is doubtful. The credit of this Government will depend more on a punctual performance of her engagements, than on any other circumstance. Now I very much doubt the ability of this country to pay the interest of her debts at four per cent. the installments of the foreign debt as they shall fall due, provide for the current expenses of the Government, and make that reasonable provision for extraordinary occurrences which is dictated by prudence, and should never be omitted when a calculation is formed.

The rage for speculating here is violent, beyond every idea you can imagine; the Government will therefore do well to determine the great question of Finance as early as may consist with a knowledge of the subject.

The increasing prosperity of this Country will give the most sincere pleasure to all its friends. As an evidence of it I need only observe, that Bills on London are now to be purchased in the three great commercial towns of Boston, New-York and Philadelphia, at par: twelve months since, they sold at an advance of seven per cent. In many instances, I am told, the specie is ordered out.

[Stockbridge, Massachusetts] *Western Star*, 26 January; reprinted at Norwich, Connecticut. The editors believe this is a paraphrase of a Sedgwick letter.

From New York

Original Communications

The subject of the *Western Territory* is referred to *The Secretary of the Treasury*—who is to prepare and report a system for the sale of the unappropriated Lands.

A Committee of conference is chosen to determine on the mode of taking up the unfinished business of the last session—If it is taken up *de novo*, new Bills on every subject may be originated—and that respecting the permanent residence will be lost, and the whole ground to be travelled over again—and this indeed will be the case, let it be brought forward in what shape it will—I wish it might sleep for a score of years, or so.

The Committee on that part of THE PRESIDENT's speech respecting the south-western frontiers informed the House, that they were ready to report—This occasioned the doors of the gallery to be shut—but as they did not long remain so, I am suspicious the business was recommitted. Time will determine.

The report of *The Secretary of the Treasury* will be out on Friday—it is contained in about 20 sheets folio—What will be its fate is uncertain; but my opinion is, that the plans will be adopted. There are some in both Houses who are opposed to funding the debt at more than *three per cent*. The report is a most masterly production—The Secretary is one of those characters, which are created for the great exigencies of nations.

Mr. MADISON and Mr. PARKER arrived today—we have 19 Senators, and 46 Representatives present.

[Boston] *Massachusetts Centinel*, 30 January; reprinted in Portland, Maine, and Portsmouth, New Hampshire. Because of the mention of the "20 sheets folio," the editors believe this was written by John Fenno.

OTHER DOCUMENTS

George Duffield to John Adams. ALS, Adams Family Manuscript Trust, MHi. Written from Philadelphia. For more on Bailey and his counterfeiting-proof method, see *DHFFC* 8:73–84.

Introduces the bearer, Francis Bailey, whose counterfeit-proof method of printing may prove useful for printing public securities; "I would entreat your Interest in his favour" in any application Bailey may make to Congress.

Robert Gilchrist, James Miller, John Hopkins, George Catlett, and William Gray to Edmund Pendleton. ALS, hand of Gilchrist, Washington Papers, DLC. Written from Port Royal, Virginia; addressed to "Edmundsbury," Caroline County, Virginia; carried by Dr. David Murrow.

Office seeking: Dr. David Morrow for the marine hospital at Norfolk, Virginia; they recommended him to Page, with whom they are not acquainted, so they ask that Pendleton vouch for them, that Page "may put confidence in what we put our names to."

Ebenezer Hazard to Jeremy Belknap. ALS, Belknap Papers, MHi. Addressed to Boston; carried by Mr. Barratt. For the full text, see *MHSC*, (5th series) 3:210.

"Wingate is very kind in the Permission he has given you: I shall probably take some Liberties with him, & may be with my friend, Col. Langdon, who now *keeps* [*lives*] with me, as the New England Phrase is."

John Henry, Joshua Seney, Daniel Carroll, William Smith, and Michael Jenifer Stone to Governor John Eager Howard. ALS, hand of Stone, State

Papers, Maryland State Archives, Annapolis. Place to which addressed not indicated. For the enclosed address, see *PGW* 5:25–26.

"We have the Honor to inclose to your Excellency the Answer of the President of the United States to the address of the Legislature of Maryland which was presented to him by the attending Members of the Senate and the House of Representatives from Maryland on Tuesday last."

James Kinsey to Elias Boudinot. ALS, Emmet Collection, NN. Place from which written not indicated.

Acknowledges receipt of a copy of Hamilton's report on public credit, which he will share with their friends.

Governor William Livingston to John Jay. New Jersey Historical Society *Proceedings* 52(1934):158. Written from Elizabethtown, New Jersey.

Office seeking: forwards five sealed letters from Robert Strettel Jones to "the Representatives in Congress of this State," regarding his application for an office.

Thomas McKean to John Adams. ALS, Adams Family Manuscript Trust, MHi. Written from Philadelphia.

Introduces the bearer, Francis Bailey, of whose counterfeit-proof method of printing securities, certificates, and other public papers "no patent could secure him much benefit from"; he therefore seeks "employment from Congress in the line of his business so long as he may deserve it, as the only reward for his discovery"; solicits Adams's patronage on Bailey's behalf.

Samuel Meredith to Henry Hill. ALS, John Jay Smith Collection, PPL at PHi. Addressed to Philadelphia.

Acknowledges letter delivered by Fitzsimons that day; supposes Congress will soon make an appropriation for the civil list.

Edmund Pendleton to James Madison. No copy known; acknowledged in Madison to Pendleton, 4 March. Date is approximate, based on Henry Lee to Madison, 25 January.

Letter of introduction for David Morrow.

George Thatcher to Sarah Thatcher. ALS, Thatcher Family Papers, MHi; place to which addressed not indicated.

Does not remember two weeks passing, during his absences from home, without his writing home, "but last saturday & sunday I hapned to be too busy, & could not get time to write"; expects a letter from her that evening; wishes he could join her and her guests, Silas and Temperance Lee, but "for our comfort we have the prospect of a much shorter Session than was expected when I left home—For now it seems the general opinion Congress will adjourn ~~by~~ in April"; inquires of the children: is Sally "crazy" or Phillips "babyish"? "Guard him, my dear, from all such—Be decisive with him," with "mildness and moderation"; listen to Phillips read a little; do the children sit at table with her?

William Samuel Johnson, Diary. Johnson Papers, CtHi. "Visits."

THURSDAY, 21 JANUARY 1790

Cold (Johnson)

William Bradford, Jr. to Elias Boudinot

Your second of the 14th. did not reach me untill Tuesday night. The information contained in the ~~letter~~ paper which was enclosed, had arrived before: but with all the lights that are yet given to us, the nature of the System proposed by Mr. H[*amilton*]. is not understood. The first arrival of the news had a considerable effect on the public securities—they sold @ 9/. but have since fallen & can be had at 8/6. If they should be funded, they will scarcely exceed 10 or 12/. There is but little money to meet the debt that will immediately be set afloat: & if any considerable funds are put into the hands of Commissioners for purchasing up these papers, the debt may be considerably sunk at a small expence. I presume that the system has been the subject of much conversation among you—What do your bretheren in Congress think of it—& is there any probability that it will be adopted either in whole or in part in the present session? The sooner the public mind is at rest, the sooner, these papers come to a settled value, the better for the Country. Every hour it is delayed, the rising & falling of Certificates, does a deal of mischief, and already produces a spirit of Gambling & all the stock-jobbing tricks that we read of in England. Many persons besides brokers, buy in order to take advantage of some bubble they intend to raise, & sell to persons whom they afterwards alarm & induce to sell out at under price. As the Nation must one day adopt the measure of ~~redeeming~~ funding them, is it not wisdom to do it early?

We have some stout advocates here for discrimination; in time, they may have an influence on the public mind, but the system, if formed now, altho' it[*s*] operation should be postponed till next year, will be unalterable & the public honor of America will be safe.

***

ALS, Wallace Papers, PHi. Written from Philadelphia. The omitted text relates to private business, the progress of the Pennsylvania constitutional convention, wife Susan's headache, and "our good mamma [*Hannah Boudinot*]," who "we expect . . . is with you."

Elbridge Gerry to John Jay

Mr. Gerry, with his respects to the Secretary of State, encloses two letters the substance of which has this morning been communicated to the President of the United States, and relates to some American prisoners at Algiers. The President has desired that the papers may be enclosed to the Secretary of State, and is disposed to do whatever may be requisite on his part to afford relief to the unhappy sufferers: adding at the same time, that by letters from Mr. Jefferson dated in August last, our Bankers at Holland had given information of their having money in their hands appropriated amongst other purposes, to the one mentioned.

[Enclosures]

James Anderson to Thomas Russell

Greenock, Scotland, 4 October 1789

I wrote to you the other day by the Ship Lucretia, and by this same opportunity, recommending the owners of the vessels to your address.

I now take the liberty of enclosing copy of a letter which I lately received from Mr. [*Charles*] Logie the british Consul at Algiers [*ca. 1785–1793*], written in answer to an application I had made to him respecting the ransom of one Robertson,[1] a young man who was taken in an American Vessel, and is now a Slave at Algiers. As it concerns the general cause of humanity, I hope that by laying it before the proper authority you may contribute to the relief of a number of miserable men. The whole sum wanted for their redemption cannot be an object of hesitation to the States of America.

Perhaps there would be an impropriety in publishing Mr. Logie's letter in Newspapers, but you are at full liberty to make every other use of it that you think may operate to the relief of the poor prisoners. Wishing you success in your endeavours to serve them.

Charles Logie to James Anderson

Algiers, 24 June 1789

I had great pleasure in receiving your letter and shall ever remember the happy and friendly hours we have spent together.

Robertson as well as the rest of the American prisoners here, have received every act of friendship in my power, and it was through my application to the American Embassador at Madrid [*William Carmichael*] that they got a daily allowance from Congress. I have also forwarded their Memorial to our Minister and backed it with every thing I could say, and have wrote to Mr. Dempster and Lord Fife[2] very strongly about them. But it is out of any bodys power to obtain his ransom under the price fixed, and this he knows himself very well. The plan of lodging his ransom money at Gibraltar will be attended with a loss on the exchange. If lodged in Drummond and Co[*mpan*]ys. Bank in London, my bills on them will be attended with no loss whatever, and as an act of humanity I shall not charge a Commission or any other expence. About four hundred and fifty pounds I should judge would pay for his ransom and fees at most it will not exceed five hundred pounds sterling. That sum must be lodged at Drummonds, and his friends may depend upon my not drawing for more than the just sum, which Robertson shall see paid, and the sooner it is done the better as we are threatened with the plague again. Messrs. Drummonds will advise me when the money is lodged and they will forward any letters they may have for the poor people here.

If you can by writing to your friends in America be of any service to those poor people, God will reward you for it. I can say they are all good worthy people and in a most dismal situation. There are fourteen prisoners in all, Americans, English, Scotch & Irish, all taken in American Vessels, and all Slaves as subjects of the States of America.

[*P. S.*] Mr. Anderson is informed that Robertson's friends are in low circumstances and unable to raise any thing near the sum demanded, and that their only hopes are in the American Congress.

Copy, Domestic Letters, Miscellaneous Correspondence, State Department Records, Record Group 59, DNA. Gerry's cover letter was dated from the House of Representatives. The copying clerk included a statement that Logie's letter was in answer to a letter Anderson wrote him "at the request of the friends" of Robertson. For background on the government's efforts to redeem the Algerine captives, see *DHFFC* 2:425–29, 8:1–3.

[1] John Robertson, mariner of the *Dauphin* taken captive in 1785, was one of fifteen who signed the 1788 petition to Congress that was probably the one submitted to the FFC on 14 May 1790 (*DHFFC* 2:435, 445, 448, 8:4).

[2] George Dempster (1735–1818) was a Scottish lawyer who supported the American cause as a member of Parliament (1762–90). James Duff, second Earl of Fife (1729–1809) also served in Parliament (1754–90).

Frederick Muhlenberg to Tench Coxe

I am sorry I have it not in my power to send a Copy of the Bill for securing to Authors & Inventors the Benefits arising from their writings or Invention—there being not a single one left in the Clerks Office, I think however I have one at Philada. amongst my papers & have directed my Son to examine them, & if he finds it to deliver the same to you immediately. The Question whether the Business left unfinished the last Session shall be taken up de novo, or in the Stage we left it has not yet been decided. A joint Committee of both Houses are now considering the Subject, but from the strong Attachment many of the Members have to parliamentary forms & proceedings, altho' in many Respects differently constituted I am inclined to think the Business will have to comence anew. If so a Committee will be appointed to report a new Bill, which probably will be the same which was reported the last Session. I doubt whether it will pass in the early Stage of the present Session, as soon however as it is reported, if any material Alterations should take place, I shall comunicate the same to You. Not having the Bill before me I cannot make any Remarks thereon.

I comunicated Your Letter to Col. Wadsworth & he was much pleased with the Contents & promised to write to You on the Subiect.

The Report of the Secretary of the Trea[sur]y. has caused much Speculation. I fear he has estimated the State Debt lower than they actually are—as yet it seems to be pretty generally approved of. Tomorrow Morning it is to come from the press, & if I can obtain a Copy before this Letter goes off I shall transmit it to You.

ALS, Coxe Papers, PHi. Addressed to Philadelphia.

Henry Wynkoop to Reading Beatty

No, I do not mean to limit my Corespondence with You to once in two weeks, but You shall hear from me not only once, but if You desire it, five times in the week.

The papers enclosed will, in some Measure gratify Your Curiosity, respecting Mr. Hamilton's Report, affording some of the general outlines, of the Plan.

The Secretary of the War Department, this day reported the Organization of the Militia, this is likewise a Measure, which, if it can be effectually carried into execution, will have an Influence on the Community, not only regarding its Defense and Security but likewise the establishment of domestic Manufactures, beyond what can be conceived, the Report is ordered to be printed, & if practicable, will also be transmitted to You for the Information of the people of Bucks.

Yes Sir, the gallery doors have been shut, it was done this day,[1] this is a Circumstance, which tho' seldom, must necessarily occur sometimes, and when it does will always create a variety of Conjectures abroad.

The election of the Representatives of North Carolina is fixed the fore part of February, one of their Senators [Hawkins] is here.

The eastern papers this day inform us that the Assembly of Rode-Island have agreed to call a Convention.

The existence or nonexistence of the Bill respecting the federal Seat depends on the Report of the Committee of Conference appointed yesterday and the Determination of the two houses thereon.

Here is no Snow at present, [*lined out*] yet Peter Wynkoop Sat out this morning in A Sleigh for Esopus [*Kingston*] which had brought some Members of the State Legislature down & was said had good Sleighing to Hackinsak [*New Jersey*].

After having gratified Your Curiosity, You will by some Means forward the enclosed to Vreden's berg.[2]

ALS, Wynkoop Papers, PDoBHi. Place to which addressed not indicated. Written in the evening.

[1] The House met in secret session on the subject of the secretary of war's report on the Indian department and western frontiers, which led to the Military Establishment Act [HR-50a] and the Indian Treaty Act [HR-50b].

[2] Wynkoop's large farm near Newtown in Bucks County, Pennsylvania.

Other Documents

Elias Boudinot to Mary ("Polly") Hetfield. FC:dft, Stimson-Boudinot Collection, NjP. Hetfield received this letter on 24 January (William Bradford, Jr. to Boudinot, 25 January).

Advises her about romantic love and her courtship; "you should consult your own Sentiments & Inclinations as a preparatory Step, without which every other should be in vain"; "it will be found in the End, that the Religion of Jesus Christ, is the only certain Road to real Happiness Here or hereafter"; has enclosed her letter in one to her mother (Mary Hetfield), which he will send the next day.

William Few to Governor Edward Telfair. No copy known; mentioned as read on 9 March, Georgia Executive Council Journal, G-Ar.

Nathaniel Gorham to Henry Knox. ALS, Knox Papers, Gilder Lehrman Collection, NHi. Written from Boston.

Suggests that Hamilton's funding plan may be construed so as to remove the people's fear of a land tax; "do suggest the business in such manner as you know very well how to do—I have been led to hope that the transfer of our Bonds for the benefit of the Nation may be a part of the ~~Land~~ plan—but this I sugguest to you only to make such use of as you think proper."

James Madison to James Madison, Sr. ALS, Presidential Letters Collection, University of Iowa, Iowa City. Addressed to Orange County, Virginia. For the full text, see *PJM* 13:1-3.

Describes his recent illness, which "took the form of a Dysentery," and slow journey to New York; spent a week in Georgetown under the care of Dr. David Stuart; is presently recovered "and have regained my flesh"; incloses newspaper with outline of Hamilton's funding plan; "I have not been here long eno' to collect the particulars of it"; there seem to be doubts of its being fully accepted by Congress; but "I can form no opinion, the members being generally reserved in communicating their views"; relays news from abroad; encloses experimental seeds for his brothers; is "extremely anxious" for news of mother's health, which he awaits with every mail.

Louis Guillaume Otto to Comte de Montmorin. Copy, in French, Henry Adams Transcripts, DLC. For the Dobbyn petition, see *DHFFC* 8:196–98. Otto's letters included in *DHFFC* were usually written over the course of days, and even weeks, following the day they were begun.
    French immigration to the United States; reports that an Irishman named (Hannibal William) Dobbyn has petitioned Congress to purchase public lands that he wished to sell to fellow countrymen whom he would transport to the United States.

Josiah Thacher to George Thatcher. ALS, Chamberlain Collection, MB. Written from Boston.
    "Agreeably to your Request that I would name to You Some Person or Persons in the Town of Gorham [*Maine*] who would be Suitable to take the Number of the Inhabitants shou'd the Congress require the number to be taken by Towns," recommends first the selectmen; "if these are Excepted," provides a list of men "Suitable to this Business."

George Washington to Thomas Jefferson. ALS, Jefferson Papers, DLC. Place to which addressed not indicated. For the full text, see *PGW* 5:29–31.
    "It was the opinion of Congress, that, after the division of all the business of a domestic nature" among the three executive departments, the duties of the department of state "might be performed by the same Person, who should have the charge of conducting the Department of foreign Affairs"; if the "experiment" proves differently, does not doubt a further division of the duties will enable it to be performed by one man.

George Washington, Diary. Washington Papers, MiD-B.
    Senators Ellsworth, Paterson, Elmer, Bassett, and Hawkins and Representatives Sherman, Cadwalader, Clymer, Hartley, Hiester, Smith (Md.), and Jackson dined at the President's.

Fallacy Detected, by the Evidence of Facts; or, Considerations on the Impolicy and Injustice of a Compulsory Reduction of the Interest on the Publick Debt in a Letter to a Member of Congress (Philadelphia, 1790). Advertisements for the pamphlet indicate that it was published on 21 January (*PP*, 23 January). The editors have concluded from the length and tone of the pamphlet that the reference to its being a "Letter to a Member of Congress" is a literary device. There is no evidence that any member read it, although Boudinot was asked if he had (From Charles Pettit, 27 January, below). For the text, see Evans 23060.

FRIDAY, 22 JANUARY 1790

Fine (Johnson)

William Widgery to George Thatcher

I have thought of What you wish me to inform you respecting Sutable Persons for Enumerating the people in each Town or District, but as I have not yet been able to hear what plan Congress proposes to adopt for that purpose, I am not able to in form you, as for the Select men doing the Business it is out of the question if Congress had power to Call on them for in your District there are more Townships settleing in which there are no Selectmen, than Towns in which there are Selectmen—therefor you Would not Get more than two thirds of the people if it is thought best by Congress to appoint a Committy in Each District, you are perhaps a better Judge than my Self you have a person in your Eye for the County of york, in Lincoln Doct. [*Daniel*] Conant—if in Each County thay will answer the Same. if the States are not all as we are divided in to Districts that will make a Dificalty, in that Case the Members of Each State may adopt a plan for there own State as to that Particular matter. in our State the matter would be Easy by District. I do not Expect to be at Boston this Sessions on account of my wife being very Ill of a fevor—therefore when you write me Direct it to Newglocester, I wish to hear from you as often as you Can make it Convenient. and Shall only Say as Joseph did to the Butler remember me when it is well with the[e].[1]

ALS, Chamberlain Collection, MB. Written from New Gloucester, Maine.

[1] Genesis 40:14.

Isaac Stephens to Mr. Stephens

Arrived the Spanish Courier from Spain. The Spanish Consul had before wrote to his broker in Spain, to get the money he had advanced us Americans in Algiers; and Mr. [*William*] Carmichael, the American Ambassador, told him that he had not received any money from Congress, for above two years, and could not answer the bill at present, which was about thirteen hundred dollars, for advancing two years pay for us; and on the return of the broker's letter to the Consul, he said that he could not advance our monthly pay: on that account we must suffer greatly for the want of it. We hope that as soon as Mr. Carmichael is informed of the matter, he will order the pay still to continue; for it not only hurts the character of the United States, but deprives us of a considerable support.

NYDG, 22 January, from [Boston] *Independent Chronicle,* 14 January; reprinted at Portland, Maine; Windsor, Vermont; Pittsfield and Stockbridge, Massachusetts; New York City (*NYWM* and *NYP,* 23 January, *NYDA,* 28 January); Philadelphia; Edenton and Fayetteville, North Carolina; and Charleston, South Carolina. Written from Algiers, dated 13 September 1789. The recipient identified in the source as Stephens' brother may have been William W. Stephens, also a Boston ship master at this time (*PTJ* 14:352).

OTHER DOCUMENTS

Jacquelin Ambler to James Madison. ALS, Madison Papers, DLC. Written from Richmond, Virginia; postmarked 6 February. For the full text, see *PJM* 13:3.
   Hopes to hear of Madison's recovery; encloses letter for delivery to Page, who left home before it could reach him.

Elias Boudinot to Charles Pettit. No copy known; acknowledged in Pettit to Boudinot, 27 January.

Richard Cranch to John Adams. ALS, Adams Family Manuscript Trust, MHi. Written from Boston.
   Introduces the bearer, Nathan Read, who wishes to submit "Drafts of Machines of his invention" to a congressional committee "to obtain a Patent, or such other encouragement as may enable him to carry them into execution for the publick Benefit"; recommends Read "to your Notice and Friendship."

SATURDAY, 23 JANUARY 1790

Warm (Johnson)

Pierce Butler to Rev. Robert Smith

This letter will be handed to You by the reverend Mr. Keating,[1] to whom I request Your friendly attention; he is a stranger in the land, as Our forefathers were. Tho' Mr. Keating is not of Your church I persuade myself that he will not, on that account meet with less attention from You. It would be repugnant to my opinion of Mr. [*Robert*] Smith, an opinion formed from long experience, to entertain a doubt on that head. However narrow the road may be represented to be, it is assuredly broad enough for both You and Mr. Keating. The kingdom of heaven is like unto the center of the compass in one sense: he that goes East & he that goes West may arrive equally soon and at the same point. If the throne of grace is reserved only for christians what is to become of Asia, Affrica, part of Europe, and part of America, yet nearer; If none but one denomination of Christians are to be admitted to the throne of mercy, for what purpose were the rest of mankind created? Such tenets might have their advocates in the dark ages of Ignorance and superstition, but in the present age must meet with contempt. He that worships God in sincerity of heart: is just in his dealing with man, doing as he wou'd be done by, is the good Samaritan whether he be Jew or Gentile. such I trust is Mr. Keating, & as such I can safely assure him of Your friendship. He goes to Carolina for the purpose of gathering together the scattered of his own flock & to lead them in the way they shou'd walk.

I felt exceedingly for Your sufferings on Your voyage home. I hope the fright did not injure Mrs. [*Anna Maria Tilghman*] Smith's health.

FC, Butler Letterbook, ScU.

[1] Thomas Keating (d. 1793) was a priest assigned to St. Mary's Church, the first permanent Roman Catholic parish in Charleston, South Carolina.

Nathaniel Gorham to Theodore Sedgwick

By the Post this evening we expect the budget on finance [*report on public credit*]—various are the opinions respecting it—The holders of State paper are very desirous that a general assumption may be a part of it—but Antis. will universally oppose such a measure and the[y] have so much alarmed the Country People with the idea of a Land tax—that if the consent of the States are necessary. the approbation of this will never be obtained unless the fears of the People relative to this Land tax is removed—if that is done—I think there will be no dificulty in carrying the measure—some suppose that the transfer of our Bonds[1] will be made a condition—If that is thought proper—I have no personal objection for I conceive that it will be for our interest that it should be so. ***

ALS, Sedgwick Papers, MHi. Written from Boston. The omitted text relates to state representative John Gardiner's controversial initiatives to reform the legal profession.

[1] See Gorham to Sedgwick, 12 January, above.

George R. Minot to George Thatcher

The boundaries between the Federal and State Governments, the establishment of which may be supposed to be affected by the assumption of the State debts, is undoubtedly an object intimately connected with the happiness of the people. Many persons, including even men of property & whose numbers are increasing since the Constitutional powers of Congress seem to be out of danger, appear to reason in this simple but rational manner.

The acknowledged end of Govt. is the good of the governed, or the people. They are the best judges of this good when they can act with understanding, and are therefore the only judges. In this sense the maxim applies that the voice of the people is the voice of reason or of God. It is very difficult to discover this voice but there was once a remarkable period in this country when it could not be mistaken. This was at the commencement of the Revolution. The late war was a war of sentiment or an opposition to future evils, which could be realized only by reasoning upon the [*lined out*] use & extent of powers then exercised in a degree too trifling, to deserve the name of a grievance. The reasons of their opposition were printed in plain language, and handed to every individual. Every man read them at his leisure, & thought about them at his work. When called to fight, he fought because he would not pay taxes unless he voted them by his Representative, and because he would not obey laws made by an authority over which he had no controul by the constitutional means of election &c.

The people prevailed, & established a right to carry their own principles into exercise. At what expense we all know. They agreed upon a Govt. which they were in hopes ~~would~~ would afford them the enjoyment of their rights and equal protection. But it was found, that the means of drawing money from the people to pay a debt they had contracted by going to war, were inefficient. They tried to supply this defect by an Impost, but were not all wise enough to agree to it. Another mode was attempted to remedy this evil. And a convention was called *for this purpose*. Their report surprized every body, because it embraced more objects than this. The human understanding could not foresee what would be the final extent & operation of the principles this system contained; human vanity pretended to, only in a few instances. The state Conventions could not but ratify it, as civil war, which was then raging in Msstts. would otherwise gain ground. But their ratifications were attended with doubts, fears, & proposed amendments, wherever they did any thing more than reading it as we read a news paper. When it came into operation all good men were for allowing it a fair experiment; but every day alarmed them with some construction wch. was never thought of in the State Conventions, or some contradiction of what all parties there supposed to be agreed facts.

Under these circumstances, untill that Govt. is settled, and we know what it is, how far ought we to resign our confidence to it? it has been always supposed to have powers eno', as nothing is witheld which it's framers required, and there has been found by experience, as yet, nothing short of what they intended to give: but the contrary perhaps has happened. We have the state Governments existing, like an old Standard, in tatters, which rather show their honours than their powers. They are acknowledged to be subordinate. Shall we pull them quite down, lest they should serve upon occasion for the people to rally by? If such an apprehension existed, it would be the best argument for keeping them up.

Where the purse & the Sword is secured there can be no cause for contending, becaus for an increase of power. And no objection can be made to a number of centinels, to see that these are used as they were designed to be. If these give a false alarm, we may justly suppose, the consequences will fall on themselves.

The change in our govt. was not effected by a proportionate change in the habits of the people: it seems therefore, as there is no long standing prejudices to support it, that it more than common pains should be used, to exhibit it always in such a light, as to address the reason of the people This would best be done by indulging them in every guard which they might desire, as it would shew a confidence that nothing was wished for, or done wch. would not bear inspection.

I do not believe much in the incompatibility of the Federal & State excises. How easy would it be, for instance, for one to take articles of trade, and the other such articles as are commonly the objects of Stamp duties, or the produce of the Country, as Cyder &c. As to our State debt, the amount is so large, that I do not see any way of its being paid but by the assumption, and that would leave little to quarrel about on the score of Excises. In short, if, on the other hand, party ideas extend no farther than the moderate exercise of constitutional powers in the federal Govt. I do not believe that there will be any dangerous opposition on the other.

ALS, Fogg Autograph Collection, MeHi. Written from Boston.

Roger Sherman to Simeon Baldwin

I have the pleasure of transmiting to you the Report of the Secretary of the Treasury for your perusal, and the perusal of the rest of the citizens of New Haven and especially the public creditors. among whom are Samuel Bishop, David Austin, & Timothy Jones Esquires & Doctr. [Samuel] Wales. I had but one to Spare, & thought it would be as convenient to lodge it in your office [New Haven city clerk] for the use of the citizens as any place.

I also have enclosed of the United States Gazette [*GUS*].

P. S. Congress have not yet acted on the report, but have referred it to a Committee of the Whole.

ALS, Sherman Collection, CtY.

Cotton Tufts to John Adams

***

We have had a long Debate on the Right of ~~certain~~ Persons holding ~~off~~ certain offices under the National Government retaining a Seat in the Legislature—The House have decided against the Right—the Senate [*lined out*] in Favour of Jona. Jackson Esqr. (Marshall) ~~holding~~ continuing his Seat in the Senate—it is considered as a *great Question*—The Herald has published the Debates of Senate on the Subject in a very unfair Manner—They were handed to the Printer by Mr. [*David*] ~~Austin~~. or ~~S. Limon~~ [*Samuel*] Lim—n taken from their memory—The Speech of the former delivered in Senate, was prepared & read [*lined out*] and no doubt was printed with correctness—He has no doubt established his Popularity by this Measure and it will probably be further increased [*?*] before the Session ends by uniting with mr. Jno. Gard—r [*John Gardiner*] in his Plan for the Reform of the Law & its Professors.

[*P. S.*] Mr. Nathan Reed will be the Bearer of this who is a Gentleman of great Ingenuity. Bror. [*Richard*] Cranch will give you [*lined out*] his Character more fully in a Letter to the Vice President.

ALS, Adams Family Manuscript Trust, MHi. Written from Boston; carried by Nathan Read.

OTHER DOCUMENTS

Henry Merttins Bird to George Washington. ALS, Miscellaneous Letters, Miscellaneous Correspondence, State Department Records, Record Group 59, DNA. Written from Charleston, South Carolina.

Mentions Izard and Smith (S.C.) as references for a London merchant house offering its services to secure loans for the United States in Europe.

Daniel Cony to George Thatcher. ALS, Chamberlain Collection, MB. Written from Boston.

Has received in the mail additional pages of the House Journal; asks Thatcher's opinion of the probability of Congress's assumption of the states' war debts; inquires what "further measures, on our part, are necessary" to get a post office at Hallowell, Maine.

William Eustis to Henry Knox. ALS, Knox Papers, Gilder Lehrman Collection, NHi. Written from Boston.

Reviews handling of pension claims of disabled soldiers by Massachusetts; many disabled veterans in Massachusetts ought to be added to the federal pension list despite statutes of limitation or they will become charges of the state; asks if necessary to apply to Congress; has mentioned it to Ames, who "may not be able to attend to all the circumstances."

Benjamin Huntington to William Ellery. No copy known; acknowledged in Ellery to Huntington, 2 February.

William Maclay to John Nicholson. No copy known; acknowledged in Nicholson to Maclay, 28 January.

John Warren to George Thatcher. ALS, Chamberlain Collection, MB. Written from Boston.

Introduces and recommends the bearer, Nathan Read, who intends to lay before Thatcher plans for various inventions for which he seeks a patent; solicits Thatcher's support.

Oliver Wolcott, Jr. to Chauncey Goodrich. ALS, Wolcott Papers, CtHi. Addressed to Hartford, Connecticut. For a partial text, see *Wolcott* 1:35.

"The general Ideas of the [*funding*] system meet with approbation, some gentlemen suppose three ℔ Cent Interest would content the public Creditors—the great question will be about the funds, and in case the State Debts shall be assumed, it is certain that the objects of revenue will be extended much farther than will be possible under the local arrangements."

SUNDAY, 24 JANUARY 1790

Snow (Johnson)

Abigail Adams to Mary Cranch

*** How long they [*Congress*] will set this Session I cannot pretend to say, but rather think they will rise early in the Spring. *** I never rode so little as I have done since I resided here ~~in the~~ There are no pleasant rides no, variety of scenes round New York, unless you cross ferrys over to long Island or to the Jerseys. I have however enjoyd a greater share of Health than I have for some years past & been less afflicted with the Complaint which used to allarm as well as distress me.

***

I could give an account of visiting and receiving visits, but in that there is so little variety that one Letter only might contain the whole History. For Instance on Monday Evenings Mrs. Adams Receives company. That is her Rooms are lighted & put in order. Servants & Gentleman and Ladies, as many as inclination curiosity or Fashion tempts come out to make their Bow & Curtzy, take coffe & Tea chat an half hour, or longer, and then return to Town again on Tuesday the same Ceremony is performed at Lady [*Elizabeth*] Temples on Wednesday at Mrs. [*Lucy*] Knox's, on Thursdays at Mrs. [*Sarah*] Jay's and on Fryday at Mrs. Washingtons, so that if any person has so little to employ themselves in as to want an amusement five Evenings in a week, they may find it at one or other of these places. to Mrs. Washingtons I usually go as often as once a fortnight, and to the others occasionally.

***

ALS, Abigail Adams Letters, MWA. Misdated 1789. Written from "Richmond Hill," outside New York City; addressed to Braintree, Massachusetts. The omitted text relates to family news. For the full text, see *Abigail Adams*, pp. 7–9.

William Cranch to John Adams

I wrote you some time ago, & desired Mr. [*James*] Lovell, who told me he should see Mr. Ames before he left Dedham, to forward it by him. Your Son Tom writes me that you have not recieved it. I shall enquire of Lovell what he did with it. ***

Our Legislature is now sitting. A question has arisen, "whether persons holding offices under the national Government similar to those prohibited by our State Constitution, have a right to hold their seats in our Legislature." A joint Committee was chosen, who reported that they had no right. The Report was not accepted by the Senate. the numbers were 13 to 11. The house accepted the Report by a majority of 137 to 24. However, the Senate still think that they have the sole right to judge of the qualifications of their own members, & are determined to pay no regard to the judgment of the House. The Consequence is that Mr. [*Christopher*] Gore has quitted his seat in the house, while Mr. [*Jonathan*] Jackson remains still in the Senate.

***

ALS, Adams Family Manuscript Trust, MHi. Written from Boston; answered 14 March. The omitted text relates to Massachusetts politics, especially John Gardiner's efforts for legal reform.

Thomas Dwight to Theodore Sedgwick

***

It is a very pleasing consideration to me, that propositions are made for funding the public debt & that the Secretary among other things has proposed an assumption of the State debts—I believe with you, that 3 ℔ Cent is as much as can be provided for as ints. by imposts & Excises, if more can safely be collected in this way, and the creditors will not reloan at that rate, more perhaps might be given them, but altho it is the duty of the Legislature to make every provision in their power for doing public creditors perfect justice yet it is not their duty to take any measures which by risquing the existence of the Governt. would also put in risque the principal as well as interest of their debts. dry taxation at this time, would in my opinion, blow up a fire which it might not be easy to quench the people have many of them been led to believe that an adoption of the Constitution would be attended with modes of collecting money very different from those which they have hitherto complained of as grievances—to most of the common people any provision for the appreciation of public securities will be disagreeable—they have seen them sported it with, by speculators while many of the original owners have not received one fifth part of the nominal value—the populace never reason very refinedly, they do not nor will they see the justice of the measures taken to establish public credit—so that if it was be established it ought perhaps to be done in the easiest possible manner to the people not by land taxes.

***

ALS, Sedgwick Papers, MHi. Written from Springfield, Massachusetts. The omitted text ridicules a proposal that the state legislature abolish titles and concludes that Sedgwick's family is said to be "in tolerable health."

Christopher Gore to Rufus King

The consequences that will flow from an assumption of the State Debts, by the United States, are not more desird by the latter, then dreaded by this Commonwealth—the antifederalists think, the advantages, to be deriv'd to the State, from a retention of the debt, are so great and important, that they stand ready to accede to any terms which the creditors may propose—A Committee, consisting of a majority of antis, have now under consideration a revision of the excise law, and the propriety of mortgaging this revenue to the creditors—hitherto this committee has been restrain'd, by the creditors themselves, from reporting—I really fear whether 4. per Cent will satisfy their demands, and think it not improbable, they may endeavor to make terms with the State.

If Congress cannot do better for them, than pay an interest at that rate—the business must be manag'd with great address to secure the cordial accession, on the part of the creditors of Massachusetts—Those, who, heretofore, have been oppos'd, to making a permanent provision, for the support of public credit, are now very desirous of doing it, that thereby their own importance may be increas'd, and the national government embarrass'd—The creditors are numerous & important, and are so attach'd to property that we have reason to fear they woud change sides rather than lose any share of this blessing—a less rate of interest than 4 per Cent, you may rest assurd will never be acceded to by nine tenths of the creditors in Massachusetts—consider the great holders in this town, [*James*] Bowdoin, [*Samuel, Jr.*] Phillips, [*Samuel*] Breck [*Jonathan, Sr.?*] Mason, & Moses Gill—and think if they will accede to any thing less then 4—and if this pill must not be gilded to insure success.

ALS, King Papers, NHi. Written from Boston; postmarked.

Thomas Hartley to Jasper Yeates

Since my last—we have been chiefly engaged in Committees but there is much Business under way.

The Committees of both Houses have reported that the unfinished Business of last Session is dismissed—and must be commenced de novo.

I was one of the Committee and advocated a different Principle but was over-ruled I am inclined to think that the Houses will adopt the Sentiments of their Committees and then the Bill about Germantown [*Seat of Government Bill HR-25*] will be lost.

There is scarcely a Hope that we can renew the Question for any Part of Pennsylvania this Session—The Eastern People are satisfied with New York and the Southern Gentlemen say they have no Objection to stay here until the Census is taken and then it will appear that the Banks of Potomack are about the Center of Population—so that we shall drop between two Stools for the present—I shall not forget our Interests but really they are in a bad way at this Juncture.

I immagine effectual Measures will be taken to establish public Credit—I sent you the Laws of the last Session last Week[1] I wish they may come safe to Hand.

ALS, Yeates Papers, PHi. Addressed to Lancaster, Pennsylvania; franked; postmarked 25 January; answered 1 February.

[1] Francis Childs and John Swaine, *Acts Passed at a Congress* . . . (New York, 1789).

Benjamin Lincoln to Theodore Sedgwick

I had the honour the last evening of receiving your favour of the 16th.

I have seen the out lines of the Secretarys bugit [*report on public credit*] and learned some of the observations made upon it, I cannot fully subscribe to either. I will first mention my objections to his propositions of delaying the assumption of the debts of the several States by the Union. The State debts are as much the debts of the United States as are those which assume that name They are for services performed for, and supplies given to the Union, at their request, and under the most absolute assurances of payment by themselves. Afterwards it became a part of the System that each State should pay the debts of the United States of a certain description and charge the United States with the amount. This ordinance of Congress passed after the debt was contracted and without the consent of the creditor. Had the several States complied with the wishes of Congress and the expectation of the creditors no complaints would have been made this however they have not done Although they have referred their accounts to Congress in which the whole is discharged, and pray an allowance of their acounts. An allowance is not yet made Congress therefore have it now in their power without injury to any to do justice to the whole and satisfy the creditors of the several States by receiving the paper of which they are now possessed and offering for it their own. If Congress should neglect the assumption of the State debts immediately they will with their eyes open suffer the different States, if their inclination to do it continues, to injure those very citizens who of all men in the Union have a right to expect justice, for they are in general those who performed personal service, and who first stepped forth with their property and at an hour when the contest was doubtful. It would be unjust to leave such creditors one moment longer in the hands of some of the States. This State has practised towards their creditors the most wanton injustice suffer me to point you to one instance of it among many. They contracted to pay a certain sum of money in January 1784 an other sum in January 17845 and one other sum in January 1786 and the interest untill paid. Notwithstanding their promise of payment at those periods they did not tax for the sum ~~due~~ for the first payment untill after it became due and when they did offer a tax for the discharge of the debt due in 84 & 1785 care was taken that the sum voted should be less than the sums to be paid and so it was in an after tax said to be for the redemption of the notes due in Jany. 1786 this was done with the express design of depreciating those securities as some members were hardy enough to say On the notes to be paid ~~to be paid~~ in the years 1784 & 1785 the interest was stopped in April 1785 and on those to be discharged in 1786 the interest was stopped in April the same year and thus has the matter remained although it is found that the taxes issued for the payment of those notes will not embrace the whole by about one hundred thousand pounds Besides the collectors have been indulged in a delay of Collecting this tax from the year 1784 to this time and untill the notes by the management of Government have depreciated from fifteen shillings in the pound to six & Eight pence need I give you any stronger proof [*of*] the wanton injustice of this State towards its creditors Can it be consistent with the justice of the United States longer to permit such inequity and especially when it is considered that they were the original contractors that the debt was originally their own and that they now have it in their power to do that justice so long sought for in vain from the State. I think longer to neglect the assumption of the State debts would be [*lined out*] impolitic in Congress [*lined out*] at the least The public creditors are among the first people of property they are among those who are the most attached to a firm and an energetic government and they are also among those on whose shoulders the constitution must rest in circumstances of confusion or it will fall to the ground and the people into confusion Is it policy for the United States to do a thing which m[*ust*] necessarily sour the minds of its best Ci[*tizens*] and probably ~~totally to~~ detach them from the interest of the Union forever determi[*ned*] for your self paint in your own mind [*the*] confusion which must be produced if [*the*] State creditors now unite with those whose only fears are that the several governments will be swallowed up by the general one If the creditors of this State should unite with the people of this class and an attem[*pt*] in the present feeble state of the general government should be made to establish themselves ~~on the product~~ on the ruins of it, which God forbid they should, you can better pai[*nt*] to your own mind the horrors of such an event than I can describe.

I am not less satisfied with the justice and policy of the measure of a reloan at three ℔ Cent—The propositi[*on*] will never engage the attention of the credi[*tors*] in general it will excite a new clamou[*r*] among the creditors and this at a time when there is the highest probability that 4 ℔ cent would give very general satisfaction—Three ℔ Cent will sacrifice one part of the United States to an other This measure if insisted on will ruin man[*y*] of your constituents—What will be the complexion of things when it is known that four and five ℔ Cent is to be paid on the European debt and that one proposition in the present system is to borrow at five ℔ Cent Are the pretentions of the old creditors less than those who may now come forward to the aid of government will they do it if they can lodge their money any where better.

But why should I press these things so fully on you I will stop lest you should suppose it possible for me to think you are an abettor of the three ℔ Cent—If these should be your sentiments I should feel more for you than I was ever brought to feel for I know that as an honest man you will support ~~your sentiments~~ them at every hazard I know at the same time what your enemies may say that the less interest the less value the principal the less value the principal the easier the debt for the western lands can be paid—I wish you had never been connected with them—You will do right—may Heaven direct you and bless the dear partner of you[r] life & the and the tender plants.

ALS, Sedgwick Papers, MHi. Written from Boston. Beneath the dateline Lincoln wrote, *"Confidential to be burnt when read."*

James Madison to Thomas Jefferson

A dysenteric attack at Georgetown with its effects retarded my journey so much that I did not arrive here till a few days ago. I am free at present from the original complaint, but a little out of order with the piles generated by that or the medicine it required.

***

The business of Congs. is as yet merely in embryo. The principal subjects before them are the plans of revenue and the Militia, reported by Hamilton & Knox. That of the latter is not yet printed, and being long is very imperfectly understood.[1] The other has scarcely been long enough from the press to be looked over. It is too voluminous to be sent entire by the mail. I will by the next mail commence a transmission in fractions. Being in possession at present of a single copy only I can not avail myself of this opportunity for the purpose. You will find a sketch of the plan in one of the Newspapers herewith inclosed. Nothing has passed either in Congs. or in conversation from which a Conjecture can be formed of the fate of the Report. Previous to its being made, the avidity for stock had raised it from a few shillings to 8/ or 10/. in the pound, and emissaries are still exploring the interior & distant parts of the Union in order to take advantage of the ignorance of holders. Of late the price is stationary, or fluctuating between the sums last mentioned. From this suspence it would seem as if doubts were entertained concerning the success of the plan in all its parts.

I take for granted that You will, known before the receipt of this, have known the ultimate determination of the President on your appointment. All that I am able to say on the subject is that a universal anxiety is expressed for your acceptance; and to repeat my declarations that such an event will be more conducive to the general good, and perhaps to the very objects of your interest you have in view in Europe, than your return to your former station.[2]

I do not find that any late information has been recd. with regard to the Revolution in France. It seems to be still unhappily forced to struggle with the adventitious evils of public scarcity, in addition to those naturally thrown in its way by antient prejudices and hostile interests. ***

ALS, Madison Papers, DLC. Received 12 February. The omitted text relates to the disposition of items Jefferson mailed from France in care of Madison and news of wheat prices in France.

[1] Knox's report on the arrangement of the militia was presented to the House on 21 January, when three hundred copies were ordered to be printed; see *DHFFC* 5:1435–57.

[2] The same day this letter was received at Monticello (12 February), Jefferson received an "Address of Welcome" from his neighbors, the citizens of Albemarle County, Virginia, in the drafting of which Madison may have played a role. Congratulatory addresses were customary on occasions such as Jefferson's return from his long diplomatic service in Europe. The editors of *PTJ*, however, discern an important political motive and characterize it as "belonging to a calculated campaign" to persuade their county's favorite son to accept appointment as secretary of state. Given Madison's influence in the administration's offer of the post and his pressure on the reluctant Jefferson to accept, the editors of *PTJ* believe Madison "would scarcely have avoided discussing" the subject with local political leaders while he was in the neighborhood consulting with Jefferson prior to leaving for the second session in late December 1789. For more, see *PTJ* 16:167–71.

Robert Morris to George Harrison

Mr. Hamiltons Report is printed I have read it with attention and find it an excellent performance that will do great honor to His abilities There are however some points which he aims at that in my opinion will operate differently from his expectations, particularly, the Reduction of interest, for altho he offers Compensation to the Holders of Public Securities they will not believe in Western Lands or distant annuities half so much as they would in Six ℔ Cent ready Money, and I believe those propositions and the Debates that will ensue, will Keep back that rise in the value of the Securities which He wishes to take place. Upon the whole I think you may set out on your jaunt[1] whenever you find yourself so disposed, and the letters already written respecting the object of your pursuit will answer untill you get into North Carolina, but I will, after I see a little farther into the *mill Stone* write to you again under Cover to Ben Harrison of Richmond and when you leave that place leave with him your farther address.

ALS, Brinton Coxe Papers, PHi. Addressed to Philadelphia; answered 26 January.

[1] Harrison was one of several speculators who traveled to the South and interior parts of the country to buy up securities before widespread knowledge of or confidence in Hamilton's funding plan raised their value.

Peter Muhlenberg to Benjamin Rush

On Friday last I forwarded the Report of The Secretary of The Treasury, imediately after it left the Press; I have since found that a Sheet was wanting, which I now enclose to You, to complete the whole—Last Evening I was Honord with Your favor of the 21st. The communications shall be attended to—Your information, That the Funding System has many Friends in New York is perfectly right, but it is a doubtful question, whether they encrease or diminish; I have hitherto heard nothing to induce a change of my Sentiments—after a perusal of the report I wish much to have your Opinion—In the report the whole debt is stated at a little more than 79 Mill[*ion*]s. but it ought to be remembred, that the State Debt, as well as the unliquidated Claims, are not fully ascertaind, but only the *Probable* Amount is given, which may, and in my humble opinion does vary much from the real amount—I am now, more than ever, convinced, that either a discrimination or a reduction of Interest must take place; For tho' I am well assurd that the Citizens of Pensylvania will submit as chearfully as any others, to pay Their proportion of Taxes, toward the support of Public Credit yet when it is known, That all the Money arising both from the impost & excise is hardly sufficient to pay the Annual Interest on the Public Securities, I am afraid that chearfullness, will give way to other feelings, especially when it is considered, that a War, or some other untoward event, may totally derange the plan, and force our Revenues into another Chan[*nel*].

Another consequence, which I dreaded & foresaw will inevitably ensue, The whole of The Money The State can possibly raise at present, will be required to carry The funding System into effect; consequently every other salutary measure recommended by The Supreme Executive will be defeated, unless Resolutions without Money, will defend the Frontiers—create a well regulated Militia & establish Schools—postroads &c. &c. I will say no more on the subject at present, The report will probably be taken up this Week, Tho' it is the general Opinion That time will be given for a full consideration before any thing decisive is done—I mean to propose some Queries, but shall withhold them until my Friends, have had an Oppertunity to peruse & form Their Opinion on The Report.

ALS, Gratz Collection, PHi. Addressed to Philadelphia.

Samuel Phillips, Jr. to Benjamin Goodhue

I am under very great obligations for your interesting communications of the measures proposed by Mr. Hamilton; I have as yet had oppy. to give the reading of your favor only to two or three Judicious friends, and they are very much gratified with the intelligence: They consider him as having calculated his measures upon an extensive & noble scale, such an one as will do honor to the Legislature of a Nation on whom the eyes of the World are fixed, to patronize—he appears to have raised himself above the influence

of objects comparatively small which becloud & bewilder minds of narrow
comprehension & under the influence of false biass, and to have attended
solely to the enquiry—What is honest & right? what will wipe away the
reproach with which the glory of the American Revolution has been stained?
what will attach the bulk of the best Citizens to thier Government, and
establish it's credit in such a manner as to ensure success to it's future applications if it should ever have occasion to make them.

The rate of Interest proper to be allowed is a great question—I believe
the original holders, this way, expect 4 pr. cent. generally so far as I have had
an Oppy. of hearing them express thier sentiments, the purchasers might
be content with less, very well—If the proportion of the latter is so small
compared with the former as I am told Mr. Hamilton estimates, viz. ¼—or
rather that ¼ only of the public debt is in the hands of purchasers, (and
Treasurers [*Leonard*] Jarvis & [*Alexander*] Hodgdon, I am informed, have
expressed an opinion that a less proportion of the State debt has been transfered) a regard to the former class & to the abilities of the U.S. will doubtless
decide the question.

Here I was intercepted by company and before the male closes can only
subjoin a request that you would keep the enclosed, till applied for, & that
you would afford Mr. Lakeman your advice about the business he may consult you on.

[*P. S.*] I expect to leave Senate next saturday ~~for~~ for some days—how long
is not certain—shd. wish that yr. letters of a private nature may not be directed to me as President [*of the state senate*].

ALS, Letters to Goodhue, NNS. Written from Boston, on "Sabth. eve."

William Smith (Md.) to Otho H. Williams

I am now to acknowledge receipt of yr. Several favors dated the 10th,
14th & 16th Instant.

In answer to the queries contained in the first, I can only Say, that, public
Securities fluctuate here as else where, and *yet* are governed by public opinion
only, Congress not having hitherto expressed any Sentiment, on that head.
The present Cash price, as far as I am able to collect, is 8/6 or 9/ on the principle & 5/ for the interest, or *indents*. I now inclose you the Secretarys Report
[*on public credit*], which together with the Presidents Speech at the opening
the Session, are the only public papers on which any opinion can be formed.
I expect, Indeed I Know, that there will be a diversity of Sentiments on this
Subject in both houses, it is said that the Eastern Members will be in favor
of Supporting public credit; if so, the probability is, that paper will rise.

but I question if it will Soon exceed 10/ on the principle, & you had best in the first Instance draw yr. Interest to Jany. 88. which I can do for you if you please. After thursday Next, I will be able to give you more full information on this head.

I have looked over your remarks on the Collection law [*HR-11*], &ca. from which I have taken some notes, & agreeable to your request, delivered them to the Secretary. I find there are many applications for relief, under those laws & expect there will be a recommendation for a general revision.

The inclosed *bill* for £600. L. Money (in yr. last) I presented yesterday for Acceptance, which was duly hon[*ore*]d. And at Maturity, will transmit you the treasurers rec[*eip*]t. for the amount. It is not at all necessary that you Should make any appology, for desiring me to Negotiate any of your transactions here, it will be no inconvenience nor trouble to me, & Shall always be attended to.

You have in one of the inclosed papers a part of the Secy. at Wars, Militia plan. the whole will Shortly be printed.

The Pennsilvanians brought forward a question which involved in it the old debate relative to the seat of government. *They wished* in both in both houses, to take up the business left unfinished when the Congress adjourned last Septemr. Just as it then *Stood*; as the Southern States were thinly represented they could with great care have fixed on Germantown. A conference of both houses took place, on this business & they finally agreed to Report, that all the business depending before the house at the Adjournment, was done away, & must be taken up de Novo. This Report I have no doubt will be Agreed to in both houses. & the federal Seat will remain in Statu quo, till near the end of the Session.

ALS, Williams Papers, MdHi. Addressed to Baltimore.

James Sullivan to Elbridge Gerry

I had your Letter of the 16th by the post last evening. I never expected that the Commissioners would have made a treaty with the [*Creek*] Indians; a Standing Army is necessary in the opinion of some men to Govern the people. our session of the General Court has had nothing more important before it than the question of the disqualification of the officers of the united States to hold Seats in the Legislature their right was advocated by the old officers of the Army. and by others who are Evidently dependent or Expectant on the General Government. the papers inclosed will give you the decision.

ALS, Gerry Papers, MHi. Written from Boston; postmarked.

George Thatcher to Sarah Thatcher

It has been very melancholly times at our house this week—poor Mrs. Chadwell[1] has lost her oldest daughter; she died on thursday morning & was buried yesterday in the afternoon. She was just entered her eleventh year; a lively, sprightly, active girl—forward in reading, writing and womanly accomplishments—her temper & disposition were mild and amiable—the whole house were charmed with her, & greatly lament her untimely death— It is not more than twelve, or thirteen months since Mrs. Chadwell lost her youngest child, about the age of our Sally—She is almost disconsolate, I am told, for I have not seen her since wednesday—It is not usual for women here to attend the funeral of their nearest relations to the Grave—Little after five o Clock the corps was put into a coach, & notice given to those who attended the funeral; we went to the door, & steped into carriages, & were drove to the burying ground—we then got out & followed the corps, but without much order, to the grave—As soon as we got to the grave, the Minister, who was a churchman, began the funeral service—which lasted till a moment or two after the corps was put into the grave—About the middle of the Service I observed a man, whom I took to be a conductor, take up some earth on a Spade, which he held in his hand directly over the grave, till the minister came to the words we commit "earth to earth, dust to dust & ashes to ashes"—at the pronouncing of which words—the con- ductor droped the earth from his spade on the coffin at three several times as the words were uttered—This was all the earth thrown into the grave while we were there—When the funeral service was ended, we went to our carriages & returned to the house, where each one was served with a glass of wine—And then those who did not belong to the house went home—I think there were four Coaches in all.

Yours of the 9th. inst. came to hand last evening—with a short note from Tempe [*Temperance Lee*]—*She sais tis terrible times in the Jerseys*[2]—You may tell her she must not laugh too soon—her time is coming.

Kiss the dear children.

ALS, Thatcher Family Papers, MHi. Place to which addressed not indicated.

[1] The City Directory lists a Benjamin Chadwell, "sailing master," as residing in Thatcher's boardinghouse at 47 Broad Street in 1789.

[2] This may be a reference to morning sickness or some other symptom of early pregnancy; on 7 September 1790 Sarah gave birth to their third child, George. See George to Sarah Thatcher, 31 January, below.

Thomas B. Wait to George Thatcher

Your Letter of the 10th. inst. is now before me—The substance of which, as it respects Capt. M__ [*Joseph McLellan*], I had before mentioned in presence of thre[e] of the town. When he made the assertion, I took the liberty to contradict it in very plain terms; and then mentioned the circumstance of your writing to him first—that you continued to write as long as any information of importance could be communicated, &c. as recited in your Letter.

I suspected, and to some few had suggested, the cause of Stephen Hall's bitterness. The *Observer*, a writer, who first appeared in the Hartford paper, has drawn his character most accurately. You will find it in his observations upon *disappointed Seekers*.[1]

Your good friend Rebecca Childs was at a few evenings since at Mr. Hall's house. In her hearing your reputation was handled with the very roughest of his fingers. Unfortunately, however for poor Stephen, it was but a few months before, that he had heaped encomiums most lavishly upon you, and this too in the presence of Miss Childs. She heard him attentively—then reverted to his Eulogiums; and concluded with asking in a tone of severity, rather than of curiosity, what was the cause of this astonishing revolution in his sentiments concerning you? But he was *"Dumb, and opened not his mouth."*[2]
***

[*P. S.*] Do inquire about the Eastern Post. there is none appointed. Remember Chamberlain—he is a good man; and the the post master gen. is acquainted with him, as they have lived in the same town at the same time.

ALS, Chamberlain Collection, MB. Written from Portland, Maine.

---

[1] See Observer No. I, 12 October 1789, above.
[2] Psalms 38:13.

OTHER DOCUMENTS

Stephen Austin to Jeremiah Wadsworth. ALS, Wadsworth Papers, CtHi. Written from Philadelphia; franked; postmarked 25 January.
   Asks to request from John Lamb, collector at New York City, an account of the quantity of bar, sheet, and shot lead imported in 1789; he will pay all expenses (for clerk, etc.) and will make similar inquiries of the other ports; their comparison with his weekly domestic production will help determine whether to seek a protective duty.

Elbridge Gerry to John Bacon. No copy known; docketed on Bacon to Gerry, 17 August and 18 November 1789.

James Madison to Edward Carrington. No copy known; mentioned in Madison to Carrington, 2 February, and acknowledged in Carrington to Madison, 5 February.

Governor Thomas Mifflin to John Langdon. ALS, Langdon Papers, NhPoA. Written from Philadelphia; marked "Answer'd."
"The Solicitations of Friends particularly of old brother Soldiers seldom fail to produce a Letter recommendatory if not of their Business at least of themselves"; solicits Langdon's attention and assistance on behalf of Jonas Simonds, inspector of the customs in Philadelphia, who visits New York to seek "an Encrease of Allowance for himself and his Associates most of them Officers of the late Army."

Theodore Sedgwick to Nathaniel Gorham. No copy known; acknowledged in Gorham to Sedgwick, 30 January.

James Sullivan to John Langdon. ALS, Langdon Papers, NhPoA. Written from Boston.
Encloses newspapers.

George Thatcher to Jeremiah Hill. No copy known; acknowledged in Hill to Thatcher, 13 February.

George Thatcher to Thomas Robinson. FC, Thatcher Family Papers, MHi. Addressed to Robinson as "Chairman of Committee"; place to which addressed not indicated. For the full text and background on the petition, see DHFFC 8:416–17.
Acknowledges receipt, on the evening of 23 January, of Robinson's letter dated 11 January and of the petition of Portland merchants, which Thatcher will present to the House at "the earliest opportunity, the ensuing week."

George Thatcher to David Sewall. No copy known; acknowledged in Sewall to Thatcher, 6 February.

Jeremiah Wadsworth to Theodore Hopkins. No copy known; acknowledged in Hopkins to Wadsworth, 16 March.

Jeremiah Wadsworth to Catherine Wadsworth. ALS, Wadsworth Papers, CtHi. Place to which addressed not indicated.
Acknowledges receipt of personal items from home, requests others,

promises to procure books, and requests son Daniel to ask Mr. Hinsdale if he wants some Madeira.

George Washington to Joseph Willard. FC:lbk, Washington Papers, DLC. Sent to "Cambridge University," Massachusetts. For background and the full text, see *PGW* 4:503–5n.

Recommends Willard make known to the Massachusetts delegation in Congress Harvard's "wishes" regarding the erection of a marine hospital in the neighborhood of the college.

William Samuel Johnson, Diary. Johnson Papers, CtHi.
"St. Pauls."

MONDAY, 25 JANUARY 1790

Fine (Johnson)

Benjamin Goodhue to Samuel Phillips, Jr.

I send you the report of the Secry. which is just publish'd, I suppose it will not be considered for some days to come, for the members will want some time to digest it, I am of the same opinion respecting the probable adoption of its most material parts as when I last wrote, Securities have fallen to 7/9 to 8/ partly owing to the scarcity of money and partly owing to a doubt of the interest's being fixed at a higher rate then 3 ℔ Ct., there is a report of Genl. Knox relative to the militia upon the most expensive plan imaginable and which I hope and trust will be discarded, but yet I have my fears, for it seems We are too compliant with the views of our great Officers, espeacialy if recommended by him in whom our confidence is unbounded [*George Washington*], I believe Knox to be the most extravagant man almost [*lined out*] living—his estimate of this expence is to be nearly 400,000 Dollars a year and this he considers a trifling sum compared with the object—I assure you Sir when I find so many of our National leaders destitute of Œconomy and acting as tho' they were either strangers to the circumstances of our Constituents or inattentive to them, I am almost discouraged—I consider the busines of this session to be so important as will be likely to distribute perhaps in a [*lined out*] lasting degree those blessings or evils which depend upon a wise or ill administration of Government. God grant our measures may be such as we may enjoy the former and avoid the latter—I have been a little unwell for some days so as not to attend in Congress, but am now better.

[*P. S.*] My private opinion is that Hamiltons plan for asuming the State debts will be adopted and I rather think the interest will not much if any exceed 3 pr. Ct. for I sincerely hope We may never promise more than we shall be able religiously to perform.

My respect to friends in Senate particularly Mr. [*Stephen*] Choate I've no time to write him.

ALS, Phillips Family Collection, MHi. Place to which addressed not indicated. Internal evidence makes clear that Samuel Phillips, Jr. was the recipient.

Governor Edward Telfair to the Georgia Delegation

In obedience to a resolution of both branches of the Legislature, I have the honor to transmit their Address to the President of the United States to be presented by any two or more of you in the name of the General Assembly of this State.

FC:lbk, Georgia Executive Council Journal, G-Ar. Written from the State House, Augusta, Georgia. The Georgia delegation presented the Address on 18 March.

Peter Van Schaak to Theodore Sedgwick

The Wheels of your Government I hope will move with more Facility, than those of your Stage did in going down—I am however happy to find your Safe Arrival announced by your taking your Seat in the House of Representatives of the United States, one of the most august Assemblies in my Opinion in the World. Pray dont forget your Promise of sometimes letting Us hear what you are about. As you and Mr. Silvester have pretty nearly the Same Connections in this Part of the Country You can relieve each other in the Burthen of communications—The Speech, and the Addresses[1] are very pleasing to Me—the Sound of *Government* is a ~~pleasing~~ grateful one to my Ears. That alone can produce the good Fruits you laboured for in ~~yo~~ the arduous Struggle.

We are still without Snow, consequently with very little Communication with Berkshire. I trust however that you hear from Home often. The Star visits us regularly and rises into Character—You must assist it in shedding its Rays with more Brightness—But qure. who writes under the Signature of Cornelius?[2] or is it but a Sham Attack. The Epigram is not without Smartness or perhaps Pertness.[3]

***

Pray what is the Rate of Exchange between N. York & London—a Line on this Subject too when you are at Leisure will oblige Me—this I fancy you must often hear mentioned.

My best Regards to Benson.

[*P. S.*] Do send the inclosed Safe.

ALS, Sedgwick Papers, MHi. Place from which written not indicated.

[1] Washington's state of the union address of 8 January and the Senate and House replies of 11 and 12 January.

[2] Cornelius was the pen name of the author of an article on assumption that appeared in the [Stockbridge, Massachusetts] *Western Star*, 19 January. He continued to publish pieces as late as September, eliciting several replies.

[3] Printed under 19 January, above.

Oliver Whipple to John Langdon

I have taken the Freedom to address you, and to inclose to your Care, three Advertisments, for the Sale of some Lands at Kennebeck [*Maine*], I would take it as a Favour, if you will imploy some trusty man to put up the Advertisments, one at the Markett, and the others, at the most public Taverns in the City. I must now Sr. intreat your Interest and Influence in a Matter, which I presume will soon take Place, The Excise is an Object that will early ingross the Attention of Congress, and is vested in them by the Constitution, Officers of Course will be appointed to collect the Excise, if you Sr. will be pleased to hand in my Name (as a suitable person to execute the Office) To the President & Senate, when the affair is upon the Carpet, I shall esteem it as the highest Favor, and shall never dishonour your Nomination.

As to the Politicks of our State a Word may not be unpleasing, on the Meeting of the [*General*] Court, almost the first Question was, wether President [*John*] Sullivan could Constitutionally hold the Chair, while he was a District Judge. This Question was postponed from Day to Day, and in the ~~Case~~ Course of the Sessions, was determined that it should be postponed for Consideration to next Sessions, tho' had a Discision on the Point, been early urged, I believe it would have been determined against him, so we see that a Man can draw pay as district Judge & President at the same Time—the General Court are Still Siting, what will be further produced by them I can not say, *** The Season now approaches, in which we begin to cast about for some Person to rule over us, Mr. Sullivan, has signified to the General Court that they must look out for some other Person to fill the Chair, after the Expiration of this Year; it is now a Scene of Speculation, Brother [*John*] Pickering & Judge [*Josiah*] Bartlet, (who is lately appointed Chief Justice) begin to prick up their Ears, in persuit of the *Game*, perhaps they may be[*gin to*] tire in the Chase, which would certainly be the Case, was you upon the

Ground, I do therefore wish as do many others, that you will let me know as early as possible if you mean to retire from Congress before the next Election, in June, for if that can be once certified to the People your Election will inevitably take Place, as President of our State, a few Lines to me on the this Subject will be very agreeable, to me & others who wish Sr. to give you every Support.

P. S. Dear Sr. as we shall soon have Ministers appointed for foreign Courts, & Secretaries of Course, it would be very pleasing to me, to act in the latter Capacity, could I be appointed; my ambition to serve the States would prompt my Exertions to such Degree, that I know I should give great Satisfaction, *This in Confidence.*

***

ALS, Langdon Papers, NhPoA. Written and postmarked 30 January from Portsmouth, New Hampshire. The omitted text relates to state politics.

[*Jeremiah Wadsworth,*] The Observer—No. XVI

The re-establishment of national credit, a measure both of justice and sound policy

We must expect the people will be alive to all those national measures which have a direct influence on their property; this I consider not as an evil, but a great support of government, for give them time to be informed, and the whole weight of their influence will come in to aid the measures of a just and politic administration. The pain of acquiring property, and the benefits which result from possessing it, will make a prudent man careful how it is taken from his hand—Avarice degrades human nature, but a love of property is a political virtue; remove this motive and civilized society, will be destroyed. An adequate provision for the debt of the nation, and for a fixed public credit, is a subject which vastly engages attention. Some diversity of sentiment is not half as strange, as that so many are united, and can think and converse amicably; neither is this diversity any evidence of dishonest intentions on either part. The particular situation of American credit, and the unhappy consequences of its past decline, have been sufficient to perplex the opinions of many worthy citizens. They are willing to be just even at the expence of all superfluities; but having only little property and that hardly earned, and thinking greater taxation needed to retrieve national credit, than will eventually be found necessary; there is a strong temptation to say, let the scene end as it hath begun.

Accustomed to see American paper of low value they have forgot, that a vast number of citizens, relying on the honesty of their country, deposited the whole savings of their industry, and dependance of their families; and that these very people or their children are now in depressed circumstances, and kept from despair, by a hope of returning justice in their country. Many hundreds of planters who had sold their lands, that they might locate property more advantageously for a numerous family, were caught in that unlucky moment when business stagnated, and a frontier situation was dangerous; all these became public creditors.

The most honest merchants, whose feelings forbid them to violate the laws of their country, limiting the high price of foreign articles, thought it more patriotic to consecrate their property to its defence. The estate of many thousand orphans, hath been deposited in the public treasury, by those who had their patrimony in trust.

A prodigious number of private funds sacred to religion and science, have been loaned to the public.

The price of the soldiers fatigue, limbs and life is yet unpaid to him. When the nation needed every exertion of its subjects, and could make no pay, the most industrious and patriotic farmers sold their provisions for the public faith: but I will not go on with this recapitulation of sufferers, for I know that principle, and the possibility of what can be done; and not passionate feelings, must form the public mind on this subject, and be the ultimate ratio of justice.

An objection against restoring credit, in the minds of some, is that the debt hath passed from the original creditors, at a low price, and that a fulfilment of the public promises would not benefit the sufferers.

That considerable sums have been sold at a low price, and passed into circulation is a fact; but these are only a small part of the aggregate debt. As little sums of money compared with the whole cash of the country, make a great show at the raffling table, in passing several times perhaps, thro' every hand of the gambling circle: So it is a small proportion of the national paper, which hath made the show in circulation. The speculation in paper hath been a kind of gambling, artificially kept up between distant parts; a few sagacious ones have been fortunate, and many have been losers. Thus circumstanced, by many times passing and repassing a small proportion of the public paper hath made a great appearance; and those securities which have circulated most, have much sound and little substance, being many of them liable to a tenfold deduction by scaling. The great weight of debt is still in the hands of the original holders, men who loaned or did service for the country from noble motives, who were conscious that the nation received from them an equivalent for its promise—men who had rather brave some distress in their private circumstances, than sell their just claim for a trifle; who were determined either to realize a moderate compensation, or die with the reflection that they had become poor in a good cause, and with a right to have this inscription over them, "here lies the man who sacrificed his all to support American liberty and sovereignty."

What can the supreme legislature say to such men, or to their children when supplicating their remembrance? Shall they be told the sum is great and there will be some difficulty in devising the means? This is allowed, but a reply is ready, is there not more difficulty and distress, in having the whole borne by a few than by the nation at large?

Among those who have alienated their public bonds, there is a variety of cases; a few have been obliged by necessity, from the tardiness of the national faith; the lot of such is hard and unfortunate—if wishing and trying to devise could give them relief, every benevolent spirit would join in the exertion; but I do not know it to be possible and may the rewarder of virtuous suffering do them right.

But this is not the case with all who have alienated their national paper. Many have done it on the principles and for the purposes of speculation; and have no reason to murmer at the consequences.

Many by improving the price of their sale in some lucrative business, have realized a greater sum, than the parent holders will ever receive from the public by the most favorable reinstatement of credit, which can be supposed; such persons may speak much of their loss, but have no right to wrangle with the event.

It is well known that the war called up a set of characters, in various departments, and in several kinds of speculation, who were calculated to thrive by public confusion, but not by persevering industry; these men held considerable sums of national paper, which they have since alienated. If the public had at that time paid them in coin, it would long since have gone from their hands, and been in possession of the very persons, who now hold their public bonds. Men calculated to gain by such overturns of society as happened in the American war, and destitute of œconomy and hard industry; must fall into decline on the restoration of order, and peace. The poor are subjects of our humane commiseration, tho' imprudence be the cause of their poverty; but such as would have scattered their property, if the nation had early paid them in dollars of Mexico, have no just rights to clamour against a re-establishment of public credit. The measures of a nation cannot be accommodated to the situation, of one or a hundred imprudent subjects; and to attempt it would be injustice to a ten fold greater number, who have a sacred claim on public truth.

A power to alienate property, is one of the rights of man, which government ought not to invade either directly or indirectly by any of its measures. Suppose I hold a government bond for 100 dollars, fairly obtained; is not such bond my own property? Have I not the same right to alienate this, as any other kind of property? Am I not my own judge of the time, place, and price of exchange in sale? Every man knows best his own opportunities, and may advance his interest by selling at a large discount, and this hath been done by many who have sold. For government to interpose arbitrarily in these matters is destroying its own credit, and an indirect way of defrauding those who patiently depended on the public truth. A power of alienating and transfering is one consideration which gives value to any kind of property, had there been more traffick in national paper, it would always have brought a greater price. So long as much the greater part of the public obligations remains with the original loaners; as the transferals which have taken place were without fraud; considering also that in many instances, it was more advantageous for the seller to alienate than to retain his property; I cannot determine that it is either just or politic for government to intermeddle in the matter.

It is not possible for a nation, or any branch of its executive to overlook all the private bargains of jockies, speculators and dunces—No rule of right can be ascertained—the expence of attempting it would bring a new debt on the country, ten fold greater than all the savings which can be made; these people must do their own business; if they practice knavery the law is open, and the judges of the land will punish them. The faith of a nation is sacred, and its measures ought to be stable, and not diverted from their course by a little traffick in public paper.

It is now from seven to fifteen years since the national paper was issued; in a period of this length, nature and the necessary changes of society, in any country, will produce a considerable revolution of property; and I believe it to be a fact, that a less proportion of this paper, than of any other kind of property which can be named, hath changed its owners. Even in improved lands, which are the most stable kind of property; fix upon a number of contiguous acres in any inhabited part of America, of value equal to the national paper when it issued, and we shall find a greater proportion of these lands than of the national and State debts, hath been alienated and passed over to other owners; this appears to me an irrefragable evidence, that there hath been in the body of the people, notwithstanding all which hath taken place, a serious dependence on the public faith, and that it is still their expectation it will be re-established. In the sale of these lands, there have been many unprofitable bargains to the sellers; and many who alienated have spent the whole amount in folly; but these are matters in which government cannot safely interfere—business, commerce and the exchange of property must have their course. One quarter of the bargains made are detrimental to one, and some of them to both parties; they were made in folly, but for national policy particularly to inspect them would be greater folly, and a most unmanageable and endless business.

The considerations suggested in this paper, with many others which I may hint in future, lead me to suppose, notwithstanding all the objections I have ever heard, that the re-establishment of public credit, is a measure of justice due to the creditors, and that it hath always been expected by the most honest part of the community, and by those persons best acquainted with the nature, operation, and events of political society.

In my next number, I will endeavor to shew, that the restoration of credit which justice claims, is also a measure of sound national policy, and the only possible means of preventing very extreme evils.

[Hartford, Connecticut] *American Mercury*, 25 January. For information on The Observer series, its authorship, and reprintings, see the location note to The Observer, No. I, 12 October, above.

[*William Maclay,*] A Citizen of Pennsylvania

An Account of the Funding System of Pennsylvania,
addressed to the Congress of the United States

Immediately after the peace, some members of the General Assembly turned their attention towards paying off the public debts due to the citizens of that state, being fully convinced that under the then existing confederation, it never could be done by Congress. When the mass of debt due to the citizens was contemplated, it struck them, that the whole *could not* be paid, and from the manner in which the greater part came into the hands of the then holders, it appeared highly improper that the whole *should be* paid. Mens minds were then familiar with the different scales of depreciation both of continental money and loan-office certificates.[1] It was resolved therefore to promote a plan, to pay off the interest due to original holders, and to open the land-office for the reception of the alienated certificates in the purchase of lands. The plan actually took place with regard to the depreciation certificates. But in order to extend the scheme to extinguish all the alienated certificates at once, and to interest the holders of them in lands, which would bind them still faster to the interests of the country, and promote new settlements, it was determined to purchase the residue of the state from the Indians, and to open the land-office for the whole, in one grand lottery, where many prizes, in the way of rich tracts of land, might be obtained without any risk of blanks. The purchase was made and the lottery took place; but unfortunately the patrons of the original scheme had in the mean while lost their seats in the House. It is painful to enumerate the arts and management by which the assembly of 1785 were induced to pass a funding law, giving full interest on the nominal amount to the holders of certificates indiscriminately. This starved the land-office, for rapacity itself must have been more than satisfied. Certificates seldom had been as high as two shillings in the pound before that period. At the time of passing the law, and for some time after, they were not more than two and six pence.

The man that laid out £100.0.0 specie, in certificates, got to the nominal amount of 800.0.0, and of course drew 48 per annum on the same. The state of Pennsylvania has paid, or stands pledged to pay, four years interest on all her funded certificates. Every holder of such certificates, purchased at or before the passing of the funding law, has cleared on the original sum laid out and on the interest on that sum, above fifty per cent. over the original sum, and has the certificates into the bargain. To make this more plain, one hundred pounds brought eight hundred in certificates, the interest on which for four years amounted to 192, from which deduct the original hundred with four years interest amounting to 124, and there remained 68.0.0 *clear* but *unlawful* gain, as the laws allow but 6 per cent. for the use of money, and the certificates still remain unsatisfied in the hands of the purchasers.

The distress which this funding system brought upon Pennsylvania, by checking its agriculture and commerce and driving her citizens into the wilderness, or other states, shall be the subject of another paper.

FG, 25 January; reprinted at New York City (*NYP*, 2 February) and Baltimore. Maclay sent this piece to Benjamin Rush on 16 January. No followup essay appeared in *FG*.

---

[1] Old Continental Money was issued by the Continental Congress between 1775 and 1780, at which time it was depreciated at a rate of forty dollars to one Spanish milled (gold) dollar, and cancelled by new currency issued at an exchange rate of one-twentieth, or forty Continental dollars to two "new emission" dollars (*JCC* 16:263–64; *Purse*, pp. 50–51).

OTHER DOCUMENTS

William Bradford, Jr. to Elias Boudinot. ALS, Wallace Papers, PHi. Place from which written not indicated.
"I had last night the pleasure of hearing of your welfare by an unfinished letter which the post brought me"; believes there are prospects for selling Boudinot's "poor mansion" at Elizabeth "particularly so near the seat of the federal govt."; "[*Francis*] Hopkinson is pretty well as to bodily health—but his mind is still shattered & his *perfect* recovery doubtful. I presume you will be obliged to pass an act for appointing two Judges for this district, (in case he should continue in his present state), and authorising either to act. There does not seem any power in any part of the Gov[*ernment*]. to remove a judge who is incapacitated by accident, or as lawyers express it—by the act of god, from discharging the duties of his office."

Benjamin Goodhue to Michael Hodge. ALS, Ebenezer Stone Papers, MSaE. Place to which addressed not indicated. For the full text, see *EIHC* 84(April 1948):147–48.
Encloses Hamilton's report on public credit, "which please to communicate

to the Gentn. of Newburyport"; the House will not consider it for some days; interest proposed will be between three and four percent, more likely the former.

Henry Lee to James Madison. ALS, Madison Papers, DLC. Written from "Stratford Hall," Westmoreland County, Virginia. For the full text, see *PJM* 13:5.
  Office seeking: the bearer, Dr. David Morrow, who "understands that naval hospitals will be established & wishes to resume his old employment."

Azor Orne to Benjamin Goodhue. ALS, Letters to Goodhue, NNS. Written from Boston. For the full text, see *DHFFC* 8:143–44.
  Describes conditions in the fisheries and commits himself to pressing the Massachusetts legislature to petition Congress for their relief.

John Adams, Diary. Adams Family Manuscript Trust, MHi. These remarks appear on the verso of the page on which Adams made his entry for 25 January. They may have been written then or at some other time.
  "Interest, Corruption, Prejudice, Error, Ignorance. Causes of wrong Judgments. have not these Causes, as much Influence in one assembly, as in two? if either or all of these Causes should prevail, over Reason, Justice, and the public good in one assembly, is not a Revision of the subject in another a probable means of correcting false decree?"

George Washington, Diary. Washington Papers, MiD-B. For the full text, see *DGW* 6:13.
  Scott, Hartley, and White introduced Francis Bailey to the President.

NYMP, 25 January. Wister Butler Papers, PHi. Annotated by Butler to indicate the article for which he retained the issue.
  "Equity" (from the [Boston] *Independent Chronicle*, 14 January), on discrimination.

TUESDAY, 26 JANUARY 1790

Thaw Rain (Johnson)

Elias Boudinot to Governor William Livingston

I spoke to our Clerk and found that the deficiency in the Votes sent you, took its rise from the Circumstance I mentioned to you.

To prevent you the Trouble of sewing them together the Clerk has given me a set for your Excellency bound in a folio Volume, which I now do myself the honor of sending by this Opportunity.

ALS, Livingston Papers, MHi. Addressed to Elizabeth, New Jersey.

Jeremiah Hill to George Thatcher

I returned from Boston last Evening when I received yours of the 3d & 10th. inst. Thank you kindly for your Information respecting impost Matters, it corresponds perfectly with the information I have recd. at Boston &c. for News I must refer you to last Saturdays [*Massachusetts*] Centinal where you will find that our Legislature are stricking out a large field of Business for the present Session—according to Custom it is very probable they will begin soon to taper off and at the End bring forth a M—e [*Mouse*][1] The *famous* Town meeting[2] (I was just a going to say infamous) lately held at Portland is a matter of speculation among the Speculators or brokers in Politicks. I understand that they have had or are about having another meeting to take under Consideration, not "the late Act of Congress" but the late Acts of the former Meeting. hem! hem! quid tum?[3] I consulted with Brother [*Benjamin*] Lincoln when at Boston about the coasting Act in particular & he informed me that Congress had that Business under Consideration again by way of Revision—I shall depend on your giving me the earliest Intelligence of all Occurrences more especially what relates to the Revenue. That is a matter you know that lays near my heart. I called to see our friend [*James*] Freeman & he presented me with a number of very pious rational Pamphlets on the divine Unity—the Logos &c.

I shall write to the Secretary [*Hamilton*] by the next Post & shall inclose a Receipt for the money I paid into the bank and at the same time advise him of the Receipt you have for me Which I wish you to deliver him. you see your Receipt is inclosed—I think the Collection Law authorises the Collectors to purchase Scales, Weights, Measures &c. for the Use of the District,[4] but if I read right it must be done under the Direction of the Treasury. I wish you to mention this Matter to the Secy. I have wrote him on the Subject but have received no Answer likewise I mentioned to him the necessity of having a Boat in this Port. I hate to be always applying to others for these things.

Adieu at present you shall soon hear again from your Friend.

ALS, Chamberlain Collection, MB. Written from Biddeford, Maine; postmarked Portsmouth, New Hampshire, 28 January.

---

[1] Mountains will be in labor and the birth will be a funny little mouse (Horace, *Ars Poetica*, 139).

[2]The reference is either to the meeting of 22 December 1789, which passed the petition of the Merchants and other Inhabitants of Portland and forwarded it to Ames, or the meeting of 11 January 1790, rescinding the order to have the petition presented by Ames. For the controversy surrounding these proceedings, see *DHFFC* 8:412–17.
   [3]What next?
   [4][HR-11], section 5.

Governor Samuel Huntington to the Connecticut Representatives

I learn from the Newspapers that the Secretary of the Treasury hath made his Report on the Important Subject of the Finnances, ~~& I wish to be I Shall be happy to~~ I Shall be happy to recieve as early Intelligence as may be, of the proceedings of Congress on So Interesting a Subject, from time to time.

You Gentlemen are Sensible that the people of this State feel themselves Interested in the ~~pr~~[*lined out*]dings of Congress, & many of them have a pecular desire to know all the Measures adopted by the National Assembly Such Information from their Representatives will not ~~only~~ merely gratify curiosity, but fullfill the expectations of many of your Constituents, & may be of Special Service to the Citizens of this State.

FC:dft, U.S. Congress Papers, MiU-C. Written from Norwich, Connecticut.

George Partridge to Alexander Hodgdon

As the report of the Secretary of the Treasury Department, proposes among other things, An Assumption of the Debts of the several States, the consideration of this report may probably bring into view the comparative exertions which have been made by ~~the such~~ states to discharge or reduce these Debts, that I may be better able to throw light on this subject, I wish you would transmit to me, as soon as may be, a Schedule of the taxes which have been laid by our Legislature since the revolution; distinguishing those which, by the tax Acts, were receivable in paper, and also the several kinds of paper in which they were receivable. as it may be more important to have this Schedule soon then to have it minute & particular, I wish you would forward it by the next post after ~~you~~ the receipt of this Letter.

ALS, Emmet Collection, NN. Place to which addressed not indicated.

From Our Correspondents at New York

We have expectations that Rhode-Island will come into the Union without the adoption of any measures which may wear the face of coertion.

The report of the Secretary at War, proposes an expense beyond my idea of the present ability of the country.

Some will doubtless oppose the assumption of the state debts by the General Government, I am however much mistaken if the People can be roused to an opposition to this measure. In my opinion, a settlement of the accounts of individual states with the United States is chimerical: because it will raise the amount of the national debt beyond the ability of provision by the Government; because as yet no ratio of apportionment is provided, and because the citizens of this country almost universally believe that the states to which they belong, are in advance beyond their respective proportions.

[Stockbridge, Massachusetts] *Western Star*, 2 February.

Newspaper Article

A correspondent who attended at the house of representatives yesterday, informs us, that in the committee of the house on the bill for enumerating the inhabitants of the United States, Mr. Livermore proposed a very considerable amendment to that part where it is enacted that every male or female, of 21 years of age, shall be obliged to render a true account of the number of persons, &c. in their families. Mr. Livermore moved, that the word *female* be struck out, and gave for his reason that it would be sometimes indelicate in a marshal to ask a young lady how old she was, or make *too strict* enquiry. The amendment was agreed to.

Before the house adjourned, a message was received from the Senate, communicating a letter from G. D. E.[1] a citizen of Genoa, directed to the Most Illustrious and Honorable the Congress of the United States of America, offering to secure to them a Truce with the States of Barbary and Tunis, for the moderate sum of 500,000l. per annum; which proposal occasioned much entertainment to the house.[2]

NYDG, 27 January.

[1] Gaetano Drago di Domenico's letter is printed in *DHFFC* 1:227–28n. For background on the Genoese merchant's intervention respecting Algerine prisoners, see *DHFFC* 1:227–28n, 2:425–49, 8:1–2.

[2] *NYDG*, 28 January, reported that "we are requested to contradict" this paragraph "as no such business appears upon the minutes of the House."

OTHER DOCUMENTS

Edward Bangs to George Thatcher. ALS, Chamberlain Collection, MB. Written from Worcester, Massachusetts.

"Blessed be the Congress for these are good times"; all eyes are turned to Congress for news "& for every thing else, even for our virtue & our industry"; Allen of Worcester, who had intended to accompany Thatcher in the state as far as Hartford, is a strong supporter of Congress; has heard Allen say that the members' travel allowance was "given that they might travel with dignity—If still they will travel in a stage coach they ought to be contentment with stage coach fare," and singled out Thatcher as an example of this claim; suggests Thatcher take the opportunity "to say something yourself" on the subject; reminds Thatcher of Bangs's request for law books; regards to Ames.

Joseph Barnard to George Thatcher. ALS, Chamberlain Collection, MB. Written from Portsmouth, New Hampshire; postmarked.
    Begs Thatcher to intervene with Postmaster General Samuel Osgood for Barnard's salary for the past two quarters.

Oliver Ellsworth and William Samuel Johnson to Governor Samuel Huntington. No copy known; acknowledged in Huntington to Ellsworth and Johnson, 6 February.

Edward Fox to Andrew Craigie. ALS, Craigie Papers, MWA. Written from Philadelphia; postmarked.
    Is "astonished" at the "outrageous act of public fraud" Hamilton, "a man who realy seems to understand the true Interests of the Government as he seems to do," commits in his report by offering only four percent interest; "Clymer is the man you take him to be—with a tolerable education he is a meer Mule. A fixed party man. Illiberal to a very uncommon degree, and I believe an utter enemy to public credit. As to Fitz—the plan of the Secretary seems to be his plan—other than he wished a Voluntary offer to be made by the Creditors"; thinks a commission for settling Morris's accounts "must be filled with some person or persons of *Dignity*."

Governor Samuel Huntington to Benjamin Huntington. FC, hand of S. Huntington, Lane Memorial Collection, CtY. Written from Norwich, Connecticut.
    Wishes to receive complete copy of Hamilton's report on public credit "by the first conveyance"; "the communications of the proceedings of Congress which you propose to make, will be very acceptable," in particular, information about the probability of the President's proclaiming a national fast day in the spring.

Justus Mitchell to Roger Sherman. ALS, Sherman Papers, DLC. Written from New Canaan, Connecticut.
Sherman's family is well; encloses letters for forwarding; "I esteem it, a great favor, to have you write often"; "people seem to be satisfied with the federal Government."

Benjamin Rush to John Adams. ALS, Adams Family Manuscript Trust, MHi. Written from Philadelphia.
Office seeking: the bearer, Andrew Brown, who "has been instrumental in a newspaper in circulating federal sentiments" for some appointment under the federal government.

Roger Sherman to Simeon Baldwin. ALS, Sherman Collection, CtY. Place to which addressed not indicated; received 29 January.
Delivered personal letter for Baldwin and advised recipient on the legal business it contained; North Carolina Act [HR-36] passed in COWH that day; encloses the day's *NYDG*; "what is most [*blotted out*] worthy of notice is the Poem at the head of the 2d. page" ("The Lawyer's Prayer").

George Thatcher to Henry Bass. No copy known; acknowledged in Bass to Thatcher, 6 March.

Abishai C. Thomas to John Gray Blount. ALS, John Gray Blount Papers, Nc-Ar. Misdated 1789. For the full text, see *Blount* 1:459–61. Place to which addressed not indicated.
Hawkins intended to write a postscript, but was too late; Congress is "going headlong" in preparing for the operation of federal revenue laws in North Carolina; wonders how "the D[*evil*]" it will know where to fix ports of entry and delivery; "if we had our H[*ugh*]. W[*illiamson*]. among them they might go on with some propriety but certain I am they must now act without the necessary information"; plans to attend the House on 27 January for second reading; Williamson and Johnston are expected any moment; Williamson's infant son (Charles) is a fine boy and his wife (Maria Apthorpe Williamson) is very well.

George Washington, Diary. Washington Papers, MiD-B. For the full text, see *DGW* 6:17.
The Vice President and Speaker of the House were among "numerous and respectable" attendees at the President's levee.

WEDNESDAY, 27 JANUARY 1790

Snow (Johnson)

Pierce Butler to Joseph Habersham

I have seen with much satisfaction Your name among the dissenters to the sale of the Western lands.[1] It is ~~is~~ an additional proof of Your Patriotism and nice sense of right. I am not equal to the description of the Injury the measure will cause to Georgia with the general Government, or the effect it had on the Members of both houses. Had Your Legislature done as the Legislatures of all the other states did, that is ceded Your Western Lands, Georgia would, I am persuaded, have had effectual aid against Indians or any other Enemys that could present themselves: but now I believe if the Indians over-run the Country there will not be one soldier sent to their Relief. I have heretofore exerted my small abilities in Council [*Senate*] to serve Georgia,[2] but however sincerely I regard many of her Citizens I must now remain silent when the Interests of that Country is the subject before us. The imprudent Measure of the majority of Your Legislature will involve Georgia in double difficulties, if not done away by a speedy repeal of the act, for within the boundaries mentioned much of the Chikesaw Lands are included; & these are guaranteed to them by the U.S. at a treaty made with them in 1785.[3] Of course the Federal Governmt. will be obliged, (& their humanity & sense of Justice dispose them to it) to interfere in favor of the Indians. What a situation then has an imprudent majority brought the Country into!

I lament it sincerely. It is not only a great injury to the Country, but materially effects the whole Southern Interest in Congress. I thought better of Mr. [*Governor Edward*] Telfair than that he would have given his assent to the bill. I wish, as a real friend to the Interests & happiness of Georgia that the Legislature cou'd be called to repeal that rash act; then would You have effectual support from here in Men & money. Can it not be done?

FC, Butler Letterbook, ScU.

---

[1] A reference to the Georgia legislature's act of December 1789, granting preemption rights to more than fifteen million acres of its western territory to the Yazoo Land Companies; see George Walton to John Adams, 20 January, above.

[2] Although Butler represented South Carolina in the Senate, he had substantial landed interests in Georgia's Altamaha River delta. By 1790, he owned seventeen hundred acres of cotton plantations spread across the barrier island of St. Simon, and an additional fifteen hundred acres planted with rice further upriver, across from Darien (*Butler*, pp. 106, 120).

[3] The Treaty of Hopewell with the Chickasaws (one of three Hopewell treaties with southern Indian nations signed in the winter of 1785–86) extended federal protection over Chickasaw lands in present-day central and northern Mississippi, covering much of the land offered to the Yazoo companies. For the text of the treaty, see *DHFFC* 2:177–80.

Elias Hasket Derby to Benjamin Goodhue

I have yours by the Stage & in answer say that 'till now from your letter & what I see in the paper I thought that we had a Government that would not be for ever on the Wing *in making laws* one Day & altering them the Next what I mean by this is that the Article of Tea for Instance was fixt @ 6 Cents which Impost on that Article was thought to be high—it bares too hard & for this reason it is an article imported from India—the Impost is laid after all the Ships are on their Voyages & no Merchant has it in his power to Counteract any of his orders—had the Merchant on the Continent have known of the Impost before their Ships sail'd—I do believe that at least 5 out of the 10 sail of Ships wld. not have gone the Voyage or not have taken Cargo's of Teas for this Market—There is three Ships of this State from the Hither [*West*] Indies gone to Canton [*China*] more than was expected—the Quantity of Tea the coming season will much exceed the Consumption so that the importer will not have it in his power to raise it—but must pay that Impost out of his own pocket this trade for the length of those Voyages—ought to be view'd different from European or West India Importers—I see by the paper & your letter to the [*Insurance*] Office that 12 Cents on Bohea & other Tea in that proportion is Mention'd—perhaps I may have my fears a little rais'd on this Matter—but it is my real opinion that if I have to pay the 12 Cents that a Cargo sold in Boston will not fetch the Impost & the cost in Canton—& for this reason that if 2000 Chests is as much as a years consumption & there is 5000 at Market how is it possible it should unless there is a Market to carry it to which is not the case—& I fear will injure those concern'd exceedingly—unless they go to smugling which no doubt will hereafter be the case if the Impost is equal to the cost of the Goods. how is a Merchant ever to make a calculation to be depended on—I was in hopes that the Government had a disposition to raise the Credit of the Continent—but barely mentioning 3 or even 4 pr. Ct. is enough to make me Judge other ways—for who will believe that the 4 pr. Ct. will be paid more honestly than the 6 an Honest Man will pay as far as he can & the rest when he is able—suppose Government from time hence should want Money who would ever put the least confidence in them—the scheme of the Wild Lands if there is not a confidence to be plac'd in the Government after I have got the Lands for one third of my debt what reason have I to think that Congress will put so high a Tax on that Land as to take the other two thirds of my debt.

FC:lbk, Derby Shipping Papers, MSaE. Written from Salem, Massachusetts. For Derby's petition on the issue in this letter, see *DHFFC* 8:403–11.

Samuel Henshaw to Theodore Sedgwick

I am happy to find by yours of the 16th. inst. that you have taken your seat in Congress—I wish you an agreeable Session.

You ask, whether, in my opinion, Congress can pay 4 per Ct. In[*tere*]st. on the Prin[*ciple*]. of the National debt, besides reserving enough for contingent demands? I am not sufficiently acquainted with the productive resources of the Union to give a peremptory & decided opinion. But I much doubt the ability of Congress to carry such a Scheme into effect—The revenue from Impost & Excise will never do it even on paper; unless it is laid so high as to be intolerable, and then it will destroy itself—Perhaps the Impost has been more productive than the Secy. had reason to expect—But it does not from thence follow, in my mind, that the Impost will long continue to be equally productive. The Merchantile part of the community are the nicest calculators in the world, & infinitely more eagle eyed than any other order of Men—And when any new scheme is adopted that affects their business, they will punctually comply 'till they have thoroughly learned all the official examinations & modes of doing Business, and then if every cargo dont yield less & less revenue, I am mistaken.

If the Secy. should calculate that the revenue will increase, in any tolerable proportion to the population of our Country, He will, I beleive, find himself in an error—Our own manufactures will soon greatly check our Importations; and unless we can create a new world, or find a better market than I have any Idea of, to take of[*f*] the surplusage produce of our farms, we shall soon get into a fixed habit of living much more within ourselves; and shall consequently consume less of foreign produce, and of course pay less Impost & Excise—A direct tax, therefore, on our lands must make good the difficiency—This Idea is big with horror to the honest Yeomanry of Mass[*achuse*]tts. And I very much doubt whether we could, at this Moment, get a Vote in our Genl. Court to surrender the State Debt into the hands of Congress, unless they can be assured, before hand, that Congress will not lay a land tax upon them—Congress Assessors, & Congress Collectors, already, sound terribly in their ears—And, my Friend, I have no scruple in saying, That Congress cannot pay 4 per Cent, & support their Governmt. without laying a very considerable land tax—and such a tax will be submitted to with a very ill grace.

Is not 3 per Cent abundently sufficient for the generallity of the present holders of public Securities? I think it is—For there is not a single purchaser but what will, at that rate, receive 6 per Ct. Inst. for the money actually paid; and by far the greater part will receive 24 per Cent. Is not this doing as great Justice as such purchasers can, without a blush, demand? And is not the public opinion, throughout the Union, against doing greater? And is it not, my Freind, in human wisdom, to make a discrimination between the purchaser & the original holder? It is my opinion, suddenly formed I confess, That if Congress should throw out a proposition for reloaning the whole debt at 3 per Ct. and make ample provision for the semiannual payment thereof—and make no provision for the payment of the Interest on obligations not thus reloaned, that 99 out of a 100 of the purchasers would instantly comply—Those few who hold the Securities they originally drew, would hang back, and would, I dare venture to say, petition Congress on the Subject before they would reloan at 3 per Ct.—And here, in my Mind, would be a fair opening for a righteous discrimination. For Congress might then, if they did not give them more than 3 per Ct., make up their loss, or nearly so, by a generous grant of lands. And I beleive all the World would say AMEN.

Since writing the foregoing I find, by the papers, that the Secy. proposes to raise the Impost very considerably on wines, foreign Spirits & other articles, If the intentions is to help the morals of the people by discouraging the use of those liquors, the plan may be good; but if an increase of revenue is intended the plan will not answer.

For you may rely on it, that if such high Duties (for high they are, for this young Country, tho they may be low compared with those paid in older & richer ones,) do not introduce smuggleing, they will prevent importations.

But I shall tire your patience. The Subject of the Fishery will be attended to by the general Court & a representation thereof made to Congress—Exports must also be regulated.

The Impost Act, & especially the coasting Act must be infinitely better guarded or frauds will soon be practised—At present, indeed, there is no check but the oath of the party concerned—at least so far as it respects Goods *not* weighed, guaged or measured—For if the packages &c. agree with the manifest, and nothing is easier, it is enough—The *Contents* are not examined—the Oath is sufficient for *that*—and therefore no further care is taken—This mode of doing business cannot last long.

Shall you lay an Excise this Session? How will it be collected? Will Comptrollers of Districts be appointed? And will a friend of yours stand any chance to serve himself & his Country in the revenue department? And had He better get Letters in his favour from Govr. [*James*] Bowdoin & others?

Good Night—And may God Almighty bless you.

ALS, Sedgwick Papers, MHi. Written from Boston.

Charles Pettit to Elias Boudinot

It was not till yesterday Afternoon that I recd. yr. Favour of the 22d. and I intended to have give you an hour or two today in Observations on the

Secretary's Report tho' I did not get the Pamphlet till late this Afternoon My reading of it has hitherto been confined to the dedached publications in Dunlap & Claypoole's Paper.[1] Other Business has engaged me till it is now too late to offer you by this Post, any Thoughts on the Plan, other than in General that it is far short of my Ideas of Justice to the Public Creditors, & if persisted in must work an Oppressive Loss to the original Holders of Securities—They are certainly intitled to 6 ℅ Ct. according to the original Contract, so long as the Principal remains at a Market price under 100 ℅ Cent. Whenever the Princ[ipa]l. comes up to that Mark or higher it will be an Evidence that the Market Rate of Interest is lower. Government may then reduce the Interest with propriety to as low a rate as they can contract a new Loan upon. Till then the Reduction of the Int[eres]t. would be an arbitrary & unjust Act which has no example but in Despotism.

But I shall say more on this Subject when I have Leisure. Mean Time, I will not impute evil Design to the Secretary—His reasoning on the Subject, and the Principles he States as his Rule are so just & proper, that I am constrained to impute what I deem erroneous in his System, to a misapprehension of Facts, and of the Circumstances existing in this Country, which differ widely from those of the Countries from which he draws Experience. His Inferences therefore I think are not deducible from our Circumstances. A strong Evidence of the Truth of my Observation is that Stock, tho' below 50 ℅ Cent at the Promulgation of the Plan, is still lower now, which shews that its Influence thus far is damping rather then reviving to public Credit.

Permit me to give you the Trouble of sending the inclosed to Major [William] Popham at Ch. Justice [Richard] Morris's. As Col. [Anthony Walton?] White resides out of Town I feared that it might be delayed at the Post Office, or I would not have troubled you with it.

Have you seen a Pamphlet intitled Falacy detected &c.[2] You will find so excellent Remarks in it applicable to the Subject of funding the Debt.

ALS, AMs 779/1, PPRF. Written from Philadelphia; franked; postmarked 28 January.

---

[1] John Dunlap and David C. Claypoole's *PP* printed Hamilton's report on public credit serially between 26–30 January.
[2] See *Fallacy Detected . . . In A Letter to a Member of Congress*, calendared under 21 January, above.

Letter from New York

You say "the political campaign I presume is about opening," &c.— it hath commenced, and herewith you will receive a typographical transcript (*the Report of the Secretary of the Treasury, containing 50 folio pages*) of the first point blank shot, of any considerable materiality, made by the chief engineer. It is thought by some that the elevation is rather high, while others suppose that were there to be a discharge from each piece in the whole park of artillery, none could be more central. It is probable that the system will, in general, be adopted. It is likely there will be a struggle to fix upon the rate of Interest—some are for three, others for six per cent, and many for an intermediate sum, but where the majority will be is uncertain.

[Worcester] *Massachusetts Spy*, 4 February; reprinted at Pittsfield and Springfield, Massachusetts, and Hartford and New Haven, Connecticut.

OTHER DOCUMENTS

Abraham Baldwin to Governor Edward Telfair. No copy known; mentioned as read on 19 March in Georgia Executive Council Minutes, G-Ar.

Royal Flint to Enos Hitchcock. ALS, Miscellaneous Collection, RHi. Addressed to Providence, Rhode Island.
    The opinions of Representatives will be "greatly divided" on Hamilton's funding plan, but "the most probable conjecture" is that it will be adopted.

Nathaniel Gist to James Madison. ALS, Madison Papers, DLC. Written from Buckingham County, Virginia. For the full text, see *PJM* 13:9–10.
    Asks about the status of "the business you were good enough to undertake to transact for me in Congress" (probably relating to Gist's expenses as an agent to the Cherokees in the Revolutionary War); if further information is needed, refers Madison to the President; enquires about the advisability of traveling to New York.

Benjamin Goodhue to Stephen Goodhue. ALS, Goodhue Family Papers, MSaE. Addressed to Salem, Massachusetts; franked.
    Discusses agricultural improvements recommended to him by Wynkoop; Hamilton's report on public credit will not be taken up for several days; "I cannot say how far it may be adopted"; thinks Congress will assume the states' debts and pay between three and four percent interest.

Stephen Goodhue to Benjamin Goodhue. FC:lbk, Goodhue Family Papers, MSaE. Written from Salem, Massachusetts.
    Trusts that Congress, "Composd of Judicious upright thinking men," will do justice to both Debtors and Creditors under a funding system; the "easy" rate at which creditors obtained their securities "I hope will be Considered"; "Fanny" (Frances Goodhue), the children, and all friends are well; G. (George, Sr.? [1740–1815]) Crowninshield "desired me to

mention it to you he had said Some Thing to you before you left home I did not ask him what"; Hamilton's proposed additional duties make those concerned in the India trade and distilled spirits "very uneasy"; while assumption gives general satisfaction, hopes Congress will consider that the present holders of securities are "mostly men of property" and whether or not they came by their securities by purchasing them cheap from the "Common & poorer Sort who must now pay at a high rate."

Nathaniel Gorham to Theodore Sedgwick. ALS, Sedgwick Papers, MHi. Written from Boston.
    Replies to the latter part of Sedgwick's letter of 16 January regarding alteration of the Massachusetts legislature's contract with him and Oliver Phelps over the purchase of the Genessee Tract; public "generally pleased" with Hamilton's report on public credit; "if it should be thought proper in the progress of the business that any of the States should make certain surrenders or compensation for the assumption—I should think it a fortunate circumstance to have our Bonds transfered to the Union—do write me by every Post as I shall in general do to you."

Henry Sherburne Langdon to John Langdon. ALS, Langdon Papers, NhPoA. Written from Portsmouth, New Hampshire.
    Reports on state business; Henry's father, Woodbury Langdon, has received brother John Langdon's letter and will write by the next post.

Benjamin Lincoln to Theodore Sedgwick. ALS, Sedgwick Papers, MHi. Written from Boston.
    Funding the assumed states' debts at three percent "will raise the D—l [*devil*]"; four percent "will unite, pretty generally all the creditors"; will be "very unhappy" if Sedgwick supported three percent.

Philip Schuyler to Jeremiah Olney. ALS, Shepley Library Collection, RHi. Addressed to Providence, Rhode Island; franked; postmarked 31 January.
    Was indisposed from waiting on the President until lately, on the subject of Olney's letter (the collectorship of Providence), delivered by John Singer Dexter; Washington's stated rule "never to engage himself" was the answer he expected "from a Gentleman of his Caution and prudence"; expects Olney will be nominated, "in which case you will certainly receive the appointment"; recommends applying to the President by letter; Hamilton will support it; the Schuyler family is well; his own "fits" of the gout "tho more frequent are less Severe"; Rhode Island's ratification "will deliver us from many serious embarrassments"; promises "any exertions" to promote Olney's interests.

Henry Sewall to George Thatcher. ALS, Chamberlain Collection, MB. Written from Hallowell, Maine. For a partial text, see Laurel Thatcher Ulrich, *A Midwife's Tale* (New York, 1990), pp. 119–20.

Commences a correspondence, confident that the balance of valuable information exchanged will be in Sewall's favor; reports on local weather and Col. Joseph North's trial (for rape); hopes "you will be able to gratify our wishes respecting the port of Kennebeck, and the extension of the post road to Hallowell"; requests enclosed letter be forwarded to "our friend" (Samuel) Loudon.

Caleb Strong to Moses Bliss. ALS, Charles P. Greenough Papers, MHi. Addressed to Springfield, Massachusetts; franked; postmarked.

Has enquired unsuccessfully "at every book Store in New York" for a set of the *Reports* of Sir Edward Coke (British jurist [1552–1634]); will give notice if any come in; will enquire for any other books Bliss wishes, but "at present there are few law Books at any of the Stores"; would be "much more happy" if he could convey his wishes for a "lucrative Feby. Court" in person; regards to "Brother [*Simeon*] Strong and the rest of the Fraternity."

George Thatcher to David Sewall. No copy known; acknowledged in Sewall to Thatcher, 6 February.

William Samuel Johnson, Diary. Johnson Papers, CtHi.

"Visits."

[Hartford] *Connecticut Courant*, 4 February, from a New York City printing not found; also reprinted at Providence, Rhode Island.

"The Debates of Congress are republished in all the papers of the United States, with an avidity which shews that the printers consider them as highly interesting to their readers. This is deriving political wisdom from the fountain head."

THURSDAY, 28 JANUARY 1790

Snow. Raw. (Johnson)

Samuel Goodwin to George Thatcher

The Peopl up Kennebeck river is Very uneasey that there is no, Port for forein Vessells To enter & Deliver. on Kennebeck river[1] where they have settled; about at 140 miles, up it from its mouth; as the river runs; & have spread out on each Side thereof at a Great Distance and about 20 thousand people, including both Sides, men women & childreen, & incressing—Continually, altho A Cold Clemet; the Expence in Geting Goods, from Wiscasset. will Cost more then the freight from boston, & that is well-Known; also they think hard, that the Post Rider doth not Goe up Kennebeck rever as fair as the Court house & as high as Fort Western [*Augusta*]: about 15. or 16 miles. above the Court house in Pownalborough: the Head of Navagation is above the Court house at the hooke about 12 miles: but when the frishet is up Sloops Can Goe to Fort Western. in Hallowell at which Town oppiset to said Fort Western is A Court Keep: & at the head of Navagation is much busness don & often in the summer there is 10 & 12 Sale of Vessells in a day passes by the Court house A Going up Kennebeck river To the head of Navagation: or Near it: therefore the Peopl Says, the Post Rider aught to Goe as fair as Fort Western; which is much Wanted & from, there & at the Court house in Pownalborough on Kennebeck river Letters Can be sent to the back settlements and above A 100 miles, up Kennebeck river—and to Penobscut, River &c. as there is a Road, from Fort Hallefax over to Penobscut river. which is now: Traveled both Winter & Summer: and there being such A large Number of People up the Great River Kennebeck & each Side thereof Who expends Large Quantitys of Duteable Goods: & so pays a large Tax: ought to have some Notice: Taken of them & favours Granted, them, in Propotion to others.

[*P. S.*] N. B. The Towns of Bath: and Pownalborough on Kennebeck river To be Ports of Entree and Delivere, Georgetown; Woolwich; Topsham; Bowdoinham; Pittston and Hallowell To be Ports of Delivere; which will be a General bennefit to the publick and prevent Smugling.

There is 15 Towns on Kennebeck river in corporation Vizt. Georgetown, 1 Bath, 2 Woolwich, 3 Pownalborough, 4 Topsham, 5 Bowdoinham, 6 Bowdoin, 7 Pittston, 8 Hollowell; 9 Vassallborough, 10 Winslow, 11 Fairfield 12 Cannan 13 Norrigewalk 14 Winthrop; 15

Plantation [*torn*] incorporated Vizt. Washington: 1 [*torn*] a 100 familys in it as I am informed Hancock 2: [*torn*]les 3 Beckerstown 4 Jones plantation 5 Sterlington 6, Smithfield 7: New Sandwich. 8. 7 mill Brook 9: 1200 settlements up Little Norregewalk or Sandy river the Names I forgot 10 & 11: Wesserunsick 12 Goshen 13: Chostas settlement back of Winslow on A Road that leads over to Penobsecut begins 5 mile from Kennebeck river 14: then Belltown Comes within 5 mile of Kennebeck river, if east Side, back of Pittston 15 Then all alonge on the west Side of Sagadahock or Androscoggin river in the County of Lincoln on the west Side of Kennebeck river is Settled all thease Parts you are acquanted with—on Sheepscut river is [*lined out*] 3 towns incorporated & the east Side of Pownalborough runs from Kennebeck river over to Sheepscut river makes A part of 4 Vizt. Boothbay; 1 Edeholm;

2. Newcastle, 3. the east Side of Pownalborough A part of 4: & part of Woolwich menaussag Bay &c. &c.

ALS, Thatcher Papers, MeHi. Written from Pownalborough, Maine. This letter was probably not sent when it was written but was enclosed in another dated 16 April and postmarked B(oston?), 9 May (Thatcher Papers, MeHi; franked).

[1] For Maine's ports of entry and delivery, see the Collection Act [HR-11], *DHFFC* 4:310.

Richard Bland Lee to [*Charles Lee*]

I yesterday spoke to the Secretary of the Treasury on the subject of the Bank-notes which he has directed to be received in payment of the duties.[1] He told me that he had some doubts with regard to the authority he possessed of making this arrangement; but conceived that, he being bound to cause the public Revenue to be remitted in some way or other, it was his duty to select the most safe and easy mode, and especially such an one, as would render it unnecessary to send the specie from the distant parts of the Union to the seat of government. And that his practice in this respect was sanctioned by a similar practice in G. Britain, where, tho' ~~there is no~~ he has not yet found any express Law for the purpose, he is informed that it is the [*lined out*] custom to use Bank notes for the transmission of the Revenue to the public Treasury. But notwithstanding this opinion relative to his authority—derived from a construction of the duties assigned to him, as there is nothing express in the Laws to Justify his practice, it has been and is his intention to lay the subject before the Legislature in the course of the present session, that provision may be expressly made for this object, either in the mode at present used or in some other manner: and that in conformity to this intention he had only made a temporary arrangement with the Banks. But tho' he has some doubts touching his authority, he says that he is most decidedly convinced of the policy of the measure. For without such a circulation Taxation could not be carried to any extent without proving in the highest degree burthensome and oppressive—by drawing from every part of the Union that specie which is essential to the support of industry—and tendering the circulation of the capital of the country, which ought to be kept in constant action, languid and stagnant—in it's various passages to and from the seat of government. How far a paper medium should be admitted in any country is a very nice point to determine, as it is perhaps impracticable to ascertain the precise quantity which may be necessary to aid industry by a brisk circulation without operating the banishment of the precious metals. But to such an extent a paper convertible into money must always be found useful. He conceives that the banishment of specie from ~~any~~ a country depends more on the state of it's Trade than any other circumstance. If the balance of Trade be against a Country it will necessarily deprive it of its specie. If the balance be in favor of a country ~~it~~ a paper circulation can have no other effect than to stimulate and promote industry as is evinced by the experience of G. Britain—and even in a Country where the balance is against it—it may prove a valuable substitute for that specie which must necessarily be carried out of it. On the whole he thinks that the remitting of the Revenue in Bank notes serves rather to keep the specie in it's natural state of circulation, than to banish it from any part of the Union: for the Revenue must be sent either in specie or paper to the Treasury of the United States. As to prostituting Bills of exchange in lieu of Bank-notes this is using one paper instead of another—and using a paper difficult on most—and impracticable on many occasions to be negotiated—and at the same time rendering the fiscal transactions complex and intricate. Another advantage results that by giving the Bank-notes an extensive circulation, it enables the Banks to aid the government more completely on emergent occasions—as in proportion to the distance at which their paper circulates from home, its quantity may be greater—and the probability of an attack on their credit less. It is his decided opinion that the finances cannot be administered without the aid of a Bank—a national Bank he would prefer. And tho' as to the present case the Law imposing duties seems to call for the payment of them in actual specie this appears in his mind rather to be a provision against the paper money circulating in some of the States than an exclusion of a paper the Representative of specie—and which at any instant may be be converted into specie. I must confess that these reasons if I had any doubts on the subject before has in a great measure removed them. The Secretary seems to have acted in the best manner that the circumstances of the case would permit. For the expence & inconvenience of sending the specie to ~~and from~~ the seat of Government would have been immense. And it is not probable that the Bank notes will circulate farther than between Merchant and Merchant—and that only in proportion to the duties that each may have to pay: As the poeple in general have a great horror at any thing like paper money. It may be justice to the Secretary to communicate these reasons to such persons who may have doubts relative to the propriety of his conduct. Next Monday se'night we take into consideration his Report.

ALS, Colburn Collection, MHi. Place to which addressed not indicated. The recipient was identified by the subject of the letter and the fact that Charles Lee's letters from his brother were sold and therefore are found in autograph collections.

[1] In a circular letter of 22 September 1789, Hamilton directed the nation's customs collectors, including Charles Lee, to accept notes payable on demand or in thirty days by the

Bank of New York or Philadelphia's Bank of North America, as equivalent to specie in the payment of duties; see *PAH* 5:394–95.

Robert Morris to John Nicholson

I received your letter by Mr. [*Francis*] Bayly and shall most chearfully give such aid to his pursuit as the ~~the~~ Importance of his discovery Merits—And it appears to me to be very Important.

Genl. Schuyler has requested me to write for a Copy of the Election Law of Pensylvania, He is in the Legislature of New York and appointed upon a Committee to bring in a bill for the regulation of their General Elections, and as I always Contemplate you in the Character of a Gentn. desirous of promoting Public service, I ask you upon that principle to send me the Law He Wants.

ALS, Gratz Collection, PHi. Addressed to Philadelphia; franked; postmarked; received 30 January. For background on Francis Bailey's "pursuit," anti-counterfeiting punches, see *DHFFC* 8:73–84.

William Smith (Md.) to Otho H. Williams

The Secretarys report [*on public credit*] having been taken into consideration as the order of this day, was, after Some debate, postponed to next Monday week.

If opinion may any be hazarded, from the sentiments that were offerd, on this Subject, I am inclined to believe, that a very great Majority in this house, are favorably disposed to Support Public credit. But however that may be, *Finals*,[1] are on the decline *here*, whatever may be the Cause; I am told they have been sold as low as 7/6; I do not conceive this arises from a want of confidence in government, but from some other motive. perhaps the mere influence of ~~Sp~~ Speculators, or the want of Cash. Capt. Campbell *now here*, & who I believe goes homeward tomorrow morning, can probably give you better information than I can, as I presume he has mixed with the holders of that Species of property. I would be glad, *occasionaly* to hear, the Sentiments of my fellow Citizens on the principal points in the Secys. Report. The consolidating the State debts, I apprehend, will not be acceptable. However Should that be the case, it Strikes me, from the tenor of the report, that Maryland, will have an [*lined out*] undoubted right, to Charge Vanstaphorsts debt to the United States.[2] This however at least, may be a Subject worthy of consideration,

and I would only observe, that I have not heard it Suggested from any
other quarter.

***

ALS, Williams Papers, MdHi. Place to which addressed not indicated. The omitted text
includes a request to serve as administrator for the estate of W. Mathews, in case of his death,
since Smith was "by far his largest creditor."

[1] Final settlement certificates amounting to over $14,700,000 were issued by federal com-
missioners under an act of February 1782, for consolidating and liquidating all civilian and
military debts that had been contracted, mostly in the form of non interest bearing promis-
sory notes issued by the army's quartermaster and commissary departments.

[2] Maryland's debt to the Amsterdam banking partners Jacob and Nicholas Van Staphorst
had a long and controversial history. In March 1781, with Cornwallis's army marching northward poised to strike into Maryland, that state's legislature authorized the negotiation of an
emergency loan in Europe to purchase war supplies. The terms of the contracts subsequently
signed with the Van Staphorsts were perceived as obligating the state to repay the principal
and interest with a fixed annual supply of tobacco priced at a fixed rate of exchange that, by
1783, was depressed well below market value. The state refused to honor the contracts and the
Van Staphorsts declined to modify their terms, despite the efforts of various state committees
and arbitration commissions (involving, among others, future Senators Carroll and King).
By early 1790, as Smith's letter indicates, the proposed assumption of the states' war debts
seemed to offer a resolution by removing Maryland's obligation to devise a final settlement.
But that resolution was not reached before *Van Staphorst v. Maryland*, the first case docketed
in the U.S. Supreme Court, resulted in an out of court settlement in early 1792, by which
Maryland agreed to pay a sum with U.S. securities from its treasury (*DHSCUS* 5:7–20).

Paine Wingate to Timothy Pickering

*** I have received no letter from home since I came on; nor any from
Salem [*Massachusetts*] lately. I forwarded your letters according to desire, &
shall be very glad to forward any letters to you that may come to me. Verry
little business has yet been compleated in congress. No confident opinion
can be formed what will be the determination of congress respecting the
public credit. It needs no great penetration to foresee very perplexing difficulties in this matter—The act of the state of Rhode Island passed Jany. 17
for calling a convention to meet on the first monday of march has been
communicated to the Senate this day with a verry respectful letter from the
governor to the President & a desire that the suspension of the Tonnage &
Impost laws may be still prolonged in favour of that State.[1] I hope that we
shall soon see the union of the thirteen states compleated, I shall be happy to
hear from you at all times. As it is probable that you will soon leave Philadelphia, it is uncertain when I shall write to you again. I suppose that the
most convenient way of convey letters to you will be by enclosing them to
Major [*Samuel*] Hodgdon in future.

ALS, Pickering Papers, MHi. Addressed to Wilkes Barre, Pennsylvania, to the care of Major Samuel Hodgdon, Philadelphia; franked; postmarked. For the full text, see *Wingate* 2:347–48. The omitted text relates to Pickering's recovery of a private debt in western Massachusetts with the legal assistance of Sedgwick, who promised to write soon.

[1] Governor John Collins's cover letter to George Washington, dated 18 January, and the Rhode Island Act [HR-71] are printed in *DHFFC* 6:1539–41.

Henry Wynkoop to Reading Beatty

The papers acompanyed will inform you of the News & Polliticks here, except that A Letter was this day delivered Congress by the Secretary of the President [*Tobias Lear*], from the Governor of Rode-Island acompanyed with an Act of Legislature of that State appointing the first monday in February for the people to elect Representatives in Convention to meet the first monday in March.[1]

This being the day apointed for discussing the Report of the Secretary of the Treasury on the establishment of the Credit of the United States, the Subject was introduced by a Motion for postponement to next monday week, this occasioned some Conversation which appeared exceedingly interesting to a very crowded Gallery, the Motion was agreed to.

If You have not sent that Report [*on public credit*] to Newtown [*Pennsylvania*], send it with the papers to Vreden's Berg for the perusal of Cousin Gerardus [*Wynkoop*] & Abram Dubois one of whom I shall request to see it deposited with Linton; You will see that Fenno in his paper of yesterday has begun it's publication;[2] I wish You to inform Yourself as You have Opertunity with intelligent people, how this Plan is relished, expect it will afford abundant Matter for polittical Disquisition, indeed it's Importance requires it, and as it is A Subject on which Congress should have the fullest Information, it is no ways probable it's Discussion will be precipitated.

Mamma [*Sarah Newkirk (Mrs. Henry) Wynkoop*] has discovered an inclination of visiting Newyork, in Case there should be good Sleighing, & should Your Busyness permit You to acompany her & gratify Your Curiosity in seeing the National Legislature & hearing their Debates, shall be very willing to bare your Expences, this tho' is a Matter must be left to You & her to manage.

ALS, Wynkoop Papers, PDoBHi. Place to which addressed not indicated.

[1] See *DHFFC* 6:1539–41 for the Rhode Island letter and act.
[2] John Fenno's serial printing of Hamilton's report on public credit in *GUS* ran from 27 January to 17 February, and resumed from 24–27 February.

[John Nicholson] to *[William Maclay]*

I RECEIVED your favour of the 23d inst. covering the statement of the secretary of the treasury, and his plan, as reported—as a composition, I think it a performance of great merit.

He has certainly said, all that could be said in favour of every thing he proposes, and in the most forcible manner—some little inaccuracies there are in the calculations—the most considerable I have observed is, that in provision for the interest of the domestic debt, the loan-office debt of 3,459,000, accruing from September 1777, till March 1778, is reduced to 2,538,572 dollars, altho' the interest is payable in specie on the nominal sum; this would be very proper if the provision were making for the discharge of the capital, but so far as relates to the *interest,* it is to all intents a specie debt; therefore near a million should be added to his amount of the domestic debt. He hath also omitted   that part of the loan-office debt, is at 4 per cent. per annum, I mean the certificates for prizes in the first class of the United States lottery;[1] the amount of which were 250,000 dollars: but a part of the prizes belonged to the state, and a part only of that sum is out, as a debt to be provided for; there are some other trivial matters, perhaps errors of the press.

His suppositious statement hath I conceive, been made upon rather an imperfect idea. I conclude that his object therein, was as much as possible, to prevent the national debt from being swelled up with the balances due to the respective states, and at the same time, that he would apportion a part on the states, so as to reduce it, he wished to leave no balances due from states.

I think his idea would be more complete by the following process. Ascertain the respective balances due to the several states in the way he proposes, then by the ratio of representation, or such other, as might be adopted: find which state had in that comparative view the smallest balance due to it—then by *proportion*—as that state's *representation* or other ratio is to its whole balance, so is the representation, or ratio of the whole union to a sum, which being quotaed, by the same proportion on the other states respectively, and charged to them severally will diminish the aggregate of the balances by that amount; that is, bringing them as low as they can be reduced, without throwing some state in arrears; which I think with him would be throwing the debt into a desperate situation, and ought to be avoided. On my first reading his report, I thought by transferring the debts of debtor states, to the credit of creditor states in a certain ratio, that he meant to pay off the balances to the forward states, by assignments on the delinquent states: And that the word "*increase*" in the next line was an error of the press, for "*decrease*;" but the schedule shows it to be otherwise.

I shall confine this letter to the subject of his report, as it affects the accounts between individual and the United States.

First. I think the general principle of the settlement so far, as relates to the states' claims on the one side, and the advances from the federal treasury on the other, a good one; and the only way in which justice can be done.

Secondly. The appropriation of funds, for discharging the interest of the balances, should be attended to as soon as any other debt, except to individual original creditors.

Thirdly. I do not like diminishing the debt, by appointing a part of these balances on the new United States; the whole amount of these and every other debt, should be taken together as the aggregate price of our freedom and independence; and although the exertions of Rhode-Island hitherto, would enable the government of the union, to manage their quota of these balances, and leave a surplus towards their share in the other debts and incumbrances, yet there is also *Vermont* and *Kentuckey*, who should contribute their proportion, which would lessen the quota of each in the whole aggregate debt, as aforesaid; they should both, and by the late act of Virginia,[2] the latter must when admitted into the union, be bound to contribute their respective shares, but it can never be obtained from them in quotas, any more than the balances can be recovered from delinquent states, indeed there is in the constitution no power to compel it: And the United States, cannot even lay an additional duty in those places, to equalize them with the other states, who will have been charged quotas of this general debt, because it is prohibited by the constitution, which requires that all duties be equal throughout the United States.

Another argument against this, is the delay that it would occasion in the arrangements of the finances, before any provision could be made for the states who were in advance: All the accounts of every individual state must be previously settled; without which, it could not be ascertained what proportion the balances bore to each other, nor what was the aggregate of all the balances; so that a single accident in the delay of settlement with an individual state, would prevent justice being done to those where it was due, and a few delinquent states might protract the business guilty; after this, should all be done, still there would be a delay of justice, till a rule of apportionment were agreed upon, and this if taken upon other than conjectural grounds, (the result of which, might be deemed unequal and unjustly by some of the states, and lay the foundation for future uneasiness) would cost besides the delay of time, more money than would go a good way towards discharging all the balances.

But there is another reason more forcible than all the rest. I agree with him that the balances due to states, should not be assignable;[3] I also agree with him that the debt of the United States should not be *unduly increased*, but it should be just what it really is and no more.

Now, the large balances not being assignable, which would be due to the several states, would operate as a powerful cement to the union of the United States, and a strong support to the government of the same: It would be adding the all prevailing motive of interest to duty, for they would consider that the payment of their own debt, depended upon the existence and support of this government, and their power to levy and collect necessary revenues. I therefore think that the balances with the states severally should be formed out of the difference between which they have respectively received, and what they have paid, or assumed for the general and particular defence against the common enemy.

Fourthly. I am still farther from approving the idea that the United States should take upon them, the payment of balances due by particular states, because it would be unjust and impolitic, and would be highly injurious to Pennsylvania: The arguments he makes use of, to shew the interferences of state and continental revenue systems, will likewise apply, though in a less degree to the states raising any revenues whatever, either for their support, as for the useful purpose of improvements: because they may interfere with continental ones, and destroy the state government, which may indeed, have been one object in view.

The fanaticism towards the new government which has prevailed, will decline in proportion as the people feel the pressure of taxes, laid on them by it, and although, with the states themselves, it will require the same sum, yet it will require the like sum *only*, and no more, and this they may levy and collect in such a way, as that the people shall feel it less, and be better able to bear it, for on account of the different situations and conditions of different states, the objects of reverence [*revenue*] are diverse, some articles will bear more in one state, and others more in an other: There be some states that are either familiarized to, or possess particular branches of revenue exclusively, these can be attended to, by the state themselves, while the constitution prevents the general government, from laying any other, or greater duty in one state, than in another, there duties, &c. must be equal.

The general government should not be over anxious of displaying their power, in levying and collecting taxes to pay debts which others are bound to pay, and they are not. And moreover if the money they do owe, be paid to the states, they will be enabled to discharge their own debts therewith without any tax for that purpose on the people at all.

Next, it rewards delinquency, and punishes the forward states for their exertions, whereas the contrary policy should ever prevail; let us see this exemplified—From the secretary's statement, there appears due by Massachusetts above five millions, New-Hampshire 3/10 of a million, by Connecticut near two million, New-York a little beyond one million, New-Jersey almost 8/10 of a million, Pennsylvania 2 1/5 millions (though in fact the sum is far less), Maryland 8/10 a million, Virginia above 3 1/2 millions, North-Carolina (a large sum), South-Carolina near 5 1/2 millions, Georgia and Rhode-Island _____, making in all about 25 millions of dollars, at 6 per cent. *the rate promised in the act for settling with the states*;[4] this will require an annual revenue of a million and an half to pay the annual interest.

This revenue when in the treasury, should in justice be paid towards the discharge of the balances, or the interest of the balances of the states, in proportion to the amount due to them respectively: And it is the summit of injustice to observe any other rule, it will dissatisfy the states, such as Pennsylvania and several others, who have large balances due to them, to be contributing their share annually of 1 1/2 million, or any other given sum to be applied towards these balances due to the several states, when they see it given out to others who have less due to them, and they getting little or none of it: But this dissatisfaction will be augmented, and greatly increased, when they see those states who have contributed least to the common cause, get the more in proportion, and they put off with least, because they have exerted themselves most, and so redeemed most of their debt.

I see the states have not sent forward, nor hath the secretary notified that the bills of credit [*paper money*] emitted since the war, by many of the states, are not included in the estimate of 25 millions. The redemption of this by the states would continue to require considerable revenues for the use of the several states, at least for some time to come; so that the difficulty would still exist, even on his own plan.

After all, the only way, the United States *can* take these debts is by bidding higher for them, and giving them better funds, than they at present rest upon; I hope they would not descend to tamper with the different states, to induce them to break their faith, that they might be thereby enabled to possess themselves of the evidence of their debt. I have enclosed a copy of the report I hinted at in a former letter,* from this you will see, that the remains of her state debt is better funded than is proposed, or can possibly be done at present, or for a considerable time to come by the United States; the holder of these securities therefore will prefer them to the proposed loan; while the creditors of delinquent states will subscribe; by this means we shall still have our own debt to pay, and to contribute our proportion to the revenues, to make up the other also. But I must break off for the present.

May God direct the councils of America to what is just, equitable and honourable.

[*Enclosure*]

*This was a statement laid before Council by the Comptroller General, whereof the following is a copy, *viz.*

Statement of sundries from the accounts of Pennsylvania,
required by an act of [the state's Supreme Executive] Council of 23 November, 1789

	Dol.	[90*t*]hs.
I. Aggregate amount of the principal of the depreciation certificates granted to the officers and soldiers of the army and military hospital, in pursuance of the several laws of this Commonwealth.	1,403,723	57
II. Ditto of certificates granted per act June 1st. 1780 for supplies for the army, other than specific supplies continental money. Equal to	34,183	59
III. Ditto of certificates granted for horses for the army in the year 1780.	90,336	03
IV. Ditto of certificates of funded debt, granted for all other debts of the state not paid off, but certified with interest.	478,352	10.

V. Amount of such expenditures and engagements of Pennsylvania since the commencement of the late war, as are chargeable to the United States, arranged and ascertained 10,219,878 unsettled, or not yet arranged, nor the value of the items paid in continental money, ascertained by the scale of depreciation, say 5,000,000   35,279,878

Note. Certificates of liquidated debt and loan office certificates of the United States, redeemed by this state, are not included in the above.

The funds appropriated either in whole or in part to pay the principal or interest of the above are as follows, *viz.*

I. 1st. The one third of the principal of the depreciation certificates, paid off in bills of credit of the emission of April 1781, on application of the holder.

2d. The whole of the forfeited estates, unsold before December 1780, appropriated as a fund to redeem both principal and interest.

3d. The tract of land in Pennsylvania, bounded on the north by donation lands, on the west, by the western boundary of the state, and on the south and east, by the river Ohio and Alleghaney, excepting the two reserved tracts thereout, at Mackingtosh and opposite to Pittsburgh on the aforesaid river Ohio, appropriated as a fund to redeem both principal and interest.[5]

4th. The excise on spirituous liquors, was appropriated to pay the annual interest to them, who had not alienated their certificates when this fund was assigned, and until they had themselves drawn the first year's interest thereon.

5th. A sum was granted out of impost duties not exceeding £ 25097 19 3 to pay up a year's arrear of such interest in aid of the excise.

6th. And lastly, these certificates principal and interest funded, or unfunded, were made receivable in the Land Office for lands sold by the Commonwealth.

II. The certificates granted per act of June 1780, were discharged by payments at the treasury shortly after they were granted, of which public notice was given, that all might come in, or they were made receivable in the taxes then collecting, and such as neglected the one or other of these means of redemption, may and do now receive payment of the principal at the state treasury.

III. 1st. The certificates granted for horses were receivable also in the taxes collecting at the time they were granted.

2d. And to such as were not redeemed in that way the principal and interest is paid from the treasury upon their application.

IV. 1st. The aggregate fund of taxes, and the arrears of taxes and imposts is *inter alia*[6] appropriated to the payment of the interest of the certificates of funded debt.

2d. They are receivable at the land office in common with depreciation certificates, for city lots, and for other lands sold by the commonwealth.

V. The claims of the Commonwealth against the United States, have generally been already discharged out of the taxes and other revenues of the Commonwealth. Such as have not, are comprized under one other of the preceeding heads, or are included in our estimated sum of about £   for which there have yet been no certificates, but which the parties, on settlement will be entitled to receive.

Comtroller General's-office, Jan. 28th, 1790

FJ, 3 February; a draft in the hand of Nicholson in Nicholson Papers, PHarH, is the basis on which the editors determined the writer and recipient of this letter. The letter is introduced by a note to the editor, signed "A. B. C.," in which Nicholson stated, "The following copies which I obtained of two letters, addressed from a gentleman to his correspondent, a member of congress, in New-York; being of a public and interesting nature, on the subject of the late report of the secretary of the treasury, are offered you for publication" (AN, hand of Nicholson, Nicholson Papers, PHarH).

---

[1] In order to raise money for the upcoming military campaigns of 1777 without resorting to another emission of paper money, the Continental Congress created the "United States Lottery" on 18 November 1776. Four classes of one hundred thousand tickets each, costing from ten dollars (for the first class) to forty dollars (for the fourth class) were to be drawn at intervals. Purchasers (called "adventurers") could claim their winnings by accepting loan office certificates payable in five years at four percent interest, or by revolving their prize money into the next class of ticket purchases. The first drawing was delayed by more than a year to May 1778, and the subsequent history was equally troubled. The lottery's first accounts were settled by a congressional resolution of 21 December 1782, which paid off all unclaimed winning tickets at an exchange rate of one dollar specie for every forty dollars of prize money (*JCC* 6:959–61; *LDC* 5:xxvii–xxviii, 571–72n).

[2] Virginia's "Act concerning the erection of the district of Kentuckey into an independent State," passed 18 December 1789, stipulated that the proposed state "shall take upon itself a just proportion of the debts of the United States" (Hening 13:78).

[3] That is not transferable to another holder.

[4] The ordinance agreed to on 7 May 1787 (*JCC* 32:262–66).

[5] Designated "depreciation lands," this territory was set aside by the Pennsylvania legislature in March 1783 for holders of "certificates of depreciation" (notes issued to soldiers of the Pennsylvania Line, to compensate for the depreciation of the continental currency in which they had been paid). The state redeemed these certificates by offering their equivalent value either in "depreciation lands" or in revenue from the lands' sale.

[6] Among others.

Other Documents

Pierce Butler to John McQueen. FC:lbk, Butler Papers, PHi. Addressed to Savannah, Georgia.

> Wishes McQueen could settle his affairs in Georgia and come to New York City as a member of Congress; expects that all claims against Butler will be settled that year; complains that the Georgia legislature's "impudence" (in selling the Yazoo lands) has been very injurious "& frustrated our plans for the relief of the State"; Mary Middleton Butler has been ill and is still much indisposed.

William Constable to Gouverneur Morris. FC:lbk, Constable-Pierrepont Collection, NN. Marked "Copied ℔ pkt."

> Believes Hamilton's report on public credit, ordered to be taken up in the House that day, will be postponed; "the Opinions of the Members are very various"; he and Robert Morris will write by the mail packet.

Philip Schuyler to John B. Schuyler. ALS, Schuyler Papers, NN. Addressed to Saratoga, New York; misdated 28 February; franked; postmarked 31 January; received 3 February.

> Has sent Hamilton's report on public credit to General (Abraham) Ten Broeck, with a request to give it to John Schuyler; attention to it will "enable You to converse with precision on a subject so Interesting to your Country"; the weather is mild, and he fears for the winter crops; "Your Mama [*Catherine*] is sincerely tired of this place," but is "perfectly in health, as are all the rest of every Branch of the family"; he has enjoyed better health than in some time.

William Samuel Johnson, Diary. Johnson Papers, CtHi.

> "Visits."

George Washington, Diary. Washington Papers, MiD-B. For the full text, see *DGW* 6:23.

> The Vice President, Hamilton, Senators Schuyler, Morris, Izard, Dalton, Butler, Representatives Smith (S.C.), Stone, Schureman, Fitzsimons, Sedgwick, Huger, and Madison dined at the President's.

NYWM, 30 January.
Johnston of North Carolina arrived at New York "from that Republic."

Letter from a Member of Congress. [Providence, Rhode Island] *United States Chronicle*, 4 February; reprinted at Boston. For the act, see *DHFFC* 6:1540–41.
Today the act of the General Assembly for calling a ratification convention was read in the House of Representatives and a committee appointed on it; will give early notice of the proceedings.

Letter from Charleston, South Carolina. *NYDA*, 16 February; reprinted at Providence, Rhode Island.
Indigo has not done as well as rice, which is abundant; rivers are low and it is difficult to get rice to Tidewater to supply Europe where the demand is considerable; "Machines for boating out the rice, and ploughs, are coming very rapidly into fashion, and from this circumstance alone we may predict that any future importation of slaves will be rendered unnecessary, as the far greater part of the labour will be saved."

FRIDAY, 29 JANUARY 1790

Cold (Johnson)

George Clymer to Tench Coxe

The conversation I mentioned produced yesterday a motion from one of the committee which was agreed to—that by a clause in the bill [*Patents Act HR-41*] they give effectual encouragement to to the introduction of Arts from foreign countries. It is impossible to say what may be the fate of such a Clause in any subsequent stage; and perhaps after all it might not be necessary—for upon considering the subject more fully I cannot help thinking but that the protection given to the invention would go the introduction—for upon application for a patent it might be sufficient to shew that the subject was new in the Country—as such it must be an invention unless proof is brought to the contrary—and how can proof be made. I would not therefore speak of any thing I wished a patent for as introduced only—Turn this matter in your mind, as I will further in mine.

ALS, Coxe Papers, PHi. Written in the morning; addressed to Philadelphia; frank lined out; carried by Mr. (Henry?) Manly.

Patrick Henry to Richard Henry Lee

After thanking you as I do most sincerely for your Communications previous to your Recess, I beg Leave again to trouble you on the Subject of General [*Joseph*] Martin's Application for the Agency of Indian Affairs to the South—This I do at his most earnest Request. Indeed the Allegations agt. him[1] seem to call for some Vindication of his Conduct which would be easily effected but for the great Distance from the Seat of Goverment—You will see by the Papers which I inclose that he has brot. on an Enquiry into his Conduct & how it has terminated—& that Govr. [*Alexander*] Martin has written to the President in his Favor—& has sent to Genl. Martin a copy of what he wrote—I shall here relate the Substance of his Communication to me when I was last in the Executive, & while he acted as Superintendant for this State of Indian Affairs—He (Genl. Martin) informed me [*Alexander*] McGilvray had several Times sent him Word to make him a Visit & carry on a Correspondence, & at length wrote him a Letter which he put into my Hands, the Substance of which was as above—He desired my Opinion on the Matter. I encouraged him so far to cultivate McGilvray as, if possible, to fathom his Veiws & keep the Indians from our People. at the same Time by Means of the Indians or others to discover the Extent & Nature of McGilvrays Connections with the Spaniards. I am satisfy'd Mr. Martin proceeded in this Idea; for he quickly satisfy'd me of the Spanish Policy respecting the Indians, sending me a Commission given to a Creek Indian by the Spanish Governor constituting him an Officer—How necessary it must be to discover these & similar Practices with the Indian Tribes, it is easy to see; & that the Interest of the U. States & of this State required, & that McGilvray's ill Designs if he had any should be turned agt. him. Genl. Martins Conduct so far as I could discern in that Affair was really praise worthy. He frequently gave me Intelligence of Creek Indian Affairs, & of the Intercourse between other Indians & the Spaniards that was interesting—I am satisfyed the Correspondence as above took its Origin as I have stated, & that General Martin in no Respect turned it to the Prejudice of any American State or citizen on the Contrary that he made it subservient to the Purpose of gaining usefull Intelligence—How cruel then is it thus to blast the Reputation of a public Servant, whose Employment in a peculiar Manner exposed him to the Hatred & Malevolence of the many Intruders on Indian Rights; & these indeed I believe he has constantly opposed as they are constantly attacking him in one shape or other.

Pardon me Sir for reiterating this Affair. I meant never to say any more of it; But Genl. Martin asks it of me as a Peice of Justice to his Character, & that which no other Person could so properly state as myself.

If any other Correspondence ever existed between Martin & McGilvray I never knew of it, or had the least Reason to suspect that the former swerved from his Duty in it but on the contrary had the best Veiws as I think—As I troubled you formerly on this Subject, I thot. it best thro' you to say thus much in Justification of one to whom I do think great Injustice has been done respecting this Affair.

I wish it were in my Power to tell you of any thing by Way of News worth your Hearing—I live too much secluded, & at this Season there is but little Intercourse here—No Doubt you will hear of me or my Doings in the Georgia Purchase.[2] All the Companys together get 15,000,000 Acres it is said—I am a Partner in one. And I own to you that some late Occurrences in Politics first suggested the Thought For if our present System grows into Tyranny is not a Frontier Position most eligible? And a central one most to be dreaded? Is the Seat of federal Goverment desirable in any other Veiw than the Goodness of that Govermt.? I do indeed suppose that these Specula-tions of mine relate to Times when you & I shall be gone off the Stage; But it is natural for us both to feel Anxiety for our numerous Familys, besides the Concern common to every Citizen—I am refining perhaps too much & looking to a Period too distant in my Estimate of Things—This is an Error Speculative men often fall into, their Calculations being founded in Theorys & not on the actual State of Things—The last can be known only by beholding & mixing with the Actors in the principal Scenes of Business. A Comfortable prospect of the Issue of the new System would fix me here for Life. A contrary one, sends me southwestward—It may be that in some Leisure moment you may give me your Thoughts on our public Affairs & their Tendencys—In the Business of the lately proposed Amendments [*to the Constitution*], I see no Ground to hope for Good. but the contrary. Your Friends think themselves under great Obligations to you for your noble Exertions altho' they were not successfull.

P. S. I have just recd. a Copy of An Act of Assembly of No. Carolina for ceding to Congress all the Territory on the western Waters or nearly all, together with the People[3]—So many Reservations of Land Rights are con-tained in the Act, that I fancy little will remain for Congress. But indeed I am astonished that the Depravity of which marks this Transaction—Care-full as they have been to save all just Rights (& I believe more) in the Lands, they have violated every Right of Citizenship; For as I hear no Convention of the People ceded was had to consult on the Subject of this Transfer, but they & their Country are voted away to Congress by a Majority of the Leg-islature of the old State of In this this, the District ceded had comparatively a very small Number—If this Proceeding is countenanced by Congress, it will form a precedent alarming as I think, & strongly tending to establish this Belief that State Goverments are not to be trusted; Besides the Invita-tion it will give to Intrigue & Faction—But if Congress accepts the Cession will they not sanction the most manifest Violation of Rights that can be committed—For expatriation of a Part of the Community is not a Power included among those exercised by Assemblys in America convened for ordinary Legislation. If then the Act of Cession is unconstitutional can Congress derive any Right under it.

I hear the Number of People ceded is more than 20,000 of all ages. Perhaps near 30.

ALS, Franklin Collection, CtY. Written from Prince Edward County, Virginia; enclosures unknown; received when Lee arrived at New York on 11 April (Lee to Henry, 10 June). The identification of the recipient is based on the subject matter of and reference to Lee's letters to Henry dated 14 and 27 September 1789 (DHFFC 17:1541–43, 1625–26) as well as Henry's regards to Lee's son Ludwell (omitted here).

[1] On 8 November 1788, while serving as Congress's agent for Indian affairs in the Southern Department, Joseph Martin addressed a private letter to Creek chief Alexander McGillivray, transmitting certain congressional resolutions relating to Indian matters. Intercepted by a troop of Georgia militia commanded by future Representative Mathews, the letter was submitted to the state legislature, which concluded that Martin's correspondence was inappropriate and was evidence of his being "treacherously leagued with the savage tribes" (PGW 1:385n). The findings were sent to Washington and to the legislature of North Carolina, of which Martin was a citizen. Martin sought vindication for his conduct, and in December 1789 the North Carolina legislature absolved him of any culpability. Its report was sent to George Washington under a cover letter by Governor Alexander Martin (no relation) dated 18 January; see PGW 5:16–18. Joseph Martin would later claim that the harm done by his correspondence was deliberately falsified by Bennett Ballew, whose "Complaints" (see DHFFC 2:199–201) were "Set on by Savier [Sevier]" in order to support his own appointment as superintendent to the Southern Indians (Martin to Patrick Henry, 18 January 1791, William Wirt Henry Papers, ViHi).

[2] Patrick Henry was a principal associate of the Virginia Yazoo Company, one of three companies of speculators to whom the Georgia legislature sold the preemption right to purchase Indian lands in present-day Mississippi and Alabama under an act of 21 December 1789.

[3] The text of North Carolina's act appears in the North Carolina Cession Act [S-7]; see DHFFC 6:1544–47.

Michael Hodge to Benjamin Goodhue

Your much esteemed favr. of the 18th. instant, I duly recieved, for which together with its inclosure I kindly thank you, the communications were intirely new and consequently interesting to the Gentlemen of this Town, who were not a little gratified, by the manner of your noticing them, and you may be assured, that it will always be pleasing to them, to be made acquainted with the earliest intelligence of what is doing in Congress, for my own part, I shall always esteem it an honr. to be the medium thro which such intelligence shall pass, they Generally seem to admire the talents which the Secy. of the Treasury posseses, and intirely willing to acquiesce in the plan of Finance which he has offered, that of taking the State debts, and a continental excise, instead of the several State excises, is a very favorite object with them, and will consequently be highly agreable.

In the collection of the revenue at this district We have had no uncommon dificulty to Encounter, Our Merchants, are as well disposed here, I believe, as in any district in the Union, and as promptly & chearfully pay up their duties; they as is natural to men, in their pursuit consult their own Interest, they have been trying different districts to make their Entries in, in order I suppose to see if they can obtain any greater indulgence, better than one quarter of our Vessels with dutied articles have been Entered in other districts, which makes a very considerable reduction, in the Surveyors department, and as that officer, from the nature of his office, if he strickly fulfills the duty of it, must be most ~~obnox~~ exposed to the reproaches as well as Temptations of the ill designing it never could be the intention of Congress to make an inspector's place more lucrative, than the Surveyor, under whose direction he is placed, which I think, is equal if not superior here, for the time past, could the Surveyors have the weighing and Guaging with power of deputation when necessary, would I think place them in a much more eligible situation in all the ports in this state (Boston excepted) and no dimunition of the revenue caused thereby, should it appear to you reasonable and consistent with the Surveyors duty, I will thank you to Endeavour the promoting of it, in this Town it can be attended to, without [*torn*] any part of Duty whatever—an uncommon favorable winter we have experienced so far, a general time of health prevails among us. ***

ALS, Letters to Goodhue, NNS. Written from Newburyport, Massachusetts. For the omitted text, see Hodge to Goodhue, 5 February, n. 2, below.

[*John Nicholson*] to [*William Maclay*]

I CLOSED my letter yesterday on account of the post, before I had closed all the observations I intended upon the subject concerning which I was writing. I shall therefore send you a line or two more, representing my ideas of the injustice and impolicy of the debts due by particular states being taken up by the United States and funded, as it will influence the property of individuals interested therein.

The debts due by the same state are differently funded, and payment and redemption differently provided for them, hence they command various prices in the market; but in different states the variation is much greater, insomuch that in some states the market price, or current value, was from one quarter of a dollar to 2/6 in the pound, a few weeks ago. I need not represent to you the *topsy turvy* effect of such a proposition on the different species of this kind of property of the same state, and of different states, and the confusion and *scramble* that would ensue. It would bear some semblance to the effects of a sovereign act to abolish and destroy all individual and appropriate right, past and present, to private property; leaving it all to be owned in future by those, who could get and take most into their possession. In a conclusion of this kind, such as had formerly earned and merited most, would generally get least. Objects of speculation will occur, where inordinate gains may be made in purchases and sales; but so far from promoting the occasions and multiplying the objects amongst a society; it should ever be the care of a wise administration in finance, as much as possible to guard against them. Property should ever be the reward of industry, and when it can be obtained on cheaper terms, agriculture and husbandry, manufactures, and mechanics, and other useful arts will be neglected; for property and the desire of gain is the main spring that sets them all in motion.

It has also a pernicious effect on the morale of the people, it hebetates and weakens that innate sense of justice which God hath implanted in every man, so useful in society, to secure the property of individuals to their own exclusive emolument and use. This feature alone in the proposition, pregnant with many and complicated evils, ought to prevent its being adopted by the government of the United States.

FJ, 3 February; a draft in the hand of Nicholson is in Nicholson Papers, PHarH. Written from Philadelphia. This letter was introduced with the same statement that precedes Nicholson to Maclay, 28 January, above.

Newspaper Article

A Correspondent requests us to inform the public, that by a letter from New-York, of the 29th of January, from a gentleman of good information, he is advised, that it appears to be the sense of both Houses of Congress, that the Acts of Congress, subjecting the citizens of this State to foreign tonnage and foreign duties, would be suspended in consequence of the request of the Legislature of this State, and their declaration that there was every reason to hope that this State would in a short time accede to the Federal Government: and that it is of the utmost importance that members from this State should go forward as soon as possible, as reports of a most interesting nature are under the consideration of Congress, and will probably be decided upon this session, which it is expected may be protracted until May or June next, which will give this State an opportunity of being represented in Congress.

Our Correspondent hopes that his fellow-citizens will not by slighting the repeated indulgence of Congress, provoke the resentment of the United States; but at the approaching Town-meetings must make such provision as that the New Government may be immediately embraced: And he further hopes, that this State may be represented in Congress, and assist with its councils in matters now on the carpet which are highly interesting to this State, and which will probably be decided upon this session.

[Rhode Island] *Newport Herald*, 4 February. Printed in italics.

OTHER DOCUMENTS

Abigail Adams to Hannah Quincy Storer. ALS, Adams Family Manuscript Trust, MHi. Written from "Richmond Hill," outside New York City; place to which addressed not indicated.
"I think it probable that congress will rise early in the Spring."

Joshua Brackett to John Langdon. ALS, Langdon Papers, NhPoA. Written from Portsmouth, New Hampshire.
Apologizes for not corresponding for so long; state legislators have inquired if Langdon intends to resign from the Senate in the spring; if so, he would be elected governor; "I replied that you had absolutely determined to return to Portsmouth in April or May, and would not go to New York again"; legislature has not ceded the lighthouse or Fort William and Mary to Congress, "therefore I do not suppose any thing can be done by you at present in the *matter* we talked about" (probably an appointment to office); does not expect to hear from Langdon often, because of the business of Congress; Langdon's family is well.

James Brown to John Brown. ALS, Brown Collection, CtY. Written from Danville, Kentucky; marked "To be put into the post Office."
Acknowledges receipt that morning of an (unlocated) letter from John sent in care of Col. (Benjamin) Logan; protests against reports of dissipation prejudicial to James's character; will not dare to justify "The levities of my too foolishly unbridled tongue," but reproaches himself for "the Intemperate licences of my words," while asking "Can you pardon a weakness which you never felt?"

George Cross to Pierce Butler. ALS, Butler Papers, PHi. Written from Charleston, South Carolina.
Thanks for the "Politeness" and "sincerity" of Butler's willingness to support Cross's earlier application for an appointment in the "Naval Department"; as the government's arrangement of a navy "is still at some distance," asks for Butler's influence in procuring the infirm Edward Weyman's post as port surveyor at Charleston.

William Davies to Governor Beverley Randolph. ALS, Executive Papers, Vi. Place to which addressed not indicated.

Regarding the settlement of Virginia's accounts with the federal government, the Virginia delegation is "fearful" of applying to Congress "for a longer time for the admission of evidence" since the state has complained so often "on this head" that she must proceed with caution "and without her appearing active in the business at all"; North Carolina's recent accession to the Union and cession of territory "seem to render an application by her the most promising of success"; since the business properly belongs with the House, it will be necessary to await the arrival of North Carolina's Representatives.

Samuel Emery to George Thatcher. ALS, Thatcher Papers, MeHi. Written from Savannah, Georgia. The letter mentioned has not been located.

"If you have my letter on light Houses & Pilotage by you & you think it expedient you may erase my Name and give it to the Secretary of the Treasury or whoever has the inspection of that department"; asks Thatcher to write him, care of Charleston or Savannah, whether the House committee on bankruptcy has reported "& what the prospects are—How the Debt of the United States stands, [*and*] as much of Publick affairs as your business will admit"; asks for Boston newspapers.

Arthur Lee to Charles Lee. ALS, Special Collections, Stanford University, Stanford, California. Addressed to Alexandria, Virginia; franked; postmarked 31 January.

Two vessels have been dispatched to buy up public securities in the Carolinas and Georgia, where their price is low; "There is reason to beleive that Robt. M[*orri*]s. is deep in these Speculations though [*William*] Constables house is the ostensible agent. It is probable that what he speculates in will succeed as far as Congress can give it efficacy"; if the public takes alarm at the rate of speculation, he doubts whether any funding plan will succeed.

Governor Beverley Randolph to Virginia Representatives. FC:lbk, Executive Papers, Vi. Written from Richmond, Virginia. The enclosures included a map of the Potomac River and the Virginia Assembly's resolution of 14 December 1789, a letter to Randolph from the president and directors of the Potowmack Company, dated 16 January, and a broadside from Alexandria and Georgetown residents dated 7 December 1789. The enclosures have not been located. Randolph's letter and other copies of the enclosures, except for the map, are printed with documents relating to the Residence Act [S-12] in *DHFFC* 6:1782–87.

Forwards enclosed papers, to be delivered by Matthew Anderson; would

have written to the Senators as well, but they were not expected at New
York City soon.

George Washington, Diary. Washington Papers, MiD-B. For the full text,
see *DGW* 6:24.
 Samuel Johnston of North Carolina paid his respects to Washington during the latter's morning horseback ride; the Vice President came at 3 P.M.
to introduce Justice (William) Cushing to the President.

From Philadelphia. [Wilmington] *Delaware Gazette*, 6 February.
 Clymer was elected a vice president of the Pennsylvania Society for the
Encouragement of Manufacturing.

SATURDAY, 30 JANUARY 1790

Fine (Johnson)

William Bradford, Jr. to Elias Boudinot

I am exceedingly obliged to you for the two reports which you sent to
me this week. Marsden [*John Marsden Pintard?*] who brought that of Genl.
Knox [*on the militia*], arrived in full health, went to the Assembly at night
lodged at the Tavern & rolled off early yesterday morning. I have not had
time or patience to get thro' the evolution of the General's System—nor
to bestow as much attention on that of the Secretary of the Treasury as it
seems to merit. One thing strikes the public creditors here—& that is, that
however it may be disguised, the system he proposes does not quadrate with
his principles—it is not a discharge of the public engagements—& the
creditor will in effect be compelled to accept less interest than was promised
him or go without any. There is no probability of there being any surplus to
pay the adventurous. If the idea of the rate of interest being soon lowered,
be well grounded, (they enquire,) why not borrow at that interest & pay off
the public creditors who are intitled to six? If the reduction be *necessary* the
public necessity, say they, ought to be *clearly* shown. Some would have the
security in the hands of original ~~lende~~ holders funded at six, & the rest at
four ℔ Cent. But in addition to the arguments used by the Secretary against
discrimination the ~~exper~~ following facts drawn from an experiment of that
kind in our State may furnish some instruction. In the beginning of 1781,
the depreciation certificates were issued. There being no funds for payment
of any interest, nor any adequate to their redemption, the soldiers soon
parted with them at a low rate, & even many of the Officers did the same.

In 1782 or 3, It was computed that there could not be more than £50,000 in the hands of the original holders. It was determined that these should be funded, & great expectations were formed of the benifits that would arise to the original holders from this measure. The only criterion to distinguish whether they had be been alienated was the oath of the party, or if he was dead, of some other person. A strange scene soon turned up. Soldiers from all quarters appeared before the Comptroller with their certificates, & instead of fifty, no less than Two hundred & sixty thousand pounds were funded—more than ½ of the whole debt. The truth is, the alienated certificates found their way back into the soldiers hands, & fraud defeated a system that was founded on a breach of public faith. The consequence was accordingly—as a discrimination had once been made it might be made again: & the original holders could not sell their certificates for more 6d. in the pounds more than those which were not funded at all on a paymt. of interest. Similar consequences would take following in the case of the U.S. could similar folly be supposed to actuate their measures.

Upon the subject of Naturalization, I have only one or two things to observe. We admit that a man by his own act can become the member of a one state, and renounce his allegiance to that with which he was connected before. The doctrine of perpetual allegiance in case of birth is too monstrous to be any longer endured—If therefore you define the terms upon which a man becomes a citizen ought not the acts by which a man may expatriate himself, be also declared? Again, what is to be the situation of Children? Are they to follow the condition of their parents—or is their birth place to be their country. If an Alien (having minor children), becomes naturalized, what is the situation of his children who are incapable of taking the oath of Allegiance? Can they inherit if their father dies—Can they hold lands &c. If an Alien has children born here, shall they [*lined out*] be natural born subjects, or according to the jus Albinatus[1] are they foreigners as their father is? If the birth place is the criterion of citizenship, what is the situation of children of Citizens born abroad. The statutes of England cannot affect this matter.

***

I have been conning over the tables of Annuities.[2] I think an attentive consideration of them, is the best lecture upon mortality, and Price upon Annuities more convincing then Sherlock on Death.[3] When the grave is made the subject of strict calculation, and even interested Caution states it but a few years distant, the matter is brought home, & the shortness of time is proved by most in the most forcible manner. As to the Tontines, I abhor them. I have no inclination to be yoked with two or three score of people all of whom are interested in each others death, & looking out with a vulture's eye to see when a life drops.

***

I have not be so well as usual—but am beginning to be well again. Susan [*Boudinot Bradford*] has also had a bad cold which has disturbed her at night, but has not confined her in the day. It is breaking & going off. ***

ALS, James T. Mitchell Collection, PHi. Written from Philadelphia. The omitted text relates to developments at Pennsylvania's constitutional convention and to a lawsuit involving Boudinot and a Mr. Williamson.

[1] An old French law pertaining to the disposal of lands upon an alien's death.

[2] Schedules F and G submitted with Hamilton's report on public credit were tables showing the annuities available to eligible subscribers to the national debt; schedule H showed the annuity table for a proposed tontine, a lottery system in which the total benefits from the initial capital invested by a group of subscribers was awarded to the sole survivor. See *DHFFC* 5:789–92.

[3] Richard Price's *Observations . . . on schemes for providing annuities* was published in 1771. William Sherlock (ca. 1641–1707), English divine, authored the widely read *Practical Discourse Concerning Death*, which enjoyed at least one American printing during the colonial period (Williamsburg, Va., 1744).

George Rogers Clark to John Brown

Since my last to you, of the 20th of August, nothing very material, that is new, hath transpired among us. The Indians continue to destroy the people as usual. Poor Owings is at last taken and burnt at the Weaugh.[1] I doubt, Sir, you will smile at the contents of this letter, as it may appear to border a little on the marvellous, when I inform you of an invention that will give a new turn to the face of things throughout the Western country.

Frequently navigating those rivers in the course of the War, with various kinds of vessels,[2] I was led to believe that great improvement might be made, which I was determined to study, when I should have leisure to apply myself. But at the period, Mr. Rumsey[3] and others amused us with vessels so constructed as to answer every desirable purpose. This I believed they would have done, having a similar idea myself. They failing, I again resumed the study, and soon found that it was necessary to make myself master of the mechanical powers, which I did, and to my astonishment, found that by a combination of those powers properly applied, that a boat of any size, with a small given force, (either by men or horses on board,) would be forced against a stream that no number of oars applied in the common way, could move her. I was highly pleased with the discovery for sometime, but viewing the simplicity of the machine, I got discouraged, supposing it impossible but that every mechanical genius that turned his attention that way must know it, and that it had been tried and found not to answer the purpose. Not being able to discover any defect, and further to satisfy myself, I had the machine actually made on a small scale and proved every conjecture beyond a doubt. It moves any number of oars you choose to apply, with more regularity and despatch than men can possibly do. By multiplying the powers, the velocity of a vessel so fixed, will be as great as possible for it to pass through the water. I am not good at description, otherwise I should attempt to give you a draught of this machine, and not wishing others, that are capable, to see it, I hope you will excuse me. What I wish you would do for me, is, to get a resolution of Congress in my favor, granting me the sole use of those vessels for fourteen years, throughout the Continent. I have already contracted for a boat of the size I wish, and within a month from the time I receive such a resolution, I will set her to work. Then all doubts respecting the expeditious navigation of those rivers will immediately vanish. The experiment is already made, and you need be in no doubt about it. I have raised every objection against it that my ingenuity could possibly suggest, without being able to find a fault. With the small one I have, I can make every experiment I could wish to make. The request, if granted, may perhaps make me some amends for my public losses. Pray honor me with an answer to this letter as soon as possible.

[Frankfort, Kentucky] *Commonwealth*, 25 July 1838. Written from Beargrass Creek (five miles east of Louisville, Kentucky), site of Clark's home, "Locust Grove."

---

[1] Probably Lower Wea, the Wea Indian town south of present-day Terre Haute, Indiana.

[2] The famous expedition that Clark led in 1778–79 against posts held by the British and their Indian allies in Illinois Country (present-day Ohio, Indiana, and Illinois) heavily utilized navigation of the Ohio, Wabash, and Mississippi rivers in longboats, operable by oars and capable of shooting rapids.

[3] For more on James Rumsey and his experiments with steam powered inland navigation, see *DHFFC* 8:39–40.

Samuel Henshaw to Theodore Sedgwick

Your's of the 19th. Inst. inclosing the Statement of the Treasury of N. York, I recd. last Wednesday evening—I wish every State Treasury was in as happy a situation—Will not New-York oppose the general Assumption? And what opposition will there be to it in Congress?

I imagine you will have a hard task to digest & adopt the Secy.'s Budget—People here do not understand it—perhaps it is because we have had but a mere glimpse of it. But the Idea of paying 4 per Ct. In[*tere*]st. and of making up the other 2 per Ct., by a grant of lands, or otherwise, is extremely painful to those who have been obliged to sell their Securities, and who expect to be obliged also to eat, and drink & wear those articles which are taxed to pay it. Indeed, I am confident, that the Holders of Securities in this quarter, are fearful, that the Principles of national faith, & Honor & Justice, which are held up by the Secy. are rather too rigid, and will operate against *his* System, & *their* Interest.

The several States will, I fear, imbibe unconquerable jealousies & prejudices against the federal Govt., if they lay so heavy a tax (no matter on what, or by what name it is called) as will be necessary to discharge the demands that will be upon them according to the Secy.'s plan. For however true it may be, in a legal Sense, that Govt. ought to pay every farthing to the present Holder, yet that they ought, in a moral Sense, is doubted by many good Men.

When the Debt was contracted both the legal and moral obligation operated in the highest degree in favour of the bona fide creditor—But Govt. not doing him Justice according to contract, did, in consequence of their neglect, oblige him to part with their paper, for which he paid a fair equivalent, for a morsel of bread! And tho the legal obligation is still on the Govt. to pay the present Holder, yet the moral obligation to do Justice to the Man whom they obliged to injure himself is also still strong upon them—and if it is not in their power to do both legal & moral Justice, the latter ought to the have the preference—If it should be said, that Govt. are under a moral obligation to pay the purchaser according to the face of the Security, it is denied, and urged, that no man, on the pure principles of morallity, has a right to demand *eight* good Dollars for *one* given; and Interest in that proportion—But if a Man by not fullfilling his fair & righteous contract, inevitably injures another, He is bound by the principles of morallity & Honor to repair the Injury, if in his power.

On the whole, I believe, it is not in the power of the federal Govt. to do strict Justice in either view—But if they establish permanent funds for the punctual payment of 3, or, at most, 3½ per Ct. Inst., they will do more universal Justice than by adopting the proposed Scheme.

Since writing the foregoing, I have recd. yours of the   I am very glad the System of finance has come forward in I shall get hold of it as soon as possible—but perhaps it will be some days first, as I am unwell & confined to my lodgings—I suppose your numerous correspondents will distract you with their contradictory opinions—Sure I am that We shall never be a quiet, happy, energetic Nation without the assumption of the whole public debt by Congress—and I am equally sure, that we shall never be a happy & flourishing people, if, in consequence of that assumption, Congress shall tax us, in this early stage of our existance, to pay an enormous Interest: But I fear your patience will be exhausted, I will not, therefore, engross any more of your precious time at present.

[*P. S.*] The attention of the people in this Town & neighbour-hood has been arested for two or three days by the appearance of a Whale in Charles river—He is above the Bridge in Cambridge Bay—Many have been the attempts to kill him, but He eludes them all. But it is thought, that He will not be able to make his escape.

Has anything been said, or like to be said, about old Continental money?

ALS, Sedgwick Papers, MHi. Written from Boston.

Samuel Johnston to James Iredell

I got to this place the 28th. and yesterday took my Seat in Congress. I found the Act for regulating the Ports in our State and enforcing the ~~Duties~~ payment of Duties & Tonnage [*North Carolina Act HR-36*] had already passed the House of Representatives and was before a Committee of the Senate, this business, which I did not expect would come forward before the arrival of our Representatives engaged my immediate attention, and tho' I find myself not so well prepared in this business as I could wish, yet, there is no preventing it's going on, they say that we are now enjoying the Benefit of the Revenue of the United States without contributing any thing on our part, that when our Representatives come forward they will agree to any amendments that may be thought necessary. Our people are obliged to pay the Tonnage Duty &c. all owing to the Folly of our Assembly in not directing the regulations of Congress to be immediately enforced in our Ports.

I waited on the President [*lined out*] the day after I came to Town, but he was abroad and I have not yet had the pleasure of seeing him. I waited on the Vice-President at his Seat in the Country this day, among other things I asked him what he thought of the Affairs of France—he thought they would end in a civil War which would probably be of long continuance—tho he gave some reasons in support of this Opinion—which appeared plausible, I hope he is mistaken.

I have not yet had time to look much about me, my time being very much engaged in getting myself settled and in paying and receiving visits of Ceremony, which begin in my Opinion to be carried to be carried to a ridiculous height, but those who are better informed think otherwise.

My Nerves have not yet quite recovered the Shock of the Waggon and I am in very good health and infinitely less fatigued than I expected to be after riding from Baltimore to this place in less than four days. the very bad Roads, and riding late at night, one night it was near twelve before we alighted at our Inn. I had forgot to mention to you that Congress has received official Notice that Rhode Island has ordered a Convention, the Assembly was equally divided and the Governor [*John Collins*] gave the casting Vote in favor of the Convention.

ALS, Charles E. Johnson Collection, Nc-Ar. Addressed to Edenton, North Carolina; franked; postmarked 31 January.

[*William Maclay*] to John Nicholson

Gospel is not truer than the enclosed Account. but who will believe our report? or by what hand shall it be revealed? if I am not misinformed, in respect of your character and independence, it will be properly placed in yours.

[*Enclosure*]

The Budget opened[1]

Objects

1st Extending the powers and influence of the Treasury.

2d Establishing the permanent Residence, of Court, and Congress, in New York

3d Securing the Revenues of the Union, to the Inhabitants of that City.

Ways & Means

Encrease the public debt by every possible method, admit all Accounts *authorized* & *unauthorized* blend the State debts with those of the Union, & that thus a pretext, ~~will~~ may be afforded, to seize all the sources of revenue, and depress the State governments. for without reducing them to insignificance, a pompous court cannot be established, and without such a Court, as a proper Machine no Government, can be properly managed, or in other Words, the People will be medling with serious Matters, unless You amuse them with triffles. fund all demands indiscriminately at the highest interest possible. but previous to this, communicate the grand Secret to all the Monied interest of New York, and to as many influential Characters in Congress, as may insure the Success of the Project. That they may by an united effort of Speculation, secure all the Certificates. Thus the Whole Union will be subsidized to the City of New York. The Revenues of the United States will flow intire into the hands of her Citizens. thus possessed of the Wealth of the Union, she will govern the Councils of the Empire. secure the Residence of the Court and Congress, and grow in power splendor and population, while there is room left on the Island [*Manhattan*], to build another House. The Idle and affluent will croud to her from all the New World, as well as many adventurers from the Old. New Loans must be opened on every pretext, in Holland and Elswhere. for the greater the Mass of public debt, the greater will be the influence of the Treasury, which has the Management of it. and all this will redound to the Emolument of the favoured city. thus shall the

Capital of the United States, in a few Years equal London or Paris, in population extent expence and dissipation. While for the agrandizement of one Spot, and One Set of Men, the National debt shall tower aloft to hundreds of Millions.

AL, Miscellaneous Collection, DLC. Addressed to Comptroller General of Pennsylvania. Maclay, who did not sign the letter, indicated in his diary that he wrote it on 30 January. Nicholson received it on 2 February and took it to Eleazer Oswald, who published it in *IG* on 6 February. For that version, which was reprinted at Boston, see *DHFFC* 9:410–11.

[1] For an interpretation of this title, see From New York, [Boston] *Massachusetts Centinel*, 10 January, above.

Andrew Moore to James Breckinridge

I can give you only a state of the Business now before us—Nothing is yet Completed. Early in the Session We receivd an Address from the President In which He recommended to our Consideration the providing for the discharge of the public debts—The defence of the Union The passing a uniform law for the Naturalization of foreigners and several other important subjects all of which are now before us[1] On the first—We have a System [*on public credit*] reported by the Secretary of the Treasury a copy of which I have transmitted to Capt. [*Henry*] Bowyer—This has become the general Topic of Conversation—When it was first read our Galleries were crouded with Speculators from every quarter of the Continent—Some of the principal Speculators have dispatcht agents To N. & S. Carolinas & to Georgia in order to purchase State Certificates in Confidence That the State debts will be assumd by the Continent—How this may be is altogether doubtfull There are Various opinions on this and indeed on the Whole System— There appears to be a Number of Advocates both in private Conversation and in the public prints for discriminating betwixt the Original holders of Certs. and purchasers They propose funding the latter at the present Market price—The Subject of General defence is not yet enterd on—The defence of our Western frontier is likewise undecided—The State of Rhode Island have by their Legislature calld a Convention a copy of the law has been laid before us Together with a Petition from the Governor[2] by the direction of the Legislature praying a Suspension of the Impost & Tonage laws so far as it respects their Vessells—they express a confidence that the Constitution will be adopted ~~th~~ by their Convention—We have a Multiplicity of [*torn*] important Business before us—The Session will prob[*ably*] be a long one as a revision of some of the laws passt last session will be necessary and also compleating the business now under Consideration—We have had no foreign news since I arrivd here.

ALS, Rockbridge Historical Society Collection, ViLxW. Place to which addressed not indicated.

[1] For Washington's first annual message, see *DHFFC* 3:252–54.
[2] Governor John Collins's letter, or "Petition," and the Rhode Island law were submitted to the House on 28 January and are printed in *DHFFC* 6:1539–41.

Theodore Sedgwick to Pamela Sedgwick

Your kind letters of the 21. & 24. I have recd. I am very happy to be informed that you have a prospect of procuring a nurse, because the fatigue you would be otherwise exposed to I feared would have been too much for your feeble frame. Your long tryed affection leaves no doubt but you will regard your health if only because it is so dear to me. Words cannot, my best beloved, express how tender and how soothing to my heart are your remembered virtues—your purity—your truth—your magnanimity. Let me beseech you to guard with care that life which allies me to such perfections.

Poor, sweet little Robert[1] how my heart bleeds for him. Is it not worth the trial to consult Doctr. Hileman? The case is too important to hesitate at any expence.

Painful to myself is the cruel seperation I suffer from almost every thing which on earth my heart holds dear and no inconsiderable portion of that pain arises from the reflection that you are less happy than I ought to make you. This I am sensible is a time when our sweet little ones most require a parents attention, to check that impatience and petulance of temper which I fear is part of the inheritance of *my* children. Eliza [*Sedgwick*], good girl is every thing I can wish her to be—prudent, discreet—sensible and considerate. the last quality will enable her to make some allowance for the petulance of her sister—Frances [*Frances Pamela Sedgwick*] too is a good girl, but she has a vivacity of temper which at her age will frequently push her into extremes of impatience, as she progresses in life, her good sense and reflection will correct, I hope, this habit, because she will feel the miserable effects of it—I will write her by this opportunity. I am very sorry I did not explain to you the reason why I extended my directions to so late a period. It was not because I did not hope and expect to be at home before summer. I believe indeed I shall pay you a visit at a much earlier period, but I fear the session will continue till the begining of may, and should we decide ultimately on the several subjects before us, I see no reason at present why congress should convene again during my political existence. Yet I fear the influence of 6. dollars a day, for I believe it has created a disposition to protract the session.

You may, my dearest and best beloved, be assured that I pay every possible attention to my health, as well in respect to exercise as diet. I eat no suppers on any occasion, and I exercise vastly more than I do at home. That life about which you have sent a tender concern will on that account become more an object of my care and attention. May those blessings you implore for me be received by you in abundant measure. may your virtues be rewarded here—My confidence in the supreme goodness assures me that they will be attended with unbounded bliss here after.

You will dearest love know the reason why you received no letters, by the last post, they were committed to the care of Mr. [*Silas*] Pepoon, who was obliged, by the breaking of the Stage to return. Adieu best beloved and know that I am your ever affect.

ALS, Sedgwick Papers, MHi. Place to which addressed not indicated. The salutation reads, "Best and Dearest creature."

¹ Their son suffered lameness because of a problem with his ankle.

Theodore Sedgwick to Theodore Sedgwick, Jr.

I have had the pleasure to receive a letter from you, I will get the scates and send them by the first opportunity and would have sent them by Mr. [*Silas*] Pepoon, had I not supposed he was out of town. I hope you have snow before now and will soon have a good parcel of wood—My sweet little fellow will I am sure so behave as to have every body speak well of him when Papa gets home. Now is the time my fellow ~~is the time~~ to get knowledge and learn to be good. Adieu! and know that you are dearly beloved by your papa.

ALS, Sedgwick Papers, MHi. Place to which addressed not indicated. The endorsement page reads, "Master Theodore." The salutation reads, "Dear little son."

OTHER DOCUMENTS

Nathaniel Gorham to Theodore Sedgwick. ALS, Sedgwick Papers, MHi. Written from Boston.

Regarding Gorham's negotiations with Massachusetts legislators for avoiding a default on the Genessee Purchase, "I shall my good Friend be willing to make every sacrafice to prevent your being involved in trouble"; asks him to "beg Mr. King by every exertion" to oppose Arthur St. Clair's Treaty of Fort Harmar with the Six Nations (ratification of which was postponed by the Senate on 22 September 1789).

John Langdon to Thomas Mifflin. No copy known; acknowledged in Mifflin to Langdon, 8 February.

William Maclay to Thomas Ruston. ALS, Coxe Papers, PHi. Addressed to Market Street, near Eighth Street, Philadelphia; franked; postmarked 31 January.

Expects the price that the state land office has put on lands on which they are considering speculating to be lowered; "in my Opinion, taking Matters on the great scale of general Advantage, the lower the better. Woods and uncultivated Wilds are of no avail to a State. Population is the great political point to be gained"; expects to be in Philadelphia in March; will correspond with his brother Samuel, a member of the state assembly, to "soon find the temper of the House"; enjoins silence about the speculation; took some pains to procure for Ruston a copy of Hamilton's report on public credit, but declines to forward it as he has seen part of it printed in the Pennsylvania newspapers, and it is bulky.

Josiah Parker to Tench Coxe and Nalbro Frazier. No copy known; acknowledged in Coxe and Frazier to Parker, 4 February.

William Paterson to Euphemia Paterson. ALS, Paterson Papers, NjR. Addressed to New Brunswick, New Jersey; carried by Col. (John) Bayard. For a partial text, see Somerset County [New Jersey] *Historical Quarterly* 5(1913):185.

Is astonished at not receiving "so much as a Line" from her, through John Bayard; "I have written at least three Letters to your one since I have been at this place; when all Things considered the Reverse ought to have been the Case. But, perhaps, your Time has been so much taken up with Business"; outlines his ideas for renting out their farm in Raritan, but "Before a final Agreement perhaps, you had better write to me the Terms"; meditation on the recent death of their neighbor Col. Azariah Dunham (1718–90); "How transient is every Thing in this World—the Days of the brightest are but short, emit a momentary Blaze, and then set in Night. May we all be prepared for a better World, whose Happiness will be one eternal Day, and where every Tear will be wiped away from every Eye" (Revelation 21:4).

Alexander White to Horatio Gates. ALS, Emmet Collection, NN. Place to which addressed not indicated. Recipient identified from internal evidence.

Encloses letter for forwarding to "Giusippi"; wrote to Gates after his arrival, and since then has sent Adam Stephen a copy of Hamilton's report on public credit, "for your joint perusal and opinion"; refers him to the newspapers for Knox's report on the militia; "I should be happy in receiving your Animadversions on that, and every other important subject."

Letter from New York. [Rhode Island] *Providence Gazette*, 6 February; reprinted at Boston; Norwich, Connecticut; New York City (*NYMP*, 20 February); Philadelphia; Winchester, Virginia; and Augusta, Georgia.

"I congratulate you very sincerely on your prospect of a return to the path of honour, and the road to happiness—to a participation of the blessings which we enjoy under the New Constitution of the states."

SUNDAY, 31 JANUARY 1790

Fine (Johnson)

John Fenno to Joseph Ward

*** As to the Secy.'s report [*on public credit*]—it will occasion much debate—but will I think be substantially adopted—Ames' motion[1] being adopted by a considerable majority is symptomatic of the Debts' being funded—I suspect the present posture of affairs will rather encrease, than abate your perplexity respecting future speculations—as to Grayson & Lee's Letter[2] you may depend it has sunk them in the view of their own party in virginia—I was told this by members from that State—besides it was contrary to the declaration of the Latter in Senate.

*** I have the pleasure to inform you that last week I begun printing the Journals of Congress for the present Session—this will be of some service to me—my friends in Congress are many—and my subscribers encrease daily—your approbation of my labors is a prop to my spirits—my engagements are arduous—but my health continues pretty so so—tho some say I am thin— ***

ALS, Ward Papers, ICHi. Addressed to "Land Office, Boston"; carried by J(ohn Foster?) Williams. For the full text, see *AASP* 89(1979):356–58.

[1] On 28 January, the COWH agreed to a motion by Ames to postpone debate on Hamilton's report on public credit until 8 February, earlier than any of the other dates proposed in substitute motions.

[2] For Senators Grayson and Lee's official letter to the speaker of Virginia's House of Delegates, 28 September 1789, see *DHFFC* 17:1634.

Thomas Hartley to Jasper Yeates

Since my last nothing very singular has happened—Congress has been divided into Committees preparing Business—and we are getting pretty well under way.

The Report of the Secretary of the Treasury will draw our attention and that of the public very much in the Course of the next week—it is very probable we shall take it under Consideration—weeks will be consumed in the Discussion—I wish we may have a happy Issue.

Certificates have suffered a little within these few Days. but in my opinion without any Cause—I think that the Funds and Abilities of the United States are so fully adequate to the Discharge of the Interest that nothing need be feared.

I shall be glad to have a History of your late Circuit. ***

ALS, Yeates Papers, PHi. Addressed to Lancaster, Pennsylvania; franked; postmarked; answered 3 February. Newspaper enclosed.

Joseph Pierce to Benjamin Goodhue

I thank you for yr. letter of 8th Inst. Our general Court are now seting—have chosen a Committee to revise the Excise Law—which they have no occasion to spend their own time & constituents money about—it has been an oppresive thing to the Trade of this State to continue it after the power of laying duties was given to the Continent—It will now I presume be assumed by Congress and if it can be so managed as not to hazard the Constitution may be made a great blessing to this Country by for by excising *heavily* Spiritous & Vinous Liquors—and a great sum may be raised—and the Morals of the people [*illegible*] for at present the Cheapness of Spiritous Liquors is a Curse on the Country.

The Plans of the Secry. of the Treasury so far as they are made known to us are pretty generally approved of—there are some who do not like the assuming the State debts—they think it a Strong string to pull upon [*lined out*] toward a consolidation of the States—how far it may have that effect time only can discover.

P. S. Mr. [*John*] Templeman & Mr. Brown have both been so obliging as to shew me yr. Letters & for which I thank you.

ALS, Letters to Goodhue, NNS. Written from Boston.

Rufus Putnam to the Ohio Company at Marietta, Ohio

***

When I left Marietta [*Ohio*] I had no Idea that any farther Divisions to the proprietors would take place till the whole business of the purches was compleated,[1] for it was well known then that there ware very great deficenses in the payments into our Treasurey and to go into the division of Lands which might never be our property, appears to me improper, but Gentlemen I will Dwell no Longer on probabilities, it is now certain that more than two hundred Subscribers will Totally fail in payment, and that we must give up a part of the lands contracted for, what terms we shall obtain or what part of the purches will be given up is at present altogather unsertain[2]—I arrived here but last evening and therfore have had no oppertunity to Sound the members of Congress, but as the Securities are risin to Eight (and have ben as high as nine) Shilings on the pound and will probbally rise higher no man in his sences will make himself responsable for the Ballance due to Congress on the risque of Selling the forfited Shares—I have no reason to doubt but Congress will Settle with the Company on reasonable terms[3] but when there terms are known Should they be other wise you may rest asured that I Shall not agree to them. till your opinion has been consulted, in the mean time I must request that you will Suspend all further Division of lands till our business with Congress is compleated. ***

ALS, Hoar Collection, MH. Addressed to Griffin Greene at Marietta, Ohio, via the post-master at Pittsburgh who "is requested to forward this by the first Trusty hand"; contents to be communicated to the "Agents and Proprietors" of the Ohio Company.

[1] In July 1787 Congress authorized the board of treasury to sell millions of acres of public lands in the Northwest Territory on credit to the Ohio Company of Associates, a corporation formed primarily of former officers of the Continental Army and land speculators from New England. The company and the board closed the deal in October. There would be eight payments of $500,000 each in either specie or public securities for approximately five million acres: one payment due immediately, one when the federal government had completed its survey of the lands, and the remaining six over the course of the following three years. The federal government was to issue the deed, or letters patent, once it had received the first two payments; in the meantime the Company was authorized to occupy and improve 750,000 acres without benefit of deed. The company sold shares rather than land to settlers and land speculators with the idea that the land would be distributed once the contract was completed (Jeffrey L. Pasley, "Private Access and Public Power," Kenneth R. Bowling and Donald R. Kennon, eds., The House and the Senate in the 1790s: Petitioning, Lobbying, and Institutional Development [Athens, Ohio, 2002], pp. 78–80).
[2] In 1789 the company declared as forfeit the shares of subscribers who had not paid. This sharp drop in expected revenue, along with the rise in the cost of public securities, made it impossible for the company to meet the terms of the 1787 contract. Putnam had come to New York City to save what he could (H. Z. Williams, The History of Washington County, Ohio [Cleveland, 1881], pp. 89–90).
[3] In 1792 Congress passed an act authorizing the President to issue a deed for the 750,000 acres in exchange for the $500,000 payment made in 1787 and offering the company several options to buy the rest (Pasley, "Private Access," pp. 84–85).

Theodore Sedgwick to Henry Van Schaack

Your kind favor of the 25th. I have had the pleasure to receive—I shall at all times with pleasure communicate such information on the important subjects before congress as may give you ~~pleasure~~ satisfaction.

The accession of Rhode island is in my mind no longer a doubtful event. Vermont too had not her stupid Jealousy prevented, might very soon have become a member of the union.

On the wise and prudent measures of the present session will depend the future respectability and welfare of this country, and indeed principally on the measures which may be adopted relative to funding the national debt. with respect to which these four great questions are most material. 1. whether there shall be any discrimination between the orig[ina]l. holders and the purchasers of the securities? 2. shall the interest already due be converted into capital? 3. shall the State debts be assumed? & 4. what shall be the rate of interest? With regard to the two first there will I hope in our house be very small divisions in favor of a discrimination and against funding the interest. The third will probably be warmly contested, the opponents may be divided into two classes, those who are actuated by local considerations as belonging to states whose debts are comparatively small & those who fear an excess of power in the national government. For my own part so important do I consider the assumption, and so essential to our national existence that I had rather see the debt destroyed by a spunge[1] than, than to consent to the funding that part of it which is now denominated national independently of the other.

The fourth question is highly important, and a determination on it, should depend on the a cool and deliberate calculation, not of on the ability of the people but on the ability of the government. Every hypothesis on the effect of national arrangements of finance by arguments *a priori*, will probably be found falacious, Experience not of others but our own being the only certain *data* from which consequences may be drawn with any degree of certainty.

You have doubtless seen Mr. H[amilton']s. report. The 3rd. proposition will be probably most generally accepted by the subscribers, This proposition contains an offer of nearly 5 per cent interest. The whole debt will amount to about 80,000,000. dollars, The question then to be determined, and it is a very serious one, can we with any degree of moral certainty determine that the government will possess an ability to fulfill engagements founded on this idea, at the same time making that provision which every government should, and every wise Government secures for unforeseen accidents? In my opinion the real security and efficiency of the government will depend more on a precise and punctual performance of its engagements than on every other circumstance combined.

***

ALS, Sedgwick Papers, MHi. Place to which addressed not indicated.

[1] A legal cancellation of a debt.

Abigail Adams Smith to Elizabeth Norton

***

We expect that Congress will adjourn in the spring. and Mamma intends if they do, to spend her summer at Braintree. ***

*** the manner of visiting here is not so well calculated to promote intimacies and sociability as in Boston, but when you are obliged to keep up an extensive visitting acquaintance—it may be done with less inconvenience here most of the Ladies whose Husbands are in Publick offices have their particular day on which they are at home to receive Company—at all other times they are at liberty to refuse them selvs if they choose. and they are *obliged* to keep up such an extensive acquaintance as would take up their whole time otherwise you may return a dosen of thease visits in an evening—it is not expected (if you find the family at home) that you will set more than a quarter of an Hour. and if you do not a Card answers every purpose—in this way you will readily suppose that one cannot form intimate acquaintances ***

ALS, Christopher Cranch Papers, MHi. Written from "Richmond Hill," outside New York City; addressed to Weymouth, Massachusetts; carried by Thomas Boylston Adams. The omitted text discusses Thomas Adams's departure from "Richmond Hill" the next day and news of other family and friends.

George Thatcher to Josiah Thatcher

Yours of the 21st. inst. came to hand last evening—And I thank you for your attention to the subject I mentioned to you last fall—Tho the plan I had in view, when I wished to be informed of some suitable persons, in each Town, to assist in taking a Census, is not likely to be adopted by Congress.

Congress has proposed a Census shall be taken by the Marshalls—each having power to appoint as many assistants as he may think expedient, within his district, seting off to each assistant his sub-district These assistants to report to the Marshalls—and the Marshalls to the President of the United States.

I transmit you herewith the Report of the Secretary of the Treasury.

I hope you have recieved the concluding sheets of the Journals of the last Sessions of the House of Representatives[1]—I forwarded them some time ago.

The consideration of the before mentioned Report, is to be the order of the day on monday after next—It begins to be a subject of much speculation, and about which there are various opinions.

The members of Congress seem to differ, in opinion, on the ~~subject~~ rate of Interest that should be allowed on the national domestic debt, from six, to two per cent—any Notes and observations you may think important on this subject, will be very acceptable—it is allowed by all to be of the last consequence to America—and certainly demands the most serious & mature deliberation. It appears to me to involve this question—whether the State debt of Massachusetts shall be paid or not? for if that should not be assumed, by the Union, it appears to me very doubtfull whether it can ever be discharged—And some members of Congress, as also some states, are opposed to a general assumption.

ALS, Thatcher Family Papers, MHi. Place to which addressed not indicated.

[1] The journals of both houses were periodically printed. These printings, or signatures, were bound together when complete.

[George Thatcher] to [Daniel Cony]

By the papers from Boston, last evening, it appears you are like to have your attention pretty well engaged this session. Another reform in the system of law and its professors is going forward[1]—I will not take it upon me to say either the law, or its practitioners, do not need it, but I really hope, sometime or other, to see both the General Court and the people at large, easy and satisfied upon this subject; for I must confess there have been so many *changes* and *alterations*, (whether *reformations* or not I will not say) in the laws of Massachusetts, within five or six years, that I dont know when I am right and when I am wrong. Indeed I have frequently told people, who came to me for advice, that it was not in my power to direct them: And I declare that I dont know any state or kingdom, where the laws have undergone so many changes, in so short a time, as the Massachusetts—about a year ago there passed a law, to be in force for three years, if I recollect right, from June. This has but just begun to operate and people begin to understand it. But from what I can collect out of the paper, Mr. [John] Gardiner's great object is to destroy what he denominates *Bar Calls*—and what is commonly called *Bar Meetings*[2]—Now I do not know what he has discovered so very injurious to the publick, or individuals, in these meetings; as far as I have been acquainted with them, in the Eastern Counties, they appear to me as mighty harmless creatures—and I should not imagine that all ever held in this part of the Commonwealth, have done so much hurt as a mouse would do in a mill in ten minutes—and yet I should hardly think it demands a parliamentary interposition to exterminate mice from the face of the earth.

[Boston] *Herald of Freedom*, 9 February. Although this piece is headed "from a gentleman in the district of Maine," and Thatcher was in New York by this time, the correspondents' identities, the letter's date, and the circumstances surrounding its publication are established beyond doubt by Cony's letter to Thatcher, 13 February, below, and are corroborated by several contemporary references (notably Cony's earlier acknowledgment in his letter to Thatcher, 7 February; David Sewall to Thatcher, 22 February; Jeremiah Hill to Thatcher, 21 February; and most explicitly in John Gardiner's reply, 11 February, below).

---

[1] The reference is to John Gardiner's crusade to correct perceived abuses in the state's legal profession; see Ames to William Tudor, 17 January, n. 1, above.

[2] Among other things, Gardiner's proposals targeted these supposed secret meetings of lawyers, where legal procedures and fees were fixed.

From New York

Judge [*William*] CUSHING arrived here on Thursday—and to-morrow the Supreme Judicial Court of the United States will be opened in this city, by the Chief Justice [*John Jay*], Judge CUSHING, and Judge [*James*] WILSON.

It is thought a majority of Congress will be in favour of funding the debt, and that the basis at least of the system is laid in the Secretary's plan. This will be a highly interesting and important question, and on its decision hangs the fate of the government.

The annual expense of the Plan of National Legionary Militia, as reported by the Secretary at War, will be near 400,000 dollars. It appears beautiful on paper, but from what I hear, it will not be adopted.

Last Thursday arrived in this city from North-Carolina, the Hon. SAMUEL JOHNSTON, Senator of the United States from that Republick.

[Boston] *Massachusetts Centinel*, 10 February; reprinted at Portland, Maine, and Portsmouth, New Hampshire.

Letter from Baltimore

I received your letter in which you request information in what light the Secretary's Report is viewed here: It has not yet been so fully examined as to produce a decided opinion on the merits of the different propositions; but it has thus far made very favorable impressions—and I am confident it will be approved of in proportion as it is examined. The truths it contains are great and interesting, and will bear the test of the strictest scrutiny, while truth and justice are applauded by men.

There are many considerations which give my mind perfect confidence and satisfaction on the subject of the public debt—some of them I will mention.

1st. The security of property is one of the first objects for which government is instituted—and it would be a most flagrant infraction of the Constitution of the United States should Congress injure the property of a very numerous and respectable class of the citizens by a violation of public contracts.

2d. It is sound policy in government to be honest—They cannot otherwise be respected—and it would be in vain for them to pass laws to secure good morals and make subjects and citizens honest, should they themselves set an example of public injustice and fraud.

3d. Those who know the characters which compose the Legislature of the Union are satisfied that they never will be influenced by the maxims and principles which have stamped infamy on the name of Rhode Island. Could no dependence be placed on the personal characters of the Gentlemen in Congress, the scorn, reproach, and misery, which Rhode Island has suffered by her dishonest policy would sufficiently warn them against the consequences of a violation of public faith.

We rest assured that no law respecting the debt will pass both Houses, and have the sanction of the President, which is not founded in that righteousness which exalteth a nation.[1] The Constitution—the characters which compose Congress—the resolution which was past last session—the President's speech—and the answers to it—and the report of the Secretary of the Treasury, authorise most perfect confidence in the measures of government.

GUS, 6 February; reprinted at Windsor and Bennington, Vermont; Boston and Pittsfield, Massachusetts; Newport, Rhode Island; Hartford, Middletown, and New London, Connecticut; and Wilmington, Delaware.

[1] Proverbs 14:34.

Letter from New York

You ask my opinion on the probability of the state debts being assumed by the Union. This is a subject that I cannot speak upon with so much certainty as I wish I could; and, at present, can only say, that I rather think the assumption will take place—but more from necessity than any other principle—there being some states, as well as some members of Congress, very much opposed to the measure. However, if Congress takes the productive part of the excise they must also take the debts—It will be very hard—as well as like the Egyptian severity[1] to take the excise from the states, and yet require them to pay their respective debts.

[Boston] Herald of Freedom, 9 February; reprinted at Hartford, Connecticut; Philadelphia; and Baltimore.

[1] Probably an allusion to Exodus 5:7–8, relating Pharaoh's order that the Hebrews be forced to produce the same number of bricks without any longer being supplied with the straw to make them.

Letter from New York

Thursday was appointed to take into consideration the report of the Secretary of the Treasury; and a motion was made for postponing it till Monday week. This brought up several gentlemen who were for putting it off for three or four months, to give time for the Legislatures of the States to be consulted upon the subject. They began to be of opinion that a discrimination must take place between original holders, and speculating purchasers: The former were honestly entitled to twenty shillings on the pound; but the latter no more than what they bona fide gave for their securities, with the interest on that sum. And should it be found that a discrimination is impracticable, the whole ought to be reduced to the average price at which they have passed, in the course of trade, since their first emission.

At present it is impossible to say what will be the determination of Congress upon this subject—There are various opinions. Some are for funding them at six per cent.—others at four; and many for three—while two, and two and an half find advocates. Those who are for six per cent. or what is equivalent thereto (as the several propositions in the Secretary's report are accounted) say the honour and credit of the nation depend on Congress punctually fulfilling all former promises, according to their letter and obvious meaning—But such as contend for low interest are of opinion, that the faith and credit of the United States will hereafter depend altogether upon a punctual discharge and honest fulfilment of the promises Congress shall now and hereafter make—without regarding what has been heretofore done. For instance—if Congress fund the debt at three per cent. or even a lower interest, and punctually pay that interest as it becomes due, without any deviation or omission whatever, the credit of the nation, both at home and abroad, will be in higher repute than if they were to promise six per cent. and finally pay a less sum.

The United States are beginning the world, and from this time will be considered as a nation, with power to execute their engagements: Heretofore they have not been viewed in that light even by their own citizens. And how often has it been said by foreign nations, that America had no Head with whom they might enter into national engagements, under just expectations of their fulfilment: Therefore every thing depends upon the punctual discharge of the promises Congress now enter into. The character of America is now framing; and it will result from what she now says and now does. What was promised and done under the confederation will no more enter into her national character hereafter, than the freaks and wild sallies of youth do that of manhood, when all the actions of the latter period are regulated by the most rigid maxims of morality and religion.

Is there any probability that the resources of America are adequate to an interest of six per cent. on the whole debt, including the State debts? And can there be any reason assigned why the State debts should not be put on the same footing with the Continental? Certainly there cannot. Then to promise six, or any other per cent. beyond the resources of America, is the most direct and certain way to prevent her gaining credit and reputation, either with foreigners or with her own citizens.

[Portland, Maine] *Cumberland Gazette*, 15 February. Printed in italics. This is probably from a letter written by Thatcher to the newspaper's editor, Thomas B. Wait.

OTHER DOCUMENTS

Thomas Crafts, Jr. to John Adams. ALS, Adams Family Manuscript Trust, MHi. Written from Boston.
Office seeking: Martin Brimmer Sohier (?) for lieutenant or captain in regiments to be added to the federal army and anything "in the Civil line" for himself.

Alexander Hamilton to George Washington. ALS, misfiled at 1799, Miscellaneous Letters, Miscellaneous Correspondence, State Department Records, Record Group 59, DNA. For the full text, see *PAH* 26:510–11.
As directed, has asked Schuyler about Rev. Samuel Kirkland's fidelity and judgment (as missionary to the Oneida Indians); Schuyler questions his judgment and recommends instead that of James Deane who can be in New York City in twelve days.

Jeremiah Hill to George Thatcher. ALS, Chamberlain Collection, MB. Place from which written not indicated.
Speculates on the origins of good and evil; on "domestic Matters," a Portland, Maine, merchant tried to clear out a vessel on a recent Saturday, found the collector out of town, "and made a very *pious* harangue on the Occasion."

Benjamin Huntington to Anne Huntington. No copy known; acknowledged in Anne to Benjamin Huntington, 8 February.

Henry Knox to William Eustis. FC:dft, Knox Papers, Gilder Lehrman Collection, NHi.
After canvassing several members, has determined it would be impracticable at that time to alter the rules for obtaining an invalid pension; Knox's plan for the militia seems principally objected to for its expense.

John Langdon to Hopley Yeaton. No copy known; acknowledged in Yeaton to Langdon, 3 April.

James Madison to John Dawson. No copy known; acknowledged in Dawson to Madison, 26 February and 14 March.

James Madison to Eliza House Trist. ALS, Mss. 1231, Pierpont Morgan Library, New York City. Place to which addressed not indicated. For the full text, see *PJM* 13:11–12.
  Wrote a letter last week, which has been detained by the carrier, Mr. (Francis) Bailey; if Edmund Randolph requires a longer stay in New York, "He will not be able to get admittance into our family, nor can I give him recommendations to any other place. The town is unusually full at this particular moment; the Legislature of the State being added to the federal Stock of guests"; prays for Jefferson's remaining in America, "for public and private reasons"; asks her to give Jefferson "my pedometer," which he forgot in Philadelphia when last there.

Theodore Sedgwick to Benjamin Lincoln. No copy known; acknowledged in Lincoln to Sedgwick, 7 February.

Abigail Adams Smith to Lucy Cranch. ALS, Cranch Papers, MHi. Written from "Richmond Hill," outside New York City; addressed to Braintree, Massachusetts; carried by Thomas Boylston Adams.
  The family had a "very agreeable visit" with brother Thomas at "Richmond Hill"; "he has been danceing amongst the Ladies and has been much approved"; they have had a beautiful winter, "very fine" for two months, with never more than one inch of snowfall at a time and temperatures almost as mild as April.

Silas Talbot to George Washington. Copy, Gilder Lehrman Collection, NHi. Written from Johnstown, New York. For the full text, see *PGW* 5:74–75.
  Office seeking: has been informed by a member of Congress "that new arrangements will probably take place in some or all of the principal Harbours," and that "there will likely be a Harbourmaster appointed to each post"; seeks this post at New York City if it is created.

George Thatcher to Joseph Storer. No copy known; acknowledged in Storer to Thatcher, 17 February.

George Thatcher to Sarah Thatcher. ALS, Thatcher Family Papers, MHi. Place to which addressed not indicated.

Such pleasant weather, for the past five weeks he has worn a cloak or surtout only twice, "tho I walk more or less every day"; not enough snow for
sleighing; "I hope you pass the winter comfortably. The *little illness you &
Tempe [Temperance Lee]* complain of I do not apprehend to be very dangerous"; enquires of molasses and pork he had sent home a day or two after
he left Boston, about 20 December.

JANUARY 1790 UNDATED

Robert Ballard to James Madison

The Secretary of the Treasury has wrote the Officers of this Port, for the
exact Sum, each Officer has received, up to the first of January.

I hope the Secretary is of Opinion that our Fees are too small and that he
will lay a Statement thereof before Congress, for Their Consideration.

I have estimated on a frugal Plan the Sum I must expend for the Support of my Family, and find it will considerably exceed the Sum my Fees
produces, for the same time—a circumstance I am persuaded the Rulers of
my Country will not permit.

The Attention I am necessarely obliged to pay to the Inspectors, Weigher,
Measurer, Guager, and measuring the Vessells, ascertaining the Tonnage and
recording it, obliges me to keep a clerk, and such a One as requires large Wages.

The Nature of my Office makes me acquinted with most of the Masters
of Vessells, as well Coasters as Foreigners—They all agree that the Officers
Fees are so trifling that they scarcely feel them, and the coasting Gentlemen
laugh at us, and tell *me*: I do their Business for nothing, which is really the
case! For Instance, a Boston Vessel arrives with a Cargo of Onions Potatoes
&ca. &ca. that fills a Manifest, as long as my Arm, which I am to record,
examine the Vessel, receive the Inspector's Report and compare it with the
Manifest, and enter it in my Book, agreeing or disagreeing, as the case may
be—for all this Trouble, I do not receive on an average more than 18. Cents.
Vessells from the adjoining States I receive nothing from, Or the Vessells
trading up this extensive [Chesapeake] Bay. And Sir, I will venture to say:
They are the Vessells that will attempt smuggling—I am obliged to search
and attend them. Surely then the Labourer is worthy of Hire. Another Piece
of Service is particularly hard on the Surveyor: He is obliged to measure and
ascertain the Tonnage of all foreign Vessells, record the same, and transmit
a copy thereof to the Collector, for all Which trouble, he does not receive
One Farthing. I have it from a Number of Masters of Vessells, that in the
Ports of England they demand and receive Four Dollars and a half, for every
American Vessel the Surveyor measures.

The Surveyor incurs a heavy Expence for Books, Paper, and blank Manifests. I have already wrote Two Rheams of writing Paper. And I calculate my Expences for Stationary and Printers Bills, at nothing less than Thirty Pounds per Year—The Law does not secure a Return of this Money. There are other Circumstances to shew that the Surveyor has not an adequete proportion of Fees for Services he must render, if he regards his Duty, and his Country's Good. I have at an early period discovered a Zealous Attachment for the Wellfare of my Country. I have been unfortunate, and am honoured With a Commission by Our Truly Honourable and Worthy President. The Office on my part shall be executed with Fidelity.

I trust Sir, from Your own Observations, and what little Light I may have thrown on the Subject, that You will rather Coincide with me, that the Ratio of Fees to the Surveyor, are unequal to the Services he must perform. In that case permit me Sir, to sollicit Your Patronage and Aid, With each branch of the Legislature for further Allowances in Fees. Inclosed I will take the Liberty of discribing what I think *at Least* the Surveyor deserves.

The Collector of this Port [*Otho H. Williams*] is very anxious, that each Officer shou'd collect his own Fees. I am sattisfied it should be so, provided the Law secures the Officers in such a Manner, that they may not be deprived of their Fees.

Knowing the goodness of your heart, to act and explain on all occasions for the best, I have taken the liberty to address you on this subject. Sir, I cannot l[*torn*] on the present fees—my family *accustomed to live well* must be Stinted. I am sure the Proportion of fees I have laid to each sized Vessell, cannot be objected to by any Owner.

One Case more I will suggest. A Vessell arrives from a Forreign Port, the Surveyor performs all his Duty of receiving a Manifest recording it, examines the Vessell, Measures her, Ascertains Tonage, records it also, & passes a Certificate to the Collector, & receives *only* five Shillings—The Collector & Naval Officer Divide Five Dollars besides Perquisite fees.

LS, last two paragraphs in the hand of Ballard, Madison Papers, DLC. Written from Baltimore. For the enclosure, see *PJM*, 13:14. The letter is undated but was written in response to Hamilton's circular of 20 January (*PAH* 6:204). It is possible that Ballard wrote it later in the second session. He repeated his request to Madison in the third session.

George Washington, Summary of Joseph Martin to Benjamin Hawkins

Encloses the report of a Comee. of the Assembly of No. Carolina, which had been appointed to examine into a corrispondence between him and Mr. [*Alexander*] McGillivray, by which he stands acquitted of any intention to injure the U. States, or any of them. Enforms him that from tolerable good information he has just heard that the Chickasaw Nation had made a stroke at the Chicamages [*Chickamauga*] Indians & were driving all before them— That several Women & Children of the latter had run into the Inhabitants of little river for Refuge—That he shall set out for that County in a few days and as soon as the particulars can be known will give information of them. Wishes to know whether Congress approves of this War or not—thinks he can easily stop it if it does not meet their approbation—But adds their wars with one another may be the means of Peace to our frontiers—requests a hint on the subject by way of Richmond, directed to the care of the Postmaster there.

No copy of letter known; summary from George Washington, Diary, 15 February, MiD-B. Written from Smith River, Virginia, at or near present-day Martinsville. For background, see *PGW* 1:384–85n. This letter was shown to Washington by Knox, who had obtained it from Hawkins. A second letter from Lardner Clark to Hawkins, dated Nashville, Tennessee, 8 September 1789, was also shown to Washington, who summarized it as follows:

Mentions that the loose and disorderly people that first settled the District in which he is remove as government (by means of the Superior Court) is extended amongst them and supplied by persons of better character & Morals—That the Spanish Governor of Louisiana [*Esteban Miró*] is holding out every lure to envite the Citizens of the United States to settle under that Government—That a Doctor [*James*] White who has been sometime at New Orleans does not seem to like the Government and discourages our Settlers from Migrating to it till it can at least be seen what Measures the Government of the Union will take respecting the Navigation of the Mississippi—That Conventions which it had been proposed to hold in Kentucky, and other Districts of the Western Country for the purpose of Addressing the old Congress on this subject had been proposed for the same reason—That there was no appearance of giving up the Post of the Natches to the U. States though it was within their Territory, on the Contrary Roman Catholick Churches were built there & provision made for newly arrived Priests—That the Spanish Governor has said that it is not want of Land that make them oppose our Settlements or which causes them to withhold the Navigation of the Missisipi from us, but because they do not like our advancing in such numbers, & so fast upon them—In short, they act under the operation of fear and Jealousy, though they will not acknowledge these to be the motives for their conduct—That it had been reported through the Western Settlements that Mr. [*Don Diego de*] Gardoqui had invited them to put themselves under the Spanish government with assurances of Peace & Trade as consequences of it—and that Governor by Proclamation had invited them to become Inhabitants of Louisiana—That any person (he is informed) may take produce to New Orleans paying 15 pr. Ct. Duty to the King—That the Force (Military) in the two Floridas consist of two Regiments of 600 Men each and he is told a third is ordered to be raised to consist entirely of Spaniards by birth—That the District in which he is populates fast and will soon make a State—And as the Navigation of the Missisipi is essential to them, it must be obtained by treaty or by force, or they must connect themselves with the Spaniards—That it is not supposed, the two Floridas & Louisiana contain more than 20,000 Souls—That the distance from Nashville to New Orleans by Land (wch. he has travelled) is abt. 450 or 500 Miles and not a Mountain and hardly a hill in the way—That this year he supposes they will make 300 Hhds. of Tobacco—for wch. 3½d. only is given when the Spaniard gets 10 dollars pr Hd wt (Summary, *PGW* 6:31–33.)

The governor's proclamation mentioned in this letter was issued in New Orleans by Esteban Miró on 20 April 1789. It offered free passage and land to Americans settling in and swearing allegiance to Spanish Louisiana, guaranteed religious freedom while limiting public worship to Catholics, and extended the same trading privileges enjoyed by other subjects of the Spanish crown in the colony). The letter's author, Lardner Clark (d. 1801), was a leading merchant of Nashville, Tennessee, where he resettled from Philadelphia in 1786 ("Lardner Clark, Nashville's First Merchant and Foremost Citizen," *Tennessee History* 3[1917]:28–133).

OTHER DOCUMENTS

George Thatcher to Samuel Nasson. No copies known; two letters acknowledged in Nasson to Thatcher, 2 March.

Daniel Hiester, Account Book. PRHi.
    Purchased three copies of the report on public credit, presumably for his constituents and in addition to those he received as a member.

February 1790

Rain (Johnson)

Pierce Butler to James Seagrove

I am looking with anxiety for a letter from You. I have great dependance on Your activity. You have had an oppy. of making Yourself once more an independant Man. I hope it is so. I send You with this the report of the Secretary of the Treasury; when You have read it send it to Captn. [*Roger Parker*] Saunders. Public securities fall here owing to two circumstances; many persons purchased largely on a credit; pay day is come round and they have not the cash; many that were purchasers have diverted their speculations to State Indts.: hence the cause of the sudden fall of Continental securities from 10/ to 6/6. I have no doubt that the ~~the~~ Continental debt will be funded this session, but at what rate I can not determine: some are for 6 pr. Ct.; others, the more numerous, for 4; many for 3. The state debts will not be consolidated this session—that however need make no difference in Your plans.

***

The conduct of the majority of Your Legislature[1] has raised such a violent opposition to any measure for the support & defence of Georgia. that I might as well think of turning the tide, as checking the sentiments that prevail. You would have had troops before this day & a fortress at St. Marys, but for the conduct of the Majority of Your State. The Legislature will not now *hear* of any expenditures for Georgia.

I could negociate a loan for the State of Georgia, in Europe & for Individuals of that State guaranteed by the state; or a number of Individuals joining in a bond, but while there is such a majority, I wou'd propose no measure to them. I have latcly had some offers on this head from Italy;[2] they were made to me individually for Congress, or Individual States. I certainly shou'd have exerted myself for Georgia if dependance cou'd be put on the Legislature.

FC, Butler Letterbook, ScU. The omitted text relates to a personal business transaction. For the full text, see *Butler Letters*, pp. 4–5.

[1] A reference to Georgia's Yazoo land sale; see George Walton to John Adams, 20 January, above.

[2] There is no documentation of such an offer. Butler was receiving correspondence in late 1789 from the Genoese merchant Gaetano Drago di Domenico, who represented a syndicate of Genoese merchants; see *DHFFC* 17:1594–95.

Isaac Coles to Thomas Read

I received the enclosed Letter under cover to me from your nephew who desired me to forward it to you with all possible dispatch, and shall be happy to render any Service in my Power to ~~render more convenient~~ make any Communications between you more convenient.

The Secretary of the Treasury has reported a Plan for the support of public Credit, the Operation of which altho' not taken into consideration by Congress has appreciated the Public Securities very much in this Place, they have sold as high as 9/5d in the pound—but beleive they have fallen within these few Days—however the Brokers here have it in their Power to make them rise or fall as may suit their Interest—And large Sums are now on their Way to the Southern States to purchase their Public-Paper—the Report contemplates an Assumpsion of the State Debts by the General Government—this I should suppose will be deferr'd 'till the Sense of the States can be obtaind—However it is the prevailing Opinion here that Public & State Securities will be put on such a footing as to render them of much greater Value than they have hitherto been—And I have it from undoubted Authority that our Credit in Holland is equal to any State in Europe. I have sent you the Report of the Secretary at War for the general Arrangement of the Militia,[1] I should suppose it will undergo material alterations—I have also sent you three of the New York Papers, and will shortly send you the Journals—there is *almost* a Certainty that Rhode Island will come into the Confœderation.

The Government seems to be gaining Ground very fast in this Quarter of the Union.

The Session I think will be long and perhaps may be the last of this Congress—I don't think that we shall adjourn before July or August, in the mean Time shall be happy to hear from you, & will give you all the Information in my Power.

ALS, Edward Coles Papers, NjP; given to Coles in 1837 by the Virginia historian Hugh B. Grigsby. Place to which addressed not indicated. Although the recipient's name does not appear on the letter, Grigsby noted on the endorsement page that it was "addressed to Col. Th. Reed."

[1] For the report, see *DHFFC* 5:1435–57.

William Webb to George Thatcher

I take the liberty to write you on the following subject, being requested by A number of the Inhabitance of the town of Bath, who think it will be necessary for yr. Hon. to be acquainted with the opinion of the people in general on this River [*Kennebec*], respecting the operation of that Law of the United States, which prohibits Foreign Vessels from unloading in this district. This prohibition has Sir become a general Complaint not only of the Merchants and Traders but Also of the Inhabitance in general on this River, who conceive they shall be greatly Aggreived if Congress shou'd not think it Consistant to grant them the liberty of the Foreign Trade. But, as in the first establishment of Revenue Systems imperfections and inconveniences will naturally present themselves in practice, which cou'd not have been foreseen in their formation. they therefore flatter themselves that Congress will take the Matter into their Consideration. In relyg. on yr. Hon. Goodness to forward the Matter as early this meetg. [*of*] Congress as may be convenient, not doubting but you [*will*] use yr. endeavours & so far give yr. Opinion in their favour [*as yo*]u may think Consistant with the public Welfare.

Altho the Complaints of Merchants &c. respectg. the Laws, are not Always infallible indications of defects, yet I cannot but join them in opinion on this subject, as it is Certain that if Foreign Vessels are not permitted to unload in this district it will be a great detriment to the people on this River.

I have heard it as the opinion of many that Wiscasset ought to have the preference to this Port (if either) for the foreign Trade or rather for foreign Vessels to unload at, as it was Supposed a greater Number of foreign Vessels loaded at the Port of Wiscasset.

But by what information I can get, more than double the number of Foreign Vessels took there Cargoes from this district than at the Port of Wiscasset. The year Past, and many more wou'd have been here after lumber cou'd they have brought a Cargo & unloaded it here.

ALS, Chamberlain Collection, MB. Written from "Collectors Office District of Bath."

Pelatiah Webster to William Samuel Johnson

I have been Reading Mr. Hamiltons report to Congress I perfectly agree with him in the animated encomiums he bestows on public credit, & all his detail of its uses, but think his mode of obtaining it by no means adequate to the end proposed. indeed his principles & Effects, or his premisses & conclusions appear to me to be of very different natures, & totally incapable of Connexion or even consistency. I will give you Some instances.

1 he says the only way to maintain public credit is by *Good Faith.* by a *punctual performance of contracts.* Yet he peremptorily refuses to pay the real Supporters of the War Such Sums as are duly & Justly owing to them, by the Most Solemn *contracts* that can be Expressed, & which he allows have not been *fully* paid, & which Every body Else knows have not been paid, bey[*on*]d. an *Eighth part.*

he says 2 When a breaches of public Engagemts. have happen'd, the way to palliate them is to make reparation, as Soon as that can be done, but he possitively refuses to make any reparation to those who have Sufferd. damages by the breach, & insists on paying the money provided for this purpose, to Strangers who never Sufferd. any damages at all or any how even merited the money.

he says 3 When necessity appears, we ought to be perfectly assured of it's *reality*, before we yield to it, but he proposes to pay 20 Million Dollrs. to people who never Earned them, on pretence of a necessity that will vanish on the Least degree of Examination before the Mirrour of Common sense.

he says 4. the public Debt is the price of Liberty. it certainly is So as to the part due to the real Supporters of the war, which he *will not pay*, but it certainly is not so, as to the part claim'd by the purchasers of certificates who, as Such, never contributed any thing to the purchase of Liberty but these he *will pay.*

he says. 5. The public faith has been pledged for the public debt, & with *Solemnities* which give peculiar form to the obligation but 'tis notorious to Every body that these Solemnities have indeed been pledged to the real Supporters of the War, whom he *will not pay*, but niver were pledged to the Spec[*ulator*]s. whom he *will pay.*

he says. 6. the case of the Seller of certificates is a hard one, that he has a complaint of injury, & claim of redress from Govt. Yet he will not Suffer Govt. to repair that injury. & redress the wrong, but will pay the Speculator, because the original hardship was occasiond. by Govt. in wh. the Speculator had no Agency. Surely a Jesuit wd. be ashamed of this Logick.[1] The fact as it stands in nature is as plain as day light, viz. when bills of public credit depreciate, the public faith is broken, & the party that Suffers, is injured by Govt., but appreciating these bills to full vallue, is no redress of that injury in any case but this one. viz. when the bills remain in the hands of the original holder, in every other case Such appreciation is Injurious to the public because it Lays a burden on the public, to pay money that never was merited by any valluable consideration paid for it. When the public faith is broken, & the party is Injured, there is no possible way of mending & redressing the one or the other but by paying to the *party Injured* the damage he has Sustain'd—it is well known in what light the promises contain'd in such bills have been uniformly view'd by congress: [*in*] all Our States, and all the States in Europe, no plan was Ever before heard of to mend them by an appreciation, which most manifestly adds to the mischief without the Least Shadow of remedy. Except in the Single case of the original holder.

he says 7. discriminating & paying the original holders will be injurious to them, in [*that*] they will be injured by receiving their whole Debt, instead of a part of it.

his opinion Seems to be. 8. that 'tis a Great benefit to us to have the certificates rise. that we may have the blessing of paying abt. 10 Million Dollars to foreigners who have purchased certificates for abt. 2½ Million dollrs. which they paid to Americans for them i.e. to realize a clear profit of 7½ Million Dollrs. ~~clear profit~~ to them.

he says 9. that all advances of Congress to particular States, and all monies, articles, & expenditures furnishd. &c. by particular States, chargeable to Congress shod. be Liquidated to *Specie Vallue* but the payments made to the real Supporters of the war, Shall not be Liquidated to *Specie Vallue*, but the depreciated paper with which they were paid Shall be charged to them at *nominal Vallue* i.e. they Shall be charged 20/ for Every 2/6. paid to them.

he says. 10. the Wistern Lands Shod. be Sold at 20 Cts. ℔ acre, which will please or Gratify nobody, but will be a [*torn*] Sacrifice of that promise[*d*] Interest; but this is [*not the*] worst of it, it will cost the States more to defend the Extensive & thin Settled frontiers produced by this Measure, than all the money wh. the Sale wd. produce besides keeping up an Eternal fret with the Indians—our Settlements of the Western Lands ought to be pushed out in Close columns, which wd. not be Easily insulted, & might be Easily defended—& in that case the Sales wd. be very productive—in fine there is no End to Exceptions to that Result, 'tis really the most unnatural, wild & incoherent production that I ever See composed by any man who had any pretensions to Genius or even common Sense which will most certainly appear if any attempt is made to carry it into Execution, Right will operate Easy, but wrong can never be forced with[*ou*]t. infinite difficulty, & Little use.

I have no Exuse for this Long letter but that the subject is Extremely Important, in vita hominis nulla Cunctatio Larga.[2] you may shew it if you please to Mr. Sherman or any body. I Sent you some time Since. my Essay on seat of fed. Government & Shod. Send you my plea for the poor soldiers.[3] but the printer Says he has Send one to the delegates & Senators of Each State. I wish your Sentiments &c. if you have Time.

ALS, Johnson Papers, CtHi. Written from Philadelphia; franked; postmarked.

[1] In the eighteenth century, "Jesuitical logic" referred to a type of casuistry said to be practiced by the Jesuit order of Catholic priests.

[2] In the lifetime of a man there can be no profuse delay.

[3] For Webster's *Essay on the Seat of the Federal Government* and *Plea for the Poor Soldiers*, see Addendum, volume 22; the latter is calendared under 14 January, above.

[*Jeremiah Wadsworth,*] The Observer—No. XVII

The re-establishment of public credit, a measure of sound policy

In my last number I considered the re-establishment of public credit, as a measure of justice to the national and state creditors. It may also be inquired, is it a measure of policy? An advantage to the creditors is apparent; but will this advantage be equal to the injury which must happen to the people at large by such an attempt? If the measure will be mutually advantageous, all ground for questioning is gone, and having no alternative, we must proceed in the most wise and œconomical manner to provide funds; but if it will be destructive to the people, if justice and policy are opposed, the question yet remains to be new traced, and solved on political grounds.

There is an old adage, "honesty is the best policy" to which I have not known an exception. The wisdom which instituted the connexions, dependences and wants of society, doth not commonly, if ever, suffer an opposition between the moral duty and worldly good, either of individuals or communities. But as the question in consideration is too consequential to be risked on a maxim, more frequently spoken than felt, we must call up probable consequences to determine it.

In measures of policy, we find men have varying opinions; this chiefly arises from different degrees of information, and from a different limitation of the questions, on which a judgment is formed. Those who espouse various opinions, before they become warm in debate, ought mutually to communicate every information, and examine the whole extent and all the consequences of the question to be decided.

Is it good policy, or for the benefit of the people at large to restore American credit? Two persons of the same honesty, may give a different answer to this question, from the different limitations which they affix to it in their own minds. One considers its present operation, without regard to distant and national consequences, his education and connexions in business do not enable him to comprehend these, without very particular information; he appeals to the present moment only, and thinks it is better for himself and for a majority of his neighbours, not to pay, than it is to pay taxes; he knows not the purposes for which public credit are necessary, nor the great benefits which will accrue by its restoration, to agriculture, commerce, and manufactures; he sees no present danger from foreign enemies, and thinks not best to restore it. Another person is acquainted with these subjects, and knows that by avoiding a present small evil, we risk the danger of a thousand which are greater, and perhaps also our very national existence.

The consequences of a depreciated credit have been too recently felt, to need a very particular description. War is a complication of calamities to the best appointed nation; to one destitute of finance and credit, it is almost certain ruin. Your late war began in a sacred enthusiasm, breathed forth from heaven on the great body of people, which supplied a thousand wants, and gave a circulation to a paper without foundation. As this enthusiasm abated, the public distress began, and half the mischief we indured, arose more from want of credit, than from the policy or power of Great Britain. A nation who can pay only in promises, which are but half believed, loses a power over its own internal resources.

Was it not a want of credit which often nearly disbanded your army? Was it not this which obliged you to execute every measure in the most expensive manner? When you had brought into the field, a military force, of one third the appointed compliment? Was it not a want of credit which obliged you to create a more numerous and more devouring host of purchasers, and retainers on the public supplies, and even to convert your town officers into gentlemen of the public departments? Why was your army but half filled, which caused a protraction of the war? Not from a want of brave and hardy men; but by a want of credit. Hence arose the necessity of those vexatious calls on the militia, at a season of the year most ruinous to the farmer, and which was a greater drawback on his interest, than all the taxes he was called to pay. It is true these things are passed, and we hope never to see another war; the wish is pious and pacific, but wishing is not fighting, and will never defend our country. The principles of ambition and violence still exist in the world, and the nations have not yet beat their swords into ploughshares; little crossings of interest, may be strangely aggravated into bloody contention. The way to prevent war is a constant preparation to repel; so good a country as this without credit and a system of defence, is a strong temptation to the avarice and ambition of the world.

Should the United States by any unforeseen event be drawn into war, how without an established credit are they to make defence? The richest nation in Europe cannot support war without having recourse to credit, and much less can these States do it. Past events will not be soon forgot; and if your promises are not fulfilled in some reasonable way, where are the men who will again loan their property to the public? Where is the farmer or manufacturer who will sell you his provision or cloathing; or the soldier who will risk his life for paper, when they know it is the custom of the people, after danger is past, to forget their engagements? Had another war overtaken these States before the organization of our present government, defence would have been impossible; with a treasury destitute of money and credit, we could not have enlisted, cloathed and fed five thousand troops. Many private citizens were more capable of levying successful war than the whole union; a nest of pirates might have destroyed our whole trade, and laid many of our sea ports under contribution, and there was no public capacity to repel them. Our present government begins to be revered abroad, but deny them the means of establishing credit, and we sink back to ignominy and a state of danger.

Suffer me next, to recall your attention from the danger of a foreign war, without credit to support it; to consider the evils which may arise within ourselves from the same cause. A people destitute of credit are in emminent and constant danger of being enslaved, by such bold usurpers, as may wish to wrest from them their properties. By a late insurrection [*Shays' Rebellion*], New-England was actually threatened, and I pray that the other States may notice the warning. Tho' Massachusetts was the seat of insurgency, the same spirit wrought in the neighbouring States, and all wise men considered it as a common evil. The insurgents had doubtless some real grievances, which might have been redressed by a proper application; but instead of this they put themselves under the guidance of mad, base, and weak leaders. While we pitied the people we were obliged to condemn their cause. The serious consequences and ending of this affair are well known. Had that insurrection been headed by a man of ambition, intrigue, extensive popularity and wealth, it would probably have overturned the government of New-England, and laid a foundation for some kind of dominion most dangerous for our liberties.

Were it either prudent or necessary, I could name you many great characters in America, who, if virtue had not prevented, might have regalized themselves and families, and formed a civil constitution in violence, suited to their own interests, and to their adherents in success. The very same people who are jealous for their privileges, in the hour of consideration; at a time of madness and insurrection will give them all away; and in this very manner many free nations have lost their liberty. Had such a thing been attempted by one, or by a coalition of a few great and popular characters; neither Congress, nor the State assemblies, who were wholly destitute of credit, could have repelled them. It ought to be a first maxim of policy with a free republic, to preserve an unspotted faith, by which they may command their own resources, either against foreign invasion or domestic insurrection, and purchase foreign assistance.

The terrors of a despotic prince, and the influence of a nobility devoted to his will, may with little credit, draw out the resources of his kingdom; but I trust the American republic, will never have such terrors or nobility; she must depend on the virtue and information of her citizens, and the purity of her national character. Patriotism is a sacred name! And I believe there is more of it in this, than any other country, and the way to preserve it is to uphold national credit. Patriotism doth not consist in a few men giving their all for public purposes, in the hour of danger, and without an expectation of being reimbursed: If it doth, wait to the time of trial, and an experiment will prove that we have few patriots. To be willing to contribute a just proportion, and pay an equal share in the public expence—to be honest and assist our government in being honest; is to be a patriot.

A fixed credit is the only means for œconomy in national expences, which is another reason for its re-establishment.

Certain expences to a large amount are unavoidable in every nation; and these will be doubled on the people, as they are obliged to make payment, by a lax and depreciated credit. I have inculcated in my former numbers, that high nominal taxation imposed on the principles of depreciation, is eventually paid by a great part of the people nearly equal to silver and gold. A suspicious credit always operates against the people; all bargaining for the public is on disadvantageous terms; the man who deals with them considers a risk, and acts from the same motive as he makes hazard in a lottery; a derangement runs thro' all public officers; it prevents responsibility and punctuality in all national concerns; and when an honest man has the care of the people's interests, he expects to manage them with loss; and an idea is gradually spread in the minds of men, that there is no evil in robbing the public.

Foreign nations, and merchants are eagle-eyed to discern the debilitated power of the country, and are not afraid to offend its majesty by abusing its subjects—commerce languishes, produce is low, and the farmer eventually pays the bill of national loss.

If the national debt be neglected, still there must be provision made for certain expences; an infeebled credit will greatly increase these, and I believe to as great a sum, as would be necessary to fund the debt honorably, and support all other expences on the principles of a punctual regard to public faith.

A man who is slack, and has obtained a reputation of being worse than his promise, lives poor at great expence; it is the same with a nation, only in greater degree. The false man may be compelled by law, but the slack nation cannot; these things are considered by those who deal with them, and they are treated in character.

Tho' my paper be already too long, there is one among many other considerations, which I cannot omit mentioning.

A violation of national promises, or tardiness in fulfilling them, hath a destructive influence on the morality of the people.

When the legislature of a nation sport with their engagements, every lesser corporation catches the same spirit and practice. The private citizen argues in self justification, if our lawgivers violate the promises of a nation; if the greatest and most informed men will defraud for the public, because they have power; I may do the same with impunity when an occasion presents. A depreciated public credit in its various operations, for a series of years, hath done more to disseminate these dangerous sentiments, than all the institutions of science and religion have done to retard them.

Let government beware of that corruption in principle and manners, which by increasing, will prove its ruin.

[Hartford, Connecticut] *American Mercury*, 1 February. For information on The Observer series, its authorship, and reprintings, see the location note to The Observer, No. 1, 12 October, above.

OTHER DOCUMENTS

William Constable to Garrett Cottringer. FC:lbk, Constable-Pierrepont Collection, NN.

Has no doubt that Hamilton's proposed funding system will be adopted.

Andrew Craigie to Daniel Parker. FC:dft, Craigie Papers, MWA. Sent on the London packet. The letter is undated but must have been written between 1 and 6 February because it mentions that Hamilton's report is to be taken up on "Monday next," which was 8 February, the date the House agreed to on 28 January.

Morris has advised William Constable "not to authorise" a purchase of the federal debt, at the present; encloses a copy of Hamilton's report on public credit, to be shared with Samuel Rogers; there will be opposition to it from supporters of six percent and three percent interest, respectively; Rogers will inform Parker of Morris's "Opinion respecting the intentions of Goverment"; Morris is surprised that no further letters of credit have been sent from Europe and that Roger's letters "*seem* very little acquainted with the nature of his Negotiations abroad."

John Debrett to Thomas Lloyd. ALS, Lloyd Papers, American Catholic Historical Society, Philadelphia. Written from Piccadilly, London.

Has not heard of an intention to reprint *CR* in London, nor does he think it would serve any useful purpose.

Michael Kaltessen to Pierce Butler. ALS, Butler Papers, PHi. Written from Charleston, South Carolina; postmarked.

Office seeking: commandant of Fort Johnson, the South Carolina legislature having resolved to instruct its congressional delegation to offer it to the federal government.

Robert Morris to Gouverneur Morris. ALS, G. Morris Papers, NNC. Place to which addressed not indicated. A coded message appears at the end of the letter. Encloses a copy of Robert Morris's letter of 2 January.

Left Philadelphia on 18 January, and his family was well; "I saw your Uncle *Isaac* [*Gouverneur*] this Morning"; Robert's hosts, the Constables, have just lost their newborn but Mrs. Constable is recovering "and I hope soon to see her down stairs"; Jefferson has not arrived yet; "my patience is put to a pretty severe Tryal by this incident, as you may readily suppose"; is again engaged in the settlement of his accounts with the Secret Committee "and have no doubt but this desirable object will be Accomplished during the present Session of Congress, this business with that in the Senate Occupy my time & attention very fully."

Wilhem and Jon Willink to John Adams. ALS, Adams Family Manuscript Trust, MHi. Written from Amsterdam.

Hopes Adams will be "a favourable interpretor" of their recent transaction involving the transfer to their "house" of part of the United States' debt to France.

Oliver Wolcott, Jr. to Oliver Wolcott, Sr. ALS, Wolcott Papers, CtHi. Addressed to Litchfield, Connecticut; marked "Paid." For a partial text, see *Wolcott* 1:37.

Hamilton's report on public credit "meets with as much approbation as could have been expected"; some think the interest rate too high, others think it so low that the creditors will not subscribe; "Many apprehend that it will tend to a consolidation of the Government': thinks it will be adopted without any substantial variation.

Hopley Yeaton to John Langdon. ALS, Langdon Papers, NhPoA. Written from Portsmouth, New Hampshire.

Is happy to hear that Langdon is in good health; reports on state government proceedings, as Langdon requested; Langdon's family in good health.

TUESDAY, 2 FEBRUARY 1790

Cool (Johnson)

William Ellery to Benjamin Huntington

I have received your letter of the 23d. of last month with the News papers and thank you for them. I have written two letters to you before this, the receipt whereof please to acknowledge in your next if you should have received them.

The Secretaries of the Treasury and War have exerted themselves and displayed great abilities in their reports if the goodness of systems is proportionate to their strengths. I have not had [*lined out*] an opportunity of forming judgment of them other wise as yet and when I shall have studied them I am not sure that I shall understand them. Military systems I am not acquainted with, and finance is of a nature so complicated that to comprehend it requires more real physical skill and mathematical knowledge than I am possessed of. I have run over that part of Genl. Knox's plan which is contained in the papers you sent me and am so apprehensive that it may alarm the Quakers in our State that I shall not offer it to the printer for publication. Military service even by substitute you know is repugnant to their religious sentiments, a plan therefore which requires personal service must greatly alarm them; and the people in general have been so long unaccustomed to military discipline that a plan less severe would I imagine at first shock their feelings. There has not been a training on this Island since the peace, and we are Islanders who are exposed to the insults of any petty pirate, for the want of discipline, and the proper apparatus of defence are unable to resist even a feeble invader. The national defence, as well as that of each State, ought to be provided for, and the militia of the country must be its defence, for notwithstanding the mass of opinion in Europe may be in favour of standing armies, I presume that it will not be the sentiment of Congress. But what institutions would be the most beneficial I leave to the wisdom of Federal Councils. That establishment which would best answer the purpose with the least expence, and the least injury to the spirit and temper of the people would appear to me to be the most eligible.

I have read the summary of Mr. Hamiltons report,[1] and I like the honest ground he proceeds upon. The establishment of public credit is certainly right as this renders the payment of the interest of the public debt necessary, and to execute this sufficient funds must be established; but whether it would be best that Congress should assume the State debts incurred by the late war or not I am not at present able to determine. That this measure would promote peace in this State I have no doubts—for there is in this State a considerable sum which has not been delivered into the Treasury for paper, and the holders of it will be always striving to obtain an administration that will more secure them from the forfeiture of their securities and make provision for an honest payment of them, and there will be a party who will always strenuously oppose them; so that unless the State debts are assumed by the U.S. we shall probably be forever in hot water. To procure a fund for this purpose without distressing and impeding commerce, which would eventually defeat the fund, is the great difficulty; but without doubt the System of the Secry. of the Treasury has provided a fund which will not interrupt the commerce, nor hurt the feelings of the citizens of the U.S. The business of funding debts, annuities, and tontines we have not been used to; and notwithstanding any clamour against taxation we have never as yet paid any worth mentioning.

In short we have been so little accustomed to system, and have lived so much at loose, that we are scared out of [*lined out*] our wits at the sight of a long military, or financeering report. The former looks like a confounded great standing army threatening us with slavery, and the latter like a vast despot who fiercely demands the earnings of our industry, and will involve us in poverty and distress.

Time and conversation will calm our apprehensions and we shall in a few years be no more afraid of either of them than [*illegible*] Siberian is of a Tartar.

We have long been acquainted with the military abilities of the Secry. of war, and it affords me much satisfaction to see at the head of the Treasury a gentleman who appears to be so attentive to the business of his department, and so able to perform it.

I have given to Mr. Partridge the best account of the state of parties here, that I can obtain at present. In the course of the next week I shall be able to determine what will be the result of the Convention. The Delegates will I am afreid will be nearly equal. I hope the majourity will be in favour of the New Constitution. If the Feds should fail it will not be from a want of the most strenuous exertion.

ALS, Benjamin Huntington Correspondence, 1772–1790, R-Ar. Written from Newport, Rhode Island.

[1] Summary View of the Report of the Secretary of the Treasury, 20 January, above.

Oliver Ellsworth to George Washington

Should you think proper to nominate a person from the State of Connecticut to the office of a Judge in the Western Territory, in the room of General [*Samuel Holden*] Parsons, permit me to name for your consideration Majr. William Judd; of whom you probably have some knowledge from his having had the honor of serving in the late American Army. The appointment would be acceptable to him, and I beleive his services would be satisfactory to the Publick. He was liberally educated and regularly bred to the profession of the law, in which he has had the advantage of near twenty years practice. He is respectable in his profession, of a fair moral character and active in his zeal for the honor and interest of the United States.

AT, Washington Papers, DLC.

Daniel Hiester to John Nicholson

I have recd. Yours by Mr. [*Francis*] Baily and am in hopes he will succeed in his application. Judge Burke is one (Indeed I believe Chairman) of his Committee and very much in his favour, the report will be made tomorrow.[1]

It has been mentioned to me that the Accounts of our State, have not all been transmitted Yet to this place for settlement with the united States. the time of sending them for that purpose elapsed some days ago, but as the Commissioners from one or two States that have their Accots. here, but have them not in that order that they can finally deliver them they are keeping the Board of Commissioners employd (or at least are craving more time). If therefore Your remaining Accounts can be send on within a few days, they will probably be recd. upon the footing of those I mentioned and make a direct Application to Congress for admitting them Unnecessary—such an application I wish on more than one accot. could be avoided.

We have nothing new here that is of any Consequence. Yesterday I moved for a Committee to bring in a bill further to provide for the Invalid Pensioners of the United States [*HR-80*]. If from Your Acquaintance with the situation of those unfortunate persons You will be so good as to furnish me with any usefull remarks You will oblige me.

I have now to beg You will pardon my suggestions respecting the accounts, and believe them to proceed (as they really do) from the best intentions of Your friend.

ALS, Gratz Collection, PHi. Addressed to "Comptroller General &c. &c.," Philadelphia; franked; postmarked; received 4 February.

[1]For the background and legislative history of the Bailey Bill [HR-44], see *DHFFC* 8:73–84.

William Maclay to John Nicholson

I write You many letters, but this You must Submit to, as I want, all the information You can give. pray how much is the State Debt of Pennsylvania? and of what articles does it consist? let me be well informed on this Subject. It is very possible that some of the delegation may be furnished with this account. I wish you, however to furnish me with it also.

The amount of Certificates taken up by the land office, will also be agreeable. in short I cannot pretend to say what Paper estimate I may want. I would therefore wish for all you can give. it is thought that the burthen of debate will be in the house of Representatives. but even admitting this, I do not wish to be an Idle Spectator.

ALS, Gratz Collection, PHi. Addressed to "Comptroller Genl. of Pennsylvania"; franked; postmarked; received 5 February; "promised to find" in answer of 7 February.

Nicholas Pike to Benjamin Goodhue

I am requested by the friends of the Person [*Anna Treat*] mentioned in the enclosed Petition[1] to beg the favor of your presenting & enforcing it with your Influence. They inform me that General Knox is able to give all the necessary information upon the Subject.

I am not acquainted with the Old Lady: but am informed She is a very worthy Person, & is now suffering with the extremity of Poverty, & has no friends able to assist her. I am so well acquainted with your benevolent & Philanthropic Disposition, that, in order to your assisting the miserable & afflicted, I am sensible you only need to have pointed out in what manner you can do it, I shall therefore say no more on the Subject, only that the Person in Question is an Inhabitant of Haverhill in our County.

Permit me, my dear Friend, to propose a Case of Conscience—Suppose a Person, who was a zealous promoter of the late Revolution, had, early in the War, loaned the Public all he was worth, relying on their promise to pay him honestly at the Rate of 6 ℔ Cent. &c. Has any Body of Men, however respectable, a *constitutional* Right to pay that debt, or any part of it, in any other Commodity than what they promised to pay or to reduce the Rate of Interest, without the Creditor's Consent? You will perhaps suspect I am interested in the Matter. I confess it, & possibly my Self-Interest may have blinded me; for I cannot conceive of the affirmation.

In 1776 I sold Goods to Congress to the Amount of more than £1000, & soon afterwards, at the Importunity of our Genl. Court, I loaned them all the Money I could possibly raise, which consolidated at about £550: As I was not then, nor have been since in a Money-getting way, only about sufficient to support myself, I depended on those Sums to support me provided I should survive my Ability to provide for my family by my Labour.

But we have it here that it is in contemplation to pay off part of the Debt in Western Lands, & not only so, but to reduce the Rate of Interest; but I cannot think Congress will do it, unless they are fully satisfied they have a constitutional Right to it.

I do not write this in a complaining Temper; for that would ill become either a Revolutionist or Federalist, both of which I profess myself to be; but

I wish to be better informed, than I am at present, respecting the Justice & Constitutionality of such a Plan.

I hope you will pardon my frequent Intrusions.

ALS, Letters to Goodhue, NNS. Written from Newburyport, Massachusetts.

[1] For background on the petition of Anna Treat, see *DHFFC* 7:257–58.

Alexander White to Horatio Gates

I write this under circumstances which prevents my saying more than that I expect it will accompany the Report of the Secretary at War on the subject of the Militia, which I send for the perusal, and ad animadversion of yourself, and General [*Adam*] Stephen I have had no letters yet from you, and few from my District.

What is become of Grayson.[1]

Have you had any Winter—the ground here had scarcely been covered with Snow, and very little frost.

ALS, Emmet Collection, NN. Addressed to "Traveller's Rest," Berkeley County, West Virginia; franked; postmarked.

[1] Grayson was too ill to get to New York for the second session of the FFC and died at Dumfries, Virginia, on 12 March.

New York Correspondent

Since I wrote you last I have seen Mr. [*Andrew*] ELLICOTT, the Geographer of the United States, who is lately returned from his survey of the Western Boundary of the cessions of New-York and Massachusetts. To effect the business he was obliged to go into the British territory. There are some facts ascertained by him, which are interesting to the people of America, and I therefore communicate them. He says, it is evident that the intention of the British is manifest not at present to relinquish the Posts which they hold within the United States.[1] This I presume will not be a foundation for WAR, for that nation will not, in my opinion, be so frantic as to attempt to put their possessions in America on the event of a war with this country. At present our Government is unsettled, and WHETHER IT WILL FURNISH DURATION OR THE CONTRARY, WILL DEPEND ON THE RESULT OF THE PRESENT SESSION OF CONGRESS. Should the measures adopted be such as are directed by wisdom and sound policy, prudence will dictate to the Minister of Great Britain the necessity of abandoning her stations within the limits of this Government.

Mr. ELLICOTT relates another fact, for which I do not feel any pain. It is, that the settlers on the west side of the Lakes,[2] (a great proportion of whom are emigrants from the United States) experience every species of misery that can be conceived; that he was for many days incapable of procuring a single mouthful of meat or bread, and was obliged to subsist on potatoes alone.

All letters from Rhode-Island announce that the adoption of the American Constitution by that state has now become certain, and that all ideas of serious opposition are abandoned. Governour [*John*] *Collins* has written the PRESIDENT a letter highly federal, which has been communicated to Congress,[3] the probable result of which will be a further indulgence to Rhode-Island, 'till the [*ratification*] Convention of that state may have time for deliberation.

The advocates for a discrimination between the original holders and purchasers of Publick Securities, will I trust be very few. In fact, every principle, if not of justice, of sound policy, is against it. The great question is, SHALL THE DEBTS OF THE INDIVIDUAL STATES BE ASSUMED? THIS MEASURE IS SO INDISPENSABLE TO THE BENEFICIAL OPERATIONS OF THE GOVERNMENT, SO ESSENTIAL TO THE WELFARE OF THE PEOPLE, AND SO INSEPERABLE FROM THE EXECUTION OF JUSTICE, THAT, INDEPENDENT OF IT, I WOULD NEVER CONSENT TO ANY SYSTEM OF FUNDING WHATEVER.

Two facts I have ascertained since I came here, in which the interests of the United States in general, and the eastern in particular, are interested—1st, That the coarse woollen and linen cloths which have this year been exported from Connecticut to the Southern states, have there a decided preference given to them, both on account of the quality and price, to European manufactures of the same kind—and 2dly, That the quantities exported have been considerable. It is however true, that the want of great capitals in our dealers, will to a considerable degree balance what would be otherwise the natural effect of that preference.

[Stockbridge, Massachusetts] *Western Star*, 9 February; reprinted at Boston (partial) and Pittsfield, Massachusetts; Providence, Rhode Island; Norwich, Connecticut; New York City (*NYDA*, 16 February); Philadelphia and York, Pennsylvania; and Winchester, Virginia.

[1] Although obligated to withdraw all its military from American territory under the Treaty of Paris of 1783, Great Britain maintained a number of frontier outposts along the New York State and Northwest Territory boundaries with Canada: Ogdensburg, Oswego, and Niagara, New York; Erie, Pennsylvania; Sandusky, Ohio; and Detroit. They were not wholly relinquished until 1796, under Jay's Treaty of 1794.

[2] Ellicott would have encountered numerous settlements of displaced American loyalists in his journey west of Niagara to that part of Ontario, Canada, occupying the isthmus between lakes Ontario and Erie.

[3] Dated 18 January 1790, the letter was sent to Congress by the President on 28 January; the letter and the enclosed act of the Rhode Island legislature are printed in *DHFFC* 6:1539–41.

OTHER DOCUMENTS

John Adams to Benjamin Rush. Alexander Biddle, *Old Family Letters* (Philadelphia, 1892), pp. 54–55. Place to which addressed not indicated.
    Disagrees with Rush's proposals arguing against education in Latin and Greek; thanks for introduction of Andrew Brown "to whom I wish success"; congratulations on new state constitution; regrets the course of the French Revolution.

William Constable to Alexander Ellice. FC:lbk, Constable-Pierrepont Collection, NN.
    When Hamilton's funding plan is taken up in the House on 9 February, "it will undergo considerable Animadversions & experience great Opposition—but must in the End be adopted."

Tench Coxe and Nalbro Frazier to Thomas Hartley. FC:lbk, Coxe Papers, PHi. Written from Philadelphia.
    Asks to receive from Parker and forward to them the amount of an enclosed one hundred dollar note, in Philadelphia bank notes.

William Few to Governor Edward Telfair. No copy known; mentioned as read on 17 March in Georgia Executive Council Journal, G-Ar.

John Langdon to Joshua Martin. No copy known; acknowledged in Martin to Langdon, 12 February.

John Langdon to Hopley Yeaton. No copy known; acknowledged in Yeaton to Langdon, 12 February.

James Madison to Edward Carrington. ALS, Roberts Autograph Collection, PHC. Place to which addressed not indicated. For the full text, see *PJM* 13:14–15, which identified the recipient based on the letter's reference to federal marshals and the census, the subject of the non-extant letter Madison wrote Carrington on 24 January.
    Has sent to James Innes one copy each of Hamilton's report on public credit and Knox's plan for the militia, with a request he share them with Carrington; sending multiple copies would add too much to the bulk of the mail; it is "impossible" to know the fate of Hamilton's report; regarding Knox's plan, "the expence, if nothing else, is a millstone about it"; reports no progress on the Enumeration Act as it relates to federal

marshals; John Blair and Edmund Randolph arrived the day before, "and the [*Supreme*] Court to which they belong was opened to day."

John S. Sherburne to John Langdon. ALS, Langdon Papers, NhPoA. Written from Portmouth, New Hampshire.
  Thanks for the newspapers; forwards the *New Hampshire Spy*; reports on state politics; "Let me hear from you as often as possible."

George Washington, Diary. Washington Papers, MiD-B.
  Bland visited the President.

[Litchfield, Connecticut] *Weekly Monitor*, 2 February.
  Parodies Williamson's recent attack against the study of foreign languages, particularly Greek and Latin, by claiming that that branch of learning is like "imported articles of finery" that only distract citizens while "our great business is to plant corn and feed pork," and by pointing to innumerable instances of individuals in public service who were ignorant of the sciences.

From New York. *NYDG*, 3 February.
  The Supreme Court met, with "some of the Members of Congress, and a number of respectable citizens, also" in attendance.

Letter from Boston. *GUS*, 17 February; reprinted at Wilmington, Delaware.
  Hamilton's report on public credit is "a most masterly performance," which "will be generally acceptable when it is rightly understood," "his reasoning *** is incontestible"; "should Congress adopt his plans *** the credit of this country will eclipse all the boasted powers of Europe."

Letter from New York. [Portland, Maine] *Cumberland Gazette*, 22 February; reprinted at Boston.
  "The blustering of the big, bombastick word thrumster [*John Gardiner*], from Pownalborough, against the Professors of the Law, is here considered, as an attack against the federal Government over the backs of the Lawyers—and is reprobated accordingly. I hope the Legislature will treat his innovations as they deserve—and rescue your rulers from the imputations which they lie under of attending to the rhapsodies of this monstrous dealer in repetition, nonsense and utopianism."

WEDNESDAY, 3 FEBRUARY 1790

Very Cold (Johnson)

Josiah Burr to Jeremiah Wadsworth

Your two favours pr. post have come to hand & agreebly to your desire I have enclosed an Answer to Mr. Ames' Queries, an history of the linen business for the Secretary of the treasury & an Invoice of the Osnabrigs[1] in the hands of Mess[er]s. Watson & Greenleaf. I hope they may be sold so as to make you payment in part.
***

I have tried but cannot find any Metheglin[2] to be sold in town equal to that I sent Mrs. [*Mehitable Russell*] Wadsworth. I have still in my Cellar about two dozen of the same kind, half of which is at your service & shall be put up & sent to you by the first boat.

Your extract from the laws of N[*ew*]. York will convince any one that Messs. [*Nathaniel*] Gorham & [*Oliver*] Phelps can make no valid conveyance of Lands in the state of N. York except they & their wives execute the deeds within that state &c.—their conveyance to me therefore is no better than a *bond for* a deed & does not give a clear & valid title; in this situation I look up to you for advice. Messs. Gorham & Phelps cannot, will not surely hesitate in giving a moment when the thing is clearly proved that the deeds executed here are not sufficient.

I am sensible that Mr. P[*helps*]. is fond of maneuvring & that it is almost impossible to keep him to a fixed point in any thing—but this [*is*] a matter that does not admit of evasion.

I have written to them urging an imediate meeting of the company & as soon as it is convened I shall propose to remove into York State for the purpose of completing the deeds, if you think of any thing more that can be done to expedite the business, I will thank you to acquaint me—They are now at Boston endeavouring to negociate with the general Court.[3] the report of the Secretary of the Treasury proposing to Congress an Assumption of all the state Debts, will doubtless influence the decision for if all the state debts be assumed by Congress, Massachusetts would be more benefited by taking back the proffered lands & reserving them for the future exigencies of their government, than by applying them at the present time to the reduction of their state debt.

Should the proposals of Messs. Gorham & Phelps be accepted by the general Court, or should they dispose of the unlaidout lands to any person or persons we then should have a clear right to insist on an imediate location of our whole share, but should they not, we [*lined out*] have no right at present except to our proportion of what is already laid out, & shall not probably obtain more without making a sacrifice of some part.

P. S. The paper designed for the secretary of Treasury is not directed not being much used to the courtly stile I feared being guilty of some impropriety in the address, will you be kind enough to supply the deficiency.

ALS, Wadsworth Papers, CtHi. Written from New Haven, Connecticut.

[1] A type of linen named for Osnabrück, Germany, a center of the linen trade since the Middle Ages.

[2] A spiced honey based liquor used as a restorative.

[3] Nathaniel Gorham and Oliver Phelps were renegotiating with the Massachusetts legislature or General Court the terms of their 1788 purchase of the six million acre Genessee Tract in western New York State. (Under a 1786 agreement, Massachusetts held title while New York retained sovereignty over the land.) The renegotiation was necessitated by that winter's dramatic rise in the market value of the state's securities, with which the two land speculators had intended to pay the £300,000 purchase price in three annual instalments at drastically depreciated levels (the equivalent of $175,000, or three cents an acre). After threatening to default on their last two payments, Gorham and Phelps brokered a plan with the Massachusetts legislature in March, returning the western two-thirds of the tract in exchange for their undisputed title to the remaining eastern third (*Westward Expansion*, pp. 253–54). For further information about the Gorham-Phelps tract, in which Wadsworth and Sedgwick were involved, see *DHFFC* 8:191–96.

Jonathan Davis and Son to George Thatcher

As Inhabitants & People concerned in Trade on this River [*Kennebeck*], we take the liberty of Soliciting your attention to a Short statement of the Apparent partial Injuries which the Settlers of our Infant Country, has and will sustain, by the operation of that part of the Collection Act [*HR-11*] so called which prohibits Foreign Vessels, from delivering their Cargoes at any Port on Kennebeck, and we can we beleive, venture to assure you, that our sentiments on this Subject are perfectly Congenial to the opinion of the Inhabitants in General of this River, and of far the greatest part of this Country—The resort of Foreign Vessels to Kennebeck has been very considerable for this Thirty Years past, except when prohibited, before the late War there were annually one or two large Mast Ships, loaded here & a number of Timber Ships, they came out generally with a Ballast of Salt or Coals a small assortment of Goods & some Cash, with those Articles they procured Cargoes of Lumber from the People of the River, who were much benefitted by the trade, since the War several circumstances has contributed, in some measure to prevent so many from coming here, foreigners has been cautious of adventuring this way on account of the unsettled state of the Trade of this Country in general, and for two Years a State prohibitary law prevented their coming intirely[1] since the removal of that difficulty, the trade with Foreigners has been gradually appreciating, there has been every Season Three or four foreigners Loaded here, and from June 1789 to the time when the Collection Law began its operation, there was seven English Vessels, entered & loaded at this Port, and probably some were prevented in the latter part of the Season, hearing of the prohibition it has we understand been supposed that the allowing Foreign Vessels to unlade at Wisscasset, would accommodate the People of this River, and it has been suggested, that but few foreigners have ever frequented here compared with the number which loads at Wisscasset with respect to the first supposition, we would observe that Cargoes of Lumber being in themselves of but little value at the places, from which they are first Exported, will render the expence of Transporting it to Wisscassett, or of a Vessell going first to Wisscassett and then coming round here after a cargo, such as would effectually preclude us from any great share in a Trade with Foreigners while our Neighbours on Sheeps Cut [*Sheepscot River*], would have the most manifest advantage over us. with respect to the prevailing Idea that Wisscasset, has been & would ever be (admitting the Laws to be equal) the Port to which Foreign Vessels would principally resort, we concieve it Groundless, and that Experience will prove the falsity of it we recollect only two Vessels under Foreign Colours, that loaded at Wisscasset during the last Season, and it is a fact that previous to the War, there never was an equal number loaded there as here & of those foreign Vessels that usually loaded there, the Cargoes have been generally procured in the first instance on Kennebeck.

The Lumber procured on this River, Exceeds by far in quantity what is procured in or adjacent to any other Port in this Commonwealth, and the cutting of it becomes equally the Interest & resource of new Settlers, of which there annually arrives great numbers on this River. The cutting of the Lumber answers them the double purpose of clearing the land, and furnishing them with Immediate Supplies of provisions, which generally they must otherwise suffer for, they are now deprived of the most profitable means of disposing of their Lumber and in case of their Transporting it to Wisscassett for sale the expence of such transportation is allowed to be equal, to one fifth part of its original value, besides the additional Ill convenience of brin[g]ing the goods received, for the sale of the Lumber back to this place, which must very considerably, enhance the prices of heavy Goods, such as Salt Coals provisions &c.—We have had the honor of seeing a Letter from you to the Honorable Wm. Lithgow Junr. Esquire, bearing date Augt. 22d. last,[2] in which you say that the designating particular Ports for Foreigners to unload at was done in order to guard more effectually against the Revenues being defrauded, but as this observation respects Kennebeck it appears to be the prevailing opinion that it will produce no good effect, and possibly a very contrary one to that Expected. having now a Port of Entry and delivery for American Vessels from foreign ports, and a Port of Entry only for Foreign Bottoms. It will become the Interest of the Inhabitants of this River, to endeavor to conceal any Goods which a Foreign Vessel, might have on board arriving here, which Goods might otherwise prevent her stay, and consequently deprive us, of the benefit of her purchasing a Cargo. you observe to the Honble. Wm. Lithgow Junr. that when the present objections are fairly examined, you presume they will not have the weight, as was first imagined, as the restriction is only on Vessels coming with Goods, for Vessels owned by Foreigners may enter at Bath & go to any place on the River & take in a Cargo.

But we have scarcely an Instance where a foreign Vessel comes out without some Cargo (never indeed with one of any considerable amount) as the purchase of a load of Lumber requires but a small sum. and indeed the small [*lined out*] value of a Cargo which could be procured here, and the trifling freight which Lumber generally pays either to the West Indies or Europe has always rendered it necessary to make some advantage on the sale of the Articles to purchase the Cargo with. and also that the Vessel should be subject to no expence in removal from one place to the other Therefore we do not concieve, that our having a Port of Entry for Foreign Vessels & not of delivery will be of any considerable advantage as we think there will scarcely be an instance of a Vessels coming from a Foreign Port, for a Cargo, without any Goods, nor will the object of procuring a Cargo of Lumber on this River, be sufficient to induce them, to come here after previously unloading their Goods at any Port of delivery—You observe in your Letter already referred to, that when you found that Bath & Wisscassett would not both be made Ports of Delivery for Foreigners, you thought from the present state of those Ports & from their situation to the Country & to each other, that it would best accommodate the Merchants & Country round about the two Ports to permit Vessels owned by Foreigners to unlade at the latter.

In answer we beg leave to say that we do not conceive that Wisscasset, being a Port of Delivery will accommodate the Merchants at all, nor the Inhabitants of this River in general, but in a very but in a small degree. The Inhabitants living in Sheeps Cut River will have such evident advantages over them in the sale of their Lumber & the Transportation of such Articles as they will receive in payment for it as will no doubt prevent any considerable trade from being carried on between the People of Kennebeck and Forcigners unlading & arriving at Wisscassett.

The Country on the Banks & adjacent to Kennebank depending on supplies from the Vessels that has heretofore frequented there is very large & the Inhabitants numerous, while on the contrary Sheepscut River is but of a Small extent to its source, and the People but few in number, compared with the extent & population of this River, and the numerous Settlements formed adjacent to its Banks.

We have now Sir explained to you, as far as in our power the sentiments of the People of Kennebeck River as well as our own on the subject of the prohibition alluded to and must beg your excuse for troubling you with this lengthy detail. convinced as we are of the importance of your time; The propriety & expediency of a Petition from the Inhabitants of this River to Congress, has been repeatedly suggested, it has hitherto been neglected, on the presumption that an alteration would be made in our favor at the present Session without it, by allowing Vessels owned by Foreigners to discharge their Cargoes at Bath, it has been mentioned as your own opinion that such an alteration would without Doubt be easily effected.

Should you Sir notwithstanding conceive such an alteration as proper and find a necessity for a Petition to enforce it we will venture to assert, that there would be scarcely a Man in this Country, who would not chearfully subscribe his name to it, nor an Inhabitant on this River—who would not feel himself particularly interested in its success.

ALS, Wolcott Papers, CtHi. Written from Bath, Maine.

---

[1] In June 1785 Massachusetts passed a navigation act to encourage American shipping: no products of the state could be exported in vessels owned in whole or in part by British subjects, and all foreign vessels were required to pay tonnage duties. This discrimination against foreign shipping was suspended in 1786 after the French protested to Congress that it was a violation of the Treaty of Amity and Commerce and other states refused to join Massachusetts in its attempt to retaliate against anti-American British trade laws (Merrill Jensen, *The New Nation* [New York, 1950], pp. 292–93, 297).

[2] Thatcher to William Lithgow, Jr., 22 August 1789, has not been located.

Elias Hasket Derby to Benjamin Goodhue

I would express to you my feelings on an affair that more immediately concerns me than any other Merchant in this State. If I say too much on the subject I hope you will pardon me, but if what I say is just I doubt not you will give me a candid hearing & endeavour to have such provision made as may quiet my fears. I have one ship that sail'd last season for Canton to load with Teas for this market, & I have two more that are gone thither, contrary to my expectations, from Bombay. There are likewise two other ships belonging to this State gone from the Isle of France [*Mauritius*] to Canton; all of which, if no accident happen to them, will load with Teas for this State, & will be here, I should suppose, about June next. Those vessels with what I hear are coming to the other States will make eleven or twelve sail, which in my estimation will bring Tea enough for two years consumption at least.

I do not expect, nor wish to be free from paying my *full* proportion of the public burden, but I do wish that the impost may be regulated in such a manner that it may not prove ruinous to me. Suppose that 2000 chests of Bohea Tea are the yearly consumption, and there are 4000 at market how can the Importer raise the price of it in proportion to the extraordinary impost talk'd of, unless he can reship a part of it to another market, and as I know of no other, I think he will be oblig'd to pay the Impost out of his own pocket. There were but two of the above vessels belonging to this State design'd for Canton, when they sail'd from hence—but owing to their making ruinous voyages to the Hither Indies, they took freights for Canton. The Merchant in this trade is not on a footing with his neighbour in another, & I do think the trade ought to be consider'd in a different light. The Impost is laid since those vessels sail'd, & their owners cannot make the least alterations in his importations, which is not the case in the European or West-India trade. Had the Merchants on the Continent have been aware of the intended impost I do believe that at least 6 of the 12 Sail now gone to Canton would not have gone thither—& if they had their orders would have been quite different from what they were, & their Captains would have taken freights for Europe, rather than ~~have~~ ruin their owners by coming here. It is generally said the consumer will pay the Impost, this may be true where the quantity of goods imported is less than the demand, but when it greatly exceeds the demand the Importer must pay it himself. I do believe that should the Ship arrive from Canton to this market the Tea could not be sold for the intended impost & one half its cost in Canton. I will not trouble you further on this subject, trusting that some thing will be done, either by delaying the time of the Impost's taking place, or ~~something~~ that will put me on a footing with my Neighbours in another trade.

At the time of Lexington battle, I loan'd to Government a large proportion of the supplies for the Army & took their obligations for those articles at their specie value, which obligations I have now by me, and it appears to me that those debts are as justly due to me as those on any private contract. To have the foreign debt on a better footing than the domestick, or to reduce the interest to 3 or 4 pr. Cent without the consent of the holders of the public securities will not in my opinion tend to raise the credit of Government, & I believe that I speak the sentiments of the public creditors in general in this quarter. With respect to the public securities I am sensible that I must share the same fate with the other creditors of Government & for that reason will say no more on the subject but leave it to some one of better abilities. I have also written to Mr. Ames & the above is a copy of my letter to him. Accept my thanks for the deposition you sent me.

LS, Letters to Goodhue, NNS; FC:lbk, Derby Shipping Papers, MSaE.

John Hobby to George Thatcher

I received your very obliging letter of the 17th. Ult. for which please to accept my sincere thanks, and be asured the friendly disposition you have been kind enough to manifest for the promotion of my interest relative to the probable determination of Congress on the interesting subject of Finance demands the warmest expressions of gratitude. As a public creditor I must confess I feel not a little disappointed to find the Secretaries report to Congress respecting our revennue so unfavorable & inadequate to the demands of the public for the regular payment of the annual interest of her debt, especially at the low rate of 4 ℀ Ct. The effects of which I fear will be extremely fatal to that class of Citizens who have either loaned their Monies or become creditors to the public by the most excruciating sufferings in her service—as to *speculators* I suppose they, in general will not be materially affected in *their* interest wheather Congress fund the National Debt at 3 Or 6 ℀ Ct. But ~~with~~ if 3 ℀ Ct. only shoud. finally be established, I fear those of us who have *earned our bread by the sweat of our brow*[1] must sit down contented at most with one half the nominal amount of our demands—however you will please to pardon the freedom with which I have delivered my sentiments on a subject to which I woud. not pretend to the least acquaintance—and altho I feel myself interested as a Creditor to the public, I have the satisfaction to declare, that from the moment I left her service I established within myself as a fixed principle chearfully to submit to all the determinations of Congress for the general good of our country, however my own private Interest might be affected thereby—nothing has transpired in th[is] quarter worthy of your attention—you will see by the Boston papers Mr. John Gar[di]ners exertions in our Genl. Court respecting the Gentlemen of the Barr—If its agreeable I coud. wish you to keep in view the subject I disclosed to you at my last interview at Boston—perhaps if Congress embrace the State Debts with the Continental some arrangements may take place to affect this Port—I have been prevailed on to accept of an appointment as Deputy Marshal by the particular desire of Judge [*David*] Sewall which I believe will not be very profitable—I must pray you to excuse all errors, as I do not pretend to accuracy with my corrispondants.

ALS, Chamberlain Collection, MB. Written from Portland, Maine.

[1] Genesis 3:19.

Gouverneur Morris to Robert Morris

*** I have now another Plan for this thing [*repaying the French debt*] which if fairly set a going will give more Profit with less risque and is in every

Respect, I think, excellent. I will not now explain it. If any Person were on the Spot duly authorized to act for the United States I am absolutely certain that with Great Gain to America and without any Loss to france it could be fully effected My present Idea is greatly conformable to what is contained in yours of the 17th. of July.

I am not at all surprized at what you say in yours of the tenth of September relative to the Squabble with Mr. [*Don Diego*] Gardoqui. I have long entertained of that Gentleman the Opinion which you express. To this Hour I have not received any Answer to my Letters from Mr. [*Michael*] Carmichael. I suppose he will make a similar Complaint. The Spanish Court have given such precise Orders for intercepting dangerous Correspondences with this Country that every Letter is opened and most of them destroyed I beleive.

*** You tell me that you will reside at Morrisania if I will build a Bridge.[1] I shall be happy to hear that you are there placed but as to the Bridge it must be taken ad referendum.[2] I have not Money for more needful Purposes, and if—
***

FC:lbk, Gouverneur Morris Papers, DLC. Written from Paris.

[1]"Morrisania" was Gouverneur's ancestral estate in the Bronx, New York, managed by his nephew James Morris. The bridge would have connected it with Manhattan over the Harlem River.
[2]To be further considered.

James Sullivan to Elbridge Gerry

I had yours by the post last Saturday. There is a Comet which the Astronomers say affects our atmosphere about this Time and we are all in a quarell. I went [*to*] get a paper of tomorrow to send you but could not obtain it [*Thomas*] Adams Says he will send you one. you have seen the Sentiment advanced by the President of N.H.[1] in the [*Independent*] Chronicle of tomorrow you see a pece called the Examiner which I have written.[2] the paper treats the goodman with great virulence, but I know not the writers.

In the [*Boston*] Gazette Extraordinary you have a dispute about the reception of the President.[3] how long this is to continue I know not.

You have seen our Controversy respecting the federal officers holding a seat in the House. G. [*Christopher Gore*] has resigned with an Intention to be [*lined out*] re elected[4] how this will go I know not we have realy come to a serious controversy on the point whether the States have ceased to be free &c. I tremble for the Consequences. the Persons who advance the idea that the States have ceased to be States are very imprudent. men who are moved by Principles of Interest only are much raised against the Impost it is heavy on some of them. the [*treasury*] secretaries plan is far from giving them Ease. the men of Principle would Support the Government. but if they are disaffected they will withdraw the support which is much needed God only knows where it will end but all prudent men; all who Love their Country will try to avert the Storm.

[*P. S.*] I wish you to do me the favour to inquire whether there is any thing & what due to Samuel Rogers an officer in Harry Jacksons Regiment he was killed in the Seige of Cornwallis.[5]

John Gardner is reforming the Law abusing every Body and has Sued the Printer of the Herald [*of Freedom*] for abusing him.[6]

ALS, Gerry Papers, MHi. Written from Boston.

[1] The speech to the New Hampshire legislature delivered by James's older brother, President (Governor) John Sullivan, on 29 December 1789, was widely reported and commented upon for its controversial interpretation of state sovereignty. Without resigning the office of governor, Sullivan had accepted appointment as a federal district judge and excused his dual office holding on the grounds that the state government had "*been changed by the voice of the people, who have agreed that their safety depended on their relinquishing many of the powers*" to "*a General Government,*" and that "*from that event,* THIS CEASED TO BE A FREE, SOVEREIGN, AND INDEPENDENT STATE" ([Boston] *Independent Chronicle*, 4 February). See Oliver Whipple to John Langdon, 25 January, above.

[2] In his essay "The Examiner, No. II," Sullivan gently criticized his brother's misconstruing the nature of federalism (*Independent Chronicle*, 4 February).

[3] The controversy surrounding Governor John Hancock's billing the legislature for the banquet he gave in honor of Washington's visit in the previous October.

[4] See Newspaper Article, *Independent Chronicle*, 18 February, below.

[5] Rogers, commissioned first lieutenant in 1777, transferred to Henry Jackson's Continental Regiment in 1779 (designated the 9th Massachusetts Regiment in 1781) in which he served until his death at Yorktown on 20 October 1781.

[6] At noon on 3 February, in Boston, Edmund Freeman was arrested on a warrant John Gardiner had obtained for criminal libel in claiming that Gardiner had murdered his wife by cruelty. A jury refused to convict after a public debate on freedom of speech (*Independent Chronicle*, 4 February; Van Beck Hall, *Politics without Parties, Massachusetts, 1780–1791* [London, 1972], p. 328).

John Wendell to Elbridge Gerry

***

I·observe you are silent on Politicks. I dont doubt the Wisdom of Congress will do the best for the Good of the Union I find the Plans of the Secy. of Treasy. are not acceptable to People at large—they May Answer his own and his friends Purposes who may possess the public Securitys but not to discriminate between the original Holders of & Supporters of public Credit from the Speculators who have depreciated it on purpose to ingross them is a Solecism in politicks—It may appear hard at first sight that Governmt.

Does not support its own Promises—but where is the End of the Promise—
I have 25,000 Dollars of Old Emission for every One of which I have a
Special promise that it shall be equal to a Spanish Milld. Dollar And the
Journal of Congress evidence that the Faith of and even the Soil of the States
are pledged for their Redemption And the Addresses of Congress from the
Pulpits and every Channel of Communication calld on the People to support
their Credit in Decr. 1778 and in March Congress reduced them ~~them~~ selves
to 40 for 1 while they were current with Us at 20 for 1—Again Sir He says
the Possessors shd. not have sold their Birth Right for a Mess of Pottage,[1]
but this is a Deception.

The Possessors originally gave them Credt. from public Good, and kept
them until the Faith of Govt. was [*illegible*] even to a Proverb, and the Distress of the Times with the Want of Business Obliged many of the Holders
to sell them because Congress took no Modes of making them serviceable or
Creditable and from the very same Principal that the Old or New Emission
Money depreciated, the other Securities have done, but I am for making
the bona fide Original Holders good with Six p. Ct. Interest in Specie but
Speculators ought to be made good only from their Purchases in Equity—
Otherways I think Congress shd. Let them rise and Fall upon their own
Bassis as heretofore—though I wish Justice may be to the origl. Holders,
I have reason to believe foriegners are greatly interested in them I know a
Gentleman in Statia [*St. Eustatius*] who has many Thousands of Contl. Secu-
rities and has Wrote to my Son abt. them.

Foreigners do not expect to have them appreciated to their Value or even
to 5/ in the 20/—Stock Jobbing will become a Science soon, the Financiers
Plans for Redemption will not please the People at large but the Additional
Duties on Luxuries will suit, but Congress must make the Mode of Payment
of the Revenue more easy than at present for the Trade cant find Money to
do it.

ALS, Gerry Papers, MHi. Written from Portsmouth, New Hampshire; postmarked Boston, 3 February. The omitted text relates to Gerry's delivery of letters between Wendell and
Captain Phillips, a Boston born retired British army officer.

[1] An allusion to Genesis 25:31–34.

Letter from Boston

You have obliged me by the copy of Mr. Hamilton's system of finance—
he has so well digested and explained his plan, that I am of opinion the
opposition to it must be feeble, and cannot prevail so far as to effect any
material alterations—the creditors in Massachusetts will cheerfully accede

to his propositions; but will universally revolt at a reduction of the interest below *four* pr. cent.

They are confident Mr. Hamilton's abilities are adequate to carrying his ideas into effect, with advantage to the community; and in particular that they will serve to create a beneficial medium, very much wanted, to put in motion the industry of the country—the constitution of this State was preserved in the late rebellion,[1] through the exertions of the public creditors—and they contributed most essentially to the establishment of the general government—in this view, it appears of the last importance to the liberties of the people, which are inseparably connected with the constitution, to consolidate and secure the attachment of so influential a part of the community.

GUS, 13 February; reprinted at Fredericksburg, Virginia.

[1] Shays' Rebellion.

Letter from Boston

I thank you for the Secretary's Report. I like it—and believe the House won't mend it—therefore wish it may be adopted; at least, that Congress may not make any alterations, but such as the Secretary shall approve—that he may *feel* his responsibility, and exert himself accordingly. I like a HEAD to every department, and that every *head* should have ample powers, and be *responsible*. Such a system of government will at once be EFFICIENT AND FREE. You will see by our papers the influence of certain volatile and giddy characters—their inconsistency and folly keep the ignorant members gaping, and waste the time of the Court [*legislature*], which ought to be employed in important business. Such conduct serves to evince the importance and necessity of the General Government. How wretched would be our situation without it.

GUS, 20 February; reprinted at Philadelphia; Winchester, Virginia; and Charleston, South Carolina.

OTHER DOCUMENTS

Stephen Austin to Jeremiah Wadsworth. ALS, Wadsworth Papers, CtHi. Written from Philadelphia; carried by Henry Drinker.
Entrusts the bearer, Henry Drinker, with $563 in gold, the balance due Wadsworth on his account with Austin (Drinker was in New York City as part of the delegation delivering the Quaker antislavery petitions); if

Congress is still sitting on 15 May, by which time Austin hopes to arrive in New York, intends to "Lay a State of Our productions [*of lead*] before them with a Petition for a Protecting duty"; proposes to contract with Wadsworth to furnish as much of the linen as possible (needed to wrap the lead shot).

Pierce Butler to Edward Butler. FC, Butler Letterbook, ScU. For the full text, see *Butler Letters*, pp. 5–7.

Rebukes nephew Edward for his disregard of "my pecuniary situation" in failing to remit purchase money for horses Butler had procured and sent on his own credit; when pressing for repayment, the creditor was "insolently affrontive; so much so that had I been able to have discharged his demand I should have kicked him out of my house"; "had I been in my former affluence your deficiency wou'd have been of no moment"; Edward never seeks advice from Butler and when "from my affection for you and tender regard for the memory of your Dear father [*Thomas*] I obtruded" advice, Edward still followed his own inclination; has acted "in the midst of my difficulties and distresses the part of a Parent to you."

William Constable to Gouverneur Morris. FC:lbk, Constable-Pierrepont Collection, NN.

Is "totally at a loss" how to proceed with buying up American securities abroad, since Robert Morris "who is here with me will not undertake to advise"; believes Hamilton's report on public credit will be adopted "after much battling"; "Our friend [*R. Morris*] promises that when the Bill [*Funding Act HR-63*] comes up to the senate He will apprise me when to strike."

James Fairlie to Philip Schuyler. ALS, Schuyler Papers, NN. Written from Albany, New York.

A small meeting of a number of their friends has decided to run Abraham Ten Broeck for federal Representative (against Van Rensselaer).

Benjamin Goodhue to John Fisk. No copy known; acknowledged in Fisk to Goodhue, 15 February.

Jeremiah Hill to George Thatcher. ALS, Chamberlain Collection, MB. Written from Biddeford, Maine; postmarked Portsmouth, New Hampshire, 5 February.

Comments on the nature of mystery; conveys Thatcher family news.

Benjamin Lincoln to Otho H. Williams. AL, Williams Papers, MdHi. Written from Boston; addressed to Collector for the Port of Baltimore. The author is identified on the endorsement sheet.

While in New York City, conversed with Hamilton on the defects and needed revision of the Collection Act [HR-11]; has received a letter from John Lamb, suggesting they petition Congress on collectors' fees; "it is humiliating to petition. I have therefore suggested the propriety of attempting relief by applying to our members in Congress respectively and engage them in our interest."

Roger Sherman to Rebecca Sherman. Excerpt of three page ALS, *Collector* 59(1946):item 2648. The ellipses are in the source.

"Discussing personal and family affairs, mentioning certain new medicines, and giving some interesting details of the cost of living in New York when it was the capital of the nation. '. . . I have a large bed & curtains round it, in the room where I keep a fire, I give at the rate of 7/6 for oak & 11/3 for walnut wood by the half cord, lawful money. I give 5 dollars a week for board, and have a waiter to do what I want done in that way. . . . I have got a new medicine for the toothake & other disorders . . . I have also the name of a person on long Island who cures cancers.'"

George Thatcher to Benjamin Chadbourn. No copy known; acknowledged in Chadbourn to Thatcher, 17 February.

Jeremiah Wadsworth to George Lang & Co. of Dublin, Ireland. No copy known; acknowledged in Lang to Wadsworth, 28 May (Wadsworth Papers, CtHi).

Encloses introductions, including of the bearer, Michael Bull.

Jeremiah Wadsworth to Harriet Wadsworth. ANS, John Trumbull Papers, CtY. Addressed to Hartford, Connecticut; franked; postmarked. The unlocated enclosures apparently relate to courtship.

"I am very well have just now received such a Volume of Letters that I cant find time [*to*] add More than my advice to think cooly on the inclosed letters before you Answer—remembering always that Your happiness is my highest wish & that I am affectionately Yours."

Paine Wingate to John Tucker, Sr. No copy known; acknowledged in Tucker to Wingate, 27 March.

William Samuel Johnson, Diary. Johnson Papers, CtHi.
"Visits."

NYDA, 3 February. Wister Butler Papers, PHi. Annotated by Butler to indicate the article for which he retained the issue.

James Duane's speech to the grand jury of the federal district of New York (2 February) on the powers of the court and federal jurisdiction.

Anonymous to Mr. Fenno. *GUS*, 3 February, edited by John Fenno; reprinted at Concord, New Hampshire; Lansingburgh, New York; Philadelphia; and Baltimore.

Introducing an extract about the debates of Congress contained in a letter from London dated 2 November 1789 (see *DHFFC* 17:1704–6), which he submitted for publication because the "remarks are dictated with candor, and perhaps may not be deemed uninteresting."

Thursday, 4 February 1790

Rain Ice (Johnson)

William Irvine to John Nicholson

***

I hope & entertain very little doubt now, but the Constitution of Penna. will be a pretty good one—I am not so sanguine, respecting the schemes proposed in the Report of the Secretary of the treasury—but probably that may be so altered as to answer the purposes better than I now expect—notwithstanding the high repute that Gentleman is in, & the probability of a majority to support his plans, in the national Legislature, yet, it is so complex, and there is such a wonderfull diversity of opinion out of doors, that I presume that body will be pretty cautious how they adopt a matter of such unbounded magnitude—and which in its consequences must determine the fate of the Nation—I believe the printers here are very squeamish about publishing any thing opposed in the smallest degree to the Report—a person under the signature Honestus,[1] has ventured to advance a few observations—and the printer as you will see has pushed it among advertisements in the back ground as if rather ashamed of it—an assumption of the state debts is too bare faced to be treated with so much moderation as honestus at least for the present passes it by—and yet I fear it will be a favorite object with too many—sundry states know not what to do with their debts—individuals, or members of Congress of others that do, wish a consolodation of the Government as well as the debt, & consider that one will tend to facilitate the other thus great exertions will be made to accomplish this point—let us hope that all may end well, tho there is to much reason to be apprehensive; if we may Judge of the future from the past it affords hope—in bringing about the revolution every man looked in a streight line, & pressed forward to gain the object. now all is speculation, & finess [*lined out*], not only in money matters, but in politics.

ALS, History of Finance Collection, Beinecke Library, CtY. Place to which addressed not indicated. The omitted text relates to a private business transaction.

[1] *NYDA*, 3 February.

Samuel Johnston to James Iredell

I am just returned from dining at the Presidents with a very respectable Company, the Vice President, the Judges of the Supreme Court & Attorney General of the United States, the Secretary at War and a number of others The President enquired particularly after you and spoke of you in a manner that gave me great pleasure on my return home this evening I had the pleasure of finding your Letters of the 20th of January, I am very thankfull to you for your friendly attention but it is no more than I expected from you.

The Act for enforcing the Collection of the Impost in our State [*North Carolina Act*] had past the House of Representatives and was on the third reading in the Senate before I got to this place, so that I had only an Opportunity of getting a few alterations inserted in it, the President will probably give his Assent to it to morrow, as soon as it is printed I will send forward a Copy to you.

You will receive your Sugar & Medicines by Jacksons Vessel I mist the Opportunity by a few minutes of sending your Books, your Hat is not yet bespoke but shall be soon. I have my health very well except some remains of my cold.

Pray write to me often.

P. S. I have not yet leisure to write to anyone but you & Mrs. [*Frances*] Johnston.

ALS, Iredell Papers, NcD. Addressed to Edenton, North Carolina; franked.

James Madison to Thomas Jefferson

Your favor of the 9th. of Jany. inclosing one of Sepr. last[1] did not get to hand till a few days ago. The idea which the latter evolves is a great one, and suggests many interesting reflections to legislators; particularly when contracting and providing for public debts. Whether it can be received in the extent your reasonings give it, is a question which I ought to turn more in my thoughts than I have yet been able to do, before I should be justified in making up a full opinion on it. My first thoughts lead me though coinciding with many of yours, lead me to view the doctrine as not in *all* respects compatible with the course of human affairs. I will endeavor to sketch the grounds of my skepticism.

"As the earth belongs to the living, not to the dead, a living generation can bind itself only: In every society the will of the majority binds the whole: According to the laws of mortality, a majority of those ripe at any moment for the exercise of their will do not live beyond nineteen years: To that term then is limited the validity of *every* act of the Society: nor can any act be continued beyond this term without a positive [*four or five words lined out*] by the without an express Nor within that limitation, can any declaration of the public will be valid which is not *express*." This I understand to be the outline of the argument.

The acts of a political Society may be divided into three classes.

1. The fundamental Constitution of the Government.

2. Laws involving stipulations which render them irrevocable at the will of the Legislature

3. Laws involving no such irrevocable quality.

However applicable in Theory the doctrine may be to a Constitution, in [*it*] seems liable in practice to some very powerful objections. Would not a Government expiring of necessity so often revised become too mutable to retain those prejudices in its favor which antiquity inspires, and which are perhaps a salutary aid to the most rational Government in the most enlightened age? Would not such a periodical revision ingender pernicious factions that might not otherwise come into existence? Would not, in fine, a Government depending for its existence beyond a fixed date, on some positive and authentic vote of the intervention of the Society itself, be too subject to the casualty and consequences of an actual interregnum?

In the 2d. class, exceptions at least to the doctrine seem to be requisite both in Theory and practice.

If the earth be the gift of nature to the living their title can extend to the earth in its natural State only. The *improvements* made by the dead form a charge against the living which who take the benefit of them. This charge can no otherwise be satisfyed than by executing the will of the dead accompanying the improvements.

Debts may be incurred for purposes which interest the unborn, as well as the living: such are debts for repelling a conquest, the evils of which descend through many generations. Debts may even be incurred principally for the benefit of posterity: such perhaps is the present debt of the U. States, which far exceeds any burdens which the present generation could justly well apprehend for itself. The term of 19 years might not be sufficient for discharging the debts in either of these cases.

There seems then to be a foundation in the nature of things, in the relation which one generation bears to another, for the *descent* of obligations from one to another. Equity requires it. Mutual good is promoted by it. All that is indispensable in adjusting the account between the dead & the living is to see that the debits against the latter do not exceed the advances made by the former. Few of the incumbrances entailed on Nations would bear a liquidation even on principle.

The objections to the doctrine as applied to the 3d. class of acts may perhaps be merely practical. But in that view they appear to be of great force.

Unless such laws should be kept in force by new acts regularly anticipating the end of the term, all the rights depending on positive laws, that is, most of the rights of property would become absolutely defunct; and the most violent struggles be generated between those interested in reviving and those interested in new-modelling the former State of property. Nor would events of this kind be improbable. The obstacles to the passage of laws which render a power to repeal as less security agst. oppression than an opportunity to reject, would here render the inferior to an opportunity of rejecting, as a security agst. oppression, would here render an opportunity of rejecting, an insecure provision agst. anarchy. add, that the possibility of an event so hazardous to the rights of property could not fail to depreciate its value; that the approach of the crisis would increase this effect; that the [*lined out*] frequent return of periods superseding all the obligations depending on antecedent laws & usages, must by weak[*en*]ing the source of reverence for those obligations, co-operate with motives to licentiousness already too powerful; and that the uncertainty incident to such a state of things would on one side discourage the steady exertions of industry produced by permanent laws, and on the other, give a disproportionate advantage to the more, over the less, sagacious and interprizing part of the Society.

I find no relief from these consequences, but in the received doctrine that a tacit assent may be given to established Constitutions and laws, and that this assent is to be inferred, where at least in most cases may be inferred, where no positive dissent appears. It seems less impracticable to remedy, by wise plans of Government, the dangerous operation of this doctrine, than to find a remedy for the difficulties inseparable from the other.

May it not be questioned whether it be possible to exclude wholly the idea of tacit assent, without subverting the foundation of civil Society? on what principle does the voice of the majority bind the minority? It does not result I conceive from the law of nature, but from compact founded on conveniency. a greater proportion might be required by the fundamental constitution of a Society if it were judged eligible. Prior then to the establishment of this principle, *unanimity* was necessary; and strict Theory at all times pre-supposes the assent of every member to the establishment of the rule itself. If this assent can not be given tacitly, or be not implied where no positive evidence forbids, ~~no persons attaining ripe age would not our~~ persons born in Society would not on attaining ripe age be bound by acts [*lined out*] of the Majority; and either a *unanimous* repetition of every law would be necessary on the accession of new members, or an express assent ~~of these be obtained~~ must be obtained from these to the rule by which the voice of the Majority is made the voice of the whole.

If the observations I have hazarded be not misapplied, it follows that a limitation of the validity of national acts to the computed life of a nation, is in some instances not required by Theory, and in others cannot be accomodated to practice. The observations are not meant however to impeach either the utility of the principle in some particular cases; or the general importance of it in the eye of the philosophical Legislator. on the contrary it would give me singular pleasure to see it first announced in the proceedings of the U. States, and always kept in their view, as a salutary curb on the living generation from imposing unjust or unnecessary burdens on their successors. But this is a pleasure which I have little hope of enjoying. The spirit of philosophical legislation has never reached some parts of the Union, and is by no means the fashion here, either within or without Congress. The evils suffered & feared from weakness in Government, and licentiousness in the people, have turned the attention more towards the means of strengthening the former, than of narrowing its extent in the minds of the latter. Besides this, it is so much easier to espy the little difficulties immediately incident to every great plan, than to comprehend its general and remote benefits, that our hemisphere must be still more enlightened before many of the sublime truths which are seen ~~through~~ thro' the medium of Philosophy, become visible to the naked eye of the ordinary Politician.

ALS, Jefferson Papers, DLC. For comment on the text of this and a later revision, see *PTJ* 16:146–50.

[1] For Jefferson's letter of 6 September 1789, see *DHFFC* 17:1477–79.

John Sergeant to Theodore Sedgwick

Inclosed I send you Capt. Yokes[1] petition. he is now in Town. sends his most dutifull respects to you, begs your Interest in his cause. We have procured as much evidence as the nature of the Case will admit. I have no doubt of the justice of his claim, and of the perticular service he performed in the western expedition, fully believe the fatigues he underwent greatly injured his Constitution. he was absent seven months, thinks himself entitled to Captains pay. you will please to take the most favourable oppertunity to introduce his memorial. as soon as any thing favourable turns up, you will please to communicate it in a line to me. Genl. Schuyler has been consulted in this business, has promised his influence, if you have leasure, you will please to consult with him. Esqr. [*Timothy*] Edwards recommends Yokes going down to New York with his petition. he has no money to bear the expense and is much averse to business of this sort. but if you think his success will depend on his his being present—you will please to write me the first post.

I would earnestly solisit your influence in favour of Mr. James Deen [*Deane*], that he be appointed by Congress superintendant for Indian Affairs in the Northern department. he is a gentle man of the greatest integrity and uprightness; considering the connection the Six nations have with the British I have heard that the appointment is a subject of contemplation. I am sure it would greatly serve the Intrest of the Genesee Company. it is intirely aside from the business of Missionaries to meddle too much in politicks among Indians. it is disagreeable to them that they should be made use of as public Interpreters when others can be obtained.

I have lately made your dear family a visit they are all well. I would wish to mention a little matter of business to you. you will recollect that it has been long talked of to build a new school house at the west end of the Town Street. I would wish to promote it to the utmost of my ability. Wish Sir you would communicate to Mrs. [*Pamela*] Sedgwick what you would subscribe towards it. perhaps we should find difficulty to be at the expense of a house with two Rooms. when we might build one with one Room.

[*P. S.*] N. B. I thought best to send Genl. [*John*] Sullavans letter. he made a mistake in writing his certificate on the back of a Coppy of Mr. [*Samuel*] Kirklands Certificate which I sent him. I took Wimpel affidavit myself. he was ready & willing to give oath to it. but as it was difficult to find a justice—I thought it unnecessary.[2]

ALS, Sedgwick Papers, MHi. Written from Stockbridge, Massachusetts.

[1] Alias of Jehoiakim McToksin, a Stockbridge Indian who had served on John Sullivan's western campaign of 1779; see *DHFFC* 7:6–7.

[2] The Sedgwick Papers at MHi contain the following two documents: an affidavit of Hendrick Wempel (by his mark), dated Mohawk Town, Montgomery County, New York, 21 January 1790, that while en route from Tioga Point to Oneida, he (Wempel) personally witnessed the defacement by water of General John Sullivan's certificate compensating McToksin for his service during the expedition of 1779; and a "certificate" of Rev. Samuel Kirkland, dated Stockbridge, Massachusetts, 13 January 1789, that McToksin, alias Capt. Yokun, served very actively during Sullivan's 1779 Expedition but was not paid.

Sir John Temple to Francis Osborne, Duke of Leeds

***

Inclosed is also a Report from the Treasury department, submitted to Congress for the further improvement of the Revenue, & for funding the Public debts &ca. This Report proposes many things of great Magnitude, and will probably employ Congress for some months before it shall be finally disposed of. I also inclose a Plan proposed by the Secretary at War for a general Militia-Establishment throughout the states; It will no doubt attract the attention of Military men on both sides the Atlantic, but I do not apprehend that it will be adopted by Congress at least not without great Modification. A very improper quotation from Baron [*Frederick William von*] Stubens public letter written when he was Inspector General of the Armies of these states will at once catch the Eye of all who read the said plan vizt. *"aided by our Sworn Enimies settled on our extreme left."*[1] which can mean no other than his Majestys dominions, but it is explained by the Secretary at War as meaning only that description of British Subjects, the loyalists or Refugees from this Country, settled in Canada and Nova Scotia. The said quotation is Nevertheless disliked by every body here, and will no doubt, be expunged the Report whenever it shall come under the consideration of Congress.

I am informed that Congress will, in a few days, deliberate upon a proposed general Naturalization bill, in which among others the loyalists, or Refugees from this Country, will be admitted to Naturalization and all proscription be taken off, so as that they may return to this Country at pleasure; This, several members of Congress have told me, is intended to Manifest to Great Britain their Wishes that perfect friendship may take place between the two Countries, and that every thing concerning the late contest may be done away and forgotten; I hope and think that such a Naturalization bill will pass, and that all proscription will be compleatly done away.

The Supreme Federal Court opened in this City yesterday, in which Court it is to be Supposed every foreigner may now obtain Justice.

May I still hope that your Grace will consider my contingent expences in this Country. I have been at a constant considerable expence for all Publications, Laws of different states and of Congress, Newspapers, Books, Pamphlets &ca. to gain all possible information to enable me to do my duty faithfully, and to send such laws, Books, papers &ca. to your Grace. and I humbly hope that your Grace will take into consideration the Expence I have been constantly at for Stationary & Postage, and for printing documents &ca. for I have never yet touched a farthing of Fees or other emolument more than my Salary, which Salary I am now obliged to dispose of, by Exchange at 4 ℔ Cent under par, and my house Rent is raised to £ 270 ℔ Ann. These, with what a Copying Clerk heretofore cost me, has been heavy upon me, and have obliged me to lessen the scale of my mode & Manner of living in an hospitable way to all the Members of Congress, and to the Many, Many, officers & Subjects of his Majesty, who have circulated through these states, a Mode & Manner of living that I shd. never have fallen into but to do honor to the Station I am placed in, and to conciliate the good Will & friendship of the people to Great Britain, in the same Way as the French, Dutch, & Spanish Ministers did to conciliate this People to their respective Countries; and I will be confident in saying that I effected that purpose, at least equal to either of those foreign Ministers; but I beg pardon for trespasing so much on your Grace upon this Subject, for if it does not appear just & reasonable that I shd. be considered for the real contingent expences which I have been at, I am sure all that I can say will not induce your Grace to grant it.

ALS, Foreign Office 4/8 pp. 129–30, PRO. Place to which addressed not indicated.

[1] Quoted in Knox's Plan for the Militia of 18 January (*DHFFC* 5:1454), from *A Letter on the Subject of an Established Militia* (New York, 1784).

Henry Wynkoop to Reading Beatty

The papers acompanying will afford You the general News & Polliticks of this place, this day was spent on the Naturalization & enumeration Bills, much Conversation was had but nothing done respecting the enumeration the Southern Gentlemen are disposed to cast every Obstacle in its way, while those from the eastward generally are disposed to forward it. Hope to hear by next Post wether You will favour us with a Visit & acompany Mamma [*Sarah Newkirk Wynkoop*], indeed I do not think at this Season of the Year she ought to attempt coming without some person to acompany her; the River as yet is as clear of Ice as if it was Summer.

ALS, Wynkoop Papers, PDoBHi. Place to which addressed not indicated.

Letter from a Member of Congress to a Philadelphian

Monday next will be an important day—the friends of discrimination, it is generally believed, will be ashamed to show their faces. Their doctrine, since the report of the Secretary was published, has become very unpopular.

I send this by Mr. __. The practice of closing the Mail, in this city, the evening before its departure from the post-office, proves very inconvenient to us, and must finally do great injury to the revenue.

FG, 9 February; reprinted at Carlisle, Pennsylvania, and Fredericksburg, Virginia.

OTHER DOCUMENTS

Peter Allaire, Occurrences from 4 January to 3 February. Written in New York on 4 February. Copy, Foreign Office 4/7, pp. 263–64, PRO. Place to which addressed not indicated. The Occurrences were dispatches written for the British Foreign Office through the intermediary Sir George Yonge. No documentary evidence has been located to support Allaire's claim about deputies from Kentucky.

Reports on military preparations on the frontier, Rhode Island ratification prospects, the Supreme Court's convening, and Virginia's terms for Kentucky's admission as a state; "they have sent deputies to Congress who are now here."

Moses Austin to Jeremiah Wadsworth. ALS, Wadsworth Papers, CtHi. Written from Richmond, Virginia; franked; postmarked.

That day shipped ten tons of lead shot to New York City; upon its arrival, Wadsworth may choose to examine "the first shot made in America with american lead & bagg'd in American linen"; will soon be able to furnish a great quantity of lead shot, when a protective duty "we hope will not be thought improper"; "Its' universally said that an imbargo" is early expected from Congress; asks Wadsworth's opinion about it.

Connecticut Representatives to Governor Samuel Huntington. Summary and excerpt of three page ALS, hand of Sherman, *Goodspeed's Catalog* 561(1970):item 233B. The ellipses are in the source.

"The five Connecticut representatives write in reply to a request from Gov. Huntington: 'We are sensible that "the people of Connecticut feel themselves interested in the doings of Congress and have a peculiar desire to know all the measures adopted by the National Assembly." All that are not of a secret nature are published daily in the news papers. . . . If Your Excellency will point out any mode by which we can more fully make these communications to the people of our State we shall chearfully embrace it.' The letter continues on the 'doings' of Congress, mentioning the report of the Secretary of the Treasury and the treaty with the Creek Indians, ('hitherto . . . considered as secret')."

Tench Coxe and Nalbro Frazier to Josiah Parker. FC:lbk, Coxe Papers, PHi. Written from Philadelphia.

Have drawn on Hartley for one hundred dollar note, for which they hope Parker will make prompt payment.

Andrew Craigie to Samuel Rogers. FC, Craigie Papers, MWA. Place to which addressed not indicated.

Expresses "very little Doubt" of Hamilton's report on public credit being adopted over "some Opposition"; "many Gentlemen are against the Assumption of the state Debts—others again are against any kind of Reduction of Interest ~~from~~ & some are for a reduction of interest ~~from~~ to 3 Pr. Cent"; Morris advises William Constable against purchasing government securities at present "from an Opinion that, in a few Weeks they will be lower."

Andrew Ellicott: Memorandum on Latitudes. Copy of ms., hand of Madison, Madison Papers, DLC. For the full text and Madison's annotations, see *PJM* 13:26. The dating is based on Madison's docketing. Ellicott made these measurements under the commission he had been given by Washington on 5 September 1789, to execute Congress's resolution on the survey of the western boundary of New York, dated 26 August of that year. Both the manuscript, which Madison forwarded to Jefferson, and the copy he retained for himself (Madison Papers, DLC) contain annotations that Madison added, concerning magnetic variation.

Latitude and longitude (from the meridian of Philadelphia) for Fort Erie, Fort Niagara, Niagara Falls, and the west end of Lake Ontario.

Thomas Fitzsimons to Benjamin Rush. Excerpt of four page ALS, *Collector* 59(1946):item 479. The ellipsis is in the source. The editors believe the source inaccurately transcribed the manuscript.

". . . his [*Hamilton's*] plan does not Correspond with his reasoning. I have allways thot he Resined too much to fill his present Station with propriety in many transactions—and perhaps all others—plain dealing is best in many transactions—and perhaps all others—plain dealing is best he has formed his Scheme upon Maxims that apply very well in other Countrys but they do not and Cannot apply in this till our Circumstances & habits are very different."

John Langdon to Hopley Yeaton. No copy known; acknowledged in Yeaton to Langdon, 16 February.

Roger Sherman to Simeon Baldwin. ALS, Sherman Collection, CtY. Place to which addressed not indicated. For more on Collins's petition, see *DHFFC* 7:84–85.

Relays news about his sons John and Isaac and forwards letter to John's wife; enquires about ongoing dispute in his home church, in which he esteems and supports Reverend Jonathan Edwards [*Jr.*]; will enclose next Saturday's paper; in a postscript, advises Pitman Collins to submit claim to Auditor Oliver Wolcott if legal provisions are made for it; otherwise, "application must be made by Petition to Congress. depositions & other vouchers will be admitted in evidence, & no expence attend it, except to the agent he may employ. A member will present his Petition without pay & do what may be necessary for its passing Congress."

Michael Jenifer Stone to Walter Stone. ALS, Stone Papers, DLC. Addressed to Port Tobacco, Maryland; franked; postmarked.
    "Nothing new—My Health I think has mended—My Friends all neglect me."

George Thatcher to David Sewall. No copy known; acknowledged in Sewall to Thatcher, 11 March.

Joseph Tucker to George Thatcher. ALS, Thatcher Papers, MeHi. Written from York, Maine.
    Is preparing to leave for New York City on the business of the agents for settling the accounts of the Massachusetts troops (stationed at West Point after the war); enquires whether the first of next month would be a "proper time" to apply to Congress, considering the other important business before it; asks for reply by the next post; enquires the likelihood of excise taxes, his appointment as their collector for York County, and "Your influence in the affair."

Anthony Wayne to Catharine Greene. ALS, incomplete, Wayne Papers, PHi. Place from which written not indicated.
    Asks Greene to be his advocate with the President "& your other friends in power" for any appointment when she deems proper.

George Washington, Diary. Washington Papers, MiD-B.
    The Vice President; Attorney General; Supreme Court Justices Jay, Cushing, Wilson, and Blair; Secretaries Hamilton and Knox; and Senators Johns[t]on and Hawkins dined with the President.

NYJ, 4 February.
    If Congress declares that state officials cannot hold seats in it, Judge Leonard and Sheriff Partridge will have to leave.

FRIDAY, 5 FEBRUARY 1790

Cold (Johnson)

Aedanus Burke to Samuel Bryan

I received your kind favor by Mr. [*Francis*] Baily, and have paid every attention in my power to his affairs. I was chairman of a Committee who yesterday
reported favorably respecting his device, & the matter is in such a train as he
approves of. I have to return you my thanks for the attention you have bestowed on the Commission of mine, which you were so obliging as to engage
in.[1] If the papers you transmited to Charleston are now there, I had rather they
would remain there until I return. I will therefore write to a friend of mine
there, to call on your Correspondent & obtain the packet, till my return home.

I have seen Col. [*Eleazer*] Oswald, and I regret that his independant Spirit
involves him in new difficulties[2]—What passed in the Senate in the affair you
allude to was thus—Mr. R. H. Lee offered to the Senate a proposition that Measures should be adopted to compel persons indebted to the publick, or who had
been entrusted with publick monies to come forward and settle their accounts
in a given time. I think it was nine months. Upon this, and before the Motion
could be seconded, the Gentleman you speak of, Mr. Morris, started up in great
wrath, and said that he considered the motion as leveled purposely against
himself, and on this head, retorted some warm expressions—Mr. Lee replied,
that he did not conceive the motion could fairly bear any such interpretation—
but that on such occasions he had ever been unfortunate—He said about 25
years ago (or thereabouts) ~~Ago~~ he made a similar motion in the Legislature of
Virginia, to have it ascertained what sums were due to the publick, and how
much of it was in the Treasury—The delicacy of the Treasurer was hurt, for he
considered the motion as an attack on him[3]—And the motion was not carried,
but in some time afterwards it was discovered that this same Treasurer had with
some of the publick money, bribed sundry members who opposed Mr. Lee.

This is the purport of what passed—as I have heard from some members
who were present—I shd. have observed, that the Members of the Senate
seeing Mr. Morris in a passion and resenting the motion as a personal attack,
to prevent perhaps a very disagreeable contention, Mr. Lee's motion was not
seconded—and of course is not on the Journals—~~Mr. Morris S~~.

ALS, Miscellaneous Letters, Miscellaneous Correspondence, State Department Records,
Record Group 59, DNA. The conclusion of this letter was written on 10 February and is
printed under that date, below.

---

[1] Bryan solicited responses to Burke's questionnaire regarding the constitutional revolution of 1787–88; see *DHFFC* 17:1728–38.

[2] Morris brought a libel suit against Oswald in response to pieces in Oswald's *IG* relating to Morris's unsettled accounts; see Impartial, 30 December 1789, above.

[3] John Robinson (1706–66) was speaker of the Virginia House of Burgesses and treasurer of the colony from 1738 until his death. Lee moved unsuccessfully for an investigation of the treasury in 1760 and 1763. Lee's suspicions proved correct; Robinson's estate owed the colonial treasury about $250,000.

Edward Carrington to James Madison

I am favored with yours of the 24. Ult. and am much releived by it from apprehensions that your indisposition, of which I had heard by several hands, was of so serious a Nature, as, at least to detain you on the way longer than it has. I hope you have perfectly recovered.

I thank you for your remarks upon my appointment under the fedl. Govt. I shall never pretend to an intire indifference upon the point of emolument for such services as my Country may think proper to require of me, but feel a consciousness that in any solicitude which is felt upon such occasions, a desire to be enabled to discharge the duties demanded will have its due share. Had it been the pleasure of the President or consistent with his plans, to nominate me to any other Station, I should not have declined the Task, but my pretensions to public Notice are not in my own opinion high. And if the Office confered already is rendered practicable I shall not be dissatisfied.

I have seen the Sketch of the plan for supporting the public Credit which has been published, but will not at present hazard an opinion upon it. Upon this subject I will however say in general terms, that substantial measures ought soon to be adopted. Procrastination not only will accumulate the public burthens, but will add to the difficulties of providing for them. The Enemies of the Government will consider it as a concession that ~~the~~ its powers in this respect ought not to be exercised, whilst its Freinds will become diffident as to its merits. The consequence must be, that at a later day, the former will be more bold in resisting, and the latter less firm in supporting it. I firmly beleive that an early exercise of the fullest powers of the Government in all its parts as far as the public exigencies require would reconcile its Enemies, and confirm its Freinds. Here the former would find its operation more mild and salutary than they have been made to beleive, and the latter would have their expectations realized.

The demands abroad have given an extraordinary rise to the prices of all grains here. Wheat is now at 8/. ℔ bushl. and Corn 15/. ℔ Barrel.

P. S. I suppose you have seen the reasons of the Majority of the Senate for postponing the Amendments—but lest you should not they are now inclosed.

ALS, Madison Papers, DLC. Written from Richmond, Virginia. Carrington enclosed the [Richmond] *Virginia Independent Chronicle*, 13 January, which published a statement by eight members of the majority in the Virginia Senate who on 12 December 1789 voted to postpone until the following session consideration of the third, eighth, eleventh, and twelfth Amendments to the Constitution that had been proposed by the FFC (now the first, sixth, ninth, and tenth articles of the Bill of Rights) and agreed to in the state's House of Delegates on 30 November 1789. The statement argued that the postponed Amendments inadequately addressed the desires of Virginians as expressed in the amendments their ratifying convention had proposed to the Constitution.

Michael Hodge to Benjamin Goodhue

Your favour inclosing the report of the Secretary [*on public credit*] came duly to hand, for which I sincerely thank you, I have and am communicating it agreable to your wishes, it is Universally Esteemed as a master piece of composition the principles held forth in it are as generally admired, the restrictions in the Act[1] are tho't by some to be too severe and too multiplyed, particularly respecting ardent Spirits, but upon the whole I rather think it whould carry a Major Vote, it certainly will with a little modifying of the Legislature, We in the Customs here still continue in the round of Duty, quite peaceably have as yet met with no considerable interruption, and I think Trade flourishes—We have nothing new to tell you, except, that the Spanish ship has been got off, and Safely moored again at the Wharf contrary to every ones expectation, and less damaged than was feared,[2] Your communications are very kindly received here, the Gentlemen, desire their Compliments to be presented you, with their thanks, and express their wishes that you would continue your kind communications, as often as will be convenient to you, it gives great Satisfaction I can assure you.

ALS, Letters to Goodhue, NNS. Written from Newburyport, Massachusetts.

[1] Hamilton's report included a very detailed proposed act to increase the duties on imported distilled spirits and also to lay an excise on domestically produced spirits. See *DHFFC* 5:799–822.

[2] In his letter to Goodhue dated 29 January, Hodge reported that the ship, built at Newburyport but owned by Spaniards, had run aground in attempting to pass the bar.

John Hooker to Caleb Strong

It seems to be universally agreed that the Secretarys Report [*on public credit*] discovers great Labor & reflection, & in fact does him much Honor— For my own part, I am very sensible it is a subject which I am utterly unacquainted with, & therefore cannot pretend to form any fixed Judgment upon it—The applause it recieves, from most people makes me suppose it very deserving—& the Secretary is certainly very ingenious & plausible in his reasonings—Finance, is a Science which seems to be quite in its Infancy in this Country, if we may judge from the ill-management which has taken place in our Revenue matters heretofore—the greater will be the Honor therefore if the Secretary's report should be approved by the Legislature, and his schemes should prove successful—If the whole debt can be placed on such Funds that the Interest will be punctually paid, it will be a fortunate Circumstance for us—whether the plans he has devised for the reduction of the Interest, which is what I suppose he really aims at by his different ~~plans~~ proposals will be acceded to by the public Creditors, is I suppose somewhat doubtful—The rate of Interest has been so long established at 6 pr. Ct. that they will not consent to reduce it to 4- or 4½, unless they can see some very substantial reasons for doing it—there must be I suppose punctuality in the payment of the Interest & a plenty of a circulating Medium—Perhaps they have such Confidence in the present Govt., that they will not hesitate in trusting to its Assurances—If they do, the securities themselves will rise to their full value & be equal to Cash.

From the little I have seen of your transactions this session I imagine you will have a very long one—The idea of a certain & handsome Compensation with most persons would go far towards a balance to the disagreable circumstance of being abroad from one's Family—But when united with the Honor of discharging acceptably an important Office, there is I believe hardly any that would not be pleased with the Situation—or at least they would submit to it with the resignation of a Philosopher—and I shrewdly suspect, after the four years experiment, provided you retain the Smiles of Father [*John*] Carnes & others of our most weighty Characters, it will appear rather more eligible to keep on in the same mode of Life, than to return to the drudgery of attending our petty Courts—especially if you consider the wonderful reform which is shortly to take place in our Laws & Lawyers— Under Mr. [*John*] Gardners plastic Hand our Laws are to become such, that no one is in any Case to doubt—which lops off at once all profits under the head of *Advice*—In the next place, Students are to gain all their knowledge from attendg. Courts & taking Minutes of all Cases—there goes *Tuition*— No Lawyer, is to act as a Justice, or take any fees for travel and Attendance in any Cases, & to take an Oath, which I suppose is to prevent his committing any sin for the rest of his Life—What miserable Creatures he will shortly make of us, we are trembling to hear.

*** —present my compliments to Mr. Ames.

ALS, formerly at MSonHi. Written from Springfield, Massachusetts. The omitted text relates news of the state legislature and local weather conditions.

Hugh Williamson to George Washington

Mr. Williamson has taken the Liberty, in the enclosed Paper to mention the Names of Gentlemen who as he conceives would discharge the Duties of the Offices affixed to their several Names with Reputation.
In Wilmington Col. [*James*] Read is now Collector &
    Jno. Walker is Naval Officer
In Newbern Capt. [*John*] Daves is now Collector
at Beaufort Col. [*John*] Easton has long been Collector or Naval Officer.
In Washington Capt. [*Nathan*] Keis is now Collector.
In Edenton. Thos. Benbury is now Collector &
    Michl. Payne is Naval Officer.
It appears strange that neither Navl. Officer nor Surveyor are to be appointed in so considerable a Port of Entry. 330 Vessels entered there in 1787. No other Person offering who is better qualifyed to discharge the Ð various Duties of that Office (Collector) perhaps it might be given at present to one or 'tother of the Officers named.
    Cambden is a new Port.
Genl. Isaac Gregory is recommended as a Gentleman whose Character as Soldier and Citizen stands high in the universal Esteem of his fellow Citizens. He is a Man of respectable Property; has the full Confidence of his Country and is the constant Enemy to public Officers suspected of corrupt practices.
    The Gentlemen mentioned for Surveyor in the Ports of Delivery belonging to Edenton and Cambden Districts are the most respectable Characters in the Vicinity not concerned in Trade who would probably be willing to accept of such an Office.
    There are two or three Blanks either because Mr. Williamson does not at present recollect the Name of any Person living near the Port or does not know any Person there whom he can recommend according to his Ideas of Propriety.

[*Enclosure*]
For the several Ports in North Carolina
the following Officers are humbly submitted.

Wilmington
James Reed	Collector
John Walker	Naval Officer
Thomas Callender	Surveyor

Swansbro'

Newbern
John Daves	Collector
Beaufort John Easton	Surveyor

Washington
Nathan Keais   Collector
Edenton

Murfreesborough	Hardy Murfree.	Surveyor
Windsor	[*William*] Benson	Do.
Skewankey	Henry Hunter	Do.
Wynton	Thomas Wynn	Do.
Bennetts Creek	John Baker	Do.
Hertford	Joshua Skinner Jnr.	
Plymouth	Levi Blount	

AL, Washington Papers, DLC. Written in the P.M. The same day, Washington sent this list to North Carolina's Senators (*DGW* 6:28), who apparently used it to compile their own list on 8 February (calendared under that date, below).

Paine Wingate to Jeremy Belknap

I have received your favour of January 13th. and agreeably to your desire have forwarded your enclosure to Mr. [*Mathew*] Carey. His [*American*] Museum will accompany this, which I have read with pleasure and think the most valuable production of the kind which I have seen printed in America. The Bill for securing the copy right to authors is now before the house of Representatives. I have not seen it and cannot judge of any imperfections that may be in it. I shall very gladly contribute whatever is my power to have it amply safe to reward the labours & ingenuity of the literati; but I can easily conceive the difficulty of guarding against the evils which you suggest without infringing on the right which the public possesses of making use of quotations, extracts &c. from printed books. I hope however that the privilege & encouragement to Authors will be the best that the nature of the case will admit, & that it will spedily be completed to your satisfaction. Since I wrote to you last the current price of securities has rather dwindled. I am told they now sell for about 7/6d. on the pound. This may have arisen from other causes than mearly the want of confidence in the {public} faith. It will be a considerable time {before} Congress can decide on this perplexing {and} important business; but next monday {it will} be taken up by the house of Representatives and perhaps some conjecture may be formed from the disposition which will then appear. It appears to me that matters have gone so far wrong that it is not an easy thing to find the right way out, and that men of the most upright intentions who would wish to unite justice with policy, may judge & act very differently—I rather think on the whole that the public creditors will receive as good as half the nominal value of their securities, if not more, & that there can be no discrimination between the original holders & the speculators, however deserving the one may be more than the other. Very little business has yet been compleated in Congress. We go *slow* fast enough. I have nothing remarkable to add—I desire my compliments to Mrs. Belknap & parson [*John*] Clarke.

ALS, Belknap Papers, MHi. Addressed to Boston. The upper right corner of the second page is cut out; the missing words, in wavy brackets here, are from *Wingate* 2:348–49. Belknap's dealings with Carey may have involved the advertising and sales of his *History of New Hampshire* (3 vols., 1784–92).

Newspaper Article

Congress is now deeply immersed in public affairs—and truly important are the objects that await their deliberations—the great machine of government for this extensive empire being set in motion, the adjustment of its various movements so as to produce the best good of the whole, appears to be the great concern, and to call forth the united wisdom, patience and persevering investigation, of the great national Legislature of the United States.

[Connecticut] *Norwich Packet*, 5 February.

Late Accounts from New York

The Secretary of the Treasury has made his Report. The principal objects of the report in which the public mind is interested, are the assumption of the State Debts, and the proposed rate of interest at FOUR per cent. The former will I presume be adopted, the last is doubtful. The credit of this Government will depend more on a punctual performance of her engagements, than on any other circumstance. Now I very much doubt the ability of this country to pay the interest of her debts at four per cent. the installments of the foreign debt as they shall fall due, provide for the current expenses of the Government, and make that reasonable provision for extraordinary occurrences which is dictated by prudence, and should never be omitted when a calculation is formed.

[Connecticut] *Norwich Packet*, 5 February.

OTHER DOCUMENTS

Manassah Cutler to Benjamin Goodhue. ALS, Letters to Goodhue, NNS. Written from Ipswich, Massachusetts; postmarked.
    Office seeking: Rufus Putnam to succeed Samuel H. Parsons as judge of the Northwest Territory; the Ohio Company "conceives they have a right

to expect some attention to the Massachusetts in the appointment of those Officers, as a considerable proportion of the settlers are from this State"; encloses letter for Putnam to be forwarded in care of Richard Platt.

Walter Jones to James Madison. ALS, Madison Papers, DLC. Written from Virginia.

Has heard little of Congress's proceedings; supposes direct taxation will be unavoidable; "if they are imposed, it is probable you will have a hard Struggle against the perseverance, address & partiality of our northern Brethren"; supports payment of British debts under the Treaty of Paris (1783), but believes "Some mode Should be adopted to Suspend their Execution, until the Compliance of the other party."

Robert Morris to John Nicholson. Listing of ALS, *Henkels Catalog* 6(1892): item 419 and Dawson's Book Shop Catalog 192(1945):item 223.

James Pemberton to Benjamin Franklin. ALS, Franklin Papers, PPAmP. Place to and from which written not indicated; sent by post. An identical version (in Senate Records, DNA) accompanied Franklin's submission of the petition referred to; see *DHFFC* 8:324. Pemberton's heavily amended draft is in Pennsylvania Abolition Society Papers, PHi.

Encloses copies of the petition of the Pennsylvania Abolition Society for Franklin's signature and forwarding to the President of the Senate and Speaker of the House, with request it be presented to their respective bodies and printed in their minutes.

Richard R. Saltonstall to Thomas Jefferson. ALS, Washington Papers, DLC. Office seeking: something under him; refers Jefferson to William Samuel Johnson, who has promised to mention Saltonstall to him.

William Samuel Johnson, Diary. Johnson Papers, CtHi.
"Levee."

[Connecticut] *Norwich Packet*, 5 February.
"The Debates of Congress are republished in all the papers of the United States, with an avidity which shews that the printers consider them as highly interesting to their readers. This is deriving political wisdom from the fountain head."

GUS, 6 February.
Boudinot and Hartley admitted and sworn as counselors before the Supreme Court.

NYDA, 10 February.
   Benson, Laurance, Sedgwick, Smith (S.C.), Jackson, Ames, and Thatcher
admitted to practice before the Supreme Court.

SATURDAY, 6 FEBRUARY 1790

Cold (Johnson)

Governor Samuel Huntington to Oliver Ellsworth and William Samuel Johnson

I am favoured with your letter of the 26th. Ulto. enclosing a Copy of the
Report of the Secretary of the Treasury, on the subject of funding the public
Debt.
   I observe the Secretary avails himself of the experience of the old Kingdoms in Europe, & most of the modes they have adopted in funding, but
have not had leisure fully to peruse his Report.
   The magnitude & importance of the subject must doubtless engage the
attention of Congress & is probably the most interesting to the Nation,
that can properly come before them the present Session: I shall be happy to
receive the earliest information of the sense of Congress upon the various
parts of the Report, in their progress from time to time.
   You Gentlemen are sensible that many good Citizens in this State, & indeed most of the people, feel themselves deeply interested in the proceedings
& Regulations of Congress, & wish to receive early intelligence of all their
Acts & Doings, which with propriety may be communicated.
   It is expedient that I should be informed, whether there be a probability,
or not, that the President will issue his Proclamation for a General Fast the
ensuing Spring.

   LS, Johnson Papers, CtHi. Written from Norwich, Connecticut.

James Jackson to an Unknown Recipient

I had the honor of your favor dated at Augusta previous to my sailing
from Savannah; but had not time to answer it from that place. I now seize
one of the first opportunities to thank you for it, and to assure you that a
correspondence with so old a Friend will be highly desireable.
   I reached this a few days after Congress had been in session, and after,
rather, a violent passage. I found however, that nothing had been done, and
that I was full time enough to receive my share of the abuse our Cession act[1]

has met with, and to be present at the discussion of Indian Affairs. The doors having been continually shut on this last head, prevents my being explicit; but every thing in our House, after great opposition, is in our favor as far as the business has yet proceeded. I fear however, our influence in the Senate: some of our warmest Friends having taken miff at our fatal law & left us. Had Georgia but acted prudently & avoided it; I know not any thing we could have asked, but would have been granted. The report of the Commissioners[2] was as much with us, as if it had been penned by our own Executive Majestrate.

We have now subjects of the greatest magnitude before us. The reports of the secretaries of the Treasury and War departments, the former on Finance & the funding system, the last on the subject of Militia service. The publick mind has been greatly agitated with both. The former I suppose, has given rise to speculations superior to any before us since the famous South Sea scheme.[3] The Bank of New York has even been drained of specie for those purchases, and sent of[f] to different parts of the Union to purchase State securities: which are by Hamiltons system to be placed on the same Footing with those of the Union & to draw interest alike. I am at present of opinion that it will not be the interest of Georgia to adopt this consolidation plan. At present our Audited Certificates draw no interest & are redeemab[le] at our own pleasure. with the addition of interest our Debt will become so much larger, & we shall have a superior power for our Creditor; who may in an ill humour pour down a torrent of those Certificates on us for immediate payment. This is one view of the business. another light in which it is consider[ed] is, that the whole debt shall be consolidated, and the respective States be altogether discharged & that the principal & interest of the whole Debt shall be generally defrayed. Here again Georgia would suffer. Many of the states have their Millions out: Virginia & South Carolina particularly. Georgia is not so much in Debt, & has superior resources to any of them. Her Western & other unlocated lands & her funds in the Treasury, will undoubtedly clear her, & leave her in very pretty circumstances after. Of course, this Plan would oblige her to pay not her own Debt; but the Debt of other states, and that at an advanced ratio to what she was charged during the War. I have written jointly with General Matthews to the Governor on this head.[4] it is so important to us, that altho we had no official right to demand his opinion, we conceived it, contrary to the idea of our Colleague, to be our duty—I wish to have his sentiment, as the Legislature is not in session, & I will request yours with the publick opinion on both, that & the Militia Report. we have sent them to the Governor, from whom no doubt you can procure them. Could you, if he should not answer us by any means draw his sentiments, I shall be highly obliged to you. I am afraid that the Theory of Knox's Militia plan is too refined, & that there is scarcely virtue sufficient to carry it into operation. We have likewise had warm work with the Census or enumeration law & I have had almost to wrangle with the Eastern Members; a Mr. Sedgwick from Massachusets in particular. His illiberality led him to tax Georgia with being over represented, that her Representatives knew it, and for that reason wished to delay the business. I replied, that the state of Georgia as little deserved his illiberal assertions, as that I knew she would despise them. that as an individual to w[*hom*] they were addressed I equally treated them [*with*] disdain. that they were calculated for the [*people*] of his state, and not for the floor of Congress—they would not have persuaded any other [*people*] than his own. This law is not yet gone through, it has taken up a deal of time and will require as much more. I expect [*he*] will begin again, he may rely on as good as [*he*] brings, & at present the ballance is on my [*side*].

*** I wish to hear from you as early as possible, [*Capt. Cornelius*] Schermerhorn I suppose will be long enough at Savannah for your answer to reach me by him. Do write me all the Augusta intelligence. Apropos! remember me to Dr. Powell. Mr. Beckley our Clerk I find was his intimate acquaintance, he likewise begs his regards.

***

[*P. S.*] N. B. The speculations on the securities will have a good effect in some cases. it will defeat [*Thomas*] Washington & Co.,[5] or I am mistaken—raise our state funds in value; & pour in a flood of present cash: but it is not hard to discover that it will be a temporary benefit only. The speculators are chiefly near this City, & this Cash will as speedily find its way back to pay the Interest of those very Certificates, which on account of their holders would center altogether near the seat of Government in fact they would become a drain to our specie—If the plan should not take, many of them have burnt their fingers, which I pray God they may. they certainly have ruined many in south Carolina & Georgia. I do not like it on another principle—It is evident & our late act shews, we ought not to be left too much to ourselves: still I would always preserve as much weight in the State Governments as would prove a check to Arbitrary stride [?] on the part of the Union. This consolidating plan is calculated to throw more power in the scale of the latter, by making more people interested in its welfare, & diminishing their dependence on the different states.

Should Washington come your way Ill thank you to [*go*] at him again for me.

[*P. P. S.*] I shall apply for admittance in the Supreme Court on Monday next as a Counsellor or Barrister.

RC, Rare Book 39002, vol. 11:738, CSmH. Place to which addressed not indicated. The omitted text relates to a private lawsuit.

---

[1] The act of 21 December 1789. See George Walton to John Adams, 20 January, above.

[2] For the Report of the Commissioners for Southern Indians, 17 November 1789, see

DHFFC 2:210–41. The report, highly critical of Creek intransigence, was laid before the Senate on 11 January.

[3] The South Sea Bubble was the name applied to the financial scheme by which the British South Sea Company attempted to buy up the national debt in 1720. The speculation collapsed, and its name became a symbol for the dangers of stock speculation.

[4] See Mathews and Jackson to Governor Edward Telfair on this date, immediately below.

[5] Thomas Washington (d. April 1791), who changed his surname from Walsh and settled in Savannah, Georgia, after the Revolutionary War, used his position as Georgia commissioner for confiscated loyalist estates to become the state's most prominent land speculator. Despite bankruptcy in 1788, he became involved in the Yazoo land fraud and was later hanged for counterfeiting South Carolina currency. Jackson, commander of the Georgia Legionary corps in which Thomas Washington had served as a major during the war, referred to him as "the famous speculator, but a good soldier" (Lilla M. Hawes, ed., "Manuscript Papers of James Jackson, 1781–1798," *Georgia Historical Quarterly* 37[March 1953]:80; Lamplugh, pp. 35–36; *McGillivray*, p. 292).

George Mathews and James Jackson to Governor Edward Telfair

INCLOSED we have the honor to send you the Reports of the Secretary of the Treasury Department, one part of which, the consolidation of the State Debts with those of the Union, is of so much importance to Georgia, that we are induced to request an official communication thereon. It is true, as we have been informed by our colleague [*Baldwin*], that we have no right to call on you as the Representatives of the State Legislature, but being the Representatives of the People constituting that Legislature, and who will be ultimately affected by the decision, we have conceived it our duty to make this application: In the light it at present appears to us, we view the measure as contrary to the interest of the state, setting its policy entirely aside. We have struggled to get this part of the Report postponed, until the sense of the respective states, on this subject can be ascertained, in vain; but we hope to have time to receive your answer previous to a final decision.

We likewise do ourselves the honor of inclosing the Report of the Secretary of the War Department on the militia establishment.

[Georgia] *Augusta Chronicle*, 10 July 1790. According to the Georgia Executive Council Journal, the letter, which is not extant, was received on 17 March.

William Paterson to Euphemia Paterson

Your Letter, my dear Affy, of the 3d. of this Month, has this Moment come to Hand. I have no Objection to the Rule you have laid down in Order to determine our Affection for each other, namely, the Number of Letters, which we respectively write—It is much in my Favor, and clearly proves, that I love you three Times as much as you do me, since I write three Letters to your one. I have no Doubt on my Part, that my Affection for you is of such a Nature, that neither Time nor Distance will lessen it; the Reverse is the Fact; for I can truly say, that my Love increases with the years, and at this Moment glows with more Fervor than it did on my Wedding Day. I trust, it is the same with you—I shall endeavour to be with you toward the latter End of this or Beginning of next Month.

I rejoice, that my dear little Children are well; their Happiness stands high in my Mind—I have a thousand Anxieties about them. Their own Mama [*Cornelia Bell Paterson*] could not be more attentive and affectionate to them than you are—I hope they will ever retain a grateful & warm Remembrance of your motherly Care and Tenderness.

I would rather that Mr. Sebring should have the Farm than either of the others—I shall have no Objection to Summer Grain being put in the low Land, if it be necessary.

I have not heard of any News—indeed I go out but little—I am fond of my room—reading and Business keep me employed. I always had an Aversion to going out in Winter. To Day, however, I shall dine at Mr. [*Louis Guillaume*] Otto's—The Card says, *"to celebrate the Alliance"*—On such an Occasion an Excuse would not well pass. there is much Entertainment in the dining Way at present, in this City; you may judge, I have no less than 4 or 5 Invitations for Tuesday next, to say Nothing of the other Days. I intend to resume the Rule I laid down for my Conduct last Summer to find an Apology.

8 OClock in the Evening.

I have just returned from Mr. Otto's—fine Times, Dinner after 5—but it was to celebrate the Alliance—On my Return, I found a Letter from you, my dear Affy, another from my sweet Cornelia [*Paterson*], and a third from my good Colo. [*John*] Bayard. Poor Susan [*Kearny*], heigh ho! sick at Heart— The Doctor [*John Richardson Bayard Rodgers*] will make her a good Husband—They have my best Wishes; I hope and believe they will be happy.

Adieu and Adieu—

ALS, Paterson Papers, NjP. Addressed to New Brunswick, New Jersey.

Theodore Sedgwick to Pamela Sedgwick

You do not know how much I was disappointed on Wednesday in not having the pleasure to receive a single line from home. Mr. Jacob called on me this morning and said he saw you and that you informed him that the family was all well, and perticularly observed that little Kitty [*Catherine Maria*] appeared to grow finely. As he said nothing about poor little Roberts lameness I ardently hope it is not so alarming as when you wrote me. Had you known how extreamly grateful to me would have been a single line, had it contained no more than these words, "Pamela Sedgwick" you certainly would not have omitted writing. But best beloved of my soul I mean not to recriminate, nor to complain. I will be satisfyed in the assurance that I have an unrivalled interest in your good heart.

I believe you will think me very unpardonable, when I inform you that I have not yet seen good Mrs. [*Theodosia*] Burr, though I have proposed several times to pay her a visit yet something has always intervened to prevent my intentions.

On Monday we shall enter on the all important subject of funding the national debt. There as yet seems no union of minds nor any certainty of the event on any one great question. As soon as the event of that discussion will permit me, I hope to have it in my power to pay a short visit to my dear family. I know indeed of no other business which need long keep congress together. At present I am of opinion the session will not continue longer than till may. I have many letters by this post to write to my friends in Massa. should I get time I shall however write one to Eliza [*Mason Sedgwick*]. Pray let me know very perticularly your state of health & that of all the family.

ALS, Sedgwick Papers, MHi.

David Sewall to George Thatcher

Since my Comeing here I have been favoured with yours of the 24th. & 27th. Ultimo. For Which I thank you. The Secretary of the Treasurys Report is a masterly performance, I have once read it, but it will take various readings to Comprehend it—If funds can be procured to Certainly insure the punctual paiment of the Interest—The Credit of the U.S. will be established and Secured—But I have not Sufficient Data to form a fixed opinion in the Premises—the Supposed Revennue of the Post office is far beyond any Conception I had of the matter if its real amount is as loose as Stated[1]—The making it a sinking fund, and from Time to time appropriating it to purchase up the Securities for Sale at market will be an excellent provision[2]—I had some Ideas, that the appropriations for 1789. [*Appropriations Act HR-32*] were not for more than two months of the Judicial department, which was the Reason of my Expressing the Business in the manner I did in the authority I sent you—The draft has been duly honoured—Should it be a provision made for the residue & the mistake you mention, be ratified, I will be so kind to do the necessary to procure the Residue—For I Suppose that if the money is placed in the Treasury for a Certain purpose it will remain there, until it is actually taken from there, and no advantage remain to the U.S. from its being there detained   As to News We have none.

ALS, Foster Collection, MHi. Written from Boston. The omitted text includes reports on John Gardiner's legal reform movement, other Massachusetts and New Hampshire politics, and local weather.

[1] Hamilton's report on public credit estimated it at not less than $100,000 (*DHFFC* 5:773).

[2] Hamilton proposed and Congress established a fund (Sinking Fund Act [HR-101]) consisting of the unappropriated surplus impost and tonnage duties; its purpose was to reduce the public debt by purchasing it at market value, thus reducing the debt.

Caleb Strong to Nathan Dane

I have not heard of your taking a Seat in the Senate of Massachusetts but I hope and presume that will be the Case before this arrives at Boston—We are impatient to hear the Proceedings of the General Court and it is likely you feel as much interested in the Measures adopted by Congress—they proceed as you will suppose by slow Steps and have not as yet adopted any very important Resolutions—the Subject of Mr. Hamiltons Report in a good Measure engrosses the Attention of our Politicians, it will be taken up in the House next Monday unless further postponed which I think is not likely to happen—the Question whether the State Debts shall be assumed will give an Oppertunity to play off many learned & laboured Speeches, but I think it most likely that the Affirmative of the Question will prevail—as our Debt is the largest in the Union and a considerable part of it was incurred for Services which tho' designed for the General Benefit, the Continent has been backward to recognize, perhaps the Measure will be as agreeable to the Massachusetts as to any of the States but some Gentlemen from those States which are the least in Debt are of the opinion that as the Debts were incurred for the Service of the United States they ought to be the Debts of the Union, and that an Assumption is necessary to prevent Disputes between the Genl. & State Governments, and that the Creditors of the State Governments if the same provision is not made for their Debts as for the Demands against the Continent, will continually complain and endeavour to defeat the Operation of the Revenue Laws—Another great Question will be the Rate of Interest, it is supposed by some that the promise of Interest recommended by Hamilton is beyond the Abilities of the Government and that a lower Interest will be most beneficial even to the Creditors themselves others affirm that we can pay an Interest of 6 ℔ Cent and that the people are so strongly impressed with the Idea that the publick Contracts ought to be fulfilled, that they will cheerfully submit to any heavy Taxes for that purpose, but I am not certain that those who are of this Opinion learnt it in that part of the Country where I live[1]—The Supreme Court of the U.S. is now sitting here and have appointed Mr. [*John, Jr.*] Tucker their Clerk—I have written several Times to Mr. [*Samuel, Jr.*] Phillips and have received no Answer I presume therefore he is sick if he is at Boston pray give my Love to him and let me know whether he is like to recover, remember me too with Expressions of Regard to your other Colleagues from Essex—Mr. Sedgwick has this Moment come into the Room and desires me to give his Love to you.

ALS, Wetmore Family, CtY. Place to which addressed not indicated.

[1] Hampshire County, Massachusetts, was the hotbed of Shays' Rebellion for tax relief in 1786–87.

John Trumbull to John Adams

*** I shall now take up a more important subject, and in return for the advice received, (for I do not choose to be in any Man's debt) address some hints to the Vice-President, relative to his own political situation, & the Strictures made upon his conduct by his Enemies. I shall ask no excuse for my assurance, & am certain my motive needs no Apology.

Be it remembered then, that the Vice-President is a native of New England, & that the inhabitants of the Southern States are not yet entirely cured of their local jealousies—that without any considerable advantages from the pride of family, or the favours of fortune, he has raised himself to that eminent station, solely by his personal merit, & the importance of his public services—& that this circumstance has provoked the pride & raised the envy of many of the Southern Aristocrats, who suppose themselves born to greatness, & cannot bear to be eclipsed by merit only—That this Party are endeavouring to represent his character in an unfavorable light, & if possible prevent his ever rising to the first office in the States, whenever a vacancy shall happen. The obloquy they have endeavoured to raise against him, as having deserted his republican principles, & become fond of the splendor, & titles of monarchical Courts, is well known, & needs no remark, because it has nearly subsided in the New England States, where his character is known & justly appreciated—it may perhaps still be a subject of unjust censure in the southern States—But must there at length subside, as their people, who are an age behind us in political knowledge, become convinced of the necessity of energy in the executive Department. But they attempt an attack on another ground, & endeavour to render him unpopular in the Senate, the principal theatre on which his political talents can now be exerted. They assert that the Constitution gives the President of the Senate no right to mingle in their debates—that he can on no occasion with propriety offer his sentiments at large, except when he is requested to give information respecting the affairs of foreign courts, which have fallen under his personal observation, or when in case of an equi-vote, he states his reasons on giving his casting voice. They add that as a public Speaker, the talents in which he excells all others, are force of argument & strength of language, approaching to sarcasm, and expressive of some degree of contempt for the opinions & reasonings of his adversaries— that in consequence, whenever he mingles in debate, he offends those whose sentiments he opposes—while the party he supports are not always pleased, as his idea of the necessity of affording his assistance is a tacit reflection on them, as incompetent advocates of a good cause—that he who mingles in debate subjects himself, to frequent retorts from his opposers, places himself on the same ground with his inferiors in rank, appears too much like the leader of a Party, & renders it more difficult for him to support the dignity of the chair, & preserve order & regularity in the debate—while he gives his enemies frequent opportunity by reporting casual expressions, which have fallen in the warmth of argument, to misrepresent his opinions & designs, with little danger of detection—as the doors of the Senate are always shut.

Of the truth or justice of these remarks I am no judge—but I have heard them so frequently made, & sometimes by men who I am sure are not unfriendly, and in every other respect have the highest esteem for your abilities & character, that I thought it my duty to communicate them—especially as on so delicate a subject it was doubtful whether You would hear of them in any other way—I should have chosen to hint them in a personal interview, but my business has disappointed me of a visit to New York, which I had intended in the course of this winter.

I congratulate You on the favorable Prospect of the firm establishment of our Government—The proceedings of the last Session are generally approved—The clamours attempted to be raised on the subject of Salaries have died away and our most sensible men would rather see an augmentation in one or two instances than a considerable diminution in any.

Vesting in the President the power of removing all officers in the executive department is a most important amendment of the Constitution in the only part in which I ever thought an amendment essential, or a defect absolutely necessary to be supplied. The other proposed amendments are very harmless at least—The Article, which establishes the right of Trial by jury in all cases at common law, I should object against as holding out a false light, because in many cases, it must be absurd, if not impossible to carry it, into execution—but the very objection shows that it is not dangerous.

The establishment of Fœderal Courts entirely separate from those of the States was another measure of equal importance the effect will not be immediately seen, but will be eventually of the highest consequence. In a word, though there are sundry members of Congress, whose opinions on Government have never advanced beyond the crude ideas of pure Democracy, which we imbibed at the beginning of the Revolution, the Majority appears sufficiently enlightened to carry every necessary measure, for establishing an energetic Government, armed with power for our Protection & Defence.

ALS, Adams Family Manuscript Trust, MHi. Written from Hartford, Connecticut. The omitted portion relates to Trumbull's law practice and health.

Newspaper Article

Saturday last, the 6th instant, being the anniversary of the *Alliance between France and the United States*, we are informed, it was celebrated by the *Chargé des Affaires* [*Louis Guillaume Otto*] *of his Most Christian Majesty*, who gave an entertainment to his Excellency the Vice-President, the Honorable the Senate, the Speaker of the House of Representatives, the Chief Justice, and the Heads of the great Departments of the United States—to his Excellency the Governor [*George Clinton*], and the Honorable the Chancellor of the State of New-York [*Robert R. Livingston*], and to the Diplomatic Body, and Foreigners of distinction.

After dinner the following toasts were introduced.

1. The Alliance.
2. The King, the National Assembly, and the People of France.
3. The President, the Congress, and the People of the United States.
4. The King of Spain.
5. The United Netherlands.
6. The King of Sweden.
7. The Cincinnati and the Soldiers of both Countries who have fought in support of the Alliance and of Independence.
8. Mr. Jefferson and the preceding Plenipontentiaries of the United States in France.
9. The Count de Moustier[1] and the preceding Plenipotentiaries of France in the United States.
10. The Marquis de la Fayette, and all those who cherish the connection of the two countries.
11. May the encrease of our commercial intercourse daily confirm the alliance.
12. May the advantages of a free, consolidated and efficient government be felt in both countries.
13. Perpetuity to the Alliance. Let us be rivals in Wisdom only and in National Honor!

NYDA, 8 February.

[1] Eleanor-François-Elie, comte de Moustier (1751–1817), resided in New York City as the French minister to the United States from January 1788 until his return to France in October 1789.

OTHER DOCUMENTS

Tench Coxe and Nalbro Frazier to Josiah Parker. FC:lbk, Coxe Papers, PHi. Written from Philadelphia.

> After looking more carefully into their accounts, finds an additional twelve pounds due from Parker, for which they have also drawn drafts on Hartley which they hope Parker will pay "at Sight"; for balance due on teas and nankeens, "You may give Col. Hartley any part of it you can spare"; if Parker provides a description of his mills, its outbuildings, etc., they will advertise for "a good tenant."

George Thatcher to Joseph Barnard. No copy known; acknowledged in Barnard to Thatcher, 19 February.

Jeremiah Wadsworth to Barnabas Deane. ALS, Silas Deane Papers, CtHi. Addressed to Hartford, Connecticut; franked; postmarked.

> "It is yet doubtfull if the Secretarys report [*on public credit*] will be adopted—but I think before the Session ends there will be additional duties therefore good pay should be had for rum"; reports crop prices and advises on mercantile matters; Morris thinks Silas Deane's accounts "will have a larger Ballance due him"; will send word.

[Rhode Island] *Providence Gazette*, 6 February.

> "By Advices from New-York, of a late Date, we learn, that in Consequence of the Representation from our Legislature that this State would probably soon accede to the General Government, there is a fair Prospect of our obtaining a farther Indulgence with Respect to the Payment of foreign Tonnage and Duties."

SUNDAY, 7 FEBRUARY 1790

Cold (Johnson)

Fisher Ames to William Tudor

I thank you for your esteemed favour by the mail. The attempts of Mr. __ [*John Gardiner*] may not demolish the bar, but they serve to prolong the silly prejudice against them. His whimsical violence, and overdoing the matter, may perhaps disgust even prejudice, and turn the current a little the other way against the persecutors. I suppose the world will not allow the lawyers to compare their persecutions with those of the primitive Christians.

I perceive our General Court have a fondness for paying debts, and Mr.

Edes's paper[1] complains of the hardship and danger of having them paid by a foreign government, for whom, and at whose special instance they were contracted. No doubt these people would claim repayment of the United States. How is that to be reconciled to the project of keeping the debt alive, as a good thing, and a nurse to the sovereignty of the state. Or would it be expected that the state should get paid by the U.S. and refuse to pay the creditors afterwards? For payment would destroy this good thing the debt. I should think our people mad if they should finally oppose the assumption of the state debts, which has clogged industry, kept the state poor and uneasy, and kindled one rebellion [Shays'], and will banish the farmers to the western woods.

I have actually sought for the Bath Memoirs[2] for Mrs. [Delia Jarvis] Tudor's memorandum, hitherto without success. The book is not in the New York [Society] library, where I went to inquire for it. If possible, I will send the information she desires. Please to present my most respectful regards to her. A young Mr. Martin Hoffman is now in Boston, and I promised to give him letters of introduction, but shamefully forgot it. You will see him, however, I presume, as his agreeable mother says she is acquainted with you. Permit me to hope that you will introduce him to the good folks, whom he may wish to see. I told him in particular that I would write to [Christopher] Gore.

To-morrow we are going to turn financiers—scarce a head in New York that is not ready to burst with a plan. The issue is very doubtful, as many oppose the assumption of the state debts, and others propose to offer the creditors three per cent. which I presume they would reject with indignation. ***

MHSC, ser. 2, 8(1826):321. The omitted postscript relates to a court case and the state judiciary.

---

[1] Benjamin Edes edited the *Boston Gazette*.
[2] Robert Pierce, *Bath Memoirs, Or, Observations in Three and Forty Years Practice at the Bath, What Cures Have Been There Wrought . . .* (Bristol, England, 1697).

William Bradford to Elias Boudinot

***

I am sorry your time is so much engrossed, that you find it difficult to write. but you seem to be cutting out business enough for yourselves, and Congress will sit much longer than was expected before it can all be finished. The public debt must be a weighty subject, and I think an embarrassing one on the enlarged plan [*for public credit*] of the Secretary. I find the objections to comprehending the State debts very numerous; and it seems the general opinion here that it will not succeed. But as far as I can learn, the funding of the rest is generally expected & desired.

***

ALS, Wallace Papers, PHi. Written from Philadelphia. The omitted text reports on Pennsylvania's state constitutional convention and refers Boudinot to John Marsden Pintard for delivery of an act for incorporating Philadelphia and for family news.

Lambert Cadwalader to Levi Hollingsworth

I have recd. your Letter of the 3d Inst. and am much pleased with the Information you have given me respecting the Experiments made on Mr. [*James*] Rumseys[1] Principles; I sincerely wish the Grist and other Mills you mention, to be constructed on similar Principles, may answer equally well; as the Success will not only reflect Honor on our Country, but be of considerable Benefit in reducing the Expence of manufact[*uring*] the most valuable Article of the Exports of Pennsylvania—I shall not fail to lay your Letter before the Committee tomorrow.

The [*Patents*] Bill is in considerable Forwardness and will be presented to the House in a few Days—The Committee ~~being~~ desirous of making it as perfect as possible have applied themselves to the Business with great Assiduity and the moment it is completed, it will be reported. It is impossible to say when the House will be at leisure to take it up, as tomorrow is the Day appointed, ~~on which~~ for considering the Report of the Secretary of the Treasury respecting the funding the public Debts—But you may rely on our Endeavouring to have the Business brought on as early as possible.

ALS, Hollingsworth Papers, PHi.

[1] For more on Rumsey, see *DHFFC* 8:39–72 passim.

Daniel Cony to George Thatcher

Your favour of the 31. ulto. was rec'd last ev'ning enclosing the report of the Secretary of Treasury, which Subject is the topic of Conversation in this Town.

Tis generally acknowledged that Mr. Hambliton has discovered an ingenious mind, a liberal System, and a magnanimous policy; how far it will be adopted you can guess, better than I. Saml. Adams, together with a number of our old, *genuine old* 75 patriots, are much opposed to a transfer of our State debt, But if Congress takes the best and most productive part of the Excise (which by the way tis acknowledged by all they have a right to) necessity will compel us to an adoption of the measure, a measure which I believe for my Self, will not prove So mischievous and distructive as Some affect to represent—for I confess tis my oppinion that a greater *Curse* may befall our *State government*, than that of exonerating her Self of a *debt* no less than a million & a half; and I will venture to guess that a majority of her citizens will be of my oppinion in less than a year.

***

ALS, Chamberlain Collection, MB. Written from Boston. The omitted text relates to John Gardiner's proposed judicial reforms and the state gubernatorial election and requests "Do continue to write."

Benjamin Goodhue to Stephen Goodhue

Yours of the 27th. Ulto. I recd. I find people are one with respect to the interest to be allowed, just as they are concern'd in securities—I understand those who have got large quantities, think that paying 3 or 4 ℔ Ct. is so far a breach of promise, that they bellow loudly on the occasion; it seems to me those Kind of folks would not care if the divil had all the rest if they could be benefited by it, they do not consider the great increase of duty which will be necessary to provide even for 3 or 4—I hear that they have understood that I and the chief of my Colleagues are against an high interest and grumble very much on the occasion, it is true that We are all from the Massachusetts. one or two excepted have much the same sentiment as to the rate of interest and are for measuring it by the Scale of our abilities, and not run headlong into such an excess of duties as will endanger the welfare of the Government and must issue in a breach of public engagements.

Tomorrow We enter on the business but the result I cannot hardly guess—I am satisfied a load of Indian Corn will do in Europe and therefore the Brig will I suppose go with such a Cargo I suppose it will be better to say but little what my sentiments are upon the subject of interest but I understood that I. Derby[1] was a good deal warm but that W[illiam]. Gray attack'd him and said 3 was enough.

ALS, Goodhue Family Papers, MSaE. Place to which addressed not indicated.

[1] Probably John Derby (1740–1812), a prosperous sea captain and merchant of Salem, Massachusetts, like his older brother Elias Hasket Derby.

Benjamin Goodhue to Insurance Offices

I have nothing interesting to inform you of, as the great business of the Secrys. report [*on public credit*] has not yet been taken into consideration, tomorrow it is to be taken up, when from the discussion which will be had on the subject, those measures which will probably result, will begin to unfold, that from the reservedness hitherto observed by the members, as yet furnishes no evidence scarsely for conjecture—the Assumption of the State debts however I am aware will be strongly opposed, tho' I am not without hopes it will eventually obtain, for as it appears to me We are so circumstanced, that we cannot with justice provide for the one to the neglect of the other, for the provision which will be made for the support of the Continental debt without assuming the State debts, will be taking away or so far interfere with the only support upon which our State Creditors can have any dependence that I presume no partiality of this Kind will ever be adopted, as reconsilable with either the principles of justice or National policy.

ALS, Goodhue Letters, NNS. Addressed to Salem, Massachusetts; franked; postmarked.

Thomas Hartley to Jasper Yeates

***

The Courts have lately been rather unproductive—The New Constitution of the united States and that which is intended to be formed in Pennsylvania will I trust give Confidence and Contracts must follow.

There is a high probability that there were will be great Emigrations from Europe in the Spring.

The Splendor of the new Government begins to be pretty conspicuous on the other Side the Ocean—& our Enemies seem to decrease it is astonishing what strong Prejudices were established there against us.

Dueling has been much abused and has often falln into improper Hands.

The appeal is an awful and I might say a sacred one—There are very few Instances in human affairs w[h]ere the Measure can be justified—It is flying in the Face of God and Law.

The two intended Combatants have got well over the Business—Impertinence and Indiscretion will have their Quarrels—in spight of all that can be said or done.

I will answer you respecting Timothey in a few Days—I left my orders with Mr. Burd[1] as I came through Philadelphia to issue my Distringasses.[2]

The funding System is to come forward to Morrow—I believe some of the great Leaders are prepared for Action—I shall give you an Account of the Process.

***

ALS, Yeates Papers, PHi. Addressed to Lancaster, Pennsylvania; franked; postmarked; answered 27 February.

[1] Probably Edward Burd, prothonotary of the Pennsylvania Supreme Court.
[2] A legal writ.

Jeremiah Hill to George Thatcher

You have doubtless heard of the dreadful Jealousey in a number of the pious good People of the different States against the federal Officers having a Seat in the State legislatures. President [*Governor John*] Sullivan in his Speech to the Legislature of New hampshire says,[1] to this purport "that they had ceased to be a free, Independent & Sovereign Government" which has given a dreadful Alarm to tender Consciences, I mean, such as believe in the doctrine of Bug-bears, Hocus pocus Jack with a Lanthorn Ghosts,[2] Spirits, Apparitions &c. &c.—I suppose the President to be a Unitarian, does not believe in *three being one* or rather *twelve* being *one* and *one* being *twelve.* but you know persons of a different sort of Abilities can see into Misteries of this nature, therefore I rather wish that the President as well as others of the same Class, woud take the Advice of brother Paul, "Him that is weak in the faith receive ye,"[3] but not with doubtful disputations fine spun niceties are with some the same as mistical Jargon & answers no better purpose in Society than talking Logic to an Ass. or casting Pearls before Swine—However I leave this Sort of Stuff and notice domestic Matters, There are a number here that wish a Post Office in this place, we have heard that Judge [*David*] Sewall has mentioned it to you or some of his friends at Congress if there are any prerequisites such as petitioning or the like if you will let us know, *the time when, the place where, and the manner how,* it will be complyed with, I wish you to write me your Ideas on this Head.

The Weather here for several days past has been very cold, ***

I think I told you that when I was at Boston I was introduced by my Friend Judge [*James*] Sullivan to the french Consul [*Philippe-André-Joseph de Letombe*] and among other things he requested me to find him the current price of our Lumber here, he wanted to acquaint his Country Men with it to introduce there coming here for it I hope this will be a port for foreigners &c., it appears hard to me to be denied there is upwards of forty Vessells belonging to this District, which of course makes it a district of some Consequence although the Sea Coasts are long—I have not had a line from you since the 10th Ulto.—Notwithstanding I shall keep scribling about something sometimes Sense, Sometimes nonsense, sometimes prose & sometimes verse, as the Spirit shall give me Utterance but ever subscribe your Friend in Spirit & in Truth.

ALS, Chamberlain Collection, MB. Written from Biddeford, Maine. The omitted text reports shipping news.

[1] Speech of 29 December 1789; see James Sullivan to Gerry, 3 February, n. 1, above.
[2] Mischievous spirits, cheating conjurations, and Halloween ghosts.
[3] Romans 14:1

Jonathan Jackson to Fisher Ames

I wrote you hastily by the last post—and intended to have made a few observations upon the report of Mr. Hamilton [*on public credit*] but my remissness to be in season for the Office prevented me then. Indeed I am so totally uninterested personally in such speculations I am not sure I have any business to give an opinion upon them—unless in being only a looker on upon the game it may be presumed some parts of it may be viewed by me with more temper & moderation.

Mr. Hamilton has certainly done himself personally great honour by his report—all agree it is ingenious or in the language of London *clever*. I am pleased that he has adopted so fully the sentiments of Adam Smith [*Wealth of Nations*] as he has—it will serve to disseminate them more fully here, and it will create him just applause & our Country deserved honour in Europe—where we have unfortunately lost a reputation it is full time we should be repairing.

As far as my observation has extended few appear to be alarmed at the reduction of interest to 4 ℔ Ct. for as to the residue being paid in Western lands most here I have met with would consider them of equal value in the moon—the highest at wch. I have heard them appreciated is 1/8 for the 6/8 proposed to be paid in them—I am not sure if Congress should put the interest at 3 ℔ Ct. that it would go down.

I wish Mr. Hamilton had proposed a general excise, not only to divide some of the Duties proposed that they might be less felt by individuals in the payment, and less temptation given for smuggling by charging some articles so high upon the importation of them—but also that our legislatures might have all occasion removed for their dabbling in what appears by experience they are quite unequal to—that is collecting excises, while the Executive of the Government is so feeble, & while they are surrounded by neighbours who think it their interest not to cooperate with them.

Besides which—it seems to me Excises must be brought forward in aid of your other impositions, to secure a sufficiency for the performance of your promises & full support of your credit—Perhaps your Secry. may have left Excises for the *act* & *deed* of Congress (that he might not appear to dictate too much) should they agree to the assumption of the State Debts—A measure I hope you will not split upon—for it is to be considered in a much higher veiw then a mere question of finance—It appears to me a principal hinge upon which will turn the stability of your new government—some here would kick at it if they dared, and if they could make it unpopular would stir up breeze—but fortunately some of these—such as the bald pated Doctr. [*Charles Jarvis*] on the Boston seat—and the bald

pated Genl. [*William Heath*] at Roxb[*ur*]y. & some others are so far interested in both kinds of Securities, that Interest may, tho' nothing else would,
stifle their lust for popularity and leading a mob—Besides Mr. Secry. "has
come York shire over us"[1]—as the saying is—by not referring the question to our legislatures, whether he shall assume the State debts or not—
which ~~debt~~ question I hope to God! Congress may never be brought to
put to the several assemblies—for if they ~~are~~ should be half so cross as I
fear a majority of our's are at present, they would give it I presume a flat
negative.

Your Sessions I think must be lengthy and the subjects before you still
momentous—I hope the majority will act with consistency and with vigour—and not spoil the measures already gone into by timidity—I am
sensible in a government so popular as ours—if not in every one, the general
opinion must be consulted and in a great measure conformed to—But it
behoves every gentleman situated as you are critically to distinguish the
opinions thrown out by the snarlers and bawlers in our gazettes & our Assemblies from the Good sense of the public at large.

I did not intend to have extended myself to another sheet—but finding
since my last that the fears I had then expressed were not without foundation
I thought it best to confirm them to you.

A day or two since one of our Executive Council [*John Hastings*] took me
aside & suggested whether it would not be best to originate some motion in
the present sessions of the Assembly for them to sanction the Enumeration
of the Inhabitants and order some aid to Congress in the execution of it—for
he said he fear'd it was becoming or would be made unpopular—I told him
that certainly I would not move in such a business for I hoped that Congress
were sufficient for their own affairs—if they must depend as formerly upon
the assistance of State Legislatures, their ordinances as heretofore would be
very uncertain & their power very inefficient—the gentleman who is from
Hamps[*hi*]re. County appeared very sincere in his apprehensions, & added
that he did not mean I should appear in such a motion—Genl. Cobb is in
opinion with me that it is best ~~for Congress~~ to make no recurrence to the
state legislatures for their interference—I hope the act of Congress will
permit the enumeration to be taken in Districts as large as Counties at least
by a single man—Cobb offers & has half agreed to take his own County
if not all the old Colony[2]—my brother—senator [*David*] Sexton (a good
man) has this day offered his services for part of our western Counties—
I wish Congress may add a little more allowance for the assistants, and I
think good men may be engaged throughout this State to undertake the
Census.

Please to remember me with respect & esteem to Colo. Wadsworth

& Mr. Trumbull to Mr. Dalton Mr. Sedgwick & all of my acquaintance among you.

ALS, Sedgwick Papers, MHi. Written from Boston; postmarked Boston, 8 February. A dated notation in an unknown hand is evidence that the letter was among Sedgwick's papers by May 1831.

---

[1]Bamboozled by his shrewdness: a phrase derived from the proverbial wiliness of the people of Yorkshire, England.

[2]David Cobb resided in Bristol County. The "old colony"—Plymouth Colony was separate from Massachusetts Bay until 1691—was the area composed in 1790 of Bristol, Plymouth, Barnstable, Dukes, and Nantucket counties.

Samuel Johnston to James Iredell

It is now near nine O'Clock at night when the Mail will be closed, so that I have only time to tell you that I have just this minute received a ~~Letter~~ Message from the President by Major [*William*] Jackson to inquire of me whether you will accept the Office of Associate Judge in the Supreme Fœderal Court and to inform of his intention to appoint you to that Office in the place of Mr. [*Robert Hanson*] Harrison who has resigned, on which I sincerely congratulate you and hope to have the pleasure of forwarding your Commission by the next Post.

ALS, Charles E. Johnson Collection, Nc-Ar. Addressed to Edenton, North Carolina; franked; postmarked.

Tobias Lear to James Madison

In obedience to the command of the President of the United States, I have the honor to enclose you a letter from Peyton Short Esquire resigning his Commission of Collector of the Port of Louisville in Kentucky, and to request that you will be so good as to consult with Mr. Brown, and any other Gentlemen from Virginia who are acquainted with characters in that part of the Country, upon a suitable person to supply the place of Mr. Short, and let the President know the result of your consultation this evening, as he intends to give in the nominations to the Senate to-morrow.

FC:lbk, Washington Papers, DLC.

Benjamin Lincoln to Theodore Sedgwick

I had, the last evening, the pleasure of receiving Your Esteemed favour of the 31st. Ulto. nothing could have made me more happy than the information that you had no other connexion with Gorham & Phelps in the western lands than being their a bonds man I wish the matter was justly settled the General Court have the business now under consideration and will it is probable point out some mode for an adjustment.[1]

Permit me to make some observations on the subject of interest—It is a subject in which I am deeply interested in I therefore shall probably view it in a light too partial. I will endeavour however to do the subject justice I have very little [*lined out*] before my letter must go to the post office the hints will consequently be rude and undigested I must think as I write, and write as I think.

If you are for three ℔ Cent interest, it arises, if I take your ideas, not from a conviction that it is right abstractly considered but that it is as much as the people have ability to pay and that an attempt to urge them farther will destroy the efficiency and respectability of Government. You know my dear sir that in a Government like ours tottering in feeble infancy it has but a choice of difficulties with which it must contend. On the one side its best friends and ablest supporters after sacrificing one third of their property to their darling object a firm and an energetic [*lined out*] government are looking earnestly for a security of the other two thirds [*lined out*] There are others for 3 ℔ Cent interest whose only view is to form such a contract as the people can comply with ~~with punctuality~~ with punctually—and thereby secure the honour and dignity of government.

The matter now seems to be reduced to these two points whether we shall ~~adopt~~ place the debts of the United States and with them the debts of the different States at an interest of three pr. Cent and thereby risk the disaffection of the holders of the public securities and ~~thereby~~ render the existence of the government or not very problematical; or whether you will place the interest at four ℔ Cent and thereby effectually attach to your new and infant government a very great able body of men in each State men on whom I am confident the present constitution must lean for support One of these propositions must yield to the other the question now is which ought to be sacrificed I think the former *must go over the dam* for if we embrace it, we embrace a proposition which will produce certain evils at a time when experiment alone can determine whether any good will arise from the measure or not We are sure no good will arise from it if we can rely on the calculations of our financier. I think we ought to rely on them, and mutilate his system as little as possible and not do as we have always done in this State so mangle any financing system as at last we had no person who would father the brat or who would be responsible that it would be useful in after life.

I think the four ℔ Cent interest should be adopted because it is coming much nearer to the just [*lined out*] expectations of the public creditors and will be nearer to the original contract because if the debt is fully funded and at four ℔ Cent the securities will very soon become important to us as a medium, if in this way they are to be useful the advantage will be one fourth more than if the debt shall be funded at three ℔ Cent In this view of the matter, that our debt will finally serve us as a medium, great good may be expected it will promote our commerce, advance our manufacturing, and give vigour and success to our husbandry.

We cast very differently respecting the proportion of the debt which will fall upon this State you say 200,000 annually I make it by my calculation to be 138,750 You may suppose that this State by the impost will pay more than its proportion of the public debt I believe that is not the case. If we [*lined out*] consume as little of foreign produce as other States we pay no more of than our proportion of the debt about 1/8 when we consider the saving made in our State compared with the neighbouring States by the use of New England rum instead of west India molasses instead of Sugar and Cider instead of the wine used in the Southern States the large proportion of articles we manufacture for our selves compared with the southern States it will leave I think if any way a ballance in our favour—The consumer of the goods must pay the duties on them eventually so that if we do not consume an over proportion of foreign produce we shall bear an equal proportion of the [*lined out*] burden only.

ALS, Sedgwick Papers, MHi. Written from Boston.

---

[1] For this issue see Josiah Burr to Jeremiah Wadsworth, 3 February, above.

James Madison to Tobias Lear

I have consulted with Mr. Brown on the subject of a Successor to Mr. [*Peyton*] Short. He is apprehensive that the reasons which induced Mr. S. to decline his appointment will have the same weight with any other person who could be recommended. He names Col. Richard Taylor as worthy of the appointment, and as not more likely to follow the example of Mr. Short, than any other fit person within his knowledge. I am acquainted with this gentleman and consider him as perfectly trust worthy. He held formerly a similar office on the Ohio when the trade of that Country was regulated by the State of Virginia.

ALS, Washington Papers, DLC.

Robert Morris to George Harrison

Mr. [*Garrett*] Cottringer informs that you departed from Philadelphia last Wednesday, therefore I suppose this letter will find you at Richmond if not sooner.

Yours of the 26th of Jany. came duely to hand but I did not reply immediately because my engagements employed my time very fully and indeed
they Continue to do so, for I am settling Accounts in the forenoon and forced
whether I will or no, to dine in Company almost every day, but this last
course will I hope Soon be over, I think my Public Accounts will be Settled
in the course of this & the next Month in the mean time I shall present a
Memorial to the President, Senate & House of Representatives which will
find its way into the Public Prints and if you keep a look out you will see it
by & by. The Public Securities have been Sold here at 7/6 in the pound that
is for final Settlements, Loan office Certificates and Nourses Certificates and
5/9 in the pound for Indents or Facilities but they seem rather to hold up
again, however the Debates of tomorrow may produce some alteration if the
Report of the Secy. [*on public credit*] be taken into Serious debate & it is the
day fixed for it In the course of next Week I intend to write to you again
but I give it as a general Rule if you can buy Loan office Certificates or Final
Settlements at 6/8d in the Pound, you will do well & Indents at 5/ but be
very carefull that all you purchase are genuine. I do not know how to inform
you as to the detection of Counterfeits, that was the principal object of your
journey to this City and I thought you had accomplished it.

ALS, Brinton Coxe Papers, PHi. Received in Baltimore.

Louis Guillaume Otto to Comte de Montmorin

Although, by the nature of my functions and the scantiness of my means, I
could not act as an ambassador in this country, and the state of public affairs
in France obliges me to maintain a strict economy, I could not refrain from
returning the polite gestures I receive from time to time from the principal
characters in the American government. In order to show them my appreciation in a more impressive way, I hosted a dinner yesterday to celebrate
the anniversary of the Alliance. I invited all the Senators, the Vice President
of the United States, and the heads of the great departments of Congress. I
had the satisfaction of receiving for the most part very flattering responses
and Mr. Jay himself wrote me "that he would celebrate with the greatest
pleasure an event *that has been of the greatest benefit to the United States.*" Others
responded that they hoped the grand epoch would always be, for their fellow
countrymen, a great source of gratitude and would become the basis for an
indissoluble tie between the two Nations. The Vice President postponed a
dinner that he had already arranged for the same day, and the Senators expressed the great satisfaction they felt with my sentiments regarding the alliance. To conform to the customs of the country, I proposed *toasts*, of which
I have the honor of attaching the translations here. The last, which relates

to the endurance of the Alliance, was repeated with a degree of enthusiasm admittedly inflamed by the wine, and the words *Esto perpetua*,[1] that some Senators added, were a sign of joy. As they attach great importance here to those types of patriotic *toasts*, the printers have come to request copies, which I could not refuse. I know too well the ground on which I stand, to allow myself to be dazzled by the demonstrations; they show only that, all things being equal and other interests not intervening, the heads of this Government will cherish an Alliance that even the greatest detractors of France can not help thinking of as the cornerstone of the independence of the United States. We spent the entire evening smoking and giving patriotic toasts. Mr. Jay, who did not leave until 10 o'clock, proposed the following prayer, which was welcomed with feeling: "May His Most Christian Majesty [*Louis XVI*] preserve all the prerogatives and all the powers consistent with the liberty and welfare of his people." Since it is only at table that Americans permit themselves any emotional effusions, I hope, Sir, that in the actual scarcity of public events, you will hear with indulgence these details, of little interest under any other points of view. I have had the satisfaction of hearing so many members of the Government say that they were surprised the President did not celebrate the important event that contributed more than so many others to the independence of the United States and that their compatriots had taken the greatest advantage available to them from our Alliance to celebrate the anniversary with public rejoicing.

The residence occupied by the comte de Moustier being the most beautiful and most spacious in New York, the President of the United States, being very poorly housed for someone of his rank, has desired for a long time to rent it. The comte de Moustier even seemed disposed, before departing, to give it to him, but the President's extreme reserve prevented every discussion of the subject. Only after some days did Mr. Jefferson's rumor about (Moustier's) assignment to Constantinople induce the President to make some inquiries. At first he sent the house's owner [*Alexander Macomb*] and then his private secretary [*Tobias Lear*] to request the sacrifice of my exchanging residences with him, on condition of compensating the comte de Moustier for extraordinary expenses that he had incurred inside the house. I was only partially authorized to begin the negotiation, but it was hard to refuse the first Magistrate of the United States without hurting his pride and without making myself disagreeable to the public who greatly desire the President to appear more lustrous. It even seemed to me that it was my duty to give in to the man who, under the modest title of President, enjoys several prerogatives of royalty. Therefore I consented to everything except the compensations, which the Secretary whom Monsieur the Count de Moustier left here, can agree to with that of the President. It is possible, however, that the Minister will suffer losses, but this case being extraordinary and one of a kind, I have good reason to presume the [*French*] Court will have regard for that sacrifice when circumstances permit. The exchange of houses with so eminent a character, which had to be handled very carefully, was accompanied with many difficulties and some special expenses which, in the belief I had that a refusal would have been very displeasing, I would calculate as nothing if I were entirely free of any apprehension of its being disapproved. The singularity of my position in this regard will perhaps merit some indulgence.

Copy, in French, Henry Adams Transcripts, DLC. Otto's letters included in *DHFFC* were usually written over the course of days, and even weeks, following the day they were begun.

[1] May it last forever.

George Thatcher to Sarah Thatcher

This is only to ask you to accept of two or three Lines, as it is impossible for me to give you any more at this time—I have been writing ever since morning, & have not got through with my correspondents, & it is now almost sunset.

Yours of the 23d. Jany. came to hand on wednesday evening—I rejoice to hear you are so well as to keep about house; much better I dont expect yet.

I feel most gratefull to our friends Mr. [*Nathaniel*] & Mrs. [*Abigail*] Fosdick for their kind visit; & particularly for her tarrying with you some days—I think her little son & Phillips will have a fine playing spell—I long to see them—Is Sally as wild as ever?

I have read our Honord. Fathers [*Samuel Phillips Savage*] Letter to you and wrote him—If he only considers how much time I had in Boston, & my wish to arrive at New-York by the meeting of Congress, I think he would have wrote you a different Letter.

***

ALS, Thatcher Family Papers, MHi. Place to which addressed not indicated. The omitted text mentions a letter Thatcher received from Silas Lee.

Henry Van Schaak to Theodore Sedgwick

Your letter of the 16th of last month I did not receive until last month [*week?*]. I thank you for it on the Score of friendship as well as for the political information it contains—A politi[*ci*]on and a friend in the same person is a phe[*no*]me[*n*]on—As you are not too proud to take hints from your Country friends I will from time to time suggest what I may think expedient to facilitate the operation of the government. I took this liberty with a gentleman Senator [*Schuyler*] from the State of New York in the last Session of Congress who has treated my letters with a degree of neglect which I not only feel for the present but it has taken such hold of me that I shall not easily forget it—This Senator and I went hand in hand in the politics of their State as well as in those on the great Scale and I have some grounds to flatter myself that I was of some service to get good men chosen both in the General and that State Government—Enough of this. You will please to bear it in your mind constantly that I expect *from great men* proper attentions when I write to them. Tell your members of Congress from *me*, and that to be surely will will have great weight, that they must take every oppertunity to write to their Country friends about every beneficial measure that is likely to take effect in this Session—no pains or trouble should be spared to make early favorable impressions among the great body of the people—Every progress that you make in the great the important business of a general assumption of the State Debts ought to be known early that the people may be led into a knowledge of this measure so as to be convinced of its necessity—From the moment that you mentioned this matter my mind was struck with the fullest conviction of its utility, & the more I have contemplated the subject the further I have been led th into a belief that the existance of the government in some measure depends on its taking place. Before I received your letter the Secretarys report [*on public credit*] was put into my hands—The Subject of the Report is an important one—that it is complicated and difficult to be understook, while we are in our infancy in the knowledge of Finance, is not to be wondered at. After the first reading of the report I found myself as ignorant as Uncle Toby[1] confessed himself to be to his Brother to be about *Infinity prurience liberty necessity* &ca. "I was puzzled to death" I understood it "no more than my horse" My mind was "like a smoke-Jack." I however gave it a second and third reading by which means I am gaining ground and I know now more about our National affairs than I ever did before—some parts of the Report must remain obscure until the subject is fully explained—The four ℔ Cent is too high at this juncture—The house I hope will modify this a little—But how will the public creditors relish a reduction? Some attention must be paid to them I should suppose.

Some thought them a culpable class of men—They now appear meritorious and in so important a point of view as not to be soured or disobliged.

The Secretary in his report makes it self evident to discerning minds that the State Debts ought and must be assumed by the National Govt. his intentions would have Government I wonder he did not make an estimate of the difference of Expense whether they are collected by fourteen different Governments or one. However plain this may be to you and me we know hundreds of people in this County who need more to convince them than the report as it now Stands. It is true this subject has been well handled in the Tablet[2] and by other occasional writers but those ~~are~~ it is presumeable have not been ~~so~~ generally read because the ~~object of the~~ assumption was then considered an object to be at a great distance—I viewed it as such; because I thought things were not ripe for it. I own to you that I shall not be altogether at heart easy until the measure is fully accomplished. ***

What are your accounts from our capital? I hope the good people there continue stedfast in their faith that the General Government is the only road to political Salvation in this Country. If this Sheet anchor is suffered to slip where shall we land? Pray husband your time so well as that you may write me frequently long letters—I am full of hope but not altogether without inquietudes ~~upon~~ about our political situation—when you write inter nos the contents of your letters shall be inviolably kept secret—when your intentions are otherwise you will find that I shall be industrious to promulgate what ought to be known abroad and make the best use of your information in my power. I have not been at Stockbridge [*Massachusetts*] since I wrote you last—In the course of this or next week we will make a visit. Have you recived my letter? In future, if you write by ~~write~~ the way of Kinderhook [*New York*] direct to the care of Mr. Alexander McMechin Merchant there who is prompt in forwarding Letters. My wife [*Jane Holland Van Schaack*] and Peggy join me in wishing that you may increase in political fame and *moral rectitude*—Remember me to all there who care for your sincere friend. [*P. S.*] Let me entreat you to write as often and to as many of your friends as your leisure will admit of. I have my reasons for this you may be sure or I wod. not make this troublesome request.

Having a little more time than I expected I should have when I concluded above I cannot forbear ~~of~~ expressing to you the great satisfaction I feel upon the fall of Exchange. It was at par when you wrote me—a Gentleman from New York since you wrote me tells me that it was from 2½ to 4 below par when he left it. Are we not from these pleasing circumstance to conclude that we are not so much Indebted in Great Brittain as we were led to believe from General reports or in other words are we not so happily Circumstanced as that our Exports exceed the Imports from what we formerly called the mother Country—My commercial knowledge is too limited to trace this ~~source~~ alteration to its true source—I fondly flatter myself that this change is one of the many good Effects that have already flowed from the establishment of the New Government. The influence of the Government I think is [*lined out*] discernable in the narrow Sphere I move in—It is evident to me that the raw materials of our Country which can be manufactured here are growing daily in [*lined out*] greater demand. Iron flax and wool are as much called for as wheat—My friends the Shakers[3] make greater proficiencies than any other Class of Men I know about here. And are extending of these manufactures daily beyond what could have been concived a few months past. They have of late made me some Andirons equal in substance and neatness to any imported ones that I ever saw—They have dyed Yarn for a large Carpet for me which is to be wove Scotch fashion at Lenox. When we meet ~~you~~ at Pittsfield you will see my house nearly furnished in the homespun way—chairs Tables andirons Tongs & Shovels Bed Curtains Carpets &ca.—Pray interest yourself to get me a handsome premium from Government that I may go on. In all your proceedings let the first object of ~~your~~ the attention of Government be to encour[a]ge the farmer—let that useful class of men be considered as the Gentlemen of the Country—I suppose you are ready to laugh at me heartily and will tell me that I am selfish. Be it remembered that when I am endeavouring to raise your Character I rank you among those who are wellwishers to the Landed Interest. I wish my business would allow me to slip down to New York to have a few hours converse with you—I wod. pester you with a thousand questions—Why is not the Communication from the General Government with the Country more frequent? The proceedings of Congress ought to be known with all expedition. The [torn] I mean those who are within the limits of my knowledge [torn] favourably disposed to depend upon the General Governm[ent] for their political happiness. I hope the bad Effects of the Compensation bill [Salaries-Legislative Act] are almost done away and that nothing further of that kind may make its appearance.

ALS, Sedgwick Papers, MHi. Written from Pittsfield, Massachusetts. The omitted text relates to state politics and John Gardiner's judicial reforms.

[1] The main character's military minded uncle in Laurence Sterne's *Tristram Shandy* (1759–67).
[2] A column in *GUS*.
[3] The Shakers (or Shaking Quakers) were a communitarian and millenarian Christian sect who first assembled in England in the 1770s. The Shaker village at Hancock, Massachusetts (now part of Pittsfield), was established in 1783, the third of nineteen founded throughout New England, New York, and the Ohio River valley by 1836.

Peter Van Schaak to Henry Van Schaack

***

Genl. Schuyler informs me that he has wrote to You & analysed Hamilton's Report [on public credit]—and he asks my Opinion upon that important Subject—I give it as my Opinion that it is in my Apprehension unexceptionable. The Adoption of it is I believe pretty certain. Public Credit will rest on a Sure Basis, because founded on public Justice & good Faith. Hamilton seems to have profited by the Practice of the Wisest European Nations, England especially. His Language relative to the Funds is the more intelligible to me from my having been a Witness to the Business of buying, Selling & transfering Stock in the *Market*.[1] Sedgwick tells me the Business will resolve itself into four Points 1 Whether there shall be any *Discrimination* 2 Shall the Interest due be converted into Capital 3 Shall the State Debts be assumed & &c. What shall be the Rate of Interest? ~~with Regard~~ he is for the Affirmation in every one of these Points—the two first he thinks will be generally agreed to—Not so the third & fourth. The Accession of Rhode Island he thinks next to certain, And the Vermont Business is to be taken up very soon: N. York is a most important Theater just now—the Genl. Govt. seems to carry all before it—The criminal Code [*Punishment of Crimes Act S-6*] is to be taken up as is the Militia Arrangement very soon—The terms of the Law will hang over evil Doers. My Hopes of Wise Measures are very strong. Never was there a Country I believe where the public Offices of State were filled with such Talents. The Supreme & District Courts are opened, in the latter the Grand Jury are now Sitting. I long to see the Judge's Charge. I have now but one Wish and that is that the *Country* may see the Measures pursued in their true Light. They will suspect that the Funding of the public Debt is to enrich Individuals—that may be the Consequence but not the Motive—What else can be done? The Virgin Murmurs of the New Govt. like the Virgin Treaty of the late Congress should be pure & inviolate. Much Specie is expected and with Good Reason from foreign Countries as soon as public Credit is established.

ALS, Van Schaack Collection, NNC. The recipient noted the letter was written from Kinderhook, New York; place to which addressed not indicated.

[1] Peter Van Schaack was a loyalist who resided in London from 1778 until 1785, when New York allowed him to return.

Thomas B. Wait to George Thatcher

When the inhabitants of this town had assembled to recieve the report of their Committee *of Grievances* [*on the Collection HR-11 and Coasting HR-16 acts*]—five or six, of the 15 or 20 present, were opposed to the report—Col. John Waite, Brother John Frothingham, Thomas Motley and T[*homas*]. B. W[*aite*]. expressed their opinions freely on the subject; and attempted, at first by reasoning, and afterwards by ridicule, to convince the scanty majority of their error. And altho' neither Reason or ridicule, had, at the time, any apparent effect, yet, finally the latter worked a *wonder*! The two Oxnards, our friends George, Davis Codman, &c. &c. joined in opinion with the minority, and said so much, and laughed so much more, that the Majority were fairly sickened and ashamed. For near a week, however, they seemed undetermined in what manner to effect a Retreat—being under strong apprehensions for their *rear*. But at length this expedient was hit upon: The chairman of the Committee, appointed by the town to forward the Petition, gave out, that he was dissatisfied with the vote for directing it to Mr. Ames, and declared publickly that he would not forwarded it to any man but Geo. Thatcher Esq. "This ~~was~~ is a hard case, to be sure," said the majority; ~~but~~ "What ~~was~~ is to be done? Why call another meeting, and e'en sanction the perverse intentions of the stubborn minded Chairman:" for it was clearly impossible to forward the Petition in any other manner, or by any other person!!! "Fudge—Fudge—Fudge."[1] Thus much in answer to your inquiry, "How it happened, &c."[2]

I have perused the Report of Secretary Knox [*on the militia*]: It is calculated to form the several States of the Union into a nation of *Soldiers*; but, as *Citizens*, I fear it will operate injuriously to our countrymen. At the age of eighteen, the morals of youth are unfixed—permanent habits of honour, honesty and industry are not established—the passions are warm and ungovernable: This, therefore, is, in my opinion, a very improper ~~time~~ period of life to take young men from under the care and tuition of their Parents Masters or Guardians, and throw them ~~for the~~ for the unreasonable term of 30 days, into the proposed annual encampments—where they will be exposed at once to all the follies, the indiscretions, and the vices of an army.

The proposed period of thirty days will operate as an enormous tax on the Nation—The Secretary supposes the advanced Corps to consist of 30,000 men, the expences of whom, in Cloathing, rations, camp equipage, &c. will amt. to   400,000 dol.
But he has wisely omitted to say any thing ~~of~~ respecting the value of their time, which, at 3/ pr. day, its very lowest value, will amt. to   450,000 dol. more
~~Add~~ To this may be added for each individual on an average, at least five days, which must necessarily be employed in preparing for, travelling to, and returning from the Encampment—   750,000 dol.
Here then is ~~a~~ an annual Tax of   925,000 dollars!!!
A very handsome sum for "*should[er]ing a firelock*."
~~Mr. Secretary proposes that the American~~
Mr. Secretary recommends that his proposed ration of Soldiers should

be divided into Legions—each Legion to consist of about 3000—of whom 250, are to be officers—These are to receive their commissions or warrants immediately or mediately from the President of the United States, who, by the Constitution, will at the same time be the Captain general of the American forces: Thus, every twelfth man, from 18 to 60, throughout the United States will receive particular favours, and consequently will feel ~~themselves~~ himself under particular obligations to the *Captain general President* of the Nation. This will throw a weight into the *Executive Scale*, for which it will puzzle the great Mr. Adams himself to find a balance.[3]

To conclude the whole, Mr. Secretary very modestly ~~recommends~~ advises that all the proposed Commissions be given to himself and Brother Officers, and that they be annually & generously paid for receiving them. Huzza! for the Cincinnati![4]

After all—I have read the Report but once—and then cursorily—When I shall have thoroughly perused it—heard more, and thought more about it, I shall be better able ~~to learn~~ determine whether, in its consequences, it will be good or ill. If, upon the whole, it should be calculated to prevent more evil than it will produce (which, by they way, I very much doubt)—why then I shall make no further objections to its ~~being adoption~~ But, on the contrary, shall wish it to be adopted, & to continue in operation till some other system shall be found, productive of more *good*, and that shall be attended with less *Evil*. Men, and the measures of men, are but a composition of imperfections—when we are making a selection, therefore, from either, we are to look, not for that which is *perfect*, but for that which is the *least imperfect*. Possibly Mr. Secretary Knox's Report belongs to the latter description, ~~but~~ I will inquire further.

I have seen a sketch of Secretary Hamilton's Report [*on public credit*]—on which I dare not make a single observation. The greatness, the extensiveness of his views, astonish and confound me.

ALS, Chamberlain Collection, MB. Written from Portland, Maine.

---

[1] In this context, "nonsense, nonsense, nonsense."

[2] For the Petition of the Merchants and Other Inhabitants of Portland, Maine, see *DHFFC* 8:412–18.

[3] An allusion to Adams's well known preoccupation with balance of power theory.

[4] The Society of the Cincinnati, a national fraternal organization with state chapters, was founded by Continental Army officers in May 1783. Behind its hereditary membership and chartered purpose of providing support to impoverished members, critics spied a tendency towards a native aristocracy and a conspiracy to channel undue influence and economic benefits to veteran officers. See Markus Hünemörder, *The Society of the Cincinnati: Conspiracy and Distrust in Early America* (New York, 2006).

Letter from Virginia to a Philadelphia Merchant

Secretary Hamilton's scheme [*on public credit*] does not meet the approbation of many people in this country. The reducing the interest to four per cent. we conceive is too partial, ever to take place at this juncture; should it be the case, there can be no future dependence. Next year they may reduce it to two per cent. and the year following they may, by the same unjustifiable measure, make a *bonfire* of the principal, together with the public *honor and credit* of the United States. Surely our Congress cannot consent to a measure in every point of view so erronious; they must be too well acquainted with the great importance and necessity of establishing, on the firmest basis, public credit and public faith, the best and only security of pubic and private confidence.

NYP, 27 February.

OTHER DOCUMENTS

William Constable to Gouverneur Morris. FC:lbk, Constable-Pierrepont Collection, NN.

Robert Morris "is getting on with the settlement of his [*public*] accts.—I think Smoothly—Day light begins to Appear thro' the Gloom—but his pecuniary Embarrassments are great indeed & seem to daily increase"; had to send some bills to Boston because they would not sell in New York City, "in Consequence of his being Concerned."

Benjamin Goodhue to William Heath. ALS, Heath Papers, MHi. Addressed to the "Council Chamber," Boston; franked; postmarked. Covers forwarded letter (unlocated) from Bland.

"Congress tomorrow enter upon the important discussion of the Secrys. report [*on public credit*], but what will be the result of measures in consequence thereof is almost impossible to conjecture—perhaps it is a crisis, in which the interest and happines of our Country may be deeply involved, God grant us wisdom and integrity, in our public councills."

Benjamin Goodhue to Joseph Pierce. No copy known; acknowledged in Pierce to Goodhue, 3 March.

William Maclay to John Nicholson. No copy known; listed in H. C. Van Schaack's scrapbook "Autographic History of the American Revolution" at NHi as among the letters in the now dispersed volume two of that scrapbook.

James Madison to Thomas Jefferson. ALS, Madison Papers, DLC. Place to which addressed not indicated; received 6 March. For the full text, see *PJM* 13:31–32. The editors dated this letter by virtue of Madison's remark in it that his most recent letter (4 February) had gone by the "last mail." For the mail schedule, see 6 January, above.

The newspapers Madison has been sending convey "the complexion" of politics, especially regarding public credit, on which there is a "great variety" of sentiments; asks Jefferson to enquire of news from Paris about George Washington Greene, on behalf of his mother, Catharine "Kitty" Greene; "every one who mentions the subject of your appointment to me, seems to have much solicitude for your undertaking it."

Theodore Sedgwick to Samuel Henshaw. No copy known; acknowledged in Henshaw to Sedgwick, 14 February.

George Thatcher to Samuel Phillips Savage. No copy known; acknowledged and quoted in Savage to Thatcher, 17 February.

George Thatcher to David Sewall. No copy known; acknowledged in Sewall to Thatcher, 11 March.

Monday, 8 February 1790

Cold (Johnson)

Benjamin Hawkins to John Gray Blount

I have been in hopes for some days past that I should be able to send you some information respecting the report of the Secretary of the Treasury, But it is this day for the first time to be taken up in the house of representatives, and the members have observed great silence, so that even a probable opinion cannot be now formed. I shall send you the U.S. gazett [*GUS*] with a note twice a week hence forward.

All your friends have enquired after you with a degree of affection which is affecting to me Miss Marshall is well, she says you did not answer her letter, which discouraged her from writing to any other of her Carolina friends in answer to this letter—so that I have been injured by your neglect. all of this amiable family are in this house in queen street, Mr. & Mrs. Remaque are well and their little babe capable of prattling a little. Mr. Van Burken [*Pieter Johan Van Berckel*] and his daughter are living in the house formerly the property of Doctr. [*Charles*] McKnight up the North River I have been twice there to see them—it has been conjectured by some near friends that Mr. [*Louis Guillaume*] Otto was making love there, and it is also believed, that his discontinuing his visits has given umbrage some where. He is by report to be married to Miss Creavecoeur daughter of Mr. St. John. Mr. [*René Charles Mathurin*] de la Forest is well he has one little daughter he often asks after you can you send forward a deed for the 1,000 acres of land to his son. Blount Hawkins de la Forest dulot.

You will see by the price Currt. the high price of wheat. Corn will consequently be very high as every bushel of the former will be shiped from the middle States—Have you not a great quantity on Tar river? I know some orders are given here for purchasing a quantity, probably on Roanoke, or your river, on speculation. We have laid before the Senate the Act of Cession of our State, it is committed, and this day we are to meet the Committee to give some information respecting it, do I pray you write to me freely and confidentially on any of your prospects. I have had an occasion to name you once or twice in a manner as you deserve. We shall be embarrassed with the Indian business, and shall want some very Confidential man in that quarter. The Judiciary system will be extended very soon to North Carolina, I am one of the Committee on the bill [*North Carolina Judiciary Bill S-10*], and we wait untill, the Committee on the Cession report.

AL, John Gray Blount Papers, Nc-Ar. Place to which addressed not indicated. On the reverse of the last page of this letter, Williamson wrote a separate letter to Blount on the same day. It is printed below.

Patrick Henry to Richard Henry Lee

A few days ago I wrote you a letter of some length; and among other things I mentioned Genl. [*Joseph*] Martin and his affairs about which I have given you so much trouble. It is with reluctance I mention his business so often. It should have ended with the first mention of it had not accusations against him been brought forth. It seemed necessary for his vindication, and in some measure for those who had recommended him, that the charges should be refuted. You should have been spared the trouble of this had I not entirely forgot to enclose in my last the papers I now send herewith. I beg you to make just such use of them as may serve to wipe away the aspersions thrown on the person intended to be ruined in the public opinion. You will find the same party also endeavoured to ruin his son, Wm. Martin, by accusing him of joining the Indians in their murdering parties. Will you be so good as communicate what relates to Genl. Martin to our Friend Col. Grayson, as also the Hints I drop on the subject of the No. Carolina cession.

The more I think of this the more dangerous it appears. I am told the people ceded are 30,000 Souls. Some say more and some less. These people placed under a military government together with the troops which may and will be placed there, will give an energy and force to northern councils in a part of the country very convenient for the views of consolidation, if such shall govern. The geography of the place renders the proceeding dangerous in the extreme to this country and to all the Southern States. These observations go not to the right of ceding a people to Congress with their consent signified in a Constitutional way, viz.: by a free convention of the people. Whether our rulers will deem this right of the people to be consulted on such an occasion worth preserving or whether it shall with so many other popular rights be yielded up, I know not. But to me it is evident that the right in question is one of the most valuable. Indeed without its full admission, it seems no political right whatever can exist. My conjecture is that the leading characters in the district are silenced by the receipt or expectation of certain things, more flattering than the struggle for rights, which promise nothing but an equality, which ambition abhors. a precedent of cession like the present will go great lengths by and by.

Whenever you have leisure to Touch upon this point, or upon any other you will give me very high gratification.

[P. S.] N.B. If this cession is permitted, the country from the [*Great*] Lakes to Georgia is under congressional power. Is not this cause of alarm?

Patrick Henry 3:415–17. The ALS was listed in *Henkels Catalog* No. 1021(1910):item 344. Written from Prince Edward County, Virginia; received when Lee arrived at New York on 11 April (R. H. Lee to Patrick Henry, 10 June, volume 19). Enclosures not located.

Anne Huntington to Benjamin Huntington

The Last letter I recd. from you was dated 31st Jany. by which I am informd. you are recovering slowly from your disorder I was in hopes you had perfectly recoverd. but as you justly observe Patience and Resignation to Providence is our duty.

I have been taking the Bark[1] prepared in a different manner from what I have ever taken it. and I have gained Strength my fever is not so high as it has been but I have at this time a Chill coming on which makes my hand tremble so that I can write but very poorly the last Letter I wrote you I never expected to write another I had been raising matter that appeard. the same as that which comes from a boil and was very low and faint I am of the same mind I was then as to what my disorder is but how long this feble thread of life is to be extended and for what purpose God only knows I am as happy as

I can be with my infirmities in your absence our Family are all well except me. I want to write a very long letter but am not able.

ALS, Huntington Papers, CtHi. Written from Norwich, Connecticut; franked; received 18 February; answered 20 February.

[1] The bark of the cinchona tree (also known as Peruvian Bark or Jesuit's Bark) became available in North America as a medical treatment in the 1720s. The basis for quinine, it was used for recurring fevers and other symptoms similar to malaria (*Drinker*, p. 144n).

Robert Laidler to [*Michael Jenifer Stone*]

I observe in Greens paper[1] that the President has recommended to the Senate and House of Representatives to take into their consideration the Post-Office and Post Roads that the intercourse between the distinct parts of our Country might be facilitated by a due attention to the same. When last I had the pleasure of conversing with you on the danger to which Ferry-keepers are expos'd from the Laws of Maryland, you were so obliging to say shou'd the Post-Roads &c. come under the notice of Congress that you wou'd use your influence to have some Clause inserted relative to Publick Ferry's which wou'd in future secure them against any Law heretofore made by re-quiring that all Ferry-keepers shou'd be Licenc'd by their respective County Courts and fin'd shou'd they not keep such Boats and hands as the Courts directed and give a speedy passage to all such persons as shou'd apply for the same unless they were first inform'd that they were runing from Justice.

As I am so much Interested, I have no doubt your goodness will excuse my Solicitude on this occasion—And may I hope in the Multiplicity of your other avocations you will not be unmindful of your promise?

ALS, Stone Papers, MdHi. Place from which written not indicated. The recipient has been assumed from the location of the document.

[1] Frederick and Samuel Green's [Annapolis] *Maryland Gazette*.

William Maclay to John Nicholson

This was a day of Much expectation, and the Galleries of the Representative Chamber ~~was~~ were much crouded. The Business however ended with laying Sundry Resolutions on the Speaker's Table, which are to be printed and will be the Subject of future discussion. I have inclosed You Copies.[1]

Two Peices[2] are likewise inclosed, which some People here wish You to send to the Freeman's Journal or some other Paper for publication. please to send me one or Two of the Papers containing them. You are however at liberty to suppress them, if any great impropriety should appear in One or either of them. They may do but little good. but it is expected they will tend to correct some Errors. I need not mention to You. that nothing need be said about the Author.

P. S. cannot expect the Copies of the Resolutions to be correct. certificates instantly rose.

ALS, Gratz Collection, PHi. Addressed to Comptroller General of the State of Pennsylvania; franked; postmarked.

---

[1] Transcripts of Smith's (S.C.) and Fitzsimons' resolutions of this date, in Maclay's hand, are with this letter in the Gratz Collection, PHi. The resolutions as printed in *NYDA* are in *DHFFC* 5:823, 839–43. Those proposed by Fitzsimons became the basis of the Funding Act and are printed below.

[2] For these pieces, see 20 February, below.

Robert Morris to George Washington

The Memorial which you will find enclosed herewith, Speaks so plain a Language as not to stand need of Explanation, and the Occasion such as not to require Appology. The request which it contains being supported by considerations of Public Justice, will I am sure from that Motive, meet your favour.

ALS, Miscellaneous Letters, Miscellaneous Correspondence, State Department Records, Record Group 59, DNA. For the enclosures and the history of Morris's petition, see *DHFFC* 8:663–75.

Roger Sherman to Justus Mitchell

I received your letter of the 26th January. Am glad to hear that sister Sherman [*Martha Sherman Mitchell*] & your family are well & that her goods came so safe to hand, as to the small expence of sending them to [*from?*] New York she is very welcome to it, I shall not take any thing for it—and I shall always be ready to render her & the rest of the family any service in my power. ***

I suppose that moral good or evil consists not in dormant principles, but voluntary exercises, that regeneration simply considered is not a moral virtue, but the holy exercises that flow from it are—And on the other hand no propensities in animal nature are in themselves sinful, if not i[*n*]dulged contrary to law. That moral good consists in right exercises of the natural power & principles of the soul, in setting the affections on right objects, &c. and moral evil in placing the affections on wrong objects And mankind having the power of free agency are justly accountable for the exercise of their natural powers, and that any indisposition [*not?*] to do what they know to be their duty can be no excuse for not doing it.

I have enquired of several Book sellers what abatement they will make from their retail price for taking a considerable number; all the answer I can get is that they will sell as low as they can possibly afford If I had a list of the Books wanted I could let you know whether they are to be had & the price.

FC, Sherman Papers, DLC.

Hugh Williamson to John Gray Blount

Not knowing a Word of what is written on tother Side & therefore not vouching for it, because I would not vouch for what is said by a congressional Man as such, I have only to inform you, what probably you know viz. that the Return of the Quantity of Land entered in Glascows Office[1] is not come to Hand.

Col. Hamilton has laid before Congress a System that opens a new ~~System~~ Train of Speculation and will furnish Substance for at least one Weeks Debate in Congress. To Day it is taken up in a Committee of the Whole. Much good may it do them. North Carolina having on the floor no Rep. I did not propose saying Reptiles but Representatives she may shun the Blame of any wrong that may be done. And the odds may be taken at two to one that some will be done if any Steps are taken according to the proposed Plan. You cannot doubt who it was who wrote so fair a Hand.

AL, on back sheet of Benjamin Hawkins to Blount, John Gray Blount Papers, Nc-Ar.

[1] James Glasgow was North Carolina's secretary of state.

[*Jeremiah Wadsworth,*] The Observer—No. XVIII

The report of the Secretary of the Treasury, being now before the public, contains information which must remove the reluctance of some, who doubted the propriety of funding the debt, and re-establishing public credit. Insidious means have been used to lead the people into an opinion, that a great part of the domestic national debt, has been purchased by foreigners at its lowest price.

In Boston, it has been published, and said to be under the sanction of a member of Congress, that "the national debt is five eights owned by foreigners, and is thus registered in the treasury of the United States." I much question whether any member of Congress ever gave such information, and suppose it rather a fabrication of design; but if it be true he is corrected by the treasury report.

Many insinuations of the same nature circulate, and cause a fear in some minds, that their country will be sacrificed to the emolument of a few rich foreigners. The Secretary's report furnishes means to detect these misrepresentations—any person holding national securitiés or bonds, may have their amount registered in the treasury books, the original bonds are given up, and an account opened between the United States and the creditor, to whom is given a new certificate of the amount due to him. The debt thus modelled is called the registered debt. Many of our citizens have registered their national paper, and it is well known that all purchased for foreigners or to send abroad on adventure, hath been entered on the treasury books in this manner.

By the Secretary's report we find that the whole domestic debt of the United States, is

	Dollars	Cents.
	42,414,085	94
The whole registered debt is,	4,598,462	78

The registered debt is not one ninth part of the whole, and only a part of this is owned by foreigners.

Several gentlemen of veracity, who are professionally acquainted with the circulation of paper, and the manner of its negociation, inform me that by enquiry at the register office, three months past, considerable less than 3,000,000 dollars had been registered on account of foreigners—but suppose three millions of dollars is the sum, this is but one fourteenth part of the national debt—The debt of the particular States hath not to my knowledge, unless it be within a few weeks past, ever been purchased for foreign adventure, and if this be considered as part of the national debt, which it ought to be both in justice and policy, not more than one twenty seventh part of the whole is vested in foreign owners, and a considerable proportion of this was taken by them, either in payment of debts due, or at a price of purchase much higher than it has been in the country.

Some persons have laboriously circulated an idea, of a prodigious foreign sale of paper, to prejudice the minds of the people against a funding system, but I think such attempts base and dishonest; even allow the facts, such as they wish to represent, it would be unfortunate for the country, but is no substantial argument against funding the debt. Justice stands on fixed principles, and not on a man's complexion, the tone of his voice, or the country in which he was born. Other things being alike, that which is justice to a native citizen is also justice to a foreigner.

The quantity of registered debt, is also some guide in determining the sum, which hath been alienated by the original holders at a low price. The brokers and great speculators in paper, in the middle States; where most of this traffic hath been managed, have registered in the treasury much the larger part of the sums purchased by them, and the whole of this we see to be a sum, comparatively small.

The alienations which have taken place between citizens removed from the course of speculation, have generally been at a price much nearer the original value. Continued examination of this subject gives me new conviction, that the alienations which have happened are far less than many suppose. I do not mention this as supposing it a matter which ought to influence in the provision of funds, but if ease can be given, in consistency with truth, to those persons whose opinion is different from mine, they ought to receive it.

In the Secretary's report there is an argument for the re-establishment of national credit, which I do not remember to have before seen publicly noticed—he says, "The effect, which the funding of the public debt, on right principles, would have upon landed property, is one of the circumstances attending such an arrangement, which has been least attended to, tho it deserves the most particular attention. The present depreciated state of that species of property is a serious calamity. The value of cultivated lands in most of the States, has fallen since the revolution from 35 to 50 per cent. In those farthest south the decrease is still more considerable. Indeed if the representations continually received from that quarter, may be credited, lands there will command no price, which may not be deemed an almost total sacrifice. This decrease in the value of lands ought, in a great measure, to be attributed to the scarcity of money. Consequently whatever produces an augmentation of the monied capital of the country, must have a proportional effect in raising that value. The beneficial tendency of a funded debt, in this respect, has been manifested by the most decisive experience in Great-Britain." The evil here mentioned is most sensibly felt, and has come near ruining many thousands of our small planters, and if a remedy be possible it ought to be immediately applied. The opening of an immense new territory is the cause, which hath been commonly assigned; this may have its influence, but is not proportioned to so great an effect. The scarcity of money is a cause greater and more immediately operating. To give a value to fixed or landed property, there must be a certain proportion of property, in its nature negotiable, such is money, and the principal in public funds, which by its credit, is received as money. The destruction of negotiable property, instantly lowers the value of landed property. When business stagnated by the commencement of war, the whole negotiable property of the people was thrown into the hands of the public, and has in effect been anihilated by the failure of credit. At the return of peace, habit and other causes, for a short season preserved a decent price, but the depreciation of lands soon took place and is now become extreme. Unless a remedy can be in part effected, by the measures recommended, the saleable value of the farmers property is half destroyed. The argument addresses itself strongly to the policy and interest of all our planters who feel the evil. If a small number of people were to be benefitted, it would be less material, but the class of citizens whose case we are now considering, contains nine parts, in ten, of the whole people.

[Hartford, Connecticut] *American Mercury*, 8 February. For information on The Observer series, its authorship, and reprintings, see the location note to The Observer, No. I, 12 October, above.

Thomas Fitzsimons, Resolutions

[*1*] Resolved, That adequate provision ought to be made for fulfilling the engagements of the United States in respect to their foreign debt.

[*2*] Resolved, That permanent funds ought to be appropriated for the payment of interest on, and the gradual discharge of the domestic debt of the United States.

[*3*] Resolved, That the arrears of interest, including indents issued in payment thereof, ought to be provided for on the same terms with the principal of the said debt.

[*4*] Resolved, That the debts of the respective States ought, with the consent of the creditors, to be assumed and provided for by the United States.

[*5*] Resolved, that it is adviseable to endeavour to effect a new modification of the domestic debt, including that of the particular States, with the voluntary consent of the creditors, by a loan, upon terms mutually beneficial to them and to the United States.

[*6*] Resolved, that for the purpose expressed in the last preceding resolution, subscriptions towards a loan ought to be opened, to the amount of the said domestic debt; including that of the respective States, upon the terms following, to wit:

That for every hundred dollars subscribed, payable in the said debt (as well interest as principal) the subscriber be entitled, at his option, either

To have two thirds funded at an annuity, or yearly interest of six per cent. redeemable at the pleasure of the government, by payment of the principal; and to receive the other third in lands in the Western Territory, at the rate of twenty cents per acre. Or,

To have the whole sum funded at an annuity or yearly interest of four per cent. irredeemable by any payment exceeding five dollars per annum on account of both principal and interest; and to receive, as a compensation for the reduction of interest, fifteen dollars and eighty cents, payable in lands, as in the preceding case. Or

To have sixty-six dollars and two-thirds of a dollar funded immediately, at an annuity, or yearly interest of six per cent. irredeemable by any payment exceeding four dollars and two-thirds of a dollar per annum, on account both of principal and interest; and to have, at the end of ten years, twenty-six dollars and eighty eight cents, funded at the like interest and rate of redemption. Or,

To have an annuity for the remainder of life, upon the contingency of living to a given age, not less distant than ten years, computing interest at four per cent.

Or, To have an annuity for the remainder of life, upon the contingency of the survivorship of the youngest of two persons, computing interest, in this case also, at four per cent.

[7] Resolved, that immediate provision ought to be made for the present debt of the United States; and that the faith of government ought to be pledged to make provision, at the next session, for so much of the debts of the respective States, as shall have been subscribed upon any of the terms expressed in the last resolution.

[8] Resolved, that the funds which shall be appropriated according to the second of the foregoing resolutions, be applied, in the first place, to the payment of interest on the sums subscribed towards the proposed loan; and that if any part of the said domestic debt shall remain unsubscribed, the surplus of the said funds be applied, by a temporary appropriation, to the payment of interest on the unsubscribed part, so as not to exceed, for the present, four per cent. per annum; but this limitation shall not be understood to impair the right of the non-subscribing creditors to the residue of the interest on their respective debts: And in case the aforesaid surplus should prove insufficient to pay the non-subscribing creditors, at the aforesaid rate of four per cent. that the faith of government to be pledged to make good such deficiency.

NYDA, 9 February.

Newspaper Article

The curiosity of the spectators, in the galleries, had been highly excited, as they expected to hear some able debates; but, as soon as it was carried to read the report, which would take up several hours, the citizens disappeared in an instant.

It is expected that the remainder of the report will be read to morrow; after which it is probable, that either Mr. Smith's or Mr. Fitzsimons's method will be adopted.

NYDG, 9 February.

[*John Nicholson*] to [*William Maclay*]

I SHALL according to your request, continue to send you my observations upon the report of the secretary of the treasury.

His prefatory declarations on the importance of public credit, are no less true than elegant and judicious. In every view of the subject, honesty is the best policy. Interest as well as morality, justice and national character requires it: for it is of great advantage to be able to buy *cheap*, or borrow on *good terms*.

Having stated the importance of *public credit*, he enquires by what means it is to be effected. The answer he gives, is so just that none will dispute it, and so plain that every one may understand it. *It consists in good faith and a punctual performance of contracts.* It is curious that a position so plain in theory, should in practice be so difficult, as to be mistaken, even by men of the first abilities. He goes on to shew the dependence of *public credit*, upon *public faith*, and the importance thereof both from negative and positive arguments; and by reflection on the particular situation of America, and the causes which originated the various obligations entered into, and which yet remain to be discharged, shews what additional force the obligations derive therefrom. He justly entitles it *"The price of liberty."*

I do not like his reflections on our former national character, nor his palliation of the past infractions of engagements, with which he charges the United States, by ascribing it partly to inexperience in the subject of finance. It is a common, but not the less unworthy practice, for individuals to depreciate the performance of others, in order to enhance the value of their own, and to prostrate the former, that they may erect the latter upon its ruins.

I shall in the course of this letter make a few reflections, to rescue the United States from the unfavourable character given of them by him; and on comparing that part with the observations which I shall take occasion to make upon the financial path he proposes to the government to tread in, you will probably conclude, that I am of opinion the charges of infractions of engagements, and ignorance of finance, will not apply so fully to the past, as to the proposed administration.

As an historian treating of the "price of our freedom," one would have expected, he would not have omitted any part of the purchase of it, especially that part which carried us through the most bloody and perilous period of the contest. But as a financier, it was certainly his duty to have omitted no part not already discharged, but to have stated faithfully their engagements to the government, in order that those engagements might be fulfilled. For although the possessors of particular classes might fare the better, that others were kept out of sight; yet it behoves the government to attend equally to all her obligations. Breach of faith is like a breach of the commandments, "he that offendeth in one point is guilty of all." He who, though he deals fairly with one, cheats and betrays others, will never be esteemed an honest man.

As the secretary hath not done it fully, I shall state all the obligations of the United States, from their first union to the establishment of the present government, so far as they have not been discharged, but exist against the United States, and which good faith requires should be fulfilled according to the engagements severally and respectively.

To take these up in the order of time, in which they were made, it will be necessary to recur to that early period, when the several states, theretofore British colonies, united in one common council, to deliberate on their joint situation, and determined on the great alternative, between submitting to abject slavery attempted by the nation they had been accustomed to regard as their parent, or defend themselves by arms. When the latter was gloriously preferred, the means of defence were yet to be provided. An army must be raised, accoutred, armed, fed and clothed, and all the concomitant expences paid. The several provinces had little or no money. The congress could have none. Their situation is well represented by that honourable body, in their circular address to the states. "Armies were then to be raised, paid and supplied, money became necessary for these purposes, of your own there was but little, the little that was spread among you could be collected only by taxes, and to this end, regular governments were essential, of these you were also destitute." Let us at this stage of the business have supposed our present financier introduced with all his supereminent abilities. What could he do? What would he have done? So circumstanced, could he have done better than was done? "Having (saith the congress) no other resource, but the natural value and wealth of this fertile country, bills of credit were issued on the credit of this bank, and your faith was 'pledged for their redemption';"[1] and on the 22d June, 1775, they "resolved that a sum not exceeding two million of Spanish milled dollars be emitted by the congress in bills of credit for the defence of America. Resolved that the confederated colonies be pledged for the redemption of the bills now directed to be emitted;" and on the 23d, "Resolved that the form of the bills be as follows—*Continental currency* No. __ dollars. This bill entitles the bearer to receive __ SPANISH MILLED DOLLARS, *as the value thereof in* GOLD *or* SILVER, *according to the resolutions of the congress, held at Philadelphia, &c.*"[2]

The encreasing demands afterwards, and the want of other revenues, compelled future additional emissions, from time to time, until there had been upwards of 200 millions emitted in bills of the same tenor. Although in the decline of the current value of these bills, the dependence upon them alone, and the extreme exigency, would demand every reasonable promise, that could add to their value; so very careful was the government to avoid entangling us with promises, that could not when the time for their performance came, be fulfilled, and so involving the states in a breach of faith, that there was no time of payment promised to the holders of these bills; and the amount already redeemed, within the limited time, exceeds the whole sum engaged to be redeemed by a particular period. No breach of faith hath ensued, nor is the present government by the engagements of the former, involved in any embarrassment in point of time. But when the question was raised, whether they should be redeemed at all, or whether the obligation of congress should be broken, (as now attempted) we read their virtuous abhorrence of the latter idea through all the stages of its depreciation.

Has there been at the time of issue, or afterwards, more said, and more frequently in favor of the paper medium afterwards issued under their authority, commonly called *certificates*, which are now held up to the eye of government with quotations in favor of them exclusively? See journals of congress, December 29th, 1778, "Whereas a report hath circulated in divers parts of America, that congress would not redeem the bills of credit issued by them to defray the expences of the war, but would suffer them to sink in the hands of the holder, whereby the value of the said bills is in the opinion of many of the good people of these states depreciated, and lest the silence of congress might give strength to the said report, resolved that the said report is false and derogatory to the honour of congress."[3] A circular letter to the states, agreed to in congress, September 13th, 1779, represents "that a national debt was unavoidably created, and the amount of it as follows.

	Dol.	90ths.
Bills emitted and circulating,	159,948,880	
Monies borrowed before 1st March, 1778, the interest of which is payable in France,	7,545,196	67
Monies borrowed since 1st March, 1778, the interest of which is payable here,	26,188,909	
Money due abroad not exactly known, the balances not having been transmitted supposed to be about	4,000,000	

Having thus given you (say that honorable body) a short and plain state of your debt, we shall proceed to make a few remarks on the depreciation of the currency to which we intreat your attention." They then go on to state the causes of depreciation, and the ability of the country to pay the debt. They say "admitting the whole national debt of the United States would be 300,000,000 dollars, there are at present 3,000,000 of inhabitants in the thirteen states; 300 million of dollars divided among 3 millions of people, would give to each person 100 dollars. Is there an individual in America unable in the course of 18, or 20 years to pay it again? suppose the whole debt assessed, as it ought to be, on the inhabitants in proportion to their respective estates, what would then be the share of the poorer people, perhaps not ten dollars." Several arguments are then drawn from the increased populations, which will take place, the resources of unfettered commerce, and from the consideration that the paper money will remain in the country, and therefore can always be paid in its redemption.

They proceed then under three heads to enquire,

"1st. Whether and in what manner, the faith of the United States has been pledged for the redemption of their bills.

2d. Whether they have put themselves in a political capacity to redeem them: And,

3d. Whether admitting the two former propositions, there is any reason, to apprehend a wanton violation of the public faith."

The first and second questions are fully established in the affirmative, by conclusive arguments.

On the third head they say, "It is with great regret and reluctance, that we can prevail upon ourselves, to take the least notice of a question, which involves in it a doubt so injurious to the honour and dignity of America." They proceed thus, "We should pay an ill compliment to the understanding and honour of every true American, were we to adduce many arguments to shew the baseness or bad policy of violating our national faith, or omitting to pursue the measures necessary to preserve it. A bankrupt, faithless republic, would be a novelty in the political world, and appear among reputable nations like a common prostitute among chaste and reputable matrons. The pride of America revolts from the idea, her citizens know for what purposes these emissions were made, and have repeatedly plighted their faith for the redemption of them. Knowing the value of national character, and impressed with a due sense of the immutable laws of justice and honour, it is impossible that America should think without horror of the execrable deed."[4]

Many other such resolutions might be quoted, but the foregoing are sufficient. To the honour of congress, and the late government of the union, they never by any subsequent act tarnished the character of America, by a violation of these sacred engagements. So far from that were their acts, that they called afterwards upon the states, by a requisition (of which Pennsylvania paid her full proportion) for their respective shares of the amount of these bills.

The debts of the former government were assumed by the constitution of the present, and an express provision therein, as the secretary observes, that there should be no violation of contracts. To call these bills unliquidated debts, and redeem them at any given rate of depreciation, is not only a breach of all these solemn engagements, but a violation of the constitution. It is therefore proposed to the government, and they are now to decide on the important question, whether they will infringe the constitution and violate public faith, or let it alone.

I am aware that many have entertained an idea, that the old congress had reduced the rate of redemption of these bills to forty for one. This idea is erroneous and unfounded. By an act passed 18th March, 1780, they allowed specie, or these bills, to be received in certain taxes, at the rate of one of the former for forty of the latter; but neither their faith to the holders, nor their obligation of redemption of the bills were infringed thereby, in form nor effect; nor did it injure their current value. At the time that act was passed, according to the rate of depreciation by the scale in Pennsylvania, they were current at 61½ for one, to which they had risen from 47½ for one in the preceding month; and it is observable, that so far from this act depreciating the bills, the progress of depreciation was in some degree stopped. They remained at the same exchange in the market the next month, and in the succeeding one, grew a little better.

Having said thus much of the *bills of credit* which were emitted to carry on the war; I shall proceed to the next means adopted by the government for that purpose.

As no taxes could then be demanded, the particular governments not being established upon the principles of the revolution, the only way to obtain the use of the same bills of credit for government again after they had passed from the treasury in payments, and so prevent the increase in quantity, and the consequent depreciation in the current value, was to borrow the bills from those who held them; and to induce them, interest was promised to be paid annually, and the principal to be repaid in three years from the date of lending. Upon these principles continental loan offices were first established by an act of congress, October 3d, 1776. "Resolved that *five millions of continental dollars*, be immediately borrowed for the use of the United States at the annual interest of 4 per cent per annum.* Then the faith of the United States be pledged to the *lenders* for the payment of the sums to be borrowed, and the interest arising thereon, and that certificates be given to the lenders

---

*This was afterwards raised to 6 per cent. per annum.

in the form following, viz. No. ___ *the United States of America acknowledge the receipt of ___ dollars from ___ which they promise to pay to the said ___ or bearer on the ___ day of ___ with interest annually at the rate of 4 per cent. per annum, agreeable to a resolution of the United States passed, &c.*"[5]

"That the several sums of money to be borrowed shall be repaid at the office, where the same was lent at the expiration of three years, and that the annual interest shall likewise be paid."[6]

AFTER this sum was obtained on loan, farther sums were directed to be borrowed, from time to time, on the same terms, and like certificates given, to as great an amount as possible. In the year 1779, when the first loans were falling due, the congress saw that manifest injustice would be done to those early lenders, if they were paid off according to the terms of the loan in the *continental dollars lent*, at the low current value at which they then passed; they therefore entered into a resolution, that the interest should be paid in an increased quantity of the continental bills, proportioned to the increase of the quantity of bills emitted subsequent to the date of the respective loans. They also resolved, that the lenders, at their election, might continue their money in the funds at interest, until the quantity of continental bills of credit in circulation, should not be greater than it was at the time of lending. This although strictly just, was of great consequence to the lender, for the borrower might in strict compliance with their engagement, have paid off all these loans when they became due, in the continental money they received, which could have been done at a very little expence.

As the depreciation of the bill still increased, that the lenders might have their doubts about its fluctuating value, and their being compelled to take payment therein, entirely removed, a new engagement on the part of the United States is entered into. Congress by an act passed June 28th, 1780, promise and engage to pay off the principal and interest of the loan-office certificates in *specie*, having regard to the current value of the bills when the loans were made, according to a certain schedule formed for that purpose, upon very generous principles to the lenders; and to such as were loaned between September 1777, and March 1778, payment of the interest at 6 per cent. per annum was promised in specie, or in what was equivalent, in bills on France. This engagement recognized on the other part by all who preferred *specie* to *continental money*, altered the terms of the contract. No day was fixed under this last act for the payment of either principal or interest. Thus, so far as respects this loan-office debt, the late government hath not involved the present in any difficulties about promises which cannot be performed; and yet in their whole conduct manifested an upright disposition.

I find indeed by the secretary's statement, that under the loan opened for *specie* to be repaid in three years, there is a debt of about £. 42,000. I am not certain how this arose. Actual specie, I believe was not lent upon the terms of the loan. I rather think this sum was granted for the depreciation of Hazen's and other independent corps; if so, I believe the interest was paid regularly on these under the late administration of finance; but however that may be, as the time of payment promised is already past, there is no alternative, but on the one hand make immediate provision for discharge of the interest, and of the principal to such as desire it, or on the other suffer the public faith to be broken. I am glad the sum is so trifling. It may be easily paid off.

I agree with the secretary of the treasury, that, where there is no day of payment of the principal fixed, congress have a right to chuse their own time of payment, and in like manner with the interest, where there are no stated periods at which payment is promised, it may be discharged when convenient; and being done at any time, no breach of faith can be charged on the government.

The next means of supporting the war, was, by borrowing money in Europe. For the purpose of paying for arms and warlike stores, money was obtained early from France. The first monies I think were received as early as January 1777.

This was also a fund for paying the interest on the domestic loans. The honourable and magnanimous conduct of the government of France towards America, should make a deep, lasting and favourable impression towards her in every American. They took us by the hand when we were yet young as a nation, and beset with dangers on all sides. She generously opened her purse; lent us from time to time, what she could spare, and when the day we had promised to make payment was come about, instead of insisting on an exact performance, she came forward, forgave the past interest altogether, and fixed new and distant periods for the payment of the principal; nor did her good offices end here, when she had given us all, she could conveniently spare, she interposed her responsibility for us, and became our surety to those who had money to lend. The payment of the interest of this debt annually (which I find hath fallen in arrears) and the instalments of the principal, as they become payable, cannot be delayed or neglected without a breach of national faith.

Of the debts due by the United States to the States respectively, I have already written fully in my letters of the 28th and 29th ult.

The next species of obligation which remains to be discharged by the United States, grew out of the insufficiency of the former means. At the close of the war, on settlement of the accounts, for pay, services and supplies of the army, large balances appeared to be due by the United States. There was no money in the treasury, therefore these could not then be discharged: so it was determined by the government, at settlement of every account, to issue to the creditor a certificate on interest for the balance due. This paper, issued on the faith of the United States, was made payable to bearer, and was of the following form. *No. ___ dated ___ On the final settlement of an account between the United States and ___ there appeared to be due to him the sum of ___ dollars: I do therefore certify, that the said sum is payable with interest at 6 per cent. from the ___ to the said ___ or bearer."* And, as in the other cases, no time was fixed or promised for payment either of the principal or interest.

After the certificates last mentioned had been issued some time, and arrears of interest were accumulated, another paper medium, or species of obligation called *indents*, were struck on the faith of the United States without interest, for the arrears of interest on the certificates aforesaid to the 1st of January, 1788. No time of payment was promised to the holders of these. Their redemption was provided for by requisitions on the states. The form of the indent was as follows, viz. *"No. ___ The bearer hereof is entitled to ___ dollars and ___ ninetieths of a dollar, which will be received for taxes on any requisition agreeably to the act of congress of ___."*

There remains yet another kind of obligation to be performed by the United States, that in the order of time, in which the faith was given, should have been mentioned first: the original holders of certificates, may not only plead the faith of the United States pledged for the redemption of these certificates, in common with other holders; they may also insist upon a contract entered into, and solemnly ratified with the United States before these certificates existed. Under the solemn engagement of payment, they rendered their services, or furnished their supplies, they possess the evidences that payment hath not yet been made them. If the last mentioned obligation were only equal to the former, the original holders possessing both, would have a twofold right; but there is no equality between the two. The one is a legal; the other is also a moral obligation and more equitable. No arguments are necessary to this belief, there is something in every man's breast, that bears witness to the truth of it, unless his conscience and judgment be very much beclouded by large purchases and speculations in certificates.

The secretary's combat with his idea of *discrimination*, puts me in mind of some of the engagements of Don Quixote. It is humorous to see him pursue, run down, and buffet a creature which can make no resistance. Does *discrimination* imply, that purchasers shall not be paid according to the faith of the United States pledged for the payment of what they purchased? Then am I as much averse from discrimination as himself, perhaps more so. He is for *discriminating* in his sense of the word between the promise and the performance; I am not. I think where 6 per cent. hath been promised, it is a direct violation of public faith, to discharge that engagement with any thing short of 6 per cent. It is the same principle, exactly applied to the capital and extended a little farther. If one penny engaged to be paid, can be taken off, from either principal or interest, then may either of them be reduced to any thing by the same rule.

If the term *discrimination* be offensive, I would use the word *preference.* Here I am sure we cannot differ; for I would just use the same preference in the revenues that he proposes, only that, instead of giving this preference to such as subscribed to his loan, and leaving the *fag end,* if any such end would remain, to those who retained the present evidences of the debt, I would be for allowing the original holders this preference.

It may indeed be a question with the legislature of the union, whether they will not on principles of equity open an audit for a limited time under certain regulations, for making up to those who have parted with their certificates the depreciation thereon, as was done by the continental bills of credit to the army; that is, the difference between the current value of the certificates *when they were issued,* and the balances due them at settlement respectively. As they have by parting with these certificates imposed an obligation on the government to pay the holders of them the sum therein expressed, they can have no legal demand; but it certainly deserves consideration whether they have not an equitable one. Policy, I conceive would dictate, that this, together with a preference to original holders, should be granted. Public credit will ever succeed public justice. It is of great importance, to be able at all times to purchase *cheap,* and *borrow* on good terms; will the secretary's plan produce this effect? If we should have a demand for men, for money and for supplies again, we will suppose an application made to those who contributed formerly. They are again asked, and nothing but the faith of government can be given. What would be the answer of those people who have heretofore generously parted with all they could spare? They would refuse their money, their provisions and other supplies, impressed with the recollection of the treatment they received for their last contributions, or if they complied at all it would be at a greatly advanced price in order that they might secure to themselves a compensation. Let us now suppose an application of a familiar nature to be made to purchasers of certificates, for whom such great exertions are proposed to the injury of the others, their answer would be "Our own business is so profitable that we cannot lose time by going into the service of the public. That, although we have money we keep it to buy up at a low rate the securities of government *after they are given,* and therefore to lend them would be defeating our own interest. That, as for provisions and other supplies, we raise and produce none, we make our living in another way, but if all these can be got on certificates from those who have them, your having no money, will be to our advantage; we shall purchase the evidences of these debts at least as much below the nominal sum, as the price you are obliged to give is beyond the real value, and this we shall gain out of you; perhaps we may gain as heretofore we have from the original possessors likewise."

Having stated my ideas of the various debts and contracts of the United

States which exist against them, I shall in a short recapitulation lay the amount thereof, as nearly as I can, respectively before you.

Of the bills of credit the amount emitted was   200,062,775.

By the register's accounts of November 1st, 1785, of the payments made on account of the sinking fund requisition, there was redeemed

88,171,412

Since that time near a million and an half hath been paid by Pennsylvania; no credit was given to the state of Connecticut, a comparatively small sum to New-York and Virginia, and none from the states southward of that, so that the whole of what they may have paid since the date of said account and what they may have on hand ready to be paid, may be set at

25,000,000

113,871,412

Leaves a balance to be redeemed
of the bills of credit   86,891,363

Amount of the loan office debt. The specie value of these loans I am sorry to find hath not yet been ascertained. The register's statement informs that the value they are estimated at, was found by taking the medium of the loans made in each month. This may be either above or below the truth, as the quantity was more or less at one time of the month than another. In a matter of such consequence it is probable precision will be attained as soon as possible. The said estimate exclusive of loans between 1st September 1777, and 1st March is

8,934,230

Loaned within the period
last mentioned equal to
2,538,572 dollars specie, but
the interest payable in specie
on the nominal sum   3,459,000

12,393,230

Deduct specie amount can-
celled and registered   365,983

Balance   12,027,247

Loan-office certificates is-
sued in 1781 for specie   112,704 15

Amount to the credit of foreign officers in the late army, the interest
whereof is payable in Europe   186,427 69

Certificates issued by the commissioner
of army accounts, and the other several
commissioners including such certified

debts, &c. as are on the funded books of the United States	16,947,882	42
	29,274,261	36
Redeemed and cancelled by land, military stores and other property sold	960,915	44
	28,313,345	82
Amount of the French, Dutch and Spanish loans	10,070,307	

The indents or facilities forthe discharge of the interest of the domestic debt until the 1st January, 1788. The aggregate of interest to 31st December, 1790, deducting the indents redeemed, is stated to be 13,030,168 28 from which deduct 3 years interest on 28,126,918 13 leaves to be redeemed   7,967,322 87

The balances due to the respective states in specie will be somewhere about   60,000,000

Total   193,242,338 79

The citizen who is solicitous for the honour and national character of America, and takes a view of these engagements and their amount, will on reflection feel grateful towards the past administrations who, although they were obliged from the exigency of the times, and the importance of the contest for that prize which is now secured to us, to contract such a debt, were not so inconsiderate as to make promises which their successors could not perform: they looked forward to the future character of the nation, which they knew would be wounded if to obtain any temporary views either for the public or themselves, any obligations were made which could not be discharged *when the time promised for payment came*, therefore no such time was fixed. How will the measures now proposed suffer by contrast? Under no such public pressure or necessity, these engagements are to be wantonly violated and a principle established by which they may at any time be reduced to nothing. New engagements without necessity are likewise to be entered into, that cannot and if made will not be performed, according to promise. No new promises should now be made, it should now be our sole care to provide for and keep those which have been entered into. The revenues the secretary proposes are on the whole I think the most proper, perhaps with a duty somewhat lower, more might be collected. The duty proposed on coffee is too high, it hath become a necessary article of life among the poor as well as the more wealthy. So far as these duties operate as a tax upon sumptuary articles it is doubly beneficial—on ardent spirits it is trebly so. He hath set the impost and

excise after deducting 360,600 dollars for the expence of collecting and drawbacks on excise at the
Annual sum of   dollars   2,843,400

I fear they will not be so productive as he imagines. It should be well ascertained by experience that they would neat that sum before engagements in the present state of affairs were entered into to pay that sum with them annually; in short, as I said before, I see no reason why any new promises should now be entered into with any of the creditors at all, these already made are sufficient. Let the revenues be appropriated, *first*, to the support of government, this should have the *preference* of all others, for unless government be supported, it cannot exist, *second*, to the payment, as it becomes payable of what is contracted to be paid at particular periods, *third*, to the original owners of certificates, the interest of their certificates, or, if you please, the interest of the balances due to them for their wages, their money and their supplies, *fourth*, to redeem such debts against the United States as are at an exorbitant interest, beginning with the highest first, *fifth*, as the revenues are liberated by the discharge of some debts, and increased by improvement in collection, by time and by increasing population and commerce that the excess be applied to the discharge of the interest of the debts from the United States to particular states, and when it became more than sufficient for this purpose that the government should appropriate the surplus to discharge the interest to such other creditors, as merited the next attention, directing the treasurer to make payment of the monies as they came to his hands in the order of appropriations, under proper regulations; and that in the mean time as soon as possible the western lands should be exposed to sale for prompt payment, at the most they would bring in gold and silver, or the respective securities for which they should be sold; and that to this end a certain tract should be appropriated to be sold as aforesaid, for the redemption of continental bills of credit, another tract to be sold as aforesaid, for the redemption of certificates, and another for the redemption of indents or facilities. These sales would rapidly redeem the debt without any other taxes on the people, and at the same time would gradually increase the current value more and more until the government would be in a situation to take them up and pay them.

In this view of the subject, I will give you my ideas what should now be done with the proposed annual revenues of the United States.

Admit the annual amount to be	2,500,000
Appropriate to the support of government	600,000
Balance	1,900,000

Appropriate to
1st Annual interest of foreign loans   304,996 87

2d Annual instalment to be paid of
the principal   462,962 96

These will no doubt be wanted in grain in the present exigency of the French government, who being engaged in an important object for liberty themselves, should claim the more attention.

Annual interest payable annually in
France to foreign offices   11,185 66

The specie loan-office certificates
promised to be paid in three years   112,704 15

Interest from January 1788
two years   13,542 45
                                                          126,246 66
                                                          _____
                                                          905,392 15
      Leaves of the revenues   994,607 85

          Appropriate to pay

The interest of the original holders who apply with
their own certificates as in the case of the depreciation debt in Pennsylvania, estimated at 16⅓ millions
dollars the annual interest is   990,000
                                                          _____
        Excess   4,607 85

Appropriate this excess towards redeeming the debt which is upon an interest of above 10 per cent. per annum; in the second year this excess would be considerably increased so as to enable the government to offer payment of the principal, of a considerable part of these loans made between September 1777, and March 1778, or reduce the interest to better terms at the option of the holder. This I conceive should be done as fast as the government was enabled, beginning with the loans made in the month of February first, when the interest is highest, and so taking them backwards in order month by month, or even by parts of a month, if the revenue would not embrace a whole one, beginning at the last part first, for the reasons aforesaid.

When the surplus was liberated from these objects, the next appropriation of the excess, which would be increasing not only because the demands were lessened, but because of the increase of the revenue as mentioned before, should be to pay up the year's arrears of interest to original holders. The means for discharging the arrears of interest and the instalments of the principal of the foreign loans, shall be noticed hereafter. There is a farther reason why the appropriation of the revenues and payment of them in such order as the government would direct should be preferred to entering into new obligations, about paying at any fixed time, and that is, the duties and imposts are and may be expected to be granted only for a limited time, to promise therefore, that a temporary revenue shall discharge a perennial demand, is a hazard to which *public faith* ought not now to be exposed.

The holders of alienated certificates, who have knowledge enough to see that whatever promises are made, there will not be money enough to pay all, that in the general scramble for the money as it comes in, some will not be paid; must think that although this will eventually produce a *discrimination* indeed between the creditors who are paid, and those who are not paid, that they will by their attention, be of the former class, and perhaps turn even the necessities of the latter to their advantage.

Upon a review of what I have written, I find this letter already so long, I shall reserve what I have farther to say for a future occasion.

FJ, 10, 17 February. Written from Philadelphia. A draft is in the John Nicholson Papers, PHarH. The printed version of the letter is preceded by the following introductory paragraph, signed "A. B. C.": "YOU were kind enough to publish the copies of two letters, sent you last week. I have to request the same for the inclosed, written by the same person, and addressed to the same gentleman."

[1] For the 13 September 1779 circular address, see *DHFFC* 5:830–39.
[2] For these resolutions, see *JCC* 2:103, 106.
[3] For the resolution, see *JCC* 12:1261.
[4] For the 13 September 1779 circular address, see *DHFFC* 5:830–39.
[5] For the resolution, see *JCC* 5:845.
[6] This concludes the portion of the letter that was printed on 10 February.

OTHER DOCUMENTS

David S. Franks to Thomas Jefferson. ALS, Washington Papers, DLC. Place to which addressed not indicated. For a partial text, see *PTJ* 16:158.
    Office seeking: clerk in the state department; some members of Congress have given assurance of promoting his application.

Benjamin Hawkins and Samuel Johnston to George Washington. AN, hand of Johnston, Washington Papers, DLC. Dated on docket.
    Repeats Williamson's list of recommended nominees (5 February, above), adding, for surveyors: Hugh Knox at Nixontown, Thomas Williams at Indian Town, Elias Albertson at Newbiggen Creek, and Edmund Sawyer at Pasquotank River Bridge.

Thomas Mifflin to John Langdon. ALS, Langdon Papers, NhPoA. Written from Philadelphia.
    Office seeking: Francis Mentges for a military appointment, or else a civil post; in doing so, Mifflin avails himself of the "privilege" extended to him in Langdon's letter of 30 January; had advised Mentges "to explain himself fully to you and have given him Assurances that you will do every thing for ~~them~~ him which Propriety & Friendship can justify."

Robert Morris to John Adams. LS, Petitions and Memorials: Various subjects, SR, DNA. Printed in *DHFFC* 8:669. Encloses his petition to Congress.

Robert Morris, Petition to the President, Senate, and House of Representatives. Printed in *DHFFC* 3:291–93 and 8:667–68. The only extant manuscript version, the one sent to Washington, is in Miscellaneous Letters, Miscellaneous Correspondence, State Department Records, Record Group 59, DNA.

Samuel Whittemore to Benjamin Goodhue. ALS, Letters to Goodhue, NNS. Written from Gloucester, Massachusetts.
> Replies to Goodhue's request, "when I saw you last," to know the amount of Whittemore's fees as surveyor: $123.25, "a small Sum considering the duty Required"; by Hamilton's report on public credit, thinks it probable there will be a "new arrangment of Officers," and in that case asks to be remembered by Goodhue.

Oliver Wolcott, Sr. to Oliver Wolcott, Jr. ALS, Wolcott Papers, CtHi. Written from Litchfield, Connecticut. The letter was sent no earlier than 9 February, the date of a postscript.
> "You will present my Compliments to Mr. Ellsworth, who has been so complaisant as to send me the Secretary of the Treays. Report [*on public credit*]—he has Askd. my Opinion upon the Subject of it. I had rather indeed he should have askd. any other Service of me—my Opinion can be but of little Aid to his own—But he is entituled to a decent Acknowledgment of his Letter, which I shall take some other Oppertunity to Answer."

William Samuel Johnson, Diary. Johnson Papers, CtHi.
> "In House."

William Smith (S.C.), Certificate. NS by Burke, Records of the Supreme Court, DNA. Burke provided this document to Smith, who filed it in support of his application to be admitted as a counselor to the bar of the Supreme Court on this date. For the full text, see *DHSCUS* 1:543.
> Certifies that Smith had practiced as a counselor and attorney before the South Carolina Supreme Court for at least three years.

NYDA, 10 February.
> Benson, Laurance, Sedgwick, Smith (S.C.), Jackson, Ames, and Thatcher admitted and sworn as counselors before the Supreme Court.

TUESDAY, 9 FEBRUARY 1790

Cold (Johnson); *Still and very cold* (J. B. Johnson)

William Samuel Johnson to [*Pelatiah Webster*]

I thank you very sincerely for yr. favour of the 1st. Instt. & the several Pamphlets you have favour'd me with on publick Affairs. They always abound in just & sensible & important Observations & throw much light upon the several subjects on which you treat. I have read them all with pleasure & improvement Upon the subject of the last[1] however which is now in agitation I can get you no Opinion as my Rule is where I am to decide in a public Character to form no Conclusive Opinion till I have heard & read all I can meet with upon the subject & revolved the whole in my own Mind till the hour of decision arrives. The Report of the Secrety. of the Treasy. is ~~the~~ now the subject of animated Debate in the H. of Representatives & will no doubt hereafter be so in the Senate, when I shall have heard the whole I will decide with all the impartiality I can I congratulate you on the fair prospect you have of obtaining a good Constitution of Governmt. in Pensilvania.

FC:dft, Johnson Papers, CtHi. Place to which addressed not indicated. The recipient was identified from the fact that this letter is a response to Webster's letter of 1 February, above.

[1] *A Plea for the Poor Soldiers*, which related to discrimination between public creditors.

William Maclay to John Nicholson

The History of this day's proceedings in the House of Representatives is but Short. Mr. Smith [*S.C.*] withdrew his Resolutions [*on public credit*], and Mr. Fitzsimons's were taken up, and the first adopted Nem. Con.[1] Jackson moved a general Postpone of the rest, seconded by Gen. [*Peter*] Muhlenberg. this was lost by a heavy Majority. The second was taken up. Mr. Scott moved an amendment. "As soon as the same is ascertained, and duly liquidated" The debate lasted untill near the hour of adjournment. The Committee rose, and the House adjourned. without any decision.

I will take repeated Opportunities of forwarding to You every Movement of Congress, that You may have it in Your power to watch over the interests of Pennsylvania. The Copy of Yesterday was scratched in the Utmost haste, I therefore send you a printed One.[2] pray let me hear often from you.

ALS, The Gilder Lehrman Collection, on Deposit at the New York Historical Society, New York. [GLC 2504.29] Place to which addressed not indicated.

[1] Nemine contradicente: with no one dissenting.
[2] Smith's (S.C.) and Fitzsimons' resolutions (printed under 8 February, above); see Maclay to Nicholson, 8 February, n. 1, above.

Theodore Sedgwick to Pamela Sedgwick

By Parson [*Samuel*] Kirkland who goes tomorrow I cannot omit to write you a single line altho in the house and during an interesting debate on the subject of funding the national debt. Every thing will depend on the result of this deliberation. There is no opinion which can possibly be holden on the subject that is not within the walls of the house. There is even a party who openly declare against any funding at all. I see that our court is adjourned till the third tuesday of march, if possible consistant with my duty I will then attend.

ALS, Sedgwick Papers, MHi. Place to which addressed not indicated.

William Smith (Md.) to Otho H. Williams

I have duly recd. your Several Communications with the inclosures[1] for the Secy. which have been attended to, and carefully delivered; No report has yet been made relative to the Collection & Impost laws &ca. Numerous memorials & papers have been reffered to the Secy. on that Subject, & Some of the Collectors, from different quarters are here, and I am told make loud complaints, also the Collr. of this port [*John Lamb*]. Perhaps, if you could Spare the time & your health will permit it might be well for you to Spend a fortnight here when that business is taken up—The inclosed [*news*] paper will give you the State of public business, this day will probably decide [*lined out*] the fate of Public credit, I mean the Sense of our house will be clearly shewn, which I think will be decidedly in favor of funding the public debt, *Without discrimination.* my next, will give you more full information on this Subject—*** I will at some other time take notice of our funding State law, from the Slight View I have taken of it, it appears unfavorable to me.[2]

ALS, Williams Papers, MdHi. Addressed to Baltimore. The omitted text relates to business affairs.

[1] Probably Williams's letter to Hamilton, 2 February, with enclosed abstracts on the past and projected emoluments of Baltimore revenue officers (*PAH* 6:241–44.)
[2] The Funding Act passed by the Maryland legislature on 25 December 1789 was

William Smith and His Grandson, by Charles Willson Peale, 1741–1827, oil on canvas, 1788. William Smith (Md.), a widower, is shown with his cherished grandson Robert Smith Williams (1786–93), the eldest son of Mary and Otho Holland Williams, outside Williams's country estate Eutaw, four miles from downtown Baltimore. By combining classical columns and pediments with books and evidence of agricultural pursuits, Peale's iconic vision linked public service and the eighteenth-century domestic ideal. (Virginia Museum of Fine Arts, Richmond. Museum purchase with funds provided by The Robert G. Cabell III and Maude Morgan Cabell Foundation and The Arthur and Margaret Glasgow Fund.)

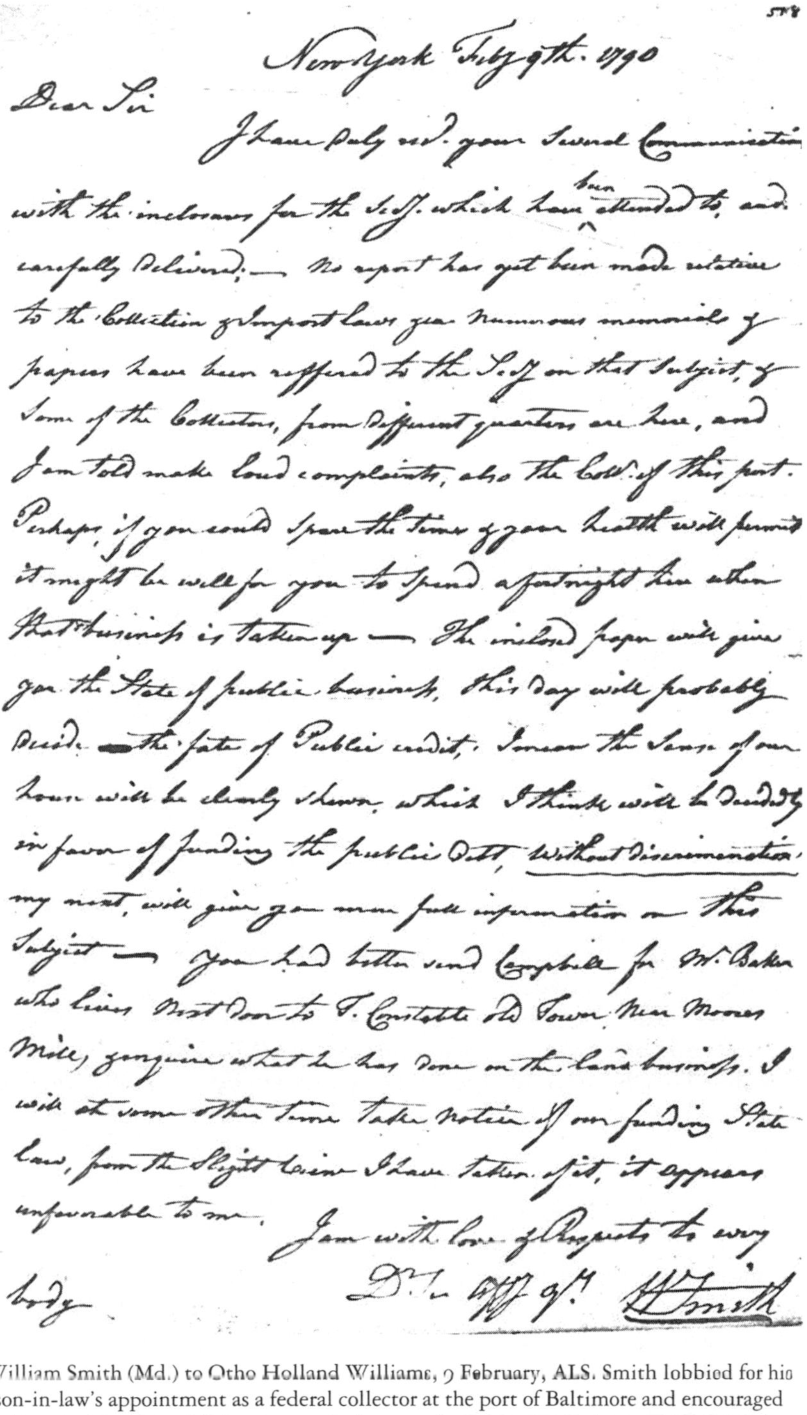
578

New York Feby 9th. 1790

Dear Sir

I have duly recd. your Second Communication with the inclosures for the Secy. which have been attended to, and carefully delivered;— No report has yet been made relative to the Collection of Import laws yet Numerous memorials & papers have been reffered to the Secy on that Subject, & Some of the Collectors, from different quarters are here, and I am told make loud complaints, also the Collr. of this port. Perhaps if you could Spare the time & your health will permit it might be well for you to Spend a fortnight here when that business is taken up — The inclosed paper will give you the State of public business, this day will probably decide the fate of Public credit, I mean the Sense of our house will be clearly shewn, which I think will be decidedly in favor of funding the public Debt, without discrimination. my next, will give you more full information on this Subject — You had better send Campbell for Mr. Baker who lives Next Door to T. Constable old Town near Moores Mill, & enquire what he has done on the land business. I will at some other time take notice of our funding State law, from the Slight view I have taken of it, it appears unfavorable to me.

I am with love & Respects to every body

Dr. Sr. Affy. Yrs.

W Smith

William Smith (Md.) to Otho Holland Williams, 9 February, ALS. Smith lobbied for his son-in-law's appointment as a federal collector at the port of Baltimore and encouraged him to maintain a visible presence at the seat of government during revenue-related debates. They remained each other's principal confidant in a voluminous correspondence throughout the First Congress. (Courtesy of the Maryland Historical Society.)

characterized by its lenient treatment of state debtors (such as allowing them to pay by installments).

OTHER DOCUMENTS

John Adams to John Quincy Adams. ALS, Adams Family Manuscript Trust, MHi. Place to which addressed not indicated.
>   Advice on legal career; encloses copy of Fitzsimons' "Motions" (see 8 February, above), regarding public credit.

Bernard Hubley to George Washington. ALS, Washington Papers, DLC. Written from Northumberland, Pennsylvania. For the full text, see *PGW* 5:113–16.
>   Office seeking: anything anywhere in the United States; lists Maclay, the Muhlenbergs, and Hartley as references.

William Samuel Johnson, Diary. Johnson Papers, CtHi.
>   "Visits."

NYDA, 11 February.
>   Paterson admitted and sworn as a counselor before the Supreme Court.

WEDNESDAY, 10 FEBRUARY 1790

Cold (Johnson); *Very cold, clear and windy* (J. B. Johnson)

Aedanus Burke to Samuel Bryan

Mr. Morris has memorialed Congress to appoint Commissioners for inspecting his accts.[1] his identical petition I put in the hands of our friend in an hour afterwards—he will tell you a pleasant story of the circumstance, and a great many other things relating to affair of [*Robert*] Morris Vs. [*Eleazer*] Oswald.[2] This Entre Nous. Oswald and [*Francis*] Baily go out of Town in five or Six days and will tell you all the News. I should have wrote immediately in answer to your kind Letter, but that I was in daily expectation of one or other of those Gentlemen going out of Town daily. I shall here mention once for all, that I shall be ever happy to render you any service in my power, or treat your friend with my best attention. I do not mean to flatter you when I say frankly that the manly independant Spirit which you displayed on a very critical occasion do you honour[3] It is but doing you justice to tell you that your sagacity has anticipated every observation made on a certain subject on either side of the Atlantic. I have seen sundry publications written in France on this subject—who if they knew you as well as I do, and dealt candidly would make an acknowledgment of their obligations to you.

ALS, Miscellaneous Letters, Miscellaneous Correspondence, State Department Records, Record Group 59, DNA. This is a postscript to a letter dated 5 February and printed above.

[1] See *DHFFC* 8:663–75.
[2] See Morris to Gouverneur Morris, 2 January, above.
[3] Likely a reference to Bryan's eighteen essays opposing ratification of the Constitution and signed "Centinel"; see *DHROC* 13:326–28.

Pierce Butler to James Iredell

I was favored with your letter by Gov. [*Samuel*] Johnston. I thank you for making me acquainted with so amiable a man. It gave me much satisfaction to see him on the floor of the Senate. Indeed the Southern interest needs some such characters to take care of it. I should have been happy to have had you in Congress. The Union will no longer be deprived of your aid, and the benefit of your abilities. You have this day been nominated by the President, and unanimously appointed by the Senate to a seat on the Supreme Federal Bench. I congratulate the States on the appointment, and you on this mark of their well-merited opinion of you. I please myself with the expectation of seeing you soon here. I think you will save the lives of your children by bringing them here. Provisions, and every thing, but house rent, is cheaper here than with you. It is probable you will find it more convenient and eligible to settle your family somewhere to the North than keep them at Edenton [*North Carolina*]. The House of Representatives are busily employed in doing something with the public debt. I think it will be provided for, &c., &c.

Iredell 2:280. Place to which addressed not indicated.

John Cogdell to Pierce Butler

I have Reced. your kind favour, and have to thank you for the attention you paid to mine that was So long before it Reach'd you; I am Now to Acquaint you that from the present mode of doing the business of the Office, as it So Complext & tedious with such methods pointed Out to me to keep my books, and so many Accounts of different kinds to make out and to be Returnd to the Treasurer Once a month and Every three months; I am also to be at every expence of Stationary, and the hire of an Office &ca. after al my trouble and expence the income will be about One hundred dollars to Support all this   as all Licenced Vessels from the Northward, are on Such a footing that they pay little or Nothing, and when they wish to Return they Can do so by the Licence they have for the Twelve months—unless Something more is done for an Office at the Out Posts of Southern States it it will not be worth any Persons while to hold it.

I have wrote to the Controler [*Nicholas Eveleigh*] & Treasurer [*secretary of the treasury?*], that I do Resign my Office on the above princaples, if any thing better can be done so as to keep a Clerk and pay Me for my trouble, Other wise I cannot think of holding it longer, we Cannot do business here for So very little as they do at the Out posts of the Northern States.

ALS, Butler Papers, PHi. Written from Georgetown, South Carolina.

Benjamin Goodhue to Michael Hodge

I inclose you a news paper which will serve to shew you, how far We have enter'd upon the consideration of the Secrys. report [*on public credit*]—A number of resolutions are submited to the House which embrace the great principles of the report, in order to collect the sentiments of the House upon the great outlines which are to constitute the measure which may finaly be adopted—the first resolution was adopted without much debate, upon the second, a motion was made, that has in view, the scaling the securities and making a discrimination between the present and original holders the discussion of which took up the whole of yesterday and to day and is not yet been decided upon—I think there is no probibility of its obtainin, as it must if just be found totaly impracticable—I have waited upon the Secry. relative to the foreign Tonage many of our Vessels have been obliged to pay in the S. States in consequence of their not having a license and he joins in sentiment with me that a restitution ought to be made, and he promises me he will in his report which he is directed to make of the inconveniences in our Revenue laws, not forget it the mode of refering subjects which concern any department to the head of such department is adopted in preference to brin[g]ing them as they may occur immediately before Congress upon the supposition that sistem will thereby be more probably preserv'd in our administration.

I am with respect to the Gentlemen of N[ewbury]port.

ALS, Ebenezer Stone Papers, MSaE. Place to which addressed not indicated.

Thomas Hartley to John Nicholson

I would have wrote you long since but expected to have been able ere now to give you some satisfactory Information upon the Business of Finance—in this I am still deficient.

Sundry Propositions were brought forward on Monday—the first one was passed upon yesterday by a large Majority—upon the second we have been arguing upon all Day or rather we have been contending about an amendment to it.[1]

There is a strong Disposition in the House to support public Credit— There may be some danger of going too far.

The Assumption of the State Debts will be a very Serious Question, I wish to have a Line from you from th upon that Head.

If the Debts should be funded and an Offer be made to the Holders of the Certificates of an Alternative—the taken Alternative ought not to be delusive—There were will be much Argument on this Subject—I will (so far as I can) occasionally write to you and shall always be happy to hear from you. ***

P. S. The Amendment was negatived.

ALS, Miscellaneous Manuscripts, NHi. Addressed to Comptroller General of Pennsylvania at Philadelphia; franked; postmarked; received 12 February. The omitted text relates to Hartley's fees for a legal procedure.

[1] Scott's amendment to Fitzsimons' second resolution of 8 February called for an immediate discharge of the public debt (*DHFFC* 5:840 and 8 February, above).

Caleb Strong to Samuel Phillips, Jr.

Yesterday the President sent a Message to the Senate concerning the disputed Line between the United States & the Province of New Brunswick at the eastern Limits of our State, accompanied by a Number of Papers among which were Govr. [*John*] Hancocks Letter to Governr. [*John*] Parr and his and Govr. [*Thomas*] Carletons Answers the Report of our Comissioners Genls. [*Benjamin*] Lincoln & Knox the Affidavits of Mr. [*John*] Mitchell & [*Nathan*] Jones & several other papers,[1] requesting our Advice what Measures are proper to be taken, the Message and Papers were this Day committed, the former Congress had referred these or other papers on the same Subject to the then Secretary of foreign Affairs who had reported that the Minister at the Court of London should be directed to propose to the Government of Gt. Brittain that the Dispute should be settled by Commissioners to be named on each part, this Report was accepted & the Ministers instructed accordingly. Mr. Adams made that proposal to the British Court as he informs me but received no Answer—from several of the Papers it is probable the British Ministry intend to insist strenuously on their Claims, and from some of them it seems that the Lands between the two Rivers whose whose Names are controverted were granted previous to the late War by the Province of New Brunswick Nova Scotia, I am told that the Genl. Court have

had the Subject before them in the Course of the present Session If any new
Lights have appeared or any Communications to the President are intended,
I should think it expedient to address him as soon as may be—I am Chairman of the Committee and will endeavour to delay the Report untill I can
hear from you—Business of this Kind is inserted only on the secret Journals
of the Senate, and therefore it would be improper to make the Contents
of this Letter publick, however I wish you to shew it to our Friends Mr.
[*Nathaniel*] Welles & Mr. [*Nathan*] Dane and pray them and be persuaded
yourself to write me concerning this Business.

Be kind enough to assure Judge [*William*] Cushing & the family where
you live of my ardent Wishes for their Happiness.

ALS, Phillips Family Collection, MHi. Place to which addressed not indicated. Strong's
letter to Nathan Dane, of the same date (calendared below), indicates this letter was written
and posted before the delivery of that evening's mail.

[1] The various papers submitted with Washington's message to the Senate on 9 February
are in *DHFFC* 2:362–86.

From Our Correspondents at New York

The citizens of Massachusetts have been exhausted by the extra exertions
of their government in the common cause; and notwithstanding all the advances they have made, they NOW OWE ONE FIFTH OF ALL THE STATE DEBTS.
How those who are attempting to defeat the assumption expect to obtain
satisfaction, is beyond my conception. Contiguous to the state of New-York,
which has no debt, and possesses an immense extent of fertile and uncultivated lands, this wild and extravagant policy would appear to be the result
of a wish to empty the commonwealth of its most valuable commodity; its
industrious inhabitants. But every age of the world has abounded in men
whose happiness seemed to depend on the degree of political confusion they
were capable of producing.

The pretended motive of their conduct is an apprehension that the *assumption* will in the event tend to a *consolidation* of the powers of government.
Do these men really believe that to attach to the state governments the affections of the people, it will be necessary to continue to load them with a
burden of taxes, which has already produced insurrections?[1] Strange indeed
is that political opinion, that a government to be beloved must constantly
be felt by acts of oppression.

[Stockbridge, Massachusetts] *Western Star*, 16 February; reprinted at Northampton, Massachusetts, and Hartford, Connecticut.

[1] Shays' Rebellion, for example.

From New York

This day the question on Mr. SCOTT's amendment was taken, and determined in the NEGATIVE, only two appearing in favour of it. This amendment was debated two days, and when negatived, was immediately followed by a motion of a similar import, offered by JUDGE BURKE, which was laid on the table, and will be debated to-morrow. I think it will share the same fate with the other—and indeed to me it appears, that Mr. FITZSIMONS' Resolutions[1] *will be adopted.*

The opposers of the SECRETARY's Report [*on public credit*] advocate, in general, *scaling, reliquidation, discrimination, procrastination,* and nobody can tell what. Mr. GERRY made a most excellent speech this day, and in a most masterly manner exploded the doctrine of discrimination between *foreign* and *domestick creditors, original holders* and *assignees,* and vindicated the rights and merits of those patriots who had so long confided in the faith and honour of the country, in a manner highly to the credit of his understanding and liberality.

[Boston] *Massachusetts Centinel,* 20 February; reprinted at Portland, Maine; Portsmouth, New Hampshire; and Providence, Rhode Island.

[1] See 8 February, above.

OTHER DOCUMENTS

Nathaniel Barrett to Andrew Craigie. ALS, Craigie Papers, MWA. Written from Boston; addressed to Craigie "at Mrs. [*Sarah*] Lorings."
  Enquires what Sedgwick or the Congress think respecting consulates "& why no mention is made of them in the resolves on foreign Supports [*Foreign Intercourse Bill HR-35*]—whether it is defer'd till Mr. J[*efferson*]'s Arrival or designedly omitted."

William Cavenough to James Madison. ALS, Montague Collection, NN. Written from William Street (New York City), No. 66. For the full text, see *PJM* 13:31.
  Although unknown to Madison, presumes on his reputation as a "Gentleman of Humanity" for the "one thing now that can save me from total destruction"; begs "an Interview with you at your Lodgings, or elsewhere, at any Hour, in the Course of this Week, most Convenient to yourself, when I shall fully explain myself"; assures him "I am Not a Mean low bad Man"; besides testimonials, "there are Gentlemen here of your Acquaintance, who will speak to you in my favor."

Daniel Cony to George Thatcher. ALS, Chamberlain Collection, MB. Written from Boston.

Encloses Massachusetts state legislature's report on revising excise laws; it "will undoubtedly *push* the Excise as far as practicable until Congress have agreed to the Assumption" of the states' war debts; it has resolved to appoint an agent for settling the state's claims against the United States, which he thinks will be Nathan Dane.

William Cumming to Samuel Johnston. LS, Washington Papers, DLC. Written from Edenton, North Carolina.

Office seeking: his nephew, John Hamilton, as federal attorney for the North Carolina district.

Stephen Goodhue to Benjamin Goodhue. FC:lbk, Goodhue Family Papers, MSaE.

Speculators have been active throughout the countryside buying up "old Continental Money"; hopes Congress will not make any promises for funding that it cannot perform "without over burdning the Community at large"; the deterioration of trade and the fisheries and proposed additional impost duties have increased "murmurs" since Goodhue's departure; thinks lessening all government salaries would "give Some Satisfaction."

Benjamin Goodhue to Samuel Phillips, Jr. No copy known; acknowledged in Phillips to Goodhue, 28 February.

James Madison to George Lee Turberville. No copy known; acknowledged in Turberville to Madison, 7 April.

Roger Sherman to Simeon Baldwin. ALS, Sherman Collection, CtY. Addressed to New Haven, Connecticut; franked; postmarked.

Encloses newspapers; summarizes progress on Hamilton's report on public credit and some rules of the Supreme Court; is "in health."

Caleb Strong to Nathan Dane. ALS, Wetmore Family Collection, CtY. Addressed to Boston; franked.

Has written to Samuel Phillips, Jr., earlier that day, regarding Massachusetts' northeast boundary dispute with Great Britain, "but upon reading the [*Massachusetts*] Centinel which has just come in I find Mr. Phillips is absent from the Senate on Account of ill health, and it is probable therefore that I shall not receive an answer from him in Season"; asks that any related communications from the state legislature be sent to the President, and that Dane and Nathaniel Wells "write me concerning it—I shall endeavour to delay the Report of the Comittee untill I hear from you"; as it concerns the Senate's executive proceedings, there would be an "Indelicacy" in making its contents public.

George Thatcher to Thomas Robison. No copy known; acknowledged in Robison to Thatcher, 5 March.

Joseph Whipple to John Langdon. ALS, Langdon Papers, NhPoA; FC:dft, Sturgis Family Papers, MHi. Written from Portsmouth, New Hampshire.
   Reports state legislature's proceedings; supposes Langdon "must have heard of every Sentiment that has been disclosd" on the precedent of multiple office holding by the state governor; has been approached "in a very Serious manner by a deputation" of state legislators, concerning whether Langdon would resign his seat in Congress before June and whether he would accept the governorship if elected; gave his affirmative opinion and said he has "heard you Say you Shoud resign your Seat," but "coud go no farther without your consent"; "I beg you will be as explicit as possible."

Francis Willis, Jr. to Thomas Jefferson. ALS, Washington Papers, DLC. Written from York, Virginia. For a partial text, see *PTJ* 16:165–66.
   Office seeking: William Reynolds as state department clerk; mentions Page as reference.

Minutes of St. John's College. [Annapolis] *Maryland Gazette*, 11 March.
   Charles Carroll appointed to a committee for accepting nominations for principal of St. John's College and for writing to Dr. Richard Price and others in Great Britain to solicit recommendations.

THURSDAY, 11 FEBRUARY 1790

Cold (Johnson); *A very cold day* (J. B. Johnson)

Benjamin Hawkins to William Blount

Mr. [*James*] Iredell is appointed one of the associate Justices, The committee will on tomorrow report on the [*North Carolina*] Cession, it is received favourably in common conversation. The sale of the Georgia Lands will probably involve the [*illegible*] in difficulties. You know too well the disposition of the Indians to leave us any roome to expect that they can without arms be prevailed on to [*relinqu*]ish so great a part of their claims.

AN, John Gray Blount Papers, Nc-Ar. Addressed to Washington, North Carolina; franked; postmarked.

Samuel Johnston to James Iredell

I have the pleasure to inform you that yesterday your Nomination to a Seat on the Bench of the Supreme Court of the United States was unanimously approved of by the Senate, it was necessary, as you was not generally known to the Members, that some Member should inform them of your qualifications to execute that Office, this your friend Major Butler did in a manner which did honor to himself and to you, a Member from New Hampshire said that tho he had the greatest Confidence in ~~who~~ the Honor of the Gentleman from South Carolina he wished to hear the Sentiments of the Gentlemen from the State where you resided, upon this Mr. Hawkins confirmed what Majr. Butler had said and added something of his own, the Senate were then perfectly satisfied.

I have got your Hat and will send it by Swift, who it is expected will sail on Sunday.

The Weather here begins to be very severe, tho clear. I do not find any inconvenience from it on the contrary I have hitherto kept my health much better than I had any reason to expect, and have not touched any kind of Medicine since I left home.

ALS, Charles E. Johnson Collection, Nc-Ar. Addressed to Edenton, North Carolina; franked; answered.

John Pemberton to James Pemberton

Our Address[1] was read this morning, but the house was not full. they gather late. & few appeared to give much attention more was given to Conversation & News Papers. sometime after a pretty many members assembled, & a Debate ensued whether it should not be entered upon, or referred to be read again to morrow & then referred to a Comittee. this & some entering upon the merits, took up about ½ hour. the southern members seem very averse to a prohibition of the wicked traffick. Jackson a member from Georgia was very warm, devoid of good manners, & wanted to lessen our weight in the scale of Citizens. that we did not appear in the time of the strugle nor Aid in the Glorious revolution. that we scattered Daily Pamphlets, representing Negroes packed togr. as Tobacco in a Hogshead.[2] Indeed was very Violent & abusive. Another hoped that the Gentlemen upon reconsidering the matter would withdraw their Memorial representing how Deeply it would affect many Individuals as feeling & humane as themselves—One member gave it as his Opinion that if only 2 or 3 members of Civil society had proposed a matter of General Concernment it ought to be treated with Consideration. That this did not Concern the Quakers solely but many others were of like mind. & therefore worthy Notice. Divers spoke in favor. Jackson said if the Quakers had entered into a subscription & formed a Bank to Compensate the Loss some would sustain, they might with some face come forward. but he heard no Argument used for so speedy a Consideration, but that the Quakers were in the Galery. I hope no Disadvantage will attend its being deferred. & we may be again in the Gallery. & some time will be for taking opp. with some of these Violent men.

The Petition from the Abolition Society in Philada. not yet come to the speakers hands—I wish it here. E. Boudinot apprehends an Aplication to the society here would be useful they might point out to the Comittee some mode that they might Adopt. & it would have been well that a Copy had been sent there.

We left the house when our Matter was over.

*** All our Com[*pan*]y. well[3] S[*amuel*]. Emlen better than he has been a Considerable time his Love to thee. his Wife [*Sarah Mott Emlen*] & children.

We are this Afternoon to Inspect the Militia Bill [*HR-81*]. E. Boudinot thinks it will bring heavy sufferings upon frds.[4] & those fr[*ien*]dly. to our society would be Glad to be strengthened By some Notice of it. The poor Natives situation claims the attention of some Members who Consider their safety to [*blotted out by seal*] tho' little handed to them but the Cruelty of [*blotted out by seal*] the Indns.; An Army is like, its said, to be raised but E. B[*oudinot*]. thinks it is as much to Curb Wicked Whites, as to Injure the Natives.

ALS, Pennsylvania Abolition Society Papers, PHi. Addressed to Philadelphia. The omitted text relates to the writer's private business concerns.

[1] The petition of the Philadelphia Yearly Meeting of Friends specifically, which was presented simultaneously with the petition of the New York Yearly Meeting of Friends; for background, see *DHFFC* 8:314–38.

[2] Probably a reference to the broadside of the Pennsylvania Abolition Society, printed under 17 March 1790, volume 19.

[3] In addition to John Pemberton and Warner Mifflin, the other Philadelphia Quakers who accompanied the petition to the seat of government were: Nicholas Waln (1742–1813), John Parrish, Jr. (1729–95), William Savary (1750–1804), Henry Drinker (1734–1809), Benjamin Clarke, Abraham Gibbons (1741–98), Jacob Lindley (1744–1816), Samuel Emlen, Sr. (1730–99), and John Haydock (AN, Names of Friends appointed to attend the application to Congress respecting slavery, &c. 2d. mo. 1790, Pemberton Papers, PHi).

[4] Quakers refer to each other and are often referred to by non-Quakers as "Friends," for their membership in the "Society of Friends."

George Washington to Edmund Randolph

I have weighed with deliberate attention the contents of your letter of yesterday;[1] and altho' that consideration may result in an approbation of the ideas therein suggested; yet I do not, at present, feel myself authorized to give a sanction to the measures which you propose. For, as the Constitution of the United States, and the Laws made under it, must mark the line of my official conduct, I could not justify my taking a single step in any matter which appeared to me to require their agency, without its being first obtained; and so far as I have been able to form a judgment upon the objects held up to view in your letter, they cannot be effected without the operation of a Law.

As an Act must necessarily be passed to extend the Judicial Power of the United States to the State of North Carolina, it appears to me that a clause might be there introduced to establishe that uniformity and precision in the business of the United States in each district, which you observe is highly proper to be effected, and to make such other regulations as may be thought necessary. I, however, only suggest this idea to you, that you may, if you think proper, mention it to such members of the Senate and House of Representatives as are acquainted with the subject, and thereby have the matter brought to view whenever the above mentioned Act shall be under consideration.

FC:lbk, Washington Papers, DLC.

[1] No copy of this letter is known to exist.

Y. Z. to Messrs. Printers

THE arguments I heard this day used in Congress, by a Gentleman from Virginia [*Madison*] I do not clearly understand—If I do it was to this purpose: that I, an original creditor of the United States should receive thirty shillings in the pound for my debt: In this sense, in the first place, I paid the certificates or evidence of my debt, to a creditor of mine in the State of New-York, at twenty shillings in the pound. If I understand him, that creditor is to refund ten shillings of the twenty to the United States, who are again to pay it to me. Pray Messrs. Printers explain this Hocus Pocus Humbug piece of business to your constant reader.

NYDA, 12 February.

[*John Gardiner*] to George Thatcher

THE extract from your letter to the Hon. DANIEL CONEY, Esq.[1] which appeared in the *Herald of Freedom*, of the 9th inst. as "from a gentleman in the District of *Maine*, to his friend in *Boston*," appears to be as nervous in

style as important in matter. You are pleased to say that you "should hardly think it demands a parliamentary interposition to exterminate *mice* from the face of the earth." Mr. G[*ardiner*]. never presumed to compare that *"Order,"* of which he confesses you are a respectable brother, to such mischievous vermin, nor did he ever harbour the most distant idea, that it would be for the benefit of society to exterminate an *"Order"* which he publickly declared he thought under *due restrictions and regulations,* absolutely necessary in all free governments. *Vermin* of all kinds, he confesses, he is willing should be exterminated, for the good of society, and that by any and every means—for
"Sportsmen say
No vermin *can demand fair play."* [*Jonathan*] SWIFT.
But if Mr. G. is to be destroyed, he confesses he would rather fall by a lion, than be gnawed to death by such pernicious vermin.

Why are you so anxious to know whether it is probable that Mr. H[*ancock*]. will be again chosen Governour, and what are the dispositions of the people towards that gentleman? If you will credit my assurances, you will rest satisfied that Mr. H. lives in the affectionate esteem of all true whigs and friends of his country—notwithstanding the spiteful, envious, malignant, and rancorous writhings and contorsions of the whole family of LACO;[2] and, that it is more than probable that he will, again and again, experience the confidence of his fellow-citizens, and, while he lives, continue to fill the chair of the Commonwealth of Massachusetts.

[Boston] *Massachusetts Centinel,* 13 February. Subscribed "Boston, Marlboro-Street." For background on the subject of this letter—Gardiner's crusade to reform the bar—see Ames to William Tudor, 17 January, n. 1, above. The letter's author is identified on the basis of its content, the assertions of several correspondents (David Sewall to Thatcher, 22 February; Daniel Cony to Thatcher, 24 February), and the fact that it was requested to be inserted in the *Massachusetts Centinel* by J. G. (whose initials nevertheless appear to have been transposed in the closing). Buccinator (trumpeter) also hints at Gardiner's authorship in his poem lampooning this letter, printed as "the Law-Reformer's Object, or the Cat let out of the Bag" ([Boston] *Massachusetts Centinel,* 17 February).

[1] See Thatcher to Daniel Cony, 31 January, above.
[2] Laco was the pseudonym used by Stephen Higginson when he attacked John Hancock in a series of articles that appeared in the press during February and March 1789. They were later published as a pamphlet entitled *The Writings of Laco* (Boston, 1789).

Letter from Newport, Rhode Island

At present our island and state may not improperly be called the *Botany Bay*[1] of America; the receptacle of the seditious, the disaffected, and the bankrupts of other states, an Augean stable,[2] whose accumulated filth will take some modern Hercules at least thirty years to clear away; for we are still in hopes there is virtue and magnanimity enough among us to remove some time or another, the mass of pollution collected in this state in the course of the last six years. The sons of Belial[3] are numerous amongst us, tho' there are some hopes of their reformation in as much as Dr. I— T— [*John Taylor*] and Co. have published some letters in which they assert that should the general government be *wisely* and *prudently* administered they make no doubt its subjects may be the richest and happiest people on earth, which (says T—) is my sincere prayer. &c. What a lovely, immaculate creature is this Dr. I— T—, and lo! he prayeth!

NYDA, 20 February. This "extract of a letter" is actually a summary of Buccinator (Latin for trumpeter), published in the [Rhode Island] *Newport Herald*, 4 February.

---

[1] An early Australian convict settlement that by 1790 had become synonymous with anything of a criminal and uncivilized nature.
[2] King Augeas's stable of oxen, which Hercules (as one of his mythic labors) cleansed by diverting a river through it.
[3] 1 Samuel 2:12; lawless and rebellious people.

OTHER DOCUMENTS

Governor William Livingston to John Jay. ALS, Jay Collection, NNC. Written from Elizabethtown, New Jersey.
> "From your extensive acquaintance with the Eastern members in Congress I don't know any person that could probably more easily procure me a Quintal of Dumbfish by their means than yourself."

Robert Morris to William Constable. ALS, Lee-Kohns Collection, NN.
> "I have occasion this day for a little more Money than I have by me"; asks to borrow $250, for which he encloses a note "which I will pay when due from monies I am soon to receive in this City."

William Paterson to Euphemia Paterson. ALS, Paterson Papers, NjR. Addressed to New Brunswick, New Jersey; franked; postmarked 14 February. Paterson's brother-in-law Anthony Walton White would petition the FFC on 10 March for settlement of his Revolutionary War accounts; see *DHFFC* 7:544.
> Asks "why accuse me of neglect"; attributes her complaints to "the warmth of your affection and love"; nothing new to report; the House is "deeply engaged" on the funding system, "about which there is much diversity of sentiment"; Dr. John Richardson Bayard Rodgers visited on Sunday but Paterson told him nothing about Susan (Kearny); that same day, also visited with Anthony Walton White; in Paterson's last letter to Col. John Bayard, discussed "our deliberations with respect to your

brother [*Anthony Walton White*]"; enquires of son Billy's schooling; "pray keep him employed."

Jeremiah Wadsworth to Charles Pettit. No copy known; acknowledged in Pettit to Wadsworth, 16 February.

William Samuel Johnson, Diary. Johnson Papers, CtHi.
   "Dind. G. [*Dined at General*] Knoxs."

George Washington, Diary. Washington Papers, MiD-B.
   Leonard, Grout, Huntington, Sturges, Silvester, Sinnickson, Gale, Bland, Parker, and Moore dined at the President's.

FRIDAY, 12 FEBRUARY 1790

Cold (Johnson); *Cold and clear* (J. B. Johnson)

Thomas Fitzsimons to Tench Coxe

I should have Answered your Obliging Letter of the 6th. before now. but that I expected to be able to give some Information that would be Usefull. ~~Nothing however has Occurred~~

The State of Pensylvania and Many of its Citizens in their private Capacity are deeply interested in the present Subject of our deliberation [*the report on public credit*]. we progress so slowly in it that as Yet Little can Appear except the great diversity of Opinions Amg. the Members—foreseeing that it would be Necessary to bring the Substance of the Secys. Plan. before the Committee of the Whole in a Shape that would be Likely to take Seperate questions on them. I prepared the Resolutions[1] Which you have seen printed & Which were received. but as yet the first only has been determined on. Mr. Madison Yesterday proposed an Amendment [*on discrimination*].[2] the discussion of which I expect will take up 2 or 3 days—I sent it to Philada. to be published for Genl. Information so that I need not Repeat it. but I cannot help Adding that he prefaced it by an Address Which would do honor to his [*lined out*] Philanthrophy & Ability before Any Assembly on Earth—I suspect Notwithstanding that his Plan ~~will~~ When Examined will be found Impracticable. if it were not he would Certainly be supported by the disinterested part of the legislature Under present Appearances—no Opinion Can be formed as to the Ultimate Issue of the business Generally—the Representatives of Every state being divided and the Views of the states extreamly discordant the Assumption of the State debts is a Condition with

some for any provision Whatever with others it is Reproprated [*reprobated?*],
& another Consider a Reduction of the Interest on the Whole debt to 3 ℔
Ct. as the Utmost that ought to be done the truth is the Subject is not Very
well Understood but it will be ably discussed. & Conviction brot. to the
mind of some Who only want good Information to direct their Judgement.

The last post brot. me the Report of the Committee of our [*state constitutional*] Convention and as farr as I have yet had oppy. of Considering it
I like it extreamly. the Mode of Chusing Senators & the limittation in the
office of Governor. Appear the most exceptionable. I am told the former
may undergo some alteration. but even if it should not I do not Apprehend
so much from it as it stands as I find others do the office of Chief Magistrate
Will under it be of Very high Importance and it will be unfortunate Indeed
If the first Choice is not a prudent one. I hope the powers Attached to it will
Strike the people so forcibly that they will see the Necessity of Chuse[*in*]g.
a Man of Character & ability.

I Read that part of your Letter to Mr. Clymer which Respected your
Machinary[3] ~~in~~ to the success of which you have Mine & his good wishes. it
will be highly Important to the state and I hope there will be no difficulty in
Obtaing. an Association sufficient to carry on the Manufacture to considerable extent If the business of the present session of Congress terminates as
it ought it will thro into Circulation a Very considerable Addition to our
present Capital—a part of which will beyond doubt be Employd in Objects
of that Kind—I do not Mean by this that funding the domestic debt would
of itself have that Effect but all the purchases of foreigners in these funds
will [*lined out*] certainly be an Addition.

The prices of Country produce with the Low rate of Exch[*ang*]e. will enrich us Extreamly & happens at a favorable time to encourage Industry—I
long to hear from Europe—to know among other things Whether the Markets there will warrant the prices given on this side.

The letter Respecting Solomons Estate, shall be transmitted to the other
Adminsrs. with directions to take Advice upon it—that of the [*Philadelphia*]
Committee of Merchts. was handed to the Post Master Genl. [*Samuel Osgood*]
but Mr. [*William*] Bingham did not Chuse to Add his Signature—the post
office bill [*HR-42*] has been drafted some days & only Waits for the Inspection of the Committee.

ALS, Coxe Papers, PHi. Addressed to Philadelphia; franked; postmarked 14 February.

---

[1] See 8 February, above.
[2] See *DHFFC* 5:840n.
[3] Coxe to Clymer, 17 January, above, relating to George Parkinson's adaptation of a water
mill.

William Maclay to John Nicholson

Madison whose obstinate Silence for some time past had raised the public expectation, opened Yesterday. I lost the forepart of his speech. but the following was the Ground he took. the 2d proposition being still before the Committee of the Whole house. That a Chancery power of dealing distributive Justice, was inherent in Government. provided they became not Judges in their own cause, the United States owe the whole debt. then the only question is to Whom shall payment be made? An Original holder admits of no doubt. he presented a Resolution that the Whole debt should be funded. and in Cases where the Evidences of the debt were in different hands, from those who performed the Service, such holders should be settled with at the highest market price. and the balance revert to the Original holder, who performed the Service. he was feebly opposed by Boudinot and some others, who admitted the Principles to be just but called it impossible. That the original Holder could not be traced &ca. this seems far from impossible nor does it appear to me likely to be attended with much difficulty. if You had a little leisure I think you could place this in a clear point of View.

The officers Soldiers &ca. to whom residuary balances might be found due, might be referred to the Western Territory for payment. this would not fail of giving them satisfaction, for anything which they may get, would come unlooked for.

The paper containing, the Budget opened,[1] came to my hands Yesterday. it was read with great avidity by the Members of Congress. I will thank You for the papers containing some other peices. and am in much Haste.

P. S. the Committee rose without putting the question on Madison's Motion, I hope to give You his Whole Speech, and the Result of his Motion in my next.

ALS, Boudinot Correspondence, Record Group 256, Presbyterian Historical Society, Philadelphia. Addressed to "Comptroller Genl. of the State of Pennsylvania"; franked; postmarked 14 February; received 16 February.

[1] For this piece, which Maclay authored, see Maclay to John Nicholson, 30 January, above.

OTHER DOCUMENTS

John Beckley to an Unknown Recipient. AL, Miscellaneous Letters, Miscellaneous Correspondence, State Department Records, Record Group 59, DNA. Printed in *DHFFC* 8:603.

Relating to supplying certified copies of the acts of Congress.

Meletiah Jordan to George Thatcher. ALS, Chamberlain Collection, MB.

Written from Frenchman's Bay, Maine; postmarked Portsmouth, New Hampshire, [April 10?].

    Asks for Thatcher's support against complaints brought against Jordan as collector.

Joshua Martin to John Langdon. ALS, Langdon Papers, NhPoA. Written from Portsmouth, New Hampshire.

    Private mercantile news; spent previous evening as guest of Mrs. Elizabeth and Eliza Langdon, who are well.

Jeremiah Olney to Alexander Hamilton. FC:dft, Olney Papers, RHi. Written from Providence, Rhode Island. For the full text, see *PAH* 6:263–64.

    "Could any thing Come from Congress or Influential Characters in New York to their Friends here in time to lay before the [*state ratification*] Convention—it would have the Happiest Effect."

Benjamin Rush to John Adams. ALS, Adams Family Manuscript Trust, MHi. Written from Philadelphia; franked; postmarked 15 February; answered 17 February.

    "I cannot help loving and respecting you. You were my first preceptor in [*lined out*] the Science of goverment"; "I learned further from you, to despise public opinion"; his personal partiality for French, Italian, and Spanish "is one of the reasons of my having quarrelled with the dead languages of Greece & Rome"; expresses his current apathy towards and detachment from public affairs.

Roger Sherman to Rebecca Sherman. ALS, Sherman Collection, CtY. Place to which addressed not indicated.

    Has heard from son John and forwarded letters from him; son Isaac seeks a federal appointment; has written to them both at Savannah, Georgia, twice and will a third time at Charleston, South Carolina; Congress is considering the payment of interest on the public debt "and I believe justice as far as may be will be done."

Michael Jenifer Stone to Walter Stone. ALS, Stone Papers, MdHi. Place to which addressed not indicated. The recipient's identity is based on M. J. Stone to W. Stone, 12 March. Harrison (1745–90), chief justice of Maryland since 1781, declined a nomination as an associate justice of the Supreme Court pending a trip to New York, at Washington's suggestion, to discuss with members of Congress some of the changes Harrison hoped would be made to the Judiciary Act. He left Port Tobacco, Maryland, on 14 January

1790 but was detained by ill health and turned back at Bladensburg, Maryland, on 21 January. He returned to Port Tobacco, where he died on 2 April (*PGW* 4:101–2). See also *DHFFC* 17:1810.

Is sorry to hear that Robert Hanson Harrison took sick en route to New York; "Had I thought my coming with him was of the importance you Suggest I believe I should have Sacraficed Publick *Duty* to private Friendship"; knows that Walter meant no ill by the suggestion, "But I beg you to reflect what affect it must have upon a Heart like mine if it admitted the Justice of your remarks"; has written to Harrison and hopes he may help him; expects him to be well in the spring.

Stephen Waite and Abner Bagley to George Thatcher. ALS, Thatcher Papers, MeHi. Written from Portland, Maine; franked. For the full text, see *DHFFC* 8:442.

Cover letter to (unlocated) petition of the weighers, measurers, and gaugers of Portland and Falmouth, Maine, seeking increased compensation.

Hopley Yeaton to John Langdon. ALS, Langdon Papers, NhPoA. Written from Portsmouth, New Hampshire.

Langdon's family is well; asks Langdon to remember him in public business.

NYJ, 18 February. *NYDG*, 13 February, reported a less complete version; reprinted at Charleston, South Carolina, and elsewhere.

Several Oneida Indians, accompanied by Rev. Samuel Kirkland, arrived in New York to transact some business with Congress, "the GREAT COUNCIL-FIRE of the United States."

Letter from Liverpool. *NYDG*, 5 April (the date on which members of Congress would have seen it).

"Wheat and flour have both declined in price" and "We do not conceive that there was any real scarcity of grain either in this kingdom or France."

SATURDAY, 13 FEBRUARY 1790

Cold (Johnson); *Cold and clear and fine weather* (J. B. Johnson)

Pierce Butler to John McPherson

Your kind favor of the 30th. of Octbr. did not reach my hands till last Month. I feel very sensibly the value of Your friendship which I trust I shall never forfeit by any private or publick deficiency.

I am much honored by the repeated marks of confidence and regard I experience from Prince William's Parish.[1] It is my unceasing desire to render them any service in my power and to exert the little abilities Providence has been pleased to bestow on me in promoting their interest. With these feelings I would assuredly, as their Representative attend the Convention, if the Fœderal Legislature did not require my attendance here. We are now in session and shall continue I am of opinion 'till July. Were I to leave Senate I should be chargeable, and perhaps charged too with a desertion of the trust the State reposed in me: I must therefore request You will apologise to the parish for me. I enclose to You my resignation to be forwarded to the Governor.[2] If I saw the smallest probability of Congress adjourning in time I shou'd not resign but on the contrary return and attend the Convention. Seeing no prospect of the former it becomes my duty to timely inform the Parish of it, that they may not lose a voice on so important an occasion.

I find You did not go to Columbia [*South Carolina*]. The upper country Members suffered themselves to be duped there by docking off all pay. I always thought two Dollars too much but some pay is necessary. Suppose a Dollar. In the present infant state of the Country it is right and proper. If nothing is given, many good Men who might be [*the*] choice of their Neighbours are excluded because they have not sufficient to bear their own expences without distressing their families. This measure then is actually narrowing the people's choice. It is not the best men that we must now look out for but the few [?] Men that can best afford the expence of attending the Legislature. In England the Members were for a long time payed for their attendance: when the Country became so as not to need it they gave it up.

I hope nothing will prevent You from attending in Convention. Two things ought to be well regarded in framing a new Constitution. Representation generally and the mode of Electing. By Representation I mean the Equalizing on just principles the Representation and not allowing to Charleston the preposterous Representation she now has which gives Her an unjust Ascendancy on all the measures of Government.[3] Attempts will be made and ably supported to halve the Representation generally but that will not in the least remedy the Evil. Charleston would still have an unjust proportion as according to the number other parishes had. It appears to me that if Charleston has ten Members for the two parishes she can not in reason complain. If the other parishes have two thirds or three fifths of their present number it would appear to me pretty just. Charleston I am sure cou'd have no just cause for complaint yet I know much will be urged against such a proportion by the Gentlemen from Charleston but the Country Gentlemen should persevere and be steady The next thing to be regarded is the number of Senators and the mode of electing them. I am of opinion that it wou'd be better to increase the number of Senators and indisputably keep the Election in the people. Advocates will not be wanting to have them elected by Electors chosen by the People. this does not meet my Judgement. I am strong in opinion that the people should have a voice immediately in the choice of every person who is to legislate for them. These two main objects well guarded there can be no lasting Evil to apprehend, because after trying the new Constitution if any defects appear or inconveniences felt the Voice of the two Houses can remedy it; provideded You do not give the Governor an absolute negative, that is a right to negative a Law agreed to by both Houses. I think I would give him a suspending power, but if after a given number of days if two thirds of the two Houses were agreed it should pass into an Act. I am of opinion he should be elected for three or four Years, and be eligible to Re-Election for as many Years more. I would give him no privy Council which destroys Responsibility.

***

Ever since the receipt of Your Letter I have been looking out for Horses to answer Your description but I cannot meet with one. Such Horses are not to be had here for any money. I have not been able to get any other than common Horses for my own Carriage that I have employed every Horse dealer here and in Philadelphia to get Horses for You and myself. I am told Virginia is the only place to get really fine Horses from. They are scarcer here than I have ever known them to be. There is not in New York but one pr. of real handsome Carriage horses and they come from Virginia.

I will still be on the look out. I sent a pr. of ordinary hacks to my Nephew [*Edward Butler*] They were not such as would suit You.

Congress is now busily employed on the subject of funding the Debt of the United States. I send You some News papers in which You will see the Debates.

FC, Butler Letterbook, ScU. The omitted text conveys greetings to friends. For the full text, see *Butler Letters*, pp. 10–13.

---

[1] Prince William Parish, the mainland neck between the Combahee and Coosawatchie Swamp rivers (part of present-day Hampton County, South Carolina), had elected Butler to represent it at the state's constitutional convention, scheduled to begin in May. McPherson was another delegate who did attend from Prince William.

[2] Butler's enclosed letter to Governor Charles Pinckney was dated 19 February and is printed under that date, below.

[3] South Carolina's constitution of 1778 perpetuated Charleston's disproportionate dominance of the legislature dating from colonial times and embodied in its first constitution of 1776. The Charleston electoral district was allotted thirteen seats out of twenty-nine in the Senate and ninety-six seats in the 202-seat House. The two parishes, St. Philip and St. Michaels, that made up the city of Charleston were allowed thirty state representatives. By 1790, the "upper country" districts made up eighty percent of the state's population but only thirty-seven percent of the apportionment in the House.

Daniel Cony to George Thatcher

I enclose the Herald [*of Freedom*] printed in this Town last Tuesday, as also the [*Massachusetts*] Centinel printed to day, by which you will See that I took the liberty of permitting the publication of an Extract or two from your Letter of the 31 Ulto.

I have freequently been Solicited to publish certain parts of your Letters but have generally declined, knowing that you held a publick appointment, and that thus circumstanced I have presumed you did not wish to take a decisive part in our State politics.

The Extracts published in the last Tuesday's paper were examined by two or three of our freinds, who were of oppinion that the publishing them could not possibly injure you. as the observasions contained therein were express'd with so much Candour. The Letter was read by a few of the members of the general Court, Some of whom I Suppose must have inform'd him [*John Gardiner*] that you wrote it, but who I do not know.

I am exceeding Sorry that from So [*lined out*] trivial a circumstance your name is handed to the publick, tho' Sure I am that it will neither injure you or effect in the lest degree the object designed.

How he affects to know that you are anxious about the future Election of *governour Hancock*, am totally at a loss to guess, for I can positively declare for my Self—that I do not recollect that among all the Letters I ever recd. from you, that you have in any Instance expressed an oppinion on that Subject.

Mr. G̶a̶r̶d̶r̶. [*Gardiner*] Seems disposed to attack every Body who may not join in his Extravagant measures and appears to wish to overturn every thing in existence "nor there Stops" but if his Slanderous breath could do it, would disturb the "Sacred Ashes of the Dead." in last Thursdays [*Independent*] *Chronicle* you will See Some just o̶b̶s̶e̶r̶ Strictures on Gardiner conduct, under the Signature of "junius."

The general oppinion here is that the great noise & bluster made by this *inovator* will Soon evaporate in ___.

I rec'd by this ev'nings mail Genl. Knox's militia Plan, for which I return you my Sincere thanks. I have little or nothing to do with militia matters therefore can Say Nothing respecting the System myself. But the oppinion of many is that it won't do at present. that the expence will be disgustfull.

The general Court have done very Little business yet, probably will Set about a fortnight or three weeks longer.

ALS, Chamberlain Collection, MB. Written from Boston.

Jeremiah Hill to George Thatcher

Yours of the 19th. & 24th Ulto. were received by the last Mail, in the latter you tell me that you have sent to Judge [*David*] Sewall & [*Nathaniel*] Wells each a Copy of the Report of the Secretary [*on public credit*]; I should have been very happy to have received one of the same but I suppose you did not then recollect that I was in the Revenue department, and that I laid Claim to communications of that kind prior to almost any body—I have been called upon by the Secretary of the Treasury for an accurate account of the Emoluments that have accrued to me under the present Regulations from the time of the ~~Orgizanation~~ Organization of the Custom House here to the first of January last past, viz. 4 month & 19 days, I have made out my Statement, the Amount of which is 187. Dol. 41 Cts. which amounts to 1.33 Cents pr. day, all expences Stationary &c. are included which are very great because the duty required is very great. we are obliged to make a weekly return, a monthly Schedule of liquidated bonds and a quarterly abstract of every particular with proper vouchers &c.—If a deputy Door Keeper [*of the House*] deserves two Dollars pr. day because they have the most important Matters of State committed to them think ye, that the Collectors of the revenue don't deserve more than 1. Dol. 33 Cts. pr. day who have the very *Semina Vitæ*[1] of the Union committed to them? However, you know I never complain but am always thankful & contented with whatever my Friends think is best—I read your Letter of the 19th. to our *wise Neighbour, cause why* and I assure you he *nodded* his most *gratious assent* to the funding the Continental Debt at three pr. Cent as well as the assumption of the States debts, and fully agreed with you that punctual Performances were more advantageous than more liberal but ineffectual Engagments, but when I came to the Proposition of some to pay of the Continental Debt at 6 pr. Cent and let the States debts go, he looked very Sowre, ~~but~~ *stroked down his face, looked very wise, but as he was always willing to support Government, he must submit & supposed Government was right, and would do what was best, he had blamed them formerly but was convinced of his Error,* but when I came to the last clause of the sentence where You said the numbers were few he held up his *head* & gave *a majestic Smile.* You say some call it unjust for the Union to assume the States debts, because some States are more in debt than others, were not the States debts contracted in Consequence of the War? if so, it was unjust for any one State to run in debt for that purpose more than others If any State was in debt on any other account the Union ought not to assume it, but if it was a crime or any state was to blame for contracting a Debt to support the public Cause, more than others, upon the same Principles every particular person who served in the field or advanced Property more than his Neighbour was equally culpable, & consequently ought not to be paid I think there is as much Reason in the one Case as in the other—I mean to go to Portland next week if weather permits, I want to know the Substance of the Portland Petition.[2] I think they are rather ashamed of it.

I Judge from Physiognomy, and you know that I have some Knowledge in that branch of Science, and I will venture to prophesy that it will sleep with my friend Millar till the general Resurection of such Matters & things.

You want to know what we are doing here I tell you, last Tuesday we had a very fine Assembly, I put on my dancing Shoes & cut capers like a *popet* [*puppet*], you perhaps may want to know the particular Company, ~~but~~ that is to much for me, but I assure you there were near forty in number, I think Eighteen Couple stood up to dance at one time— ***

ALS, Chamberlain Collection, MB. Written from Biddeford, Maine; postmarked Portsmouth, New Hampshire. The omitted text recounts an anecdote concerning tobacco chewing.

---

[1] The seed of life.
[2] The petition of the Merchants and other Inhabitants of Portland, adopted on 26 December 1789; see *DHFFC* 8:412–14.

Theodore Sedgwick to Peter Van Schaack

I will conform to your wish signifyed by Mr. Sylvester to write in larger characters and with darker ink ~~I will obey~~, but to write more legibly is hardly in my power.

We progress very slowly in the important business before us. unacquainted as we are with the subject of finance, the peculiar circumstances of our debt, the diversity and in some instances the opposition of interests which exist will these causes inevitably involve us in great perplexity. Our embarrassments are encreased by a proposition made on thursday to discriminate between the original holders and the present possessors of securities. Mr. Madison the author of this possesses a great reputation, in public estimation for integrity, & talents, he has too the aid of long experience. That to adopt his ideas would be a most violent breach of public faith, and would be impracticable in the execution, and would, also, infinitely ~~multiply~~ extend the evils of speculation, by multiplying its objects, there can in my opinion be no doubt; and there is as little that it will tend to render inveterate and perpetual parties on this touchy business. It is the more astonishing that Mr. M. who was the author of the address in 1783,[1] and after the conclusion of the war, in which the doctrine of discrimination is reprobated in pointed and unequivocal language, should now take ground so entirely different. It is a subject of vast delicacy as well as importance and what will be the result is some what uncertain, tho' I hope and believe his ~~doctrine will~~ proposition will be rejected.
[*P. S.*] Your watch cost 16/.

ALS, Sedgwick Papers, MHi. Addressed to Kinderhook, New York; carried by Mr. Witbeck.

[1] Congress's Address to the States, passed 26 April 1783, is printed in full in *PJM* 6:488–98. For the passage refuting discrimination, see *DHFFC* 5:844–47.

William Smith (S.C.) to Edward Rutledge

Your attendance at Columbia [*South Carolina*] has deprived me of the pleasure of your Correspondance for some time past, which I hope will soon be renewed.

The House have agreed to postpone the Banky. Law for the prest. We are now very busy on the funding Plan–an importt. & interesting Subject—Two days ago some Petitions were presented to the House from the Quakers of Phila. & N.Y. praying an abolition of the Slave Trade[1]—we thought it proper in the first instance to oppose even the commitmt. of them—our opposn. was ineffectual—the members who wished a committ. have however assured me that it was done purely out of complimt. to the Petitioners & that they are sensible the House cannot in any respect interfere, except as to the duty of 10 dollrs.[2] We protested in the strongest terms agst. even committg. them because the prayer was unconstitl. & it being proposed to refer them to a member from each State, we informed the house that on due consideration the Delegates from So. Cara. & Georgia had resolved not to sit on such Committee. The Quakers [*who*] presented the Petitions were in the gallery [*torn*] trimming.

I have to inform Mr. [*William*] Drayton that the Supreme Court have not fixed any thing as to the dress of the Courts, & that each District Court is to fix establish its own Seal. They have fixed the Seals of the Supreme Court & Circuit Courts according to the mode I suggested to Mr. Jay, as he yesterday informed me. You will see them in the papers—The Ch. Justice & Mr. [*William*] Cushing are to ride the Eastern Circuit—Mr. [*James*] Wilson & [*John*] Blair the Middle—Your Brother [*John, Sr.*] & Mr. [*James*] Iredell (appointed vice Mr. [*Robert Hanson*] Harrison, resigned) the Southern. I have been admitted a Counsellor, they have seperated the business of Counsellor & Attorney.

We had a great deal of warm debate two days about these cursed negro Petitions, & I think we so effectually tired them out members out & embarassed them that they will not be in a hurry to bring the subject on again. Mr. Izard & Maj. Butler were in the house during the debate—the former you may suppose was a not little displeased.

I find you had a short Session at Columbia—I was delighted with the vote withholding pay—it will have admirable effects.

The great question of discrimination is now before the House—Burke first moved it, I opposed it; before I had finished my speech, he withdrew the motion, which was renewed by Madison & will occasion considerabl. debate, but will be rejected—the assumption of the State Debts measures conside. warm opposition—the Event is uncertain, but I think will be carried. I wish the Legisle. of our state had come to some vote on the subject.

Mrs. [*Charlotte*] Smith is getting better—She has been much indisposed. my Son [*Thomas Loughton*] is hearty.

ALS, Smith Papers, ScHi. Addressed to Charleston, South Carolina; franked.

[1] See *DHFFC* 8:322–24.
[2] The Constitution's Article I, section 9, forbade Congress from prohibiting the slave trade prior to 1808, but empowered it to tax the importation of persons up to ten dollars per head.

Newspaper Article

A correspondent observes that a report is in circulation, that the *New System of Finance* lately promulgated, had its origin at a meeting of quarter masters general, and their deputies, commissaries of stores and other attendants on the armies of the United States. The truth of this report is not vouched for, but probability certainly would induce one to think it possible at least; as we are convinced those gentlemen have not amassed such fortunes, as the like officers in the British army have done: By this admirable stroke of ingenuity they will become the richest men in the United States, as more certificates are issued in their names, than to all the Virginia line.

Another wicked insinuation (but which is too glaring to be credited) is whispered about, that several governors of the United States, in conjunction with the late Financier and some wealthy contractors, are at the bottom of this new arrangement; and that on a moderate calculation, the following gentlemen will be benefitted somewhere near the following; no small addition to those gentlemen, who it is presumed already possess a genteel competency.

His Excellency Gov. Clinton   5 mil. dol.
Robert Morris, Esq.;   18 do. do.
Jeremiah Wadsworth, Esq.:   9 do. do.

It will readily occur, that in all the states pretty lucrative douceurs will tumble into the laps of very many meritorious and deserving characters.

NYDA, 13 February; reprinted at Charleston, South Carolina.

From Our Correspondents at New York

Congress go on very slowly in the business of funding the debt. The longer it is delayed, the more will men's minds divide on the subject. This is the great business on which the future respectability of the Government must depend. On Thursday Mr. MADISON made a motion, the object of which was to discriminate between the original holders and the present possessors of publick securities. This motion I presume cannot take effect, because it will be a most open and flagrant breach of publick faith, solemnly pledged—because it will be impracticable to discover who were the original holders—and because it would open a door for infinite speculations with the original and pretended original holders.

[Stockbridge, Massachusetts] *Western Star*, 23 February, paraphrasing Sedgwick to Van Schaak of 13 February.

OTHER DOCUMENTS

Edward Bangs to George Thatcher. ALS, Chamberlain Collection, MB. Written from Worcester, Massachusetts.

Is not "discouraged, nor too proud to continue writing to you, altho my last long impertinent epistle has brought me none in return"; reminds Thatcher, "if you should get a little leasure," to purchase and send him "your laws of Congress," and any "second hand & cheap" law books, but no garden seeds "for you are an improper person to be entrusted with such business—Indeed you are incapable"; asks if Hannibal Dobbyn's offer to purchase western lands will be of "any Considerable consequence" to the public debt, or his proposed settlements "advance our future revenue?"

Jeremy Belknap to John Adams. ALS, Adams Family Manuscript Trust, MHi. Written from Boston; addressed to "Dr. Adams."

Introduces Manasseh Cutler, "whose Character in the botanical Line is doubtless known to you"; his concern in establishing "a permanent foundation for Literature" in the lands of the Ohio Company "will give him consequence in your Eye"; asks Adams for such advice and assistance as "you are both able & willing to afford" Cutler.

William Constable to Garrett Cottringer. FC:lbk, Constable-Pierrepont Collection, NN.

Hopes Madison's "proposition for Discrimination will have an effect in lowering your Market & alarming so that People may be disposed to sell at reasonable Rates on time."

William Constable to Benjamin Harrison. FC:lbk, Constable-Pierrepont Collection, NN.

Finals and indents have fallen at New York City in consequence of doubts about the adoption of Hamilton's plan; "Maddison has contributed not a little by his proposition"; is not afraid however and believes all will go right; if he was not so pushed he would purchase deeply.

William Constable to John Richard. FC:lbk, Constable-Pierrepont Collection, NN. For background on the subject of this letter, see *DHFFC* 7:663–65.

The treasury department has finished auditing most of Morris's accounts (as chair of the Continental Congress's secret committees of trade and correspondence).

Benjamin Huntington to William Ellery. No copy known; acknowledged in Ellery to Huntington, 8 March.

Samuel Johnston to James Iredell. ALS, Charles E. Johnson Collection, Nc-Ar. Addressed to Edenton, North Carolina; answered. For a partial text, see *Iredell* 2:280–81.

Sends Iredell's hat and books, as well as "all the News papers I have by," which he asks to be distributed first to "my friend [*Abraham*] Hodge" and then others "as you may think proper"; Hamilton's report on public credit "occupies the principal Attention of Congress"; Madison supported his proposed discrimination among public creditors by "a very elegant speech of considerable length," which Boudinot and others opposed "by a variety of plausible Arguments"; thanks for the "Friendly attention" to his family, and for promise to write by every post, which "will afford me the most sensible gratification"; "I write to you as often as I can but really I meet with so many interruptions that I find it difficult to write any thing to the purpose"; asks for first name of (William) Benson, whom he will "mention" to the President for surveyor of Windsor, North Carolina.

William Paterson to Euphemia Paterson. ALS, Paterson Papers, NjR. Place to which addressed not indicated; carried by Mr. Young.

Reports that he is well; gossips about family and friends; "We are just getting fairly into Business in the Senate. When we shall rise it is impossible to say; not, however, before the 1st. of May, unless we make greater Progress in Business than I expect we shall. This will break in very much upon my Plan with Respect to the Spring and Summer Courts in West Jersey, which I proposed to attend."

Walter Rutherfurd to John Rutherfurd. FC:dft, Rutherfurd Papers, NHi.
"Many long Speeches we have had" in the House on Hamilton's report
on public credit; Madison spoke on discrimination on Thursday "very
lengthy, and ably"; "Speculators have been sadly abused particularly by
Jackson. and Scot in a very long Speech, I [*have*] been been thrice at the
House. yesterday the Quakers broke in upon them. here the northern and
southern members were in Opposition: the Question was to prevent the
Trade, and the debate turned on, whether the Congress had right to in-
terfere by the Constitution"; "another match in Congress soon expected.
Mr. Page to Miss [*Margaret*] Lowther—called handsome. he has nine
Children"; regarding "Genl. Reid. shall see Boudinot about his Rights.
doubt if he'll sell on Credit."

George Searle to George Thatcher. ALS, Thatcher Papers, MeHi. Written
from Newburyport, Massachusetts.
His shipment of bricks and pickled fish to a buyer in Charleston, South
Carolina, was forced to pay the foreign impost rate because it had first
passed through St. Domingue (Haiti); asks that the sum be remitted and
a regulation made "in this particular to prevent the like evil in future."

Theodore Sedgwick to Henry Van Schaack. No copy known; acknowledged
in Van Schaack to Sedgwick, 25 February.

Roger Sherman to David Austin. No copy known; acknowledged in Austin
to Sherman, 25 February.

Jeremiah Wadsworth to Josiah Burr. No copy known; acknowledged in Burr
to Wadsworth, 18 February.

SUNDAY, 14 FEBRUARY 1790

Snow (Johnson); *Cold and some snow, thickly overcast* (J. B. Johnson)

John Chaloner to Jeremiah Wadsworth

*** I had a few days past occasion to make some remarks on the Auction
business, which I was told when I was solicitted for it, was for Mr. Hamilton;
who had in view to bring it under the regulation of the new Goverment &
to raise a Revenue therefrom[1]—this performance was done in haste & I am
told is lodgd with Col. Hamilton, if he has it in contemplation I should be

happy in contributeing any information relative thereto that he might wish to receive. if it was taken by the new Goverment & laid open to as many persons of Character that could obtain publick Confidence I doubt not but it would be productive of a very large Revenue— ***

ALS, Wadsworth Papers, CtHi. Written from Philadelphia. The omitted text relates to private business transactions.

---

[1] Hamilton's report of 4 March, on additional sources of revenue, included a one percent tax on sales at auction. No "remarks" on the subject by Chaloner to Hamilton are known to exist, but a letter from Philadelphia collector Sharp Delany, dated 18 January, suggested a two percent tax would yield $100,000 annually (*PAH* 6:185).

Thomas Hartley to Jasper Yeates

I received your Favor of the 7th. inst. I am sorry for the Loss of the Child but am very happy to hear that Mrs. [*Sarah Burd*] Yeates is safe and likely to do well.

Our Friends in [*Pennsylvania's constitutional*] Convention have had a troublesome Job, I wish the Fruits of their Labour may be such as their Constituents hoped for—I presume the Convention will soon rise.

We have had the Secretarys Report [*on public credit*] under Consideration—but our Progress has not been very great but yet perhaps full as much as could have been reasonably expected.

Mr. Madison made a Strange Motion on Thursday—which he enforced with a Speech of one hour and three Quarters length of the finest Language I almost ever heard—but many Persons were very much surprized at the Nature of his Motion—and thought it had more the Scent of the Chamber Lamp than generally appears in his Productions—in short that it was not founded upon practical Life.

The honesty of his Mind or Ambition has prompted him to the Attempt, but his Motion will I immagine fall to the Ground.

There are many Things in human aff Life which are wished for—but not practicable from the Nature of Worldly Affairs—Certificates have I am told fallen since that Speech, but [*lined out*] as the Change is merely the Whim or Caprice of the Moment I am inclined to think there is no solid Ground for it—nay I beleve as I have before hinted the Motion when the Question is put [*lined out*] will go to [*illegible*].

We shall have much difficulty in the Report, but we must go through with it—several of the Principles in it will require alteration.

I hope your Next Courts will be better I wish the [*Pennsylvania*] Circuit Courts were fixed at the same Time as last Spring—do communicate this Idea to Mr. Bard to be mentioned to their Honors.

ALS, Yeates Papers, PHi. Addressed to Lancaster, Pennsylvania; franked; postmarked; answered 27 February.

Samuel Henshaw to Theodore Sedgwick

Your favour of the 7th. Inst. is recd. and I thank you for it—but am not able to answer it—You mention, that you have recd. mine of the 30th. ult. but do not acknowledge the receipt of the one I wrote you the week before—I hope it has not miscarried as there were some things in it, that I would not wish any body but my Friend, should see—If it has come to hand, I would thank you to give me your opinion, by next post, on those suggestions contained in it, that relate immediately to your Friend.[1]

*** I have not yet read the Secys'. plan [*on public credit*]—nor have I been able too—There are various opinions concerning it—But I am not able to give you proper information as I have been confined ever since the plan has been generally read & digested—Mr. Stephen Higginson was to see me the other evening—I asked his opinion of it—He liked it generally—But was fearful it was too rigid, prompt, & energetic for this early period of our political existance.

You observe That the Secy. is very Sanguine, that He can carry his Scheme into effect without a direct Tax—If He can, I doubt the Justice of it—But I am as sanguine as He can be, that his Scheme is not within the ability of the people. If the Commerce of this State is to be taxed with £220,000 annually, it will be annihilated—and the public faith, & public creditors, will go to the Devil together.

Farewell—May wisdom & patriotism lead my Friend into the paths of truth & righteousness.

ALS, Sedgwick Papers, MHi. Written from Boston; postmarked. The omitted text relates to Henshaw's poor health.

---

[1] See Henshaw to Sedgwick, 27 January, above.

James Madison to Thomas Jefferson

We proceed slowly in business. The Report of Mr. Hamilton has been, of late, the principal subject of debate. On the foreign debt the vote has been unanimous. On the domestic, a reduction of the transferred principal has been brought into view by several arguments and propositions. My idea is that there should be no interference of the public in favour of the public either as to principal or interest, but that the highest market price only should be allowed to the purchasers, and the balance be applied to solace the original sufferers, whose claims were not in conscience extinguished by a *forced* payment in *depreciated* certificates. The equity of this proposition is not contested. Its impracticability will be urged as an insuperable objection. I am aware of the difficulties of the plan, but believe they might be removed by one-half the exertion that will be used to collect and colour them.

A bill for a census [*Enumeration Act*] has passed the House of Representatives, and is with the Senate. It contained a schedule for ascertaining the component classes of the Society, a kind of information extremely requisite to the Legislator, and much wanted for the science of Political Economy. A repetition of it every ten years would hereafter afford a most curious and instructive assemblage of facts. It was thrown out by the Senate as a waste of trouble and supplying materials for idle people to make a book.[1] Judge by this little experiment of the reception likely to be given to so great an idea as that explained in your letter of September.[2]

PTJ 16:183–84, from Madison, *Letters,* 1:507.

[1] Among federal marshals, who were responsible for taking the first census, at least one did in fact encourage his deputies to approach the task with more latitude than was prescribed by the Enumeration Act. On 1 July, Robert Forsyth sent Col. Richard Call his appointment as census taker for Richmond County, Georgia, along with "a form (such as I think will do) for the head of the Book you may use in taking down the Residents; it is rather more particular than the act; but the trouble will be much the same to you, and some advantages may be derived from taking the Census agreeably thereto." In addition, he recommended that every other page be left blank for recording more specific information about places of residence (ALS, Forsyth Papers, NcD).

[2] The principle that the earth belongs to the living and not to the dead; see Jefferson to Madison, 6 September 1789, *DHFFC* 17:1477–79.

Charles Pettit to Elias Boudinot

The great hopes I had entertained of seeing a well digested practical plan of finance, adapted to our circumstances, are mortifyingly damped. Still, however, I am strongly inclined to believe that the *intentions* of the Secretary [*Hamilton*] are honest & praiseworthy. I shall not now repeat to you my reasons for this belief, having, if my memory is just, mentioned those reasons to you in a former letter. But errors, in a business of this kind, may be equally injurious whether they flow from mere mistake, or from evil intention.

A proper system of finance is so important a part of the grand political system of Government, that the latter, however well constructed in other respects, must be defective & subject to destructive disorders, in proportion as the former is defective or erroneous. Systems of finance, however, are of modern invention, or rather of modern discovery, and their elementary principles, however simple & plain when fairly investigated, have been so little explored & thoroughly examined, that a competent knowledge of their rise in practice, is little is yet scarcely discernable in the conduct of the Government in any of the European States. Even in England, where the science of finance seems to be best understood, their funding system is not yet purged of all its errors; but it has attained a degree of perfection sufficient to give us so great light on the subject, as to enable us to form a better system than theirs, if we duly attend to the principles deducible from their practice. A system of finance may be likened to a complex machine, the component parts of which must be adapted to each other in such manner as to perform their respective functions in due proportion and in regular order. To construct such a machine, requires a previous knowledge of the principles by which its operations are governed. The powers with which, & by which, the several parts will operate, upon & be operated upon one another, and the combined effects of the whole must be perceived previously to their being formed & put together. And in proportion to the degree of accuracy with which they are perceived, and the degree of Judgment & Skill in adapting each of the component parts to the performance of its proper functions, in giving them a due proportion to each other, and adapting the whole to its proper Object, will the machine work well or ill, and be attended with advantage or disadvantage to the proprietor. Each of the parts, considered abstractly, may be good, and yet if they be not accomodated to each other, the machine will either not move at all, or move heavily, perhaps destructively. The machine, moreover, must be duly proportioned to the force of the propelling power which is to give it motion. If this power be limited, the whole machine, in all its parts, should be regulated by such limitation. the wheels & pendulum of a clock, for instance, must not exceed a due proportion to the power of the weight, or spring.

I can readily subscribe to an opinion that the Secretary has competent abilities to become as perfectly skilled in this or any other Science, as the human mind is capable of attaining to—I will also acknowledge that he has made considerable progress in the science of Finance; but at the same time I cannot but think the specimen he has given us shews that he has yet much to learn before he will construct a system properly adapted to our national circumstances. The model he has exhibited appears to me to be crude, and the parts so disproportioned and ill adapted to each other as to destroy its capacity of acting either regularly or safely. I find there are people in New York & other places who perceive its defects and are beginning to point them out. Three or four of Dunlap & Claypoole's papers of last week, contain Remarks on the Subject, which I think worthy of notice;[1] and this morning I have seen an essay, extracted from Mr. Fenno's Gazette, under the signature of a "Jerseyman"[2] which contains many just Sentiments. The more the plan is considered, the more liable to objections it will be found. To adopt it as it is, appears to me more dangerous than to let it remain under consideration a while. It is a subject of the utmost importance to the well being of the United States, & the credit & stability of the Government, and therefore merits mature consideration. The throng of business in which the members of Congress are involved hardly admits of their giving the subject a full & fair investigation & discussion in a few days or weeks—In a little Time they will probably collect much information from without doors which may give them material assistance. The Secretary himself, will, I doubt not, obtain farther light, and I should hope his candor would induce him to suggest alterations, if he should perceive the propriety of them.

The best treatise I have ever met with on this Subject is contained in Mr. Gale's three essays, dated in 1782, 1783 & 1786.[3] I procured them last summer at [*James*] Rivington's. I wish every Member of Congress would read & understand them; but they are so dry and unentertaining, that the study would be tedious to a Mind not thirsty for information of this kind. This writer has reduced in my Mind to settled opinions, established by incontestible proofs and mathematical demonstrations, what were previously but floating Notions which I believed to be just, but was unable to trace fully to immutable principles. I think I can perceive in the Secretarys plan, that he has read these Essays, but not thoroughly digested the truths they contain. My *anxiety* on this subject may be increased by the suggestions of interest as a public creditor, which, however, is much less that that of many others, and much less than is imputed to me; but I do veryly believe that my *opinions* would ~~would~~ be the same if I was not a public creditor at all. I have carefully examined the principles on which my opinions are founded, & ~~compared them with~~ find them established by the best experience I can find recorded. I have also examined every argument I could meet with either for or against those opinions; and after rejecting all which do not fairly apply to the public interest, abstractly considered, I find my opinions more strongly confirmed. Wherever I find the interest of an individual, whether as a public creditor or otherwise, opposed to the general interest, I reject the former, or make it yield to the latter, because, in a well regulated Government no incompatibility of this kind can exist; the line of honesty and justice must necessarily be the fair line of boundary to both, and therefore cannot be invaded by either without injury to both.

ALS, AMs 779/1, PPRF. Written from Philadelphia.

---

[1]On 8, 9, 11, and 13 February, John Dunlap and David C. Claypoole's *PP* printed the four part "Remarks on the Report of the Secretary of the Treasury" by S. T.

[2]"A Jersey Man" appeared in John Fenno's *GUS* on 6 February.

[3]*On the Nature and Principles of Publick Credit*, a series of three essays by Samuel Gale

(1748–1826), an economist who had served as assistant paymaster for the British army in North America in the 1770s.

William Smith (Md.) to Otho H. Williams

Notwithstanding, I daily expected to hear the Melancholy news, of the death, of a much respected & old experienced friend, by the sp seperation of Doct. Boyd from us,[1] your letter of the 4th Instant, which gave me the intelligence, brought to my mind, all those gloomy sensations, which Naturaly occur, on those solemn occasions; I most affectionatly and Sincerely condole with all his friends on the loss they have Sustained. I think however *his exit*, a very desireable conclusion of this transitory Scene he retained his Senses to the last moment, without excrutiating pain, *or much regret*; maintaining the rational hope, & faith, of a Sincere Christian. May we all live the life of the Righteous, that our latter end, may be like his.

***

We have had Ten days of Serene, Steady, cold weather, which I hope is favorable to yr. health, & from yr. last letter I expect you will be perfectly restored.

***

Continental paper remains in Statu quo, at 7.6 in the Pound for final Settlements & 5/6 for Indents. Congress has not hitherto made much progress in the funding Business the last two days being lost by the Consideration of a petition from the Quakers on the Subject of Slavery, which was finally refferd to a Special committee; *We have only resolved* that Adequate provision Ought to be made for paying the foreign Debt. To the second resolution proposed, Namely, that funds Shall be provided for paying the ~~Domestic~~ Interest on the Domestick debt &ca. Mr. Madison, proposed an Amendment, to this effect. "That Original holders of Certificates Shall be paid the Rate of 6 ℔ Cent on the full Nominal Value, that, the present holders by *purchase*, Shall be allowed at the rate of the present market price, & the difference paid to the Original Owners." This Motion he introduced by a very masterly Speech, enforcing the Justice of the Measure. However, notwithstanding the equity & Justice of that mode of Settlement, I am of opinion at present, no discrimination will, or can take place from the impractabillity of doing Strict Justice in that mode.

I expect the public Domestic debt, will be funded, *the principal & interest consolidated*, but at what Interest I cant Say, I question, if there is any Material departure from the Secretarys report [*on public credit*], but youll Observe this is only matter of opinion. If I am right in my Conjecture, public Securities will probably Settle down at 10/ or 12/6 in the pound, but that must be after Some time, which will be necessary to gain Confidence.

***

ALS, Williams Papers, MdHi. Place to which addressed not indicated. The omitted text relates to friends and personal finances at home.

[1] Dr. John Boyd (b. ca. 1730) died in Baltimore on 4 February 1790. The 1757 Princeton graduate practiced medicine in Annapolis, where he held many offices during the early revolutionary movement.

James Sullivan to John Langdon

We have neither politicks or news here. even party contests, and Election-eering squables are not seen for more than two months past.

We have however a Constitutional question before our Supreme Court which may have very serious consequences. we had an Impost Law made in 1786. an Act made June 1789 provided that the Impost Law should be continued in force untill an Act of that nature made by Congress should begin to Operate. large Sums have been collected and Secured. Some Seizures have been made upon a Supposition of the Legallity of this measure. but a question is now agitated, whether the Impost acts of the Several States did not cease as Soon as Congress met, because the Government of the united States has the exclusive right of making Impost Laws. if it should be decided in favour of this proposition we must give up the Vessels Seized, [*lined out*] and refund the large Sums which our Collectors have levied. this will beyond all doubt disturb that harmony which every good man wishes to see continued between the General Government and those of the particular States. the threatning by the Claimants of decrees of Circuit Courts & the Terrors of the General Government has no tendency to prevent uneasiness. I wish you to Consider whether it would not be prudent for Congress. to heal this difficulty by a Resolve Recognizing the Right of the Several states so far as the same was Exercised before the Law of the union began to operate.

ALS, Langdon Papers, NhPoA. Written from Boston.

George Thatcher to Stephen Hall

You have heretofore professed a great friendship towards me; you always accosted me under the most endearing terms of affection, such as my old friend—my dear friend, my good friend &c. &c. And your conduct corresponded to your professions—I on my part, called you my friend; & I also professed friendship towards you—and I do not recollect any instance wherein my conduct was repugnant to my professions.

When this has been the apparent connection between two persons, and one, of a sudden, exhibits; both in conduct and conversation, the reverse; the other has a right to demand an explanation.

Now, Sir, I take you to be a man of honor & a christian—the principles of the former prohibet your injuring your friend, while those of the latter enjoin upon you to do good to them who do evil to you, & to speak well of those who revile you—take your choice then—and declare yourself openly, my friend, or my enemy.

I take you to be a man of independence who will not servily court the favour of any man—such I declare to you I have always felt myself—after premising thus much Let me tell you plainly, because this only is the Language of friendship—that I have been informed you have again & again—and in different companies, in public as well as private endeavoured to injure my character & reputation—Now I will not say this is true—indeed, I am led to hope that it is all a falsehood, but I have such evidence of its Truth that I feel myself bound to acquaint you of it; that you may either avow it and assigne your reasons; or disavow it, & thereby restore in my mind that trust & confidence I have heretofore placed in your declaration of Friendship—You will observe I have addressed you by the epithet of dear friend—by such we formerly addressed each other; I am sensible of nothing on my part that dictates to my feelings that it is improper; & it remains for you to determine the question, while I, once more, subscribe myself, my dear friend, Your friend & humble Sert.

FC, Thatcher Family Papers, MHi. For the background of this letter, see Hall's reply, 24 February, below.

George Thatcher to Sarah Thatcher

Last evening I recieved, at the same instant, eleven Letters; and almost the first opened was one from Tempe [*Temperance Hedge*], dated the third inst. This, among other things, informed me "that [*son*] Phillips was not gone to Portland [*Maine*], & that you had concluded not to send him"—I could not tell what to make of it, because it was couched in such a manner as to contain an idea of my having been informed that you had entertained thoughts of sending him there—At first I imagined that you had wrote about it in some former Letter which had not reached me, & what confirmed me in this idea was that I had not recieved any Letter from you for ten days before—I went on in reading my Letters and the last I opened was from friend [*Jeremiah*

Hill?] inclosing yours of the 31st. of Jany. This explained the mystery I was led into by Tempe's—And I confess, that I almost wish you had let Phillips have gone to Portland, with Mr. [*Nathaniel*] Fosdick, if he had tarried but a week or fortnight—His family is not large, & the trouble would be trifling, as they have no children smaller than Phillips—I should not have valued paying his board, & Schooling.

I begin to think that as soon as I get home I shall put him some where to school—I dont know yet where—it is too far for him to go to the falls, or on the other side of the [*Saco*] river; & if I put him from home I had rather he would go twenty or thirty miles than not—He is almost five years old, which is about the time for him to begin to read, & write.

I should be glad to have him schooled under my own eye, if possible.

I am glad to hear our friend Ruthy Emerson is with you—keep her as long as you can. I suppose Tempe will be soon for cleaving to her husband—when you will be alone—I really should have been rejoiced if Mr. [*Silas*] Lee could have setled nearer to us than Wiscassett—but we can not complain.

I have had no Letter from Mr. Lee since he was at Biddeford—but I hear by a Letter from Judge [*David*] Sewall, & another from Mr. [*James?*] Freeman, that he was in Boston about eight days ago, & would soon return to the eastward.

As you are unwell, & writing may be disagreeable, I would not have you attempt to write me so often as usual—once in a fortnight will be as often as I shall expect to hear from you, hereafter.

ALS, Thatcher Family Papers, MHi. Place to which addressed not indicated.

Jeremiah Wadsworth to Harriet Wadsworth

I last night received your letter with the enclosure true it is not precisely such an one as I thought it—but previous to its being wrote I was asked to consent to a project which I did & you may be assured he intends to be more explicit answer the letter inclosed in the same friendly stile by this means the correspondance may be carried on without injury to either for if it ends only in Friendship it will put it in your power to ~~be~~ act without reserve and you will be compleatly at liberty to finish with friendship only or to Do otherwise as shall suit you my love to all the family I have been interupted to day & could not write them.

ALS, John Trumbull Papers, CtY. Place to which addressed not indicated.

William Wetmore to Benjamin Goodhue

I do not give you the trouble of this letter, because I suppose myself qualified to communicate my new ideas upon that wch. I intend shall be the subject of it; but solely that I may satisfy my own mind, on the score of our old acquaintance & friendship, which I always recollect with great pleasure. You are now a Member of Congress & must desire all just information, respecting the subjects wch. may come before you; but on whom shall you rely for it? not upon the interested man or the [*office*] seeker: and if I know my own views, I am neither of those, except that I am interested for the honour & glory of my country at large, & especially of her legislators, at the dawn, if you will allow me to use the expression, of her greatness. Every trifling observation, or straining after popularity, or apparent desire of following instead of leading the mass of people, to proper measures, wounds my feelings as sensibly as if I were myself guilty of the fault. You will understand me when I refer you to Fenno's paper of the 30th. jany. where one member of Congress, wishes to read the news papers; in order to acquire ideas I suppose of what is right & wrong, or to collect from them the opinions of the people—as if the news papers, were the book of reason & nature & truth. Another wishes Congress to remove to the banks of the Potowmac, in order to settle plans of finance in profound secrecy, & to prevent by buying & selling a particular article of merchandize, which such a secret expedition, especially if undertaken in the night time, would with out doubt I suppose accomplish.[1] These triflings will I fear disgrace us. But what should we not all feel, if for such reasons as these, we should the restoration of public Credit should be neglected even for a moment? And yet it is whispered here that, at least, it will be delayed; that objections & very plausible ones too, may be raised by those who perhaps may wish to purchase the public securities; or may want the revenue to maintain their friends, creatures and dependents, in offices & places already created or that may be created, in which they may be sharers of the profits; or may be hawking after popularity to secure their places: The rate of Interest may be objected to; so may the assumption of the State debts & many other points, & it will be impossible to distinguish, between objections that come only from the head; & those that spring from the heart; but that from such Sources as these jealousies will consequently arise, the present members may lose their seats & the affection & enthusiasm towards the Genl. Govt. be cooled & perhaps turned to another object; A very honest man of Essex, who during the war loaned some money to Congress, attacked me very abruptly the other day, with, well! what do you think of your friend Goodhue now; they tell me, he is for allowing me only 3 per cent, for my money—I always thought him an honest man; and I think so still, replied I, even if he is for the 3 per cent, which however I know nothing about—but if he is for that rate of interest he has good reasons for it I am very sure. He concluded with another, well! I see what they are all after & I believe the people begin to see it too! I reasoned with him & endeavoured to cool him down & to wait with patience, 'till the subject should be taken up in Congress. I write in confidence & give you this out of a thousand anecdotes of the kind, which I might put upon paper, to give you some idea of the jealousies that are spreading—which can be in no other way counteracted by Congress, than by decisive measures, immediately adopted, about the public debt, as well of the United States, as of the several states. The *people* are waiting for the doings of Congress, to be determined in their minds upon the propriety of the measure to be adopted: And I am as confident as I ever was of any point in my life, that this is the moment for Congress to make a general arrangement for both species of debt—the people universally expect it, & are daily inquiring in all parts of the Country, what Congress intend to do, & the topic of conversation with all ranks, is that the Genl. Govt. must take the excise, & of Course the State debt, because no state excise can operate equally, but partially & fraudulently—some members of our Genl. Court are however endeavouring to support an idea, that it is best for us to keep the debt, & continue our excise, & make proper provision for the interest, in order to attach the Creditors to the Govt. & support its sovereignty & independence & because if Congress leaves the debt, upon us, they must leave the Excise; but it is by no means a popular business, notwithstanding the labour bestowed upon it by [*Charles*] Jarvis, [*John*] Gardiner, [*Samuel*] Lyman [*Daniel*] Coney, & Co. & they are evidently I think losing ground in it; [*Ebenezer*] *Pierce* of Partridgefield a popular man with that party is for continuing or amending our Excise act; but he told me this day that he did not see what could be done with it, & he wished we could know whether Congress would take the debt, or what they intended to do about it in short all persons are anxious to have this question setled—And from what I can collect, I think it very probable that the G. Court, will rise without voting a tax, or doing any thing about the excise, notwithstanding the public talk of some who affect to believe the contrary. and this on acco. of the uncertainty whether Congress will assume the debt, which the majority of them as well as the people at large, at *heart* desire, however they may sometimes hold a different *language*. If Congress make a partial arrangement, & leave the State debts upon the individual Govts., for the present, it will only be postponing the evil day, for come it will; & in the mean time the seeds of caballing about them are sown, clashing of jurisdiction & interest arises, frauds upon the revenue multiply, and an intire new system becomes necessary; whereas if a general arrangement now takes place, it will meet the wishes of the people,

& be as universally acceptable as the Secretary's ~~rept~~ report [*on public credit*]; which is speaking as strong language as I can speak.

As to the rate of Interest, the Secretary's plan if adopted will be acceded to, perhaps some large stock holders, & some purchasers at a low price would be content with a lower rate—but a lower rate would not, I am confident from what I hear, bring in a majority of the Creditors with us; I could mention many large Creditors by actual loans to Govt. whom you well know (Gov. [*James*] Bowdoin among others) who can be hardly persuaded to subscribe to the secretary's plan & I have heard them declare, that they will not subscribe to 3 per cent nor to any thing short of what the Secretary proposes they hold securities for money actually lent to the Govt., to many instances of which I am personally knowing; and they consider a part of their property sacrificed, even by the proposed scheme; and *as they think*, without any necessity for it, & a sacrifice as they say which the old Congress never did & never would call upon them to make; the resources of the country being as they think sufficient to pay 6. I will not tire your patience any longer by enumerating the common reasons against reducing the interest; they will naturally occur to you; nor will I say any thing upon the popularity of the Secretary's plan because that ought not & I know would not influence you. I have not heard any encomiums of Secy. Knox's [*militia*] plan to make a nation of boxing fellows; but as I am not a military man, perhaps I am not so likely to hear these encomiums, if they exist, & perhaps I do not feel the necessity of a "strong corrective arm" & the expence of 400,000 Dols. annually as I ought.

If the Secretary's plan of excise shd. be adopted, Collectors and inspectors will be appointed—I suppose—perhaps too it will be thought best to appoint officers to receive the subscriptions to the proposed loans, as well in the district of main[e], as elsewhere—in either of these cases I shall be obliged, if you can give me some early information—as Mr. Saml. Waldo, a brother in law of mine, would propose himself for a Candidate—he is married & setled at Portland He has had a regular education in an accompting house & is a young man, whose abilities & character are unquestionable—& who can obtain a recommendation from the first people here—he has been setled in Portland about a year—his father lived there & the family is much beloved there—if you can render him any services, you will oblige me as well as him—in the mean time, you will be so good as ~~to~~ not to mention those views of his to any one.

ALS, Letters to Goodhue, NNS. Written from Boston.

---

[1] Seney and Jackson, respectively, were the two speakers alluded to, according to the account of their speeches of 28 January in *GUS*, 30 January; see *DHFFC* 12:103.

Letter from a Citizen of Massachusetts at New York

Congress, at this moment, are involved in the labyrinth of Finance; and if they find the "clue" that will finally lead them through its windings, it will certainly be much to their honour. The same doubts, perplexities, and discordant opinions, the same chaos of hints, motions, plans, and systems, which have confounded and disgraced our house of representatives on past occasions, (for I presume nothing of this nature appears at present) is visible here—I mean in Milton's language, that the darkness is visible,[1] for, as to the light hitherto, it would puzzle a Herschell[2] to discern it with his best constructed tellescope. If the "souls of men" have been tried by the revolution, and "the summer soldier and sunshine patriot"[3] have been so often conspicuous in the war, the honour and consistency of some of our boasted "federalists" will be as effectually tried by this intricate measure of funding the public debt. It would afford you most excellent amusement, to observe the twistings and wreathings, of certain characters among your old and decided friends of government, and your high-flying federalists, on this unfortunate question. Madison, the great Madison, for this has been the epithet, I think, by which this gentleman of the long robe[4] has been lately distinguished, has been converted it is said by Gen. H—'s publications in the Boston Chronicle,[5] and after a profound silence of a few days, has at last appeared the warm and open advocate of "discrimination." The "honest and independent" Sed—ck too has broke through the cobweb texture of our "*saccred*" engagements, and now talks of three per centum, on the face of the note, as an adequate, and equitable, compensation at least for speculators. What will be said by the zealots of the insurance-offices to these astonishing Phenomena,
> *how will they rave, and fume, and fret, and chafe,*
> *And swear, not* Addison *himself is safe.*[6]

This is the fact with *these*—But Gerry, the hunted Gerry, moves along the same firm manly solid whig he always has been, despising the little arts, and confounding the feeble arguments of his ancient persecutors.

It is thought however upon the whole, that this confusion of the elements will settle in the general adoption of Hamilton's plan.

Apropos—Have you seen Knox's plan for the Militia—I have heard it said, that if you send a "good doctor" to a place, however healthy before, that you will soon find disorders enough—So the instant you make a Secretary of War, let him alone to cut out business for his office—This scheme, however, is too barefaced and ridiculous not to be exploded by the very party for whose sake it was constructed.

Boston Gazette, 22 February; reprinted at Providence, Rhode Island, and Norwich, Connecticut.

[1] Line 60, book one of *Paradise Lost* (1667) by the Puritan poet and essayist John Milton (1608–74).

[2] Sir William Herschel (1738–1822), royal astronomer to George III.

[3] From the opening lines of Thomas Paine's *American Crisis*, a series of sixteen papers published periodically throughout the Revolutionary War to boost morale. The first, which appeared over Paine's familiar pseudonym "Common Sense," was dated 23 December 1776, three days before the American victory at Trenton, New Jersey.

[4] A reference to the legal profession.

[5] William Heath penned several pro-discrimination public opinion pieces that appeared under the pseudonym Equity ([Boston] *Independent Chronicle*, between 24 December 1789 and 11 February 1790).

[6] From the "Epistle to Dr. Arbuthnot" by British poet Alexander Pope.

From New York

We have a packet in from London to-day—All quiet in France, and going on in their National Assembly with great dispatch and harmony.

To-morrow an interesting debate is expected on Mr. MADISON's scheme to pay the purchasers of Securities the highest average market price; and those who sold them the remainder. A plan that will give immortality to speculation; and make sharpers, swindlers and tricksters swarm through the land like the locusts of Egypt.[1] *Nemo omnibus horris sapit.*[2]

Those who have a knack at anticipation, tell, that on the question of assumption of the State debts, the numbers will be—for it 30, against it 29—so close as that—however, the weight of argument will prove the preponderating principle. I think that the fate of the government is suspended on a right decision on this important question.

[Boston] *Massachusetts Centinel*, 24 February; reprinted at Portsmouth, New Hampshire.

[1] Exodus 10:4–15.
[2] "No one is wise to all the horrors."

Letter from New York

Monday last was the day assigned for the House of Representatives to take up the subject of Finance; and they accordingly went into a committee of the whole. Mr. Fitzsimons then presented to the committee the several Resolutions I sent you inclosed in my last—(*see the first page of this paper.*) The first of these, respecting an adequate provision for the discharge of the foreign debt, was unanimously adopted. To the second, several amendments were proposed, and the committee continued to debate upon it till Thursday; when Mr. Madison, after a speech of an hour, moved to amend the proposition, and that it should read thus: *Resolved, That adequate funds ought to be provided for paying the interest and principal of the domestic debt, as the same shall be liquidated; and that in such liquidation the present holders of publick securities, which have been alienated, shall be settled with according to the highest market rate of said securities; and that the balance of the same, due from the publick, be paid in just proportion to the original holders of the said securities.*

The speech that introduced this motion was a masterly piece of investigation. When Mr. Madison set down, it being late in the day, the committee rose. Friday was taken up in hearing the petitions from several societies of Quakers, praying for the abolition of slavery; and then the House adjourned to Monday. So that there has been no opportunity for any body to attempt an answer to the arguments of Mr. Madison. His speech makes a prodigious buzing among the Speculators; for its object is to effect substantial justice, and give to every man his due. The greatest objection I have heard against the proposed amendment is, that it is impracticable: now this is, will appear after a more thorough examination of the subject. Some appear to be outrageous—say it is the height of iniquity; and declare that if iniquity is to be established by law, it ought to be in such a manner as that the publick may receive an equivalent. Whereas, by the proposed amendment, the publick will gain nothing; for what will be taken from speculators, who purchased the securities at five or six shillings on the pound, will be paid to those who sold them for that sum: Therefore they would rather have a general *depreciation scale* adopted, and let all fair alike. Then, say they, the publick would gain something by it. But it ought also to be observed, that in this case, the publick will only gain what the original holders actually loose; while the speculators loose nothing.

[Portland, Maine] *Cumberland Gazette,* 1 March. This is probably from a letter written by Thatcher to the newspaper's editor, Thomas B. Wait.

OTHER DOCUMENTS

Stephen Austin to Jeremiah Wadsworth. ALS, Wadsworth Papers, CtHi. Written from Philadelphia; postmarked 15 February.

Does not doubt that lead shot manufacturing will require as much linen (for wrapping) as Wadsworth may wish to supply; reminds him of the request to collector John Lamb for the amount of lead imported into New York in 1789.

John Carroll to Daniel Carroll. ALS, Washington Papers, DLC. Written from Baltimore.

Quotes letter from (John?) Thorpe recommending Alexander Sloan for United States consul to Civitavecchia, Italy; "I beg you to mention this application in its proper place, & give it in writing, that it may be remembered."

Andrew Ellicott to Sarah Ellicott. ALS, Ellicott Papers, DLC. Place to which addressed not indicated.

Speaker Muhlenberg and Governor George Clinton "have constantly had me to dine with them—The Western Land Office business I expect will be come forward in a few days."

Thomas Fitzsimons to Benjamin Rush. Combined summary and excerpt of seven page ALS from *Charles Hamilton Catalog* 7(1955):item 66, and an excerpt from *Parke-Bernet Catalog* 468(1943):item 98. The ellipsis is in the source.

An "analysis of the political" and financial "situation in the United States, with particular reference to the ideas of James Madison, and very lengthy explanation of precisely how his own views on the public debt differ from those of Dr. Rush"; "'And tho Mr. Madison has done honor to his feelings as a man, he has forfeited all character, & and that of a legislator by advocating the measure [*discriminating among public creditors*] . . .'."

Thomas Jefferson to James Madison. ALS, Madison Papers, DLC. Written from "Monticello," Albemarle County, Virginia; franked; postmarked Richmond, 18 February. For the full text, see *PJM* 13:41–42.

Asks Madison to explain to Washington the reasons for Jefferson's postponed departure for New York; was "greatly alarmed" by report of Madison's "attack" of illness at Georgetown, Maryland (present-day Washington, D.C.); asks for advice on where to lodge in New York and requests that Madison find him a temporary place to stay; directs him to send the information about lodgings to Mary House in Philadelphia.

William Maclay to John Nicholson. Combined summary and excerpt of two page ALS from *Argosy Catalog* 448(1959):item 377, and *Henkels Catalog* 1201(1917):item 544. The ellipsis is in the source. Enclosed in the letter was a parody about the resolve, which Nicholson gave to *IG*, where it appeared on 27 March; see volume 19.

"'A Resolve passed both Houses [*15 April 1789*] for Mr. [*Samuel*] Osgood, the proprietor of the House formerly occupied by the President of Congress, to put the same and the furniture thereof in condition for the temporary accomodation of the President of the United States. . . . Osgood recd. already about 11,000 dollars, and the bills are said not all to be come in'"; also mentions "Hamilton, and Madison."

James Madison to Edward Carrington. No copy known; acknowledged in Carrington to Madison, 2 March.

Philip Schuyler to John B. Schuyler. ALS, Schuyler Papers, NN. Addressed to Saratoga, New York.
    It is believed Hamilton's report on public credit will be generally adopted.

Theodore Sedgwick to Benjamin Lincoln. No copy known; acknowledged in Lincoln to Sedgwick, 26 February.

Theodore Sedgwick to David Sewall. No copy known; mentioned in Sewall to Thatcher, 11 March.

James Sullivan to Elbridge Gerry. ALS, Gerry Papers, MHi. Written from Boston; postmarked 17 March; answered 15 May.
    Raises the same issue as in his letter to Langdon of this date, above; if Massachusetts state imposts collected before 6 August 1789 are deemed illegal, providing refunds "I beleive will make an uneasiness between the Government of the united States and that of this State"; "Whether Congress may interpose and by a recognition of the Right of the Several States put an End to this disagreeable controversy you can Judge better than I can, but unless something is done there may be very disagreeable consequences."

George Thatcher to Daniel Cony. No copy known; acknowledged in Cony to Thatcher, 24 February.

George Thatcher to Jeremiah Hill. No copy known; acknowledged in Hill to Thatcher, 24 February.

William Samuel Johnson, Diary. Johnson Papers, CtHi.
    "St. Pauls."

MONDAY, 15 FEBRUARY 1790

Rain (Johnson);
Remarkable change from cold to warm and overcast (J. B. Johnson)

Jabez Bowen to John Adams

I doubt not but You have been inform'd that our Genl. Assembly have order'd a Convention to be called to meet a[t] South-Kingston the first Monday of March. the Delegates were Chosen the 8th. of this Month and from the Returns we Count Thirty Two Federals and Thirty Eight Antis—so that the Battle will go hard against us if some methods cannot be hit upon to affoard us some help. as I hinted in a former Letter so I repeat it in this, if Congress would take up the Letter that was sent from our General Assembly[1] and give them a firm and Spirited Reply it would be of great service. they might let them know that Congress Consider the Teritory of Rd. Island as a part of the United States that if a part of the present Inhabitants did not Choose to Live under the Federal Government they would be permitted to sell Their Estates &c. but that the people of Rd. Island must of necessity be united with the Rest of the American States. The same wicked disposition continues among the Leaders as heretofore and Congress can do nothing that is good or praise worthy but every of their Acts and [are] found fault with.

We shall do every thing in our power *per fac aut nefas*[2] to accomplish our ends—as we really look on the people as Dluded and facinated at present, and seem determined to oppose with Forc of Arms every effort that can be made for the Establishing the Federal Government, if a firm arm could be laid on us to let them feel and see that Congress was Determined that something should be done and that soon it would have a good Effect.

The present plan of the oposition is to adjourn the Convention to September by which time they say Congress will do so many unjust things that several of the great States will be ready to Revol, and that Rd. Island remaning a Free & Independent State will put her self at their head. &c. with many other Extravigant plans.

On the whole if something could be sent on from Congress to look as if it was spontaneously done addressed to the Convention I really believe it would have a great weight in producing a favourable determination of the Question.

ALS, Adams Family Manuscript Trust, MHi. Written from Providence, Rhode Island; answered 27 February.

[1] The letter, which committed Rhode Island to conform to the federal government's commercial regulations and discharge its share of the public debt despite its remaining outside

the union, was transmitted to Congress by Washington on 26 September 1789. See *DHFFC* 8:396–98.

²Through right or wrong; justly or unjustly.

Oliver Ellsworth to Ephraim Kirby

I was seasonable & faithful in my application for you to the Judges of the Supreme Court, & probably should have been succesful had not Judge Cushing brot. along with him Mr. [*John*] Tucker for the same birth. He had served with reputation as Clerk of the Supreme Court in Massachusetts, & being on the spot & well patronized he obtained the appointment. If any door should hereafter open that I can at once serve you & the publick I shall be happy to do it.

ALS, Ephraim Kirby Papers, NcD. Addressed to Litchfield, Connecticut; franked; postmarked 17 February.

John Fisk to Benjamin Goodhue

Yours of the 3d. Instant Incloseing the Report of the Secretary of War [*on the militia*] came safe to hand, the Gentlemen of the Town have seen it, but I find the plann is not agreeable to the People, it has but few advocates, They say firstly that 70 days in the Three last years of an Apprentice the only years that there time is Profitable to the Master, or Parent, is more than they can losse. secondly, that Young men taken from there Business, & going into Camp, will Acquire such a habit of Idleness, that it will be allmost Imposeable to Eredicate it, & make them Serviceable as before, & will have attendancey to Corrupt there Moralls. Thirdly that the great Expence that will Accure to goverment now at peace, & not in a Capacity to pay there present debts, no not the Interest should be a sufficient Bar to the mode. the Idea of Discrimnation in goverment Debts, with the low Interest propos'd by Mr. Hambleton with the great Salary to officers of goverment Creates much Uneasiness. there has much been said, about the additional Impost, it bears hard on the Importer, also respecting the paying Foreign tunnage on our Vessels to the Southern States, which we think not Just, nor the Intention of Congress, & exspect to have a refund.

You know my Oppinion respecting goverment, but sir all men do not think as we do, I hope & Trust that the United wisdom of the Continent in Congress will Enact such salutary and Equal laws, as will keep the mindes of the people quiet and at the same time Establish [*lined out*] a Permanent Goverment, & with such funds as will Inabil them to Estabish Publick Credit.

LS, Letters to Goodhue, NNS. Written from Salem, Massachusetts.

Benjamin Goodhue to Insurance Offices

We have had under consideration for the week past the subject of our national debt, but have come to no material resolution respecting it, Mr. Madison came forward on Thursday in a long speech in favr. of a discrimination between the original holders and the present possessors, that is the original holders who still hold their securities are to receive the sum or be consider'd equal to what they express, those ~~who hold~~ held by purchase are to be considered equal to the highest market price, that is for instance 10/. and the original Owner of whom they were purchased to be entitled to the other 10/—a motion to this purport is now before us, but I cannot suppose that a principal of this Kind which according to my apprehensions, strikes at the root of public credit can ever obtain, for surely no one will ever purchase a security which the Government has made transferable, if any advantage is to be taken of such transfer so as to impair the obligation, and without their being made transferable when Government has occasion in consequence of great exertions to issue promisary obligations, they could never answer any purpose—therefore for us to take any advantage of this transfer, which was authorised in the very face of the obligations, is to me a direct violation of public engagement, and distructive of every principal of public credit, the original holders who have parted with them are to be pitied and if our circumstances admited, perhaps in many cases they ought to have a further consideration but not at the expence of our plighted obligations—beside I presume the scheme will be found altogether impracticable, for in a variety of cases very large sums where given out to Agents either in the name of the Agent or in some fictitious name, as it was supposed of no consequence as they were made payable to the bearer—there are such a variety of opinions on the subject of funding our national debt and it is attended with so many perplexities, that it will probably enough put on from time to time a variety of appearances, before it comes to issue, and what will be the issue is impossible to say, tho perhaps it is most likely we shall rest down finaly not far from the plan which the Secry. [*of the treasury*] has reported, I have ever considered it incumbent on us to view our obligations as valid and that National faith National honour, and National interest forbids us to view them less obligatory in consequence of their depreciation. and that We ought to provide for them as far as the abilities of our government will in prudence warrant, how far this will carry us is a matter of opinion—some suppose we can pay 6 per Ct. tho' I believe there are few of this number, others that what the Secry. has reported is the extent of our abilities and I believe this number is the majority of which I at present am one, and others suppose 3 ⅌ Ct. is as much as we can with certainty discharge, I confess I have been rather of this opinion, but yet I shall be willing to go to what ever lengths our circumstances will admit, tho' I cannot suppose our abilities so great as some imagine, or that prudence would dictate so high a rate of duties as materialy to affect our commerce or cause so general a complaint as to disturb the quietude of our government, there is therefore a discretion to be used, that we provide for our creditors as far forth as our abilities will admit and at the same time to be cautious that We do not exceed it—I think the Secry's. report does credit to his abilities and attention, and perhaps his general principles are such as it will be wise for us to adopt—the rate of duties he proposes and the act for collecting them have not yet been much attended to, they will I think when they come under consideration require a close attention, and be ~~stripd~~ stript of those embarrasments with which it is incumber'd as much as the nature of the thing will admit—on subjects of the Kind in which we are now engaged almost every person has more or less turn'd his attention and as it [is] of so interesting a nature I should be gratified with any observations which my friends should make ~~out~~—I Know its impossible to please all, I have no private interest in view and I am determined to make the happiness of my Constituents so far as ~~they are and~~ is consistent with the National dignity and welfare of my Country the line of my conduct, and I hope they will have candour to suppose if I should differ in opinion from any of them, that this difference does not proceed from any impure motive in their representative.

I have thus been explicit as to the view I have of this interesting bussines. I am not sanguine that my ideas are well formed, however conscious I may be of the rectitude of my designs; if I err I shall be pleased with a refutation of my errors. I mean to do right all circumstances considered and hope our measures will eventualy be productive of National dignity and prosperity.

ALS, Goodhue Letters, NNS. Addressed to Salem, Massachusetts. On the same day, Goodhue wrote a shorter version of this letter to Michael Hodge. That letter concludes with a postscript, which reads in part: "Perhaps it may not be amiss to say that I am not the holder of one farthing of securities either Continental or State and therefore I hope the part which I may take in this bussines will not be imputed to any impure motives" (ALS, Ebenezer Stone Papers, MSaE. Place to which addressed not indicated).

John Nicholson to Thomas Hartley

I recd. your favor of the   Instant covering the Resolutions offered to the house by Mr. Fitzimmons[1] I suppose Mr. Scott's motion was not serious but designed to expose the other following resolutions respecting a loan for modifying the public debt for that in fact would be a new Liquidation as they both intend a reduction of the debt, and if any is to be taken off from the first engagement to the creditors it is certainly better to take it from the principal than the interest for the following reasons It would diminish his present annual income less and leave a less burthensome capital debt on the public 2d. it would then be less likely to be parted with by Americans and transfered to foreigners because the market rate of interest is higher in this Country and lower in Europe by getting into the hands of foreigners the annual payment of Interest would be a direct annual drain of cash from this Country & the principal a very heavy one. It may be said they would leave the value of the principal in the Country before they could possess themselves of the debt but a capital at 4 ℔ Cent in a Country where the market rate of interest is and will continue from the nature of things above or at least as high as 6 ℔ Cent will never sell at its nominal value even if it rested on the most stable basis and unexceptionable funds but the hand that can once prune off a part or mo[d]ify its engagements after they are made will ever leave an impression that they may do the same again and this risque will also reduce the market price of the debt 3d. if the part that is to be deducted from the creditor be taken from the principal it will be done at once and however disagreeable it may be yet time will diminish and wear off the act of injustice and ~~be~~ it will in time be forgot but by taking it from the rate of interest the creditor will be reminded periodically of the act of injustice of government so oft as he receives his annual interest at 4 ℔ Ct. or whatever else it might afterwards be reduced to for a debt where 6 ℔ Cent was once promised.

If The Legislature of the Union should attempt a reduction of either the principal or interest of the debt by any modification of it as it is called it would not eventually bind the government for there is a still higher act in its favor than any Congress can pass and that is the constitution itself, And which must finally prevail, and will even if such an act should pass for the present—~~There is something~~ it could not dissolve the obligation a future legislature would be bound upon application to make up what was taken off. There is something in the attempt to impose upon the creditors by pretending an Equivalent for the reduction of interest that adds insult to the injury—There would be something in a law of the kind proposed even worse than breach of faith and violation of engagement there is also insult added by pressing an equivalent to the creditors for what is taken off. this is a truth that cannot be veiled over so as to impose even the shallowest understanding—In order to give it a fair trial let the revenues without any preference be appropriated in the aggregate to pay the interest to those who hold the present evidences at the rate and upon the terms which they now are held and to those who may subscribe one or other of the loans upon the terms proposed and see if there will be a single creditor will subscribe to any of them he will keep the paper he has and will ridicule the offer It is the money not the having his debt redeemable that would influence the creditor in his choice the use of the money ~~would induce~~ to every american who hath use for money in trade or other business is worth more than 6 ℔ Cent so that he would prefer having his capital if he could get it and if he were not in business himself he would readily have it lent upon the best security to others at 6 ℔ Ct. per ann. would the officers of government or would the secretary of the Treasury prefer having the debt accrueing for salary or wages funded at 4 or even at 6 ℔ Ct.? the capital irredeemable to being paid the principal as it becomes due if they would and I think it ought to be proposed to all such as advocate the measure but altho a paralell case it would be almost too great a punishment to insult them with the alternative that unless they chose to chuse that they should get nothing. After all the arguments and propositions which may be used & made the zest of the business is who shall have the money. The annual revenue is set at 2,800,000 Doll. by the secretary he hath overrated the duties upon distilleries and several other articles which will either be thrown out in the legislature or if passed in the law will never be collected I think the revenues should be set at about 2½ mill. annually this revenue is not sufficient to pay all the debts at once and therefore the question recurs who shall have it and therefore some preference must be given Altho those who have heretofore served the late Government either in the civil or military departments, many of whom are not paid would naturally have a preference to those whose services to the Government whether in the civil or military have been since or are now to be required the engagements to both were alike in their form & nature and the former have a preference in Justice from the priority of the [*illegible*] and yet the principal and interest of this would require such a sum as would be out of the power of the government to pay, And to take away the present support of government would also be injuring their claims the payment of which depends on the Existence of that government which cannot subsist without support—and again it is of the last importance that the faith of the government should not be broken, wherefore the first appropriation of the revenues should be to the support of government next to those payments that were promised to be made at particular periods as they become payable after that to those who in the order of merit would come first I mean such as served the public in time of calamity personally or by supplies And are not yet paid so far forth as they hold in their own hands the evidence of these services which were given at settlement granted on the faith of government and made payable to bearer for such as have parted therewith have under the promise last mentioned imposed an obligation to pay them altho no time is mentioned when it shall be done—Let not those who performed the services be ranked with other holders of certificates who became such voluntarily by purchase at a low rate on account of the difference between them and specie in every mans mind & on and of the fund and indefinite time of payment—as holder

of Certificates they in common with Others have a claim on the public faith
for payment when it can conveniently be done but they have Also a much
more meretorious claim one that existed before the existence of these certificates and which is not yet discharged that is the promise of payment, as
that cannot all be made at once to original holders the interest should be first
paid and the revenues appropriated to this purpose in the next place, lest the
revenues should not yield according to expectation I think no new promise
of payment should be made but let the revenues be thus appropriated and
the Treasurer under certain regulations be directed to make payment of the
monies according to the appropriations as they come in, if there is money
they will be paid if there be not, promise will not pay them, and there is no
need to entangle the government with new engagements Especially with
an uncertain and untried revenue. But there is a never failing sinking fund
in the hands of Government which should be brought immediately into
operation, the western lands should be sold not merely for 20 Cents but for
what they will bring payable in gold and silver or the Evidences of the debt
appropriating different traits for the different species of evidences according
to their value whether bills of credit indents or Certificates the sale of old
Continental money of lands near our frontiers would not only bring in vast
sums of it but being held principally by the eastern people where they are
ready to live would form a settlement which would make us an excellent barrier, this would be redeeming them according to good faith I have given you
my thoughts on a subject of great importance, I am not for discriminating
in cases where there is no difference All those in the same situation should
fare alike—but the people see an attempt to confound classes of creditors
that are widely different in situation and stand in different relation to the
government, and by mixing them together it will work an act of Injustice
to those best intitled—The practicability of separate provision is questioned
I have had the execution of a similar measure with the depreciation debt of
Penna. and know it is not only practicable but with some alteration easy.

FC:lbk, Nicholson Papers, PHarH. Heading the first page of this letter in the letterbook,
Nicholson wrote, "N. B. sundry other similar letters were wrote to my friends in Congress
about that time of which I have not copies."

---

[1] See 8 February, above.

John Pemberton to James Pemberton

*** I send my wifes [*Hannah Zane Pemberton*] Letter open that thou may
peruse it besides the Books mentioned there, it would be right to send the
following, if to be had, the [*House*] Comittee appointed desiring all the

Information they can obtain[1]—I am concerned to hear just now, that On J. Adams presenting our Adress[2]—it was read with great Opposition to it from Butler & Izard. & these so fiery that there was little said in Opposition to them this throws a Damp as J. Langdon on 7th. day [*13 February*] told some frds. there would be a large Majority in favor of it. I have not heard whether the other petitions were read or not. I am sorry so many are leaving their work. it will make it more heavy & discouraging to such who remain.

[*Enclosure*]

A few of the Queries of the Privy Council Gt. Britain to the Legislature in the Wt. Indies.

& their Answers from thence.

Notes on the two reports from the Comittee of Assembly in Jamaica.

Beaufoy's speech 18. 6 mo. 1788 in a Comittee of the whole house On a bill for regulating the Conveyance of Negroes from Africa to the West indies &c.[3]

Act of the Assembly of Granada. 4. 11 mo. 1788.[4]

An Adress on the proposed Bill for the Abolition of the slave trade

Wilberforce's Propositions—13. 5 mo. 1789[5]—

Queries put by the Abolition society in London. for Information from such who were acq[*uain*]ted. with the trade &c.

ALS, Pennsylvania Abolition Society Papers, PHi. Addressed to Philadelphia; carried by Henry Drinker.

[1] The enclosure sought duplicate copies of many of the titles Pemberton apparently had supplied to the committee this day. See Books Sent to the Committee, *DHFFC* 8:328.

[2] Probably the petition of the Philadelphia Yearly meeting of Friends (Quakers specifically), rather than those of the New York Yearly meeting or the Pennsylvania Abolition Society, all presented and read in the Senate this day. For the petitions and background, see *DHFFC* 8:314–38.

[3] Henry Beaufoy (d. 1795), the son of a Quaker merchant, delivered his famous speech in a committee of Parliament on 18 June 1788.

[4] Probably "An Act for the better Protection and promoting the Increase and Population of Slaves," passed by the legislature of the British Caribbean colony of Grenada on 3 November 1788 (*The Laws of Grenada, from the Year 1763, to the year 1805 . . .* by George Smith, Esq. [London, 1808]).

[5] William Wilberforce (1759–1833), Britain's most noted antislavery reformer, delivered a three and a half hour long speech before the House of Commons on 12 May 1789, during which he moved twelve resolutions condemning the slave trade.

Don Pedro to Mr. Greenleaf

THE exertions of the people denominated Quakers in endeavouring to bring about the abolition of slavery, seems to engage the attention of every class of citizens, and agitates the public mind to a degree, that may in the end prove inauspicious to that harmony, which now happily exists in the United States. How far the Quakers are entitled to praise for their conduct, I shall not here make a question—how far their activity may be called laudable—how far their intrusion on the Congress of the United States, to bear hard on some parts of the Constitution, in direct opposition to the wishes, and interests, of a respectable part of the community—and at a time, when their sect will not be injured by any decisions of Congress—how far they are to be praised, for wishing to strip their fellow citizens of their property, without offering a compensation, are matters, which every man will determine for himself—Of this, however, I am convinced, that they do not discover a proper respect for that body, to whom they have presented their memorial, for when they were attending in the galleries, the Chaplain of Congress proceeding to prayer, and contrary to the usual practice in their meeting-houses, they continued *sitting with their heads covered*—I should not have taken notice of these things, had not the great professional sanctity of the Quakers, led me to expect to see in them a greater share of decorum, and reverence, upon all occasions, when the Father of Spirits is petitioned to shower down on the human race every good thing.

NYJ, 18 February, edited by Thomas Greenleaf. The piece was headed by a note to the editor from A Customer, requesting that the enclosed piece be printed in the next issue.

Letter from Philadelphia

I found fault latterly with my correspondents in New-York, for not answering letters by the return-post, and they have informed me it is in a great measure owing to a regulation of the post-master of that place, by which the mail is closed *at 9 o'clock in the evening*, although it does not leave the city until 8 o'clock *the next morning.*

This regulation deprives us in a great degree of the advantages we expected to derive from *a daily post*, and at the same time diminishes the revenue of the Post-Office; for instance, if the southern Mail does not arrive at New-York until the evening, there is not time to answer letters and a post is lost, and we cannot get the debates of Congress which are usually in the next mornings papers, until the second post after they are published. This is considered as an inconvenience and real injury both to the merchants and community at large, and obliges people to look out for private conveyances to send their letters. We have also to lament the very great irregularity in the carriage of the Mail to the southward of this City.

GUS, 24 February; reprinted at Philadelphia.

Letter from Jamaica

Emancipation of the blacks seems to be the popular phrenzy of the day in Great-Britain. Every weaver and day-laborer in that island talks in favor thereof, not considering that the situation of our negroes is in almost every respect preferable to their own. After all that has been said of our country, ten times worse punishments are inflicted upon free born Englishmen in the capacity of soldiers (or rather slaves) in St. James's park, and elsewhere, than were ever inflicted upon slaves in Jamaica. Punish them when they commit faults, we do; and so also do we punish freemen. Most of those gentlemen who have been active in promoting the emancipation of slaves, are least acquainted with these countries, or the condition of slavery. It is observable throughout all the creation, that there are inferior classes of all animals; and it is clear that black men are an inferior race of human creatures, infinitely inferior to the red Indians of America: certain it is they are the only men who traffick publicly in human flesh. But whatever their condition [*may*] be, they should be treated with humanity, and no one dares say that their usage is otherwise in this Island. The Jamaica Negroes, it is well known, even in this hot country, meet after their work is over, and are able and willing to dance for hours in actions and attitudes as violent as they are indecent. On the contrary, the day-laborer in England retires late to bed, dejected and fatigued with the severe labor that he must undergo in order to procure a livelihood. It is probable there will soon be accounts published in England, that the West-India planters cut off *both the hands* of all their field negroes, and the *feet* of their house slaves.

NYDA, 22 March (the date on which members of Congress would have seen it).

OTHER DOCUMENTS

Benjamin Goodhue to Stephen Goodhue. ALS, Goodhue Family Papers, MSaE. Addressed to Salem, Massachusetts; franked; postmarked 14 February. Congress engaged in the funding debate; discrimination "can never obtain"; "I mean in the whole of this bussines to do what I think is just and honourable to our Country at the same time having reference to the abilities of the people let it please or displease, I know its imposible to please all, therefore to do what I think right is the surest way of satisfying my own mind and perhaps as likely a method of pleasing others."

Ralph Izard to Governor Charles Pinckney. ALS, U.S. Relations with S.C., Sc. Addressed to "His Excellency the Governor of the State of South Carolina." Declines election as St. James Goose Creek Parish's delegate to the state constitutional convention in May, "as I do not think it probable that Congress will adjourn before that time."

Melatiah Jordan to George Thatcher. ALS, Thatcher Papers, MeHi. Written from Union River, Maine; postmarked Boston, 17 March.

His enemies' only possible objection to him as collector at Frenchman's Bay is that he lives in nearby Union River; "to fulfill all and Every Point of the Laws," will relocate to the center of Frenchman's Bay in May; wrote on 24 December 1789 with the names of the three "Princible men" of every town in his collection district, "according to your Request."

John Langdon to Joshua Brackett. ALS, Sturgis Family Papers, MH. Addressed to Portsmouth, New Hampshire; franked; postmarked 17 February; received by the last post (13 February).

Relations between Governor John Sullivan and the state legislature "afford Matter for Considerable Conversation here"; regarding the governorship, "I would not Interfere with Mr. [*John*] Pickerin[*g*] or my Brother [*Woodbury*] by any means, But rather than it should go out of Town I would Accept of it for I fully intend to Return in the Spring and my Present Intention is not to attend Congress any more after this Session"; Congress has entered on "the Important Object" of establishing national credit; refers him to newspapers for the outlines; "there is nothing of a Particular Nature worth minuting"; "P. S. It is of Consequence that the President [*governor*] of the State should be out of Portsmouth, by all means let me have one line as soon as may be."

Peter Muhlenberg to Samuel A. Otis. AN, Records of the Secretary: Concerning printing, Senate Records, DNA. Printed in *DHFFC* 8:746.

Has been authorized to receive money due Henry Kammerer for supplying paper to the Senate.

George Olney to George Washington. ALS, Washington Papers, DLC. Written from Providence, Rhode Island. For the full text, see *PGW* 5:147–49.

Office seeking: naval officer at Providence, Rhode Island; lists Strong, Wingate, Dalton, Baldwin, A. Foster, and Ames, who have been written to on his behalf, as references; has written to Johnson to whom he is known personally, and also to Morris who knows about his service as receiver of continental taxes for Rhode Island.

Jeremiah Olney to Philip Schuyler. FC:dft, Shepley Library Collection, RHi. Written from Providence, Rhode Island.

Office seeking: acknowledges Schuyler's "promtitude in Support" of his appointment (as collector of Providence); had intended to press for his appointment in person, but his duties as invalid pension commissioner for Rhode Island will prevent it; retains "full Hopes that my Friends in New York will go as far to Serve me as Shall be consistant with the Strictest Rules of propriety and the public Good"; elections for the state's ratification convention are unpromising; is happy to hear that Schuyler's gout is less painful.

Samuel A. Otis to Peter Muhlenberg. AN, Records of the Secretary: Concerning printing, Senate Records, DNA. Printed in *DHFFC* 8:746–47.
   Will apply to Hamilton to settle Henry Kammerer's account for supplying paper to the Senate as soon as new Appropriations Act [HR-47] is passed.

Louis Guillaume Otto to Comte de Montmorin. Copy, in French, Henry Adams Transcripts, DLC. Received 10 May; copy forwarded in a letter to Jacques Necker on 6 June. Otto's letters included in *DHFFC* were usually written over the course of days, and even weeks, following the day they were begun.
   Difficult transportation from the interior because of the moderate winter's lack of snow threatens a scarcity of wheat and grains, which some parts of the Continent are asking Congress to embargo; the more enlightened Americans think it that it would be useless, that the prices are artificially high, and that when the farmers find they have reached their highest price, they will open their granaries; Carolina's rice harvest is abundant but the high price of other foodstuffs has rather affected it, so that it does not seem it will help the French market; Wadsworth has written Otto of the usefulness of rice, and said that while supplying the French army during the war, he often blended grains of rice and corn without the soldiers realizing it; he intends to make some enquiries (on the use of rice) of which he promises to communicate the results to Otto; the threat of a scarcity in England has led (on 2 December 1789) to a repeal of its Order in Council prohibiting the importation of American wheat; the sloop of war announcing the repeal was the first British warship seen in New York since the end of the war; it exchanged salutes with the fort (Battery) and its officers were presented to the President; some politicians strive to attribute the expedition to other motives, but their conjectures seem entirely baseless.

William Paterson to Euphemia Paterson. ALS, Paterson Papers, NjR. Addressed to New Brunswick, New Jersey.
   Acknowledges her letter of 11 February, "just come to Hand"; wrote her by Mr. Young, who was to set off on 14 February; dined with Anthony Walton White, also on the 14th; has seen Susan Kearny's "Swain" (Dr. John R. B. Rodgers) only once since they began their courtship; "I shall

call on him To-Day"; would like to see the correspondence between them; "It must be a pleasing Reflection, that all Parties approve the Match, and that Love goes Hand in Hand with Duty"; daughter Cornelia should write more often; has received only one letter from her since being in New York City.

James Pemberton to Frederick A. Muhlenberg. FC:dft, Pennsylvania Abolition Society Papers, PHi. Place from which written not indicated. Printed in *DHFFC* 8:328.

Covers fifty-eight copies of the Pennsylvania Abolition Society's petition for distribution to the members of the House.

Adam Tunno to Pierce Butler. ALS, Butler Papers, PHi. Written from Charleston, South Carolina.

Office seeking: recommends John Mitchell as surveyor of Charleston, to succeed the dying incumbent, Edward Weyman; his appointment would be agreeable to "the Mercantile Body in general from whom a recommendation gos to your self & Mr. Izard."

Minutes of Trinity Church. Ms, quoted in *Iconography* 5:1262.

Church vestry votes appropriation of the pew opposite the President's for the use of the governor and members of Congress.

TUESDAY, 16 FEBRUARY 1790

Rain (Johnson); *Mild and overcast* (J. B. Johnson)

Brown & Francis to John Adams

We are Sorry to Inform You that the Members of the Convention of this State as Chose on Munday the 8th Inst. to Consider and Determin on the New Constitution are by a Majority of about 8 or 10, Ante Feddural Viz. about Thirty Deligates for the Adoption of the Constitution and about Forty Against it & for Continuing out of the Union and will we Suppose Adjourn the Convention to Some Futer Day Expecting theirby to Gain the Election of Antefedderal Members to the Genl. Assembley at the Annuel Town Meetings in April and theirby keep out of the Union An Other Year. We have had the most Sanguine Expectations of their being a Suffitient Number of Feddural Members Appointed to Adopt the Constitution, but the post from the Southard has Blasted our Sanguwine Expectations and Indeed the Towns around us Turnd out much more Antefeddural then we had Reason to Expect. What can be Done? we hartely wish for Something from Congress or the Members their of to the Governour & Compy. of this State in time to be Laid before the Convention which may prevent their puting of the Joining the Union aney Longer; may not an Answer be given to the Letter from the General Assembley of this State at their Sessions in Septemb. Last to Congress,[1] Couched in Such terms as the Convention may theirby be Convinced that Congress will not be Dallied with aney Longer but that Some Decissive Measures will be tacon by Congress if the convention will not Adopt the Constitution So as to Join the Genl. Government without Further Delay. May not Congress Say with propriety that they have Raised and Secured Very large Sums of Mony from the States in the Union by the Impost Law and that from Good Information the Laws of this State are such that no Spetia will be Raised from its Impost Act the paper Money being a Tender at Fifteen for one by which means the State will be Obloiged to make up Its Defitiencey by a Direct Tax on the Estates & poles of the Inhabitents, or may not Congress with propriety Write the Govr. & compy. that the Finances of the Union may be So much Deranged and Obstructed by this States Remaining out of the Union that the Seaport Towns & others which may Join them Will be Recd. into the Union on their Applycation and Impost Officers Appointed and Supported by Congress.

In short Aney Method that Can be thought of by Congress or Aney Individuall Members theirof which may Tend to git the Convention which is to meet at South Kingstown on the 1st. Munday of March Next, to Adopt the Constitution will be perticulerly Agreeable to the Fedderals of the State.

ALS, Adams Family Manuscript Trust, MHi. Written from Providence, Rhode Island.

[1] See Jabez Bowen to John Adams, 15 February, n. 1, above.

Thomas Dwight to Theodore Sedgwick

Your favor, with the report of the Secretary [*on public credit*], I have received since my return from Boston for which I sincerely thank you—however the plans suggested may be approved or condemned all seem to join in the eulogium on Mr. Hamiltons abilities—I was not long enough in Boston to find out the general opinion in regard to his propositions—they will not certainly be pleasing to our Lt. G. [*Samuel Adams*] or his party—he is passionately opposed to the assumption of the State debts. & I believe it may be said to any thing and every thing which is the consequence of the operation of our new Govt.—the mode of taking the census & the appointment of national officers to do it. are made the subjects of contention and detestation by that party—how far they will carry opposition—I will not pretend to say but there are some threatenings which I presume will never be carried into effect.

There is now an almost universal outcry against our excises—petitions without number have been proffered from corporations as well as individuals for the repeal of these laws—but it is said altho a repeal of the acts will take place that it will not be without a substitute differing only in the mode of collection—a sole appropriation of imposts and excises to national purposes is devoutly to be wished—partial ones are now deprecated by every honest man and even *honest men* are now habituating themselves to every impos possible evasion of the laws imposing them. such habits may eventually have too much influence on any national system of excise which may be hereafter adopted.

Our friend Mr. [*Samuel*] Henshaw has been dangerously ill at Boston, but is now recovering—The public papers will have informed you of the *truly noble efforts* of Mr. [*John*] Gardiner to free his country from the iron hands of tyrannical lawyers—but as his gun is charged with wad only—the profession will not suffer much unless by fright at the noise—however the people may curse the profession it is not the less true that we are indebted principally to that class of men for the knowledge *of our own rights* as well as for their the defence and preservation of them.

ALS, Sedgwick Papers, MHi. Written from Springfield, Massachusetts.

Benjamin Huntington to Governor Samuel Huntington

It is with Pleasure that I can say that [*blotted out*] of the Subject of Discrimination between the original holders and Present Possessors of Continental Securities is not likely to find many friends in the House of Representatives The last week was Spent on the Subject and Monday & Tuesday the Present week has been taken up on the Debate untill every body, but Superrogating Orators, is Tired with the Argument and by a Number of Gentlemen, taking minutes I Expect the Subject will be much longer hained and hobby-horsed.[1]

Mr. Maddison's Speech which appears in the New York Packett of this Day[2] is a Subject of much Conversation it Occasion a fall in the Value of Certificates for two or three Days but Since Some Speeches in opposition to him have been Delivered the Paper Securities have been at a Stand and now are Rising such is the Instability of the Populace and the Knavery of the Speculators!

By the Inclosed Papers will be seen what are the Commotions in Europe and that a Spirit of Independence seems to prevail to an astonishing Degree. [P. S.] Col. Bland & Mr. D. Carrold have very kindly Enquired after your health & Wellfare and Desire their Respects to you Col. Bland in Particular presents his very best Regards &c.

ALS, Betts Collection, CtY. Marked "Private"; addressed to Connecticut; received 24 February; answered 27 February.

<hr/>

[1] No members' notes of House debates are extant for the second session.
[2] *NYP*, 16 February, reprinted Madison's important speech of 11 February from *NYDG*, 15 February. See *DHFFC* 12:278–82.

John Nivison to Josiah Parker

At the request of one of your constituents Capt. John Brown, I have taken the liberty to inclose you a Certificate on a subject in which he is apprehensive of some difficulty.

The case is, he took out a Register for his Sloop under the Act of Congress and gave Bond to return the same according to the tenor of that Act[1]—He sold the Sloop and indeavored to regain his register which was deposited in the Custom House in Port au Prince [*Haiti*], that he might be enabled to deliver it to our Collector [*William Lindsay*] within eight days after his return agreeable to the Law—but to his great injury & surprise he was refused; he then made application to the Judge of the Admiralty who referred his Petition to the Kings Attorney, by whom he was also refused & was consequently compelled to return without it—all these circumstances he has communicated to the Collector in order to indemnify him; the Collector alledges he is without power to relieve and promises to transmit the papers to the Secretary of the Treasury and to wait his answer. Capt. Brown hopes your representation to the Secretary will have such effect as to obviate further trouble on t[he] subject—by procuring an order to the Collector directing that no suit shall be instituted on the Bond, which will otherwise be certainly done—On this occasion I am informed by Capt. B. that the same political motives operate with the French to preserve the Sloop's Register that influence our government to require a return of it—the Sloop became a french bottom, and of such registers were delivered out of the Office—it might be made use of by the same Sloop or some other of like dimensions in prejudice to the French Flag we wish the return of the Register to prevent its application to any other Vessel.

In consequence of these circumstances Capt. Brown's case is particularly hard He must either lose the sale of his Vessel for which purpose she was built, or he must suffer under his Bond—I hope his affidavit and the other papers so clearly prove that there was an anxiety, on his part to comply with our law and not the least design of fraud, that he may be relieved and put to no further trouble or expence—If entire relief cannot be granted, perhaps possibly the Register might be secured after a proper representation from the French Consul—& in that case a suspension of the Suit might be serviceable—*You see the Federal powers are much dredded.*

I have no news worth communicating except that Mrs. [*Mary Pierce*] Parker and your Daughter are very well.

When any thing occurs worth your attention you shall hear from me—as soon as you may have done any thing, if in your power for Capt. Brown please make it known with the news from Congress.

N. B. Cullen removed suddenly to North Carolina, no money yet received for you, I shall continue my endeavor to get it.

Copy, Miscellaneous Letters, Miscellaneous Correspondence, State Department Records, Record Group 59, DNA. Place from which written not indicated; docketed, in part, by Jefferson. The enclosed certificate was Brown's deposition before Nivison of this same date and in the same location. Parker evidently forwarded these two documents to Hamilton, who enclosed them to Jefferson on 20 April, with other supporting documentation supplied to him by Collector Lindsay. Jefferson then furnished all the papers to Silvanus Bourn, the United States consul at Hispaniola (Haiti), on 24 August, as the basis for a formal protest to the French government there (*PTJ* 16:353–54, 17:417).

------

[1] Clauses two and eight, respectively, of the Coasting Act [HR-16].

John Pemberton to James Pemberton

Being informed that John Haworth proposes to set out for Philadelphia to morrow morning, take the oppo. to acknowledge the Receipt of thy Acceptible favor of 14th. Inst. delivered on this afternoon by Miers Fisher, it is Acceptable to hear my Dear Wife [*Hannah*] is as well as usual, I wrote her last evening & thee also a few lines, ℔ our freind H[*enry*]. Drinker who with all our Com[*pan*]y. except 4 of us set out this morning on their return,[1] we feel blank by their absence, but the End of our Embassy does not seem compleated. We had this day an Interview with some of the Natives of our land, the Oneida Nation,[2] & was an Oppertunity as moving & affecting as any since I left home, their situation is much to be Comisserated. Our Friend John Murray invited them to Diner with Samuel Kirkland a Presbyterian Minister their Interpreter who appears a thoughtful Man, after diner we spent upwards of two hours in a solid weighty Oppo.; they were informed that we were Men of the same peaceable principles with Wm. Penn & the early setlers of Pensylvania, & had transmitted to us from our forefathers the Friendship & kindness which subsisted between them & the Indians, & also the kindness of the Indians to the First setlers, & desired a sence hereof might be transmitted to future generations. & for such kindness we Could not but love the Natives. & that tho' we were not

Men in Government. & therefore did not desire them to inform us their business yet as Brethren were willing they should speak freely if they had any thing upon their Minds, they then were very open. & represented their situation, that they were subject to many tryals, & that perhaps they might be Suffered to be afflicted because they had not pleased the Great spirit in their lives & Conduct. they said they were weak & were overcome also by temptation, they looked at the flourishing state of the white people & were ready to apprehend the Great Spirit loved the white People more, because they were better, yet they saw the white People did not all do right. Their Minds were often sad when they considered the Increase of the White people, that their lands were setled & they hedged up. & knew not what would become of them in time. Perhaps the Great Spirit saw fit they should suffer. the white People had often spoke good words to them. & when the Calamity of the warr came on desired them to be quiet & take no part. & had often said they loved the Indians, but they thot. if it was so they would allot some land for them that could not be taken from them. & when all their land was gone from them they should then know if the white people did really love them. for them they would pity & take Care of them. they said they understood we had come to plead the Cause of the Black People who were made slaves of, which gave them pleasure, for that all men ought to be free, but said they knew not but the white people would in time make slaves of them. & much more they Delivered in a very solid Affecting Manner. that excited near Sympathy & Brotherly feeling with them. & divers freinds in their turn had something solid & proper to Comunicate which reached their Understandings & caused the usual Note of Approbation Uha, Uha. I beleive the Interpreter Did his part faithfully. there were 9 Indians. One white man who was taken Captive about 33 Years past & is Adopted into their Tribe, & the Interpreter. & about 12 white present at this Conferrence. at the Close we Distribute or gave for Distribution 11 Bandannoe Hankercheefs as a small Testimony of our Love which they reced. kindly & we parted with shaking hands. this Interview with these Afflicted people gave us satisfaction who are deserted by our Brethren, & I beleive would have claimed thier feeling & sympathy had they been present & I apprehend W[*illiam*]. Savory did not go away fully easy. I hear the Comittee[3] is to meet to morrow morning, we found on searching today a Box of Pamplets from the Abolition Society in London to that here which had laid Dormant & unopened. & Contain'd sutable peices for Distribution & seem like to find use for some of Barclays Apologys[4] which I sent hither a few days before leaving home which I took of Jos. James—& sent hither for sale on my Accot. but some of the frds. now gone thot., the meetg. for Suffs.[5] shd. be Accountable for what are Dispersed—& Edmund Prior says J. James may send 30. of them which

I mentd. in my letter to Jno. Wilson yesterday & expect he will call upon Joseph. Oppo. has not yet been taken with Jackson nor Smith [S.C.], which Warner [Mifflin] has in Veiw, [lined out].

If we are not called upon by the Comittee & after some further Visits to the senators we feel our Minds released shall be willing to return home. & by the end of the week may be better able to Determine.

[P. S.] S[amuel]. Emlens love to thee & please to Convey Notice of Love to his Wife [Sarah] & Children he is Well. Warner has a Cold but moves about with Diligence. Jno. Parrish also well. his Love to thee. his Wife [Abigail] &c.

I have not yet heard whether the Memorial⁶ Designed to be sent to the Vice has reached his hands—it was not recd. on yt. day & was not read I beleive yesterday.

ALS, Pennsylvania Abolition Society Papers, PHi. Addressed to Philadelphia; carried by (Philadelphia spice merchant) John Haworth, "who is desired to deliver it soon"; received 18 February; answered 19 February by post. The editors have elected to print this letter in its entirety because it is a rare expression of Indian concerns at the dawn of Indian-federal relations. Although the Quakers' interview with the Oneida did not involve Congress or individual congressmen, the letter's content and tone offer insights into what congressmen probably heard from other Native Americans visiting the seat of government, most notably the Creek delegation that would negotiate the Treaty of New York that summer.

[1] Of the eleven man delegation of Quakers who accompanied the Philadelphia Yearly Meeting's antislavery petition to New York City, the four who remained until 23 March were John Pemberton, Warner Mifflin, Samuel Emlen, Jr., and John Parrish. Responsibility for lobbying the FFC on the subject of the petitions devolved onto these four joined, less conspicuously, by New York City Quakers. On 18 February, the New York Manumission Society—much of whose membership overlapped with the New York Yearly Meeting (Quakers)—appointed a committee of three to confer with the state's delegation in Congress on the subject of the slave trade. There is no record of their subsequent activities (Minutes, Manumission Society of New York, NHi).

[2] In the first week of February the Oneida delegation had arrived in New York City to meet with New York State authorities and make an unsuccessful attempt to secure an increase in the $600 annuity fraudulently negotiated under the Treaty of Fort Schuyler in September 1788. See George Beckwith, Conversations with Different Persons, August 1790 Undated, n. 1, volume 20.

[3] The House committee to which was referred the three antislavery petitions on 12 February.

[4] Robert Barclay (1648–90) was an early Quaker writer whose Apology (1678) became the standard exposition of Quaker belief.

[5] The Quaker meeting for sufferings began as a body for seeking legal redress from persecution in seventeenth century England and evolved into an administrative organ for the oversight of certain social concerns.

[6] The Pennsylvania Abolition Society petitions to the House and Senate were sent to New York City after the delegation of Quakers had already arrived there from Philadelphia. The Senate petition, under separate cover to Adams dated 9 February (DHFFC 8:324), was presented on 15 February.

Samuel Phillips, Jr. to Benjamin Goodhue

Your kind Favor accompanied with Mr. Hamilton's report [*on public credit*] & another of the 27th. enclosing two papers containing the latter part of Knox's Report [*on the militia*], came safe to hand—The letter which you mention to have been forwarded by the preceeding post, enclosing papers which gave an account of the first part of his Report did not reach me. To these I should have returned an answer before, but have been so unwell as to leave my Seat in Senate & retire home where I have been three weeks nearly: Mr. Hamiltons System contains so much important matter that I dont wonder the members choose to digest the subject well, before they make up their judgment upon it, but I hope they will not wait to know the opinion of their Constituents before they decide: The advantage which Gentlemen in Congress possess for judging on these great questions, after mutual consultation & full discussion, even supposing them to be no more capable of it than others when they go from home, must induce a confidence of the people in the wisdom of their decisions, so long as they retain an opinion of their Integrity, which I trust will be the case for a great while yet to come—Had the Convention who framed the [*federal*] Constitution waited to know the sentiments of people abroad, it is not probable that you would have been now administering it, or that the wished for period would have soon arrived.

Will not Congress themselves, find it expedient to pay considerable Respect to the sentiments of their Secretary, particularly in the Treasury, at least so far as to be cautious of deviations from the measures he has proposed which he does not approve of, for when the system is so far altered, he wont consider himself responsible for the success of it, but if like some others, may be willing to see it defeated, to justify his own predictions; at least we may rationally doubt whether there would be that solicitude & those exertions to ensure success to a System diverse from his own, ~~as~~ which would take place for the support of his own measures.

The consequences of hesitation & delay in this business are justly noticed by the Secretary, and they are of a very serious nature.

As to the rate of Interest, altho' on the one hand we should ~~guard~~ in promissing, guard against exceeding our ability to perform, yet, we ought to come near to what we have a rational probability and moral certainty of being able to accomplish—It is observed that the present Congress have exhibited pretty high sentiments of the Resources of the United States in the Act of compensations [*Salaries-Legislative Act*], & it is not doubted but they will be consistent— If the duties proposed by the Secretary will be productive at the rate he has estimated them, the Interest which he has recommended cannot be oppressive.
***

ALS, Letters to Goodhue, NNS. Written from Andover, Massachusetts. The omitted text asks Goodhue to forward an enclosed letter to whomever he might engage to negotiate with a paper manufacturer that Phillips was trying to hire for his papermill. The Phillips and Houghton Papermill was established in 1788 on the Shawsheen River in Andover, Massachusetts, on the site of a gunpowder mill Phillips began in 1776.

Thomas Rodney to George Read

I Contend That Cæsar Rodney[1] has not been paid for his Services in Congress Nor for five hundred pounds Which he advanced in 1776 for a Tun of Powder for the State—That the House of Assembly in March 1776—Directed him to Sue Vinings Ex[ecuto]rs. and that the Members in favour of this Measure declared he Must do that or Make [himself] accountable for the ballance due from Vining's estate. That after conversing with Doct[or] [Vin]ing Exr. he Made himself Chargeable [illegible] that ballance and that in consequence of this the Assembly drew orders on him—That it appears by his Accts. that he paid More than £1553.18.6 towards that ballance in the Year 1776 and before he received any part of it from Mr. Vinings Exrs. That You & Judge [Thomas] McKean, and Governor [John] McKinley and Judge [William] Killen were in the House of Assembly in 1776. were Acquainted with the State of our Finances and [torn] [illegible] these Transactions. Must My Sisters Estate loose all this Money or Must I expose the private and confidential Letters of Yourself, Judge McKean & Conlonel Hazlett[2] respecting those Measures which were then thought ~~improper~~ and Still May be, imp[r]oper to communicate to the public—Consider what I have Suffered already rather than ~~ds~~ disclose those Communications which were confidential—But can You & the other gentlemen Su[e] the Estate of a aman whose [Con]duct You then all approved of [one line torn and illegible] which were necessary in deffence of the Country. Will you permit prejudices founded on the little and inevitable incidents of a great event, prevent Your doing what is Just and right on Such an Occasion—Can you be thus governed by things that Should rest no where but in the bosoms of the weak & Ignorant and Yet think Your self a wise and good Man? How Much would it appe[ar] otherwise if I was to disclose [half line torn and illegible] refered to—When it is too late for you [torn] [illegible] which confidential Trust, Virtue, Justice and Wis[d]om require a Moment May arrive when reflecting on the Omission Will Sit heavy on Your Mind But Whatever weight this may have with you I Shall rest assured that I have evidenced a due regard for the Trust reposed in Me by My brother as well as a due regard to the confidential communications of other public Servants for the welfare of their Common Country.
It cannot be a Secret to You that the persons Who Controle the legislature

and Administer the Government at present are Most of them Young and inexperienced and all of them Unacquainted with the public Measures in the early part of the War, and Much less acquainted with those that preceeded it [*half a line torn*] [*ju*]stice without knowledge, with the [*half a line torn and illegible*] [*pre*]judice hanging about [*torn*] —Can You [*torn*] Transactions of Such Importance will be Transmitted to posterity without being Accompanied with the Truth? I have in Some Measure Taken care that they Shall not that posterity whose Judgment will feel less prejudice May Judge with propriety.

[*P. S.*] And be[*illegible*] [*torn*] than My brothers reputation and Estate Shall Suffer in the Manner threatened by the present determinations respecting his conduct I will appeal openly and publickly to the wisdom and Judgement of America, and Accompany that appeal with Such Documents as will place his Conduct in its True light. and clear it from those ~~base~~ Secret Sugestions which have been basely Circulated against it by internal inemies for the vindictive purpose of Injuring his Reputation & Estate.

FC:dft, Rodney Papers, Historical Society of Delaware, Wilmington. The letter is torn and blotted at the fold and the top and bottom edges and may not have been sent.

[1] Caesar Rodney (1728–84), older brother of Thomas Rodney, was a lifelong planter of Kent County, Delaware, which he represented in the colonial and state Assembly from 1761 to 1776. An early leader of the state's revolutionary movement, he attended the Stamp Act Congress in 1765, the Continental Congress, 1774–76 (where he signed the Declaration of Independence), and ended the Revolutionary War as major general of the state militia. He served as associate justice of the supreme court, 1766–77, and governor, 1778–81, and died while serving as Speaker of the state Legislative Council's 1783–84 session.

[2] John Haslet (ca. 1727–1777) was a native of Ireland who immigrated to America in 1757. By 1764 he had settled in Milford, Delaware, where he became both pastor and physician. He served as colonel of Delaware's sole Continental Army regiment from 1776 until his death at Princeton in 1777.

William Smith (Md.) to Otho H. Williams

I yesterday inclosed you the N.Y. Papers which contained the latest European News. those of this morning is a contin[*u*]ance of the horrible Situation, the inhabitants of Flanders, Brabant, &ca. are in,[1] And although the Emperor [*Joseph II*] seems at last disposed to yield to their first demands, the people will not now accept of those terms which at first they demanded; In this respect their Situation is Similar to that of America at the commencement of our revolution. I wish them the same Success.

No question is yet taken, on the motion for discrimination; yesterday there were Several able Speeches, of considerable length, in opposition to that doctrine, *Ames* in particular delivered a very Sensible & animated Speech on that Side. This day I expect Mr. Madison will reply assisted by Scott & Some others—The house will be more divided on this question than I at first apprehended and it will probably be some days before it is decided although, I do not think a Single Member has or will alter his opinion. The whole of the Senate have attended in our house for Several days past to hear the debates, & as many of the Citizens as could possibly croud into the gallerys. Instant all ranks seem much Agitated by this question.

I expected to have heard the Sentiments of some of my friends at Baltimore on this Subject, *for that purpose*, besides the Secrys. report [*on public credit*], which I inclosed to you, I sent one to Mr. [*Alexander*] Lawson, to be communicated generaly, but I have been hitherto disapointed, not, even in the Baltimore papers, do I See a Single Polititian Step forth for or against. I expected at least an outcry against the consolidating the State debts with the Domestic debt of the U.S.

ALS, Williams Papers, MdHi. Place to which addressed not indicated.

[1] A reference to the suppression of the Brabant Revolution which broke out in 1789 in the Austrian Netherlands (present-day Belgium and Luxembourg) in response to the centralizing and secularizing reforms of its Habsburg ruler, Joseph II. The short lived revolt, which centered on the province of Brabant, resulted in the establishment of a United States of Belgium in January 1790. Lack of support from the neighboring Dutch Republic and a string of military successes by Joseph's successor Leopold II led to the revolt's total suppression by year's end.

Richard Stockton to Elias Boudinot

*** The Secretary's report is the subject of much speculation—Various are the opinions and objections which it has produced—one party think he does not go far eno. in support of public faith—an other that he goes too far and for sounding words gives up Substantial good—of this last class are the *discriminators*—But the good sense of the more discerning; See in the plan he lays down see the happy medium which while on the one hand it supports public credit—on the other hand avoids those difficulties and embarrassments which would certainly attend a literal performance of the contract—I have not yet seen the whole of the report—but as far as I have read I think it is a performance which will do honor to the American Financier—it is replete with great sentiments finely expressed.

ALS, American Bible Society Boudinot Collection, NjP. Written from "Morven," outside Princeton, New Jersey; carried by Mary ("Polly") Hetfield. Part of the omitted text refers to two unlocated letters of unknown date from Boudinot to Stockton, one accompanying books Boudinot had purchased for him, and the other relating to private legal business.

OTHER DOCUMENTS

Edward Bangs to George Thatcher. ALS, Chamberlain Collection, MB. Written from Worcester, Massachusetts.

Notes the high cost of domestic printings of the Bible, compared with British imports, whose printers may receive government salaries; "unless government give encouragement, in some proper way, to one or two printers here; *they* will always be our printers of the bible"; "a prohibition of their importation is easy"; asks Congress's power to prevent too many printers from dividing and spoiling the market; "I wish you would communicate this subject to mr. Ames & a few others, without making it very public at present; & let me know your sentiments."

William Davies to Governor Beverley Randolph. ALS, Executive Papers, Vi. Addressed to the "Governor of Virginia"; postmarked; docketed "Done Mar. 8. 90."

Has consulted with the North Carolina commissioner (Abishai Thomas) and Mathews from Georgia on the time for producing evidence of the state's accounts with the federal government; Mathews is "rather inclined to wait [*for*] fortuitous events in course of the session, than to make any direct application to Congress"; has also communicated with Virginia's members "from time to time," particularly Madison, "who has entered into the business with some zeal, and assures me he will watch every opportunity of doing something effectual," which he thinks will be during the debate on assumption.

Samuel Emerson to George Thatcher. ALS, Chamberlain Collection, MB. Written from Wells, Maine.

Hints to Congress, "who are our political guardians," that merchants would be benefitted by establishing a post office at Kennebunk; "However, I am happy in knowing the best good of the people [*is*] at your heart & that your attention is always given to the promotion of the interest of your constituents"; in a postscript, wonders if John Gardiner's "present pursuit" (to reform the legal profession) is aimed at securing Thatcher's seat in the second federal election; "if the *Order* [*i.e., lawyers?*] should give him their influence to get rid of trouble, perhaps it may prove a deep-laid plan."

John Montgomery to John Adams. ALS, Adams Family Manuscript Trust, MHi. Written from Boston. Philadelphia merchant Robert Montgomery established the brothers' mercantile house in Alicante in 1776 and was appointed U.S. consul there in 1793 (Priscilla H. Roberts and James N. Tull, "Moroccan Sultan Sidi Muhammad Ibn Abdullah's Diplomatic Initiatives toward the United States, 1777–1786," *Proceedings of the American Philosophic Society*, vol. 143, 2[June 1999]:246).

Office seeking: forwards the (unlocated) application, and adds his own recommendation, for his brother Robert's appointment (as United States consul at Alicante, Spain).

James Pemberton to John Adams. ALS, Adams Family Manuscript Trust, MHi. Written from Philadelphia. Printed with enclosures in *DHFFC* 8:329–31, 332. The FC:dft, Pennsylvania Abolition Society Papers, PHi, includes the crossed out salutation "Respected Friend."

Cover letter enclosing copies of an "Address and Plan" from the Pennsylvania Abolition Society for distribution to the Senators.

Charles Pettit to Jeremiah Wadsworth. ALS, Wadsworth Papers, CtHi. Written from Philadelphia; franked; postmarked 19 February.

Background of Nathanael Greene's unsettled public accounts (largely repeating Pettit's letter of 16 March 1788, included in Hamilton's report of 26 December 1791 on Catharine Greene's petition, and printed in *DHFFC* 7:530–32); criticizes Wadsworth's letters for failure to include more political news, or "If you were too indolent, or too much thronged with business," to enclose some published essay and pamphlets.

George Thatcher to Thomas Roberson. FC, Thatcher Family Papers, MHi. For the full text, see *DHFFC* 8:417.

Relating to the Coasting Act.

William Samuel Johnson, Diary. Johnson Papers, CtHi.

"In Senate. Dind. [*Dined with*] Boudinot."

Letter from Augusta, Georgia. *NYDA*, 12 March (the date on which members of Congress would have seen it); reprinted at Charleston, South Carolina.

"The whole world seems to be running patent mad"; even here "at the extremity of the United States we have also our steam-engine mongers and perpetual-motion-men."

WEDNESDAY, 17 FEBRUARY 1790

Rain (Johnson);
Damp and mild. A thunderstorm last night (J. B. Johnson)

John Adams to Benjamin Rush

I had heard, before I recd. your Letter of the 12th, of your new Engagements in the Colledge[1] added to your extensive Practice and other virtuous Pursuits: and therefore was at no loss to account for your long Silence.

I have no Pretensions to the Merit of your manly and successful opposition to the Constitution of Pensilvania: but I am very willing to be responsible for. any Consequences of its Rejection. I have never despised public opinion deliberately. if I have ever expressed myself lightly of it, it was in haste and with out caution. on the contrary It is always to be respected and treated with decency, even when in Error: but never to be made the Rule of Action against Conscience, it is seldom, and only in small Matters to be followed, implicitly. it is a Wave of the Sea in a Storm in the Gulph Stream, except when it is the Result of methodical Councils or secret Influence. It Should be guided and aided, as well as informed by those who are in Possession of all the Secrets of the State. in no nation that ever yet existed, were all the Facts known to the whole Body or even a Majority of the People, which were essential to the formation of a right Judgment of public affairs. The history of this Country for the last thirty years, affords as many proofs of this Truth as that of any other Nation. how many times, both at home and abroad have our affairs been in situations, that none but Madmen would have thought proper to be published in detail to the People.

You are not the only one, who has Seen and felt The Jealousy Envy and Ingratitude of Friends.

"I love my friend as well as you

But why Should he obstruct my view"[2]

contains a Truth, which has laid the foundation for every Despotism and every Absolute Monarchy on Earth. it is this Sentiment, which ruins every Democracy and every Aristocracy, and every possible Mixture of both, and renders a mediating Power, an invincible Equilibrium between them indispensible. never yet was a Band of Heroes or Patriots able to bear the Sight of any one of them constantly at their head, if they Saw any opening to avoid it. Emulation almost the only Principle of Activity, (except Hunger [*lined out*] and Lust) is the Cause of all the Wars Seditions and Parties in the World. What is most astonishing is, that We Should be so ignorant of it, or inattentive to it. and that We should not See, that an independent Executive Power, able at all times to overrule these Rivalries, is absolutely necessary.

The charming Picture you give me of your Domestic Felicity, delights my inmost soul: but revives in me a lively regret for the ten years of my Life that I lost. when I left my Children to grow up without a Father.

There are two Parties my friend, who have united in some degree, to obscure the fame of the old Whiggs. The Tories. are one, and the Young Fry is the other. By the latter I mean a sett of young Gentlemen who have come out of Colledge Since the Revolution, and are Candidates for fame. There is a Sett of Men in this Country, who have hazarded too much, laboured too much, suffered too much, and Succeeded too well, ever to be forgiven. Some of these unfortunately are not men of large Views and comprehensive Information, and have adopted destructive systems of Policy. Were it not for this last Consideration, you would hear their Cause pleaded in accents that would make Impressions on every honest human heart.

You, my dear Sir, enjoy the Esteem of the honest and enlightened and are perhaps more usefully and happily employed than others in places of more Eclat. There is no Man however that I should see with more Pleasure in public Life, especially in Congress.

With a Knowledge of the modern Languages it is so easy to acquire the ancient, and the ancient are so great a step towards the Acquisition of the Modern, that I cannot help, putting in a Word more in favour of Greek and Latin.

[*P. S.*] I forbid you, on pain of what shall fall thereon from giving me a Title in your Letters. I Scorn, disdain, despise, (take which Word You will) all Titles.

ALS, Rush Papers, DLC. Written from "Richmond Hill," outside New York City. The date is from the FC:lbk, Adams Family Manuscript Trust, MHi.

---

[1] Rush was devoting much of his time to composing and delivering classroom lectures, having been appointed professor of the theory and practice of medicine at the College of Philadelphia on 24 October 1789 (*Rush* 1:530, 532n).

[2] A paraphrase of "Verses on the Death of Dr. Swift" (1731), by the British author, critic, political figure, and ecclesiastic Jonathan Swift (1667–1745).

Abraham Baldwin to Joel Barlow

I have felt myself in great suspence during our long expectation of the British packet, and in greater disappointment on her arrival, not to hear a word from you. your last letters raised our hopes so much de summa re.[1] that it was just a coming, that you must know our anxiety to hear it is finished.

You must know we have had brought before us a law providing for a uniform mode of naturalization &c. This required two years residence to become a citizen, hold lands &c. One Praum[2] got up and convinced them that they knew nothing about their own acts, and that they had every reason to suppose from the operation of their own acts, that there must actually be aliens at this time holders of lands in their western territory, that the common law of particular states respecting aliens holding lands, was not common law to that territory, and that their positive regulations admitted of aliens holding land there, and provided for their descent intestacy &c. The bill was recommitted, and was yesterday reported to us again in much better form. After three months residence, taking the oaths to government and that they mean to reside here &c. they shall be capable of holding and conveying lands; and after two years be citizens in full: Provided nothing in this act shall prejudice the right of aliens who may now have rights to lands &c.

Whether it will pass in its present form is uncertain. it has not been much discussed as yet, I have heard no objection as yet to the proviso. but that is all that is to be expected, foreigners who now own land will probably hold it; but after passing the law probably it will be confined to those who come here and swear they mean to be residents &c. Finals are about 7/9 facilities 6/3 They are doubtful how the great questions before us will be decided. I sent you Hamilton's report [*on public credit*] two weeks ago. 1 Resolve to provide for the foreign debt was agreed to without debate.[3] On the 2d providing for the domestic debt Madison proposed discrimination &c. which read for yourself the question has not been taken. I expect two thirds will be against him. you see we are just beginning, how it will work is uncertain. Adieu.

AL, Baldwin Family Collection, CtY. Place to which addressed not indicated.

[1] "About the great matter," possibly relating to Barlow's sale of Scioto Company lands in the Northwest Territory.
[2] "Praum" was a family nickname for Baldwin.
[3] See Fitzsimons, Resolutions, 8 February, above.

Benjamin Chadbourn to George Thatcher

I feel myself under particular obligation to you for your favour of the third Instant with the public prints therein included—and altho' I feel myself happy in my ritirement from the busy scenes of political life, yet as I am embarked in the ship, it gives me great pleasure to know of her prosperity in weathering the Cape. *** I view the gentlemen who compose the Congress to be equal to any that could be found among the people for wisdom and integrity, but when I consider the importance of the business before them, that is to say, in laying a foundation for national character, and national happiness, ~~where~~ When there are such different interests to be attended to in such an extensive continent as compose our Union I may say as is said in another case "who is sufficient for these things"[1]—I feel myself happy in placing confidence in the wisdom and integrity of congress, not doubting but all their determinations will be upon such principles, as will be conducive for the happiness of the people at large—As to the discrimination [*among public creditors*] so much talked of, would be very right, if human wisdom could make it, but I can't see how it is possible but that there would be danger in attempting to separate the tares from the wheat; that there would be danger of plucking up the wheat with the tares; that is, I suppose many honest creditors would be cut short, & many artful speculators git the whole of their demands; heretofore it has been my decisive opinion that is a matter that government ought never to interfere in—perhaps three ℔ Cent may be as likely to do equal justice as any that can be projected—For a government to promise more than can be performed, is bringing it into contempt—I should rather the whole domestic debt should rest upon the old promise, than for congress to make any [*blot*] one that cannot be fully complied with—I have seen [*the*] Secretary of the treasury's report to congress, it looks plausible upon paper, and I earnestly pray if it is adopted the operation of it may exceed the most sanguine expectation for the purpose for which it is intended—Dear Sir you may be assur'd it gives me great pleasure in my advanced age to see this Empire founded upon truth & justice hoping every individual who composes it, in their various stations & employments in life may reap the happy effects of it—I hope you won't conceive that I mean to dictate, or so much as to advise, I only write my thoughts to you as a friend—I think the burden you have upon you intitles you to the well wishes of your constituents, of whom I claim a share mine you have—wishing you, and every member of Congress that happiness which is the natural result of having served yr. country, hoping when you have leisure you will favour me with a further correspondence.

ALS, Chamberlain Collection, MB. Written from Berwick, Maine; postmarked Portsmouth, New Hampshire, 19 February. The omitted text recounts the author's political beliefs and role during the American Revolution.

[1] 2 Corinthians 2:16.

John Nicholson to Thomas Hartley

I wrote you on the 15th. and now take the liberty of enclosing you copies of a number of letters to a friend in Congress on the important business before you setting forth my ideas upon the subject[1] everyone will agree that if public faith may be kept on as easy terms as it may be broken the observance of it should be prefered. Whether the plan I have held out does not promise fairest for it I shall submit—In opening the Credit therein refered to anything would be Acceptable if therefore a tract of the Western Country were appropriated for the payment of the depreciation of the Certificates with proper regulation the act of injustice would not embarrass the public funds nor add to the burthens of taxes.

Inclosed is 28 doll. which please Accept for the business in Lancaster with the charge I owe you.

FC:lbk, Nicholson Papers, PHarH. Place from which written not indicated.

[1] Per Nicholson's notation, at the bottom of the letter, these were the letters to Maclay, dated 28 and 29 January and 8 February, above.

Samuel P. Savage to George Thatcher

Your Letter of the 7th. Instant I this Day recevd from Boston by Captain Jos. [*Joseph Savage*], who arrived here from Springfield last Fryday & designs for West Point ~~from~~ to morrow or next day; this goes by him as far as Springfield.

I had one Letter from Sally [*Sarah Thatcher*] since that you brought and was in hopes to have seen my dear little Name sake [*Samuel Phillips Savage Thatcher*] before this time, accompanied by Mr. [*Silas*] Lee & his Lady [*Temperance*], but the Badness of Slaying preventes her coming with Mr. Lee; I fortunately had the Oppy. of seeing him at Boston, he had only time to make a Short Visit to his father from Saturday Evening until monday morning, when on ~~the~~ much the coldest day we have have had this year, he set out to see his dear little wife, as he expresses it.

The Apology you make for not calling on us in your to N. York is fully equal to the pain you gave me for the neglect.

I never heard a political Opinion of yours that I was so much surprised with, as the One in your Letters "that you do not hesitate to give it as your Opinion, that if it *be practicable*, a Discrimination between original holders & Speculators of publick Securities ought to take place and while the former recieves according to the face of their Securities, the latter may content themselves on receiving an Equivalent for what they gave for them." and ~~further~~ to support wh. you observed that on "public measures are *just* or *unjust, only* as they relate to the good of the whole or the great Majority. Is it not better that one man perish, than that the Whole nation perish?"[1] and I say he that ruleth over men.[2] This Idea of yours of Virtue and Vise is truly and to the hub ~~those~~ that of the late infamous T. H__n.[3]

If this is the principle by which the World are governed the Freedom of an Indian is infinitely superior, and I am sure much less expensive. every man has a right to that he purchased or labored for; it is his own, & if he is

a member of a ~~free~~ Society, ~~into which he voluntarily entered for~~ he expects
& has an equal right w[*it*]h. every member to the protection of his person
& property Government have no more right to divest him of it, without a
valuable Consideration, than a common highway man. ~~The Nation of~~ England in the late Contest with America acted on this principle, and thot by
~~ensale~~slaving America, their Nation might be benefited. was this right—
~~according to~~ your hypotheses ~~it was~~ undoubtedly it was (as the pretended
motive was the holders good), but ~~as it turned out it was political Vice or~~
~~folly, but~~ and had it succeeded, tho rivers of blood was shed in the Attempt,
it would a glorious piece of political Virtue but happy for mankind at large
it—like its motive, proved as great a piece of political folly or Evil as the
Sun ever saw.

But, for a moment let ~~me~~ us ~~see,~~ examine whether on the principal of
strict Justice—I mean righteousness—whether a nation or a man, for my
Idea of Justice applies equally. whether any difference can or should be made
in paying a Note or Bond to A the original Drawer or to B who purchased
it of his Neighbour C—both of which was drawn by X for similar Articles
purchased at the same time?

There is and ever will be in the nature of things, ~~my dr. Sir,~~ are ~~infinite~~
a difference between right & wrong—virtue and Vice, and it is impossible
by any Means whatever to alter them, you may as soon change the Nature
of heat and cold, they are eternally & essentially different—a Govermt. or
a Man who promises me 100 £ and allows me 6 ℀ Ct. Intt. till paid—if
when demanded will not pay me but 75 £ & but 3 ℀ Ct. Int.—unless he
be a bankrupt is a Villain & deserves a halter. and if Govt. owe more than it
can pay let the World know it, but we know it does not. ~~it is very poss~~ every
body knows it cannot at present pay the Debts, and not but Fools expect it.
we know it can annally pay some part of the Intt. say 1/2 or 2/3—but to
accommode these matters wd. not Virtue blink at the proposal that the holders of Securities should for a qtr. Intt. ~~make~~ oblige them to take [*lined out*] If
Words have determinate Meanings—this act may as well be stilld virtuous
or vicious, even tho establishd by a Law. but the faith of such a Govermt. in
future will ever have and richly deserve the Name of R.I. Govt. and every
man who 2 from 4 sd. Shun it as he would the plague.

I w[*it*]h. you own that that Justice demanded a discrimination between
the original Holders of Govt. Securities and Speculators. but on a cool review
of the matter I think very differently. When Govt. issued their paper Securities, they passd at par wh. Silver of [*or*] Gold, ~~but~~ and so passed for some
time, but the Demands for the wars being so great, and the fears continually encreasing by the Arrival of the Enemy's Fleets & Armies, the people
began to think and the Same Sum would not supply the same Effects it had
heretofore done, the emence sums required to furnish Supplies, at length

brought the value of Securities so low, they were scarce worth accepting, and the arose to such a Sum, that it was thot so great by some that it never could be pd. and every man who bought or received Notes at that Day, acted as Men do at a Game of Hazards. and I ask you whether at that day you would have ~~given~~ risked 3/ for a pound has it even entered his Mind that Govt. would have not pd. him the sum & Int. promised. it was a Lottery of 20 to 1. if Brittian did not conquer, & during the Contest it ever was more than an even Chance she would, considering her Strength & amazg. resourses. and 2/6 was in fact as full a proportion for 20/ as 19/11 was at the beginning.

Goverment made a Scale for adjusting the Value and with Congress & this State it was never lower than 75 for one.

***

FC:dft, Savage Papers, MHi. Written from Weston, Massachusetts. The author's identity is based on the handwriting. The omitted text is random theological meditations.

---

[1]John 11:50.
[2]In a footnote Savage expands the quote from 2 Samuel 23:3, ". . . must be just ruling in the fear of God."
[3]Thomas Hutchinson (1711–80), the last royal governor of Massachusetts (1771–74), whose unpopularity was a rallying point for Boston's revolutionary movement. Savage seems to be alluding to his reputation for political amorality.

Pamela Sedgwick to Theodore Sedgwick

I am favour with yours my Best Beloved Friend of Feb'y. the 6 by the Last post—I think my last letters will account to you for my long Silens—of this you my dear will ~~ever~~ Rest assured that writeing to you will ever be a Grateful employment to me so Long as I can fondly Pleas my self with the thought that my letters will give you one pleasant Sensation. You kindly enquire after my health—I am Tollerably well except a could which I have constantly had more or less of ever since I began to go about the House ~~The~~ as yet I have not made abroad. I hope to do that soon tho when I have no kind friend to invite me out—I can quietly remain at home where my Little family seem to affoard me full employ—I have been so long of Little use to them that their demands upon me seem to be Greatly augmented—I often lament the Poorness of my Constitution as that ever deprives me of that Power that would render me Usefull—"I can soundly Sleep the night away and Just do nothing all the day"[1]—Poor Robert [*Sedgwick*] I Thinks remains much as he has Been—If the Doctr. Call to look at him this week I shall desire him to make a Statement of his Case and Inclose It to you and beg the favor of you to Consult some of the Faculty in N. York upon It—Miss Frances [*Sedgwick*] Grows fast on to a Womans Statture—I have heard much said in Commendation of the Bethleham School[2] I could wish you my dear to make some enquiries Respecting it if you can with convenience— ***

By this Time I suppose you are Engaged in Business of importance and If you adopt any System so extensive and Complicated as the secretarys Report [*on public credit*], I think it must Cost you Great Labour and Pains at any Rate If you can unite in a matter so important, I think It will be next to a Miricle—Doctr. [*Erastus*] Sergeant desires his compliments to you and informs that theay are now forming a Plan for a School House upon the plain and as you have heretofore Proposed to be at part of the expence wishes to know what Proportion of It you would agree to.

I have not been able as yet to get a Statement from Doctr. [*Oliver*] Patterridge of Roberts case he promises to do It next week and I shall enclose It to you—I am very sorry you have not found Leisure my dear to call on the Poor dear afflicted Mrs. [*Theodosia Prevost*] Burr—It is often times Consoleing To the Miserable to meet with a simppathiseing friend and many Times softens our hearts to go to the house of Mourning.

As every Circumstance that concerns you my love is interesting to me you will permit me to ask you whare you Lodge and If you are agreeably Situated—may divine wisdom be a light to your Steps and almighty Goodness Protect you from every evil.

ALS, Sedgwick Papers, MHi. Written from Stockbridge, Massachusetts. The omitted text relates to provisions for "Cousine Betsey's" upbringing in the Sedgwick household and the difficulty of placing her as a servant elsewhere.

[1] From the poem "An Epitaph" by Matthew Prior (1664–1721).
[2] Founded by Moravians in 1742, the Female Seminary in Bethlehem, Pennsylvania, provided instruction in both academic disciplines and domestic skills. It opened its doors to non-Moravians in 1785 and added a boarding school two years later.

William Smith (Md.) to Otho H. Williams

I have only to tell you that the question on Discrimination, is not yet taken, nor do I expect it will be determined in all this week, A number of Speeches have been delivered on both sides of the question, many more will yet be made, Mr. Madison lays by, to Sum up the whole, that Shall be offered against his amendment; & refute the arguments if he can. *that side* of the question, appears to have gained Some friends, but I Still am of opinion the Majority is on the other Side—perhaps a Still more deficult question, will be the Anuity on Interest to be allowed on the funded paper, on this question there are a Variety of Sentiments, even so great as from three to Six ℔ Cent.

ALS, Williams Papers, MdHi. Place to which addressed not indicated. Written in the evening.

Joseph Storer to George Thatcher

Your favor of the 31st of Jany. last duely came to hand for which I am much obliged to you and in answer to which I would acquaint you that I am one of those who are anxious to know what Congress are like to do with public securities.

I believe if a discrimination could take place it would be more just than any other mode. but suppose that hardly possible, therefore, as I take it all must be on the same foundation.

As to funding the debt at three or four, per cent, I suppose it would be as well as any other way whatever, but it is probable that Congress has discussed the matter before now—I find that Public securities are about the same in New York as they are here, they are and will be subject to rise & fall till they are established on a better foundation.

Should Congress assume the State debts it might have a tendancy to prevent some of the States defrauding their creditors of their just dues &c.

I would wish to mention one disadvantage we labour under in this place i.e. in not having a Post Office established between Portsmouth [*New Hampshire*] and Portland [*Maine*] as this is a place of very considerable Trade.

Hope Sir you will think of the matter, as on you we depend as our Guardian and Protector believing that you have at heart the good of your constituents.

We have nothing new in this quarter at present but if I should meet with anything worth notice will communicate it, in the mean time shall always esteem it a particular honour in hearing from you as often as convenient.

ALS, Chamberlain Collection, MB. Written from Kennebunk, Maine; postmarked Portsmouth, New Hampshire, 18 February.

OTHER DOCUMENTS

Daniel Cony to George Thatcher. ALS, Chamberlain Collection, MB. Written from Boston.

Reports state senate's debate and vote in favor of establishing a college in Cumberland County (Maine); John Gardiner's newspaper pieces (advocating legal reform) are universally censured; encloses a newspaper and promises to continue writing every post.

Nathan Dane to Caleb Strong. ALS, Strong Papers, MSonHi. Written from Boston. Dane received the appointment mentioned in the letter.

State legislative business, including John Gardiner's legal reform proposal; congressional news is "here considered as very important and Interesting"; the rate of interest on the funded debt and the assumption of the states' war debts "are esteemed the two principal questions"; public sentiment varies; asks whether the board of commissioners for settling accounts among the states has commenced its duties, since the state legislature has agreed to appoint an agent to it; regards to Dalton and Sedgwick.

Foreigner to James Madison. Ms., Madison Papers, NN. Place from which written not indicated. For the full text, see *PJM* 13:42–45.
Argues that Madison's proposal for a discrimination between original holders of the public debt and assignees violated Madison's 1783 Address to the States (*PJM* 6:488–94); if the proposal prevails, asks "in what light will American faith be viewed in Europe," especially by "Hollanders" who held large amounts of the debt on the assurance of American public officials "that the assignees stood on a footing not less eligible than the original claimant."

Nathaniel Gorham to Theodore Sedgwick. ALS, Sedgwick Papers, MHi. Written from Boston.
Cannot fully answer Sedgwick's question in his last letter, "but I think I can say that the assumption of the State debts will please most people," also the lowering of the interest, although the securities "holders will probably be displeased"; asks Sedgwick to contact Hannibal Dobbyn "& send him to us to [*torn*] his purchas of Land"; asks to be written to more frequently.

John Nicholson to James Madison. ALS, Madison Papers, DLC; FC:dft, Nicholson Papers, PHarH. Written from Philadelphia. For the full text, see *PJM* 13:45. The enclosures are the same as those Nicholson sent to Hartley on the same date, above.
Encloses copies of letters he wrote "to a friend in Congress" (see Nicholson to Maclay, 28, 29 January, 8 February, above); is convinced of the "*practicability*" of discriminating between securities holders; he has implemented a similar plan for Pennsylvania, "and with a few alterations it might be done with great exactness and very little difficulty."

Michael Jenifer Stone to Walter Stone. ALS, William Briscoe Stone Papers, NcD. Place to which addressed not indicated. The recipient's identification is based on the format of the salutation ("Dear Brother," employed in other letters to Walter) and the fact that there is no evidence of any FFC letters to his brother John.
"We are warmly Engaged about discrimination—and how it will terminate I know not—But I believe it will be sound—Just—and—Impracticable. I am tolerably well" and Frederick (Stone) is very well.

George Thatcher to Joseph Tucker. No copy known; acknowledged in Tucker to Thatcher, 6 March.

Letter from New York. [Portland, Maine] *Cumberland Gazette*, 1 March. This is probably from a letter written by Thatcher to the newspaper's editor, Thomas B. Wait.

Doubts whether Madison's motion on discrimination will be voted on sooner than two or three days.

THURSDAY, 18 FEBRUARY 1790

Foggy (Johnson); *Very moderate weather* (J. B. Johnson)

William Constable to Gouverneur Morris

*** several Persons who hold Securities begin to be alarmed, & were it not for the Philada. Publications Respecting the Debts due by R[*obert*]. M[*orris*]. to the Continent wh. have made such Impressions to his prejudice I shoud be able to make Considerable purchases, but this Constantly operates against me—please God We shall have these Accots. finally settled before the breaking up of the present session—& be able to prove the Infamy of the Authors, some of whom by the bye will I apprehend be shewn to have abused their trust, at least We have grounds for so believing as there are none of the Accounts of their Office yet settled or lodged with the proper Departments—Inclosed you have Mr. Morris' Memorial[1]—It has already had an effect & is the first step to Reinstating him in the good Opinion of his Fellow Citizens whose Confidence He will 'ere long as fully possess as ever—indeed woud He agree at this Moment to accept their is no doubt He woud be elected Governor of Pennsylvania—wh. at present He refuses to stand for.

***

FC:lbk, Constable-Pierrepont Collection, NN. Sent by the Hull, England, packet.

---

[1] For the legislative history of Morris's petition for the settlement of his public accounts as superintendent of finance, presented on 8 February, see *DHFFC* 8:663–75.

Samuel Johnston to James Iredell

It is now seven OClock in the evening and the Post I have been waiting ever since 4. the Hour when it usually arrives with great impatience, as the Mail Closes at Nine I can delay no longer for fear of omitting an Opportunity of letting you and my other freinds know that I continue well, the weather is so remarkably mild that I have been out to day without a great Coat without finding any inconvenience.

After the adjournment of the Senate this morning I attended the Debates in the house of Representatives, I was very much pleased with part, for he had been some time up before I came in, of a Speech from my freind Madison, the Subject was a proposition of his own, to make a discrimination between the Original holders of Certificates and Purchasers, that those who held Certificates which were originally granted to them should be permitted to Fund them at their full Value, that purchasers should be permitted to fund at the highest market Price and that the Surplus should be funded for the benefit of the Original holder who had sold. The debates on this Subject will yet continue for some time, when they are closed I will send them forward to you, if justice is done to the Speakers in taking down what ~~they~~ fell from them correctly, you will be ~~greatly~~ agreeably entertained, I should have been very happy to have had you along with me during some of the debates.

Be pleased to inform our freinds that Grain is high here & rising, but still higher in Pennsylvania and Maryland Certificates and even our Officers & Soldier's Certificates are selling here at 8/ in the pound, there were many long faces in the Gallery to day while Mr. Madison was speaking.

*** I expect you will receive your Commission[1] by this Post, pray the enclosed Letters to Mr. [*William*] McKenzie and my brother [*John Johnston*] as soon as you can get an Opportunity.

ALS, Preston Davie Collection, Southern History Collection, NcU. Addressed to Edenton, North Carolina; docketed "Ansd." The omitted text sends greetings to family and friends.

[1] As Supreme Court justice.

Benjamin Rush to James Madison

I expected that the establishment of the federal Goverment, and the reformation of the Constitution of Pennsylvania would have gratified all my wishes for the prosperity of my Country, and have left me to enjoy in private life the pleasures of science and professional pursuits. But I find I cannot be an indifferent Spectator of the great Question [*discrimination*] which now agitates your house. It involves in it the honor and Safety of the United States. The p[*art you*] have taken in it accords so perfectly with Op[*inio*]ns that I have entertained After mature investigation for four years upon that Subject, that I should do my feelings great violence if I did not do homage to the integrity, and independance you have lately discovered in your proposition to do *strict justice* in funding the debts of the United States.

The enemies of your motion concur in its being agreeable to *just* feelings, but they say that reason alone should decide upon all great Questions of National policy. this is a new doctrine in Morals & Metaphysicks. In matters of *right* & *wrong feeling* alone should be our Guide. What would be the state of morals [*lined out*] in our World if mankind were to be led only by the slow, and feeble Operations of reason? To renounce *feeling* upon the present Question, is to desert the standard of heaven implanted in the human breast. Nineteen out of twenty of the citizens of Pennsylvania will in a short time follow you in your motion. It is true they cannot all reason upon it—~~they~~ but their feelings in favor of justice are in some instances *excruciating.* Never have I heard more rage expressed against the Oppressors of our Country during the late War, than I daily hear against the Men who by the Secretary's report [*on public credit*] are to reap all the benefits of the revolution, at the expence of the greatest part of the Virtue & property that purchased it.

I am not more satisfied that theft & murder are contrary to the divine commands, & to the Order of Society, than that the report of the Secretary involves in it a breach of the fundamental principles of justice.

If the interest upon our National Debt were to be paid to the purchasers of Certificates ~~by~~ out of the mines of Brasil or Peru, without a single tax extorted from our citizens for that purpose, I think I could prove that the measure would ruin our country.

I could fill a Volume with facts & Anecdotes of the Characters of those Men who now hold the greatest part of the Alienated Certificates of this state. Many of them are not worthy of the priviledges of Citizenship in the United States.

The principal design of this letter is to suggest to you that your Success in carrying your motion will be ensured by *delay.* The members of our Convention & Assembly (a great majority of whom think with you) will soon ~~return~~ [*leave*] our city, & spread your principles & fee[*lings*] thro' the Country. The clamors in conseque[*nce*] of information being carried home to our farmers, will be *loud—violent—*& *universal.*

I have only to request that you would conceal my name in mentioning the Contents of this letter. I have taken no part in the Controversy in this city—and wish to continue a Spectator of its progress & issue.

Mr. Peter Muhlenberg will convey an ~~Ack~~ Acknowledgement from you of the receipt of this letter, if your leisure should not permit you to answer it. P. S. A regard to what is falsely called *National honor* in G. Britain, produced the independance of America.

ALS, Madison Papers, DLC. Written from Philadelphia. For the full text, see *PJM* 13:45–47.

Theodore Sedgwick to Pamela Sedgwick

I had the pleasure to receive your favor this morning which came by the post last evening. It gave me the most sincere pleasure, and perticularly as it contained information that sweet little Robert's case is less alarming than when you wrote last. I shall not fail of consulting as soon as possible some of the most respected of the [*medical*] faculty. and by the next post will write you such information as I may be able to give.

This letter is wrote in the house.

ALS, Sedgwick Papers, MHi. Place to which addressed not indicated.

Henry Wynkoop to Reading Beatty

Your Reasons offered in the Letter of sunday last, for not coming forward as was urged by me are perfectly right, yet feel sorry you could not comply with propriety, as the importance of the Debates, then suggested, have since been fully verified; I beleive I mentioned in my last the Proposition of Mr. Madison to introduce a discrimination between the original holders & present posessors of public Securities, this has been the Subject of Debate ever since & is yet undecided, the principal Advocates for this Measure are Madison, Jackson, White & Lee, those in opposition, are Ames, Hartley, Lawrence, Boudinot, Benson & Wadsworth, the House being anctious to have this Matter fully discussed, the Question has not been urged & the Gentlemen have come forward fully prepared with their Arguments on both sides, Mr. Boudinot yesterday spoke more than two hours & Mr. Madison this day was up near that time, perhaps tomorrow may close this important Debate; You could not have been here at any one time, since the existence of the Government, when Your curiosity would have been more highly gratified, tho' perhaps You might be more comfortably acomodated with a Seat in the Gallerey; Shall look for You on tuesday & think You had best take Your Seats at Morton's[1] in the first Stage wherein You can be comfortable, because finding seats vacant in the Mail Stage is uncertain & should You be disappointed You will wait for the next more comfortably at home than at Trenton [*New Jersey*].

ALS, Wynkoop Papers, PDoBHi. Place to which addressed not indicated.

[1] A tavern on the busy road between Bristol, Pennsylvania, and the Delaware River ferry crossing to Trenton (*Cutler* 1:430).

Newspaper Article

A correspondent observes, that however "nice" the Legislature of Massachusetts may be, in excluding their Federal Officers, yet we have authority to assert, that letters from some of our Members in Congress, have approved of the determination of our House of Representatives; and the proceedings of the town on the letter of Mr. G.[1] must evidently show, that the inhabitants approved of the proceedings of the [*General*] Court—as his arguments in favor of his *eligibility*, were not even noticed by his constituents.

[Boston] *Independent Chronicle*, 18 February.

---

[1] On 4 February, Christopher Gore, United States attorney for Massachusetts, wrote a letter to Boston's town meeting explaining his reasons for resigning from the Massachusetts House of Representatives on 29 January. Unable to agree to a joint resolution on the question of dual federal-state office holding, the House had voted overwhelmingly (137 to 24) on 21 January against allowing federal officers to sit in that body. While claiming that his seat was not explicitly declared vacant thereby, and notwithstanding his personal and legal opinion to the contrary, Gore felt that the controversy had impaired his ability effectively to serve the town. On 10 February the town meeting acknowledged the letter and thanked Gore for his services ([Boston] *Independent Chronicle*, 28 January; [Boston] *Massachusetts Centinel*, 13 February).

Newspaper Article

A correspondent observes, that notwithstanding the indecent (*speculator*) squibs at a respectable member from Vir. [*Madison*] he cannot help wishing him success—To do justice is a heavenly attribute; and if a plan can be adopted, by which the decrepit soldiers, and the widows and the orphans of those whose constitutions were impaired in the glorious contest, and are since dead, can have their certificates made good, *their* blessings will attend the successful advocate, and the universal cry will be, that however intricate and embarrassing has been the situation of the United States, they have now interwoven the celestial principles of justice and humanity in their judgments, which will run down their streets like a mighty flood.[1]

NYJ, 18 February.

---

[1] A paraphrase of Isaiah 2:28.

OTHER DOCUMENTS

Josiah Burr to Jeremiah Wadsworth. ALS, Wadsworth Papers, CtHi. Written from New Haven, Connecticut; carried by Captain Clarke, "with Box."

Does not anticipate that Nathaniel Gorham and Oliver Phelps's difficulties (regarding their Genessee Purchase) "should be attended with the loss of our share or even any part of it"; should Gorham and Phelps prove unable to provide a deed, imagines that the New York legislature "would on proper application authorize a location to be made within the purchased territory"; Wadsworth's nephew will be in New York in about three weeks, with details relating to the Genessee business.

Edward Fox to Andrew Craigie. ALS, Craigie Papers, MWA. Written from Philadelphia; postmarked 19 February.

Cannot account for Madison's conduct over discrimination; "I am told he is honest: sensible & well informed—and yet he holds principles, such as, Clymer ought to hold: who is neither one nor the other"; thinks nothing will be decided this session; "perhaps this is best, as we may possibly have a better set, after next election'" although he does not expect "that any Stir will be made here"; people are "at a loss which rascal to admire most. Hamilton, Scott, or Madison"; supposes Madison's conduct is a sign that he and Hamilton "must have had some difference"; asks Craigie to feel out Morris about the likelihood of Fox's appointment as commissioner for settling accounts.

William Maclay to [*John Nicholson*]. Combined excerpt of one page ALS, *Henkels Catalog* 946(1906):item 225, 1057(1912):item 352. Place to which addressed not indicated. The ellipses are in the source. The editors have identified Nicholson as the recipient because the context is similar to several other letters Maclay wrote Nicholson during the spring of 1790 (all of which were sold on the autograph market), and because the letters to Maclay's other correspondent of the period, Benjamin Rush, are all accounted for.

"The question is not yet put on Madison's motion. Ames and the New Yorkers showed want of temper this day. They had called in the beginning of the debate on Madison to show a single case in history that would apply. He fairly beat them on this ground. They then flew to matter of right founded on strict law and disclaimed all precedent. He claimed the field of victory, and put them in mind of their challenging him to meet them on this ground. He has certainly gained considerably, but it is yet very doubtful. The whole city, or nearly so, support the Secretary's report. This would not avail, if the members were free from the bias of private interest. . . . The members from our State have hitherto been silent, but several of them will support Madison, . . ."

Samuel A. Otis to John Adams. ANS, Adams Family Manuscript Trust, MHi.
"I intended to have observed to your Excellency, that upon what was intimated yesterday, I have induced the Clerk of the H. of Representatives [*torn*] to join me, in authenticating & publi[*shing*] copies of the acts of Congress, until the further orders of Goverment."

William Smith (Md.) to Otho H. Williams. ALS, Williams Papers, MdHi. Addressed to Baltimore; written in the evening.
"No decision yet on the question of discrimination This day Mr. Madison reply'd to those, who had opposed his amendment, *in a masterly manner*, time must Shew the result of this interesting debate, I however think it will be determined, against the amendment, abt. *thirty* to twenty four"; private business.

Jeremiah Wadsworth to Catherine Wadsworth. ALS, Wadsworth Papers, CtHi. Place to which addressed not indicated.
Will not be able either to go to Philadelphia or return home; progress is very slow; we "talk much, decide on nothing and are very cross"; is disappointed there is no snow; "there is nothing new or entertaining to write you about"; there are no plays and he has not been to the dancing assembly; has danced once at Leffert's with Fanny (Frances Crèvecoeur), who is to be married to Louis Guillaume Otto.

John B. Johnson, Diary. NNC.
Attended Congress in the afternoon.

George Washington, Diary. Washington Papers, MiD-B.
The postmaster general and Representatives Boudinot, Griffin, Coles, Gerry, and White, with their wives, dined at the President's.

NYJ, 18 February.
Since the House started debating Hamilton's report on public credit, "the gallaries have every day been crouded—and all the vacant chairs within the bar filled with respectable personages."

Letter from Pittsburgh. *NYDA*, 13 March (the date on which it would have been seen by members of Congress); reprinted at Providence, Rhode Island; New York City (*NYDG*, 27 March; *NYP*, 30 March); and Baltimore.
"Every inducement is held forth by the Louisiana Spanards to prevail upon our western settlers to cross the Mississippi and become subjects

of their government. *** as she [*Spain*] dreads nothing more than an enterprising, active nation in the vicinity of her Mexican settlements."

FRIDAY, 19 FEBRUARY 1790

Very Fine (Johnson); *An almost summer day* (J. B. Johnson)

Pierce Butler to Governor Charles Pinckney

I find there is not the smallest probability that Congress will adjourn so as to admit of my returning to Carolina to attend the [*state constitutional*] Convention; and the business before Congress being of too important a nature for Carolina to dispence with the absence of any of Her Members, I am, though reluctantly, constrained to relinquish the honor that Prince William's Parish intended me—I request that Your Excellency will give directions to have a Writ Issued in time that the Parish may not lose a Voice in Convention.

ALS, Legislative Papers, Sc. Addressed to South Carolina.

Ralph Izard to Gabriel Manigault

*** Congress is at present engaged in some very important objects. The Report of the Secretary of the Treasury is before the House of Representatives, where I suppose it will continue some Weeks before it is sent to us. Mr. Madison, and his friends contend that the present holders of securities should be paid only what they gave for them with the Interest, & that the difference between that Sum, & Twenty Shillings in the Pound ought to be paid to the original holders from whom they were purchased. This appears to be an inadmissable doctrine, which would tend to destroy all future credit. Some are for ~~funding~~ the assumption of the State Debts, & some against it: and there are Advocates for 3, 4, 5, & 6 pr. Cent. It is difficult at present to form a decisive opinion; but I am inclined to think that the State Debts will be assumed, & combined with the Continental Debt, & that the whole will be funded at three, or four pr. Cent. Perhaps 3 pr. Cent. for five or six years, & four pr. Cent. from that time. Perhaps also the Western Lands may be reserved as a Sinking Fund. I tell you what I think will be done. Possibly it may be only because it is conformable to my wishes. You have never given me any information respecting the election at Goose Creek, which I expected you would have done. Mr. [*John*] Owen has written that Mr.

[*Edward*] Ellington told him I was elected. Taking it for granted that his information was true, I have written to the Governor to decline serving.[1] I now enclose the Letter, which you will be pleased to seal, & deliver to him. In addition to the reason which I mentioned to you in my last Letter, it will not be consistent with my duty to leave Congress, & there is no probability of an adjournment taking place before the meeting of the Convention. I beg the favour of you to mention that reason to the Gentlemen of the Parish with my Compliments; & express to them my grateful sense of the honor they have done me. My Colleague tells me that he agrees with me in opinion, & that he intends sending his resignation likewise to the Governor.

P. S. I am informed by Letters from Charleston that Mr. [*Edward*] Weyman is dangerously ill, & several applications have been made to me to procure his Office for Mr. Stephen Drayton. In my opinion [*Peter*] Bonnetheau would execute the Office better. Will you learn from him whether he would wish to be Surveyor, if the Office should become vacant?

ALS, Izard Papers, ScU. Addressed to Charleston, South Carolina. The beginning of the letter relates to the state constitution and legislature. Part of the postscript was written on 25 February and is printed under that date, below.

[1] See Izard to Governor Charles Pinckney, 15 February, above.

William Maclay to John Nicholson

I recived your letter of the 17th this Morning before Senate met. and had an Opportunity of putting, the pieces which were inclosed into the hands of Sundry Members. There is such a spirit of Volatility and dissipation of thought, with many men, that you cannot get them to read any performance of the length of a column in a news paper, with attention. unless you can engage them with novelty, or something of a laughable nature. their minds seem to revolt at the Idea of seriousness, and still more at any thing which requires thought or calls for calculation. Two readers of this class soon returned the papers. some others have taken them home, to peruse them at leisure.

The Accounts of the Treasury have been sent to Us to the end of last Year, in a Cursory View of them I noted the following Warrants & Payments.

To Mr. [*Tobias*] Lear for Compensation. to the President—			To Royal Flint for temporary residence furniture &ca.	
No. 75	1000	Doll	No. 118	5000
77	2000	Do.	136	500
78	1000		141	1000
80	3500		147	1500
81	200			8000 Doll.

omitted	300
95	1000
140	1000
149	2000
150	1500
157	2000
	15,500

There may be more payments made last year under the Above heads which I may have omitted in casting my Eye over the Account. as many other Payments were made to this Flint for Cloathing. but I am certain of the foregoing. What Warrants have been drawn on the Treasury this year I do not know officially but the common Observation is, by a certain Class of People that the 25,000 will fall greatly short &ca. it is likewise said the furniture &ca. will be 11,000 or 12,000. but even at 8,000 which was paid last Year, at different times, and without any remark of it's being in full. The good Woman's complaint is well founded.[1] please to destroy and disregard my former letter on this Subject, as it is less accurate than this. tho equally true as to me having heard the Sums from those Who had attended more minutely to the business than I did. indeed You may destroy this and all my letters as none of them are worth keeping. and as they are all wrote to you in intire confidence. no question is Yet put on Madison's Motion. I consider all this as lost time. for he will loose it. and I fear he had committed himself, in some of his Arguments, so as not to have left himself room to sit in, on future Occasions. It really seems as if the public were to be plundered by common consent, and all the difference was Who should have the spoil. The Persons Who have been in possession of alienated certificates for 3 or 4 years past have generally cleared money on them. and Yet these are the People for whom we must ruin the public. but I must Stop.

ALS, Gratz Collection, PHi. Addressed to "Comptroller Genl. of the State of Pennsylvania"; franked; postmarked 21 February; received and answered 24 February.

[1] This is a reference to the newspaper piece that Maclay wrote and sent to Nicholson; see 14 February, above.

Benjamin Rush to Thomas Fitzsimons

While You condemn the legislator in Mr. Maddison, I will admire in him the honest man. I have ever tho't that the *heart* is a better centinel of what is just than the *head*—and I would as soon believe in the grossest Absurdity in Gullivers travels,[1] as admit any thing to be impracticable in legislation that is perfectly ~~right~~ just. The Abbe [*Guillaume*] Raynell in complaining that

Americans deprived Columbus of the honor of having a Continent called by his name, remarks that it was a fatal presage ~~of~~ that America was to be the theatre of future Acts of injustice.[2] Your funding System is to be one of them, and however much it may be gilded by the splendid and imposing names of honourable policy, &c. it will rank hereafter with the murder of the innocent inhabitants of South America by the Spaniards—with the [*lined out*] Slavery of the Africans by our Southern states, and with the ravages committed by Great Britain upon property & life in America during the late War. All these Acts had their *Secretaries* to propose and defend them & they were all advocated upon the principles of policy—necessity—or National honor. But ~~they~~ they have all left a stain upon our Country & Upon human Nature.

I feel so much hurt at the indignity done by your proposed Act to justice & humanity, that I [*lined out*] now wish I had never consented to any One Act of the revolution. Passive Submission to Great Britain would have been Sublime Virtue compared with the adoption of the Secretary's report.

Mr. [*Alexander*] Wilcox objects to that part of Mr. Maddison's Motion which proposes to ~~pay~~ refund the original holder his losses upon his Certificates. Three ℔ Cent he says to the purchaser would satisfy every body.

The Universal Cry here is to pay the present original holders 6 ℔ Cent.

This is the last testimony I shall bear against your proposed System of ~~nati~~ honourable fraud and oppression.

ALS, The Gilder Lehrman Collection, on Deposit at the New York Historical Society, New York. [GLC 7874] Docketed by Rush, "Feb. 17. 1790. Intended to have been sent to Mr. Fitzsimons."

[1] Jonathan Swift's satirical fantasy, published in 1726.
[2] Raynal (1713–96), a defrocked priest and radical political philosopher, published his six volume *Philosophical and Political History of the Settlement and Trade of the Europeans in the East and West Indies* in French in 1770. Although banned in France and placed on the Catholic Index of Forbidden Books, it went through thirty editions before 1789.

Paine Wingate to Samuel Hodgdon

I have received your favours, one of the 19 Ultimo, & the other of the 15 Instant, with the enclosures which I have delivered agreeably to your desire. The last I this day deliverd in person, the other I forwarded by an early conveyance. I thank you for the kind offer of services & shall be likely some times to trouble you with my requests, and in return shall be very ready to render you the like service. I am very glad to hear from Mr. [*Timothy*] Pickering's family that they are well. I desire my Love to him & that you would let him know that I have received his letter of Jany. 26 by Mr. Andrew Brown whom I shall chearfully befriend If there is opportunity. I have not heard from home or from Salem [*Massachusetts*] lately & have nothing particularly to write to Mr. Pickering. The house of Representatives have already spent four days on Mr. Madison's motion for a discrimination & probably the question will take up one or two more days; yet it is not doubted but a great majority of the house are against it. I hope that we shall unite justice & sound policy in support of the national credit; but I assure you that the mode in which it can be best done is a very perplexing question. I believe that if our resources were adequate to the purpose, there would be a general disposition to comply fully with the former promises of government to all its creditors; but in our present situation, how to preserve our credit & give satisfaction to our creditors is not an easy task. The discussion of this subject will yet require considerable time, and it is not worth while for me to conjecture what will be the result. I will only add that it is my opinion that the public credit will be better than it has been. You will perhaps think that this is saying very little. I wish I could say more. I will enclose to you a news paper, though possibly it may contain nothing new.

ALS, Pickering Papers, MHi. Place to which addressed not indicated; received 21 February.

Newspaper Article

The hon. Messrs. Lee and Grayson Senators to Congress from Virginia, have lately wrote two spirited Letters to the Legislature of that State, wherein they observe that nothing on their part has been omitted to procure the success of those radical Amendments to the Constitution as approved by their Legislature; and that "if a persevering application to Congress, from the States that have desired such Amendments should fail of its object, they are disposed to think, reasoning from causes to effects, that unless a dangerous apathy should invade the public mind, it will not be many years before a constitutional number of Legislatures will be found to *demand* a convention for the purpose"—How far such ideas agree with those of the people of this consolidated empire; our correspondent leaves to the decision of the reader.

[Connecticut] *Norwich Packet*, 19 February. Lee's and Grayson's letters are printed in *DHFFC* 17:1634–35.

OTHER DOCUMENTS

John Adams to James Pemberton. ALS, Pennsylvania Abolition Society Papers, PHi. Addressed to Philadelphia; franked; postmarked 21 February; received 23 February. For the full text, see *DHFFC* 8:332.

Has delivered "Addresses and Plans" to Senators.

Joseph Barnard to [*George Thatcher*]. ALS, Thatcher Papers, MeHi. Written from Portsmouth, New Hampshire. Recipient verified from context of Barnard to Thatcher, 26 January, above.

> Has received an order from the postmaster general for $300; thanks for "Attention you paid to My Letter" and "kindness."

Elias Boudinot to Samuel W. Stockton. No copy known; acknowledged in Stockton to Boudinot, 23 February.

Tristram Dalton to Josiah Little. ALS, Dalton Papers, MSaE. Addressed to Newbury, Massachusetts. A postscript dated 21 February is calendared under that date.

> Advises on the legal standing of Little's land claims in Vermont, in dispute between New Hampshire and New York State; relates Senator Johnson's opinion of the validity of the grants made there; promises to send New York's bill on the matter; asks for business advice relating to his land in Dalton Township, New Hampshire, upon which he has consulted with Jacob Bayley.

Woodbury Langdon to John Langdon. ALS, Langdon Papers, NhPoA. Written from Portsmouth, New Hampshire.

> Has received Langdon's "several Letters"; reports on Langdon's mercantile interests; the petition of the merchants and traders of Portsmouth, on trade policy and the location of the federal district court, "will I hope be forwarded next Week" (see *DHFFC* 8:185–86, 353–54); heard that Langdon has been informed of the proceedings of the state legislature; enquires of the residence and circumstances of Archibald Mercer, who is indebted to Woodbury.

Governor Thomas Mifflin to John Langdon. ALS, Langdon Papers, NhPoA. Written from Philadelphia.

> Office seeking: recommends and seeks Langdon's aid for Benjamin Elliot for surveyor "of one of the Districts on the River Ohio."

George Thatcher to Nathaniel Barrell. No copy known; acknowledged in Barrell to Thatcher, 11 March, which indicates Thatcher's letter was written over the course of 19–21 February.

William Samuel Johnson, Diary. Johnson Papers, CtHi.
> "Dind. [*Dined at the*] Kings."

Letter from Kentucky to Pittsburgh. *GUS*, 5 May, from a non-extant 17 April issue of the *Pittsburgh Gazette*; also reprinted at Boston, New York City (*NYDG*, 6 May), and Charleston, South Carolina.

Reports Indian depredations on settlers in Kentucky in the previous December and January; wishes the information made public.

SATURDAY, 20 FEBRUARY 1790

Cloudy (Johnson); *Overcast p.m. and very rainy* (J. B. Johnson)

Fisher Ames to Welcome Arnold

I ought before this date to have expressed my gratitude for your esteemed favour by the mail—Please to accept my apology for my neglect—For several weeks public business here has required an unremitted attention, and I have not supposed that any thing which I could communicate would be earlier news than you get regularly by the post I cannot, however, at this time forbear to express the degree in which I feel myself interested in the proceedings of your approaching Convention—I shall rejoice to see the forms of the Union completed—and if the measures of this Session of Congress should terminate in a prudent and honourable provision for public credit, I shall dismiss any fears for the permanency and tranquility of the Government—It will be our fault if we are not the most prosperous and respectable people in the world—and Rhode Island has good cause to expect a full share of the blessings of such a Govt.—I understand, however, that the passions which have hitherto resisted the spirit of union have not subsided, and that a majority of antifeds will meet in Convention. I hear this with regret—If argument can have effect, I shall expect the adoption. But I fear that it will be as it has been before—and that a dead majority will resist reason and public good with silent obstinacy—Considerations drawn from the power of the united states by restrictive acts to hamper the industry & trade of your state would not be regarded—But the plan of the Secretary [*on public credit*] affords an Argument more upon a level with their views—The scheme of adjusting accts. between the U.S. & individual states presents to your people a solid & very alluring advantage. It is equally beneficial to creditor states who will now get their due, & to debtor states who will get their debts paid for them by the U.S. I do not allude to the assumption of the state debts—tho' that is connected with the subject—but to the Supposititious statement of such accts. Rhode Island I suppose will prove a Creditor & may expect that this will procure an annual sum from the public Treasury sufficient to pay the

expences of civil Govt. and to save your people from taxes on that score—
Nor have they cause to fear direct assessments by the U.S. For it cannot be
expected that the landed interest which predominates in Congress, will
abuse this source of taxation—nor is it easy to devise a mode, according to
the rules of the constitution, which will admit of excessive impositions—If
for instance a tax of so much per acre should be imposed, your state would
pay less than any state in the Union, the land being in proportion to other
property more valuable than that of any other state—I suppose that you will
sit in Convention—I wish you all imaginable success.

[*P. S.*] I ought to have observed that I have not the least expectation that
a land tax will be laid.

ALS, Rhode Island Manuscripts, RPB. Place to which addressed not indicated; received
3 March.

David Austin to Roger Sherman

I thank you for your kind favr. of the 13th Instant which came safe to
hand, I purchased one of the Secretarys Reports [*on public credit*] of Mr. Beers,[1]
and have paid some attention to it—It gives me sinsible pleasure to observe
the high sense of obligation which he manifests in his preamble to establish
that Righteousness which exalteth a nation,[2] after mentioning a Number of
obligations in a Political view he very Justly mentions a Moral obligation
as the greatest—you inform me that there is a diversity of opinions on what
terms & rate of Interest a loan shall [*be*] opened for the domestic Debts, and
wish my opinion on the Subject—when I observe that depth of penetration
discoverable in the Secretarys Report, I feel a reluctance in giving my opinion, from a consciousness of my being unacquainted with such important
matters, It has been so long since I have received any benifit of the principal
on Interest of my property loaned to the United States & of my unliquidated
claim, I think I should for my self acquiese in the proposals of the Secretary,
giving the Creditors their choise of the methods proposed by him. whether
that part of the Continental Debt which has been loaned at Six per Cent,
and the time of payment has long since Elapsed, (and the Creditors many
of them, have suffered greatly, for want of some part of the principal or Interest) Ought not to be continued at the existing rate of interest untill the
Principal can be paid by Government, at which time it will (in my Opinion)
be strictly Just to fix any rate of Interest they shall please, or redeem those
Securities by paying the principal? I only suggest for your consideration—
with respect to assuming the State debts I am fully of your Opinion on the
Subject, and I see no impropriety even if a Small tax should be necessary in
as much at a very considerable one will be necessary in each State in order to

pay their particular Debts, unless the several States have a demand against
the united States sufficient to discharge the Debts of the particular States
upon a Settlement, which by the Secretarys Report, seems to be the case in
some Instances if I understand it—I have full confidence in the wisdom and
Integrity of Congress under the present Constitution which vests them with
sufficient power to carry their Resolutions into Efect, that they will support
an Eficient & Righteous Government I doubt not.
    ***

ALS, Sherman Papers, CtY. Written from New Haven, Connecticut. The omitted text
relates to religion and church administration.

¹ Isaac Beers (1742–1813), bookseller in New Haven, Connecticut.
² Proverbs 14:34.

Samuel Henshaw to Theodore Sedgwick

By your favour of the 7th. Instant, you seem to apprehend, that now is
the *solemn crisis*—that on the Doings of the present moment depend the
respectability & permanency of the federal Govt. Agreed! Congress ought,
therefore, to make haste slowly—to tread firmly, but cautiously—They
have a great, enlightened & jealous people to govern—A people, zealous
of their rights & properties. A people who have not yet got rid of local &
State prejudices, and who have not yet seen & felt so much of the beneficial
effects of the federal Govt. as to be wedded to it in love! And if Congress
should NOW adopt any important Measure that is repugnant to the general
Sense & feelings of the people, it would throw them into a very unhappy
situation—But I have too much confidence in the wisdom, patriotism &
moderation of Congress to suppose they will act hastily on any Subject that
involves the Fate of the Union! Prudent Legislators will always pay a great
regard to the general Sentiments of a well informed People—and especially
at in the first moments of their political existance.
    I know not but the Secy.'s plan [*on public credit*] is a good one—And, as
far as I have contemplated it, I think it does him honor as a Man of Genius—But as you observe it is founded in our inability to pay the In[*tere*]st.
agreeably to contract—Now if that inability will justify the Govt. in reducing it to the point of ability—For unless it is as low as that, the Govt.
must again violate their faith—And this would be worse than doing nothing—But what is the point of ability? This is the great question—And it
appears to me that it cannot be yet answered—We have not had sufficient
experience of our productive resources to determine with any tolerable degree of certainty—and on a question of such magnitude we ought not to

depend too much on suppositions & abstract ~~specu~~ calculations—But if the Secy.'s plan is the best that can be devised, and was I convinced of it, I should much doubt the policy of an immediate adoption—It is New, & of infinite Importance, and the opinions of people concerning it are various—Let them have time to examine it thoroughly, and if it is the best plan that can be exhibited, the general voice will undoubtedly be in its favour; and all will be quiet & happy under it—But should it not be the best, a little delay will give opportunity to our sage politicians & Financeers to point out its defects, & to introduce those alterations that may be necessary to perfect the system.

And to induce Congress to make haste slowly, let them recollect, that the people are more apprehensive of danger from the great federal Officers— *the Heads of departments*, than from every other quarter—The Militia plan as brought forward by the Secy. for the department of war is extremely unpopular here—At Salem, last week, they were about erecting a Stage with intention of burning thereon the Secy.'s effigy & the plan together—Should Congress adopt this System, I would not advise the Secy. at war to review the "advanced corps" of Massachusetts! He makes the annual expence to the united States to be 384,440 dollars, but He makes no allowance for loss of time—30,000 non commissioned Officers & soldiers to lose one twelfth part of their time is no inconsiderable object—besides the 1000s and 1000s of days that would be idled away by spectators—And will not this system operate greatly to the disadvantage of the Northern States, in loss of time as blacks are out of the question?

I am clear with you, that to cement the Union, to give force & energy to the federal Govt. an assumption of the State debts must take place. Untill this is done, we shall be a miserably divided, distracted People—State duties or Excises will be adopted, & will interfere with each other, & with the federal collections also—and will eventually ruin the revenue—Your Secy. [*Hamilton*] may make as many calculations as He pleases, yet if He cannot prevent the States from laying an excise on imported articles, I venture to predict that He will not be able to support the Govt. and pay two per Cent Inst. It does, therefore, appear to me that Congress ought, or that the supreme fedl. Judges ought, immediately to determine whether the State Legislatures have, or have not, a right, agreeably to the fedl. constitution, to lay any impositions or Duties whatever on imported articles? And I hope to GOD they will determine in the negative, even if they force a construction— Our State are now new modelling an Excise Act; it will play the devil with our citizens and finally learn them, & force them, to cheat State & Continent.

I have regained my Health so far as that I intend to go out on Monday next—Our Genl. Court have not perfected any business of consequence, nor will they ever, while [*John*] Gardiner & [*William*] Bacon are in the House.

ALS, Sedgwick Papers, MHi. Written from Boston.

Andrew Moore to Arthur Campbell

I have frequently wrote to you by the way of Winchester [*Virginia*]. But have recieved no Answer from you or any of my Acquaintances—I Suppose the post Neglects forwarding them—I have little or no news—The Secretary of the Treasury's Report has engrosst the Whole of our Attention for some time past—A proposition brought forward by Madison has been under discussion for some [*da*]ys and is not yet decided He proposes funding the [*en*]tire debt now in the hands of the Original holders at Six per cent Interest—Those certificates in the hands of Purchasers at the Present highest Market price (suppose ten shillings) bearing six per cent Interest—The Ballance to be paid to the Original holders—I have inclosd some of the papers Which will give you some Idea of the present state of this Business They also contain some of the most Interesting foreign Intelligence lately received. I am not at Liberty to make any Communications on the Subject of Western defence as yet—I may however assure you I think something effectual will be done—We have now before us a great deal of Business—The Session I expect will continue to May or June—We shall be Obligd to revise & Amend the Impost Law and probably the Judicial System before We rise—We have hitherto proceeded with a great deal of Coolness in our deliberations, The Seat for the permanent residence of Congress Will not be tak[*en into*] Consideration I expect this session.

ALS, Draper Collection, WHi. Addressed to Washington County, Virginia; franked; postmarked 23 February; sent to the care of the printer Augustine Davis at Richmond, Virginia, who endorsed the letter: "The Bearer of this left at this Office, two letters for to be sent to N. York, which were ~~forwarded~~ sent by the Mail this morning. A. Davis. P. Office, Richmond, March 5th. 1790."

Theodore Sedgwick to Pamela Sedgwick

The hasty scrawl you will receive by Mr. [*Samuel*] Kirkland you will please to pardon. they were wrote in great haste, and when my mind could not be detached from the important subject which was then discussing in the house.

Our progress here is very slow—Mr. Madison has made a motion in the house for discriminating between the original holders and the present possessors of the public securities. nor have we yet come even to a decision on it. It is very clear that it cannot succeed, but there will be a greater number for it than was at first apprehended. To this question will follow the great and important one of the assumption of the state debts, which will meet great, but I hope not successful oposition. It is now reduced nearly to a certainty that our state on a final settlement will be in circumstances as eligible as any in the union. This alone will create a great degree of opposition, for no state will probably be more an object of jealousy than Massachusetts, when unincumbered by those embarrassments, by which she is at present oppressed.

I have not yet had it in my power to call on the surgeons in this town in regard to the case of our sweet little Robert. I shall do it however so as to write you on the subject by the next post which you will receive with this.

Three weeks from next tuesday our court sits. It will depend on the progress we make in the report of the secretary of the treasury whether I shall then be at home or not. This important subject I dare not leave unfinished. I hope it will be in your power to procure a nurse for poor little Kitty [*Catharine Maria*]. but I confess this wish is not so much founded on her account as on yours.

Adieu! dearest and best beloved of my heart—Be assured that you continue to reign sole mistress of my affections.

ALS, Sedgwick Papers, MHi. Place to which addressed not indicated.

Theodore Sedgwick to Theodore Sedgwick, Jr.

Why do you not write to Papa? Let me know how you do, and what you do; how often you go to play how often to school and how often to work. tell me how little Harry and little Robert are, how mamma, and little Kitty [*Catharine Maria*] get along, how mom Bet[1] is, whether the new man is good, how the hay Setts, whether you have any more pigs, whether the hogs are well taken care of, whether you have any sheep fating, and all about & about it. But above every thing do not forget to be a good boy—Farewell.

ALS, Sedgwick Papers, MHi. Place to which addressed not indicated (probably enclosed in Theodore to Pamela Sedgwick, of the same date, above).

[1] The Sedgwicks' free Black house servant was still popularly known as Mumbet after changing her name to Elizabeth Freeman (ca. 1744–1829) upon winning her freedom in the lawsuit *Brom and Bett v. Ashley*, which helped to establish the unconstitutionality of slavery in Massachusetts in 1781. Sedgwick was Mumbet's lawyer in the case, and she was his family's beloved servant thereafter until her death (Arthur Zilversmit, "Quok Walker, Mumbet, and the Abolition of Slavery in Massachusetts," *WMQ*, 3rd ser., 25[Oct. 1968]:618–22).

[*William Maclay*,] Letter to the Printer

I AM an old soldier, and an Irishman. This I tell you at once by way of subscribing my letter; for by letting you know before who I am, you may soon guess what I will be after.

I followed the fortunes of the great Washington thro' all the wars; and hearing of his glory in New-York—heaven be praised, for she has a knack of doing things handsomely—aye, in New-York, where he used to be cursed regimentally, and on field-days, by whole brigades, that there his honors should be shed upon him. To New-York, however, I came; and the first thing I wanted to see, was some of the laws made by my old General; for as I had been long under his command, I did not want to disobey orders now. I soon got one of them, but could not understand it well—There was a string of names at the end of it, and among the rest, one *Vice*. Now I knew *Vice* in camp to be, drunkenness, swearing and some other things, which used to befall us when we happened to be well fed for a day or two, and had nothing else to do. But cousin Patrick coming by told me, that this *Vice* never was in camp, but that it was a man that took the room or place of my General, who they now call President. What! and before his face too? says I. Where was the man to take his place when our frost-bitten toes looked thro' our ragged shoes—in the Jersies, or at Brandywine, or Germantown, or Monmouth, or York-Town? He for a—I was just going to curse, and call names, but Pat stopped me; and it was a thousand pities, for I never was in a finer humor for it. Well, Pat, says I, coming a little to myself, how shall I contrive to see him? And will there ever any thing more be done for us, poor soldiers? As to seeing him, says Pat, I believe that must be out of the question. He is now in the hands of fine folks, who do not like to admit any body who has not new shoes, and is not as neat about the heels as a pin; and I doubt, in your present trim, you would not pass muster. But then brave times are coming on: the certificates will all be paid off at there full amount; and money will be so plenty, especially among those who have taken care to provide themselves well with them, at a proper time, that they will be able to live at their ease, and give generous prices to you, and to every body else that will work for them. And as for the trifle of taxes that will fall to the share of any individual man, to make them up, a clever fellow would not have his name told for it. Pat, says I, these fine folks would spoil our General if they could. He never was a greater man, than when he rode among us with his dusty boots. They may hide him from us, but they never can make him hate or despise us, though we may have a patched shoe, or a ragged stocking. As to other matters, Pat, you must have your finger in the pie, or you never would talk so. If our earnings are to procure ease and affluence to any, it ought to be to ourselves. To work for our money a second time, and pay taxes a third time for it, won't do, Pat. No, no, Pat, it will never do. I guessed you meant some mischief, when you, and a set of rooks, used to be following us, poor soldiers, like a pack of wolves, or a flight of ravens, to prey upon our distresses. Was it for this you used to give us such friendly advice—O, take any thing for your certificates; they'll follow the continental money—they'll not be worth a farthing—And now to be served such a dog's trick—to be told to work and pay taxes for them, Pat—by—But I believe, Mr. Printer, it would not do to swear in a newspaper—and I'm not a fine writer, and can't give you a whole chapter on my feelings. Pat surely had some feelings too; for I did not know that I had got my stick elevated a tone or too higher than a presented musket, till I saw him edging off to get out of the reach of it.

Now, Mr. Printer, to have lost my youth, my health, my strength and pay—to have become the heir of aches and pains, hunger and nakedness, would not grieve me. A belief, that the virtues and sufferings of the American army would be had in grateful rememberance, should have been my consolation; but to see luxury and riot rise on our hard earnings, while misery is our lot—a brave heart cannot bear the contrast! Farewell! But if there be word of truth in what Pat says, you Congress, and all the world, shall hear from me.

> *IG*, 20 February; reprinted at Newburyport, Massachusetts. Maclay sent the manuscript of this piece to John Nicholson in a letter dated 8 February, above.

[*William Maclay,*] Letter to the Printer

It cannot have escaped an attentive observer, that some individuals have endeavored to model the Constitution of the United States to the standard of the British monarchy. This is a matter far from being impossible—it needs but the overcharging of some features, and the lessening or obscuring of others. The first step to a work of this kind, would be, to swallow up the state Legislatures in the federal Government. The Judiciary of the United States is considered, by some, as capable of producing a like effect, with regard to the state Judiciaries. The Report from the Treasury, on the subject of finance, copies after a British nation, and if pursued in its full extent, cannot fail of soon overwhelming us with masses of irredeemable debt. Men, who lay it down as a maxim, that England is the happiest and best governed spot on the globe, will not consider themselves as criminal in endeavoring to place their country in the same situation. Doing it, however, by indirect means, seems to need an apology—Nor will it do to tell enlightened Americans, that thus children are beguiled into health, by imposing physic upon them instead of food. Such state physicians will always be suspected of having an eye to the loaves and fishes, which are generally dealt out with a bountiful hand in royal governments. The cost, however, should be well counted, before systems of such magnitude are attempted. Several serious questions will arise—for instance—Are we able to support a civil list of a million sterling a year? Can, or will we bear the exactions of the miriads of retainers to the law, and the protractions of causes for ages, that attend the practice in England? Her criminal jurisprudence, indeed, never should be mentioned without a tribute of praise to its excellence. Shall we, in our infancy, adopt a system of finance, which will at one stroke reduce us to the beggary of borrowing every shilling we may want on any emergency, while our whole resources are mortgaged to a set of speculators, for the support of riot and dissipation?

Public faith—public credit—inviolable observation of contracts—the fairest names in the social catalogue—have in all ages been brought forward to cover the grossest enormities; thereby verifying what has been said of rigid law, SUMMUM JUS, SUMMA INJURIA;[1] and have ever called for the interposition of the supreme power, as a correcting chancery, to remedy the evils which have been engrafted by accidents and artifices upon them.

The Jewish jubilee,[2] of divine origin, had this for its object. The Roman secession to the Aventine mount,[3] gives us a clear example of it. But to descend to modern times—The Legislature of Great-Britain, in the present century, deranged the course of the law respecting contracts, in the affair of the South Sea Company. Debts were discharged, on payment of ten per cent. Sureties acquitted, and the law-suits discontinued, by act of Parliament. And perhaps no occasion ever existed, that would more fully justify the exercise of such chancery in government, as the present one in the United States.

Whether a splendid government, with all the retainers to, and trappings of, royalty, be for the advantage of the governed, is a question which ought be fully settled, before any imitations or innovations take place. Men, who have given grave opinions on the prosperity of nations, seem to refer the whole to the mass of productive labor carried on among any people. Whether a court, such as the head of a great empire is generally surrounded with, is a likely place to produce such qualifications, may justly be doubted. In such places, men sacrifice every thing to appearance: they soar above common life; and the domestic habits of industry and frugality are forgotten. Examples from such high sources cannot fail of imitation; and the contagion may be spread far a[nd] wide.

Should, however, such a misfortune ever befall America, we have a sure resource in the different state Legislatures. Here the seeds of genuine republicanism have flourished, and brought forth fruit—and here they are still cherished. Let not, however, the different state governments be wanting to themselves, but fill, with firmness and decision, the stations assigned them in the general arrangement of the empire. For this purpose, let them instruct and direct the conduct of their Senators, in the Senate of the United States.

Thus will the confidence of the people, in the federal government, receive additional strength, and the interests of republicanism a further security and support.

IG, 20 February; reprinted at Newburyport, Massachusetts. Maclay sent the manuscript of this piece to John Nicholson in a letter dated 8 February, above.

[1] Rigorous application of the law causes rigorous injustice.

[2] The jubilee year in ancient Israel occurred every fifty years. At that time there was a compulsory restoration of hereditary properties to their original owners or their legal heirs, as well as the emancipation of certain servants.

[3] The secession occurred when, in order to force Rome to accept their views, the plebeians left public and political life and withdrew to Aventine, one of the seven hills outside the city.

Letter from New York to Philadelphia

The subject of a discrimination between the public creditors, agitates all descriptions of people in this city; and Mr. Madison's motion, "to settle with the present possessors of the public securities according to the average rate they now bear in the market, and to pay the difference between that and the nominal amount, to the original holders," has been attacked with all the virulence of party, and the utmost malevolence of interested opposition. Within doors, and without, every attempt is made to render it odious; and the language of opposition is addressed to all the motives that can influence the human heart, whether of hope, fear, or interest. The justice and practicability of the measure have been arraigned, and it is declared to be unconstitutional, unprecedented, destructive of public credit, repugnant to the public mind, iniquitous, and finally impossible. I shall, therefore, my friend, proceed to consider it under all these several and formidable grounds of objection, and see whether it be not possible to evince the verity of the proposition upon the great principles of public justice and public honor.

The unconstitutionality of the measure is inferred from that clause in the Constitution, which declares, "that all debts contracted, and engagements entered into, before the adoption of this Constitution, shall be *as valid* against the United States, under this Constitution, as under the Confederation:" And which is called a recognition of debts; but in my opinion is nothing more than to say, that they should stand in "*statu quo*," precisely as they were, without being *more* or *less* valid against the present government, than against the former. Indeed, the idea of a recognition of debts as contended for, would involve the monstrous absurdity of inhibiting the Legislature from all enquiry into the nature of the debt, and compel full payment to the nominal amount of all the old paper money now in being, to the amount of from eighty to one hundred millions of dollars. Nor would the absurdity end here, because in denying the right of legislative discretion, a fundamental provision of the Constitution, and upon which must depend every hope of the public creditor, would be defeated, to wit, the second clause of the 8th section of the first article—by which the power "to pay the debts and provide for the general welfare of the United States," is conjunctly given; clearly and absolutely providing that in devising a mode for this great object, the legislative discretion shall be freely used as to all the considerations of public justice and public honor on which it shall depend. How far these considerations will be affected remains to be enquired, having regard to all the other formidable objections which I have before noticed. The nature of the public debt in its origin, has not I apprehend been duly adverted to, otherwise the position that the present certificates on the evidences of a debt in the hands of the present possessors, would not be taken, for I cannot but regard them as the secondary and depreciated evidences of a debt justly due to the original holder, who held and still holds a primary right to that debt, upon an evidence which the public could never divest him of, I mean the discharge of the brave soldier who had faithfully rendered his military service, and the certificate of the honest planter or farmer, who zealously contributed his property to support the war—and to say that the public, who arbitrarily called in these primary evidences, and issued the present certificates, which I denominate "secondary and depreciated paper evidences of a debt originally due," are thereby exonerated from the claim of the original holder, to make good that depreciation, is to confound the distinctions of right and wrong, and prostrate every principle of justice. The *prima facia* evidence of a debt to the present holders, being thus, I think, fully refuted, let us ask, what obligation of equity the public are under to them? Can it result from the fairness of the transaction between them and the original holders, or from the fulness and sufficiency of the consideration paid? for surely fraud, and want of consideration, are as much objects of enquiry before the Supreme Legislative Council of the nation, as before any Judge or Chancellor whatsoever.

In general, it cannot be denied, that necessity on the one hand, and the arts of speculators on the other, induced the original holder to part with his certificate at one eighth or one tenth of its nominal value, and in most cases *a supresso veri*, or concealment of the truth, has been practiced, such as that the soldier would never receive any thing but the paper certificate for his debt; that the public had neither ability or power to pay the nominal amount; that the paper certificate was only meant to pay 2s. 6d. in the pound, in full discharge of the debt, and that that being the established price no more could be obtained, or would be given; again all provision for the payment of the interest, and every act of government for raising the credit of the securities, was carefully concealed or artfully misrepresented to the view of the war-worn veteran. In some, very rare instances indeed, the purchaser may have been fair, and between all intermediate purchasers it may be regarded as speculation opposed to speculation. But it has been said that the speculators purchased at a risk which depended on nothing less than a revolution in government—surely, however, those who advance this argument do not see its tendency, for if the risk of purchase depended on a revolution, surely the possession of the original holder was at equal risk, and the act of government, which gave him the certificate, a cruel and nefarious deception; this argument, however, is not just, because the two or three years interest due on the certificates at the time they issued, was generally equal in value to the sum given both for principal and interest, and therefore nothing was risked. Again the transferable property, which was given to the securities, by an act of the government, is much relied on in favor of the present holders, but as I conceive without reason; two facts, are certain, one that this property could not be necessary to the certificate in the hands of the original holder so long as he retained it; the other that the price of the securities did not rise, and has never been influenced by that consideration; on the contrary let me ask, whether if none of the securities had ever been transferred, the value of them would not have been always beyond what it ever was or now is? Indeed, I believe, the current interest would have produced nearly as much to the original holder, as both principal and interest have since done. It has been suggested too, that foreigners have purchased to large amount in the domestic debt, upon solemn assurances and certificates from public Ministers, Presidents of Congress, &c. that the certificates were alienable and would be as obligatory in the hands of purchasers as if original holders; this fact, however, is not well founded, that certificates to the effect mentioned, may have been granted, I will not deny, but that foreigners have in any instance been deceived by them, will, I think, clearly appear not to have happened—from two considerations, both well established, the one that the domestic debt never sold in Europe for a price any thing nearly equal to the foreign debt, and the other, that in the purchases made here, the agents of those purchases have all acted upon a secret reservation that in case the debt should be redeemed at nominal value in the hands of the present holders, they should receive a proportionate commission or share of profit; and in some instances, it is well known, that loans of money have been made on a credit of 3, 4, or 5 years with security, and a reserved condition that the lender should receive half the profit of a speculation in the domestic debt of the United States, which might arise, beyond a fixed rate of purchase. If these things bespeak a deception on the part of the government against the foreign purchasers, or rather speculators, then indeed may public credit be in danger from their opinion; but if not, I will ask for a serious answer to the enquiry, what is the public opinion at home? and what danger there is to public credit among our own citizens, from the adoption of Mr Madison's motion? Those who assert what the public mind is from what they experience of that mind in the meridian of this city, deserve not to be estimated as statesmen or politicians; and perhaps we may be led to excuse the temerity of their counsels, from the ignorance which conceived them. Public opinion, I will venture to assert, is in favor of the proposed measure, and let him who doubts it, recur to the national character and prejudices of the American people: Ask the planters, farmers, and yeomanry of your country, to pay their taxes, and contribute their several proportions to discharge the public debt and satisfy the present holders, and they will demand of you, in a plain, but nervous stile, Are these the men who fought our battles, who spilt their blood, and nobly purchased the liberties of their country? or, are they the speculators who have deceived the poor soldier, and gotten for a song the evidences of his hard earnings? perhaps too, many of these people are of the description of those who fought to enslave us. If so, we disdain the idea, and reject with horror the suggestion that this first act of our independent government, is to be marked with black ingratitude and injustice to our defenders, preservers and deliverers. But bring to us, the meritorious sufferers, those, who have never yet experienced ought but contumely and injustice, from that country, which they saved by their valor, bring them, and we will gladly contribute to the uttermost farthing, for their payment and reward.

That such would be the language of my countrymen, is, I hold, too congenial with American feelings and principles to be doubted. We have not yet reached that point of apathy, which, in private life, converts into deadly enmity, friendship for the man who can be no longer serviceable. If then, such be the public sentiment, will it be doubted that in any future contingency, the government may rest with perfect security, on the cheerful contributions of its citizens, as well of personal service as of property, to supply every demand there may be occasion to make. Indeed, the record of public gratitude and justice, will be so indelibly marked on the mind of each citizen, that he will transmit it with the history of the revolution, amidst the atchievments of the war worn soldier, to his children, and childrens children, until the tradition shall become sacred and immutable.

But no objection to the measure I have advocated, is, perhaps, less founded, than that which calls it unprecedented; the history of nations, abounds with instances of it, and none more so than those of commercial countries, particularly Genoa, Venice, France, Holland and England. In the last mentioned country, a memorable instance happened in the year 1713, in the reign of Queen Anne, when all the alienations and transfers of public securities in the civil list department to the amount of 500,000L sterling, were declared void, and those who had purchased at 3, 4, or 5 for one, were compelled to relinquish to the original holder, upon his paying what he had received with interest at 6 per cent. a case, which is so fully and absolutely in point, as to preclude all possibility of refutation.

But I fear that I have been already too prolix, for the bounds of an ordinary letter, and ill therefore hasten to conclude it, but not without observing that all objections founded on the supposed impracticability of the measure, are mere arbitrary assumptions, and cannot be determined until the principle is detailed into those modifications, which the various contingencies it is designed to embrace, may demand; and that even if it should be found too difficult in toto, it will most assuredly admit of none so far as respects the army debt.

IG, 27 February. The editors believe that this is the letter sent to John Nicholson by William Irvine on 21 February.

OTHER DOCUMENTS

Abigail Adams to Mary Cranch. ALS, Abigail Adams Papers, MWA. Written from "Richmond Hill," outside New York City; addressed to Braintree, Massachusetts. For the full text, see *Abigail Adams*, pp. 36–39.

It is thought that the House will vote on discriminating between securities holders tomorrow, when she intends to attend the debates with Ruth Dalton, Sarah Jay, and Hannah Cushing; Smith (S.C.) "is one of the first from that State, & I might add, from the Southern States"; Ames, Sedgwick, and Gerry "are all ~~write~~ right upon this Question & make a conspicuous figure in the debates"; presumes next they will take up assumption of the states' war debts, "and here I apprehend warm work, and much opposition"; believes "it will terminate in the General Good."

John Baptista Ashe to John Gray Blount. ALS, John Gray Blount Papers, Nc-Ar. Addressed to Washington, North Carolina.

Congratulates Blount on the election of his friend Williamson; reports his own election by a majority of 202.

John Baylor to James Madison. ALS, Madison Papers, DLC. Written from New Market, Virginia. Printed in *DHFFC* 7:545.

Concerning the settlement of brother George's Revolutionary War accounts.

Richard Curson to Horatio Gates. ALS, Gates Papers, NHi. Written from Baltimore; addressed to "Travelers Rest," Berkeley County, West Virginia.

William Seton writes Curson that the debates on Hamilton's report on public credit have been very warm both in and out of the House, although the prevailing opinion is that there will be no discrimination among security holders, that principal and interest will be funded at four percent, and that the report will be adopted nearly in full.

Thomas Fitzsimons to Thomas Ruston. ALS, Coxe Papers, PHi. Addressed to Ruston as "Presidt. Manufactureg. Society."

Recommends the bearer, Mr. Byrne, for employment with the Philadelphia Cotton Manufactory.

Benjamin Goodhue to Nicholas Pike. No copy known; acknowledged in Pike to Goodhue, 1 March.

Ebenezer Hazard to Thomas Jefferson. ALS, Washington Papers, DLC. For a partial text, see *PTJ* 16:188.

Office seeking: chief clerk of the state department; Langdon particularly advises him to seek it.

Benjamin Huntington to Anne Huntington. No copy known; indicated in endorsement of Anne Huntington to Benjamin Huntington, 8 March.

Caleb Strong to David Sewall. No copy known; mentioned in Sewall to Thatcher, 11 March.

SUNDAY, 21 FEBRUARY 1790

Drizzly (Johnson); *Overcast* (J. B. Johnson)

Nathaniel Barrell to George Thatcher

***

But now for your letter. I can assure you the expectations of the people are as great as they were in your first sessions, and as divided as they then were—there are some who wish you to do justice according to the true definition of the word, by following the strait line, agreeable to the simple sense it will bear—to do which, these say, you must fund the debt at six ℗ Cent, or according to the face of governmental security's. the question is not whether 4 ℗ Cent be too high, or too low—they say if you take it upon yourselvs to fund the debt under 6 ℗ Ct., you depart from justice and good policy—and assume a power you have no right to—that if you have my note for six per cent interest, it is not in my power to oblige you to take four per cent; which ought to be your guide in these matters. they say, that if you were as careful to do justice to the public creditors, as you were to procure for yourselvs large compensations, the Revenue would be sufficient, for the discharge of the interest, & support of Goverment, without any adition to it—and that if you would even now, *reduce* your compensations to a *moderate allowance*—lay aside for the present, the *sinecures*, those *unnecessary district Courts* &c. in a short time, it would be in the power of Congress to pay of[*f*] the national debt—after which, they might have new funds at four percent—but untill then, they cannot in justice reduce the interest, without the consent of the public creditors. I hope Congress will assume the several state debts, even tho they should not think proper to fund them at more than four percent, but in that case, to come near to justice, they ought to pay up the interest to 1791.

I am sorry my dear friend, from the hints you thro out, that the question with Congress is not what is right? but what is too high an interest or what may be promis'd wth. the greatest probability of performance—in this juvenile state of Goverment we are too apt to contract, & confine our Ideas, to the present appearance of things—but if we allow ourselvs to look forward a little without being invested with the talents of prophecy, we may say, when our sinking funds come to opperate and we become honest—there is not only a base probability, but a morral certainty, that we shall be able to make good all our honest engagements. when we look back and see the rise and fall of Empires, & Kingdoms, we find they succeeded no further than they kept pace with justice and if they departed from that, they crumbled away, till they became what we now see them.

You say some are opposed to an assumption of the state debts, "because say they, some states have very large debts, while others have small ones." these objections do not proceed from an attachment to the rule I have been contending for—those gentlemen are not honest enough to say how this comes about—if they would speak out, according to that rule, we might hear them say, that by a course of Chicanery, and injustice, some States have evaded providing their proportion of men & money agreable to a recommendation of Congress during the Warr, by which iniquitous means they avoided large, and by similar means since, have discharg'd those small debts—and are now free—while the Massachusetts have at all times exerted themselves even beyond their abilities, and by such exertions, have accumulated an emense debt, which justice now says those States ought to pay their proportion off. I agree with you in thinking that some of those who oppose an assumption of the state debts, are holders of large sums in continental securitys, which is the cause of their opposition—Mrs. [*Sally*] Barrell joins with the girls in respects—I am wth. proper remembrance to your brother Colleagues—Your old friend &c.
P. S. pray let me hear from you soon.

ALS, Chamberlain Collection, MB. Written from York, Maine; postmarked Portsmouth, New Hampshire, 26 (?) February. The omitted text praises the *General Dictionary, Historical and Critical* (London edition, 1734–41) of Pierre Bayle (1647–1706), which Barrell recommends Thatcher acquire for himself in New York, "and not insist on my complying with my promise to let you have."

William Irvine to John Nicholson

Fourteen days have elapsed since Mr. Madisons motion for discrimination was made, and little else has been agitated in Congress during that time—it will probably be decided tomorrow or next day, as is supposed negatively, but this in my opinion will not prove that there are a majority of that body against any kind of discrimination, on the contrary I am persuaded sundry will vote against this motion because it does not go far enough, others have different schemes, and some reserve themselves, it is said to see whether the State debts are or not to be assumed, if not, that they will become as strenuous for reducing the debt or rather against any funding system whatever, as they are now against discrimination.

I believe there are but few who have any fixed principles, for after the long discussion that has taken place, there is no clear or divided majority for any plan.

Many are for adopting the Secretarys Report without any enquiry or investigation, or calculation of the resources; Some of these must be secretly opposed to public credit, tho they are most loud in support of it, I am led to this opinion by my knowledge of the information which some of them possess and a supposition therefore, that they must know the resources are not adequate to pay the interest of the whole debt, even at 4 per cent, when augmented to 100,000,000 Drs., which it must be by assuming the several state debts, of course a Spunge, in a few years must wipe away all stains—or a new Revolution perhaps—much has ben said about the impracticability of a discrimination, if I was as clear that it would be politic as I am that it is practicable I would at once pronounce in favor of the measure—nay I am not certain but a new investigation of the claimants actual or Just right to the securities might be well worth the attempt, without any discrimination between present & original holders as I am persuaded, many Certificates have been obtained by fraud, and others unduly encreased—admit that it would be unjust, impolitic, or what not for the Government either to reduce the Capital, or discriminate, yet if fraud can be proven, the whole world will allow and approve of detection & punishment, as the most honorable & Just measure—In what ever way the present question is decided, I fear public credit, is in a precarious situation in some stage of the business I take it, that a more pointed proposition for a reduction will be brought forward, but should all kind of reduction or discrimination be rejected, and the Secretarys plan fully adopted, will that support public credit? I answer the question myself & say that no Man in his senses will believe that these States can raise by any and all possible revenue, upwards of 6,000,000 Dollars annually—this I grant is not a direct answer—but I wish to see it demonstrated that less will do—and I will venture to pronounce that members will act a strange and improper part if they Vote for a measure of this importance til they have the most perfect information of the sum wanted and how it can be raised, however these inconsistencies & imprudencies are not novel.

You have doubtless seen the plan proposed by the Secretary at War, for a National Militia—I intended troubling you with some observations on it but am interupted, and shall not therefore have time by this days post—beside I know not whether it may not be as well to condemn it, in gross as by particular strictures—I think it expensive (much more so than the estimate accompanying it admits) that it would teach the youth Idleness & extravagance &ca. &c. & wont make soldiers of them.
P. S.
The interuption mentioned in the close of my letter, was occasioned by a young Gentleman coming into my room and putting the inclosed piece or letter into my hand—which he read (I have not) and signified a wish that it might be published in a Philadelphia paper as he did not like to be known as an author here.

The printers it seems are quite squeamish, so much so that young Men are afraid to offer almost the simplest thing imaginable, for fear of being exposed.

It strikes me that this piece does not contain any thing but such as any printer would be glad of to occupy a page in his paper—when you read it and discover nothing improper to be sent, to a press, as a letter, for publication, I shall be obligd. by your doing so, provided however that there is nothing improper in this request—if there is, be so good as to return it by the next post, and if it is published send me two or three papers—it is not mine, nor is it a members, of Congress. I think every investigation that is in decent language on this very interesting subject, ought to be freely disseminated.

ALS, Gratz Collection, PHi. Addressed to Philadelphia; franked; postmarked; received 24 February. Nicholson forwarded the enclosed piece to Eleazer Oswald, editor of *IG*.

George Thatcher to Sarah Thatcher

I have recieved no Letter from you the week past, but as I did not much expect any I am not disappointed—I suppose that Tempe & Silas [*Lee*] are about leaving Biddeford, or will in the course of the ensuing week—I have had no Letter from Silas during his tarry at Boston—I would write to him if I knew where he was.

I am more & more anxious about your being alone, & hope some good friend or other will fall in with you & cheer up your spirits till my return.

We have had spring like weather the week past—The week before was the only cold weather I have felt since I arrived to this city—There has not been so much as one days good Sleighing in this City this winter.

I wish I could see our dear children & kiss them as much as I want to—do they enjoy good health? are they good natured & quiet?

I forgot before I left home to give you all a caution against fire—you know this is always upper most in my mind when I am at home; & it haunts me much more now I am from home.

Take care to burn all the chimnies in rainy weather—Take care of your candles when you go into the Celler just before you go to bed for should fire take there you would all be a sleep before it could be discovered, and get so much a head as to render it impossible to extinguish it, or escape from the flames.

On very windy, dry days, of which there are many in the spring of the year, let somebody look frequently on the House to see if any sparks light there— in the evenings also be mindfull how you carry a candle into the chambers, & especially in the closets where there are cloaths hanging—The upper part of the house is so full of partitions of boards that in half an hour or less the fire would rage beyound a possibility of extinguishment—When any body goes into plac[es] where cloaths, or dry combustables are hanging—with a candle—within ten minutes after somebody ought to look into the same place in the dark—because then the smallest spark will discover itself—I know you will be carefull for your own sake as for your dear husbands.

ALS, Thatcher Family Papers, MHi. Place to which addressed not indicated.

George Thatcher to William Webb

Your favour of the 1st. inst. came to hand three days ago. To which I beg leave to answer, that I am fully sensible of the injuries the inhabitants at large, as well as the Merchants & Traders, upon Kennebeck River will sustain by the exclusion of vessells owned by foreigners, from delivering their Cargoes at Bath—And I endeavoured once and again, towards the close of last Session for Leave to bring in a Bill to the House to remidy the inconvenience, but was not successfull—I do not dispair, however, of accomplishing so necessary an object this Session. The Secretary of the Treasury has recieved Letters from all the Collectors thro' the United States, and it is probable from you among the rest, stating to him the imperfections of the Revenue Laws; and early this Session he was directed to arrange the amendments, he should think necessary from such statements, and lay them before the House. I have also conversed with him myself, particularly upon the expediency of making Bath & Frenchmans Bay ports of Delivery for vessells owned by foreigners—And he confessed to me there were good reasons in favour of the former; and I have very little doubt but he will report the desired amendment—I have frequently conversed with the members of the House upon this subject, and have their assurance of assistance when it comes before them.

In this and all other matters respecting the district of Maine you may rest satisfied of my exertions so far as the measures are not opposed to any principle necessary to be observed for the general wellfare of the United States at large.

Another subject I wish to bring to your mind, & for your opinion upon it—That is the expediency of a post office at Bath—I have wrote to D[*ummer*]. Sewall Esqr. upon this subject, but have had no answer—I am, at present of opinion, that, upon the new arrangement of the General Post-Office, an office will be very convenient some where in Bath—And shall thank you for your opinion of some suitable person for Post-master—It must be some person whose usual business will not lead him much from home, as it will be necessary for him to be at his office at the established hours of the arrival of the mail—And the emoluments of the office cannot be very great.

FC, Thatcher Family Papers, MHi.

OTHER DOCUMENTS

Joseph Barrell to Samuel B. Webb. ALS, Barrell Papers, CtY. Written from Boston.

> Madison's proposal for discriminating between security holders proves "the old proverb that 'Great men are not always wise'," and the complexities of it as observed by the secretary of the treasury should prove its folly even to Madison, unless he is actuated by popularity.

John Carnes to George Thatcher. ALS, Chamberlain Collection, MB. Place from which written not indicated. Dated "Lords Day Evening."

> Relates efforts for settlement of Thatcher's accounts with Massachusetts and news of the Massachusetts legislative session; the newspapers "give You all the information You can expect"; hopes "something will be done to establish public Credit," as Massachusetts legislators have "been a long while upon it"; "we are anxious to know what you are like to do, and we wou'd outdo you if we could"; in a postscript, sends regards to the Massachusetts delegation.

Daniel Cony to George Thatcher. ALS, Chamberlain Collection, MB. Written from Boston.

"We hear that *Consolidation* has been Toasted at a *public dinner* in N. York, which has caused a little, a little, a little Speculation, amongst __ however and wherefore—and so forth—possibly—but we don't know—perhaps—had there not better be a little inquirery—this matter deserves a some attention—the Americans ain't fools"; was disappointed in not hearing from Thatcher; will write to him as often as he can while in Boston; news of the state legislature.

Tristram Dalton to Josiah Little. ALS, Dalton Papers, MSaE. Addressed to Newbury, Massachusetts. This is a postscript to a letter begun on 19 February and calendared under that date.

Has gone with Jacob Bayley "to the proper offices to negotiate his business—and offered him any assistance that he might want while in Town"; will try to see him again tomorrow; the treasury department officers, "with some of whom his business lieth, are Men of application—knowledge & Industry"; further advice on the legal standing of Little's land claims in Vermont; will consult with Bayley about building roads through Dalton, New Hampshire.

Jeremiah Hill to George Thatcher. ALS, Chamberlain Collection, MB. Written from Biddeford, Maine. For the Portland Merchants' petition, see *DHFFC* 8:412–14.

People at Portland "very much chagrined" about the port collector's low compensation after expenses; they "would not find fault" if his annual compensation amounted to $750; is astonished that the Portland merchants' petition (of 29 December 1789) "should represent such awful Calculations, Matters & things to Congress, where accurate Calculations must detect them"; the secretary of the treasury's report on it "must glare them in the face like Death"; had intended to comment on Thatcher's letter to Daniel Cony (printed in the *Herald of Freedom*; see 31 January, above) and John Gardiner's response (printed in [Boston] *Massachusetts Centinel*; see 11 February, above), upon which "there is a great deal said."

John Langdon to Joseph Whipple. ALS, Sturgis Family Papers, MH. Addressed to Portsmouth, New Hampshire; franked; postmarked.

Has just received Whipple's letter of 10 February; repeats statement in his letter to Joshua Brackett, 15 February, regarding his willingness to be elected governor and his intention to resign from the Senate before June.

Walter Livingston to Robert Livingston, Jr. ALS, Roosevelt Library, Hyde Park, New York. Addressed to "Manor Livingston," comprising parts of present-day Dutchess and Columbia counties, New York; postmarked; a second postmark indicates the letter was miscarried to Philadelphia.

King and Sedgwick met with Hamilton, James Duane, and Brockholst Livingston at Walter Livingston's house for two hours on Friday, 19 February, as informal legal counsel in a property law case brought by Robert Livingston; they would convene again.

Dummer Sewall to George Thatcher. ALS, Thatcher Papers, MeHi. Written from Bath, Maine; franked.

Argues the necessity of a post office in Bath for speedy communication between the seat of government and the port's revenue officers, a coastal post road further east, and weekly mail delivery to Hallowell.

Theodore Sedgwick to Nathaniel Gorham. No copy known; acknowledged in Gorham to Sedgwick, 28 February.

Theodore Sedgwick to Benjamin Lincoln. No copy known; mentioned in Lincoln to Sedgwick, 3 March.

Theodore Sedgwick to Henry Van Schaack. No copy known; acknowledged in Van Schaack to Sedgwick, 10 March.

George Thatcher to Daniel Cony. No copy known; acknowledged in Cony to Thatcher, 27–28 February.

George Thatcher to Jeremiah Hill. No copy known; acknowledged in Hill to Thatcher, 3 March.

Otho H. Williams to [Benjamin Lincoln]. FC:dft, Williams Papers, MdHi. Written from Baltimore. This draft fills the blank pages of Lincoln's letter to Williams, 3 February, the endorsement sheet of which identifies Lincoln as the recipient.

John Lamb has written proposing to petition jointly on collectors' "emoluments," and to meet in New York City; "I am far from being disposed to the making of any *solicitations* about the matter"; has already spoken with Hamilton about "the unreasonableness of the Services required of Collectors, by the Present impost System, and the incompetency of the reward"; expects Hamilton will relay it to Congress; is thankful his personal situation does not require him to petition for employment; "I agree with you that it is humiliating."

William Samuel Johnson, Diary. Johnson Papers, CtHi.
"St. Pauls."

From New York. [Boston] *Massachusetts Centinel*, 3 March.
Believes discrimination between securities holders will be rejected by the
House the next day; "I think it involves the fate of the Constitution. I say
the Constitution—for should they determine a discrimination, away goes
the whole debt—our national character–and all hopes of future credit:
But I have no apprehension."

MONDAY, 22 FEBRUARY 1790

Rain (Johnson); *Some rain. Very mild* (J. B. Johnson)

Benjamin Goodhue to Samuel Phillips, Jr.

I am extreamly sorry to find by the public papers, that from indisposition, you have been obliged to quit your place in the Senate I sincerely hope
it may be but for a short period, tho' I must confess my fears have been for
a long time, that your rigid attention to your public and private bussines
was too great for your Constitution to sustain, and I think you must be fully
satisfied with the truth of the observation and I trust it may ~~in future~~ have
its deserved influence on your future conduct.

We have been this week past, and have yet come to no decission, on a
motion for making a discrimination between Original holders and present
possessors of securities, in this way, those in the hands of the Original pos-
sesor to have the full, those in the hands of purchasers to have the highest
market price say 10/ and the other 10/ to be paid to the original proprietor—this motion has much plausebility in its favour, but as it strikes at
the root of national faith, credit and policy, can never obtain the sanction of
the legislature, it has Madison for its supporter and perhaps when it is determined, which I expect will be this day, there may be 10 or 15 votes for the
affirmative, it is true the case of those who from necessity parted with their
securities for small sum, ~~and as~~ are entitled to our compassion and generosity, and if our abilities admited ought to be ~~releif~~ releived, but not at the
expence of our public engagements, the subject of funding the debt I clearly
see will take up a long time before any decissive measures are adopted, and
what they will be is altogether uncertain, I am fearfull the opposition to
the assumption of the State debts, will be so great, as to prevent its taking
effect this session, tho' I am not without hope—I am inclined to believe,
that nothing will induce them to the measure, but the impracticability of

availing ourselves of proper resources, while simular modes of revenue exist necessarily in the State Governments for providing for their own debts, under this idea, will it not be wise for Massachusetts to continue her excise, as a means of accomplishing the object.*

I wish if you find yourself in sufficient health, you would give me your thoughts on the momentous bussines in which We are engaged.

[P. S.] I have not yet heard or seen anything of Mr. Lakeman.

*Since writing the above I find by conversation with Mr. Hamilton, that he fully joins me in opinion on the continuence of State Excises for the above purpose, and was glad I had urged the measure, therefore if you can it may not be amiss to write some members of the General Court, on the subject but Keep our names out of sight.

ALS, Phillips Family Papers, MHi. Place to which addressed not indicated.

Daniel Hiester to John Nicholson

I reced. Yours in favour of Mr. [*John*] Baird by Mr. [*Arthur*] St. Clair yesterday, and wish it may fall in my way to render him a Service. I have long esteemed him a worthy man, and am Assured he has qualified himself for such an Appointmt.

Mr. Madisons Motion [*for discrimination*] was this day rejected by a great Majority. the Committee proceeded to declare that the Arrearage of Interest shod. be funded on the same terms with the Principal by a still greater Majority, and from what has happened I am led to think, had it not been moved for the Committee to rise the funding the State debts wod. have passed with equal Facility that subject will probably be determined tomorrow if it is I will inform You of it ℣ first opporty.

ALS, Nicholson Papers, PHarH. Addressed to Philadelphia; franked; postmarked 23 February; received 25 February.

Peter Muhlenberg to Benjamin Rush

This day Mr. Madisons Motion was Negativd by a considerable Majority; and we are now on the resolution relative to the assumption of the State Debts on the issue of this, the fate of The System will much depend.

I have but just time, before the closing of The Mail to forward the enclosd.

[*Enclosure*]

The following Subjects are hereby recomended to Mr. Trumbull as highly proper, to be transmitted, upon Canvas to posterity as part of the History of The American Revolution.[1]

I.

A Speculator in Certificates riding in a Chariot and four over an American Soldier, who is unable to move out of his way, in consequence of the loss of one of his Legs.

II.

An American Major in Livery, waiting at the Table of a Man, who was the Barkeeper of a Tavern in the year 1774, and who has acquired an estate of 1500£ a year by buying Officers & Soldiers Certificates at 2/6 in the pound.

III.

An old Serjeant who survivd the Wounds he receivd in the attack upon Stony point, under General [*Anthony*] Wayne, driven from the door of a Tory Merchant, who bought his Certificate. The Serjeant appears in the humble posture of a Beggar points to his Wounds, and asks only for a loaf of Bread The Merchant seems to say to him, "begone you Dog—you now enjoy the reward of your rebellion."

IV.

An American Lieutenant selling his Watch & Shoebuckles for half price to raise a little cash, to pay his proportion of the interest due on a Certificate, which he sold to a Captain in the Brittish refugee Corps, that hung Captn. Huddy on the Jersey shore.[2]

V.

A Sheriffs sale at which 39 farms are sold at the [*lined out*] sale bought for funded Certificates for half price by two New York & Philada. Speculators, and the wretched owners of them of driven with a single Horse & Cow to Kentuke & Niagara.

VI.

An American Major General, who sold his Certificates for 2/6 in the pound in the year 1784 dying with a broken Heart in an American Goal.

VII.

A Widow Lady who sold a Certificate of £1000 for 200£ standing over a Washtub in the Kitchen of a Broker who receives 40£ a year on her Certificate.

8.

Mr. M-d-n [*Madison*] pleading the cause of Justice & Humanity in Congress, an Angel whispering in his ear, and a Groupe of Widows Orphans & decrepid Soldiers, contemplating him with ineffable delight.

9.

Genl. W-n, holding in his hand, His Farewell to The Army,[3] & lamenting even the Act of Congress for Alienating the Certificates of His beloved Army without allowing an equivalent for them.

ALS, Gratz Collection, PHi. Addressed to Philadelphia; franked; postmarked 23 February. Enclosure in Muhlenberg's hand, John Trumbull Papers, CtY. The editors confirmed that the document at Yale had been enclosed with this letter by comparing numbers on both documents placed there after they were removed from Rush's Papers in the nineteenth century and before they were sold at auction in 1943 and 1944. Although the enclosure is headed with the phrase "for the Phil. Indepent. Gazetteer" in an unknown contemporary hand, no newspaper printing has been found.

[1] John Trumbull's proposed series of paintings of the American Revolution was first advertised in *GUS* on 23 January, and subscriptions to the engravings solicited at three guineas per print. Thirteen scenes were initially proposed: the battles of Bunker Hill, Quebec, and Princeton; the British surrenders at Trenton, Saratoga, and Yorktown; the signing of the Declaration of Independence, the treaty with France in 1778, and the Peace Treaty of 1783; the British evacuation of New York later that year; and Washington's triumphal procession through Trenton in 1789 and inauguration at Federal Hall. Fenno published a broadside on 2 April (Evans 22946) advertising a fourteenth installment that would depict the Battle of Eutaw Springs. The first two paintings were already being engraved in Europe when Trumbull announced the series. Disappointed with the response, Trumbull completed only the *Battle of Princeton* before abandoning the project in 1794 when he sailed to Europe as secretary to John Jay in his treaty negotiations with Great Britain. The next five scenes listed above were the only others ever to be completed.

[2] The capture and subsequent execution of New Jersey militia captain Joseph Huddy while on parole and waiting to be exchanged by the Associated Loyalists in 1782 was a breach of protocol that became a byword for British perfidy and the victimization of the common soldier.

[3] Washington issued his paternal and optimistic "Farewell Address" to the Army as his final Orders from headquarters near Princeton, New Jersey, on 2 November 1783. It closed with the wish "that he was really able to be usefull to them all in future life" and that "he can only again offer in their behalf his recommendations to their grateful Country" (Transcript, Washington Papers, DLC).

David Sewall to George Thatcher

My last I think was from Boston since which I am returned, and about the middle of this Week I expect to depart for Witscassett—I hear nothing as yet respecting the several queries I gave you—and what I Wrote the Vice President, save that a Bill describing Crimes and Punishments had by the News Paper Intelligence passed the Senate—I wish that this Bill may fully Solve my doubts—But unless something is done to it in the House beyond what the Senate did—from what I hear it will be in my humble Opinion deficient—for [*lined out*] want of Some explicit provision respecting the mode of [*lined out*] carrying Sentence into Execution upon Persons Capitally Convicted—Are they to be beheaded, shot, drowned Hanged, or Burt, &c. &c. This Idea may at first appear unnecessary—you will say perhaps that Hanging has been the common mode of Execution, and doubtless that will be adopted. Be it So But then is it not Easy for the Legislature to Say so & in case they say nothing about it and the Court should order the Convict to be Shot, will it be Illegal—I am informed that no provision is made respecting the Death Warrant—when the Bill passd. the Senate, altho' the matter was urged—The very Reasons given for not making such provision carry with me very cogent arguments that It ought to be made—That the Senate differed among themselves—Some Supposed the President had the Power of Course and others that it was Incident to the Court Who gave Sentence.

The President has the power of Pardoning—But if the Court can legally Issue Warrant for Execution—They may very easily prevent the Exercise of this Constitutional Power—especially in the remote parts of the Union—A short day after Conviction ~~will~~ assignd for Execution will make a Pardon too late. I was in expe[c]tation of having something upon this Subject before my departure Eastward—But unless it comes by the Post tomorrow—my Expectations will be ended for the present—I find Mr. G. [*John Gardiner*] Intentions in his Bustle for a Reforme—are now pretty generally understood—I find in a late *Centinel* He addresses you respecting a paragraff in a Letter it is said you Wrote to Docr. [*Daniel*] Cony[1] His Reform Bills have hitherto come to a poor market I do not learn that any one has got to a 3rd. Reading in the House *** I find from the Congressional Intelligence that you presented Po[r]tland Petition,[2] notwithstanding it was by your Suggestions addressed to Brother Ames—The Report of the Secretary [*on public credit*] upon a 2d. Reading strikes me more agreably [*lined out*] than it did at First—indeed I did not fully understand him—nor perhaps do I now—My decided opinion is, in favour of an assumption of the State debts Incurred on the Common Account—The arguments adduced by the Secretary are conclusive—And that it is for the Interest of the States Severally—and the U.S. conjunctly that it should be Spedily effected—Whether it is in the Power of Congress ~~of~~ at this time to fund the Whole at the present Interest, with a Rational Prospect of punctually complying with paimt. of Int. I am unable to say—But certainly Congress can more readily call forth the Resorces for this purpose than to make a partition between the Several States, of the Resources—The latter method will certainly tend to an Interference, in some of the Important Branches of Revennue and of course a competition between State & continental creditors—I wish you may be directed to do in this, and the many other important matters that necessarily arise, for the Union, What will be most conducive to their essential Interest.
***

ALS, Autograph Collection, MHi. Written from York, Maine; postmarked Portsmouth, New Hampshire, 23 February. The omitted text relates to state judicial business and local weather.

[1]The Letter to Thatcher inserted at the request of "J. G." and dated 11 February (above), appeared in the [Boston] *Massachusetts Centinel*, 13 February. Thatcher's letter to Cony, to which it in part replies, is printed under 31 January, above.

[2] The petition of the merchants and other inhabitants of Portland, Maine, presented in the House on 26 January; see *DHFFC* 8:412–18.

William Smith (Md.) to Otho H. Williams

The following resolutions, have been passed, in committee of the whole house. Viz. Resolved, That adequate provision ought to be made for fulfilling the engagements of the U.S., in respect to their foreign debt.

Resolved, that permanent funds ought to be appropriated for the payment of interest on, & the gradual discharge of the domestic debt of the United States. Resolved, that the arrears of Interest, including indents issued in payment thereof, ought to be provided for on the same terms with the principal of the said debt.

Thus far, have we got & no further; The motion for a discrimination was rejected by a great majority, not more than twelve, or thirteen in favor of that amendment. To morrow comes on the question. "That the debts of the Respective States ought to be with the consent of the creditors. to be assumed & provided for by the United States"; on this question we will be more divided; I have seen or heard no opinion from our State on [t]his head. Whatever may be the determination. I discover that those Politicians, who prevented the Maryland Assembly from complying With the requisitions of Congress, made in 1787, whereby Indents were made receivable for the respective quota of each States *interest* due the U.S. have done an irreparable injury to us. And that finally we will be obliged to make good that deficiency, in Specie this will give a great advantage to those States who were so Judicious as to comply.

A few days past a British Sloop of war arrived at this port; Various are the conjectures on this event. All I Know for certain, is that the commander brought a large Packet for Sir John Temple, & An other for the President, which he Says, he was directed to deliver to *Sir John* with positive instructions that he should See, the same deliverd by *him*, into the Presidents hands, & this he has done—It is Supposed these dispatches are for Lord Dorchester & that [*lined out*] Canada, not being accessible at this Season through St. Lawrence the British Minister has availed himself of communicating through this channell—others Suppose that it is nothing more than to announce to the United States, that the British ports are open for Ama. [*American*] wheat, but this would not, I think have been so long concealed—Let us Suppose, That the purport of those dispatches, are to order the [*lined out*] British posts within the limits of the U.S. to be evacuated, & to offer us an Advantagious commercial treaty.

ALS, Williams Papers, MdHi. Place to which addressed not indicated.

Governor Edward Telfair to the Georgia Delegation

I have reason to expect a reply to my Address to you of the 15th. day of December last past, in a short time; a due observance of the communication above alluded to, is of much importance to this State, and doubt not of your exertions in the execution thereof.

The Secretaries of the Treasury and War Departments have made communications to me, which are replied to; copies of them are herewith transmitted, by which you will be competent to judge of the objects presented for consideration.

The interest of this State will require serious reflections on the measures that will present themselves to view in the course of the deliberations of the present Session of Congress. each State has the indubitable right, and will doubtless exercise it, of applying the respective funds and resources belonging thereto, to the discharge of the domestic debt thereof; and a departure therefrom, would be a manifest injury to this State.

The debts of the United States may be said to be divided into two seperate and distinct claims. the foreign debt, it would appear, must be provided for in gold or silver, or funded on that principle. the payment of the annual interest, appears to be all that will be in the power of Congress for some time; this measure will, no doubt, present itself to view.

The domestic debt, presents itself, under a variety of complicated forms; to draw a conclusion thereon, it will be best to have retrospect to the nature and origin of the same; for the expenditures of the late war, Congress emitted from time to time large sums in bills of Credit, which were applied to various exigencies of Government, in the course of the contest, depreciation took place thereon; and continued from period to period, until they were totally rejected, and here it may be remarked, that every person who held the aforesaid bills, contributed (according to the sum in his hands, and the length of time in his possession) to the sinking of the same, or, in fact, it operated as a Tax, falling most burthensome on him in whose hands it sunk: during this complicated state of national concern many individual injuries did arise, that from the nature of the case were unavoidable.

The outstanding securities of the United States, have arisen from the exigencies of Government, before and since the reduction of the paper bills of Credit, and become a debt on the United States: a question now arises, on the best and most equitable mode of taking up and providing for the same; were the securities in the hands of the Original holders, the redemption thereof would appear to claim a liberal provision on the part of Congress; this being evidently not the case, and by recurring to the foregoing clause, you will find great difficulty in making arrangements on that head, so as to extend equal justice to all: two plans present themselves on this occasion for redemption;

the one, by quota on the several States; the other to provide for the interest annually, and to avail of national expedients in taking up the same.

The sense of the General Assembly on the territorial rights of the State, is so fully ascertained, by the Act of the last Session [*the Yazoo sale*], that it is altogether unnecessary for me to comment thereon. the Confiscations of this State were made in the face of an enemy consisting of at least double the number of her Citizens, those acts were of a local nature, and in this State were revenged by bloodshed, the unrelenting depredations of war and all the cruelty of oppressive tyranny, and these funds have been and are applied to the State emergencies to which they of right belong.

The communication of the Honorable William Few Esq. of the 12fth. Ultimo, on the subject of Indian affairs will be understood by the inclosed dispatches[1] which comprehend all I have been able to collect on the head, and will readily point out to you, that a negotiator in the first instance together with other necessary appointments might be best calculated for the present conjuncture.

[Enclosures]
[To Henry Knox, 16 February]

The delay of a reply to your communication of the 24th. November last arose from doubts that existed respecting the disposition of the Creeks towards the Citizens of this State; it is now near four months since these Indians have desisted from every species of hostility, and are daily evincing their friendly intentions by an amiable intercourse with the remote settlers, and from present appearances I have reason to hope that they will not attempt future depredations. If contrary to expectation they should depart from the present tenor of their conduct, no time shall be lost in giving the necessary information.

The regulation of Commerce with the Indian tribes ought to be governed by one uniform system, as well as that of fit and qualified persons being appointed to superintend such commercial regulations as Congress may deem best calculated to promote confidence and secure harmony between the Citizens and Indians.

[To Alexander Hamilton, 19 February]

Your Communication of the 26th September last came to hand on the 17th. December thereafter. the Executive order thereon, with the reports of the respective Officers are herewith transmitted: You will observe by that of the Auditor, that the derangement of the finances of this State will preclude me for some considerable time from making any Statement that can lead to the information required.

Till of late we have been in a State of warfare or apprehension since the close of the late war—troops were raised for the common defence, that since only been discharged a few days and the payment thereof not yet completed—considerable advances made by the Citizens, as well as services performed by them in defence of the State also remain for future liquidation.

Notwithstanding the present derangement I have every reason to hope, that the funds and resources of this State will prove adequate to the extinguishment of her domestic debt, at least so far as to prevent any burthensome taxation for the accomplishment thereof.

FC, Georgia Executive Council Journal, G-Ar; a duplicate of the cover letter was sent to the delegation on 17 March. Written from State House, Augusta, Georgia. The letter appeared in [Georgia] *Augusta Chronicle*, 10 July. The communication by Hamilton referred to by Telfair is probably Hamilton's circular to the governors of the states dated 21 November 1789, reminding them of his letter of 26 September requesting a statement of the amount of federal public securities in state treasuries (*PAH* 5:411, 534–35).

---

[1] Not identified.

OTHER DOCUMENTS

Elias Boudinot to William Bradford, Jr. No copy known; mentioned in Charles Pettit to Boudinot, 25 February.

Nicholas Eveleigh to Tench Coxe. ALS, Coxe Papers, PHi. Addressed to Philadelphia; franked by Hamilton; postmarked 23 February.
   The question of discriminating between securities holders is expected to be decided this day; expects it will not be carried; in postscript, reports the question "is just this moment decided, minority 11."

Thomas Fitzsimons to Tench Coxe. ALS, Coxe Papers, PHi. Addressed to Philadelphia; franked; postscript written in the afternoon; postmarked 23 February.
   Will dedicate the "first leisure I have" to reply to the important subject of Coxe's last letter of 15 February; expects motion on discrimination between securities holders will be decided that day; the present letter is only to enclose the Patents Act, "that if anything Occurs to you respecting it I may benefit of your Good Advice"; a postscript reports the assumption of the states' war debts would be taken up the next day.

Benjamin Goodhue to Michael Hodge. ALS, Ebenezer Stone Papers, MSaE. Place to which addressed not indicated. For the full text, see *EIHC* 84(April 1948):150.
   Expects question on discrimination between securities holders will be decided that day, with no prospect of passing; provides New York City prices of goods and securities.

Thomas Hartley to Jasper Yeates. ALS, Yeates Papers, PHi. Addressed to
Lancaster, Pennsylvania; franked; postmarked 23 February; answered 27 February.

> The motion to discriminate between securities holders was just that mo-
> ment defeated, 30 to 13; second (of Fitzsimons' resolutions of 8 February)
> agreed to unanimously "and we are now again under way"; the arguments
> on funding have been lengthy, "but the out lines are by this Time better un-
> derstood. we expect more business hereafter"; intends to be home in April.

George Thatcher to David Sewall. No copy known; acknowledged in Sewall
to Thatcher, 11 March.

Jeremiah Wadsworth to John Chaloner. ALS, Chaloner and White Papers,
PHi. Addressed to Philadelphia; franked; postmarked 23 February.

> Urgently requests information respecting some business venture involving
> them, Hamilton, and John B. Church; "I do not know what project Col.
> Hamilton has about Vendues for the truth is I do not see him once in a Week
> as I wish to avoid seeing him till I can give him some satisfactory answer to
> the questions that he too often asks me respecting the concern with you."

William Webb to George Thatcher. ALS, Chamberlain Collection, MB.
Written from Bath, Maine.

> Office seeking: Dummer Sewall for postmaster of Bath; if appointed, the
> proximity of his residence would enable Webb to forward his returns as
> collector at Bath more conveniently.

Manasseh Cutler, Diary. Cutler Papers, IEN.

> "Called on a number of my friends. Delivered Letters. Attended debates
> in Congress, very much entertained. The Hall appears superb. After
> diner, waited on several members of Congress."

Letter from New York. *PP*, 26 February; reprinted at Baltimore.

> The question of discriminating between securities holders was rejected,
> only eleven voting in favor; the second and third resolutions were then
> carried; the fourth resolution, for assuming the states' war debts, "is the
> next to be considered."

Letter from New York. *PP*, 26 February; reprinted at Baltimore and Winchester, Virginia.

> The "grand question" for discriminating between securities holders was
> rejected that day, 47 to 11; the next day the House will take up as-
> sumption of the states' war debts, "which no doubt will bring on a very

warm debate—the general expectation is that it will not be agreed to this session."

TUESDAY, 23 FEBRUARY 1790

Rain (Johnson); *Some rain, muggy and close* (J. B. Johnson)

Edward Fox to Andrew Craigie

***

The speeches of Messrs. Sedgwick, Smith [*S.C.*] & Aims, have done considerable service to the cause of public Credit here: they have cleared up many doubts, and oblige some of our clamourous ones to be silent. How can Madisons conduct be accounted for? It is said he is honest and well informed, and that he possesses considerable abilities. These things being true, make a very strange character, when they are compared with his conduct upon the business before the Legislature [*on discrimination*].

Are you acquainted with Sedgwick? Is he an influential Man at head Quarters? He is a distant relative of my wife's [*Elizabeth Sargent Fey*]—and altho' he does not know me, yet he might possibly befriend me, if in his power.
***

ALS, Craigie Papers, MWA. Written from Philadelphia; postmarked 24 February.

Richard Bland Lee to Charles Lee

I have received your letter of the 31st. Ultimo—and had answered it ~~and~~ but have lately discovered that I neglected to send my letter.

Since writing that letter we have been busily engaged in discussing the principles of the Secretary's report [*on public credit*]. One great preliminary question introduced and supported by Mr. Madison in the most eloquent and able manner was to make such a discrimination between the original holders who had alienated their claims, and the *present* possessors of the debt, as to give to the latter the highest *market* price at which the public Securities had sold—consoli~~at~~dating these with the interest which had accrued on the principal in their possession and ~~unpaid~~ was unpaid so as to make a new principal bearing an interest of 6 per Cent.—and to restore to the original holders the balancce which balance to bear a like rate of interest This proposition was finally rejected by a great majority.

We are now employed in discussing another leading feature of the report, the assumption of the state debts by the U. States. From the explanations which have taken place, I have no doubt in my mind that this part of the

Secretary's plan will be agreed to—tho' it will be distasteful to some of the states, probably to Virginia: all that we shall be able to do will be to secure to our state such a settlement of her accounts, as will intitle her to a proper credit for her expenditures. during the late War. And if we can obtain a settlement on liberal and just principles the state will certainly be a gainer, so far as pecuniary considerations have weight; and the poeple will probably be relieved from direct taxes—For the Eastern states are almost unanimously opposed to direct taxation, and the late insurrection in that state[1] has been attributed to the attempt of the government to raise money in that war. And direct taxes are more or less odious in all the states. Consequently other means of raising a revenue will be resorted to—and probably the indirect sources may be so extended as to produce the sum wanted—The duties on imports, Mr. Hamilton's inspection plan, the Post office, and a tax in the nature of stamp duties—may possibly furnish the adequate revenue.

The spirit of liberty seems to be extending over the European World. The Brabantes are likely to be successful in their atte[*mpt*] to throw off the Yoke of the Emper[*or*][2] The Poeple of Spain seem to be catching the spirit of their neighbours.

The crops of grain are very defective in Great Britain. A British sloop of war arrived here a few days ago—and brought with her the act of the Court of London taking off the prohibition of the importation of American wheat. Wheat is very high in England. And such are the European demands for grain—that it is probable the price will continue high for some years, when we take into [*lined out*] view the present convulsed state of that part the Globe—So that in my opinion that we cannot at this time extend the cultivation of grain too far—And it is my advice to cultivate as much corn and other spring grain as possible—and to take the best care of the Winter crops: and if Tobacco should be in a great measure relinquished by the poeple in general, our crops will be increased in their value two ways—the price of grain will be very high—let the crop be what it will and that of Tobacco will be enhanced if the quantity made is lessened. It might perhaps be prudent to impress these ideas on the poeple—as such a [*c*]ourse will certainly terminate to their advantage. I hope you will soon have the survey of our joint speculation made—so that I may immediately comply with my contract with Mr. Arthur Lee.

***

ALS, Custis-Lee Papers, DLC. Place to which addressed not indicated. The recipient has been identified by the handwriting of the endorsement. The omitted text is advice for planting.

[1] Shays' Rebellion.
[2] Brabant was one of the seven provinces that made up the Austrian Netherlands of the

Holy Roman Emperor Joseph II. In October 1789 the Brabants revolted against Joseph's statist reforms. They declared their independence as the United States of Belgium on 11 January 1790; the revolt was suppressed by year's end.

John Pemberton to James Pemberton

I wrote my Dear Wife [*Hannah Zane Pemberton*] on first day in which I acknowledged the Receipt of thy favor of 16th. Inst. & yesterday thy further favor of the 18th. came to hand. I wish Our friends who met with so much difficulty on their return had taken advice & continued here.[1] & tho' some might rejoyce at their Departure, there are others who have expressed sorrow—One of the Delegates said there was a loss in their absence. apprehending while we were together there was a aid. We who remain were affected in hearing the last evening, that the Senate had agreed to accept the Temptation held out to the Congress by the state of North Carolina.[2] there were but two who appeared to Oppose it. Bassett & Wyngate, the first was earnest they sent a message to the lower house. with this Account. This made a stir this morning & renewed our request to divers members to be on their guard & not to act as the senate had done, but there is too much reason to fear it will be adopted. but when men are guided by the Wisdom which is Earthly & sensual. what can be expected. the Eastern Members are very desirous that Vermont shall be Acknowledged. apprehending it will throw' a weight in thier scale. & so are in danger of joining the Southern proposal too much like Scratch me & I will scratch thee. They erected a state to the westward where they guarded agst. there being any Slaves. & now the senate has acceeded to the No. Ca. proposal in which is this Clause "Provided always that no regulation made or to be made by Congress shall tend to emancipate slaves." Once declare all men are by nature free. & then declare men shall not be made free. Much pains has been taken to expose their Inconsistency. but self ends & party views warps aside however Friends must Console themselves, in this, they have done what they could. Some of the members friendly to the Cause say there is an overuling power & what we have in view will be effected in kind. As the Comittee app[*ointe*]d. in Consequence of the Adresses[3] proposed to meet again to morrow morning to agree upon their report it is probable it may be proposed to the House to morrow after which we may be better able to determine our departure. yet wish to be present at the Debate upon the result of the Comittee, & also upon the Carolina proposal.

It was a singular favor our freinds escaped without having their bones broken & also from being drowned. I expect it brought some questioning whether they did well in leaving N. York. We have wanted the Adresses

printed here, but not yet got it done. tho' it would remove missapprehen-
sions from some of the Inhabitants who seem alarmed with Apprehension
we are soliciting for all slaves to be set immediately free.

What may be done in the militia law is Uncertain, the report from the
secretary [*on public credit*] takes up much time. Divers men here tell us we
need not fear but care will be taken respecting our religious Society, & also
respecting other tender People.[4]

W[*arner*]. M[*ifflin*]. & J[*ohn*]. Parrish Dined with M[*iers*]. Fisher at the
French Consuls [*St. Jean de Crèvecoeur*] yesterday & spent several hours there
much to their satisfaction. ***

ALS, Pennsylvania Abolition Society Papers, PHi. Addressed to Second Street, Philadelphia; postmarked; received 26 February. The omitted text relates to friends' health, missionary efforts in Europe, and Quaker administrative affairs.

[1] Pemberton here refers to the seven members of the Quaker delegation who accompanied
the petition to New York City and then returned to Pennsylvania immediately after the
petition was referred to committee.
[2] On 22 February, the Senate agreed to a committee report proposing the acceptance of
North Carolina's cession of the territory that became Tennessee "upon the Conditions therein
contained" (*DHFFC* 6:1544–51).
[3] The antislavery petitions; see *DHFFC* 8:314–38.
[4] Members of the peace churches.

Annis Boudinot Stockton to Elias Boudinot

***

Make my most tender regards to my dear sister [*Hannah Stockton Boudinot*],
whom I hope enjoys her health at new york this winter for tho a very moderate one, I think it more trying to a delicate Constitution than a severely
Cold one.

Deluged in politics, I suppose you never can find a moments time to let
such little folks as your sister, have a line from you Concerning state affairs
or any other—as you know, I am a little blasted with the flame of patriotism,
I can not but wish to know a little of what is going forward. I wish supplying the poets Corner—with one little matter or other, would bring me fenos
paper[1]—it would chear many a dull hour, in reading what I should have
so often the pleasure of seeing your name and the efforts you make to serve
your Country—Dicky [*Richard Stockton, Jr.*] takes the papers but between
him and capt. [*Samuel*] pintard, and their hurry to file them—I never get
a sight of them—but Joking [?] a part about the poetry—I will thank you
if you would make enquiry of Mr. Feno, wether they could be had to a year

back—if they could I shoud strive hard but I would take them—they are by far the best papers on the Continent in my opinion— ***

ALS, Boudinot Collection, NjP. Written from Princeton, New Jersey; franked; answered.

[1] Although not referred to by that name in John Fenno's *GUS*, the "Poet's Corner" was a standard feature of many newspapers in which poetry, *bon mots*, and other purely literary submissions were printed.

Samuel W. Stockton to Elias Boudinot

***

I have lately heard that you have gained an encreased reputation among the *Quakers* for your assiste. on their petition agt. the *Slave trade* &c.—dont forget to forward by Mr. Cox[1] or perhaps sooner the late numbers of the Congres[*siona*]l. Register—I have recd. the 18th. I expect there will be warmer debates on the question of assuming the State debts & *the lowering the Int. to 4 ⅌ Cent. or* recd. *1/3d. of the principal in back lands*—I hope there will be found many & able advocates agt. the last measure—as *it is not a fair equivalent*—The small creditors would be absolutely *robbed* by it—as they never could make any option of taking western lands—suppose one to pos- sess a *capital* only of 600 Dol. he must accept 200 of it in Back lands wch. wd. never at any rate answer any purpose to look after at such a distance—& with respect to the large Creditors, it is also *compulsory* & not optional—But the measure is totally *unconstitutional* with out a fair equivalent—The interest is as much a part of *the contract* as the principal—& they can as justly take from the one as the other But *"all contracts* under the former govermts. are held sacred"[2]—How would the *federal Judges on oath then*, on the question being brought before them say—They must declare *the law* which shd. go counter to this *Constitution null & void*—If we could but permit our new governmt. to be without one *Stain* on its national character, how it would delight every good & liberal minded man—& how beneficial to the govermt. itself—the lowering the interest to 4 per Cent, at a future day, when our necessities call for another loan wd. cost the govermt. 12 ⅌ Cent as the *risk of paymt. would be so much* greater, after one breach of contract, the *premium* on borrowg., wd. of course be so *much higher.* But *how inconsistent* wd. the new govermt. be with itself—They have ordered a *new Register of the public Securities* to as many as please under a *new & specified promise* of *paying 6 ⅌ Cent.* interest. Continental money & all our former *faux pas* we may resolve into the defects of our old governmt.—but do not let the *new* be *infected* wth. them—consider of *future consequences & be wise in time.* I have written hastily & have no time to read it—therefore take it as it is—The little *woman* [*Catherine Cox Stockton?*]

in the straw is bravely, and her little son also & send much love & greet-
ing—she says her boy is so like her old *gray headed* brother, And she having
a *presentiment* some how or other, (as nurses & women in the straw are apt to
have) that [*he*] will be a *very clever fellow,* that is now determined, he shall be
named *Elias Boudinot,* that, when all your grey hairs have become perfectly
white & your age makes you hobble in your gait, You may, if you please, use
him as a *cane* to walk with to Church for he has at part[*icula*]r. times, *exactly
your Sunday mouth.*

ALS, Stimson Boudinot Collection, NjP. Written from Trenton, New Jersey; to be carried
by Mr. Cox but sent by post instead. The omitted text relates to Boudinot's business affairs.

[1] Stockton had assumed when writing the letter that it would be carried to New York by
Cox, probably his father-in-law John Cox or a member of his immediate family.
[2] A paraphrase of the first paragraph of Article VI of the Constitution.

Letter from New York

In my last I expressed my astonishment at the conduct of some of our
high flying Federalists, on the subject of Finance—Madison's ill conceived
system, will to-morrow be consigned to everlasting repose.[1] There appears a
fixed and determined majority against it. The adoption of it would have implied the utmost injustice, as well as the extreme of folly in the public Councils of his country: For how can it be otherwise, when the party becomes the
Judges in the cause depending? Congress have the right only of finding the
means, the *principles* and *terms* of performance, are beyond the power of any
Government, in every contract. We complain, as it were instinctively, of the
tediousness of our public deliberations in almost every state in the Union.
But the slowest of them move with the rapidity of a Comet, in comparison
with those of the Federal Head. It would be a good rule if the speeches of
gentlemen, like the sales of an auction, were to be struck off by an inch of
candle. Upon the subject of discrimination, the argument rests on but few
points; yet, what would you think of a speech of two hours, when, perhaps,
the session of the day is but three? If you read what is published, you will find
that these speeches are but the copies of each other as to substance, though
the manner may be widely different; In fact, we seem to be enchanted to a
spot. We talk a great deal; but we advance not forward. Hamilton's plan has
been before Congress three weeks, and we are not even in the title page. At
this rate, the Lord only knows when we shall get thro' it. Some of our orators
remind me of the Dutchman, who in celebrating the literary accomplishments of his father, said he was certainly the greatest writer of the age—for
he had published seven folios already. I like Goodhue extremely. His longest

effort does not exceed the time which another takes for his preface, and yet, I know not whether he has not said everything to the purpose which the subject will admit.

The rate of interest appears to me the only question, and, here we shall find a strange contrariety of sentiment among the members: but when the final settlement of our final certificates will take place, it is not even within the reach of conjecture—Perhaps, *cum prima hirundine*;[2] Perhaps, But I will not even surmise; I hope, however, before the solstice. For the long declamations of some of the gentlemen in hot weather would be truly insufferable.

Boston Gazette, 1 March; reprinted in whole or in part in Providence, Rhode Island; Norwich and New London, Connecticut; and Lansingburgh, New York.

[1] The prediction regarding Madison's motion on discrimination suggests that this letter is misdated; it may have been written on 21 February.
[2] The first swallow (does not make a summer).

OTHER DOCUMENTS

Samuel Johnston to James Iredell. No copy known; mentioned in Johnston to Iredell, 24 February.

Abigail Rogers to Daniel Denison Rogers. ALS, Miscellaneous Collection, MHi. Addressed to Petersburg, Virginia; postmarked 7 March. This letter, which was written over the course of two weeks, is also the source of a calendar entry dated 7 March, below.
    "Bland is exceeding sick, with the Gout, poor Gentleman! his groans, at times, calls forth every sympathetic feeling"; attended House debates the day before, but "there was not any distinguished Caracters that spoke."

Charles Storer to John Adams. ALS, Adams Family Manuscript Trust, MHi. Written from Troy, New York; answered 20 March.
    Office seeking: first secretary to the secretary of state.

Willing, Morris, & Swanwick to John Langdon. ALS, Langdon Papers, NhPoA. Written from Philadelphia.
    Hopes Congress, by restoring public credit, will be exalted "in the Minds of all Reasonable and Just Men."

Manasseh Cutler, Diary. Cutler Papers, IEN.
    "Attended Debates."

WEDNESDAY, 24 FEBRUARY 1790

Rain (Johnson); *Rain. Clear. Cloudy. Evening windy* (J. B. Johnson)

George Clymer to Timothy Pickering

I made ineffectual attempts 'till the third day to enter Chaos—the Assemblage of old Congress papers—Mr. [*Roger*] Alden the keeper of Chaos on search could not discover the paper you desire—It then occurred to me That the shortest way would be to write to one of the Judges who passed the decree,[1] and accordingly by this post I have addressed a letter to Mr. [*David*] Brearley at Trenton to requesting him, to save time, to inform you of the truth of the fact relative to the story of the letter recommendation said to have accompanied the decree of Trenton—this I make no doubt he will do—The mail just on the point of closing.

ALS, Pickering Papers, MHi. Place to which addressed not indicated. The letter is apparently misdated 23 February.

[1] The Wyoming Valley on the East Branch of the Susquehannah River above present-day Wilkes-Barre had been the object of competing and sometimes violent jurisdiction and land title claims between Pennsylvania and Connecticut since the early 1760s. In December 1782 a federal court convened at Trenton, New Jersey, under Article IX of the Articles of Confederation, decreed in favor of Pennsylvania's jurisdiction over the contested Wyoming Territory. In 1787 the Pennsylvania legislature adopted the Wyoming Act, confirming land titles granted by Connecticut in the disputed area. The issue heated up in early 1790 when the Pennsylvania legislature debated and then, on 1 April, repealed the Wyoming Act.

Manasseh Cutler to Oliver Everett

I arrived in this city on Sunday, on Monday attended the debates in Congress. The most of last week was taken up with a very unexpected motion from Mr. Madison, for making a discrimination between original holders and purchasers of securities. A motion of this kind from a member of less consequence than Mr. M. would have been smiled at, but his character gave it importance. The principal speakers were engaged in the debates. I was, however, so unfortunate as to hear very little from the first characters, as the subject was nearly exhausted, and left to the bickerings of some of the smaller folks. On taking the question Mr. M. had the mortification, which he appeared sensibly to feel, to be in a minority—only 13 for the motion. The next question was the funding the domestic debt. It was contested, but none of the great characters arose. It passed in the affirmative by a very great majority.

The next question, which employed yesterday and this day, was on the assumption of the State Debts. This was held up as a most important question, involving in it the whole system of the Secretary of the Treasury, and in its consequences materially affecting the very existence of the Union. All the great characters were engaged, and much ability and eloquence was displayed.

Mr. Gerry ably defended the assumption on anti-federal ground. His principal arguments were that if the State debts were not assumed, the States being absolutely unable, at present, to secure funds for the payment of their debts, would become less popular and less important in the view of the people. The State creditors would feel themselves injured, while they were neglected, and the Continental provided for, and their wish and exertions would be to diminish the State and exercise the Continental powers. And that if the States should ever find it necessary to oppose the General Government, a heavy debt and the charge of a violated faith would frustrate all their attempts. The most violent and clamorous opposer of the assumption was Mr. Stone, of Maryland. Although the question is not yet taken, there is not the smallest doubt of its being carried in the affirmative. Just before the Committee rose this afternoon, there appeared evidently to be a coalescence of parties, in consequence of an amendment proposed by Mr. Madison, that the credits as well as the debts of the States should be assumed, and a final settlement of accounts, between all the States from the commencement of the war, be adjusted. It is, however, not improbable that it may be several days before the question is taken. If this question passes in the affirmative, there seems to be little doubt of the adoption of the whole system of the Secretary of the Treasury.

***

Cutler 1:458–60. The omitted text includes a request for information about the status of Nathaniel Gorham's and Oliver Phelps's Genessee Purchase, "from a probability that if I was furnished with the present state of their Purchase it may be of some advantage in securing the influence of some members in Congress in accomplishing our wishes," that is, renegotiating the terms of Cutler's Ohio Company purchase of 1787.

Benjamin Goodhue to Michael Hodge

The motion for a discrimination was negatived by a great majority—the subject of assuming the State debts is now under discussion. I am in great hopes it will obtain, tho' it will be with great difficulty—for it is pretty evident the House are is near equly divided. God grant it may take effect, for I concive, justice policy and every consideration which will advance the future prosperity of these United States, requires, that those debts incurr'd for the attainment of our Independence whether in the hands of State or

Continental creditors should stand on the same footing and receive a supply from one common fountain.

ALS, Ebenezer Stone Papers, MSaE. Place to which written not indicated.

Stephen Hall to George Thatcher

By the Post I have just received your favor of the 14 Inst. It contains a declaration & an implicit charge; together with a demand of an Answer to that charge. Most readily I obey your Commands. You say You have been informed that I "have again & again, & in different companies, in publick as well as private endeavoured to injure" your "character & reputation" That You have been thus informed I believe; but that I have thus endeavoured, I absolutely and positively deny, and in my turn call upon You to declare your Author and on the very just principles, on which you reason in your letter, demand of You your Informant.

You also suggest as your own sentiment that I have acted an unfriendly part towards You. On what you ground your opinion I know not. If on information only, I have given You a full answer as to the justness of it; if on any thing else, I must guess at it. I know of nothing, neither can I guess at anything, on which You could ground such an opinion, unless it be on a publication of Mr. Waite's,[1] that was expressly designed to injure me, which however rebounded on himself, & perhaps extended to You: but for this I am not accountable, neither do I wish to be, as it conveyed Ideas absolutely false; on which subject I have spoken to Mr. Waite, who in the presence of Mrs. [Mary Cotton] Hall did not pretend to deny the design I have imputed to it, but only to palliate. You doubtless know the Article I refer to. It is that, in which I am in a very peculiar manner mentioned as seconding & strongly supporting a motion to forward a petition from the Town of Portland to Congress to the care of Mr. Ames. The fact is, Such a motion was made; but the Idea was novel to me, for I k[n]ew not that such a thing was even in contemplation. Several Gentlemen urged the expediency & propriety of it for reasons that were to me convincing. I therefore, on the Moderator's asking if the motion was seconded, briefly recapitulated what they had said, and seconded the motion, which was adopted by a Vote nearly unanimous. I know of nothing unfriendly in all this. I acted from a sense of duty & fidelity to the Town, and not from any peculiar regard to Mr. Ames, or disregard to You. Such a sense I trust ever will influence me in my conduct without favor or affection. The article referred to therefore can be no just ground for You to think me unfriendly. From what other cause, than those I have mentioned, your suggestion can arise, is out of my power even to guess. I can add no more therefore on the subject till I know whence your Information came, & who your Informant is.

ALS, Chamberlain Collection, MB. Written from Portland, Maine, and postmarked there on 26 February.

[1] Probably the notice printed in Thomas B. Wait's [Portland, Maine] *Cumberland Gazette* non extant 4 January issue (reprinted in the [Boston] *Massachusetts Centinel*, 16 January), which stated that the motion to forward Portland's petition "was made, and strongly supported by STEPHEN HALL."

Jeremiah Hill to George Thatcher

Yours of the 14th. instant came to hand by this days post, which I read with pleasure. when I came to Mr. Madison's proposition for a discrimination, I thought it pointed to something good, perhaps not so literally considered in itself but good of necessity, if practicable—But when I came to read that "some begin to declare in favor of scaling the whole" I was instantly inspired, I longed to make a *Speach* & proclaim the glad tidings of Salvation to this Young Empire—*Facts* always appears to me to be stubborn things: I think it was in '76 Congress *put out* a continental Lottery consisting of four Classes, this was only a polite mode of borrowing Money, I with some Others formed a small Company & put in forty dollars, then in Estimation as good as Silver, as we were fortunate in the first Class we put our prize into the second & so on till the last, when we drew 148 dol. the *fortune* of our 40 good ones put in first—we sent our Prize Tickets to Boston to get into personal Possession of our good Luck the Officer there, (by this time it was '79) scaled our prize down to 3¾ dols. and sent us a final Settlement, or Certificate of the same import which at that time would have sold for perhaps half a Dollar in Specie, all the fortunate adventurers forced the same, as there was no discrimination no one complained, at least I heard no complaint, some said it was honest, some said it was for the public Good, others called it a political Manœuvre & so they wrap'd it up—People in general were much in favor of Scaling the old Continental Money and when it died I believe it had very few Mourners, though many followed it to the Grave—Congress then made a Scale of depreciation, & I believe every State in the Union did the same; Let me Ask, is the Circumstances of the United States so altered that the same causes will not produce the same Effects? can that be said to be unjust or wicked in a nation that in effect produces Happiness and Prosperity to that nation? Can that be unjust or wicked to day which was not so Yesterday? I will mention one more fact existing in this State, the Excise is the chief Resourse the State has, The Treasurer gives orders for one Quarter

Part of the Interest of the State debt on the Excise, yet these orders were sold when I was at Boston for 12/9 on the pound, now, pray tell me by analysis of Reason when this State will pay the other three Quarters of the Interest and Principal? When the Recourses of a State will not support the Government & pay its Interest it is in fact in a State of Bankruptcy as much as a Merchant who by imprudence or misfortune is unable to pay his debts, in the Latter Case every one is content to take his dividend; & what Reason can be offered why the Creditors of a Government should not average such Resources as the Government can make? What the United States has heretofore done, (tho' they scale the whole) will not be look'd upon [*as*] criminal or iniquitous any more than a Merchant will be called roguish who fails by Misfortune. the Cause was of necessity the effect is of Course.

ALS, Chamberlain Collection, MB. Written from Biddeford, Maine, in the evening; post-marked Portsmouth, New Hampshire, 26 February.

Samuel Johnston to James Iredell

I wrote to you yesterday by a Vessel of Jackson's which I hope you will receive.

The House of Representatives have come to a Resolution to Fund the Foreign and Domestick Debts and are now Debating on the propriety of Funding all the State Debts, this last measure meets with considerable Opposition, but I am inclined to believe, as far as I am at present capable of Judging, that it will be ultimately adopted, the great difficulty seems to rest on the ways & means, but, your favorite, the Secretary of the Treasury, whose application is as indefatigable as his Genius is extensive, encourages us to hope that they may be found, I wish to God he may not be too sanguine, we cannot be too cautious of any future breach of Faith.

I am sorry to hear of your Brother's indisposition,[1] I fear without more prudence than young men generally possess, he will experience a premature old age.

I should be quite well if it was not for that complaint in my head which I have so long complained of and that is no worse than usual. Mr. Hawkins desires his best respects to you I have prevailed on Mrs. [*Penelope*] Dawson to [*write?*] Billy [*William Johnston Dawson*] tho she says he is a lazy Fellow and I cant help thinking that she is half right as I have not received a line from him.

Pray give my love to Mrs. [*Hannah Johnston*] Iredell, kiss the Children for me and tell Annie [*Frances Cathcart Johnston*] I love her dearly, perhaps as well as ever any other husband likes his wife & better than many do.

ALS, Charles E. Johnson Collection, Nc-Ar. Addressed to Edenton, North Carolina; franked.

[1] Thomas Iredell (1761–post 1796) immigrated to North Carolina from England in 1784, heavily in debt and a source of constant concern to James and their mother, Margaret McCullough Iredell, who followed her sons to North Carolina in 1790.

The War-Worn Soldier to Mr. Russell

AN old Soldier, who, "in the times that tried men's souls,"[1] risked his life in defence of his country, would inform the speculating gentry, that, notwithstanding all their railing, he feels himself under g[reat] obligations to the Hon. Mr. MADISON, for stepping forward in the cause of publick justice, and in vindication of the claims of the defenders of our country, whom necessity obliged to sell their notes, received for services in the field, at 2/. for 20/. If the country is to make good those notes, who ought to receive the benefit? Certainly the original holder, who bore the heats and burdens of the day—and who placed his country in the situation thus to do justice, and not the person, who, taking advantage of the necessity of the soldier, and knowing that he *must* sell his note or *starve*, would not give him but 2/. for 20/. Do the speculating gentry wish that the poor soldier, &c. shall still be taxed to pay the interest on the very notes he sold, which will amount to three times as much as he got for them? If they do, it is happy there is a MADISON, who, fearless of the wreathing of bloodsuckers will step forward, and boldly vindicate the rights of the widow and orphan, the original creditor, and The War-Worn Soldier.

[Boston] *Massachusetts Centinel*, 24 February, edited by Benjamin Russell; reprinted at Exeter and Portsmouth, New Hampshire.

[1] From the famous first line of Thomas Paine's first *American Crisis* essay (December 1776).

Original Communications from New York

Congress have come to no further decisions on the subject of the Secretary's Report [*on public credit*]. The *Assumption of the State Debts* was further discussed this day. Mr. SEDGWICK advocated the measure in a very nervous and ingenious speech—he has thought much on the subject, and did great justice to it; and from the apparent disposition of the House, I anticipated a very cordial adoption of the Resolution: But Mr. MADISON, after expressing in the fullest terms his approbation of the idea as contained in the Secretary's Report, proposed an amendment to the Resolution, by adding a clause to this effect—"Provided, *That the whole expenses of the several States, whether discharged, or existing in negotiable, or other evidences, shall be taken into account—and the respective liquidated balances form the object of the assumption.*" Some desultory conversation ensued on this motion—and the Committee rose without a decision; so that the business of Finance stands as it was left yesterday.

The Post-Office Bill [HR-42] was read the second time—and the Naturalization Bill was discussed in Committee of the whole, without completing it.

When the assumption of the State debts was brought forward yesterday, Mr. GERRY distinguished himself greatly by the able manner in which he handled the subject. I was particularly pleased with the ideas in the following remarks, "That the assumption would be perfectly consistent with the Constitution—the debts were incurred for the general defence—the States acted as agents on behalf of the Continent." Was surprised that gentlemen should suppose that the measure would involve the annihilation of the State Governments. He compared the State and General Governments to one great machine, in which small wheels are as necessary as large ones—destroy either and the destruction of the machine, as to all its essential purposes, follows—He considered the measure important to the *preservation* of the State Governments—for if the debts should not be assumed by Congress, a clamour would be raised against the State Governments for not doing justice—they would be considered as oppressive, and will depreciate in the estimation of the citizens. If the General Government should hereafter oppress the States, they will (in case their debts are now assumed) be in a better situation to defend themselves, being relieved from such a load of debt—for "out of debt—out of danger" is an old and a true saying. He added many more observations which time will not permit me to detail—Upon the whole, I have no doubt that the debts will be assumed.

[Boston] *Massachusetts Centinel*, 6 March; reprinted at Worcester, Massachusetts, and Exeter, New Hampshire.

Letter from New York

The motion made by Mr. MADISON for a discrimination was on Monday negatived, as might have been supposed, by a large majority, there being but 13 in favour of it out of 49 members present. We are now on the great subject of assuming the State Debts, and I am much encouraged from present appearances, that it will obtain, though it seems pretty evident the House will be almost equally divided on this great question. Many gentlemen, who I take for granted, will be opposed to the measure, at this time, acknowledge it is what must necessarily take place at some time or other. God grant we may not delay this essential measure to the establishment of our national concord, justice and credit.

[Boston] *Massachusetts Centinel*, 6 March.

From Correspondents at New York

For the two days past the assumption of the State Debts has been in debate—so far as it is possible to judge at present, from the weight of argument there is every reason to believe that the proposition for that purpose will take effect. Indeed, those who oppose it, I believe must be convinced that eventually the measure must be adopted; their arguments therefore seem only to point at delay.

[Stockbridge, Massachusetts] *Western Star*, 9 March. The first sentence is a paraphrase of Sedgwick's letter of this date to Peter Van Schaack, calendared below.

OTHER DOCUMENTS

George Clymer to David Brearly. No copy known; mentioned in Clymer to Timothy Pickering, above.

Daniel Cony to George Thatcher. ALS, Chamberlain Collection, MB. Written from Boston.
    Thanks him for sheets of "Journals of Congress"; John Gardiner's newspaper piece (see [*John Gardiner*] to George Thatcher, 11 February, above) "is universally condemnd" in Boston as evidence of "a low mean, Sordid, and grovelling disposition"; encloses the day's newspapers.

Nicholas Gilman to Daniel Gilman. No copy known; acknowledged in Daniel Gilman to Nicholas Gilman, 6 March.

Thomas Hartley to Tench Coxe. ALS, Coxe Papers, PHi. Place to which addressed not indicated.
    Received Coxe's letter of 21 February "last night at ten oclock"; Madison's motion for discriminating between securities holders was, "as I expected," defeated; they are now considering the resolution for assuming the states' war debts, "and I confess it is one of the most difficult Questions I ever had to decide upon"; is inclined to think it will pass; enquires whether the state constitutional convention has finished "the great Business" yet.

Charles Pettit to Elias Boudinot. No copy known; mentioned in Pettit to Boudinot, 25 February.

Benjamin Rush to John Adams. ALS, Adams Family Manuscript Trust, MHi. Written from Philadelphia.
Agrees with Adams's remarks on "the 'young fry' who are now crouding into the Councils of our Country" and laments with him that "your old friends" of 1776 are as forgotten as the dead; describes the history of his exclusion from state politics; would have accepted a diplomatic appointment under the new federal government, "but the time is past."

Theodore Sedgwick to Peter Van Schaack. ALS, Sedgwick Papers, MHi. Addressed to Kinderhook, New York; franked; postmarked.
For two days the House has debated the assumption of the states' war debts and "so far as I can judge the event will correspond with my wishes"; "the weight of argument is infinitely in favor of the proposition"; it is "a bond of union."

George Thatcher to Daniel Davis. No copy known; acknowledged in Joseph McLellan and John Fox to Thatcher, 27 March.

Alexander White to Governor Beverley Randolph. ALS, Executive Papers, Vi. Addressed to His Excellency The Governor of Virginia; franked; postmarked; read (in Council?) on 12 March.
Acknowledges receipt on 20 February of Randolph's letter dated 29 January, directed to "the Representatives of Virginia in Congress with the enclosures accompanied by a Chart or Plan of the River Potowmack," which will be laid before Congress "as soon as it can, with propriety, be done"; the delegation has asked White to write and sign this letter.

Hugh Williamson to John Gray Blount. ALS, John Gray Blount Papers, Nc-Ar. Addressed to Washington, North Carolina.
"Try to buy up all you can" of "Old Continental Money" and certificates up to four hundred for one dollar of state money, as well as certain state certificates; he will take an equal share in them with Blount, and "will dispose of them here as fast as you can send them on."

Manasseh Cutler, Diary. Cutler Papers, IEN.
"Attended debates. called on Mr. Strong."

Letter from New York. [Charleston, South Carolina] *City Gazette*, 12 March.
The Senate has "discountenanced" the antislavery petitions "in explicit terms, for there was not one member for referring"; the House committee's members "promise to make such a report against the petition as

your delegates wish"; has sent the secretary's report on public credit; the assumption of the states' war debts will take place.

THURSDAY, 25 FEBRUARY 1790

Windy (Johnson)

Ralph Izard to Gabriel Manigault

I have just received my Letters by [*Capt. Thomas*] Snell. Among them one signed by a considerable number of the principal Merchants in Charleston, strongly recommending Col. [*John*] Mitchell as a Successor to [*Edward*] Weyman, should there be a vacancy. I think it proper to comply with their wishes, in a matter in which they are so much interested. It will be better therefore that you say nothing to [*Peter*] Bonnetheau on the subject. The business respecting the assumption of the State Debts has been well debated in the House of Representatives, & I think will certainly be agreed to. In the Senate there will undoubtedly be a majority in favour of the measure. The question will yet undergo a discussion of several days before it is brought to us. As soon as it is, I will inform you of it, as I know it is of considerable importance both to you, & your Brother [*Joseph*]. If no opportunity offers by Water, I will write to you by the Post.

ALS, Izard Papers, ScU. This is part of a postscript to a letter begun on 19 February and printed under that date, above.

Louis Guillaume Otto to Comte de Montmorin

The debates of the House of Representatives are becoming daily more interesting. The public flocks there in crowds to hear the interests most dear to the nation decided. The Speaker of the House, having noticed me in the gallery, had the sergeant at arms invite me to take a seat in the inner part of the hall where up to that time only the Senators, the heads of departments, and the justices had been admitted. The Resident [*minister*] of Holland [*Franco Petrus van Berckel*] enjoys the same advantage exclusive of the charge d'affaires of Spain and other foreign employees. Probably they believed it proper to invite the agents of nations essentially interested in it to be present at the debates on the public debt. From now on, I will be properly situated to follow the deliberations of Congress more regularly and to make a more detailed report to you about them.

The Northern delegates have been agitating for some time in order to obtain a more complete representation in Congress. They maintain that their population exceeds by nearly a quarter the number which was attributed to it in the first formation of the new government. Accordingly, they insist on a new census to be made by order of Congress. The Southern delegates, who are only too weak as it is, do their best to thwart a measure which will not fail to give to the Northerners still more preponderance than before. It [*the Enumeration Act*] has been adopted, however, by a great majority and the President is going to name immediately the commissioners charged to get the necessary returns in each state.

Another question divided the House for some days. It was the matter of determining whether the salaries of ministers in foreign countries should be fixed by the President *with* or *without* the consent of the Senate. The majority decided for the prerogative of the President and to enable him to discharge this function, they granted him the sum of 40,000 dollars or 210,000 tournois. The smallness of this sum proves sufficiently that the intention of Congress is not to maintain many ministers in foreign countries. In taking up this question again, Congress has reduced this sum to 30,000 dollars or 157,500 tournois.

The constitutional amendments proposed by Congress have not had, My Lord, all the success this assembly seemed to expect from them. The Senate of Virginia is in this respect the most intractable of all the legislative bodies. It has put off to next year the consideration of four articles which appear to it absolutely inadmissible, and it pushed its opposition to the point of publishing a protest[1] against these amendments which it calls insidious and fitted to dazzle the people without sheltering them from the *encroachments* and from the *despotism of Congress.* This protest is the strongest document which has appeared yet against the general government and it has caused much sensation; They believe, however, that it is the last effort of a dying faction which will soon be silenced by the moderation and prudence of Congress. In Rhode Island these amendments have produced a better effect. The upper house of the legislature has just given its consent to the convocation of a convention to examine the Federal Constitution and to bring this state finally under the new American Government. Vermont appears also very well disposed, but the commissioners have not been able to agree with those of New York concerning the guarantee of about 469,000 acres which the Vermonters have encroached upon and which they fear they will be forced to restore by a decision of the Supreme Court of Congress which from now on will deal definitively with all the differences between the respective states. In spite of this difficulty, the New York legislature occupies itself seriously with the emancipation of this small state of which the proximity to Canada and the intrigues of Lord Dorchester make the defection feared.[2]

The consolidation of the states under a single head would meet with fewer difficulties, My Lord, if the imprudence of some ardent Federalists did not reveal from time to time the secret of Congress, which is to despoil gradually the individual legislatures and to consolidate its government under the guise of the greatest moderation. General [*John*] Sullivan, president of New Hampshire, having been appointed federal judge, the legislature of this state decreed that in spite of this nomination he could continue the functions of president. The minority protested, and General Sullivan to justify the decree of the legislature published a manifesto[3] in which he tried to prove that since the establishment of the new government, it was absurd to maintain this jealousy and this distinction between it and the particular legislatures; that in taking the oath of allegiance, Americans had put an end to these differences; that all the power of the union emanated henceforth from a single center and that the particular legislatures were themselves only dependencies of Congress. This imprudent declaration from a man who has always played a role in the North makes the Antifederalists complain loudly. Writers under the names of *Brutus* and *Cassius*[4] exhort the people to be suspicious of a government which by the admission even of a notable Federalist makes a game of trespassing upon the sovereignty of the particular states. They accuse the lawyers of being the principal authors of federalism because they hold the principal government posts and, to avenge themselves, they propose a general reform of the laws and a reorganization of justice which would make this profession entirely useless. A moving speech delivered by a Mr. [*John*] Gardener in the Massachusetts legislature depicts the lawyers in the most odious colors. He proposes the destruction of this pest of society and the substitution for the barbarous laws of England of a simple code which will be within the reach of everybody and which will demand on the part of the judges no other qualities than honesty and good sense. The moment appeared favorable. They named a committee to make a report on it; but either because the reform is subject to too many inconveniences or the influence of the lawyers has, on this occasion as on so many others, triumphed over the impotence of their adversaries, this motion has had no result. Mr. Gardiner was passed off as an incendiary who delights in disorder. Finally, no other trace remains from the imprudence of General Sullivan than a greater distrust on the part of the Antifederalists and, on the opposite side, a greater attention to not creating new embarrassments by ill-timed declamations.

O'Dwyer, pp. 420–23. Answered 2 July. Otto's letters included in *DHFFC* were usually written over the course of days, and even weeks, following the day they were begun.

---

[1] The protest of the state Senate's majority, dated 12 December 1789; see Edward Carrington to Madison, 5 February, n. 1, above.

[2]Through the lobbying efforts of the prominent Allen brothers (Ethan, Eli, and Levi), Canada's Governor Guy Carleton (Lord Dorchester) exempted the independent Republic of Vermont from Britain's Order in Council of 1786 that prohibited direct trade between Canada and the United States. By 1788 Vermont enjoyed unimpeded trade with Canada (except in furs and peltry) via Lake Champlain and the Richelieu River. That year, the Allens began lobbying Canada and Britain to secure those economic gains through an overt and permanent political alliance. Carleton was the conduit of such overtures until early 1789, when Eli Allen went to England as Vermont's "agent" and as late as March 1790 petitioned for a commercial and military treaty. In April the ministry effectively closed the door to that option, owing in part to fear of alienating the United States in the looming confrontation with Spain over the Nootka Sound affair (Charles R. Ritcheson, *Aftermath of the Revolution* [New York, 1969], pp. 153–58; John J. Duffy, et al., eds., *Ethan Allen and His Kin: Correspondence, 1772–1819* [2 vols., Hanover, N.H., 1998], p. 261). See also *DHFFC* 15:524.

[3]Speech of 29 December 1789; see James Sullivan to Gerry, 3 February, n. 1, above.

[4]Pseudonyms adopted from the two figures most closely associated with the attempt to restore the Roman republic by assassinating the tyrant Julius Caesar in 44 B.C.: Marcus Junius Brutus (85?–42 B.C.) and Gaius Cassius Longinus (d. 42 B.C.). Specific "Brutus" essays fitting Otto's description appeared in [Boston] *Independent Chronicle*, 4 and 8 February.

John Page to St. George Tucker

Quis?[1] by T. T. T. [*Thomas Tudor Tucker*] M. D.
In Gravity clad,
He has nought in his Head,
   But Visions of Nobles & Kings,
With Commons below,
   Who respectfully bow,
   And worship the dignified *Things*
       The Answer Impromptu by P[*age*].
I'll tell in a Trice—
   'Tis Old Daddy *Vice*
Who carries of Pride an Ass-load;
   Who turns up his Nose
   Wherever he goes
With Vanity swell'd like a Toad
Dr. Tucker
Your Brother has been drawn out by me into a Walk to Parnassus[2]—in the House of R—s he just now gave me the *Quis?* to which I replied as above.

I can only add that when I have more Leisure I will send you more of his Productions.

Riddle mocking the aristocratic pretensions of Vice President John Adams, written on the House floor by John Page and Thomas Tudor Tucker, enclosed in Page to St. George Tucker, 25 February. (Courtesy of the Swem Library, College of William and Mary, Williamsburg, Virginia.)

ALS, Tucker-Coleman Papers, ViW. Place to which addressed not indicated. On the reverse of the letter, St. George Tucker composed a bawdy exchange in the same poetic format, including some stanzas he credits to "W. N," possibly their mutual friend William Nelson.

[1] The motif "Quis?" ("Who?") was frequently employed by Page and Tucker in their playful exchanges of rhymed riddles, to challenge the recipient to identify the subject satirized (in this case, the Vice President, a favorite target).

[2] A mountain near Delphi, thought by the ancient Greeks to be the abode of the muses, most especially poetry and music.

John Adams by Charles Willson Peale, 1741–1827, oil on canvas. Thought to have been painted during the early years of Congress's stay in Philadelphia, Peale's portrayal is of a distinctly humble Adams, in vivid contrast to the ego lampooned in Page and Tucker's doggerel and suggested in John Singleton Copley's magisterial portrait of 1783 (see *DHFFC* 9:98). (Courtesy of Independence National Historical Park, Philadelphia.)

Theodore Sedgwick to Pamela Sedgwick

I have had the pleasure, best beloved of my heart, of receiving your letter by the last post. On the case of dear little Robert [*Sedgwick*], I have consulted two of the most eminent surgeons in this city. They both say it is impossible to form an opinion which may be relyed on without seeing him, & They both agree that it probably is not incurable unless the bone is diseased. that it is not probable the bone is diseased, because if it was it would be very painful. they say they have frequently seen children whose ancles were disordered by the issuing of the Juices from the joints. and have never known any instance where an attempt to cure has been made without effect. On the whole therefore I am of opinion that it will be worth the attempt to bring him down here as soon as the [*Hudson*] river opens.

Let me again intreat my best beloved to regard her health. The reflection that my absence renders you less happy than you would otherwise be gives me great pain.

I have made perticular enquiry about the schools at Bethlehem [*Pennsylvania*], and my information is such as is very agreable. They teach reading, writing, arithmetic, geography, needle work and in short every thing substantially useful. At the same time the utmost attention is paid to purity of morals and decency of conduct And the whole of the annual expence is not more than 100 dollars. I am therefore of opinion that Miss Frances [*Sedgwick*] should be soon sent there.

With regard to cousin Betsy I am sorry she cannot be happy at our house. Should she incline to go to her aunt Cooks & she be willing to receive her, I could possibly have no objection but I could not consent, unless because it was your pleasure, that she should there be considered as a boarder. As to what you may think it proper in that or any other case to do for her in that as in every thing else I have the utmost confidence in your prudence and discretion.

I spent the whole of yesterday morning untill 2 oClock in the after noon with my dear freind Mrs. [*Theodosia Prevost*] Burr. She is the very picture of Maloncholy, and her distress appeared by my company to be augmented. She however, assured me that the company of those few of real freinds, who could feel for her distress, and who would with sympathy hear her complains, tended to assuage the bitterness of her anguish. Indeed, my love, though I was greatly pained by the interview, yet I have pleasure in the reflection. She complains like one voluntarily wedded to woe. To me she said, "do not my dearest freind do not attempt to suppress the flowing of my tears nor to hide your own mine indeed are selfish, but they are companions of relief, yours are disinterested, they are an evidence of your virtue, this world has some thing yet in it which commands my respect" She enquired tenderly after your health and after that of little Kitty [*Catherine Maria Sedgwick*]. You have got said she an angel for a wife, god "grant that she and your children" she could add no more. After some moments pause, she became more composed. and she ~~had~~ added, "I too some little time since had the company of angels—angel daughters, but they are flown, while I, O my god, am here." At another time she said, you my friend have lost children, but you know not, you cannot imagine from thence the severity of my loss. Mine too have died in infancy, this though at the time I thought heavy I now consider as nothing. My lovely cherubs, and she looked up as if to see them, rendered perfect that I might ~~consider~~ know the perfection of misery.[1] And poor Bartow,[2] from him I have heard nothing nor dare I enquire. and yet I live can you tell me how it is that my heart is not yet broken. When I came away, she said, "and will you leave me, well I am sure I have no demand on you to render you miserable, but call as often as you can sacrifice your own happiness to alleviate the misery of a friend." she requested me perticularly to present you with her affece. regards. I shall write you again by the Thursdays post. Adieu! dear creature & know I am sincerely your affect.

ALS, Sedgwick Papers, MHi. Place to which addressed not indicated.

[1] The three daughters from Theodosia's first marriage who survived infancy all died in the 1780s, two within a year of each other at age sixteen.
[2] John Bartow Prevost (1766–1825), Theodosia's oldest son by her first marriage. She was apparently in touch with her other surviving child from her first marriage, Augustine James Frederick Prevost (b. 1767) .

William Smith (Md.) to Otho H. Williams

We have not made the Smallest advance, in the funding System, Since I last wrote you, but are Stopt Short At the resolution for assuming the State Debts, by the United States. This has been the Subject of debate for many days, And contrary to my expectations at the first out set of this business; I now perceive the resolution will be carried, *I think*, by a considerable Majority, my objection to the plan, is that it is very Unexpected in the different & [*lined out*] States, may alarm thier fears, & give rise to groundless apprehensions. The amot. of the resolution is "That Such of the State Creditors, who choose to exch[*ang*]e their Securities for that of the U.S. Shall have their debt funded by the U.S. *equaly with all other creditors of the U.S.*" only no provision is to be made for payment of *their* Interest before 1792—The Represents. from Maryland, are totally in the dark on this Subject So far as relates to the Sentiments of their Constituents I believe however we will be unanimous in the Negative. Virginia will concur with Us, South Carola. & Several other States have instructed their members to Vote for the Measure—I am convinced the business is premature & am fearfull it will be attended with injurious consequences. which a delay might prevent.

P. S. I am long without a letter from Baltimore & anxious to hear you are all Well.

ALS, Williams Papers, MdHi. Place to which addressed not indicated.

Henry Van Schaack to Theodore Sedgwick

Your letter of the 13 Instant came to me three days ago I thank you for it—continue as time and leisure will admit of it, to convey to me the progressive steps Congress take in the Funding System—without the entire Establishment of public credit every thing will be at loose ends. The speech of Mr. M[adison]. upon the subject of discrimination is as extraordinary as unexpected—The design of the Orator appears to me is to establish his popularity among a certain discription of people within the antient Dominion upon whom probably depends his re-election to a seat in Congress—Time I hope will unfold clearly his designs & hope the good sense of the people will discern that characters coming forward, at this late day, for a discrimination are actuated by motives inconsistant with the public good. In this part of the Commonwealth [western Massachusetts] I am of opinion this object of iniquity and ill policy will be rejected by the people at large—The opposition you give to the measure will do you credit and your ultimately voting for the national 4 ℔ Cent Interest must be advocated by every friend to his Country—There are many here more friendly to 3 than 4 ℔ Ct.: but I trust we have few among us who will condemn their representative for voting for the latter if the former cannot be obtained. Our people, I firmly beleive, are ripe for reciving the funding System in toto as the Secy. has detailed to the house. I wish your Members who are opposed to Maddison upon great questions wod. pay less Deference to him than they do when they rise to reply to him—Scarc[e] one gets up ~~but lauds~~ to answer but pays some evident tribute to his great abilities—This you may be sure exalts his character—I want to see him confronted with evident marks of equality—The Author of the address in 1783[1] ought to be Exposed for his opposite conduct now—Let me see your name frequently in opposition to this man—Watch him and by all means probe him to the bottom where he is vulnerable. His disappointment in the last Session, I fancy, makes him anxious to display his talents on some subjects to regain the consequence he at first supported in the national assembly. So much for M. May he and every one else opposed to a funding System, founded in justice, meet with a disappointments proportionably to the measure of their iniquity.

I have since my last letter more and more contemplated the Secretarys report [*on public credit*]—The further I consider the Subject the better I am satisfied that its object is of so much consequence as to ensure to this Country great political advantages. I have been a good deal abroad this winter the Report has been my constant companion—If people of my level wod. take half the pains that I have taken the people wod. be better informed than they are—In this District I made use of it among the leading Anties where the System met with a very favorable attention. The people there and here I am persuaded are disposed to give the Government a full and complete trial in every department. The Report from the war office for a Militia Establishment I have also advocated and made proselytes of some zealous opposers ~~of it~~ to it. The next Compensation Bill I hope will make ample provision for all faithful Servants as well out as in Congress in that case I trust great care will be taken of me. I wod. premise before that takes place that you let Congress know that 2 dollars for Every 25 Miles travel is sufficient for me. and that in future they allow themselves no more than 3 dollars for that distance I do not in consience believe that I am a dollar in 25 Miles travel less than you and others are—I mean of the lower house—The upper members may have 4 dollars for 26½ Miles travel.

***

If you knew my anxiety about the assumption of the State Debts you wod. take every oppertunity to write me. Without this is done I am persuaded the provisions for ~~a~~ Revenue will be clogged with great embarrassments—I hope and I fear alternately about this important matter—adieu I am called upon to conclude all here join in affectionate regards.

Remember me most respectfully to the Great men of our acquaintance in Congress.

[*P.S.*] Will you be so good as tell Silvester that I am anxious to have an answer from him to the letter I wrote him.

ALS, Sedgwick Papers, MHi. Place from which written not indicated; franked. The omitted text relates to the Massachusetts legislature's handling of the state debt and the controversy surrounding Governor John Hancock's billing the legislature for the banquet he gave in honor of Washington's visit to Boston the previous October.

[1] The Confederation Congress's Address to the States on 26 April 1783, written by Madison, was a clear acknowledgment of the nation's fiscal debt and commitment to discharge it. Part of this address is printed in *DHFFC* 5:844–47; for the full text, see *PJM* 6:487–98.

OTHER DOCUMENTS

Stephen Austin to Jeremiah Wadsworth. ALS, Wadsworth Papers, CtHi. Written from Philadelphia; franked; postmarked 26 February.

Directions respecting Wadsworth's contract to supply linen (for wrapping lead shot).

Constantine Freeman to George Thatcher. ALS, C. P. Greenough Papers, MHi. Written from Quebec; carried by Jacob (?) LeRoy.

Has had no success searching for records regarding a land patent in Maine; as Thatcher requested, will forward copies of such papers if any are found; thanks for procuring son Ezekial Freeman a clerkship in the auditor's office.

Matthew McConnell to Andrew Craigie. ALS, Craigie Papers, MWA. Written from Philadelphia; postmarked 26 February.

Received Craigie's letter of 21 February "last evening"; believes Pennsylvania Representatives "about equally divided" on the question of assuming the states' war debts; "I was well informed this day that Mr. Boudinot had written that he was against their assumption, but rather than lose the great question of funding this Session he would vote for them; (These things between ourselves)"; encloses "some remarks" he had privately printed last October and circulated among three or four persons; would have "no objections if you think worth while to shew them to Mr. Emes [*Ames*]."

Charles Pettit to Elias Boudinot. AL, AMs 779/1, PPRF. Place from which written not indicated; franked; postmarked 26 February. Author identified by the endorsement.

Has heard that the assumption of "facilities" (indents), as part of arrearages of interest, was agreed to; thinks both had better been left out "for the present, if it proves any impediment to the funds affording 6 per centum on the principal."

Isaiah Thomas to George Thatcher. ALS, Fogg Collection, MeHi. Place from which written not indicated.

Has subscribed for Thatcher to Noah Webster's *Collection of Essays* (Boston, 1790); wants to print Bibles and thinks Congress should grant a privilege, and that only those who are privileged should be allowed to do it; Edward Bangs has written Thatcher on this; asks his opinion.

Hopley Yeaton to John Langdon. ALS, Langdon Papers, NhPoA. Written from Portsmouth, New Hampshire.

Langdon's family and friends are well; reports on state election.

Manasseh Cutler, Diary. Cutler Papers, IEN.

"Waited this Morning on the Vice-President. Went up in a Hackney Coach, and spent an hour. Delivered letters."

William Samuel Johnson, Diary. Johnson Papers, CtHi.

"Visits."

Letter from London. *NYJ*, 26 April (the date on which members of Congress would have seen it); reprinted at Winchester, Virginia.

Several gentlemen gathered at the Maryland Coffee House on 11 February to celebrate Washington's birthday.

FRIDAY, 26 FEBRUARY 1790

Fine (Johnson)

Michael Hodge to Benjamin Goodhue

Yours of the 15th instant has been duly received, and communicated to the Gentlemen in Town, who appear to be much gratified by your perticular attention to them, and desire me in their name, to thank you, and to express their wishes for a continuance of your informations, which are very interesting to them at this time, your Sentiments upon the discriminating plan, offered by Mr. Madison has the applause of every one, who has seen them, by many who are not possessed of one farthing of the public certificates, and who cannot be said, to be tinctured with prejudice, for my part I am pleased to See so many great characters in Congress reprobating the plan, and sincerely hope that it will at last settle down, much on the principles held out by the Secy. in his report [*on public credit*], which by the bye is universally (amongst us) acknowledged, to be a Master piece, his plan for funding the debt, has the applause of all, with whom I have had any communications, the Act respecting the collection of the excised articles,[1] does not meet with similar approbation, those concerned in Trade say that so many difficulties, occasioned by so many formalitys are thrown in their way, that it will deter many from being either Importers or retailers of Wines or Spirits—no dificulties has as yet occurred in the revenue department in this Town, punctual payments have been made, of all the bonds that have become due, and a general acquiescence in and observance of the revenue laws does really take place in this Town, and will, I doubt not continue to be so, I cannot discover any Disposition to do otherwise—exceeding dull times with us, for this month past, no business to transact, looking out for arrivals daily, but none appearing, have had a very moderate winter, and a fine healthy season.

ALS, Letters to Goodhue, NNS. Written from Newburyport, Massachusetts.

---

[1] Hamilton proposed such an act as part of his report on public credit; see *DHFFC* 5:799–822.

Benjamin Lincoln to Theodore Sedgwick

Your very acceptable favour of the 14th instant came by saturday nights post Should have acknowledged my obligations for it before but was in the country on its arrival.

Although it may be painful for us to disagree on a matter so interesting to me and my family as is the funding of the State debts by the Union at an interest at four ℔ cent at the least Yet you may be assured that if we never unite in our sentiments on this point I shall nevertheless esteem you my *honest* friend and grant you at all times the same right of determining for your self and of adhearing to your own opinion as I claim for my self. And I will ~~always~~ pray that you may always have sufficient light properly to direct you in the discharge of the important duties now incumbent on you.

I hope the secretary of the treasury will be suffered to make one experiment at the least he is confident that he can execute his own system He certainly is possessed of the best information and I am quite willing to risk the little which I shall have exposed on the success plans if they are not ruined by *amendments.*

Mr. Madison I hope is an honest man. I am sorry that he ever brought his mind into a state so servile as it seems to have been in when he wrote a certain letter[1] His propositions [*on discrimination*] are odious here they will not be executed, or can they, with equal justice to all. I hope and trust that *all* will be brought to adopt the Secy. Report.

Our General Court is yet sitting If we come of with a more negative session it will be well for us I am affraid that ours is not that agreeable fate. Being more yours than I can express.

ALS, Sedgwick Papers, MHi. Written from Boston.

[1] "Address and Recommendation to the States," 26 April 1783, drafted by Madison; for the full text, see *PJM* 6:487–98, for a partial text, see *DHFFC* 5:844–47.

John Page to St. George Tucker

Quæ? [*who?*]

With Modesty sweet:
    In Virtue compleat,
Her Gentleness charms ev'ry Age:
    No longer I'll dwell;
    Her Merits to tell,
Would surely require a *Page.*

Answer Impromptu

Without Loss of Time,
  In Prose or in Rhyme,
Who e'er in New-York late has been,
  May readily tell
  As I can fulwell
Th'amiable Maiden you mean—
  Miss [*Margaret*] Lowther the Fair,
  Beyond all compare,
Whose Charms must enrapture e'en Age
  Her Praise to define
  You rightly decline
She'll be known to late Times in her *Page*.

Yr. Brother just now gave me the Query above, whilst we were at our Table in the House of R—s & I returned him the Answer—He has now queried me with a Quis & a Quæ. I suppose he will next with a Quid—take Notice, this does not interrupt our Attention to Business—for I arose between my 1st. & 2d. Stanza & reproved the [*torn*]tion [*of*] the Committee. [P. S.] [*torn*] [*William?*] Nelson are Approved to *Dodsley*[1] I shall send you as much more.

ALS, Coleman-Tucker Papers, ViW. Place to which addressed not indicated.

---

[1] This and later mentions of "my Dodsley" or "our Dodsley" refer to the ongoing collection of verses exchanged among Page, St. George Tucker, his brother the congressman, and occasionally William Nelson, written in a style inspired by the British poet and satirist Robert Dodsley (1703–64). In 1790 the New York printer Hugh Gaine published an edition of Dodsley's *Œconomy of Human Life*.

Pamela Sedgwick to Theodore Sedgwick

I received my dearest Mr. Sedgwick Too short Letter from you by Parson [*Samuel*] Kirkland I have only To lament that the Hurry of Business Prevents you from affoarding some few moments more of your Time in writeing for my Pleasure and amusement—The time that can be spent for the Benefit of the Public I should most willingly resign To their Sole use and [*lined out*] Emollument—But Truly I am not so good as I should be nor will I make any Great Pretentions to Public Spirit I am very willing to leve that Virtue to the Fathers of our Infant Nation and let them Bustle and wranggle about the Interest of their Country at their Leisure If I can Still a Squalling Infant and Settle a matter of Great Contention amoung a Company of unruly Boys—I feel my self as happy and as Great as an Empress—Doctr. [*Oliver*] Patterridge has made I think a very accurate Statement of Roberts

Case I could wish it might be handed to Some Reputable Surgeon as Soon as may be—I dare not be very Sanguine in my expectations of Seing you on the Third Thursday of March Ardently as I wish to bid you welcome to Stockbridge—I could hardly consent that you should Submit To a Conveyance from N. York in a Stage When speaking within the Bounds of humane Provabillety the roads will be Intollerable.

The Family are all well the Children wish to be kindly rememberd to Pappa.

ALS, Sedgwick Papers, MHi. Written from Stockbridge, Massachusetts.

William Smith (S.C.) to Edward Rutledge

Your letter arived yesterday. I wish I had leisure to answer it fully at present but it is out of my power—your very affectionate congratulations & wishes have made impressions on me which pages would be necessary to communicate to you & which I should (hurried as I am) be unable to express—give me then credit for every sentiment of gratitude which your expressions require on my part.

Snell arrived very opportunely—we were on the subject of the assumption of the State Debts—Tucker was opposed to it in our house, & Major Butler in the Senate—the proceedgs. of our State have put things to rights,[1] & I have reason to hope the measure will be carried—it appears to me a glorious thing for So. Cara.—Mr. Izard communicated your Letter—[*John*] Kean was present when it was read—we think you are mistaken in the supposed amount of our Credits & ultimate Ballance which will fall far Short of £700,000. Kean has undertaken to explain the matter to you. I am delighted with the Columbia project & the compleat triumph our friends have had—the Ge{neral} & yourself deserve the thanks of every goo{d cit} izen for your exertion{s}[2] I am Sure I give mine most cordially. persevere, my worthy friend, for I am confident the future happiness & honor of our State depend on rescui{ng} the conduct of public affairs from persons who appear no [*torn*] deserves [*torn*] & I hope no Gentleman of the Law will stir a question so dangerous to the welfare of our country—The members of Congress have never expressed any opinion unfavorable to the Installmt. Law,[3] whenever I have had an opportunity of introducing the subject, I have taken great pains to reconcile them to it & so successfully that every person I have spoken to have agreed with me that it was necessary & that it is not agst. the Constitution. Some time ago I recd. a Letter from John Nutt[4] abusing the Law terribly—I ansd. him & explained The matter so satisfactorily that in his reply he confessed himself persuaded that the measure was proper & even advantageous to the British Creditors.

I shall endeavour to write you more fully by [*John*] Motley or Snell.

The opposition to the assumption comes chiefly from Maryland & Virginia—Pensya. Massa. ~~Ch~~ Connecticut pretty unanimous for it, also—the better part of the New York Delegation—all So. Cara.—part of N. Hampe.—part of Jersey—Georgia dubious.

We had a conside. debate on a plan of discriminatn. but the measure had few s{upporte}rs. after the question {of Assumption is disposed of} the amot. of interest will create warm {debate}—but I beleive the Secretary's plan will go down—the Secretary says he has resources ready for the State Debts, without recurring to direct Taxation, but he thinks they ought not to be brought forward at present for fear of alarming.

[*P. S.*] Mrs. S. [*Charlotte Izard Smith*] has been much indisposed but is recovering—my Son [*Thomas Loughton*] is well. Mrs. S. feels very sensibly ~~of~~ Mrs. [*Henrietta Middleton Rutledge*]'s congratulns. & requests her best respects to which please to add mine—Your Son [*Henry Middleton*] is well & improves daily.

ALS, Smith Papers, ScHi. Addressed to Charleston, South Carolina; franked. A postscript dated 27 February is printed below. The words in curly braces are from *SCHM* 69(1968): 104–6.

¹ Thomas Snell's packet carried to the South Carolina delegation a concurrent resolution from the state legislature, dated 19 January, instructing them to vote for assumption.

² The "Columbia project" may refer to the recent vote on assumption, taken by the state legislature then meeting at Columbia, South Carolina (see n. 1, above), or it may refer to the recent election of delegates to the state's constitutional convention scheduled to convene in Columbia on 10 May. The election returns were formally announced on 30 January and listed Gen. Charles C. Pinckney, Rutledge, and many other of Smith's "friends" among the delegates expected to affirm the state's "low country" or tidewater interests against "upcountry" demands for more equitable apportionment ([Charleston] *State Gazette of South Carolina*, 15 February).

³ "An Act to regulate the payment and recovery of debts . . .," passed by the South Carolina legislature on 4 November 1788, allowed for repayment in installments over a five year period of debts contracted before 1787. It could be interpreted as a violation of Article I, section 10 of the Constitution, which forbids states from impairing the obligation of contracts, as well as of the treaty of 1783.

⁴ A London merchant and banker, who served as the longtime agent for the Smith family in England.

Richard Stockton to Elias Boudinot

I enclose you a letter for Mr. [*John Marsden*] Pintard which you will please to take care of—I acknowledge the receipt of two letters from you—one by Mr. [*Samuel?*] Sterret—the other by John Stockton—I am much obliged by your attention in letting me know the issue of the important question which has engrossed the attention of your house as well as of the public for some time past—Since it has turned out as it has I am glad it was brought forward—the sentiments breathed by a majority of the house will do honor to the new goverment both at home and abroad—The [Am]erican name has risen fast for a few months—but this will (if I mistake not) add many cubits to her Stature—I was never more convinced of the weakness of the cause of those who advocated for a discrimination than in reading the Speech of Mr. M[adison].—For a Man of his superior Character he supported the cause he espoused (in my weak apprehension) very faintly—But he is not to blame—Ability cannot supply the want of solid principles—please to remember me to all friends.

ALS, American Bible Society, Boudinot Collection, NjP. Written from "Morven," the family estate in Princeton, New Jersey; franked.

Samuel Vaughan, Jr. to James Madison

With this letter you will receive a Pamphlet, you was so obliging as to lend me, & which from inadvertency I never returned. I was much surprised on opening my things here to find it among them.

I congratulate you most heartily on the facility you are likely to meet with in the various objects of the Legislature. It was always my opinion that you might be bolder, particularly in your commertial System. Fostering of Prejudices is fostering of future Evils; & without a necessity, if these Prejudices are not religious ones, & if measures do not affect the Purses of the People. All the Arguments in favor of Civil Liberty apply with equal force in the case of Commercial freedom. Indeed more is to be said in favor of the first then the last. A restriction in Civil Liberty may give energy to a government, & turn to the Aggrandisement of the Family at the Head of it. But Commercial restrictions can add neither to the means, Magnificence or Energy of a Government; & of Evils that arise from them, surely it is no small one to keep alive the resentments of Nations against each other. If we examine the fact I believe we shall find not a single instance in which a Nation has clearly benefited by them. I will not except the famous [British] Navigation Act: for the supposed advantages or ends gained by it, may either with equal justice be attributed to other causes, or may be produced without this one of Restriction. Take for instance that of National Defence. Those who live by you will surely fight for you; & that which is admitted in Armies, should & may be made to be equally Legal in Marines, viz. Recruits from all Nations indiscriminately. The Custom is different in the two Cases at present, because Nations had Pyracy to guard against; but now that this Danger is removed, the declaration of a Single Protector might establish the custom in the one as is in the other case. Indeed to go farther, I shall not be surprised if

I live to see the Body of Marines like the Amazons[1] of old become a distinct Nation independant of all others, altho' owing their very Existence to them.

Excuse me for troubling you with a Political Speculation when you are pestered so much with them otherwise. I have been insensibly lead on, for I had no intention of it, both as I believe we fundamentally agree in Principle tho' not in opinion respecting Measures; & as I think the Light & Reason that has opened on the World will produce a Reformation in Measures soon enough for the good of Humanity.

Remember me to Mr. Page & Mr. White, & any other friends of mine that may be with you.

ALS, Madison Papers, DLC. Written from St. James's, Jamaica; carried by Mr. Yates.

[1] The itinerant female warriors of Greek legend.

The Type-Nostrum

The maxim's held by all mankind,
That Quacks in ev'ry trade we find;
And yet how few are on their guard—
Pretenders seldom miss reward:
E'en Senates—form'd of learned sages—
Have been be-quack'd, in former ages.
All hail ye labor-hating crew,
Who keeping *novelty* in view,
Mankind bewilder and surprize,
To see with *your's*—not their *own eyes*.
Yet spight of nostrum, pill and powder,
The knell of death was never louder.
    But nostrum, hid in *broken steel*,
To benefit the common weal—
May justly make a stoic feel.
Yet B—[1] says no mortal snout,
Can scent this wondrous secret out—
And ev'n C— [*Congress*] seem to think,
That he can make such strokes in ink,
As shall defy all future cheats,
T'enrich themselves by counterfeits.
Hence Patents "ready cut and dry"—
Confirm the maxim in my eye:
While B—'s meer *chance medly stroke*,
Prove wit and genius all a joke!

GUS, 27 February. The piece was introduced by a note: "MR. FENNO, Being in the gallery this day, the rapidity of certain movements, gave rise to the following, which please to publish, and oblige, S." A nostrum, in this sense, is a panacea or quack remedy.

---

[1] Francis Bailey (1735–1815), a Philadelphia printer, who petitioned the House on 29 January for patent protection for his method of producing counterfeit-proof print type. The poem's satirical tone is in the spirit of some members' reception of Hamilton's report that day, recommending a bill described by Livermore as preventing an anticounterfeiting method from being counterfeited (*DHFFC* 12:580). For more, see *DHFFC* 8:73–84.

OTHER DOCUMENTS

Jacob Broom to John Langdon. ALS, Langdon Papers, NhPoA. Written from Wilmington, North Carolina.

"As our Commercial regulations are now uniform thro'out the United States, the Coasting Trade has is become more worthy of attention"; asks for recommendation of merchants at ports "to the Eastward" with whom he may safely trade.

John Dawson to James Madison. ALS, Madison Papers, DLC. Written from Richmond, Virginia.

Hamilton's report on public credit and Knox's on the militia have "given rise to a variety of opinions"; Hamilton's report especially "is not thought altogether orthodox in this place"; asks for any information which may prevent Anthony Singleton, the sinking fund agent in Virginia, from "being playd on by the Speculators who have always the earliest information intelligence" as a result of public securities' fluctuating prices.

John Fitch to William Samuel Johnson. ALS, Fitch Papers, DLC. Written from Philadelphia. Recipient's identity based on content and context of Johnson's letter to Fitch, 20 January.

Too "engaged in the Boat" to come to New York; asks for Johnson's interest on behalf of himself and Henry Voight, for appointments to the Mint, and whether Johnson would provide recommendations to accompany their petition to the President; if only one appointment is to be made, recommends Voight as more capable.

Horatio Gates to Jonathan Trumbull. ALS, Dreer Collection, PHi. Written from "Travellers Rest," Berkeley County, West Virginia; franked; postmarked Baltimore, 7 March.

Encloses letter to Trumbull's brother John for forwarding; "all Honest thinking Men seem satisfied with the Conduct of their Delegates"; inevitably, some are disappointed, "but such opposition will only serve to fix

Government on a Firmer Foundation"; hopes it may be "as Firmly Fixed as the Allegheny Mountain, & Stand as long."

William Paterson to Euphemia Paterson. ALS, Paterson Papers, NjR. Place to which addressed not indicated.

Must postpone his return home from the next day to the end of the following week; roads are "scarcely passable"; is serving on three committees "which will take up my Time for about a Week; one of them, perhaps, longer"; two of the committees, appointed that day, "will keep pretty closely to business"; was in Elizabethtown on court business from Monday to Wednesday; took an hour to go from Elizabethtown Point to Elizabethtown; will answer a letter from daughter Cornelia "by this Opportunity"; inquires about purchasing provisions for home; is pleased with son Billy's schooling, which the weather will probably suspend until mid-May; dined with Walton (Anthony Walton White) on 14 February, but has not seen him since; "the Roads have been too bad to stir out."

Roger Sherman to Rebecca Sherman. ALS, Foster Collection, MHi. Mistakenly dated from New Haven rather than New York; place to which addressed not indicated.

Sends directions for the use of leather ("I want a good handsome pair of home made gloves") and gold tincture (for treating toothaches) that he has purchased for home; is not certain if William Cushing and wife will be able to stop at New Haven to visit; believes the session will be longer than he expected; the funding business "goes on slow"; may return home once "by water" during the session; "I would have you write as often as is convenient."

Samuel Storer to John Langdon. ALS, Langdon Papers, NhPoA. Written from Portsmouth, New Hampshire, and postmarked there on 2 March.

Langdon's friends "in this Quarter" are "Anxious" to know about his intention to leave Congress; is convinced he would have been elected governor "Unanimously"; doubts the truth of a rumor that Langdon plans to return to Portsmouth in the spring to oversee construction of two ships, either for the navy or the India trade, "which report is very pleasing to the People"; Langdon's family is well; regards to Tobias Lear.

Thomas Thompson to John Langdon. ALS, Langdon Papers, NhPoA. Written from Portsmouth, New Hampshire. For background on the Portsmouth district court petition, see *DHFFC* 8:185–86.

Asks "to be Honour'd with a line" in a leisure moment; Langdon is much wished for as governor; his family is well; inquires about purchasing home goods from New York or Philadelphia; wishes Congress would establish a sinking fund for its paper money; "a Petition is on foot to Congress from this Town concerning the District Court—our Trade &c. which will be forwarded you when Signed by a Sufficient number—but they are very tardy in this, as in all other Busness of this nature"; regards to Wingate, Livermore, and Gilman.

Dudley Atkins Tyng to George Thatcher. ALS, Chamberlain Collection, MB. Written from Newburyport, Massachusetts.

Regrets the lapse in their former correspondence, "which had been so useful and honorary to me"; asks Thatcher to "pack up old Newspapers now & then for me—It will look as if I kept up a connection with the great World" and to give an enclosure to "Mr. J. who is now in New-York," about whom Thatcher might "recollect a little Conversation between us, as you passed through Newbury"; solicits his attention on [*Jonathan*] Jackson's behalf, "and if any Thing should be on Foot for his Relief, for God's sake lend a helping Hand."

Manasseh Cutler, Diary. Cutler Papers, IEN.

"Invited to Dine with the Vice President. Mr. Reed [*Nathan Read*] went with me in a Hackney Coach. Returned in the evening. Very agreeable. Colonel [*William S.*] Smith and Lady [*Abigail*] present."

William Samuel Johnson, Diary. Johnson Papers, CtHi.

"Levee. Visits."

SATURDAY, 27 FEBRUARY 1790

Cool (Johnson)

John Adams to Jabez Bowen

Your letter of the 15th never reached me till yesterday I condole with you in the unfavorable aspect of your elections: but still hope that your people will cool upon reflection and that a majority of the convention may be induced to accept the constitution. It is in vain to enquire what Congress may or can do; at present they can do nothing. The awful object before them, I mean the national debt, monopolizes the attention of Congress to such a degree that untill some system is digested no member of either house will be able to attend to any thing else. When the affair of Rhode Island shall be taken up, there will be twenty different plans proposed, time must be spent in examination discussion and deliberation.

He must be less than a thinking being who can be at a loss to foresee what Congress will ultimately do with Rhode Island, if she obstinately refuses to come in—But it would not be prudent in me to predict it The opposition of Rhode Island to the impost seems to have been the instrument which providence thought fit to use for the great purpose of establishing the present constitution:[1] I sincerely hope their infatuation may not oblige the United states to take severe measures at their expence to convince the people that their interests are in the power of their neighbours and to gain strength to the New government by punishing its rash opposers. I must finally say to you in confidence that I beleive Congress will never beg or pray or exhort your Antis to come in. They will leave them at perfect liberty—and whenever they take any steps it will not be till injuries shall be multiplied and their just resentment approved by all the world.

FC:lbk, Adams Family Manuscript Trust, MHi. Sent to Providence, Rhode Island.

[1] Congress's inability to levy impost duties that would ensure a federal revenue independent of state requisitions was seen as a major shortcoming of the Articles of Confederation virtually from its inception. The proposal for such an impost was on the table when the Articles became effective on 1 March 1781, at which time it became a proposed amendment requiring unanimous ratification by the states. Rhode Island alone refused to ratify, after which Virginia rescinded its ratification in December 1782, killing the initiative. In April 1783 a second amendment for a federal impost was sent to the states for ratification, over Rhode Island's solitary negative, but was defeated by unacceptable conditions imposed by Pennsylvania and New York (*DHROC* 1:140, 146–48; *DHFFC* 10:2–3n).

John Adams to Francis Adrian Van der Kemp

Your agreable Letter of the 9. Jan. has lain too long unanswered. Mr. Mappa,[1] I should be happy to present to the President and to Serve in any other Way in my Power.

Your Criticisms upon "the defence"[2] deserve more Consideration than I have time to give them.

***

I will candidly confess, that an hereditary Senate, [*lined out*] without an hereditary Executive, would diminish the Prerogatives of the President and the Liberties of the People. But I contend that hereditary descent in both, when controuled by an independent Representation of the People, is better than corrupted, turbulent and bloody Elections. and the Knowledge You have of the human heart will concur with your Knowledge of the History of nations to convince you that Elections of Presidents, & Senators, cannot be long conducted in a populous, oppulent and commercial Nation, without Corruption, Sedition and Civil War.

A Discourse upon Fœderative Republicks and an History of the American Revolution, are both Undertakings too extensive for my Forces, unless I should retire from all Employments public and private, and devote the Remainder of my Life to writing.

***

How far it will be proper for the President to interpose, in your favour in your affair in Holland, I pretend not to say. My Advice is that you write to the President, Stating the whole of the Facts and requesting his assistance by his Minister, as far as may be proper. it will probably produce an Instruction to assist you at least in a private way.

I was Surprized to find that you had given Such particular Attention to my Volumes, and am much flattered with your favourable opinion and ingenious Compliments. The Necessity of Reaction to counterpoise Action, is pursued further than it ever was before in any Age or Language that I know of. The opinion is as ancient as Zeno as We learn from Diogenes Laertius[3] I think this may be asserted without Hesitation that every Example in History proves that Peace, & Liberty, can be united only by the Equilibrium of three Branches, because there is not one Example to be found of Peaceful Liberty without it. and it is not to be wondered at because human Passions are all insatiable—They will move and increase in motion untill they are united. this ~~quatity~~ quality in Men explains all the Phænomena in Government.

I am flattered in Letters from Europe, with Compliments that the Science of Government has not been so much improved Since the Writings of Montesquieu &c. But notwithstanding this, the Books will not be much read. So far from flattering they offend the Passions and counteract the Views of all Parties—of Courts Kings and Ministers—of Senates Aristocrates and all the Pride of noble Blood—and of Democrates and all the Licentious Rabbles, who wish to fish in troubled Waters. a Wish for Unlimited Power is the ~~Wish~~ natural Passion of each of these orders, and no Doctrine Pleases but that which flatters the ruling Passion.

Whether human Reason will ever get the better of all these Prejudices and be able to govern Such Passions I know not. I will never cease to preach my favourite Doctrine, untill I die.

ALS, Letters of John Adams, PHi. Place to which addressed not indicated. The omitted text includes factual clarifications of his *Defense* and comments on the American Revolution and his reluctance to support independence "untill Hostilities commenced."

[1]On 9 January, Van der Kemp wrote Adams a letter of introduction for Adam Gerard Mappa, whom the Dutch minister could not introduce because Mappa was officially *non grata* to his home government (Adams Family Manuscript Trust, MHi).

[2] Adams's *Defense of the Constitutions of the United States* (New York, 1787).
[3] The Greek biographer Diogenes Laertius (early third century A.D.) cited Zeno of Elea (ca. 490–430 B.C.) in his *Lives of Eminent Philosophers*. Zeno's teachings on the motion and rest of bodies refuted the existence of genuinely separate units in any plurality, for which Aristotle considered him the inventor of dialectic.

Fisher Ames to Nathaniel Appleton

I paid immediate attention to Mr. [*Ebenezer*] Prout's subject—I first applied at the Auditor's [*Oliver Wolcott, Jr.*] office without success—then I desired information of Mr. [*Joseph*] Howell the Commissioner of Army Accounts His Answer is inclosed. I have since called upon the Comptroller [*Nicholas Eveleigh*], who informs me that the ordinance of Congress limiting the period of exhibiting claims will not admit an examination of the acct.[1] Nothing remains but a petition to Congress praying that the acct. may be passed that ordinance notwithstanding—Many petitions have been presented which express a similar request—But no decision has yet been made as to the point of admitting excluded claims—If Mr. Prout should think fit to petition for relief, I shall be ready to pay proper attention to the business—If Congress should not interpose, many worthy claimants will suffer loss, and on the other hand it is difficult to open the door again without opening it for a throng of obscure and improper demands—you will, however, do me the favour to assure Mr. Prout of my readiness to serve him.

We are still occupied with the business of assuming the debts of the states—A motion to limit the assumption to the surplus of a state's debt more than it's quota was rejected by two to one. It seems to be very probable that the measure will be adopted. In that event, you have, I suppose contemplated the revival of the Loan Offices for the purpose of procuring the return of the debt.

ALS, Colburn Collection, Bostonian Society, MHi. Addressed to Boston; franked; postmarked 28 February. The enclosures, which included "Mr. Prout's papers," have not been found.

[1] Prout sought his pay as a clerk to the commissary for British prisoners held in Massachusetts. For the acts of limitation barring the claim, see *DHFFC* 7:588–89. For Hamilton's report on Prout's 3 November 1791 petition, see *PAH* 13:200–201. The petitioner was probably Ebenezer Prout (1752–95) of Boston, rather than his father, also Ebenezer Prout (1719–1804), a Boston merchant.

Thomas Dwight to Theodore Sedgwick

We had heared of the report of the Secretary at war, respecting a national militia, but knew nothing of the principles of it, until I was favoured with the whole plan by you—to most of the people it would in my opinion, if adopted, be extremely disagreeable were it to be attended with no accumulation of debt; but with an annual expence of so great a sum as is proposed, you would set the whole body into a flame which would not be easily extinguished—we are told that at the Eastward it is a subject of bitter cursing and condemnation, not of antifederalists only. but the generality of the people.

You will perceive Sir. that in N. Hampshire the alarm is sounded in regard to an assumption of the State Debts—and that they are led to believe such a measure would be attended with consequences destructive of their liberties—what manner of men they are in that State who patronize and inculcate these sentiments, I know not, but in our Comm[*unit*]y. so far as I can inform myself—the party is composed of men who, (almost unexceptionably) expect to derive benefit from the importance of the State Govt. by offices which are in its gift—all influence and power given to the Genl. Govt. is estimated as so much taken from the individual ones, and many of our *great little folks* dread a reduction to that state of insignificance which they are fearfully anticipating, and from which many of them never would have emerged, but by the follies and passions of the people.

Mr. Scots proposal in Congress for *discrimination*[1] is spoken of by our anti's as the only one to the purpose and of course his speeches are complimented as the very best Mr. Maddisons project[2] finds hardly a single advocate in this quarter—indeed so far as I can form an opinion there is an almost universal expectation that the Secys. system will be the groundwork of the acts of Congress in regard to the debt—should Mr. M—s proposals go into operation, I shall immediately lose all pride for my Country and will never consider it as a blessing that I was born in America—no one disputes the greatness of Mr. M—n nor have I heared his integrity called in question—all seem to be puzzled to investigate the source from whence his projects arise—if he aims at popularity, never did a great man more fatally misjudge.

You will excuse me for the liberties I take in saying any thing and every thing to you about public men and measures—I hope never to be guilty of making a business of complaining of & reprobating either the one or the other to every body.

We expect daily to have the fountains of scurrility and abuse opened on the subject of State elections—the law reformer [*John Gardiner*] has been the bone at which the scribblers have gnawed for some time—but as the man and his measures are both hanged on the same gallows—they will I believe say little more about either.

ALS, Sedgwick Papers, MHi. Written from Springfield, Massachusetts.

[1] On 9 February Scott proposed that Congress discriminate among creditors as to the merit of their claims, paring down a claim "if on enquiry it is found that the ostensible demand is double what ought in justice to be paid."

[2] Madison's 11 February motion to discriminate between original and secondary holders of federal certificates.

James Madison to James Madison, Sr.

I have not yet recd. a single line from Orange since I left it. The letter from my brother [*Ambrose?*] when at Alexa. is the only written information that I have had the pleasure of, A few lines from Mr. [*George?*] Hite excepted. These gave me an account of my sisters marriage,[1] and added that about that period my mother [*Nelly Conway Madison*] was better. I am anxious to hear more on that subject, and indulge my hopes that her health will yet be re-established.

The papers inclosed at different times will have shewn the state of the business before Congs. The proposition for compromizing the matter between original sufferers & the Stockjobbers, after being long agitated was rejected by considerable majority, less perhaps from a denial of the justice of the measure, than a supposition of its impracticability. The idea is much better relished I find in the Country at large, than it was in this City. The subject now before Congs. is the proposed assumption of the State debts. Opinions are much divided on it, and the result can not be foretold. These difficulties and discussions seem to have produced here a suspence of the public opinion. Stock has been stationary in consequence of it at about 7/. in the pound. I am afraid that the people at a distance from information will continue to be a prey to those who have about the public Councils, and communicate with emissaries all over the Continent. I wish it were possible to defend the uninformed from these impositions. The best they can do is not to deal with speculators, but to await patiently the event.

I find by a letter from Mr. Jefferson that grain is getting as high in Virga. as here. The run on our market from Europe seems to be increasing. If the alarm be not artificial in France England &c. which can not be altogether the case, it is probable that the price will be high for several years.

ALS, Madison Papers, DLC. Place to which addressed not indicated.

[1] Sarah Catlett Madison (1764–1843) married Thomas Macon (1765–1838), of Orange County, Virginia, on 30 January.

Samuel A. Otis to William Smith (of Boston)

I wrote you by wednesdays post since which no progress is made in the funding system The fact is Madison heads a party to embarrass the assumption of the State debts, after much opposition I am however induced to think it will obtain—The opinion of some upon the rate of interest, is, that the original promise of six p. Ct. should remain unimpaired, but to pay no ~~faster~~ more than revenue will admit if, if sufficient to pay four, or only three pay that now, and the remainder as ability will be afforded—This say they would shew an honest intention, and being all that the public can do, will probably give satisfaction—The question is of so much magnitude that the House view it with circumspection, and will hear and combat every proposition.

I have enclosed the papers to Harry [*Harrison Gray Otis*], but suppose your own come regularly.

I have a disposition to make the most of things for the benefit of my family, but it would not be will for me to be seen much in business, as my office might be injured thereby; I am however of opinion that something might be made by underwriting if I could by lodging a sum with a confidential friend, induce him to take prudent sums from—I will thank you for a candid opinion upon this subject.

The whole world seem to be innovating in regard to their governments, but I am not sure they will exchange for the better.

The prospect of accession by the State of R.I. is unfavorable, there are restless & abandoned men there who want curbing, but I know not when it will take place.
***

ALS, Smith-Carter Papers, MHi. Addressed to Boston.

Benjamin Rush to James Madison

In answer to your polite letter, I have only to repeat my congratulations to you for the honor you have done to the claims of justice and patriotism by your motion [*on discrimination*]. The Small number of the minority that rose to support it, does not lessen its merit. The decision upon that great question will leave a stain upon our Country which no time nor declammation can ever wipe away. History will decide very differently upon it. [*lined out*] Perhaps in the course of our lives we may hear it reprobated by the very men who have been its advocates, for I take it for granted that the whole of the Certificates will be bought up by foreigners as soon as they reach their nominal value, and then the people of America will Speak One language upon this Subject. Such a decision I am sure would not have taken place had the Congress been seated on the Banks of the Delaware or Potowmac. Public Opinion is a Species of influence—and this I [*lined out*] well know has been exerted too successfully in New York on some of your members. The desertion of principles, that the clamors of Speculators have created in

New York in [*lined out*] your house, has given me a melancholly proof that we want much of the Spirit & dignity of true republicans in our Country.

The weight of reason—morality—and even religion is so great on your Side of the question, that I ~~feel~~ wonder ~~at~~ that a man of any character should have opposed it. The same arguments ~~that~~ would justify the African Slave trade, that were used against you viz. National honor pledged to the African Company,[1] and political necessity; and the man who can receive 4 or 6 ℔ cent on an £100 for which he gave only ten, without inviting the man from whom he obtained this unequal bargain to share in the immense profit which has accrued upon it, is but a few degrees removed from that State of mind which would lead to highway robbery.[2]

Mr. Miller the bookseller of London[3] gave Dr. Robertson £500 for his history of Scotland[4]—but such was its reputation that the bookseller made several thousand pounds by the Sale of it. As a compensation to Dr. Robertson for the unequal bargain Mr. Miller [*lined out*] had made with him, he sent him every year ~~for every year~~ as long as he lived Afterwards a pipe of Madeira Wine. This was natural justice. Its Obligations are infinitely more binding upon Congress in the case lately before them.

In reviewing the decision upon your motion, I feel disposed to wish that my name was blotted out from having [*lined out*] contributed a single mite towards the american revolution. We have effected a deliverance from the national injustice of Great Britain, to be *subjugated* by a mighty Act of national injustice by the United States.

It is amusing to hear Gentlemen talk of the "public blessing" of a debt contracted to foreigners & a few american Speculators of four or five millions of dollars a year. Nothing fundamentally *unjust*, can ever produce happiness in its issue. It will lay the foundation of an Aristocracy in our Country. It will change the property of nine tenths of the freeholders of the States, and it will be a lasting monument of the [*lined out*] efficacy of idleness—speculation & fraud Above industry Œconomy & integrity ~~to~~ in obtaining wealth & independence. Nor is this all. It will be a beacon to deter Other nations & future generations from attempting to better their situations, for it clearly establishes this proposition, that revolutions like party Spirit, are the rage of *many* for the benefit of a *few*. The Abbe [*Guillaume*] Raynell in speaking of the name of America being derived from Americus instead of Columbus, says "it was a presage that America was to be the theatre of future Acts of injustice."[5] The extirpation of the ~~Spaniards~~ Indians by the Spaniards in South America—the importation of slaves into the southern states—and even the depradations committed upon our country by the British Army during the late war, are not more striking proofs of the truth of that observation than the establishment of the principles of the Speculators in the rejection of your motion in Congress.

Good men sigh and deplore in Secret the [*lined out*] measures which are expected to follow that unfortunate event. you are happy in having your name upon record as an enemy to it. I am not [*lined out*] called upon to give a public Opinion upon it, nor do I feel disposed to ~~object to~~ oppose it, as I have often done Vice & error in the public papers, but I shall leave a testimony upon record against it for the information of my Children—for ~~with them only~~ they ~~by~~ are the only part of posterity by whom I wish to be remembered, or known hereafter.

Our Country people are as yet uninformed or deceived in this important business. *Delay—delay—delay* therefore will do wonders for you.

The combined influence of British agents—[*lined out*] New York tories and antifederalists—and New York aristocratical whigs upon the Councils of the United States, have long ago led me to wish that the Seat of Congress was on the Delaware—the Susquehannah or the Potowmac. The sooner this question is determined the better.

I have only to request that these broken tho'ts may rest in your own bosom.

P. S. The extracts contained in the enclosed pamphflet shew that mankind are growing wise upon the Subject of penal laws.[6]

The report of your Secretary of War [*on the militia*] seems to indicate a retrograde progress upon the Subject of murder by War. He seems to consider man as created not to cultivate the earth—or to be happy in any of the pursuits of civilized life, but to *carry a musquet*—to *wear a regimental* coat—& *to kill or be killed*. It is better to prevent wars, than to learn the Art of carrying them on successfully. For the purpose let military Shews (so fascinating to young people) be rare—and if possible let the military character be stripped of its glare—and even rendered unpopular. Half the money demanded by general Knox's report spent in establishing free Schools, & in teaching our young people industry & morality, would extirpate war for ever from the United States. The ~~successful of the~~ successful issue of the late war under a thousand disadvantages that can never occur again, proves that militia establishments in the *time of peace* are wholly unnecessary. We lose the Attainment of great Objects by not attempting them. The preamble of a single law ~~be~~ of Congress declaring in strong terms the folly & Absurdity as well as inhumanity of war, would be do more good than a thousand Volumes written against it. A proposition from the United States to some of the Courts of Europe to concur in the appointment of Umpires to decide national disputes without appealing to Arms, would be considered as Utopian at present, but it would be successful in 40, or 50 years. Truths resemble trees—some ripen in a short time—while others require half a century ~~to~~ or more to bring them to perfection. But the Seeds of the latter must be planted, as well as of the former, by *some body*. To plant a forest tree says Dr. Johnson[7] is the most *disinterested* Act of benevolence a man can perform, for it is impossible for him to live long eno' Afterwards, to enjoy any benefit from his labor. To sow the seed of a truth, or of a revolution, in favor of human happiness that requires many years to ripen it, is equally a mark of disinterested benevolence. The Seeds of truth differ from the seeds of plants in one particular. None of them are *ever lost*. ~~They~~ [*lined out*] Like matter they are indestructable in their very nature. They produce fruit in Other ages or Countries. The Seeds of the american revolution were sown in the reign of Charles the first. The Seeds of the reformation were sown in England in the reign of Henry the IVth. The Seeds of the present humane & enlightened policy upon the Subject of the Slavery of the Negroes, were sown in Pennsylvania near 20 years ago. many other instances of a distant & improbable connection between the first proposition, & the Accomplishment of events might be mentioned. Your extensive reading & observation will naturally suggest them. To oppose popular prejudices, or to propose plans of human happiness that cannot be perfected in the course of a single life, I know subjects a man to the imputation of being a Speculator, but as long as his Speculations are not in the blood or limbs of poor Soldiers, there can be no disgrace in them here, or remorse from them hereafter.

Excuse the length of this postscript. My ~~pen~~ heart ran away with me—& my pen followed it.

ALS, Madison Papers, DLC. Written from Philadelphia; franked; postmarked.

[1] Great Britain's Royal African Company (also known as the Guinea Company), chartered in 1672, enjoyed a monopoly on the British trade in African slaves until 1698.

[2] Much of the language of this paragraph comes from a piece that Rush wrote for the *Pennsylvania Mercury* but never published (PPL at PHi).

[3] The influential publisher Andrew Millar (1705–68) was the leading commercial force behind many voices of the Scottish Enlightenment. He was the first person in Britain to litigate for the legal protection of copyright (*Annual Newsletter of the Centre for the History of the Book*, Autumn 2004, pp. 5–6).

[4] William Robertson (1721–93) was a Scottish churchman who became "historiographer to the King." His two volume *History of Scotland during the Reigns of Queen Mary and King James VI* was published in London in 1759.

[5] Paraphrased from Volume 2, Book II of Abbé Raynal's *History of the . . . West Indies*.

[6] Probably Rush's *Extracts and Remarks on the Subject of Punishment and Reformation of Criminals* (Philadelphia, 1790).

[7] Dr. Samuel Johnson (1709–84) was the premier literary scholar and lexicographer of England's Augustan Age.

William Smith (S.C.) to Edward Rutledge

The question of assumption still under debate—various amendments are proposed by Madison, White &ca. to embarass the business—White's amendmt. was lost by a great majority—Madison has proposed another which if agreed to will blow up the whole business—the difficulties are great—& after all, the State Creditors will receive nothing for two years. The new England people are against the Amend. warmly—they want no payment from Debtor to Creditor States—they say let Congress pay the State ~~Creditors~~ Debts, & on a final settlement of accounts pay the Creditor States whatever ballance they may be entitled to, out of the fœderal Treasury. The amendment requires that ballances shall be paid from Dr. to Cr. States, & if it is carried, I fear, the friends to the assumption will then vote against it.

In my next {I hope} to inform you of our Success—we shall opp{ose? t}he propo{sition} {torn}ly even tho our people shod. {get} nothing for two years, yet {they would} be in a better plight than if they depended on the State, for there appears no disposition there to do them any Justice. The Virginians tell us that unless their amendmts. take place, the Creditor States will never receive their ballances—this is not improbable.

ALS, Smith Papers, ScHi. This is a postscript to a letter begun on 26 February, above. The words in curly braces are from *SCHM* 69(1968):107.

Caleb Strong to Nathan Dane

I thank you heartily for your two Letters of the 17th. & 20th. Instant the latter of which I have just recd. they contain more Information touching the Subjects before Congress than all the Rest I have received from Massachusetts, I have just now enquired of Mr. [*John Taylor*] Gilman the Commissioner how they proceed in their Business, he informs me that they are now considering the Claims of New Jersey, Mr. [*Abraham*] Clark as agent from that State is [*lined out*] attending here; Mr. Gilman says that after he has finished, the Commissioners will probably be able to attend to the Demands of our State but he cannot ascertain the Time when that will happen, I am glad that the Genl. Court have agreed to choose an Agent, we heretofore supposed that Mr. [*Samuel*] Osgood would be able to do the Business, and as the Genl. Court might object to the Expence of an Agency, and Mr. Osgoods Demands would not probably be great, we thought they might readily agree to choose him, but I am better pleased if they propose to make Choice of a Person who need not be diverted from the Business by other Objects, I have strong Suspicions, partly indeed from what Mr. Osgood has informed me that our Claims are not in a very good Situation, and that much Attention will be necessary to obtain Justice for the State.

From the Votes already taken in the House it is probable that a considerable Majority will be in favour of an Assumption of the State Debts, but Mr.

Madison wishes to make some qualifying Terms which many others are not pleased with, you will see his last Motion in this Days paper, the Advocates for an Assumption I think are increasing from the Idea, that it is impracticable to carry into Effect a Revenue System of the Genl. Government while the several States by different Modes are making provision for their own Creditors, who indeed are as much entitled to Consideration & Payment as the Creditors of the Genl. Government—I know have been told before that some few Persons have been indiscreet enough to express their Wishes of a compleat Consolidation of the States [*lined out*], the Scheme is so absurd that I wonder any reasonable Man should either vindicate or be alarmed by it—President Sullivans Speech[1] is not mentioned here as an Evidence of his Judgment or Discretion, the Truth of it may very well be questioned the several States have never possessed compleat Sovereignty as the Power of making peace & War has since the Revolution been vested in the Genl. Government, but no one doubted of their Sovereignty to certain Purposes, their Powers it is true are considerably diminished by the new Constitution, but still they are uncontroulable in the Exercise of internal Legislation & the administration of Justice—I am confident that Sir Wm. Temple in his Acct. of the United Provinces[2] [*lined out*] represents that the Sovereignty is sometimes said to be in the Assembly of the States General. but that there are also marks of Sovereignty not only in the Provincial States but also in many of the Cities of which those States are composed, those Cities having "the power of exercising Judicature & levying Money" Their is nothing absurd in the Idea that a Government may be sovereign to some purposes & not to all—several Instances of this kind might be mentioned in other Countries, and I presume it will be the Case in this so long as the States continue to be united—but I have said enough & perhaps too much on this Subject for while I complain of others preaching about it I am turning Preacher myself.

Be kind enough to let me know whether Mr. [*Samuel, Jr.*] Phillips has recovered his health and if not what his Distemper and Situation are, I have too much Interest in him not to be anxious for his Welfare.

[*P. S.*] I enclose a letter to Mr. [*Abel*] Wilder as he may be gone from Boston—if that is the Case be good enough to cover it and direct it to him.

ALS, Wetmore Family Collection, CtY. Place to which addressed not indicated.

[1] New Hampshire President (Governor) John Sullivan's controversial speech of 29 December 1789 proposed that the states ceased to be sovereign with the ratification of the Constitution; consequently a conflict of interest between state and federal officeholders was not possible.

[2] Sir William Temple (1628–99), British diplomat and historian, authored *Observations upon the United Provinces of the Netherlands* (1696).

Paine Wingate to Mary Wingate Wiggin

Though you are often hearing from me by my letters to your Mother, to Mr. [*Andrew*] Wiggin, and to others, yet I believe that it will be some satisfaction to you to recieve from me one of your own. When we are absent at a considerable distance & for some time, a letter is something like a short visit, though not so agreeable as a personal interview & conversation. When we cannot have what we most wish for, the next desireable object is to be embraced. I should be very happy to see you and my family & friends at Stratham [*New Hampshire*]; but since my situation at present deprives me of that pleasure, and probably will for some months to come, I esteem it a very great privelege that I can so conveniently & frequently write to & hear from you & them. I have had it in my intention for a considerable time to write to you & have promised it in my letters to your mother, but one thing & another has hertofore prevented me. I can assure you that you are dayly present in my mind and always have my tender affection & concern. You know that I am a fond parent to my children and am ever anxious for their welfare and happiness & you have a full share with the rest. I am sorry to hear that you have been so much afflicted this winter with the toothach. I was in hopes that the extracting of one last fall would have relieved you; but you must endeavour to bear with patience those troubles which are allotted in life. We have great reason to be thankful for those blessings we do enjoy, though they may be mixed with some troubles. If we look round among our fellow creatures how many do we see whose situation is not so comfortable as ours? Indeed how few are there with whom we should be willing to exchange? This, and the consideration of the many desireable enjoyments we have should lead to contentment and inspire us with gratitude. In the ways of religion & virtue we may have peace of mind & a chearful hope of future happiness. Religion if we rightly understand it will not deprive us of any innocent enjoyments of life. It will not fill us with fear & gloom as some would represent it, but with love & peace. It very much consists in love to God & the Saviour & benevolence to our fellow men & sobriety with regard to or ourselves. In these duties there is nothing hard or mysterious; nothing but what tends to make us chearful & happy in this life as well as the next. I am very glad to hear that Harriet [*Wiggin*] was relieved from relieved from her late indisposition. Poor child! I do not wonder that she should be unwell in cutting so many of her large teeth. I hope that she is now well & will be long spared for a comfort to you. You will remember that Polly Wiggin is now at an age in which she is capable of much useful instruction & improvement & I hope that you will be a good & discreet mother to your children. You will perhaps begin to think that my letter is too much taken up in lessons of instruction, rather than in affording you some amusement & entertainment. I will therefore dwell no longer on the subject & believe that you will receive what I have said as a mark of my sincere affection for you. I begin now to think that it is doubtful whether I shall get home quite so soon as I expected. I thought when I left home that it was likely I might return in May. We may possibly; but if Congress should not adjourn until June or the first of July, I think we shall not meet again until the march after. For my part I shall be glad to be at home whenever I can; though I have enjoyed my health here unusually well; & am tollerably contented. We have considerable amusements as well as business, and company enough at all times. I spend a good deal of time necessarily in writing, & some in reading. I have a very pleasant chamber & fire by myself where I can retire out of company as I please, when not attending in Congress. But as my eyesight fails me by candle light I always spend my evenings in company either at home or abroad. I have very little female acquaintance. No family in which I am intimate & where I can go as I chuse without ceremony as I used to your Aunt [*Hannah Veazie?*] Wingate's. But I live more like a stranger which does not perfectly suit me. I cannot tell much about fashions, but so far as I observe there is no material [*alter*]ations between this & last year. I am told there has been fine sleighing in New Hampshire. I hope you have been able to improve it in visiting your mother often & your other friends. I dont know but Sally [*Wingate*] will think I have forgotten her, as I have not written to her yet or mentioned her very often; but she may be assured that I remember her with much affection & intend to write to her as soon as I well can. If there is any thing which you wish for, that I can buy here before I return I will procure it for you with pleasure. I suppose any thing of the silver kind is rather dearer here than at the Eastward as workmanship costs more; but perhaps some sorts of plaited ware, such as Salts, peper casters &c. may be as cheaper or cheaper. If you or your mother should desire any of these I will buy them if I can & you or she ~~desire it~~ will write me word. When I return I purpose to give you more if there should be any thing you wish for towards your furniture.

ALS, Wingate Papers, MH. Place to which addressed not indicated.

Oliver Wolcott, Jr. to Nathan Strong

Congress are proceeding in their deliberations on the Secretarys report. the Northern states seem generally to favour the plan. in Virginia & some other States, there is a determined and stubborn opposition. they fear a consolidation of the government, and also that if their State debts are assumed ~~that~~ all the securities will be purchased by foreigners & by their neighbours. they say that the system ~~of~~ for raising revenues by imposts operates unequally, they being the greatest consumers; that to remedy this inequality by a land tax will render such establishments necessary, as will render the general government formidable. that though the assumption will be a temporary relief, by causing the revenues to be expended where they are collected, yet in the end it will operate to them like a foreign debt, as they know the dispositions of their people will be to sell every thing which will produce money. these arguments have weight upon the principles of the gentlemen who urge them, but the contrary ideas by being founded upon the most undeniable principles of general policy, will gain ground & obtain a majority in the United States.

The worst circumstance attending our affairs, arises from the great variety of prejudices & manners in the United States, if they shall not shortly be assimulated, I fear that disagreable consequences will ensue.
***
I firmly believe that the United States, will never appoint more respectable men to seats in Congress, than the present and yet the observation made by a ~~Swedish~~ statesman to his son, is in many instances deplorably ~~true~~ verified—"Nescis, mi fili, parva cum sapientia regitur mundus."[1]

ALS, Wolcott Papers, CtHi. Place to which addressed not indicated. The letter may never have been sent; the date is from Wolcott's docket. The omitted text discusses the general hypocrisy of the public councils, where "a sufficient degree of the tribunitian spirit prevails." For the full text, see *Wolcott* 1:39–40.

[1] "You do not know, my son, with how little wisdom the world is governed." Axel Oxenstierna (1583–1654), lord high chancellor of Sweden from 1612 until his death, wrote this in a letter to his son, one of the negotiators at the Treaty of Westphalia (1648), ending the Thirty Years War.

Newspaper Article

The Old Soldier, whom *necessity alone* obliged to sell his pay, is happy that it is so great and so good a man, who has stepped forth, the champion of publick justice, publick faith, and publick honour. While the publick creditor, and the warworn Soldier can see
"*A* MADISON *above the rest,*
Pouring from his narrow chest,
More than Greek or Roman sense,
Floods of Truth *and Eloquence,*"
They will rest satisfied that his persevering endeavours will be crowned with success. "*If you wish to be a prosperous nation*" said our beloved Chief, "*do justice to your late army*"[1]—It is that justice which Mr. MADISON is now vindicating.

[Boston] *Massachusetts Centinel*, 27 February.

[1] A paraphrase of George Washington's 1783 Address to the States.

Letter from Charleston, South Carolina

The late impost laid by congress on salt, it is thought will operate partially and unequally, at least in these southern states. The greatest consumption of the salt is among that class of citizens that reside in the interior and
frontier parts of the state, who generally are very poor: A bushel of salt that
will cost a farmer, in the vicinity of the coast, one shilling, will cost a farmer
residing higher up from one dollar to fourteen shillings sterling, in proportion to the remoteness of his situation from the sea ports. And it is to be
remembered that the proprietor of 100 negroes, will not in the course of one
year, consume more salt than the man who owns 100 head of cattle, which,
in value is in the proportion of 5000l to 250l.

NYDA, 13 March; reprinted at Philadelphia, Baltimore, and Charleston, South Carolina.

Letter from New York

If I mistake not, my last ended towards the close of the debate on the
motion for a discrimination between original holders of securities and the
holders by purchase. The question on this motion was taken the day after
I wrote you, and carried against the discrimination by a majority of about
thirty five to fourteen. Then it was moved to amend the Resolution to read
as follows—*Resolved. That permanent funds ought to be appropriated for the support
of the civil and military establishments of the United States, and that the surplus of
the revenues of the United States, ought to be applied in just proportion to the discharge
of the interest of the domestick debt.* This finding but few supporters was soon
negatived: and it was moved, *That the monies arising from the sales of the Lands
belonging to the United States, be appropriated to the payment of the domestick debt—
But this motion was not seconded.*

[Portland, Maine] *Cumberland Gazette*, 15 March. This is probably from a letter written
by Thatcher to the newspaper's editor, Thomas B. Wait.

OTHER DOCUMENTS

Pierce Butler to Reverend Weeden Butler. ALS, Butler Letters, Uk. Addressed to Cheyne Walk, Chelsea, near London; postmarked 3 March; postmarked London, 26 April; answered "May and 1 June."
    Has sent a set of "Our Journals of last Session," in care of Mr. Richards,
    who sailed on Christmas Eve and whom he recommends on the basis
    of their "short acquaintance"; "He is a West Indian, yet a friend to the
    rights of Man"; Butler will introduce himself to Captain Edmonstone, to

whom he is indebted; Mrs. Butler "has been more than usualy indisposed of late—I thank God She is better"; "We are here thank God, in perfect peace and tranquility, there is not on Earth a more orderly Govermnt. than that of the United states at present"; Congress is "busily occupied" with funding and assumption; "I trust We shall soon get to rights and become a great People."

Daniel Cony to George Thatcher. ALS, Chamberlain Collection, MB. Written from Boston; received 6 March. A postscript dated 28 February is calendared under that date, below.

Reports the week's proceedings in the state legislature, including its support for establishing a college in Cumberland County (Maine), although no funds were yet provided; John Gardiner's legal reforms will come to nothing this session; Nathan Dane is appointed agent for the state's claims against the United States.

John Hamilton to John Steele. ALS, Steele Papers, NcU. Written from Edenton, North Carolina; addressed to Steele "in Congress." For the full text, see *DHFFE* 4:361.

Office seeking: federal district attorney; congratulations on election.

James Madison to George Nicholas. No copy known; acknowledged in Nicholas to Madison, 3 May.

Governor Alexander Martin to George Washington. Written from Rockingham, North Carolina. ALS, Washington Papers, DLC. For the full text, see *PGW* 5:183–85.

Office seeking: James Iredell for district judge; is sure he will be unanimously recommended by North Carolina's Senators and Representatives, who also are well acquainted with the probable candidates for officers of the court for the North Carolina district.

John Page to Edmund Pendleton. No copy known; acknowledged in Pendleton to Page, 15 March.

Roger Sherman to Simeon Baldwin. ALS, Sherman Collection, CtY. Addressed to New Haven, Connecticut; franked; postmarked 28 February.

Encloses that day's newspaper; requests copies of certain New Haven laws; believes there will be a majority for assumption of the states' war debts, as "the debts must follow the funds."

George Thatcher to Stephen Waite and Abner Bagley. FC, Thatcher Family Papers, MHi. For the full text, see *DHFFC* 8:442–43.

Received their letter dated 12 February on 24 February; reports on the status and prospects of their petition for increased fees for the weighers, gaugers, and measurers of the Portland district; notes his difficulty in explaining the contradiction between this petition and one from the town of Portland to the House complaining that the fees are too high.

A. B. & C. [Hartford, Connecticut] *American Mercury*, 8 March. Written from Farmington, Connecticut.

Includes a passing reference to Madison's discrimination proposal as "worse than the *disease*."

Credentials for the North Carolina Delegation. Governors' Letterbooks, Nc-Ar.

Issued to Ashe, Bloodworth, Steele, and Williamson as a followup to their election on 4–5 February; Sevier received his following the 8–9 March election in the western district (present-day Tennessee).

SUNDAY, 28 FEBRUARY 1790

Windy (Johnson)

Manasseh Cutler to Oliver Everett

Congress are still on the question, whether the State debts shall be assumed. In my letter of Wednesday last I mentioned Madison's amendment.

On Thursday Mr. White moved a proviso to Madison's amendment, viz: "Provided, such assumption shall not exceed the sum which any state may have advanced above its just proportion, as the same shall appear upon its liquidation." This produced a debate, which continued until just before the adjournment on Friday, when the question on this amendment was taken, and passed in the negative. During these debates there appeared to be some changes in the opinion of members respecting the question of assumption, which rendered it more difficult to form a judgment how it would issue. When White's motion was negatived (which seemed to have been originally intended to embarrass, and, if possible, prevent the assumption), Madison moved an amendment to his own, which was long, but found to contain in substance no more, than that there should be a liquidation of accounts with the States, within a certain period of time, should be made on the principle of enumeration, making that the rule of adjustment. This amendment will probably take up much more time, and postpone the general question. Some gentlemen say Madison is in fact opposed to assumption; others that he has only in view a particular modification in favor of his own State. I must confess it appears to me somewhat problematical, but, on the whole, I think he is in favor. Our members, I believe, are all in favor, except Grout, who, I observed, has taken care to be wrong on every question taken in Congress since I have attended the debates. Several of them have made great exertions. Sedgwick and Goodhue have distinguished themselves, but Gerry has gone beyond them, in displaying a clear and extensive knowledge of the subject, and tracing the probable consequences. He has certainly done himself much credit in the view of the Federalists. Ames has not said much in the House, but I believe has been very active abroad. Indeed, at this stage of the business, I believe the friends to the assumption depend more on management out of doors than within, and I believe, firmly, will out-general their opponents.

Many of the speeches in the House have been truly Ciceronian, but some of them far below par; the latter description of speeches are put into the hands of some pretty able cobbler to mend, before they go to the press, which will account for that tolerably decent appearance they make in the papers. As the mail will be closed in a few minutes I must desist.

Cutler 1:460–61. Place to which addressed not indicated.

Thomas Fitzsimons to Tench Coxe

I usually dedicate sunday Morng. for answering such of my friends letters; as the Avocations of the Week prevent my doing ~~in the Week~~ at other times and this I hope will apologise for my not Replying to your first favor sooner I have this Morng. been favored with a 3d Letter from you Sir and will pay particular attention to that part which Respects the bill Referred to the letter for Mr. [*Nicholas*] Eveleigh was handed to him Imm[*ediatel*]y.—We have yet made very Little progress in our finance business, haveing only Agreed to the three 1st propositions one of which admitted of No dispute. the Subject of discrimination Occupyd us for 6 days. and on the question 11 Members only appeared in favor of it—Indeed I believe Compliment to the mover Influenced most of these for as the Subject was Reasoned upon, it seemed to be abandoned by those who had been its most Strenuous advocates—it was found that Nothing like Justice Could have been done to those who suffered by the Rejection. that the Original holder in Possession—~~whear~~ whose debt would be Rendered less Valuable by the Example wd. be Injured the Enormous Expence & delay that would attend the operation And the unfavorable point of View in which the character of the New Government would be placed in the Eye of other Nations—if You have taken the pains to Read the debates on this Subject, tho they are but Imperfectly detailed they will at least Suggest the Reasons upon Which the Majority Voted the assumption of the state debts appears to me to be a Much more difficult Subject and one less understood both within doors & without those others—upon the first View if adopted it appears to operate very unequally. So. Ca. who will Contribute about ½₀ to the Revenue will be releived of Near ¼ of the whole debt—I believe there is no other state to which the inequality is will so Strikeg. apply—but it is sufficiently so in many to Create a Strong Repugnance to the Measure fortunately the Circumstances are not fully Known to [lined out] the Gen[eralit]y. of the opposers of it or I beleive the thing would be hopeless—I say fortunately—for I am persuaded if the assumption does not take place there will be no provision for the other part of the debt which I should Consider as unfortunate. Indeed if after holding out the expectations we have done we should fail in Makeing a permanent provision No Reliance could be had on future promises. the debt would fall as low as it ever had been before. And We should be a further prey of to foreign Speculators who at some More favorable period would Reap the Abundant Advant[ag]e. of our Neglect while our Character & Consequence was prostrated to the Earth— As Matters stand at present there can be no doubt but some of the States have Contributed More than their proportion to the the Genl. expence of the Warr—and it is Needless to look for any Compensation on that account to the delinquent states the only Chance there is of obtaining [lined out] it is from the treasury of the U.S.—after being Collected by a Genl. Revenue—I Confess this is a very distant one: yet it *may* take place. and the chance of it Added to the other advantages would I believe render it Eligible.

The other Advantages would be the Additional Strength & Consistency it would give to the Governmt. the Releivg. the people generally from the burthen of direct taxation the appearance of Justice it would do by payg. the Creditors of the States as well of the U.S. for the Supplys for Common defence—and by this Means Reconcileing the Inhabitants of every part of the Union to a System which will otherways Operate very partially inasmuch as Very Little of the domestic debt other than the State debts exists So. of Maryland. on this question Pensylva. holds the ballance and may incline it to either scale at pleasure. it is highly Important to her that the debts of the U.S. should be funded And not very prejudicial if the state debts shd. be Assumed—We are trying to make some Advance of our Situation—but I Cannot be Sanguine of our Success—for my own part I will Vote for the Assumption but if Lost will Contend Strenuously for Providing for the other part of the debt.

If our Assembly should persevere in their Scheme of districts for fœderal Representatives. I am afraid it would deprive the City of its share of

Representation & Introduce some Improper Members—I am not sure how-ever Whether another Choice on the plan of the former [*election*] would not hazard every thing—I am told that great Jealousys have been instilled into the minds of the Western people on Acct. of the Residence by some of ourselves who were so Vain as to suppose they Acquired Consequence by their Representations & so weak as not to See that they were duped from the outset in the Susq[*uehann*]a. business[1]—it is a little Surprizeing that experience has not Suggested the Importe. of Commercial Representation, to the people of Pensylva. it is the thing in Every Legislature most to be Regretted—I have scribbled over My paper, under so Many Interruptions that it will Require an Apology—I hope you will Excuse it.

ALS, Coxe Papers, PHi. Dated at "The post offc."; place to which addressed not indicated; mistakenly docketed by Coxe as dated 28 March.

[1] A reference to the September 1789 debate over the location of the federal seat of government and the anger of western Pennylvanians at most of the Pennsylvania delegation for voting against a Susquehanna River site.

Thomas Hartley to Jasper Yeates

Two Posts have passed without my Hearing from you—I hope my dear Friend that neither you, nor any of your Family have met with any further Mishap—Indeed I have been somewhat anxious on that Score—yet trust that the next Post will inform me that you are all well.

The Report of the Secretary of the Treasury is contended Inch by Inch. Mr. Madison seems opposed to it—and manages his Opposition with great Address—he is generally on the popular side.

Some of your Friends are in an aukward Situation—Whether we shall assume the State Debts—contracted in carrying on the war—and have only the General Government to lay the Taxes for the discharge of the same or let the State Debts remain as they are is the Question. The Enormity of the Sum frightens me—some States will be against any System at this Time for paying the public Debts, unless this Measure takes place—Necessity may perhaps oblige some of us to do what in ~~some~~ a degree may be against our Inclinations—however I shall not yet draw any Conclusion.

Many strong Arguments are used on both Sides—I wish we may determine right.

The other Business goes on slowly—& Congress will have to sit many Months—I shall as I have mentioned in my last go Home in April—I wish the Circuit Courts may be at the same Time as last Spring.

ALS, Yeates Papers, PHi. Addressed to Lancaster, Pennsylvania; franked; postmarked.

Samuel Henshaw to Theodore Sedgwick

I am unhappy to find by yours of the 21st. "That the assumption of the State Debts, grows more & more doubtful"—After the proposition was brought forward & supported by the Secy. I felt almost certain of its adoption and if it does not take place, I hope no funding System at all, will be established—And those who are in favour of the assumption, ought to [*uni*]te against it making provision for paymt. of the Interest on any part of the debt, unless the whole is provided for—Indeed, my dear Friend, I am more, & more convinced, that NOW is the Important CRISIS! I do not beleive that America ever saw a more critical moment than the present—And if Congress are greatly divided on the great national questions before them, they will distract the people, & give opportunity to the State incendiaries to set the Union in a flame!

Madisons motion for a discrimination for cannot be said to be popular here, tho it has some advocates—It is the most ineligible Scheme I have yet heard of—Your arguments against it, as printed in [*John*] Fenno's paper [*GUS*], have done you much honor.

But my Freind, I begin to be apprehensive, that, as so much is said in Congress about discrimination, reliquidation &c. &c. the next step will be, to annihilate the whole debt! For if you cannot find a way to pay the debt, that is just & equitable, you will too soon find people, who will say, that a debt so circumstanced ought never to be paid. For Heaven's sake! be more united, or shut your Galleries—& your Doors, and let us hear nothing from you, 'till your whole funding System is compleated.

When you honor me with another Letter direct it to me at N[*orth*]. H[*ampton*]. to be left at Springfield.

Shall I again ask you, because you have not yet answered, "will a Freind of yours stand any chance for an appointment under the excise act? And had He better get Govr. [*James*] Bowdoine to write to the President, in his favour? Will the excise be soon adopted?"

I am going to ride out of Town to day, and therefore can only write you enough to let you know I have recd. yours.

ALS, Sedgwick Papers, MHi. Written from Boston.

Jeremiah Hill to George Thatcher

I will tell you a short Story this morning & then make some Application—Moses Brown an opulent Quaker in the State of Rhode Island in the beginning of the War belonged to their general Assembly, and being somewhat torified the Assembly call'd upon him to know whether, if the

Enemy were coming out upon the Country & he knew it he would give the Information, Moses told them he wanted time to consider, after a short pause, he said it would depend on the Quantity of Blood he thought would be shed, that is, if he thought the least blood would be shed by giving the Information he would do, *e contra*, he would not. By way of Application let us consider whether it will be doing the most Justice to the Nation to pay the public Securities at their nominal Value, make a discrimination, or scale the whole. there is in my Opinion a good deal of distinction to be made between public Justice & private Justice—I do not pretend to be a political Metaphysician, but I can spel an hard name as well as most School Boys so I will let that matter go and say If stubborn facts prove any thing (which I treated you in my last) the first Proposition in the Application is inadmissible—the Second, is said to be dangerous if not impracticable ergo consequentia sequitur is that the third is least dangerous ~~most~~ practicable, & most Just considered in a national view—but perhaps you will say, what Business have you to dictate Politicians? you'are an executive officer & it is enough for you to Obey your Order, very true, I did but speak—but let the Matter go as it will.

P. S. your Children are getting better of the Meazels My daughter Polly is enlisted as an Aid de Camp to Mrs. [?] Thatcher, Term unknown, that is [*illegible*] politely speaking during pleasure.

ALS, Chamberlain Collection, MB. Written from Biddeford, Maine; postmarked Portsmouth, New Hampshire, 2 March.

Benjamin Huntington to Anne Huntington

By a letter from Hary [*Henry*] & two others from Gurdon & George [*Huntington*] by the last Post I have learned from you that you are much in the same Ill State of health as for a month passd. which is not Surprizing but I hope your Case is not Desperate but be that as it will, I know it is my duty to Trust you in the hands of a faithful Creator who will take us all out of this world when he Pleaseth. I hope your confidence in the great Redeemer of Mankind will be well grounded and unshaken—I cannot say when I shall come home but Hope to see you in May or June and that you will before that Recover your Health.

My own health is nearly the same as when I mentioned to you that I was slowly Recovering I attend Congress every Day where there are good Fires but cannot attend Meeting on Sundays being so much Troubled with the Rheumatism that I cannot Endure sitting in the Cold but hope to get the better of it in a Short Time.

I am deprived of a great Satisfaction which I should take (were it possible) to see you and spend the Time in Admi[*ni*]string some Degree of comfort to you in your sickness but we must be contented with the Allotments of Providence to whose divine Protection you are most heartily Recommended.

ALS, Huntington Papers, CtHi. Addressed to Norwich, Connecticut; franked; postmarked.

William Irvine to John Nicholson

Two days since I was favored with your letter without date, tho from circumstances it must be a late one; The letter signed I. W.[1] was not designed I believe to have any effect in bringing about an actual discrimination, at least it was not expected by the auther as far as I can learn, but he has sundry objects in view, one to prepare for counteracting impressions that may be made against the late Army, by some very unhandsome expressions to thier prejudice on the floor of Congress, in drawing comparisons between them and Speculators—not only unhandsome, but untrue The main object however, I believe is to oppose an immediate assumption of the state debts, and to intimidate farther or new Speculations, as the Auther knows that many not very distant, from the helm, are deeply engaged, or at least thier friends are—you will probably have the trouble of a second letter soon. the inclosed papers will shew you the present state of the business in Congress—There seems at this moment a little hessitation about the Assumption, unless it should be adopted tomorrow or next day, this is the moment, to make objections, but if the Committee ever should, when the Bill is taken up it may be at least modified. at present I am apprehensive there are a majority for swallowing the whole, & apparently none more avoritious for the bait than your Representatives, at least a majority of them—it would seem as if all communication was cut off, if any thing is published or written in other parts of the Country they are not republished here, and if Gentlemen get letters they are either afraid or ashamed to divulge the contents—opposite sentiments to the officers of government, or to Congress collectively are quite unfashionable here—and the Man that will hazard them, will only bring himself into disrepute & perhaps trouble, with even a remote chance of answering any purpose—this is.

[*P. S.*] Mr. Madison's, amendments, to the Resolution for assuming the State debts must at least embarrass, & stop the career, & perhaps bring about a suspension.

ALS, Gratz Collection, PHi. Addressed to Philadelphia; received and answered on 2 March.

[1] This is a reference to the "Letter from New York to Philadelphia" that Irvine sent Nicholson on 21 February. Only the undated postscript is extant.

William Smith (S.C.) to Edward Rutledge

I wrote my worthy friend a hasty Letter yesterday by [*Captain William*] Elliott—a little leisure on Sunday affords me an opporty. of writing more particularly—The Bankrupt Law is laid asleep by general acquiescence—a motion was made at the beginning of the Session to re-appoint a Committee to bring in a Bankt. Law, but on my opposition was withdrawn—other important matters have thrown it entirely out of view. You will remember when Ramsay & I had such a contest last year,[1] he & his friends said there was no cause of apprehension that his Sentiments respecting Slavery could prejudice So. Car. in Congress because the Constitn. put it out of the power of that body to interfere in any respect for 20 years—those who were better acquainted with human nature knew that some indirect attempt to interpose would be made within that period & that it was not prudent to trust our interests to men of Ramsays description: Some days ago several very urgent [*pe*]titions & memorials were laid before Congress on the Subject of Slavery, ~~pressing Con~~ some measures conducive to a speedy emancipation & a regulatn. of the Slave Trade in the interim. On motion to commit the Petitions, I urged the improp[*riet*]y. of committing Petitions which contained an applicatn. for an infraction of the Constitution—I was supported by Burke—Tucker, Baldwin & Jackson—but alass—how weak a resistance against the whole house—the Petitions were committed—we called the Yeas & Nays & protested loudly against the measure—~~d~~ a Committee of a member from each State was proposed—we declared we thought the measure so violent an attack on the Constitn. & our particular rights that So. Car. & Georgia would not sit on the Committee—so the Petitions were referred to a Committee of seven. The galleries were thronged with the Quakers who had presented the Petitions—they had the impud[*enc*]e. to express a wish to be admitted within the house, but were told it wod. not be granted—their appearance had a manifest influence on those members who apprehended the loss of their Election if they displeased the Quakers who vote by System;[2] ~~& who~~ they theref[*or*]e. [*lined out*] voted for the Commitment without wishing to take any step in the business—our early & violent opposition had This good effect it convinced the house that So. Car. & Georga. look with a jealous eye on any measure in which the negroes are at all concerned—we did not admit that even after 1808 Congress would be authorized to prohibit the importation, but that the clause was inserted for greater Caution & to quiet the minds of our people—we assured them that whenever Congress should directly or indirectly attempt any measure levelled at our particular rights in this respect, they must expect a revolt in those States, which wod. never Submit to it, & that the most violent opposition would be given to every step which might appear to interfere in any manner with our negro property. We maintained a debate for two days at a time when the members were exceedingly desirous of proceeding to the Secretary's Report; they became so tired of the discussion that they heartily damned the Quakers & their Petitions & seemed so sick of this little sample of what they might hereafter look for that they declared to us that we were unnecessarily alarmed, ~~for~~ that they had not the most distant ide[*a*] of interfering, & they only wished to commit the Petitions out of complim[*en*]t. to the Quakers. We did not lose the opporty. of trimming the Quakers in the gallery pretty soundly. The Committee have adjourned from time to time I suspect to tire out the Quakers who remained here to urge the business—I long to see the report: ~~they'll make~~ two days ago one of their leading men of the name of [*Warner*] Mifflin a great fellow near seven foot high stalked into my parlour & sat two hours—we endeavoured to convert each other in vain—when I got tired of him I asked him if he had seen friend Izard—he said no, but wished to see him—so I sent him there—about an hour after, I called on Mr. Izard to ride & found him & the Quaker in close debate attacking each other with Texts of Scripture—Major Butler was there, & we all three fell foul of friend Mifflin who was glad to make a retreat; he asked us all to dine with their Society that day, but we were engaged.

Sumpter arrived day before yesterday; I have not seen him—Tucker was opposed to the Assumption of the State Debts before he heard of the resolutions[3]—he says he will vote for it now; but, tho' in the course of the debate much has been said respecting So. Car. & her enormous debt, he has not opened his mouth, tho from his being so long in Congress, he is better able than any of us to explain the matter—the whole burden has fallen on myself & Burke ~~& myself~~, who has behaved exceedingly well hitherto in this business: he has taken a decided part & come forward manfully. This remark abot. T. is entre nous.

What does the Legislature wish to do with Fort Johnson—is it meant that Congress shall establish a Post there? do our Citizens require that? I should rather have thought they would see such an establishmt. with a jealous eye.

The Cession of the Light-house[4] is clogged with a condition that the members in general won't like, tho it appears but reasonable—I wish you'd send me a correct statement of the Expences attending the building &ca. Col. [*John*] Mitchell will do it, if you require him.

The General [*Charles Cotesworth Pinckney*], our worthy friend, has so much business on his hands that I don't expect a correspondance with him—I wish however to be informed whether he ever received a Letter I wrote to him last Summer & to which I recd. no answer—will you be so good as to ask him—He is a gentleman for whom I entertain the highest respect & regard & indeed no ~~little~~ small degree of gratitude for great Kindness rendered me in the professional [*w*]ay when I was very young at the Bar & wanted the assistance of a friend—I shall therefore be always happy [*torn*] opportunity of testifying my acknowledgmts.—I am restrained from writing, least it Should interfere with his occupations.

You were too kind, my good Sir, in condescending to make apologies for not having written sooner on the Bankt. Law: I am well acquainted with the multitude of your avocations & have often considered with astonishment the happy facility with which you got thro them all. [*John*] Kean called on me yesterday & shewed me some memorandums for Mr. Izard, in answer to your last. Your Exertions on this occasion may be of considerable advantage to our State—I cannot but lament sometimes that circumstances restrain you from relinquishing the planting business & the Profession of the Law— I wish to see you (notwithstg. my sorrow at your quittg. the Bar) entirely at liberty to attend to matters of government: we want a man like you to watch over our interests—one whose attention to politics shall not be diverted to other objects—who is there now at home who considers himself responsible for public measures—what is every man's business, is no man's—for gods sake take the most early Steps in bringing forward our Claims—the neglect of it will be highly injurious & eternally prejudicial to our interests. I have another wish—I must impart it to you—It is probable in my opinion that by the next Constitution of our State the Governors will either be re-eligible or will not be disqualified in so short a period as at present, & that the person who shall be first elected will continue (as in New York & other states) for a considerable number of years in office—shod. that person be an improper one, which is not unlikely in these days when fit men stand aloof, what a misfortune it will be to the Country! now my most sincere wish is my dear Sir, that you would make this Sacrifice to your country & allow yourself to be elected Governor—your fellow-citizens w[*ill*] confer their blessings on you & every thing else which gratitude can bestow. Then indeed the new state constitution will be a real Treasure to us—then we shall have at the helm one no less Zealous for the honor & happiness of the republic than able to carry into operation those measures which will ensure them—Think seriously of this! should I succeed in persuading you to make this Sacrifice for the happiness & prosperity of So. Cara. I should reckon myself among those who may say, I have done the State some service.[5]

ALS, Smith Papers, ScHi. Place to which addressed not indicated.

[1] For the heated contest between Smith and David Ramsay for the right to represent Charleston, South Carolina, in the FFC, see *DHFFE* 1:173–98; for the disputed election result, see *DHFFC* 8:541–54.

[2] Meaning, as a bloc.

[3] On 19 January, the South Carolina House of Representatives instructed its congressional delegation to vote for assumption.

[4] Located on James Island, at the southern mouth of Charleston harbor.

[5] Shakespeare's *Othello*, Act V, scene 2.

George Thatcher to Sarah Thatcher

***

I expect to be able, some time in march, to forward to you some money—I have wrote to a friend in Boston to know whether I may draw on the Treasurer for what is due me there—and as soon as I ~~am~~ hear that I may, I shall forward an order to our good friend [*Thomas*] Dakin to recieve it & transmit it to you. In several of your letters, especially, the two last you complain much of the shortness of mine—To which I can only say, that as this shortness does not arise from a want of Love or affection I am not disposed to deny the fact; but plead the great variety of objects that are constantly demanding my attention—to each of which I endeavour to give a due portion of my time.

Ever since I first engaged in public Business I have made it a rule to spend the morning in reading unless some necessary business took me off. The afternoons & evenings in walking visiting, or reading as I feel disposed—and Sunday, to my correspondence—And as often as I am at leisure in Congress I write to somebody or other.

Kiss our dear little children, & tell them how dearly their papa loves them, as well as their mamma.

ALS, Thatcher Family Papers, MHi. Place to which addressed not indicated. The omitted text relates to Silas Lee's recovery from measles, concern for their children ("the meazles generally seize them more severely than grown people—And it is more difficult to manage them"), and inquiries about the purchase of a bed.

[*Otho H. Williams*] to [*William Smith (Md.)*]

THE silence of the citizens of this state, on political subjects, is the effect, I really believe, of their reliance on the integrity and ability of their representatives, to secure to them all the blessings which the constitution they have adopted has for its object. All the conversations of a public nature which I have attended to, have expressed or implied this confidence in the strongest terms.

The system of finance, proposed by the Secretary of the Treasury, has here also been for some time a subject of general conversation: It has its patrons and its opposers; but not being considered as any thing more, in its present form, than a mere compilation of principles, propositions and arguments, submitted to the consideration of the general legislature, the people content themselves with an assurance that the most critical investigation will supercede a judicious determination; and that whatever the laws of their country shall prescribe, will be the best rule of their political conduct. Indeed I am convinced that there are some who carry their delicacy so far as to observe a silence on dubious points, lest, by exciting a general opinion (which might ultimately be opposite to the views of government) discontents might follow which would be attended with unfavorable consequences.

The ability and composure with which the first propositions, relative to the funding system, have been discussed in the house of delegates [*Representatives*], afford a pleasing hope that neither *prepossession* nor *prejudice* will have any share in the *adoption* or *rejection* of any part of the secretary's plan. The secretary, no doubt, courts an honest fame, and therefore must prefer a rigid scrutiny of his principles to a tacit adoption of his measures.

I assume not the task of criticizing so splendid a performance, but there are *parts* of it which I cannot reconcile to my ideas of JUSTICE, EQUITY, and an HONORABLE POLICY; words which in characters of gold should forever shine in the front of the *capital*—whilst INTEGRITY should grace each *public department*, and ABILITY distinguish the exchequer.

Contemplating the public debt, the Secretary says—"It is agreed on all hands that that part of the debt which has been contracted abroad, and is denominated the *foreign debt*, ought to be provided for according to the precise terms of the contracts." Certainly! It is agreed on all hands that all the just debts of the United States *ought to be provided for*—every just demand ought to be discharged—every reasonable claim should be duly regarded—and recompence, as far as possible, ought to be made for injuries sustained in the common cause. But the imbecility of the old government, and a multitude of consequent circumstances, have put it out of the power of the new one to render compleat justice in all cases.

It is to be lamented that even the discrimination, proposed by Mr. Madison, is not practicable. Honest citizens and heroic patriots, who are impoverished by the predicament, have only the consolation of knowing that their merits and actions, are commemorated by the wisest and best of their countrymen. The arguments in the House of Delegates reveal a congeniality of sentiment on the subject, which I am persuaded would have been more general if the mode in which the principle was to operate had not been exceptionable. It was, however, an amiable error. The claims of the possessors of public securities will remain undiminished (unless by due payment) so long as the public faith shall remain inviolate. The unfortunate who suffered by the revolution have claims also, but they address themselves to the humanity, not to the justice, of government. If once the dictates of generosity be allowed, in administration, to precede the decrees of justice, the delight of the former attribute will for ever find occasions to supercede the decorum of the latter.

Every one knows that the certificates granted under the old government were made transferable, *intentionally*, to appreciate their value, by thus *inviting the guaranty of the wealthy*, and thereby increasing the weight of interest in the scale of the union. Interest is the strongest cement of, at least, political friendship; and government made no bad bargain when it bartered (upon that principle) the remnant of an useless army for the substantial influence of opulent citizens. Nor do I conceive that any reproach ought to reflect on the latter for accepting the conditions—they were not always the most flattering: and the soldier, who, at any time, refused the market price for the evidence of his claim against the government, manifested no greater confidence in it than the citizen who made him the offer. I, myself, have been a soldier, and have not prostituted the character by any imputed means: "Mrs. Speculator" neither controuls my opinion by the prerogatives of wife, nor the wiles of a mistress; I am free to pronounce that he who *holds*, and he who *buys* a certificate, act precisely upon the same plan, of making the most of it.

It were ungrateful, perhaps, to enquire what motives, besides friendship to these states, induced foreigners to contribute to the means of maintaining our independence. Motives of interest in individuals, or of policy in nations, ought not to diminish the weight of our obligations, or to lessen our sense of the favors conferred. But what consideration could confer an obligation of an *higher* nature than the voluntary contributions of the *staff of life*, or the *sinews of war*? What *greater* sacrifice could be offered at the shrine of liberty, than an effusion of blood generously shed in its cause. Yet these are the claims which the Secretary proposes to except from the equitable proposition first contemplated by his plan; an exception not justifiable upon any supposed cause *but necessary*: and necessity would equally affect the claims of all.

While candour confesses that the holders of certificates are, by transfer, invested with all the rights of original creditors, and common honesty will not admit that strict justice can make any discrimination between either of these and a foreign creditor, I cannot suppress my astonishment at the views of the Secretary; who, by incontestible arguments, banishes the idea of one discrimination, at the same instant that he introduces another not less exceptionable in its form or iniquitous in its principles. NECESSITY makes *no* discrimination; if the idea of coertion is the motive for giving a preferrence to foreigners, to what extent may it not operate? POWER may enforce, equally, the discharge of original and transferred obligations; and foreigners are not without the *means* to purchase the whole of our debt, and the *power* to make us pay it. I say *to make us*, on a presumption that the advantage of our commerce, and the wealth of our cities (which are at their mercy) are more than equivalent to the utmost of our debts. I can have no apprehension of a permanent loss of territory, while the scales of public justice are held by an impartial legislature, and each part of the union is sure of an equal regard.

THE debt of the United States is the price of their sovereignty. As a constant admonition against prodigality, it is the guarantee of their independence. In this sense, if in any, "the public debt is a public blessing." The career of extravagance which ensued the peace, was soon checked by this consideration; and it happily produced a reformation, not only in manners and morals, but even in government itself. To complete the design of this revolution, to accomplish all its views, and substantially to secure the happy consequences that are expected to result from its perfection, is the business of the present session. Congress have yet to perform a task of the highest concern to the nation; and whoever has been accustomed to feel an interest in its prosperity, must be anxious at the present moment.

With too small a stake to account for my fears, and with no party connection to bias my judgement, I feel the solicitude of a patriot upon the occasion: this must be my apology for adventuring upon grounds, which I tread with more trepidation than I once did fields of common hostility. Finance is the most difficult theme of politics, and I am conscious of my incapacity to discuss the subject; yet as the suggestions of the simplest citizen, if respectful, may not be unworthy of the attention of the profoundest statesman, I will venture candidly to communicate my reflections.

The scheme of the Secretary of the Treasury is a display of splendid abilities, and merits the applause it has met with. If I do not think it perfect, I differ not from its author in a general sentiment, whatever diversity of opinion we may entertain on particular parts.

After a general statement of the national debt, comprehending an estimate of the respective state debts, and calculating interest at six per cent to the end of the year 1790, the Secretary states "the interesting problem." It is, Whether the United States have "ability to pay upwards of 4,000,000 dollars per ano. besides the current expenses?" Of this the Secretary is so very doubtful, that he "hopes, and even expects, that the domestic creditors will cheerfully concur in such modifications of their claims, on fair and equitable principles, as will facilitate to the government an arrangement, substantial, durable, and satisfactory to the community." The Secretary professes not to lose sight of those fundamental "principles of good faith, which dictate that every practicable exertion ought to be made, scrupulously to fulfil the engagements of the government; and that no change in the rights of its creditors ought to be attempted, without their voluntary consent; and that this consent ought to be voluntary in *fact*, as well as in *name*: consequently that every proposal of a change ought to be in the shape of an appeal to their reason and to their interest—*not* to their necessities. "To this end, the Secretary adds, it is requisite that a fair equivalent should be offered for what may be asked to be given up, and unquestionable security for the remainder. Without this, continues the Secretary, an alteration, consistently with the credit and honor of the nation, would be impracticable." In all this I coincide most sincerely. But, according to my calculations, there is nothing offered to the domestic creditor, in complete conformity to these principles—no just appeal to his *reason* or his *interest*—no *fair equivalent* for what is required to be given up—no *unquestionable security* for the remainder. Consequently the propositions of the Secretary cannot be insisted on, consistently with the credit and honor of the nation. The propositions contained in his scheme are mere commutations, offered in lieu of something which ought to be of greater value.

Is not this confessed by the supposed incapacity of government to discharge its just debts, while the proferred means are presumed to be equivalent to the just claims of its creditors. I cannot reconcile the seeming paradox. This political creed will prevent my being of the number of the elect; and, unhappily for me, although I am an *original* and a *fair* creditor, and have never swerved from the true faith of a patriot, the only alternative left me is a hope of receiving two-thirds of my just claim, for *future interest only*, "out of a temporary appropriation of the surplus of the revenue which may remain," after satisfying all other demands. There is no design to operate on *my necessities*, but it is expedient for the government to reserve 100,000 dollars per annum (the product of the post office) for the purpose of reducing the public debt *by purchase*. Here, indeed, an alternative presents itself; and if the NATIONAL BROKERS will pay ready money, such is the prospect of public credit, I will avail myself of the first opportunity to deal with them. They will not offer me less, even if they have no competitors, than an equivalent to say capital at *four per cent.* The *balance* I will resign to their *justice*, and trust to the *generosity* of government for future retribution.

By a subsequent statement of the interest, at *four percent.* of the foreign and domestic debts, it appears to be the opinion of the Secretary that the sum to be provided, in addition to what the current service will require, is

	2,239,163	9
The expences of the current services of the year, at	600,000	
Amounting to	*Dols.* 2,839,163	9

Which sum may, the Secretary thinks, be obtained from the present duties on imports and tonnage, with the additions which may be made on *wines, spirits,* including those distilled within the United States, *teas* and *coffee.*

Whatever dependence the Secretary places on these additional duties, he says, that "should the *increase* of the duties tend to a *decrease* of the consumption of those articles, the effect would be in every respect desireable." The advantages he predicts are—ease to individuals; a favourable balance of trade; the substitution of cider and malt liquors in place of distilled spirits; benefit to agriculture, and a *new* productive source of revenue.

It has been a matter of surprise to many that the Secretary should place a reliance upon the production of a fund, the uncertainty of which he deems a recommendation of it. But it is evident the Secretary was not unconscious of the necessity of looking forward to *new* and *productive sources*. His opinion, that "these articles are amongst the most difficult objects of an illicit trade," is controverted by the notorious circumstance of our being supplied at this time, by means of a foreign illicit trade, with some of those articles, in sufficient quantities to reduce the price in our markets.

As a further testimony of the precariousness of the means proposed by the Secretary, I may be pardoned for quoting his report once more. "But a duty, the precautions for the collection of which should terminate with the *landing* of the goods, as is essentially the case in the existing system, could not with safety be carried to the extent which is contemplated. The only expedient which has been discovered for conciliating high duties with a safe collection, is the establishment of a *second*, or interior scrutiny." These reflections lead to the introduction of an *excise law*, in the shape of a bill for the repeal and revision of the present impost law.

Whatever recommendation may be derived in favour of this new law, from the circumstance of its having been "tried with success," there is no absolute certainty of its effect when applied according to the constitution and to the intention of the Secretary, as a mode of equal and uniform taxation in all the states. It is not, I presume, satisfactory to the constitution, that Congress enact laws *intending* an equitable operation: If they do not actually operate equally, they ought not to be continued. Wherefore it is necessary that experiments should be made of every proposed expedient to create a revenue, before the laws for that purpose are made *perpetual*; and before they become *the permanent basis of public credit*.

We all know that a man may be indebted to a greater amount than his capital, may have his whole estate mortgaged, and his notes, "without any definite period of redemption," circulating below their nominal value; and yet while he acts honestly, is industrious, and pays in proportion as he acquires the means, he is not *only indulged* by his creditors, but *trusted* and respected by others. But if, in a misplaced confidence in untried resources, he should call his creditors together, insist that they should all compound with him, except a favoured few; that they should allow him his own terms and time for payment, and *cheerfully* consent to receive four per cent. interest, instead of six: or that he would give a preference to those that would comply, and divide the residue of his *temporary* funds, if any, among the least indulgent, reserving however to himself the issues of a certain estate to diminish his debts *by purchase*. Such a man would justly incur the suspicion of his best friends. If he should give acceptances for interest, even upon his own terms, and should fail at the day of payment, what would be his condition? Worse, unquestionably more pitiable and detestable, than if he had at first declared his bankruptcy or disowned his debts. How much more creditable and honourable would it have been, for him to have persevered in more prudent and certain measures to discharge his debts, or at least to have preserved his credit?

I confess that I do not comprehend the magick of the funding systems, sufficiently to know why, like a charm, they should, more than everything else, conciliate the public confidence. My greatest apprehension of the ruin of public credit, is excited by the very circumstance upon which some appear to have an implicit reliance. I may be deemed an infidel in politics, but my mind is nevertheless susceptible of the true faith, whenever it shall be demonstrated to me.

There is, I conceive, this material difference between postponing the funding system to a convenient time, and adopting it immediately: The domestic creditors, so long as their claims are unimpaired, will take less umbrage at a preference being given to foreigners, as to relation of payment, or even as to the mode; and it is to be expected that they will be content with a *proportion* of their interest, if the revenues will not afford a full discharge. They will be ready, upon all occasions, to favour the government, and to facilitate the payment of the taxes, by receiving their paper, which may be circulated by measures of the Treasury, or of a national bank, as successfully without a new modification of claims otherwise. While they confide in the justice of the government, they will be ready on all emergencies to suspend their claims; and their inclinations, uniting with their interests, will combine them with the rest of the community in every expedient to promote the general happiness, and in preservation of independence.

On the other hand, if the principles of justice are violated, or made subservient to political expediency; if the most numerous class of public creditors are compelled to compromise, and there should happen a default on the part of the government, what confidence could thereafter be expected? what further favor from the public creditors? would not friends and foes equally despair of the success of the experiment, which has brought the science of government so near to perfection in a land of freedom? And what are the consequences that might be expected to follow?

On the first assault of an enemy, we should be found without friends; our commerce obstructed; our resources cut off; our citizens in confusion; and the nation convulsed. Then, indeed, the *majesty of the people*, like the mock-majesty of the stage, would be an amusement to speculators. The tragedy, for a while, would command the attention of nations; and the catastrophe, at last, excite the sympathy of the world. Ages unborn would read, with regret, the history of a people, who, at the instant they were endowed with every blessing, risked all on the fatal issue of a precipitate measure; a measure which exposed themselves to ruin, and deprived their posterity of the fair inheritance of a government, the most perfect ever known upon earth.

My contemplations lead me to this conclusion, that there is less probability of establishing public credit, upon a permanent and substantial foundation, by the *immediate* adoption of the measures proposed in the report of the Secretary, than there would be making "every practicable exertion" first by way of experiment. Credit is not better supported by positive promises, than by absolute payments; nor would the punctual discharge of interest, at 4 per cent. on *a funded capital,* be deemed a greater evidence of *public justice,* than a partial three per cent. per annum on an *undiminished claim.* Creditors would not unwillingly wait the results of expedients to prove the utmost ability of the nation; nor would the evidences of their claims depreciate so much under a prospect of complete satisfaction at a future day, as under any of the circumstances proposed. If every measure of government should manifest a disposition to render all the justice that the *tried-resources* of the states could afford, what creditor would not patiently abide the determination of its honest endeavours? In the last resort a compromise, if necessary, would be attended with no defection. An uniformity of sentiment would happily unite all our citizens in a strict adherence to the principles of the union, and in a zealous defence of the general government.

The most satisfactory evidence which Congress could give of an intention to render justice in proportion to their powers and resources, would be the enacting of laws to comprehend, at once, every subject of taxation which the constitution admits of; and to consolidate the whole production, not excepting that of the post-office, into one general fund. The foundation of a system being once established, government might, with less difficulty, *enhance* or *diminish* the specific taxes, as exigencies might require. This would afford a substantial and permanent fund for the support of the credit of the nation, whilst auxiliary means might be devised for diminishing its debt. I am so well convinced that means are not wanting to the extinction of the whole that I cannot resist the persuasion that the Secretary has many expedients in reserve. Among those, which I have heard suggested, there is none more universally approved, or that would be more generally conform to the temper of the times, than a state lottery upon an extensive scale. Sacrifices to such a scheme would, *in reality, be voluntary,* and a large deduction might be made of interest, provided the principal, which might constitute each prize, were so funded as to yield a perpetual annuity to the adventurer.

I have been more tedious than I intended; and will close with assuring you, that in all events, I shall invariably adhere to the true interest of my country, to which I am not unwilling to sacrifice even my opinion.

NYDG, 8, 12 March. Written from Maryland. The newspaper entitled the letter, "Abstract of an Answer to a Letter from a Gentleman in a public Station to a private Citizen." The editors based their identification of the sender and recipient first, on Smith's letter to Williams of 16 February, complaining about the silence of his constituents regarding the report on public credit, and second, on Williams's letter to Philip Thomas, 17 March, Williams Papers, MdHi.

OTHER DOCUMENTS

John Adams to Messrs. Brown & Francis. ALS, John Brown Collection, RHi; FC:lbk, Adams Family Manuscript Trust, MHi. Addressed to Providence, Rhode Island.

> Received their letter of 16 February on 23 February; asks if the "Antis" of Rhode Island think Congress will petition them to come into the Union, or that the President will send an ambassador to negotiate their accession; Congress does not feel authorized to treat them as anything other than foreigners "and extend all Laws to them as such"; this will inconvenience the friends of the federal government as well as the Antifederalists; "But you know in all national Calamities, the Same Fortune attends the good and the Evil the Just and unjust."

John Adams to William Ellery. FC:lbk, Adams Family Manuscript Trust, MHi. Sent to Newport, Rhode Island.

> Despite the unfavorable prospects, hopes Rhode Island will ratify the Constitution, "as it will not be possible much longer to extend that lenity and indulgence, which has been hitherto granted"; asks if Rhode Island's "Anti's" maintain "secret communications" with those of Virginia and Boston, as is rumored; the national debt "engages all attention," by the end of which "some thing must be done" regarding Rhode Island; promises to be a better correspondent.

Nathaniel Barrell, Jr. to John Langdon. ALS, Langdon Papers, NhPoA. Written from Basse-terre, Guadeloupe.

> "The Eyes of Politicians are fixed on America to see how the federal constitution fits."

Daniel Cony to George Thatcher. ALS, Chamberlain Collection, MB. This is a postscript to Cony's letter of 27 February, calendared under that date, above.

> Expresses satisfaction with the observations in Thatcher's (unlocated) letter of 21 February, which put the publication mentioned in Cony's letter of 13 February "in its proper point of light, that is of too little consequence to merit your displeasure."

Mary Cranch to Abigail Adams. ALS, incomplete, Adams Family Manuscript Trust, MHi. Written from Braintree, Massachusetts.

Cousin William Cranch has written Henry Knox in care of John Adams, asking for a job as a gunsmith; asks Abigail "to mention the thing when you think it will do the best."

Royal Flint to Nathaniel Appleton. ALS, Colborn Collection, MHi. Addressed to Boston; postmarked.
Although many members of Congress think Hamilton's funding plan will be difficult to execute, Flint thinks it will be adopted "without material alterations"; "the arrangements respecting the mode of conducting the new Loans are not yet contemplated. It will be discussed in Congress long before it is put into a train of operation. Nothing will be done in haste"; believes letters to "your friends" are enough to secure Appleton's appointment to office; attendance at New York City is not necessary, except "it will gratify you to hear the debates of Congress."

Nathaniel Gorham to Theodore Sedgwick. ALS, Sedgwick Papers, MHi. Written "Sunday evening" from Charlestown, Massachusetts.
Reports the Massachusetts legislature's measures regarding Gorham's Genessee Purchase; will ask Benjamin Lincoln to lobby state senators, "as I learn from him that you have written to him on the subject"; as he cannot come to New York City, asks "if you will se[e] the mutual Friend who mentiond. the probability of a good contract"; "if you are at Liberty mention the name of the Friend as by that I may possibly form some judgment"; if someone is needed there, asks him to write for Oliver Phelps.

James Madison to Walter Jones. No copy known; acknowledged in Jones to Madison, 25 March.

Peter Muhlenberg to Benjamin Rush. Excerpt and summary of three page ALS, *The Collector* 59(1946):item J 1228. The ellipsis is in the source. Addressed to Philadelphia; franked; postmarked.
"'If the State Debts were Liquidated and ascertain'd, some good reasons, perhaps, might be given for the assumption. . . .' It would be unjust, however, to put on an equal footing those states which have paid most of their quota and those which have not. He mentions the recent census taken in Pennsylvania and the increased number of Representatives."

Samuel Phillips, Jr. to Benjamin Goodhue. ALS, Letters to Goodhue, NNS. Written from Boston.
Asks Goodhue's further assistance in procuring an employee for Phillips's papermill "as soon as your public engagements will permit"; encloses

a "Report" (probably on a new state excise act) which he hopes Goodhue will keep secret after showing it to Strong; "we hope to prevent it's acceptance, but can't answer for it"; state legislative business; believes that more uneasiness than he had expected would be generated among "a very respectable number of our very substantial men" if the interest on domestic debt is reduced below four percent; reports Nathan Cushing's appointment to the state supreme court.

Benjamin Rush to Elias Boudinot. ALS, Rush Family Papers, NjP. Written from Philadelphia.

Encloses letter for Hannah Stockton Boudinot and "extracts" (probably his *Extracts and Remarks on the Subject of Punishment and Reformation of Prisoners* [Philadelphia, 1790]), which he wishes "published in New York & circulated throughout the world"; Knox's plan for the militia "is very unpopular in Pennsylvania"; paraphrases the antiwar sentiments of his letter to Madison dated 27 February.

Caleb Strong to Theodore Foster. ALS, Foster Papers, RHi. Addressed to Providence, Rhode Island; misdated 29 February; franked; postmarked; received 7 March.

Has forwarded a letter enclosed in Foster's last; based on "Our Accounts" from Rhode Islanders, prospect of their ratifying the Constitution is favorable; if the convention adjourns without ratifying, "the Government here will be justified even to the discerning People in Rhode Island in pursuing measures that in other Circumstances might be thought Severe"; [*P. S.*] Sedgwick sends his regards.

George Thatcher to Daniel Cony. No copy known; acknowledged in Cony to Thatcher, 6 March.

George Washington to James Madison. ALS, Straus Collection, NjP. Dated "Sunday Morning." For the full text, see *PJM* 13:70–71.

Returns Jefferson's letter to Madison of 14 February regarding acceptance of post of secretary of state; is glad he accepted "but sorry it is so repugnant to his own inclination that it is done."

William Samuel Johnson, Diary. Johnson Papers, CtHi.
"St. Pauls."

FEBRUARY 1790 UNDATED

Pierce Butler to John Houston

I can not easily express how greatly the late rash Act[1] of a Majority of your Legislature has injured the Interests of Georgia with the General Governmt. Having allowed myself to take an active part in the concerns of that State I feel hurt by that measure: Just as we had brought things to bear here for the future security and benefit of Georgia; when Troops were preparing to be sent to defend the State and secure the tranquility of it, unfortunately for that Country the Account of the sale of the Western Lands arrived. This truly impolitick step gave such general disgust, that we should as soon have got Congress to throw money into the Sea as agree to a Vote of Credit for the defence of Georgia: When will that distressed State cease to be the sport of intrigue and design, or to have her dearest interests sold at a market! It is high time to wrest the Governmt. out of the hands of designing men; whose own Egrandisement is paramont to every other object. I know Your attachment to the true Interests of the Country. I know the well placed confidence of your fellow Citizens in that attachment: Exert then, my dear Sir, as you regard your Country. Exert Your Abilities and influence to call together the Legislature in order to get them to repeal the rash Act, otherwise You must be left a prey to Eternal foes—to the insolence of [*Alexander*] McGuilvery and the Intrigues of His Counsillors. By the sale of the Lands on the present plan Georgia will advantage little. By a cession to Congress she will gain much. Security to the Planter encourages Emigration and consequently encreases Your Representation and importance in the Fœderal Governmt. In short every beneficial Effect is to be expected from the adoption of one, and every Evil to Georgia from the other. Exert yourself then, as you regard your Country and the peace and prosperity of it to get the Legislature called in order to recind the imprudent Act. What in the name of Common Sense, what solid Advantage can Georgia derive from the Sale of Her western Lands on the present plan? Can the payment of a few thousand Dollars of your State Debt be put in competition with the protection and security of the Country. The stationing of Troops in Georgia would not only bring a great addition of money into circulation, but give such confidence as to encourage new settlers, and of course rapidly encrease the wealth and strength of the State.

The benefit flowing from one, and the Evils resulting from the other are too evident to need Elucidation: God grant that the one may be adopted and the other rejected. I really am attached to Georgia, and if I had not one foot of Land in the Country I would serve her with the same zeal that influences me at present in trying to promote her welfare; but the late conduct of a

Majority of your Legislature Seals my lips. I cannot advocate such a measure. Disapproving of it I lament the step in silence.

FC, Butler Letterbook, ScU.

[1] The act of 21 December 1789 regarding the Yazoo land purchases; see George Walton to John Adams, 20 January, n. 1, above.

Pelatiah Webster to William Samuel Johnson

I Inclose you a Set of my Essays, Except the third which was printed in a newspaper,[1] [*lined out*] they were wrote when no inducement of Interest or passion Operated at all to divert the Conclusions from their Natural principles, nor any Occasions offerd. for giving birth to any Sinister considerations Whatever, perhaps running over them again (for you have Seen them all before) may be of Some use in forming a Judgment upon proper principles at a time When the winds & Currents of Interest, party, prejidice &c. all Spend their force to bend the mind towards their Several favorite Conclusions &c. to warp the Judgement from the Grand point of unbiassed truth. The real vallue, nature & operation of Money. the Nature & use & properties of Paper Credit—the Absurdity of Appreciating depreciated paper—the Nature of Taxation or drawing money from the people at Large & Issuing it out again into Genl. Circulation—The disavantages of too much or too little circulating cash—The Importance of the Great Staples of our wealth, & the Care with which they Shod. be saved nursed, protected & Encouraged &c. you'l find Among the Subjects of Very carefull discussion.
P. S. Wrote some Strictures & Theses to Mr. Sherman. which I desired him to Shew You. dated feby. 22d.

ALS, Johnson Papers, CtHi. Place from which written not indicated; sent by post.

[1] Webster's seven *Essays on Free Trade and Finance*, published at Philadelphia between 1779 and 1785. All but the third appeared as pamphlets; these are Evans 16670, 16671, 17064–65, 18301, and 19367.

Remarks on the Slave Trade

Extracted from the AMERICAN MUSEUM, *for May,* 1789

IT must afford great pleasure to every true friend to liberty, to find the case of the unhappy Africans engrosses the general attention of the humane, in many parts of Europe: but we do not recollect to have met with a more striking illustration of the barbarity of the slave trade, than in a small pamphlet lately published by a society at Plymouth, in Great Britain; from which the Pennsylvania society for promoting the abolition of slavery have taken the following extracts, and have added a copy of the plate, which accompanied it.[1] Perhaps a more powerful mode of conviction could not have been adopted, than is displayed in this small piece. Here is presented to our view, one of the most horrid spectacles—a number of human creatures, packed, side by side, almost like herrings in a barrel, and reduced nearly to the state of being buried alive, with just air enough to preserve a degree of life sufficient to make them sensible of all the horrors of their situation. To every person, who has ever been at sea, it must present a scene of wretchedness in the extreme; for, with every comfort, which room, air, variety of nourishment, and careful cleanliness can yield, it is still a wearisome and irksome state. What then must it be to those, who are not only deprived of the necessaries of life, but confined down, the greater part of the voyage, to the same posture, with scarcely the privilege of turning from one painful side to the other, and subjected to all the nauseous consequences arising from sea-sickness, and other disorders, unavoidable amongst such a number of forlorn wretches? Where is the human being, that can picture to himself this scene of woe, without at the same time execrating a trade, which spreads misery and desolation wherever it appears? Where is the man of real benevolence, who will not join heart and hand, in opposing this barbarous, this iniquitous traffic?

Philadelphia, May 29, 1789

THE above plate represents the lower deck of an African ship, of two hundred and ninety-seven tons burden, with the slaves stowed on it, in the proportion of not quite one to a ton.

In the men's apartment, the space, allowed to each, is six feet in length, by sixteen inches in breadth. The boys are each allowed five feet, by fourteen inches. The women, five feet ten inches, by sixteen inches; and the girls, four feet by one foot, each. The perpendicular height, between the decks, is five feet eight inches.

The men are fastened together, two and two, by handcuffs on their wrists, and by irons rivetted on their legs—they are brought up on the main deck every day, about eight o'clock, and, as each pair ascend, a strong chain, fastened by ringbolts to the deck, is passed through their shackles; a precaution absolutely necessary, to prevent insurrections. In this state, if the weather is favourable, they are permitted to remain about one third part of the twenty-four hours, and during this interval they are fed, and their apartment below is cleaned, but when the weather is bad, even these indulgences cannot be granted them, and they are only permitted to come up in small companies of about ten at a time, to be fed, where, after remaining a quarter of an hour, each mess is obliged to give place to the next, in rotation.

It may perhaps be conceived, from the crouded state, in which the slaves appear in this plate, that an unusual and exaggerated instance has been produced; this, however, is so far from being the case, that no ship, if her intended cargo can be procured, ever carries a less number than one to a ton, and the usual practice has been, to carry nearly double that number. The bill, which has passed this last session of parliament,[2] only restricts the carriage to five slaves for three tons: and the Brooks, of Liverpool, a capital ship, from which the above sketch was proportioned, did, in one voyage, actually carry six hundred and nine slaves, which is more than double the number that appear in the plate. The mode of stowing them was as follows: platforms, or wide shelves, were erected between the decks, extending so far from the sides towards the middle of the vessel, as to be capable of containing four additional rows of slaves, by which means the perpendicular height above each tier, after allowing for the beams and platforms, was reduced to two feet six inches, so that they could not even sit in an erect posture; besides which, in the men's apartment, instead of four rows, five were stowed, by placing the heads of one between the thighs of another. All the horrors of this situation are still multiplied in the smaller vessels. The Kitty, of one hundred and thirty-seven tons, had only one foot ten inches; and the Venus, of one hundred and forty-six tons, only one foot nine inches perpendicular height, above each layer.

The above mode of carrying the slaves, however, is only one, among a thousand other miseries, which those unhappy and devoted creatures suffer, from this disgraceful traffic of the human species, which, in every part of its progress, exhibits scenes, that strike us with horror and indignation. If we regard the first stage of it, on the continent of Africa, we find, that a hundred thousand slaves are annually produced there for exportation, the greatest part of whom consists of innocent persons, torn from their dearest friends and connexions, sometimes by force, and sometimes by treachery. Of these, experience has shewn, that forty-five thousand perish, either in the dreadful mode of conveyance before described, or within two years after their arrival at the plantations, before they are seasoned to the climate. Those who unhappily survive these hardships, are destined, like beasts of burden, to exhaust their lives in the unremitting labours of slavery, without recompense, and without hope.

It is said by the well-wishers to this trade, that the suppression of it will destroy a great nursery for seamen, and annihilate a very considerable source of commercial profit. In answer to these objections, mr. Clarkson,[3] in his admirable treatise on the impolicy of the trade, lays down two positions, which he has proved from the most incontestible authority—First, that so far from being a nursery, it has been constantly and regularly a grave for our seamen; for, that in this traffic only, more men perish in one year, than in all the other trades of Great Britain in two years.

And, secondly, that the balance of the trade, from its extreme precarious-ness and uncertainty, is so notoriously against the merchants, that if all of the vessels, employed in it, were the property of one man, he would infal-libly, at the end of their voyages, find himself a loser.

As then the cruelty and inhumanity of this trade must be universally admitted and lamented, and as the policy or impolicy of its abolition is a question, which the wisdom of the legislature must ultimately decide upon, and which it can only be enabled to form a just estimate of, by the most thorough investigation of all its relations and dependencies; it becomes the indispensable duty of every friend to humanity, however his speculations may have led him to conclude on the political tendency of the measure, to stand forward, and assist the committees, either by producing such facts as he may himself be acquainted with, or by subscribing, to enable them to procure and transmit to the legislature, such evidence as will tend to throw the necessary lights on the subject. And people would do well to consider, that it does not often fall to the lot of individuals, to have an opportunity of performing so important a moral and religious duty, as that of endeavouring to put an end to a practice, which may, without exaggeration, be stiled one of the greatest evils at this day existing upon the earth.

By the Plymouth committee,

W. ELFORD,[4] chairman

Broadside, Pennsylvania Abolition Society Papers, PHi. The editors are printing this broadside because of a remark in John Pemberton to James Pemberton, 11 February, above, that Jackson had seen a pamphlet showing enslaved Blacks packed together like "Tobacco in a Hogshead." No other known document fits that description as closely as the extracts of a "small pamphlet" reproduced in broadside form by the Pennsylvania Abolition Society in May 1789. The February 1790 dating is based on the supposition that Jackson saw the pamphlet at this time, perhaps from among the literature the Quaker antislavery petitioners brought with them to New York.

---

[1]The Plymouth Society was one of the numerous local societies organized in 1788 throughout the United Kingdom by the country's leading antislavery activist and lobby-ist, Thomas Clarkson (1760–1846). Late in that year, the Society succeeded in dramatizing the horrific conditions of Britain's slave trade by producing a diagram of the main stowage deck of the slave ship *Brookes*, out of Liverpool, which operated between Africa's Gold Coast (present-day Ghana) and Jamaica. The society sent a plate of the diagram to Clarkson, who immediately recognized the publicity value of the image and modified it to include the floor plan and cross section of each deck, along with explanatory comments. The revised diagram, printed as more than seven thousand broadsides and reproduced in newspapers, books, and pamphlets that circulated throughout the Atlantic world, reportedly made Tsar Alexander I nauseous and was deliberately not shown to France's Louis XVI for fear of the same reaction. It "remains one of the most widely reproduced political graphics of all time" (Adam Hochschild, *Bury the Chains: Prophets and Rebels in the Fight to Free an Empire's Slaves* [Boston, 2005], pp. 155–56, 183, 317). For the Pennsylvania Abolition Society's adaptation of the Plymouth Society's original diagram, see the illustration at 17 March, volume 19.

²"An Act to regulate, for a limited Time, the shipping and Carrying Slaves in *British* Vessels from the Coast of *Africa*," 28 George III, cap. 54, passed in 1788.

³Clarkson's *Essay on the Impolicy of the African Slave Trade* [London, 1788].

⁴Sir William Elford (1749–1837) was co-owner of the Plymouth Bank, founded in 1773.

Letter from New York

You ask my opinion of the expediency of sending an Agent or Agents to settle the account between the state and the union. In answer, make it the business of one man and he will be likely to attend to it, but if you depend upon the members of Congress they must neglect their business in the legislature.

Some of our delegation have written to their friends to have Mr. [*Samuel*] Osgood appointed by the state—I believe him to be a gentleman of integrity and abilities; but you will consider him a citizen of this state—that his interest is here, and that he has other business to take off his mind and attention.

I will suggest to your consideration Mr. [*Nathan*] DANE, of whom it is here said that he has a peculiar talent in sifting out justice from among old and intricate resolutions of Congress—forgive me, the wisdom of the legislature is sufficient.

[Boston] *Herald of Freedom*, 16 February.

Letter to a Friend

The Secretary's report is couched in what is called the *elegant stile*. I wish to impress it on your mind, that such a stile is altogether unintelligible to nine tenths of readers. The use of Latin derivatives and abstract propositions renders the ideas incomprehensible to mere English readers. It is the modern corruption of stile, and a great misfortune to our language, to *generalize* ideas, until they become so indefinite that readers and hearers have no distinct notion of what is read or delivered. This is the fact with respect to the report. Common readers, of good sense and honest hearts, do not understand it, and are apt to suspect it contains mischief.

The report has great merit—it discovers great attention to the subject and great zeal in the public cause. Besides, the arguments in the beginning are unanswerable. But I am bold in censuring the stile, and am sorry annuities and tontines form any part of the proposition.

[Hartford, Connecticut] *American Mercury*, 1 March.

Letter from Wilmington, North Carolina

Accounts from Georgia mention, that one of the acts of their last legislature, granting the right of pre-emption of a certain part of their western territory to the North-Carolina, South-Carolina, and Virginia companies, has been, and still is pretty severely animadverted upon by the Georgians; some entertaining the idea that the Spaniards have an inclination to purchase this western territory from these companies, and people in general not considering that their legislature are of their own chusing, and of consequence, all their legal and constitutional acts binding upon them.

NYDA, 5 March; reprinted at Hartford, Connecticut; Charleston, South Carolina; and elsewhere.

Letter from New York

It is said that purchasers have gone from hence with cash to the southern states, to buy the certificates or debts of the states, for less than their real value; a measure big with mischief and injustice, which ought, by all possible means, to be checked. The public securities of the United States, and the debts of the different states, are considered of equal value, and are fluctuating in value between seven and nine shillings in the pound.

The question for calling a Convention, to take into consideration the Federal Constitution, passed the Lower House of the state of Rhode-Island by a majority of five; the Senate being equally divided, the Governor [*John Collins*] gave the casting vote in its favor.

[Georgia] *Augusta Chronicle*, 13 March.

Letter from Quebec

The posts we consider as the key to the fur trade—from which trade Great-Britain derives her principal revenue in this province; though it is not always equally productive. This object is greatly coveted by the people of the States; but whenever it shall fall into their hands, they will be very much disappointed—for a spirit of rivalship will lead adventurers into such schemes of competition, and out bidding of each other, as will eventually ruin the trade—and as to any advantage it would be to their government, I can conceive of none. Our merchants under the strictest regulations that our government can impose, are often sufferers by their speculations in this business. With respect to relinquishing the posts I see no symtom of it.

GUS, 26 May; reprinted at Baltimore.

OTHER DOCUMENTS

William Brown and John Hopkins to John Adams. Ms., Adams Family Manuscript Trust, MHi. Place from which written not indicated. Date supplied by the Manuscript Trust.

On Jay's advice, petitions for release from jail.

Arthur Lee to [*Thomas Lee Shippen?*]. ALS, incomplete, Shippen Family Papers, DLC. While the editors cannot be certain that the recipient was Shippen, the evidence strongly supports this conclusion: the document's location in the Shippen Papers and the fact that Adams and Jefferson considered the recipient a friend, as Shippen knew both from his European travels. Less certain is the letter's date. Jefferson's acceptance of the office of secretary of state was known at New York City by the end of February. Congressional harmony broke down in early March as the COWH debate on assumption dragged on.

"The conduct of public affairs goes on as harmoniously both in & out of Congress as can be expected. Which is much owing to the wisdom & prudence of the President & the universal confidence in his patriotism & judgment. Mr. Jefferson, I think, stands next in the public esteem, & will be received here with very particular respect & attention."

Warner Mifflin to Abiel Foster. [Philadelphia] *American Museum* 8(August 1790):65. Written sometime between 16 February and 4 March. Printed in *DHFFC* 8:331–32.

Urges Foster's committee to report promptly and favorably on Quaker antislavery petitions.

1–14 March 1790

Snow Rain (Johnson)

Richard Bassett to George Read

Your very long absence from this place, Occasions Much enquiry, and is the Subject of some Animadversion—I have Anxiously expected to see you every day for this two weeks. I hope the delay is not Occasioned by bad health—One great & important Question on the funding business has been Determined in the House of Representatives in a Committee of the whole, to wit, that there should be no discrimination between original Creditors & present holders—This Determination took place against the Sentiments of our Friend Maddison, who no doubt must be a little Mortified thereat, as he labored the point in a Most Masterly Manner, & appeared to have it Much at heart & I must own in My poor Opinion had reason Justice, & every Sentiment on his side, which ought to have acted as a Stimulous to have induced a different decission—whether he will come forward with his proposition for discrimination again before the House, cant say, but should Suppose he would not as the Majority appeared large against him—The Present great Question before them is, whether the State Debts Shall be assumed or Not great Diversity of opinion prevails on this Subject, and I fear an improper Determination will take place—The Eastern people seeming to be determined, unless they can carry the assumption of the State debts, that they will fund none—and it appears to me that as long as we continue to Sit at this place, we Most assuredly shall have whatever they Contend for, imposed upon us, be it right or wrong—from what I can discover & learn respecting the State Claims to the East, if the now favorite Measure is Adopted, poor little Delaware will have Saddled upon her between two or three Hundred Thousand Dollars More, than her former Supposed Quota—This will never do, but how to help it is the Question—do come forward & lend us your aid, I feel my own Weakness, upon Subjects of this Kind in a very Eminent degree, and therefore want your aid—Eastern Polliticks & Eastern Men will prevail in our government—They evidently begin to feel their own weight & importance—And Shew it in every Step—North Carolina has come forward with a Curious Cession of Western Territory—and Annexed thereto, are a parcel of the Most curious and Extraordinary Conditions I ever behold—I inclosed them for your perusal[1]—This cession I opposed with all my Might in Senate, but to Little purpose, have been Making all the head I can against it with the Members of the other branch, but with what Success, time must determine, I have too much reason to fear, the Same Interest will preponderate there, that did with us—Rhoad Island it is said will not come in, that there is a Majority of 12. against it—The Eastern Men hear are exerting all possible influence to bring them in, from this motive principally & alone I fear, to give a Clearar decided Majority—Inclosed is a paper or two to which I refer you, for the News of the day—for God Sake come along, I cannot Stay hear Much Longer without you.

ALS, Richard S. Rodney Collection of Read Papers, Historical Society of Delaware, Wilmington.

[1] North Carolina's act ceding what would become Tennessee was incorporated in its entirety into the North Carolina Cession Act; see *DHFFC* 6:1544–48. Among the "curious" conditions Bassett alludes to was a provision for preventing Congress from legislating the emancipation of enslaved Blacks.

Stephen Higginson to John Adams

***

The Report of the Secretary of the treasury has much engaged the attention of our Assembly, & of the people abroad. it is very generally admired; & men of information, I find, grow more attached to it upon reflection. the rate of interest proposed, the assumption of the State Debts & adjustment of Accounts between the States & the Union, & the distinction made between foreign & domestic Creditors are very generally pleasing. there are some however both within & without doors, who would wish to embarrass the System. They use every exertion to create an opposition to it; but they have hitherto failed of making any impression, & will not be able, I trust, to urge the legislature to any disagreeable points. the acquisition of Mr. [*Nathan*] Dane, by a vacancy in the [*Massachusetts*] Senate, has given Them new hopes; & their Efforts will be renewed in the way of Amendments,[1] if not [*lined out*] by a remonstrance against assuming the State Debts. They mean, it is said, to create an opposition in the national Senate, upon whom they expect to make an impression, They being chosen by the state legislatures. This mode of opposition, it is said, was recommended by Mr. [*R. H.*] Lee; & to make it more efficacious will be systematically pursued in all the States. to favour

thier Views, Mr. Dane has reported an amendment, by which the Senators are to be chosen all at the same time in future, for the term of ~~two~~ *four* years, & subject to a recall by an order from their Constituents. whether this will pass the two houses, appears very uncertain; but the principle of action, & the object in View is very apparent. what may be the effect upon any of your members, should it pass, you will have an oppy. of observing; but every new evidence of the disposition from which such propositions originate, will certainly serve to strengthen the hands of the Union. by such conduct people are taught to look up to the federal Government, for safety & protection; & the importance of the state legislatures will be thereby lessened in the Eyes of the people.
***

I have been considering the Secretarys proposal of new duties, & his mode of collecting Them.[2] the amount of the duties, & the novelty & energy of the collection seemed rather alarming at first; but they are both necessary to the object in view. to lessen the rate, will render the means incompetent to the End; & to abate of the vigour, proposed in his mode of collection, may entirely defeat the whole System. accustomed to Laws, weak in their principles & loose in their construction, & to modes of collection feeble & irregular, habits of Evasion have been here too generally contracted. it is idle to depend on the personal honour or patriotism of those who are to pay. firmness & force may be absolutely necessary to secure a due collection; They are the more so, because of the habits alluded to. the great difficulty is to have the System efficient without distressing Our trade, by drawing the Duty from the Importer before he can have received it from the retailer or consumer, or by establishing such Checks as will retard & obstruct Business. The former will increase an Evil now too generally felt, the want of capital; &, as the Bill now stands may create uneasiness. the latter can be obviated only by an attentive discharge of the inspectors duty, in giving every facility compatible with a regular collection, & consistent with the principles of the Bill. Should it be executed with attention & address, no injurious obstructions need take place; nor should I apprehend, in that case, any great clamour or uneasiness. very much will depend upon the executive Officers, especially in the outsett.
***

ALS, Adams Family Manuscript Trust, MHi. Written from Boston. For the full text, see *AHA* 1(1896):772–76. The omitted text relates to state judiciary appointments, Higginson's application for a revenue appointment, and state fiscal policies. For samples of antifederalist sentiment in the state, Higginson refers Adams to enclosed speeches by Benjamin Austin, Jr., and Thomas Dawes, Jr.

---

[1]On 29 January 1790, the day it approved ten of the proposed constitutional Amendments that had been submitted by the FFC to the state legislatures for ratification, the

Massachusetts Senate appointed three members to a joint committee for considering additional Amendments; the House appointed its members four days later. Nathan Dane presented the committee's recommendations to the Senate. Its twelve additional Amendments included empowering Congress to establish "a uniform rule of inhabitancy or settlement of the poor," guaranteeing a republican form of government to districts ceded to the federal government, giving states a veto power over the military establishment in peacetime, and giving states the power to pay federal Representatives and Senators and to recall their Senators. The only proposed Amendment relating to fiscal affairs provided that certain tax sources be reserved exclusively to the states, except in time of national emergency. The joint committee report died in the Senate without being acted on ([Boston] *Independent Chronicle*, 4 March supplement; John P. Kaminski, "The Making of the Bill of Rights, 1787–1792," in Stephen L. Schechter and Richard B. Bernstein, eds., *Contexts of the Bill of Rights* [Albany, N.Y., 1990], pp. 54–57).

[2] Hamilton's report on public credit included the draft of a bill imposing higher impost and new excise duties, primarily on distilled spirits, to be surveyed and collected by inspectors (*DHFFC* 5:770–72, 799–823).

Louis Guillaume Otto to Conte de Montmorin

The debates on the financial plan proposed by the Secretary of the Treasury constantly agitate the House of Representatives as people had good reason to expect. This question had always been considered as the touchstone of the new American Government. Parties form and become embittered; dispassionate arguments give way to personalities; and it is difficult to regain the calmness and the moderation which had formerly characterized the deliberations of Congress. To put aside a discussion which was disagreeable to them, some members tried at first to have it adjourned from one moment to the other and a Georgian [*Jackson*] even proposed to put it off to the month of May in order to have time to receive instructions from his constituents. After having had all the indulgence which prudence recommended for these delays, the majority has finally taken up the financial plan.

In my dispatch No. 11, I had the honor, My Lord, to give you a detailed account of the principal articles of this plan which does honor to the wisdom and patriotism of Mr. Hamilton; but too much impatience on the part of this Secretary to get it adopted almost without deliberation has been prejudicial from the beginning to his interests and to those of the public creditors. He has been suspected with considerable ground of having written his own panegyrics in the gazettes, the most exaggerated of which appeared in Connecticut before the plan could be known there.[1] This palpable anachronism has been severely criticized by a writer known by the name of *Independent Observer*[2] who does not fear to call his plan precipitate and futile. Be that as it may, the House of Representatives has discussed three great questions which form the basis of this plan.

The first concerns the reimbursement of the foreign debt which they have unanimously resolved to pay at the terms which have been stipulated while above all reserving to themselves to fund the heaviest debts by means of new loans at more moderate interest.

The second question was much more difficult to deal with; it related to the reimbursement of the domestic creditors. In my dispatch No. 11 and in several other parts of my correspondence, I have taken care, My Lord, to explain the difficulties which embarrass this branch of the public debt of the United States. The creditors having been paid during and after the war in negotiable contracts, a large party composed of all the original creditors who have sold their contracts at a low price have constantly shown themselves opposed to the reimbursement of this debt. Mr. Hamilton, for his part, has proposed to buy these contracts back *at par* in spite of the depreciation which they have successively undergone. It would be useless to quote the arguments which were used on both sides for or against this reimbursement. I shall mention only a strange discussion raised by Mr. Gerry, delegate from Massachusetts, who since the beginning of the Revolution has not ceased to speak and act to the prejudice of France. Without being provoked in any way, he ventured to say that the credit of American citizens or the domestic debt had a character infinitely more sacred than that of His Majesty because it represented services rendered, while the credit of the King had been rather the price of the efforts that the Americans had made to advance the prospects of France by detaching from England colonies whose growing greatness gave her some umbrage. "It is astonishing," he added, "that they have converted into loan what in all justice ought to have been considered as a simple subsidy which a powerful King cannot refrain from giving to a weak republic which waged war for his interests."[3] This favorite theme of Mr. Gerry had the success which it has always met with in Congress; many voices were raised against a doctrine false in itself and entirely misplaced on this occasion. Some Southern delegates, always friends of France, took the opportunity to recall the generosity, disinterestedness and good dispositions of the King and of the French nation toward the United States, dispositions which were manifested at all times during the war and which since the peace had constantly led the government of Versailles to favor the Americans. There was not a single member on the side of Mr. Gerry, who in his usual way was satisfied with having shot an arrow without caring about the wound he could have caused. However, to show off before his friends he had his opinion printed the next day in all the gazettes.[4] For my part, I was grateful to him for having unawares given Congress an opportunity to praise France and to record in the journals a remarkable testimony of its gratitude.

They concerned themselves up to that point only with the propriety of paying the contracts to the *holders* at par or with some reductions. No one had mentioned the *original* proprietors of these securities when Mr. Madison, representative of Virginia and the most eloquent and capable member, rose to broach an opinion which threw the whole House into the greatest ferment. After having exposed the injustice there would be in making the military and other public creditors who through distress had sold their certificates at a very low price pay considerable taxes in order to rebuy these same certificates at par from the present possessors, he proposed to make a distinction between the original purchasers and the speculators; to reimburse the former at par and to give the latter the highest current price of those securities while reserving the right to pay the surplus to the first purchasers who had sold at a low price. He supported this motion with several examples drawn from the history of England and in part from what had been done by the French Government with regard to the bills of Canada.[5] This proposition, perfectly equitable by every standpoint, for five days met with the most violent opposition on the part of the delegates whose constituents had bought many of these certificates and had hoped thereby to absorb a large share of the revenue of the United States. It was called *infamous*, and they exhausted all the odious expressions to put it aside and to prevent the House from listening to it. As to the public, that of New York composed almost entirely of speculators whose agents had been even in Georgia to buy contracts, was generally indignant with Mr. Madison. Some spread doubts about his talents and his integrity; others affected to believe that the bad state of his health had weakened his judgment. After having stood all the fire of his adversaries, this orator rose a second time[6] and in the best speech which has ever been made in America and which even his adversaries could not help admiring, showed the necessity, utility and justice of the measure he had proposed. But an all-powerful interest acted against him. He was able to bring only twelve members to his side and it was decided by a large majority that the *present holders* of the public securities should be reimbursed at *par.*

Congress having thus established the principle that the notes of the former Congress payable to the bearer should be paid, one could reasonably infer that its intention was also to rebuy the paper money, the terms of which included the same engagement as the certificates. The Pennsylvanians, who possess an immense quantity of this paper, were the first to grasp this analogy and they presented a request to Congress urging it to see to this reimbursement.[7] It is hardly probable that this assembly will consider that claim; at least it is demonstrated that it could not do so efficaciously. The claimants quote, in the same way as the French possessors of the paper money, the circular letter of Mr. Jay in which he said that "if America did not fulfill engagements so sacred, she would appear among nations as a prostitute and would be covered with ignominy."

The third question with which Congress is occupied is not less ticklish than the preceding. It is the matter of charging this assembly with all the particular debts of the states and consequently of consolidating in one sum all the domestic debts. This measure is the most important of all in order to attain finally that *unity* of government which the instigators of federalism have always had in view and which has always been so difficult for them till now to bring about. After long debates in which the Antifederalists proved very violent, it was adopted by a majority of thirty-one to twenty-six; but the delegates of North Carolina, arriving in Congress only a few days afterwards, urgently demanded that a question of this importance which would be of great concern to their state be reconsidered, and they left no stone unturned so that it is very uncertain now if after the reconsideration a majority will be formed again in favor of this consolidation of the debts.

O'Dwyer, pp. 432–26. Otto's letters included in *DHFFC* were usually written over the course of days, and even weeks, following the day they were begun.

[1] A reference to the Observer essays, authored by Wadsworth, and originally published in the [Hartford, Connecticut] *American Mercury*, October 1789–February 1790.

[2] The first Independent Observer essay appeared in *NYDG* on 10 February.

[3] Otto here either paraphrases the *NYDG* account dated 12 February or provides original reporting for part of Gerry's speech on 10 February (*DHFFC* 12:243).

[4] On 13 February, *NYDG* provided a lengthy clarification of its previous day's report of Gerry's remarks on 10 February (*DHFFC* 12:243–44n).

[5] Madison made reference to at least two precedents in his speech of 18 February (*DHFFC* 12:425–26). The only episode from the history of England cited in the extant text of the speech was the British government's default on its civil list in 1713, when Parliament ruled that original creditors could redeem their alienated certificates of debt from assignees for the actual price paid plus interest. At the close of the French and Indian War fifty years later, British speculators bought up vast quantities of certificates of debt from Canadian creditors of the French government, who were later reimbursed part of the nominal value according to negotiations carried out between the French and British governments. See *DHFFC* 12:278–82, 419–27.

[6] Madison's speech of 18 February. His first speech was on 11 February.

[7] While the Petition of the Public Creditors of Pennsylvania presented to the House on 28 August 1789 mentioned paper money, Otto is clearly referring to the Petition of Richard Wells and Josiah Hart, which urged Congress to include continental currency as part of the public debt to be discharged. Presented on 1 March, it quoted extensively from Congress's circular letter to the states signed by President John Jay on 13 September 1779 (*JCC* 15:1052–62). For the petitions, see *DHFFC* 8:258–68.

Nicholas Pike to Benjamin Goodhue

I was this Evening honored with your favor of the 20th. Ult. & the friendly proffers of your Service overwhelm me with a Sense of my Obligations.

Sensible of the weight of Public Business you have on your Mind, I felt guilty in troubling you with private Affairs. & so far from thinking myself neglected, I had no Reason to expect you could find leisure to answer them at all.

I have seen your Sentiments respecting the Public debt in the Papers, & have the honor to be of your Opinion. & it is matter of surprize, with every one I have conversed with, that Gentlemen of Sense should reason as some do in Congress. Many thought the Secretary [*Hamilton*], though they revered his abilities, very wide from the Mark; but, Messrs. Burk, Maddison, &c. have gone far beyond him, & for my own part, am unable to conceive how any *honest* Man can argue in the manner they do: however, as it is too extensive a Subject for a Letter, I will drop it for the present I will acquaint the friends of Mrs. Treat with your exertions to serve them,[1] notwithstanding the unfavourable prospect respecting the final Result.

I should not trouble you any further respecting the P[*ost*]. O[*ffice*]. had I not lately discovered that there are several Expectants of *that* in particular, as well as of the new Offices which are likely to be created in the Collection of the Excise. That Mr. D—n [*Dalton*] has been applied to, & has engaged his Influence for the P.O. in particular—and that Influence is making with several other Gentlemen for the same.

Although Mr. D. has been very kind in serving me in several Instances, yet I never applied to him on this Occasion, because I knew he had nearer Connexions, & therefore no reason to think I could obtain his Influence.

You, Sir, are the only friend I can rely on in Congress, & if you succeed, so much greater will be my Obligations, as you will, I doubt not, have numbers to oppose you.

Now, I beg to suggest to you, whether it would be *indelicate* (for I am not a proper Judge of the propriety of it) for you to propose the Question to Mr. [*Samuel*] Osgood, in the present Stage of the Business, whether it is probable there will be a Change of the Deputy in this place, & if so, to mention your friend, as I conceive the first applicant, ceteris paribus,[2] will stand the fairest Chance—and whether it ~~would~~ would be *proper* for me to write him on the subject. I do not mean to dictate, & hope you will not suppose it: but wish to leave it to your wisdom & discretion to conduct the matter as you shall think best.

Among those who are making Interest for this & some other of the Offices is Mr. William Pike Mercht. & to do him Justice, he has a fund of good sense, a very good Education, & a fair Character, although unfortunate in Trade.

ALS, Letters to Goodhue, NNS. Written from Newburyport, Massachusetts.

[1] Anna Treat's petition to Congress for poverty relief had the support of many influential people in Goodhue's district, including Pike and other creditors. For background on the petition, which Goodhue presented to the House on 15 February (unaware—like Pike—that Treat had died two weeks earlier), see *DHFFC* 7:256–58.

[2] All other things being equal.

Pelatiah Webster to William Samuel Johnson

Recd. your favr. of 9th. Ult. ℔ post. & am pleased and Obliged by your favorable Sentiments, & the Complaisant things you write if I coud. possess fine Qualities as well as you can describe them, I Shd. feel Self exalted without a blush but the description must arise out of the possession as it's only Source & this gives me a Sort of mortifying pleasure of admiring What I have mighty little right to Claim—I will however add some observations. which I hope your fertile Genius will form into Something usefull. When I wrote my Seven Essays on Finance & my plea for the Soldiers,[1] the facts & Sentiments did not Exist which have Since arisen with great force either to inform or prejudice the mind, My tho'ts were Original & grounded ma[i]nly on Such natural principles as I conceived at the time, ought to govern the decision. I then conceived that *Justice. Natural Fitness & public utility* were the Great principles the deep & sure foundation on which Every nation ought to ground the whole doctrine of Finance i.e. all calculations of ways & means of Supply & all adjustments & Liquidations of Expenditure—I tho't that the vast Importance of these principles were so universally acknoliged. & So Severely felt that, like Genuine virtue or Beauty, nothing more coud. be necessary to insure their being loved & Chosen, but to bring them fairly into view in their own native colors. I had no Idea that any man coud. assume the assurance to offer to the public a System of finance full of inconsistencies. with no connexion between the premisses & conclusions of it. the Grand object of Which is a needless & Shameless as well as most ruinous violation of national Justice, i.e. witholding from the noble deliverers of our Country the benefits of a public contract (the most Solemn & Sacred that ever was or coud. be made by men under the inspection of heaven) & Supported by the most acknoleged Merit, Supplies & Services render'd to the Country by the Claimants. Levying the money due to them on the Labor of our industrious Citizens, & paying it to idle Speculators, who never Earned it or payd for it—& Where the Said System proposes payment it docks off one third of the Acknoleged debt under the Cobweb covering of Slimsey & Childish pretences, holds out modes & arrangments, unintelligible Idle uninviting & ridiculous enough & in Short Backs & distorts the whole frame in favr. of a Small Class of Speculators by no means popular Generally invidious, & Whose real claim to either public usefulness or public favr. is as Small as that of any originators whatever who are within the protection of the Law. but what adds greatly to my astonishment & mortification is to hear that Such a System Shod. receive countenance in our Most dignifyed public councils. I can hardly beleive my Eyes when I read Such argts. as these viz. that original holders of Certificates shall not be paid because Some of them (perhaps one in a thousand) cant be found or Cant be discriminated, I tho't it very plain that Every demandant of a debt must bring his proof. & if he fails. he loses his debt but never Imagined this was an argt. why those who *coud. bring proof* shod. not recover their debts—that the most meritorious citizens who claim debts of acknoleged rights Shod. not be paid more than 2/6 in the pound—because Some of them have managed their 2/6 so well as in the Course of Seven years origination to have made 20/ out of it—because Some of them cod. Spend their money imprudently if they were paid—because some Sold their certificates. because they distrusted the public faith (which Every body did at the time)—because all that sold, were not compell'd by necessity—because paying the original Creditor wd. do him more damage than payg. the money (due to him) to the Speculator—because all the depredations of war cou'd not be made up to the Sufferers—because paying them original creditors wd. be more Troublesome than paying the Speculators—because foreigners had become Speculators to amt. of many millions in our public Securities, & must have their enormous profits Secured to them, because f the original Creditors were injured by their Country, not by the Specu[*lators*]—because the public faith must be rend[*ered*] Safe to the Speculators, by Sacrificing the [*blot*] acknoleged public Justice due to the origl. Creditors (as they all own that both cant be paid)—because the Speculators who bot. 2/6 only, & paid for no more must be considerd. as intitled to 28/ from the Govt. (for So much every certificate of 20/ with the interest will amt. to at this time)—because the public Securities must be consider'd as Transferd. on the principle of Commission assignments, tho' the case runs into an Extreme far beyound the reason of that principle. & Totally Subversive of it—I beg your indulgence to this Long Epistle pray don't read any further than you find matter worth reading.

ALS, Johnson Papers, CtHi. Written from Philadelphia; sent by post; docketed as answered.

[1] See Webster to Johnson, 1 February and February 1790 Undated, above. *A Plea for the Poor Soldiers* is calendared under 14 January, above. For the text, see Addendum, volume 22.

OTHER DOCUMENTS

William Constable to Joel Barlow. FC:lbk, Constable-Pierrepont Collection, NN.
  Manasseh Cutler and Rufus Putnam are in New York City, and "a few days will determine our Measures" regarding the Ohio Company.

Tench Coxe to Thomas Hartley. FC:lbk, Coxe Papers, PHi. Written from Philadelphia.

Asks Hartley to oversee a financial transaction with the Bank of New York, and to deliver enclosed letter to Ellsworth with directions to forward it to (David?) Gelston, whom Ellsworth knows.

Elbridge Gerry to Henry Knox. AN, Knox Papers, Gilder Lehrman Collection, NHi.

Enquires what if anything is due to First Lieutenant Samuel Rogers of Henry Jackson's (Ninth Massachusetts) regiment, killed at Yorktown on 20 October 1781.

Benjamin Goodhue to Michael Hodge. ALS, Ebenezer Stone Papers, MSaE.

The House is still debating assumption "and tho no decission is yet had, or will be soon had; from what has been said, and from the rejection of a motion for postponing the assumption till the Accounts are adjusted and the balances ascertained by a majority of two to one, I think the appearance is favourable, that the measure will take effect under some modification or other."

Levi Hollingsworth to Benjamin Contee. FC, Hollingsworth Letterbook, PHi. Written from Philadelphia.

"I am really sorry you did not give me an opportunity of seeing you when in this City on the 27th. So soon as I ~~could~~ rose I went to the Indian Queen [*Tavern*] but you was gone."

James Madison to Henry Lee. No copy known; acknowledged in Lee to Madison, 13 March.

Robert Morris to George Harrison. ALS, Brinton Coxe Papers, PHi. Place to which addressed not indicated.

"The House Spend much time before they decide on any point" of the report on public credit; William Constable will soon send instructions to Harrison regarding the state debts of North and South Carolina; hopes William White (Morris's brother-in-law?) will provide "some money" for Morris's "Blankets" to serve as "a Fund for You to Work with."

Philip Pendleton to James Madison. ALS, Madison Papers, DLC. Written from Berkeley, West Virginia. For the full text, see *PJM* 13:71.

Office seeking: Samuel H. Parsons' seat as judge of the Western Territory; solicits "your kind offices with the President," including delivery of enclosed letter of application; "the great number of the Citizens of this State who have become adventurers in that Country will certainly warrant an Appointment of one of the Judges at least from Virginia"; has also written "my freind" White for support.

William Robinson, Jr. to John Langdon. ALS, Langdon Papers, NhPoA. Written from Philadelphia.
They have not corresponded for "a considerable Time"; encloses a copy of the new Pennsylvania constitution for Langdon's "Opinion & Remarks."

Roger Sherman to David Austin. FC:dft, Sherman Papers, CtY. Sherman docketed this copy as "Minutes of a Letter to D. Austin." Dr. Charles Chauncey (1705–87), Congregational minister of Boston's First Church from 1727 until his death, authored the proto-Universalist tract *Salvation for All Men* in 1782.
Thanks Austin for his letter of 20 February and its information about their "Society" (White Haven Church) in New Haven, Connecticut; has heard many good, orthodox and pious preachers while in New York, "but I have found none that in all respects suit me better than Dr. [*Jonathan*] Edwards"; fears that Dr. Chauncey's sentiments are "very errrounious, & if believed will tend to relax the restraints on vice arising from the threatnings of the divine law. against impenitent Sinners"; "I think we are as much bound to believe the threatnings, as the promise of the Gospel."

Samuel Whittemore to George Washington. ALS, Washington Papers, DLC. Written from Gloucester, Massachusetts; franked; postmarked Boston, 7 March. For the full text, see *PGW* 5:195–96.
Office seeking: some office other than his present one of surveyor at Gloucester; had not thought it necessary to solicit the patronage of any congressman prior to being overlooked for naval officer there.

Theodore Woodbridge to Jonathan Trumbull. FC:dft, Woodbridge Papers, CtHi. Place from which written not indicated. Dating based on acknowledgment in Trumbull to Woodbridge, 20 March.
A few days before, saw Madison's proposal for discriminating between original and subsequent securities holders, and "as far as I have conversed with the Judicious and disinterested they judge it wise & just."

William Samuel Johnson, Diary. Johnson Papers, CtHi.
"At Vice Presidts."

TUESDAY, 2 MARCH 1790

Warm (Johnson)

Edward Carrington to James Madison

Upon coming to Town a few days ago I had the pleasure to receive yrs. of the 2d. & 14th. Ult. From Colo. [*James*] Innes I have also had the perusal of the reports of the Secretaries of the Treasury and War departments. I have not as yet been able to give either so thorough an examination as to enable me to give a decided opinion upon it—the former indeed is extensive and complicated; it also takes up many principles which are new to the Finances of this Country. Upon the slight view I have however been able to take of it, it appears well calculated to place the public Credit on a permanent and good footing. The Tax proposed on Country Stills would at first seem to have an unpopular cast, but when it is considered with ~~that~~ those laid on ~~Stills~~ Spirits distilled from foreign productions, and those on imported Spirits, it is certainly calculated to give a decided advantage to the country Stills. Indeed ardent Spirits are so pernicious that they ought to be highly Taxed even where they are distilled from our own produce. as to the plan for a National Militia it may be unfortunate that none can be adopted promising great advantage without an expence that will be thought too expensive by the people—we have only to weigh this agt. the benefits of a certain and firm defence on which we rely without that more expensive and odious one depending on standing Armies.

I am much obliged by your communication upon the subject of your Motion, the mode of treating the public Dt. is a point upon which there are various opinions, & I shall give you mine with ~~that~~ candour ~~which is highly proper on the occasion~~. I own I cannot see the justice or good policy of a discrimination of any kind. It was known when the paper issued that the finances of the United States, would not admit of a Compliance such as the face of the paper held out, yet the original Creditors would insist on the issues—this was the case with the Army rather in a Mutinous manner[1]—since this the paper has been a subject of Speculation, at prices which were governed by the confidence or difidence of the sellers & purchasers in a faithful redemption, and the latter have demanded a premium for their hazards— Any Measure of the sort must necessary injure the public credit which with me is the most important consideration of all. After [*lined out*] one instance of a discrimination, since you are still to give out paper, is it to be expected, that a depretiation will not take place [*lined out*] upon an apprehension that the same thing will be done again? Should it be said that adequate funds will now be provided, to this it may be answered that the descerning will perhaps be able to judge of the consequences of such a circumstance, but the ignorant will not—they will judge from former events, and will be as much speculated upon as ever. your plan of an Alternate payment of the difference to the original sufferers, in my mind presents very great mischeif to the community—it may be supposed that my partialities for that class of Creditors who were of the Army is great, as indeed it really is, but yet I know them, and I will undertake to say that had they been paid off in Gold & Silver, they would, with a few exceptions, have parted with it with as little benefit to themselves as they did the paper—they have from necessity now betaken themselves to useful employments—let it once be announced that a resettlement is to be had with them, they will quit these employments in quest of it, they will for a while be lost, as to any good purposes to the community, and will at length get as little for the second issues of paper as they did for the first. these considerations I give you as they occur—they are however inferior ones when compared with that of the public credit. I never held any of this paper except what the public issued to me, and a remittance that I received in them in place of Bills of exchange when I was in New York—the former I sold to the public at about 2/6 in the pound for Western Lands—the latter I sold immediately on their coming up, for about what they cost.

I have but an imperfect idea of the plan for the enumeration of the people. it may however be made very practicable in other States & yet be otherwise in this—where the State officers can be employed [*lined out*] as assistants they will be able to do it for much less than those who are to be employed for this purpose alone—our Comrs. of the Taxes could have done this business better than any others from their acquaintance with the families in the course of their other duty—a Law of this State however prohibits their being set about it.[2] add to these considerations that Virginia comprehends vast Tracts of Country amongst the mountains even over the Allegany, which are rough and but thinly settled.

ALS, Madison Papers, DLC. Written from Richmond, Virginia.

[1] This may be a broad reference to the Continental Army's disaffection on the subject of back pay in 1783. Or more specifically, Carrington may be alluding to the Newburgh Mutiny of March 1783 when an extra-legal meeting of army officers attempted to "assume a bolder tone" with Congress on the subject of their unliquidated accounts, by warning "that in any political event, the army has its alternatives." Washington defused the threat by formally convening a general meeting of officers who repudiated their comrades' subversive action while repeating their appeal for a liquidation of all army accounts. About $11,000,000 in final settlement certificates were subsequently issued to the troops by the paymaster general (*JCC* 24:297, 310; E. James Ferguson, *The Power of the Purse* [Chapel Hill, N.C., 1961], pp. 161–64, 179–80).

[2] Since adopting "An Act for raising a supply of money for publick exigencies" in October

1777, Virginia forbade its tax collectors from engaging in certain activities that might gener-
ate a conflict of interest. Among these were holding another public office (Hening 9:349–52).

Samuel Nasson to George Thatcher

* * *

I hartely Joyn with you in the Observation in one of them that the best
way of defusing Usefull Knowladge is by keeping up the Schools but am as
much supprised that it should ever enter into the mind of any Gentelman
that it would be best to put them in the hands of Congress if that should
be the case I have been more Decaved then I thought I was for I allways
thought that the Ins[*ti*]tution of Schools with a Number of other small
matters (such as appointing Fence Vewers hog reaves Pound keepers Cullers
of Staves Survaors of lumber &c.) would have been left in the hands of our
own State Secry. but if it must be so I am Content rather Congress should
appoint School masters then not to have any but let me ask you why you
hasten to Consoladate the whole so soon Methinks you are out in your Poli-
tick Pay the states debts why it looks dark to me as your funding them will
be why has not the Same upror been about the securitys when in the hands
of the poor soldier it is plane then A few would not have made Such large
fountains out of the poor and perhaps Bleeding Soldiers how can it be right
that he which sold his Notes of one hundred pounds for Ten should now be
obliged to Swett Even Blood to pay the Ninety he he was Cheated out of by
Some Viliane who in the war was afrad to Turn out and Stand a Mark for
the Enemey to shoot at I Say after the many Sleepless Night and weriysome
days of hard Labour and loss of half his Blood to Earn them then had them
taken away by Some winkd. at Robler; and be obliged to Pay the full ~~Some~~
Sum again to redeem by allmost Starving his dear wife and Tender Offspring
forbid it. O. my Guardians at Congress let me and mine yet live and if you
want me once more to fight your Battels I am ready all though I am Coverd
all ready with wounds then perhaps look up to that God that once and again
Saved him in the midst of Blood and Carnage and Cries forbid it Greacious
Haven and fall beneath the Burden O. my freind is or is not this but a fairst
Discription of many who once we Calld. our Brother and sayd. if he Ever
returnd from the war we would Endevour to make him happy how does this
agree with our former speachers better for the poor unfortainate man had he
Burnt his Notes then to redeem them at this rate Stop Says Some Standing
by. where is your Public faith you must keep that So Say I. but I Say it is a
word without meaning or Ells why have not all the Nations that have made
peace one with another keept. they did as long as it was for their Intrest and
then set ~~fourth~~ forth the dogs of War with all thir fury.

But I Stop least I should offend.

I see in the paper you sent me that the Jews have Pertitioned the Assembly of France.[1]

I admire thir Languge with which they adress that Assembly and hope that they may Suceead I feel for that people Scattered throughout the World Once I think they ware Naurallized in England what might the Affeccts be if they had Some incouragement in our new world. you know they Carry wealth with them. might it not be of sarvice if they ware Allowd to Settel in the old pr[ovince]. of Main think and Think again before you Trust them and after beaing Convinced that thay would be servicable then Move that they have liberty to hold lands.

***

[P. S.] N. B. Sinc I began this letter I heard a Rumore that Capt. [Richard] Trevett would soon be dropt ~~for~~ from beaing Navile offiser I suppose that Judge [David] Sewall will interpose but I think that family has annough.

I Never Beged Posts of Honour or Profit but you know how my situvation in York is well suted for Pleasure or Business Some undoubtely has as Greate pertntion to Publick favour and Rewards as the U— formerly many has done that for their Countery that they never did that is Exposed ther lives and if they return home alive it was not Because they never had ben in dangour.

My Complements to Col. Grout I should Esteem it a favour to be Taken Notice of by him if you have a favourable Opertunity Please To Give my Kine Respects to your Brother [Samuel] Otis and trust to him that if it would not be two much be neath his Dignity I ~~Sould~~ Should be raised two Degrees higher then at present if he woud do me the honour of a Short Letter.

ALS, Chamberlain Collection, MB. Written from York, Maine. The omitted text discusses Nasson's faith in Providence.

---

[1] Acting on the overwhelming mandate of a citywide referendum, the city of Paris appealed for enfranchising French Jews in an address presented to the National Assembly on 25 February 1790. Full civil rights were not bestowed until September 1791.

John Pemberton to James Pemberton

I mentioned in my last to my dear Hannah [Pemberton] the receipt of thine of 21st. Ulto. The Comittee met on 7th. day [Saturday] last & formed the heads of the report they proposed to make & find each member was privately to Consider them & at their next meeting to morrow to make their remarks. having thro' M[iers]. F[isher]. procured in Confidence a Copy of those heads some remarks are made thereon and delivered to C[ol]. Hartley one of the members from Pensylvania. & diligent W[arner]. M[ifflin]. has wrote to the Comittee to be presented to morrow. It is sorrowful to observe & cannot but feel for the Comittee, that human fears too much prevail. They see the Subject I trust in a proper light yet have not firmness to bring forth their prospects. they fear that the Southern delegates will rise in a flame, & so temporise, they propose to finish their business to morrow so as to throw' it before the house, but I doubt it. I believe they are in general favorable to the Cause of humanity, yet want if possible to please the opposite side. It is no wonder when human Wisdom & human prudence governs the mind if we do not succeed. I trust we have endeavored to fulfill our appointment & must leave the event to him who can Confound the Wisdom of the Wise.[1] & affect his gracious purposes—we have had oppy. & some repeatedly with the members of Congress generally, these opps. have had I trust a salutary effect. & find them more free, the more freedom is used. 3 of the Eastern called & spent upwards of 2 hours with us last evening. & 4 dined with us on 7th. day & more were invited but were previously engaged. [*Daniel*] Carrol from Maryland, [*Abiel*] Foster the Chairman of the Comittee, Bassett & Schurman. Izard & Smith from Carolina were invited. & had they not been engaged would have come. W. M. had for the first time an interview with them & had much free Comunication. & adjourned to a future time. Jackson has had a bad fit of the pluresy & not yet out that I hear of. I told his Friend Stone yesterday it was a Duty to visit the sick & might be a proper time to visit him, but he said not Mr. Jackson. There are agents here from the Muskingham to solicit a force to protect them from the Indians.[2] I am glad to find that the members we have conversed with have a just Idea of those back people, & hope caution will be exercised, yet as dear J. Woolman said, "the wisest in human Policy shall be the greatest fools,"[3] so these men may be warped aside by solicitation. I was disappointed in not having a letter ℔ Post eveng. of 7th. day hope for one this evening. I want to be at home. if we could hear the report of the Comittee if a Discussion was referred for some weeks we might return & others come. tho' it would be agreable [*torn*] Discussion was immediately entered into on its presentment I think it would be useful a Number of Friends attended when this happened. F. Bailey seems like to get his business effected.[4] its a Curious discovery, & will be useful.

It does not seem likely we shall leave N. York this week. My Comp[*anio*]ns. pretty well. Warner is not free of a Cold yet not Confined, is the most Comfortable of any of us. tho' the most laborious he is fitted for it. not easily daunted. & very persevering & yet with prudence. We attend generally at the [*Federal*] Hall at the time of their meeting to shew ourselves & to remind them we are waiting upon them. & Warner Seldom misses their breaking up to catch oppy. as well as in Visits to their appartments. Fnds. here are kind. & Individuals ready to join us in Visits, but &c. I hear the Stage in which G. Boune[5] went was also overset, he hurt somewhat. & One man dangerously. The roads may be better by the time of our return.

***

ALS, Pennsylvania Abolition Society Papers, PHi. Addressed to Second Street, Philadelphia; postmarked; received 4 March; answered 7 March. The omitted postscript, mostly salutations, includes expressions of concern for Hannah Pemberton's health.

[1] 1 Corinthians 1:19.

[2] Pemberton probably refers to the various communications that had arrived at the seat of government in the days immediately preceding and were forwarded by Washington to the House on 1 March, from the militia commander of Harrison County, Virginia, across the Ohio River from the mouth of the Muskingum River. For Col. John Duval's report summarizing the threat to and seeking protection for Virginia's far northwest counties at the beginning of the new warmaking season, see *PGW* 5:180–81.

[3] From a letter of 4 January 1770, recorded in chapter twenty of the famous *Journal* (1774) by the New Jersey Quaker mystic John Woolman (1720–72).

[4] For background on Francis Bailey's FFC petition seeking patent protection for an anti-counterfeiting method, see *DHFFC* 8:73–84.

[5] Probably George Bowne, one of the delegation of the New York Yearly Meeting of Friends (Quakers) that joined their Philadelphia counterparts in the early lobbying for the antislavery petitions.

Edmund Randolph to James Madison

We arrived last night after much fatigue to ourselves and horses. Indeed I have not been free from a fever since Wednesday last.

From the small opporty., which I had, to ascertain the opinion of Phila. on the subject of your motion [*for discrimination*], I am inclined to believe, that if the holders of ~~stock~~ securities, the merchants and others, associated with them, or dependent on them, were excluded, the suffrage would be in favor of the measure. I had a conversation with a gentleman, whom I thought from his complexion and connections to be in sentiment with me; but to my surprize he advocated your plan not only upon your principles, but upon that of tories, as he's says, being possessed of them.

~~When~~ I found here Capt. Heard, who married Genl. Morgan's daughter.[1] He informed me, that the people of our Frederick [*County, Virginia*] were very anxious to see your speech; and that a large majority of them, perhaps ¾ were in favor of the partition between the original & actual holders. Tell Mr. White, that I magnified his exertions to his constituent, altho' I differed from him in judgment. I will gather in Alex[*andri*]a. & Fred[*ericksbur*]g. what I can, and shall inform you from the latter.

ALS, Madison Papers, DLC. Written from Baltimore.

[1] James Heard (d. 1831), of Frederick, Maryland, married Betsey, daughter of Daniel Morgan, in 1785.

William Smith (S.C.) to Edward Rutledge

I saw Sumpter yesterday—he says he was a few days in Columbia [*South Carolina*] & reprobates the meeting of the Legislature at that abominable place.

He was against the assumption of the State Debts before he arrived, but now seems to hesitate since he has heard of the resolutns. of our Legisl[*ature*].[1]

I am told Tucker says he has no objection to vote for the measure as it is the wish of the Legislature, but that he doesn't think himself bound to obey instructions from a *Legislature*: he moved last session the amendmt. to the Constitution "that the people had a right to instruct their represents." but the *Legislat*[*ur*]*e*. (it appears) have not! Sumpter seconded him.

Yesterday Madison withdrew his last amendmt. (the first was agreed to without debate) he then proposed another, which was to assume the state debts as they stood in 1783—this is meant to please Virginia which has paid off a part of her debt & he wants the State to receive payment from the continent of the sum actually paid by her—but as other states have likewise sunk part of their debts & paid the interest regularly which ought also to be refunded, the amount, if revived, would add twenty millions more to the account. It met with such general opposition yesterday that I beleive he will withdraw it to day.

ALS, Smith Papers, ScHi. The first part of this letter was written on 28 February and is printed under that date.

[1] Instructing the congressional delegation to vote for assumption.

OTHER DOCUMENTS

John Dawson to Tench Coxe. ALS, Coxe Papers, PHi. Written from Richmond, Virginia; place to which addressed not indicated.

"I fear that by the time you receive this, youll hear of the death of our friend Grayson who has been confind at Dumfries [*Virginia*] for some time, & whose imprudence in his diet increasd with his disorder—should this event happen I know not who we shall appoint in his place, willing to serve."

Rufus King, Elbridge Gerry, and Henry Knox to Nathaniel Tracy. FC, hand of William Knox, Knox Papers, Gilder Lehrman Collection, NHi. Place to which addressed not indicated. On 22 March the House received Tracy's petition for a bankruptcy law; see *DHFFC* 8:86–89.

Advises Tracy to avoid paying one of his many creditors; "if the payment of that sum would have the desirable effect of liberating you from all your present embarrassments, difficult as it is at this time to pay the specie we would do everything in our power to effect it"; offer to pay Tracy's expenses while at Hartford, Connecticut; have written an appeal to the creditor's friends at Boston.

Manasseh Cutler, Diary. Cutler Papers, IEN.
    Dined with Goodhue.

Massachusetts Resolution on Invalid Pensions, Resolves and Acts, M-Ar.
    Representatives asked to move in the House for an extension of the dead-
    line for applying for invalid pensions and that Massachusetts be entitled
    to a new inspection and return of its invalid pensioners.

NYDG, 2 March. Wister Butler Papers, PHi. Annotated by Butler to indicate the article for which he retained the issue. For the petitions cited, see
DHFFC 8:264–65 and 260–64, respectively.
    Petition of Richard Wells and Josiah Hart (presented 1 March), and peti-
    tion of the public creditors of Pennsylvania (presented 31 August 1789).

Letter from Rhode Island to New London. [New London] *Connecticut Gazette*,
5 March; reprinted at New York City (*NYDA*, 11 March; *NYP*, 13 March)
and Edenton, North Carolina.
    The Constitution will not be adopted at the ratification convention now
    sitting; an adjournment for several weeks is expected; T. Foster was un-
    successfully nominated for secretary.

WEDNESDAY, 3 MARCH 1790

Windy Cold (Johnson)

Fisher Ames to William Tudor

We have not decided upon the assumption of the state debts. __ [*Madison*]
hangs heavy on us. If he is a friend, he is more troublesome than a declared
foe. He is so much a Virginian; so afraid that the mob will cry out, *crucify
him*;[1] sees Patrick Henry's shade at his bedside every night; fears so much
the eastern confederacy, and perhaps thinks it unpleasant to come in as an
auxiliary to support another's plan; that he has kept himself wrapt up in
mystery, and starts new objections daily. I hope a favourable event. But the
work goes on heavily and slowly.

MHSC, ser. 2, 8(1826):322. In his 1854 edition of his father's papers, Seth Ames dated this letter 8 March.

[1] The mob's cry condemning Jesus (Mark 15:13–14).

Aedanus Burke to Samuel Bryan

Your very friendly Letter inclosing the package intended for me, on the idea that I was in Charleston, came to hand about an hour ago. I cannot tell you how much I feel my self indebted to you, for your trouble and attention to a certain buisiness[1]—all I have to say is, that to be able to be of service to you, or any friend of yours, will be pleasurable to me. I shall pay the most particular regard to your request relative to a certain publication and it's author.[2] I love truth and merit too well not to feel how much our country is obliged, as well as enlightned by your bold spirit and foresight.

I write this in haste as Col. [*Eleazer*] Oswald is waiting and to set off in a few hours. In my next I shall answer your Letter more particularly. Our friend Col. O__d. Will inform you of every thing going forward here on every subject. Congress is daily engaged on the Report of Mr. Hamilton. I know no man in either house, who is not totally at a Loss on this important subject—Funding the debt is the word at present, but no one can tell wh. way it will end. Funding the debt may, or may not be, a blessing, or a curse to the people of America, for ought I dare say, at present. But this I sincerely regret. It will add strength and power to that faction that brought about the late 2d. revolution, and it will make their princely fortunes. You may judge that I stand in a particular situation not agreeable to me. for my time at present is entirely taken up ~~from~~ with buisiness while I long for a little retiremt.

ALS, Miscellaneous Letters, Miscellaneous Correspondence, State Department Records, Record Group 59, DNA. Place to which addressed not indicated.

[1] Burke had asked Bryan to answer a detailed questionnaire on the constitutional "revolution" of 1787–88 as it occurred in Pennsylvania; see *DHFFC* 17:1728–38.
[2] Probably a reference to Bryan's eighteen influential Antifederalist "Centinel" essays regarding the proposed Constitution that were published between 5 October 1787 and 9 April 1788. Bryan revived the essay series during the first federal election in the fall of 1788 and again a year later during the public debate about a new constitution for Pennsylvania. See *DHROC* 13:326–28.

Pierce Butler to Archibald Maclaine

Since I last wrote to you I have been favored with Your two acceptable letters of the 20th of december and 8th of February. I sincerely wish that your own private Interest could be benefitted as much by your coming to Congress as Your Country's wou'd for indeed the southern Interest calls loudly for some such Men as you here. Your senators are at length on the floor. Govr. Johnston is a very amiable and desirable associate and indeed so is Coll. Hawkins. I hope your Representatives may be Men of abilities and business. The Eastern states have a great advantage in the latter for all their Members are men of application & well acquainted with the rotine of business. The house of Representatives are busily engaged with the Secretary's report; they have been for several days debating the propriety of assuming the States debts. The Speaker yesterday gave the casting vote for postponing it for the present. I think Mr. [George] Hooper is now as well off in not having bought in.

I have strong doubts of the propriety of the measure at the present stage of the Union. My apprehensions of lasting harmony are awakened by the self-interestedness of the Eastern States. You will have heard before this reaches You of the appointment of Mr. [James] Iredal to a seat on the bench of the Supreme Court. I was happy in the oppy. of being instrumental in obtaining the appointment [as] Justice. Mr. Hawkins left nothing undone to serve Mr. Iredel & he did materially serve him.

The appointments in the Customs for No. Carolina are all made. I shd. have exerted myself in obtaining your wish respecting the appointments had not your senators been on the floor & made out the list as it now stands. I could not interfere with them.

It is generally agreed in Congress that the judiciary must undergo alterations when the system is before Senate I will attend to the observation you honored me with. I have spoke with Your Senators respecting the appointment of Mr. Hays [John Hay] as Atty. General of the Federal Court they think well of him, but at the same time speak of Mr. Alfred Moore.

The Senate have accepted the territorial session of No. Carolina We are trying to hurry on the bill for fixing the places & times of holding courts in Your State, so that they may commence this spring. ***

FC, Butler Letterbook, ScU. The omitted text relates to business affairs. For the full text, see *Butler Letters*, pp. 15–17.

George Clymer to Tench Coxe

I received yours of the 28 [*February*] but last night and would have conferred on the subject of the patent bill with the committee but am this morning kept in doors by a little cold and fever—Tomorrow I may see them.

The assumption makes no progress—there is much talk but no conviction on either side—the inequalities between the states already too great and which there is scarce a prospect of seeing eventually levelled would certainly be encreased by it—it is on this account apparently wrong but a clashing taxation will be inconvenient if not ruinous—As to our own state the measure is in itself indifferent to it, and nothing may be considered in it but its natural fitness and propriety—I question however whether it will be possible to give reason the fairest play—the recollection, that one of the states to be benefitted has been an open enemy and the other a treacherous friend may have a little influence with us.[1] Yesterday there was a stay of execution till the Secretary of treasury should report the extraordinary ways and means. I begin to wish a truce with this affair which has most unreasonably stopped all the business of the union—In all such points it is often better to suffer opinion silently to mature with time than to attempt force conviction against the will—As to Messieurs the Speculators in the continental certificates I doubt not their clear-sightedness on one side of this question—they are also as clear that they ought to have their full 6 ⅌ cent in ready cash—they some people however are not quite so enlightened.

At the opening of the session the president recommended the encouragement of such domestic manufactures as were important towards the defence of the country—a reference was made to the Secretary—Your *report* of the state of the Gunpowder making in Penna. which I shall take the liberty of publishing here, will be I believe more to the purpose than any he can make.[2]

ALS, Coxe Papers, PHi. Written in the morning; addressed to Philadelphia; franked; postmarked.

[1] Perhaps a reference to Massachusetts and Virginia, respectively, and their roles in the fight over the location of the federal seat of government in August and September 1789.
[2] The brief report appeared in *NYDG*, 5 March (see below).

Jeremiah Hill to George Thatcher

Yours of the 21st. Ulto. came to hand by this days post, I am Glad to hear that we are like to have a post office in this Town, I have read your Letter to "Father [*Daniel*] Hooper." I think the old Gentleman is pleased.

If I said that there were "upwards of forty sail of Vessels in the District of Biddeford &c. that follow the foreign Trade" I said wrong, there is upwards of forty sail belonging to this district in the whole, but about half of them are employ'd in the coasting business—whether it is an hardship or not to exclude foreigners, is for you to say—I state facts, id est,[1] we do not enjoy that Priviledge which other districts enjoy—Whether it is good Policy to exclude Foreigners from bringing goods to America, is or may be a matter under Consideration.

To encourage our own trade & navigation is in fact essential to our own Interest.

To make Mice Rats & Rats Musquashes [*muskrats*] is very easy, it requires no more that no [?] nominate & by and with advice to appoint an *Adam* or as we moderns say a *Plenipotentary* to new name them, it is very common now a days for things to acquire a new name by *Custom*, the same as we often acquire title by occupancy—My Heart sang Praises when I heard of Father Wingate's being Proselyted from the worship of the Creature to that of the Creator—I shall acquaint our Parson with the Information the first Opportunity, I can assure you that our Parson begins to be in Charity with the true Worshipers, who worship the father in Spirit & in truth— ***
P. S. one of the inclosed came to my hand too late for the last post.

ALS, Chamberlain Collection, MB. Written from Biddeford, Maine; postmarked Portsmouth, New Hampshire, 5 March. The omitted text relates to friends in Maine.

[1] That is.

Benjamin Lincoln to Theodore Sedgwick

In obedience to yours of the 21st. Ulto. Say that Mr. M— ~~projection~~ project[1] here is considered in a very unfavourable point of light; The proposition is not calculated to meet the public smile. He should have come forward, if popularity was his aim, with power in one hand and a scale in the other here the people at *large* would have got what the public creditors should lose but by his mad scheme none are to be benefitted by it but a few whom the public eye have so long seen in distress ~~untill~~ that the sight is quite familiar to them—They now do not *pass by even on the other side.*
***

Mr. Dane is going to settle our old acct.[2] I hope he will confine himself to his proper business I am affraid he will not If he was the father of some late proposed amendments more properly called alterations in the federal constitution.

ALS, Sedgwick Papers, MHi. Written from Boston; postmarked. The omitted text discusses Nathaniel Gorham's and Oliver Phelps's negotiations with the state legislature to modify their contract for the Genessee Purchase, probably to the satisfaction of all investors.

[1] Madison's proposal on discrimination.

[2] On 4 March, just weeks after Nathan Dane's election as state senator for Essex County, Massachusetts, Gov. John Hancock appointed him agent "to arrange & enforce" Massachusetts' claims against the United States, "& as far as you may find it expedient to support & advocate the same" before the commissioners for settling accounts with the states, in accordance with a resolution of the state legislature passed on 23 February (Dane Manuscript Collection, Beverly Historical Society, Massachusetts).

Joseph Pierce to Benjamin Goodhue

I recd. your kind Letter of 7 past and skim'd. it as requested, I thank you for the information it contained—We hear, & by the papers, see that you have very hard work at Congress on the Secry.'s Report—Mr. Maddisons speech has surprized many people here—to be sure it has verified the saying "that great men are not always wise"[1]—If Mr. M. had happened to look into Rousseaus System of Education—I think the 4th Vol. abt. the 248 page & on he could have seen something useful, & that might have given his thoughts a different turn[2]—he has been answering ably—I suppose before this his ~~question~~ motion has been decided.

Our General Court rise this week they have done little else than make a new excise Law & altering the Rates which many doubt they had no right to do—you will undoubtedly see that clause of the Constitution (amongst others) which says all duties shall be uniform throughout the United Stats[3] complied with if it is not attended to in time, the greatest confusion must follow.

***

ALS, Letters to Goodhue, NNS. Written from Boston.

[1] Madison's speech of either 11 or 18 February on discrimination among public creditors; the Biblical reference is to Job 32:9.

[2] By 1790, seven four-volume editions of *Émile* had been published, the most famous being the Paris edition of Jean Neaulme in 1762. The first English edition was in 1793.

[3] Section 8, paragraph 1.

William Smith (S.C.) to John F. Grimke

I had the pleasure of hearing from you the other day by a Letter in which you request my assistance to Serve poor [*John*] Mitchell. I have seen with Satisfaction that you advocate his cause, because I think your recommendation will add weight to those of the Merchants which have been sent to me & which I have laid before the President. I beleive the impressions on the President's mind are not the most favorable from a recollection of the Colo.'s conduct Some years ago at Philada. & from his abandonment of his wife, a measure which a man so uxurious & domestic as the President does not approve of. These are conjectures of mine which have arisen from Some conversation I had with the President when I presented him the Letter from the Merchants & which you had better not suggest to any one; I endeavoured to remove these impressions, by assurances that the Colol. was considerably reformed &ca. I also communicated your recommendation & Stated to him that the most respectable merchants approved of the appointmt. &

Seemed desirous of it. he answered that gentlemen could not refuse their signature on these occasions & that the Col. had not formerly shewn himself capable of managing his own affairs, but that he would take the matter into his consideration—don't mention these circumses. as they may be painful to our poor brother. I have heard no complaints from any of the States of the Magistrates having neglected to take the oath prescribed by the fœderal Constitution: I will however, inquire into the matter & see what can be done—at present our minds are so intent on matters of finance & particularly the State Debts that we can't allow ourselves to think of any thing else; There is considerable opposition to this measure, which takes a new Shape every day & makes the Event dubious—indeed the prospect of Success changes daily & there is no saying with certainty what will be the Issue; yet I can't help thinking it is so necessary to do compleat Justice & to cement the Union of the States & to systematize the national finances that a majority of the Members will finally ask for it.

I give you joy on your safe return from Columbia & wish you had brought all the offices & records with you.

I thank you for your Kind congratulations—Mrs. S. is recovered & our Son is hearty.

[*P. S.*] Your Brother Burke[1] is become very pleasant—a great speaker, & often entertaining, with humorous strokes of fancy.

ALS, Emmet Collection, NN. Addressed to Charleston, South Carolina; franked.

---

[1] Grimke and Burke served together on the South Carolina court of sessions and common pleas.

Adam Stephen to James Madison

We were Sorry to hear of your being taken ill at George Town [*Maryland, present-day Washington, D.C.*], but rejoiced to see you correcting the Schedule of the Census at New york.

Mr. Hamilton has discovered great extent of Comprehension in his Report—He with great facility develops and simplifies the most Complicated Subjects—The funding the debts of the Individual States with the Others, is a masterly Stroke of Policy, and will establishe The Federal Government in the Hearts of the People—The Resources of the Nation stand more Clear, to be adapted to General purposes, as the Excegencies of Govermt. may require—Reflecting on the feeble Attempts of the different States to establish a Revenue, and observing them repealing or Altering the laws every Session, and giving so great advantage to Sheriff or Collector to prey upon the Poor, makes me in Some Measure apply to Hamilton what Mr. Pope did to the Immortal Newton—

Resources and Revenue Laws lay hid in Night
'Twas said Let Hamilton be! and all was right.[1]

The Report has already advanced the Credit of the Nation, and It is the general Wish of the people within my Circle, that it may be adopted.

The expostulations of Potowmack[2] will make their appearance, after the Treasury and Militia Business is finishd. Extract "are we to be told says Mr. Sedgewick that a Respectable State would not have adopted the Constitution, had they known the proceedings of this House to day"[3]—Are Mr. Sedgwicks Organs of hearing so delicate, that they cannot bear being impressd with the truth? If the language displeases; remove the Cause, and the Effects will cease: Let mutual Attention and Concessions take place, Civilities will follow, and matters of Government will go on Smoothly and with Ease.

ALS, Madison Papers, DLC. Written from Martinsburg, West Virginia.

[1] A paraphrase of Alexander Pope's (1688–1744) famous epitaph in honor of Sir Isaac Newton (1642–1727) for unlocking the laws of physics.

[2] The broadside *The Expostulations of Potowmac* (Martinsburg, W.Va., 1790) was the final effort in the Potomac Interest's library of propaganda for attracting the federal seat of government. It was authored by Stephen, who enclosed a copy to Madison in his letter of 25 April, volume 19.

[3] A paraphrase of Sedgwick's rejoinder to Madison's controversial avowal of Virginia's position on the Seat of Government Bill, spoken before the Committee of the Whole House and a crowded House gallery during the heated debate of 3 September 1789 (*DHFFC* 11:1413).

Letter from Boston

There is however much anti-federalism in the [*Massachusetts*] house; and **** [*Nathan Dane*] has brought forward in the senate, a budget of alterations to the federal constitution. One of which is that the members of Congress, shall depend on the legislatures of the states for their pay, and the quantum of it—blessed effect of individual folly! To suppose that one set of the servants of the people, should make wages for another—and a higher set too! If our legislature should adopt this *mess*, I hope that Congress will send out an amendment that the pay of the state legislatures, shall be stated by the representatives of the union.

GUS, 13 March; reprinted at Exeter, New Hampshire; Windsor, Vermont; and Salem, Massachusetts.

OTHER DOCUMENTS

William Constable to Gouverneur Morris. FC:lbk, Constable-Pierrepont Collection, NN.

> The funding plan may be postponed until the next session because of opposition to the assumption of the states' war debts, "whose advocates are determined to reject the whole if these are not adopted"; believes the assumption will take place.

Andrew Craigie to Horace Johnson. FC:dft, Craigie Papers, MWA.

> "At present it is rather uncertain whether the adoption of the State Debts will take place."

Stephen Goodhue to Benjamin Goodhue. FC:lbk, Goodhue Family Papers, MSaE. Written from Salem, Massachusetts.

> "Fanny" (Frances Goodhue) and children are well.

Benjamin Huntington to William Ellery. No copy known; acknowledged in Ellery to Huntington, 28 March, as the beginning of a letter concluded on 8 March.

Christopher Leffingwell to Benjamin Huntington. ALS, Benjamin Huntington Correspondence, 1772–1790, R-Ar. Written from Norwich, Connecticut; franked; postmarked; answered 14 March. (Leffingwell's news about Arnold was rumor; he was tending to his mercantile affairs in St. John, New Brunswick, Canada, while his wife Peggy Shippen Arnold [1760–1804] visited family in Philadelphia, by way of New York City, between November 1789 and April 1790 [Willard M. Wallace, *Traitorous Hero* (Freeport, N.Y., 1954), p. 294]).

> Asks assistance in recovering a debt from Benedict Arnold, whom Leffingwell has heard was in New York City en route to Philadelphia; wife Anne Huntington is "much as when you left home the rest of the Family well"; asks if Jedidiah Huntington can receive a better appointment than collector at New London, which Leffingwell wishes for himself; details scandal of Norwich sheriff's dereliction of duty (news important to Huntington, as the town's mayor, 1784–96).

William Pinkney to James Pemberton. ALS, Pennsylvania Abolition Society Papers, PHi. Written from Lower Ferry of the Susquehannah, Cecil County, Maryland; addressed to Philadelphia; received 7 March; answered 9 March.

> News of antislavery debate in the Maryland legislature; does not anticipate, "from Recollection of the Constitution," that Congress is empowered

to do much on the antislavery petition; "Our Delegate (Mr. Stone) is not, I perceive, become more liberal by being a Member of Congress. I am sorry for it. I wish his Opposition had been more directed agt. the Measure itself than the persons who petitioned. Tis really strange that any Contest shd. arise about the Reference to a Committee! Till that is done & a Report made the Subject is not in a Train of Đ Discussion. I never knew a Reference refused where a Petition contained nothing scandalous or indecent."

Walter Rutherfurd to John Rutherfurd. AL, Rutherfurd Papers, NHi. Addressed to "Tranquillity," in Independence, New Jersey; carried by Robert Morris of New Jersey. The conclusion of the letter was written on 7 March and is printed below.
    House debate on Hamilton's report on public credit will probably be very tedious; "it is a Comedy to hear [*William*] Duer, especially if Maddison is mentioned."

Jeremiah Wadsworth to Alexander Hamilton. ANS, Wadsworth Papers, CtHi. Dating and name of recipient based on Hamilton to Joseph Howell, Jr., 3 March, *PAH* 6:285.
    Requests a check to pay the people who apprehended Adonijah and Francis Crane, accused of counterfeiting federal securities; statement dated 5 March acknowledging receipt of $500 included.

From New York. [Boston] *Massachusetts Centinel*, 13 March. (Byline date of 10 March was corrected in the same newspaper on 17 March.)
    House will be nearly equally divided on the assumption of the states' war debts; "very great majority" think it must be adopted "before any considerable time elapses"; all but one of the Massachusetts members are for it.

Letter from New York. [Portland, Maine] *Cumberland Gazette*, 15 March.
    Summarizes progress on resolutions on funding; the House "thought it not proper to go into a committee" of the whole until Hamilton had complied with the resolution of the previous day for a report on funds applicable to funding the states' debts, if assumed.

Warner Mifflin to Abiel Foster. [Philadelphia] *American Museum* 8(August 1790):65. For the full text, see *DHFFC* 8:331–32.
    Describes the religious motivation of the Quaker antislavery petitioners and defends their authority for advocating on behalf of enslaved Blacks; urges the committee to report on their petitions as early as possible.

THURSDAY, 4 MARCH 1790

Cold (Johnson)

Samuel Johnston to James Iredell

Your Letter of the 10th. of February I had the pleasure of receiving on thursday evening last after I had sent my letters to the Post Office and the Mail was closed, which is always done at nine. You will know before this time the reason why you did not get my Letters by Jackson's Vessell and how much I was vexed at the disappointment. I am ~~the~~ glad that your Sugar and Medicines came safe, I hope before this you will have reserved by Swift your Books and Hat.

I am very much obliged to you for your information with respect to my Family it afforded me great relief from apprehensions which arose from Mrs. [*Frances Cathcart*] Johnston's not having written, I am very happy to hear that my Sister [*Hannah*] was so much better. ***

I received a Letter from Colo. Ashe informing me that he and the Doctor [*Williamson*] were elected.

A Bill has this day been read a second time and passed unanimously in the Senate for accepting the Cession of our Western Territory. as soon as this Bill is enacted into a Law, the Act for extending the Judiciary of the United States to North Carolina will be brought forward. The House of Representatives are still deliberating on the Report of the Secretary of the Treasury.

A general Inspection of Commodities under the Laws & Officers of the United States is talked of and a Committee of the Senate, a member from each State, appointed to consider of this Subject under an Idea of regulating Exports.

It is now past seven and the post is not yet come in I have just left the President's where I had the pleasure of dining with almost every member of the Senate, we had some excellent Champaigne and after it, I had the honor of drinking coffee with his Lady a most amiable Woman, if I live much longer I beleive I shall at last be reconciled to the Company of old Women for her sake, a Circumstance which I once thought impossible, I had found them generally so sensorious & envious that I could never bear their Company, this among other reasons made me marry a Woman much younger than myself lest I should hate her when she grew old but I now ~~may~~ verily beleive that there are some good old Women.

It is now near the time of closing the Mail and the post is not yet arrived. I must therefore conclude.

ALS, Iredell Papers, NcD. Place to which addressed not indicated. The omitted text relates to the health of family and friends.

Henry Lee to James Madison

Since your illness at Georgetown [*Maryland, present-day Washington, D.C.*]
I have heard nothing of you, only that you had so far recovered as to proceed,
until yesterday, when a gentleman from Alexandria [*Virginia*] told me that
you had taken your seat in Congress.

This information gave me pleasure, as it seemed to communicate your
complete recovery, as well as because it assured me that you was executing
your duty at a time which seems big with important consequences to our
country. It is very much to be lamented that all in legislative trust were not
where they ought to be. The infirmitys to which old age is subject especially
in the winter season, has detained Col. [*Richard II.*] Lee & poor Grayson has
been constantly ill—It is said that he must very soon quit us for ever. Indeed as long as Congress continue in a northern climate, I think the spring
& summer should be your period of session, or absence in many members
must take place from respect to their health.

I have seen the report of the secretary of the treasury on the subject of
finance. It is certainly impossible for any one with my limited information
to judge with Tolerable justice on a subject so complex.

Defective as it appears to me to be in its principles, it yet may be worthy
of congressional approbation for public bodies as well as individuals always
act wisely in my opinion, when they do the best in their power, altho that
best may not be in itself the most proper.

In this view then the report may be praise worthy—in any other I am
confident it is abhorrent to political wisdom & not strictly consonant to justice—Certainly the original holders of certificates merit in every vicissitude
of the public paper distinction from the ~~transferred~~ assignees of the certificates & if the supreme power shall consider it expedient & right to treat the
latter as depreciated in value, it cannot be just that the former should meet
the same fate—much plausible argument I am well aware may be [*us*]ed by
ingenious men against this position, but when examined accurately I think
it will appear to be absolutely sophistry & inadmissible.

This is only one of the many objectionable parts of the proposed system.

But my opposition to it proceeds on ground more material. I never can
think the funding scheme wise & proper in any nation, if the common good
is the supreme point to which all their consultations & doings tend—It is
no doubt political to establish this system where the govt. is in the hands of
one or a few, because it draws to the support of the govt. a numerous class
of the people from the strongest Motive of human action, viz. self interest.

But where the people are really free & mean to be so, where the govt. is
absolutely their own property, political tricks of this kind are abominable
& dangerous in their effects—If they succeed completely national debts

will be encouraged by wanton expeditions, wars & useless expences. This encrease of the peoples burthen, will in exact proportion encrease the operation & influence of the principle & the one will continue to cherish the other, untill the weight of oppression shall force the people to recur to first principles, or the Government shall have changed hands.

Funding systems belong to arbitrary governments, they are not congenial to the true spirit of general, common freedom—they are [blot] excellent means to change the latter into the former.

However then in theory the mischeif & wickedness of such policy is plain to my mind, I confess my disapprobation of it is heightened by recurrence to the experience of nations. It is not in my power to trace the practice of communitys on this subject with accuracy, nor can it be done generally within the limits which my dislike to scribbling prescribes always to my letters.

Already this has reached my common boundary, but having given my opinion with respect to this *pitiful* plan, I will exceed my ordinary limits & view the subject experimentally in the case of G. Britain.

I prefer this nation as the exemplum not only because their history ~~of this nation~~ is more familiar to me than that of any other modern people, but because it is the polar star of the advocates for the funding system & because it conveys the plainest & strongest testimony of the pomp & vice of this fashionable scheme.

Contentions for the crown, wars with France for a feather & with other european potentates at various periods for straws or for what is commonly called the ballance of power plunged that people into debt—small at first but so large that direct taxes could not be assessed at once, in conjunction with their impost, so as to meet the debt.

It became them to pay, or to secure payment satisfactory to their creditors. Inhabiting [lined out] an island & habituated to commerce, they readily determined that credit was all important to them, that it would serve them instead of principal & extent of territory—Wonderful indeed have been their exertions, & astonishing the event.

To the workings of their unbounded commerce are they entirely indebted for the success of a system wicked in its beginning suitable (if at all suitable) only to nations whose situation genius & habits direct them to commercial pursuits, & which must terminate in national bankruptcy.

But admitting this issue to be doubtless as it respects Britain, how can america expect to flourish under a system calculated only for commercial society—we thank heaven are by situation genius & habit agricultural, & our commerce ought to be considered only as the hand maid of our agriculture—The preeminence of the last I trust will be ever distinguished by all the regulations of our general govt.—If this should not be the case, a change may be worked in our national character which will debase us as men, & destroy us as a people.

God forbid the event, I ardently pray that the U. States may to the latest ages continue to possess the character & enjoy the blessings of tillers of the earth.

In this light then, how will funding systems square with their interest.

In the first place they will draw a great part of the circulating cash from the proper channels, cultivation of soil & commerce, & appropriate it in a line unproductive to the community—For altho individuals may amass princely fortunes by stock-jobbing, yet in the encrease of their wealth the national income receives not the addition of a penny—Reverse is the case where the farmer adds to his capital & where the merchant by fair commerce encreases his stock in trade—Each of them add to the national income, in as much as they add to their own. Then will a wise honest people by their laws establish a mode of appropriating one third of the circulating cash of the community inproductively to the society.

I think not, truth & reason condemns such policy every where, but especially in America.

As you encourage this artificial use of money, in so much do you starve the real uses of money & in the same proportion do you absolutely diminish the ability of your people to pay towards the support of govt.

A complete investigation of this subject in this point of view only would I think be sufficient to demonstrate the error of the secretarys report.

But let us touch upon the effects of funding systems as they operate on the moral character of the people.

Habit is second nature, a long course in vitious habits will corrupt the best heart—What can be denominated the habit of supporting life, subsisting family &c. by buying & selling in the funds, when contrasted with the habit of performing the same object by tilling the earth. Avarice, deception falsehood & constant over-reaching belong to the first, while contentment, moderation, hospitality, frugality & a love to mankind result from the last. Ought not then the U. States possessing extensive & fertile territory abominate the policy, which in addition to other evils, depretiates the morals of their citizens.

The subject is important & cannot be entered on without a copious discharge of the mind—I have given proof of this myself, for when I began, I did not mean to use five minutes of your time. Then I will stop & promise no more to [*lined out*] write of funds or funding systems.

I am not interested, only in common with my fellow citizens, & individually I care not what fiscal policy is pursued—I cannot give you any opinion with tolerable precision on the feelings of our people towards the genl.

govt. Living in very retired part of the country & mixing only with a few neighbors I have little oppertunity of knowing the general mind.

While on the last session of Assembly, I was impressed with a beleif that the enmity was rather encreasing, than otherwise.

The debates of your house during this session, I have not seen on any subject, but have heard that as far as your intentions have been discovered they are not esteemed on this side of the potomac.

It seems to me that you must introduce real taxation & bring the seat of govt. near the center of territory, or we southern people must be slaves in effect, or cut the Gordian knot at once.

By these two measures we shall be greatly assisted & may be able to bear up, till our encrease in inhabitants may place us nearer equality.

Another political involuntary flight. I ask pardon.

You have seen Mr. Jefferson or may have heard from him on the subject of the great falls[1]—Prospect as delineated by him to me gloomy—He has done all in his power, to promote our views & is entitled to our grateful thanks.

Ware houses are building on the place but nothing material can be done without 3000 £.—The sum is small & certainly might be raised in Newyork.

The object is great, very great indeed—As Tontine days are coming again, perhaps some of these paper gentry would become part owners.

Wadsworth is a man of enterprize & full of gold.

Mrs. [*Matilda*] Lees health is worse & worse, I begin to fear the worst.

ALS, Madison Papers, DLC. Written from "Stratford Hall," Westmoreland County, Virginia. A postscript relating to the Second Federal Election in Virginia is printed with that section in Correspondence: Third Session.

---

[1] Madison had invested with Lee in a five hundred acre tract on the south bank of the Potomac at Great Falls, Virginia, where Lee envisioned the rise of a manufacturing town he called Matildaville. In response to Lee's solicitations in the summer of 1789, Jefferson encouraged European investment in the project (*PTJ* 15:526); his "gloomy" prospects must have related to the investments rather than his opinion of the project's future.

James Madison to Edmund Pendleton

Your recommendation of Docr. [*David*] Morrow was handed me some time ago. I need not tell you that I shall always rely on your vouchers for merit, or that I shall equally be pleased with opportunities of forwarding your wishes.

The only act of much consequence which the present Session has yet produced, is one for enumerating the Inhabitants as the basis of a reapportionment of the Representation. The House of Reps. has been cheifly employed of late on the Report of the Secy. of the Treasury. As it has been printed in all the Newspapers I take for granted that it must have fallen under your eye. The plan which it proposes is in general well digested, and illustrated & supported by very able reasoning. It has not however met with universal concurrence in every part. I have myself been of the number who could not suppress objections. I have not been able to persuade myself that the transactions between the U.S. and those whose services were most instrumental in saving their country, did in fact extinguish the claims of the latter on the justice of the former; or that there must not be something radically wrong in suffering those who rendered a bona fide consideration to lose ⅞ of their dues, and those who have no particular merit towards their Country, to gain 7 or 8 times as much as they advanced. In pursuance of this view of the subject a proposition was made for redressing in some degree the inequality. After much discussion, a large majority was in the negative. The subject at present before a Committee of the whole, is the proposed assumption of the State debts. On this, Opinions seem to be pretty equally divided. Virga. is endeavoring to incorporate with the measure some effectual provision for a final settlement and payment of balances among the States. Even with this ingredient, the project will neither be just nor palatable, if the assumption be referred to the present epoch, and by that means deprives the States who have done most, of the benifit of their exertions. We have accordingly made an effort but without success to refer the assumption to the State of the debts at the close of the war. This would probably add ⅓ more to the amount of the Debts, but would more than compensate for this by rendering the measure more just & satisfactory. A simple unqualified assumption of the existing debts would bear peculiarly hard on Virginia. She has paid I believe a greater part of her quotas since the peace than Massts. She suffered far more during the war. It is agreed that she will not be less a Creditor on the final settlement, yet if such an assumption were to take place she would pay towards the discharge of the debts, in the proportion of ⅕ and receive back to her Creditor Citizens ⅐ or ⅛, whilst Massts. would pay not more than ⅐ or ⅛, and receive back not less than ⅕. The case of S. Carola. is a still stronger contrast. In answer to this inequality we are referred to the final liquidation for which provision may be made. But this may *possibly* never take place. It will *probably* be at some distance. The payment of the balances among the States will be a fresh source of delay & difficulties. The merits of the plan independently of the question of equity, are also controvertible, tho' on the other side there are advantages which have considerable weight.

We have no late information from Europe more than what the Newspapers contain. France seems likely to carry thro' the great work in which she has been laboring. The Austrian Netherlands have caught the flame, and with arms in their hands have renounced the Goverment of the Emperor [*Joseph II*] for ever. Even the letharthy of Spain begins to awake at the voice of liberty which is summoning her neighbors to its standard. All Europe must by degrees be aroused to the recollection and assertion of the rights of ~~man~~ human nature. Your good will to Mankind will be gratified with this prospect, and your pleasure as an American be enhanced by the reflection that the light which is chasing darkness & despotism from the old world, is but an emanation from that which has procured and succeeded the establishment of liberty in the New.

ALS, Madison Papers, DLC.

Robert Morris to Mary Morris

Your affectionate letter of the 27th Ult. came safe & in due course, by which I find Govr. [*Edmund*] Randolph had bad roads and was longer in delivering mine to you than if it had gone by Post. I knew from him that he prefers Philada. to New York but He cannot give us a Casting Vote. I am beginning to feel some Peoples Pulse on that point but as yet, no judgement can be formed as far as I know the matter is against our hopes. but more of this when We meet.

*** Tom [*Morris*] dined in Company with me yesterday at Mr. [*Daniel*] McCormicks but My Packet & Post letters requiring my presence to send them off, I left him making very Merry there. I am now just come from dining at the Presidents, they like their New Quarters exceedingly & live well,[1] I executed your Commands both to Mrs. Washington & to Miss [*Eleanor "Nelly" Parke*] Custis. This is a very Cold day here & I suppose the same with you perhaps it may make Ice in the Delaware. My Shoes are nearly wore Out if Mr. [*Garrett*] Cottringer can meet a good opportunity you may send me a pair as I think there are several pair in readiness.

Remember me to your Mother[2] and give my Love to her, tell her that Mr. [*George*] Meade has been treating with me about buying the House She lives in but he will not give the Value & so we are off.

ALS, Morris Papers, CSmH. Addressed to Philadelphia. The salutation reads, "My Dearest Friend & Companion." The omitted text discusses the failed courtship of a family friend, advising, "we must leave her to the effects of future disapointments to produce those Sensations in her mind which lead People to Contemplate the Vanity, folly & uncertainty of Human Affections & pursuits."

---

[1] Dissatisfied with the inadequate space and dignity of the Cherry Street residence they had occupied from the beginning of the first session, on 23 February the Washingtons and their retinue moved into new quarters leased from Alexander Macomb at 39–41 Broadway. The four story Macomb Mansion, with fifty-six feet of frontage on lower Broadway and an uninterrupted rear vista of the Hudson, was considered one of the grandest residences in America when it was built in 1787–88 and was already known for a tradition of gracious

hospitality set by its previous occupants, the French ambassador the Comte de Moustier and his successor, Louis Guillaume Otto (*DGW* 6:26n).

[2]Esther Hewlings Newman White (d. 1790) of Philadelphia was the mother of Mary Morris and Bishop William White by her second marriage, to Thomas White, in 1747 (*Drinker* 3:2230).

John Page to St. George Tucker

Your Brother's [*Thomas Tudor Tucker*] *quis*? & *quæ*? I sent you in my two last,[1] in this I would have sent his *Quid*? but it is not fit to be trusted by Post when we meet you shall see it—I now send you the original first Piece which I extracted from him—The occasion of it I think was some Ladies desiring him to make an Acrostic on them he wrought the one within which you see is *The Beaver* so that whatever Lady presents it to another presents an Acrostic on herself & hence it is called the acrostic transfereable—Miss [*Margaret*] Lowther presents her Compts. to you.

ALS, Tucker-Coleman Papers, ViW.

[1]See Page to St. George Tucker, 25 and 26 February, above.

Theodore Sedgwick to Pamela Sedgwick

With your favor of the 26th ult., my dearest love, I had the pleasure to recieve this day, Doctr. [*Oliver*] Partridge's state of the case of dear sweet little Robert and I am the more pleased because from it I hope his complaint not quite so thretning as before I considered it. I shall not fail tomorrow to call on the gentlemen I have before consulted on this subject and will write you more fully respecting it.

I am sorry my dearest love that you have cause to complain of my negligence in writing, but your candor will permit you to make a proper allowance for it. Ever since I have been in town I have been deeply engaged on a most interesting subject. I am very well persuaded that unless the state debts shall be assumed the benefits which the friends of the Government expected from the adoption of the constitution would not ~~to~~ be ~~expected~~ realised. Every ~~art~~ obstacle which art and address are able to produce are thrown in the way, yet I trust our efforts will eventually be crowned with success. Mr. Madison who is the leader of the opposition is an apostate from all his former principles. Whether he is really a convert to antifederalism—whether he is actuated by the mean and base motive of acquiring popularity in his own state that he may fill the place of Senator which will probably be soon vacant by the death of Grayson, or whether he means to put himself at the head of the discontented in America time will discover. The last, however, I do not suspect, because I have ever considered him as a very timid man. Deprived of his aid the party would be weak and inefficient.

*** ~~Perhaps~~ I have got thro a resolve for allowing Capt. Yoke 120 dollars,[1] and it is refered to the committee of appropriations to provide for the payment. While he is there perhaps he had better inclose me an order for the money. Will you mention this subject to your Brother Mr. [*John*] Sergeant?

Even yet my best beloved I do not dispair of seeing you by the siting of our court. this however will depend on the determination on the great question. It will I believe be put by monday at the furthrest. Should it pass in the negative I shall consider myself bound to continue here untill the subject of funding shall be discussed, and shall consider it my duty to defeat any plan with which the ~~funding~~ assumption shall not be connected.

ALS, Sedgwick Papers, MHi. Place to which addressed not indicated. The omitted text relates to local town business. The letter is continued on 6 and 7 March, below.

[1] For background on the petition of Jehoiakim McToksin ("Capt. Yoke"), see *DHFFC* 7:6–7.

Henry Wynkoop to Reading Beatty

The Assumption of the State Debts is yet undecided the day before yesterday the Debate was suspended in order to obtain from the Secretary of the Treasury a Report on the aditional Resources required in case the Adoption of the State Debts should succeed, this Report was made this day & is limited to aditional Imposts on luxurious articles of consumption except Salt on which likewise six aditional Cents is proposed,[1] 100 Coppies of this Report are ordered to be printed for the Use of the Members, of course it is not probable the Question will be taken before some time next week.

For the News of the place & Debates of Congress refer You to the papers.

Mama [*Sarah Newkirk Wynkoop*] is in no want of Visitors, this evening we have drank tea, I belive for the first time, this week with the family, but has not yet seen the Hall, the Congress or paid her respects to Mrs. [*Martha*] Washington, a Task she wishes to perform & yet is in fear of it, wether it will yet be undertaken & how performed I do not know.

The weather is again as cold aparently as any time this winter.

ALS, Wynkoop Papers, PDoBHi. Place to which addressed not indicated.

[1] The report is printed in *DHFFC* 5:852–55.

Machiavel to Mr. Greenleaf

I beg the favor of a corner in your Journal, to convey a word of instruction to Executive Officers—I should begin with a Secretary of State, but as no such officer has yet appeared within the vortex of the New-York newspapers, the next in rotation is a S—y, or first lord of the T—y. If this officer has a superficial knowledge of Greek and Latin, a small smattering of mercantile affairs, and great abundance of law quibbling, with a smart knack at lying and defamation, he will exactly suit. Indeed I have always heard it said, that Financiers should understand Algebra and Fluxions; but the deficiency in these sciences may be made up by the assistance of some Scotch teacher,[1] who will devote a couple of hours every morning to instruct the young minister; another couple of hours should be devoted to *writing for newspapers* in praise of HIMSELF and his systems. But (*N. B.*) he must take care to send this for publication to another town, in order that he may avoid detection, and it would be wrong to write letters to himself, as Lord George Gordon did.[2]

Thus he will be locked up for four hours every morning, studying with his tutor and writing for the newspapers, whilst his creatures will report, that he is deeply immersed in the business of the nation; and he must appear in the streets but seldom, and then let him take care to look down on the pavement as if lost in thought profound. It is pretty picking to get three or four thousand dollars per year for scribbling for newspapers. He must make a thousand promises to get his adherents into lucrative employments, and of all things keep up a good face to the brokers of all religions. The remainder of this lesson I shall reserve for another occasion.

N. B. He must never argue from true principles. In my next I will instruct him how to prove, that the only way of making money circulate over America, to encourage agriculture, is to collect every six-pence into his own hands, and never let it depart thence.[3]

NYJ, 4 March; edited by Thomas Greenleaf. The editors are publishing this piece because the similarity of its rhetoric to William Maclay's diary suggests his authorship. The pseudonym as well as instructional format are intended to evoke Niccolo Machiavelli (1469–1527), the Renaissance Florentine statesman and political theorist whose *Prince* (1532) is regarded as a textbook on the amoral means of achieving and maintaining political power.

[1] A reference to the Scottish Enlightenment of the first half of the eighteenth century that produced a large body of influential writings. Most prominent among those associated with it are David Hume and Adam Smith.

[2] George, Lord Gordon (1751–93) was acquitted for his role behind London's anti-Catholic "Gordon Riots" of 1780. In 1787, however, the British government finally succeeded in convicting the country's most notorious agitator in a celebrated trial for allegedly authoring a pamphlet addressed to himself, in the name of some jailed prisoners, that was ruled as a libel against the integrity of British judges (Christopher Hibbert, *King Mob: The Story of Lord George Gordon and the Riots of 1780* [London, 1958], p. 161).

[3] Greenleaf reported in his 18 March issue that he had received Machiavel's second piece and would publish it in an extraordinary issue on 25 March. In that issue he informed his readers that he did not have room to include it. It was apparently never published.

A Free Citizen to the Officers and Soldiers of the Late Army of the United States

BRETHREN and FELLOW CITIZENS,

It is with pain that I come forward in behalf of the rights of justice, in opposition to those who, under peculiar circumstances, voted against the amendment of that great statesman, Mr. Madison, last Monday, which was ably supported by his colleagues on the board basis of equity.

I call on the majority, for one of the facts, unanswered, introduced by Mr. Scott; he offered to prove—that hundreds were obliged to give receipts, previous to their receiving certificates, as vouchers for the contractor, which when obtained were applied to the contractor's use.

There are [those] who advocate the appeal to the courts of judicature, to redress frauds! Common sense revolts at the subterfuge.

The opposition calls for authorities—they are produced, and by a dint of sophistry, it is attempted to prove them not in point, reprobating quotations from Europe. The same Massachu. gentleman with his address, appeals to the country he condemns to establish his creed; he remarks the wicked reign of Henry the 8th, and Charles the 2d, who shut up the exchequer; William paid 14 per cent. on annuities, and at the rate of 10 and 12 per cent. interest, but by good faith, in 5 or 6 years money fell to 5 per cent. interest. In endeavoring to prove, that there is not a debt subsisting against the public in favor of the soldiers, who have sold-out, he proceeds—"Let us ask what will be the effect? Is this what was expected under the new constitution? Did we expect it? Is there one here who has not told the people, that an end would be put to tender acts, paper money, and the ruinous effects of government's interposition?[1] The learned Marquis Beccaria's opinion is in these forcibly words—"In every humane society, there is an essay continually tending to confer on one part the height of power and happiness, and to reduce the other to the extreme of weakness and misery; the intent of good laws is to oppose this effort, and to diffuse their influence universally and equally."[2] If the soldier has to redeem his note, gave him for 20s. and sold at 2s. and 6d. for the benefit of the speculator, it is injustice on every rational principle, and time will evince the reality, and its dangerous effects. The very persons who were in the enemy's lines during the war, declare, they will cheerfully pay to the soldier their proportionate part; for, say they, *their virtues plead loudly for justice*. What would have been the opinion of that illustrious soldier, the late General Baron de Kalb, who, struck with amazement at the Roman fortitude of the troops at the southward, in his letter to the Chevalier de la Luzerne, the French Minister Plenipotentiary of Aug. 14, 1780, says—"You may judge of the virtues of our small army, from the following fact: We have for several days lived on nothing but peaches; and I have not hear a complaint? There has been no desertion," *Dr. Ramsey's 2d vol.*[3]

The singular abuse of the prophecies respecting Jacob and Esau, made by a member from New Hampshire,[4] of the latter selling his birth-right, obliges me to have recourse to sacred writ.

Genesis 25th chapter, and 29th verse—And Jacob sod pottage, and Esau came from the field, and he was faint.

30th. And Esau said to Jacob, feed me, I pray thee, with that same red pottage, for I am faint: therefore was his name called Edom.

31. And Jacob said, sell me this day, thy birth right.

32. And Esau said, behold I am at the point to die, & what profit shall this birth right do to me.

33. And Jacob said, swear to me this day; and he swear unto him: and he sold his birth right unto Jacob.

For the consequences that followed I beg leave to refer to the learned Dr. Newton, in his dissertation on the prophecies;[5] recommending caution to the honest mind of the judge [*Burke*] from South Carolina, as it equally militates against that doctrine.

My friends, when an address was circulated in the cantonment of the late army, in March, 1783, to assume a bolder tone, and change the milk and water style of your memorials for justice, agreeable to promise, the commander in chief, apprehensive of the author's influence, issued orders, that the general and field officers, and a representation of the staff of the army, to assemble at the new building, to hear the report of the committee from the army to Congress, who were to devise what further measures ought to be adopted as most rational and best calculated to attain the just and important object in view, and report their deliberations to the commander in chief.[6]

On which the second address made its appearance, exploring your hard situation and ill treatment: upon this the general meets the officers, makes his speech, pledges himself to see ample justice done the army, requests them to rely on the plighted faith of their country, and place a full confidence in the purity of the intentions of Congress, and effectual measures would be pursued to do ample justice for your faithful and meritorious services. In his circular letter he says, "Where is the man to be found who wishes to remain indebted for the defence of his own person and property, to the exertions, the bravery, and the blood of others, without making one generous effort to pay the debt of honor and gratitude? In what part of the continent shall we find any man, or body of men, who would not blush to stand up and propose measures purposely calculated to rob the soldier of his stipend, and the public creditor of his due."[7]

Alas! Cruel, thrice cruel—the rulers have thrown your demands on the dung-hill, there to perish for your reward!

I close with this sacred verse:

"Hear the word of the Lord, ye children of Isreal, for the Lord hath a controversy with the inhabitants of the land, because there is no truth, nor mercy in the land."[8]

NYJ, 4 March.

---

[1] Ames's speech of 15 February included these references to British history (*DHFFC* 12:343–44).

[2] Cesare Beccaria (1738–94), Italian social thinker and founder of the modern science of penology. His most famous work, *On Crimes and Punishment* (1764), denounced the irrational use of punishment.

[3] David Ramsay, *History of the Revolution in South Carolina* (2 vols., Trenton, N.J., 1785), 2:139. Johann "Baron" de Kalb (1721–80) was a French army volunteer in the Continental Army from 1777 until his death following the battle of Camden.

[4] Livermore's speech of 19 February; see *DHFFC* 12:450).

[5] Sir Isaac Newton (1642–1727), perhaps the most famous British mathematician and natural philosopher (physicist), enlarged his researches and discoveries on the workings of nature to include the workings of providence in such published works as *Observations upon the Prophecies of Daniel and the Apocalypse of St. John* (1733).

[6] These instructions were included in Washington's general orders for 11 March 1783, calling for a representative meeting of officers to preempt mutinous proceedings at the Continental Army's main cantonment at Newburgh, New York (see Edward Carrington to Madison, n. 1, 2 March, above). The orders, and the anonymous "second address" and Washington's "speech," both referred to below, are printed in *JCC* 24:297–99, 306–10.

[7] From Washington's circular letter to the state governments, Newburgh, New York, 8 June 1783.

[8] Hosea 4:1.

Newspaper Article

Yesterday March 4, was the anniversary of the first meeting of the two houses of the supreme legislature of the United States, as organized under the federal government; a day, that every friend to the peace, union and happiness of mankind it is hoped will have reason sincerely to celebrate to the latest ages, as auspicious to the interests of this country. If July 4th, 1776 is commemorated by all true Americans as the date of their emancipation from the fangs of foreign dominion, no less ought the 4th of March 1788 {*1789*} to be recognized in all our public registers as that which saved us from intestine divisions, a contracted spirit of partial interests between individual states; and from being dupes to the politics of such European nations as, being our rivals in the commercial world, wished to profit by our civil feuds, and thus prevent the good effects of a revolution, which as it originated in the true spirit of virtuous patriotism, promises a new and improved æra in the history of civilized man.

NYDA, 5 March; reprinted at Philadelphia and Charleston, South Carolina.

Newspaper Article

Thursday last was the anniversary of the first meeting of Congress under the new constitution—a day to be remembered with peculiar pleasure by all the friends to the civil rights—the property, happiness and future glory of these rising States—on that auspicious day, we received the surest pledge of enjoying and perpetuating the invaluable acquisitions of "*Peace, Liberty, and Safety.*" Then old anarch's kingdom fell—and our country invigorated in her councils, and animated by her prospects commenced anew, her career in the road of empire, fame, and honor.

GUS, 6 March; reprinted at Salem, Massachusetts; New Haven, Connecticut; Philadelphia; Baltimore; and Winchester, Virginia.

Other Documents

William Irvine to John Nicholson. Summary of ALS from *Henkels Catalog* 1439(1930):item 187.
    Assumption of state debts.

William Short to Thomas Jefferson. ALS, Jefferson Papers, DLC. Written from Paris. For the full text, see *PTJ* 16:202–4.
    Asks Jefferson to intervene with Congress concerning his compensation.

Michael Jenifer Stone to Walter Stone. ALS, Gratz Collection, PHi. Addressed to Charles County, Maryland; franked; postmarked 7 March.
    Is happy to receive Walter's letters, "and so as you would give me Facts I do not Care how many reflections you *add*"; is in good health; is happy Congress has "cooled" on Hamilton's report on public credit, "and we shall probably do right."

Richard Wells to Henry Wynkoop. ALS, Petitions and Memorials, HR, DNA. Written from Philadelphia. For the full text and background on Wells's petition, see *DHFFC* 8:42–43, 57–60.
    Encloses and paraphrases a petition to strike out the sixth section of the Patents Bill [HR-41], granting patent protection to the first importer of foreign inventions; suggests withholding such protection for a year.

Manasseh Cutler, Diary. Cutler Papers, IEN.
  Drank tea at Ames's.

George Washington, Diary. Washington Papers, MiD-B.
  The Vice President, Langdon, Wingate, Dalton, Strong, Ellsworth, Schuy-
  ler, King, Paterson, Morris, Maclay, Bassett, Henry, Johnston, Hawkins,
  Izard, Butler, and Few dined at the President's.

FRIDAY, 5 MARCH 1790

Cool (Johnson)

Thomas Fitzsimons to Tench Coxe

The bill for promoteing Usefull Arts has been so farr Gone thro. as to be
nere Engrossed—& will probably go to the senate in a day or two. Many
alterations in Stile & some in Substance has been made—Among which are
some Suggested in your Letter to me the 6th Section allowing to Importers
was left out. the Constitutional power being Questionable—but if it ~~was~~
~~Was~~ is not the inconvenience is too Manifest of Admitring Patents. in such
Cases except some better guards could be provided—Indeed on Consideration the bill altogether was found to be Very imperfect—yet we preferrd
Makeing some Amendments to Recommitting which might prevent any
one the Subject passing this Session. I dislike Very much the decision by
Referrees since we have struck out of the bill the Appeal to a tryal by Jury—I
hope however the Senate will Correct our Errors & as they have no business
before them. they will have time to Consider the subject which is Very Important—We have been stopped in our decision on the Secy.'s Report for
some days in Waiting to Know from him the Objects upon which he Relyd
for Raising the Revenue to pay Interest on the State debts If Assumed—I
inclose his return but cannot say how farr they will Reconcile the opinions of
those opposed to that assumption—I believe the decision cannot be delayd
much longer—that it will be Agreed to in Committee but that the final
agreemt. will depend upon the No. Carolina members Who are expected
very soon—this whole business is so Irksome, to some & so little understood
by most that we have allready Consumed too great a portion of our time in
it—I find our assembly are divided in opinion abt. the mode of Chuseing
their Representatives in Congress—that is a Subject which I hope You will
attend to—I fear Very much that the Sense of Common danger which heretofore Kept the Republicans together is now Considered as done Away—&
that no concert will be established to obtain the fruits of Past exertions—I

wish you would take the trouble to Inquire & advise me the Cost of Erecting our Light house in the 1st Instance by some Estimates before us it would seem that we were going fast into Extravagancys which our funds will not warrant—I see the Comptr. Genl. is Involved in a dispute with the assembly which I fear will not terminate to their honor.[1]

ALS, Coxe Papers, PHi. Place to which addressed not indicated.

[1] Throughout early 1790 John Nicholson, long a target of Pennsylvanian "Republican" (anti-Constitutionalist) abuse, was under investigation by the state's executive council on suspicion of improprieties regarding pension payments made as state comptroller general since 1782. The investigation concluded with a council vote on 14 April, holding Nicholson responsible for overpayments. Accusations of his embezzling state money circulated until 1794, when he resigned following a failed impeachment attempt (Robert Arbuckle, *Pennsylvania Speculator . . . John Nicholson, 1757–1800* [University Park, Pa., 1975], pp. 47–60).

Josiah Parker to Alexander Hamilton

Queries
Should not the Collectors office for the District of Norfolk & Portsmouth [*Virginia*], be removeable to any Part of the District, which the Secy. of the Treasury might direct, as from the exposed Situation of the Town of Norfolk in case of Invasion, neither public Monies or Papers would be secure.

Would it not be better establishd at Portsmouth as more convenient to Suffolk & Smithfield which are ports of delivery only—& Vessells arriving in Nansemond River or Pagan Creek, might delay the time of entry in case of Norfolk Rivers beeing frose over which some times happen—or if not would it not be proper that one of the offices should be kept at Portsmouth or some officer establishd there—that Town owns more Sea Vessells than Norfolk—but Norfolk haveing the Foreign Merchants settled there Causes Foreign Vessells to resort to it.

Should not all Vessells bound up James River be obliged not only to Stop & report at Norfolk or Portsmouth but take an inspector on board at the Vessells expence—the State of Virginia would not allow an office of entry at Bermuda Hundd. knowing it would introduce clandestine measures. Hampton should only be a port of entry—as Vessells of burden cannot go in—None belong there but Pilot boats & Craft; and Hampton Road which is 4 or 5 Miles from the Town is a dangerous road Stead.

There is an inlet makes into Lynhaven bay which has deepend so much within a few years as to admit small sea vessells, would it not be necessary to have a Searcher at Kempsville which is a little Town at the Head of the East Branch of Elizabeth River in the County of Princiss Anne. he would be a Check to any clandestine business, which might be carried on

in Lynhaven—The officers on the Eastern Shore wish their Ports open to
Foreign Vessells—but I think many ports should be shut to them, in order
that the Crafting business might be advantaged, but if the ports remain
in general open to them I must request those on the Eastern Shore as well
as Smithfield & Suffolk should be allowed to admit them, I can prove that
a Ship [lined out] unloading & loading at Norfolk will save expence to the
proprietor in preference to going up James River, & the only reason that
causes the Foreign Merchants who live at Petersburg & Richmond to order
their Ships going up James River instead of Stoping below is, that they Pay
their own Seamen instead of our Craftmen, (See Statement).

Portsmouth has Petitioned Congress for a Collector to be establishd
there,[1] but I beleive if the Naval officer or Collector was to reside there it
would cease their inquietude if either it might be better for the Collector
as he is not fixed as to Property in either & the Naval officer is in Norfolk.

The Collector complains of his Commissions being too low [lined out] if
the Collector at Bermuda Hundd. receives as much duty it is not proper that
his Commission Should be more—[lined out] the Collector & Surveyor both
complain that their duty is much more than that of the Naval officer who
deserves less, and has little or no expence & very little trouble.

Excuse these observations & if any thing Should occur to you in which I
can give further information it will give me pleasure to offer it.

ALS, Wolcott Papers, CtHi.

[1] See DHFFC 8:402.

Letter from New York to Philadelphia

Since my last on the subject of Mr. Madison's motion, a question has been
taken upon it in committee of the whole House, when there appeared for
the motion 15, against it 32. You will not, however, suppose that all those
who voted against it are opposed to a discrimination, on the contrary many
declared that they voted so because they thought the proposition did not go
far enough; and I strongly suspect that there will yet be found a majority
for it, when the business is resumed in the House, so that the national honor
and justice may still be rescued from the violation that awaits it, and the
evidence of public gratitude, perpetuated to the view of admiring posterity, in the just reward of the most virtuous and patriot army the world has
ever seen. But the precipitation with which the business is hurried, seems
to indicate a fixed determination in some, as well within *certain* doors as
without, to cram down the Secretary's report in toto, and at all events, if
they can accomplish it; and it will no doubt surprise you to be told that

a question was taken, with not more than an hours discussion, by which the whole arrears of interest on the public debt, amounting to 13 millions and upwards, is consolidated with the principal and made a part thereof, whereby, the holders of this part of the debt, are to receive compound interest, so that the holder of a certificate for 100l. lent the public, say in January 1776, will now receive 11l. per annum, instead of a rate of six per cent. and stranger still, a motion to postpone or pass over that question, until other parts of the report could be discussed, did not even meet with a second. Are the honest and industrious yeomanry of Pennsylvania prepared to pay the new taxes which systems like this will demand of them? if not, tell them, in the seaman's phrase, to work double tides, against their task masters come to exact the avails of their hard labours, and put it in the pocket of some city speculator, or unprincipled tory, who can now make more successful pillage upon them, than he had ever courage to attempt in the darkest days of desolation and havoc, during the war. I trust, however, that this picture may not be realised, and that the public opinion will interpose to check the precipitancy of measures calculated to produce the most dreadful evils. But, whence and wherefore, you will say, this precipitancy? To which I answer, from the east, and from one state south [*South Carolina*], that state debts may be assumed, and the public debt again augmented 30 millions more. Nay, would you believe, that the temerity of some men had led them to declare, that the assumption of the state debts was the ultimatum upon which alone they would consent to provide for any part of the public debt? thus violating that sacred duty, which, in their representative character, they owe to the people of the United States at large, and sacrificing the general good, to local, private, and partial interests, and that too on a question in which neither the national faith or honor is concerned.

As yet this question is undecided; but the haste with which it is perused, has betrayed its patrons into difficulties which will I think finally defeat the measure; for even yet no question has been taken on the rate of interest that shall be allowed to the public creditors, or whether the present rate of six per cent shall be reduced; upon which questions alone can it be determined what will be the amount of debt that must be provided for. Again, no discussion or enquiry has yet been had, either into the practicability or productiveness of the funds which the Secretary has so neatly delineated upon paper; and by which enquiries alone it can be ascertained, what amount of debt the ability and resources of the United States are equal to pay. If, therefore, the rate of interest shall not be reduced, which, upon principles of public justice, I hold it cannot; and if upon enquiry the Secretary's proposed funds are found impracticable, or over-rated, as I am certain they must, then will the infatuation of an unqualified assumption of the state debts, appear in the strongest light. At present, however, all is smooth with some—assume the state debts as they now stand—burn books and accounts—reduce the rate of interest on the whole mass of public debt to three per cent.—make no discrimination or composition whatever in favor of the original holders—open loan subscriptions upon the modifications proposed by the Secretary—and compel subscriptions, by withholding any provision for non-subscribers—and then, let it be sung how easy and happy we shall be, if those troublesome fellows called the people, will but let us alone.

Such indeed, my friend, is the creed of politics with some men, I fear with too many. But a truce to such reflections—Perhaps my suspicions are too much alive. I wish that it may ultimately appear they are so.

I will now proceed, as you request, to hazard a few thoughts on this question of assumption generally, which you will already perceive I consider as inexpedient. I think it moreover unjust, because it will occasion the necessity of a reduction of the rate of interest, and thus operate a manifest injustice to the present existing creditors of the United States, as well as to the state creditors; nor is it less unjust to the creditor states themselves, since it is well known that in the present unliquidated state of the accounts between the United States and the individual states, no ascertainment can be had of the just balance due to a creditor state, and of consequence no appropriation can be made or security given for the payment of that balance at a future day; whilst in the mean time the citizens of a creditor state who have been heavily taxed to pay their own debt, must now be as heavily taxed to pay the debts of a debtor state whose citizens have never been taxed at all, thus rewarding the delinquent and punishing the meritorious; and even a promise of future payment is too precarious for the creditor states to trust in, as we have daily experience with how much facility political tenets are changed, and with what dexterity that political opiate, called necessity, in the hands of a state physician, can be applied to put asleep all future claims, although an humble and injured creditor state, should ever be so hardy to raise its voice in the demand of justice, from an *energetic* and *consolidated* national government. I have said that this assumption will occasion the necessity of reducing the rate of interest, and thus I prove it. By the Secretary's estimate, the amount of the present foreign and domestic debt is 54,124,464 dollars, to which add, he says, 25 millions for the state debts, but I presume it will be nearer the mark to say 30 millions, will make 84,124,464 dollars, the annual interest of which at six per cent (allowing the interest on the foreign debt according to contract only) will amount to 4,887,443 dollars, to which add 600,000 doll. for the support of government, and there will be the enormous sum of 5,487,443 dollars to be raised off the people of the United States, annually; compare this with the means of raising it, which the Secretary proposes, and you will find the whole amount (supposing the funds to be as practicable and productive as he states) is only 2,839,163 dollars, as opposed to the debt of the Union, and 1,000,000 dollars additional (by his estimate of yesterday, and of which I send you a copy) as opposed to the state debts, leaving a deficiency of 1,684,280 dollars, which must be annually supplied, and can be only done by direct taxes, since every source of excise and impost is stretched to the utmost by the Secretary himself. But he has said, and the friends of his plan follow him, that direct taxes must not be attempted. What then results, but the necessity of reducing the rate of interest in order to accommodate the debt to the ability of the people? I would now ask, whether this reduction of interest is not a violation of the public faith? And if so, can it be justified upon a self-created plea of necessity, arising from the assumption of the state debts? In my opinion it cannot; nor will it be sufficient to say, that since the resources of the Union have fallen within the power of the general government, they must therefore provide for the state debts. It is well known that some of the states are, and have been, in the use of direct taxation for several years past, and the people well contented to comply with the demands of their own Legislatures; but will they be so under the demands of the National Legislature? I think not, and that those who argue the contrary have a very limited idea of the genius and character of the American people—But this leads me to consider the expediency of the proposed assumption, on which ground the arguments of the Secretary have been re-echoed by the patrons of his plan. It is said that there will be opposite systems, a competition for resources; distinct and incompatible provisions; injury to the state creditors; and finally, disunion, discord and faction; that the present public debt may be rendered a public blessing; and that a small direct tax, say a land tax, is necessary to impress the minds of the people with a sense of their interest in, and relation to the general government. Happily, however, the wisdom of a Solon[1] is not necessary, to expose the fallacy of this reasoning; indeed, the last argument is too absurd; for, if the people feel an interest in, and affection for their immediate local governments, will that be lessened or increased by the encroachments of a government, which they are in the habit of viewing as foreign and hostile to their own? But why resort to direct taxes merely to teach the people this important truth, when the Secretary proposes to meet the whole mass of public debt, including the assumption, without it. Surely, here is something of inconsistency. Again, why is so much said about contrary systems of impost and excise, when it is known that all the states have relinquished both, except one or two, and that they will probably do so, if the state debts are suffered to remain as they are. In respect to direct taxation, should there be a necessity to recur to that, I am decidedly of opinion, that the exercise of the power will be best confided to the state Legislatures, since there are numerous objects of taxation, as well as various means of collection, which their local circumstances would admit of, but which could never be provided for in a general, uniform, and national law, applicable only to the states col-lectively, and not individually; not to mention the difficulty and expence of collection by the general government in those states which have drawn a line of distinction and disqualification between their officers and those of the general government. How far the present public debt can be rendered a public blessing, I will leave to the disciple of Machaivel[2] to demonstrate, although I believe no one here, who is indifferent and disinterested, can re-sist the conviction that it has already become a public curse. I beg you will excuse the incongruity of this hasty epistle.

IG, 13 March. Because John Nicholson regularly used Eleazer Oswald's newspaper as a publication medium, the editors believe that this piece could have been a letter to him.

[1] Solon (639–559 B.C.) was an Athenian statesman whose timely constitutional and eco-nomic reforms in a critical period made his name a synonym for wisdom and compromise.
[2] See location note for Machiavel to Mr. Greenleaf, 4 March, above.

Newspaper Article

The President of the United States having recommended to Congress a legislative encouragement for producing, among ourselves, the various articles of manufacture conducive to the defence of the country, it may be satisfactory to learn the actual state of one of these manufactories in Penn-sylvania, as it appears in the following extract of a letter from thence:

"Being directed by the manufacturing board, lately, to take upon me a share of an extensive report, in which gun-powder was an article, I was much pleased and surprized to find that we have twenty-one powder-mills, capable of making six hundred and twenty-five tons per annum: that they retail at 37s. 6d. per quarter of 25 lb. and offer to sell, in quantities, under 6l per cwt. and that the English prices after deducting the bounty of 4s. 6d. is 75s. 6d. sterling, or 6l. 6s. 10d. currency, per cwt. English powder is now nearly done with here, and one year will entirely exclude it. I am convinced this essentially necessary manufacture, besides ensuring defence, is worth above 200,000 dollars. It has surprized me as much as the paper-mills."

NYDG, 5 March; reprinted at Philadelphia and Annapolis, Maryland. See Clymer to Coxe, 3 March, above.

OTHER DOCUMENTS

Joshua Brackett to John Langdon. ALS, Langdon Papers, NhPoA. Written from Portsmouth, New Hampshire.

　　Reports on state elections; encloses two recent newspapers; could not find a suitable bottle for mailing the ointment Langdon had requested for his

"Itching"; advises him to send to an apothecary for the extract of lead, "which is what I used to give you."

Andrew Craigie to Daniel Parker. FC:dft, Craigie Papers, MWA. Sent to London, by the sloop of war *Echo*; duplicate sent the same day on the packet boat.
    Morris advises against purchasing continental securities, satisfied that the state debts will be assumed and that the price of the former will drop.

James Monroe to James Madison. ALS, Madison Papers, DLC. Written from Richmond, Virginia; postmarked 4 March. For the full text, see *PJM* 13:91–92.
    Apologizes for late payment for a joint land purchase from John Taylor in Mohawk Valley, New York; Jefferson will leave town in a day or two for New York; public credit is the only subject of debate in Richmond; is not sufficiently acquainted with Hamilton's various plans, but "a superficial view" has not led him to assent to any; "tis hardly possible to devise any plan free from exception."

Thomas Robison to George Thatcher. ALS, Chamberlain Collection, MB. Written from Portland, Maine; franked.
    "I am honored with your very Obliging favour of the 10 Ult. would have done myself the pleasure to have answer'd it ere now, had I not let different Gentlemen had it to peruse. They seem Well pleased with Your attention, *as well as me*! although we have no Vessels under the perdicament you describe."

Walter Rutherfurd to John Rutherfurd. AL, Rutherfurd Papers, NHi. Addressed to "Tranquillity," in Independence, New Jersey; "Favored by Mr. R[obert]. Morris [of New Jersey]." Continues a letter begun on 3 March, above.
    Governor George Clinton has used his influence to pass the state law for building a "Government House" (to serve as a presidential residence); Hamilton's funding plan would "reduce the Jersey taxes to a Triffle"; the Southern members are "warmly" opposed to it.

Theodore Sedgwick to Thomas Dwight. No copy known; acknowledged in Dwight to Sedgwick, 14 March.

Pamela Sedgwick to Theodore Sedgwick. ALS, Sedgwick Papers, MHi. Written from Stockbridge, Massachusetts. (Daniel Defoe's [1660?–1731] *Robinson Crusoe* was first published in 1719; Arnaud Berquin's (1749–91) two volume work *L'Ami des Enfants* was published in French at Geneva, Switzerland, in 1782 and translated into English the next year.)

Always looks forward to a letter from "my Belovd. friend"; reports on the children; son Theodore hopes "Poppa will Purchase Robinson Crusoe and the Childs friend for him"; hopes the next post will bring word "that you have got so far throu your Business that I may have the pleasure of Seeing you for a few days"; begs him not to take the stage, whose safety she distrusts "at this Season"; hopes this is the last letter he will receive from her "until I can press you To my heart."

Philip Theobald to George Thatcher. ALS, Chamberlain Collection, MB. Written from Pownalboro, Maine; postmarked Boston, 8 April.
    Seeks additional aid from Thatcher in recovering money owed him by Mr. Hesshuyzen.

SATURDAY, 6 MARCH 1790

Rain (Johnson)

Henry Bass to George Thatcher

I recd. your kind letter of the 26th Jany. in which you direct the mode of my proceeding in order to obtain a new Certificate in lieu of that which is lost—and have agreeable to your advice Inclosed it to Fisher Ames Esqr. a Petition to Congress (as under cover) I have left it unsealed for your perusal, after which If you think it will probably answer my design: please to seal & deliver it. I doubt not your endeavours in Congress. that it may be effectual. P. S. Mr. [*John*] Waite who lost my certificate is now at New York. please to take his affidavit. word it in such a manner as will corroborate w[*ha*]t. I have asworn in my Petition, & will be suitable to accompany it.

ALS, Chamberlain Collection, MB. Written from Boston. For more information about the petition and the petitioner, Thatcher's brother-in-law, see *DHFFC* 8:255–57.

Theodorick Bland to [*St. George Tucker*]

I was yesterday favord with your agreeable letter enclosing two for the Boys[1] which I deliverd to them—I have the Satisfaction to inform you they are both well—I am myself Just risen from a fit of the Gout which attacked me a day or two before the atty. Genl. left this Place, and exerted its utmost violence on my hands feet Knees and Elbows for about ten days it has however spared my head—and I thank God has left that in a Better Situation than it has been for twelve months preceeding—so that it is now more than

four weeks since I have been obliged to bleed or Cup—Thus do I begin
to entertain hopes that I shall again enjoy good health—thus much for
myself—The federal Councils move with a Slow and Cautious Step—but
a Politician of no great depth may easily see what is likely to be the Issue
of the Fiscal arrangements of the Present System—Absorption of revenue
will Certainly follow Assumption of debt—so that our State governments
will have little else to do than to eat drink and be merry—all this I think
I foresaw would be the case for how are states to be managed who have not
nor ever will make any exertions to pay the debts contracted in a common
cause—while the Citizens of others are taxd up to the teeth for that purpose—again Consolidation follows power—power has been given with a
liberal hand—how then is consolidation to be with held—some feeble attempts to keep it back may now be made by those who gave the power—but
I see tis in vain it may be a sort of apology for the moments of Liberality
but what avails it—I see I must either go with the tide of Power or become
again a Rebel—which is the best at my time of life? You wish to have the
secretary's Budget [*report on public credit*]—it is too large to enclose in a ~~paper~~
letter—and I have only one which is my Text Book in Congress—But by
this time the Atty. Genl. & Mr. [*John*] Blair are arrived and they carried
each a copy with them—the Second or Subsidiary Budget is come out to
Encompass the Assumption and fundg. of the State debts[2] of this there were
no more copies Struck but sufficient for the members of both houses—it
consists of additional Imposts on *Pepper Salt* Rum Wine Sugar Melasses &c.
&c. to a little more than one million—I have enclosed you the last Paper—
tis but a Barren one but may be Intcresting to you as you will see the roll of
the Regt. of Lawyers enlisted to serve at the federal Bar. ***
P. S. we are told here that poor Grayson is so ill on the road that his life is
despaird of—shd. he die—I mean to become a Candidate to be his Successor
in the Senate—if you can give me a lift with your Honble. Friends in the
Executive—Shd. that event take place I shall Esteem it a favor—but do not
mention this Subject unless the Event shd. actually take place.

ALS, Tucker-Coleman Papers, ViW. Place to which addressed not indicated. The identification of the recipient is based on the letter's existence among Tucker's papers and the fact
that the closing parallels the one that Bland used in his other letters to Tucker.

[1] Theodorick Bland Randolph and his younger brother John "of Roanoke."
[2] For the 4 March report, see *DHFFC* 5:852–55.

William Constable to Joel Barlow

*** [*Samuel*] Broome wrote Colo. Hamilton acquainting him of your
success, this I fear will Operate strongly against us. He declines reporting

on Scribas Memorial[1] assigning for reason that Congress only mean that He shoud report some general System for the Sale of the Western Lands—I apprehend this is not his true reason for defering his report—however I am of opinion that Cutler[2] shoud memorial Congress for an Abatemt. in price on the Lands wh. they Have purchased & wh. I have no doubt they will grant—if We We obtain our Object in this Way—Scribas Memorial is popular with the Members—they conceive that He is to bring over Germans.

I made choice of him as least likely to excite suspicion & at present none is Entertained but I fear that the News wh. may be recd. by the Pkt.[3] magnifying the quantity sold & the prices Obtained as is always the Case with reports, which will sett them all up in Arms. & furnish a New Argument to the Enemies of the funding System. ***

FC:lbk, Constable-Pierrepont Collection, NN. A second copy was sent on 24 March via Philadelphia. The omitted text relates to the settlement of French immigrants on Scioto Company land in Ohio.

[1] For background on George Scriba's petition, see *DHFFC* 8:198–99.
[2] That is, the Ohio Company, for which Rev. Manasseh Cutler was the lobbyist to Congress. He spent two months (21 February–23 April) at New York in 1790 lobbying for such an abatement but, recognizing that Congress's attention could not easily be diverted from the debate over public credit, he withheld a petition until the Second Congress. See Jeffrey L. Pasley, "Private Access and Public Power," in Kenneth R. Bowling and Donald R. Kennon, *The House and Senate in the 1790s* (Athens, Ohio, 2002), pp. 78–87.
[3] Presumably one of the packet ships that carried mail to and from Europe.

William Constable to Thomas Truxton

*** Mr. Morris who is here has written You—He has nearly got thro' the settlemt. of his Public Accots. & after all the Calumny of his Enemies the Contint. will be in his Debt—He has Memorial'd Congress for a Committee to report on his administration,[1] I have Conversed with Maddison who is One of the Members Appointed for the Business who tells me that Mr. Morris with 5,000,000 Dlrs. carrd. on the War to more effect, paid & Clothed a larger army & rendered more Services than his Predecessors in office had done for 4 times the Amot.—his Enemies begin to hide their heads & as a proof of the Opinion wh. his fellow Citizens entertain of him. He can be Governor [*of Pennsylvania*] if He will Accept—but this He declines. ***

FC:lbk, Constable-Pierrepont Collection, NN.

[1] For the petition, see *DHFFC* 8:667–69.

Jeremiah Hill to George Thatcher

In some of my late letters I gave you some Tracts respecting the Domestic debt, I have read the Arguments of Mr. Scott, Mr. Madison and others, I think there are some facts which I have not mentioned in my former Letters, neither have I heard them mentioned by any one in Congress, and as I think they are of weight in the Scale, I will now mention them [*lined out*] the *poor Soldiers* are said by many to be the great Sufferers in Consequence of the public Securities being depreciated; whom Mr. Maddison seems to be principally aiming at in his discrimination Scheme. but be it remembered, that when the army was raised for three Years & during the War in the latter part of 1776, & first of 1777, the Congress gave a bounty of twenty Dollars, and the Commonwealth of Massachusetts in addition gave their Quota 20 £ each more, here is 26 £ good money paid down. they also had their Monthly pay nominally and at the End of the three Years (for they were mostly enlisted for that Term) this Commonwealth put their Monthly nominal pay on the Scale & gave them a Consolidated note for the Depreciation—upon a Scale of Justice, was not all this pretty good monthly pay? but hear what follows in the latter part of 1779 & the first of 1780 the Army must be raised again at least recruited. this Commonwealth proportioned the Quota required of them by Congress, on the several Towns, according to their Taxes, & recommended classing,[1] of which Biddeford had to raise eleven the Town in Town Meeting raised one and then agreed to class for the remainder, ten. the Class I belonged to was obliged to give 130 £ some indeed did not give so much, but I believe they averaged at 80, or 90 £, & I think that that was about the average price throughout the Commonwealth, & the reason offered by the Soldier was that the public pay was good for nothing and they would not go except the Class would make them whole (as they called it) I might have told you the Class I belonded to, paid one third part down in hard Specie & stock at Cash price & the other part annually as it became due, other classes did near about the same, some Classes gave 40/ specie pr. month during the Term they should be gone. I am informed that the Town of Andover gave each Man required of them twenty heifer Calves and obligated themselves to raise them free of expence to the Soldier for three years which was the term enlisted for. now these are facts which I dare venture to say can be made manifest, not only by the several Towns ~~by~~ but by the public Books, for every Town was call'd on to send in what price they gave, in order to average the whole. now pray tell me when is the great Reason in favor of making the *poor Soldier* good? The Officers indeed had no bounty but those who continued to the Close of the war had the Commutation, and those who resigned before that Period, are denied any compensation already. see, the fate of Millers Petition[2]—there is indeed some Soldiers & some Citizens who doubtless will suffer if scaling comes in fashion and they will suffer if it does not; for there is no discrimination in Taxation or a Revenue System—You recollect how the Sailors served poor old Jonah when the Ship was in danger,[3] but remember he was provided for—You may perhaps think I am running wild or am a[s] *crazy* as ever *Jonathan* was[4]—but I tell you, I *speak the words of truth & soberness*[5]—I believe it is near ten O. C. P. M. & Miss [*Mary Emery*] Hill is teasing me to go to Bed so I bid you—Good Night.

ALS, Chamberlain Collection, MB. Written from Biddeford, Maine. The omitted post-script includes assurances that Sarah Thatcher, "the Children, & Eben are all well."

---

[1] Classing was a method for filling assigned troop quotas from among existing local militia units, according to procedures established by the individual states. The mechanics of classing are described in Van Schaack to Sedgwick, 10 March, n. 1, below. Hill refers more specifically to the practice whereby a class could hire a substitute to meet its quota. The process operated as a type of bounty for purchasing indentured servitude and, as Hill's subsequent description suggests, contributed significantly to the spiraling costs and inefficiency of the recruitment system (James Kirby Martin, ed., *Ordinary Courage: The Revolutionary War Adventures of Joseph Plumb Martin* [New York, 1993], pp. 38–39; James D. Scudieri, "The Continentals: A comparative analysis of a late eighteenth-century standing army, 1775–83," [Ph.D. diss., City University of New York, 1993], pp. 45–52).

[2] For background on the petition of Thatcher's constituent Lemuel Miller, seeking commutation (or conversion of the service pension for qualified Continental Army officers, from half pay for life to full pay for five years), see *DHFFC* 7:146.

[3] Jonah's shipmates cast lots to determine who was responsible for drawing down God's wrath in a storm at sea. After the lot fell to Jonah, they immediately quieted the tempest by casting him overboard. Even then, God preserved Jonah for three days in the belly of a great fish (Jonah 1:4–17).

[4] Crazy Jonathan was the pseudonym employed by Thatcher in a series of nine essays published in 1787, arguing the importance of separating church and state. It subsequently became a nickname sometimes used for Thatcher by his Maine friends.

[5] Acts 26:25.

Benjamin Huntington to Anne Huntington

By a line from Harry [*Henry Huntington*] by last Post I was very happy to hear you had been more comfortable than usual I hope you are really in better health than when I left home I have sent you half a Dozen of best Madeira by Capt. Parker and would have you send for more if needed or for anything I can Procure for your health or Comfort I hope you are mistaken in your Conclusion that you shall not recover. Mrs. Harding[1] tells me her Sister Rockwell was [on]ce Supposed to be in a fixed Consumption but Recovered; it has been the Case with many others who have recovered & I hope to see you again in Perfect health—Our lives are but short at the longest; but to have useful Lives cut off before they are arrived to the Age of Man ~~seems~~ is a most afflicting loss to friends and to the Public; ~~but~~ the tender Thread is so easily broken that none of us even in the Meridian of life and vigor of health can presume with Safety on an hour's Continuance in this World we ought to wait with Patience our appointed Time and be ready at the Call of heaven to leave these Tabernacles of Clay[2] which must be shaken off at some Time or other it's not best for us to know when, nor is it ~~our~~ our Duty to be Gloomy at the Thoughts of Mortality a Christian's life may be Chereful and I think ought to be so; we ought to spend this life in Praising the Deity which is by no means a Melancholly Employment.

To leave you in a Declining State as I supposed I did when I parted with you was to me a most painful Circumstance I anticipated the heaviest bereavement I could Conceive of among human losses. I am now much Encouraged concerning your Recovery & hope on my Return to find you able to Ride out for your health and to have as many happy Days in carrying you abroad as I have had.

ALS, Huntington Papers, CtHi. Addressed to Norwich, Connecticut; carried by Capt. Parker.

[1] Probably Ruth, the second wife of Seth Harding, who married in 1760 and ran the boardinghouse at 59 Water Street where Huntington resided with Sherman during the FFC's stay at New York City (James L. Howard, *Seth Harding: Mariner* [New Haven, Conn., 1930], p. 4).
[2] Job 4:19.

Benjamin Huntington to Governor Samuel Huntington

By the Inclosed Papers your Excellency will have two Reports which are not yet Acted upon the first is no other than an additional Estimate of Necessary appropriations of Money for the Services and Expences of the Current year which were not Included in the Secretaries former Report & for which Provision must be made.[1]

The Second is the Secretary's Report of Articles from which (in his opinion) the necessary funds may be drawn for payment of Interest on Debts of Individual States if Assumed according to the Modification proposed by him in his Report of the 9th of Jany. Passd. as also an Abstract of the Proceeds of the Duties on Impost & Tonnage to the 31st of December last which Rises higher than was generally Expected and will amount if the Same proportion holds to the 15th of August next to Near two Million of Dollars.[2]

The Plan for Assuming the Debts of the Particular States meets with opposition but is Strongly urged by many. The Reasons Pro and con are Published in all the Papers in the Debates of the House. The National Debt (if those of Particular States are assumed) will be large, but the mode of Payment will be facilitated by uniting the Resources of the Country to an

Uniform mode of Collection, Whereas an Interfearance of Taxation for the Several Demands of the General and State Governments may and doubtless will take place unless the Assumption is adopted. The Assumption would be an Immediate Relief (from the Commencement of its opperation) to the People of the Individual States against their Burthen of Internal Debts contracted for the benefit of the United States, and the mode of Collection under the General Government being from Resources which cannot be made use of by Particular States nor drawn out with the Same advantage as may be done by the United States will certainly lay the Burden on the most proper objects and of Taxation and Relieve the more Indigent members of the Community. Whether the State of Connecticut would gain or loose by the assumption is what I cannot Determine Every State in the Union fully believes She has advanced much beyond her Proportion for the United States and that her Particular Debt is Incurred for Services and Advances for the common Defence, but as to our State I cannot Even Conjecture how the Proportion will appear in a Settlement of the whole.

Some Gentlemen object to an Assumption that it will make the General Government too Important and by Absorbing and Engrossing the Greatest Concern of the States and leaving them in the unimportant Predicament of having nothing on hand but the Small Affairs of their Internal Police to manage. I think the weight of this objection may appear from Comparing the Distresses of a Man deeply in Debt with the Happiness of one out of Debt and not liable to the Insolent Demands of a haughty Creditor.

ALS, Smith Collection, NjMoHP. Addressed to Governor of Connecticut; received 11 March; answered 24 April.

[1] For Hamilton's report on further appropriations, 2 March, see *DHFFC* 4:110–30.
[2] For Hamilton's report on additional sources of revenue and abstract on impost and tonnage, 4 March, see *DHFFC* 5:852–55.

Theodore Sedgwick to Pamela Sedgwick

It is now Saturday and nothing decisive is yet done. I am extreamly sorry that Fenno's paper [*GUS*] is got so far behind in the very important subject [*assumption*], now before the house. It is a subject on which the people much want to be instructed, and many arts I fear are used to deceive them. The Gentlemen who take the lead in these debates in general prepare their speeches for the press and Fenno cannot deny the insertion. This is not the case with me, for I will never put myself in a situation to feel a dependence on any printer. I have been obliged by the perticular appointment of the gentlemen in favor of assumption, to take a principal part in the debates. and I am persuaded that if Fenno is able to do Justice to the subject my opinions will not be unacceptable to my constituents and the people in general. This however has hitherto & I hope will continue to be a secondary consideration with me.

I still continue, my dearest life, to enjoy my health as well and I think better than usual when I have been from home. I have indeed been more than commonly attentive to exercise. I have not excepting on the business of consultation, spent more than 4 or 5 evenings abroad since I have been in town. and those only in small circles. I pray you my dearest and best beloved be equally attentive to the preservation of your precious Health.

Just now some Handkerchiefs were brought here for sale, they are musling, and thinking them pretty I purchased 4 for the best beloved of my heart.
***

ALS, Sedgwick Papers, MHi. Place to which addressed not indicated. This text continues a letter begun on 4 March, above, and concluded on 7 March, below. The omitted text describes a visit the previous night with a family friend at "Mr. Penfields" (possibly Daniel Pennfield, merchant, at 193 Water Street in New York City).

Roger Sherman to Governor Samuel Huntington

The proceedings of Congress being daily published in the news papers, your Excellency has I conceive been fully informed of the progress they have made in the public business, Several new laws have passed both Houses, & have been approved by the President, there are a number of Bills that have been formed & passed one or other of the Houses that are yet unfinished. A Bill passed the Senate yesterday accepting a large Cession of western territory made by the State of North-Carolina, 'tis said it contains about 18 millions of Acres exclusive of the Grants that have been made in it by that State—The report of the Secretary has been under consideration for some time respecting a provision for the national debt. There has been a long debate respecting a discrimination between the Securities in the hands of the original creditors and those which have been tranfered—but it was finally decided by a large majority against a discrimination, the motives were that the Securities were by government made transferable, & payable to the bearer, and therefore the tranfer vested the whole property in the purchaser, if there was no fraud or compulsion. That they were in the early Stages of the loans many of them purchased at par. in a way of commerce or in payment of debts, and others at So Small a discount. as to be equal to the full value considering all circumstances. that the very low rate at which they Sold commenced about the time of issuing the final Settlement certificates to the Army, and were chiefly confined to the Army Securities, so that no common market price could be fixed without great inequality & injustice in many Instances, and a particular inquiry into the circumstances of every case would be impracticable; besides the public faith had been pledged after the transfers in most of the cases of Speculation. by issuing new Securities to the purchasers in their own names, to the amount of about 5 million dollars; upward of 3 millions of which were registered to foreigners in their own names. It was therefore concluded that government could do nothing to impair or alter the contracts consistent with good faith. The assumption of the debts of the Several States incurred for the common defence during the late war, is now under consideration. The Secretary of the Treasury has been directed to report what funds can be provided for them in case they Should be assumed, his report is contained in one of the enclosed papers.[1] He Supposes that Sufficient provision may be made for the whole debt without resorting to direct taxation; if So—I think it must be an advantage to all the States, as well as to the creditors. Some have Suggested that it will tend to increase the power of the federal government & lessen the importance of the State governments, but I dont See how it can operate in that manner, the constitutions are so framed that the government of the united States & those of the particular States are friendly, & not hostile, to each other, their jurisdictions being distinct, & respecting different objects, & both Standing upon the broad basis of the people, will act for *their* benefit in their respective Spheres without any interference. and the more Strength each have to attain their ends of their Institutions the better for both, and for the people at large.

I have ever been of opinion that the Governments of the particular States ought to be Supported in their full vigour, as the Security of the civil & domestic rights of the people more immediately depend on them, that their local interests & customs can be best regulated and Supported by their own laws; and the principal advantages of the federal government, is, to protect the Several States in the enjoyment of those rights, against foreign invasion, and to preserve peace & and a beneficial intercourse between each other, and to protect & regulate their commerce with foreign nations. I shall be always happy to receive your Excellency's Instructions respecting any public affairs in the transaction of which I may be concerned.

ALS, The Gilder Lehrman Collection, on Deposit at the New York Historical Society, New York. [GLC4841] Place to which addressed not indicated; received 11 March.

[1]The report is printed in *DHFFC* 5:852–55. It was presented to the House on 4 March and began to appear in newspapers shortly thereafter (for example, *GUS*, 6 March).

Roger Sherman to Rebecca Sherman.

I received Your letter of the 1st. Instant Judge Cushing & his Lady are yet here, they propose going to Middletown by the next Stage[1]—I am glad to hear that you are in better health—Carpets are 5/6 this currency for a yard Square I Shall Send you one as Soon as I draw Some money. I wish to be informed what Size will Suit. If the children make more gloves than will Sell at New Haven they may put up Some in dozens & Send them here—I will leave them to be Sold with a wholesale merchant that I deal with who may Sell them at the same price as imported ones—If Martin Skins[2] can be procured as cheap as you mention it might be well to manufacture Muffs & Tippets for Sale—I Should be glad to have 8 or 10 pound of the Pea Coffee Sent ground, in papers to contain one or two pounds each, it is well liked here, tho' none of the family knew that it was not imported Coffee, nor Should I wish to have any thing Said about what you Send here Mrs. Polock[3] is desirous to buy some of it. She knows what it is made of, I wish to know how much a pound it can be afforded at. I Shall Send my clothes home to wash. it has cost me but three quarters of a dollar for washing here—I believe it would be for Your health to come to New York after the ways are well Settled, you may come with our horse & Chaise & [sons] Roger or Oliver may come with you. it will be less expence than for me to come home considering the loss of time—Capt. Abraham Bradley & Capt. [Daniel] Bonticure are now here. Congress have under consideration the assumption of the debts of the States I believe there will be a great majority for assuming them, & then the Interest will be punctually paid in hard money. Mr. Davis has sold all the Sacramental Sermons that I left with him—I wish to have 6 more Sent & 3 or 4 Paulinus's letters to Scripturista[4]—Send my linen drawers when you Send the green Box—I would not have you give your Self much trouble to See Judge C[ushing]. & Lady, but be prepared. you would be pleased with their conversation, but I Suppose they will make no Stay in town. but go out with the Stage.

I believe I Shall get a new coat made here—the Taylor will have 11/6 lawful for making it—you will See that my Society tax[5] is paid & make Dr. [Jonathan] Edwards Some presents, give him what Support you can within the circle of your acquaintance. his continuance with us is a matter of great importance in my mind. I am in Health.

ALS, Sherman Collection, CtY. Place to which addressed not indicated.

[1] Justice William Cushing and his wife Hannah (Phillips) frequently vacationed at her hometown of Middletown, Connecticut.

[2] The pelt of the weasel-like marten.

[3] The wife of Isaac Polluck, who operated the boardinghouse at 37 Broad Street where Sherman resided.

[4] *A Letter to Scripturista: Containing, some remarks on his answer to Paulinus's three questions* (New Haven, Conn., 1760), by Joseph Bellamy (1719–90), dealt with the governance and authority of the New England Congregational churches.

[5] In Connecticut and Rhode Island, the tax that was levied for the support of the local minister.

Joseph Tucker to George Thatcher

Your favour of the 17th Ultimo came Safe to hand and I am exceedingly Obliged to you for the trouble you have in my Affairs & must pay you in good wishes—before this reaches you, Mr. Madison's Motion [*for discrimination*] will be Either received or rejected, whatever fate may attend it, he appears to me to be Inspired with a love of Justice—and Should he fail of accomplishing his wish, in my mind he ought to be revered by his Country as a friend to the Rights of mankind, Neither do I think there is anything (excepting Interest) that can withstand Such cogent Arguments as he makes use of—Should Congress, refuse to Interfere in behalf of those Soldiers, who have Suffered, and bled, for their Country, whose wounds, have given them peace, then poverty a Number of the Citizens of the United States Wealth, God—who is a God of Justice will not Suffer any body of Men even Congress themselves to Escape with Impunity, if they Violate it, nor will he Smile on their Councils.

The Securities these poor Soldiers, received at the disolution of the Army, were forced on them—they were obliged to take them or nothing, while they remain'd in the hands of the Original proprietors, we hear nothing about the paying of them, or making of them good, but on the Contrary that they never would be paid, how is the language changed now, let us look back a little See the Soldier retiring from the field at the dismission of the Army, his whole Wardrobe, on his back, his family, which he left at home, he finds in the jaws of famine, no possible means of relief—but by disposing of his Securities, to those who laid in Ambush—to watch his wants, and to hoop over his distress—it has brought to this, that he must either let his family perish—or Sell those Certificates for the paltry Sum of 2/6 on the pound, must that Soldier be Taxed to make them good to the now holder to the Amount of twenty Shillings on the pound, if so he may have Set others free but he has made himself a Slave to all intents and purposes—and in Vain may Congress, or there Chaplains, offer up prayers, and Incence on their Alters if these Sacrafices are mingled with the blood and Sweat of there Army—the beleif of the Army, was that the United States wished to do them Justice, and that their Inability was all that prevented, but pray what would they now think should they find themselves Totally neglected—If paying those that have purchased double, what they gave for them are not Sufficient let them have three fold, but think a little for the Soldier—Want now Extends her naked arms for Comfort, & redress, the Indigent, and fatherless, are now become your Suitors, they have no other friends on Earth to resort to for Comfort, or relief, to protect the hard Earnings of there fathers from the hands rapine and oppression—Should Congress prefer the Interests of a few Individuals to the Voice of Justice, and the Cry of humanity, they may seek repentance hereafter Carefully and with tears but they will not find it—And as mr. Madison beautifully Says that was their a Tribunal on Earth Capable of doing it they would Compel the Americans to do Justice to their Army.

Instead of taking the Europeans for an Example, they should be taken for a Warning, many of the members have made mention of the measures of Charles, the Second, William the Conqueror,[1] &c. &c.—why those times mentioned they differed as much from us as our Complexions does from Moors—the very great Esteem I have for you and your uprightness and unshaken honesty makes me Certain that which ever way you may Vote it will be on a full conviction you are doing right.

I Shall take your advice and not come to New York till some time in April.

[*P. S.*] Sir

Excuse the writing and the Inacuracies in the Within as I have not time to look over it or Correct it.

[*P. P. S.*] Make my Compliments to friend Van Ranselaer tell him I hope he will do right.

ALS, Chamberlain Collection, MB. Written from York, Maine.

[1] In a lengthy speech on 15 February, on discrimination among domestic creditors, Ames made reference to public credit policies of Charles II (1630–85), king of Great Britain from 1660, and William III (1650–1702), king from 1689. Tucker evidently confused the latter with William I, the Conqueror (1027?–1087), king of England from his invasion in 1066.

Hugh Williamson to Governor Alexander Martin

The last Letters from Edenton inclose me a State of the Poll by which it appears that I have been elected to represent the State in Congress. If by accepting this appointment I was necessarily unable to discharge the Duties of Agent in settling the public Accounts I certainly should not accept, but I think that by having a Seat in Congress I shall be the better able to serve the State on the Subject of Accounts. Congress will hardly sit above two months longer—there will then be a long adjournment. During the Recess the more weighty Part of our Accounts may be gone over. While Congress is in Session we may probably find it necessary to have a Law *requiring* or *enabling* the general Commissioners to admit certain new Claims or to pass others that may have been litigated; By having a Seat in Congress I can the better explain the Necessity of such a Measure. I wish it may be understood that I shall not consider myself entitled to draw Pay from the State while I am serving in Congress. And that I shall nevertheless keep a steady Eye on our Accounts and render Col. Thomas every Assistance he may need.[1]

A Measure has lately been attempted in Congress and is now under Consideration which demands the utmost Exertions of our State, it claims your Attention. The Object is to assume the Debts of the several States and fund them. According to this Plan the State or its Citizens will only draw Interest and receive Credit for the Amount of the Certificates now in Circulation, future Contingencies only can reach the amount of the Certificates already sunk or called in. Now it happens that N. Carola. has sunk a much greater Share of her domestic Debt than most of the other States and I hold it to be ~~absolutely~~ proper and necessary that we obtain a plenary Credit, before one other Step is taken for the Amount of what we have sunk since the Peace. Will you be so good as desire the Comptroller [*Francis Child*] forthwith to inform you of the Amount of all the Certificates that have been taken up by the Sale of vacant Lands of confiscated Property or by Taxes, also the Amount as nearly as he can determine of all the Certificates now in Circulation, distinguishing those of 1786.[2] This Return you will be pleased to forward as soon as possible I need not assure your Excellency that no possible Exertion of mine shall be wanting to relieve my fellow Citizens from direct Taxes or to obtain for the State an ample Credit.

ALS, Governors' Papers, Nc-Ar. Addressed to "Gov. &c. N. Carolina."

[1] Williamson and Abishai Thomas had served since 1788 as agents for North Carolina in settling its revolutionary accounts with the "general" (that is, federal) commissioners for settling accounts among the states. See *DHFFC* 14:754–56.

[2] In December 1785 North Carolina adopted "An Act to empower Commissioners to liquidate the Accounts of Officers and Soldiers of the Continental Line of this State." It empowered the commissioners to issue each individual two certificates, one payable immediately and one in the future with interest. So much fraud occurred involving the resulting "Certificates of 1786" that in 1789, when the state passed an act to pay off its domestic debt, it declined to accept the certificates in payment of the tax required by the act.

Paine Wingate to Jeremy Belknap

I received your favours, one of Feb. 13. by Mr. [*Manasseh*] Cutler, and the other of Feb. 17. pr. Post and agreeably to your request forwarded the enclosed papers to Mr. [*Matthew*] Carey. I now enclose to you a bill reported to the house of representatives for securing to authors their copy-right &c. It has not yet been considered, & probably will not be passed by Congress for some time as other matters of considerable moment are now before them. Whenever it shall come before the Senate, (unless the provisions you mention in your letter & which I think are very reasonable, should be inserted in the other house), I will endeavour so far as I have any influence to obtain the amendments.

In your letter by Mr. Cutler you ask of me a service I am poorly able to

perform. I commonly have to write in a hurry & suggest my thoughts in a
very imperfect manner—I never was a member of the legislature in New
Hampshire, unless the Congress at Exeter in 1779 could be called one,[1]
where I attended not long & have had but little opportunity of knowing
the public proceedings of that State respecting Vermont. The ground on
which N.H. considered the territory on the west of Con[*necticu*]t. river, (as
I have understood it) ~~was~~ to belong to them was that after running the line
between Massa. & N.H. New Hampshire was directed to keep up the garrison & protect the frontiers on that side of the river & Govr. Wentworth[2]
was by his instructions permitted to grant the lands there which implyed
the right of Jurisdiction. But when the King in council annexed that part to
N.Y., it was supposed the jurisdiction was legally changed, and the Eastern
part of N.H. had no great objection as by this time they began to be jealous
that the Western parts by their increase would soon overballance & govern
the politicks of the Eastern, without affording aids to the government sufficient to compensate for that inconvenience. Those on the Eastern side of
Cont. river & near it had a different interest & wish. They wanted the western side of the river to add to their strength & importance. Of course, when
Vermont disgusted with N.Y. for their abuses of them were determind not
to submit to their government & N.H. not being desirous to keep them, at
the revolution they set up for independency. Still the Eastern side of the river
were struggling to have them annexed to N.H. To effect this they claimed
a right to indepen[*den*]cy also. This they grounded on a principle, that by
breaking off from G.B. they were reduced to a state of nature & had a right
to form a social compact in any manner that was for their own convenience
& interest. But their principle object was to induce N.H. to claim & receive
the~~r~~ Vermonters as a part of the~~m~~ State. The Eastern part of Vermont wished
for this also. But if they could not joyn N.H., they wished to have two tier
of towns on the Eastern side of the river to joyn them in order that the seat
of government and the weight of numbers might be on the Eastern Side of
the green mountains. This is the light in which I have considered the proceedings respecting Vermont. Genl. [*Benjamin*] Bellows of Walpole & many
others in N.H. can give you a much more circumstantial & correct account
of the matter.[3] I have now the pleasure to inform you that the commissioners of N.Y. & Vermont are at this time in treaty & probably will in a few
days adjust their disputes & the latter it is expected will during the present
session of congress be admitted as an independent State in the union.[4] As to
the confiscation of Estates, I suppose you mean in N.H. I know very little
about them. I can neither tell you who were the promoters or opposers of
that business. I have always heard that the confiscations in N.H. instead
of being an advantage, were a considerable expence to the State. No body
reaped any profit by them unless the trustees who had the opportunity of

paying themselves very well for their services. I am very glad to find that you are prosecuting your design of writing a history of N.H. I wish you health & spirit to go through the laborious task & that you may meet with a just reward for your toils by the grateful approbation of the public & an extensive sale of your history—The funding system goes on very slow, but I presume it will be accomplished. you will see by the newspapers what is doing better than I can tell you.

ALS, Belknap Papers, MHi. Place to which addressed not indicated.

[1] A convention for proposing measures to stabilize currency and fix commodity prices was held in Exeter, New Hampshire, on 3 November 1779.

[2] John Wentworth (1737–1820) served as the last royal governor of colonial New Hampshire, 1767–75.

[3] Wingate's account succinctly describes the short lived history of the Eastern Union of thirty-eight New Hampshire towns along the Connecticut River, which formally acknowledged themselves part of Vermont from February 1781 until the Union was dissolved in February 1782 (Richard F. Upton, *Revolutionary New Hampshire* [1936; reprint, Port Washington, N.Y., 1970], pp. 192–96). Benjamin Bellows (1740–1802), a longtime colonial and state legislator of Walpole, New Hampshire, held a state militia general's commission from 1781 to 1792. He voted to ratify the Constitution at the state convention and served as a presidential elector in the first federal election (*DHFFE* 1:854).

[4] For background on the progress of negotiations between Vermont and New York in 1789–90, paving the way for Vermont's admission as a state in 1791, see *DHFFC* 16:1114–15.

OTHER DOCUMENTS

Joseph Anthony, Sr. to Nicholas Gilman. ALS, Miscellaneous Collection, MHi. Written from Philadelphia; postmarked 8 March. On the same day, Anthony wrote a letter with the same message to John Langdon (ALS, Langdon Papers, NhPoA). The writer was a former business partner of Gibbs, who was Channing's brother-in-law.

Office seeking: Walter Channing for collector of Newport, Rhode Island, based on "Recent Inteligence" that Rhode Island "will shortly Join the Union"; is strongly recommended by George Gibbs of Newport; asks Gilman to mention the matter to those senators "with whom you have an Intimacy" as well as to the "President General."

Joseph Anthony, Sr. to Robert Morris. ALS, Washington Papers, DLC. Written from Philadelphia; franked; postmarked. Most of the letter substantially repeats Anthony's other two letters of this date, above.

There is no other Senator to whom he could have written "that could have the Same Access to the President & afford Equal Prospect of Success."

John Barry to James Nicholson. Copy, Barry-Hayes Collection, Independence Seaport Museum, Philadelphia. Written from "Strawberry Hill," in

Fairmont Park, outside Philadelphia. For background on the petition attempt described in this letter, see *DHFFC* 7:438–43.

Received Nicholson's letter of 1 March yesterday; will join in joint petition for compensation for Continental Navy officers; advises collecting as many officers as possible in New York and assigning a committee to draft the petition; "the more Officers their is there the more weight it will have for at least each one will have ~~his~~ a Friend"; will come to New York himself as soon as the roads permit and intends to bring John Green and Alexander Murray with him.

Elias Boudinot to Samuel W. Stockton. No copy known; acknowledged in Stockton to Boudinot, 13 March.

George Clymer to Timothy Pickering. ALS, Pickering Papers, MHi. Place to which addressed not indicated.

Discusses the state politics of land speculation in Northampton County, Clymer's role as state legislator and land speculator, and the involvement of Morris and Samuel Meredith among others; summarized on the docket as the "Wyoming Affair."

Daniel Cony to George Thatcher. ALS, Chamberlain Collection, MB. Written from Boston.

Discusses the state legislature's mixed support for a college in Cumberland County (Maine); is happy to hear Thatcher's opinion on "*Consolidation*" [*of the states*]; agrees perfectly "that all those who either wish or fear Such an event, will rest with the good Deacon, long e're *it* takes place"; there has been no obvious electioneering for state offices in Boston, much to its credit; forbears urging a post road to Hallowell (Maine), "having heretofore exausted the Subject."

Daniel Gilman to Nicholas Gilman. ALS, Archives, NhD. Written from Boston.

Received Nicholas's letter of 24 February on 4 March; public securities are rising in expectation of Congress's funding all the debt, including assuming the states' war debts; "will you be so kind as to informe me" of the probability of an assumption, so that he might know whether to invest brother Nathaniel's money in final settlement certificates or state debt notes; numerous vessels from England reported headed back to the Southern states to purchase flour and grain; considering "our poor people begin to complain—will it not be necessary to lay an embargo upon it"?

Ebenezer Hazard to Jeremy Belknap. ALS. Belknap Papers, MHi. Place to which addressed not indicated.

> Sends antislavery literature (some of the same distributed and evidently acquired from the Quaker antislavery petitioners in town); "Congress will probably put the ten Dollars pr. head on Negroes imported, this Session"; doubts the post office will be able to generate the income predicted, although the new postmaster general (Samuel Osgood) "has fairly *committed* himself, as they say. the fact is (inter nos) that he knows nothing about the Business, & I am told he does not take proper Pains to be informed"; a House committee reported the Post Office Bill [HR-42] "without even consulting him about it: I have been applied to for my remarks on it: these things look oddly."

William Samuel Johnson to Timothy Pickering. Copy, authenticity attested by Samuel Hodgdon, Pickering Papers, MHi; FC:dft, Johnson Papers, CtHi. Addressed to Philadelphia.

> Has received Pickering's letter of 3 March "just now" and has only a few minutes to reply to Pickering's query; supplies his legal opinion against the Pennsylvania legislature's threatened repeal of the Wyoming bill, its 1787 act confirming the titles granted by Connecticut in the Wyoming Valley.

Samuel Johnston to James Iredell. ALS, Iredell Papers, NcD. Place to which addressed not indicated.

> Encloses newspapers of that day; saw (Penelope Johnston) Dawson the day before; "I continue pretty well my Cough is much better and I begin to recover my flesh"; suspects Iredell has already written to Washington regarding his appointment to the Supreme Court, and advises him to write also to "your friend" Butler, "who acted a very friendly part on that occasion"; New England members had supported some competitor, "but I cannot discover who it was"; John Skinner is in New York City.

Edmund Randolph to James Madison. ALS, Madison Papers, DLC. Written from Fredericksburg, Virginia. For the full text, see *PJM* 13:92–93.

> Public opinion in Georgetown, Maryland (present-day Washington, D.C.), and Alexandria and Fredericksburg, Virginia, is against Madison's proposed discrimination, although George Mason supports it; cannot read public opinion on assumption, except for Charles Lee, who is against it; "the sentiments of the *Jersey man* [*Boudinot?*] have been spoken of in terms of praise"; found Grayson recovering in Dumfries, with "hopes of a restoration"; Jefferson expected in Fredericksburg daily, en route to New York.

GUS, 6 March.

Boudinot and Hartley were admitted as counselors before the Supreme Court on 5 February; Benson, Laurance, Sedgwick, Smith (S.C.), Jackson, Ames, and Thatcher on 8 February; and Paterson on 9 February.

Letter from Philadelphia. *NYDA*, 12 March; reprinted at New York City (*NYWM*, 13 March); Charleston, South Carolina; and elsewhere.

Denounces the call for an embargo on exportation of grain and flour, against a scarcity invented by speculators; as an alternative, proposes raising a subscription for supplying the poor for three months at a moderate price.

NYJ, 22 April.

The Grand Lodge of Masons of Georgia appointed Jackson to a committee to consult with other state grand lodges about a national convention to establish a "Supreme Grand Lodge of the United States."

Sunday, 7 March 1790

Blustering (Johnson)

Abigail Adams to Cotton Tufts

*** I am sorry to find your Legislature acting a part so derogatory to their Honour and interest, and so little agreeable to what I know your Sentiment are. It must be painfull to you to See Such a combination to destroy all order, & overthrow the constitution, the proposed amendments I Sincerely hope for the Honour of the State, will be successfully combatted. how can these people all of whom have Solemnly Sworn to Support the constitution come forward with proposals which Strike a deadly blow at the vitals of it, but I trust they will be dissapointed Mr. M——n [*Madison*] is not acting a much better part here, only a more artfull and coverd one. the more I See of Mankind, and of their views and designs, (the more Sick I am of publick Life) and the less worthy do they appear to me, and the less deserving of the Sacrifices which Honest men make to Serve them. I think from what I can hear & see the Assumption of the State debts much more uncertain than I conceived a week ago—but time must determine there are some person who think the Stability of the general Government rests upon that one point.
***

ALS, Miscellaneous Manuscripts, DLC. Addressed to Weymouth near Boston; franked; postmarked. The omitted text relates to a purchase of land near the Adams's home in Quincy, Massachusetts, and the health of son Thomas.

John Carnes to Benjamin Goodhue

The assumption of the State Debts is so important a matter that it cant but engage the attention of every Man that is a lover of his Country, and capable of judging & determining; but the sentiments of Gentlemen are very different, and the fear of a consolidation is the reason that some of your Friends have not wrote You more fully, & oftner; but I confess that this has not been my excuse, but the want of time, there being so many important matters under consideration in our House.

In answer to your favour recd. the last Evening, I wou'd inform you, that the Judges of the Supreme Court, judge [*Nathaniel Peaslee*] Serjeant in particular, think & say, that the assumption is the only way to prevent a consolidation; and wish earnestly for it.

The Merchants in Town, and the more sensible Members of our House, are much in favour of it, & have been uneasy lest it shou'd not take place; & the improbability has been lately publickly mentioned. The Secretary [*Hamilton*] it is thought has done himself great Honour, and that his Plan cannot be alter'd for the better, and must be adopted; and we are glad to find that all our worthy Gentlemen at Congress are in favour of it, saving Mr. Grout, and we dont wonder at that. I hope Sir that You will continue to distinguish Yourself. By the Papers, & Letters from your Friends, You have come to the knowledge of many matters that have been before our General Court, which will rise, if we can compleat the important matter of [*Nathaniel*] Gorham & [*Oliver*] Phelps, in a few Days. But for one I am not satisfied with it. *Art is discoverable.* Our indebtedness to You is great on account of the attention You have paid to our matter, and we rest satisfied as it is in your hands, knowing that it cant be in better. And we heartily thank You. It being Lords-Day Evening is my Apology for not enlarging, but when I get Home I shall write more fully & more frequently, and give You a particular Account of what was, or may turn up in our County.

P.S. Mr. Otis's amiable Daughter [*Abigail*] is supposed to be a Dying.

ALS, Letters to Goodhue, NNS. Written from Boston.

George Clymer to Tench Coxe

Being for some days indisposed my attendance at Congress has been remiss—I however learn that the patent bill [*HR-41*] having been called up, the clause to protect the importation of machinery has been thrown out. I had indeed foreboded as much, for on pressing it on some of the Committee as necessary to be supported in the house, I found they had altered sentiments upon it—I trust as you have some improvements in the construction of what you proposed to [*specify*] that they will avail in such measure as still to encourage your undertaking. I can only say that upon this occasion I truly regret the failure of that advantage you had a right to propose to yourself.

If your manufacturing committee have gone through the report[1]—it would be a great satisfaction to me to have some outlines of it—I mean the heads of articles only ~~the~~ and the estimated value—such information given to the Secretary of the Treasury would be kept for his own use, and no one be the better for it—If you have a leisure five minutes you will oblige me in a few words on this subject. The Assumption still lies—I do not pretend to know whether it will be carried or not—or if carried whether it will be by dint[?] of votes or firm effect of judgment.

ALS, Coxe Papers, PHi. Written on "Sunday afternoon"; addressed to Philadelphia; franked; postmarked. The date was determined from the docket.

[1] The Pennsylvania Society for the Encouragement of Manufactures and the Useful Arts, established at Philadelphia in 1787 may have been reviewing the report on public credit.

George Clymer to Henry Hill

Nothing as hard as writing letters where nothing is to be said, and yet I have always a desire of writing to my friends—but so it has happened that I have seldom been able to spin out any subject but what has arisen from the circumstance of domestic concerns, on little matters of business, ever since my two terms of exile, ~~or ba~~ I will not call it banishment to this place. This may appear strange, such barrenness at the great political head quarters! but nothing is more repugnant to my feelings than to deal either in the past, the theme of every common news paper, or to put forth vague conjectures of the future, in which kind of wisdom one man, generally speaking, is as well qualified as another.

You see then, upon my reduced plan, little is left me but common occurrences—and for those in the town of New York, for some reasons, not, perhaps, much to the credit of my temper or my philosophy, I have less feeling than for the transactions at Grand Cairo [*Egypt*]—I seldom know, for example, who is dead in the Broad way or married in Queen street, and if I by chance arrive at this knowledge, it makes but little impression on me at first and is soon lost—the New Yorkers and I are ~~nearly~~ on an equal footing—mutual civility without a grain of good liking between us—I speak as a Pennsylvanian—In short, my immediate duties excepted, in which I suppose I have a common attention, all my cares my sollicitudes my affections turn towards home—for this I constantly sigh. You must therefore take this only as a letter of enquiry and friendship to know what you are now about, and what you are to be about, and to demonstrate how much I am Yours &c.

ALS, Signers Collection, N. Place to which addressed not indicated.

John Fenno to Joseph Ward

*** It will give you pleasure to be informed that my subscribers have encreased much of late, I reckon a Thousand at present—and in addition to the Journals of the Senate Mr. Otis has promised me other business.

You will see by the papers how we are going on—there is a bare majority in favour of the Assumption—at present—and it is tho't that it will be finally carried—there is a great party opposed to any Funding System—but as they are divided in their Sentiments, & none of them appear to have any plan, when their Speechifications are out, & they are properly fatigued, the Secretary's System will be adopted—at least this is my opinion—there is a decided Majority of the Senate in favor of the Assumption—Securities appear to be stationary—Finals & Indents, the last price I heard quoted were 7/6— & 5/10 to 6/ ***

ALS, Ward Papers, ICHi. Addressed to Land Office, State Street, Boston; carried by Capt. George Lane (d. 1805, of Charlestown, Massachusetts). For the full text, see *AASP* 89(1979):358–59. The omitted text relates to family letters, friends, and the value of securities.

Thomas Fitzsimons to Benjamin Rush

I am Uneasy at being so long without a Letter from You least any thing in my Correspondence or Conduct should be the Occasion of it—If it has I have been guilty without intention—I Receive with pleasure Your Observations or strictures and tho I May not allways Conform to your good advice it is not therefore Lost upon me—people not Immy. Concernd in Public affairs have oppy. of Judgeing which those who are have not. but on the other hand those within have Views of Subjects which others Must be Strangers to. You must at least acknowledge that we have not been precipatate in our business of finance 4 Weeks tomorrow since we took it up. and as yet have got but to the 3d. proposition & As farr as I am Yet Informed the diversity of Opinion without is not much less than it is within doors—it is a subject in which private interest is so much interwoven that it is difficult to Judge how farr Mens Opinions are Influenced by that Consideration—I had A letter last week from Mr. [*William*] Findley (with a Copy of the [*new Pennsylvania*]

Constitution) Very sensible but very Guarded. he has hazarded No opinion either upon the Constitution or the Subject upon which we are engaged [*assumption of the state debts*]. tho a Letter I wrote to him called for it in the latter except yours I have not An Opinion from any friend at Philada. by a Leter to our Speaker I am Led to believe that the Next Elections for Representatives in this Legislature will be in districts and in that case I think it highly probable the Commerce of Pennslva. May be without a Single Representative.

I suppose the Constitution will be Agreed to in August Nearly as published—in which Case your Next Election will be an Important [*torn*]—I do not understand that any mea[*seal*] is Likely to be taken about the [*seal*] Governor & if so we may set out under very Unfavorable Auspices. Mr. Morris's Accounts will soon be settled—& the event will prove the Wickedness of his Enemys—he is endeavoring to obbtain a Review of the Administration of the finances under his Management which I hope he will Accomplish—If I have not the please. of hearing from you soon, my apprehension of havg. offended you will be Confirmed. I can Acquit myself of any intention of that sort.

ALS, privately owned in 1983. Addressed to Philadelphia.

William Maclay to Benjamin Rush

For some time past I have delivered You up to the Correspondence of Genl. [*Peter*] Muhlenberg but not in so Absolute a Manner, but that I reserved the right of writing to You now and then and claiming the right of a few lines in Answer.

The Secretary of the Treasury, has made such large demands on Us lately, as seem to have put the Subject of the federal Residence, (at least in a permanent point of View) intirely out of our heads. for at the rate he goes on. he will not leave Us a penny to build a pig Stye. let alone a federal Town. Our thoughts on that Subject, seem now turned to an adjournment to Philada. without saying a Word about permanency. This was the Idea adopted by some of Us a Year ago, and perhaps We were wrong in departing from it. This I however give you in confidence. I have seen our New [*state*] Constitution, and for my part would not alter a pin in it. not that I approve of the Whole of it. but I think it high time we had something stable to rest on. for surely we have been long enough afloat on this Subject. one great point remains to be settled to secure happiness to Pennsylvania. You will know that I mean a Proper Character to fill the Chair of Government. nine Years is a long Term, and I think it Two to one, that the Person who carries the first Election, will hold it for that period. over & above the influence of Office, voting against a Man who has held an ~~Office~~ appointment. carries with it an

Idea of Striping, and with some delicate minds even of robbing, a Man, of What he has a kind of right to. much therefore does it concern Us to set out with a good Man. The Country will be divided. & the great Weight of the City will certainly determine it. if they only mind to be unanimous.

ALS, Rush Papers, DLC. Addressed to Third Street, Philadelphia; franked; postmarked.

James Madison to Benjamin Rush

Although your last favor of the 27 Feby. does not require any particular answer, I can not let this occasional correspondence drop without thanking you for so interesting a supplement to your former remarks on the subject [*discrimination*] lately decided in the House of Representatives. It not only gives me pleasure but strengthens my conviction, to find my sentiments ratified by those of enlightened and disinterested judges. If we are to take for the criterion of truth, a majority of suffrages they ~~must~~ ought be gathered from those philosophical and patriotic Citizens who cultivate their reason, apart from every scene that can disturb its operations, or expose it to the influence of the passions. The advantage enjoyed by public bodies in the light struck out by the collision of debate, is but too often overbalanced by the heat proceeding from the same source~~, to which might be added~~. Many other sources of involuntary error might be added. It is no reflection on Congress to admit for one, the ~~unanimous opinion~~ united voice of the place where they may happen to deliberate. Nothing is more contagious than opinion, especially on questions which ~~are~~ being susceptible of very different glosses, ~~and which of course~~ beget in the mind a distrust of itself. It is extremely difficult also, ~~to withold the respect due to the public opinion from~~ to avoid confounding the local with the public opinion, & to withold the respect due to the latter, from the fallacious specimen exhibited by the former. Without looking therefore beyond innocent causes of fallibility, I can retain the sentiments which produced the late motion[1] ~~relative to th~~ notwithstanding the disproportion of numbers by which it was out voted; especially when I can fortify them with such reflections as your two favors have communicated. Indeed, it seems scarcely possible for me ever to be persuaded that there is not something radically immoral, and consequently impolitic, in suffering ~~those rewards due to those who defenders of their Country to be reaped by~~ the rewards due for the ~~gallant~~ most valuable of all considerations, the defence of liberty, to be transferred from the gallant Earners of them to that class of people who now take their places. It is equally inconceivable, if the new Constitution was really calculated to attain more perfect justice, that an exposition can be right, which confirms & enforces the most flagrant [*lined out*] injustice that ever took place under the old.

I must add my thanks for the little pamphlet covered by your last.[2] I have for some time been a thorough believer in the doctrine which it exemplifies and about & am not unapprized of the obligation which in common with other proselytes, I am under to the lessons of your pen.

FC:dft, Madison Papers, DLC. The ALS, privately owned in 1961, is printed in *PJM* 13:93–94; it varies slightly from the draft.

[1] At a later date Madison placed an asterisk at this point in the draft and noted in the left margin: "*to divide the payment of the pub. debt, between the original & purchasing holders of certificates."

[2] The unidentified pamphlet concerned penal law; Rush's only significant known writing published in pamphlet form in 1790 was his *Inquiry into the Effects of Spirituous Liquors*.

Henry Marchant to John Adams

It is mortifying to be beat in a good Cause, without Sense or Argument, but merely by Self-Will and vile Principles—Our Convention sat all the last Week—Our News-Papers I suppose will give You the particulars—It was with Difficulty I could get a Motion for the main Question upon the Journalls—An Adjournment was determined upon by the Anties before They met Us, in Their private Conventions: And They held nocturnal Conventions the whole Week, for the Purpose of carrying Their own Measures, [*lined out*] and for settling Their Arangements for the Genl. Election—The Dep. Gov. Owens [*Daniel Owen*] President of the Convention, did not hesitate to say out of Doors, That an Adjournment of the Convention was necessary to insure Their Election—He is proposed for Govr.—[*John*] Collins having been Their weak Tool long enough—O—s is a Man of more Subtilty—a profound Hypocrite—at the Gen. Assembly after the Vote for calling a Convention; He took me by the Hand, and altho' He had voted against it, He declared I could not more rejoice than He did—He had voted as He he had done He said, because the People round Him were averse to the Measure as yet, but were coming over fast; And He had no Doubt the Constitution would be adopted as soon as the Convention met—Yet He now came with the greatest Zeal for an Adjournment—He still holds up the Idea that it will soon be adopted.

The great Objection which had been made by one of Their Leaders—Jona. Haszard a Delegate in the former Congress—was the Mode of proportioning the Tax by Numbers, instead of the former Method—The Word Tax, partial Tax &c. sounded in the Ears of the People, had been alarming; but when an Amendment for that Purpose was brought forward—His own Party failed Him; and We had a Majority of six for the Mode fixed by the Constitution—They were now left without any formidable Objections—We took Notice that there had been a Number of Things suggested out of Doors, which we were surprised, none would now further, or even mention—In short They were beat out of all Their strong Holds—We agreed to Their Bill of Rights, copied nearly from New York, and Their Amendments taken mostly from New York, with Their Darling Paper Money Amendment copied from our dear Sister North Carolina.[1]

What was now left, but that we should Adopt the Constitution? It must be sent to the People, for the Consideration of the Towns! And I expect next to hear the Amendments must be sent to Congress, to see if They will agree to adopt Them, previous to Our adopting the Constitution—And this will be the sine qua non, of many.

Their majority when we met was twelve agt. the Constitution—Could We have brought on the Question, I presume we should have been beat by four—wheather We shall succeed in getting that four is uncertain—They had Instructions from Their Town to vote for the Constitution, but a few Days before the Convention met; and were directed not to vote for any adjournment, without the greatest Necessity; and then not beyond the first of April. But They paid no attention to Their Instructions, How They may yet be opperated upon is uncertain—I have done giving, for I have almost lost my Hopes of Success—Misery will fall upon the Merchantile Interest, and upon poor Newport most heavily—wood & Flower will rise to an extravagant Price—The Farmer will not begin to feel till next Fall, unless Congress provide otherwise—Pray Sir, what must become of Us? what more can we do, if the Constitution is not adopted at the adjournment of the Convention the 24th. of May And what will be the Measures of Congress in that Case? If we adopt the Constitution The Anties hope to be able to send forward their own Creatures; and expect The Recommendation of Their Senators &c. will be sufficient to procure Appointments to Their own peculiar Friends.

I fear Congress may adjourn, before They may be able to pass the proper Bills for collecting the Revenue &c. &c. should We adopt the Constitution the last of May: For it must be sometime in June, before Our Assembly will meet to choose Senators &c.—Will there be a Necessity that Our Senators &c. should be appointed and be in Congress, previous to Congress's passing the necessary Bills and making all the proper Arangements? I wish to be advised hereon—I had the Honor to write You Sir the 19th. of Decr. and 18th. of Jany. last—I could wish barely to know They were recd. We want the best Advice. What we may *fear*, what *We* may *hope* should we fail at last.

ALS, Adams Family Manuscript Trust, MHi. Written from Newport, Rhode Island.

[1] For the New York amendments, see *DHFFC* 4:19–26. The 1788 North Carolina ratification convention proposed that a declaration of rights with twenty provisions be added to the Constitution. It also proposed twenty-six amendments to the body of the Constitution, the

twenty-fifth of which related to paper dollars. The 1789 convention asked Congress to add it to the Constitution along with seven other proposed amendments; see *DHFFC* 12:871–72.

Andrew Moore to Robert Gamble

I received yor Letter dated Fredericksburgh 22d Ultimo—The first I have receivd Since I arrivd at this place—The Report which you mention the Receipt of In Your Letter Has almost wholly Engrosst our attention From the time it was presented—And Very little progress made—We have Resolv'd on making Provision for the payment of the Interest & Gradual Redemption of the Principal of the foreign debt and the debts of the United States—The Rate of Interest is not yet determind I think I mentiond in my last letter to you A Proposition made Whilst the above Resolution was under discussion For discriminating between Certificates in the Hands of Original Holders and those in the Hands of Purchasers—This Proposition has been Negativ'd by a Considerable Majority We have now under Consideration The assumption of the State debts (I dont know but I mentiond this in my last However I may repeat it) I will State to you The Reasons as chiefly Urg'd pro & con—Those in favour of the assumption. Say (& Truly I believe) That the Exertions of the States during the War Were unequal That some of them By their ~~extraordinary~~ extraordinary Exertions have incurd a debt for exceeding their just proportion They conceive that justice Requires That the expence ought to be Equally ~~by~~ born by all the States—As every Exertion may be suppos'd for the promotion of the General Cause They Consider the assuming the State debts as Calculated to do them justice— In order to Obviate this Difficulty It was propos'd To Set on foot a finall Liquidation off all the Claims of the different States And To Resolve to pay ~~to pay~~ to the States Which on such a liquidation had paid more than their proportion Such terms As They might appear to be Entituled to—And ɇ in the same manner that The other debts were provided for—This Proposition has been Negativ'd—It has been Objected against the Assumption—That It will tend to Increase the Influence of the General Government—That The Operation of the System with Respect to those debts agreeably to the Report Will be unequal That The States Which have paid ~~on~~ the Most of their states Debts Will not Receive the Credits To Which they are justly intitled at the time of making the Asstn. [*assumption*] That this by the plan Is postpond for an Adjustment Which probably Will never take place—Mr. Madison Propos'd That The Certificates in the Possession of States Which had been Collected by Tax—Should be loand & the Interest paid in the Same manner of those in the hands of Citizens This was Negativd—It has also been Objected to the System That Our Resources are inadequate to the Redemption—Unless We Embarrass trade or have Recourse to direct Taxes—By an Order passt a few days ago The Secretary was Requird to lay before the House Those Resources To Which He refers in his Report—for the purpose of Discharging the Interest & Redeeming the Principal of the State debts—He has Complied with the Request[1] As nearly as I can Recollect He pro[*po*]ses An Additional per Cent duty on all Goods Imported Also an Additional Tonnage—An additional Duty on Coffee Choce. Spices On Rum On Molasses One half Cent On Salt six cents addition & Some others This Report does not Satisfy my mind altho He pledges himself The product of the proposed Duties will be Adequate to the purpose—I think the state Debt far Exceed his Statement—And I think our Resources will be insufficient—Unless We impose a direct tax A Power Which I never Wish to see exercisd Only in Case of Necessity—I think the States are more Competent to this Business And can in laying their Tax More Effectually Accomodate it to the Conveniency of the Citizens—Should the United Government be able to Raise More Money by Duties than is necessary to discharge their present Engagements—The Ballance may be applied in just proportions to the Discharge of the Respective state debts In the Mean time They may avail themselves of direct taxes in such Mode & Extent they think proper— To morrow I expect this Question Will be decided Its fate is doubtfull—I rather think It will be Adopted.

The little State of Rhode Island Continues Obstinate Notwithstanding Their Assurances In the Petition presented to us Praying a suspension of the Tonnage law With Respect to them[2]—There is still a majority against adopting the Constitution—I hope We shall take Measures with her That will be more Effectual—The Cession ~~ma~~ of Western territory made by North Carolina Was yesterday accepted in the Senate It is now before us— And I suppose We shall concur.

I inclos'd to you in my last all the foreign News—An Arm'd frigate from England Arrivd here a few days ago, On her Way to No[*va*]. Scota. she Informs That One hundred & ~~fourty~~ two Sail of Vessels are on their Way from that kingdom for Wheat & flour—A Merchant in this City Yesterday Receivd Orders from a Conside. House in London Countermanding Orders lately Receivd for purchasing Wheat & flour The Reasons as assignd Are that from an Unaccountable Influx of thos Articles (He does not know how or from where) The Market is Glutted—This I expect is only a piece of Management—In order to lower the price. We have passt a Bill Establishing a uniform Mode of Naturalization—A Bill Securing to Authors & Inventors the Exclusive Right of Using or Venting their Respective productions—An Act Vesting the Judges &c. in Admiralty with Power to Remitt fines incur'd under the Impost law under particular Circumstances—~~And~~ no others that I recollect—The Session I suppose will Continue to June or July—perhaps longer—We have had the most favourable Winter ever known in this Country by the oldest Inhabitants—We have not had a snow to ly Twenty four hours—A few Days past has been as Warm As We usually have in April—I have Wrote in great haste—Youll Discover this in reading.

ALS, Claiborne Papers, ViHi. Addressed to Staunton, Virginia, via Winchester, Virginia; franked; postmarked. The letter is dated 9 March, but is postmarked 7 March.

[1] For the report, see *DHFFC* 5:852–55.
[2] For the petitions, see *DHFFC* 8:389–96.

Peter Muhlenberg to Benjamin Rush

I am Honord with your favor of the 3d instant & shall take the earliest Opportunity, of making the necessary enquires of Commodore [*James*] Nicholson, relative to Wm. Hays—I am much obligd to you, for the different communications &c. Enclosd, I transmit The additional report of The Secretary, providing for the assumption of the State Debts; not a Word of direct taxation in the whole—tis only doubling the impost &ca. & the revenue is created; sufficient to answer every purpose—which proves at least, That the fears of The House entertaind during the last Session were ill founded, when it was generally believd, the raising of the impost too high would introduce smuggling, and injure our Revenues—But tho' there is a bare possibility of carrying into effect those propositions, still it is certain that the revenues, even then would be very insufficient—The Assumption of the State Debts is not yet decided on, & The issue is still doubtfull If those Gentlemen who advocate the measure, would candidly inform us, what They understand by State Debts, many Difficulties would be removd; Some of The Eastern Members tell us—That some of The States, since the peace, have extinguishd part of the National Debt; That for this They ought to have no Credit, That it only proves, The Delinquent States, had exerted themselves beyond Thier Abilities before the peace, & therefore could not exert themselves equally with others, afterwards This Doctrine I believe, would not be relishd very well in Pensylvania, & some other States; It is said indeed, that this was the intention of The Secretary—and the proof advanced to support this Opinion is—That The State of Virginia has redeemd near three Million out of five—but The Treasurer [*Samuel Meredith*] calculates only what is still due, without paying any regard to what the State has paid—On the other hand, a Member from S.C. [*Burke*] informd us He should vote for it, tho' He conceivd a National Bankruptcy would ensue, & the whole would blow up—I confess Candidly, that notwithstanding all the pains I have taken to inform myself; I do not see my way clear—If the assumption was to take place, when the State Debts are ascertaind—& such only should be asertaind as were Authorisd; Then I should vote for it with out hesitation—I expect that the Question will be decided to Morrow or next day.

ALS, Society Miscellaneous Collection, PHi. Addressed to Philadelphia; franked; postmarked.

William Smith (Md.) to Otho H. Williams

I Recd. yours of the 28th Ulto. yesterday evening, *with the inclosure*, which I sent this morning to the Printer for publication[1]—I find you have not touched on the question depending at this time before Congress; I mean the assumption of the State debts, *by the United States* which is not yet determined; but was postponed. two or three days ago, untill the Secry. Should report the ways & means, to provide for the payment therof, *if they Should be assumed*. The Report you have in one of the inclosed papers, Perhaps this business may be again taken up, tomorrow or next day, what may finally be the fate of the proposition, is dificult to determine. The House is much devided. The Eastern Members (except N. Hampshire) *for*, the Southern (except So. Carolina) *against*, the measure the middle States devided. If it pass in our house, I have reason to believe a great Majority in the Senate are in favor of Assumption. you Shall hear from me When the question is decided, although even that will not be final, for it is expected the Members from No. C. who are daily expected, will be opposed to the Assumption & they will undoubtedly be here before the Bill pass into a law.

ALS, Williams Papers, MdHi. Addressed to Baltimore.

[1] See Williams to Smith, 28 February, above, printed in *NYDG*, 8 and 12 March.

James Sullivan to Elbridge Gerry

I am two Letters in your debt, and am much more under obligation for your obliging correspondence.

The Argument you made has been nearly all published in our papers already. and it is universally agreed agreed that you have done your Country much service, and yourself much honor. The idea of discrimination in the redemption of public securities is generally reprobated here. Judge [*Francis*] Dana & General [*William*] Heath are the only respectable Advocates for the plan that I know of amongst us. The former does not say much on the subject, the Latter writes incessantly. the productions under the Signature of

Equity are his.[1] I have been myself of opinion that the most perfect equity would be done by making a discrimination but on attempting to form a plan I found myself unequal to the task, and became conceited enough to beleive that no one could Succeed better, and upon the whole have concluded that we had better suffer Speculators to make money than to risque our National faith & Character. This was the conclusion of the whole matter with me more than a year ago. I have never thought Madison serious in his Motion [*on discrimination*]. I believe him to be a man of Ability, and cannot but suppose that he must have known his plan to be impracticable I have therefore Set him down in my mind as playing the politician, and as making a motion which he did not wish to Succeed in ~~in~~, merely to Subvert the Scheme of Burke and Scott.[2]

I know not what we are about here. our General Court are divided into two parties they are called Federalists, and Antifederalists, the former are for making provision to pay the State debt though they are some of them for giving the General Government Constructive powers while they Limit the Commonwealth to authoritys Expressed: the Latter hold the reverse of this opinion, and yet by their ~~oposition~~ opposition to the performance of public promises they will effect what the highest Consolidators are wishing for. Mr. [*John*] Bacon of Stockbridge has the lead in opposing the payment of warrants and due bills in the Treasury, and his Argument end in the extreme of discrimination. the vote to pay off warrants and due bills indiscriminately was negatived by a majority of one only. the public Creditors in and out of the Legislature openly declare that they look to the General Government alone for their debts, and the idea of suing the Commonwealth in the federal District Court ~~it~~ is ~~mue~~ too frequently mentioned. one man ([*John*] Stone the Bridgebuilder) Sent a Letter to the House a day or two ago informing them that he Should Sue the State in the district Court. it was read but *not resented.*

There is no process provided by the General Government for Suing States, nor can they be amenable as States, perhaps there may be an attempt, and when there is one a civil war will be the Consequence.

Our papers have nothing in them but the debates in Congress therefore I do not trouble you with them.

ALS, Gerry Papers, MHi. Written from Boston.

[1] Heath's pro-discrimination public opinion pieces appeared in *IC* between 24 December 1789 and 11 February 1790.
[2] Burke's and Scott's proposed amendments are printed in *DHFFC* 5:840, n. 4.

George Thatcher to Sarah Thatcher

I have several of Mr. [*Silas*] Lee's Letters before me—which give an account of his doings at Boston, his return to Biddeford & his full recovery from the Meazels—Also that on the 24th. of Feby. when his last was dated, our dear children were, in his & the Doctors opinion, by no means dangerous tho the meazels were about turning—I am not, however, altogether out of fear, because they are not wholly out of danger—Mr. Lee's full recovery, & the childrens prospect of being soon out of danger, with his information that you begin to eat corn'd beef & pork with a good apitite I assure you, have released my mind from a mountain of anxiety.

I am sorry we are disappointed in geting a Bed—but it could not be helped; & I am glad you have got a Bed-stead—The remainder of the money I suppose you will find very necessary—I was informed, by the last mail, that I have between eighty & ninety dollars in Boston which wait my orders—I have accordingly drawn on the Treasurer for fifty dollars to be sent to me as soon as possible; as I have not recieved any since my arrival to this City; I do not expect to draw any here for my pay till I am about seting off for home.

There will remain about thirty five dollars that I can spare—which I shall appropriate to purchase a Bed & beding as far as it will go, unless you need it for other uses before I can get home.

***

ALS, Thatcher Family Papers, MHi. Place to which addressed not indicated. The omitted text details arrangements for purchasing a bed in New York.

Paine Wingate to Timothy Pickering

I yesterday received your letter of the 3d Instant with the enclosures. I immediately called on Dr. Johnson and left your letter to him, but he was not at home and I have no opportunity of knowing his sentiments, as it is likely unless I write by the post this evening my letter will not find you at Philadelphia. I am sorry for the perplexities which attend your part of the country; but should suppose that the Legislature of your state would never repeal the law you mention.[1] The Legislature of N. York have lately passed a law to empower commissioners on their part to give up to Vermont the claims of certain citizens to lands granted to them in that country; and upon this cession of claims the Vermonters suppose themself perfectly safe to come into the union. But if N.Y. can when they please repeal this law & their citizens have a right to claim their former grants, where is the safety or significancy of such a treaty as they now are about to establish? I believe their is no danger of Genl. Knox's militia plan being adopted. What plan the committee of the house of Representatives who have the matter under consideration will report I can not tell. I should think that at present there will be but little necessary more than has been practiced in Massachusetts for some years past—But if we must have a well disciplined militia I should think that your plan[2] would answer the purpose with much less disgust & expence to the country than that proposed by the Secretary at war—I am glad you have got thro' the task of forming a Constitution & hope you will experience the good fruits of it notwithstanding any imperfections which are inseperable from humane wisdom. I do not suppose that Congress are infallible tho' we go on in business much slower than you did, Nothing is yet determined respecting the national debt nor will be I think for some time. I conclude you have had all the news I can give you on that subject—I begin to think that we shall not see an end to the present session so soon as I hoped for. I had a letter from home dated Feb. 22d. when my family was well. Have not heard from Salem [*Massachusetts*] lately.

ALS, Pickering Papers, MHi. Addressed to Wilkes-Barre, Pennsylvania; postmarked.

[1] On 28 March 1787 Pennsylvania passed "An act for . . . confirming to . . . Connecticut claimants . . ." who had actually resided in 1782 on lands within Pennsylvania granted to them by Connecticut. The act was repealed on 1 April 1790.
[2] Pickering's *Easy Plan of Discipline for a Militia* was widely used in the Continental Army as a training manual from 1775 until it was replaced in 1779 by his friend Baron von Steuben's official *Regulations for the Order and Discipline of the Troops*, which was used until the War of 1812.

Letter from Providence, Rhode Island

Alas for poor Rhode-Island! doomed still to experience the evils attendant on anarchy and misrule.

The delegates of this place are just returned from South-Kingstown, the convention having risen last evening at ten o'clock, without accomplishing the important business of their appointment. The convention stands adjourned to the 24th of May, then to meet at Newport—which favourite measure was carried by a majority of 1. Every objection raised against the general government was clearly obviated; but antifederalism, obstinacy and ignorance, were triumphant. A committee was early appointed to draft and report a bill of rights, and amendments to the constitution: The former, I am told, is nearly a copy of the Virginia bill[1]—the latter are said to have been collected chiefly from amendments proposed by other states. Where any thing *new* has been introduced, stupidity is the characteristic feature. The old game of handing these to *the people*, is once more to be played; and yet no mode is pointed out whereby their sentiments are to be collected. An adjournment till after our election, is intended to serve the purposes of party, and obtain a re election of the powers that be, or others of similar character.

It is much to be lamented, that an exemption from foreign impost and tonnage was ever asked for or granted. The first indulgence afforded our antifeds an opportunity to dispose of their fall produce, and they must be made to *feel*, before they can be brought to a sense of duty.

GUS, 20 March; reprinted at Elizabethtown, New Jersey; Philadelphia; Annapolis, Maryland; Fredericksburg, Virginia; and Edenton, North Carolina.

[1] For the Declaration of Rights that Virginia proposed be added to the Constitution, see *DHFFC* 4:15–17.

OTHER DOCUMENTS

Oliver Ellsworth to Abigail Ellsworth. ALS, Ellsworth Papers, CtHi. Addressed to "Nabby Ellsworth," Windsor, Connecticut; franked; postmarked. George Pitkin (1729–1806) of Hartford, Connecticut, was a colonel in the state militia.

Is glad to hear their children are recovering from the measles; cautions against their taking cold; "As to the negro girl," is still negotiating terms with Col. Pitkin; in conversation, agreed to be responsible for her support "should she come to want" after freeing her at the age of twenty-five; thinks they may get her for free, considering the "risk" they are assuming, but would pay up to £10 if Abigail agrees after seeing the girl.

Thomas Hartley to Jasper Yeates. ALS, Yeates Papers, PHi. Addressed to Lancaster, Pennsylvania; franked; postmarked.

Is happy they agree that discrimination between securities holders "would have been impolitic and I think impracticable"; the "battle" over assumption resumes tomorrow and the outcome is doubtful; will write again soon on that subject; discusses provisions in the new Pennsylvania constitution regarding the judiciary.

Samuel Johnston to Francis Child. No copy known; acknowledged in Child to Johnston, 20 May.

Silas Lee to George Thatcher. ALS, Chamberlain Collection, MB. Written from Wiscasset, Maine.

Thatcher's children were just recovering from a "disorder" when he saw them last (on 26 February); local court news; Betsey King (King's half sister) is living with the Lees.

New York March 7. 1790.

Dear Mrs Ellsworth

I rec'd your Letter by the last Post & Nabby's the Post before — & am very glad to hear that two of the Children are nearly thro' the Measles — The others I hope will have them equally favourable. You will I am sure be very cautious to prevent their taking cold which is often attended with fatal consequences. —

———— As to the negro girl I came to no agreement with Col. Pettibone about her. In the little conversation we had I told him I should not take her as a slave for life but to hold only till she should be 25 years of age, which he seemed to approve of. He will expect to be freed from her support should she come to want after her term of service shall be expired; this we must agree to & take the risk upon our selves.

Oliver Ellsworth to Abigail Ellsworth, 7 March, ALS, p.1. Congressmen's letters home reveal an abiding interest in the details of household management. Ellsworth's letters during the First Congress are rare; this letter to his wife "Nabby" is largely devoted to negotiating the hiring of a "negro girl" from her owner. (Courtesy of the Connecticut Historical Society.)

Oliver Ellsworth and Abigail Wolcott Ellsworth, by Ralph Earl, 1751–1801, oil on canvas,
1792. The family homestead in Windsor, Connecticut, shares the center of the painting
with a copy of the Constitution, which Ellsworth helped to frame (although he was not
present to sign) and later defended in the press, voted to ratify at the state convention, and
fleshed out as the principal author of the Judiciary Act. (Wadsworth Atheneum Museum of
Art, Hartford, Connecticut / Art Resource, NY.)

Samuel Meredith to Henry Hill. ALS, John Jay Smith Collection, PPL at
PHi. Addressed to Philadelphia.
    Hamilton's "second report" (of 4 March on sources of additional revenue)
    "may from enquiry be acted upon in about a Week, or ten days."

Samuel A. Otis to Mr. [*Henry, Jr.?*] Remsen. Transcript of ALS, *Nate's Autographs,* 8 May 2002, item 254.
    "I am greatly obliged to you for remembering me to your kinsman about
    the house in Kingstreet. I don't know that he asks out of proportion with
    others but he asks more than I think it provident to give. I think I must
    take a house somewhere out of town. If it should lie in your way to get

me the family House on Long Island I should prefer it—My family is small and I should have no objection to taking it, your unkle or father [*Henry Remsen, Sr.*] reserving a room or two. I am in no hurry for a house, only, when the family arrangements are made, & the place is to be let, an intimation thereof will oblige."

A. Rogers to Daniel D. Rogers. ALS, Miscellaneous Collection, MHi. Addressed to Petersburg, Virginia. The beginning of this letter was written on 23 February and is calendared under that date in volume 18.
   "Bland, is so well as to walk about he came in to see me yesterday"; "poor gentleman his sufferings have been extreem."

Walter Rutherfurd to John Rutherfurd. AL, Rutherfurd Papers, NHi. Written in the evening; addressed to "Tranquillity," in Independence, New Jersey; carried by Robert Morris of New Jersey. Continues a letter begun on 3 March, above. The page including this day's entry is badly torn.
   "Have had a [*torn*] with Boudinot."

Theodore Sedgwick to Samuel Henshaw. No copy known; acknowledged in Henshaw to Sedgwick, 19 March.

Theodore Sedgwick to Pamela Sedgwick. ALS, Sedgwick Papers, MHi. Place to which addressed not indicated. Concludes a letter begun on 4 March and continued 6 March, above.
   "Sunday. Yesterday the house did not sit and we are as we were. On Wednesday I shall again write you, should it be out of my power to go home."

George Thatcher to Thomas Robison. FC, Thatcher Family Papers, MHi.
   Encloses secretary of the treasury's report of 4 March on revenue sources to pay the interest on any state debt assumed; if assumption takes place, it is probable any change in the existing revenue laws would not go into effect until the end of the year or the beginning of next year.

George Thatcher to David Sewall. No copy known; acknowledged in D. Sewall to Thatcher, 20 March.
   "In yours of the 7th. is this Phraze, when mentioning the filling the S[*upreme*]. J[*udicial*]. Court. 'The Nomination of four Gentn. to fill one office was noted here as a Novelty.'"

Hugh Williamson to Governor Alexander Martin. No copy known; acknowledged in Martin to Williamson, 25 May.

From New York. [Boston] *Massachusetts Centinel*, 17 March; reprinted at Portland, Maine; Exeter and Portsmouth, New Hampshire; and Providence, Rhode Island.

> Virginia, Maryland, and a part of Pennsylvania oppose assumption of the states' war debts because little of it is theirs; there is a bare majority in favor of the measure, the outcome of which is uncertain; discussion of the troops to be raised for defending the southwestern frontier against "the depredations of the savages" was the reason, it is said, for clearing the galleries.

Letter from a Member of Congress. [New Hampshire] *Concord Herald*, 30 March.

> Congress is engaged in funding the domestic debt; there will be an excise, some additional impost duties, but no direct tax; assumes the state debts will be assumed; New Hampshire will not be injured: "our State will be in a happy situation with respect to taxes in future."

Letter from Kentucky. *NYP*, 20 May, from a non-extant Winchester, Virginia, newspaper of 24 April.

> The Shawnee Indians have captured and carried off fourteen men besides women and children.

MONDAY, 8 MARCH 1790

Cold (Johnson)

Elias Boudinot to Charles Pettit

The delay in answering your very useful Favours of the   has been occasioned by the continual engagements ~~occasioned by~~ the important business before Congress have produced, as also an expectation of being able of giving you some certainty with regard to the Issue—I have been greatly obliged by the particularity of your Letters and the enclosures—for altho they have not entirely met the Objections & difficulties attending this Business, for want of your knowing the Turn the argument takes in the House, yet they have been a considerable Source of Information—The Opposition to the assumption of the State Debts, is very considerable & respectable, yet I am still of Opinion it will be carried, ~~and I also~~ tho it will be by a very small Majority indeed—perhaps I may be mistaken—I also believe it to be a prudent & politic Measure—The arguments in its Favour are founded on the Justice of the demand—That the States have been but the Agents of Congress in Contracting the Debts, that for our comon Cause, which by the Confederation was to be paid out of one comon Treasury—That therefore the publick Faith is as much pledged for these as for the federal Debt—That not to do it, is an Injury to the federal Creditors, as it will be raising an impenetrable Phalanx of State Creditors, who will be continually opposing the Payment of Interest to them, & claiming the first resources of the States for their own Use—That it will be productive of Parties in Congress & the Government, by State Creditors forcing themselves into Congress for this Purpose &c. &c. But what weighs very heavy in my Mind, I am convinced that without it we shall not have any Debt whatever funded at this Session, which I think will greatly endanger the peace of the Government. To Judge of this Matter rightly, you must be made acquainted with the Situation & views of the House—The opposers of the Assumption, are divided into several Classes—a small Party wish to apply a Spunge[1] to all the Debts of the Union—a larger number are very desirous of delay in Funding, [*lined out*] in hopes of something turning up to justify lessening the Debt by some Means or other—a few are very desirous of any Measure that will prevent a Settlement ~~of the Debt~~ between the ~~U.S.~~ several States—Some are violently attached to a compleat discrimination among the Creditors, from an Enmity to Speculators—[*lined out*] and a greater number violently oppose the assumption from Principle or local Interests—These are ready to Join a considerable part of the supposed Majority who are bound from their State Politics to oppose any funding System that does not comprehend the State Debts, by which means the advocates for a Funding System, who are now two thirds of the House, would on a reconciliation taking Place (on the assumption being negatived) ~~from a strong Majority~~ dwindle down to ~~an indifferent~~ small Minority of the whole—It is a universal Idea that adequate funds are to be provided to secure 4 ℔ C. to all the Creditors of the Union Subscribers & non Subscribers and to leave further Provision for the 2 ℔ C. to Non Subscribers to ~~the~~ a future Legislature, where the Production of the Funds will be certainly known—all agree that 6 ℔ C. is due, but most think that if we can fund & pay 4 ℔ C. with certainty, it is as far as we dare to go at present, but by no means to do any Thing that will render the payment to Non Subscribers of 4 ℔ Ct. uncertain or to injure their demand for the remaining 2 ℔ Ct.

FC:dft, AMs 779/1, PPRF. According to Pettit's acknowledgment on 14 March, the last three paragraphs of this letter were written on 9 March. They are printed under that date.

---

[1] To cancel or wipe out a debt without payment.

William Ellery to Benjamin Huntington

I have received all the letters you have written to me which could have come to hand by this time.

In answer to that of the 13th of February I would observe that the Militia system of the Secretary of War has not been made [*lined out*] publick; because it was thought it might hurt the cause of federalism; especially among the Quakers;[1] and as you have not desired my sentiments upon it I have thought it prudent to say little or nothing about it. Some plan of national defense is certainly necessary, and that which will be the least burthensome and expensive, and most agreeable to the spirit and manners of the people, will in general be the most suitable to adopt. I coincide with you in opinion respecting the probable effects of the Secretary's plan. I presume that no plan of militia regulations will be fixed upon this Session. Your whole time will be taken up I imagin in contriving and establishing a system for funding the public debt. I have not as yet seen Mr. Maddison's plan. If a discrimination can be possibly made which will satisfy the origl. holders of securities, and the present possessors of them, and a considerable saving be made to the public it ought to be made. It cannot be expected that the great council of the nation should split hairs. De minimis non curat lex,[2] and the trouble of making discriminations, should not be suffered to outweigh the public Interest. I trust that no system of finance will be determined upon until Congress shall be sure of sufficient funds for discharging the Interest of the debt they shall contract to pay. If they should fail here the whole [*lined out*] fabrick of public credit, however speciously and ingeniously it may be built, will tumble into ruin. You have time enough to consult about and wisdom enough to form a plan for establishing a plan public credit, which shall be satisfactory to the people at large. To please every one is impossible. We are informed that your house have, by a large Majority, determined against making any discrimination between the Original and present holders of public securities, that you are upon that part of the Secretary's report which respects the assumption of the State Debts, and that no debt prior to the commencement of the war will be considered as a part thereof because, I suppose, the admission of debts which accrued before that period well might too much enhance the aggregate debt.

You have heard of the Act of this State forfeiting such of the State securities, given for articles furnished during the war, which were not exchanged for paper bills at par by certain periods.[3] Some persons in consequence of that Act received Paper in exchange for their Securities and delivered them up into the Treasury of the State, [*lined out*] and others refused to exchange them, and still hold their Securities. Will an estimate be made of the specie value of the paper received by the first, and the difference between that and the Specie value of their Securities be considered as a part of this State's Debt? and will the Securities which have not been delivered up come within the description of and considered as State debt? Upon the principles of Justice I think that they, who, for fear of loosing the whole of their debt, received in fact but a part only, ought to have the deficiency made up to them; and that they who still hold their securities ought to receive their full value. It would be hard indeed if the last should loose their whole debt; because they refused to submit to a most iniquitous law.

When the New Constitution shall be adopted the Fed's will do every thing in their power to prevent an Antifedl. Election to Congress—The Constitutionvention, after sitting only one week, have adjourned to the fourth monday in May next to meet in this town.

It was the determination of the Feds to force the Antis to a decision on the Constitution but they could not effect it. When they failed in that point they moved for an adjournment to the last monday in March; but could not succede, they then tried for the fourth monday in April, here they failed also, they represented that the State would suffer great injury if the Constitution was not adopted before the time limited for the suspension of the navigation act of the U.S. as it respects this State;[4] that the trade of the State would be ruined, a great number of its inhabits. be thrown out of employed, and in a word that we should be involved in the deepest distress; but it was to no purpose, the Antis must have a *bill* of rights, and a long string of Amendments to lay before the freemen at the annual Town-meetings for proving the Genl. Officers on the third wednesday in April next, then the time for planting Indian Corn would be at hand, that the merchants would be able on application to Congress to procure another revival of the suspension act &c. &c., and in short an adjournment could not be attainment obtained than to a shorter period than that I have mentioned. The Antis [*lined out*] carried their bill of rights and twenty amendments, exclusive of the proposed amendments proposed by Congress all which except the first they approved. The bill of rights is I am informed innocent enough. Their Amendments are made up of the Amendments proposed by No. Carolina, No. Carolina, and some other States. In the course of the debate on the Constitution they made but few objections, reserving to them a place in their Amendments—On every question which they considered as important, and which they had settled in their private meetings they carried a majority from four or five to twelve. Some others they lost by a small majority. What will be the result of the next meeting of the Convention it is impossible to say, it has hitherto been the design of the Antis to amuse Congress and the Feds, and in my opinion they will continue to do it until Congress shall take some measures that will make them feel more sensibly than will the operation of the navigation Act. If Congress have a right to comprehend this State in the exercise of their general government, and were to declare that they had such right, and would exercise it unless the State acceded to the Union it would have a powerful effect—this and an annihilation of our State jurisdiction, and a division of the State they are more afraid of than a requisition of our quota of this public debt, the loss of this States share in the profits of the Western territory; or any thing else.

The Feds will endeavour to gain some of them over to their side between this and the next meeting of the Convention, and to lessen their numbers in the legislature at the election in April but exitus in dubio est.[5]

I have recd. a letter from the Secretary of the Treasury in which he advises me that he will advance a thousand dollars towards my salary on the settlement of my accounts at the Treasury, and to authorize a person by a proper power of Attorney to receive the advance on my account at the time I send forward my accounts. I send them forward by this post, and have taken the freedom to authorize you by a power of Attorney which I now inclose [to] receive the money for me. I cannot conceive that any objection can lie to the power; if any objection should be made to it please to frame me and send it to me immediately first assuring yourself that it will be approved when executed. When you have received the money, send me three hundred dollars by the first packet, and keep the rest until I shall give further directions about it. My accounts are in such order that they can be settled at once, and there will be a balance due me after the payment of the Thousd. dollars of nearly seven hundred dollars; so that if the any thing should interrupt an immediate settlement of my accounts the sum you are authorized to receive may be paid at once with the greatest safety.

Besides receiving a reward for your trouble in negotiating this business your attention to it will much oblige Your friend & hble. servant.

P. S. Urge a speedy paymt. my situation requires it.

ALS, Benjamin Huntington Correspondence, 1772–1790, R-Ar. Written from Newport, Rhode Island; received 18 March; answered 23 March "by Capt. [*James*] Brown with 300 Dollars." Huntington's reply was drafted on the bottom of the last page of this letter and is calendared under 23 March, volume 19.

[1] Secretary of War Knox's comprehensive plan for the regulation of the states' militias when called into federal service, which proposed the universal mandatory enrollment of males between eighteen and sixty and raised the possibility of exempting principal magistrates, judges, clergymen, "and perhaps some religious sects" (*DHFFC* 5:1448) was presented to the House on 21 January. It was bound to meet the resistance of the historically pacifist Quakers.

[2] Law does not concern itself with trifles.

[3] "An Act for paying off the whole of the State Securities," adopted in March 1789.

[4] A section of the North Carolina Act [HR-36] dealt with Rhode Island's ongoing separation from the union by extending until 1 April 1790 "and no longer" the provision in a first session Collection Act [HR-23] that exempted the state from the burden of paying foreign impost and tonnage rates (*DHFFC* 6:1534).

[5] The result is in doubt.

Benjamin Goodhue to Michael Hodge

The subject of Assumption has been suspended for some days past, to give time to the Secry. to report the provision,[1] should it take effect, this was order'd to be done to obviate the fear of direct taxation, tho' it is not improbable, the opposers of the measure might expect an addition of strength by the ~~unpalatabb~~ unpalatableness of some sources of revenue which might be reported—I expect the subject will be renew'd to day—the opposition rather increases, and leaves the event more doubtfull then appearances seem'd the other day to indicate.

I recd. yours of 26th Ulto. and am sensibly impressed with the good opinion they have bestow'd on my public intentions.

ALS, Ebenezer Stone Papers, MSaE. Place to which addressed not indicated.

[1] Additional sources of revenue for paying the interest on the states' assumed debts were detailed in Hamilton's report of 4 March.

James Madison to Thomas Jefferson

The newspapers will have shewn you the late proceedings of the House of Representatives. The present subject of deliberation is the proposed assumption of the State debts. Opinions are nearly balanced on it. My own is no otherwise favorable to the measure than as it may tend to secure a final settlement and *payment* of balances among the States. An assumption even under such circumstances is liable to powerful objections. In the form proposed that object would be impeded by the measure, because it interests South Carolina and Massachusetts, who are to be chiefly relieved, against such a settlement and payment. The immediate operation of the plan would be peculiarly hard on Virginia. I think, also, that an increase of the federal debt will not only prolong the evil, but be further objectionable as augmenting a trust already sufficiently great for the virtue and number of the federal Legislature.

PJM 13:94–95, from Madison, *Letters* 1:511. Place to which addressed not indicated; received at Philadelphia on 17 March (*PTJ* 16:213n).

John Pemberton to James Pemberton

I have wrote my dr. Wife [*Hannah Zane Pemberton*] to which refer & have sent the Congressional Register in which is Contained part of the Debates when the Adresses were read. As it is probable a Comittee may be appointed sometime but when I know not such delays are made. I have thot. some sections of the Law made in Pensa. abt. 30 Years past to regulate respecting Vessels bringing German passengers[1] might throw some light to the Comittee. There are so many persons passing back & forward expect a Conveyance may be found sometime this Week.

This goes ℔ Henry Vanderwerf who is desirous to get into some employ in Philada. in the writing way, & wish he may get with a steady friend. My Compns. I expect will write or have wrote—They are Industrious the effect must be less.

ALS, Pennsylvania Abolition Society Papers, PHi. Addressed to Philadelphia; carried by Henry Vanderwerf.

---

[1] "An Act for the Prohibiting the Importation of Germans or Other Passengers in too Great Numbers in Any One Vessell," passed by the Pennsylvania colonial assembly in January 1750, and a supplemental act passed in May 1765, sought to ameliorate shipboard conditions by regulating space allotments and food, and by requiring that families not be separated.

John Pemberton, Notes on Speeches in Congress on the Slave Trade

Shurmen [*Sherman*]. after smiths [*S.C.*] speech. stood up & said he thought it was very wrong to Abuse People that had not permission to Answer in that house for themselves.
Gerry Vindicated our Memorial tho' apprehended some exceptions might be respecting some parts of that from the Abolition Society.

Moore from Virga., also abusive, & mean—yet towards his Close expressed he was for Stoping the trade.

Warner [*Mifflin*] has made some remarks upon his Invectives.

ALS, Pennsylvania Abolition Society Papers, PHi. Date based on content.

John Pemberton to James Pemberton

I wrote thee a few lines this morning ℔ H[*enry*]. Vanderwerf & referred for further information to my letter to my dear Hannah [*Zane Pemberton*] & the Congressional Register sent her which contains the debates in part of the House of Delegates On the 2d Reading of our Address—we waited on several members this morning, & urged a proposal for 2d. Reading of the Report of the Comittee[1] which was motioned by Thos. Hartley. but some members one after another presented private Petitions for Allowances or Claims for supposed services during the Warr, however Hartley repeated his

motion & was seconded by divers members. but E. Boudinot to avoid Altercation proposed the first 2d day[2] in the next month being appointed for the
Discussion. Some from the southward proposed & Insisted if Considered at
all shd. not be before 1st. 2d day 5th mo. & Jackson uttered much reflection
& scurrility representing we Acted Inconsistent with our profession that our
Adress was Inconsistent & big with dreadful evils, its tendency being to promote Insurrections & bloodshed. & persecution agst. the southern states. &
much to this purpose. & smith from S.C. much like him, only more gaurded,
but very Censorious. Gerry took them up. & so did J. Vining Very masterly.
& turned all their Arguments backward. & if what they aledged was true the
sooner it was Discussed the better. & that no Delay should be given but An
Immediate Discussion entered into. Gerry thot. it very Unreasonable that
such reflections shd. be Cast upon the people Called Quakers—representing
the frds. who brot. the Memorial had taken divers opps. with the Comittee
& allways appeared Reasonable. & that he thot. more was Contained in the
Memorial signed by B. Franklin for them to object to.[3] then Jackson said
he did not mean to Cast unreasonable Reflections upon frds.—& said he
Admired that B. F. who had been On the Convention & knew so well the
Disposition of the southern states that he Could not reconcille his signing
Such a paper unless his Age had weakened his faculties. There was about two
hours taken up in Disputation. Jackson, Smith Stone. & Burke being in the
Opposition. Vining, Boudinot. Hartley Gerry. Fitzsimons & some others in
our favor & it was evident the Opposition was much Weakened. afer divers
propositions it was Concluded to take the matter up to morrow week—The
snare of leaning to please Men was very evident in the Disputations of this
day. for Smith & Jackson particularly objected to the foreparts of the Report
reasoning the Danger of enforcing such a position. as it was plain to them
& would be to any reasonable Man that their saying what Congress could
not do until 1808.[4] Implied that then they might set every Slave On the
Continent free. & this sentiment would Create great Discontent to the so.
ward. Had we not been here the presentment of the Report would have been
delayed. & had we not been here. it does not seem probable it would have
been revived this day. Nor perhaps for a Considerable time. & there appears
a Necessity of still attending to the subject to its Close. If Committed the
Next week, it is Necessary to watch the Bill &c. I say this much to shew
the Necessity of some frds. being here. & it is scarce Brotherly that we shd.
be detained—& not released By other Brethren. I think there were but 4
frds. of this City attended with us today. tho' in many respects are very kind.
& some as have heretofore said, when we Call upon them willing to join in
Visits to the Members.

I thot. Some little Accot. of this days proceedings would be Acceptable.

ALS, Pennsylvania Abolition Society Papers, PHi. Addressed to Second Street, Philadelphia; postmarked.

---

[1] For the committee report on the antislavery petitions, presented to the House on 5 March, see *DHFFC* 8:335–37.

[2] Quaker practice at the time expressed days and months as ordinal units (e.g., Sunday as "First Day"), rejecting the English language's names because they are based on pagan usage.

[3] The petition ("memorial") of the Pennsylvania Abolition Society was signed by its president, Benjamin Franklin, and unlike its companion petitions from Quaker yearly meetings, it sought the outright abolition of slavery. For the petition, see *DHFFC* 8:324–26.

[4] Article 1, section 9 of the Constitution prevented Congress from prohibiting the importation of slaves prior to 1808.

Epes Sargent to Benjamin Goodhue

I thank you very sincerely for your kind favour and the report [*on public credit*] of Mr. H[*amilton*].; it is far beyond the inferior praise I can bestow, comprehending great wisdom, justice and policy every measure of this kind carried into effect, tis visible diminishes the importance and necessity of the State Governments; of course you are prepared to expect opposition to its being adopted; the plan to be pursued however is of such a nature as to go forward and bear down all opposition; the Class of public Creditors is so large and influential, that its quite apparent if government support the one, interest will urge to support the other; opinion may be considered as strong, but of all motives interest under some disguise will prove the strongest.

The District Court have sat at Salem, and acquitted the two Captains charged with not producing ~~two~~ true manifests; I am not yet informed of the principle on which they were cleared, your Salem Friends will doubtless write you, I have been obliged to prosecute two Masters for the same offence in this port to be tried in June; if these actions like the Salem ones should fail; I think I shall have but done my duty; this good at least will grow out of it, wch. has been a difficult point to establish, for a pretended or real ignorance has prevailed on the important distinction held up by Law between manifests and entries; the one has been blended and confounded with the other; from a practise heretofore observed of looking for safety in a port entry, when every other effort has failed this was the dernier resort: these with similar usage in foreign ports has obstructed the observance of this wholesome regulation: I consider it a striking merit of the Revenue Law and have laboured its attention: goods of bulk admit of deviations where the quantity cannot be expected to be ascertained, and in these cases I have not been exact to note the differences, but goods to be delivered by tale [*tally*] can admit of no mistake, except designed ones.

According to the desire of Mr. H. I forwarded him a particular statement of the fees I have received from Augt. 15 to Jany., amounting to 158 dollars in this Sum was included the registers emollments and licenses for Vessells under 20 Tons, wch. can never appear again in any coming period.

The transaction referred to in the inclosed letter will explain itself, the Person[1] recommended to your notice is well known to me, and in my opinion is possesed of those rare and solid good qualities of firmness, moderation, fidelity punctuality and a sensible mind. Col. P.'s influence is by no means inconsiderable.

ALS, Letters to Goodhue, NNS. Written from Gloucester, Massachusetts.

---

[1] Rufus Putnam, who was closely involved with members of the Sargent family in the development of the Northwest Territory, would be nominated as federal judge of the territory on 30 March.

OTHER DOCUMENTS

Fisher Ames to William Tudor. Misdated in *Ames* 1:729. See Ames to Tudor, 3 March, above.

Silas Cooke to Samuel Johnston. Copy, Iredell Papers, NcD. Cooke copied this letter into his letter to James Iredell, 15 March, volume 19.
    Office seeking: clerk for the federal court in North Carolina; could have solicited aid from other of his friends in Congress, but applies solely to Johnston; alternatively, seeks Johnston's influence on his behalf with the federal judge for the state, if the appointment of clerk is to be made by that officer.

Richard Curson to Horatio Gates. ALS, Gates Papers, NHi. Written from Baltimore; addressed to Berkeley, West Virginia.
    C. Carroll has just left for Congress.

William Ellery to Alexander Hamilton. FC, Ellery Letterbooks, Newport Historical Society, Rhode Island. For the full text, see *PAH* 26:522–23.
    Has given Huntington a power of attorney to receive treasury's advance of $1,000 on Ellery's salary (as continental loan officer), pending the settlement of his accounts.

William Finnie to Horatio Gates. ALS, Emmet Collection, NN. Place to which addressed not indicated. For background on the petition Finnie was promoting in New York at this time, see *DHFFC* 7:464–67.

"Your friend" Morris and many others there "are strong advocates in my favor"; will remain there another four weeks; he may be written in care of White.

Benjamin Goodhue to Stephen Goodhue. No copy known; acknowledged in Stephen to Benjamin Goodhue, 17 March.

Benjamin Huntington to William Ellery. No copy known; acknowledged in Ellery to Huntington, 28 March.

Daniel Hiester, Account Book. PRHi.
Dined with the Pennsylvania delegation at Simmons's Tavern.

Letter from Hartford, Connecticut. *NYDA*, 15 March.
A Private Citizen (*Connecticut Courant*, 25 February), apparently a foreigner, has "recommended a wise scheme for paying the national debt"; his proposals consist of seven propositions, subdivided into nineteen; "It would puzzle Doctor Faustus himself to make any thing of more than half of them." (Dr. Faust or Faustus was a character who supposedly sold his soul to the devil in return for supernatural powers.)

TUESDAY, 9 MARCH 1790

Very Cold (Johnson)

John Adams to John Trumbull

Coll. [*David*] Humphreys, at the Levee, this morning, delivered me your kind Letter of Feb. 6, for the favour of which you cannot imagine how much I am obliged to you—not less delighted with your frank communications respecting your own affairs, than Satisfyed with your friendly cautions to me, I shall make a kind of Commentary, or at least serve marginal Notes upon both. I rejoice in your health, and your Success at the Bar as well as in your Learning and Fidelity to your Clients. You are building on a Rock that will never fail you. But I must repeat my request that you attend to Air and Exercise, and that you do not avoid a share in public Life—the last however is less the Dictate of Affection to you, then of Regard to the Public and myself, for I can give you no Encouragement from Experiance to hope for any Thing but Care and Labour. I will Say no more concerning yourself at present: but come to the Observations that relate to me. You talk of my Enemies: but I assure you I have *none*. I am the Ennemy of no Man living; and I know of none who is an Ennemy to me. I have injured no Man alive—I have not intentionally offended any Man: and I know not that I have actually offended any. This I think gives me a right to Say that I have not an Ennemy. But "The V. P. is a Native of New England." To this Charge, I plead guilty the fault is irreparable, and I am reconciled to the Punishment which New England has already joined the southern States, in inflicting, for it, and to such as I knew they will hereafter join in inflicting. God Save me from myself and my Friends is a Proverbial Prayer, and no Spaniard had ever more reason to offer it up than I have. "The V. P. has no considerable Advantages from the Pride of Family." This I deny. My Father was an honest Man, a Lover of his Country, and an independent Spirit, and the Example of that Father, inspired me with the greatest Pride of my Life, and has contributed to support me, among roaring Billows yawning Gulphs and burning Fevers. I must dilate, a little upon this important Subject. My Father Grand Father, Great Grand father and Great Great Grand father, were all Inhabitants of Braintree and all independent Country Gentlemen—I mean officers in the Militia and Deacons in the Church. I am the first who has degenerated from the Virtues of the House so far, as not to have been an officer in the Militia nor a Deacon. The Line I have described makes about 160 Years, in which no Bankruptcy was ever committed no Widow or orphan was ever defrauded no Redemptioner intervened and no Debt was ever contracted in England. Let others Say as much. My Father was a Farmer and a Tradesman, all the rest were farmers I know and Tradesmen I believe—and the greatest fault, I ever found with any of them was that they did not educate me to their Farms and Trades. My Mother was a Boylston one of the richest Families in the Massachusetts for above an hundred Years, and certainly not obscure, Since Harvard Colledge is indebted to it for very generous Donations and all Christendom for Inoculation for the Small Pox.[1]

But although I am proud of my Family, I should be very much mortified, if I thought that I enjoyed any share of public or private Esteem, Admiration or Consideration, for the Virtues of my Ancestors. By my own Actions I wish to be tried. But The V. P. has had no Considerable Favours of Fortune. This I deny, and boldly affirm that he has been the most fortunate Man in America without Exception. in the public service, he has escaped death in more shapes than any Man, not excepting any officer of the army. He has escaped Death, in stormy Seas, leaky ships, threatning Diseases Cannon Balls and private Daggers, with a long train of [*illegible*] But if by Fortune is meant private Property, his paternal Estate and his own acquisitions before he turned Fool and Politician would outweigh the Ballance of many of those, who ride with Six horses owned in England or Elswhere. But is it not provoking, that the V. P. should be abused for the obscurity of his Birth and the smallness of his Fortune; and at the same time abused for telling People that they have Prejudies in favour of Birth and Fortune?

When I Said I had no Ennemy, I did not mean to deny that I was envied—but Envy is not Enmity. But Envy need not labour to prevent me from being President. there is no danger. The President is happily likely to live longer than the V. P.—and if it Should be otherwise ordered, the V. P. has no desire to be P. He would retire to his Farm with more pleasure than ever he accepted any public office. Whether this is believed or not is a matter of Indifference at present. The World may possibly be convinced of it, by unequivocal Proofs, sooner than they imagine. The accusation of "fondness for the Splendor of monarchical Courts" has no Effect on me. I started fairly with my Countrymen. I published to the World with my name, my honest sentiments of Government, with the Reasons on which they were founded, at great length in three solid perhaps ponderous Volumes.[2] these opinions are not changed, and if my Countrymen dissapprove them, they are perfectly at Liberty to reject them and their Author together. I will neither falsify nor dissemble my Opinions on that Subject, if it were to obtain all the Gold of Ophyr,[3] added to Presidencies or Royalties.

The other charge is less founded. I have never given my sentiment at large upon any question, but once. Then I asked leave, and it was granted, seemingly with Pleasure. it was upon the great Question of the Presidents Power of Removal, at other times I have only occasionally asked a question or made a Single observation, and that but Seldom—if these are faults they are easily corrected, for I have no Desire ever to open my mouth again, upon any questions. I am So far, from a desire of talking that I have never in any one Instance given my Reasons, for my Judgment in any of those many Cases in which the senate has been equally divided, and in which I suppose no Man would call in question my right of discussing the question at large.

No my Friend—The observations you have heard are only Revivals of old grumblings when I was a Member of Congress from 1774 to 1778— or they may be observations on private Conversation—When I have company of friends at my own Table, and I feel very easy and happy, I sometimes hear such Strange sentiments, as arrouse me to some earnestness and perhaps warmth of Expression, and without meaning or thinking of offence to any Mortal, I may have hurt the Feelings of some of the Company. Your Friend Mrs. [Abigail] Adams sometimes objects to me on this head.

You are the first who has ever hinted to me, that any Exception has ever been taken in senate—excepting about ten months ago Mr. Gerry mentioned to me that he had heard something of this kind hinted in Conversation.

To be candid with you, the situation I am in, is too inactive and insignificant for my disposition, and I care not how soon I quit it. while in it, however I wish to do my Duty, and avoid giving just offence and you cannot oblige me more than by communicating to me, with the same Confidence and openness, whatever you hear objected to my Conduct.

I mentioned to you three Volumes, and wish to know whether I have ever sent you a sett of them? if not, and I could find a Conveyance I would beg your acceptance of one, for I wish to know your sentiments of it.

P. S. Encore. All their Arts or rather absurdities, cannot make me unpopular. I am, and they know it, more popular in their own States than they are. I was so fourteen Years ago, and by means of their own Constituents forced Numbers of them to vote with me, much against their Inclinations.[4] The Lyes that have been inculcated in the Southern States do me good, one was that I never came to Senate but with Six horses, and often with an Escort of twelve horsemen. There is, much too large a Proportion of both Houses who from Ignorance, Timidity or positive Antifœderalism, vote for Measures which you and I know would Subvert the Constitution. These are Sure to find me in their Way. What am I to do? Act a low Cunning? a dirty Craft? a vile Hypocricy? a base dissimulation? You know me too well to believe it possible. Your Informers my Friend are young Men, who knew not Joseph.[5] or Tories who are associated with them. John Adams has done Services for North America, of which no Man is ignorant, and which cannot be forgotten. They appear to be least of all known and felt in New England. The southern Gentlemen I must confess have shewn a better disposition to do me Justice then New Englandmen have. The two Men who envy me most[6] as you must know if you reflect, have Elections in New England much in their Power, and these have used their Influence in both Houses of Congress, to cramp me, more than the southern Gentlemen have.

This is confidential, you see wholly, I mean the whole Letter.

ALS, AMs 1052/19.2, PPRF. Place to which addressed not indicated.

---

[1] The wealthy Boston merchant Nicholas Boylston (1716–71) bequeathed £1500 to establish Harvard's first professorship of rhetoric and oratory. Against much opposition, Dr. Zabdiel Boylston (1679–1766) successfully performed the first smallpox inoculations in America during an epidemic in Boston in 1721.

[2] Adams's *Defense of the Constitutions of the United States* was first published in London in three volumes throughout the course of 1787.

[3] Also Ophir, a legendary land, thought to be part of Arabia, noted for its gold (I Kings 9:26–28).

[4] A reference to Adams's pivotal role in securing the 2 July 1776 vote to declare the colonies independent of Great Britain.

[5] An expression for young upstarts, taken from the biblical description of the new Pharaoh who did not know his predecessor's relationship of trust with the Hebrew Joseph (Exodus 1:8).

[6] John Hancock and Samuel Adams, the sitting governor and lieutenant governor, respectively, of Massachusetts, were the major forces in state politics. Adams identifies "H." and "A." as his major detractors in his letter to Trumbull of 12 March, below.

John Avery, Jr. to George Thatcher

Your favor by the last post I have had the pleasure of receiving, I wrote you a few days ago that your account was passed the General Court and that a Warrant was also made out[1]—I have mentioned the matter respecting the pay to the Treasurer and he informs me that he shall pay your order on sight I am much pleased that Congress have determined that no discrimination shall take place in payment of their debts—I am not concerned in public securities nor never was—but Justitia fiat ruat cœlum[2]—As to the payment of State debts, in my very humble opinion, the several States are competent to pay their own debts, and let them do it in their own way; perhaps it may give greater satisfaction in the end—not that I think that a consolidation of the Government will take place, even if Congress should assume the State debts; for it will be the interest of the General Government to support the several States in their sovereignty and independence & so it will be the interest of the several States to support the federal Government and while they move harmoniously—We shall be the happiest people in the world, but if there should ever by [be] clashing between them anarchy and confusion will be the consequence—therefore I hope the greatest care will be taken to prevent it, or rather the most judicious steps taken to maintain the Union & cement it by the strongest ties of affection—And my friend as we are now in our infancy therefore we ought to use the greatest œconomy in all our affairs.

ALS, Chamberlain Collection, MB. Written from Boston.

[1] For Thatcher's service in the Confederation Congress.
[2] Let justice be done, tho' the heavens crumble.

Theodorick Bland to Patrick Henry

The friendly wish with which your obliging favor of the 8th. ultimo was concluded for my health was but just realized after a severe fit of the gout, when your friendly and agreable letter reached me. Scarce had I began my career of Politics in the great Sanhedrin[1] when that fell Monster seized my hands and feet, knees and elbows where he wreaked his vengeance for near a fortnight—but, I thank God, has spared my head, and left it in a better condition state than it has been for ten months past, being now free of vertigo—and I once more enjoy the pleasing hope of a good state of health with only semi annual returns of that painful crisis of other disorders.

The transactions of Congress, from the first days of its commencing its operations to this hour, has confirmed me in the opinion which I entertained on the day of its adoption by our State—viz. that the power in whom was vested the sword and the purse and a paramount authority could have no competitor—from that moment I have bounded my hopes to the single object of securing (in terrorem)[2] the great and essential rights of person from the encroachments of Power—so far as to authorise resistance when they should be either openly attacked or insidiously undermined—This is the polar star of my politics. The sacrifice of state rights has in my opinion been offered up, and has already bled its vital drops—let those who led it to the altar bring thither their repentance as an atonement. I find they are beginning to be astonished at their own work and every step which the Federal Government takes shakes that resolution which they so fully possessed at the adoption, and they, like the stormy ocean when it returns to a calm, wonder at the ruin they have made. Having sworn to support the constitution, I feel myself impelled on all occasions to try how far its energy may be made useful for the preservation of peace and harmony. to this [*lined out*] point are all my secondary views directed. Clashing powers and interfering jurisdictions appear to me the weak side of our incongruous machine—well am I aware that from strong collisions sparks are generated, which will inevitably light up a flame unquenchable—but (perhaps) with blood—you will not then be surprised to find me on every occasion (except where the great rights of man are concerned) on the side of Energy and consolidation—for I [*lined out*] never was a milk and water politician—and government with all its essential powers once assumed over so extended a dominion, I am firmly convinced, must either fall into anarchy or be supported with vigor. The first is an unbridled monster, and the second may peradventure be restrained—of two evils then let us choose the least. Thus have I explained to you, my dear Sir, the principles by which my political conduct is activated—happy shall I be if they meet your approbation—for next to that of my own conscience the approbation of the good man and the virtuous patriot is the first of wish of my heart.

You will no doubt have heard of, and have seen, the secretary of the treasury's report, which has engrossed almost the whole attention of Congress. That body have agreed to the funding the foreign debt according to the stipulations at the time of borrowing, they have also agreed to fund both the principal and interest of the domestic debt of the United States, and have this day in a committee of the whole come to a resolution to assume the state debts which are also to be funded, the States to have credit for such parts of their debt as they have paid in interest, or extinguished by their own exertions, which are to be liquidated, and the balance of the C[*redito*]r. States carried to their credit and of the D[*ebto*]r. States placed to their debits—the quantum of interest is not ascertained, there are various modifications proposed, but it appears to me evident that the principles laid down must be violated by any thing short of 6 ⅌ ct. I fear that the *America fides*[3] is not yet ripe for such a process, and that a blot or stain will still be suffered to remain on it. I find that the boldest advisers of instituting a government to do complete justice, shrink from the idea of completing the work which they themselves started to do.

Your idea of the North Carolina cession strikes me forcibly, and alarms me not a little. It is an innovation on those rights which are in my eye the most sacred that a republican man possesses, and I fear the pretended acquiescence of the people thus disfranchised, is nothing more than the acquiescence of a party wishing to be aggrandized at the expence of those over whom they are to rule—Their acceptance however has gone down in the senate as I am informed with[4] opposition and I believe without examination. I congratulate you on the purchase you have made in Georgia[5] which I hope will turn out to your most sanguine expectations, and be not only a provision for your family, but an asylum from tyranny whenever it may arise or become oppressive to that freedom which I know you so highly prise, and for which you have so long been a firm and unshaken advocate. Believe me, dear Sir, that except hearing of your happiness and welfare, nothing will afford me more pleasure than frequently hearing from you, and participating in those sentiments on political subjects which flow with such spontaniety from you & which may peradventure correct those erroneous ones, which the court air & my own imbecility may produce in me.

Ms. transcript, Rives Papers, DLC. Place to which addressed not indicated. According to *American Book Prices Current*, 27(1911):782, the three page ALS sold in 1910 for six dollars. An earlier transcript at ViHi is incomplete.

[1] The ancient Hebrew supreme council and high court of justice.
[2] As a warning.
[3] American faith.
[4] In *Patrick Henry*, this word is "without."
[5] Henry had invested in the Virginia Yazoo Company.

Elias Boudinot to Charles Pettit

Since writing the above, we have spent part of another day on a desultory argumt. on the same Subject—but I think if any Thing the Subject is rather more in the dark & uncertain as to the Event.

There are more real Objectives at bottom & behind the Curtain agt. the Funding at all, then I could have ever supposed, tho' the detail is made the ostensible Reasons—The whole Business goes on very heavily and I am not certain of the Event.

It is remarkable, that every Member of the Union (except N. Carolina) is on the floor of Congress, so that it will have a full Consideration.

FC:dft, AMs 779/1, PPRF. The first part of this letter was written on 8 March and is printed under that date, above.

Jabez Bowen to John Adams

Your favour of the 27th. ulto. came safe to hand yesterday.

I attended the Convention last week and after choosing a President &c. we heard the Constitution Read by paragraps with the objections which were verry few and of no great importance, and were fully answered a Committe was then appointed to draw a Bill of Rights with such Amendments as they Thot necessary which they Reported and after the necessary discussion they were Received. A Motion was then made to Adjourn, which was carrid by a Majority of Nine. The Bill of Rights with the amendments were ordered to be Printed and sent out to the people to be considerd of by them at the Anual Town Meetings to be held on the third Monday of April and the Convention Adjorned to the Twenty fourth day of May.

We are not much disappointed in the event but much Mortify'd; more especially as we cannot see any end to our sufferings, if good arose to the Ud. States from our opposition to the five per Cent Impost.[1] I fancy your Excellency will be obliged to Rack your Invention to point out the advantages that can possibly arise to the United or to this particular State from our late determination.

We had five old Tories in the Convention who would keep a Day of Thanksgiving on hearing that the Federal Government was dissolved, and some of the principle officers carred away prisoners to Babilon[2] alias G[reat]. B[ritain]. we had many of Desperate Circumstances and the principle heads of the Papermoney faction, all ad[ded] their strength together made the Collam to firm [cut out] broken and these same people never will come so long as they can possibly keep a Majority [cut out] the convention We are almost discouraged from makeing further Exertions. our best Citizens are looking out to dispose of their property and to Remove out of the Government. the Restrictions on Trade will fall intirely on our Friends at which the oposers of the Fedl. Government will be well pleased so that on the whole we begin to turn our Eyes back on the Country that we left and must all turn Tories, for any thing I can see.

Be so kind Sir as to let the President know how our Convention has ended and that the Friends of the Federal goverment are in desponding Circumstances, at present.

We would willingly Receve the necessary Officers for Collecting the Impost; if Congress would Order them to be appointed.

P. S. as the Freemen at large are to take up the Amendments on the 17th of

April I cannot help reminding you that it will be a good oppertunity for an Remonstrance or Adress from Congress to the People, stateing the Reasons for their Adopting & the probable Consequences of their Rejection.

ALS, Adams Family Manuscript Trust, MHi. Written from Providence, Rhode Island; answered 20 March.

---

[1] Rhode Island refused to ratify the 1781 Amendment to the Articles of Confederation that gave Congress the power to impose a five percent tariff. The state ratified a similar 1783 Amendment but only if Congress (and all the states) agreed to changes in it, primarily for the benefit of Rhode Island.

[2] An allusion to the ancient Israelites exiled during the "Babylonian Captivity" in the sixth century B.C.

John Pemberton to James Pemberton

It was after 3. oClock this evening before thy Acceptable letter of 7th. Inst. came to hand. As I sent ℔ H[enry]. Vanderwerf a Copy of the Report presented by the Comittee On the subject of our adress. I expect thou may see it this eveng. I agree with thee that any Regulation is like a Compromise & what I object to notwithstanding I sent for a copy of the regulation respecting German passengers thinking if Nothing more could be obtained this would Amount to a prohibition. smith from S.C. yesterday adverted to this & reprobated the Idea.

The meetg. for Suffs.[1] was held here this day & was a solid meeting & frds. were stirred up to Unite with us from Pensylvania & An adition made to the former appointment If this business is Attended to as it ought to be it does not appear likely frds. will be released for weeks to Come. for the Opposition will Contrive all ways to make delay to wear out our Patience M. F.[2] might have shewn thee the heads of the Report. & there is little Variation from it.

I find the dear Women have a prospect opened to them Respecting leaveing the City, I doubt not their being directed aright they would be welcome to our Grey horses but I think less horses would suit better & be more likely to be Accomodated in their journey. I wish to be at home to Assist them & my dear Wife [Hannah Zane Pemberton] for whom I have much sympathy & that increased By Receipt of her letter this evening. My dr. love to her & the dr. frds.

Burke yesterday after having reprobated the Report & saying he had wrote his Constituents that the Congress would take No Notice of it Confessed he was himself against slavery but spoke the sentiments of those who appointed him. & indeed all the opposers made poorly out. Abuse & Malevolence was most of their Speeches. besides those presentd in my last. Page & Madison from Virga. spoke well on our Cause.

ALS, Pennsylvania Abolition Society Papers, PHi. Addressed to Second Street, Philadelphia; carried by John Davis. For background on this petition attempt and related documents referred to below, see *DHFFC* 8:314–38.

[1] The Quaker "meeting for sufferings."

[2] Miers Fisher, an active behind the scenes antislavery advocate, who frequently visited the seat of government on other legal business related to his Philadelphia clientele, seems to be credited here with circulating John Pemberton's outline of the select committee's draft report, printed in *DHFFC* 8:333–34.

Richard Peters to Thomas Fitzsimons

I saw a Letter of yours to [*William*] Lewis & am obliged by your desiring him to communicate it. I was at a Loss to determine on several matters we had before us at the Time I wrote to Mr. [*Peter*] Muhlenburg & wished for Information which on some Points I have since obtained. It is now generally agreed that the old Plan of choosing [*federal*] Representatives shall be again adopted & of Course the Law must again be temporary. If a permanent Law was to be enacted we should adopt some Mode of making Nominations to save the Trouble and Expense [*of*] Conference, & if it could be done now it would be better; but I see not that it can as the Terms will not admit of it. I wished to know how the Connecticut Plan[1] or any other on this Head was approved of & should have wrote to some of my Eastern Friends but that I feared we could not do anything of the Sort as the Nominations are made for a succeeding choice at a precedent Election. If you know of anything that will make our Bill better inform me of it.

As to your Plans of Finance the Opinions here are as various as at New York. The Assumption of the State Debts is pleasing to many but its Antagonists are not a few. A direct continental Land Tax is supposed to be the consequence & tho' I see not that this would be wrong our People are sick of Land Taxes. We shall have nothing else however to carry on our State Government for it seems all our Sources in another way are or will be seized on by federal Financiers. We are turning our attention to a [*state*] Tax *** You are my Oracle on fiscal Subjects—communicate some of your Thoughts about the Plan we ought to persue. I often miss you but never more than on this Subject in which we are most distressingly wanting in our House. I wish I could say however this was the only Deficiency.

The subject of Roads & Navigation I have pushed these two Years & I think now it has laid deep Hold of our House who had never before a just Idea either of its Practicability or Consequence. The Explanations we had made last year have opened Peoples Eyes & we are now about persuing them so as to complete every species of Information. One Point I thought would have been ascertained by actual Surveys & Documents was that which has Reference to

the federal Seat, to wit, that the great Route from the western world must be thro' Pennsilvania where it can be carried thro' better Waters & a shorter Distance. Much has been done towards establishing Proofs of it & a short Time will put it beyond a Doubt. Now I am on this Subject I recollect a Passage in your letter which alludes to Jealousies respecting the Eastern Members of our State [*congressional delegation*]. I am convinced the Noise made about this flowed more from Artifice than Conviction. The Persons who brought it forward wished to hang Terrors round the Minds of the Delegates from this Quarter which might induce them in case the Point came up again, under a false Delicacy, to abandon the Idea of Residence in the Eastern Part of the State. Who does not wish that it should be somewhere in Pennsilvania at all Events? & on this Account local Objects should be sacrificed. But are we on the Eastern Border to be blamed for Endeavors to have it near us more than the western Gentlemen who wish it fixed so as to accommodate themselves?[2]
***

I agree in your Ideas that mutual Communications will be useful & I heartily concur in the Plan. But do not think I expect you will take up Time much engaged unless it be absolutely necessary. Therefore whatever you may think of my Jealousy on this Head it only amounted to a Distinction between hearing from you *sometimes & not at all*. Among Lovers moderate Jealousy—not that of Othello[3]—is a Proof of Love. Why should it not also evidence Friendship?

[*P. S.*] *** You know better than I do the necessity of taking care of the Police of our Port. We cannot pay our Health Officers, Wardens, &c. It would be wise in Congress when they take away Revenue to attend to the Offices necessarily supported by it. This would make the States easier under the Deprivation.

PMHB 8:108–10. Written from Philadelphia. The omitted text relates to state revenue, the Wyoming Valley controversy, John Nicholson's affairs, and, in the postscript, a request for testimonials about the effect of vendue laws in New York.

[1] Connecticut's first federal election for Representatives proceeded upon a two tiered popular process in use since the Confederation period. Voters in each town selected twelve nominees in a preliminary election. The twelve statewide front runners were then listed, in order of votes received, on a ticket from which voters selected the five winners in the second stage of the election. Pennsylvania's first federal election act, on the other hand, provided for a single state wide election, and was passed over the opposition of the assemblymen from the western counties, the "Constitutionalist" (pro-state constitution and generally antifederalist) minority.

[2] Peters is referring to the outrage expressed by residents of western Pennsylvania after a majority of the delegation, led by Morris, worked against placing the seat of federal government on the Susquehanna River in September 1789; see Peters to William Lewis, 4 October 1789, *DHFFC* 17:1669.

[3] Shakespeare's Othello murdered his wife Desdemona out of jealousy.

Letter from Boston

It is the duty of those persons who deprecate a consolidation, or general governmental assumption of our state debt, now to come forward and exert themselves to obtain a tax, which will be competent to the end proposed. However, it may appear to some, a consolidation is destructive of us as a free people, and the moment it is adopted, the liberties of our country fall a sacrifice. By paying our own state debt we shall baffle the designs of those men who are wishing to bring about this consolidation, as they know that while the several states maintain their own credit, the people will confide in them, and will be ever anxious to support them.

NYDA, 15 March.

Other Documents

John Barry to Seth Harding. ALS, Barry-Hayes Collection, Independence Seaport Museum, Philadelphia. Written from "Strawberry Hill," Fairmont Park, Philadelphia; place to which addressed not indicated. For background on the petition effort mentioned, see *DHFFC* 7:438–43.
    Is encouraged by the prospects of their petition effort; encloses affidavit of Harding's service.

Edward Fox to Andrew Craigie. ALS, Craigie Papers, MWA. Written from Philadelphia; postmarked.
    "Our Comptroller [*John Nicholson*] is among the strangest characters you ever knew—he has drawn Madison into a correspondence: But I suppose Madison's whole view must be to obtain some information as to our public accounts and funds. Nicholson's wishes are very like to those brought forward by Madison, but not quite so honest. He is for paying original holders now—purchasers when *we can better afford it*, and in the mean Time let them purchase Lands."

Thomas Hartley to Jasper Yeates. ALS, Yeates Papers, PHi. Addressed to Lancaster, Pennsylvania; franked.
    Requires $500 "in order to observe a punctuality in some of my affairs"; directions for procuring the money; finds that his congressional pay will nearly pay the expenses for himself and family, without being "extravagant"; "as I have few Friends in Human Life," entrusts the task to no one else; the question of assumption is expected to be decided that day.

Thomas Hartley to Jasper Yeates. ALS, Yeates Papers, PHi. Addressed to Lancaster, Pennsylvania. Written at 2 P.M.; franked; postmarked.

"The Assumption of the State Debts has just now been agreed to by 31 to 26. and we are now proceeding with the other Resolutions—I am Sir in Haste."

Jeremiah Hill to George Thatcher. ALS, Chamberlain Collection, MB. Written from Biddeford, Maine; postmarked Portsmouth, New Hampshire, 12 March.

If the clergy aimed less "at alluring the Passions rather than touching the Senses of rational Creatures," thinks they would soon see "the Great advantages that would [*lined out*] result from the Establishment of public Teachers of Piety, Religion, & Morality"; "give my kind Love to our Brother Wingate, chear his Heart, strengthen his hands, & encourage his ~~Heart~~ Soul."

Andrew Moore to Robert Gamble. See 7 March, above.

Louis Guillaume Otto to Comte de Montmorin. Copy, in French, Henry Adams Transcripts, DLC. Received 2 July. Otto's letters included in *DHFFC* were usually written over the course of days, and even weeks, following the day they were begun. For background on the petition of Pennsylvania's Richard Wells and Josiah Hart, presented in the House on 1 March 1790, see *DHFFC* 8:264–68; for Leray de Chaumont's mission in America, see Benjamin Franklin to Chaumont, 31 October 1789.

Attending the debates, has noticed that some influential members may not be opposed to the claims that French merchants have made, so far ineffectively, to be redeemed for the paper money that they have left on deposit with the consulates; has been at the point of confirming their thinking in this regard, but has been prevented by numerous considerations; because the value of the deposits can only be determined by the date, which in consequence of the bad faith of the agents was often made after their receipt, their devaluation would be great and prejudicial to French merchants; although any reimbursement would be better than the worthless paper money, wonders whether Congress might not ultimately redeem its paper money, and whether the example of the Pennsylvanians' petition on the subject might not be followed by other states; the question has generally been covered with difficulties, and even supposing the effectiveness of a direct appeal to Congress, one risks hurting the French merchants more than helping them; suggests entrusting the French creditors' interests to a special agent; mentions Jacques-Donatien Leray de Chaumont (fils), who has already been invested with a commission of this type, and is on the verge of returning to France; if Otto is given instructions in this regard, hopes he will be left some latitude to act according to circumstances, "which, in a country like this, are subject to infinite variations."

William Smith (Md.) to Otho H. Williams. ALS, Williams Papers, MdHi. Addressed to Baltimore; franked; postmarked.
> "The question was Just now decided in a Committee of the whole house 'Shall the U.S. assume the debts of the individual states.' Thirty one for the proposition, Twenty Six against it. we have now proceeded to the Ratio of Interest, where we may probably Stop a day or Two."

George Thatcher to David Sewall. No copy known; acknowledged in D. Sewall to Thatcher, 20 March.

George Washington, Diary. Washington Papers, MiD-B.
> "Many members of Congress" attended the President's levee.

Letter from New York. *FG*, 11 March; reprinted at Carlisle and Philadelphia, Pennsylvania.
> Question on assumption passed 31 to 26, about 1 P.M.

Letter from Philadelphia. *NYDA*, 13 March.
> The increasing scarcity and cost of firewood "indicates the absolute necessity of attending in future to the coal mines of this country"; "Besides the saving of our timber for more valuable uses," jobs would be created "and the price of wood kept within bounds"; "the coal mines on the James River [*Virginia*] are inexhaustible and we have undoubtedly others nearer home, which might be broke up at a triffling expence."

WEDNESDAY, 10 MARCH 1790

Cold (Johnson)

Abraham Baldwin to Joel Barlow

Your long and friendly letter of the 30th novr. was received a few days ago; the packet sailed before I knew it. [*Royal*] Flynt tells me he wrote you fully, which is better than I could have done, for our politicks have confined me so much for several weeks, that I have scarcely known what any body else was saying or doing. De summa re,[1] your observations are good, and as usual judicious. Praum[2] swears he will do all in his power to give them ample scope. If you have recieved the report of the secretary [*Hamilton*] which I sent you some time since, you must see that it will be a favorite measure to do as much as possible for the disposal of lands, and that the price is to be 20 cents. It is now referred to the secretary to report a uniform mode for the disposal of the lands in the western territory, as soon as that is done I will avail myself of the first opportunity to see what can be done de summa re. there was an application made to the old cong. by George Morgan for about 2 million acres on the Missisippi directly opposite the mouth of the Missouri,[3] the French settlers at Kaskaskias [*Illinois*] are on that tract they were to be quieted by a survey of 200 acres to each, which woud take but a small part, and leave the rest to the company. This location was considered as among the best, there are very few indians upon it, and a settlement might be carried on immediately. all the preliminaries to this business were adjusted, and just as he was on the point of closing, the offers for a settlement on the other side of the Missisippi beguiled him off,[4] and the Kaskaskia tract is now open. This joins the Wabash tract, and doubtless both might be taken if it was thought proper, I have conversed with him generally on the subject of your letter, he said there were no associates, but that he had determined to send Bang Slabang[5] to join you on that business, and that he was now making out the papers. He had empowered [*Brissot de*] Warville, but he believed he had done nothing. He has not come to any explanation on the subject, but has sent for the extracts from your letter, containing the necessary directions &c.

[*Nathaniel*] Gorham has given up his Genesee contracts and taken only one third upon different terms. There is no doubt but the two thirds may be got on very reasonable terms of the state [*Massachusetts*]. The Connecticut lands you know might be got on very easy terms. I mention these only to impress upon your mind an idea which you do not seem to have, that Flynt's contract,[6] or any body's else is nothing, for a better contract can be made now than ever was made before. I will try it the moment the plan is agreed upon, and send you the necessary documents without delay, whether he chooses to join or not. you may then sell for Praum or any body else that offers, as you think best There should be a petition to Cong. immediately, but I believe it will go faster in the present train.

So much on the subject in general, but to follow your good example and come to one proposition, the tract I expect to send you titles for is the George Morgan tract of two millions. if Royal chooses to join the Wabash tract and will get titles for it well and good, if not I will let him alone. Nothing shall defeat this but the secretary's reporting an impracticable forbidding plan, which I cannot think he will be stupid enough to do. You readily see that to attempt to petition and contract with Cong. when they have no plan yet digested would only occasion jealousies and probably longer delays than the other mode, I trust it will not be long before the secy. reports, and probably the result of it will be that the business will be put into his hands to contract for the sale of them at 20 or 25 cents. I told you in my last the state of the naturalization bill, in Praum's house the clause prohibiting aliens to hold real estate &c. was struck out altogether, and the subject left precisely as it was before, no bar to any body's holding western territory. But on their coming to settle on their lands, though the title to their lands would be good, they would have to apply for admission to citizenship. this would be very easy, one short bill would carry through a whole raft of them. what alterations it will undergo in the other house is uncertain, I am informed their plan is to make the business progressive, that in so many months they shall be citizens so far as to be able to hold lands; in so many more they shall be able to vote, and in such a time, say two years, enjoy all the rights of citizenship. many of us were [*of*] opinion that it was undoubtedly our policy to break down all bars to aliens holding landed estate, but our power is only to pass a uniform rule of naturalization but not to legislate about aliens holding lands. It is doubtful what form it will finally take, I will inclose it as soon as it is finished. what more have I to say to you de summa re? you see my expectation rather is, that Royal will say nothing more about it, but pursue his own measures. if so I shall make use of some other name for the other tract and send it to you as soon as possible, but if he should bring forward his sooner and in better shape, you will surely make the most of it you can for yourself.

The Reb [*Dudley Baldwin*] writes me this week that the girl [*Ruth Barlow*] never was fatter & happier in her life, and that women never feel better than when their husbands are away. we have had the question of assuming state debts today 31 for 26 against. finals with two years interest upon them sell now at 7/6 facilities or indents of interest from 5/6 to 6/. wheat is about 11/ in Philadelphia, superfine flour 55/ a barrel. it is rather falling, probably wheat will be as low as 9/. If I could think of any thing else you wished to know I would tell you, when I have more leisure I will think better. Adieu.

AL, Baldwin Family Collection, CtY. Addressed to the care of Henry Broomfield, 1 Size Lane, London; received 1 May.

---

[1] Concerning the most important thing.

[2] A family nickname for Baldwin.

[3] On 28 August 1788 the Confederation Congress authorized its board of treasury to proceed with a contract with George Morgan and Associates for the purchase of federal lands, some of which had been settled prior to 1783 by foreigners who now professed themselves to be citizens of the United States (*JCC* 34:467–68). See the Northwest Territory Act [S-17], *DHFFC* 6:1563–1607. Morgan had long been interested in the area. In 1766 he built and supplied stores at Kaskaskia, Cahokia, and Fort Chartres on the Mississippi River in the Illinois Country. That enterprise had failed by 1768.

⁴Morgan's colonization scheme, under the patronage of Spanish Louisiana, at New Madrid, Missouri. See *DHFFC* 15:134–36.

⁵A nickname for some unknown person.

⁶In 1789 the Scioto Associates—among whom Flint, like Barlow, was a shareholder—purchased a large number of delinquent shares in the Associates' parent Ohio Company, whose contract with the government required payment of one dollar an acre. One month after this letter, Flint formally became one of three trustees for the execution of the Scioto contract (Shaw Livermore, *Early American Land Companies* [New York, 1939; reprinted 1968], pp. 140–41).

Benjamin Goodhue to Michael Hodge

Yesterday in a Committee of the whole House the question of the Assumption obtain'd by 31 to 26 so that including the Chairman, there were 32 out of 58 members pre[se]nt, in favr. of the question, this bussines has yet various stages to pass through and the opposers will doubtless take every oppy. that may present for defeating the measure, and propably they may calculate upon additional strength by the arrival of the North Carolina members who are soon expected, so that altho' the question has thus obtain'd in the first instance, it is by no means put beyond hazzard as to its final issue—We are now upon the subsequent resolutions relative to the terms proposed for reloaning, and I am of opinion those reported by the Secry. may probably in substance, be agreed to.

[P. S.] A Mr. [*Josiah*] Little of Newbury [*Massachusetts*] who was concern'd in the [*Continental Army's*] Commissary department, desired, I would inform if any board was instituted to settle such accounts, I wish you to inform him the Treasury board have cognizance thereof.

ALS, Ebenezer Stone Papers, MSaE. Place to which addressed not indicated.

Archibald Maclaine to James Iredell

***

While I rejoice upon the public account as well as yours, I must lament that the duty of your office is so severe—I am persuaded that the present court system cannot last, without amendment; and so I have wrote our friend Johnston about two days ago. From your situation, you will of course ride the Southern district with Mr. [*John*] Routledge, and to ride through the three Southern states twice a year, and return home, would be enough in all conscience, without attending twice a year at the seat of government. I do not believe any [*a*]lteration will take place [*this*] Session; but I think the view to acco[*torn*] liti[*torn*] must in this instance give place to several additional [*torn*].

If our representatives would go on and do [th]eir duty (I hear nothing of Bloodworth yet) I should have hopes that courts would be established here, so that N. Carolina would begin the circuit—Should the first be held in Newbern perhaps this might not be much out of your way; but as the first in S. Carolina will be at Columbia, our first court will probably be at a distance from the sea coast; & I flatter myself (pardon the presumption) that Fayetteville will be the place. It will be impossible however, as the courts in S. Carolina and Georgia are directed to be held at particular times, so to fix ours to correspond with them, and not at the same time to interfere with the Superior courts of the State. When your Honors are met, and the lawyers upon the State circuit, you will have none to apply for admission to practice, except perhaps some county court attornies I should have told you that I do not know the road to Columbia, but I will inquire and inform you.

***

ALS, Charles E. Johnson Collection, Nc-Ar. Written from Wilmington, North Carolina; addressed to Edenton, North Carolina; docketed "Ansd." The editors believe that the suggestions in this letter could reflect those in a no longer extant letter to Johnston. The omitted text congratulates Iredell on his appointment, made by the President "spontaneously" without "the agency" of Johnston.

Edmund Randolph to James Madison

***

Yesterday I saw Colo. [*James*] Innes. He informs us, that the discrimination proposed by you is not more palatable in Richmond, than in the other towns. Some of the leading antifederal Names in amherst (C-b-ll) and another of the same stamp in Culpeper (Str-th-r)[1] are endeavouring to turn *the* motion against its author. But the temper of Va. is not yet known, and Mr. Francis Corbin, who left us this morning, is of opinion, that the bulk of the country will testify their approbation thro' the conduct of the next assembly. I am irritated, when I hear the various insinuations, which the advocates for the plan are exposed to. But the purity of motive ~~must make~~ will prove a sufficient shield against calumny.

There is not an individual, whom I have seen, friendly to the assumption of the state debts.

I am interrupted by company.

LS, Madison Papers, DLC. Written from Williamsburg, Virginia. For the full text, see *PJM* 13:96–97. The omitted text relates to personal and family health.

[1] William Cabell, Sr. (1730–98) and French Strother (1733–1800).

Benjamin Rush to James Madison

I once knew a Swedish Clergyman in this city, who told me that when he preached in the Country, he always studied his Congregation *first*, and *Afterwards* his sermon. Something like this Should ~~always~~ be done by legislators. They should perfectly understand the character of the people whom they represent, and Afterwards suit their laws to their habits and principles. I suspect the present Congress have neglected this ~~business~~ important part of their duty. They appear as if they were legislating for British subjects, and for a ~~great~~ nation whose whole business was to be, WAR—hence the Sacrifices that are called for of justice—gratitude—and national interest to public credit. After all the encomiums upon it—what is it? An Ability to borrow money. But for what? why only for the purpose of carrying on unjust and offensive wars—for where wars are just & necessary—Supplies may always be obtained by annual taxes ~~sufficient to~~ from a free people. Loans (says Genl. Chatteleaux in his treatise upon national felicity[1]) were introduced into Europe only to enable ~~the~~ ambitious kings [*lined out*] to carry on wars without the Consent of their subjects. But in a republic, where wars must always be wars of the *whole* people, loans ~~may always~~ will be ~~for~~ rendered unnecessary by taxes equal to the exigencies of the state. Under all the disadvantages of a weak Confederation, and corrupted state Governments the United States during the late war ~~really~~ nearly at one time realized this Attribute of a republican Government. Under a Constitution like the present, I am sure the most expensive war might be carried on by annual Contributions provided it met with the Consent of a great majority of the people.

The provision which our Congress is making for future Wars by Acts of Supererogation, reminds me of the Conduct of the Earl of Warrington[2] who in the marriage Settlement of his daughter stipulated for ~~an Amount~~ a pension of £500 a year for her in case she should commit Adultery, & be divorced for it from her husband. Our distance from Europe ~~will~~ is a Security against four out of five of the chances & causes of War. Besides peace is the business and interest of republics. Why then provide for war, at the annual ~~expense~~ waste of four millions of dollars a year? especially when this Sum will cut the Sinews of our Country, and thereby render ~~a~~ a just war impracticable.

The people of Pennsylvania have caught the alarm. It has been proposed out of doors by some members of our Assembly to instruct their Senators to vote against the Secretary's report. 99 out [*of*] an 100 of our Country Citizens I am well informed are opposed to it, & if it ~~is~~ be adopted a change of every member from Pennsylvania who votes for it will take place at the next election. As you failed of doing justice to the Army & original Creditors, what do you think of saving the Sum due to them to the United States by proposing 3 ℥ Cent upon the whole debt? Very few certificates are in the hands of original holders, and of those who hold them, most of them lent their money at A time when it was received by them in a depre[c]iated state equal to 100 ꝑ cent. Those who hold certificates for Services or produce were paid at a time when Specie was depreciated above 200 ꝑ cent—of Course their Certificates were conformed to that low Value of money. Unless the public mind is quieted by discrimination, or an interest of 3 ꝑ cent, a total change of the representation in Congress will I suspect take place thro'out the Union. Happy will it be for Us if a contrary measure does not end in a dissolution of our goverment. To inculcate these sentiments I know is considered as "Devilish peoplish" in New York—But—the people must & will be obeyed in this business.

Let us not overvalue public credit. It is to nations, what private Credit, & loan offices are to individuals. It begets debt—extravagance—vice—& bankruptcy. But further—if we mean to negociate loans with Success hereafter, let us not exhaust all the taxable resources of our Country. we shall borrow twice as easily if we pay 3, as if we pay 6 ꝑ cent upon our present debt, for the lenders of money [*lined out*] depend more upon the Ability, than upon ~~the~~ the integrity of all Countries to pay debts, & this Ability will be doubled by paying only 3 ꝑ cent.

I sicken every time I contemplate the European Vices that the Secretary's gambling report will necessarily introduce into our infant republic.

In five years, the whole debt if funded at four or even five ꝑ cent will probably center in London, or Amsterdam. what difference will it make to ~~an~~ the American farmers whether 4 millions of their dollars are sent out of the Country every year to support the dignity of the British parliamt., or the public Credit of the United States? The wars of the Crusades in my Opinion do not place the human Understanding in a more Absurd point of light, than the present Opinions of your house on the Subject of public Credit.

ALS, Madison Papers, DLC. Written from Philadelphia.

[1] François Jean, marquis de Chastellux (1734–88) was a French philosophe whose popu larity in America derived from his travel writings while serving here with the French army from 1779 to 1782. The English version of his *Essay on Public Happiness* was published in London in 1774.

[2] Henry Booth, earl of Warrington (1652–94), chancellor of the exchequer under William III.

John Tracy to John Langdon

Your civilities and attention to me, and your offers of services to me when you last passed through this Town emboldens me to write you on a subject truly interesting to my Family—I need not picture to you my Situation before the Revolution and my present very distressed circumstances, neither, need I introduce my Character to you—all of which I flatter myself you are perfectly acquainted with—I have a handsome real Estate will'd to my Children by my Father. but no personal property to support it. it is scarcely sufficient to defray the Taxes. the distresses of my Family at times almost discourage me; can I look to the Fathers of my Country for employ—The Sacrifices I made in supporting the late Revolution encourages me. to effect which I beg your Influence—my wishes are that my very worthy Friend Major [*Michael*] Hodge the present Surveyor of this Port may be promoted to the office of Excise Master for this district—the county of Essex being divided into two districts—and that I may succeed Major Hodge in his office—I flatter myself that my Industry and attention to the Revenue will give Satisfaction on and risque my Honor and Reputation that there is no man in the County better calculated for an Excise Officer than the Gentleman proposed—I have wrote more fully to my Friend Mr. Dalton at different Times to which I refer you. I would thank you if you would present my most respectfull compliments to your Honble. Colleague and to the Honble. Mr. Livermore and Mr. Gilman I should esteem as a very great favour if they would interest themselves in my behalf I should write them, but my present acquaintance with them is such that I cannot take the Liberty.

ALS, Langdon Papers, NhPoA. Written from Newburyport, Massachusetts.

Jonathan Trumbull to Theodore Woodbridge

I have received your favr. of the 1st. Instant—The Proposition of Mr. Madison on Discrimination has received a very lengthy candid & dispassionate Discussion—on all its merits—& has been decided against its admission—on principles which you will see by attendg. to the Debates, which are publisg. in all the newspapers—The Merits of the sufferers are universally admitted on all Hands—but it was thot. Justice & retribution could not be obtained in that Way—The Decision was made by a very large Majority—more than ⅔ds of the Members voting again[s]t the Question—Con[s]idring this great Majority & the principles which actuated it—I hope the public Mind will be quieted on the subject—& that the immediate Sufferers will con[s]ider the Sacrifice as one part of the pri[c]e of those Blessings which we have in p[r]ospect.

ALS, Woodbridge Papers, CtHi. Addressed to Glastonbury, Connecticut, via Hartford; franked; postmarked.

Henry Van Schaak to Theodore Sedgwick

Your favor of the 21 of Feby. and the Militia plan reached me only last Evening. I have read the Report, but by no means with the satisfaction that I expected I should. Is it possible that an american of so much experience as the Secy. [*Knox*] has should so far mistake this business? Surely he ought to have known the genius and temper of his countrymen better than to bring forward to an enligh[*te*]ned people a System whereby they are liable to serve for a length of time in the Militia before they are entitled to the rights of Citizenship in the country of their nativity and after all this to be liable to be draughted to serve 3 years as Soldiers in a Southern climate—~~Surely~~ this never will go down in the Eastern States whatever effect it may have in other parts of the union—I am the more hurt at this business on account of the implied approbation of the President—I dread every appearence that may lessen his popularity—If he has Enemies in this part of the Union and they make proper use of the Report I am persuaded many people will not think so highly of him as they now deservedly do. I cod. wish that it never might be warmly discussed in ~~the~~ [*lined out*] Congress but die as easy a Death as possible. The Sexion business in the Secy. at Wars ~~business~~ report will revive the idea of classing[1]—This is a sore that will admit of little rubbing before it bleeds afresh—People have too lately immerged out of the difficulties ~~of~~ which classing has brought upon them to be volunteers for a perpetuity ~~in the a~~ which ~~place~~ the present plan holds out. It will not do for an Eastern Member to support it depend on it.

I was told a day or two ago by a Gentleman that Colo. William Lyman said in Compy. at Boston that you had expressed yourself last Spring at Springfield that you felt yourself less responsible to the people in your present situation than you did when you belonged to our State Legislature. This surely cannot be true.

I have seen papers as late as the 4th March by wh. I find that the assumption of the State debts goes on slowly—The 4 ℀ Ct. Interest will also undergo a Severe discussion. [*illegible*]

In haste.

ALS, Sedgwick Papers, MHi. Written from Pittsfield, Massachusetts.

---

[1] Under Knox's militia plan, submitted to Congress on 21 January, all the companies in his proposed advanced corps and main corps (comprising all men between eighteen and forty-five) would be divided into sections of twelve men each. When the militia was to be called up, the assigned troop quota would be filled by a given number of men per section. In the failure of any volunteers to come forward from their respective section, (or "association of sections" if the quota demanded fewer than one man per section), sections could either recruit from one another's surplus of volunteers or "detach" the required number by an

"indiscriminate draught." In either case, the furnished quota was to be paid for by the remaining members of their respective sections (*DHFFC* 5:1441–42). For this system's resemblance to the "classing" practiced during the Revolutionary War, see Jeremiah Hill to Thatcher, 6 March, n. 1, above.

Virginia to New-England, New-York, Pennsylvania, and Carolina

Dear Sisters,

I have seen your familiar epistle,[1] and really thought it must be the production of some enemy to the whole family. Under these impressions, I expected to see you all in an uproar calling on the printer for the author. I conceived that your own credit, as well as the reputation of the family, required it; but by your silence you have convinced me that it is your own. Ah sisters! however treacherous your memories are, the world recollects when your cries of murder, rape, starve, reverberated from pole to pole[2]—and it is with a bleeding heart I recollect what numbers of my sons fell in your defence. What can my dear sisters mean? why am I twited in the teeth with many of my farms being untenanted—that I boast of the largeness of my purse—and such envious, malicious raving, as sheweth what termagants my sisters are. I can tell them, that so many of my farms would not have been untenanted, if great numbers of my sons had not fell in their defence. And as for my being in debt, it is a proof that I have had credit—little thanks are due to those who never had credit that they owe nothing. But I suppose my sisters think they have cured all, by their great condescension in allowing some merit to my son George [*Washington*]. To be sure they shall have credit for that, but I can tell them that my sons Dickey [*R. H. Lee*], Bill [*Grayson*] and James [*Madison*], too, are not to be browbeaten or frightened by any of their blustering boys. I once thought that some of you, my dear sisters, were very religious; but methinks you seem disposed to convince the world that it is otherwise. Your levity, your wit and freedom with omnipotence, is big with impiety. It is blasphemous, and would have exposed strict civilized heathens to capital punishment. What do my sisters want? they have shared my bread with me when they were in want. I have given up a most important and valuable part of my farm for the benefit of the whole family.[3] Has any of my sons begged favours and courted exalted places and high employment? Where is it that the aching heart is throbbing for sounding titles? and where does the sentiment of well born originate? Where is the thirst for the distinction of birth and blood, which has made tyrants of a few, while the multitude drag ignominious chains? Look at home, my dear sisters, before you upbraid me. You may, if you please, make a comparison between the best of your sons and mine during the conflict when all our farms[4] were proscribed. And you may, if you please, add to my disgrace, by publishing a true state of the expenditure from each of our purses to pay the public debt, and to support the copartnery—this, as things are now organized, is easily done, and this will fairly shew whether a local, partial, and parsimonious spirit did not govern in the clamour upon the proposed tax upon m*****s [*molasses*].

Ah, sisters! my sons are in a great measure proscribed from a right to take any of the lands which I threw into the common stock.[5] You will retort that my sons will not come because they must not bring their negroes. Ay sisters! this is against the copartnery—the interest of the company requires that the land should be free at least to all the parties—but while my sons are kept from the market, your sons may perhaps purchase cheaper, and you have the choice of land more in your power. What allow the iniquitous, the abominable slave trade to be carried on under the law of the land in some places, and proscribe others from a right to bring their property with them, when perhaps the intention and design that many wou'd have in going there, would be to enable them to emancipate their poor slaves with propriety. So it is urged, that a poor ignorant slave, who has not learned to provide for himself, and is totally ignorant of the arts which a designing world will impose upon him, is in a better condition under the care of a good master than he is like to be in on his own account.

[Richmond] *Virginia Independent Chronicle*, 10 March; reprinted at Boston; Hartford and Litchfield, Connecticut; New York City (*GUS*, 27 March); Baltimore; Fredericksburg, Virginia; and Edenton, North Carolina.

---

[1] Printed under 14 January, above. For a similar reply, see V. to N.E. N.Y. P. and C., 5 June, volume 19.

[2] A reference to New England's call for assistance in the days after the battles of Lexington and Concord, perhaps the most celebrated response to which was the rapid deployment of Daniel Morgan's troop of Virginia riflemen in June 1775.

[3] In January 1781 Virginia offered to cede to the Confederation Congress all its holdings (by royal charter) north of the Ohio River. Congress accepted in September 1783, and in March 1784 what became the states of Ohio, Indiana, Illinois, Michigan, Wisconsin, and part of Minnesota was added to the public domain as the Northwest Territory.

[4] A Familiar Epistle had used "farm" as a metaphor for "state."

[5] The Ordinance of 1787, which established the jurisdiction and civil rights of the Northwest Territory (Virginia's western cession), contained a famous provision outlawing slavery in the Territory.

From New York

You will observe, by the papers, that the State Debts are to be assumed—31 to 26: Those who are in opposition to the measure, depend on defeating the vote of the Committee [*of the Whole*], when the members from N. Carolina arrive; whom they suppose will vote with *them*; but if they *all* should, it will make barely an equality—the Speaker's vote being reckoned above. The Chairman did not vote, and one Member was absent, I believe a *nay*.

The rate of interest was, in effect, determined to-day, by the adoption of the first alternative, viz.—To fund *two thirds* at 6 per cent. and receive Western Lands for the other third. The irredeemable principle in the second alternative, was contested, and the Committee finally rose without deciding upon it—Mr. AMES distinguished himself greatly on this proposition. I think the Secretary's whole plan will be adopted. The field that opens upon you, as its principles are unfolded, is boundless; and reason appears in her element in supporting his system.

[Boston] *Massachusetts Centinel*, 20 March; reprinted at Portland, Maine; Portsmouth, New Hampshire; Salem, Massachusetts; and Providence, Rhode Island.

Letter from a Boston Tobacconist

I thank you for the newspapers you sent by Mr. B—. I have looked over the Report of the Secretary of the Treasury, made the 4th instant, wherein he says, "that the funds requisite towards the payment of the interest on the debts of the individual states may be obtained from the articles of sugar, molasses, snuff, salt, &c. &c." This scheme of the Secretary's, has induced me to contract my plan of going largely into the manufacturing of tobacco and snuff, which I mentioned to you when I was last in your city. My reasons I trust, are such, as will vindicate me in your opinion from any charge of in-ability, when you have considered the matter properly, and weighed every circumstance as seriously as I have done. Of all the variety of duties proposed by the Secretary, none has appeared to me more exceptionable, than 10 cents per lb. upon snuff, and 6 cents per lb. upon tobacco, manufactured within the United States, and were it even practicable to raise the revenue he sup-poses from this article, still the attempt must be condemned as a measure tending to destroy the infant manufactures of the country; but how much more will it be reprobated by the southern planters, and by every member of Congress, when they shall be convinced that it is not only an imaginary scheme but a deceptious one. For, the instant a law passes to lay such an exorbitant duty on manufactured tobacco and snuff, that instant will the few persons already engaged in the business drop it, and turn their money into some other channel, for my own part I am resolved to drop it as soon as I hear the result of the deliberations of Congress on the subject, should those be in favor of the duty. Indeed, I have little doubt, should the Secretary's plan be adopted, that government will be involved in many inextricable difficulties, the manufactures will be destroyed and the supposed revenue may be looked for in the moon.

Some of my neighbors have observed, that had the Secretary proposed half a cent per lb. on snuff, and ten cents per gallon on molasses, he would have raised an host of enemies to the eastward and northward, which must have affected his interest with the majority in Congress, and you know our members have carried all before them since the establishment of the present constitution. It was therefore good policy of the Secretary not to provoke them by laying a higher duty on molasses, and with regard to the Southern members, as they are so much in the minority, he had the less to fear from their opposition; hence he has ventured to overload the staple commodity of Virginia and Maryland, &c.

I hope the Senate, however, will check this extravagant scheme of taxing our own manufactures, should it even pass through the House of Representatives.

You complain of our members "that they support the Secretary's systems, however absurd and impracticable." I am sorry to hear this, but I must beg leave to differ with you in some respects, for I know some members, who will not hesitate to reject every *deceptious proposition* that may be offered for their consideration, of which nature I consider that which has been the subject of this letter.

Respecting the advantages of a drawback, held out by the Secretary to manufacturers who export manufactured tobacco; he must first get laws enacted in Europe to permit our landing there; had he proposed a drawback upon printed callicoes exported to Manchester [*England*], it would not have appeared more extraordinary to me. I shall not trouble you further at present on this subject, but request you to inform me how the business goes on. I received a letter from our friend L——, of Philadelphia, who informs me that the manufacturers there entertain nearly the same opinions on this business that I have been just expressing to you.

NYDA, 26 March; reprinted at Richmond, Virginia.

Letter from Marietta, Ohio

The Indians have been very peaceble in this quarter since August last, no person has been molested within two hundred miles of this since that time—About 500 miles below, they are continually doing mischief, and in my opinion, nothing short of the sword will ever stop the infernal barbarity of the Shawanese and Wabash tribes. The winter has been very mild. Our surveyors have just returned from the extreme parts of the [*Ohio Company*] purchase, their accounts of the land are very favorable. We have had very little snow, not more than three inches at any one time. Our settlement has now become So strong that we are under no apprehension of being disturbed the ensuing season by the savages. We are making very large improvements, and expect to raise plentiful supplies of corn and other provisions for the next year. Settlers come on full as fast as is for the interest of the company, and if more had come on last fall we should have met with difficulty in the procuring provisions for them. So great has been the demand for corn, wheat, tobacco, butter pork, &c. to supply the Spaniards at New Orleans, that rich settlements in Westmoreland and Washington counties [*Pennsylvania*] are almost drained of provisions. These articles have risen 60 per cent, since last October: corn is now 3s. 6d. and flour 30s. per barrel.

NYDA, 8 May; reprinted at Exeter, New Hampshire; Newburyport and Pittsfield, Massachusetts; Providence, Rhode Island; York and Philadelphia, Pennsylvania; Baltimore; Alexandria, Virginia; and probably elsewhere.

Warner Mifflin to [*William Smith (S.C.)*]

RESPECTED FRIEND,

I Hope I may address thee thus, without offence. I cannot foresee how any can be given, when I feel as I do towards thee: in truth I feel respect for thee; then there is safety as to that; and why thou art not my friend, I cannot conceive. I love thee—I wish thee well—and would not injure thee knowingly more than I would myself; then why is it not proper to stile thee my friend? I think I ought not to have an enemy in the world. I never have been offended with thee—not even so much as ever to remember (that I can call to mind) when in thy company what thou hadst said about quakers. Then "the wounds of a friend are faithful—when the kisses of an enemy are deceitful."[1] I know I am thy friend. On this ground I hope thou wilt consider me, and not be angry with me.

I therefore having this hope, and feeling my mind engaged toward thee; think it right to open myself to thee in this manner, as it does not seem agreeable to thee to receive a visit from me; rather put it off to visit me at my quarters: but this has not been the case, though it would have been agreeable.

Thou mayest be doubtful that my coming will corrupt thy servants: this I would wish carefully to guard against, not to make them restless or dissatisfied in their condition. Though I am fully satisfied, many of that people have understanding sufficient to know it is unjust on every principle thus to treat their colour; yet I uniformly recommend to them wherever occasion occurs, to submit in patience to their situation, resigning their cause to God Almighty, that he may do with and for them, according to his will. On this principle I have prevailed on some to return to their masters, when I have seen them near an hundred miles off. They have returned with a letter from me, and I have received the thanks of their masters therefor. And as far as I know, this is the conduct of the quakers generally, to advise the negroes to remain quiet, be honest and faithful in their service.

I have had a prejudiced education in favour of negro holding, and was largely bound thereto by interest; and never would have given up mine, I believe, if I could have concieved I might have got to heaven, (as I believe there is such a place) and have kept them; but did believe, and yet do, that let me have done what I would otherways, the main avenues to that kingdom, would have been effectually shut against me; for with what reason could I have expected it, when continuing in the open violation of the law and commandment of the high God, viz. "Thou shalt love the Lord thy God, with all thy heart, soul, and strength, and thy neighbour as thyself."[2] This command I understand to include all the sons and daughters of men, of all nations, colours, and languages: and if I do manifestly act so differently from this of loving my neighbour as myself, that I should hold them as my property, and leave them as such to be divided among my children, as cattle and horses, endeared husbands and wives separated, mothers torn from their tender offspring, I believe my love to God, let me profess what I might, would be no more than the sounding brass, and tinkling cymbal.[3] Let me have offered thousands of lambs, or ten thousand rivers of oil, shall I give the very fruit of my body for the sin of my soul,[4] it would have been unavailing, while I was so very short in doing justly, loving mercy, and walking humbly before God, which is what I firmly believe he yet calls for, and what he shews unto the workmanship of his hands, and is what he expects, ere they shall be in favour with him. And therefore, being one who, having experienced the terrors of the Lord for this sin, and through his adorable mercy and goodness, been made partaker of a portion of his joy and peace for yielding obedience to the teachings of his divine grace, am willing in the ability afforded, to persuade my countrymen and fellow mortals, fully believing that light on this subject is come into the world, craving that they may not choose darkness, rather than light, by continuing in deeds of iniquity.

I hope thou wilt bear with me. I desire not to offend thee. Believe me to be thy friend: then I think thou wilt allow me the freedom taken. We both, I presume acknowledge the being of a God; that he is the Creator of all things; that he created man in the image of himself, and gave him dominion over all other creatures; that he created him for a purpose of his own glory; and from thence that we shall agree, that he is the great Father of the family of mankind. This, I take for granted, we shall agree in, as I hope we shall in the authenticity of the sacred writings of the scriptures: if so, then we may unite, that the great Father, as a safety to his children, has declared, "that at the hand of every man's brother, will he require the life of man."[5] This, together with the command, first, "to love the Lord thy God, &c. and thy neighbour as thyself," is a wall of security and safe preservation for all such as live in the fear of God, and believe that he will finally bring them to account for their actions and doings in this world, and reward every one according to what their deeds may have been. God Almighty grant, if it be his holy will, that this belief may not be the subtil intrigues of satan, get out of fashion with any of our rulers. When the aforesaid fear takes place, it will also beget a care to the fulfilling the injunction of our blessed Lord, viz. "whatsoever ye would, that other men should do unto you, do you even so unto them."[6] This puts the former out of dispute, if any doubt had arisen, respecting the propriety of owning people of another nation, as our neighbours; now, as soon as we do acknowledge them to be men, then we are immediately put under the Son's obligation. And further to enforce the necessity hereof, though he was the Son of God, yet he confessed that whosoever did the will of his Father, the same (though he might have a black skin) is his brother, &c. and pointed out in forcible language, that an injury done to such, was to be considerd as done to himself. And we find it repeated, that on this was grounded the dreadful sentence, "depart from me, I know you not"[7] Oh! what would a thousand worlds like this, do then for us!

Thus I consider all men to stand on the footing as brethren, and bound by the aforesaid obligations; and that nothing short of a special divine commission, will, or has ever authorized in any age, the violation thereof, without incurring the supreme displeasure; and that this never was granted against men, but for their sins, iniquities, and transgression of the laws of heaven, and then never to perpetuate slavery from one generation to another, I do believe, since men had an existence, which would be to make the innocent suffer for the guilty. Thus stands my belief as to myself, which I do not wish to impose on any man, but by conviction, if I might be instrumental thereto. Then how this would persecute—I am at a loss to see—or how any motion, we have made, can be so. I think that the persecution lies on the other side, in wanting the federal government to sanction what I believe nine-tenths of the citizens of America reprobate. (here I speak largely—however within bounds in my judgment) that is, the infamous slave trade. Now if the Carolinas and Georgia have this trade open to themselves, unembarrassed by the federal government, where is the persecution? no attempt being made to take from them the negroes that they have, I am at a loss to discover what this charge can arise from, except it is, that a belief is professed that the practice of slavery is oppressive and inhuman: to be sure, this is held up not only by quakers, but by men of all ranks, and different nations: yet if individuals can reconcile it to themselves, and to their Maker, I am for men to judge for themselves; and as to this, under the peculiar circumstances of things, if congress had unquestionably the power to emancipate all the slaves in America, I should be sorry to see them pass an act for their immediate liberation: although I firmly believe the Almighty will, in his own way and time, bring their deliverance about. I also believe if it be done in favour to us and them, it will be by gradation—by the minds of men becoming more and more enlightened; and as obedience is yielded, and keeps pace with knowledge, the work may be brought about in safety. But if we should be found fighting, as it were, against the Almighty, this may procure his displeasure, so as to produce something dreadful to us; his power being the same as when he made a pathway in the great deep, by dividing the waters thereof, for his people to go through:[8] yea, equal to what it was in the creation, when he said, "let it be," and it was so,[9] and the world we inhabit came forth into being. Oh! may we reverence and adore this power, that we may be preserved in the favour thereof: for should our conduct produce the reverse, even one day may bring amazement and horror to us. I feel for the southern people with much sympathy, and lament their condition, believing nothing short of the power of the highest can deliver them from their difficulties (I mean the whites); and oh! that he might be reverently sought for by them.

I trust, my conduct for these sixteen years, has given convincing proof to the world, of the sincerity of my professions, as held up in the foregoing communication; having not only liberated those I had of my own, but run a considerable risk, in liberating those that belonged to an estate, to which I was executor, as also in making restitution to such as I had held, and in purchasing those that had belonged to the family, to make free—this I do not mention in a boasting way—but just to confirm my belief, respecting the iniquity of this practice: and if all I have done, or can yet do, may be a means of wiping off from me the stains of guilt, on account of this injured people, I shall think it a great favour: wherein I do much desire also, to remove in the Lord's way and time the guilt from our nation: for this cause, my concern is great, to stop, as much as can be done with competency, the wicked, barbarous, inhuman, and devilish trade to Africa for slaves. What theft, what robbery, what murder to exceed this! my belief none is, or can be acted under the sun: wherein the accomplices, aiders, and abettors are proportionably guilty; and though it were sanctioned by the laws of all the nations of the earth, yet will it never receive the royal signet of the King of kings; but surely do I believe his indignation thereat will be more and more conspicuous, till he burst the bands of all those laws and decrees that countenance it.

For, my friend, let us just reason on this subject a little; did ever the people of Africa injure us in any sense? then why should we desire to so grievously afflict them? I think to persons of sense and humanity it is scarcely needful to say any more, than mention this subject. Indeed I feel so, that I can scarcely bear to reflect on it. I told my wife in a letter the other day, if she and I were so seized, and on our way to the West Indies expecting to be sold one on one island, and the other on another—Oh horrible, horrible indeed! thus I feel; how can I help it? it is disagreeable to me to have those sensations—I cannot help them—and so am constrained to plead with others.

I have a particular regard to thee, and believe, if thou had been willing to a further acquaintance, it would have terminated in as much satisfaction to thyself; however, be that as it may, I wish thy temporal and eternal happiness, and am thy friend.

American Museum, August 1790. Written from William Shotwell's (an ironmonger at the corner of Queen and Beekman streets, according to the 1789 New York City Directory). The editors believe this letter, addressed to "___ ___, member of the house of representatives of the united states, for the state of South Carolina," was the letter that Mifflin sent to Smith on 15 March (John Pemberton to James Pemberton, 16 March). Mifflin later sent a copy to Benjamin Rush, noting that it "was deliv'd Smith when in his seat, in Congress, about the middle part of the debates on the slave subject" (19 June, Rush Papers, PPL at PHi). In addition, Smith was the only South Carolina Representative Mifflin is known to have lobbied at his home, as described in the second paragraph. Brissot de Warville, in his famous *New Travels in the United States*, reprinted much of the letter in his native France the next year, followed by German, Dutch, and Swedish editions throughout the remainder of the decade.

[1] Proverbs 27:6.
[2] Mark 12:30–31.
[3] 1 Corinthians 13:1.
[4] Micah 6:7.
[5] Genesis 9:5.
[6] Matthew 7:12.
[7] A paraphrase of Matthew 7:23.
[8] Exodus 14:21–22.
[9] From Genesis 1.

OTHER DOCUMENTS

Elias Boudinot to Samuel W. Stockton. No copy known; acknowledged in Stockton to Boudinot, 15 April.

Benjamin Goodhue to Stephen Goodhue. ALS, Goodhue Family Papers, MSaE. Addressed to Salem, Massachusetts; franked; postmarked.
    Substantially repeats Goodhue to Hodge of this date, above; "the weather is as cold as [*it*] has been this winter."

Matthew McConnell to Andrew Craigie. ALS, Craigie Papers, MWA. Written in the evening; postmarked Philadelphia, 11 March.
    Believes Ashe and Williamson "will be right" on the subject of assumption; does not know how far the North Carolina members will feel governed by the state ratification convention's proposed Amendment against the measure.

James Madison to Edward Carrington. No copy known; acknowledged in Carrington to Madison, 27 March.

Peter Muhlenberg to Benjamin Rush. Excerpt and summaries of one page ALS, *Collector* 56(1942–43):item 468, 59(1946):item J 1229.
"Regarding the question of the assumption by the Government of State Debts and votes given in Committee, Ayes, 31, Noes, 26. the outcome [*on assumption*] in the House is doubtful. '. . . We are now endeavouring to fix the rate of Interest in which Opinion seems to vary more than on the Assumption.' He includes clippings from the March 9th N.Y. Daily Advertiser."

John Pickering to John Langdon. ALS, Langdon Papers, NhPoA. Written from Portsmouth, New Hampshire.
Report on public credit engrosses "our Politicians" no less than it does Congress; the proposal for assumption is so disliked by the legislature that they voted no account of the state's debts should be transmitted to Congress; reports on New Hampshire politics; Langdon's family and friends there are well.

James Trimble to Peter Lloyd. ALS, Supreme Executive Council Records, PHarH. Written to and from Philadelphia. Under his signature, Trimble (1754–1837), a deputy secretary of Pennsylvania's Supreme Executive Council, indicates that he writes for Charles Biddle (1745–1821), the Council's secretary.
In compliance with Maclay's request for "the several Inspection Laws of this State," asks that he be furnished with copies of the laws passed in the second and third sessions of the thirteenth Assembly, as well as the law relating to flour, passed 5 April 1781.

Jeremiah Wadsworth to Harriet Wadsworth. ALS, Wadsworth Papers, CtHi. Addressed to Hartford, Connecticut; franked; postmarked.
The coldest weather of the winter has struck; "Uncles Trumbull" (John and Jonathan) are well, "but we are prisoners here for I know not how long"; has no time to write to the rest of the family; asks about her progress with French—"can you think French"; saw Frances de Crèvecoeur the day before; "good morning my dear I must go to my daily labor"; P. S. has written to son Daniel "to send Giant—but he may let it alone till He hears from me again."

Thomas B. Wait to George Thatcher. ALS, Chamberlain Collection, MB. Place from which written not indicated. The "former conduct" mentioned relates to a petition attempt described in *DHFFC* 8:412–17.

Relates a discussion on parental roles in childrearing and seeks Thatcher's opinion; Joseph McLellan and others are about to petition the President that Nathaniel Fosdick performs his duties as collector at Portland, Maine, too "strictly and conscientiously" and "is therefore 'disagreeable to the people'"; "their former conduct has sunk them as low as H——ll; and this last undertaking, should they pursue and compleat it, will seal their D——mna——n!!!"

Stephen Waite and Abner Bagley to George Thatcher. ALS, Chamberlain Collection, MB. Written from Portland, Maine; franked. For background on the petitions mentioned, see *DHFFC* 8:411–14, 442–43.

Agrees with Thatcher's letter of 27 February, that the exorbitant fees complained of in the Petition of the Merchants and Other Inhabitants of Portland, Maine, applied only to those of the collector and surveyor; many think the fees of the weighers and gaugers too low, as the collector would probably admit if the secretary of the treasury asked.

Letter from New York. [Philadelphia] *Pennsylvania Journal*, 13 March; reprinted at Baltimore.

Reports the previous day's vote for assumption and that day's COWH resolution to adopt Hamilton's alternative for funding two-thirds of the debt at six percent and the remaining third in Western Territory lands at the rate of twenty cents an acre.

Letter from New York. *PP*, 16 March; reprinted at New York City (*NYDG*, 20 March); Wilmington, Delaware; Baltimore; and Winchester, Virginia.

In response to enquiries, judges "from the complexion of the House" that Hamilton's report on public credit will be adopted "without any material alteration."

Letter from New York. [Portland, Maine] *Cumberland Gazette*, 22 March. This is probably from a letter written by Thatcher to the newspaper's editor, Thomas B. Wait. For the resolutions quoted, see *DHFFC* 5:856–57, nos. 4–6.

Reports verbatim COWH resolutions from the previous day on Hamilton's report on public credit.

Thursday, 11 March 1790
Deep Snow (Johnson)

Nathaniel Barrell to George Thatcher

I wrote you a few days ago, since which am favord with yours of 19th. continued to 21st. Ulto.—yes my friend, I perceive the subject of finance and establishing Revenue System is truly interesting to the Citizens of America, your observations on that subject coincide with mine—'tis natural to think from a cursory view of the matter, the fear of changing for the worse is what keeps the people obedient to the Laws, and so soon as designing men can persuade them 'tis for their interest, they will attempt another revolution. much has been said by your friend Madason in favor of discrimination—to me it appears his plan is indigested and impractable—the sufferings and merrits of the Soldiers have been magnified beyond bounds—I am surprisd that no one in congress has represented that matter in a true light. I think it would not be difficult to prove they have been amply rewarded even tho they receive no further compensation for their services. the majority of those who have gone from these parts, were men of neither property nor respectability, much in debt—some of them wretchedly indigent—but by becoming soldiers they have dischargd their debts & returnd to their abodes in easy circumstances & respectable, farr above what they could attain, or expect, had it not been for the warr, and I believe when you look around in the compass of your own observation you'll agree with me they have sufferd as little if not less than any of us—perhaps upon investigation it will appear they have been more benefited than any class of men among us, and almost the only men who have gaind by the revolution—I could tell of my sufferings and dangers that way—boast of the fatigueing marches—cold & hunger, when necessaty obligd me, in an enemy's country, to feed on raw pork—the inclemency of the season when the snow was my bed—no covering but a blanket no Canopy but the heavens—of the groans of dying & wounded men &c. was I to stop here the picture would be dreadful—but to do justice I must say, that even then, amidst these hard stripes, the pleasing satisfaction of knowing I was serving my Country, doing my duty, was an ample reward—to say nothing of the pleasure enjoyd on return to camp, and the danger past, upon a retrospect view of the perils escap'd, over a chearful glass, or in company with a kind landlady—a source of Joy which to this day is not exhausted—realitys which I myself can talk of even now. These arc hints to build upon, and as much as should be said within the compass of a letter—but says you, there are pleasures which cannot be enjoyd by the mercinary hireling, or the avaricious speculator.

I am extremly pleasd with the masterly speech of Mr. Ames[1] in answer to Mr. Madason, and tho I see he might have said more, yet I am persuaded, there is not a word wanting—it is a compleat reply to evry thing said on that subject, and deserve to be written in letters of gold—but I would not be understood as tho I thought there was no merit in what Mr. Madason advanc'd. I do think at first sight there is the appearance of justice and cool reasoning in his argument, and that it is the product of a benevolent mind—but upon deliberate thought, his plan to me is not well digested—and I am clear in saying, is utterly impracticable. Much has been said with respect to the domestic debt—if a discrimination could be made I can see how justice might be done to all—but to me it appears impossible to bring this about ~~in~~ in that case, the first class we ought to attend to, is the Widdow & fatherless, whose property was early applyd, as they thot, for the benefit of their country—how will you do justice to them? many of whom have sufferd & died in the most indigent circumstances, while the survivors are mouldering away in corroding penury and distressing want—how can these be compensated? As to the speculators, a thought should not be lost on them—they are the source of depreciation those from whome all injustice has taken its rise, and no wrong can be done them even if compeld to take the lowest market. what injury can those suffer whose origin are the dregs of creation and the scum of iniquity? you know my friend I am of no class, neither an original holder or a purchaser, consequently my sentiments ought to be the most disinterested.

Well my friend—but what think you of the general Court? are you pleas'd with theire doings? if you are, it seems they are not so with yours—strange it is that we should be so little acquainted with ourselves—see the power of envy upon our minds—and often, how dreadfull are its effects? do you think any Government can be form'd to their likeing? can you think they will be satisfied with the additional amendments now propos'd? No my dear friend, unless you can swallow up the revenue by granting them as large compensations as you allow'd yourselves, and vesting them with supreme power, greater than you yourselves enjoy you may rely upon it, they will not cease to spy defects in the System—there are to be found in that group, those whose ambition was insatiable as Cesars[2] was when he said he had rather be the first man in an obscure Village than the second in Rome.

Dont you mean to take some steps to prevent a famine among us? for if flower be eight dollars & a quarter now in the City of New York, and the demand be so great abroad as we are told, depend upon it, if a stop is not put to exportation, three months hence if not before, we shall be in distressing want of bread.

What do those dispatches contain which you say came in the English Frigate to the President of the united States, is their contents still a secret?

The winter has been favorable to us, tho we have had some severe cold spels.

ALS, Chamberlain Collection, MB. Written from York, Maine.

[1] His speech of 15 February against discrimination between securities holders.
[2] Gaius Julius Caesar (100–44 B.C.), ruled as both Roman military leader and supreme civil authority despite some residual trappings of republicanism retained in such institutions as, for example, the Roman Senate, where he was ultimately assassinated for his ambition.

William Irvine to John Nicholson

Although the vote in the Committee of the whole has been carried by a majority of five for assuming the State debts I do not think it certain that it will go down in the house, twenty six is a heavy load to be dragged by thirty one, beside N. Carolina have five members coming on, all against the measure add to this it is probable that some of the majority may yet take fright & retract, for it can not be but they must be sensible of their error, at least they ought to be made so—Pennsylvania Members on this occasion support the interest of their State wonderfully; it is true they have not the effrontary to say they do, but local interests must give way to great national principles—and they now acknowledge that they do not expect any retrobution for advances over their proportion, in case the state should have advanced more than her proportion, notwithstanding one of them prevailed on the legislature last Session to repeal the land tax law, as an unnecessary burden, the State would immediately receive as much from the U. States as would defray all her expences, on account of balances coming &ca. but this is a slight inconsistency—there must be some thing more than ordinary in this matter—it is said that two Carolina Delegates, one a Senator the other a Representative, have lately purchased Certificates of that State to the amount of £50,000 at twenty pence in the pound.[1] I do not say that the Pennsylvanians have made any such speculation, but I think they might as well have the advantage as not, for if they have betrayed their trust, it is all one to their constituents what the motives were—Generals Heister and [Peter] Muhlenberg were the only two who voted against the assumption.

The Sense of the people are not known on this or almost any other point, as to the timing of your Philadelphia papers few reach this place that I can see the members got them, but there is no more heard of them, at least I can neither see nor hear of them, except Browns, most worthless thing.[2]

I well knew that the Massachusetts members, did not represent truely, their Constituents more than those of your State—as an instance, you have the Report of a Committee of their General Court—I wish to know what our

Assembly are about—some here think they will be so highly pleased with the assumption that they will vote the thanks of the house to their Delegates, for their conduct—I dare say a great majority of them will gratify their Representatives with any such reasonable compliment, still this cannot blind the bulk of the intelligent people long—the rejection of the amendment of that Article of the Constitution, for fixing the Representation at 30,000 was extraordinary,[3] for the assembly of Penna. a few well chosen strictures, at this moment, on the assumption might have great & good effects, for I am certain there is a probability of turning some about, beside it would tend to strengthen & confirm others in the opposition, & the most daring of those for it will not like to go on with only one or two of a majority—one of whom yesterday acknowledged that he knew, the people as such of his State, (Massachusets) would not approve of the assumption—but would he sacrafice, the public creditors, the best men? he asked, a few Speculators, he might have added, himself included, so common fame relates—But there are hints here that some high prerogative Men would perhaps call treason—and tho I dispise & defy them yet there is no accason to court enemies—you will therefore commit this scroll to flames.

[P. S.] The opposition to assumption will cease til N. Carolina is represented, and perhaps til the Bill is brought in.

This day, on the Resolution or clause, for making the 4 ℗ cents irredeemable; it was struck by a majority of six, to the no little surprize of the Assumption Gentry—I expect, to hear from you by tomorrow or next days post.

ALS, Gratz Collection, PHi. Place to which addressed not indicated. Docketed in the hand of Nicholson as received 14 March; as enclosing two newspapers, "deld. 1 Saml. Maclay"; and as answered. While the body of the letter was probably written on 11 March, the postscript might have been added on 12 March.

[1] On 22 November 1792, Smith wrote Henry William De Saussure:
While the subject of the Assumption was under consideration, I received one day in Congress an anonymous Letter charging the Anxiety of Mr. Izard & myself for that measure to the account of interestedness & alledging that the writer knew for a fact that we had bought Indents to the Amount of £100,000, & that unless I abandoned the Cause, he would bring to public view the proofs he had in his possession & expose my conduct to the world; *as I was conscious that neither Mr. Izard nor myself had bought Indents to the value of one farthing*, I on that very day exerted myself for the Assumption in the House more than ever in spite of the writer's proofs" (*SCHM* 70[1969]:42).
Based on the legislative history of assumption and Smith's speeches on it, the editors believe that Smith was referring to an event that occurred on 31 March or 1 April.

[2] *FG*, published by Andrew Brown.

[3] On 10 March 1790, Pennsylvania ratified all but the first two of the twelve Amendments proposed by Congress in September 1789. Its copy of the Amendments—the Bill of Rights—was alienated, probably in the manner described by the manuscript dealer Walter Benjamin: "Some fifty years ago [*ca. 1880s*] a man from Harrisburg made frequent trips to

New York carrying a large carpetbag bulging with old state papers. These he sold to C. D. Burns, Simon Gratz, Dr. T. A. Emmett [*Emmet*], and other collectors" (Charles Hamilton, *Collecting Autographs and Manuscripts* [Norman, Okla., 1961], p. 32).

Samuel Johnston to James Iredell

I wrote to you a few days agoe by the way of Norfolk [*Virginia*] acknowledging the Rect. of your Letter of the 17th. I should hope to hear from you this Evening but the severity of the weather will probably delay the Post as there is now more Snow on the ground than there has been at any time in the course of the Winter.

The Committee of the whole in the House of Representatives have voted the Assumption of the State Debts, by a Majority of five, this was strongly opposed.

The House of Representatives having taken up most of the Business recommended by the President, there has not as yet been much debating in the Senate, in some few instances where there has, it would appear that the Sentiments of the Northern or Eastern and Southern Members constantly clash, even where local Interests are out of the question, This is a thing I cannot account for, even the Lawyers from these different quarters cannot agree on the principles and construction of Law, tho they agree among themselves.
***

John Skinner is here under innoculation and in a good way Mr. Hawkins is just come from him.

I have just received your Letter of the 24th February for which I am infinitely obliged to you.

ALS, Charles E. Johnson Collection, Nc-Ar. Addressed to Edenton, North Carolina; franked. The omitted text relates news of family and friends.

Woodbury Langdon to John Langdon

Since my last I have received yours of the 22d and 25th. February, I shall pay Clark and Carlton what you desire, your Sloop is loading and will be ready I expect next Week shall give every assistance respecting her that may be necessary as to President [*governor of New Hampshire*] your Letter was quite too late for any proposal in your favor as one third of the Votes had been thrown before your Letter came besides it would have been impracticable even if it had been received before unless you had actually resigned your seat in Congress and that had been known through the State nor even then unless you had been here, however I am far from thinking it a Place either honorable or desireable to any Gentleman as it is now managed, I would not have you think of resigning your seat in Congress by any means it will be time enough to talk about that after Congress adjourns & you return but at ~~present~~ present it must not be thought of, *** the Memorials you mention'd sometime past respecting Commerce, Courts &c.[1] are prepared and signing and will be forwarded to you by next Post. I wish you would endeavor all you can to get Harry [*Henry Sherburne Langdon*] placed in some eligi~~a~~ble situation that will give him a ha[*n*]dsome support if possible as he seems to be very ~~an~~ anxious to be imploy'd which would be very pleasing to him and give him spirrits.

ALS, Langdon Papers, NhPoA. Written from Portsmouth, New Hampshire; endorsed "Answered." The omitted text details the state election.

---

[1] The petitions of the merchants and traders of Portsmouth on the location of courts and on trade policy; see *DHFFC* 8:185–86, 353–54.

William Maclay to John Nicholson

I would be much obliged to you for information; how much of the State debt of Pennsylvania is sunk. I think she cannot have much more than one Million of dollars existing State debt. By the Operation of the federal impost, thus far. it appears that Pennsylvania, (or the imports into Philadelphia) Pay about one fourth of the Whole. at this rate, should a Mass of State debt, to the amount, of 24 Millions be assumed, by Congress, our port would have to provide for Six Million of it. had we been among the delinquent States all this would be right. but I think differently on this Subject. But now to the Business of this letter. it is alledged against you, that you have brought forward, Charges on the part of Pennsylvania, against the united States that cannot be supported. One Gentleman alledged that there were not charges to the amount of more than eight Millions. I write you this in confidence, but these insinuations came from a Quarter, I did not expect. and from a Quarter that, I fear, will hurt the Credit of our State accounts. but pray go on firm and fearless, in every thing that is warrantable. I know you have your Enemies. diligence in business, you are generally allowed to possess, in an eminent degree. but this seems to be a fault fixed on your very Virtues. I pray you however, to make the Use only of this letter, which I wish you to do. namely consider it, as a friendly hint. to State and explain all Accounts against the Union with such clearness as may, if possible, put all objection, to silence— There is a cry among some People now to burn all Accounts. it is a common Observation with some People that the Accounts never can be settled.

I cannot believe that it is the interest of Pennsylvania to act so.

The Secretarys first scheme of a loan was agreed to yesterday, in a committee of the Whole Representatives. the second rejected this day. the third before them. It is very curious to hear the language of some of the very Men who are voting for the Report, damning it and Swearing it will all blow Up.[1] You will see how the adoption of the State debt was carried, by the papers. shall add no more least the Post should be gone.

ALS, Gratz Collection, PHi. Addressed to the "Comptroller Genl. of the State of Pennsylvania"; franked; postmarked; received 14 March; answered 15 March.

[1] Burke, in the debate of 10 March, "declared it would blow up" (*DHFFC* 9:216).

David Sewall to George Thatcher

This is to acknowledge the Reciept of yours of the 7th. & 22d ultimo together with the Secretary of War's Communica. to Congress [*report on the militia*]. They arived during my absence at Pownalbo. Court Which I held at Witscassett. I called upon Mrs. [*Sarah Savage*] Thatcher going and Comeing, and found her Well; the Children have got well thro the Measles, Which Mr. [*Silas*] Lee gave them upon his returne from the Westward. Mr. Lee ~~has~~ is safely housed at Witscassett and appears to be cordially recieved with his lady [*Temperance Lee*]. I found the principal Charackters there Friendly and Social. And have suggested to Mr. Lee that his amusements and enjoiments should be guided and directed, with a degree of *Temperance* Miss [*Betsy*] King went with them in the Slay. last Thursday We dined with Judge [*Thomas*] Rice Who had the principal Genls. and ladys of the Place upon Invitation to the amount of 15 or 20 and We had a very pleasant Social Evening together. The Snow is near or quite 3 feet deep in that quarter and very Stiff and Solid, which makes it Inconvenient Turning out—I find by your last as Well as by the News Papers that you have had long and ingenious debates upon discrimination But I hope they are Satisfactorily and finally Setled. I think I feel as unbiassed and as Uninterested (unless for the great Whole) as any one. I also feel desirous that such as have disposed of their public Securities for a small Consideration to relieve their necessities should be relieved. But this notwithstanding Mr. Madisons Proposition had it been adopted would have entailed the most disagreable Consequences. And could not have been caried into execution without a Violent and flagrant Violation of public faith. The next great question is the assumption of the State debts, This it Strikes me will be essentially necessary to the calling forth the resources of the States—for if the Several States are to make provision for the paiment of their debts Contracted by the War their Systems of Finance for that purpose, will be Continually thwarting the general System of Finance that is or may be adopted by Congress and also bring on a Continual bickering between the

Several State and Continental Creditors—and there is no knowing where such Bickering will Terminate. And perhaps the sooner this great Question is Setled the better: Notwithstanding it may diminish if not annihilate the Importance of a Number of small Financiers in the Several State legislatures. The amendment proposed by Mr. Madison to the 4th. Resolution at present Strikes me agreably. And as Savering of Justice and equity. And what will have a good operation upon the People of such States as have made exertions, and suppose they have few debts of their own State to discharge. Mr. Strongs of the 20 & Mr. Sedwicks of the 14th. ulto. are recieved. and to whom I shall Write by the next mail. *** The Accounts of the high price of Farrinaceas[1] food in the Southern States Strikes the People Eastward very disagrebly. As their Crops Were exceeding short the last Season, as Well in that particular, as forage—and some Persons of pretty good Judgement predict that the Succeeding Spring & Summer to Barly harvest will be the most distressing that has been known among us—and that there will be a Real Death of a Considerable quantity of Stock for want of Forage. Thus much must Suffice for this Time from your Friend & Servant.

ALS, Foster Collection, MHi. Written from York, Maine; postmarked Portsmouth, New Hampshire, 12 March. The omitted text relates to state politics.

[1] Mealy.

William Smith (Md.) to Otho H. Williams

You will have discovered by the papers I inclos'd you a few days, past, That the first part of your letter was already published, & that being the case, I sent to the press this morning the conclusion thereof.[1]

We have proceeded so far on the Secretarys Report, as "That two thirds of the Principal Shall be funded at Six p. Cent, & the other third paid in lands in the Western territory at twenty Cents p. Acre." this was agreed to by a great majority—A motion is now before the committee to Strike out all the Other Alternatives, except That which offers an interest of Six p. Cent on 66⅔ dollrs. & to have 26 Dollrs. & 88 Cents funded at the same rate of interest at the end of ten years—This motion will probably Succeed, when this business is through, I presume the Impost law will be taken up & revised.
***

ALS, Williams Papers, MdHi. Addressed to Baltimore. The omitted text relates to personal legal affairs.

[1] Williams's letter to Smith dated 28 February, above. It appeared in *NYDG* on 8 and 12 March.

Andrew Craigie to John Holker. FC:dft, Craigie Papers, MWA. For background on George Scriba's petition, see *DHFFC* 8:198–99.

Reports on encouraging news from Europe about (Joel Barlow's) western land sales and the arrival of French settlers in Philadelphia; encourages Holker to promote French migration to the West, while keeping as quiet as possible (about George Scriba's petition for land?) "because should it be immediately publickly known great injury ~~may~~ will be incurred in the arrangements we are now making with ~~the~~ Congress."

John Langdon to Hopley Yeaton. No copy known; acknowledged in Yeaton to Langdon, 3 April.

Joshua Martin to John Langdon. ALS, Langdon Papers, NhPoA. Written from Portsmouth, New Hampshire.

Sends box of saddles, as directed.

George Washington, Diary. Washington Papers, MiD-B.

Read, both Muhlenbergs, Gilman, Goodhue, Ames, Wadsworth, Trumbull, Benson, Laurance, Wynkoop, Vining, D. Carroll, Contee, Madison, Page, and Sumter dined at the President's.

FRIDAY, 12 MARCH 1790

Fine (Johnson)

John Adams to John Trumbull

Your Letter of Feb. 6 has made so deep an Impression that it may not be amiss to make a few more observations on it as it respects both of Us.
***
Let me come now to the more aukward and unpleasant Task of saying something more of myself. it is more than twenty years that the American Newspapers have been throwing out hints of the Lowness of my Birth and the obscurity of my Family. These generous and Philosophical Intimations have been carefully copied, with large additions and Decorations in the English Newspapers, and from these translated into all the Languages and Gazettes of Europe, and now they are repeated again with as much ardour as ever—if I had been the Son of an Irish, Scotch or German Redemptioner, or of a Convict transported for Felony, there could not have been more Noise about it, or a more serious and weighty affair made of it. I am the last Man

in the World who will ever claim a benefit from the ~~popular~~ Democratical and Aristocratical Prejudice in favour of Blood. But pushed as I am upon this point I will add, and Posterity will confirm it, I am the last Man in the United States, who should have any occasion for it. But if I had neither done nor suffered nor hazarded any Thing for this Country, I am one of the last Men in the United States, who ought to be ashamed of his Family or to Suffer the Smallest Reproach, Disgrace or Reflection on account of it. a Saxon Family by the Name of Adami, came over to England at the Time of the Saxon Conquest [*fifth century A.D.*], and after settling in the Country translated their Latin Name into the English Plural Adams. They have multiplied exceedingly in England, and are now Scattered in great Numbers in Lincolnshire, Essex, Devonshire, the Isle of Wight, and most other Counties in England as well as in London and Westminster. many of them are opulent, some of them Magistrates Judges &c. about the year 1628 one of the Family who was wealthy but a Non conformist, became a Member of the Plymouth Company and an Assistant in the first Charter to the Massachusetts Colony,[1] and as you may see in Prince's Chronology,[2] one of the most active, zealous and influencial Men in procuring the Resolution to transport the Patent to New England. About two years after my Ancestor came over with Eight sons and a considerable Property, Settled in ~~the Town of~~ Braintree and became an original Proprietor and a large Proprietor in that Town, and every foot of the Land he owned with great additions is now possessed by his Posterity in that Place. having been a Country Gentleman in England, and consequently a Maltster, as all the Landed Gentlemen are, he sett up a Malt House, which I have seen: as his Grandson sett up another in Boston which now belongs to the Lt. Govr. [*Samuel Adams*] a more industrious a more virtuous and irreproachable Race of People is not to be found in the World. I really never knew a vicious Man of the Breed. I have therefore good Reason to despise all the dirty Lies that are told in the Newspapers. Let this Descent be compared with the Descent of any of the Grandees of any Part of America and I shall have no Reason to blush. I have Reason to blush however for the low Cunning, the mean Craft of those who talk and Scribble upon this subject. I have cause to blush, and I do blush at the Meanness and Inconsistency of the American public for tolerating this Insolence and much more for encouraging it. But I will tell you a Fact, and the longer you live, the more you will be sensible of it, the American Families who have been conspicuous in Government have more Pride Vanity and Insolence on Account of their Birth, than the Nobility of England or France have. and it is more difficult for a new Man to conquer Envy in this Country than it is in any Country of Europe; notwithstanding all our bosted Equality and Philosophical Democracies.

The charge of deserting my Republican Principles is false. My Principles and system of Government are the same now as they ever were. And if I have ever acquiesced in Measures more democratical, it was in compliance with dire necessity, and a despair of resisting the fury of a popular Torrent created by Men as ignorant and blind in this matter as the lowest of the People. before any Government was sett up, in Jan. 1776 I wrote & printed at Philadelphia a Pamphlet, recommending a Ballance of three Independent Branches.[3] This Pamphlet Suggested to the Convention at New York their Idea of a Constitution. Mr. [*James*] Duane who was one of its framers told me as soon as it was done that it was done in Conformity nearly to my Idea in my Letter to Wythe in 1779, I drew the Plan of Government for the Massachusetts, which without me they could not have carried.[4] Though they injured themselves by departing from my Ideas with regard to a Negative in the Governor, and by giving the Election of officers of Militia to the Men. The Constitution of the United States is borrowed much too servilely from that of Massachusetts and now Pensilvania and Georgia have adopted the same, with some Improvement. I have therefore been consistant in these Principles and to that Consisten[*c*]y and Constancy America is now Indebted for all the Peace order and good Government she has. Without it she would have been at this hour in all Probability in a civil War. and if my Advice had been more exactly followed, the shame of America would have been avoided, I mean her Breaches of Faith, her Violations of Property, her Anarchy and her Dishonesty.

I can conceive of no other Reason than this, Why I am singled out to be the Subject of their eternal Clamours about my Birth. if they could find a Spot in my moral Character or political Conduct they would not harp so much upon this String. But the Principles of Government which I have always embraced and professed, as they well know are such as they now Want and as the People now feel the necessity of. They have no Chance against me in this Way. Sam. Adams, R. H. Lee P[*atrick*]. Henry and many others are so erroneous in their Principles of Government as to be now growing Unpopular, and the Tories and Yonksters [*youngsters*] think they shall soon get them out of their Way. But John Adams remains an Eye sore to be a little more particular. There is a sett of Smart Young Fellows who took their degrees at Colledge, Since the Revolution in 1774 who are now joined by the old Tories in opposition to the old Whigs. many of these latter by their Obstinate Attachment to the Ignorance and Error of the Author of Common sense [*Thomas Paine*], are giving all possible Advantages against themselves. But your Friend is not in this Predicament. and nothing remains but lies about his Birth and Conduct, to get him out of the Way. Why else am I singled out? Three Presidents of Congress, have been sons of French Refugees Farmers and Tradesmen[5]—surely not a more honourable Descent than that of an whole blooded English Family among the first settlers of the Country, constantly holding respectable landed Estates and enjoying the invariable

Esteem of their fellow Citizens. The American Ministers abroad the Chief Justice, the Ministers of State, the Governors of States the President himself have not one Iota of Advantage of me in Point of Blood. [*John*] Hancock and Washington had Splendid Fortunes. I had not. I have therefore surely bribed no Votes, nor dazzled any Man by my Wealth. I am however and have been all my Days as independent a Man as either of them and more so too because I have never been so much in debt, and have always lived more within my Income.

As to "Fondness for the Splendor of Titles" I will tell you an Anecdote. The Second Day, that I presided in Senate, last April, the two Houses enjoyned me to receive the President and Address him in Public. Upon this I arose and asked the advice of the Senate, by what Title I should address him? The Constitution had given him no Title. it either intended that he should have none: and in that Case Honour or Excellency would be as much a Violation of it as Highness or Majesty. if We now addressed him by the Title of Excellency, We should fasten that Epithet upon him and by it depress him, not only below Ambassader from abroad and his own Ambassaders, but below the Governers of Seperate States &c. upon this arose a Gentleman [*R. H. Lee*] in great Zeal, Said he was glad to hear the Proposition; that this was the precise moment to determine it: agreed in the Necessity of giving a Title that would be respectable Abroad; and moved that a Committee should be appointed to consider and report what Title should be given to the President and *Vice President.* Here was the blunder. I had Said nothing about Vice President. But can one do when We are compelled to cooperate with Men, who are no Politicians? This blunder was Seized, in order to throw the blame of Titles on me. But my shoulders are broad enough to bear it.

You Suppose me to be envyed in the Southern States more than in the Northern. here you or I are mistaken. The real Envy against me is in the Northern States, and in two Men H. and A. [*John Hancock and Samuel Adams*] and they are their Friends who raise most of the idle Conversation about me. Their are many Gentlemen in the southern states who would prevent any northern Man from ever rising high in the public Esteem if they could: but they have no Objection against me more than any other. Emulation and Rivalry, arises between South and North as well as between Individuals. these Competitions have ever been a sourse of discord, Sedition and civil War, and unless some effectual Ballance for them is provided, I dread the Consequences. We may live to see from this Cause every great popular Leader, followed by his Clann, building a Castle on a Hill, and acting the Part of a feudal Chieftain. The Age of Chivalry and Knight Errantry may come upon Us in America. The melancholly prospect of this has induced me to wish for an Executive Authority independant and able to counterpoise the Legislative, and compose all feuds.

The Idea of the Leader of a Party, is easily conceived and propagated, from the Part I have been obliged to act, in the question of the Presidents Power of Removal from office. I was unfortunately obliged to decide all those questions the Senate having been equally divided. There was all the last session about half the Senate disposed to vote for Measures that would as I thought weaken the Executive Authority, to a degree that would destroy its capacity of ballancing the Legislature, and consequently, in my Idea, overturn the best Part of the Constitution. This Principle I must pursue, tho it may give occasion to a Party to represent me as a Leader of the opposite Party. as to order in debate, I think there has never been any difficulty in preserving it. I have attended the Supream Court of Justice in Gallicia in Spain, the Parliament of Paris, the assembly and Courts of Justice in Holland, and both Houses of the British Parliament as well as Congresses, Senates Councils and Houses in America, and I never Saw more order in any one, than has been constantly observed in senate Since I sat in it.

Who your Informers were I know not—you say they are not unfriendly to me. but it is most certain they have been deceived, or they have misrepresented, for the facts they reported to you are not true. New England men, my friend, are more of Statesmen than they are of Politicians. The Old Whigs have lost much of their Influence. I am now obliged to act openly, in conformity to my invariab[l]e professed Principles, which they well know, against them. Mr. [John] Hancock Mr. Sam. Adams, Mr. R. H. Lee—P[atrick]. Henry—Govr. [George] Clinton and General [James] Warren with twenty others, with whom I acted in pulling down the British Government, are now not very cordially supporting the new Government. They mistake their own Interest as I think as well as that of their Country. This however must necessarily produce a Coldness towards me, while those against whom I acted for many Years to their mortification, altho We now Act together, you may suppose have not forgotten their ancient feelings. in this situation, public Life is not very agreable to me. I pray for long Life to the President with as much Sincerity as any Man in America. I have more pressing Motives to wish it, than any Man. I sincerely think him the Best Man for his Place in the World and I very much doubt, whether if it should be the Will of Heaven that he should die, any other Man could be found who could Support the Government. if there is any one, I would give Way to him, with Pleasure, and retire to my farm. I never will act in my present Station under any other Man than Washington. But who can We find—Mr. Jay, Mr. Jefferson Mr. Maddison. I know very well that I could carry an Election against either of them in Spight of all Intrigues and Maneuvres. Yet I would not do it, if I thought either could govern this People. But I know they could not, so as to give Satisfaction while I should be in the Country. I should find myself become all at once the Idol of a Party, my Character and services would be trumpetted to the Skies—and I should find myself forced in Spight of myself to be placed at the head of a Party. I will never be in this situation. if Circumstances should force it upon me—I will at all Events quit the Country—if I spend the rest of my Days in a Garrett in Amsterdam. thank Heaven however the President is in a vigourous Health and likely to live till the Government has a fair Tryal whether it can be supported or no. I could now quit my Place and retire without much Noise or Inconvenience, and if there is the least Uneasiness to the danger of the Government I am very willing to quit it. The System of Policy, in my Salary and in some other Things seems to have been to compell me or provoke me to retire.

I have written to you in Confidence with great freedom, because I have the highest Esteem for your Abilities and the Utmost Affection for the qualities of your heart.

ALS, AMs 1052 19.3, PPRF. Place to which addressed not indicated. The omitted text encourages Trumbull to continue training for public life, including public speaking, assuring him, "Your Gestures are no more Stiff than Elsworths and every other Connecticut Man."

[1] English Separatists (not in conformity with the official Church of England) made up the bulk of those who sailed from Plymouth, England, in July 1620 to found a colony under a patent from the Virginia Company. Beginning in 1621, the government of the religious haven they founded in Massachusetts was composed of a popularly elected governor and his "assistants."

[2] *A Chronological History of New-England* (Boston, 1736), by the Puritan divine Thomas Prince (1687–1758).

[3] The first imprint of Adams's *Thoughts on Government* (printed in *LDC* 3:399–406) was published by John Dunlap in late March 1776 from a version that Adams had included in a letter to the Virginia jurist and fellow delegate to Congress, George Wythe (1726–1806). In his *Autobiography*, begun in 1802, Adams implied that he wrote *Thoughts* at R. H. Lee's encouragement as a corrective to the alarmingly radical notions of constitutionalism that had been recently propagated by Thomas Paine's *Common Sense* (*Adams* 3:330–32).

[4] While serving as delegate for Braintree at the Massachusetts constitutional convention in September–November 1779, Adams assumed the role as a subcommittee's sole draftsman for what was ratified in June 1780, with minimal changes, as that state's still-functioning constitution.

[5] Henry Laurens (1724–92), delegate from South Carolina, John Jay, and Elias Boudinot.

Benjamin Lincoln to Fisher Ames

We are now attempting to enlarge our trade to those [*Madeira*] Islands whence we import the small Wines, we are induced to this as we can purchase them without the cash and what is Still more benefical we can procure them from the refuse of our fish provisions &c. but as the law now Stands the trade is greatly embarrassed as The bonds for the duties become due in six Months after the importation Little of the wine is used here no advantage can be obtained from a draw back in discharge of the bond for there are few instances where a Vessel makes her Voyage out with those wines & back in six months—The wish of the Merchants is that the time may be protracted before the bonds shall become due and that when the bond is to be settled that all the duties due, one the Wines which have been entered for exportation should be deducted from the bond.

ALS, Letters to Goodhue, NNS. Written from Boston; postmarked 14 March. The existence of this letter among Goodhue's papers may be the result of Ames's having shared it with his Massachusetts colleague, who some weeks later was appointed to the committee on the Collection Act [HR-82]. The bill that Goodhue presented later that session provided the solution suggested in this letter, extending from six to twelve months the due date for bonds securing the payment of duties (exceeding fifty dollars) on Madeira wines (*DHFFC* 4:420).

Andrew Moore to Arthur Campbell

I yesterday Receivd a Letter from you I receivd another on the 6th. Instant Inclosing one to the President & One to the Secretary of War—I must declare ~~my~~ myself under peculiar Obligations to you For your attention in Writing—[*lined out*] No person can be more Anxious ~~to hear~~ Nor more pleas'd Than I am In my present Situation to hear from my Acquaintances—Your Letters I Deliverd—I have frequently Wrote to you—But As my letters may have miscarried—I shall now give you a short sketch of all our proceeding—The Presidents ~~Letter~~ address to the Congress—Was immediately taken up after presented And the different Matters therein Recommended to our Consideration Were Referd to Committes Bills are now before us—On the forming a Uniform Mode of Naturalization—On the defence of our Frontiers On Securing to Authors &c. the exclusive Right of Vending or Using their Respective Inventions—A Bill is now before us Which originated and has past the Senate accepting the Cession of land propos'd by North Carolina The difficulties you suggest to me on that Subject had occurd & several others—I had proposd to move that the further consideration should be postpond untill the Representation from that state should be present I hope It will be postpond—The Report of the Secretary [*on public credit*] has chiefly engagd our attention since submitted We have made but little progress—I contemplate it as the most important most Interesting And the most complex difficult Business which has or perhaps may ever come before us—The following is as nearly the Progress as I can now Recollect—A Motion was made on its first Introduction to postpone it Untill the Representatives from North Carolina should arrive This Was negativd The forreign debt We have unanimously Resolvd to fund on the Terms of the Stipulation—When the debts of the United states were under discussion—An Amendment was propos'd by Mr. Madison—Which Was to discriminate between the Certificates in the possession of the Original Holders and those in the Possession of Purchasing—This was very ably advocated—Was long under discussion and at length Negativ'd contrary to my earnest Wish—The assumption of the States Debts has been long under Consideration—The Propriety Policy & justice of the Measure is urgd in the Report—The Objections made to its adoption Were the Inequality of the exertions made in the different states for the payment of their Citizens some having paid Nothing Other a Very considerable portion of their debts—On the other hand Was urgd the Inequality of Exertions & of course deb[t]s contracted during the War—Their exhausted Resources And Inability to pay a Proportion was made by Mr. White That so soon as the accounts of the Several states with the Continent were Adjusted—Congress should pay to each state so much As she should appear on such liquidation to have paid More Than her just proportion—This Was Negativd Mr. Madison proposd That the Certificates in the possession of the states Collected from their Citizens should be funded And the States Receive payment of Principal & Interest in the Same manner as Individuals This was Rejected And the Resolution for the Assumpsit past in the Affirmative Thirty against Twenty six—It is Thought the Representatives of North Carolina Will be against the assumption As their Convention have proposd as an amendment to the Constitution a Clause prohibitting their Interference with State debts—should They arrive in time & be oppose to the measure—It will probably be Rejected—The first of the Secretarys funding Propositions ~~has~~ is agreed to The Second Rejected The third amend~~mente~~d by Changing the Rate of Redemption to six dollars per annum—All the others I believe will be Rejected—The Assumption of the State debts has been objected to—On a Supposition (and I think Well founded) That our Resources will be inadequate to the Redemption Unless We have Recourse to direct Taxes Or to such Indirect taxes or duties as will be highly Exceptionable & Impolitic—The Secretary has been Calld on To submit to us Those funds from Which He Contemplates the Payment As stated in the Report—He has done so[1] He proposes ~~an~~ Additional duties on Imports generally—and on Enumerated Articles Wine Rum Sugar spices On Molasses half a Cent per Gallon On Salt six Cents per Bushel On process in Courts And Writings a Tax no statement of the amount—From those He pledges himself He can pay the Whole Without Recourse to direct taxes I think some of those as disagreeable and more so in some of the States Than a direct Tax impost by their state Legislature would be—I also think The Amount ~~of~~ from those Resources Would not be equal to the discharge of the Interest I think the State debts Will far exceed any Statement Which has been yet made—I have thus hastily & Confusedly stated the Reasons pro & Con for your Consideration—The Rate of Interest I suppose Will not be alterd from the Report Viz. 4 per Cent.

It is reported that the Legislature of Massechusets ~~have~~ have passt a law Imposing an Excise On Liquors Imported & distill'd—It has been passt Or is under Consideration And taken up since They Receivd the Secretarys Report[2] It is said With intent to avail themselves of those Resources Contemplated by the Secretary for federal purposes And to prevent the Adoption of the state debts a Measure to which the Citizens are Violently oppos'd Altho Advocated by their Representatives A Report prevaild here yesterday That the King of France had elop'd from paris—I cannot give you any Authority for it—It is believd by some & some not—should it be true It will Require the Utmost Exertion of the Abilities & Address of the Marquis de le fiat [*Lafayette*] to keep order & Support that discipline necessary in an Army—If true It is is probable the Revolution will not be Compleated Without Bloodshed—A Query is made Where will he go? Not to Germany His Reception would probably not be favourable To Spain? The Spirit of freedom is stifled for the Present there With the utmost difficulty—Their greatest exertions are not fully adequate to the purpose—You mention the purchase[3] in Georgia—I mentiond to you ~~in my last~~ my sentiments on this Business And my Apprehensions of the Consequences in my last letter—I hope They will be disappointd That The Legislature will Reconsider the Subject and Repeal their law—It ~~is~~ Certainly will be a Justifiable Exercise of Legislative Authority to Repeal a law obtaind by fraud & Collusion & so pregnant with Injustice—I approve of the Ideas you Suggest With Respect to Defence I conceive It would be less Expensive & more Effectual Than any other I can Contemplate—Will the Sale Alarm the Chuctaws & Chuckesas? Will not an attempt to Settle Engage them Immediately in Hostilities? Mr. [*Patrick*] Henry I am told Writes That Agents are now employd amongst Them and likely to Succeed in a friendly Negotiation Whatever information you may Receive on this subject Please to Write me—I need not suggest to you the propriety of such Communications Or the Use may be made of them—A Bill for establishing post Roads is now before us—The Power will be lodgd in the President & director general in a great Measure—Your Object I am afraid cannot yet be Accomplisht Nor on any terms short of Its bearing the entire Expence—I have in my hasty Observations Referd to the Secretarys Report—As I take it for Granted you have seen it.

The fixing on a Seat for the Permanent Seat of Congress has not yet been brought forward I believe it will not this Session—The member of Pensylvania talk of it—But I believe their Desertion last Session—From what Was thought a Pre engagement—Will prevent their Success—I receivd a Letter from Mr. [*John?*] Smith I shall Write to him by the next Opportunity.

ALS, Campbell Papers, Filson Club, Louisville, Kentucky. Addressed to Washington County, Virginia (in present-day Kentucky); sent "Via Richmond To the Care of Mr. A[*ugustine*]. Davis—Printer"; franked; postmarked.

---

[1] The 4 March 1790 report is printed in *DHFFC* 5:852–55.

[2] The Massachusetts legislature discussed the bill throughout February and on 3 March adopted it as "An Act to raise a public Revenue by Excise, and to regulate the Collection thereof." It replaced that state's 1786 act and its several revisions.

[3] For background on the Virginia Yazoo Company's purchase of seven million acres in northern present-day Mississippi (then occupied principally by Choctaws and Chickasaws), under a controversial Georgia law of December 1789, see Walton to Adams, 20 January, n. 2, above.

Hugh Williamson to John Gray Blount

You will be so good as consult Wm. Blount on the Subject of my Letter to him of this Date. viz. whether the Holders of Land to the South of the Tenessee [*River*] had best apply to congress for Leave to surrender their Lands on obtaining other Certificates for them to the same Amot. as the lands east. The increased Value of the Certificates might be an Object compared with the great uncertainty when those Lands may be come at.

We are here told that Speculators are buying up the Certificates of 1786— though they are declared by the State to be *not good*. Let me advise you not to touch them. As for the other State Securities, if you can get them in Paymt. of Debts or in Payment for Lands or on Credit or by any other honest means I think you may touch them freely if their Price is not greatly advanced above what they were when I left Home. I think it probable that they will be up to 6/ Specie for the Principle & nearly as much for the Interest, make what Allowance you think fit for Lee Way.

ALS, John Gray Blount Papers, Nc-Ar. Addressed to Washington, North Carolina; carried by Capt. Eastwood.

OTHER DOCUMENTS

John Avery to the Massachusetts Representatives. LS, Letters to Goodhue, NNS. Written from Boston. For the congressional resolution of 11 June 1788 limiting the time during which individuals could apply for invalid pensions, see *DHFFC* 7:589.

> "Inclosed you have a resolution of the General Court passed the 2d instant requesting you to move in Congress, that provision be made for all persons in this Commonwealth, who may be proper subjects for pensions, as invalids; to have leave to apply therefore, notwithstanding the time is elapsed. Which Resolve I have the honor of transmitting agreeably to their directions."

James Callaway to James Madison. ALS, Washington Papers, DLC. Written from Amherst County, Virginia. For the full text, see *PJM* 13:101.

Office seeking: excise collector or any other post in his county or district; as Madison does not know him; Madison can apply to residents of the county for information.

William Davies to Governor Beverley Randolph. ALS, Executive Papers, Vi. Addressed to the Governor of Virginia; read to the Council on 25 March.

The Virginia Representatives have asked him to report on the state accounts, supporting evidence, and "the different *desiderata* necessary to be attended to in the bill providing for the State debts"; Congress is moving in a "deliberative manner" and it "will be several weeks before the business will be so adjusted, as to know with certainty what will be done"; he has all the papers respecting the Shawnee expeditions, which the members have returned to him "without doing any thing in respect to them." (The most notable of the punitive expeditions against Britain's allies, the Shawnee, was conducted by Virginia and Kentucky militiamen under the command of George Rogers Clark in 1782.)

Thomas Jefferson to William Short. ALS, Short Papers, ViW. Written from Alexandria, Virginia. For the full text, see *PTJ* 16:228–30.

Grayson's death is expected hourly.

Thomas Lee, Jr. to Governor Beverley Randolph. ALS, Executive Papers, Vi. Written from Dumfries, Virginia; addressed to the Governor of Virginia; postmarked 14 March.

"I take this early opportunity to inform you that Colo. Greyson depa[r]ted this life to day between the hour of ten and eleven OClock."

Daniel Lyman to George Washington. ALS, Washington Papers, DLC. Written from Newport, Rhode Island. For the full text, see *PGW* 5:220–21.

Office seeking: revenue post; mentions Baldwin as reference.

Samuel Nasson to George Thatcher. ALS, Thatcher Papers, MeHi. Written from Sanford, Maine; postmarked Portsmouth, New Hampshire, 8 April.

"Your hint as to seneators and Representatives I supose was ment for those that sett with you in the Higher Courts but let me tell you the people are in as much dangour from our own littel Court [*legislature*] for if we have men in our State Leg. Bodys that do not study the good of the people how can they Choose good men for the higher Court you know I mean Seneators."

Michael Jenifer Stone to Walter Stone. ALS, Stone Papers, MdHi. Place to which addressed not indicated.

Nephew Frederick is very well; "I have been hiss'd [*at*] for a Day or two owing to too ardent an attraction to the funding sistem—I believe however that it will all end nearly as I think right—Dabling in the Funds is what I should not like."

Abishai Thomas to John Gray Blount. ALS, John Gray Blount Papers, Nc-Ar. Addressed to Washington, North Carolina; carried by Capt. Eastwood.

Thanks to Mrs. (Mary Grainger) Blount "for her very acceptable present," which arrived safely and which he shared with Williamson.

Hugh Williamson to William Blount. No copy known; mentioned in Williamson to John Gray Blount, 12 March.

William Samuel Johnson, Diary. Johnson Papers, CtHi.

"Dined at Chancellors [*Robert R. Livingston*]."

Philip Freneau, "Federal Hall." *NYDA*, 12 March; reprinted at Boston; Litchfield and Norwich, Connecticut; Philadelphia; Georgetown, Maryland (present-day Washington, D.C.); Winchester, Virginia; and Charleston, South Carolina. For the full text, see *DHFFC* 12:xv–xvi.

Poem satirizing—or celebrating—the popularity of attending House debates, enjoyed among all ranks of citizens.

Letter from Dumfries, Virginia. [Baltimore] *Maryland Journal*, 19 March; reprinted at New York City (*GUS*, 24 March) and Philadelphia.

Grayson died at Dumfries, Virginia, en route to Congress: "By the death of this gentleman the public, as well as his own family, have sustained an irreparable loss.

His abilities were equalled by few.

His integrity surpassed by none."

SATURDAY, 13 MARCH 1790

Moderate (Johnson)

Henry Lee to James Madison

Before I left home, Col. [*R. H.*] Lee being about to depart for Congress, I wrote you by him—Since my arival here I got your letr. of the 1st. March, & have had an opportunity of reading your debates in Congress.

Your motion [*on discrimination*] which underwent so much discussion & met with such a decided negative is pleasing to the landed interest in this Country, & very much disrelished by the town interest. It is substantially right indubitably, altho not consonant to the spirit of contracts between man & man. It will I suppose undergo the same fate in Congress, as all other questions will, which in any degree resist the opinions & wishes of the Northern people. This govt. which we both admired so much will I fear prove ruinous in its operation to our native state. Nothing as I said in my letr. the other day can alleviate our sufferings but the establishment of the permanent seat near the center of territory & direct taxation.

Hav[*ing writt*]en largely on politics last week [*torn*] more now on that subject. As I passed thro Dumfries yesterday poor Grayson was breathing his last—He was speechless, had been so the previous night, & before this must have paid his last debt.

[*Patrick*] Henry & yourself are named as competitors for the vacancy. But he will not (it is said) accept, & whether you will is doubtful.

I wish Mr. Henry was with you in the lower house, & in the event of your walking up stairs that he could take your place. But this is impracticable— Mr. Shorts letr. repeats what Mr. Jefferson has before communicated to me.[1]

I am very sorry that want of a small sum of money should stop the use & improvement of a spot really necessary to the trade & convenience of the people on the potomac.

ALS, Madison Papers, DLC. Written from Alexandria, Virginia.

---

[1] Probably William Short to Madison, 17 November 1789 (*PJM* 12:447–49), in which Short discussed his efforts on behalf of Madison and Lee's attempt to secure European investors for their proposed town at Great Falls, Virginia, on the Potomac River.

Robert Morris to George Harrison

*** Our State Doctors in the House of Representatives are daily at Work on the Secretarys Report, and altho the Spirits of the Public Creditors are Some times up, yet they are frequently drooping again and in fact the present State of the matter is not very pleasing to those who are the real Friends of America, because all such must wish to see the Credit of the Country fully and fairly established. Credit, public Credit, particularly is a *Jewell* so invalueable as to exceed all price. I think however that you may safely proceed in the execution of the orders you have, and if at any period. during your Absence there should be a Necessity for altering the Terms Mr. [*William*] Constable will write you the needfull.

You have enclosed a letter to George Walton Esqr. if you go for Georgia,

I suppose you know General [*Anthony*] Wayne if not give My Compliments & shew him this part of this letter whereby I request his attention to you and I know He will respect you as one Worthy Pensylvanian ought to respect another of Meritorious Character You will also make yourself known to Major [*Benjamin*] Fishbourne and if necessary make use of my Name to him. I am not satisfied with the Report on my Memorial[1] & shall call for farther proceedings thereon being, determined to root out all possibility of future suspicions and thereby cure the past & prevent future Calumnies. The Settlement of the other accounts not quite finished yet oweing to the Multiplicity of business in the public offices but all in good time it will be done and then the $470,000 Vanish.

ALS, Brinton Coxe Papers, PHi. Addressed to Philadelphia; answered 31 March. The omitted text contains advice for financing Harrison's trip through the southern states (to purchase continental and state debts).

[1] For background, see *DHFFC* 8:663–75.

Robert Morris to Mary Morris

Your letter of the 7th My dear Molly is the latest and indeed the only one which has not been acknowledged by its Contents I find you had, had your Party and that the entertainment was Satisfactory both to the Young and to the Elder Guests which is so far well, and indeed I never doubted but it would be so, because a disposition to please, when exerted as yours is upon such occasions seldom fails to succeed: but I am sorry you had the Head Ache after it. poor Miss Abby Willing,[1] the description you give of her situation is terrible She is much to be pitied and I think her time in this World has been so spent as to propose her for leaving it without much Regret. The time is approaching when I must pay you a visit if it is to be paid at all, but the Senators say I cannot be spared, indeed I have for some time past seen that the most Important business would be coming on about the time I should want leave of absence, However I tell them that at all events I must go Home and accordingly I expect the happiness of Seeing You the end of this Month, but you must not be too Sure of it, lest the Senate should refuse to grant me a leave of Absence.

The Committee of the House of Representatives have made a Report upon my Memorial[2] which Mr. Madison who was Chairman thought would Satisfy me, but it does not, and I shall either prevail on the said Committee to go further into the business or to get another Committee appointed for the purpose of making a full investigation. which is what I wish, or if they do not I will again Memorialize the House being determined to give the

Lie Compleat to all the abusive Publications that have been made on those Subjects. Here has been a Considerable fall of Snow and all New York were in Sleighs for a day & a half but the Snow is now too much Melted for a farther pursuit of that pleasure, a pleasure which the People here are very fond of, You know I hold it in Contempt & therefore I did not get into a Sleigh. I see the same fall of Snow extended to Philada. for Mr. [*Garrett*] Cottringer on the outside of his letter says it is 18 Inches deep—but notwithstanding that Depth of Snow I doubt if there was much Sleighing at Philadelphia.

How did my little Captain [*Henry Morris*] conduct himself on the Occasion. I suppose He did not this time as whilst I was in Virginia occupy himself in Wheeling snow about the Yard in a wheel-Barrow.

Lewis Morris has petitioned the Assembly of this State for a Bridge across Harlem River at Morrisania, should He succeed and I am obliged to come here next year it may not be inconvenient to take up my quarters there & in that case perhaps you may be of the party, However we must have another Tryal to Remove Congress from hence altho the success appears more doubtfull now than it did last year.

I did intend to have filled this Sheet of paper and perhaps may do it before it goes, but at present I bid you adieu & with the utmost affection Continue to be my Dear Molly yours only.

ALS, Morris Papers, CSmH. Place to which addressed not indicated. The conclusion of this letter was written on 14 March, below.

---

[1] Abigail (b. 1747), the younger sister of Morris's business associate Thomas Willing, died unmarried on 10 August 1791.
[2] See *DHFFC* 8:663–75.

Louis Guillaume Otto to Comte de Montmorin

The tendency that the United States has to draw nearer and nearer to an elective Aristocracy and even a mixed Monarchy becomes more noticeable every day; the newspapers that have so much influence in this country, being written by the most populous party, lead minds imperceptibly towards a state of things that assures the most tranquility and well-being for the Republic. I had the honor, Sir, to report to you in Dispatch No. 4, some principles that were bound to serve as the foundation for the new Constitution of Pennsylvania. This work, which took three months, has just been accomplished. As a principal innovation, one notes the establishment of *two* Legislative Chambers, of which, according to the opinion of one of the authors, the *lower* one ought to represent the *passions* of the people {*and*} the *higher* one, its *reason*. South Carolina and [*New*] Jersey, whose executive power was extremely limited, also proposed to alter their Constitutions. The first of these States has already named the Members of its Convention, the number of which, to the astonishment of everyone, given the tiny population of this state, will be 230. One will see, at last, throughout the extent of the United States, Governments of *three branches*, Monarchical, Aristocratic, and Democratic. These attempts made on a small scale are so much less troublesome when the people remodel their Constitutions with the greatest moderation. There is more tumult over an election at Westminster [*Parliament*] than there has been in America over the establishment of federal Government. To facilitate the understanding of public matters, already widespread, a federal catechism[1] was just printed in Connecticut, which will be introduced in the schools and which will contain all that will be necessary to know in order to judge soundly the operations of Congress.

Meanwhile, Sir, the affairs of the general Government are very far from being entirely without difficulties. The deliberations on finances proceed very slowly and do not yet present a favorable outcome. The amendments with which Congress had desired to sooth the individual states, are meeting with some opposition in Virginia, Pennsylvania, and Massachusetts, the most powerful states of the Confederation. The Senate of Massachusetts has, among others, proposed as *counter amendments*: "that the members of Congress will be payed and removable by the individual legislatures; that the boundaries between the judiciary power of Congress and of the States will be better defined; that it will be determined by law *in what cases* Congress will be able to require a State to execute its orders, finally, that a part of the internal taxation will be reserved exclusively for the particular [*i.e., State*] Legislatures." These counter amendments would become much more troublesome if they were adopted by the other States, but each [*acts*] acts formally in its own way and according to its special interests, so that the little agreement that reigns in this regard between the Antifederalists of the different States turns out for the benefit of Congress.

The act for a general census of the inhabitants of the United States has just passed into law, likewise the naturalization Bill that Congress was occupied with for some time. Two years of residence and the taking of an oath of allegiance will suffice to secure the rights of citizenship to foreigners. Expressly exempted are the royalist refugees who will not possess this advantage, without virtue of a special act of the [*state*] legislature that banished them.

The hopes that had been expressed for the immediate accession of Rhode Island to the new Confederation vanished very suddenly. The Antifederalists, feeling that they had the majority in the convention of that state, adroitly had a motion passed, that the questions of adjournment and amendments would be decided before the question of adoption. Without giving themselves the time to read the new Constitution or to examine any article, they proposed the day after to adjourn and to have the good people nominate a new *Convention* to draw up some amendments to this constitution. This conduct, unique in its way since there have been Conventions in America, has shocked some Federalists to the point of wanting to commit Congress to conquer Rhode Island, others have laughed, and she [*Rhode Island*] inspires pity in all sensible men. This tiny state has carried on this extravagance up to imagining that she can conserve her independence in the center of the United States and that by means of free commerce she will be able to become for them [*the United States*] what the Island of [*St.*] Eustatius is for the Antilles. The Antifederalist majority there is much too small to be able to resist for long the torrent of public opinion and the powerful motives which must persuade them to take part in the collective United States. In spite of these appearances, Congress is beginning to grow tired of all these manoeuvres which have been used to deceive their expectation and several senators are preparing an extraordinary measure, the substance of which they have communicated to me. Under penalty of the confiscation of their ships, wagons, and merchandise, and even fines and imprisonment, they propose to prohibit all communication with Rhode Island by land and water and to authorize the President of the United States to exact from this state the payment of its share of the debt contracted during the war. They are waiting for things to be ripe before passing this motion, which will probably not be done for two months and which, until then, they will keep secret to curb intrigues.

Copy, in French, Henry Adams Transcripts, DLC. Otto's letters included in *DHFFC* were usually written over the course of days, and even weeks, following the day they were begun.

[1] The "Federal Catechism" appeared in the ninth Hartford edition of Noah Webster's *American Spelling Book* (1790).

Alexander White to Horatio Gates

Your favour of 27th Ul[*tim*]o. came to hand yesterday—The Report of the Secretary of the Treasury is no doubt a great performance and upon the first reading I seemed inclined with you to adopt it in toto,[1] but on considering it as a subject to be acted upon in my Legislative Capac[*it*]y I found, or thought I found, many defects, The various inducements proposed to the Creditors for the reduction of their interest are all illusive, except the one third in Land that is a fair alternative, provided your rights are not diminished in case of refusal I do not wish To see Men basking in the Sunshine of Wealth not acquired by their own Industry. but by the Sweat and blood of their Fellow Citizens, is to me no pleasing Scene, but I would only submit to this rather than see them who had sweat and bled for their Country deprived of their stipulated hire—I was at first blush much pleased with the Assumption of the State Debts, and when they can be adjusted have yet no objection to the measure, but to suffer the Individuals who have claims against their respective States to loan them to the General Government will be attended with amazing injustice—the measure is urged principally by Massachusetts—whose Citizens are inclined to emigrate to avoid the Taxes necessary to discharge their own Debts—an undue proportion of those Debts already fall on the Southern States by the operation of the impost Law S. Carolina it is true joins in the Measure I suppose it is for the interest of that State but that Pennsylvania should support the Measure, altho their Members avow it to be unjust in its operation. particularly in their State is not so easily accounted for—The Proposition underwent a very full discussion and was at length carried by a Majority of 5—31 to 26—We expect however it will be finally lost. unless it should be so modified as to defeat the wishes of those who are now most anxious for it—I hear nothing of a Revolt in Mexico—if there have been any flying Paragraphs in the Papers they have not att[racted] general attention.

Mr. Jefferson is not arrived, he hesitated about accepting. I believe he has not yet explicitly declared his Sentiments—he has married his Daughter to a Mr. Randolph[2]—this was the last excuse I heard—We however, expect him daily I am astonished—I am astonish at the Report of my being in danger of drowning in the Susquehannah—the Weather was so calm that the Ladies sat in their Carriages in the Boats the whole way over—Mrs. [Sarah Hite] White and Polly[3] went with the Phaeton in the first Boat, and I accompanied the rest of the Family in the second, there was a small Rain during the Passage which increased after we got across shore so as to detain us all Night, during the Night and next Morning the Wind was high—The first account I had of the report I supposed it owing to some exaggerated account of our crossing the Hackinsack in which we found some difficulty from contrary Winds and Tides the Ladies all alarmed—but no damage done Indeed I believe no so large a Family never went so far long a Journey with so little delay or loss—Our House is rather small—in other respects they have everything that can be pleasing to young Minds, the politeness of the place has occasioned such attention, that they are seldom at home of an Evening without Company, and have not had time to return all their Visits. they have received—There are Assemblies once a Fortnight, and Balls once a Month to both which they were presented with Tickets soon after their arrival to to the latter. Youth and young Misses are admitted—Mrs. [Martha] Washington has her drawing Room, every Friday Evening—Mrs. [Abigail Smith] Adams every Monday, Lady [Elizabeth Bowdoin] Temple on Tuesday—Mrs. [Lucy Flucker] Knox on Wednesday—Madam de La Forrest & Mrs. [Sarah Livingston] Jay on Thursday—Music and Dancing Masters attend the Girls at home they go to no Public School—Mrs. [Abigail (Mrs.

Daniel Denison)] Rogers was among our early Visitors—she enquired very particularly for Mrs. Thompson—Mrs. White and the young Family join in respectful Compts. to you Mrs. [*Mary Valens*] Gates and Mrs. Thompson, they look forward to the time of their Return, with anxious Wishes, and consider the time they may spend at Travellers Rest as not the least pleasing part of the Scene.

P. S. This letter is for the perusal of our Friend General [*Adam*] Stephen— There was scarcely ever known so mild a Winter in this place, the greatest Snow we had fell three days ago, it was above four inches deep. and is now almost gone.

ALS, Emmet Collection NN. Place to which addressed not indicated.

¹ In its entirety.
² Jefferson's first born, Martha (1772–1836), also known as "Patsy," married Thomas Mann Randolph, Jr., on 23 February.
³ White married his second wife, Sarah Hite, in 1784. "Polly" may have been Mary Hite (b. pre-1777), probably a relation and one of the daughters of John Hite (d. 1777) of Winchester, Virginia, all of whom were "distinguished for their beauty, intelligence, and accomplishments" (Jacob Hite Family [folder], Handley Library, Winchester, Virginia). In 1790 White represented the children of John Hite in a lawsuit brought by their uncle, George Hite of Berkeley County, West Virginia (*PJM* 13:254n).

OTHER DOCUMENTS

William Constable to George Harrison. FC:lbk, Constable-Pierrepont Collection, NN.

The opinion of the members regarding Hamilton's funding plan is in a "very uncertain state"; there is no certainty that the assumption of the states' war debts will pass when the Funding Bill comes before the full House; "the senate are in general right I believe on the subject of Public Credit," but does not think that the House "mean what is fair"; their intention will be known in a few days.

William Constable to James Seagrove. FC:lbk, Constable-Pierrepont Collection, NN.

Hamilton is "so rigid that there is no Chance of his dispensing with any order Our friend W[*illiam*]. D[*uer*]. is going to quit the office" as his assistant secretary.

Andrew Craigie to Horace Johnson. FC:dft, Craigie Papers, MWA. Sent to Charleston; carried by Capt. Thomas Snell.

Mentions confidentially that, although assumption of the states' war debts passed in the COWH, it is uncertain whether it will succeed in the full House.

Benjamin Huntington to Governor Samuel Huntington. No copy known; acknowledged in Samuel to Benjamin Huntington, 24 April.

John Lansing, Jr. to Egbert Benson. Written from Albany, New York. Summary of one page ALS, *Heritage Auctions* 21[February 2006]:item 205409. "Lansing tells Benson of other letters enclosed."

Robert Morris to George Washington. ALS, Washington Papers, DLC. Marked "private." For the full text, see *PGW* 5:226.
>   Forwards letters from Maria de la Puente Miralles (of Havana, Cuba; widow of Juan de Miralles [d. 1780], first Spanish agent to the United States); after they are translated, Morris will wait on him to discuss their subject. (The subject may have related to the Miralles's finances, which Morris had offered to manage for her as early as 1781.)

Henry Remsen to Thomas Fitzsimons. ALS, Miscellaneous Manuscripts, DLC. A draft, with minor stylistic variations, is in the same collection. No such petition was ever presented to the FFC. The Confederation Congress petition Remsen refers to was presented on 17 March 1785 and referred to a committee that included future FFC members King, Johnson, and Monroe. Their report of 28 March 1785, while acknowledging the merchants' wartime losses and exertions to support public credit, lamented Congress's lack of power to make special provisions for them and referred the petition to the state legislature for action (*JCC* 28:121n, 199–200).
>   Encloses newspapers, and a Confederation Congress petition from New York City merchants, to "enable you to form a competent judgment on the claims of the petitioning Merchants of New York for relief, on account of the extra sacrifices of their property for the public service during the period of the late contest."

Samuel W. Stockton to Elias Boudinot. ALS, Stimson Boudinot Collection, NjP. Written from Trenton, New Jersey; sent per post. Boudinot's proposal of 9 March was to strike a discounted purchase of federal lands from among the options for payment offered public creditors and to substitute another option by which four percent of the interest would be funded and a certificate, payable in ten years, would be given for the other two percent (*DHFFC* 5:841).
>   Has forwarded Boudinot's money and certificates by John Noble Cumming; was pleased to see in *GUS* (10 March) his "proposal"; was "amazed" to find members opposed to it, as it approached nearer to paying the original six percent; understands it may not be popular since it will oblige people to pay more taxes—"Even in N. Jersey I suppose that doctrine

not the most popular," in either East Jersey, except among those with certificates, or West Jersey, where they have none; was glad to hear that Boudinot had kept up (John?) Cox's spirits "by often calling on him"; asks if Boudinot will be at the April sitting of court.

Caleb Strong to Nathan Dane. ALS, Dane Collection, MHi. Addressed to Boston; franked; postmarked 14 March.

Since his last letter, has not seen any of the commissioners for settling accounts between the states and the United States; yesterday asked Otis to enquire of his housemate, Commissioner John Taylor Gilman, "what prospect there was of a speedy alteration to the Accounts from Massachusetts"; Otis just informed him that Gilman suggests Dane "come forward as soon as you would be able to prepare the necessary papers"; John Kean to replace Baldwin as commissioner.

Manasseh Cutler, Diary. Cutler Papers, IEN.

"Dined at Mr. [*John*] Pintard's. very large company. several members of Congress."

Noah Webster, Diary. Webster Papers, NN.

Wadsworth arrived in Hartford, Connecticut.

Letter from Providence, Rhode Island. *NYDA*, 27 March; reprinted at Boston and Burlington, New Jersey.

If Rhode Island's next convention does not ratify the Constitution, there is no probability that the state will benefit from any further exemption from foreign impost and tonnage duties, obliging several classes of citizens either to emigrate or "starve at home."

Sunday, 14 March 1790

John Adams to Stephen Higginson

I am much obliged by your favor of the first instant with the report of the Committee: and glad to find that the bench has been filled with Characters to your satisfaction. The report of the Committee gives me concern, as it [*is*] evidence of an unquiet restless spirit as it tends to encourage Rhode Island in their obstinacy; but most of all as I fear there is too much probability that it originated in the advice you mention and is aided by some of the great folks you allude to—It is supposed to have been sett on foot in the Massachusetts to assist in raising the same spirit in Virginia, where there is at present a very general satisfaction with the national Government: though it is apprehended that this measure may revive some old uneasiness. I really fear that some of my old friends both in Virginia and Massachusetts hold not in horror as much as I do, a division of this Continent into two or three nations and have not an equal dread of Civil war. The appearance of reviving courage in this Country is very pleasing to a man as much mortified as I have been with reproaches against the Religion, morals, honor and spirit of this Country. it is rapture to see a returning disposition to respect treaties to pay debts, and to do justice by holding property sacred and obeying the Commandment "Thou shalt not steal." The worthy Clergymen throughout the United States when they pray for the Vice President petition that he may be endowed with the Spirit of his Station in this petition I most devoutly join. And the most difficult part of the spirit of his station is to abstain from medaling improperly with the executive power. For this reason you must not depend upon any activity on my part to promote your views This I can say however, that I believe your qualifications for the office you mentioned to be of the best kind and equal to those of any man, that I shall make no opposition to you personally and that whenever it may fall in my way consistent with the aforesaid spirit of my station to assist your wishes, it will give me pleasure to do it. I received some time ago a letter from you for which I was much obliged to you tho' I fear I have never answered it. The inspection of Merchandizes to be exported is one of the most important things this Country has to do. Next to the faith of treaties and the payment of debt, punctuality in the quality of merchandizes to be exported is the thing most wanted I will not say to support, but to restore the moral character of our Country. Pensylvania has derived such advantages from her inspection laws, that I wonder the Massachusetts should want any motive to follow her example. Some of the States derive such advantages from their own inspection laws and from the want of them in New England that opposition to a general law may arise from that interest. The national debt I have long thought, must be the instrument for establishing a national government, and have the pleasure now to see that the President, his ministers and a majority in the house are of the same opinion I have also the satisfaction to see that the ennemies and opposers of the Government are all of the same mind. The latter are accordingly exerting themselves against the assumption of the State debts, as the pivot upon which the general government will turn. The opposition however seems to be feeble as not supported by the voice of the people This is a favorable symptom Indeed the government appears to have had as happy an effect upon the prosperity and peace of the Country as its friends had reason to expect. It might not be too strong an expression to say that the most sanguine prophecies of its blessings and utility have been fulfilled. There are defects still in the Constitution, which if they are not supplied by degrees as it gains strength will produce evils of a serious kind.

FC:lbk, Adams Family Manuscript Trust, MHi.

John Dawson to James Madison

***

I[n] this place where most persons are dealers in public securities your plan for a discrimination in public them has been generally disapprovd of as might be expected—what is the general opinion in the State I will not pretend to say—but my own is that the difficulties attending the business form the greatest objection, and that Justice is in your favour.

For several weeks we have been in daily expectation of hearing of the death of our friend Grayson—I still hope he will recover for shoud he not I know not who we shoud appoint willing to serve, and who woud meet with the approbation of the Legislature.

***

ALS, Madison Papers, DLC. Written from Richmond, Virginia. For the full text, see *PJM* 13:106–7. The omitted text includes a request to confirm the receipt of a map of the Potomac River and "some papers" for William Davies, forwarded at the request of Governor Beverley Randolph. In December 1789 the Virginia legislature resolved that such a map should be sent to Congress with other documents related to a Potomac River location for the seat of federal government; see *DHFFC* 6:1783.

Thomas Dwight to Theodore Sedgwick

That so great obstructions should be thrown in the way of the funding system, as you represent in your favor of the 5th. inst. is to me an unexpected and mortifying consideration; I have heard the national views of most of the members of the present Congress so much spoken of, and applauded, that I had wrought myself into a belief, that partial and local advantages from legislative acts, would neither be aimed at, or sought for by them—something of this kind was, however, to be expected from a discussion of the question in regard to the established residence of the Govt. but here I had hopes it would end—opposition from men so high in reputation and influence as Mr. M[adison]. would be disagreeable in matters of lesser importance but when they [*lined out*] become obstinate in support of measures which would certainly if adopted, destroy public credit, and endanger the very existence of the government, we may very justly ascribe their conduct to motives which do not savor much of patriotism or national views. I was overjoyed when I

found the question in regard to discrimination carried in the negative by so great a majority—if an assumption of the State debts can be brought about I will sing "laus deo"[1] with as much devotion as any saint in Christendom.
***

ALS, Sedgwick Papers, MHi. Written from Springfield, Massachusetts. The conclusion of this letter was written on 15 March, and is printed in volume 19. The omitted text relates to Massachusetts politics.

[1] Praise God.

Benjamin Goodhue to Insurance Offices

The last week We went through in a Committee of the whole House, the several resolutions, which contain'd the most material principles of the Secry.'s report, and agreed to most of them, except the propositions of Annuities,[1] they will be now submited to the House for their acceptance, and if accepted will form the ground work of the funding sistem—I expect the opponents to the Assumption will be active to prevent that part of the resolutions from being accepted, and will doubtless loose no opportunity in the various stages of this bussines of defeating the measure, so that on the whole, what from the opposition to assumption in many, and the disinclination to any funding sistem whatever in others, I consider the subject to be altogether in much jeopardy, tho' we have now a majority and I hope we may continue it! this is indubitably our national crisis, and from our measures, We may date our future prospects, as they relate to the Union and government.

ALS, Goodhue Letters, NNS. Addressed to Salem, Massachusetts; franked; postmarked.

[1] For the propositions referred to, see *DHFFC* 5:842.

Benjamin Goodhue to Samuel Phillips, Jr.

*** I cannot but be much surprised, at the hesitation which prevails in the minds of some of my good friends relative to the assumption, if concord between different creditors, if interferences ~~between~~ in the exercise of different powers is to be avoided, in short if our worthy and suffering State creditors are ever to be paid, these and numberless blessings are involved in the measure, and all the contrary evils will most assuredly follow a rejection—the idea of a consolidation being the effect is establishing this absurd and unpalatable doctrine, that its necessary Massachusetts shd. be overborne with ~~healt~~ debt in order to preserve her in health and prosperity—if it should ever be the wish of Massachusetts to oppose the Genl. Government, surely she will be capacitated to oppose with vigour much more if she is unembarrass'd—I wish we may not be freightned with such bugbears— Madison would be an excellent politician if he was not so much warped by local considerations, and popular influences, but with those about him he is a dangerous foe, to those measures which soar above trifling objects, and have national advantages for their basis—perhaps the people of Massachusetts look forward to a speedy settlement of State accounts that will releive them from their present unequal burthens, and in this view, the assumption is a matter of indifference, but I beleive they are deciev'd, I hope and wish for a settlement tho' I fear they must bear the burthen a long time if this is to be the only sourse of relief—I am sensible this bussines of funding will try mens characters, and mine will be subject to much scrutiny, but I am firmly bent to pursue that line of conduct that shall appear to point to National Justice dignity and prosperity, and if its possible for me to feel myself above partial considerations and murmerings the present bussines fixes me in that situation.

***

ALS, Phillips Family Papers, MHi. Place to which addressed not indicated. The omitted text repeats Goodhue's letter to the Salem Insurance Offices, above, and discusses his role in helping to procure an employee for Phillips's paper mill.

Thomas Hartley to Jasper Yeates

I receved your Favor of the 8th. inst. and am happy to hear that Mrs. [*Sarah Burd*] Yeates is recovered—I hope you may have an agreeable Evening on the Seventeenth—I shall endeavor to be in Mind with you for a few Minutes upon that Occasion.

Your Sentiments concerning the public Debt I think are just—Some Men whose States are rather in a desperate Situation are ~~rather~~ for pushing Us too fast—They wish to induce us to lay heavy additional Duties, in short enter into very deep Taxation.

But we have resolved yesterday that we will during the present Session make full Provision by funding to pay the Interest upon the now actual Debts of the united States under certain Terms &c. & that at the next Session Provision shall be made for funding the Several State Debts—The Measure I dare say you will consider as prudent—for if we were to travel before our Means Confusion and Distruction would insue—I will on to Morrow strive to send you a Copy of the Resolutions agreed to in a Committee of the whole.

There are some Deviations from the Secretary's Report tho not unfavourable to the Creditor.

~~Some~~ more attempts will be made—but the Fine Edge has been pretty well taken off. Some of Mr. Madisons Opinions have prevailed—But when the North Carolina Delegates come on he will make another push agst. the Assumption of the State Debts.

He is certainly an extraordinary Man—and when he comes to have a sufficient Knowledge of practical Life—there will be few beyond him—As I intend to send you the Resolution to Morrow I shall conclude this Letter.

ALS, Yeates Collection, PHi. Addressed to Lancaster, Pennsylvania; franked; postmarked.

Benjamin Huntington to Anne Huntington

I Recd. no letter by the last Post from any of our Family but by a letter from the Govr. [*Samuel Huntington*] and another from Col. [*Christopher*] Leffingwell I was informed that you Remained in much the same State of health as when I left home which I think is not by any means discouraging—I am however exceedingly concerned for you but hope to see you in better health on my Return but cannot say when that will be but Expect it will be in May or June—I am in better health then when I left home, am obliged to be very careful of myself and not exposed [*torn*] to the Cold or ~~to be~~ wet We have no [*torn*] Importance—I hope & trust you will be enabled to endure with a becoming Patience the Distresses of your Infirmity & that all the Divine Dispensations towards you may be so Improved as to promote your happiness both temporal & Eternal—I am very unhappy in being separated from you at a time when you stand in greater need of my Services aid & Support than ever before.

ALS, Huntington Papers, CtHi. Addressed to Norwich, Connecticut; franked; postmarked.

Richard Bland Lee to Theodorick Lee

I have received your favor of the 7th. Instant and tho I have no splended project to recommend to you take the first opportunity of answering it. You say that Mr. Madison has not one advocate in your part of the country. This only proves that the opinion of the community differs from his. This I am convinced of that his proposition[1] was dictated by the purest motives and a solicitude to establish the credit of the U. States on the firmest basis. He thought that from a review of the late and present circumstances of the Country—that justice required that the claims ~~of~~ Against the U. States ought to be modified in the manner proposed by him. And that such a Modification was essential~~ly necessary~~ to reconcile the public mind to the taxes which would necessarily be required: and that in commencing our national existence—a sacred regard to the natural dictates of Justice and gratitude would be the direct way to obtain the confidence of our own poeple, and that of the world—tho' in so doing we should disregard maxims derived from and [*lined out*] observed with inflexible strictness by the British Nation, which, since it contracted a National debt, never was in any situation similar to that of America and therefore would not be a proper guide on this occasion. I think you mistake the nature of mankind very much th when you suppose that direct taxes will be more acceptable to the body of any poeple than indirect ones. If such is the opinion of the poeple of Virginia, they differ from the rest of the World, and may deservedly be ranked as one of the most enlightened Societies.

I have nothing to add except that I shall be happy to see you in this city— if your projects should render a visit here necessary—and will be ready to contribute all the aid in my power to farther your views. Tho' I have neither money nor in influential friends. If you come it would be prudent to leave your servant in Virginia.

ALS, Custis-Lee Family Papers, DLC. Addressed to "Sully," Loudoun County, Virginia, via Alexandria, Virginia; franked; postmarked.

---

[1] For discriminating between original and subsequent securities holders.

William Maclay to Benjamin Rush

I have received your letter of the 10th instant, the sentiments are just and perfectly in Unison with my mode of thinking. Yet, I much fear, we shall be left in the Minority. The Secretary's report, labours hard, in the house of representatives, it is carried, but carried with difficulty; and the Views of many, who vote for particular parts of it, are as discordant, as any thing you can imagine For instance, on the assumption of the State debts. I know Members who voted for it, that they might extricate the honor of their respective States. and whose next measure will be to apply the Spunge[1] to the Whole if possible. others voted for the same Measure, only that they might be enabled, to draw an Argument, from the Mass of the debt, so accumulated, against the funding altogether, on the Score of inability. In the Mean While the Secretary's Friends, are exerting themselves, to the Utmost of their power. to secure a Majority for the adoption of the Report. By the Returns of the New Impost. the Port of Philada. furnishes one fourth of the present Revenue of the Union. this places Us in a most important point of View, and forces an unwilling attention to Us. our Pennsylvania News papers are sought after, with greediness, by some Political Characters, but for different purposes, some to gain a knowledge of the Sentiments of our

Citizens. and by others to secrete & destroy them, for fear our Sentiments should be found, averse to their Views. Much however do we wish that the Voice of the public might be heard. for tho' some Men affect to despise it, I shall for my part always listen to it with pleasure. The Crisis is an important One, he that will not now speak, should allow himself, for ever hereafter, to be silent, happen what will. I for my part wish for information, & receive it with pleasure and gratitude.

ALS, Rush Papers, DLC. Addressed to Third Street, Philadelphia; franked; postmarked.

[1] To cancel or wipe out a debt without payment.

James Madison to [*Edward Carrington*]

Your favor of the 2d. inst. came to hand two days ago. Though I can not yield to the remarks on my proposition ~~in the H. of Reps.~~ I am not the less indebted for the candor which dictated them. The nature of the domestic debt will account for the diversity of opinions among those who examine it. Those who are disinterested or being interested are superior to that biass, will be materially liberal and tolerant. Those of an opposite complexion on both sides, will breathe an opposite spirit.

[*lined out*] It has appeared to me that the transactions of the public with the orig[*ina*]l. Creditors, were not an equitable and bona fide discharge of its engagements, and consequently that the original contract is [*lined out*] partly still in force in their favor. If this datum be admitted, the transaction between the origl. Creditor & the assignee, can not absolve the public from its obligation to the former. To say that the Creditor ought not to have distrusted the public is not satisfactory for two reasons, first because in many cases the alienation was the effect of ~~the same~~ necessity; secondly, because the default of the public warranted the distrust. Nor can I agree with you ~~that~~ in supposing that the probable use that would have been made of a real payment by those who parted with their depreciated one, or the probable repetition of the folly, in case the deficiency should now be made up, can diminish either the rights of the ~~Idivid~~ individual, or the obligations of the public. With respect to the latter probability however, I do not think it by any means so great as is stated. The different circumstances under which the payments would be received, seem to warrant this opinion. But it might easily have been provided, and would actually have been proposed, as a precaution agst. a second harvest of speculation on the ignorance or distrust of the creditors that the new paper should not be transferrable for a definite term, within which the receipt of the interest would have taught the holder its proper value, and have inspired him with a proper confidence in his Country—I differ from you also in supposing that a wound would have been given to public Credit. The measure not only carried equity on the face of it, but proclaimed honesty to be its motive. Will not public credit be more wounded by a *forced* re-loan in *favor* of the public? and will not the world ascribe this operation ~~either~~ to a want of ~~bounty~~ inclination either in the Government to comply strictly with its engagements, or in the people to submit to its just authority, rather than to a want of resources in the Country? and will not either of these suspicions be more unfriendly to our object, than any imputations that could have been thrown on the other measure. For my part I am convinced that the public is able to perform, its stipulations, or if the Government be *unable*, it is because the people are *unwilling*, & that this unwillingness is produced by a sentiment as natural as it is general, that there must be something wrong, radically & morally & politically wrong, in a system which transfers the reward from those who paid the most valuable of all considerations, to those who scarcely paid any consideration at all. If the public debt had never been alienated, or had been alienated for its nominal value, The whole resources of the community would have been at the disposal of the Govt. and might have been exhausted without a murmur.

I have carefully avoided throughout this business in the H. of Representatives to animadvert on the title of the actual holders, because ~~my~~ the principle of my motion did not require it, and because I did not wish to inflame popular prejudices which are already sufficiently strong. I am not the less persuaded however that in many instances, in more than could be prudently left to private litigation, the purchases have been viciated by fraud, that in most instances the equity of the ~~title is impaired~~ transaction has been impaired by the event of a valuable consideration, and that it is at least doubtful [*lined out*] whether the buyer is more entitled than the seller, to the benefits resulting from the New Government. This event was, in most cases as much out of the contemplation of both parties, as a miraculous shower of gold from heaven. Neither the confidence of the former, nor the distrust [*of*] the latter had any reference whatever to it. Where then is the merit of the confidence, or the want of it in the distrust, which are now to be appreciated by the New Government? But I forget that I am discussing a point already decided, and am writing a letter not a dissertation.

The law for enumerating the inhabitants will have been transmitted to you. It is as good as was to be got. I fear much that the execution of it will be so defective in the Southern States as to give an undue preponderancy agst. them in the Legislature. Every thing that is practicable in Virga. may I am sure be counted upon, but your efforts can not conquer impossibilities. It is of great consequence that the people should be impressed with the importance of the measure, and particularly that their attention should be turned from the contingent disadvantage, to the certain & essential advantage of a full return of their number.

The assumption of the State debts has been a subject of much discussion. Virga. has endeavored to ~~secure~~ tack to it a secure provision for justice in the ultimate settlemt. and has succeeded in part. But on the whole no provision can be made that will not leave a great uncertainty of that event. In every other view the measure is inadmissible by that State. Altho' already in advance she would be called on for further advances, Even in a political & general view there are strong objections. The practicability itself of the plan is at least questionable—In a committee of the whole the assumption was voted by a small majority. N. Carola. is still, to be added, we calculate, to the minority. The result therefore is very doubtful. The modifications of the pub[*lic*]. debt. have undergone some changes in the Com[*mitte*]e. but more with a view to simplify the debt, than to change the principle of the Secretary.

ALS, Emmet Collection, NN. Place to which addressed not indicated. Carrington is identified as the recipient by the fact that the letter is clearly an answer to his letter of 2 March, above.

James Madison to Edmund Randolph

I have recd. the few lines you dropped me from Baltimore, and daily expect those promised from Fred[*ericksbur*]g. I am made somewhat anxious on the latter point, by the indisposition under which you were travelling.

The question[1] depending at your departure was negatived by a very large majority, though less than stated in the Newspapers. The causes of this disproportion which exceeds greatly the estimate you carried with you can not be altogether explained. Some of them you will conjecture. Others, I reserve for conversation if the subject should ever enter into it. As far as I have heard, the prevailing sense of the people at large does not coincide with the decision. and that delay and other means might have produced a very different result.

The assumption of the State debts has of late employed most the H. of Reps. A majority of 5 agreed to the measure in Com[*mitte*]e. of the Whole. But it is yet to pass many defiles. and its enemies will soon be reinforced by N. Carolina. The event is consequently very doubtful. It could not be admissible to Virga. unless subservient to final justice. or so varied as to be more consistent with intermediate justice. In neither of these respects has Va. been satisfied. and the whole Delegation is agst. the measure except *Bland*!!

The *substance* of the secretary's arrangements of the Debts of the Union, has been agreed to in Come. of the Whole and will probably be agreed to by the House. The number of alternatives has been reduced for the sake of greater simplicity, and a disposition appears at present, to shorten the duration of the Debt. According to the Report, the debt wd. subsist 40 or 50 years, which, considering intermediate probabilities, amounts to a perpetuity.

[*P. S.*] Mr. Jefferson is not arrived. He has notified his acceptance & is expected here in a day or two.

ALS, Madison Papers, DLC. Place to which addressed not indicated.

[1] For discriminating between original and subsequent securities holders.

John Pemberton to James Pemberton

Yesterday I received thy favor of 10th. Inst. with an Adition of the 11th. It would have been acceptable & useful had Pickney's speech[1] &c. been ready & here for Distribution, The Paper proposed to be sent ℔ [*Richard*] Hallet is not yet reced.[2] We do not expect to promote any Compromise & have the like sentiment with thee. & divers of the members of Congress know our mind. yet apprehended if the Report was Agreed unto. & Comitted, & there was a determination to do no more than to make some regulation, I was apprehensive, that regulation Comprised in the Law respecting German passengers[3] might operate as a prohibition—I see evil men might evade every regulation. If it comes, I believe we shall not make use of it.

E. Boudinot & J. Vining told me yesterday they would Oppose any further posponement. & expect it will come on debate on 3d. day [*Tuesday*] I expect One or more friends will come from the Country to give their attendance on that day, Friends here are very respectful, but the part many took during the Warr. I believe has weakened their hands. & do not like to appear active. My kind Landlord E. P. [*Edmund Prior?*] & J[*ohn*]. Murray with W[*illiam*]. Shotwell & L[*aurence*]. Embree shew a good disposition & attention, but they have a Law under Consideration of the Legislature of this state which claims their attention.[4] My long absence & the present state of my family as well as some private Concerns. renders it very desirable to be released, but I do not feel it right to leave my Companions upon whom a great weight devolves. & who are studiously Concerned that no Oppo. might be lost to further the momentous work. Forster [*Abiel Foster*] the Chairman of the Comittee yesterday honestly Confessed that he gave the Casting Vote to the second Article of the Report. & did it with a Veiw to make the Report set easy with the Georgia S. Carolina men. & I beleive is not pleased with himself, as it did not Answer what he had in Veiw. I have wrote my dear Wife, & refer thee thereto.

This morning there was a Cry of fire about 5 o'Clock & proved to be a malt house. lately belonging Jacob Watson, which Jno. Murray and his Brother in Law had purchased, & they had provided much barley & a large Quantity of Hops to Carry on the brewing business, the brewery is saved, but the malt house at least the upper part burnt down & the Walls fallen in. Dear John has tried at several branches of business which did not seem to Answer. this had a favorable prospect which now will put them back. & Cast Discouragment: he is a Valuable Improving man. & can but sympathise with him.

Job Scott had a Close testimony this morning at the [*Quaker*] meeting here. My Companions are pretty well. & expect two of them will write ℔ this Conveyance. he is a man of some Account in New Castle County [*Delaware*] & an Acquaintance of W[*arner*]. Mifflin. let Sarah Emlen know her husband [*Samuel*] is brave. & yet patient.

ALS, Pennsylvania Abolition Society Papers, PHi. Addressed to Second Street, Philadelphia; postmarked.

[1] Pemberton was probably referring to the antislavery speech William Pinkney delivered before the Maryland House of Delegates in November 1789, which was printed as a twenty-two page pamphlet in Philadelphia in 1790 (Evans 22800). However, Pinkney also delivered an earlier, shorter antislavery speech during the legislature's second 1788 session (3 November–23 December), which was printed in the *American Museum* in July 1789.

[2] Perhaps a partner in Hallett and Brown, ironmongers at 20 Queen Street and neighbors to William Shotwell's shop at Queen and Beckman streets, which suggests an antislavery connection among Quaker ironmongers in New York City.

[3] See John to James Pemberton, 8 March (A.M.), n. 1, above.

[4] A New York act of 22 March suspended certain provisions of a 1788 "Act concerning Slaves" by permitting the sale out of state of enslaved Blacks convicted of a capital offense.

Charles Pettit to [*Elias Boudinot*]

Your favor of the 8th. & 9th. did not arrive till friday afternoon. Since that I find there are letters as late as Thursday evening. I must own I am grieved that the Assumption of the State debts has become necessary, in the opinion of so many Members of Congress whose Opinions I highly respect, to the establishment of a funding system. It may be, as you say, a prudent and politic measure as things now stand. and so would be the amputation of a limb under particular circumstances; but they are circumstances which every one would avoid if he could. Every Man, however, who is confided in by the public, is bound to act according to his own opinion & the dictates of his own conscience. His own Sense of what is right to be done must therefore govern his Vote if he acts honestly. And when the measures of Government are conducted on these principles, it is the Duty of private Citizens to acquiesce, even when they cannot fully approve the Measures. I shall therefore

yield obedience to the Laws, whatever they may be, while they are Laws, tho'
they may operate contrary to my opinions of justice and right. The Arguments in favour of this measure do not appear to me in the light in which
they seem to appear to the advocates for the Assumption. If [*the Continental
Army*] Commissaries & Quarter Masters, for instance, have received payment
from the public for the articles they have furnished, & have procured the
articles from Individuals on their private credit, the public are not bound to
discharge the debts thus contracted, even tho' the Commissary should fail
of means to pay them; nor do I know of any instance in which the United
States have paid or assumed such debts. In this case, The States have been
generally paid for the debts now to be assumed & taken off their Shoulders—
the public will therefore pay these debts twice. To pay them once is all that
the public faith is pledged for. Any State that has not been fully paid, let
her be paid. So far justice & good faith requires but no farther. It is farther
said to be necessary because the Funds are taken from the States, by which
alone they can make payment. Is this true? I think not. The funds by which
the States have heretofore made any payments to their creditors are yet
untouched, & there seems to be a disposition in the U.S. to leave them so—
direct taxes. Any of the States who have raised Money by impost, have never
got as much from it as to pay their money contributions to the Union on
Requisitions. Another argument relied is the Power & the Disposition of the
State Creditors to raise factions, to impede the movements of Government,
and to force themselves into power enough to carve for themselves. Is this
an appeal to the *Reason* or to the *Fears* of the honest part of the community?
To simplify this Argument, we must suppose the creditors of a particular
State coming forward with a claim that the United States shall pay them
what their own particular State owes them, and what the U.S. have already
paid to that State, and urging this claim with threats that if they are not
gratified they will take by force what they cannot obtain by the operation of
equity & justice. In States in which such creditors predominate, these very
creditors owe the greater part of the money themselves—that is, the fund to
pay them, ought to be made up mostly by their own contributions. If such
concessions are *necessary* on the part of Government, it is a strong evidence
that the People of the United States are less fit to govern themselves than I
had imagined. That they are necessary, or appear to be so, to the majority of
the House, I must suppose from their late determination. How they became
necessary may, one day or an other, be enquired into—I fear, indeed, it is
now too late to reject it with safety even if a majority should be convinced
of the impropriety of the measure. The idea is gone forth, & thousands,
prompted by self interest, will join in the clamor, who would not have conceived the notion if it had not be suggested to them.

I agree with you in opinion that some who have opposed this measure are against paying the public debts at all. I will own that I began to doubt my own opinions from seeing some particular names in the opposition to the assumption. The result was a reexamination & a farther confirmation that I was right—But there are also some in favor of the measure from similar motives—I shall not mention names on either side, but you will not be at much loss to know the characters—You are not therefore to count on all the Majority as favourers of an honest funding System, nor on all the minority as opposers of it.

Having made up our minds, however, that the State debts must be assumed, it becomes necessary to think of the ways & means of funding them, together with the other debts including the balances which will be found due to particular States. These will require funds vastly exceeding the means pointed out by the Secretary, even to pay 4 per cent. An internal or direct tax therefore seems to me to be necessary—Indeed I think it ought always to form a part of all systems of taxation. Other sources are but branches, of which this is the trunk and root. It is not in the nature of Things to lay taxes so as to operate equally on the citizens in the first instance, but this should nevertheless be aimed at and always adhered to as nearly as may be, and therefore if we wanted but one million a year instead of the 5 or 6 millions we now shall want, I should think it right to raise a part of it by direct taxes. This idea I know is unpopular at present, and perhaps uncourtly too, but it ought to be popular; & it is from the popular side of my notions that I draw it. As a private citizen—as a mere farmer, I find the strongest arguments in favor of it. The assumption of the State debts seems to me to create a necessity for it, and to point it out as a kind of compensation or compromise which ought not to be omitted.

The true art of taxation is to draw money from the several channels in which it circulates in as just a proportion as may be to the quantity & force of circulation in each channel—If these principles are duly observed, much greater revenues may be raised without being injuriously burthensome, than would otherwise be practicable. The farmer generally turns his money but once a year. Money therefore circulates but slowly amongst the farmers & the body of the people of the country, and a smaller portion of the whole should be drawn from that channel. In commercial Towns, money circulates more briskly & is turned more frequently; a larger portion of the whole may be drawn from that quarter. And if the channels of circulation be kept full & regular, by returning the money into circulation again as fast as it is collected, large revenues may pass through the treasury books without being injuriously burthensome. I say through the treasury books rather than through the treasury, because but a very small proportion of the money itself need, or ought to come actually into the treasury at the seat of government, nor to be checked in its career of circulation by being carried far out of its ordinary course.

This reminds me of the bank which the Secretary announces he has in contemplation. A national bank is certainly necessary, and it may be an engine of much good if it be well constructed & organized, or of much evil if it be otherwise. There is no subject of equal importance less likely to be understood by a majority of the members, & of course none in which they may be more likely to be led into dangerous errors, if either ignorance or evil designs should pervade the framing of it. I have much curiosity as well as patriotic anxiety to know the leading features of the plan for this purpose, and shall therefore be thankful to you for some communication on this Subject—If the plan be formed, I presume it neither can nor ought to be a secret.

I pray you to excuse the freedom I take with you as well in asking information as in offering my own opinions, especially when they differ from yours. I am not yet courtier enough to attempt that kind of flattery which consists in dissimulation; but in differing in opinion from others I wish to avoid giving offence.

ALS, incomplete, AMs 779/1, PPRF. Written from Philadelphia. The recipient was identified by the reference to acknowledged letters and the letter's location in a collection of Pettit-Boudinot correspondence.

Theodore Sedgwick to Pamela Sedgwick

Yesterday, my dearest love, the Committee of the whole made a report on the subject of finance to the house. This will be taken up and I should hope decided on tomorrow, in which case I shall, if the riding is not intolerable set out for home next day, yet every thing respecting the conduct of the house is uncertain.

We have had for four or five weeks a season as busy as any I have ever known in public life. A constant and painfull attention has been necessary to keep the majority united. This however has not materially affected my health, feeling however some what of those vertiginous complaints I have thought it prudent to send for a physician this morning who has just taken from me about 16 ounces of blood, and I feel quite relieved.

Perhaps I may have the pleasure to see you before this arrives—if not I shall hope it will soon be in my power to do it without neglecting my duty in the house. I shall write a few lines to each of the little children who can read. You forgot in your last to mention to me how little Robert was. The Gentlemen whom I have consulted on his case have not yet given me an answer.

It is now said Rhode Island will not adopt the constitution.

[P. S.] Mr. Jacob went out of town without calling on me.

ALS, Sedgwick Papers, MHi. Place to which addressed not indicated.

William Smith (Md.) to Otho H. Williams

***

I believe I already told you, that our house had passed a resolution for assuming the State debts, we have Since agreed to fund two thirds of the debt at Six ℔ Cent & to pay the other third in lands in the Western territory at 20 Cents ℔ Acre. The other Alternatives which you have Seen are Struck out, except that which, which Says two thirds Shall be funded at 6 ℔ Cent, *irredeemable by any payment exceeding 4⅔ Dollrs. ℔ Annum* on Accot. of both Principal and interest & to have at the end of 10 years *26 Drs. 88 Cents, funded in like manner.* Those parts of that proposition, which I have marked are Stricken out, with an intention to enlarge the 26. Drs. 88 Cents to a higher Sum in lieu of the irredeemable quality Stricken out, on which great Stress was laid, from an opinion that interest will fall in a Short time to 4 ℔ Cent. I am inclined [*to*] think that the blank will be filled up with the full third at least, perhaps more in consideration of the 10 years interest, which will on this plan be lost to the holder, Some gentln. have proposed 53⅓ Dollrs. at the end of Ten years, which includes the full interest.

On the whole I am far from thinking this business is finally settled, the very Small Majority in favor of assuming the State debts, has alarmed the friends to that measure, & if the No. Carolina Members arrive before the Bill pass thro' our house, & are against the assumption, *as is expected* the bill will be lost, Should that be the case, it will greatly derange the whole of the funding System, for I believe many members would give up the *whole*, if Thwarted in their favorite Scheme.

Nothing has transpired, relative to the dispatches brot. by the British Sloop of War, nor has there any communications been made to the Senate I am inclined to think, She brot. dispatches for Lord Dorchester, not being Able to proceed up the River St. Laurence, took this route.

I was not at the house yesterday, having been confined to my room for two days past, with a Violent head Ache, & Sore throat, last night I had a very profuse Sweat, which I think has relieved my head a good deal, but my throat still continues Sore, however on the whole I am better & hope by tomorrow or next day to be able to go out.

My objection to the assumption of the State debts at this time, is, that I think it premature. That the accots. ought to be first Settled, & the amot. ascertaind. That a delay of this business could not possibly be injurious either to the U.S. or any individual State, Because it is not proposed to make any provision for their payment, before 1792 And because every State owe debts which the U.S. ought not to pay, & it will be impossible to discriminate, And I forsee great frauds will be commited in the one way that might be avoided in the other. I however think in the end it would be Just & Right.

Be this matter Settled as it may, Maryland will have reason [*to*] Curse, those leaders in our assembly who prevented, A Sufficient Sum of old Continental, & Finals from being procured, equal to our quota, of both those Species of Money. I am inclined to think, the continental paper will be Sunk at 40 for one & the other paper we must pay for, probably in Specie this will bear very hard on Maryland, most of the other States, have acted wisely on this head & provided paper to meet the demands against them.

P. S. you have inclosed, the paper containing the Conclusion of the Maryd. letter, as I have parted with the originals to the Printers & which I presume he would not choose to return, you can furnish Dr. [*Philip*] Thomas with the paper.[1]

ALS, Williams Papers, MdHi. Place to which addressed not indicated. The omitted text directs Williams in a business transaction.

[1] *NYDG*, 12 March, published the conclusion of Williams's 28 February letter to Smith, printed above.

William P. Smith to Elias Boudinot

***

From *Fenno's* paper [*GUS*] I read your daily public proceedings. I have hitherto been pleased. But I cannot say, I should so well acquiesce in the proposed reduction of the Interest on the National Debt. I perfectly join in Sentiment with the Writer of a Paper under the signature of a *Connecticut Man* in *Fenno's* of March 3d. This must be accounted as direct a Violation of Public Faith, as any Act of our honest State Governments, since the Revol[*utio*]n. Could you obtain the *really free* consent of Creditors—It would be very well—But if they should pretend this, it will be, as they say, a forced-Put;[1] it will be—and will be justly deemed *Compulsory*—unless you can offer them the Principal, & say "Here Gentlemen is your Money, if you dont chuse it to remain in our hands, at the Interest we chuse to give You." I declare, I should prefer the payment of my Principal—What! are we become Bankrupts, & forced to compound? *Credat Judeus!*[2] If some unexceptionble Measures be not taken on this head, there is not a monied Man will trust the public in any future Emergency, be it what it may.

ALS, Boudinot Family Papers, NjR. Written from Newark, New Jersey; carried by John Noble Cumming. The omitted text relates to a legal transaction for collecting a debt for a Mrs. Woodruff.

[1] An act of distress.
[2] "Let the Jew believe that" (Horace); said of someone considered gullible or superstitious.

John Trumbull to John Adams

I have the honour of yours of the 9th. instant, & am happy to find that you are not displeased at the frankness of my communications. There are very few Persons to whom I would have written with equal freedom—Half the world are of the temper of the Italian Cardinal, described in the Spectator,[1] who kicked his Spy down stairs for telling him what the world said against him—but with such I desire to have no connection. Whatever may be the odds of Rank, merit or abilities, in a friendly correspondence, there must be an unreservedness, which assumes the appearance of equality—And were I to open a Correspondence with the Angel Gabriel, notwithstanding my deference to a superior nature, I must write with the same freedom as to a Mortal—or not write at all.

I fully believe that more has been said on the subjects I mentioned, at a distance, than at New York; Slander has her whispering-gallery, formed to increase the sound in its progress—and the distant echo of a lie is always louder than the first report.

Your distinction between Enmity & Envy is undoubtedly just—Yet the Envious are enemies of the worst kind—the most active persevering & malignant.

The People of New England have often been charged with this fault. Perhaps the charge is not strictly true. We are true Republicans, & have the strongest feelings of personal Independence & universal equality. We are led by education to be jealous of Power, & to distrust those Men, who are raised to a dignity and elevation above the general rank. We are not however generally chargeable with ingratitude in our elections, towards public services, or known merit. But the moment we have raised the Man of our choice to a rank, necessary indeed in government, but disagreeable to our eyes, ~~then~~ we wish to make him sensible of his dependence on our suffrages, to teach him to consider himself as the servant of the people, & to ascribe his elevation, not to his own merit, but to our gratuitous favour. This must be acknowleged as our general character. We hate to see great men, & endeavour to *belittle* them as much as possible. The V. P. must therefore expect to find his merits, & services depreciated among us, but may always be sure of our suffrages. We dislike an Office of such high rank, but if there must be such an one, we are satisfied with the Person, who holds it. Indeed so strong are our ideas of republican equality; that were the other world peopled only by a certain Party of New Englanders with their present feelings, they would be disgusted at the splendor of Omnipotence, & would wish to limit Almighty Power, & establish a democracy in heaven. Our most sensible & influential characters are however fully convinced of the necessity of an energetic Government, of due subordination, & of the proper checks & balances in the Administration. But most of these are Men of ambition, & can scarcely endure a superior. Indeed Ambition is universal among us—We have Presidents, not out of their leadingstrings & Vice Presidents by dozens in embrio.

The Gentlemen from the Southward may have more apparent politeness than those from New England, & would certainly be more liberal in the allowance of adequate salaries—But the People of the Southern States will never be fond of uniting their suffrages in favor of any Native of New England.

I was entertained with the account of your honest, independent & respectable ancestry. Yours is a genealogy of which a wise man may be justly proud, but not such as a Coxcomb would boast. ***

I shall hardly allow You to ascribe to the favour of fortune your frequent escapes from death and danger in the public service. It was the hand of heaven, that conducted the American Revolution, & provided & preserved the proper Instruments for our success. Providence raised a Washington & [Nathanael] Greene &c. to command our armies, & a [Benjamin] Franklyn, Jay &c. to conduct our foreign negociations. It preserved your life to accomplish the important treaty with Holland, to give Mr. Jay the necessary assistance in settling the terms of Peace with Great Britain, & to be Vice President of the United States. On this subject I own myself an enthusiast. In the late illness of the President, when we had an account, that his Physicians despaired of his recovery, I offered to ensure his life for a sixpence, because I was convinced, that America could not do without him as yet.

Your present situation, tho' as You observe it is in some degree inactive, is by no means insignificant or uninfluential. In the equal division of Parties in the Senate, You have had sundry questions of great importance to decide. Could the grand point of the President's Power of removal have been carried without your assistance & influence? Yet that very debate has left a great share of rancour in the minds of those, whose visionary plans, political ignorance & frivolous arguments, You on that occasion detected & exposed.

Solitude & retirement, at which you hint, certainly form no scene for the exercise of activity, or the acquirement of significance. All things, I firmly believe, will be & continue right. The Batteries of Slander will waste themselves in noise & smoke, or destroy themselves by being overcharged. ***

I know not that I should object to any of your opinions—Yet on one subject, on which indeed I am not certain of yours, I will venture a single remark. I am exceedingly doubtful, whether any imitation of the Pageantry of foreign Courts would, in the present age & according to the feelings of my Countrymen, contribute to strengthen the foedcral Government—Our national Character is very different from that of the Populace of Europe. What in that country "dazzles the croud & sets them all agape,"[2] excites in our Yeomen nothing but envy, contempt & ridicule. Let our Government be possessed of real strength—It will not need the aid of ostentation. We are sufficiently enlightened to detect the imposition of pageantry—& I fear our Government would gain as little benefit by it, as one of my dearest Friends, Col. H—s [*David Humphreys*], has acquired from the French Silks & Laces, in which he returned from Europe—He is happily weaning himself from that his almost only foible—and I cannot wish to see our Government dressed in his cast suits.

What may be politic on this subject in the next generation, I will not undertake to say.

I shall conclude with an observation in answer to a Query in your last letter.

Art & dissimulation are the very Antipodes to your character, & You know me too well to imagine I should recommend them. The utmost exertion of your influence and abilities, on all subjects on which the happiness of America & the force of her Government depends, in such ways as are best calculated to continue & extend that influence, & crown those abilities with deserved success, is expected by your friends & the Public. We look to You for important additions, to those services, You have already rendered to your Country, which as You justly observe can never be forgotten, & for which I trust You will find that America will not be eventually ungrateful.

ALS, Adams Family Manuscript Trust, MHi. Written from Hartford, Connecticut; answered 2 April. The omitted text discusses Trumbull's genealogy and his initial review of Adams's *Defense of the Constitutions*.

[1] *The Spectator* was an influential literary magazine published in London (1711–14) by the British essayists, poets, and politicians, Joseph Addison (1672–1719) and Sir Richard Steele (1672–1729).
[2] Book Five of John Milton's *Paradise Lost* (1667).

Sarah Henshaw Tucker to Theodore Sedgwick

I believe it a very unusual circumstance for a Lady to propose, and begin a correspondence with a Gentleman of your rank in life, but I hope the subject of this letter, with the motives that induce me to write it, will prove a sufficient apology for calling off your attention a few minutes from Bussiness or pleasures of more importance—First then accept my Grateful thanks for your polite attention to, and Friendly exertions in behalf of my Husband,[1] and let me hope that you will extend the latter to procure him a salary that will enable us to live at the seat of Goverment with reputation and give our Children such an education as you wish to bestow upon your own: it is for their advantage that I have consented to leave Boston and I hope not to have reason to repent it; but I have another favor to sollicit at the request of a Friend whose happiness and interest are very intimately connected with my own, it is the amiable and worthy Brother of Mr. Henshaw,[2] he has been extremely unfortunate for several years back, had a very handsome real estate consumed by Fire, in addition to the loss of an office as register of deeds for this [*Suffolk*] County, which was a comfortable support and has been out of Bussiness two or three Years back constantly hopeing and expecting to supply some vacancy that would afford him a moderate living but all his exertions have proved abortive he has now very nigh reduced the small patrimony left by his Father to nothing [*he*] has a very delicate constitution not able to indure hardship and if you could procure him an appointment under Goverment to remain in Boston with an income of about two Hundred or two Hundred and fifty a Year it would be doing real kindness to a man of merit and promoting the intrest of virtue and Honesty in the world for I would pledge my life for the faithful discharge of any appointment you should interrest your self to procure him and I Flatter my self your friendship for me as well as the benevolence and compassion that Marks your character will not Make you unmindful of a Man who as a Son of Misf[*ortune*] sollicited your attention in his Favor he is very well kn[*own to Mr.*] Ames and if you please you will Mention the Matter to [*torn*] is any impropriety in such a request coming from me your Friendship will apologize for it if you could devote a few of your leasure Moments to answer this.

ALS, Sedgwick Papers, MHi. Written from Boston.

[1] John Tucker, Jr., had been appointed clerk of the Supreme Court of the United States, an office he resigned in 1791; see *DHFFC* 17:1893.

[2] Joshua Henshaw (1746–1823), the older brother of Tucker's deceased first husband, Andrew Henshaw (d. 1782).

Letter from Boston

We are all fatigued out with the slowness of congressional proceedings. Too much time is wasted in long speeches upon points, to say the least not of the greatest importance; at this rate of progression, it will consume the life of Congress to decide on the Secretary's report. Not a day should be lost, as the year will be too short for the arrangements necessary in the Treasury department—and it gives a *trifling* air to the measures of government to spend so much time in debating and re-debating inconsistent propositions. The foregoing are my own sentiments—but I forbear to repeat the observations of *some* characters, who take pleasure in finding fault, and wish to sow the seeds of disaffection among the people.

GUS, 24 March; reprinted at Exeter, New Hampshire; Hartford, Litchfield, New Haven, and New London, Connecticut; Poughkeepsie, New York; Elizabethtown, New Jersey; Philadelphia; Wilmington, Delaware; Baltimore; and Winchester, Virginia.

Letter from Louisville, Kentucky

In these remote parts of the American wilderness, we are still happy to think ourselves subjects, and under the protection of the Atlantic States. How should we do otherwise? are we not your children and connected with you by every tie of consanguinity and friendship? There are no oceans to divide us, no contrariety of interests, no dissimilarity of language. We are told that persons amongst you from hence have intimated, that this country does not relish a connection with the old states. Be assured the idea is false and unsupported, and the person here would, I might say, be execrated who would suggest an idea of independence. In one word, nothing will separate this Western Territory from the Union but wrong measures at home. Let wisdom and sage experience sit at the helm and all is safe; it is both our interest and our honor to be united to you. It is true, the harmonizing *such an empire* is one of the boldest experiments that has ever been made by man, but as we have struck out a new track in other things, why may we not do the same in cementing a republic in peace and good understanding, which bids fair to be by far the most extensive of any upon the globe.

NYDA, 12 May; reprinted at Norwich, Connecticut; New York City (*NYP*, 18 May); Philadelphia; Baltimore; and Alexandria and Winchester, Virginia.

OTHER DOCUMENTS

John Adams to William Cranch. FC:lbk, Adams Family Manuscript Trust, MHi. Place to which addressed not indicated.
  Discusses the state of Massachusetts' legal profession.

Thomas Fitzsimons to Michael Hodge. ALS, Ebenezer Stone Papers, MSaE. Addressed in Goodhue's hand to Newburyport, Massachusetts; franked; postmarked. In a postscript, Goodhue writes Hodge explaining that he had mentioned Hodge's name to "my friend" Fitzsimons for assistance in posing some "interrogatories" to Nathaniel Tracy.
  "Under the Sanction of our Mutual friend" Goodhue, has inserted Hodge's name in a commission for examining Nathaniel Tracy on a matter of personal financial business; will reimburse expenses "or if I can at any time be usefull to you or your friends—I shall be happy in the Occasion."

Benjamin Goodhue to Michael Hodge. ALS, Ebenezer Stone Papers, MSaE. Place to which addressed not indicated. For the full text, see *EIHC* 84(April 1948):152–53.

Repeats almost verbatim his letter to the Salem Insurances Offices, above, concluding, "God grant We may rise superior to partial and trifling considerations."

Nathaniel Gorham to Theodore Sedgwick. ALS, Sedgwick Papers, MHi. Written from Charlestown, Massachusetts; postmarked.

Encloses letter to be delivered to Oliver Phelps, who would arrive in New York soon; describes settlement of terms with the Massachusetts legislature for retaining one third of Phelps and Gorham's original Genessee (New York) purchase; Phelps will inform him of the particulars; thanks for Sedgwick's letter and will soon reply more fully; lists state legislators who were "violently opposed," "in our favour," or "stood by us manfully."

Benjamin Huntington to Christopher Leffingwell. No copy known; noted on endorsement sheet of Leffingwell to Huntington, 3 March.

James Madison to Francis Taylor. No copy known; received 2 April. Information supplied by *PJM* 13:107.

Robert Morris to Mary Morris. ALS, Morris Papers, CSmH. This is a postscript to a letter begun on 13 March.

"Mr. Ryerson arrived last Night and on my Return from club, I received Your letter which came by him but as yet I have not seen him—by a Note which he left for me I see it is his intention to set out on his Return tomorrow but I think He will of necessity be detained untill Tuesday and if I can find time—you shall hear from me again by him."

Theodore Sedgwick to [*Ephraim*] Williams. ALS, Sedgwick Papers, MHi. Place to which addressed not indicated. The recipient's identity is based on internal evidence.

Is disappointed in not returning home when expected, but hopes to precede this letter's arrival; discusses his legal practice; presents his compliments to "the Brotherhood" (of lawyers), and supports them against the "heavy hand" of John Gardiner's legal reforms; asks Williams to inform "Brother Harry" (Henry Williams Dwight) that Sedgwick has recommended him as deputy marshal for taking the census in Berkshire County, Massachusetts.

Samuel B. Webb to Joseph Barrell. FC, Webb Papers, CtY. Sent to Boston; docketed as "Sketch of a letter."

Anticipates all state securities will reach a common market price within a few days, "as the funding System goes on well, and we have not a doubt, the Secretary's Plan, will be fully adopted, excepting some Variation respecting the Interest—the members have such a variety of opinions on that subject that it is impossible to Judge how it will be finally settled."

Paine Wingate to Samuel Hodgdon. ALS, Roberts Collection, PHC. Addressed to Philadelphia; franked; postmarked 15 March; received 17 March. For the full text, see *Wingate* 2:353–54. Poor was principal of the Ladies Academy of Philadelphia in 1792.

Forwards letter from George Williams; "nothing new here"; encloses newspapers; acknowledges Hodgdon's letter delivered by (Charles?) Stewart, whose wishes he "shall gladly promote"; enquires about John Poor of Philadelphia.

William Samuel Johnson, Diary. Johnson Papers, CtHi.
"St. P[aul's]."

Letter from Dumfries, Virginia. [Baltimore] *Maryland Journal*, 19 March; reprinted at New York City (*GUS*, 24 March), and Philadelphia.

Grayson's remains, attended "by a numerous Circle of his Acquaintance," were deposited in the family vault.

Letter from New York. [Portland, Maine] *Cumberland Gazette*, 29 March. This is probably from a letter written by Thatcher to the newspaper's editor, Thomas B. Wait.

"It is said there will be strong opposition to the assumption of the State Debts. In the Committee there were a majority of five only in favour of the measure. And though the probability is that the vote of the committee will be accepted, it is uncertain; which uncertainty is increased by the prospect of the arrival of the North Carolina Representatives, who, it is said, are instructed by their state Legislature to oppose the assumption."